The
Alexander H. Stephens Reader

ᴥ THE LOCHLAINN SEABROOK COLLECTION ᴥ

AMERICAN CIVIL WAR
Abraham Lincoln Was a Liberal, Jefferson Davis Was a Conservative: The Missing Key to Understanding the American Civil War
Confederacy 101: Amazing Facts You Never Knew About America's Oldest Political Tradition
Confederate Blood and Treasure: An Interview With Lochlainn Seabrook
Everything You Were Taught About African-Americans and the Civil War is Wrong, Ask a Southerner!
Everything You Were Taught About the Civil War is Wrong, Ask a Southerner!
Give This Book to a Yankee! A Southern Guide to the Civil War For Northerners
Lincoln's War: The Real Cause, the Real Winner, the Real Loser
The Great Yankee Coverup: What the North Doesn't Want You to Know About Lincoln's War!
The Ultimate Civil War Quiz Book: How Much Do You Really Know About America's Most Misunderstood Conflict?
Women in Gray: A Tribute to the Ladies Who Supported the Southern Confederacy

CONFEDERATE MONUMENTS
Confederate Monuments: Why Every American Should Honor Confederate Soldiers and Their Memorials

CONFEDERATE FLAG
Confederate Flag Facts: What Every American Should Know About Dixie's Southern Cross

SECESSION
All We Ask Is To Be Let Alone: The Southern Secession Fact Book

SLAVERY
Everything You Were Taught About American Slavery is Wrong, Ask a Southerner!
Slavery 101: Amazing Facts You Never Knew About America's "Peculiar Institution"

CHILDREN
Honest Jeff and Dishonest Abe: A Southern Children's Guide to the Civil War
Saddle, Sword, and Gun: A Biography of Nathan Bedford Forrest For Teens

NATHAN BEDFORD FORREST
A Rebel Born: A Defense of Nathan Bedford Forrest - Confederate General, American Legend (winner of the 2011 Jefferson Davis Historical Gold Medal)
A Rebel Born: The Screenplay (film about N.B. Forrest)
Forrest! 99 Reasons to Love Nathan Bedford Forrest
Give 'Em Hell Boys! The Complete Military Correspondence of Nathan Bedford Forrest
Nathan Bedford Forrest and African-Americans: Yankee Myth, Confederate Fact
Nathan Bedford Forrest and the Battle of Fort Pillow: Yankee Myth, Confederate Fact
Nathan Bedford Forrest and the Ku Klux Klan: Yankee Myth, Confederate Fact
Nathan Bedford Forrest: Southern Hero, American Patriot - Honoring a Confederate Icon and the Old South
Saddle, Sword, and Gun: A Biography of Nathan Bedford Forrest For Teens
The God of War: Nathan Bedford Forrest As He Was Seen By His Contemporaries
The Quotable Nathan Bedford Forrest: Selections From the Writings and Speeches of the Confederacy's Most Brilliant Cavalryman

QUOTABLE SERIES
The Quotable Alexander H. Stephens: Selections From the Writings and Speeches of the Confederacy's First Vice President
The Quotable Jefferson Davis: Selections From the Writings and Speeches of the Confederacy's First President
The Quotable Nathan Bedford Forrest: Selections From the Writings and Speeches of the Confederacy's Most Brilliant Cavalryman
The Quotable Robert E. Lee: Selections From the Writings and Speeches of the South's Most Beloved Civil War General
The Quotable Stonewall Jackson: Selections From the Writings and Speeches of the South's Most Famous General
The Unquotable Abraham Lincoln: The President's Quotes They Don't Want You To Know!

CONSTITUTIONAL HISTORY
The Articles of Confederation Explained: A Clause-by-Clause Study of America's First Constitution
The Constitution of the Confederate States of America Explained: A Clause-by-Clause Study of the South's Magna Carta

VICTORIAN CONFEDERATE LITERATURE
Rise Up and Call Them Blessed: Victorian Tributes to the Confederate Soldier, 1861-1901
The Alexander H. Stephens Reader: Excerpts From the Works of a Confederate Founding Father
The Old Rebel: Robert E. Lee As He Was Seen By His Contemporaries
Victorian Confederate Poetry: The Southern Cause in Verse, 1861-1901

ABRAHAM LINCOLN
Abraham Lincoln: The Southern View - Demythologizing America's Sixteenth President
Lincolnology: The Real Abraham Lincoln Revealed in His Own Words - A Study of Lincoln's Suppressed, Misinterpreted, and Forgotten Writings and Speeches
The Great Impersonator! 99 Reasons to Dislike Abraham Lincoln
The Unholy Crusade: Lincoln's Legacy of Destruction in the American South
The Unquotable Abraham Lincoln: The President's Quotes They Don't Want You To Know!

CIVIL WAR BATTLES
Encyclopedia of the Battle of Franklin - A Comprehensive Guide to the Conflict that Changed the Civil War
Nathan Bedford Forrest and the Battle of Fort Pillow: Yankee Myth, Confederate Fact

PARANORMAL
Carnton Plantation Ghost Stories: True Tales of the Unexplained from Tennessee's Most Haunted Civil War House!
UFOs and Aliens: The Complete Guidebook

FAMILY HISTORIES
The Blakeneys: An Etymological, Ethnological, and Genealogical Study - Uncovering the Mysterious Origins of the Blakeney Family and Name
The Caudills: An Etymological, Ethnological, and Genealogical Study - Exploring the Name and National Origins of a European-American Family
The McGavocks of Carnton Plantation: A Southern History - Celebrating One of Dixie's Most Noble Confederate Families and Their Tennessee Home

MIND, BODY, SPIRIT
Autobiography of a Non-Yogi: A Scientist's Journey From Hinduism to Christianity (Dr. Amitava Dasgupta, with Lochlainn Seabrook)
Britannia Rules: Goddess-Worship in Ancient Anglo-Celtic Society - An Academic Look at the United Kingdom's Matricentric Spiritual Past
Christ Is All and In All: Rediscovering Your Divine Nature and the Kingdom Within
Christmas Before Christianity: How the Birthday of the "Sun" Became the Birthday of the "Son"
Jesus and the Gospel of Q: Christ's Pre-Christian Teachings As Recorded in the New Testament
Jesus and the Law of Attraction: The Bible-Based Guide to Creating Perfect Health, Wealth, and Happiness Following Christ's Simple Formula
Seabrook's Bible Dictionary of Traditional and Mystical Christian Doctrines
The Bible and the Law of Attraction: 99 Teachings of Jesus, the Apostles, and the Prophets
The Book of Kelle: An Introduction to Goddess-Worship and the Great Celtic Mother-Goddess Kelle, Original Blessed Lady of Ireland
The Goddess Dictionary of Words and Phrases: Introducing a New Core Vocabulary for the Women's Spirituality Movement
The Way of Holiness: The Story of Religion and Myth From the Cave Bear Cult to Christianity

WOMEN
Aphrodite's Trade: The Hidden History of Prostitution Unveiled
Princess Diana: Modern Day Moon-Goddess - A Psychoanalytical and Mythological Look at Diana Spencer's Life, Marriage, and Death (with Dr. Jane Goldberg)
Women in Gray: A Tribute to the Ladies Who Supported the Southern Confederacy

Five-Star Books & Gifts From the Heart of the American South

SeaRavenPress.com

The Alexander H. Stephens

Reader

Excerpts From the Works of a Confederate Founding Father

COLLECTED, ARRANGED, & EDITED, WITH A FOREWORD & NOTES
BY THE "VOICE OF THE TRADITIONAL SOUTH," COLONEL

Lochlainn Seabrook

JEFFERSON DAVIS HISTORICAL GOLD MEDAL WINNER

Introduction by Charles Kelly Barrow

**Diligently Researched for the
Elucidation of the Reader**

2013

SEA RAVEN PRESS, NASHVILLE, TENNESSEE, USA

THE ALEXANDER H. STEPHENS READER

Published by
Sea Raven Press, Cassidy Ravensdale, President
PO Box 1484, Spring Hill, Tennessee 37174-1484 USA
SeaRavenPress.com • searavenpress@gmail.com

Copyright © 2018 Lochlainn Seabrook
in accordance with U.S. and international copyright laws and regulations, as stated and protected under the Berne Union for the Protection of Literary and Artistic Property (Berne Convention), and the Universal Copyright Convention (the UCC). All rights reserved under the Pan-American and International Copyright Conventions.

1st SRP paperback ed., 1st printing, January 2013; 2nd paperback ed., April 2018 • ISBN: 978-0-9858632-3-4
1st SRP hardcover ed., 1st printing, April 2018 • ISBN: 978-1-943737-67-3

ISBN: 978-0-9858632-3-4 (paperback)
Library of Congress Control Number: 2012953132

This work is the copyrighted intellectual property of Lochlainn Seabrook and has been registered with the Copyright Office at the Library of Congress in Washington, D.C., USA. No part of this work (including text, covers, drawings, photos, illustrations, maps, images, diagrams, etc.), in whole or in part, may be used, reproduced, stored in a retrieval system, or transmitted, in any form or by any means now known or hereafter invented, without written permission from the publisher. The sale, duplication, hire, lending, copying, digitalization, or reproduction of this material, in any manner or form whatsoever, is also prohibited, and is a violation of federal, civil, and digital copyright law, which provides severe civil and criminal penalties for any violations.

The Alexander H. Stephens Reader: Excerpts From the Works of a Confederate Founding Father, by Lochlainn Seabrook. Introduction by Charles Kelly Barrow. Includes an index and bibliographical references.

Front and back cover design and art, book design, layout, and interior art by Lochlainn Seabrook
All images, graphic design, graphic art, and illustrations copyright © Lochlainn Seabrook
All images selected, placed, manipulated, and/or created by Lochlainn Seabrook
Cover images and design copyright © Lochlainn Seabrook
Front cover image: Alexander H. Stephens, circa 1860s; redesigned image © Lochlainn Seabrook

The views on the American "Civil War" documented in this book are those of the publisher.

PRINTED & MANUFACTURED IN OCCUPIED TENNESSEE, FORMER CONFEDERATE STATES OF AMERICA

Dedication

To the idea of the Constitutional Confederacy, the only hope of preserving humankind from the domineering rule of liberals, socialists, Marxists, communists, dictators, kings, tyrants, monarchs, autocrats, czars, potentates, and despots.

If only Abraham Lincoln had understood and obeyed the Constitution:

"There would have been no war, no bloodshed, no sacking of towns and cities, no desolation, no billions of treasure expended, on either side, and no million of lives sacrificed in the unnatural and fratricidal strife; there would have been none of the present troubles about restoration, or reconstruction; but, instead of these lamentable scenes, a new spectacle of wonder would have been presented for the guide and instruction of the astonished Nations of the earth, greater than that exhibited after the Nullification pacification, of the matchless workings of our American Institutions of Self-Government by the people!"

Alexander Hamilton Stephens, 1868

CONTENTS

Notes to the Reader - 11
Foreword, by Lochlainn Seabrook - 15
Introduction, by Charles Kelly Barrow - 23

SECTION ONE
LETTERS, SPEECHES, RECOLLECTIONS, TESTIMONY, REVIEWERS, & THE HISTORY, 1836-1881

1 PRIVATE & PUBLIC LETTERS - 1836-1881: 31
2 PUBLIC SPEECHES - PART ONE: 1844-1860: 105
3 PUBLIC SPEECHES - PART TWO: 1861-1866: 195
4 RECOLLECTIONS OF YANKEE ARREST & IMPRISONMENT - 1865: 273
5 TESTIMONY BEFORE THE RECONSTRUCTION COMMITTEE - 1866: 291
6 RESPONSE TO REVIEWERS - 1872: 307
7 EXCERPTS FROM STEPHENS' *HISTORY OF THE U.S.* - 1874: 317

SECTION TWO
EXCERPTS FROM *A CONSTITUTIONAL VIEW OF THE LATE WAR BETWEEN THE STATES*, 1868-1870

8 LAYING THE FOUNDATION: 325
9 THE CHARACTER OF THE FEDERAL GOVERNMENT: 343
10 AMERICA'S FIRST TWO CONSTITUTIONS: 357
11 THE NATURE OF THE U.S. GOVERNMENT: 379
12 A STUDY OF THE U.S. CONSTITUTION: 411
13 HOW THE STATES UNDERSTOOD THE CONSTITUTION & THE UNION: 423
14 WEBSTER & CALHOUN ON THE U.S. CONSTITUTION: 479
15 WEBSTER, CALHOUN, & DAVIS ON THE U.S. CONSTITUTION: 513
16 ANDREW JACKSON ON THE U.S. CONSTITUTION: 529
17 THE NATURE OF THE COMPACT OF OUR UNION: 563
18 THE BEST GOVERNMENT THE WORLD EVER SAW: 591
19 GOVERNMENT, SLAVERY, & THE START OF LINCOLN'S WAR: 605
20 THE TRUTH ABOUT AMERICAN SLAVERY: 627
21 THE MISSOURI COMPROMISE OF 1820: 669
22 THE MISSOURI COMPROMISE OF 1850 - PART ONE: 697
23 THE MISSOURI COMPROMISE OF 1850 - PART TWO: 739

24 THE MYTH OF THE "IRREPRESSIBLE CONFLICT": 753
25 SECESSION & THE FORMATION OF THE C.S.A.: 783
26 THE WAR FOR SOUTHERN INDEPENDENCE - PART ONE: 815
27 THE WAR FOR SOUTHERN INDEPENDENCE - PART TWO: 855
28 THE WAR FOR SOUTHERN INDEPENDENCE - PART THREE: 895
29 THE WAR FOR SOUTHERN INDEPENDENCE - PART FOUR: 941
30 THE RESULTS OF LINCOLN'S WAR: 977

The Confederate Cabinet in Pictures - 1001
Notes - 1011
Bibliography - 1019
Index - 1025
Meet the Author - 1045

Notes to the Reader

☙ In an effort to retain the true character and meaning of Vice President Stephens' words, they have been printed here exactly as they appear in the original manuscripts, including typographical and grammatical peculiarities inherent to both Stephens and to 19th-Century American writing and speaking (including long running paragraphs, English spelling forms, and intra-sentence capitalization).
   Stephens' quotes are marked with a traditional Victorian "hand" pointer. My chapter introductions are in normal font, my explanatory comments appear in italics above Stephens' quotes, and my clarifications are in brackets within his quotes. Double-spaces separate all excerpts, sharply delineating my words from Stephens'.

☙ Where applicable I have corrected obvious typographic errors in Stephens' original manuscripts. As mentioned, at the same time I have taken great care to leave his own eccentric spellings, unusual word usage, and invented words, all intact. Brackets *always* contain my notes, unless otherwise indicated.

☙ Stephens was, by today's standards, quite long-winded and liked to exhaustively cite his sources, usually word for word and nearly always at great length. To preserve the full context of his own thoughts, as well as aid in buttressing his main argument (that secession was and is legal under the Constitution, and that therefore Lincoln's War was both immoral and illegal), I felt that, in most cases, it was of supreme importance to retain this extra text—even though it added to the length of the book.

☙ While my personal sources for Stephens' speeches only go up to 1866, the other writings I have included here (such as his letters and book excerpts) more than adequately reveal the sentiments, views, and opinions he held up until the time of his death in 1883.

☙ Those who are familiar with American history will forgive me for repeatedly spelling out and fully identifying the names of our better known historical figures, places, political parties, word and phrase meanings, and events. This I have done for my many foreign readers, most who have little knowledge of these topics; or, more likely, have procured their information of American history from erroneous pro-North sources.

❦ Two of the Victorian's most commonly used words in relation to the calender, "instant" (often abbreviated *inst.*) and "ultimo" (often abbreviated *ult.*), are unknown to modern Americans, and so are defined here: "instant" refers to the present month; "ultimo" refers to the month preceding the present month. Stephens and his colleagues made much use of these two words.

❦ In any study of the "Civil War" it is vitally important to keep in mind that the two major political parties were then the opposite of what they are today. The Democrats of the mid 19th Century were conservatives, akin to the Republican Party of today, while the Republicans of the mid 19th Century were liberals, akin to the Democratic Party of today. Thus the Confederacy's Democratic president, Jefferson Davis, was a Conservative (with libertarian leanings); the Union's Republican president, Abraham Lincoln, was a Liberal (with socialistic leanings). For more on this topic see my work: *Abraham Lincoln Was a Liberal, Jefferson Davis Was a Conservative: The Missing Key to Understanding the American Civil War*.

❦ Stephens' use of the words *Federal* and *Federation* bear explanation, as they have meant different things at different periods in history. Indeed, there is so much confusion surrounding these words that to this day they continue to be defined differently in different countries.

In the U.S. the word *federal* is an abbreviation of the original word *confederal*, and *federation* is an abbreviation of the original word *confederation*. Thus, the sense in which the Confederate Vice President used these two words is immediately clear: For 19th-Century Americans, "federal" referred to a Conservative, even Libertarian, form of government. For Stephens then, a federation was identical to a confederation or rather a confederacy: a small weak central government operating under the auspices of strong independent sovereign states—favored by men like Thomas Jefferson, Patrick Henry, and Jefferson Davis.

Again, in 19th-Century parlance, the opposite of a federation would be a *nation* (or something akin to an *empire*): an all-powerful government ruling over weak dependent states—preferred by men like John Adams, Daniel Webster, and Abraham Lincoln. Thus we would call the U.S. Federalists of Stephens' day Conservatives and the U.S. Nationalists of his day Liberals. Stephens himself sometimes also referred to his liberal foes in government as "Centralists" or "Consolidationists," due to their desire to do away with states' rights altogether and unify all political power in the central government.

(Note: Some, like George Washington, added to the lingual chaos by using the words Federal and Confederate to mean the same thing. And, as Stephens himself often complained, the definitions of these words were further jumbled when Liberals among the Founding Generation hijacked the word "Federal" [i.e., Confederal or Confederate] and changed its meaning to "National." This makes the Federalists of the 1700s akin to modern day Liberals, the opposite of the Federalists of the 1800s, who were considered Conservatives, and who, to add to the confusion, were called Antifederalists by their Liberal enemies.)

When it comes to the topic of the U.S. government, things have not changed one iota since Stephens' time. If anything, they have grown worse: today American Liberals, along with Socialists, Marxists, Collectivists, Communists, and other progressives, continue their anti-constitutional efforts to enlarge the powers of the central government and weaken those of both the states and the people. Their opponents, Conservatives and Libertarians (I count myself among them), continue their efforts to defend the Constitution and preserve what little is left of Thomas Jefferson's "Confederate Republic."

As Stephens himself predicted, the fight to preserve the constitutional government of the Founding Fathers may ultimately be in vain: as I write this, our liberal socialistic president has, in a mere four years, greatly enlarged both the powers and dominion of the Central government, further curtailed the rights of the states, created hundreds of new laws, invented dozens of new governmental positions and departments, and created more national debt than all the former U.S. presidents combined. We are indeed going backwards down the road to autarchy, empire, and dictatorship, the very things our Revolutionary ancestors gave their lives to avoid.[1] "Squinting towards monarchy," Patrick Henry rightly called it.

🐦 Lincoln's War on the American people and the Constitution can never be fully understood without a thorough knowledge of the South's perspective. As this book is only meant to be a brief introductory guide to these topics, one cannot hope to learn the complete story here. For those who are interested in additional material from Dixie's viewpoint, please see my comprehensive histories listed on pages 2 and 3.

Keep Your Body, Mind, & Spirit Vibrating at Their Highest Level

YOU CAN DO SO BY READING THE BOOKS OF

SEA RAVEN PRESS

There is nothing that will so perfectly keep your body, mind, and spirit in a healthy condition as to think wisely and positively. Hence you should not only read this book, but also the other books that we offer. They will quicken your physical, mental, and spiritual vibrations, enabling you to maintain a position in society as a healthy erudite person.

KEEP YOURSELF WELL-INFORMED!

The well-informed person is always at the head of the procession, while the ignorant, the lazy, and the unthoughtful hang onto the rear. If you are a Spiritual man or woman, do yourself a great favor: read Sea Raven Press books and stay well posted on the Truth. It is almost criminal for one to remain in ignorance while the opportunity to gain knowledge is open to all at a nominal price.

We invite you to visit our Webstore for a wide selection of wholesome, family-friendly, well-researched, educational books for all ages. You will be glad you did!

Five-Star Books & Gifts From the Heart of the American South

SeaRavenPress.com

FOREWORD
By Lochlainn Seabrook

Like President Jefferson Davis (1808-1889), most historians have relegated Vice President Alexander Hamilton Stephens (1812-1883) to the scrapheap of American history. Why? Because of their association with the Southern Confederacy, that short-lived republic that is more feared, hated, and misunderstood by Northerners and uneducated Southerners than any other. This, however, is irrational and unfair, for not only was the formation of the Southern Confederacy one of the most remarkable events in world history, both men were among the most famous, fascinating, and important American statesmen to have ever lived.

Stephens as a young man.

As I descend from the Stephens family (Edward Stephens, Alexander's 7th great-grandfather, is my 12th great-grandfather), and as I, like Stephens, am a Southern Conservative and a strict constitutionalist, I find the Confederate vice president particularly intriguing. Indeed, he was one of the great lights of the Confederate Founding Fathers, as well as a brilliant writer and a captivating orator. He was right, of course, about the importance of states' rights and the dangers of straying from the U.S. Constitution (which he called "the Ark of the Covenant of our Fathers"),[2] a view that is more relevant now than it was in his own day. And he was right about the Confederate Cause, the purpose behind the secession of the Southern states. It was, he declared until the end of his life, nothing more than an effort to "render our liberties and institutions more secure" by "rescuing, restoring, and re-establishing the Constitution." As for the War, the South took up arms, he often noted, for no other reason than a "desire to preserve constitutional liberty and perpetuate the government in its purity."[3]

He was wrong on several issues, however, most notoriously the one concerning his early view of blacks; that they were "designed by Nature" to be slaves; that they were part of a "degraded caste" meant to serve the rest of humanity in a "subordinate position." But unlike Yankee white supremacist Abraham Lincoln, Stephens based his belief on the Bible—which, from Genesis to Revelation, sanctions slavery.[4] Lincoln's racism, on the other hand, was based on his own deep seated dislike of all non-white peoples, whom he typically referred to as "inferior races."[5] (Lincoln often publicly called blacks "niggers" and Mexicans "mongrels.")[6] Besides, Lincoln could not use the Bible to justify his racism: he was a self-proclaimed atheist and anti-Christian.[7]

Since it is Stephens' alleged "racism" that pro-North historians most enjoy emphasizing, it is worth taking a moment to correct some of these myths.

To begin with, Stephens was not only a lifelong opponent of the slave trade, he was a kindly and generous slave owner who emancipated his younger slaves during Lincoln's War,[8] and supported aged black pensioners who could no longer work[9] (considered "useless" by Yankees). Indeed, he was emotionally closer to many of his own servants than he was to his white colleagues in Congress.

His servant Harry, for example, nursed his "master" through many an illness, staying with him all the way through Lincoln's fake and illegal emancipation and his needless and illicit War. Afterward, Harry continued to remain loyal during his employer's unlawful Yankee imprisonment in Boston, ultimately even taking Stephens' surname as his own.[10] Such was the trust and friendship between Stephens and his black servants that he put Harry, along with several other "slaves," in complete charge of his home and farm during his five month incarceration at Fort Warren.[11] Before his departure by train under Yankee guard, a number of Stephens' "old [black] friends" met him at the station where they shook his hand and cried bitterly at seeing him leave.[12] Of the occasion Stephens wrote:

> "The servants all wept. My grief at leaving them and home was too burning, withering, scorching for tears. That parting and that scene I can never forget."[13]

Obviously, Stephens was not the heartless, racist, slavery-loving monster that pro-North writers have always portrayed him as. He was, after all, a traditional Southern Christian who felt deep compassion and empathy for others, including African-Americans—both bonded and free.

This is why, as early as 1845, sixteen years before Lincoln's War, he publicly commented that he was "no defender of Slavery in the abstract. . . This was true then, and now, and always with me."[14] In this same speech he went on to say that:

> "Liberty always had charms for me, and I would rejoice to see all the sons of Adam's family, in every land and clime, in the enjoyment of those rights which are set forth in our Declaration of Independence as 'natural and inalienable' . . ."[15]

Not surprisingly, the Confederate vice president once noted that "many things connected with slavery did not meet with my approval but excited my disgust, abhorrence, and detestation." Among these "things" were the ban in some Southern states on educating servants and a prohibition against marriage.[16] Like most Southern slave owners, Stephens ignored such laws, both educating his servants and allowing, even encouraging, them to marry whenever possible.[17]

Despite his antebellum *political* (though not *moral*) support of slavery, Stephens always maintained that: "If Slavery does not stand upon the immutable principles of nature, as I believe it does, it must go down, and ought to go down."[18] The day eventually came, of course, when he was finally convinced that slavery did not "stand upon the immutable principles of nature." Sticking by his statement, immediately after the War he counseled the Southern people to a "full and perfect acceptation"[19] of the abolition of slavery, that its extinction should be "received and accepted as an irrevocable fact."[20]

Still, he lamented the tragic reality that in early 1861 many radical Northern abolitionists had called for a war on the South to rid her of slavery, even though the South would have eventually abolished slavery anyway—in her own time and manner. If only the North had granted the South the same privilege it had granted itself. That is, *unlimited time to demolish slavery within its own region.*[21] As Stephens stated in 1868, if the meddling North had only been more patient with Dixie, if only she had not been so quick to rush into war:

> "Other changes would certainly have been made, even to the extinction of the [Southern slavery] system, if time, with its changes, and the progress of attainments on the part of these people [African-Americans] had shown it to be proper—that is, best for both races. For if the system, as designed, was not really the best, or could not have been made the best for both races, or whenever it should have ceased to be so, it could and would have been thoroughly and radically changed, in due time, by the only proper and competent authority to act in the premises."[22]

After he became convinced that slavery was not "the best for both races," Stephens began championing the racial cause of "perfect equality with the whites," including the right of *all* African-Americans to vote[23]—something Lincoln never did.[24] Less than a year after Lincoln's War, in February 1866, Stephens told the Georgia General Assembly that

> "ample and full protection should be secured to them [blacks], so that they may stand equal before the law, in the possession and enjoyment of all rights of person, liberty and property. Many considerations claim this at your hands. Among these may be stated their fidelity in times past. They cultivated your fields, ministered to your personal wants and comforts, nursed and reared your children; and even in the hour of danger and peril they were, in the main, true to you and yours. To them we owe a debt of gratitude, as well as acts of kindness. . . . All obstacles, if there be any, should be removed, which can possibly hinder or retard, the improvement of the blacks to the extent of their capacity. All proper aid should be given to their own efforts. Channels of education should be opened up to them. Schools, and the usual means of moral and intellectual training, should be encouraged amongst them."[25]

In April 1866 he was proud to say that his state, Georgia, had passed a racial equality act the month before, which he read before the U.S. Reconstruction Committee. One of its clauses was as follows:

> . . . persons of color shall have the right to make and enforce contracts, to sue, be sued, to be parties and give evidence, to inherit, to purchase, and to have full and equal benefit of all laws and proceedings for the security of person and estate, and shall not be subjected to any other or different punishment, pain, or penalty for the commission of any act or offence than

such as are prescribed for white persons committing like acts or offences.²⁶

In 1870 Stephens noted that anyone who was for the enfranchisement of slaves before Lincoln's War was possessed of "certainly high and admirable qualities,"²⁷ while in 1871 he wrote:

> "I can [now] well see how a man could have been most conscientiously and earnestly devoted to the emancipation of the negroes in this country. No man I think was more so or could have been more so than [Southerner] Mr. [Thomas] Jefferson was. However much therefore I may have differed with others upon that question while it was a living one, yet I can now not only cordially co-operate with all such men, since that question is forever out of the way, upon all the really practical and living questions of the present and future which involve the essentials and essence of liberty itself—and the more so when I meet with men of that class, who show by their acts that they were moved by earnest convictions and devotion to what they deemed the just rights of man on the question of emancipation."²⁸

Such views were quite unlike those of Lincoln, who went to his grave refusing to grant citizenship, suffrage, or anything else to blacks.²⁹ Instead, as a lifelong member (and onetime leader) of the Yankee founded organization, the American Colonization Society, Lincoln spent his entire political career trying to deport all blacks and settle (i.e., colonize) them in foreign lands,³⁰ like South America, the Caribbean, and Africa.³¹ Stephens was entirely against black colonization.

While Stephens' early views of blacks put him in the vast minority of Southerners—after all, Dixie, to this day still America's most racially tolerant region, is where the country's abolition movement got its start³²—he was well within the majority when it came to secession. Before the War, nearly all Southerners were against disunion, including Stephens, who, while recognizing secession as an important constitutional right, violently opposed it as a solution to the South-North conflict that had been raging for decades. Only when his state seceded (January 19, 1861) after the election of anti-South, big government Liberal Lincoln did he acquiesce, dutifully but reluctantly following Georgia out of the Union. Stephens was no wild-eyed Fire-eater.

Unanimously elected into the office of the Confederacy's first vice president, he served superbly his first year. But Stephens, always the strict constitutionalist and loather of war, soon found himself revolting against several of the policies of his boss President Davis. These were chiefly the Davis administration's mishandling of financial, agricultural, and material resources, refusal to pass a tax act, denying a provision for the redemption of the issue of treasury notes, "the general disarrangement of labor," mismanagement of Southern farms, plantations, livestock, and the army's reserve corps, implementing a military draft, and suspending the writ of *habeas corpus*—the latter two which Stephens correctly considered unconstitutional.

Though far from harboring "bitterness, hostility and malignancy" toward Davis, as the press misleadingly told the public, this in-house spat between the president and vice president, like the petty squabbles between numerous Confederate military officers, helped prevent the Confederate government from forging a unified front, further allowing the U.S. to gradually overwhelm and wear down the South and her people.

After the War, Stephens and Davis were arrested at the same time and shared an uncomfortable boat ride up the eastern coast to Fort Warren in Boston Harbor. Though formerly the two had disagreed on the manner in which the Confederacy prosecuted the War, there was no outward show of ill will. Nonetheless, Stephens described the ride as "not unfriendly, but far from cordial."[33] When they were separated for the last time a few days later, the vice president recalled that Davis "said nothing but good-bye, and gave my hand a cordial squeeze; his tone evinced deep feeling and emotion."[34]

After his release from prison, Stephens was grilled before the transparently revengeful "Reconstruction Committee of Congress," then wrote and published his brilliant pro-South work: *A Constitutional View of the Late War Between the States*. In 1873 he was elected to his ninth term as a Georgia state representative (he had served eight terms in the same position before Lincoln's War). On November 4, 1882, at the end of his thirteenth term, he retired from the U.S. Congress and was elected governor of Georgia, a job that he held for only four months.

On March 4, 1883, the always frail and sickly Stephens—who had been born during the presidency of Conservative U.S. Founding Father James Madison—passed away at the age of seventy-one. At one time a penniless orphan, he never married and bore no children. To his dying day he remained a stalwart advocate of the idea of state sovereignty, which he called the "great Continental Regulator."[35] He wanted his own epitaph to read:

". . . give me liberty as secured in the constitution with all its guaranties, amongst which is the sovereignty of Georgia, or give me death."[36]

Naturally, the most accurate description of Stephens' core beliefs was the one he wrote of himself:

"No more ardent or devoted friend to the Constitution of the United States, and the principles of civil and religious liberty therein embodied and guaranteed, than I was and am, ever breathed the vital air of heaven . . ."[37]

While all traditional Americans can certainly agree with these sentiments, it is true that Stephens' antebellum views on a number of topics were indisputably incorrect.

For instance, his belief that, prior to secession, the U.S. government had "always been true to Southern interests"; his early belief that the Southern secession movement was an "attempt to overthrow the U.S. government"; his belief that blacks were culturally "inferior" and that slavery was their "natural" birthright; his belief that the North could not possibly benefit from a war with the South; his belief that Abraham Lincoln (who Stephens once said he "esteemed highly") could be trusted solely because, before the War, Lincoln had held that the "Constitution was a Compact between the States"; his belief that though he considered Lincoln's election to president a "great public calamity," the South was in "no immediate serious danger," and that Lincoln was "powerless to do any great mischief" due to the many "Constitutional checks thrown around him" (*after* the War, Stephens lamented that Lincoln was a "public usurper who was wanting in humanity, and was insincere, and cruel"); his belief that history would record that the South seceded only in an effort to "rescue the constitution from utter annihilation"; his belief that "European governments have no sympathy with either side in this struggle"; his belief that cotton was "one of the greatest elements of power, if not the greatest" the Confederacy possessed during Lincoln's War; his belief that his home state of Georgia (as well as the rest of the Southern states) would never want to secede again (as I write this, Georgia, along with the other forty-nine states, is filing a petition to secede from the U.S.); and his antebellum belief that Thomas Jefferson and other early Southerners were wrong in supporting abolition.

But we cannot fault Stephens for such opinions. At the time they were held by millions of other Americans as well, both North and South. When displayed side by side with his many virtues, his sterling Christian character, his literary and oratory brilliance, his devotion to Confederate principles, his formidable political capabilities, his loyalty to the South and the Southern Cause (devotion to the idea of the *Confederate Republic*: a constitutional government of limited powers, separation of governmental branches, enumerated rights of the people, and sovereign nation-states—an idea he referred to as "the political Messiah just born for the regeneration of the down trodden Peoples of the Earth"),[38] and his fearless love for the Constitution, his few misconceptions and mistakes pale in comparison.

Indeed, my cousin Alexander Hamilton Stephens was one of the most distinguished and accomplished individuals in world history. He truly was, as *Confederate Veteran* called him, "one of the noblest and most unselfish men America has ever known."[39] An authentic Southern gentleman, a pragmatic but emotional Georgian, and an eccentric lifelong bachelor who died preaching the hard-earned lessons of a one-time great American statesman and Confederate Founding Father: peace, justice, and equality for all.

Colonel Lochlainn Seabrook, SCV
Franklin, Williamson County, Tennessee, USA
January 2013, Civil War Sesquicentennial

INTRODUCTION
By Charles Kelly Barrow

Being a native Georgian, I am proud that such a remarkable gentleman such as Alexander Hamilton Stephens left his mark on the State that we both share and love. And I am grateful that Southern historian and fellow SCV member Lochlainn Seabrook has created the monumental detailed work that you now hold in your hand, dedicated to one of America's most significant figures.

Stephens' devotion to his beloved state of Georgia can be seen in his service to public office from 1836-1866 (interrupted during the United States Military Occupation of his State, 1861-1865). After the War, he served again from 1872-1883. Stephens served in the State House and Senate, the United States House of Representatives, as a delegate to the Georgia Secession Convention and Provisional Confederate Congress, as Vice-President of the Confederate States, the United States Senate (where, however, he was not allowed to take his seat), the United States House of Representatives again, and finally as Governor of Georgia.

Alexander Hamilton Stephens, also known as "Little Elick" due to his small frame and light weight, was born on February 11, 1812, in what is now Taliaferro County. His mother Margaret (Grier) Stephens died while he was still an infant, and his father Andrew Baskins Stephens died in 1826, when Alexander was 14. At 17 years of age, Stephens entered Franklin College (now known as the University of Georgia) and roomed with famed American surgeon and pharmacist Crawford Williamson Long. In 1832 Stephens graduated first in his class, then went on to teach school for two years before being admitted to the Bar in Crawfordville, Georgia, in 1834.

In 1836 Stephens was elected to the Georgia House of Representatives at the age of 24. The young man made history by not only helping to charter the Western and Atlantic Railroad as State owned, but for supporting the education of women. And it was Stephens who backed the chartering of Georgia Female College (Wesleyan College, the world's oldest women's college) in Macon, Georgia, in 1836. He served in the State Senate from 1840 until 1842.

He then ran for a seat in the United States House of Representatives as a Whig and won. He served in the U.S. Congress until 1859, then retired. During his tenure, he switched from the Whig Party to the Democratic Party, voted for the annexation of Texas, and opposed the War with Mexico. He supported the Compromise of 1850 with his good friend from Georgia, Robert Augustus Toombs.

Stephens was a Unionist and a strong supporter of States Rights. He was chosen to represent his county at the Georgia Secession Convention in Milledgeville, Georgia, which met on January 16, 1861. Even though he knew Georgia had the constitutional right to withdraw from the United States, he spoke against it. While opposing secession as a remedy, he believed it was a constitutional right that could be used as a last resort. What a sight it would have been to see Stephens and his best friend Toombs debating over whether or not their beloved State should secede. After the vote for secession went to the majority, Stephens pledged to support the New Republic of Georgia with his "life, fortune and his sacred honour."

Stephens served as a delegate to the convention in Montgomery, Alabama, and helped form the Confederacy's government, making him, as Mr. Seabrook calls him, one of the "Confederate Founding Fathers." Stephens asked that the new Confederate Constitution be based on the United States Constitution of 1787, with some minor changes. He had hoped to be chosen as this country's first Chief Executive Officer, but accepted the position as Vice President instead. Jefferson Davis and Alexander H. Stephens represented the views of the Southern people and they worked well together; yet, as time went on they began to disagree on several important issues. Due to Stephens' cultivated character, he offered no embarrassing opposition to the policies of the Davis administration; however, he showed that he would not compromise his convictions by refusing to attend various governmental events and functions. When he was not in Richmond on official duty, he could be found at his home "Liberty Hall" in Taliaferro County.

In the summer of 1863 Stephens sought to arrange a prisoners of war exchange program with the United States Government, but was refused. The reason? President Lincoln would not work with someone from a government he did not recognize as legitimate.

On February 3, 1865, Stephens, along with Assistant Secretary of War John A. Campbell and C.S. Senator Robert M. T. Hunter, met with Lincoln and William Henry Seward at the Hampton Roads Conference. The discussion centered around Union preservation versus Confederate independence, with one of the topics being Lincoln's "military measure," the Emancipation Proclamation. During the discussion, the upcoming Thirteenth Amendment was mentioned. Lincoln showed little interest in it, and instead told the Confederate commissioners that if the Southern States came back into the Union, for all he cared they could vote against the amendment and continue practicing slavery. Here the South had a great opportunity to rejoin the Union, defeat the Thirteenth Amendment, and preserve slavery. She did not, however, for the Southern people's main interest was, and always had been, their constitutional independence. Had it just been about slavery, they would have accepted Lincoln's offer. (The only good thing to come out of the meeting was, at Stephens' request, the release of his nephew, Captain John Alexander Stephens, who was being held at Camp Chase, Ohio.)

After the failed conference, Stephens returned to Richmond for a short time, then left for "Liberty Hall" on February 9th. He remained at "Liberty Hall" until his arrest by United States Troops on May 11, 1865. It was in Augusta, Georgia, that future U.S. President Woodrow Wilson witnessed both Davis and Stephens under heavy Federal Guard, walking together to catch their transport to Savannah, Georgia. From there, Stephens was sent to prison at Fort Warren in Boston Harbour—without charge or Writ of *Habeas Corpus*. He was released five months later, on October 13, 1865. During his incarceration, he kept a diary (now titled *Recollections of Alexander H. Stephens*) about his experiences during captivity. Upon his release he returned to "Liberty Hall," where he helped Georgia rebuild herself during "Reconstruction."

In 1866 Stephens was selected by the Georgia General Assembly to represent Georgia in the United States Senate. This position of honour was refused to him by the Radical Republicans who controlled the U.S. Senate at the time. One of the reasons Georgia chose Stephens was because of his Unionist views before the War, which they believed would now help Georgia forge a smooth transition back into the Union.

After his denial to sit in the U.S. Senate, Stephens began writing two of his greatest works: *A Constitutional View of the Late War Between the States* (he coined the phrase), and *History of the United States*. Mr. Seabrook has kindly provided excerpts from both of these books.

Another important event that transpired during this time, and probably the one most overlooked, is Stephens' testimony before the Reconstruction Committee. Here he asserted that as Georgia had complied with all that the U.S. had asked her to do, the sooner she was back in the Union the better.

In 1872 the Georgia General Assembly chose General John Brown Gordon over Stephens as their representative in the U.S. Senate. Later that year Stephens was elected to the U.S. House of Representatives and served from 1873 until he resigned on November 4, 1882. He then served as Governor of Georgia until his untimely death in Atlanta on Sunday, March 4, 1883, at the age of 71. After his interment at Atlanta's Oakland Cemetery, he was laid to rest in his front yard at "Liberty Hall."

Stephens' legacy lives on to this day. "Liberty Hall" is now a part of the Alexander H. Stephens State Historic Park. There are streets, roads, schools and even a county named after him. He has the distinction of being one of only two people to represent Georgia in Statutory Hall, located in the U.S. Capitol in Washington D.C. Perhaps the words inscribed on his monument above his grave say it best:

> "I am afraid of nothing on the earth, or above the earth, or under the earth, except to do wrong—The path of duty I shall ever endeavor to travel, 'fearing no evil' and dreading no consequences."

I, along with Mr. Seabrook and thousands of others, believe that Alexander Hamilton Stephens was a great American patriot who deserves to be remembered and whose life should be celebrated. By providing relevant examples of the Confederate Vice-President's writings and speeches—many of them unknown to the general public—Mr. Seabrook's massive work, *The Alexander H. Stephens Reader*, is a unique, timely, and much needed contribution to Southern literature that will be valued for generations to come. I am honored to be a part of it.

Charles Kelly Barrow, SCV
Griffin, Spalding County, Georgia, USA
January 2013

Mr. Barrow is Lieutenant Commander-in-Chief of the Sons of Confederate Veterans, and the author of the following popular books: *Black Confederates*, *Black Southerners in Confederate Armies*, and *Georgia's Confederate Counties*.

SECTION 1

LETTERS, SPEECHES, RECOLLECTIONS, TESTIMONY, REVIEWERS, & THE HISTORY

1836-1881

1

Private & Public Letters
1836-1881

Though Stephens wrote untold numbers of personal and public letters, many have not survived. Those that have are notable for their length, passion, clarity, forcefulness, and descriptiveness. Strangely, quite unlike fellow Southerners Robert E. Lee and Stonewall Jackson, Stephens seems to have seldom written to family relations, and having never married, he had no wife or children to correspond with. Indeed, nearly all of his surviving epistles are addressed to political colleagues, many of whom he counted as his closest friends. One exception stands out: his younger half-brother Linton Stephens, who Alexander greatly admired and with whom he forged a powerful lifelong relationship until Linton's death in 1872.

―――※※※―――

In 1836, in one of Stephens earliest known letters, the future Confederate vice president wrote the following to his friend Dr. Thomas Foster of Crawfordville, Georgia. Stephens had recently entered the halls of the Georgia state legislature:

☞ "I have, since I came here, come to the conclusion that words are—if you please—moral instruments capable of effecting much, when properly applied and directed. And it is altogether useless, at any and all times to talk, without having in view some object to effect. In legislating in Georgia, it is waste of breath for a man to talk about Greece and Rome, Scipio and Hannibal, Tyre and Carthage, or any of that learned sort of lore. If one indulges much in it, he is soon looked upon as a fool, speaking in an 'unknown tongue,' and very properly so too. Eloquence, true eloquence, is certainly in some degree an art; but in nothing more than in selecting and fitting the matter to the time, place, and circumstances. The whole generation of our young orators, instead of reading Blair for rules, Scott and Addison for figures, and [Lord] Byron and [William] Shakespeare for quotations, had better be studying their subject, and thinking to whom they are going to present it, and how they will most probably engage attention, and produce conviction in the minds of those to whom it is presented. Success in producing conviction is the object of oratory."[40]

Stephens wrote this letter to the prominent Sparta, Georgia, attorney James Thomas, whose daughter Emmaline would later (in 1852) marry Stephens' half-brother Linton Stephens. The letter is dated May 17, 1844:

☛ "Washington, D.C., May 17,1844: Dear Thomas, Your favour from Savannah was duly received yesterday and I feel greatly obliged to you for it. I was not unapprised of the movements of the Locos [Democrats] at home upon the new issue got up by Captain Tyler, nor was I at all surprised at it, as I remarked in the House. So soon as the late tariff bill 'humbug' was disposed of I had no doubt as a party, like most men when publicly condemned in the last court, they would in mass cut out for Texas! And so it seems what I predicted as a result has come to pass. But it will avail them nothing. Mr. [John] Tyler may consider that the people of this country are as much lost to all sense of national honor as he is of personal, and that they place no higher estimation upon good faith than he does, but he will find himself mistaken and will be brought to see that they do not look upon breach of faith, meanness and perfidy in the same light that he does. I wish I had time to write you a full letter upon this subject but I have not. Suffice it to say that the whole annexation project is a miserable political humbug got up as a ruse to divide and distract the Whig party at the South, or peradventure with even an ulterior view—that is the dissolution of the present Confederacy [as the United States was then referred to]. That is not yet quite free from disguise but I only believe it lies near Mr. [John C.] Calhoun's heart. And as for Tyler, he would willingly destroy a country which he has [word illegible] deceived and betrayed when he is satisfied that he can no longer be its chief ruler. He and Calhoun both know that the Senate would never prove themselves so lost to all sense of national honor and good faith as to ratify their treaty. This they know well. As for Tyler I do not know but he fool-like did think that perhaps others had as little regard for these qualities as himself and had as little abhorrence for meanness and perfidy as himself. But Calhoun knew better. It is all a trick—one of his desperate moves or strokes to produce dissention in the country for his own personal aggrandizement. But as I said, he will not succeed. [Martin] Van Buren will be nominated at Baltimore, a kind of [schism?] will ensue and the dissenters will run a Texas man for the South and Van Buren will run at the North, and the whole for the purpose if possible of driving the election to the House where they know Van Buren will be elected. For it is now the general belief that without some such trick [Henry] Clay's election is inevitable. So far as Tyler is concerned in the project it has been for his own aggrandizement. So far as Calhoun is concerned it has been done to [set?] up a Southern party. So far as the Locos are concerned—I mean by them the old Simon pures, it has been to distract the Whigs, upon the old principle 'divide and conquer.' But again I say it will not succeed. When the people of Georgia see all these facts and know everything relating to the treaty it will be by all sensible men of all parties I think universally condemned. But I have not time to give you details. You may have seen it said in the papers that he (Tyler) has actually called out our military forces and stationed two regiments on the confines of Texas and several sail in the Gulph—a virtual declaration of war—without consulting Congress. This is true, and a greater outrage upon the constitution has never been committed by any President. I should not be surprised if he is impeached. P.S. I have not got time to look over the [above?] to see if spelling is correct. Marginal P.S. [Democratic Congressman Absalom H.] Chappell is completely off, and every Whig should know it."[41]

Stephens to Georgia statesman and military officer Howell Cobb, February 27, 1845:
☛ "Steamboat [from] Wilmington [North Carolina] (near Charleston Harbour, Thursday Morning), 27 Feb. 1845. Dear Cobb, According to promise I drop you a line, though I write on the boat where I am rocked and shaken so I fear you can not read it. I have had a fine and comfortable travel so far, and expect soon to take leave of the sea and its dangers. I never had a smoother passage from Wilmington to Charleston [South Carolina]. The wind was perfectly calm and the sea at rest. Touching the stages, I ascertained that there is a daily line from Raleigh to Columbia—two horse, I was told. It leaves Raleigh at 2 p.m., and after being out two nights arrives at Columbia at 8 p.m. the third night. Another line leaves the Wilmington railroad at the breakfast house Warsaw, for Fayetteville and Columbia. That is the best route, and it gives you an opportunity of judging of the probable state of the weather—as you can pay to that place, and then if the weather threatens to be bad you can take that line. It leaves the railroad 45 miles from Wilmington; is a four horse coach, but did not look to me as if it could carry more than six. It is a small and slender looking North Carolina affair. But I can say no more."[42]

Stephens to Kentucky statesman John J. Crittenden, September 26, 1848:
☛ "Crawfordville, Ga., 26, Sep. 1848. Dear Sir: I reached home a few days ago and found your kind letter, for which I felt truly obliged to you. You have doubtless heard of the occurrence [in which Stephens was physically assaulted

and injured] which put me out of the canvass in this [state] for three weeks past and upwards. I am now recovering slowly. My right hand is still in bad condition and I fear I shall never be able to use it as formerly. I now can only scribble with my left hand—but enough of this. Our election for Congress comes off next Monday and trust we shall send you a good report. The Democrats [Conservatives] however are making a most desperate fight. But I think you may rely on Georgia for [Zachary] Taylor. It is true I can't form so satisfactory an opinion as if I had been in the field for the last few weeks. But I know we were gaining fast when I was amongst them. The whole campaign since then has rested entirely upon the shoulders of Mr. [Robert A.] Toombs, and I assure you he has done gallant service. The real [Henry] Clay men here as elsewhere I believe are doing nothing for Taylor, while many of them are openly in opposition; but I think we shall triumph notwithstanding.

"We were greatly rejoiced to hear of your great triumph in Kentucky. The Locos in Congress were making extravagant brags just before the election but I would not permit myself even to feel apprehension. Remember me kindly to Mrs. Crittenden [Maria K. Todd]. I cannot say more now and I fear that you cannot read what I have said."[43]

Stephens to James Thomas, February 13, 1850:
☛ "House Of Reps., Washington, D.C., Feb. 13, 1850. Dear Thomas, ... We have no news here at this time of interest or importance. What is to be the result of the slavery question I can not tell. I suppose however that some adjustment of it will be made—some adjustment of it for the present. But when I look to the future and consider the causes of the existing sectional discontent, their extent and nature I must confess that I see very little prospect of future peace and quiet in the public mind upon this subject. Whether a separation of the union and the organization and establishment of a Southern Confederacy would give final and ultimate security to the form of society as it exists with us, I am not prepared to say. I have no doubt if we had unity, virtue, intelligence and patriotism in all our councils, such an experiment might succeed. But unfortunately for our country at this time, we have if I am not mistaken too much demagogism and too little statesmanship. Most of the fighting resolves of our Legislatures I fear are nothing but gasconade [bluster] put forth by partisan leaders for partisan effect. If our people really mean to fight, if their minds are made up upon this alternative, they should say so, and they should make the declaration in Congress too plain to admit of equivocal readings. But if they do not intend to resort to the *ultima ratio* of all nations they should cease in that sort of braggadocio which will in end result in their own degradation. But enough. I did not commence this with any intention of giving

you a dissertation on the present crisis of public affairs."⁴⁴

Stephens to Howell Cobb, June 23, 1851:
☛ "Crawfordville, Ga., June 23, 1851. I have been extremely ill—but am now better—am able to sit up, that is all. I cannot walk out yet. I see you are going to have a bitter and heated contest. You must be wide awake with all your wits at command from the word go. No time is to be lost. You have an adroit and wily competitor. Take the stump and keep it on all suitable occasions. . . .

"In reference to the calling out of the militia, etc., maintain the right of the President and duty of the President to execute the law against all factious opposition whether in Mass. or S.C. Maintain the power to execute the fugitive slave law at the North and the power to execute the Revenue or any other law against any lawless opposition in S.C. Turn the whole force of this upon the revolutionary movement in S.C., and urge all good citizens who value law and order and the rights of liberty and property to stand by the supremacy of the law. This is the life and soul of a republic. Warn the good people of Georgia to beware of revolution—refer to France—and plant yourself against the factionists of S.C., upon the constitution of the country. The right of secession treat as an abstract question. It is but a right to change the Govt., a right of revolution, and maintain that no just cause for the exercise of such right exists. And keep the main point prominent, that the only question now is whether we should go into revolution or not. S.C. is for it. This is the point to keep prominent. I wish I had strength to write more or to give you my views more at large. Our central committee must be at work soon. There never was a more bitter contest I expect in our state than will be this fall. Our opponents will leave no stone unturned, no lie untold, and no dollar they can raise unspent. You must be up and awake."⁴⁵

Stephens to his half-brother Linton Stephens, December 10, 1851:
☛ "Washington, D.C., 10ᵗʰ December, 1851. Dear Brother, Your two letters, one of the 5ᵗʰ and the other of the 6ᵗʰ inst. were received this morning. In reply to your inquiries about the state of things here I can only say that very much to my surprise and regret I am bound to believe that a coalition has been entered into between the Southern Rights men and the Free-Soilers under the name and style of a reorganization of the Democratic party. The failure to pass the Compromise resolutions in the so-called Democratic caucus was owing to this union of opposing elements. . . .

"At this time I have no doubt that it is the determination of the small fry now at Washington, who have the control of the Democratic party North and

South, to form a perfect coalition between the two extreme wings of their respective divisions, whose ruling spirit will be, as [John C.] Calhoun said, 'the cohesive principle of public plunder.' The spoils is all they go for. But I cannot believe that the country is prepared for such corruption. I have no doubt that Southern Rights men are—such as figured in the late meeting in Milledgeville—and even the S.C. chivalry; but I do not believe that the body of our people are prepared to sanction such a foul conspiracy against their rights, interests, purposes and honor. We are now in a great crisis in our history. If the South, if Georgia, succumbs to this movement and gives in her adhesion, we are gone people. Now is the time for firmness. We must teach the tricksters that the destinies of this great country are not to be bartered away in this manner. The Whig party, so-called, put itself right in caucus. That was a great point. But there will be no national Whig convention. And I trust there will be no Whig organization kept up. The true men must get together, and act together without any regard to past party names. The contest will be between the coalitionists and the Spoilsmen [Liberals] on the one hand, and the Conservatives or Constitutional Union men on the other. It is the object here to drive Georgia into a division on the old lines. It is thought that she cannot maintain her present position. As a part of this scheme it is the earnest desire of the tricksters to keep up the Whig party. . . .

"Let the world know that we stand upon our own platform and adhere to our own principles, through weal through woe, now and forever. Georgia saved the Union last fall, and she may be the instrument in saving it again by compelling a purgation of National parties. The Whig party has already undergone the process. It remains only now to compel the Democratic organization to pass through the same or a similar lustration. Without this her work will be but half done, and the mission of the Constitutional Union party be only half accomplished."[46]

Stephens to James Thomas, February 22, 1853. This particular excerpt concerns Franklin Pierce, a Yankee Democrat (Conservative) who had been elected U.S. president a few months earlier on November 2, 1852:

☞ "Washington, D.C., Feb. 22, 1853. . . . Mr. [Franklin] Pierce is here. He keeps secluded. I am much pleased with [his] conduct so far. How I shall like his cabinet I do not know until I know who it is. But I fear he has not the nerve to stand up against the great Democratic party clamour of those who force themselves upon him. If he were a man of stern nature and principle he might do a great service to his country. I hope for the best but fear the worst. I shall give him a fair trial. I shall not factiously oppose him."[47]

Stephens to W. W. Burwell, May 7, 1854:
☛ "Washington, D.C., May 7, 1854. Dear Sir: Your letter was duly received and I feel obliged to you for it. Your lick on [Thomas H.] Benton was appropriate and was well calculated to lessen the effect of his speech with his old party. His speech by the by is very valuable in many points. Tomorrow I think we shall get the Nebraska bill up in committee. The contest will be hard and the vote close, but we have the count. How the result will be I cannot positively state. Any thing that you may feel disposed to say favourable to the measure will be very timely this week. Perhaps Franklin [Pierce] might be induced not to vote against the bill if he should be assured that the sentiments of the people of Maryland were for it. I feel a deep interest in the success of the measure as a Southern man. The issue presented by the bill is one which in the main has arrayed the free-soilers in solid ranks against the South. The moral effect of the victory on our side will have a permanent effect upon the public mind, whether any positive advantages accrue by way of the actual extension of slavery or not."[48]

Stephens to Judge Thomas W. Thomas, May 5, 1855. Thomas had written to Stephens asking him if the rumors were true that he was about to resign from Congress due to the fact that many of his friends had "gone into the secret order called Know-Nothings":
☛ "Crawfordville, Ga., 9th May, 1855. Dear Sir:—Your letter of the 5th inst. was received some days ago, and should have been answered much earlier, but for my absence from home. The rumor you mention in relation to my candidacy for re-election to Congress, is true. I have stated, and repeated on various occasions, that I was not, and did not expect to be, a candidate—the same I now say to you. The reason of this declaration on my part, was the fact, that large numbers of our old political friends seemed to be entering into new combinations with new objects, purposes, and principles of which I was not informed, and never could be according to the rules of their action and the opinions I entertain. Hence my conclusion that they had no further use for me as their representative; for I presumed they knew enough of me to be assured if they had any secret aims or objects to accomplish that they never could get my consent, even if they desired it, to become a dumb instrument to execute such a purpose. I certainly never did, and never shall, go before the people as a candidate for their suffrages with my principles in my pocket. It has been the pride of my life, heretofore, not only to make known fully and freely my sentiments upon all questions of public policy, but in vindication of those sentiments thus avowed, to meet any antagonists arrayed against them, in open and manly strife—'face to face and toe to toe.' From this rule of action by which I have up to this time been governed, I shall never depart. But you ask

me what are my opinions and views of this new party called 'Know-Nothings,' with a request that you be permitted to publish them. My opinions and views thus solicited, shall be given most cheerfully, and as fully and clearly as my time, under the pressure of business, will allow. You can do with them as you please—publish them or not, as you like. They are the views of a private citizen. I am at present, to all intents and purposes whatsoever, literally one of the people. I hold no office nor seek any, and as one of the people I shall speak to you and them on this, and on all occasions, with that frankness and independence which it becomes a freeman to bear towards his fellows. And in giving my views of 'Know-Nothingism,' I most truly say, that I really 'know nothing' about the principles, aims or objects of the party I am about to speak of—they are all kept secret—being communicated and made known only to the initiated, and not to these until after being first duly pledged and sworn. This, to me, is a very great objection to the whole organization. All political principles, which are sought to be carried out in legislation by any body or set of men in a republic, in my opinion ought to be openly avowed and publicly proclaimed. Truth never shuns the light nor shrinks from investigation—or at least it ought never to do it. Hiding places, or secret coverts, are natural resorts for error. It is, therefore, a circumstance quite sufficient to excite suspicion against the truth to see it pursuing such a course. And in republics, where free discussion and full investigation by a virtuous and intelligent people is allowed, there never can be any just grounds to fear any danger even from the greatest errors either in religion or politics. All questions, therefore, relating to the government of a free people, ought to be made known, clearly understood, fully discussed, and understandingly acted upon. Indeed, I do not believe that a republican government can last long, where this is not the case. In my opinion, no man is fit to represent a free people who has any private or secret objects, or aims, that he does not openly avow, or who is not ready and willing, at all times, when required or asked, candidly and truthfully, to proclaim to the assembled multitude not only his principles, but his views and sentiments upon all questions that may come before him in his representative capacity. It was on this basis that representative government was founded, and on this alone can it be maintained in purity and safety. And if any secret party shall ever be so far successful in this country as to bring the government in all its departments and functions under the baneful influence of its control and power, political ruin will inevitably ensue. No truth in politics can be more easily and firmly established, either by reason or from history, upon principle or authority, than this. These are my opinions candidly expressed.

"I know that many good and true men in Georgia differ from me in this particular—thousands of them, I doubt not, have joined this secret order with good intentions. Some of them have told me so, and I do not question their motives. And thousands more will, perhaps, do it with the same intentions and motives. Should it be a short-lived affair, no harm will, or may come of it. But let it succeed—let it carry all the elections, State and federal—let the natural and inevitable laws of its own organism be once fully developed—and the country will go by the board. It will go as France did. The first Jacobin club was organized in Paris on the 6th November, 1789, under the alluring name of 'the Friends of the Constitution,' quite as specious as that we now hear of 'Americans shall rule America.' Many of the best men and truest patriots in Paris joined it—and thousands of the same sort of men joined the affiliated clubs afterward—little dreaming of the deadly fangs of that viper they were nurturing in their bosoms. Many of these very men afterward went to the guillotine, by orders passed secretly in these very clubs. All legislation was settled in the clubs—members of the national assembly and convention, all of them, or most of them, were members of the clubs, for they could not otherwise be elected. And after the question was settled in the clubs, the members next day went to the nominal halls of legislation nothing but trembling automatons, to register the edicts of the 'order,' though it were to behead a monarch, or to cause the blood of the best of their own number to flow beneath the stroke of the axe. Is history of no use? Or do our people vainly imagine that Americans would not do as the French did under like circumstances? 'Is thy servant a dog that he should do this thing?' said the haughty, self-confident Hazael [the Aramaean king of the Bible]. Yet, he did all that he had been told that he would do. 'Let him that thinketh he standeth take heed lest he fall.' Human nature is the same compound of weak frailties and erring passions everywhere. Of these clubs in France, an elegant writer has said:

> 'From all other scourges which had afflicted mankind, in every age and in every nation, there had been some temporary refuge, some shelter until the storm might pass. During the heathenism of antiquity, and the barbarism of the middle ages, the temple of a god or the shrine of a saint, afforded a refuge from despotic fury or popular rage. But French Jacobins, whether native or adopted, treated with equal scorn, the sentiments of religion and the feeling of humanity; and all that man had gathered from his experience upon earth, and the revelations he hoped had been made him from the sky, to bless and adorn his mortal existence, and elevate his soul with immortal aspirations, were spurned as imposture by these fell destroyers. They would have depraved man from his humanity, as they attempted to decree God out of his universe. Not contented with France as subject for their ruthless experiments—Europe itself being too narrow for their exploits, they send their propagandists to the new world, with designs about as charitable as those with which Satan entered Eden.'

"This is but a faint picture of some of the scenes enacted by that self-same party, which was at first formed by those who styled themselves 'The Friends of the Constitution.' And where did these 'secret Councils' we now hear of, come from? Not from France, it is true—but from the land of *isms*, where *the people would have gone into anarchy long ago, if it had not been for the conservative influence of the more stable minded men of the South*? And what scene have we lately witnessed in the [ultra Liberal] Massachusetts legislature, where the new political organism has more fully developed itself than anywhere else. What are its fruits there? Under the name of 'The American Party,' they have armed themselves against the constitution of our common country which they were sworn to support—with every member of the Legislature, I believe, save eight, belonging to 'the order,' they have, by an overwhelming majority vote, deposed Judge [Edward G.] Loring, for nothing but the discharge of his official duty, in issuing a warrant as United States commissioner, to cause the arrest of the fugitive slave, [Anthony] Burns. In reviewing this most unheard-of outrage upon the constitution, the *National Intelligencer*, at Washington, says it 'shudders for the judiciary.' And if they go on as they have, well may the country 'shudder,' not only for the judiciary, but for every thing else we hold most sacred. 'If these things be done in the green tree, what may you expect in the dry.' [Emphasis added, L.S.]

"But I have been anticipating somewhat. I was on the preliminary question; that is, the secrecy which lies at the foundation of the party—that atmosphere of darkness in which 'it lives, and moves, and has its being,' and without which probably it could not exist. I do not, however, intend to stop with that. I will go further, and give, now, my opinions upon those questions which are said to be within the range of its secret objects and aims. The principles, as published, (or those principles which are attributed to the order, though no body as an organized party avow them,) have, as I understand them, two leading ideas, and two only. These are a proscription by an exclusion from office of all Catholics as a class; and a proscription of all persons of foreign birth as a class; the latter to be accomplished not only by an exclusion from office of all foreigners who are now citizens by naturalization, but to be more effectually carried out, by an abrogation of the naturalization law for the future, or such an amendment as would be virtually tantamount to it. These, as we are told, are the great ostensible objects for all this machinery—these oaths—pledges—secret signs—equivocations—denials, and what not. And what I have to say of them, is, that if these in deed and in truth be the principles thus attempted to be carried out, then I am opposed to both of them, openly and unqualifiedly.

"I am opposed to them 'in a double aspect,' both as a basis of party organization, and upon their merits as questions of public policy. As the basis of party organization, they are founded upon the very erroneous principle of looking, not to how the country shall be governed, but who shall hold the offices—not to whether we shall have wise and wholesome laws, but who shall 'rule us,' though they may bring ruin with their rule. Upon this principle, [Lyman] Trumbull, who defeated General [James] Shields for the Senate in Illinois, can be as good a 'Know-Nothing' as any man in the late 'Macon council,' though he may vote, as he doubtless will, to repeal the Fugitive Slave law, and against the admission of any slave State in the Union; while Shields, who has ever stood by the constitution, must be rejected by southern men because he was not born in the country [Shields was born in Tyrone, Ireland]. Upon this principle, a Boston atheist, who denies the inspiration of the Bible, because it sanctions slavery, is to be sustained by Georgia 'Know-Nothings' in preference to me, barely because I will not 'bow the knee to Baal,' this false political god they have set up. The only correct basis of party organization is an agreement amongst those who enter into it upon the paramount question of the day. And no party can last long without bringing disaster and ruin in its train, founded upon any other principle. The old national whig party tried the experiment, when there were radical differences of opinion on such questions, and went to pieces. The national democratic party are now trying a similar experiment, and are experiencing a similar fate. This is what is the matter with it. Its vital functions are deranged—hence that disease which now afflicts it worse than the 'dry rot.' And what we of the South now should do, is not to go into any 'Know-Nothing' mummery or mischief, as it may be, but to stand firmly by those men at the North who are true to the constitution and the Union, without regard either to their birth-place or religion. The question we should consider is not simply who 'shall rule America,' but who will vote for such measures as will best promote the interests of America, and with that the interests of mankind.

"But to pass to the other view of these principles—that is, the consideration of them as questions of public policy. With me, they both stand in no better light in this aspect than they do in the other. The first assumes temporal jurisdiction in '*forum conscientiæ*' [Latin: "forum of conscience"]—to which I am quite as much opposed as I am to the spiritual powers controlling the temporal. One is as bad as the other—both are bad. I am utterly opposed to mingling religion with politics in any way whatever; and especially am I opposed to making it a test in qualifications for civil office. Religion is a matter between a man and his Creator, with which governments should have nothing to do. In this country the constitution guarantees to every citizen the right to entertain whatever creed he pleases, or no creed at all if he is so inclined; and no other man has a right to pry into his conscience to inquire what he believes or what he does not believe. As a citizen and as a member of society, he is to be judged by his acts, and not by his creed. A Catholic, therefore, in our country, and in all countries, ought, as all other citizens, to be permitted to stand or fall in public favor and estimation upon his own individual merit. 'Every tub should stand upon its own bottom.'

"But I think of all the Christian denominations in the United States, the Catholics are the last that southern people should join in attempting to put under the ban of civil proscription. For as a church they have never warred against us or our peculiar institutions. No man can say as much of New England Baptists, Presbyterians, or Methodists; the long roll of abolition petitions with which Congress has been so much excited and agitated for years past, come not from the Catholics; their pulpits at the north are not desecrated every Sabbath with anathemas against slavery. And of the three thousand New England clergymen who sent the anti-Nebraska memorial to the Senate last year, not one was a Catholic, as I have been informed and believe. Why then should we southern men join the Puritans of the North to proscribe from office the Catholics on account of their religion? Let them and their religion be as bad as they can be, or as their accusers say they are, they cannot be worse than these same puritanical accusers, who started this persecution against them, say that we are. They say we are going to perdition for the enormous sin of holding slaves. The Pope [Pius IX], with all his followers, cannot, I suppose, even in their judgment, be going to a worse place for holding what they consider the monstrous absurdity of 'immaculate conception.' And, for my part, I would about as soon risk my chance for heaven with him, and his crowd too, as with those self-righteous hypocrites who deal out fire and brimstone so liberally upon our heads. At any rate, I have no hesitancy in declaring that I should much sooner risk my civil rights with the American Catholics, whom they are attempting to drive from office, than with them. But, sir, I am opposed to this proscription upon principle. If it is once begun, there is no telling where it will end. When faction once tastes the blood of a victim, it seldom ceases its ravages among the fold so long as a single remaining one, be the number at first ever so great, is left surviving. It was to guard against any such consequences as would certainly ensue in this country, if this effort at proscription of this sect of religionists should be successful, that wise provision to which I have alluded, was put in the fundamental law of the Union. And to maintain it intact, in letter and spirit with steadfastness at this time, I hold to be a most solemn public duty.

"And now, as to the other idea—the proscription of foreigners—and more particularly that view of it which looks to the denial of citizenship to all those who may hereafter seek a home in this country, and choose to cast their lots and destinies with us. This is a favorite idea with many who have not thought of its effects, or reflected much upon its consequences. The abrogation of the naturalization laws would not stop immigration, nor would the extension of the term of probation, to the period of twenty-one years, do it. This current of migration from east to west, this exodus of the excess of population from the old to the new world, which commenced with the settlement of this continent by Europeans, would still go on. And what would be the effect, even under the most modified form of the proposed measure—that is of an extension of the period from five to twenty-one years, before citizenship should be granted? At the end of the first twenty-one years from the commencement of the operation of the law, we should have several millions of people in our midst—men of our own race—occupying the unenviable position of being a 'degraded caste' in society, a species of serfs without the just franchise of a freeman or the needful protection due to a slave. This would be at war with all my ideas of American republicanism as I have been taught them, and gloried in them from youth up. If there be danger now to our institutions, (as some seem to imagine, but which I am far from feeling or believing,) from foreigners as a class, would not the danger be greatly enhanced by the proposed remedy? Now, it is true, they are made to bear their share of the burthens [burdens] of government, but are also permitted, after a residence of five years, and taking an oath to support the constitution, to enjoy their just participation in the privileges, honors, and immunities which it secures. Would they be less likely to be attached to the government and its principles under the operation of the present system, than they would be under the proposed one which would treat them as not much better than outcasts and outlaws? All writers of note, from the earliest to the latest, who have treated upon the elements and component parts, or members of communities and States, have pointed this out as a source of real danger—that is, having a large number of the same race not only aliens by birth, but aliens in heart and feeling in the bosom of society.

"Such was, to a great extent, the condition of the Helots in Greece—men of the same race placed in an inferior position, and forming within themselves a degraded class. I wish to see no such state of things in this country. With us at the South, it is true we have a 'degraded caste,' but it is of a race fitted by nature for their subordinate position. The negro, with us, fills that place in society and under our system of civilization for which he was designed by nature. No training can fit him for either social or political equality with his superiors; at least history furnishes us with no instance of the kind; nor does the negro with us feel any degradation in his position, because it is his natural place. But such would be the case with men of the same race and coming from the same stock as ourselves. And what appears not a little strange and singular to me in considering this late movement is, that if it did not originate with, yet it is now so generally and zealously favored by so many of those men at the North who have expended so much of their misguided philanthropy in behalf of our slaves. They have been endeavoring for years to elevate the African to equality, socially and politically, with the white man. And now, they are moving heaven and earth to degrade the white man to a condition lower than that held by the negro in the South. The Massachusetts 'Know-Nothing' Legislature passed a bill lately to amend their constitution, so as to exclude from the polls in that State hereafter all naturalized citizens, from whatever nation they may come; and yet they will allow a runaway negro slave from the South the same right to vote that they give to their own native born sons! They thus exhibit the strange paradox of warring against their own race—their own blood—even their own 'kith and kin,' it may be, while they are vainly and fanatically endeavoring to reverse the order of nature, by making the black man equal to the white. Shall we second them in any such movement? Shall we even countenance them so far as to bear the same name—to say nothing of the same pledges, pass-words, signs and symbols? Shall we affiliate and unite ourselves under the same banner, with men whose acts show them to be governed by such principles, and to be bent upon such a purpose? This is a question for southern men to consider. Others may do it if they choose; but, I tell you, I never shall; that you may set down as a 'fixed fact'—one of the fixedest of the fixed. I am not at all astonished at the rapid spread of this new sentiment at the North, or, rather, new way of giving embodiment and life to an old sentiment, long cherished by a large class of the northern people, notwithstanding the paradox. It is true[,] 'Know-Nothingism' did not originate, as I understand its origin, with the class I allude to. It commenced with the laborers and men dependent upon capital for work and employment. It sprang from the antagonism of their interests to foreigners seeking like employments, who were under-bidding them in the amount of wages. But money capitalists of that section, the men who hold the land and property in their own hands, wishing to dispense with laborers and employees, whose votes at the polls are equal to their own, seized upon this new way of effecting their old, long-cherished desire—and the more eagerly as they saw that many of the very men whom they have ever dreaded as the insuperable obstacle between them and their purpose had become the willing, though unconscious instruments of carrying that purpose out, which, from the beginning, was a desire to have a votingless population to do their work, and perform all the labor, both in city, town and country, which capital may require. And as certainly as such a law shall be passed, so far from its checking immigration, there will be whole cargoes of people from other countries brought over, and literally bought up in foreign ports, to be brought over in

American ships to supply the market for the labor throughout all the free States of the Union. The African slave trade, if reopened, would not exhibit a worse spectacle in trafficking in human flesh. And those most deluded men of the North who started this thing, and who are now aiding to accomplish the end, may find they have but kindled a flame to consume themselves. The whole *sub stratum* of northern society will soon be filled up with a class who can work, and who, though white cannot vote. This is what the would-be lords of that section have been wanting for a long time. It is a scheme with many of them to get white slaves instead of black ones. No American laborer, or man seeking employment there, who has a vote, need to expect to be retained long when his place can be more cheaply filled by a foreigner who has none. This will be the practical working of the proposed reformation. This is the philosophy of the thing. It is a blow at the ballot box. It is an insidious attack upon general suffrage. In a line with this policy, the 'Know-Nothing' governor of Connecticut [William T. Minor] has already recommended the passage of a law denying the right of voting to all who cannot read and write. And hence the great efforts which are now being made throughout the North, to influence the elections, not only there, but in spending their money in the publication of books and tracts, written by 'nobody knows who,' and scattered broadcast throughout the southern States, to influence elections here by appealing to the worst passions and strongest prejudices of our nature, not omitting those even which bad and wicked men can evoke under the sacred but prostituted name of religion.

"Unfortunately for the country, many evils, which all good men regret and deplore, exist at this time, which have a direct tendency wonderfully to aid and move forward this ill omened crusade. These relate to the appointment of so many foreigners—wholly unfit, not only to minor offices at home, but to represent our country as ministers abroad. And to the great frauds and gross abuses which at present attend the administration of our naturalization laws—these are the evils felt by the whole country, and they ought to be corrected. Not by a proscription of all foreigners, without regard to individual merits; but, in the first place, by so amending the naturalization laws as effectually to check by holding to strict accountability at the polls in our elections and prevent these frauds and abuses, and, in the second place, all those public functionaries, who, either with partisan views or from whatever motive, thus improperly confer office, whether high or low, upon undeserving foreigners, to the exclusion of native-born citizens better qualified to fill them. Another evil now felt, which ought to be remedied, is the flooding, it is said, of some of the cities with paupers and convicts from other countries. These ought all to be unconditionally excluded and prohibited from coming amongst us. There is no reason why we should be the feeders of other nations' paupers, or either the keepers or executioners of their felons—these evils can and ought to be remedied without resorting to an indiscriminate onslaught upon all who by industry, enterprise and merit may choose to better their condition in abandoning the respective dynasties of the old world in which they may have chanced to have been born, and by uniting their energies with ours, may feel a pride in advancing the prosperity, development and progress of a common country not much less dear to them than to us. Against those who thus worthily come, who quit the misruled empires of their 'fatherland,' whose hearts have been fired with the love of our ideas and our institutions, even in distant climes, I would not close the door of admission. But to all such as our fathers did at first, so I would continue most freely and generously to extend a welcome hand. We have, from such a class, nothing to fear. When, in battle or in the walks of civil life, did any such ever prove traitor or recreant to the flag or cause of his country? On what occasion have any such ever proven untrue or disloyal to the constitution?

"I will not say that no foreigner has ever been untrue to the constitution; but, as a class, they certainly have not proven themselves so to be. Indeed, *I know of but one class of people in the United States at this time that I look upon as dangerous to the country. That class are neither foreigners or Catholics—they are those natives born at the North who are disloyal to the constitution of that country which gave them birth, and under whose beneficent institutions they have been reared and nurtured.* Many of them are 'Know-Nothings.' This class of men at the North, of which the Massachusetts, New Hampshire and Connecticut 'Know-Nothing' legislatures are but samples, I consider as our worst enemies. And to put them down, I will join, as political allies now and forever, all true patriots at the North and South, whether native or adopted, Jews or Gentiles. [Emphasis added, L.S.]

"What our Georgia friends, whether whigs or democrats, who have gone into this 'new order,' are really after, or what they intend to do, I cannot imagine. Those of them whom I know, have assured me that their object is reform, both in our State and federal administrations—to put better and truer men in the places of those who now wield authority—that they have no sympathies as party men or otherwise with that class I speak of at the North, that they are for sustaining the Union platform of our State of 1850, and that the mask of secrecy will soon be removed when all will be made public. If these be their objects, and also to check the frauds and correct the abuses in the existing naturalization laws, which I have mentioned, without the indiscriminate proscription of any class of citizens on account of their birthplace or religion, then they will have my co-operation, as I have told them, in every proper and legitimate way, to effect such a reformation—not as a secretly initiated co-worker in the dark for any purpose, but as an open and bold advocate of truth in the light of day. But will they do as they say? Will they throw off the mask? That is the question. Is it possible that they will continue in political party fellowship with their 'worthy brethren' of Massachusetts, Connecticut, New Hampshire, and the entire North? Every one of whom elected to the next Congress is our deadly foe! Do they intend to continue their alliance with these open enemies of our institutions and the constitution of the country under the totally misnamed association of the 'American party,' the very principle upon which it is based being anti-American throughout?

"*True Americanism, as I have learned it, is like true Christianity—disciples in neither are confined to any nation, clime, or soil whatsoever. Americanism is not the product of the soil; it springs not from the land or the ground; it is not of the earth, or earthy; it emanates from the head and the heart; it looks upward, and onward and outward; its life and soul are those grand ideas of government which characterize our institutions, and distinguish us from all other people; and there are no two features in our system which so signally distinguish us from all other nations as free toleration of religion and the doctrine of expatriation—the right of a man to throw off his allegiance to any and every other State, prince or potentate whatsoever, and by naturalization to be incorporated as a citizen into our body politic. Both these principles are specially provided for and firmly established in our constitution.* But these American ideas which were proclaimed in 1789 by our 'sires of 76,' are by their 'sons' at this day derided and scoffed at. We are now told that 'naturalization' is a 'humbug,' and that it is an 'impossibility.' So did not our fathers think. This 'humbug' and 'impossibility' they planted in the constitution; and a vindication of the same principle was one of the causes of our second war of independence. England held that 'naturalization' was an impossible thing. She claimed the allegiance of subjects born within her realm, notwithstanding they had become citizens of this republic by our constitution and laws. She not only claimed their allegiance, but she claimed the right to search our ships upon the high seas, and take from them all such who might be found in them. It was in pursuit of this doctrine of hers—of the right of search for our 'naturalized' citizens—that the Chesapeake was fired into, which was the immediate cause of the war of 1812. Let no man then, barely because he was born in America, presume to be imbued with real and true 'Americanism,' who either ignores the direct and positive obligations of the constitution, or ignores this, one of its most striking characteristics. As well might any unbelieving sinner claim to be one of the faithful—one of the elect even—barely because he was born somewhere within the limits of Christendom. And just as well might the Jacobins, who 'decreed God out of his universe,' have dubbed their club a 'Christian Association,' because they were born on Christian soil. The genuine disciples of 'true Americanism,' like the genuine followers of the Cross, are those whose hearts are warmed and fired—purified, elevated and ennobled by those principles, doctrines and precepts which characterize their respective systems. It is for this reason that a Kamschatkan [a native Siberian], a Briton, a Jew, or a Hindoo, can be as good a Christian as any one born on 'Calvary's brow,' or where the 'Sermon on the Mount' was preached! And for the same reason an Irishman, a Frenchman, a German, or Russian, can be as thoroughly 'American' as if he had been born within the walls of the old Independence Hall itself. Which was the 'true American,' [Benedict] Arnold or [Alexander] Hamilton? The one was a native and the other was an adopted son. But to return. What do our Georgia friends intend to do? Is it not time that they had shown their hand? Do they intend to abandon the Georgia platform, and go over, 'horse, foot and dragoons,' into a political alliance with their open enemies? Is this the course marked out for themselves by any of the gallant old whigs of the 7th and 8th Congressional districts? I trust not, I hope not. But if they do not intend thus to commit themselves, is it not time to take a reckoning and see whither they are drifting? When 'the blind lead the blind' where is the hope of safety? I have been cited to the resolution which, it is said, the late Know-Nothing convention passed in Macon. This, it seems, is the only thing that the 600 delegates could bring forth after a two days' 'labor'—and of it we may well say, 'The mountains have been in labor and a ridiculous mouse is born.' It simply affirms most meekly and submissively what no man south of Mason and Dixon's line for the last thirty-five years would have ventured to deny, without justly subjecting himself to the charge of *incivism*—that is, that 'Congress has no constitutional power to intervene by excluding a new State applying for admission into the Union on the ground that the constitution of such State recognizes slavery.' This is the whole life and soul of it, unless we except the secret blade of Joab which it bears toward Kansas and Nebraska, concealed under a garb. [Emphasis added, L.S.]

"It is well known to all who are informed, that in the organic law of these territories the right of voting, while they remain territories, was given to all who had filed a declaration of intention to become citizens. This was in strict compliance with the usual practice of the government in organizing territories; and under this provision that class of persons are now entitled to vote. Kansas, in two elections under this law, has shown that an overwhelming majority of her people are in favor of slavery. Now, then, when Kansas applies for admission as a slave State, as she doubtless will, a southern 'Know-Nothing,' under this resolution can unite with his 'worthy brethren' at the North, in voting against it, upon the ground that some have voted for a constitution recognizing slavery, who had not been 'naturalized,' but had only declared their intention. For this resolution, in its very heart and core, declares that the right to establish slave institutions 'in the organization of State governments, belongs to the native and naturalized citizens,' excluding those who have only declared their intention. A more insidious attack was never made upon the principles of the Kansas and Nebraska bill. And this is to be the plank on which northern and southern 'Know-Nothings' are to stand in the rejection of Kansas. But the main objection is to the resolution. Why did it stop with a simple denial of the power of Congress to reject a State on account of slavery? Particularly when it had opened the door for the rejection of Kansas on other grounds by way of pretext. Why did it not plant itself upon the principles of the Georgia resolutions of 1850, and say what ought to be done in case of the rejection of a State by Congress because of slavery? So far from this it does not even affirm that such rejection by their 'worthy brethren' of the North would be sufficient cause for severing their party affiliation with them for it?

"Again, I would say not only to the old whigs of the 7th and 8th Congressional districts, but to all true Georgians, whether whigs or democrats, union men or fire-eaters, whither are you drifting? Will you not pause and reflect? Are we about to witness in this insane cry against foreigners and Catholics a fulfilment of the ancient Latin proverb: 'Whom the gods intend to destroy they first make mad!' The times are indeed portentous of evil. The political horizon is shrouded in darkness. No man knows whom he meets, whether he be friend or foe, except those who have the dim glare of the covered light which their secret signs impart. And how long this will be a protection even to them, is by no means certain. They have already made truth and veracity almost a byword and a reproach. When truth loses caste with any people—is no longer considered as a virtue—and its daily and hourly violation are looked upon with no concern but a jeer or a laugh, it requires very little forecast to see what will very soon be the character of that people. But, sir, come what may, I shall pursue that course which a sense of duty demands of me. While I hope for the best, I shall be prepared for the worst; and if the 'worst comes to the worst,' as it may, I shall, in common with my fellow-citizens, bear with patience my part of the common ills. They will affect me quite as little as any other citizen, for I have but little at stake; and so far as my public position and character are concerned, I shall enjoy that consolation which is to be derived from a precept taught me in early life, and which I shall ever cherish and treasure, whatever fortune betides me . . . Yours, most respectfully, Alexander H. Stephens."[49]

Stephens to Thomas W. Thomas, December 12, 1856. While having a particularly venomous debate with Know-Nothing politician Benjamin H. Hill during the 1856 presidential election, a feisty Stephens challenged him to a dual. Hill declined, a decision to which Stephens probably owed his life:

☛ "Washington, D.C., 12 Dec., 1856. Dear Thomas, Your letter from Atlanta enclosing Hill's refusal of my demand did not reach me until late last night. His reply is truly an enigma to me. I have prepared and sent to the *Constitutionalist* a short card which seems to me proper. I know no other course to pursue. What I say is short and to the point. You were perfectly right about the pistols. I should not have hesitated to fight with any weapon I could have used. I meant only to exclude the right of choosing any kind of weapon, such as rifles, broad swords, &c., on the part of the challenged party. My letter was written in great haste for the mail, and I only intended to put you on your guard on that point, as it might not have occurred to you that a rifle was too heavy for me. . . ."[50]

Stephens to J. Henly Smith, July 29, 1859, following one of Stephens' numerous popular speeches:

☛ "Crawfordville Ga., July 29th, 1859. Dear Smith, Your highly esteemed favour of the 26th was duly received. . . . I have been struck with the various comments that have been made on my speech and the sensation it seems to have produced. On the slave trade question I certainly meant to say nothing except what is clearly expressed—that was that unless we get immigration from abroad we shall have but few more slave states. This great truth seems to take the people by surprise. Some shrink from it as they would from death. Still it is as true as death. On the policy of opening the trade I said nothing, and meant to say nothing. The people must consider that for themselves. But a man has called to see me on business and I must stop."[51]

Stephens to J. Henly Smith, January 5, 1860:

☛ "Crawfordville, Ga., Jan. 5th, 1860. Dear Smith: . . . My being out of sorts in health I think is owing to the weather. We have no news. Times [are] rather hard and some complaint with the people for money. Provisions are high [priced] and property of all kinds higher than I ever knew. . . . How the honor of being a member of Congress and working and worrying oneself half to death there for the good of the people at home vanishes into thin air and becomes perfectly nothing in the estimation of one mingling with the people and seeing how little they care for such things. I had no idea that what was going on at the seat of gov[ernme]nt produced so little effect upon the public mind as it does. If I had known the fact, I think I should have quit long time ago. But enough of this. . . ."[52]

Stephens to J. Henly Smith, January 22, 1860. Stephens' distaste for disunion is in line with the vast majority of other Southerners at the time:
☛ "Crawfordville [Ga.], Jan. 22nd, 1860. Dear Smith, Your long letter of the 9th inst. was not received by me until my return the other day from Savannah, where I was at the Supreme Court for ten days. . . . In relation to the matter of Union or disunion I have only a word to say and that is, if I thought our own people, our public men and private men, were prepared for it, had the proper elements of character, stability of purpose, loyalty to principle, devotion to country, etc., I should not look upon such an alternative with the apprehension I do. The truth is I fear that if disunion should result, if by necessity it should come, we should be no better off in a new republic than we are in the present one. We should have the same or similar wrangling and confusion. Indeed if we were now to have a Southern convention to determine upon the true policy of the South either in the Union or out of it, I should expect to see just as much profitless discussion, disagreement, crimination and recrimination amongst the members of it from different States and from the same State, as we witness in the present House of Representatives between Democrats, Republicans and Americans. The troubles that now beset and environ us grow not out of the nature of our gov[ernme]nt or any real 'irrepressible conflict' between adverse interests. No such things; they grow out of the state of public opinion and the character of our public men North and South. There is a general degeneracy, confined not to one section or the other. The gov[ernme]nt in itself is good enough—the danger lies in no inherent defect in it. It is in the men who have charge of it, and the people who put such men in charge. The danger is much more radical, I fear, than the Southern people generally imagine, especially those who think disunion would be a remedy for the evils they feel. One may talk as flippantly or as seriously as one pleases of disunion, but one thing is evident to my mind, it will only render confusion worse confounded unless our people can agree upon some line of policy to be pursued and shall generally at least unite and agree to stand together in its maintenance. And if they would do this there would be no necessity for disunion. If they will not do this beforehand have we any reason to hope that they will do it afterwards? I fear not. *When the passions of men are once let loose, without control legal or moral, there is no telling to what extent of fury they may lead their victims. Republicks can only be maintained by virtue, intelligence and patriotism. We have but little public virtue, heroic virtue or patriotism now amongst our public men. They are generally selfish, looking not to country but to individual aggrandisement. There are but few now in Congress who consider anything so much as how their own votes affect them at home. This is a lamentable truth. And if we should break up, all these fellows would be striving to get the inner track of each other, each to take the lead of all the rest. It would be a race between*

demagogues to see who could pander most to the passions, prejudices and ignorance of the people, that they might profit thereby—just such a sort of thing as was seen in France, 1792, and in Mexico now. This is my apprehension. If the necessity comes I shall hope for the best; but I am by no means sanguine. I wish I were. I can but look upon the alternative as little better than jumping out of the frying pan into the fire. We would quit one set of demagogues to try another. But enough. These sentiments I give to you. They are hastily penned and not intended in this shape for anybody's use and reflection but your own."[53] [Emphasis added, L.S.]

Stephens to Dr. Henry R. Casey, March 9, 1860. Stephens here comments on the push to make him the Democratic presidential candidate in the upcoming November election, a movement that had started in the winter of 1859:
☛ "Crawfordville [Ga.], March 9th, 1860. Dear Sir: . . . This is certainly no time for the people of the South to be weakening their strength by divisions and struggles to promote or advance the aspirations of particular favorites to the office of Chief Magistrate of the Union. It is eminently a time for harmony among the friends of the [U.S.] Constitution every where, South as well as North. So far as I am individually concerned, I wish it distinctly known that I have no aspirations for that high office—none whatever; and whatever comment it may subject me to by those who do not know me, I assure you I would not of my own free choice assume its great trusts, if nothing were necessary to enable me to do so but my bare volition. Its duties, cares, anxieties and heavy responsibilities would, with me, far outweigh all fancied honors that may be supposed to attend it. . . ."[54]

Stephens to J. Henly Smith, April 14, 1860. Here Stephens reveals one of the many truths about the South and slavery; namely, that Southerners were far less interested in the slave trade than were Northerners. This is not surprising: contrary to Northern myth, the American abolition movement got its start in the South (Virginia), while both the American slave trade and slavery began in the North (Massachusetts)[55]:
☛ "Crawfordville [Ga.], April 14th, 1860. Dear Smith, I got home last night from Hancock court and found your letter of the date I forget but the one about your correspondence with the [*Southern*] *Confederacy* [newspaper]. I would advise you to write as requested. I do not know what the prospect for your pay will be; but he [James P. Hamilton, editor of the *Southern Confederacy*, Atlanta, Georgia] is a clever man personally. I would simply give him the news. He is not a disunionist per se as I understand him. He is not in favour of opening the African slave trade either, as I understand him . . . . I would advise you, if you write, neither to advocate disunion or the opening of the slave trade. The

people here [in the South] at present I believe are as much opposed to it as they are at the North; and I believe the Northern people could be induced to open it sooner than the Southern people. It would be useless to write on that subject at this time. I have nothing more to say; no time rather to say more."[56]

Stephens' reply to a letter by thirteen Macon, Georgia, men concerning the "rupture" in the Democratic Convention at Charleston, South Carolina, in 1860:

☞ "Crawfordville, Ga., May 9, 1860. Gentlemen: Your letter, of the 5th inst., was received last night, and I promptly respond to your call as clearly and fully as a heavy press of business engagements will permit. I shall endeavor to be no less pointed and explicit than candid. You do not, in my judgment, over-estimate the importance of the questions now pressing upon the public mind, growing out of the disruption of the Charleston Convention. While I was not greatly surprised at that result, considering the elements of its composition, and the general distemper of the times, still I deeply regret it, and, with you, look with intense interest to the consequences. What is done cannot be undone or amended; that must remain irrevocable. It would, therefore, be as useless, as ungracious, to indulge in any reflections, as to whose fault the rupture was owing to. Perhaps, and most probably, undue excitement and heat of passion, in pursuit of particular ends connected with the elevation or overthrow of particular rivals for preferment, more than any strong desire, guided by cool judgment, so necessary on such occasions, to advance the public good, was the real cause of the rupture. Be that as it may, however, what is now to be done, and what is the proper course to be taken? To my mind the course seems to be clear.

"A State Convention should be called at an early day—and that Convention should consider the whole subject calmly, and dispassionately, with 'the sober second thought,' and determine whether to send a representation to Richmond or to Baltimore. The correct determination of this question, as I view it, will depend upon another; and that is, whether the doctrine of Non-intervention by Congress, with Slavery in the Territories, ought to be adhered to, or abandoned by the South. This is a very grave and serious question, and ought not to be decided rashly or intemperately. No such small matters, as the promotion of this or that individual, however worthy or unworthy, ought to enter into its consideration. It is a great subject of public policy, affecting the vast interests of the present and the future. It may be unnecessary, and entirely useless, for me to obtrude my views upon this question, in advance of the meeting of such Convention, upon whom its decision may primarily devolve. I cannot, however, comply with your request, without doing so to a limited extent, at least. This, I shall do. In the first place, then, I assume, as an unquestioned and unquestionable fact, that Non-intervention, as stated, has been for many years received, recognized, and acted upon, as the settled doctrine of the South. By Non-intervention, I mean the principle, that Congress shall pass no law upon the subject of Slavery in the Territories, either for, or against it, in any way—that they shall not interfere or act upon it at all—or, in the express words of Mr. [John C.] Calhoun, the great Southern leader, that Congress shall 'leave the whole subject where the Constitution and the great principles of Self-government place it.' This has been eminently a Southern doctrine. It was announced by Mr. Calhoun, in his speech, in the Senate, on the 27th of June, 1848; and, after two years of discussion, was adopted as the basis of the adjustment finally made in 1850. It was the demand of the South, put forth by the South, and since its establishment has been again and again affirmed and re-affirmed as the settled policy of the South, by Party Conventions and State Legislatures, in every form that a people can give authoritative expression to their will and wishes. This cannot now be matter of dispute. It is history, as indelibly fixed upon the record as the fact that the Colony of Georgia was settled under the auspices of [James] Oglethorpe, or that the war of the American Revolution was fought in resistance to the unjust claim of power on the part of the British Parliament.

"I refer to this matter of history connected with the subject under consideration, barely as a starting point—to show how we stand in relation to it. It is not a new question. It has been up before, and whether rightly or wrongly, it has been decided—decided and settled just as the South asked that it should be—not, however, without great effort and a prolonged struggle. The question now is, shall the South abandon her own position in that decision and settlement? This is the question virtually presented by the action of the Seceders from the Charleston Convention, and the grounds upon which they based their action; or stated in other words, it amounts to this; whether the Southern States, after all that has taken place on the subject, should now reverse their previous course, and demand Congressional intervention for the protection of slavery in the Territories, as a condition of their remaining longer in the Union? For I take it for granted that it would be considered by all as the most mischievous folly to make the demand, unless we intend to push the issue to its ultimate and legitimate results. Shall the South, then, make this demand of Congress, and when made, in case of failure to attain it, shall she secede from the Union as a portion of her delegates (some under instructions, and some from their own free will,) seceded from the Convention, on their failure to get it granted there?

"Thus stands the naked question, as I understand it, presented by the action of the Seceders, in its full dimensions—its length, breadth, and depth, in all its magnitude.

"It is presented not to the Democratic Party alone; it is true, a Convention of that Party may first act on it, but it is presented to the country, to the whole people of the South, of all Parties. And men of all Parties should duly and timely consider it, for they may all have to take sides on it, sooner or later.

"It rises in importance high above any Party organization of the present day, and it may, and ought to, if need be, sweep them all from the board. My judgment is against the demand. If it were a new question, presented in its present light, for the first time, my views upon it might be different from what they are. It is known to you and the country, that the policy of Non-intervention, as established at the instance of the South, was no favorite one of mine. As to my position upon it, and the doctrine now revived, when they were original and open questions, as well as my present views, I will cite you to an extract from a speech made by me in Augusta, in July last, on taking final leave of my constituents. I could not restate them more clearly or more briefly. In speaking of, and reviewing this matter, I then said:

> 'And, as you all may know, it (Non-Intervention) came short of what I wished. It was, in my view, not the full measure of our rights. That required, in my judgment, the enactment by Congress, of all needful laws for the protection of slave property in the Territories, so long as the territorial condition lasted.
>
> 'But an overwhelming majority of the South was against that position. It was said that we who maintained it, yielded the whole question by yielding the jurisdiction—and that, if we conceded the power to protect, we necessarily conceded with it the power to prohibit. This, by no means, followed, in my judgment. But such was the prevailing opinion. And it was not until it was well ascertained that a large majority of the South would not ask for, or even vote for, Congressional protection, that those of us who were for it yielded to non-intervention, because, though it came short of our wishes, yet it contained no sacrifice of principle—had nothing aggressive in it, and secured, for all practical purposes, what was wanted; that is, the unrestricted right of expansion over the common public domain, as inclination, convenience, or necessity may require on the part of our people. . . .
>
> 'Thus the settlement was made—thus the record stands, and by it I am willing still to stand, as it was fully up to the demands of the South, through her Representatives at the time, though not up to my own; and as by it the right of expansion to the extent of population and capacity is amply secured.'

"In this you clearly perceive what I think of the proper course now to be taken on the same subject. While, in the beginning of this controversy, I was not favorable to the policy adopted, yet I finally yielded my assent. It was yielded to the South—to the prevailing sentiment of my own section. But it never would have been yielded if I had seen that any of our important rights, or any principle essential to our safety or security, could, by possibility, result from its operation. Nor would I now be willing to abide by it, if I saw in its practical workings any serious injury to the South likely to arise from it. All Parties in the South, after the settlement was made, gave it the sanction of their acquiescence, if not cordial approval. What, then, has occurred since to cause us to change our position in relation to it? Is it that those of the North who stood by us in the struggle from 1848 to 1850, did afterward, stand nobly by us in 1854, in taking off the old Congressional Restriction, of 1820, so as to have complete Non-Intervention throughout the length and breadth of the common public domain? Was this heroism on their part, in adhering to principle, at the hazard and peril of their political lives and fortunes, the cause of present complaint? This cannot be; for never was an Act of Congress so generally and so unanimously hailed with delight at the South, as this one was—I mean the Kansas-Nebraska Act of 1854. It was not only indorsed by all Parties in Georgia, but every one who did not agree to its just provisions, upon the subject of Slavery, was declared to be unfit to hold Party associations with any Party not hostile to the interests of the South. What, then, is the cause of complaint now? Wherein has this policy worked any injury to the South, or wherein is it likely to work any?

"The only cause of complaint I have heard is, that Non-Intervention, as established in 1850, and carried out in 1854, is not understood at the North as it is at the South; that, while we hold that, in leaving 'the whole subject where the Constitution and the great principles of Self-government place it,' the common territories are to remain open for settlement by Southern people with their slaves, until otherwise provided by a State Constitution, the friends and supporters of the same doctrine at the North maintain that, under it, the people of an organized Territory can protect or exclude slave property before the formation of a State Constitution. This opinion, or construction of theirs, is what is commonly dubbed 'Squatter Sovereignty.' Upon this point of difference in construction of what are 'the great principles of Self-government,' under the Constitution of the United States, a great deal has been said and written.

"We have heard it in the social circle—in the forum—on the hustings—and in the halls of legislation. The newspapers have literally groaned with dissertations on it. Pamphlets have been published for and against the respective sides. Congress has spent months in its discussion, and may spend as many years as they have mouths, without arriving at any more definite or satisfactory conclusion in relation to it, than Milton's perplexed spirits did upon the abstruse questions on which they held such high and prolonged debate when they reasoned—

> 'Of Providence, foreknowledge, will, and fate;
> 'Fixed fate, free will, foreknowledge, absolute,
> 'And found no end in wandering mazes lost.'

"It is not my purpose now to enter the list of these disputants. My own opinions upon the subject are known; and it is equally known that this difference of opinion, or construction, is no new thing in the history of this subject. Those who hold the doctrine that the people of the Territories, according to the great principles of Self-government, under the Constitution of the United States, can exclude Slavery by Territorial Law, and regulate slave property as all other property, held the same views they now do, when we agreed with them to stand on those terms. This fact is also historical. The South held, that under the Constitution, the Territorial Legislatures could not exclude Slavery—that it required an Act of Sovereignty to do this. Some gentlemen of the North held, as they now do, that the Territorial Legislatures could control slave property as absolutely as they could any other kind of property, and by a system of laws could virtually exclude Slavery from amongst them, or prevent its introduction if they chose.

"That point of difference it was agreed, by both sides, to leave to the Courts to settle. There was no cheat, or swindle, or fraud, or double dealing in it. It was a fair, honorable, and Constitutional adjustment of the difference. No assertion or declaration by Congress, one way or the other, could have affected the question in the least degree; for if the people, according to 'the great principles of Self-government,' under the Constitution, have the right contended for by those who espouse that side of the argument, then Congress could not and cannot deprive them of it. And if Congress did not have, or does not have, the power to exclude Slavery from a Territory, as those on our side contended, and still contend they have not, then they could not and did not confer it upon the Territorial Legislatures. We of the South held that Congress had not the power to exclude, and could not delegate a power they did not possess—also, that the people had not the power to exclude under the Constitution, and therefore the mutual agreement was to take the subject out of Congress, and leave the question of the power of the people where the Constitution had placed it—with the Courts. This is the whole of it. The question in dispute is a judicial one, and no Act of Congress, nor any resolution of any Party Convention can in any way affect it, unless we abandon the first position of Non-intervention by Congress.

"But it seems exceedingly strange to me, that the people of the South should, at this late day, begin to find fault with this Northern construction, as it is termed—especially since the decision of the Supreme Court, in the case of Dred Scott. In this connection, I may be permitted to say, that I have read with deep interest the debates of the Charleston Convention, and particularly the able, logical, and eloquent speech of the Hon. Wm. L. Yancey, of Alabama. It was, decidedly, the strongest argument I have seen on his side of the question. But its greatest power was shown in its complete answer to itself. Never did a man, with greater clearness, demonstrate that 'Squatter Sovereignty,' the bug-bear of the day, is not in the Kansas Bill, all that has been said to the contrary, notwithstanding. This, he put beyond the power of refutation. But he stopped not there—he went on, and by reference to the decision of the Supreme Court alluded to, he showed, conclusively, in a most pointed and thrilling climax, that this most frightful doctrine could not, by possibility, be in it, or in any other Territorial Bill—that it is a Constitutional impossibility. With the same master-hand he showed that the doctrine of 'Squatter Sovereignty' is not in the Cincinnati Platform; then why should we of the South now complain of Non-Intervention, or ask a change of Platform?

"What else have we to do but to insist upon our allies standing to their agreement? Would it not have been much more natural to look for flinching on their side than on ours? Why should we desire or want any other Platform of principles than that adopted at Cincinnati? If those who stood with us on it, in the contest of 1856, are willing still to stand on it, why should we not be equally willing? For my life I cannot see, unless we are determined to have a quarrel with the North anyhow on general account. If so, in behalf of common sense, let us put it upon more tenable ground! These are abundant. For our own character's sake, let us make it upon the aggressive acts of our enemies, rather than any supposed short-comings of our friends, who have stood by us so steadfastly in so many Constitutional struggles. In the name of patriotism and honor, let us not make it upon a point which may so directly subject us to the charge of breach of plighted faith. Whatever may befall us, let us ever be found, by friend or foe, as good as our word. These are my views, frankly and earnestly given.

"The great question, then, is, shall we stand by our principles, or shall we cutting loose from our moorings, where we have been safely anchored so many years, launch out again into unknown seas, upon new and perilous adventures, under the guide and pilotage of those who prove themselves to have no more fixedness of purpose or stability, as to objects or policy, than the shifting winds by which we shall be driven? Let this question be decided by the Convention, and decided with that wisdom, coolness, and forecast which becomes statesmen and patriots. As for myself, I can say, whatever may be the course of future events, my judgment in this crisis is, that we should stand by our principles 'through woe' as well as 'through weal,' and maintain them in good faith, now and always, if need be, until they, we, and the Republic, perish together in a common ruin. I see no injury that can possibly arise to us from them—not even if the Constitutional impossibility of their containing 'Squatter Sovereignty' did not exist, as has been conclusively demonstrated. For, if it did exist in them, and were all that its most ardent advocates claim for it, no serious practical danger to us could result from it.

"Even according to that doctrine, we have the unrestricted right of expansion to the extent of population. It is admitted that slavery can, and will go, under its operation, wherever the people want it. Squatters carried it to Tennessee, Kentucky, Missouri, Alabama, Mississippi, and Arkansas, without any law to protect it, and to Texas against a law prohibiting it, and they will carry it under this doctrine to all countries where climate, soil, production, and population will allow. These are the natural laws that will regulate it under Non-intervention, according to that construction; and no act of Congress can carry it into any Territory against these laws, any more than it could make the rivers run to the mountains, instead of the sea. If we have not enough of the right sort of population to compete longer with the North in the colonization of new Territories and States, this deficiency can never be supplied by any such act of Congress as that now asked for. The attempt would be as vain as that of Xerxes to control the waters of the Hellespont by whipping them in his rage.

"The times, as you intimate, do, indeed, portend evil. But I have no fears for the Institution of Slavery, either in the Union or out of it, if our people are but true to themselves—true, stable and loyal to fixed principles and settled policy; and if they are not thus true, I have little hope of anything good, whether the present Union last or a new one be formed. There is, in my judgment, nothing to fear from the 'Irrepressible Conflict' of which we hear so much. Slavery rests upon great truths, which can never be successfully assailed by reason or argument. It has grown stronger in the minds of men the more it has been discussed, and it will still grow stronger as the discussion proceeds and time rolls on. Truth is omnipotent, and must prevail! We have only to maintain the truth with firmness, and wield it aright. Our system rests upon an impregnable basis, that can and will defy all assaults from without. My greatest apprehension is from causes within—there lies the greatest danger. We have grown luxuriant in the exuberance of our well being and unparalleled prosperity. There is a tendency everywhere, not, only at the North, but at the South, to strife, dissension, disorder, and anarchy. It is against this tendency that the sober-minded and reflecting men everywhere should now be called upon to guard.

"My opinion, then, is, that delegates ought to be sent to the adjourned Convention at Baltimore. The demand made at Charleston by the Seceders ought not to be insisted upon. Harmony being restored on this point, a nomination can doubtless be made of some man whom the Party, everywhere, can support, with the same zeal, and the same ardor with which they entered and waged the contest in 1856, when the same principles were involved.

"If, in this, there be a failure, let the responsibility not rest upon us. Let our hands be clear of all blame. Let there be no cause for casting censure at our door. If, in the end, the great National Democratic Party—the strong ligament, which has so long bound and held the Union together—shaped its policy and controlled its destinies—and to which we have so often looked with a hope that seldom failed, as the only Party North on which to rely, in the most trying hours when Constitutional rights were in peril, let it not be said to us, in the midst of the disasters that may ensue, 'you did it!' In any and every event, let not the reproach of Punic faith rest upon our name. If everything else has to go down, let our untarnished honor, at least, survive the wreck. Alexander H. Stephens."[57]

Stephens' to Mr. Z. P. Landrum, of Lexington, Georgia, July 1, 1860, on the "rupture" in the democratic convention, at Baltimore, Maryland, in 1860:
☛ "Crawfordville, Ga., July 1,1860. My Dear Sir: Yours of the 26th ultimo was duly received, and I now return you an answer by the earliest mail that will bear it. But I confess my utter inability to give you any definite or satisfactory response to your several inquiries. The condition of public affairs, in my judgment, is truly deplorable, and I see but little prospect of it being bettered by any effort of patriotism on my part. Your professional practice has doubtless presented you with many cases where the symptoms indicated a malignity of disease beyond the power of medical skill. Such, you will excuse me in saying, are the symptoms of our public disorders, in my judgment, at this time. I see no remedy, can make no prescription—and can suggest nothing. The '*vis medicatrix naturæ*, [Latin: the natural restorative process of the body] is the only hope, and when this is the only hope, the best course is to leave the patient quietly to himself.

"It is useless to discuss questions relating to the origin of this state of things, or how the evils that are upon us, or the worse ones ahead now threatening, could have been avoided. The times seem to be sadly out of joint.

"In reply to what you say of my power, and that patriotism and statesmanship must 'save us, else we perish,' I can only say, with an oppressed heart, that there are periods in every Nation's history, when passions get the better of reason, when no human power can avail anything, when patriotism and statesmanship are alike submerged under the irresistible wave. At such times no power short of that which said to the troubled waters of Galilee's Sea, 'Peace, be still!' can allay the storm. This is that unseen, but all-prevailing, and all-controlling power of Providence, which shapes the fortunes of men, and guides the destiny of States. What is to be the future of this country, I cannot say. I cannot even venture a conjecture. All I can do is to indulge a hope, strong or weak, as it may be, that all may yet be well. How this is to be, I do not see; it was the prospect of the events we now have upon us, 'the shadows' of which I saw in advance of their approach, with the full conviction and consciousness that I could do nothing to avert them, that caused me to retire from that position of responsibility I had so long held, and in which I felt satisfied I could no longer be useful.

"The real evils of the times the people do not understand. It springs from no defect in their Government, from no 'Irrepressible Conflict' of interest between the two great sections of the Union, from no danger to the rights, interest, honor, or safety of either, but from the want of true patriotism on the part of our public men in all sections; from the want of devotion to the country, for the country's sake; from a want of loyalty to principle; nay, more, directly from the ambition of aspirants for place and power. This begets personal strife, prompted by jealousy and envy, and hate. These are amongst the strongest, as well as the worst passions of human nature. They are not confined to humanity; even in Heaven (it is said) they once exhibited their power and fury. If there they made devils of angels, what may we not expect them to make of men on earth? The good, the virtuous, and the wise, may look on and lament. Sometimes wise counsels may arrest and prevent most mischievous consequences, at others they are as impotent as chaff to stay the force of a storm. What influence had La Fayette's sage admonitions on the passions of the frenzied populace of France, aroused and led on by demagogues? I need not indulge, however, any longer in this strain.

"To come to particulars. I assure you I am pained and grieved at what was done at Baltimore. The Charleston Rupture was bad enough, but that at Baltimore was much worse. What the friends of Mr. [Stephen A.] Douglas meant by pressing his nomination in the face of the secession of Tennessee, Kentucky, and Virginia, to say nothing of other States, I cannot imagine. As I view the field, he has no probable chance of election. Why they should put him up to be beaten is strange to me. I cannot understand it. They certainly have not as much regard for his noble spirit, great talents, and merits as I have. Madness and folly seem to have ruled the hour. The only use or public benefit his running can be, it seems to me, is for him to carry enough Northern

Electoral votes to defeat Mr. [Abraham] Lincoln before the people, and to throw the election into the House, where his Party rival, Mr. [John C.] Breckinridge, may make him a stepping-stone in his elevation to power and place. In this way he may possibly, by his back and shoulders, enable Mr. Breckinridge to succeed in his election, and benefit the country by the defeat of Mr. Lincoln. But what honor this will be to Mr. Douglas I think it would be difficult for his friends to show. If this position had been necessary for any one, I would have assigned it to some other—some one who could, and would have rendered the country great public service, and at the same time might have been gaining and not losing public reputation himself. Again, his friends, it seems to me, must have known that his nomination, made under the circumstances that it was, could not have the power of keeping the National Organization together. It was virtually a rupture of it. The usages of the Party and its constitution, it will be said, (however the facts may be,) were violated in putting him forth as its nominee, without the concurrence of two-thirds of the Electoral votes. This will effectually produce general demoralization.

"The consequence is, we are and shall be, during the whole canvass, entirely at sea. No one will be looked to as the regularly appointed standard-bearer of the flag of the National Organization. The rupture is complete, and may be final. How that will be, the future must determine. This election, at best, can but be a scrub race between the Democratic candidates. The National Democratic Party is in the position of the old Republican Party in 1824. The same fate may be in reserve for it. That never was again re-organized, though another National Organization did spring up out of the fragments and dissolving elements of old organizations, which was sufficient, under Providence, to save our Institutions; and so it may be again.

"It is consoling to the patriot at least to indulge in the hope that such may be the case. But that the South will ever get an Act of Congress protecting slave property in the Territories, I have no idea. That those who now insist upon such an article in a National Party creed ever expect to see such an Act passed, I have no idea. For many of them say that they would not vote for such a law. And that such a law would never be of the least advantage to the South, I am well satisfied. Hence, I was, and am clear in my conviction that it was not only not patriotic, but exceedingly unwise and mischievous to insist upon such an interpolation on the old National Party Platform, and particularly at this juncture. But I will not confine my remarks to this juncture; for I verily believe that Non-intervention by Congress with Slavery in the Territories, is a proper and safe doctrine at all times. For this reason I acquiesced in it, when and as I did. Had the Party at this time continued to stand on it with Mr. Douglas, they would have carried the country by an overwhelming majority, and would have annihilated the 'Black Republican Organization,' as it is called, for all time to come. This is my opinion. As matters now stand, this great result is put almost upon the chances of the turning of a die [dice]. If Douglas can carry enough Northern States to defeat Lincoln's election in the Electoral Colleges, the contest will then come up in the House; when, if the South unite with California and Oregon, Lincoln may be defeated.

"But the seat of the Democratic member from Oregon (Mr. [Lansing] Stout) is now contested, and I have no doubt a majority in the present House will vote him out, in case the election for President shall go before that body. Then there is great danger that a strife will arise between the friends of [John] Bell and Breckinridge, in case they both be on the list of the three highest voted for by the Colleges. In that event, there will be no hope but in staving off the election until the 4th of March, when the Senate will have to make the choice under the Constitution. But in all these chances, in view of the passions and prejudices of bad men, aiming at rule and power, who does not see in advance the imminent danger at every turn, of some outbreak that may lead to revolution? Have we not fallen upon evil times, when so much has been hazarded to accomplish no object higher or worthier than the gratification of personal envy, hate, revenge, and ambition? The prospect is gloomy enough, but, my dear sir, I do not despair of the Republic; though I do not at this time see in what way anything I can do or say would be of the least benefit, yet I am not without hope that deliverance in some way is in store for us. As to whether a Douglas ticket should be run in Georgia, I can give no advice either for or against it. What those Southern States—Alabama and Louisiana—which voted for Mr. Douglas at Baltimore, as they did, meant by their course, or what they expected to accomplish by it, I do not know. I have received no explanations. What Governor [Andrew] Johnson expects to accomplish, I do not know. I have heard nothing from any of them. I see the editor of the *Constitutionalist* speaks as if he thinks the South will go for Douglas. To me, this seems little short of utter dementation. Still I may be mistaken. I only speak to you my individual opinions, formed from observations such as I can make in my quiet retreat, without mingling at all with the outside world, except through the medium of the public press. Had Douglas been nominated at Charleston (even after the Secession took place), he would have carried the South against a Richmond nomination. But at present it is impossible. The Baltimore Convention, instead of stopping the break in the levee, only made it deeper and wider. It is now, in my judgment, entirely beyond control. Nothing but a subsidence of the waters will ever arrest it. I think, moreover, that the declination of [Benjamin] Fitzpatrick, and the general enthusiasm for Breckinridge and [Joseph] Lane in the South, will greatly damage Douglas in the

North, if it does not entirely break him down there. As the prospect of his election diminishes, as it will very soon, even with those who were foolish enough to put him up as they did—thousands will abandon him to get on the winning side. Some from spite, and some from personal motives, so that in the end I should not be greatly surprised to see Lincoln elected by the people. In this state of things, so far as I am concerned, I am satisfied that the best course I can take is, to leave the whole matter with those who have undertaken the management of the crisis. Should it turn out well, no one will be more rejoiced than myself. Should it turn out badly, while I shall feel relieved of all personal responsibility—should I be in life—I shall endeavor to do whatever the dictates of patriotism may point out, whenever an occasion shall arise, when I see any prospect for doing good. At this time, I repeat, I see none. I expect, therefore, in this contest, to be perfectly silent. I see no good to be accomplished by any word that I can say. The popular fever must run its course. I do not wish any one to be influenced by my views, one way or the other. Every one should act from the dictates of his own judgment. If the 'worst comes,' and we shall be precipitated into disunion, even by what I deem unwise counsels, which is not at all improbable, I shall yield to that misfortune as to all others. My destiny is with Georgia; whatever awaits her people, awaits me, so long as I live. Whatever errors her people or her rulers commit in controlling the common destiny of all of us, I shall endeavor to bear my share of the consequences of them with that patriotism which prompts a loyal heart to go for his country, right or wrong. At present, my patriotism embraces the whole country, North and South, and I have spent the best of my days in promoting the Union, harmony, peace, rights, interests, and happiness of the whole. But if for any cause a division takes place, then Georgia will be my country; her people will be my people, and their cause will be my cause! I do trust that this division will not take place. I see no necessity for it. Still it may come. And if it does, my judgment as to the necessity of the thing, or the propriety of the course of our public men, that may induce it and hasten it, will not influence my action when the great fact is upon us.

"Excuse this long letter. It is written, as you see from its date, on Sunday. I give it to you as a sort of pious offering, not altogether unsuited to the sacredness of the day. There are occasions when attention to bodily suffering of ourselves or our friends, as well as personal cares, are not thought to be out of place on this day. Even Christ, after ministering in this way on that day, asked those about him, 'Which of you shall have an ass, or an ox fall into a pit, and will not straightway pull him out on the Sabbath day?' The illustration is good to the extent that good may be performed on Sunday. And with a consciousness that what I have said or written has been prompted by no motive, but the public good, which concerns us all so deeply, I have no further apology to offer you for this deed on the Sabbath, though I make no attempt to get the country out of its difficulties, for I see no way to do it.

"In reply to your inquiries after my health, I have to say that it is very feeble indeed. I am barely able to be up. I have quit all professional labors. I suffer from extreme debility, accompanied with vertigo. The cause or nature of the malady I do not understand. When I was at Athens, attending the Supreme Court, I consulted Dr. Moore, who thought it was brought on by exposure to the sun. I had been very much thus exposed on my farm, during the hot days in May, just before the first attack. I am on no treatment or regime, except rest and quiet.

"To your other inquiry about our National [U.S.] flag, all I can say is, that the designer of the present flag was Captain [Samuel C.] Reid, of the privateer brig, *General Armstrong*, in the war with England, in 1812. The dates and particulars I cannot give, or wherein the device of the present flag differs from the old one. The full history of the stars and stripes I expect would he entertaining if not useful. The Stars, as a matter of course, represent States. The origin of the Stripes, I think, if searched out would be found to be a little curious. All I know upon that point is, that on the 4th day of July, 1776, after the Declaration of Independence was carried, a Committee was appointed by Congress, consisting of Mr. [Thomas] Jefferson, Dr. [Benjamin] Franklin, and John Adams to prepare a device for a Seal of the United States. Each member of the Committee prepared a device, and then they combined something of the ideas of each in one they reported. Mr. Jefferson was to combine their ideas. The seal he thus reported had on one side of it the Goddess of Liberty and the Goddess of Justice, supporting a shield with six quarterings, denoting the six countries from which the Colonies had mainly been peopled, to wit: England, Scotland, Ireland, France, Germany, and Holland. The motto on this seal was '*E pluribus unum.*' This seal, as reported, or the device in full as reported, was never adopted. But in it we see the emblems in part, which are still preserved in the flag.

"The stripes or lines, which on Mr. Jefferson's original plan were to designate the six quarterings of the shield, as signs of the six countries from which our ancestors came, are now, I believe, considered as representations of the old thirteen States, and with most persons the idea of a shield is lost sight of. You perceive, that by drawing six lines or strips on a shield figure it will leave seven spaces of the original color, and of course give thirteen apparent stripes; hence the idea of their bring all intended to represent the old thirteen States. My opinion is, that this was the origin of the stripes. Mr. Jefferson's quartered shield for a seal device was seized upon as a national emblem that was put upon the flag. We now have the stars as well as the stripes. When each of these were adopted I cannot say; but the flag, as it now is, was designed by Captain Reid, as I tell you, and adopted by Congress. The first one with his device, which Congress adopted, was put over the Capitol. It was made by the wife and daughters of Captain Reid.

"Please remember me to Miss Grattan and to Mrs. Gilmer—to both give my kind regards. And though this letter is written entirely and exclusively for yourself, and not for the public, in any sense of the word, yet I have no objection to your reading it to Mrs. Gilmer if you think proper. In it she will but hear repeated several thoughts and opinions she heard from me last fall, on a memorable occasion. It was the last night Mr. Gilmer ever sat up and talked with his friends, a conversation I shall never forget, for the strong faith and confidence he then expressed, in the ultimate virtue and intelligence of the people to arrest the evil tendencies of the times, greatly strengthened my own hopes, weaker then than now. What has occurred since has not disappointed me at all. It has not even surprised me. I was expecting it, and am now expecting a much worse state of things before any wholesome reaction takes place, if it ever does.

"I must repeat to you, that what I have said is not for public use in any sense. I do not wish your own action to be governed in the least by that line which I think proper to take myself. Do as you think best. Present my kind regards to Mrs. Landrum and accept for both of you my best wishes for all the happiness this world can bestow, as well as that in a life to come, which is in reserve for the virtuous and the good. Yours truly, Alexander H. Stephens."[58]

Stephens to J. Henly Smith, November 8, 1860. Due to the Electoral College, big government lefty Abraham Lincoln was elected two days earlier with less than 50 percent of the popular vote, enraging both conservative Southerners and conservative Northerners: ☛ "Crawfordville [Ga.], Nov. 8th, 1860. Dear Smith, I got home Sunday night last—was here at the election. . . . I see by the papers received this morning that Lincoln is elected President. It does not surprise me in the least. I have been expecting it ever since the burst up at Baltimore, as you know very well. What is to be the result I cannot tell. We shall, I apprehend, have trouble. The people here are taken greatly by surprise at the result. They did not anticipate it and thought I was only indulging in unnecessary apprehensions when I told them months ago how it would most probably be. I have never been disappointed in a Presidential election since 1840. I do not feel so much oppressed in spirits at the result now actually upon us as I did months ago in looking forward to it. . . ."[59]

Stephens to J. Henly Smith, December 31, 1860. South Carolina had recently seceded from the Union due to the election of Lincoln in November:
☛ "Crawfordville [Ga.], Dec. 31st, 1860. Dear Smith, . . . I do not think that we stand in need of any new constitutional guarantees—we may hereafter if the Union should last—but at present we do not. All we now want or ought to want is a faithful administration of the gov[ernme]nt, under the present constitution with all its present obligations and guarantees. All that the South has at present just cause to complain of, and the chief ground of just complaints, is the personal liberty bill[s] of some of the non-slaveholding states. These ought to be repealed, and I doubt not if the whole South had united in asking their repeal with firmness and decision and with an honest intent to be satisfied with it when they got it that success would have crowned their efforts. Of this I am satisfied. But the truth is our ultra men do not desire any redress of these grievances. They would really obstruct indirectly any effort to that end. They are for breaking up. They are tired of the gov[ernme]nt. They have played out, dried up, and want something new. Here was all the danger or the great difficulty in the way of making any settlement or adjustment. It seems to me at present insurmountable! I do not see how it can be removed or gotten over. Our difficulties spring not from the gov[ernme]nt, its frame work or its administration so much as they do from the people, the leaders mainly. I have for now two years been impressed with the conviction that we are approaching 'the beginning of the end' of this great republic."[60]

Stephens wrote the following letter to Rudolf M. Schleiden (German minister of the Bremen Republic) on April 26, 1861, following the Battle of Fort Sumter—where Lincoln nefariously tricked the South into firing the first shot of his War on the Constitution:
☛ "Richmond, Va., 26th April, 1861. My Dear Sir: . . . No one can more deeply regret the threatening prospect of a general war between the United States and the Confederate States than I do. Such an unfortunate result, if it should occur, cannot be charged to the seeking or desire of the Confederate States government. On the contrary I feel assured in saying that every honourable means has been resorted to by the government to avoid it. Peace not only with the United States, but with all other Powers, is eminently the policy of the Confederate States. But they will have no peace with any which depends on a sacrifice of either their honor or right. Their independence with absolute jurisdiction over their own soil they will maintain at any and every hazzard.

"The bombardment of Fort Sumter was not resorted to until every effort at a peaceful adjustment of all matters of controversy with the United States had failed. This the correspondence between their Commissioners and the Secretary of State at Washington as well as the correspondence between General [Pierre G. T.] Beauregard and Mr. Secretary [Leroy P.] Walker—with which you are fully acquainted—will abundantly and clearly show.

"As to the future or any terms which our Government might grant or accept with a view to arrest further conflict, I can say nothing. I have no authority from the Confederate States government on the subject. But as a citizen desirous at all times to preserve peace, if it can be done on just and correct principles, I have no hesitancy in saying to you that the course of future events in these particulars will depend to a great extent, in my individual judgment, upon *the course to be pursued by the government of the United States. From all evidences and manifestations of their design which have reached me, it seems to be their policy to wage a war for the recapture of former possessions, looking to the ultimate coercion and subjugation of the people of the Confed. States to their power and dominion. With such an object on their part persevered in, no power on earth can arrest or prevent a most bloody conflict.* [Emphasis added, L.S.]

"If, however, such a war is not the object of the government of the U.S.—if they have any idea or disposition for an amicable adjustment of the questions in issue, then a great deal depends upon some early indication of such disposition or willingness and its communication either directly or indirectly in some authoritative way to the government of the Confederate States.

"This may be the invitation of other steps leading to a peaceful settlement. But without some such expression or indication of their designs and wishes, in the present posture of affairs I see no prospect of arresting the present tendency of events. . . .

"In relation to the Proclamation of [Confederate] President [Jefferson] Davis inviting offers for commissions in Privateer service mentioned by you in conversation, I will barely add that it was intended as a justifiable and legitimate measure in defensive warfare against the war of aggression so clearly inaugurated by the Proclamation of President Lincoln. This at least was and is my individual view of the subject."[61]

Stephens to Atlanta, Georgia, Mayor James M. Calhoun (a cousin of John C. Calhoun), September 8, 1862. The letter concerns constitutional law, martial law, and the recent suspension of Habeas Corpus *by the Confederate government:*
☛ "Richmond, Virginia, September 8th, 1862. Hon. James M. Calhoun, Atlanta, Ga.: Dear Sir:—Your letter of the 28th ult., to Hon. B[enjamin]. H. Hill, was submitted to me by him a few days ago, for my views as to the proper answer to be made to your several inquiries touching your powers and duties in the office of Civil Governor of Atlanta, to which you have been appointed by

[Confederate] General [Braxton] Bragg. I took the letter with the promise to write to you fully upon the whole subject. This, therefore, is the object of my now writing to you. I regret the delay that has occurred in the fulfilment of my promise. It has been occasioned by the press of other engagements, and I now find my time too short to write as fully as I could wish. The subject is one of great importance, and this, as well as matters of a kindred sort, have given me deep concern for some time past.

"I am not at all surprised at your being at a loss to know what your powers and duties are in your new position, and your inability to find anything in any written code of laws to enlighten you upon them. The truth is your office is unknown to the law. General Bragg had no more authority for appointing you Civil Governor of Atlanta, than I had; and I had, or have, no more authority than any street-walker in your city. Under his appointment, therefore, you can rightfully exercise no more power than if the appointment had been made by a street-walker.

"We live under a Constitution. That Constitution was made for War as well as Peace. Under that Constitution we have civil laws and military laws; laws for the civil authorities and laws for the military. The first are to be found in the Statutes at Large, and the latter in the Rules and Articles of War. But in this country there is no such thing as Martial Law, and cannot be until the Constitution is set aside—if such an evil day shall ever come upon us. All the law-making power in the Confederate States Government is vested in Congress. But Congress cannot declare Martial Law, which in its proper sense is nothing but an abrogation of all laws. If Congress cannot do it, much less can any officer of the Government, either civil on military, do it rightfully, from the highest to the lowest. Congress may, in certain cases specified, suspend the Writ of *Habeas Corpus*, but this by no means interferes with the administration of justice, so far as to deprive any party arrested of his right to a speedy and public trial by a jury, after indictment, etc. It does not lessen or weaken the right of such party to redress for an illegal arrest. It does not authorize arrests except upon oath or affirmation upon probable cause. It only secures the party beyond misadventure to appear in person to answer the charge, and prevents a release in consequence of insufficiency of proof, or other like grounds, in any preliminary inquiry as to the formality or legality of his arrest. It does not infringe or impair his other Constitutional rights. These Congress cannot impair by law. The Constitutional guarantees are above and beyond the reach or power of Congress, and much more, if it could be, above and beyond the power of any officer of the Government. Your appointment, therefore, in my opinion, is simply a nullity. You, by virtue of it, possess no rightful authority; and can exercise none. The order creating you Civil Governor of Atlanta, was a most palpable usurpation. I speak of the act only in a legal and Constitutional sense—not of the motives that prompted it. But a wise people, jealous of their rights, would do well to remember, as [Swiss-English political authority Jean-Louis de] Delolme so well expressed it, that 'such acts, so laudable when we only consider the motive of them, make a breach at which tyranny will one day enter,' if quietly submitted to too long. Now, then, my opinion is, if any one be brought before you for punishment for selling liquor to a soldier, or any other allegation, where there is no law against it, no law passed by the proper law-making power, either State or Confederate, and where, as a matter of course, you have no legal or rightful authority to punish, either by fine, or corporeally, etc., you should simply make this response to the one who brings him or her, as the case may be, that you have no jurisdiction of the matter complained of.

"A British Queen (Anne) was once urged by the Emperor of Russia to punish one of her officers for what His Majesty considered an act of indignity to his ambassador to her Court, though the officer had violated no positive law. The Queen's memorable reply was that 'she could inflict no punishment upon any, [even] the meanest of her subjects, unless warranted by the law of the land.'

"This is an example you might well imitate. For, I take it for granted that no one will pretend that any General in command of our armies, could confer upon you or anybody greater power that the ruling Sovereign of England possessed in like cases under similar circumstances. The case referred to in England gave rise to a change of the law. After that an act was passed exempting foreign ministers from arrest. So with us. If the proper discipline and good order of the army require that the sale of liquor to a soldier by a person not connected with the army should be prohibited, (which I do not mean to question in the slightest degree,) let the prohibition be declared by law, passed by Congress, with pains and penalties for a violation of it, with the mode and manner of trying the offence plainly set forth. Until this is done, no one has any authority to punish in such cases; and any one who undertakes to do it is a trespasser and a violator of the law. Soldiers in the service, as well as the officers, are subject to the Rules and Articles of War, and if they commit any offence known to the Military Code therein prescribed, they are liable to be tried and punished according to the law made for their government. If these Rules and Articles of War, or in other words, if the Military Code for the government of the army is defective in any respect, it ought to be amended by Congress. There alone the power is vested. Neither Generals nor the Provost-Marshals have any power to make, alter or modify laws, either military or civil; nor can they declare what shall be crimes, either military or civil, or establish any tribunal to punish what they may so declare. All these matters belong to Congress; and I assure you, in my opinion, nothing is more essential to the maintenance and preservation of Constitutional Liberty than that the Military be ever kept subordinate to the Civil Authorities. You thus have my views hastily, but pointedly given. Yours most respectfully, Alexander H. Stephens."[62]

Stephens to Confederate Secretary of War James A. Seddon, April 29, 1864. In this letter Stephens corrects a number of misunderstandings and discusses the current problems of the Confederate government and military, including his alleged "bitter and hostile" relationship with Jefferson Davis:

☞ "Crawfordville, Ga., April 29, 1864. Hon. James A. Seddon, Sec. of War. Dear Sir: Your letter of the 21st instant was received yesterday. In my letter of the 15th instant to Judge [John A.] Campbell, I referred in a postscript to the fact of an editor of this State having exhibited an extract of one of my communications to you, etc., barely as an explanation of the tone and manner of my speaking to him as I did on certain subjects in that letter, which without the explanation might have appeared strange and singular to him. The tone and manner alluded to were simply repeated assurances that my sole object was the public good, however strong and earnest the expressions used. I did express surprise at the editor's having the extract referred to, but no indignation. I felt none such. How the editor became possessed of that portion of my communication I did not know, and I added most truthfully that it was a matter of very little consequence to me. I saw, to my mortification, that the editor had put an erroneous construction upon my motives and feelings in using the words I did. I did not know but that others who had seen it, had put a like construction upon them, and hence I guarded myself against any such construction of my motives from any earnestness of expression in what I had said to Judge Campbell, and in explanation of my reasons for thus guarding him referred to the fact mentioned. The editor alluded to had exhibited (privately not published) the extract referred to. He showed it as evidence of my 'bitterness, hostility and malignancy' (I quote his words) against the administration. Entertaining no such feelings, or any thing kindred to them, I did not wish Judge Campbell to draw any such inference from anything I said to him upon the subjects I was writing to him about, however strong or earnest my language might be.

"I should certainly have written immediately and directly to you upon the subject, if I had attached any great importance to the matter, or had really felt anything like indignation on account of it. I am glad Judge Campbell informed you of what I said to him on this point. From what you say I can now readily account for the editor alluded to having the extract. It was doubtless furnished by some of the subordinates in the bureau of conscription to whom it was referred. You cannot possibly regret more sincerely or profoundly my disagreement with members of the administration upon some of the late measures of legislation than I do myself. And nothing could have induced me to take public position against them, but a sense of public duty arising from a strong conviction of the mischievous and dangerous tendency of those measures—founded as they were, in my judgment, upon great and radical errors. But in this, as in all differences amongst common friends in a great common cause, I assure you I was influenced by nothing except what I regarded as the public good. I was not influenced in the slightest degree by feelings of hostility or bitterness, to say nothing of malignancy, toward a single mortal who disagreed with me.

"And while I am writing to you thus frankly, I will take occasion to say that I see and hear almost daily of matters involving the deepest interest that ought to be corrected. Such at least is my judgment; and I give it to you for what it is worth. Some of these I mentioned in my letter to Judge Campbell; they relate to the waste and misuse of the tithes. With my ideas of this war, its probable duration and the manner in which it can be successfully conducted on our side, I think the greatest danger ahead of us, under the present policy, is the ultimate failure of subsistence. War, in one view, is eminently a business affair upon a large and magnificent scale; and it requires eminently business qualities to conduct it safely and successfully against such disadvantages as we labor under. But with the advantages we possess I have never doubted for a moment, but that we can wage it successfully in our defence, just as long as our enemies shall choose to prosecute it, if our resources of men and means are properly and efficiently wielded. *From the beginning I believed it would very probably be ultimately a war for our subjugation or extermination.* This opinion I gave the Virginia convention in April, 1861, as will be seen by reference to my speech before that body; and from the beginning I was for husbanding and wielding our resources with this view. No equal number of people on the face of the globe ever had superior elements of power, or internal resources for defence than we had. How the great elements of cotton and tobacco, in a financial point of view, were neglected against my early and earnest appeals, I need not now say any thing—nor need I now say any thing of other like errors as to other resources I could mention. These things are past. We have now to deal with the present, looking to the future. Our finances now are a wreck. Past all hope, in my judgment. Just where I was fully convinced they would be, and so stated repeatedly and sorrowfully two years ago, when the first [Confederate] Congress, under the permanent [Confederate] constitution, adjourned without passing a tax act, or making any provision for the redemption of the issues of treasury notes. To me the result seemed as certain and as inevitable as other results seem now if our policy is not changed. [Emphasis added, L.S.]

"To be brief and pointed, our present reliance for sustaining the war, feeding the armies, is upon the substance of the country—the agricultural productions and not the credit of the government. The tax in kind or tithe is the surest hope; that is abundant, if it be properly and wisely managed. But under present management so far from doing the good it ought it only increases the evil. It is wasting the substance of the country without supplying the army as it ought to do entirely. The tithe ought to feed the army without the expenditure of a dollar by way of purchase. This it is abundantly sufficient to do upon the most moderate estimates; and, if it were not, then our cause, if the war last two years longer, would be hopeless. For if one tenth of the food produced in the country will not support or feed the armies, how can nine tenths support or keep from want and starvation the rest of the population? I suppose the whole list of our ration-drawers does not exceed six hundred thousand. The remaining population cannot be less than seven or eight millions—perhaps more. I have not the census before me, and speak in general terms, being quite certain that my statements are within bounds. Now if one tenth of the food of the land will not support six hundred thousand men with the horses etc. they have, it is manifest that the other nine tenths cannot support the remaining seven or eight millions with the stock they must keep to produce with. The government, therefore, or those administering the government, should look to the tithe [tax] as the main hope and only sure reliance for the support of the army. With these views premised, I now come to the errors I spoke of. From what I see and hear I am at this time of the opinion that what ought to have supplied the army for twelve months will be exhausted in less than six. I allude specially to the articles of corn and wheat. In this county, small and poor as it is, thousands of bushels of tithe corn, and great amount of forage, have been fed to poor cattle, bought up in February and March for beef, while the tithe pork and bacon was uncollected through the country. Had this been used now the grasses of summer would have fattened the beef to be used then, without consuming the tithe forage for the army. This is the matter I alluded to in my letter to Judge Campbell. This, it is true, is a small matter, but what is being done here is doubtless being done elsewhere. And since that letter I have learned the fact, that five thousand bushels of tithe corn just above me have been turned over to a party to distil into whiskey, right on the railroad and within two days transportation, or three at the furthest, to [Confederate General Joseph E.] Johnston's army. And these five thousand bushels, I am informed, were turned over to the distiller upon a contract, that for the five thousand bushels of corn he was to deliver five thousand gallons of whiskey! Out of which the contractor may make not less than $125,000 in our currency. One bushel of corn in winter, it is said, will make two gallons of whiskey, and besides, it is said, that the slops from stills will fatten as much pork as the corn would if fed to hogs in its natural state. With this view the contract was worth even more to the distiller. Now, I assure you, I think this radically wrong. I refer to it with no spirit of captiousness, but for the sole purpose of having such errors corrected. This contract is a small affair compared with others on the same principle. It is to all contracts on such principles I call your attention. In the first place, the army can do better without whiskey than bread; and, in the next place, if we have corn enough to put any into whiskey, it ought to be so used in sections remote from railroads. So with all corn or forage fed to cattle or hogs to fatten them for beef or pork for the army.

"The provision crop last year was abundant for all our population for the present year, for the army and people at home, if it be economically used. But I sincerely fear it will not be next year. The policy of impressing provisions without paying market price will greatly lessen production of itself; this was the case when there was confidence in the credit of the government. But that confidence is now lost by reason of the late financial and currency acts. I assure you it is lost. People may not be as candid in telling you the truth as I am; but the fact is so, and wise men should act accordingly. I mean wise statesmen. The government cannot afford to buy provisions at the market price in treasury notes six months to come, with any expectation of ever redeeming their issues dollar for dollar in specie; and to continue to issue them with this semblance of integrity of purpose, will but result in greater mischief in the end. The tithe, therefore, should be and should have been husbanded and guarded as gold; not a grain of corn or blade of grass should have been wasted, or lost, or misapplied.

"Our production of provisions this year will be greatly lessened from another cause. That is the general disarrangement of labor, and the management of large planting interests, as well as small, under the last military act. The uncertainty of whether parties could get what is called details, has caused many to make arrangements to suit themselves; many have gone into the army rather than be conscripted; many plantations have been virtually abandoned to the negroes, without any suitable superintendent; many persons still at home, under the uncertainty of getting details, are failing to plant their usual crops. And the bare absence from home at this season of the year, in going to and returning from camp to present their papers and look after them, will tell upon the crops even if they should ultimately be detailed. I speak of what I see around me, and don't for a moment suppose I am saying this to you with any other view than to present a fact which is important for you to know.

What is the case here it is reasonable to suppose is the case elsewhere. In my judgment this organization of what is now called the reserve force is almost a farce. It would be indeed a farce if it were not for the serious consequences attending it. There will hardly be as many able-bodied men sent to the army under its operation, as there are useless drones and consumers engaged in it. As a reserved corps, to be relied on in emergency, the State militia organization would have been much more efficient, and the agricultural or other interests would not have been so much deranged by relying on that. But enough of this; I find that I am writing much more than I intended when I first set out. What I have said is with great freedom and frankness, and with a profound sense of the great interest at stake. I trust you will receive it for what it is worth simply as a matter of opinion and judgment, and as from one friend to another conferring together upon questions in which each feels a like interest.

"I hope to be in Richmond soon, when I can personally confer more at large upon these and kindred questions, if it be agreeable to you. I am at present detained on some business, connected with the public service. I hope to be able to leave in a few days. My health is much better, though not yet restored to its usual standard. With sentiments of the highest esteem, I remain, Yours, most respectfully, Alexander H. Stephens."[63]

Stephens to the Honorable Herschel V. Johnson at Sandy Grove, Georgia, June 22, 1864:
☛ "[From] Crawfordville, Georgia, 22 June, 1864. My Dear Sir:—In my letter of yesterday, long as it was, I omitted some points that ought not to be overlooked in replying to yours of the 30th ultimo. You will therefore excuse me, I trust, for resuming the subject this morning.

"The first of these omitted points, that now occurs to me, is what you say of the reason assigned by some, why [Georgia] Gov. [Joseph E.] Brown had not sent on the resolutions passed by our legislature. Why he had not sent them, I do not know. Perhaps he had, and some miscarriage of the mail attended them. Perhaps he had not, because he was not directed to send them. How this is, I do not know. But if he has not sent them, I feel confident that his motives in not doing so, or in withholding them, could not have been such as you mention some had attributed to him. The resolution expressing 'undiminished confidence' in the President [Davis], was, I think, not connected with either set of resolutions on public affairs—either the *habeas corpus* or the peace resolutions. It was a distinct and separate resolution. This is my remembrance; and, if I am right in it, he could have withheld that if he chose, and sent on the others. But then, I do not think Gov. Brown regarded either that resolution or the others in the light in which, as you say, some are inclined to think he did. I judge him by myself. I think I took as much interest in the passage of the *habeas corpus* resolutions as anybody did or could; and I assure you much greater and higher objects by far occupied, filled, and absorbed my mind, than the censure of the President. These related to the welfare of millions living, and millions unborn—transcendently beyond in importance the contracted consideration of the position or popularity of any man living or dead! Would it not be humiliating, and almost degrading to human nature, to suppose that [George] Washington, in his ever-memorable address to the army, in March, 1783—the greatest speech I have often thought, all things considered, that was ever made by man (the speech he made in reply to the anonymous appeal that had been made to the army, to take the redress of their wrongs into their own hands)—would it not, I say, be humiliating and almost degrading to human nature to suppose, that in that noblest exhibition of patriotism upon record, that Washington was influenced by no higher object than to censure or put down the supposed author of that appeal? I do not claim for Gov. Brown, or myself, the exalted position of Washington, but I give the illustration in vindication of the honor and dignity of human nature, degraded as it is, to show that upon great occasions it is possible for the mind and soul to be elevated above the low and grovelling passions, which the reason assigned for Gov. Brown's motives presupposes. And as I think it hardly probable that Armstrong (I believe that was the name of the supposed author of the appeal) entered the mind of Washington at that time, so I think it hardly probable that Gov. Brown thought of President Davis in the connection or with the view attributed to him. He of course did not approve of President Davis' agency in the passage of the act [to suspend *habeas corpus*], or his sanction of it; nor did I. This was a source of deep pain and mortification to me, and I think it was to him. I was with him a great deal. But the objects expressed by him, and certainly entertained by me, were far higher than the bare expression of this disapprobation of the President's conduct. That was not thought of by me further than as an argument, or the expression of popular feeling upon a vital question affecting public rights, it might cause him to review the subject, and induce him to change or modify his policy in reference to it. Even this incidental effect was the source of no pleasure or gratification. It was, on the contrary, disagreeable and painful. My opinion is that Gov. Brown's feelings and views upon the subject were very similar to my own. I believe, from all that I have seen of him, that he is an ardent friend of the cause—*the cause of constitutional liberty*—that his whole soul is in the contest with this object, and has been from the beginning; that his every effort and every act is made and done with a view to secure its success; that so far from courting or seeking points of controversy with the head of the confederate government, his earnest desire is and has been to keep that government on that line of policy on which alone he thinks success is attainable—success not in achieving independence only, but success in the maintenance of constitutional liberty. He is as anxious, I believe, for harmony between the action of the State and confederate governments as any man can be, but for the sake of harmony he can never surrender principles, which he thinks if surrendered will be attended with a loss of great essential rights. When he finds himself differing from the President, whether he be right or wrong in the points of difference, justice to him requires it to be said, I think, that the cause of difference is a source to him, not of gratification, but of the deepest regret and pain. I know this is the case with myself, and I believe it to be the same with him. Moreover, with regard to that resolution which it has been supposed that Gov. Brown had such opposition to—the one complimenting the President, or expressing undiminished confidence in him—I will add, that it was offered by one of the warmest advocates of the action of the majority. It was shown to me by the mover before it was introduced. I had no objection to its passage by the legislature, and I suppose that Gov. Brown had none; especially as the object stated for offering it was to rebut the charge that the majority resolutions were intended as a mere censure of the President, and got up with a view of raising a party in opposition to him. The resolution passed without a dissenting vote. This is a history of the matter. Others may think as they please; I know my objects, views, and feelings. They looked not to a reproof or censure of the President, nor to the very small and almost contemptible idea of raising a party in opposition to him and his administration. They looked to far higher, greater, nobler purposes, not unaccompanied with an ardent and, I will add, a patriotic desire to direct and guide the President and his administration to these ends and results.

"Another point in your letter of the 30th ultimo, omitted by me yesterday, was the probable extension of the *habeas corpus* suspension to the end of the next session of Congress, and probably to the end of the war. This you attribute to the tone of expression on that measure in Georgia and North Carolina. Its harshness, in your opinion, I judge from your manner of speaking of it, tended to exasperate the advocates of the measure, and had rendered them 'more tenacious,' etc. Now allow me to say to you in all frankness, candor, and sincerity, as I always write or speak to you on all subjects and on all occasions, that I think you are entirely mistaken in your views of the cause and effect in this matter. I was not at all surprised at what you stated the prospect of the question to be, but I differ entirely as to the effect of the tone of expression in Georgia and North Carolina, and Mississippi may also be added. I looked upon the act at first as only an entering wedge. Power is ever insidious in its encroachments, or at least is usually so. Give it an inch and an ell [a right-angled bend] is soon taken. Various attempts had been made to get some such policy fixed upon the country; all had failed of perfect success. This was started and had been adopted under far more favorable auspices than any of its predecessors. It was, therefore, by far the more dangerous. When error once gets foothold, it seldom ever voluntarily abandons its advantage. Power, however insidious in its approaches, is ever insolent in a position once gained. The only sure way to meet it successfully, is with a bold, unyielding defiance at the beginning. Whoever trifles with it or dallies with it at first, is certain to become its victim in the end. This was my view of this matter when I first heard of the passage of this most monstrous act. The only sure hope of preventing its principles from becoming fixed upon the country, was such an immediate, prompt, bold, and harsh, if you please, expression of popular indignation and reprobation of it as to cause, if possible, its immediate abandonment. It was no time for soft words or temporizing. Usurpation never did and never will yield to gentle suasion. Power never let[s] go its grasp, and never will upon mild entreaty. I speak to you eternal truths in all soberness. In this instance, had the Georgia delegation in Congress, and the delegations from Mississippi and North Carolina, uttered the same stern sentiments in the same stern language which their State legislatures used, and which the great body of the people everywhere felt, this monster evil—this escaped demon from the perdition of other regions—might have been expelled and driven from our Eden! I say it might have been. That was the only sure way of its ever being done. How it may now result, time must disclose. I had but little hope, when this measure first passed, that we should ever again have constitutional liberty upon this continent. This you well know. The measure, as passed, was somewhat different from what I had supposed it to be upon the first intelligence of it. This difference afforded me grounds of stronger hopes for arresting its progress—for preventing the consummation of its mischiefs. These hopes, in turn, were soon greatly weakened by seeing the opponents of the measure yielding their position, and coming to terms with its advocates. From that day to this I have had but little hope. I was not at all surprised, therefore, at what you said was the prospect before us on this question; still *while I live and breathe I shall do, and continue to do, what I can to preserve the liberties of the people from overthrow and ruin.* I have nothing to do with the motives of men; I wish this distinctly understood, not only for once, but always. I arraign no one, and pronounce judgment upon no one. I speak of things, acts, and measures, and their inevitable tendency. My deliberate opinion is, that very few men understand, know, or appreciate the nature of their acts, the character or tendency of them. Men, at best, are but grown up children. In legislatures, or other deliberate bodies, they generally act in masses; the individual is merged in the multitude; he exercises very little of his own private judgment. This is the general rule with a large majority according to my experience and observation. To assign bad motives to such, would be as cruel, as unjust. I have no disposition to do it. As well might one poor wretch be held responsible for the sins of society. But this cannot prevent or modify my judgment of the acts of the aggregate mass, the great sins of the whole, or the ruinous tendency of them. My experience has also taught me that men hardly ever understand themselves. The wisest uninspired maxim that ever was uttered, I think is this: 'Know thyself.' Millions have repeated it, and other millions still repeat it, without the slightest comprehension of its import; hence it not unfrequently happens, when the nature or tendency of one's acts are stated to him, he flares up in a passion and in a rage, because he thinks his motives have been impugned. 'Is thy servant a dog, that he should do this thing?' exclaimed Hazael [of the Bible], on such an occasion. Now I wish to be understood, as giving it as my deliberate opinion, that Hazael was perfectly honest and sincere in the passion and indignation he expressed. The difficulty or error with him was, he did not know himself. Hazael was a representative man. As I really do not believe he was actuated by bad motives at the time the prophet was speaking to him, so I am willing to admit that every one who disagrees with me upon these questions may be equally free from bad motives; hence I assign none; charge none. But that Hazael did as he did, is history; that thousands of others under like circumstances have done as he did, is history, too; and that others still under like temptation will hereafter do what they may now think they would sooner become a dog than do, will not only probably, but almost certainly be history also. *Power is corrupting. It fascinates, intoxicates, turns the brain, and changes the nature of man; it transforms those who touch and handle it. Such is its unvarying tendency. This is an eternal truth, and no wise man or people will ever disregard it. People are never in so much danger as they are when unlimited power is in the hands of those in whom they perfectly confide.* Personalities, therefore, with me, are out of the question on these great subjects. They dwindle into insignificance; and I assure you, I almost weep for the weakness, frailty, and short-sightedness of my fellow-beings, when I see and hear such motives or feelings attributed to me. [Emphasis added, L.S.]

"But I must again stop. This letter is becoming itself long, almost as long as the one of yesterday. I fear I shall bore you. I do not wish or intend to do so. What I write is, of course, for yourself only, not for the public. I do not put any injunction upon you in reference to it, however, further than the dictates of your own judgment and discretion may suggest—only one request I will make, and that is, that you will preserve what I have written that you may review it at a future day. Neither my sentiments nor my acts, on the matters under consideration, are the result of impulse or passion. I am perfectly willing that they may be laid away and turned to hereafter, in condemnation or vindication of the impropriety or wisdom of my present course, or, at least, in condemnation or vindication of my memory: for I do not feel as if my days on this earth are many [unbeknownst to Stephens at the time, he would live for another nineteen years]. The time that I shall be further perplexed with its scenes, strifes, cares, and anxieties, is, and must be short, at best. This reflection brings but little regret to me. What of future in this existence is left for me is without any personal aspiration for myself, and with very little hope for others, so far as concerns the present prospect of good government in any part of this once happy and prosperous country [the South]. Life, therefore, has but few attractions for me. While I have been here I have with free will and of my own accord labored, I think, more for the benefit of others than I have for myself, which is more than many mortals I ever knew could say of themselves. It may be presumption in me to say it of myself, but I nevertheless do say it, believing it to be true. The consciousness that it is the truth affords me more consolation and gratification than all the honors that it is in the power of man to bestow, could possibly impart. But enough. Adieu. Let me hear from you when you have leisure. Yours, truly, Alexander H. Stephens."[64]

Stephens to the Honorable Alexander J. Marshall, at Richmond, Virginia, November 4, 1864:
☞ "[From] Crawfordville, Ga., 4th Nov., 1864. My Dear Sir:—Your kind letter of the 1st instant was received yesterday. The other package referred to in it came by the same mail. I have read both with serious attention and profound interest. The defects of the old [U.S.] constitution, and the causes of disunion, are now more properly fit subjects for the speculative philosophy of the historian, than the practical objects of inquiry on the part of the living actors who have to deal with facts as they find them, and make the best of them as they arise. Wise men will, however, study the past as closely as they watch the present and guard the future. With this view your reflections are not only entertaining but useful. . . .

"Secession, with us, I regarded as one of those moral or political epidemics to which States and communities are often subject—like other epidemics of a physical character to which humanity in general is subject. It was both infectious and contagious, baffling all skill and defying all treatment. Logically speaking, there was but one real and substantial cause for it. That was the open, palpable, and avowed breach of the compact of 1787, by a number of the States at the North in the matter of rendition of fugitives from service. A compact broken by one party to it is broken as to all. This is a universal rule of law amongst all people, civilized or savage. The old Union was, therefore, virtually broken by those faithless States at the North. Other irritating causes and apprehended dangers contributed to the consummation of the result at the South. But for this cause by itself, the seceding States will ever be justified in what they did by an impartial and enlightened world. The wisdom or policy of their course looking to their own interest is not now the question. That was a matter for them to determine for themselves in view of all the consequences attending it. *What they* [the Southern states] *did they had a perfect right, moral as well as civil, to do.* States, however, are not bound even by honor to resort to the '*ultima ratio regum*' [Latin: 'the last argument of kings'], or that which may involve it, for every cause that would fully justify them in doing it. The redress of grievances of this sort may often most wisely be postponed and other methods adopted to secure their removal. Such was my view of our case as you may, perhaps, know, in the fall of 1860. *The old Union was founded upon a compact between sovereign and independent States. This compact was based upon the idea or assumption that it was for the best interests of all to be united upon its terms, each performing and discharging faithfully to all the rest the obligations imposed by it. That assumption, in my judgment, was sound and correct.* I was, therefore, not without hopes that by our adopting a different course the offending States at the North might be brought to a reconsideration of their action. Whether that view was correct can never be certainly known. A different line of policy was adopted. By that we must abide and bring it to the best results possible. If the assumption upon which the old Union was originally based was correct, of course there could not, logically, as you say, be any objection to its ultimate restoration, if all parties could be brought to a faithful discharge of their obligations under it. But, my dear sir, the actions of men in the aggregate, of communities, states or nations, are seldom governed or controlled by logic. If they had been, many of the bloody wars which fill the history of our race never would have occurred. What was more illogical than the influences that produced the crusades for the recovery of the Holy Sepulchre, or the passions that incited deadly strife on so many fields of carnage upon such a question as the real presence? Man is certainly a strange creature, and both 'fearfully and wonderfully made.' [Emphasis added, L.S.]

"Governments, philosophically considered, are but the outward coverings, the skins or shells of society, or political organisms thrown out or developed by a natural process for the protection of the inner life, according to the laws of its being. Hence the constitutions of States must grow—they can never be made—they must spring from natural development. What is to be the future of this country time must disclose upon this principle. For dead governments or defunct empires there is no resurrection. After dissolution their elements may come up in some other living form; not upon the principle, however, of reconstruction, but upon that of new assimilation. Without busying ourselves much about the future, or making efforts to shape its destinies, *the great object at present of every well-wisher to his country should be to direct all energies, moral, intellectual, and physical, to the vindication and establishment of the principle for which the war now upon us is waged on our part*—that is the ultimate absolute sovereignty of the several States. *This principle once recognized, permanently fixed and adhered to, affords the surest grounds for the hope of a lasting peace. This, and this only, so far as I can see, will prove the self-adjusting principle, the perfect regulator in the working of our present or any new system of association of States that may arise.* With this principle settled the future may well be left to take care of itself. Mutual safety, security, protection, and interest are the natural affinities that draw people or States into alliances and confederations. When these natural laws are left perfectly free in their operation, they never fail to produce their legitimate results—the peace, prosperity, and happiness of the people in whatever associations or alliances they may arrange themselves. After the long struggle of the first war of independence [i.e., the American Revolutionary War], both parties came to the conclusion that 'reciprocal advantages and mutual convenience are found by experience to be the only permanent foundation for peace and friendship between States.' [Emphasis added, L.S.]

"This great truth, found after the most painful analysis of years in the crucible of blood, was set forth in the preamble of the provisional treaty of peace. It is for the statesman a far more useful truth than was ever the fancied philosopher's stone for the alchemist. Had it been recognized and acted upon this war with its horrors, its cruelties, sufferings, and desolation never would have occurred. To illustrate:—If, after the secession of the southern States, clearly justified by the breach of faith on the part of their northern confederates, the latter States had discovered, as they seem to have done, that the Union was of so much benefit to them, they would have looked to its restoration not by force but by a correction of their own error—by renewed assurance of good faith in the future. If, after that, the seceded States had found it to their benefit and advantage, all things duly considered, to be in union on the original terms, with good faith maintained by all, they would, as naturally as every thing in the material world obeys the law of affinity, have adjusted themselves accordingly. If they had not so found it to be their interest to renew that confederation, they would have remained separate and independent, as they ought to have done. For safety, security, and self-preservation is the first law of nature with States as well as with individuals. In the latter event, whatever treaties or leagues the reciprocal advantages and mutual convenience of both or each and all required, would have been entered into and nothing more. There would have been no war—no force—but each and all would have moved on peacefully and prosperously in their own rightful spheres. The surest way to preserve the health and vigor of the physical body, is strictly to conform to the laws of its existence. The same is true of States or governments. A fundamental principle in the old Union and constitution, one of the laws of its existence, was the reserved sovereignty of the several States.

"The right to resume the exercise of all powers delegated when safety required it, was declared by Virginia in her act of ratification. *The Union was one eminently of consent. An attempt to continue it by force, violates the law of its existence. As paradox[ic]al as it appears to many, yet it is nevertheless true, that the doctrine of the reserved sovereignty of the State, under the old constitution, carrying with it the perfect right on the part of any State to secede at pleasure, subject to no control but moral obligation, was the strongest Union doctrine consistent with the preservation of liberty ever proclaimed.* . . . Governments to be strong must indeed be held together in its parts by force. The universe is held together by force, by the strongest of all forces, by Omnipotence itself; yet the power that controls its every part, preserving forever one indissoluble whole, is nothing but the simple law of attraction. This is the force that should be looked to in binding States indissolubly. This is the force that gives governments irresistable strength in the union of all their parts. . . . [Emphasis added, L.S.]

"Under its operations, (whether our present organization shall remain, or whether new ones shall take their places in whole or in part, as exigencies may arise and the interests and the affinities of the parties may determine, in the process of future assimilation,) I can but hope that the States, both South and North, will enter upon a new career of development, prosperity, and greatness, exciting increased wonder in the old world by grander achievements hereafter to be made, than any heretofore attained under the true workings of the principles of our American institutions of self-government. But I cannot continue this theme. I must stop.

"You ask my criticism on your views, as to certain amendments of the old [U.S.] constitution, and certain defects in it, which caused the present alienation and disruption of the States. My opinion, as to the origin and cause of these troubles, is that it existed more with the people than with the government; or rather it may more properly be assigned to the prejudices and passions of the people, excited, aroused, and inflamed by unprincipled, ambitious, and selfish demagogues, North and South, than to any radical defect in the constitution. The ship was strong enough, large enough, safe enough; the real difficulty was with the crew, or those of the crew who strove amongst themselves for some share in the guidance and control of the noble, stately old craft. Of course she was not perfect in all her parts, as nothing from human hands ever was or ever will be; still, in my judgment, there was in the old constitution no inherent radical defect. As expounded by [Thomas] Jefferson and the States rights men in the Kentucky and Virginia resolutions of 1798 and 1799, it was intended to, and did, in deed and in truth, establish the 'best government on earth.' This is my deliberate judgment. *So far as our troubles in their origin can be traced to the constitution, I think, without doubt, they are attributed to the consolidating tendency with which it was administered. It was the centralizing idea that carried protection into the halls of Congress; then internal improvements; and lastly, satan-like, the slavery question.* [Emphasis added, L.S.]

"*This, after being agitated there until the popular mind was greatly excited, was carried back to the northern States by their demagogues, and made the test of party organizations. In this way those States at the North, before alluded to, were brought to their open breach of faith under the constitution, and to their virtual disruption of the Union under the compact. But for the centralizing, consolidating ideas under which the constitution was administered, (not as it was made and intended to operate by the States which formed it,) these disturbing questions would never have been entertained by Congress. But for getting seats in Congress on this hobby, there would have been no such parties formed at the North; and no such breach of faith would ever have been committed, nor would any of the other evils and excitements growing out of the slavery question, which so agitated the public mind North and South, and which did so much in the hands of demagogues in both sections, in producing the actual and final rupture, ever have occurred. In this view our present troubles may be mainly attributed to this tendency in the administration of the government to centralism and consolidation.* That clause in the constitution, to which you refer, did work injuriously to the South: but that (I speak of the whole clause) was one of the compromises of the constitution. The southern States yielded that to the North in consideration of some concession, (which one I forget now,) made by them upon the subject of slavery. *That whole clause, giving Congress power to regulate commerce, was the source of more injury to southern interests than every thing else together.* This clause authorized the navigation acts under the operation of which southern importations, and their direct trade from abroad, were crippled, and soon amounted to little or nothing. The financial system adopted, centralizing the capital of the funded public debt at the North, in combination with the navigation laws, completely revolutionized commerce, or at least changed its channels and marts in the States. Charleston, before the constitution was formed, was not much, if in any degree, inferior in trade and commerce to Boston or New York. I do not recollect the statistics exactly, but all southern ports lost largely in their trade by the operation of these navigation acts. This principle was not well understood by our people; much that was attributed to the tariff, and other imaginary causes, was due to this. The monied capital was at the North; the shipping was owned at the North. The whole coast trade was secured to American bottoms. No foreign vessel was allowed to break, bulk, or unload parts of her cargo in different ports. Hence nearly all importations in foreign bottoms were thrown into New York, Boston, or Philadelphia. These became the great marts. A ship from Liverpool coming for cotton, rice, or tobacco, would first leave her cargo of imports at New York, thence sail in ballast to Savannah, Charleston, or Norfolk for her return cargo. Northern shipping, then, under the monopoly secured by the navigation laws, distributed the assorted cargoes accumulated in the great marts as the demands in other ports required. Southern cities thus became nothing but tributaries and dependencies upon those of the North. The latter grew and prospered, while the former remained stationary or declined. This is but a glance at the system. *All growing out of that clause of the constitution agreed to on compromise as stated.* [Emphasis added, L.S.]

"But these navigation laws might have been revised and amended, so as to break down this monopoly of New England shipping, if the southern members of Congress had united with those of the west upon the question, and exerted half the efforts they wasted upon many very trifling subjects. I am not prepared to say what would be the practical workings of the system, with the omission in this clause of the words 'between the States.' I should have to think about it and study it more than I now have time to do, before arriving at any opinion satisfactory even to myself upon it. *I am so much of a States rights man, however, by nature; my first impulse is strongly in favor of the opinion that it would have been better to leave that matter to the States.* Had the States retained that power under the old system, we might perhaps under it have been enabled to bring the covenant breakers to a reconsideration of their acts of bad faith, in the matter before alluded to, without resorting to secession. This power, retained by States thus confederated, might be an important and useful check in bringing delinquent members up to the full discharge of their duties and obligations under the compact. Still I could not venture a positive opinion one way or the other, without more reflection. I should, however, never favor its exercise, simply with a view to the protection of any of the mechanic arts or industrial pursuits. That whole theory, in my judgment, is radically wrong. [Emphasis added, L.S.]

"I agree with you entirely about parties and party organizations. They are the curse and bane of republics. They can exist nowhere else. They are generally considered, to some extent, the life of free institutions; at least they seem to be so to the casual observer; and yet they have never failed to be the cause of their ultimate overthrow. This is somewhat paradoxical. Perhaps they are not what they even seem to some extent to be—the life of free institutions. This, I think, is the truth; and a little analysis will show it. Free thought, free speech, and free discussion, are the life as well as soul of free institutions. Parties generally spring from these, and necessarily, under our present modes of deciding questions. They never arise, however, except when questions are to be decided by a count of votes. The freest and most enlightened discussion may exist, and progress without any party organization, until arrangements are made for marshalling the forces for a decision of the question. How then can the bad effects of this marshalling of the forces (which soon becomes so corrupt) be best guarded against, or prevented consistently with the progress of thought, interests, and welfare of society. I have thought of it a good deal recently. To my mind the remedy is now clear. It lies in a modification of the bare plurality principle, in the decision of all questions affecting the general interest of society. A larger portion than a bare half of these, who are to decide all such questions, should be required to be consentient to any decision before it is binding upon the whole. The jury trial, which has worked so well for centuries in England, and with us, requires unanimity to give validity to the verdict. This principle might, with great profit, be carried also to the halls of legislation and the forums of election. I will not undertake to say to what extent, above plurality, and short of unanimity, it could be properly carried in either. But in a resort to this principle, lies the surest guarantees against corrupt party organizations in a republic. One of the most erroneous ideas generally entertained is, that a majority barely should govern, and that any measure is right which secures the greatest good to the greatest number. This dogma, or these dogmas, are both fundamentally wrong. That society, or the body politic, should govern itself, is true. This, however, does not imply that a bare plurality should govern all the rest. If this were so, no constitutional barriers or checks would ever be proper. The objects to be aimed at in providing a proper system for society to govern itself justly, so as that the rights of each shall be secured and the common interests of all promoted, should be to require, as far as practicable, the consentient will of the whole, expressed through its proper channels, to give validity and sanction to any measure affecting the general interests or welfare of all.

"No doctrine or principle is more unjust or pernicious than that 'of the greatest good to the greatest number.' *The true rule is the greatest good to all, to each and every one, without injury to any. No one hundred men on earth have the moral right to govern any other ninety-nine men or, less number, and to make the interests of the ninety-nine, or less number, subservient to the interests of the hundred, because thereby the greatest good to the greatest number will be promoted.* Some persons on this view (not understanding it properly) attack our institutions of the subordination of the inferior race amongst us, while others defend that system upon the principle of the greatest good to the greatest number, which I am combatting. Both these classes of persons are wrong. If slavery with us rested upon this principle, which these advocates advance, it would be wrong, and ought to be abolished, while the position assumed by me above is perfectly consistent with that institution. The solution is this: The negroes amongst us, it is true, form component elements in society. But subordination from natural [cultural] inferiority is their normal condition. This does not imply, however, that they have no rights or interests that society in its government of all its members should look after. Our institutions logically rest upon the assumption, which I think demonstrably correct, that their present relation to the white race, when properly regulated by law, is best for both parties. One thing is certain, if it is not best for both, or cannot be made best for both in view of the physical, moral, and intellectual development and advancement of both, by proper regulations to be adopted by society in its government of the whole, then the institution is wrong in principle, and ought to be abandoned. The fact is, that the relation properly regulated by law is the best for both in every view of the question in my judgment. [Emphasis added, L.S.]

"This digression you will pardon. I was drawn into it only for illustration. *Society in its government should look not to the greatest good to the greatest number, but to the greatest attainable good to all without injury or detriment to any. This should be the universal rule.* The best way to secure its practical application in republics or popular governments, in my opinion, is to make approaches toward the unanimity principle, at least in legislation. How nearly perfect unanimity should be required, or what proportion of the votes in legislative bodies should be required to pass any law, I am not prepared to say. While great mischiefs grow out of the bare majority principle as our own, as well as the history of many other countries shows, very little danger need be apprehended from such modification of it as I speak of—not even if it should be extended to a requisition of perfect unanimity. All proper laws are steps in progress by society. Society can much more safely stand still awhile as a general rule, than to venture a step without a full and clear conviction that it is in the right direction. *No truth is better established than that 'the world is governed too much.'* No new law ought ever to be passed until the wants and needs of society as a whole in its progress requires it. All checks upon legislation looking to this end are not only proper, but eminently wise. With free speech, free discussion, and a free press, the power of truth, amongst an enlightened people, would not be long in bringing the general opinion of the whole body of legislators to a proper and just appreciation of any new measure or proposed advanced step in progress—quite soon enough for that prudent, safe, and stately step, that all governments should be careful to make. Many, I am fully aware, would be disposed to consider these views utterly impracticable, if not chimerical; such persons are but superficial observers. They do not understand the true philosophy of government. It is a lamentable fact, that there has been less improvement in the progress of civilization from the lights of experience in the science of government, than in any other branch of human knowledge. I have not time now to enlarge upon those views, or to fortify the positions taken. I will simply add, that those who doubt the efficient practical working of such new checks upon legislation in our systems, as I suggest, would do well to study the annals of Poland and the [Spanish] kingdom of Arragon [Aragon]. Mr. [John C.] Calhoun, in his matchless treatise upon government, has clearly shown the admirable workings of the unanimity principle, even in the election of their chief magistrate in the former of these countries for centuries. While in Arragon, to which he does not refer, history teaches that for several hundred years the Cortes, the legislative body of the kingdom, could pass no law or elect a ruler without the vote of every member in each house. The system worked well with them. Under that system, [King] Ferdinand with [Queen] Isabella reigned. Under that system, Spain reached a higher degree of civilization than any of her neighboring States. She took the lead of all Europe—and under her liberal and enlightened auspices the new western world was discovered. Let no one hastily or rashly condemn even the unanimity principle in view of this actual practical experiment as to its workings, and working well for ages. Indeed, the liberties of Arragon were never lost until the ambitious Charles V by corrupt means procured the abandonment of this principle in the Cortes. Under it, there can be no such thing as party or party organization. All must agree; all must be of the same way of thinking; all must be of the same party before any thing can be done. Without saying more on the subject, I submit these thoughts to you as the key to the surest prevention of parties in Republics.... This letter is already much too long. I have been interrupted several times since its commencement. It is not, therefore, so connected as it otherwise might have been. I trust, however, that as long and as disjointed as it is, you will not feel bored by its perusal; if, indeed, you shall be able to decipher my hieroglyphics. I hope to be in Richmond before long, when I should like to talk over these and other matters. My health is quite feeble, though it is much better than it was last fall and winter. Yours, most respectfully, Alexander H. Stephens."[65] [Emphasis added, L.S.]

In response to growing criticism that he was working at cross purposes with President Davis and the Southern Cause, Stephens addressed this letter to "the Public" on November 10, 1864:

☛ "To The Public: The following old address [given by Stephens at Crawfordville, Georgia, on July 4, 1834] is now reprinted in this form, not with any special view to its own merits, but for the purpose of self vindication. Insinuations and flings, if not direct charges, have repeatedly been made of late against me as a new light on States' Rights, in my advocacy of the doctrine of 'the ultimate absolute sovereignty of the several States' as the only sure basis of a permanent peace between the States of the old Union.

"This address was the first written political speech ever made by me. It was made while I was a student of law, and notwithstanding its many very apparent defects (of which however as a first production I am not ashamed), it clearly shows that States' Rights and State Sovereignty are no new or latter day ideas with me. For this purpose only I ask its perusal at this time by all who may be disposed to do me justice in this particular.

"It is true I was not a Nullifier. Nullification as I understood its exposition at that day claimed the right of any State, in effect, to render null and void, or inoperative within her limits, any law of Congress, and still remain within the Union. Without any desire to revive any of the questions that then divided State Rights men, I may simply add that in my judgment then and now, the reserved Sovereign Powers of the States could be properly resorted to for ultimate protection only by a full resumption of all powers delegated; in other words by secession. In this way only could the sovereign veto of a State against actual or threatened aggression be effectually and properly interposed. When thus interposed there was no constitutional power in the Central Government to command obedience by coercion.

"It is also true that I opposed secession in 1850 and 1860, as a question of policy, but not as a matter of right. The charge that I ever at any time or on any occasion uttered the sentiment that secession would be 'a crime' is entirely without the shadow of a foundation. The clear right of a State under the compact of 1787 to resume the full exercise of all her delegated powers by a withdrawal from the Union whenever her people in their deliberate and solemnly expressed judgment should determine to do so, was never questioned by me. This was the doctrine of the States' Rights party of Georgia under the lead of the illustrious and renowned Troup—the correct teachings of the Kentucky and Virginia Resolutions of 1798 and 1799. In these principles I was reared, by them I have ever been governed in my political acts, and by them I expect to live and die. Hence when Georgia seceded in 1861, even against my own judgment, I stood by her act. To her alone I owed ultimate allegiance. Her cause became my cause. Her destiny became my destiny. From that day to this that cause has engaged every energy of my heart, head and soul, and in it they will continue to be enlisted to the bitter end. Should that end be the establishment of this principle of 'the ultimate absolute sovereignty of the several States,' it will in my judgment more than compensate for the loss of blood and treasure of this war so unjustly waged against her and her confederates, great as it has been or may be. This doctrine once firmly established will, I doubt not, prove to be the self-adjusting principle—the Continental Regulator—in our present or any future systems of associations or confederations of States that may arise. I make no boast of consistency so far as party relations are concerned—these I have often changed, but principles never."⁶⁶

This letter, penned by Stephens, and signed by Confederate commissioners Robert M. T. Hunter and John A. Campbell, was written to U.S. General Ulysses S. Grant on January 30, 1865, in preparation for the Hampton Roads Conference. The meeting, proposed by the South, was designed to bring the North to the table to discuss drawing the War to an immediate close. It was the only known instance in which Lincoln met personally with, or even recognized, peace ambassadors from the Confederacy (of which there had be many previously). There can be no doubt that Lincoln only agreed to the Hampton Roads Conference because he already knew the North was on the verge of winning the War. Indeed, going into the meeting, he had already planned out his shameless plot to further weaken the Southern position by offering only one method of ending the War: "unconditional surrender," something he knew the South would never do. Thus he had nothing to lose and everything to gain from attending:

☞ "Petersburg, Va., Jan. 30, 1865. Lieut.-Gen. U. S. Grant, Commanding Armies of the United States: Sir: We desire to pass your lines under safe conduct, and to proceed to Washington to hold a conference with President Lincoln upon the subject of the existing war, and with a view of ascertaining upon what terms it may be terminated, in pursuance of the course indicated by him in his letter to Mr. [Francis P.] Blair [Sr.] of Jan. 18, 1865, of which we presume you have a copy, and if not, we wish to see you in person, if convenient, and to confer with you on the subject. Very respectfully yours, Alexander H. Stephens, J. A. Campbell, R. M. T. Hunter."⁶⁷

Stephens to General Grant, February 1, 1865:

☞ "City Point, Feb. 1, 1865. To Lieut.-Gen. Grant: Sir: We [Stephens, Hunter, and Campbell] desire to go to Washington City to confer informally with the President personally, in reference to the matters mentioned in his letter to Mr. Blair of the 18ᵗʰ of January, ult., without any personal compromise on any question in the letter. We have the permission to do so from the Authorities in Richmond. Very respectfully yours, Alexander H. Stephens."⁶⁸

This letter by Stephens (and signed by Hunter and Campbell) appears to have been written on February 2, 1865, to General Grant:

☞ "The substantial object to be attained by the informal Conference is to ascertain upon what terms the existing war can be terminated honorably. Our instructions contemplate a personal interview between President Lincoln and ourselves at Washington; but, with this explanation, we are ready to meet any person or persons that President Lincoln may appoint, at such place as he may designate. Our earnest desire is that a just and honorable peace may be agreed upon, and we are prepared to receive or to submit propositions which may possibly lead to the attainment of that end. Very respectfully yours, Alex. H. Stephens, Robert M. T. Hunter, John A. Campbell."[69]

Stephens (along with Hunter and Campbell) sent this letter to Union Major Thomas T. Eckert on February 2, 1865:
☛ "City Point, Va., Feb. 2,1865. Thomas T. Eckert, Major and A.D.C.: Major: In reply to your verbal statement that your instructions did not allow you to alter the conditions upon which a passport would be given to us, we say that we are willing to proceed to Fortress Monroe, and there to have an informal conference with any person or persons that President Lincoln may appoint, on the basis of his letter to Francis P. Blair of the 18th of January, ultimo, or upon any other terms or conditions that he may hereafter propose not inconsistent with the essential principles of Self-government and Popular Rights, upon which our institutions are founded. It is our earnest wish to ascertain, after a free interchange of ideas and information, upon what principles and terms, if any, a just and honorable peace can be established without the further effusion of blood, and to contribute our utmost efforts to accomplish such a result. We think it better to add, that in accepting your passport, we are not to be understood as committing ourselves to anything, but to carry on this informal conference with the views and feelings above expressed. Very respectfully yours, etc., Alex. H. Stephens, R. M. T. Hunter, J. A. Campbell."[70]

The Hampton Roads Conference failed, of course, just as devious Lincoln had planned. The War dragged on for another two months, and thousands more lives were lost unnecessarily. After the unsuccessful meeting, Stephens sent this letter to Confederate President Jefferson Davis on February 5, 1865. It was signed by Stephens' colleagues at the meeting, Robert M. T. Hunter and John A. Campbell:
☛ "Richmond, Va., February 5, 1865. To The President Of The Confederate States: Sir: Under your letter of appointment of the 28th ult., we proceeded to seek an 'informal conference' with Abraham Lincoln, President of the United States, upon the subject mentioned in the letter. The conference was granted, and took place on the 30th inst. [this appears to be a typo: the meeting took place on February 3, 1865], on board of a steamer in Hampton Roads, where we met President Lincoln and the Hon. Mr. [William H.] Seward, Secretary of State of the United States. It continued for several hours, and was both full and explicit.

"We learned from them that the Message of President Lincoln to the

Congress of the United States, in December last, explains clearly and distinctly his sentiments as to the terms, conditions, and method of proceeding, by which peace can be secured to the people, and we were not informed that they would be modified or altered to obtain that end. We understand from him that no terms or proposals of any treaty, or agreement, looking to an ultimate settlement, would be entertained or made by him with the Confederate States, because that would be a recognition of their existence as a separate Power, which, under no circumstances, would be done; and for like reasons that no such terms would be entertained by him from the States separately; that no extended truce or armistice (as at present advised) would be granted, without a satisfactory assurance in advance of a complete restoration of the authority of the United States over all places within the States of the Confederacy.

"That whatever consequence may follow from the reestablishment of that authority must be accepted; but that individuals, subject to pains and penalties under the laws of the United States, might rely upon a very liberal use of the power confided to him to remit those pains and penalties if peace be restored.

"During the conference the proposed [Thirteenth] Amendment to the Constitution of the United States, adopted by Congress on the 31st ult. [i.e., December 31, 1864], was brought to our notice. This Amendment declares that neither Slavery nor involuntary servitude, except for crimes, should exist within the United States, or any place within their jurisdiction, and that Congress should have power to enforce this Amendment by appropriate legislation. Of all the correspondence that preceded the conference herein mentioned, and leading to the same, you have heretofore been informed. Very respectfully, your obedient servants, Alex. H. Stephens, Robert M. T. Hunter, John A. Campbell."[71]

Stephens to his good friend James A. Stewart, July 21, 1865. At the time, Stephens was illegally imprisoned at Fort Warren, a Yankee garrison located in Boston Harbor, Massachusetts. Stephens asks for a fair trial before a jury, something no liberal Northerner wanted—or ever allowed. Why? Because it would have exposed the unconstitutionality of Lincoln's War and his many crimes. Thus Stephens was freed from prison without explanation after five months:

☞ "21st July, 1865. Mr. J. A. Stewart, Louisville, Ky.: My Dear Sir:—Yours of the 10th inst. was received to-day. Language would fail to express to you the thanks I feel for it. I cannot write to you as fully as I wish. I am suffering from rheumatism in the hand, and cannot use the pen without pain. You will please take the will for the deed.

"You understand me thoroughly, I think. I went with the State on secession from a sense of duty only. No more ardent or devoted friend to the

Constitution of the United States, and the principles of civil and religious liberty therein embodied and guaranteed, than I was and am, ever breathed the vital air of heaven; and no one can rejoice more than I at the prospect of seeing peace and prosperity restored to our once happy land. This appears from the indications of the [U.S.] President's [Andrew Johnson] policy. No one would take more pleasure in using his powers to the utmost extent in that direction, if permitted, than I should, if my counsels should be sought. I have no desire, on my own account, however, ever to have anything to do with public affairs again. But if I were at liberty, and the people should desire to know my sentiments, I should take great pleasure in giving them. Perhaps in Georgia they are in better condition to listen to me than they ever were before. I know this was the case when I was taken away; and I know my counsel was peace and the full and perfect acceptation of the new order of things. I mean the abolition of slavery.

"I am sincerely thankful to you for your letter to the President. Why I am confined here, and that too under such rigorous orders, is a mystery to me. . . . I do not understand why I, who exerted my every effort to prevent the strife, and then my every effort to end it in the speediest manner, reasonably, by peaceful adjustment of some sort, should be the victim of such sufferings as I am. This is what is strange, mysterious, and unaccountable to me. I therefore thank you for your letter to the President. You have known my course throughout. I feel assured, if I could but confer with him face to face, that I could satisfy him that I am, upon all principles of justice, entitled to parole. If, from the office I held under the Confederate organization, and which was accepted with the sole view of doing all in my power to maintain the principles of the government under the circumstances, it should be thought proper to make an example of me by trial for treason—that, it seems to me, is no reason why I should be punished as I am, in advance of the punishment first to be found to be right, by judgment of the law. My parole would be most sacredly adhered to.

"But I can say no more, except again to thank you for your letters—the one to me just received, and the one you wrote to the President. I should be glad to hear from you often.

"This I shall send to Louisville, with directions to be forwarded to Rome, Ga., in case you shall have left the former place before it reaches there. Yours truly, Alexander H. Stephens."[72]

Stephens to J. Barnett Cohen, July 4, 1866:
☛ "Crawfordville, Ga., July 4, J866. My Dear Sir: I have but a moment to thank you for your letter of the 9th June. It was a long one, it is true, and I liked

it the better for that. I have just got through reading it. It came to the office here while I was absent attending our supreme court at Milledgeville. I was gone over three weeks and only got back a few days ago. I am now going through with my correspondence which heavily accumulated during the time I was away. The labor in this particular is great, hence I can only thank you for yours. . . . Our only hope [now], the only hope for the country, is with the conservatives [then the Democrats] of the North. But outside the Democratic party at the North we have but few friends, and constitutional liberty has but few friends there outside of that organization. Hence a great deal will depend upon how they act towards the new movement. You are right about the ultimate destiny of the black race amongst us I think. But I can say no more. Kind regards to Mrs. Cohen and your father. Should I go to Charleston I shall certainly avail myself of your kind invitation."[73]

Stephens to J. Barnett Cohen, May 25, 1867:
☛ "Crawfordville, Ga., May 25, 1867. My Dear Sir: Your letter of the 20th inst. was received yesterday. . . . I am extremely weak and feeble, am suffering very much today, am hardly able to be up and scribble these lines. As a general answer . . . I will say that I do not think that the Congress plan when carried out as it will be can be successfully worked—the two races can not coexist in their proportions in this country on this basis. What is to be the end I do not know. But reason and logic lead me to the conclusion that the system cannot be worked. The wish is not father to the thought with me in this instance. Far from it! Nothing could rejoice me more than the grand spectacle that the exhibition of the successful workings of our system of self govt. would thus present to an astonished world. But I do not think any such grand, moral and even sublime result is in store for us. I do not look to any such result. While I shall do nothing to hinder it or obstruct it yet I tell you candidly that I do not think humanity capable of such a demonstration. The system in my judgment will not work. It will break down and with its breaking down all semblance even of self govt. by both races will go with it. *We are upon the verge of a consolidated centralized despotic empire. We are fast abandoning the Teutonic systems on which our institutions were based and are lapsing fast into the Asiatic system of empire.* I can say no more. What is said is for yourself only. I am ever glad to hear from you. Write to me often."[74] [Emphasis added, L.S.]

Stephens to J. Barnett Cohen, July 15, 1867:
☛ "Crawfordville, Ga., July 15, 1867. My Dear Sir: Your welcome letter of the 10th inst. was received some days ago. I have not been able to reply sooner. I am quite out of health. . . . [It] is . . . my opinion that the action of the

majority of Congress is governed by no fixed principles or settled policy. They themselves do not know what they may do. The ruling principle with them is power, and they will do anything to secure that. I think they will secure their object without resorting to [the] confiscation [policy of Liberal Pennsylvania politician Thaddeus Stevens, in which the slaves of Southern slave owners would be seized if their owners were found to have aided the Confederacy]. As I wrote to you before, I think constitutional liberty on the continent is in its last death struggles. Did you get that letter?"[75]

Stephens to James A. Stewart, August 10, 1868:
☞ "Liberty Hall, Crawfordville, Ga., 10th August, 1868. Mr. J. A. Stewart, Rome, Ga.: My Dear Sir:—Your letter of the 2nd ult. came to the office here, as you know, while I was in Atlanta defending the Columbus prisoners before the late military commission at that place. I informed you, when we met there during that trial, that your letter had been received; that it had been forwarded to me there; and that I would reply to it so soon as I should have sufficient leisure and a suitable opportunity. This promise I now fulfill; and in doing it, I can but repeat in writing substantially what I said to you verbally upon the subject.

"Your motives, in not going with your State in her act of secession, I always respected. In reference to this measure we stood together on one point—that was the impolicy of it.

"On two other points, however, we differed widely. These were, first, its rightfulness as a sovereign remedy against Federal wrongs; and, secondly, the results of its success, when resorted to, upon our institutions generally. I believed in the right—you did not!

"I believed, also, when it was resorted to (however strongly I was opposed to it as a politic or expedient remedy for then existing wrongs), that the only sure hope for the preservation of Constitutional liberty in this country, North as well South, was in the success of the measure; that is, in the successful maintenance and establishment of the principle of the sovereignty of the separate States. In this view you differed from me '*toto coelo*' [Latin: diametrically]. Your only sure hope for the same end was the failure of the cause, and the re-establishment of what you considered the legitimate national authority. The reasons and convictions by which you were governed I then fully understood. From your conversations with me before secession, and your letters to me after that event, I knew perfectly well what they were. Your motives, as I have said, I respected. Your patriotism I did not doubt. Your devotion to principles, as you understood them, I considered equal in sincerity to that of any man I ever knew. Not more so, however, than my own. My own convictions were as strong and thorough as human convictions or belief can be, that you were wrong on both the points of our disagreement referred to. A mutual tolerance of these differences preserved our friendship during the war; and it was only after repeated indications, in your letters to me pending the 'reconstruction measures' of Congress, of your great disappointment at the results, and the then general tendency of public affairs, that I took occasion to call your attention to the elaborate exposition of all these antecedent questions in the *'Constitutional View'* [Stephens' book], etc., and to ask you what you thought of it.

"The object was, that from that exposition you might perhaps, see, that it was a radical error to suppose that constitutional liberty with us could be maintained by attempting to perpetuate, by force, a Union of States voluntarily associated by compact!

"A calm review of the whole question, I thought, might bring you to a reconsideration and change of your previous opinions, and sincere convictions, as I knew them to be, as to the nature of our system of Government, and the surest means of preserving liberty under it. In this work were thoroughly discussed, those points on which we had so widely differed at the beginning of our public troubles.

"My object, as stated before, was not controversy. It was simply to impress upon your mind the great truths set forth in the work alluded to, establishing the sovereignty of the States; from a denial of which came the war with all its calamities—from which came all our present political ills—and from which, I fear, will come much greater and more disastrous ills of a like character hereafter.

"You say you have had but little time to devote to the consideration of the more explicit statement of my views on State Sovereignty submitted in my last letter for your further reflection and meditation; and then you go on to offer what you style 'desultory remarks,' to show why you refused to go with your State when she attempted to resume her delegated powers, &c.

"Now, these remarks so offered, are by no means uninteresting to me as matters of personal history, but you must allow me most respectfully to say to you, that they do not touch the great facts of the history of our country, to which your attention was at first called, and to which it was again earnestly directed.

"The reasons assigned for your not going with your State, your conscientious belief as set forth, may be quite sufficient to justify you in the judgment of all unprejudiced minds, as an honest, sincere, conscientious man; and not intentionally derelict in the discharge of any duty understood, and considered as such. They certainly so justify you in my estimation, and they so justified you in my estimation during the war. Just as I, for like considerations, perhaps, stood justified in your personal good opinion, notwithstanding the course I took in the conflict when it arose. Of this personal good opinion on your part, and even kind feelings towards me, I received evidences and testimonials of a character, and under circumstances never to be forgotten; and never to be thought of without emotions of gratitude.

"But all this has nothing to do with the great questions of the right, or wrong of secession; the right and the wrong of the war; which are so fully discussed in the book. It has nothing to do with the question of State Sovereignty, on which depends the right of secession; and with it the solution of the question, on which side, in the war that followed, is to be placed the right of the contest; and also, on which side the present evils, so seriously felt by all of us, are chargeable—on the side of secession, or on the side of those who made war to prevent it.

"Let me again ask you to re-read the book. Study it closely. Examine its array of facts—not my statement of them, but the records therein produced themselves—these enduring monuments of history. When you have done so, put to yourself these questions. Is it true that the Colonies, before their Declaration of Independence, were separate and distinct political organizations?

"Is it true, that in making the Declaration of their Independence, they voted by Colonies, and thus unanimously declared themselves to be Free and Independent (not nation) but States?

"Is it true that before this Declaration was made, a committee was raised by the Congress that made it to prepare Articles of Confederation between them as separate, distinct, sovereign States, to go into effect after the Declaration should be made?

"Is it true that these Articles of Confederation were afterwards reported and entered into, and in them it was declared:

> 'Each State retains its Sovereignty, Freedom and Independence, and every Power, Jurisdiction and Right which is not by this Confederation expressly delegated to the United States in Congress assembled'?

"Is it true that this Congress expressly declared that the allegiance of the citizens of the several States was due to the State?

"Is it true that in the Treaty of Peace, in 1783, Great Britain acknowledged the Independence and Sovereignty of each of the States separately, and by name?

"Is it true that the Supreme Court of the United States, in 1805, decided that 'on the 4th of October, 1776, (after the general Declaration of Independence on the 4th of July before,) the State of New Jersey was completely a Sovereign and Independent State, and had a right to compel the inhabitants of the State to become citizens thereof'?

"Is it true that Judge [Samuel] Chase, from the same bench, in 1796, gave forth these utterances:

> 'In June, 1776, the Convention of Virginia was a Free, Sovereign, and Independent State, and on the fourth of July, 1776, following, the United States, in Congress assembled, declared the thirteen United Colonies Free and Independent States; and that as such they had full power to levy war, conclude peace, &c. I consider this as a declaration, not that the United Colonies jointly, in a collective capacity, were Independent States, &c, but that each of them had a right to govern itself by its own authority, and its own laws without any control from any other power on earth'?

"Is it true that Chief Justice [John] Marshall, from the same bench, as late as 1824, declared that under the Confederation the States were completely Sovereign and Independent?

"If, after a thorough examination, the answer is Yes, as it must be, to each of these questions—for the proofs of the facts embraced in them, adduced in the volume referred to, are incontestable—then allow me, without submitting any more of a like character, now to ask you—barely for your reflection, and with a view to elicit an answer—if these be really the facts of history, does it avail anything against them, for you to inform me, however honestly and sincerely, that you do not believe that absolute paramount State Sovereignty ever did exist in this country, either before or after the adoption of the present Constitution? This is about the substance of what you say upon that subject.

"It is not my purpose to argue the case at this time. I simply ask if the facts be as set forth, were not your previous opinions, which are now repeated, founded in error? You say, for instance, 'the Government of the United States, as I understand it, is of the nature of an indissoluble partnership.' But is this a correct understanding of it, if the facts of its history be as set forth in the *Constitutional View*? Must not these facts be assailed and demolished, or must not this understanding be abandoned? Is not one or the other of these alternatives a logical necessity? Can opinions, theories, assumptions, or understandings of any sort be maintained against unquestionable and indisputable facts, when intellect, guided by reason is the arbiter?

"This is the view I have endeavored, and still endeavor to impress upon you. The real undeniable facts of history, and not our crude understanding of them, must prevail in this matter. Moreover, allow me to say that I do not know that I exactly comprehend what you mean by an indissoluble partnership. There is, and can be no such thing in law, as an indissoluble partnership between persons in any of the business transactions of life, much less can there be any such thing between Sovereign States or Nations.

"Again, what avail is it for you to tell me that the question of difference between the advocates of a strong Government [i.e., Liberals] and the advocates of a Government of delegated and limited powers [i.e., Conservatives] in the Convention that formed the present Constitution, was settled by that body 'ordaining a National Congress, a National Judiciary, and a National Executive,' &c, if the records taken from the Journal show directly the reverse of this to be the fact of the case, as those adduced in the volume referred to do most explicitly show? Is it or not true that the word *National* was stricken out of the draft of the proposed plan of Government, then before them, wherever it occurred, and the words 'United States,' or 'Congress' substituted in its place?

"Was not *National Legislature* stricken out and *Congress* put in its stead? Was not the meaning of the word *Congress* well understood? Did it not then and now mean an assemblage of States? *Congress*, under the first Articles of Confederation, was the meeting in council of the several separate sovereign States, through their duly appointed and accredited representatives. This well-known word, with its proper and legitimate meaning, was retained in the present Constitution. There was no change in this particular in the present Articles of Union from those of the first Confederation. *Congress* means the same now that it did before the Convention of 1787 met. It means the assemblage of sovereign States in grand council. It was known not as the National Legislature, as by some it is called, but as 'the Congress of the United States.' Under the first Articles of Union, this council of States consisted of but one house. Now it consists of two. The members of both, however, are chosen by the States, as States; and every law that has been passed since the adoption of the present Constitution, as before, is in the name and by the authority, not of a National Legislature, but expressly by the authority of 'States in Congress assembled.' Moreover, in the new arrangement it was so provided, as I have before said to you, that no law can pass, nor can any person be appointed to any high office of honor or trust, if a majority of the States vote against it. Delaware to-day, with her little over one hundred thousand population, has as much power to prevent the ultimate passage of a law, as New York with her nearly forty times that number. Are these facts or not? If facts, what becomes of your idea of the fundamental majority principle of the Government? These are the points, in all legitimate inquiry on these subjects, first to be ascertained and settled. The book referred to showed them to be incontestable facts.

"Then again, what avail is it for you to tell me that 'the power to each State at its own will and pleasure to withdraw from the Union and resume the delegated powers, was not reserved' under the Constitution, if it be true, as matter of fact, that the sovereignty of the States was not surrendered by the adoption of the Constitution? That they were sovereign before must be received as an unquestionable fact. And the bare fact that all the powers possessed by the Federal Government are by universal accord admitted to be delegated only, ought to be of itself sufficient to satisfy any one that the Paramount Authority delegating must of necessity have continued to exist. So general was this opinion in the minds of those who framed the Constitution, that nothing was said on that subject in the instrument, as it at first came from their hands. But, to quiet the apprehensions of many upon that point, it was soon after expressly stated in an amendment unanimously adopted by the States, that 'the powers not delegated to the United States by the Constitution, nor prohibited by it to the States, are reserved to the States respectively, or to the people.' This settled the question that sovereignty, the source of all political power, was reserved or retained by the States severally, under the second Articles of Union, as it had been under the first. So stated Samuel Adams when this amendment was before the Massachusetts Convention. No one in the Convention that framed the Constitution questioned the sovereign right of the States severally to secede from the first Articles of Union, though upon their face they were declared to be perpetual. Eleven States did thus, of their own will and pleasure, withdraw from the first Union, by virtue of this power or right, which was incident to their sovereignty, and entered into the new articles. The two other States left by them soon followed. The same power or right to withdraw in like manner from the second Articles of Union necessarily remained as an incident of the same sovereignty. Hence, if the facts of our history be as set forth in the book referred to, it must be admitted that the power to withdraw at pleasure was reserved to the States. Judge [Joseph] Story and Mr. [Daniel] Webster fully admitted this. All rational minds must admit it. The whole question therefore turns upon the truth of the facts of our history set forth in the book. These I cannot repeat here, but re-invite your attention to them.

"What you say about the power to disturb the domestic tranquillity, or injure the general welfare, not being reserved, I fully admit. The power wrongfully to disturb the domestic tranquillity of neighboring States, is not a natural right of Sovereignty. The powers reserved to the States were all the natural rights of nations, as established by the laws of nations; except such as were delegated to their co-States, and such as were covenanted not to be exercised by them separately, while the bond of their associated union should continue. In this respect there is not the slightest difference between the provisions of the present Constitution and the first Articles of Confederation. It was because the right to disturb the domestic tranquillity of their neighbors was not reserved to the States, and did not by nature belong to their

Sovereignty, that the Southern States so justly complained of the settled policy of many of their Northern Confederates to disturb their domestic tranquillity, and even to stir up insurrections in them.

"A great deal more I could say on the same line, but I have not time. What I have said, is sufficient to show you that nothing in your letter, now before me, bears at all upon the great questions to which I first called your attention, and which underlie the whole subject. The latter part of your letter I do endorse fully; I recognize in it a paraphrase only of what I said myself upon some occasion. I did consider the Constitution, as made by the Fathers, as embodying the best system of Government ever devised by man. While the breaches of faith on the part of some of our Northern Confederated States, were sufficient to justify a withdrawal from the Union, on the part of the Southern States, yet I did not think a withdrawal the wisest or best, or even surest policy, to obtain a redress of the grievances of which they so justly complained. The state of things then existing, sprung from no defect in the Constitution; it was the work of demagogues, both South and North; chiefly, however, at the North. I, moreover, greatly doubted if we had statesmanship enough at the South to guide our fortunes safely and successfully, in case this course should be adopted. I had the liveliest apprehensions that the end would be just what it is. These views, however, did not weaken in the least, my devotion to the great principles—the eternal truths—upon which our Government was established, and upon which, alone, you will allow me to say, in my judgment, Constitutional Liberty, on this continent, can be maintained and perpetuated. Had these principles been adhered to—if no war had been waged against the seceding States, I feel quite sure we should, sooner or later—perhaps before this time—as I have said before, have had a restoration of the whole Union, upon the same principles of voluntary agreement, that it was at first formed upon.

". . . But, with your views of the nature of the Government of the United States, you will allow me, most respectfully, to say, I do not see how you can complain of its late action, even in the enfranchisement of the blacks. If a National Congress was ordained with full power to pass all laws that they might deem proper, for the general welfare, with a National Judiciary to interpret, a National Executive, with an army and navy to execute, why has not the present Congress the perfect right to enfranchise the blacks, and place them upon a perfect equality with the whites in any respect, if they think the general welfare and domestic tranquillity require it? But, my dear Sir, without saying more, let me assure you in conclusion, that *our fathers made no such government. Further, I will add that any government in this country, administered on these principles, as ours has been for the last eight years, will and must end, in a short time, in Empire and*

Despotism. Yours truly, Alexander H. Stephens."[76] [Emphasis added, L.S.]

Stephens to J. Barnett Cohen, April 16, 1870:
☞ "Liberty Hall, Crawfordville, Ga., Apr. 16, 1870. My Dear Sir: I have wanted to write to you for some time and return you my thanks as well as acknowledgments for the papers you sent me; but the truth is I have been too unwell to do anything. When I was able to be up at all I devoted what strength I had to the completion of the 2nd vol. of my work on the war [*A Constitutional View of the Late War Between the States*]. All the writing on that as well as nearly all my other writing for twelve months and more has been done by the hands of others. It is painful to me to use the pen. But occasionally I do scribble a letter to particular friends as I am now doing and on matters of private business, but all else is done by others. I can sit up and read what is brought to me but I can not stand or walk or help myself in any way in getting about or even in dressing, without assistance of some sort. The book is now off my hands and I hope to recuperate my nervous energies to some extent though I fear I shall never be on foot again. Can you not come up and see me. You may be assured I should be highly gratified to welcome you here, not only once but often. I feel greatly obliged to you for your review of the [*Harper's Weekly*?] controversy. I take it for granted that you were the author of the piece on that subject which I saw in the *Charleston Courier*."[77]

Stephens to onetime Lincoln supporter Francis P. Blair, Sr., May 8, 1871:
☞ "Liberty Hall, Crawfordville, Ga., 8 May, 1871. My Dear Sir: Your esteemed letter of the 3rd instant written at St Louis, Mo. has just reached me—I thank you for it. . . . I can well see how a man could have been most conscientiously and earnestly devoted to the emancipation of the negroes in this country. No man I think was more so or could have been more so than [Southerner] Mr. [Thomas] Jefferson was. However much therefore I may have differed with others upon that question while it was a living one, yet I can now not only cordially co-operate with all such men, since that question is forever out of the way, upon all the really practical and living questions of the present and future which involve the essentials and essence of liberty itself—and the more so when I meet with men of that class, who show by their acts that they were moved by earnest convictions and devotion to what they deemed the just rights of man on the question of emancipation. The only real difference, as I see it, between myself and [others on this point] . . . is the question of having an affirmance of the 14th and 15th amendments. . . . Now . . . the War was over, peace was declared, the 13th amendment was ratified. Slavery was forever abolished. All the states had returned to their obligations under the

constitution. This was what the war had been waged for. At first it was waged solely with a view to compel the withdrawing states to return to their obligations under the constitution—when this was accomplished its end was attained—but under this negro slavery which was the prime exciting cause of it had been overthrown by it. It was abandoned in good faith by the returning states—these states were then certainly entitled to their seats in the Congress of States, for withdrawing from which the war had been waged against them, and which they [were assured during the while?—original editor's note] war was going on were vacant and awaiting their return. The denial of this return, and the Revolution forced by arms on their Govt. by which the 14th and 15th amendments were claimed to have been passed, was certainly a most glaring usurpation—after the war was over—after all its ends were attained and not as any thing growing out of the war. . . .

"The way is pointed out or clearly indicated in the Ky. Resolutions in the late Democratic Convention of that State, which have just reached me and with which as a whole I am greatly pleased. These Resolutions are brief but significant—they are potent not only in what they affirm but in what they do not affirm. . . . The great breaker ahead in the ranks of the Democracy is a positive affirmance of the validity of any usurpation caused by federal violence and perfidy. . . .

"*The ballot and the checks of the Constitution are the only sure safe guards of the people against the schemes of those who are now aiming at the overthrow of liberty and the establishment of a centralized Despotism in this country*. On such a program, if power can be wrested from the hands of those who are now so outrageously abusing it for their ambitious and wicked purposes, all the questions growing out of the 14th and 15th amen[dmen]ts touching either their validity or effect can be practically easily settled through the instrumentality of the Constitution without wrong to any person or interest in the Country, by those who are really devoted to the great cause of maintaining and preserving free institutions on this continent—and that is now the only real living and absorbing question. . . ."[78] [Emphasis added, L.S.]

Stephens to J. Barrett Cohen, September 18, 1881:
☞ "Liberty Hall, Crawfordville, Ga., Sept. 18, 1881. My Dear Sir: Your very highly appreciated letter of the 16th inst. with P.S. of yesterday was received today—Sunday—and as I was at leisure I enjoyed its perusal very much. Do come and see me 'immediately if not sooner.' I want to talk over divers matters with you, among other things that law argument which you sent me and which I did receive but did not have time to write you about as I wished. I have been exceedingly busy on my work—devoting all my time and strength to it.

I want to get through with it before the meeting of Congress. I will say no more now but to repeat my request for you to come as soon as you can. Drop me a postal [a] day or two before you start so I will know when to look for you."79

2

PUBLIC SPEECHES - PART 1
1844-1860

STEPHENS GAVE HUNDREDS OF SPEECHES during his life. Those in this chapter, which derive from his time as a Georgia state representative in the U.S. Congress, are excellent examples of his antebellum views. During this period he switched back and forth between political parties a number of times, from the Whigs (Liberals), to the Constitutional Union Party (which he helped found), to the Democrats (the Conservatives of the day). Throughout this process we see Stephens' innate conservatism and adherence to the Constitution increasing.

Stephens was elected to the Georgia state legislature by "general ticket." Since the laws had recently been changed—requiring candidates to be voted in by districts—some questioned the constitutionality of his right to a seat. On February 9, 1844, Stephens challenged his opponents in the Georgia state legislature in the following excerpt of his speech before the House:

☞ "The majority of the Committee of Elections, in their report, which is now under consideration, affirm that the

> 'second section of the act of apportionment is an attempt, by the introduction of a new principle, to subvert the entire system of legislation adopted by the several States of the Union, and to compel them to conform to certain rules established by Congress for their government.'

"Sir, I cannot agree with the committee in opinion that such was either the object of the act in question, or can, in any way be its consequence. If so, I should be the last to advocate the measure. I consider myself as one of those who hold the doctrine that the permanency of our institutions can only be preserved by confining the action of the State and Federal governments each to its own proper sphere; and that, while there should be no encroachment upon the rights of the States by this Government, there should also, on their part, be no disobedience or failure to perform their duties according to the terms of the constitutional compact.

". . . Sir, it is the most equal system. It is the most republican. It gives every section of the State a representative. It gives the minority in the State a voice in the National Councils. It increases the responsibility of the representative to his constituents, and better enables the constituents, from personal acquaintance and intercourse, to judge correctly of the man to whom they confide the important trust of legislating for them. But I cannot enumerate the advantages of this system at this time; I will barely, however, add that, if from no other consideration, I should be in favor of it from its conservative tendency. Under its operation, parties in the different States are more nearly balanced against themselves, and their violence is more nearly neutralized by its counteraction. This tends very much to check that high degree of excitement, which otherwise would prevail on many questions, and might be most deleterious in its consequences. To be useful and salutary, laws must have some continuance and stability. But if the opposite principle should prevail, or, if even the four larger States in the Union should adopt the general ticket mode of election, who is so careless an observer of men and things as not to see the consequences that would result?

"The representatives from each of these States, instead of being divided as they now are, so as almost to balance each other in party strength, would most probably all be on the same side of the question; and might, perhaps, be elected by only a few hundred majority in their respective States; and to the next Congress another delegation, equal in number and equally divided on the other political side, might be returned by about as large a majority the other way. The effect would be an entire change of measures; for the past admonishes, and the present speaks in language not to be misunderstood, that party rules every thing.

"Amongst the dangers to which our system of government is exposed, I consider as not the least, the effects upon the public interests of the country of those fearful shocks produced by the sudden change of such large party majorities upon this floor. The human system, in its soundest health and fullest vigor and strength, cannot long sustain its healthful action against quick transitions from the extremes of temperature. The most deeply laid and substantially built of human edifices cannot stand amidst the oscillations of an unsteady earth; nor can the government of a free people, the noblest of all human structures, remain firm, if its elements and foundation are subject to constant vibrations. Its basis is public opinion; and the elements of the human mind are not unlike those of the atmosphere about us—which, however still, and calm, and quieted today, may be roused into the whirlwind to-morrow. And as the mild air we breathe, when put into commotion, assumes all the power and terrific force of the tornado, laying waste and in ruin every thing in its desolating sweep; so with the passions, prejudices, and ambition of men, when excited and aroused into factious strife: without reason or argument to control their action, every thing relating to order, right, law, or constitution, is equally disregarded: and government itself cannot be saved from its ruthless destruction. Wise legislation should always guard against every thing tending to promote such excitements. It was in this view of this subject, and to guard, as far as possible, against the liability of such results, that the same wise statesman—the pure patriot, the sage of Montpelier [James Madison]—to whom I have before alluded, while the adoption of the Constitution was before the American people, urged upon them the necessity of establishing such checks and restraints in their government as would be a 'defence for them against their own temporary errors and delusions'—assuring them that, if the people of Athens had possessed such provident safeguards for their protection, 'they might have escaped the indelible reproach of decreeing to the same citizens the hemlock on one day and statues the next.'"[80]

During the 1844 presidential election Stephens voted for Henry Clay, a Southerner who was against the annexation of Texas. Stephens, however, was greatly in favor of the idea, as he lays out in the following speech given on July 25, 1845, before his state legislature. This address marked the beginning of his split away from the Whig Party:

☛ "For the information of those of my constituents who have not seen a history of the proceeding when the vote came to be taken, it may not be improper to state that several of the propositions alluded to in the foregoing speech were offered in the Committee of the Whole, and were each successively rejected; and against each of them I voted in their order. At length, Mr. Milton Brown, a Whig member from the State of Tennessee, presented his plan, to which reference is also made in the speech; and for this myself and seven other Southern Whigs voted, and it was carried in the committee by a vote of 109 to 99, and was finally passed in the House by a vote of 120 to 98. Had myself and the other seven Whigs referred to, voted differently upon this plan in the committee, it would likewise have been rejected by a vote of 107 to 101, and no plan would have been agreed upon. It was not until the party so largely in the majority found that they could do nothing with their favorite schemes, that they consented, or rather were reluctantly forced, to take the Whig measure or none. That measure embraced the terms upon which the Southern Whigs had put the question, from the beginning. It provides for the admission of Texas as a State, without the assumption of her debt, and with a settlement of the slave question. A copy of the resolutions of Mr. Brown are appended. Alex. H. Stephens."

Washington, D. C, 11th of February, 1845.
Resolutions offered by Mr. Brown, of Tennessee, as adopted by the House:
Resolved by the Senate and House of Representatives in Congress assembled, That Congress doth consent that the territory properly included within, and rightfully belonging to, the Republic of Texas, may be erected into a new State, to be called the State of Texas, with a republican form of government, to be adopted by the people of said Republic, by deputies in convention assembled, with the consent of the existing Government, in order that the same may be admitted as one of the States of this Union.

Section 2. And be it further resolved, That the foregoing consent of Congress is given upon the following conditions, and with the following guarantees, to wit:

1. Said State to be formed, subject to the adjustment by this Government of all questions of boundary that may arise with other Governments; and the Constitution thereof, with the proper evidence of its adoption by the people of said Republic of Texas, shall be transmitted to the President of the United States, to be laid before Congress for its final action, on or before the first day of January, one thousand eight hundred and forty-six.

2. Said State, when admitted into the Union, after ceding to the United States all public edifices, fortifications, barracks, ports and harbors, navy and navy yards, docks, magazines, arms, armaments, and all other property and means pertaining to the public defence belonging to said Republic of Texas, shall retain all the public funds, debts, taxes, and dues of every kind which may belong to, or be due and owing, said Republic; and shall also retain all the vacant and unappropriated lands lying within its limits, to be applied to the payment of the debts and liabilities of said Republic of Texas; and the residue of said lands, after discharging said debts and liabilities, to be disposed of as said State may direct; but in no event are said debts and liabilities to become a charge upon the Government of the United States.

3. New States of convenient size, not exceeding four in number, in addition to said State of Texas, and having sufficient population, may hereafter, by the consent of a State, be formed out of the territory thereof, which shall be entitled to admission under the provisions of the Federal Constitution. And such States as may be formed out of that portion of said territory lying south of thirty-six degrees thirty minutes north latitude, commonly known as the Missouri compromise line, shall be admitted into the Union with or without slavery, as the people of each State asking admission

may desire. And in such State or States as shall be formed out of said territory, north of said Missouri compromise line, slavery or involuntary servitude (except for crime) shall be prohibited.[81]

Stephens gave the following speech on June 16, 1846, in the U.S. House of Representatives. The subject is the Mexican-American War, which had recently begun. In it we see Stephens' early strong adherence to the principles of the U.S. Constitution:
☛ "I allude, Mr. Chairman, to the Mexican war; and I will state in the outset that I am not, as some gentlemen seem to be, the advocate of war in the abstract—war for war's sake. I hold all wars to be great national calamities. I do not maintain that war can or should always be avoided. I do not belong to the peace party, so called; I am no non-resistance man; I am far from holding that all wars are wrong. But I do hold that they ought never to be rushed into blindly or rashly. This *ultima ratio*—this last resort of nations to settle matters of dispute or disagreement between them, should always be avoided, when it can be done without a sacrifice of national rights or honor. And the greatest responsibility rests upon those at the head of affairs, to whom are confided the interests and destinies of a country, that they do not disregard the heavy obligations of this most important trust.

"These general principles, universally held in this age and country, I believe, to be correct, shall govern me in what I have to say upon the present occasion.

"Having thus premised, I shall proceed to the subject I propose to discuss, and shall first inquire into the true cause or origin of this war; and shall then speak of the manner and spirit with which it should be prosecuted. First, as to its cause.

"The country, Mr. Chairman, at this time, is in a strange and singular condition. We are at war with a neighboring Republic; an army of fifty thousand men has been authorized to be raised; and millions of money have been appropriated to prosecute it; and millions more will doubtless have to be raised and appropriated for the same object. And yet the country seems to be anxiously waiting information as to how this state of things has been brought about. Some seem to consider it a necessary result from the annexation of Texas, or, in other words, a war that Mexico is waging against us on account of that measure. But I intend to show, as I think I can most clearly do, that the whole affair is properly chargeable to the imprudence, indiscretion, and mismanagement of our own executive; that the war has been literally provoked when there was no necessity for it, and could have been easily avoided without any detriment to our rights, interests, or honor as a nation. Indeed, sir, I may be permitted to say, that a strange infatuation seems to have governed this administration ever since it came into power in reference to our foreign affairs;

a war with some power or other seems to have been its leading object. The assertion of untenable rights in the Oregon territory looked to, if it did not seek, a rupture with England. Happily for the country, by the interposition of the wisdom of the Senate, that question, if rumor be correct, is about to be settled. And in the discussion of this question *I wish to remind gentlemen of what they appear sometimes to forget, that the executive and his cabinet are not the country, and that it is quite possible for him and them to be wrong without putting the country in the same condition. There is a wide difference between the ministers and the sovereign. In this country sovereignty resides, not in the throne or the executive, but in the people. The administration is but the ministry; they are but public servants, and should be held to strict accountability. I hope never to see the day when the executive of this country shall be considered identical with the country itself in its foreign relations, or when any man, for scanning his acts, however severely when justly, shall on that account be charged with opposition to his country. Such is the case only where allegiance is due to a crown, where the people's rulers are their masters; but, thank God, in this country we can yet hold our rulers to an account. How long we shall be permitted or be disposed to do so I know not; but whenever we cease to do it we shall become unfit to be free.* [Emphasis added, L.S.]

"With these views and these feelings, and with this spirit, I go into the investigation of the cause of this war, the expenditure of so much money, the raising of so large and great a military force, and the breaking up of the repose of that general peace with which we have been so signally blessed for the last quarter of a century. This is the inquiry upon which I am about to enter; it is a grave and important inquiry, and one to which the attention of the people of this country should be directed; and I assert in my place, that the immediate cause of all these things, and the present unlooked-for state of affairs, is properly chargeable upon the administration; for the advance movement of our troops, or 'army of occupation,' as it is called, from Corpus Christi, on the Nueces, to Matamoras, on the Rio Grande, into a territory, to say the least of it, well known to be in dispute between Texas and Mexico; this, I say, was the immediate occasion of hostilities; and if our army had been permitted to remain at Corpus Christi, where it had been since August last, there is no evidence or reason to believe that there would have been any outbreak between our people and the Mexicans upon the frontier. This is my first proposition in considering the cause of this war, which I trust I shall be able to make perfectly clear; and then I trust I shall be able to make it appear equally clear that that step was unnecessary for any of the legitimate purposes for which the army was sent to Texas; also, that it was improper, under the circumstances, as being calculated to irritate and provoke hostilities; and further, that it was a step which the [U.S.] President [James K. Polk] was not clothed with the proper power legally and rightfully to take, without authority from Congress.

"My first proposition is, that the immediate cause of hostilities between our army and the Mexican forces, was the advance movement from Corpus Christi, upon the Nueces river, to Matamoras, upon the Rio Grande or Del Norte. And, to sustain this, I need but refer to the history of the case, given by the President himself in the documents accompanying his message to the House, when he asked us to recognize a state of war with Mexico; a singular request, by-the-by, for the President to make, when the constitution gives Congress the sole power to declare war. Perhaps some gentlemen may suppose that that clause in the constitution simply means that when the President gets us into a war, it is the business of Congress then to make it known—to declare it—or recognize the fact. This, however, is not my understanding of it. Congress alone has the right and power to engage in war. The President has the right to repel hostilities; but not by his policy with other nations to bring on and involve the country in a war without consultation with Congress.

"But to proceed with the argument and the history of the case. Soon after the passage of the resolution of annexation last year, it will be recollected that General [Zachary] Taylor, with a large portion of the army, was ordered to Texas to protect that country and its citizens from an invasion of Mexico, if any should be made or threatened. He arrived there in the month of August, and took a position at Corpus Christi, on the west bank of the Nueces, one hundred and fifty miles this side of the Rio Grande. In the meantime, the question of annexation may be considered as having been settled by the people of Texas. Her convention had been called, and her people were almost unanimous in favor of it. If Mexico had intended an invasion on account of that act, that was the time to have made it. But there was no invasion; and there is no evidence of any intention on her part to offer hostile resistance to that measure. Nor is there any evidence of any hostilities on her part until the advance movement of our army alluded to, which took place in the month of March of this year. During this interval of time, a regular correspondence seems to have been kept up between General Taylor and the War Department here, concerning the state of Mexican feeling. This correspondence accompanies the President's message. It is copious, and I take it to be a true exposition of the real state of affairs, as well as the disposition of the Mexicans during that time.

"On the 15th of August, then, in his first communication on this subject after arriving at Corpus Christi, General Taylor writes [to President Polk]:

> 'That General [Mariano] Arista was to leave Monterey on the 4th of that month for Matamoras, with fifteen hundred men, five hundred being cavalry. . . Nor do I hear that the reported concentration of troops at Matamoras is for any purpose of invasion.'

"On the 20th of August, from the same place, he wrote [to Polk]:

> 'Caravans of traders arrive occasionally from the Rio Grande, but bring no news of importance. They represent that there are no regular troops on that river, except at Matamoras; and do not seem to be aware of any preparation for a demonstration on this side of the river.'

"On the 6th of September, he wrote that:

> 'a confidential agent, despatched some days since at Matamoras, has returned, and reports that no extraordinary preparations are going forward there; that the garrison does not seem to have increased; and that our Consul is of opinion there will be no declaration of war.'

"On the 14th of September, he wrote:

> 'We have no news of interest from the frontier; [General] Arista, at the last accounts, was at Mier, but without any force; nor is there as yet any concentration of troops on the river.'

"On the 4th of October, he wrote:

> 'Mexico having as yet made no positive declaration of war, or committed any overt act of hostilities, I do not feel at liberty, under my instructions, particularly those of July 8th, to make a forward movement to the Rio Grande, without authority from the War Department.'

"On the 11th of October, he wrote:

> 'Recent arrivals from the Rio Grande bring no news or information of a different aspect from that which I reported in my last. The views expressed in previous communications relative to the pacific disposition of the border people, on both sides of the river, are continually confirmed.'

"All this time General Taylor was remaining at Corpus Christi. The propositions for annexation had been before the people of Texas, as I have said; and it was clear and well understood that that measure would be speedily consummated. And yet no demonstration was made by Mexico, and no evidence of hostilities was evinced. Nay, more, sir; so late as the 7th of January last—some time after annexation was complete, and after Texas had been admitted as a State into the Union; after that 'bloodless achievement' of so large a territory, of which the President [Polk] spoke in his annual message, had been fully accomplished; and, in deed and in truth, 'without a resort to the arm of force'—General Taylor writes from the same place, where he was still stationed, and where he should have remained:

> 'General Arista rests quiet, to see, perhaps, what success attends General [Mariano] Paredes. In this part of the country the people are in favor of peace; and I should judge, of a treaty with the United States.'

"But, on the 13th of January of this year, it will be recollected, the order was given by the [U.S.] Secretary of War [William L. Marcy] for the forward movement of the army to Matamoras. And this, as I assert, was the cause of the outbreak; for, no sooner was this known, and preparations were making for that purpose in our camp, than the temper of the people in that quarter began to change—I mean the temper of the Mexican people living in the province of Tamaulipas, on this side of the Rio Grande—and the tone of General Taylor's letters immediately changed. On the 4th of February he acknowledges the reception of the order of the 13th January; and on the 16th of February writes:

> 'Many reports will doubtless reach the Department giving exaggerated accounts of Mexican preparations to resist our advance, if not, indeed, to attempt an invasion of Texas.'

"This shows that opposition to that movement had commenced, and resistance was threatened; and this is the First intimation General Taylor gives of any hostility in that quarter on the part of the Mexicans, from the time he first arrived there, in the summer of last year—six months after he had been quietly settled at Corpus Christi, without any offer to resist, with the border people quiet, peaceable, and satisfied, desirous, as he thought, of peace and a treaty with this country—with no concentration of forces, and no disposition to fight.

"On the 8th of March General Taylor commenced his forward movement, and on the 11th the whole army left Corpus Christi for Matamoras. The next time we hear from him is on the 18th March, when he is one hundred and nineteen miles on his route. He then states, that:

> 'within the last two days our advance has met with small armed parties of Mexicans, who seemed disposed to avoid us. They were doubtless thrown out to get information of our advance.'

"The next we hear from him is the account of the 21st of March, of the resistance offered to his crossing the Little Colorado, and the protest of the

Mexicans against his proceeding to Matamoras. Further on, and just before getting to Point Isabel, he was met with a civil deputation, with the Prefect of the district of Tamaulipas at its head, 'protesting against his occupation of the country.' No attention was paid to this; his orders were imperative, and soon the buildings at Point Isabel were seen in flames, and all the inhabitants fled to Matamoras, except 'two or three inoffensive Mexicans.'

"The next we hear of General Taylor is, on the 29th of March, at his camp, on the left bank of the Rio Grande, opposite Matamoras. And now he writes:

> 'The attitude of the Mexicans is so far decidedly hostile. An interview has been held, by my direction, with the military authorities in Matamoras, but with no satisfactory result. Under this state of things, I must again and urgently call your attention to the necessity of speedily sending recruits to this army.'

"It may be well here to call the attention of the House to the notes of the interview [he] had with the Mexican authorities, to which General Taylor alluded in his last letter. From these notes I read:

> 'General [Romulo Diaz de la] Vega then stated, that he had been directed to receive such communications as [U.S.] General [William J.] Worth might present from his commanding general—going on to say, that the march of the United States troops through a part of the Mexican territory (Tamaulipas) was an act of war.' General Worth asked, 'Has Mexico declared war against the United States?' General Vega: 'No.' General Worth: 'Are the two countries still at peace?' General Vega: 'Yes.' General Vega afterward, in the interview, asked: 'Is it the intention of General Taylor to remain with his army on the left bank of the Rio Grande?' General Worth: 'Most assuredly; and there to remain until directed otherwise by his government.' General Vega remarked, that 'we felt indignation at seeing the American flag placed on the Rio Grande, a portion of the Mexican territory.'

"This interview took place on the 28th March last, soon after General Taylor's arrival opposite Matamoras; and it shows clearly the state of feeling produced by this advanced movement, and which resulted in the collision which so soon after followed. For matters now were rapidly coming to a crisis; and the next we hear from General Taylor is on the 15th April, when he writes:

> 'I have to report, that, on the 11th instant, General [Pedro de] Ampudia arrived at Matamoras with two hundred cavalry, the remainder of his force, variously estimated from two thousand to three thousand men, being some distance in rear on the route from Monterey. Immediately after assuming the

chief command, General Ampudia ordered all Americans to leave Matamoras within twenty-four hours, and repair to Victoria, a town in the interior of Tamaulipas. He had taken the same severe measure at Reynosa, on his way hither. On the 12th, I received from General Ampudia a despatch, summoning me to withdraw my force within twenty-four hours, and to fall back beyond the river Nueces. To this communication I replied on the 12th, saying that I should not retrograde from my position. Copies of this correspondence are enclosed herewith. I considered the letter of General Ampudia sufficient to warrant me in blocking up the Rio Grande, and stopping all supplies for Matamoras, orders for which have been given to the naval commander at Brazos Santiago.'

"The communication from Ampudia, to which General Taylor refers, is in the following words:

[Translation.] 'To: Senor General-in-Chief of the United States Army, Don Z.[achary] Taylor. General-in-Chief: To explain to you the many grounds for the just grievances felt by the Mexican nation, caused by the United States Government, would be a loss of time, and an insult to your good sense; I, therefore, pass at once to such explanations as I consider of absolute necessity.

'Your government, in an incredible manner—you will even permit me to say an extravagant one, if the usage or general rules established and received among all civilized nations are regarded—has not only insulted, but has exasperated the Mexican nation, bearing its Conquering banner to the left bank of the Rio Bravo del Norte; and, in this case, by explicit and definite orders of my government, which neither can, will, nor should receive new outrages, I require you, in all form, and, at latest, in the peremptory term of twenty-four hours, to break up your camp, and retire to the other bank of the Nueces river, while our governments are regulating the pending question in relation to Texas. If you insist in remaining upon the soil of the department of Tamaulipas, it will clearly result that arms, and arms alone, must decide the question; and in that case, I advise you that we accept the war to which, with so much injustice on your part, you provoke us; and that, on our part, this war shall be conducted conformably to the principles established by the most civilized nations; that is to say, that the law of nations and of war shall be the guide of my operations; trusting that on your part the same will be observed.

'With this view, I tender you the considerations due to your person and respectable office. God and Liberty! Headquarters at Matamoras, 2 o'clock, P.M., April 12, 1846. Pedro de Ampudia.'

"In this communication it will be perceived that General Ampudia did not order General Taylor to evacuate Texas—to go beyond the Sabine—but to fall back beyond the Nueces, to withdraw from what he considered the Mexican district of Tamaulipas, until the two governments should settle the pending question in relation to Texas. General Taylor's orders, however, from the War Department were positive; he was to hold his position opposite Matamoras. And what immediately ensued is well known: first, the capture of Captain [Seth] Thornton and his men; and, soon after, the ever-to-be-remembered battles of the 8th and 9th of May, which, so far as the bravery and gallantry of our officers and army is concerned, are amongst the brightest and most glorious achievements in our history. I have nothing to say against that. I have every assurance that our arms will ever be victorious, let them come in conflict with whatever foe they may; and whatever laurels or honors they may win, whether on land or the ocean, when acting in obedience to orders, I shall claim an interest in, as an addition to the common stock of American fame. But I am now giving the history of the circumstances that led to this result. I have been minute in details, in tracing it to its proper source, to show that there was no disposition on the part of Mexico evinced to invade this country or Texas on account of annexation; and if the army had remained out of the country upon the Rio Grande, which was in dispute between Texas and Mexico, both claiming it, there would have been no hostility on the part of Mexico; or, in other words, that *the cause of this war was the taking military possession of the disputed territory.* And, if further authority is wanted to establish this position, I refer to the letter of the present [U.S.] Secretary of Foreign Affairs in Mexico to Mr. [John] Slidell, of the 12th of March last. It is in that letter in which he gave the reasons of his government for refusing to receive him as a resident minister, but not as a commissioner to settle the question of boundary. [Emphasis added, L.S.] Speaking of the views and feelings of the present government of Mexico upon this subject, and their intended course toward the United States, he says:

> 'A lover of peace, she would wish to ward off this sad contingency; and, without fearing war, she would desire to avoid so great a calamity for both countries. For this she has offered herself, and will continue to offer herself, open to all honorable means of conciliation, and she anxiously desires that the present controversy may terminate in a reasonable and decorous manner.
>
> 'In the actual state of things, to say that Mexico maintains a position of quasi hostility with respect to the United States, is to add a new offence to her previous injuries. Her attitude is one of defence, because she sees herself unjustly attacked; because a portion of her territory is occupied by the forces of a nation, intent, without any right whatever, to possess itself of it; because her ports are threatened by the squadrons of the same power. Under such circumstances, is she to remain inactive, without taking measures suited to so rigorous an emergency?'

"From this it appears that, even up to the 12th of March last, it was not the intention or wish of Mexico to make war against us; and that, in the actual state of things then, to say that Mexico maintained 'a position of quasi hostility with respect to the United States,' was 'to add a new offence to her previous injuries.' Can any man doubt, then, that if our army had not been pushed forward to the Rio Grande, there would have been no hostility, resistance, or war with Mexico?

"Then, sir, was this movement necessary for any of the legitimate purposes for which our army was sent to Texas? There was no invasion threatened, there was no violence offered to the persons or property of the citizens of Texas that required this movement to give any additional protection. Beyond Corpus Christi, where the army had been stationed for six months, there were no citizens of the United States or Texas that I have ever heard of. I mean, by citizens of Texas, those who acknowledge her government, and come within the jurisdiction of her laws. Why, then, was the army, at great cost and trouble, marched over and across that 'stupendous desert between the Nueces and the Bravo' (Rio Grande), which the chairman of the Committee on Foreign Affairs stated, when he offered the resolution for the annexation of Texas, was the 'natural boundary between the Anglo-Saxon and the Mauritanian races?' Was there a man on the Rio Grande that acknowledged the jurisdiction, much less that claimed the protection, of the laws of Texas? Wherefore, then, was there any necessity for this move? Can any man offer a pretext for it but the masked design of provoking Mexico to war?

"But this move was not only unnecessary, but improper, imprudent, and unwise. For it was known that the friendly relations between this country and Mexico were interrupted; and, notwithstanding she was making no show of hostilities—her people being pacifically inclined on the border—yet she was in an irritable mood, if you please, and every thing calculated to excite either her government or her people by a wise President would have been avoided. I now speak without reference to the disputed character of that country. Even if it were admitted that the Rio Grande was the established boundary of Texas, as much so as that the St. Lawrence is the boundary between us and Canada, it was improper, under the circumstances, to send an army upon the border of a country at peace with us, and not only this, but order them to construct fortifications and mount heavy guns right opposite a peaceful town, pointing toward the main square, and ready at any moment to 'spot' any place in it. I say, sir, this was wrong, and it was calculated to provoke, to irritate, and to bring on a conflict, if it was not so designed. Suppose any nation should act so toward us, and point their guns toward any or either of our towns or cities, could any thing be done more calculated to warm the blood of the nation, or more effectually 'to prepare the hearts of our people for war?' Would we permit England or France to do so toward us, or could we do so toward them without being involved in a war? Did Mr. [Thomas] Jefferson act in this way when Louisiana was acquired? The western boundary of that country was then in dispute between us and Spain. Did Mr. Jefferson send an army of occupation to take possession of the part in dispute, or did he wait for peaceful negotiation to settle it?

"How was it with our north-eastern boundary, another case in point? For half a century and upward, the line there was in dispute between us and Great Britain, and a large extent of territory was claimed by each. Did any of our Presidents, in that long interval of time, think it necessary or proper to send an army of occupation to take possession of the disputed section? So far as necessity was concerned, the argument was much stronger in the northeast than it was upon the Rio Grande, for there were people there claiming the protection of our laws. But not only this, sir; if I am not mistaken, for some time, and even during Mr. [Martin] Van Buren's administration, a portion of that disputed country was permitted to be occupied by British troops without opposition or resistance on our part. I do not say that that was right; but it shows the great caution exercised by former Presidents, when the questions and issues of peace and war were at stake, and it would have been time enough, at least, for our troops to have made a movement when Mexican forces had attempted to seize upon the country. I venture to say, if a tenth part of the prudence, and caution, and propriety, had been exercised in the southwest that was in the northeast, there would have been no collision with Mexico; and if a tenth part of the folly and blunders of this administration in the southwest had been committed in the northeast, when that question was open, a rupture with England would have been inevitable; and we might to-day, for that small strip of territory, with an exhausted treasury and accumulated debt, be waging an unfinished war with that country.

"And I shall here, Mr. Chairman, though not exactly pertinent to the question I am discussing, take occasion to refer to that great statesman, through whose extraordinary talents and ability that long protracted and much vexed question was so advantageously to his country finally settled. And I do it from what I feel to be a sense of public duty to a man who rendered such essential service to his country, in such a critical period in the history of our foreign affairs. And the more cheerfully and willingly I do it in consequence of the many gross and foul imputations that have been attempted to be cast upon his character for his course in that matter. So far from being a fit subject for attack and detraction for his conduct in relation to that measure, he is entitled to the gratitude of the nation and the gratitude of mankind. If a man, who has the requisite ability and patriotism for so noble an achievement, is to be denounced for having brought to an honorable and peaceful settlement a question of so much difficulty as to have baffled the powers of the ablest men of this country for fifty years or upward—for doing what all our Presidents, from the days of [George] Washington down, had failed to accomplish—for saving this country from all the consequences of a protracted war, the loss of blood and treasure that would have been spent therein—for saving mankind and the civilized world from all the fearful and disastrous effects that would have been produced by the shock and collision of the two mightiest nations on earth, brought in battle array and deadly conflict against each other. I say, if, for doing all this, a man is to be denounced, assailed, and despoiled of his good name, then, indeed—'Worth is but a charter, to be mankind's distinguished martyr.'

"And then, indeed, may it be truly said that 'Republics are ungrateful.' But, sir, I do not believe this of my countrymen; I rely more upon their intelligence, their virtue, wisdom, and patriotism—more upon that liberal, high-minded, generous, and magnanimous spirit by which they are characterized. There may be some who, with the wish but without the ability to take the lead in the arduous ascent of fame's proud steep, would fain attain their ends by pulling down those above them, rather than encounter the labor and toil of honorable though hopeless competition; but I trust their number is few. They belong to that class of old—'Who have no base to bear their rising fame, but the fallen ruins of another's name.'

"In this instance, however, their object is beyond their reach. In solitary loneliness he stands high above them all—with full consciousness, perhaps, of the truth of what was said long since by one well acquainted with the passions and vices of the human heart, that—'He who ascends to mountain tops shall find, the loftiest peaks most wrapt in clouds and snow; and he who transcends or excels mankind, must look down on the hate of those below.'

"There is a majesty in true greatness which seldom fails to command the admiration of the high-minded and honorable, while it as naturally excites the envy of the ignoble, the grovelling, and the mean: just as there is a majesty in virtue which secures the love and respect of the good, but never fails to arouse the hate of the vile. . . .

"So, sir, it is with Daniel Webster. The efforts of his enemies have been as impotent as they were reckless, and their attempted aspersions will but add new lustre to his fame. I do not claim to be his defender or his eulogist; that is a distinction I do not aspire to. But we all have reason to be proud of him as an American. He has not only won immortality for himself, and taken a position amongst the greatest of the earth, but added greatly to the reputation of his country; and, in the bright constellation of gems and honors that encircle and adorn his brow, shines not least conspicuously, in my opinion, the glory of having effected the treaty of Washington. Would for the country's sake he filled the same place now that he did then—we might not be in our present embarrassment!

"But, sir, to return from this digression, for which I hope the committee will excuse me.

"I have endeavored to show that the movement of our army to the Rio Grande, the immediate occasion of hostilities, was unnecessary and improper, under the circumstances. I come now to say, what I fearlessly assert, that *the President [Polk] had no right, no power, legally, to order the military occupation of the disputed territory on the Rio Grande without authority from Congress.* He had no right or power to send the army beyond that country over which Texas had established her jurisdiction. The boundary between Texas and Mexico—I mean Texas as an independent State after her revolution—was never settled. Before the revolution the river Nueces was the southern boundary of the department of Texas. Between that river and the Rio Grande lay the districts of Tamaulipas, Coahuila, and others. During and after the revolution, a portion of this country on the south of the Nueces, about Corpus Christi, went with Texas and adhered to the new government; the other portion, lying on the Rio Grande, adhered to the old government; and though Texas, after her declaration, defined her boundary to be the Rio Grande, yet she never successfully established her jurisdiction to that extent. Between Corpus Christi and the Mexican settlements on the Rio Grande is an immense desert or waste, where nobody lives. The first settlements to the south of that unoccupied region are on the Rio Grande, or near it, and have continued subject to the laws of Mexico. The people are Mexicans or Spaniards. In proof of this I need but refer to a letter from the American camp, published in most of our newspapers, and which nobody, I presume, will venture to contradict. [Emphasis added, L.S.] The letter bears date the 21st of April last, and, speaking of the country on the Rio Grande, says:

> 'The people are all Spaniards, and the country is uninhabitable, excepting the valley of the Rio Grande, and that contains a pretty dense population; and in no part of the country are the people more loyal to the Mexican Government.'

"This country, it is true, is claimed by Texas and Mexico. It is in dispute, and was well known to be so at the time of annexation. For proof of this, I refer to Senator [Thomas H.] Benton's speech in the other House upon the Tyler treaty, in which he seems to decide the claim in favor of Mexico; for a resolution offered by him on that occasion is in these words:

Resolved, That the incorporation of the left bank of the Rio del Norte into the American Union, by virtue of a treaty with Texas, comprehending, as the said incorporation would do, a part of the Mexican departments of New Mexico, Chihuahua, Coahuila, and Tamaulipas, would be an act of direct aggression on Mexico, for all the consequences of which the United States would stand responsible.

"One of the strong objections to the Tyler treaty was that it fixed the boundary at the Rio Grande, which the resolutions that finally passed did not do.

"I refer, also, to the speech of Senator [Chester] Ashley, of Arkansas, on the resolution itself, in which he says, speaking of the resolutions submitted by himself for that purpose:

'The third speaks for itself, and enables the United States to settle the boundary between Mexico and the United States properly. And I will here add that the present boundaries of Texas, I learn from Judge [Richard] Ellis, the President of the Convention that formed the constitution of Texas, and also a member of the first Legislature under that constitution, were fixed as they now are [i.e., extending to the Rio Grande] solely and professedly with a view of having a large margin in the negotiation with Mexico, and not with the expectation of retaining them as they now exist in their statute book.'

"Again: Mr. [Andrew J.] Donelson, our Charge to Texas, or the agent sent on to effect annexation, in a communication on the 23rd of June, 1845, to Mr. [James] Buchanan, upon this subject, speaking of the country between the Nueces and the Rio Grande, says:

'That country, you are aware, has been in the possession of both parties. Texas has held in peace Corpus Christi; Mexico has held Santiago [near Point Isabel]; both parties have had occasional 'possession of Laredo and other places higher up.'"

"But it is useless to multiply authority upon this point. All this was well known at the time of the passage of the resolution of annexation; and hence the resolution was guarded so as to cover only so much territory as was 'properly included within, and rightfully belonged to the Republic of Texas,' reserving the question of boundary to be settled and adjusted between this government and Mexico by negotiation, and not by arms; and Congress positively refused to pass any measure of that sort which fixed the boundary at the Rio Grande or Del Norte; and I venture to say that no resolution so fixing the boundary could have passed this or the other House. And now what I have got to say is this:

Congress having failed to establish a boundary in that quarter, the President could not undertake to do it. *The limits or boundaries of a country can be fixed in two ways only: one is by negotiation, and the other is by the sword. The President by himself can do neither. He may make the initiative in the former case; but Congress can alone constitutionally draw the sword for any purpose.* I grant, if Mexico would not negotiate, would not treat, would not come to any understanding in a friendly manner where the dividing line should be, where their jurisdiction should end and ours commence, that we would then have a right to make a limit for ourselves, and a right, by force of arms, to establish that limit or line. But, sir, this is a right that Congress only can constitutionally exercise. The President cannot do it. That is what I assert; and I defy any man in this House to gainsay my positions. Is there any boundary line established between Texas and Mexico? Every body must say—no. Was it not expressly omitted to establish a line in the resolutions of annexation? Everybody must say—yes. Can the President, then, undertake to say where the line is or shall be, when Congress fails to speak? [Emphasis added, L.S.]

". . . But, sir, I wish to know what is the design and object of the administration as to the ends of this war. It has been brought upon us while Congress was in session without our knowledge. And I wish to know for what object, and with what spirit, they intend to prosecute it. I regret the chairman of the Committee on Military Affairs is not in his seat to answer such inquiries upon this subject as I intended to propound to him. For, occupying his position, I presume he must be in the confidence of the executive. And I hope, at some early day, he, or some other person standing in the same relation to the 'powers that be,' will inform the country upon this subject. Is the object to repel invasion, to protect Texas, to establish the Rio Grande as the boundary? or what other objects are had in view? I, sir, not only as a representative upon this floor, but as a citizen of this republic, having a common interest with others, in every thing that pertains to her interests, her rights, and her honor, wish to know if this is to be a war for conquest? And whether this is the object for which it is to be waged? If so, I protest against that part of it. I would shed no unnecessary blood; commit no unnecessary violence; allow no outrage upon the religion of Mexico; have no desecration of temples, or 'revelling in the halls of the Montezumas;' but be ready to meet the first offers of peace. I regret that General Taylor did not have the authority to accept the proffered armistice when it was tendered. In a word, I am for a restoration of peace as soon—yes, at the earliest day it can be honorably effected. I am no enemy to the extension of our domain, or the enlargement of the boundaries of the republic. Far from it. I trust the day is coming, and not far distant, when the whole continent will be ours; when our institutions shall be diffused and cherished, and republican government felt and enjoyed throughout the length and breadth and width of this land—from the far south to the extreme north, and from ocean to ocean. That this is our ultimate destiny, if wise councils prevail, I confidently believe. But it is not to be accomplished by the sword. Mr. Chairman, republics never spread by arms. We can only properly enlarge by voluntary accessions, and should only attempt to act upon our neighbors by setting them a good example. In this way only is the spirit of our institutions to be diffused as the 'leaven,' until 'the whole lump is leavened.' This has been the history of our silent but rapid progress, thus far. In this way Louisiana, with its immense domain, was acquired. In this way the Floridas were obtained. In this way we got Oregon, connecting us with the Pacific. In this way Texas, up to the Rio Grande, might have been added; and in this way the Californias, and Mexico herself in due time may be merged in one great republic. There is much said in this country of the party of progress. I profess to belong to that party; but am far from advocating that kind of progress which many of those who seem anxious to appropriate the term exclusively to themselves are using their utmost exertions to push forward. Theirs, in my opinion, is a downward progress. It is a progress of party—of excitement—of lust of power—a spirit of war—aggression—violence and licentiousness. It is a progress which, if indulged in, would soon sweep over all law—all order—and the constitution itself. . . . It is the progress of that political and moral sirocco that passed over the republics of 'olden time,' withering and blasting every thing within its pernicious and destructive range. Where liberty once was enjoyed—where the arts and sciences were cultivated—and literature flourished—philosophers taught and poets sung—and where the most majestic monuments of refinement, taste, and genius were erected, 'towers, temples, palaces, and sepulchres;' but where now—'Ruin itself stands still for lack of work, and desolation keeps unbroken sabbath.'

"Or, to come nearer home for an illustration, it is the progress of Mexico herself. Why is that heaven-favored country now so weak and impotent and faithless? Why so divided and distracted and torn to pieces in her internal policy? A few years ago she set out in the career of republicanism under auspices quite as favorable for success as this country. Her progress has been most rapid from a well-regulated, good government, formed on our own model, to the most odious military despotism. We would do well to take a lesson from her history, and grow wise by the calamities of others, without paying ourselves the melancholy price of wisdom. They lacked that high order of moral and political integrity without which no republic can stand. And it is to progress in these essential attributes of national greatness I would look; the improvement of mind; 'the increase and diffusion of knowledge amongst men;'

the erection of schools, colleges, and temples of learning; the progress of intellect over matter; the triumph of the mind over the animal propensities; the advancement of kind feelings and good will amongst the nations of the earth; the cultivation of virtue and the pursuits of industry; the bringing into subjection and subserviency to the use of man of all the elements of nature about and around us; in a word, the progress of civilization and every thing that elevates, ennobles, and dignifies man. This, Mr. Chairman, is not to be done by wars, whether foreign or domestic. Fields of blood and carnage may make men brave and heroic, but seldom tend to make nations either good, virtuous, or great."[82]

On February 12, 1847, Stephens gave the following speech before the U.S. House of Representatives. At the time a proposition had been put before the House to appropriate 3 million dollars so that President James K. Polk could finalize a treaty with Mexico:
☛ "Mr. Chairman—It is useless to attempt to disguise the fact, or to affect to be blind to the truth, that this country is now surrounded by difficulties of no ordinary magnitude, and fast approaching others, which threaten to be far greater and more perilous than any which have ever been encountered since the foundation of the government.

"It is true, the declaration was made the other day, by a distinguished senator [Lewis Cass], in his place, that he saw no dangers about, he espied nothing in the prospect to cause alarm or apprehension, and that, in his opinion, 'the sentinel upon the watchtower might sing upon his post!'

"Sir, whether this sentiment was expressed by authority, and is to be taken as the exponent of the feelings of those who are now wielding so recklessly the destinies of the nation, I know not; but to me it seems somewhat kindred to, if not the legitimate offspring of, that spirit which prompted Nero to indulge in music and dancing when Rome was in flames. . . ."

"[Now let me say this: I unhesitatingly denounce the unfair means by which President James K. Polk was elected.] But if, in the inscrutable ways of Providence, he, who has been thus fraudulently elevated to power, should be the ill-fated instrument of our chastisement, the punishment maybe just, but he will take no honor in its execution. If the result of his mischievous counsels should, in any way, prove disastrous to our institutions—the stability, harmony, and permanency of the government—which there is now abundant cause seriously to apprehend, he will certainly have no place in the grateful remembrance of mankind. Fame he will have; but it will be of the character of that which perpetuates the name of Erostratus [an ancient Greek who, for fame's sake, set fire to the temple of Artemis at Ephesus, now in modern Turkey]. And the more deeply blackened than even his, as the stately structure of this government, the temple of our liberties, is grander and more majestic than the far-famed magnificence of the Ephesian dome.

"The crisis, sir, requires not only firmness of principle, but boldness of speech. As the immortal Tully [Marcus Tullius Cicero of ancient Rome] said, in the days of Cataline, when Rome was threatened with the most imminent dangers, the time has come when the opinion of men should not be uttered by their voices only, but '*inscriptum sit in fronte unius cujusque quid de respublica sentit*'—it should even be written upon the forehead of each one what he thinks of the republic—there should be no concealment. In what I have to say, therefore, I shall use that character of speech which I think befitting the time and occasion. . . .

"[I greatly question the current policy of the Mexican-American War, and ask whether] . . . a line of military posts should now be established and defended, until our enemy shall get in a humor to treat; or whether the most desolating invasion should be pushed forward. . . .

"[I personally oppose all wars that are waged for conquest!] . . . [For, as we all well know,] free institutions never did and never will enlarge the circuit of their extent by force of arms. The history of the world abounds with many melancholy examples in illustration of the truth of this position. No principle is more dangerous to us, than that of compelling other nations to adopt our form of government. It is not only wrong in itself, but it is contrary to the whole spirit and genius of the liberty we enjoy; and, if persisted in, must inevitably result in our downfall and ruin. No instance is to be found upon record of any republic having ever entered upon such a hazardous crusade which did not end in the subversion of its own liberties, and the ultimate enslavement of its own people. And before embarking upon so dangerous an enterprise, I trust we shall have some security and guarantee that we shall at least escape the fate of those whose example we follow.

"Sir, I very much fear that the people of this country are not sufficiently awake and alive to the mischievous and ruinous schemes of those to whom they have for a time confided the management of public affairs. Mr. [James] Madison long since uttered the prophetic warning, that 'if a free people be a wise people also, they will Never Forget that the danger of surprise can never be so great as when the advocates of the prerogative of war can sheath it in a symbol of peace.' And never in our history did the times so strongly require a practical consideration of this solemn admonition. . . .

"[The Mexican-American War now being waged will inevitably lead to dreadful consequences, perhaps involving a conflict between South and North in the not too distant future. Add to this the complications of the Wilmot proviso, as well as the resolutions of the legislatures of the States of New York,

Pennsylvania, and Ohio.] They show a fixed determination on the part of the North, which is now in a majority in this House, and ever will be hereafter, that, if territory is acquired, the institutions of the South shall be forever excluded from its limits; this is to be the condition attached to the bill upon your table! What is to be the result of this matter? Will the South submit to this restriction? Will the North ultimately yield? Or shall these two great sections of the Union be arrayed against each other? When the elements of discord are fully aroused, who shall direct the storm? Who does not know how this country was shaken to its very centre by the Missouri agitation?

"Should another such a scene occur, who shall be mighty enough to prevent the most disastrous consequences? The master spirit of that day is no longer in your councils. Shall another equally great and patriotic ever be found? Let not gentlemen quiet their apprehensions by staving off this question. It has to be met, and better now than at a future day. It had better be decided now than after more blood and treasure has been spent in the pursuit of that which may ultimately be our ruin. *Upon the subject of slavery, about which so much has been said in this debate, I shall say but little. I do not think it necessary to enter into a defence of the character of the people of my section of the Union, against the arguments of those who have been pleased to denounce that institution as wicked and sinful. It is sufficient for me and for them, that the morality of that institution stands upon a basis as firm as the Bible; and by that code of morals we are content to abide until a better be furnished. Until Christianity be overthrown, and some other system of ethics be substituted, the relation of master and slave can never be regarded as an offence against the Divine laws. The character of our people speaks for itself. And a more generous, more liberal, more charitable, more benevolent, more philanthropic, and a more magnanimous people, I venture to say, are not to be found in any part of this or any other country. As to their piety, it is true they have 'none to boast of.' But they are free from that pharisaical sin of self-righteousness, which is so often displayed elsewhere [i.e., in the North], of forever thanking the Lord that they are not as other men are.* [Emphasis added, L.S.]

"But if bad counsels prevail—if all the solemn admonitions of the present and the past are disregarded—if the policy of the Administration is to be carried out—if Mexico, the 'forbidden fruit,' is to be seized at every hazard, I very much fear that those who control public affairs, in their eager pursuit after the unenviable distinction of despoiling a neighboring republic, will have the still less enviable glory of looking back upon the shattered and broken fragments of their own Confederacy [a popular name for the U.S. throughout the late 1700s and 1800s]. And instead of 'revelling in the halls of Montezuma,' or gloating over the ruins of the ancient cities of the Aztecs, they may be compelled to turn and behold in their rear another and a wider prospect of desolation, carnage, and blood.

"Mr. Chairman, it was asked by him [i.e., Jesus] who spake as man never spake, 'What shall a man be profited, if he gain the whole world and lose his own soul?' And may I not, with reverence, ask what we shall be profited as a nation, if we gain any part, or even the whole of Mexico, and lose the Union, the soul of our political existence? The Union is not only the life, but the soul of these States. It is this that gives them animation, vigor, power, prosperity, greatness, and renown; and from this alone spring our hopes of immortality as a common people."[83]

Stephens delivered the following speech on February 2, 1848, before the U.S. House of Representatives. It concerns the Mexican-American War, which was just then drawing to a close. In it Stephens defends General Zachary Taylor (soon to become America's twelfth president, and the father of future Confederate General Richard Taylor) against false charges from then U.S. President James K. Polk and others. Again, both Stephens' strict constitutionalism and his traditional conservatism are in evidence:

[Introduction by an unnamed eyewitness:] 'Mr. Stephens said he had a desire some days ago, when the question of reference of the President's message was before the Committee of the Whole on the State of the Union, to say something upon that extraordinary State paper, and some of the novel and dangerous doctrines therein very distinctly set forth as the settled policy of this Administration. But, as he was disappointed in repeated attempts to get the floor, he had abandoned the idea of any further struggle, and had made up his mind to leave the discussion of these grave and important topics in the hands of others.'

☛ "And my object in seeking the floor now arose from no change of purpose. I wish to move an amendment to the report of the committee, and I should have confined myself strictly to that amendment, but for some of the positions assumed by my honorable colleague [Howell Cobb,] who has just taken his seat. I ask the indulgence of the House, therefore, for a few moments, while I reply to those positions, and one or two others kindred to them, as briefly as justice to the subject will admit. The speech of my colleague was a labored argument to remove the responsibility, the heavy responsibility, of the existing war from the head of our Executive [President Polk]. And, if I understood him rightly, he seemed disposed to place it upon Congress—not the Congress that passed the war bill, as some before have done—but the Congress that passed the original resolutions of annexation. Amongst the defenders of the President upon this floor it is not a little interesting to the curious and speculative to see the great variety and diversity of excuses and apologies which have been offered by way of justification for his lawless abuse of power. The gentleman from Maryland [Robert M. McLane] first led off with an attempt to throw the whole burden upon Gen. [Zachary] Taylor; or at least he insisted that the removal of the troops from Corpus Christi was in accordance with the advice of that officer, and if any body was to blame for it, he was the proper person. Subsequently the same gentleman attempted to put the responsibility upon Congress for admitting Texas into the Union as a State, with her boundaries, as fixed and defined in her constitution, extending to the Rio Grande. And now my colleague would have us to understand that the fatal blunder was committed in the original act of annexation.

"Now, sir, none of these excuses or shifts will answer. The argument may be labored, the effort may be bold, but truth can never be obliterated, or even obscured by such sophistry. There it stands; the fact is upon record. There is no getting over it, or around it, or under it; and until history shall falsify the events of the past there can be no mistake as to the real paternity of this war, which gentlemen seem so anxious to have us believe is now actually in quest of an author, or in search of a father. The true cause lies at the door of your own Executive [President Polk]. He commenced it by the exercise of power never conferred upon him, and in a wanton outrage upon the constitution of his country. Upon his head rests all the responsibility, with all its force and weight, and there it will continue to rest.

"It will require no effort, Mr. Speaker, to show the utter groundlessness of the argument, so far as the action of Congress is concerned. I mean the action by which Texas was admitted as a State with her constitution, as well as, the passage of the original resolutions of annexation. I grant if Texas had never been admitted there would have been no war. But what I insist upon is that war was not a necessary consequence of annexation; that it was in no way involved in that measure as it was finally adopted. Every point had been carefully guarded. Of this the resolutions, which speak for themselves, afford sufficient evidence. But we have that which to my colleague and his side of the House should be even stronger; we have the declaration of Mr. Polk himself, after the consummation of the measure, congratulating the country upon its having been 'a bloodless achievement.' What then prevented its remaining 'a bloodless achievement?' It was the occupation of the country on the east bank of the Rio Grande by our troops, in obedience to the orders of the President. Was this order necessary and right? That is the question. The gentleman from Maryland [McLane] says that it was, because it was the duty of the President to defend the State of Texas to the limits of her boundaries as defined in her constitution when she was admitted into this Union. And he says her boundaries thus defined extended to the Rio Grande. Now, this is a matter that can be easily settled by reference to the record. Here it is. I have that constitution before me, and I find in it no such limits of boundary set forth. The preamble of that constitution is in these words:

> We, the people of the republic of Texas, acknowledging with gratitude the grace and beneficence of God in permitting us to make choice of our form of government, do, in accordance with the provisions of the joint resolution for annexing Texas to the United States, approved March first, one thousand eight hundred and forty-five, ordain and establish this constitution.

"And the third section of the thirteenth article of that constitution is in these words:

> All laws and parts of laws now in force in the republic of Texas, which are not repugnant to the Constitution of the United Slates, the joint resolutions for annexing Texas to the United States, or to the provisions of this constitution, shall continue and remain in force as the laws of this State, until they expire by their own limitation, or shall be altered by the Legislature thereof.

"This is all I find in this constitution which has any relation to boundary whatever. And there is in it not the least reference to the Rio Grande, or any other definite limit. But, says the gentleman, the Republic of Texas had a law in force which prescribed the Rio Grande as her boundary from its mouth to its source, which law was affirmed in that section of the constitution to which I have referred; and therefore the boundary with that limit was thereby affirmed. By no means; for the section itself only affirms such laws in force as were not repugnant (amongst other things) to the 'joint resolutions for annexing Texas.' What, then, is the language of the 'joint resolutions annexing Texas' upon this subject? The express condition in those resolutions, upon which annexation was to take place, is in these words:

> Said State to be formed, subject to the adjustment by this Government of all questions of boundary that may arise with other governments.

"The constitution of the State of Texas, therefore, was formed subject to this condition. Her unsettled boundary was in the very terms of the compact of union reserved for the adjustment of this Government. And if she had any law in force anterior to that time fixing the Rio Grande as her boundary, it was clearly repugnant to that condition in the joint resolutions of annexation, which left her boundary an open question for future adjustment. This to my mind seems too clear to argue. But, if further authority be wanted to corroborate my view and position, I refer to the despatches of Mr. [Andrew J.] Donelson, our *charge d'affaires* in Texas, while the question of annexation was pending there.

In a letter to Mr. [James] Buchanan, Secretary of State here, bearing date Austin, Texas, July 11, 1845, he says:

> 'Sir: You will have observed that in my correspondence with this government there has been no discussion of the question of limits between Mexico and Texas. The joint resolution of our Congress left the question an open one. And the preliminary proposition made by this Government under the auspices of the British and French Governments as the basis of a definitive treaty with Mexico, left the question in the same state.
>
> '. . . The proclamation of a truce between the two nations, founded on propositions mutually acceptable to them, leaving the question of boundary not only open, but Mexico in possession of the east bank of the Rio Grande, seemed to me inconsistent with the expectation that in defence of the claim of Texas our troops should march immediately to that river. What the Executive of Texas had determined not to fight for, but to settle by negotiation, to say the least of it, could as well be left to the United Stales on the same conditions.
>
> '. . . There are no unfavorable symptoms in the proceedings of the convention; there is a disposition in some members to resort to some action to exhibit in strong terms the expectation of Texas that the Rio Grande will be maintained as the boundary, but no provision making this a *sine qua non* in our action hereafter will be adopted. Members of all parties have assured me that I need apprehend nothing; that annexation is settled, and that the constitution will contain nothing that has not been sanctioned by numerous precedents in the constitutions of the other States of the Union.'

"These extracts, as well as the whole despatch itself, show conclusively that however much confidence Texas may have placed in the validity of her claim to the east bank of the Rio Grande, and whatever may have been the expectation on her part that her boundary would ultimately be fixed at that limit, yet she did not make its maintenance and defence up to that line a condition or *sine qua non* of annexation. This despatch, I say, shows conclusively as part of the *res gestæ* [Latin: 'things done'] the distinct understanding of Texas at the time of the formation of her constitution, that the boundary between her and Mexico was to be left open for the adjustment of this Government, according to the terms of the joint resolutions of annexation. So much for the argument of the gentleman from Maryland [McLane].

"And now, sir, I come to the position assumed by my colleague [Howell Cobb]. And it is necessary in the outset to put him right on a material point of difference between us. He says that we contend that the Nueces [River] was the proper boundary of Texas, and yet justify the position of the troops at Corpus Christi, which is on the west bank of that river. This is a radical error of the gentleman, with most of those who defend the acts of the President. We do not contend that the Nueces, or any other river, was the proper boundary of Texas. We say her boundary extended just so far as her revolution successfully extended, and no further—be that from the Sabine to the Brazos, the Colorado, the Nueces, the great desert, or any other limit. Her title to any portion of the territory depended solely upon the right of revolution. Her limits were marked by her sword; and, just so far as she had succeeded in establishing her jurisdiction, so far her limits rightfully extended, and no further. So far they were recognised by the original resolutions of annexation, and no further; and so far, after she acceded to the terms proposed, they should have been defended by our arms, if occasion had required it, and no further. It is true that Texas, as a department or district of Mexico before her revolution, was bounded by the Nueces; but after her revolution she declared her boundary to be the Rio Grande, from its mouth to its source, which included portions of the States of Tamaulipas, Coahuila, and New Mexico; and, as far as that declaration was made good by the establishment of her authority and her laws, her title was good. A portion of the State of Tamaulipas, on the west side of the Nueces, including Corpus Christi, joined in the revolution, and thereby became a constituent part of that republic. But it is equally true that the people on the other side of the great desert, that lies between the valleys of the Nueces and the Rio Grande—those occupying the country on the east bank of the Rio Grande—never did, from the best evidence we have, join in the revolution; they adhered to Mexico, and recognised her laws and her authority. This I believe neither my colleague, nor any other gentleman on this floor, will pretend to deny. Hence it was very proper for our troops to be stationed at Corpus Christi, and very improper for them, before the boundary was settled, to be sent by the President to the Rio Grande. But, my colleague asks, where was the point at which the movement of our troops, under the order of the President, became aggressive and unwarranted? I say at that very point where they left the country 'occupied by the people—the citizens of Texas'—those who obeyed her laws and recognised her authority; for, until the boundary was adjusted with Mexico, the President [Polk] had no right to do more than defend Texas to the extent of her acknowledged jurisdiction. This is the point we make, and it is too clear to admit of argument. He had no right to say that the Rio Grande should be the western limits of Texas, when Congress had expressly declined so to declare. But this he did so, while Congress was in session too, without even consulting them; and, in so doing, we say that he grossly and wantonly abused his powers, and 'unnecessarily and unconstitutionally' involved us in war with Mexico; for no man, at this day, can doubt that the removal of our army from Corpus Christi, over the desert, to the banks of the

Rio Grande, which was in the possession of the Mexicans, was the occasion of hostilities; and if this lawless measure had not been adopted, war might have been avoided. But my colleague says, again, that the intention of the President to maintain the boundary of Texas up to the Rio Grande was set forth in his message of December, 1845; and that it was known here that the troops had been ordered to the Rio Grande, and yet no effort was made to arrest their march; and, according to this, I suppose he would argue that any act of violence, or in derogation of law, is justifiable, if those who know of its progress do not attempt to arrest it. But, sir, my colleague knows that when the message of December, 1845, was delivered, we were also informed that a minister was sent to Mexico with a prospect of settling this matter by negotiation. He knows, also, that the removal of the troops from Corpus Christi was not publicly known here until long after the order was given. He knows, also, that it was utterly impossible for any man on this side of the House to get a resolution even of inquiry upon this subject, against that fixed, inflexible, dead majority, on his side, which was at all times ready, as the same party now are, to defend any act of the President, however monstrous. An attempt was made, in the month of February, by the gentleman from Massachusetts [George Ashmun,] which failed. And sir, the journals show that, even after the rumors reached here of the actual commencement of hostilities, a majority of the House voted against resolutions inquiring into the subject. These resolutions were submitted by Mr. [Jefferson] Davis, a distinguished Whig from Kentucky, and the House would not even allow them to be introduced. And yet are the Whigs of that session to be charged with the grave offence of not having made an effort to prevent Mr. Polk from doing what he did? But again, he has labored to show that Mexico was making preparations for war with the view of recovering the whole of Texas, and he has read several extracts from papers and proclamations to show this hostile intention. But he certainly forgets that, after most of these belligerent exhibitions, the authorities in Mexico agreed to receive a commissioner from this country, and to settle the dispute without a resort to arms. The commissioner, he says, was rejected under a bare pretext; and the administration of [Mexican General José Joaquín de] Herrera, which had been pacifically inclined, was overturned by [Mexican General Mariano] Paredes, with the avowed object of making war for the recovery of Texas. Now, in all this my colleague must allow me most respectfully to say he is very much at fault. Mexico never did refuse to accept a commissioner from this Government, because no commissioner was ever sent. She agreed to receive a commissioner; but our President, for reasons known perhaps only to himself and Cabinet, declined to send such an officer, but sent an envoy and minister plenipotentiary, with certain secret instructions, which have not yet seen the light, (and about which I intend to say something more before I conclude,) and Mexico refused to receive and accredit him as such, because she had not so agreed, and because she did not think, as the question then stood, she could, consistently with her honor, do so. But it was from no disposition evinced on her part to put an end to negotiation, and to resort to arms. This the correspondence with Mr. [John] Slidell, the minister sent, abundantly shows. And we have the authority of Mr. Slidell himself that other and very different causes operated in the overthrow of the administration of Herrera than those which were connected with his pacific views towards this country. In his letter to Mr. [James] Buchanan, of the 27th December, 1845, from Mexico, he says:

> 'To enable you better to decide upon the course proper to be pursued, I will endeavor to give you, in as few words as possible, some idea of the present state of things here. I will not enter into detail; for their phases vary so much from day to day, and there are so many factions and subdivisions of party, that, even if I possessed the necessary information, I could not communicate it to you within any ordinary limits. The two great divisions of party are those of the Federalists [Conservatives] and Centralists [Liberals]: the former desiring the establishment of the constitution of 1824, which, with the exception of the absence of religious toleration, was very nearly a counterpart of our own; the latter, as the name implies, advocating a consolidated government as the only one adapted to the character of the people, and possessing sufficient strength and energy to preserve their nationality. . . . The associations of General Herrera have heretofore generally been with the Federal party, and the basis of his feelings in that direction was indicated by the selection from it of a majority of the members of his cabinet; but his failure to proclaim the federative, and to throw himself frankly upon that party, soon alienated the greater portion of it, while the remainder have given him but a feeble and reluctant support; and the whole force of the Centralists, comprising nearly all the officers of the army, and almost the entire clergy, has been arrayed against him.'

"This letter of Mr. Slidell, written a few days before, shows that the overthrow of the administration of Herrera was owing mainly to the influence of domestic questions, and that hostility towards the United States had but little to do with it. Indeed, we have his own assurance that he had more hope of success with a more hostile administration. In a letter of the 17th December, 1845, he uses this language:

> 'Notwithstanding the desire which I believe the present administration (Herrera's) really entertains to adjust all their difficulties with us, so feeble

and inert is it that I am rather inclined to the opinion that the chances of a successful negotiation would be better with one more hostile, but possessing greater energy.'

"This certainly shows that Mr. Slidell did not believe that Herrera refused to accredit him as a minister plenipotentiary from any hostile motives, or any disposition to avoid an amicable settlement of the difficulty; for he said he believed the administration really entertained a desire to adjust all their difficulties with us. This, you will observe, was in the month of December, 1845, long after Almonte had demanded his passports, and declared that Mexico would consider annexation as a cause of war, and long after most of the hostile threats mentioned by my colleague. But, sir, I now call the attention of the House to the language of Mr. [Joaquín María del] Castillo y Lanzas, Minister of Foreign Affairs under the administration of Paredes himself, to show the feelings he entertained towards us. This was long after the overthrow of Herrera; it was on the 12th of March, 1846. He says, after assigning the reasons why Mr. Slidell could not be received as a minister:

'If good faith presides, as is to be supposed, over the disposition of the Government of the United States, what motive could exist for so anxiously repelling the indispensable restriction with which Mexico has acceded to the proposal spontaneously made by the former? If it was really and positively desired to tie up again the bonds of good understanding and friendship between the two nations, the way was very easy. The Mexican government offered to admit the plenipotentiary or commissioner who should come clothed with special powers to treat upon the question of Texas. . . . A lover of peace, she would wish to ward off this sad contingency; and, without fearing war, she would desire to avoid so great a calamity to both countries. For this she has offered herself, and will continue to offer herself, open to all honorable means of conciliation; and she anxiously desires that the present controversy may terminate in a reasonable and decorous manner.

'In the actual state of things, to say that Mexico maintains a position of quasi hostility with respect to the United States, is to add a new offence to her previous injuries. Her attitude is one of defence, because she has seen herself unjustly attacked; because a portion of her territory is occupied by the forces of a nation intent, without any right whatever, to possess itself of it; because her ports are threatened by the squadrons of the same power. Under such circumstances, is she to remain inactive, without taking measures suited to so rigorous an emergency?

'It is, then, not upon Mexico, seeing her present state, that it devolves to decide if the issue shall be a friendly negotiation or an open rupture. . . .

'The undersigned doubts not that he makes his excellency Mr. Slidell sensible that, in view of what is set forth in the present note, the Mexican government trusts that the Executive of the United States, in coming to the determination which it shall deem proper, will act with the deliberation and mature consideration demanded by the exceedingly grave interest involved in this very thorny question. The Mexican government, preparing for war, should circumstances require it, will keep alive its flattering hope that peace will not be disturbed on the new continent; and, in making this declaration in the face of the world, it emphatically disclaims all responsibility for the evils which may attend a struggle which it has not provoked, and which it has made every effort to avoid.'

"I have read these copious extracts to show the tone and tenor of the feelings of Paredes, who, it is said, came into power with the avowed object of making war against this Government. Does this language of his minister look as if he had any such intention? Does he not signify as great a willingness and desire to settle the matter by negotiation as Herrera did? Does he not put a question which Mr. Polk has never yet answered, either to him or this country: Why, if he was really desirous of adjusting the matter amicably, he did not comply with the only terms upon which Mexico thought she could treat consistently with her honor? Why, in other words, did he send an envoy and minister plenipotentiary instead of a commissioner, according to the terms agreed upon? I wish to know, also, where the evidence is to be found that ever our minister was insultingly and indignantly rejected? And where is the evidence that, even up to the 12th March, 1846, Mexico was making any hostile preparations, except for defence? At that time your navy was hovering on the coast of California, whither it had been sent the summer before, to be ready to seize that country when the war should break out, which the President was then so eagerly striving to provoke. A squadron was ready at any day to blockade her ports in the Gulf, while the army was then on its way to the Rio Grande. Were not all these hostile demonstrations on our part quite enough to provoke any nation, however pacifically inclined, to resistance? But, sir, to show that Mexico did not intend to commence the attack, I refer to the last letter received from Mr. Slidell on his return home: it bears date as late as the 2nd of April, 1846. This letter contained what Mr. Slidell called the manifesto of Paredes, and he says of it:

'The manifesto declares that until the National Congress shall have concluded the question no act of aggression will be committed against the United States by the Mexican Government, but that it will repel any that may be offered by them. This declaration, however, under existing circumstances, even if made in good faith, leaves a wide range of discretion; for the advance of our troops to the banks of the Rio del Norte can at anytime be made a ground for commencing hostilities.'

"And why, Mr. Speaker, did Mr. Slidell say that the advance of our troops to the banks of the Del Norte could at any time be made a ground of commencing hostilities on the part of Mexico, even though the Government there, in good faith, did not intend to make an aggression upon us? It was because he knew, as Mr. Polk knew, and you know, and I know, and every man on this floor, as well as every intelligent man in this country knows, that the people there were Mexicans, in the possession of a country where they had been born and reared, and which had been occupied by their fathers before them; that they were loyal to their Government, and attached to their homes, their laws, customs, and institutions; and that resistance would be inevitable. The advance, however, was made in the very teeth of this knowledge, and the resistance which was expected and provoked was also made. A collision of arms ensued. This is the origin of the war; and who, sir, is responsible for it? The President of the United States, who ordered that advance; he, and he only, is responsible for it. Was there any necessity for it? None whatever. There was not a single settlement of the citizens of Texas in all that country that asked for protection, as far as I have ever heard, against any threatened invasion. Our troops had been at Corpus Christi for six months, during which time all was quiet on the frontier. Moreover, Mexico had just given an assurance of her willingness to settle the matter amicably and peaceably, if a special commissioner should be sent for that purpose. She protested, as late as the 12th of March, 1846, that she did not occupy a position of even quasi hostility towards us. Why, then, was the advance ordered? There is but one answer to this question: it was to provoke resistance, and thereby involve us in a war. Had the President power rightfully, under the Constitution, to do this? I answer in this House, before the American people, and in the face of Heaven, most emphatically, he had not. The war-making power belongs to Congress and not to the Executive. Neither had the President [Polk] any power to fix or determine a boundary line which Congress had expressly declined to do. In this case Congress, in express terms and with settled purpose, left the boundary an open question. Gentlemen may turn and twist this matter as they please, for the purpose of screening the President, but all such attempts will prove utterly fruitless and unavailing; the final conclusion that he 'unnecessarily and unconstitutionally' commenced this war can never be escaped. The mark is fixed upon him as indelibly as that stamped upon the brow of Cain by the finger of God. He and his friends may say 'out, foul spot,' but it will not 'out.' From this conclusion I say there is no escape—none whatever. Not even by taking shelter under that, of all others the most miserable subterfuge, of attempting to cast the blame on the shoulders on General Taylor, that gallant and brave officer, who has won such a name for himself, and gained so much fame for his country.

"Sir, I say, of all the excuses, apologies, subterfuges, and pretexts resorted to by the advocates of the President [Polk], this will afford him the least shelter; and the attempt to throw the responsibility of this war upon him is but a part and parcel of that spirit of gross injustice with which he has been so shamefully treated by this Administration and many of its advocates. It is said that he advised the removal of the troops, and that the advance was made in pursuance of his advice. Now, let us see how this position is sustained by the record. The first order to General Taylor, directing him to enter Texas, bears date at the War Office here on the 15th day of June, 1845, and contains this language:

> 'The point of your ultimate destination is the western frontier of Texas, where you will select and occupy, on or near the Rio Grande del Norte, such a site as will consist with the health of the troops, and will be best adapted to repel invasion, and to protect what, in the event of annexation, will be our western border.'

"This was the order of Mr. [George] Bancroft, the Secretary of War, in June, 1845, directed to General Taylor, at Fort Jesup, in Louisiana, and before the army entered Texas, telling him his ultimate destination was the Rio Grande, and directing him to select and occupy a site on or near that river, as, in the event of annexation, it would be the western border or boundary of this Government. This, sir, was the first order given, and before General Taylor had given any advice; nor have we ever yet seen the reply of General Taylor to that letter. I infer from the correspondence published that he did reply to it; but, as in other matters, the great injustice has been done him of suppressing his views; for, on the 8th of July, Mr. [William L.] Marcy, Secretary of War, writes to him:

> 'In carrying out the instructions heretofore received you will be careful to avoid any acts of aggression, unless an actual state of war should exist. The Mexican forces at the posts in their possession, and which have been so, will not be disturbed so long as the relations of peace between the United States and Mexico continue.'

"And, in answer to this, General Taylor's letter is given; and a valuable paper it is, not only in vindication of his character as an officer, but as a patriot and a statesman:

> 'Head-quarters First Military Department, New Orleans, Louisiana, July 20, 1845. Sir: I respectfully acknowledge your communication of July 8,

covering instructions of the Secretary of War of the same date, relative to the Mexican settlements on this side the Rio Grande. These instructions will be closely obeyed; and the Department may rest assured that I will take no step to interrupt the friendly relations between the United States and Mexico. I am gratified at receiving these instructions, as they confirm my views as previously communicated in regard to the proper line to be occupied at present by our troops. I am, sir, very respectfully, your obedient servant, Z. Taylor, Brevet Brig. Gen. U.S.A. commanding.'

"From this it is evident that General Taylor had previously communicated to the Department some views in regard to the proper line to be occupied by our troops which did not accord with the views of the Department, as expressed in the order of the 15th June, and he was gratified at receiving the instructions of July 8, which directed him to abstain from interfering with the Mexican posts on the east side of the Rio Grande; and he assured the Department that he should take no step to interrupt the friendly relations between the United States and Mexico. With these views he took a position at Corpus Christi, and made that point his head-quarters until he received the celebrated order of the 13th January, 1846. But it is said that, in a letter of the 4th of October, 1845, he gave that fatal advice which Mr. Polk was so innocently led to follow. Now, let us see that letter, or that portion of it upon which gentlemen rely to maintain this position. It is in these words:

'It is with great deference that I make any suggestions on topics which may become matter of delicate negotiation; but if our Government, in settling the question of boundary, makes the line of the Rio Grande an ultimatum, I cannot doubt that the settlement will be greatly facilitated and hastened by our taking possession at once of one or two suitable points on or near that river.'

"Now, sir, who can mistake the character of this language? It is simply his opinion, that if our Government intended to make the Rio Grande an ultimatum in the settlement of the question of boundary, it would be as well to take possession of the country at once. He says nothing about the propriety of making that line the boundary, nor any thing about the power of Mr. Polk to fix our ultimatum as to boundary; nor does he recommend or advise him to exercise any such power. In his original orders, as I have shown, he was told that his ultimate destination would be the Rio Grande, which, in the event of annexation, would be our western boundary; and he here says, that if such is the intention of the Government the army might as well move on to its ultimate destination. Indeed, in the introductory part of the same letter of the 4th of October, he says:

'It will be recollected that the instructions of June 15, issued by Mr. Bancroft, then acting Secretary of War, directed me to select and occupy on or near the Rio Grande such a site as will consist with the health of the troops, and will be best adapted to repel invasion.'

"And the plain import of the after part which I have quoted is, that if it is still the intention of the Government to make the Rio Grande the line, the forward movement might as well be made, as it might facilitate negotiations. But, so far from advising or recommending the President to exercise such a power, he expressly says in the same letter that he should not do so without positive orders, particularly under his instructions of the 8th of July. But, sir, after General Taylor had been there a few weeks longer, and had become better acquainted with the state of things, he changed his opinion as to the tendency of a forward movement of the army to facilitate negotiations. And on the 7th of November, he wrote that, while negotiations were pending the position at Corpus Christi was the best one to be occupied. This is his language:

'The communication from the Secretary of War, dated October 16, was received and acknowledged on the 1st and 2nd instant. I purposely deferred a detailed reply to the various points embraced in that communication, until I could receive an answer to mine of October 4, which covered (at least in part) the same ground. The intelligence from Mexico, however, tends to modify in some degree the views expressed in that communication. The position now occupied by the troops may perhaps be the best while negotiations are pending, or at any rate until a disposition shall be manifested by Mexico to protract them unreasonably.'

"And now, who from all this can say that Gen. Taylor ever breathed one syllable to Mr. Polk, by way of advice to him, to exercise the extraordinary power—that power which does not belong to him—of determining what shall be the ultimatum of an unsettled boundary? That is the point. Show that he advised the President no longer to consider the boundary line between Texas and Mexico an open question, where Congress had left it, but to make the Rio Grande the line by his own executive edict, and to defend it with the arms of the country without ever consulting Congress on the subject, and then, and never till then, may he be brought in to share some of the blame in this matter. But, sir, this never can be done; and the attempt to cast the censure of this movement upon the head of that gallant old chief is an act of the grossest injustice, and is but a part and parcel of that spirit of opposition and persecution with which he has been pursued by this Administration almost ever since the commencement of this war. It is akin to that spirit which kept him 'crippled' in the summer of 1846, on the Rio Grande, without the necessary means of transportation, and then found fault with his conduct at Monterey, where the victory he achieved, considering the circumstances in which he was placed, was almost a miracle in itself. It comes from the same spirit that sought to supplant him of his command by the appointment of a Lieutenant General; that spirit that stripped him of the main body of his forces, and left him with a small handful of men, about five thousand only, and about five hundred of these regulars, the rest all volunteers, exposed on the frontier to an attack from [Mexican General Antonio López de] Santa Anna, that 'knight of the cockpit,' as the gentleman from Virginia [Henry Bedinger] might perhaps style him, with twenty thousand of the chosen soldiers of Mexico. Why this was done I know not. But I leave it for the country to determine whether it was not an act of great injustice to him and his men, to be placed thus, as it were, 'in the fore-front of a battle,' where the odds against him were so great that retreat, if not defeat, seemed inevitable.

"But, sir, the same great spirit which marks his every act did not fail him on that occasion. The resources of a keen foresight and good judgment proved him to be not only equal, but superior, to the perils of the crisis. The ever memorable night of the 22nd of February, Mr. Speaker, must have been one of the most intense suspense to that small Spartan band of devoted spirits who spent its sleepless watches resting on their arms. Contemplate them for a moment, anxiously waiting the coming dawn, when life, and fame, and every thing dear to each, were to be determined by the fate of one day's bloody action. What emotions of apprehension must have moved in the breast of the most dauntless, when the music and exulting shouts of anticipated victory ever and anon arose from the immense hosts encamped in hostile array against them! But the presiding genius of our country was there; that guardian angel which, one hundred and fifteen years before, ruled the destiny of empires at the birth of [George] Washington, was over and around that army, guarding the fortunes of her most favorite son; and the next day dawned but to witness one of the greatest achievements ever won by the valor of arms—a victory which, in the language of a resolution on your table, is unsurpassed in the military annals of the world. It is true, it cost us dearly; many gallant hearts poured out their life-blood on that eventful day; some of them, known to members of this House, I may be permitted to name. There was . . . [an Archibald] Yell, frank, bold, and generous; a [William R.] McKee, one of Kentucky's most ardent, accomplished, and chivalrous sons; a [Henry] Clay [Jr.], with a heart as pure, stern, inflexible, and patriotic, as the great sire from whom he sprung; and a [John J.] Hardin, Mr. Speaker, well known to you and to me, and many of those around me, and of whom I take this occasion to say I never knew a truer, firmer, and nobler man. These men all fell in sustaining the flag of their country against the fearful odds brought against them on the field of Buena Vista. And it was here that gallant old officer, who bore our flag on that occasion, notwithstanding he was left with such a handful of men, gained such undying honors for himself and his country. But no thanks to the Administration for it. By them he was stripped of his men and crippled in his means; and what he did was the more glorious, as it was done in spite of their neglect. But another act, emanating from the same spirit, remains to be mentioned, which deserves the indignant rebuke of the whole country. I refer to the reprimand he received for writing the well known letter to General [Edmund P.] Gaines, and the revival of the old order No. 650, which had been obsolete for years, and by which he was threatened with dismissal from service for the repetition of a similar offence.

"I must ask the indulgence of the House while I read a portion of the letter of the Secretary of War to him, enclosing a copy of his letter to General Gaines; and I affirm it to be the most insolent outrage upon the character, motives, and patriotism of a high-toned, chivalrous officer, that was ever committed in this or any other country. Hear what Mr. Polk, through his Secretary, says:

> 'Sir: I deem it proper to send to you a letter, (taken from a newspaper,) which first appeared in the New York *Morning Express*, and has since, as a matter of course, been transferred to many other journals. . . . It will in a short time be in the possession of our enemy; and, coming as it does from the General [Zachary Taylor] to whom the conduct of the war on our part was confided, it will convey most valuable information to the Mexican commander.'

"I have not time to read all the letter; but can you imagine a more wanton insult to a brave officer, who had done such service to the country, than this letter contains? It charges him with having given valuable information to the Mexican commander; in other words, of giving 'aid and comfort' to the enemy. And who is it, sir, that brings this accusation? The same man that commenced this war in violation of the Constitution of his country; the same man whose friends now seek to throw the odium of it upon General Taylor; the same man who himself gave a free pass to that same Mexican commander to enter that country to take command of her armies. And against whom is it brought? Against the old soldier, who has devoted a long life to the service of his country in the field; who was engaged in the last war with England; who gained the victories of Palo Alto, Resaca de la Palma, and Monterey; a man whose every act was glorious, and every throb of whose heart was patriotic. Ransack the annals of your country, and show me, if you can, an act more scandalous than this outrage upon the integrity and patriotism of that gallant chief. I want, sir, to see his reply to it. We have not yet been favored with it, but it has been called for by the resolution offered by the gentleman from Kentucky, (Mr. Duncan,) and I hope we shall have that at least, if we cannot get the secret instructions to Mr. Slidell. And what was that 'valuable information' which had been given to the Mexican commander, or rather which gave such offence to our Executive? Here it is, every sentence bearing the unmistakable stamp of truth, honesty, and patriotism. I wish I had time to read the whole letter. I suppose these are the parts considered particularly obnoxious, and for the repeating of which he [Taylor] was threatened with dismissal from service:

> 'I do not believe the authorities at Washington are at all satisfied with my conduct in regard to the terms of the capitulation.'

"Referring to the capitulation entered into at Monterey. And in another place, in reference to the same, he [Taylor] says:

> 'In regard to the armistice, which would have expired by limitation in a few days, we lost nothing by it, as we could not move even now had the enemy continued to occupy Saltillo; for, strange to say, the first wagon that reached me since the declaration of war was on the 2nd inst.—the same day on which I received from Washington an acknowledgment of my despatch announcing the taking of Monterey—and then I received only one hundred and thirty-five; so that I have been since May last completely crippled and arrested for the want of transportation. After raking and scraping the country for miles around Camargo, collecting every pack-mule and other means of transportation, I could bring here only eighty thousand rations, (fifteen days' supply,) with a moderate supply of ordnance, ammunition, &c; to do which all the corps had to leave behind a portion of their camp equipage necessary for their comfort, and in some instances amongst the volunteers their personal baggage.
>
> '. . . Had we been put to the alternative of taking the place by storm, (which there is no doubt we should have succeeded in doing,) we should in all probability have lost some fifty or a hundred men in killed, besides wounded, which I wished to avoid, as there appeared to be a prospect of peace, even if a distant one. I also wished to avoid the destruction of women and children, which must have been very great had the storming process been resorted to.'

"But perhaps the part most offensive to the royal ears of the inmate of the White House, is where he says:

'If we are (in the language of Mr. Polk and Gen. [Winfield] Scott) under the necessity of 'conquering a peace,' and that by taking the capital of the country, we must go to Vera Cruz, take that place, and then march on to the city of Mexico. To do so in any other direction, I consider out of the question. But, admitting that we conquer a peace by doing so, say at the end of the next twelve months, will the amount of blood and treasure which must be expended in doing so be compensated by the same?'

"This is doubtless the part that wounded deepest. But were ever prophetic words spoken more truly? After going to Vera Cruz, and marching to the capital, and taking that place, at the end of the next twelve months, is the amount of blood and treasure expended in the enterprise compensated by our victories, as glorious and brilliant as they have been? Are we any nearer a peace? It is true our army has done every thing that men could do, and more than it was expected that they could do; they have gained for themselves imperishable fame. But have they brought us any nearer a peace? And yet, for uttering this prophetic sentence, for writing the letter which contained it, General Taylor received the insolent and insulting reprimand I have read, under the preposterous pretence that he was giving valuable information to the enemy. The real burden of the grief was, that he was giving valuable information to the people of this country touching the mischievous schemes and reckless policy of their own Executive, who is at this time the greatest enemy they have. I repeat it, sir, the present Executive [Polk] is the greatest enemy the people of this country have at this time; for he is waging a war, of all others the most dangerous to a free people—a war against the Constitution of the country. But why should he have been so particular about valuable information getting to the ears of the Mexican commander? Under whose auspices but his own was that commander permitted to enter freely into that country? Was the insolence of place and power ever more audaciously exhibited than in this instance?

"Sir, I will here say a word or two on the message of the President in relation to the return of that Mexican commander, and the instructions to Mr. Slidell. I shall not moot the question of his power to withhold those instructions from this House and the people. I know we have no power to compel their production. But I submit it to this House and the people, whether it is not the exercise of Executive power bordering on 'royal prerogative,' as the eloquent gentleman from Mississippi [Patrick W. Tompkins] said the other day—to withhold from them and their representatives information so important in relation to the origin and cause of this war? I submit to them, also, whether the reason assigned for withholding them is any thing but a pretext! If they contained nothing but what was honorable, just, honest, and right, as they should, how could their publication injure our interest or cause with Mexico, or any body else? It would rather have the contrary effect, by placing us in the right and them in the wrong before the civilized world. The secret of this matter, I apprehend, is the fear of personal exposure. And he has a much better protection, I doubt not, than the precedent which he quotes affords him, in that clause of the Constitution which provides that no person 'shall be compelled in any criminal case to be a witness against himself.' I had very little hope when the resolution passed calling for those instructions that we should get them. I believed then, as I do now, that they contained secrets connected with the origin of this war that he dare not publish—not from any fear of Mexico; that is idle, absurd, and preposterous; Mexico is prostrate; she is at our mercy—but from a fear of the American people. I had quite as little hope, also, of getting the facts in relation to the return of Santa Anna. I had no idea that a man who had so repeatedly outraged and insulted the intelligence of this country and this age by the misstatement and distortion of facts well known, would make a full disclosure of all the circumstances attending a secret transaction so little to his credit as this intrigue with [General] Santa Anna. Who, sir, in this House, believes the President [Polk] in his message upon this subject? He says the order to let him 'pass' was issued 'without any understanding on the subject, direct or indirect, with Santa Anna or any other person.' I do not intend to rely upon the notorious rumors of the day—of the visit of Alexander Slidell Mackenzie [a nephew of John Slidell] to Havana—but I undertake to say that the papers accompanying this message carry upon their face internal evidence that this statement (or the impression intended to be made by it) is utterly destitute of all claims to faith and credit. The order is in these words:

> '[Private and confidential to Com. David Conner, Commanding Home Squadron.] U.S. Navy Department, May 13, 1846. Commodore: If Santa Anna endeavors to enter the Mexican ports, you will allow him to pass freely. Respectfully, yours, George Bancroft.'

"And Commodore Conner writes on the 16th of August, 1846.

> 'I have allowed him to enter without molestation, or even speaking the vessel, as I was informed by the senior English naval officer here, Capt. Lambert, she carried no cargo, and would not be allowed to take any in return. I could easily have boarded the *Arab*, but I deemed it most proper not to do so, allowing it to appear as if he had entered without my concurrence. It is now quite certain that the whole country—that is, the garrisons of every town and fortress—have declared in his favor,' &c.

"Now, is it not exceedingly strange, past all credence, that Santa Anna, with his suite, should have attempted, in the open day, to enter a port closely blockaded, and have approached so near the flag-ship of the blockading squadron as that the vessel he was in could have easily been boarded, without some understanding with Mr. Polk, 'either direct or indirect, or some other person,' that he could pass freely? Is it not strange that Mr. Polk should have sent such an order without 'some understanding, either direct or indirect, with Santa Anna or some other person,' that it was his intention to return? And how could Commodore Conner have known that the *Arab* had Santa Anna on board, unless there was 'some understanding, either direct or indirect,' between them upon this subject? The tale will not bear telling. It is one of those gross fabrications that carries its own detection on its face. According to all the rules and principles of human reason on probabilities, the honest inquirer after truth is compelled to pronounce it wholly incredible and perfectly mendacious. The President is also quite unfortunate in the reason which he says induced him to permit Santa Anna to return. For this he refers to his message in December, 1846; and the reason there assigned is, that Santa Anna was known to be opposed to monarchy, and in favor of the restoration of the constitution of 1824. Now, nothing is more notorious in relation to Mexican affairs and Mexican history than that Santa Anna was the man who overthrew the constitution of 1824, and was at the time this order was given in exile for his lawless usurpations and abuse of powers. Sir, whoever will take all these facts into consideration—the condition of Mexico, the exile of Santa Anna; the date of his permission to pass our blockade; the date of his return; the circumstances of that return, and the request of Mr. Polk for a certain extraordinary appropriation of two millions of dollars, cannot fail to come to the conclusion that there was some 'understanding, either direct or indirect, between him and Santa Anna, or some other person,' yea, some 'mystery of iniquity' in this business, which has not yet seen the light, and which he would sooner see his grave than see published to the people of this country.

"But, sir, I said upon rising that I had a motion to make before concluding, and that is, to amend the report of the committee by striking out the amendment of the gentleman from Pennsylvania [David Wilmot] proposing to raise five millions of dollars per annum by a direct tax on the personal property of the country so long as this war continues. I do it to let this House know that, for one, I do not intend to tax my constituents to carry on this war for the objects now avowed for its prosecution. After the war was recognised, and as long as the proposed objects were peace and an amicable settlement of the matters of dispute, I was for its prosecution, and was ready to vote any and all necessary means to bring it to a speedy and honorable termination; even taxation, if it should have been required, and I am so yet. But this war is now waged for conquest; the object can no longer be disguised. No man can be mistaken after reading the ultimatum in the instructions to Mr. [Nicholas P.] Trist. The President says it is waged for indemnity. Every man of sense knows it is waged for no such thing. The *sine qua non* for peace in the instructions to Mr. Trist was to take New Mexico and California and pay $15,000,000 or $20,000,000. No man can be mistaken. The reason peace was not made was because Mexico was unwilling to sell a portion of her country; and the avowed object in continuing it now is to compel and force her to make the surrender, or to take the whole of it.

"Sir, I take this earliest opportunity of saying that I shall never tax my constituents for any such object. If they wish to contribute their substance to sustain a policy so odious and detestable, so entirely at war with all the most sacred principles upon which their own Government is founded, they must send some other person here to lay the taxes. I never shall do it.

"The President [Polk] assumes (if I understand his position) that the honor and interest of this country requires us to make this demand of Mexico. Sir, I wholly dissent from any such doctrine. The honor of this country does not and cannot require us to force and compel the people of any other to sell theirs. I have, I trust, as high a regard for national honor as any man. It is the brightest gem in the chaplet of a nation's glory; and there is nothing of which I am prouder than the high character for honor this country has acquired throughout the civilized world—that code of honor which was established by [George] Washington and the men of the Revolution, and which rests upon truth, justice, and honesty, which, is the offspring of virtue and integrity, and which is seen in the length and breadth of our land, in all the evidences of art and civilization and moral advancement, and every thing that tends to elevate, dignify, and ennoble man. This is the honor of my admiration, and it is made of 'sterner,' purer, nobler 'stuff' than that aggressive and degrading, yea, odious principle now avowed of waging a war against a neighboring people to compel them to sell their country. Who is here so base as to be willing, under any circumstances, to sell his country? For myself, I can only say, if the last funeral pile of liberty were lighted, I would mount it and expire in its flames before I would be coerced by any power, however great and strong, to sell or surrender the land of my home, the place of my nativity, and the graves of my sires! Sir, the principle is not only dishonorable, but infamous. As the representative upon this floor of a high-minded and honorable constituency, I repeat, that the principle of waging war against a neighboring people to compel them to sell their country, is not only dishonorable, but disgraceful and infamous. What, shall it be said that American honor aims at nothing higher than land—than the ground on which we tread? Do we look no higher in our aspirations for honor, than do the soulless brutes? Shall we disavow the similitude of our Maker, and disgrace the very name of man? Tell it not to the world. Let not such an aspersion and reproach rest upon our name. I have heard of nations whose honor could be satisfied with gold—that glittering dust, which is so precious in the eyes, of some—but never did I expect to live to see the day when the Executive of this country should announce that our honor was such a loathsome, beastly thing, that it could not be satisfied with any achievements in arms, however brilliant and glorious, but must feed on earth—gross, vile, dirt!—and require even a prostrate foe to be robbed of mountain rocks and desert plains! I have no such notions of honor; and I have quite as little opinion of that policy which would spend fifty or a hundred millions of dollars in compelling the Mexicans to take fifteen or twenty millions for New Mexico and California, on the score of public interest. And, I repeat, I shall vote to tax my constituents for no such purpose. You already have a debt of near sixty millions of dollars, and a loan bill on your table for eighteen millions, and another one coming, according to the request of the Secretary of the Treasury, of twenty millions more. It may be that under this accumulated pressure the public credit may go down. If so, all I can say is, so let it be. Perhaps, when the business of the country begins to suffer, as it must, and the people begin to feel, as they surely will, the ruinous effects of the policy of this Administration, they will rise in their majesty and send up a rebuke to their rulers in such tones as will make them feel some of the consequences of an abuse of power, and from which there will be no escape, no shelter, not even in the dark vaults that, contain the hidden instructions to Mr. Slidell. Indeed, I have very little hope for the country until the people begin to feel; they will then reflect, they will then speak, and they will then act."[84]

The following excerpt is from Stephens' February 23, 1852, speech before the Maryland Institute at Baltimore, Maryland. The occasion was the commemoration of the birthday of George Washington, to this day considered one of the great Southern heroes in Dixie. Here Stephens pleads the case for the Washingtonian idea of nonintervention, predicting dire consequences for disregarding it:

☞ " . . . The other point I promised to allude to is the subject of our foreign relations. This is becoming a matter of grave and momentous importance for the consideration of the American people. It was a matter that the far-seeing eye of [President] Washington did not overlook. Hence his emphatic and solemn warning:

> 'Against the insidious wiles of foreign influence, (I conjure you to believe me, fellow-citizens,) the jealousy of a free people ought to be constantly awake.'

"This was the language of the patriot and sage in his last words to his countrymen. The hand that penned it has long since returned to its mother dust; but the same voice still comes from his tomb at Mount Vernon, and here this night, I invoke you, for his sake, if not for your own, to hearken to that voice. Again he says:

> 'The great rule of conduct for us in regard to foreign nations is, in extending our commercial relations, to have with them as little political connection as possible.'

"From that day to this—for more than half a century—we have followed that advice. Our motto from that time to this, in the language of Mr. [Thomas] Jefferson, has been 'Friendship with all nations—entangling alliances with none.' And I am proud to say that no American—no son of Washington, not even the most degenerate—was the first to advocate a change of this policy. It was reserved for the son of another and a distant clime—a man, too, who had abandoned his own country in the hour of her peril, to come here to teach us how to make ours great, prosperous, and powerful. For the honor of Americans, I say, be it spoken, that this first attempt to arraign the wisdom of Washington on this question of our foreign policy was made by a foreigner. Would that I could say that no American had yielded to 'the insidious wiles of his influence.' But the virus has taken effect; it is spreading through the land; and we now hear it openly proclaimed in many places, that it is time for us to assume our position amongst the nations of the earth; that it is time we had a foreign policy. What does this language mean? Is it intended by those who use it to convey the idea that we have gone on for upward of sixty years in a career of prosperity never before equalled, without any foreign policy? Was not the rule laid down by Washington, and acted on by every President from his day to this, a policy? It was a policy. *It was and is the policy of attending to our own business, and letting other-nations alone. It was and is the policy, the time-honored policy, of non-intervention. It may not be a foreign policy, but it is a Washington policy; by an observance of which we have come to be what we are—one of the first nations of the earth.* Are we to be told that it is now time for us to assume a place amongst the powers of the world? Did not our forefathers do that when they compelled Great Britain, in 1783, to acknowledge our sovereignty and independence? Had we no position amongst the great nations when France sought our alliance in 1795 and 1796, which overture was rejected? Had we no position in 1812, when we again met in combat our old enemy, and the most formidable foe then in the world? Had we no position when British fleets were driven from our seas, and her invading armies were cut down and beaten back from our shores? Were the heroic deeds of our naval officers, to whose memory a marble monument has been erected on the capital grounds, performed before we had sufficient power to be felt? Was the gallant and daring defence of your own city, which you have put in monumental remembrance on your own public square, all done without a foreign policy, and before we were enabled to take a place amongst the nations of the earth? Be not deceived my fellow countrymen, we have had a policy from the beginning. It is a good policy; it has worked well. Let us adhere to it. [Emphasis added, L.S.]

"And, above all, lend no listening ear to those who come from other countries to teach you the principles of republicanism. Yield not to the tempter. The father of your country forbids. It was in an evil hour that our great first parents touched the forbidden fruit. They were happy in their paradise; their wily enemy came from other regions. Imagine for a moment the scene, when the guardian angel of that innocent and noble pair took his last departure from them; when he was called away from his charge of watching over and protecting them. Hear the last whispers of his voice, beware of foreign influence. It was thus that Washington, our deliverer, defender, and guardian spirit, spoke to us on taking his last parting leave. Had they heeded the warning given to them, they had not fallen. May we as a nation never fall as they did!

"The right, fellow-citizens, to interfere in circumstances that might happen, I do not mean to discuss. I grant that we have all the attributes and powers of a full-grown nation, so far as our foreign relations are concerned. But the right to do a thing and the policy or propriety of doing it are quite different questions. Any man can get into a fight when he pleases. And so can we. Intervention to prevent intervention is very much like getting into a fight to prevent a fight. Intermeddlers with other people's business generally come off worsted. Be not misled [by] appeals to your sympathy. It is for no want of the profoundest sympathy for the misgoverned tribes of the race of man in all parts of the world that I speak as I do. It was for no want of sympathy for them that Washington spoke as he did. I wish that all nations had as good a government as we have. But we should not peril our own life in hopeless efforts to rescue that of others. Let us not, in a fit of misguided zeal for the liberties of mankind, lose our own. All men are not suited for constitutional free government. One of the most common of the popular errors of the day is that any people having the wish to be free also have the ability to be free. This is a great mistake. Constitutional liberty, or liberty regulated by law—the only liberty that is worth the name—is not so easily acquired. If it were, we would not to-day be the only people on earth in its enjoyment. It is true, the people of almost any nation, with a firm resolution, can overthrow the strongest of despotisms, but they can not build up a republic in its stead. This requires more than physical force. It requires virtue, intelligence, morality, patriotism, and statesmanship. Brutus and a few associates found no difficulty in removing Caesar from an imperial throne. But they did not thereby restore lost freedom to Rome. France found but little difficulty in bringing Louis the XVI to the block; but France did not thereby establish a republic. She found even less difficulty in driving Charles the X from the kingdom he had so badly governed; but she did not thereby succeed in establishing a good government for the people. Louis Philippe had in like manner in a short time to be carried to her Tarpeian Rock. It is now just four years since she made her last effort at republicanism. And what do we now behold? Louis Napoleon [III]—a President King!

"And so it will be, I fear, with all the nations of Europe, until there be a change in the minds, habits, education, and modes of thinking on the part of their people. Liberty, in their estimation, is licentiousness, lawlessness. They do not understand or appreciate its first principles. Men, to be capable of maintaining law and order in a free government, must be schooled in the elementary principles.

"Suppose the autocrat of Russia four years ago had taken sides with the exiled Louis Philippe, and we had intervened to prevent his intervention. What would have been our condition to-day? After the expenditure of millions in money, and the loss perhaps of hundreds of thousands of our bravest sons in foreign wars, we should have found the people of France shouting huzzas to the emperor in the person of the 'nephew of his uncle.' All such crusades are idle. And if to-day we should go and surround 'poor down-trodden Hungary' with a wall so high and so deep that a Russian could neither scale it nor undermine it, and leave the people of that ill-fated country to perfect 'fair play' amongst themselves, I should expect nothing with more certainty than that, in quite as short a time as France has been trying the experiment, we should have her fickle and restless population crying out for the restoration of the House of Hapsburg! Why then, again, I ask in the language of Washington,

> 'Why quit our own to stand on foreign ground? Why be interweaving our destiny with that of any part of Europe, entangle our peace and prosperity in the toils of European ambition, rivalship, interest, humor, or caprice?'

"Here, perhaps, I should stop. But there are some reflections growing out of these topics which, it seems to me, may be appropriately connected with them. It is now just one hundred and twenty years since Washington was born. What was the condition of our country then? What is it now? And what is it to be one hundred and twenty years hence, if we continue to follow that line of policy which has marked our past career? Baltimore then was hardly a hamlet; now her population is over one hundred and seventy thousand, and the canvas of her commerce whitens every sea on the face of the globe, while her productive industry turns out an annual yield of twenty millions of dollars! What is true of Baltimore in improvement and advancement is true of almost every other part of our common country—not in extent, but in a relative degree. In 1732, the population of the colonies which afterward became the United States, was less, perhaps, than two millions. The population of the United States now is over twenty-three millions. Then an unbroken wilderness extended from a border near us to the distant Pacific. The great valley of the Mississippi was reposing under the shade of her primeval forests, in which the silence of centuries remained unbroken by the voice of civilization. Now behold her teeming population, her cultivated plains, her villages, towns, and cities, springing up as if by magic, and her majestic rivers alive with her accumulating commerce. See the hundreds and thousands of emigrants annually quitting the despotisms of the old world, and taking shelter and protection in this our favored land! To these we give a hearty welcome. We offer a safe retreat for the exile, and a peaceful quiet home for the emigrant, but no theatre for foreign propagandists.

"But these are not all the subjects suitable for our contemplation on this occasion. What advancement have we made since this government was formed, in letters, in mechanic arts, in discoveries, in inventions, and in science? Consider the number and character of our schools of learning, our academies, colleges, and universities; colleges for the education of women as well as men. See what steam has done under the power and control of American genius, fostered by the influence of our free, wise, and beneficent institutions. Behold the mysterious workings of the telegraph. It was [Benjamin] Franklin's honor to 'weave his garland of the lightning's wing,' and 'with the thunder talk as friend to friend.' But it has been [Samuel F. B.] Morse's glory, in our own day, to seize the spirit of the lightning itself, and to make it the swift messenger of our thoughts. What has caused this mighty change? Need I tell you it is the spirit of our institutions? It is that government which makes us not only one people, but a people with whatever diversity of interests or pursuits having all alike security at home and abroad. That government which heretofore has looked to our own safety, welfare, peace, quiet, prosperity, and domestic tranquillity, without meddling with the affairs of others, further than to give them the influence of a noble example. Shall this state of things continue? Shall we go on in the bright career we have commenced? Have we a national immortality before us? Or is the sun of our glory soon to go down in darkness to rise no more? These are questions which will spring up in the anxious mind; but to them no answer can be given. They involve the subtle problems of human destiny. Providence has wisely veiled the future from our vision. All we have to do is with the present. Let us take care that that is done rightly, and we need not fear for what shall come after."[85]

The following excerpt is from a speech Stephens gave on December 14, 1854, before the U.S. House of Representatives. It concerns the introduction of a bill to "restore the Missouri Compromise," which would, by Federal law, prohibit slavery in the newly developing Western states. Stephens, like most other conservatives, believed that the Western states should be able to decide for themselves whether or not to accept or reject slavery; that the Federal government had no business telling the individual states what to do. After arguing for states' rights, Stephens goes on to contend in favor of the institution of slavery as it was practiced in the South. His defence here rests on philanthropy, and what he perceives as the more "civilized" attributes of European culture (compared to the more "barbaric" characteristics of African culture). He also uses crime and agricultural statistics in the South and North to fortify his position:

☞ "I believe . . . that the system of government, as adopted by the South, defining the status or relation of [the white and black] . . . races, is the best for both of them; and I am prepared to argue that question with the gentleman, here or anywhere. Take the negroes in Indiana, take them in the North generally, and compare their condition with those of the South. Take them in Africa; take them anywhere on the face of the habitable globe; and then take them in the southern States, and *the negro population of the South are better off, better fed, better clothed, better provided for, enjoy more happiness, and a higher civilization, than the same race has ever enjoyed anywhere else on the face of the world.* Could [John] Howard the [British] philanthropist [and social reformer], who has left an undying fame for his deeds of humanity, have taken the same number of Africans from their native country and raised them from their barbarous condition to that of the slaves of the South, he would have added much to that stature of immortality which, in his day, he erected to himself. It would have greatly added to that reputation, which now sanctifies his memory in the hearts and affections of mankind. [Emphasis added, L.S.]

"Look at the three millions of Africans as you find them in the South; and where is the man so cold-hearted, and cold-blooded, as would wish to put them in the condition that their forefathers were, or their kindred now are in Africa? What has done so much for these people but that which is so much denounced by inconsiderate fanatics; men and women, too, who find fault with what they know nothing about?

"Again: take our negroes, and compare their condition with that of the free negroes of the North. I have the result of the census returns before me, and from that it appears that the increase of the free people of color in the United States, from 1840 to 1850, was only ten and ninety-five hundredths *per centum.*

This shows that their condition cannot be very good, or desirable; and to this increase is to be added, too, the fugitive slaves, and those who have been emancipated. With all these sources of increase, that increase has only been ten and ninety-five hundredths *per centum.*

"Now, how is it with the [Southern] slaves—the [so-called] down-trodden, the abused, the half-starved slaves? Their increase, during the same period, was twenty-eight and fifty-eight hundredths. Is there any such result to be presented at the North, where they are free and left to themselves? How can your missionaries in philanthropy and crusaders in benevolence account for this?

"But some people say that slavery is a curse to the white man. They abandon the idea that it is a curse to the negro. They say it weakens, impoverishes, and demoralizes a State. Let us see. They say there can be no high social, moral, or material development under the institution of slavery. I have before me some statistics on this point—statistics relating to material development. But, before alluding to them, I will say upon the subject of morals, that I saw a table of crimes made out in the census office for 1850. From those statistics it appeared—I speak from memory; I have not the paper before me—that the number of convictions for crimes of every grade, in Massachusetts, the land of 'steady habits,' and where we hear so much of the immoral effects of slavery, with a population under one million, was several thousand; while in the State of Georgia, with a population not so great, the similar convictions are less than one hundred. I say, then, upon the score of crime, upon the score of morals, I am ready to compare my State with that of Massachusetts, or any one of the free States. Where, then, is the moral curse which arises from slavery?

"A few facts in reference to physical development. I had occasion, some time since, for another purpose than the present, to look a little into the statistics of Georgia, compared with those of other States. I selected the State of Ohio, because it was one of the most prosperous of the North—often styled, and, perhaps, justly too, the giant of the West. According to the census returns in 1850, Ohio had of improved lands 9,851,493 acres—Georgia had only 6,378,479 acres, the cash value of the Georgia land so improved and under culture was $95,753,445, while the cash value of the Ohio lands was returned at $358,758,603—Ohio had nearly one-third more land in a state of improvement than Georgia had, and returned at more than three times the cash value of the Georgia lands. The whole population of Ohio was 1,908,480, the whole population of Georgia, white and black, was 905,999. The population of Ohio, therefore, was more than double that of Georgia. Here we see her free labor more than double in number, working one third more land, worth, by valuation, more than three times that of Georgia. From these elements it might not be surprising to see her agricultural products greatly exceeding those of Georgia, without resorting to the 'curse of slavery' to account for it. But how stand the facts? *Ohio* produced the following articles:

Wheat: 14,487,351 bushels at 80 cents: $11,589,880
Buckwheat: 638,060 bushels at 40 cents: $255,224
Indian corn: 59,078,695 bushels at 30 cents: $17,723,608
Rye: 425, 918 bushels at 50 cents: $212,959
Barley: 354,358 bushels at 50 cents: $177,179
Oats: 13,472,742 bushels at 25 cents: $3,368,182
Peas and beans: 60,168 bushels at 1 dollar: $60,168
Irish potatoes: 5,057,769 bushels at 40 cents: $2,023,107
Sweet potatoes: 187,991 bushels at 50 cents: $93,995
Tobacco: 10,454,449 lbs. at 7 cents: $731,811
Cloverseed: 103,197 bushels at 4 dollars: $412,748
Flax: 446,932 lbs. at 10 cents: $44,693
Flaxseed: 188,880 bushels at 75 cents: $141,660
Maple sugar: 4,588,209 lbs. at 6 cents: $275,292
Molasses: 197,308 gals. at 35 cents: $69,057
Wine: 48,207 gals. at 1 dollar: $48,207
Garden products returned in money, value: $214,004
Orchard products returned in money, value: $695,921
Aggregate $38,137,695

"This list includes nearly every agricultural product of the earth in that State, except hay, which is omitted, because in Georgia there is no return for fodder, which, in that State, answers the same purpose of hay in Ohio, as food for stock. The quantity of each product produced is given from the census tables. The values run out are such as are believed to be the usual average values of each article in that State, except the products of gardens and orchards, which are taken from the tables—no other values are put upon the products in the tables. The estimate above stated is believed to be a fair one. Now let us take up the returns for *Georgia* and place upon them a like estimated average value. Here we have:

Wheat: 1,088,534 bushels at 1 dollar: $1,088,534
Indian corn: 30,080,099 bushels at 50 cents: $15,040,049
Cotton—bales: 499,091, 400 lbs. at 8 cents: $15,970,912
Rice: 38,950,691 lbs. at 4 cents: $1,558,027
Peas and beans: 1,142,011 bushels at 1 dollar: $1,142,011
Sweet potatoes: 6,986,428 bushels at 25 cents: $1,746,607
Irish potatoes: 227,378 bushels at 50 cents: $113,689
Oats: 3,820,044 bushels at 37.5 cents: $1,432,516

Cane sugar: 1,642 hhds. 1,000 lbs. at 6 cents: $98,520
Molasses: 216,150 gallons at 25 cents: $54,037
Orchard products of Georgia: $92,766
Garden products of Georgia: $76,500
Aggregate: $38,414,168

"An amount so far from falling under that of Ohio as might have been expected, actually exceeds it about a quarter of a million, without extending the Georgia list to rye, barley, tobacco, and other articles which are produced in that State. Away, then, with this prating cry about slavery paralyzing the energy of a people, and opposing the development of the resources of a country. If I were to take the statistics of any other State, and go through them in the same way, I have no reason to doubt that an equally favorable result to Georgia would follow. I took the State of Ohio, not as any disparagement to her, but to show that even in the South, where they say the soil is sterile, and the population inert, and cursed with slavery, as it is said to be, Georgia, with one half of the population, and only two thirds of the value of land, exceeds in agricultural products by one quarter of a million of dollars the great giant of the West.

"Now, then, if the people of Kansas, the people of Nebraska, or the people of any other portion of our territory, going from old Massachusetts, going from New York, or from Indiana, or from the South, learning and consulting wisdom from the past, and profiting by experience from all parts of the Union, should think it practically best for the happiness of themselves and for their posterity in the far distant future, to adopt the social institutions of Georgia in preference to those of Indiana, if they prefer the institutions of the South to those of the North, I say they should not be deprived of their right to do it, and the gentleman from Indiana, and those who act with him, should not set themselves up as judges and 'masters' to control the matter."[86]

The following speech was given by Stephens before the U.S. House of Representatives on February 19, 1856. It concerns "the Kansas contested election case," in which former Kansas Governor Andrew H. Reeder opposed the selection of Tennessee born U.S. General John W. Whitfield as delegate of the Territory of Kansas. The claim was that the law under which Whitfield had been elected was "invalid." Here we see Stephens, by then a well respected and successful lawyer, at his judicial best, defending Whitfield in his usual elaborate and dramatic manner:

☞ "I do not propose, Mr. Speaker, to say much on the subject of this resolution. It involves one of the extraordinary powers of this House, and one which ought not to be inconsiderately or rashly resorted to. I believe there is but one instance, so far as I have investigated the matter, where, in cases of contested elections, the House of Representatives has ordered the sending for persons and papers. That was the case of the New Jersey election. At that time, sir, there was no general law of the United States regulating the taking of testimony in cases of contested elections. Whether the committee in that case ever exercised any power under the resolution, I am not prepared at this time to say. I am not going to contend against the power of the House, if a proper occasion should arise, to give such authority; but we ought to inquire whether the necessity has arisen in the present case, before we do exercise this power, and particularly in relation to a Territory so distant as Kansas, putting witnesses to so great inconvenience and expenses in obeying our summons. The House is uninformed this morning by the Committee of Elections why it makes this application; and I shall, before I take my seat, move that the resolution be referred back to that committee, with instructions to report to this House the grounds on which it makes this application, or their reasons for invoking the unusual exercise of this power. Then the House and the country will be duly informed whether sufficient reasons exist why the resolution should he adopted. We, Mr. Speaker, as now advised in this House, (for it is improper to speak of what has occurred in the committee,) can only judge of the matter submitted to us by the memorial and notice given by the gentleman contesting the seat of [U.S.] General [John W.] Whitfield. [Note: Six years later, during Lincoln's War, Whitfield would serve with distinction as a Confederate general.]

"The memorial alleges the invalidity of the law under which General Whitfield, the Delegate from the Territory, now holding his seat in this House, was elected. He affirms that the Law was void—that there was no law. But how, sir, are we to judge by oral testimony as to the validity of that law? The facts which are sufficient to determine this case, I apprehend, are all of record, and accessible to us here.

"I have before me the public records of the Territory of Kansas, in which is to be found the law under which General Whitfield was elected; the members of the House can see this law. The allegation of the memorialist is, that this law is invalid and void. If so, how? in what way? for what reason? Why is it invalid? Sir, it was passed by the Legislature of Kansas, under a published law of the United States, of which we are bound to take notice; and it is itself a public law, of which we are bound officially to take notice. Yet, sir, it is now proposed to go behind that law, and to send for persons to establish its invalidity by oral testimony. How many witnesses are we to have? who are they? and what are they to prove? We have before us no specifications. Who are the witnesses we are to send for, and what are they to prove? Of course, the sitting Delegate, General Whitfield, according to all rules of courtesy, to say nothing of the members of the House, is entitled to have notice of the names of the persons to be sent for, and what it is expected to prove by them. This he is entitled to, as a matter of right, and this the House should also have, in order to judge of the competency as well as relevancy of the testimony sought to be obtained. If it is neither competent nor relevant to establish the point in issue, then why incur the delay and expense in getting it?"

[Israel Washburn of Maine speaks:] "If the gentleman will allow me, I will say, that of course, if the resolution shall be adopted, it will be within the power and discretion of the Committee of Elections not only to say what, who, and how many persons shall be sent for, but also what papers. It will be in the discretion of the Committee of Elections to determine what witnesses shall be sent for. It is a discretion that has always been intrusted to committees under such circumstances. As to how that discretion shall be used, of course witnesses can be sent for at the instance of General Whitfield as well as of [Kansas] Governor [Andrew H.] Reeder. The resolution only asks that the committee itself shall have the power and authority, in its discretion, to send for such persons and papers as they shall deem to be absolutely necessary to come to a correct conclusion upon this subject, whether those persons and papers are called for by one party or the other."

[Stephens responds:] "But, Mr. Speaker, when it is notorious that this law was passed by the Legislature in Kansas, elected under the superintendency of officers appointed by the Governor, of which we are bound to take public notice, in all matters arising under it, and when it is proposed to invalidate this law, or any other such law, by oral testimony, should not this House require that the precise character of the testimony proposed to be adduced should be specially set forth, before we consent to give the power to a committee?

"The memorial of Governor Reeder barely states that this act was illegal and void, and the election under it void. This is his case, as I understand it. But why illegal? why void? Was not the Legislature duly elected and legally organized? This, though not stated, we all know, is the ground upon which his contest rests. But can he raise that question? I have before me the journal of the Kansas Legislature. The memorialist in the case was the Governor of the Territory when the Legislature that passed that act was elected and organized, as stated by the gentleman from Missouri [John S. Phelps], and, whether rightly or not, he, the present memorialist, as Governor, judged of the election returns, and recognized the Legislature as duly and properly elected and organized. He assumed the power to judge of the election returns, and gave certificates of election to a large majority of the Council and House of Representatives. Many of the people of the Territory disputed his right to do it; but, as I have said, whether rightly or not, he assumed the power, and exercised it, to judge of the election returns, and certified to the proper election of a large majority, both in the House and Legislative Council. The election of every member, I believe, who took his seat at the organization, was certified to under the Governor s own hand or by his direction.

"Now, sir, I say, when this memorialist comes before us and asks us to send for persons and papers, without naming the parties, to prove that what he himself has officially certified to was invalid, I would hold him to a very rigid showing. Justice requires it; the peace, and repose, and quiet of the country require it.

"Sir, if a memorialist from your district had come and asked us to set aside your election because the law under which you were elected—a public act of the State of Massachusetts—was void, and nothing but such a broad allegation had been referred to a committee, would any committee have asked for power to send for persons and papers to inquire into the validity of that law? And if they had, would the House give the power upon no other showing? I apprehend not. Now, let us apply the same rule to this case as would be applied to any other."

[Walker:] "Will the gentleman from Georgia allow me to suggest a matter to him?"

[Stephens:] "Yes, sir."

[Walker:] "I have no desire to occupy the attention of the House in an argument myself upon this question; but I would be pleased to remind the gentleman from Georgia of this portion of the thirty-second section of the act organizing the Territory of Kansas:

> That the Constitution and all laws of the United States that are not locally inapplicable shall have the same force and effect in said Territory of Kansas as elsewhere within the United States, except the eighth section, &c.

"Now, I would suggest to my friend from Georgia that, as a matter of course, that clause carries with it the act of February, 1851, providing the mode and manner of taking evidence in contested election cases."

[Stephens:] "I was coming to that view of the case. As the gentleman has called my attention to it, I will say what I intended on that point here. I grant, as the gentleman from Maine says, that that law of 1851, for taking testimony in contested elections, does not, in express terms, apply to Delegates from Territories. It speaks of members of Congress; but I apprehend that Delegates come within the spirit of the law. But if not, just let us, by resolution or by bill, put them under the operation of that law, or let the committee, by order of the House, do it, and not bring hundreds of witnesses here from Kansas, at an enormous expense, to say nothing of inconvenience, delay, and trouble. Let us extend the provisions of the act of 1851 to the Territories. It seems to me that that would be the best way, if any such testimony is pertinent to this case.

"But this contestant, sir, evidently acted under that law in the beginning. This present movement can be nothing but an after-thought; for I have before me the notice which he served upon General Whitfield [in which he declared that he would contest Whitfield's right to a seat in the next Congress]. . . .

"That notice was given on the 16th of October. The election took place on the 1st. The next day (the 17th) General Whitfield [defended himself in a letter to Governor Reeder]. . . .

"General Whitfield is duly certified as having been elected in pursuance of the territorial law on the 1st day of October, 1855. It is alleged, however, in the notice served on him by the memorialist, that the law under which he was elected is invalid. The Legislature passed the law; that is not questioned; the Governor then in office [Wilson Shannon] signed it. Why, then, was it invalid and void? We come now to the real point in the case. If the House can determine the question, it can do so, it seems to me, to-day as well as at any other time."

[Dunn:] "Allow me to ask a question. Does the gentleman insist that this House has no right to inquire into the validity of the law?"

[Stephens:] "I made no such assertion."

[Dunn:] "Then I misunderstood the gentleman?"

[Stephens:] "Mr. Speaker, as I was saying when interrupted, this memorialist passed upon the election returns of the very men who passed this very law which he now says has no validity, and calls upon us to send for persons and papers to prove the invalidity of what he, in his official gubernatorial capacity, gave validity to; that is, the proper and legal organization of the Legislature. Gentlemen say that it is argued we cannot inquire into the validity of the law. I do not say that we cannot so inquire in a proper case; but this is not such a case in my opinion.

"Governor Reeder, in this case, it seems to me, is estopped from questioning the validity of the law, so far as it concerns the legality of the Legislature. He says he does so in behalf of the people of Kansas. There is nobody else here from Kansas asking us to take any notice of the matter. We have no memorialist but Governor Reeder himself. I want the House to mark this fact. I hold, then, that Governor Reeder, out of his own mouth, by his own official act, is estopped from denying the validity of the law, upon the ground that the Legislature was an illegal body of men, unauthorized to pass laws for the Territory.

"This question, Mr. Speaker, I repeat, can he decided as well to-day as after witnesses shall have been brought from Kansas. Why? Because the whole ground of objection of Governor Reeder and others, as I understand the case, against the validity of the law under which the present Delegate was elected, is, that the Legislature, which was duly recognized by Governor Reeder, and convened by him at Pawnee City, when convened at that place, adjourned their sessions to Shawnee Mission. There is no other point made; and when we are called on to send for persons and papers, we ought to know from the Committee of Elections why it is proposed that they shall be sent for. Governor Reeder can contest the election on no other ground than the one I have stated. It was a regularly elected Legislature, and recognized as such by him, so long as its sessions were held in Pawnee City. He holds that they had no power to adjourn to Shawnee Mission. That is the whole question; the Legislature is empowered to pass laws for the Territory at Pawnee City; but it loses legislative power when it sits at Shawnee Mission. The Governor sanctioned everything done at Pawnee City—at least he did not dispute their rightful power in anything done there; but he disputes the power of the Legislature when it adjourned to meet at another place. This is the question to be settled; and it may be as well settled now as at any other time. I say here, without wishing to prejudge this case, that I am as well prepared to-day to decide on that naked question, unless some gentleman will give me a new view of it—and I am open to conviction—as I shall ever be at any other time. I am clearly of the opinion, as at present advised, that the adjournment of the Legislature from one place to another did not deprive them of their capacity to pass laws; that they were as capable at Shawnee Mission as at Pawnee City to pass laws to regulate the election of Delegate to Congress. If gentlemen hold different views, I should be glad to hear them.

"When Governor Reeder vetoed the act for the removal of the Legislature, the bill was again passed, not only by the requisite majority to make it a valid law, but the question was submitted to the courts of the Territory. I have before me the opinion of the supreme court of the Territory in regard to the legality of the session of the Legislature held at Shawnee Mission. I will not consume the time of the House by reading it; but I call especial attention to the clearness, and force with which the case is handled.

[A member of the House:] "Who is it by?"

[Stephens:] "By S. D. Lecompte and Rush Elmore, and is concurred in by Mr. Isacks, who was, I think, district attorney. They argue the whole case. I have not marked the pertinent passages; I will send the opinion to the reporters, that it may be printed in full, when all can read the whole of it, as I hope they will. It is so decisive that, it seems to me 'a wayfaring man, though he be a fool, cannot err therein.' It instances the case of the Continental Congress, in 1777, when Philadelphia was threatened by the British, having adjourned its sessions to Lancaster. Nobody ever questioned its authority to do so. The British Parliament, in the time of the plague in London, left the ancient seat of legislation, and betook themselves to another place. Many instances are given from several States of the Union. Some in my own State might have been added if the traditions of her early history, as I have heard them related, be true. When Georgia was invaded by the British, or the Whigs were pressed by the Tories, the Legislature went from place to place on several occasions, and I believe some of them once got into the State of North Carolina—perhaps in my friend's [Thomas L. Clingman] district. [Laughter.] Some of their records very strangely found their way as far east as Annapolis. The legality of the proceedings of a Legislature, then, do not, I think, depend on the place where they hold their sessions, especially if it be within the limits of their jurisdiction. The validity of any law passed by Congress would not be questioned, I suppose, if Congress should be compelled by an invading enemy to go elsewhere. The city of Washington was once taken by the British. I do not think such an event will ever occur again. But if it should, and Congress should adjourn to some other place, I cannot suppose that their acts would be invalidated thereby. And I hold that the Legislature of Kansas had the power to sit just where they pleased within that Territory: they certainly have the power, in my opinion, to set at Shawnee Mission: so thought the Supreme Court of that Territory. . . .

"[In the paper by Lecompte and Elmore we find that the] . . . organic law of the Territory, sir, gave the Legislature all legislative power, under the Constitution, not inconsistent with that organic law. Well, one of the first functions of legislative power is, to determine where the body will meet. The organic law—the Kansas bill—said that Fort Leavenworth should be the temporary seat of government. The Governor himself had changed that, before the first session of the Legislature. Congress afterwards gave them the absolute power to fix the permanent seat of government. The power to fix the permanent place, of course, includes the less power of sitting, until that place should be selected, just where they please.

"I do not intend to detain this House longer upon the argument of this preliminary question; but Governor Reeder, in his message to the Legislature, vetoing their bill changing the place of sitting, stakes his case of the illegality of the subsequent acts of that body solely upon the fact that they adjourned to a place which did not meet with his approval. He, in the mean time, was removed. His successor in office, however, sanctioned the proceedings of the Legislature at Shawnee Mission; and there were passed all the laws, I believe, they now have for the protection of life, liberty, and property, in Kansas."

[Dunn, interrupting:] "I would like to ask the gentleman a question before he takes his seat. I believe that the right of a member or Delegate to a seat upon this floor is a right which belongs not to the Representative or Delegate, but a right which belongs to his constituents. Suppose, therefore, that any gentleman upon this floor should absolutely make an affidavit, or do any other act which in a court of justice might be regarded as an estoppel—short of an actual resignation, would that preclude his constituents from insisting upon his services in this Hall?"

[Stephens:] "Very well. Suppose I grant it—admit what you say—we have been here two months and upwards, and we have heard no mortal man, except Governor Reeder, questioning the right of General Whitfield. When and where have the constituents of General Whitfield spoken? Have you heard a mortal man of Kansas, except Reeder, complain of the legality and rightfulness of General Whitfield's election? If you have, when and where?"

[Dunn:] "The question which I present to the gentleman from Georgia is the question of the power of any man to estop himself of his duty to represent his constituents upon this floor."

[Stephens:] "The question was, whether anything Governor Reeder has done should jeopard the right of the constituents of General Whitfield or the people of the Territory of Kansas? I say no; but we are acting upon the memorial of A. H. Reeder, and I say A. H. Reeder is estopped. When General Whitfield's constituents speak, or the people of Kansas speak, and say that he is not their duly elected Representative or Delegate, I will give not only a respectful hearing to their memorial, but go into an investigation of it. If Governor Reeder has any constituents who will say that they ought not to be estopped by his act, I will give them a like hearing and investigation. I will take the cases as they come. We are acting now upon the memorial of ex-Governor Reeder, and it is enough for me to show that he is estopped.

"Now, as I stated before, I do not intend to detain the House. I think that, if the House were in possession of all the facts which have caused this motion, they could vote more understandingly. I therefore move that this resolution be recommitted to the Committee of Elections, with instructions to report the grounds upon which they make this application for extraordinary power, and the reasons which induce them to do it."[87]

The following excerpt is from Stephens' June 28, 1856, speech before the U.S. House of Representatives. During his discussion on the bill to admit Kansas as a state under the Topeka Constitution, he paused to give his opinion on "slavery at large," using both the U.S. Constitution and the Bible as a defense. We will note here that—from God himself to the Old Testament prophets, from Jesus to Paul—the Bible not only allows and encourages slavery, it actually demands it in several sections. Thus in defending slavery using the Bible, Stephens was only following the Christian interpretation of the Good Book as it was then understood by most Americans South and North. While modern America has condemned slavery, to this day the most learned Bible scholars and theologians are still unable to explain why, far from prohibiting or even disapproving of slavery, the Bible clearly and repeatedly condones, approves, and even requires it:

☛ ". . . Even, however, if slavery be sinful, as they [abolitionists] affirm, or their language implies, permit me here to ask, is not the sin the same whether the slave be held in Georgia, Carolina, or in Kansas? Is it any more sinful in one place than another? But are these gentlemen correct? Is African slavery, as it exists in the South, either a violation of the laws of nature, the laws of nations, or the laws of God? I maintain that it is not. It has been recognized by the laws of nations from time immemorial. [In our Constitution, the] . . . highest court in this country, the Supreme Court of the United States, has so decided the laws of nations to be. . . .

"Then as to the law of God—that law we read not only in his works about us, around us, and over us, but in that inspired Book wherein he has revealed his will to man. When we differ as to the voice of nature, or the language of God, as spoken in nature's works, we go to that great Book, the Book of books, which is the fountain of all truth. To that Book I now appeal. God, in the days of old, made a covenant with the human family—for the redemption of fallen man: that covenant is the corner-stone of the whole Christian system. Abram, afterwards called Abraham, was the man with whom that covenant was made. He was the great first head of an organized visible church here below. He believed God, and it was accounted to him for righteousness. He was indeed and in truth the father of the faithful. Abraham, sir, was a slaveholder. Nay, more, he was required to have the sign of that covenant administered to the slaves of his household."

[Mr. Campbell:] "Page, bring me a Bible."

[Mr. Stephens:] "I have one here which the gentleman can consult if he wishes. Here is the passage, Genesis 17:13. God said to Abraham:

> 13. He that is born in thy house and he that is bought with thy money must needs be circumcised; and my covenant shall be in your flesh for an everlasting covenant.

"Yes, sir, Abraham was not only a slaveholder, but a slave dealer it seems, for he bought men with his money, and yet it was with him the covenant was made by which the world was to be redeemed from the dominion of sin. And it was into his bosom in heaven that the poor man who died at the rich man's gate was borne by angels, according to the parable of the Saviour. In the 20th chapter of Exodus, the great moral law is found—that law that defines sin—the ten commandments, written by the finger of God himself upon tables of stone. In two of these commandments, the 4th and 10th, verses 10th and 17th, slavery is expressly recognized, and in none of them is there any thing against it—this is the moral law. In Leviticus we have the civil law on this subject, as given by God to Moses for the government of his chosen people in their municipal affairs. In . . . 25:44-46, I read as follows:

> 44. Both thy bondmen and thy bondmaids which thou shalt have, shall be of the heathen that are round about you; of them ye shall buy bondmen and bondmaids.
> 45. Moreover, of the children of the strangers that do sojourn among you, of them ye shall buy, and of their families that are with you which they begat in your land: and they shall be your possession.
> 46. And ye shall take them as an inheritance for your children after you, to inherit them for a possession; they shall be your bondmen forever; but over your brethren, the children of Israel, ye shall not rule one over another, with rigor.

"This was the law given to the Jews soon after they left Egypt, for their government when they should reach the land of promise. They could have had no slaves then. It authorized the introduction of slavery amongst them when they should become established in Canaan. And it is to be noted that their bondmen and bondmaids to be bought, and held for a possession and an inheritance for their children after them, were to be of the heathen round about them. Over their brethren they were not to rule with rigor. Our southern system is in strict conformity with this injunction. Men of our own blood and our own race, wherever born, or from whatever clime they come, are free and equal. We have no castes or classes amongst white men—no 'upper tendom' or 'lower tendom.' All are equals. Our slaves were taken from the heathen tribes—the barbarians of Africa. In our households they are brought within the pale of the covenant, under Christian teaching and influence; and more of them are partakers of the benefits of the gospel than ever were rendered so by missionary enterprise. The wisdom of man is foolishness—the ways of Providence are mysterious. Nor does the negro feel any sense of degradation in his condition—he is not degraded. He occupies and fills the same grade or rank in society and the State that he does in the scale of being; it is his natural place; and all things fit when nature's great first law of order is conformed to.

"Again: Job was certainly one of the best men of whom we read in the Bible. He was a large slaveholder. So, too, were Isaac and Jacob, and all the patriarchs. But, it is said, this was under the Jewish dispensation. Granted. Has any change been made since? Is any thing to be found in the New Testament against it? Nothing—not a word. Slavery existed when the gospel was preached by Christ and his Apostles, and where they preached: it was all around them. And though the Scribes and Pharisees were denounced by our

Saviour for their hypocrisy and robbing 'widows' houses,' yet not a word did He utter against slaveholding. On one occasion He was sought for by a centurion, who asked him to heal his slave, who was sick. Jesus said he would go; but the centurion objected, saying: 'Lord, I am not worthy that thou shouldst come under my roof; but speak the word only, and my servant shall be healed. For I am a man under authority, having soldiers under me; and I say to this man, go, and he goeth; and to another come, and he cometh; and to my slave, do this, and he doeth it.' Matthew 8:9. The word rendered here 'servant,' in our translation, means slave. It means just such a servant as all our slaves at the South are. I have the original Greek.

"The word in the original is *doulos*, and the meaning of this word, as given in [Edward] Robinson's Greek and English Lexicon, is this—I read from the book: 'In the family the *doulos* was one bound to serve, a slave, and was the property of his master—"a living possession," as Aristotle calls him.' And again: 'The *doulos*, therefore, was never a hired servant, the latter being called *misthios*,' etc. This is the meaning of the word, as given by Robinson, a learned doctor of divinity, as well as of laws. The centurion [a non-Christian Pagan] on that occasion said to Christ himself, 'I say to my slave do this, and he doeth it, and do Thou but speak the word, and he shall be healed.' What was the Saviour's reply? Did he tell him to go loose the bonds that fettered his fellow man? Did he tell him he was sinning against God for holding a slave? No such thing. But we are told by the inspired penman, that:

> When Jesus heard it he marvelled, and said to them that followed: Verily I say unto you, I have not found so great faith, no, not in Israel. And I say unto you that many shall come from the east and west and shall sit down with Abraham, and Isaac, and Jacob, in the kingdom of heaven. But the children of the kingdom shall be cast out into utter darkness; there shall be weeping and gnashing of teeth. And Jesus said unto the centurion, Go thy way, and as thou hast believed so be it done unto thee. And his servant [or slave] was healed in the selfsame hour.

"Was Christ a 'doughface' [i.e., a Yankee who sanctioned slavery in the South; who sympathized with the South]? Did He quail before the slave power? And if he did not rebuke the lordly centurion for speaking as he did of his authority over his slave, but healed the sick man, and said that he had not found so great faith in all Israel as he had in his master, who shall now presume, in His name, to rebuke others for exercising similar authority, or say that their faith may not be as strong as that of the centurion.

"In no place in the New Testament, sir, is slavery held up as sinful. Several of the Apostles alluded to it, but none of them—not one of them, mentions or condemns it as a relation sinful in itself, or violative of the laws of God, or even Christian duty. They enjoin the relative duties of both master and slave. Paul sent a runaway slave, Onesimus, back to Philemon, his master. He frequently alludes to slavery in his letters to the churches, but in no case speaks of it as sinful. To what he says in one of these epistles I ask special attention. It is 1st Timothy, chapter 6th, and beginning with the 1st verse:

> 1. Let as many servants (*douloi*, slaves in the original, which I have before me) as are under the yoke (that is, those who are the most abject of slaves) count their own masters worthy of all honor, that the name of God and his doctrine be not blasphemed.
> 2. And they that have believing masters, (according to modern doctrine, there can be no such thing as a slaveholding believer; so did not think Paul,) let them not despise (or neglect and not care for) them, because they are brethren; but rather do them service, because they are faithful and beloved, partakers of the benefit. These things teach and exhort.
> 3. If any man teach otherwise and consent not to wholesome words, even the words of our Lord Jesus Christ, and to the doctrine which is according to godliness:
> 4. He is proud, (or self-conceited,) knowing nothing but doting about questions and strifes of words, whereof cometh envy, strife, railings, evil surmisings.
> 5. Perverse disputings of men of corrupt minds, and destitute of the truth, supposing that gain is godliness: from such withdraw thyself.

"This language of St. Paul, the great Apostle of the Gentiles, is just as appropriate this day, in this House, as it was when he penned it eighteen hundred years ago. No man could frame a more direct reply to the doctrines of the gentleman from Ohio, [Joshua R. Giddings,] and the gentleman from Indiana, [Mr. Dunn,] than is here contained in the sacred book. What does all this strife, and envy, and railings, and 'civil war' in Kansas come from, but the Teachings of those in our day who teach otherwise than Paul taught, and 'do not consent to wholesome words, even the words of our Lord Jesus Christ?'

"Let no man, then, say that African slavery as it exists in the South, incorporated in, and sanctioned by the constitution of the United States, is in violation of either the laws of nations, the laws of nature, or the laws of God!

"And if it 'must needs be' that such an offence shall come from this source, as shall sever the ties that now unite these States together in fraternal bonds, and involve the land in civil war, then 'woe be unto them from whom the offence cometh!'"[88]

On January 6, 1857, Stephens spoke before the House of Representatives on the

Compromise of 1850 and the Kansas-Nebraska Act of 1854. In the following excerpt from that address he defines the powers of the Federal (Central) government, then goes on to express the true cause for which the South was about to take up arms against Lincoln and the North, constitutional liberty:

☞ "This, sir, is a government of limited powers. All the powers it can rightfully exercise or confer, are such as are expressly delegated in the constitution, and such as may be necessary to carry out those which are expressly named. . . . But I am asked: 'Is not the government of the United States sovereign?' and 'whether it is not the representative of the sovereignty of the people of the United States over the territories?' In reply, I state, that the government of the United States, in my judgment, is clothed with certain sovereign powers; but these powers are limited to specified objects. In the legitimate and proper exercise of these powers, to the extent of their grant, it may be considered as sovereign or supreme as any other government, just as sovereign as the Autocrat of Russia, in whom is concentrated all power; but these powers with which it is clothed, extend only to such subjects as are covered by the grant delegating them. Over all others, it has no power or authority to act at all. So far from being sovereign as to these, it is perfectly impotent. It cannot rightfully exercise any authority whatever upon any matter not committed to its charge by grant from the people of the States respectively; and it can wield the sovereign powers of the people thus delegated to it only over such subjects, and to accomplish such objects, as the people have authorized it to exercise authority upon. To this extent it is the representative, or rather the active and living embodiment of the sovereignty of the people. It is, in other words, the organ, or constitutes the channels through which their sovereignty acts on the subjects specified in the grant of its powers. But the appropriation of the public domain to one class of citizens, to the exclusion of another, is not to be found in the scope of these powers, or the objects for which they were conferred. . . . [Emphasis added, L.S.]

"But the practical point, looking to the probable prospect of any of these territories becoming slave States, dwindles into perfect insignificance in view of the principle involved. That principle is one of constitutional right and equality. Its surrender carries with it submission to unjust and unconstitutional legislation, the sole object of which would be to array this government, which claims our allegiance, in direct hostility, not only to our interests, but the very frame work of our political organizations. Who looked to the practical importance of the 'Wilmot proviso' to the South in 1850, when it was attempted to be fixed upon New Mexico and Utah, with half so much interest as they did to the principle upon which it was founded? It was the principle that was so unyieldingly resisted then. It was this principle, or the threatened action of Congress based upon it, which the whole South, with a voice almost unanimous, including the gentleman himself, then said they would not and ought not to submit to! Principles, sir, are not only outposts, but the bulwarks of all constitutional liberty; and, if these be yielded, or taken by superior force, the citadel will soon follow. A people who would maintain their rights must look to principles much more than to practical results. The independence of the United States was declared and established in the vindication of an abstract principle. Mr. [Daniel] Webster never uttered a great truth in simpler language—for which he was so much distinguished—than when he said, 'The American Revolution was fought on a preamble.' It was not the amount of the tax on tea, but the assertion (in the preamble of the bill taking off the tax) of the right in the British Parliament to tax the colonies, without representation, that our fathers resisted; and it was the principle of unjust and unconstitutional Congressional action against the institutions of all the southern States of this Union, that we, in 1850, resisted by our votes, and would have resisted by our arms if the wrong had been perpetrated. Those from the South who supported the New Mexico and Utah bills, did so because this principle of Congressional restriction was abandoned in them. It was not from any confidence, in a practical point of view, that these territories ever would be slave States. The great constitutional and essential right to be so if they chose was secured to them. That was the main point. This, at least, was the case with myself; for, when I looked out upon our vast territories of the west and northwest, I did not then, nor do I now, consider that there was or is much prospect of many of them, particularly the latter, becoming slave States. Besides the laws of climate, soil, and productions, there is another law not unobserved by me, which seemed to be quite as efficient in its prospective operations in giving a different character to their institutions, and that is the law of population. There were, at the last census, nearly twenty millions of whites in the United States, and only a fraction over three millions of blacks, or slaves. The stock from which the population of the latter class must spring, is too small to keep pace in diffusion, expansion, and settlement, with the former. The ratio is not much greater than one to seven, to say nothing of foreign immigration, and the known facts in relation to the tardiness with which slave population is pushed into new countries and frontier settlements. Hence the greater importance to the South of a rigid adherence to principles on this subject vital to them. If the slightest encroachments of power are permitted or submitted to in the territories, they may reach the States ultimately. And although I looked, and still look, upon the probabilities of Kansas being a slave State, as greater than I did New Mexico and Utah, yet I voted for the bill of 1854, with the view of maintaining the principle much more than I did to such practical results. As a southern man, considering the relation which the African bears to the white race in the southern States, as the very best condition for the greatest good of both; and as a national man, looking to the best interests of the country, the peace and harmony of the whole by a preservation of the balance of power, as far as can be, (for after all, the surest check to encroachments is the inability to make them,) I should prefer to see Kansas come into the Union as a slave State; but it was not with the view or purpose of effecting that result that I voted for the Kansas bill, any more than it was with the view or purpose of accomplishing similar results as to New Mexico and Utah that I supported the measures of 1850. It was to secure the right to come in as a slave State, if the people there so wished, and to maintain a principle, which I then thought, and still think, essential to the peace of the country and the ultimate security of the rights of the South."[89]

Stephens uttered the following words during a speech before the U.S. House of Representatives on February 12, 1859. It concerned the admission of the state of Oregon. Here Stephens took the opportunity to expose the hypocrisy of those Northerners, like Abraham Lincoln and his fellow members of the American Colonization Society, who only wanted to free black slaves in order to ship them, as "Honest Abe" put it, "back to their native land":

☛ ". . . those [Northerners and Westerners] who profess to be the exclusive friends of negroes, as they now do, so far as that constitution was concerned, voted to banish them forever from the State, just as Oregon has done. Whether this banishment be right or wrong, it is no worse in Oregon than it was in Kansas. But, on the score of humanity, *we of the South do not believe that those who, in Kansas or Oregon, banish this race from their limits, are better friends of the negro than we are*, who assign them that place among us to which by nature they are fitted, and in which they add so much more to their own happiness and comfort, besides to the common well-being of all. *We give them a reception. We give them shelter. We clothe them. We feed them. We provide for their every want, in health and in sickness, in infancy and old age. We teach them to work. We educate them in the arts of civilization, and the virtues of Christianity, much more effectually and successfully than you can ever do on the coasts of Africa. And, without any cost to the public, we render them useful to themselves and to the world.* The first lesson in civilization and Christianity to be taught to the barbarous tribes, wherever to be found, is the first great curse against the human family—that in the sweat of their face they shall eat their bread. *Under our system, our tuition, our guardianship and fostering care, these people, exciting so much misplaced philanthropy, have attained a higher degree of civilization than their race has attained anywhere else upon the face of the earth.* The Topeka [Kansas] people excluded them; they, the like neighbors we read of, went round them; we, the like good Samaritans, shun not their destitution or degradation—*we alleviate both*."[90] [Emphasis added, L.S.]

From the same February 12, 1859, speech, Stephens gave his thoughts on America's growing population, the admission of new states, and the ever increasing friction between South and North:

☛ "This progress, sir, is not to be arrested. It will go on. The end is not yet. There are persons now living who will see over a hundred million human beings within the present boundaries of the United States, to say nothing of future extension, and perhaps double the number of States we now have, should the Union last. For myself, I say to you, my southern colleagues on this floor, that I do not apprehend danger to our constitutional rights from the bare fact of increasing the number of States with institutions dissimilar to ours. The whole governmental fabric of the United States is based and founded upon the idea of dissimilarity in the institutions of the respective members. Principles, not numbers, are our protection. When these fail, we have, like all other people, who, knowing their rights, dare maintain them, nothing to rely upon but the justice of our cause, our own right arms and stout hearts. With these feelings and this basis of action, whenever any State comes and asks admission, as Oregon does, I am prepared to extend her the hand of welcome, without looking into her constitution further than to see that it is republican [Confederate] in form upon our well-known American models.

"When aggression comes, if come it ever shall, then the end draweth nigh. Then, if in my day, I shall be for resistance, open, bold, and defiant. I know of no allegiance superior to that due the hearthstones of the homestead. This I say to all. I lay no claim to any sentiment of nationality not founded upon the patriotism of a true heart, and I know of no such patriotism that does not centre at home. Like the enlarging circle upon the surface of smooth waters, however, this can and will, if unobstructed, extend to the utmost limits of a common country. Such is my nationality—such my sectionalism—such my patriotism. Our fathers of the South joined your fathers of the North in resistance to a common aggression from their fatherland [Britain]; and if they were justified in rising to right a wrong inflicted by a parent country, how much more ought we, should the necessity ever come, to stand justified before an enlightened world, in righting a wrong from even those we call brothers. That necessity, I trust, will never come.

"What is to be our future, I do not know. I have no taste for indulging in speculations about it. I would not, if I could, raise the vail that wisely conceals it from us. 'Sufficient unto the day is the evil thereof,' is a good precept in every thing pertaining to human action. The evil I would not anticipate; I would rather strive to prevent its coming; and one way, in my judgment, to prevent it, is, while here, in all things to do what is right and proper to be done under the constitution of the United States; nothing more, and nothing less. Our safety, as well as the prosperity of all parts of the country, so long as this government lasts, lies mainly in a strict conformity to the laws of its existence. Growth is one of these. The admission of new States is one of the objects expressly provided for. How are they to come in? With just such constitutions as the people in each may please to make for themselves, so it is republican in form. This is the ground the South has ever stood upon. Let us not abandon it now. It is founded upon a principle planted in the compact of Union itself; and more essential to us than all others besides; that is, the equality of the States, and the reserved right of the people of the respective States. By our system, each State, however great the number, has the absolute right to regulate all its internal affairs as she pleases, subject only to her obligations under the constitution of the United States. With this limitation, the people of Massachusetts have the perfect right to do as they please upon all matters relating to their internal policy; the people of Ohio have the right to do the same; the people of Georgia the same; of California the same; and so with all the rest.

"Such is the machinery of our theory of self-government by the people. This is the great novelty of our peculiar system, involving a principle unknown to the ancients, an idea never dreamed of by Aristotle or Plato. The union of several distinct, independent communities upon this basis, is a new principle in human governments. It is now a problem in experiment for the people of the nineteenth century upon this continent to solve. As I behold its workings in the past and at the present, while I am not sanguine, yet I am hopeful of its successful solution. The most joyous feeling of my heart is the earnest hope that it will, for the future, move on as peacefully, prosperously, and brilliantly, as it has in the past. If so, then we shall exhibit a moral and political spectacle to the world something like the prophetic vision of Ezekiel, when he saw a number of distinct beings or living creatures, each with a separate and distinct organism, having the functions of life within itself, all of one external likeness, and all, at the same time, mysteriously connected with one common animating spirit pervading the whole, so that when the common spirit moved they all moved; their appearance and their work being, as it were, a wheel in the middle of a wheel; and whithersoever the common spirit went, thither the others went, all going together; and when they went, he heard the noise of their motion like the noise of great waters, as the voice of the Almighty. Should our experiment succeed, such will be our exhibition—a machinery of government so intricate, so complicated, with so many separate and distinct parts, so many independent States, each perfect in the attributes and functions of sovereignty, within its own jurisdiction, all, nevertheless, united under the control of a common directing power for external objects and purposes, may natural enough seem novel, strange, and inexplicable to the philosophers and crowned heads of the world.

"It is for us, and those who shall come after us, to determine whether this grand experimental problem shall be worked out; not by quarrelling amongst ourselves; not by doing injustice to any; not by keeping out any particular class of States; but by each State remaining a separate and distinct political organism within itself—all bound together for general objects, under a common Federal head; as it were, a wheel within a wheel. Then the number may be multiplied without limit; and then, indeed, may the nations of the earth look on in wonder at our career; and when they hear the noise of the wheels of our progress in achievement, in development, in expansion, in glory, and renown, it may well appear to them not unlike the noise of great waters; the very voice of the Almighty—*Vox populi! Vox Dei!*" [Great applause in the galleries, and on the floor.][91]

The following excerpt is from Stephens' "farewell speech," delivered at Augusta, Georgia, July 2, 1859. The occasion was his retirement from Congress. Little did he realize at the time that soon he would not only be drawn back into politics, but he would remain in that occupation until the last day of his life:

☛ ". . . I must now take my farewell leave. My race has been run—my career is ended; whether it has been for good or for evil, the record is made up. By it, I must be judged in the future, as all others whose acts form a part, however small, in the public history. I am willing that my conduct, as it there stands, shall be squared by the Grecian's rule, that 'the course of every public man, upon all great questions, should not only be the best that was thought of by any at the time, but the very best that all subsequent disclosures shall show, could have been thought of and adopted under all the circumstances.' The rule is a rigid one; but I ask no exemption from it now, nor hereafter. Upon a review of the past up to this time, I see no cause to regret any of my acts upon any of those questions to which I have alluded; nor is there a single one of them that I would change.

"I retire from no feelings of discontent—far from it; no one ever had less cause to complain. If you are satisfied with the past I am. If any explanations are necessary to satisfy the inquiries of those who seem to think it so strange that one should voluntarily retire from a place of position and honor, I state explicitly that it is because those questions having been settled with which I had become connected, there are other pursuits more agreeable to my nature, and I do not know that I could render the public any more essential service at this time than by showing, to the extent of my example, at least, that [political] office is not the chief end of man. I do not say that I will, under no circumstances, ever hold office again, or serve the country in any emergency that may arise. That would be tantamount to a declaration of incivism, inexcusable under all circumstances. An occasion may arise when I should feel it a duty even to shoulder a musket—though I could not render much service in that way. But I do say, that there is no office under Heaven that I desire, or wish ever to hold—there is none that I should prefer to that of representative in Congress—especially from the eighth district of Georgia. In quitting that, therefore, I quit for good and in earnest—hoping and believing that no such crisis ever will come when I should be required to take active part again in public affairs. As a private citizen, I shall continue to feel the same interest in passing events, and take such part in them as all other good citizens should—nothing more. I cannot permit this occasion to go by without adding, that if, in the heat of any of those high party excitements, through which it has been my lot to pass, I have ever, at any time, said or done aught to give offence, or to wound the feelings of any one wantonly, or without cause, I do deeply regret it. It was never my intention to offend, or to give cause of offence to any, unless first offended against; and whatever instances of this kind may have occurred, I deeply regret the necessity that occasioned them; and trust that the whole, alike, may be buried in oblivion forever.

"With you, my fellow-citizens, here present, and those of my constituents absent, I leave my best wishes for long life and happiness. With our common country, I leave like good wishes, and the earnest hope for undisturbed peace and prosperity, and that our institutions, unimpaired, national and State, may long continue to bless millions, yet unborn, as they have blessed us."[92]

Now once again a private citizen, on September 1, 1860, with the possible election of anti-South, big government Liberal Abraham Lincoln looming, Stephens gave this speech at City Hall Park, Augusta, Georgia. Here he offers his support for the election of fellow Democrats (the Conservatives of the day) Stephen A. Douglas for U.S. president and Herschel V. Johnson for U.S. vice president. Stephens also predicts the coming secession of the Southern states and the War, ardently coming out against both:

☛ "Fellow-Citizens:—I appear before you in obedience to a call made on me by those whose call could not be refused. The sacrifice of personal feelings or wishes, on such occasions, is not to be taken into the account. If it were, I assure you I should not be here. I had hoped never again to be drawn into the active struggles, the strifes, and excitements of politics. The address I made on the 2nd of July, of last year, near this spot, on taking leave of you, and this District, as Representative in Congress, I intended to be the last speech of the kind I should ever make. I trusted that in no event, or under any circumstances, should I ever be called on again to mingle in public affairs. All the questions with which I had been connected in the public councils having been settled upon terms satisfactory to us—upon terms thought to be just and honorable to all sections of the Union—it was but natural to look upon that settlement as permanent, and to indulge the hope of a happy and prosperous future for the country. But how illusory are all our hopes! How changed the prospect before us now from what it was twelve months ago! Then everything was encouraging to the heart of the patriot—would that I could say the same now. Those agitating questions, then thought to be settled, have been opened up afresh, and all that was done in their settlement is attempted to be undone. You ask me what I think of the present state of the country? I told you, in the speech alluded to, that the peace and safety of the country, in my judgment, depended upon an adherence to the principles of the settlement of those questions then made. I tell you the same now. I tell you candidly and frankly that the signs of the times, as I read them, portend evils of the gravest magnitude. There is an attempt made to depart from the principles of that settlement.

"At this time, and for some months past, the tendencies have been decidedly toward National disruption, and general anarchy. This conviction is beginning to force itself upon the minds of all. Can these tendencies be checked? Can the threatened disasters be avoided or prevented? If so, how, and in what way? What course should the patriot, looking only to the public good, public peace, welfare, and safety, take in the complicated contest before us? These are questions which now crowd upon our consideration. On them I propose to address you to-night. They present a wide field for thought and reflection—abounding in subjects of deepest interest and gravest import. I can only touch upon a few of them. My physical strength will not allow me to attempt more, if, indeed, it will sustain me in the limited view I have I marked out for myself. I assume, in the outset, that the Government, as it exists, is worth preserving; nay, more, with all its errors and defects, with all its corruptions in administration, and short-comings of its officers, it is the best Government on earth, and ought to be sustained, if it can be, on the principles upon which it was founded.

"First, then, as to the duty of Democrats [Conservatives] in the approaching Presidential election; for to that Party I specially address myself. The choice of Chief Magistrate is the now pressing and absorbing issue. Greater and more momentous issues may be behind; but I wish not to lift the curtain of the future, it is with the present we now deal. For whom should Democrats vote? There are two tickets in the field claiming to be Democratic; which one is entitled to and should receive the votes of the Democrats? To this I answer, that, in my judgment, the National ticket, bearing the names of Douglas and Johnson, is the one entitled to Democratic support.

"The nominees on this ticket are the representatives of the Party, put forth according to the usages of the Party, and are the representatives of the long-established [conservative] principles of the Party. Nay, more, they are the representatives of the only principles upon which, in my judgment, the Union of the States, and the rights of all sections, can be maintained. For this reason I would urge this ticket, not only upon all Democrats, but upon all well-wishers of their country, whether called Democrats, Whigs, or Americans. Allow me briefly to notice some of the prominent objections urged against this ticket by the partisans and friends of the other ticket claiming to be the true Democratic Party.

"These relate to the manner of the nomination, the principles of the Platform, and especially to certain opinions of Mr. Douglas, whose name heads the ticket.

"First, as to the manner of the nomination. It is said he failed to get two-thirds of the votes in the Convention—that by Democratic usage from 1832 down, no candidate could be nominated without a two-third vote.

"I would not notice this point, if so much stress had not been put upon it by those who advocate the other ticket. Not only in the press, but in the speeches of leading men, and in the address to the public, put forth by the Seceders Convention's Executive Committee, this point is made prominent, and urged as one of the main reasons why Democrats should feel under no Party obligation to support the ticket of the regularly constituted Democratic Convention. In my judgment, Mr. Douglas did receive two-thirds of the votes of the Convention, according to the usages of the Party, and according to the proper construction of what is known as the two-third rule.

"It is immaterial to me whether he received the nomination according to the interpretation or construction of that rule at Charleston or not. I mean the construction that the nominees should receive two-thirds of all the Electoral votes. That construction was wrong. It was an interpolation. It was inconsistent with the clear meaning—the letter, as well as the spirit—of the rule. The letter of the rule in most, if not all the Conventions from 1832, running through 1836, 1840, 1844, 1848, 1852, and 1856, was that the nominees should receive two-thirds of all the votes cast or given in the Convention. It is immaterial whether, in point of fact, in all other Conventions, the nominees did actually receive two-thirds of the entire Electoral vote or not—there never was before such a secession as was at Charleston and Baltimore: the question is what is the right construction of the rule requiring two-thirds of the votes of the Convention to make a nomination, and when will its requisition be complied with? This principle of a two-third vote is well understood in the Parliamentary law of the country. It is fixed in the Constitution of the United States, and in the Constitution of our own State, perhaps of most of the States of the Union. It is a principle often carried into practical operation in Congress, and in our State Legislatures. For instance, in the Constitution of the United States, Article First, Section Seven, and clause two, we have this provision:

> Every Bill which shall have passed the House of Representatives and the Senate, shall, before it becomes a law, be presented to the President of the United States; If he approve, he shall sign it; but if not, he shall return it, with his objections to that House in which it shall have originated, who shall enter the objections at large on their journal, and proceed to reconsider it. If after such reconsideration, two-thirds of that House shall agree to pass the bill, it shall be sent, together with the objections, to the other House, by which it shall likewise be reconsidered, and if approved by two-thirds of that House, it shall become a law.

"Now, what has been the universal construction given to the words 'two-thirds of that House' in practical legislation? Has it been that it required two-thirds of all the members constituting the House and Senate to pass a bill over the veto of the President? Never! The construction given, from the beginning down to the present time, without an exception, was, and is, that two-thirds of those voting, in each House, may pass a bill over the Executive veto, though there be barely a quorum present and voting. Such has been the uniform construction, not of this, but another clause, which authorized the expulsion of a member of either House, by a two-third vote—two-thirds of those voting, if there be a quorum, is all that is necessary for a compliance with that clause of the Constitution. So in our own State Constitution it is provided:

> That the Governor shall have the revision of all bills passed by both Houses, before they become laws, but two-thirds of both Houses may pass a law notwithstanding his dissent.

Under this clause of our State Constitution, the construction has been uniformly given. Two-thirds of those voting in each House, if a quorum be present, is all that is required. Again, in another article of our Constitution, we have a provision for its amendment, in these words:

> No part of this Constitution shall be altered, unless a bill for that purpose, specifying the alteration intended to be made, shall have been read three times in the House of Representatives and three times in the Senate, on three several days in each House, and agreed to by two-thirds of each House, respectively; and when any such bill shall be passed, in manner aforesaid, the same shall be published at least six months previous to the next ensuing election for members of the General Assembly, and if such alterations, or any

of them so proposed, should be agreed to, in the first session thereafter, by two-thirds of each branch of the General Assembly, after the same shall have been read three times, on three separate days, in each respective House, then, and not otherwise, the same shall become a part of this Constitution.

"Under this clause, two-thirds of each branch of the General Assembly has always been held to mean two-thirds of those voting on any proposed amendment—provided a quorum were present. Some of the most important amendments that have been made to the Constitution, since its first adoption, were made by a much smaller number than two-thirds of the entire House, in either branch. The one establishing the Supreme Court was made by a vote not much over a majority in each House. If a Constitution can be thus amended—if this construction holds and obtains in all such cases, both Federal and State, why should it not be held in a similar rule, founded on similar principles in a Party Convention, especially as that Convention had adopted the rules of the House of Representatives of the United States, where always a two-third vote is held to be two-thirds of those voting on any question?

"It is immaterial with me, then, whether Mr. Douglas got two hundred and twelve, or one hundred and ninety-six, or one hundred and eighty-one and a half, or one hundred and fifty-four, as has been variously contended; in either case he got two-thirds of those voting in the Convention, as it then stood—as it was then constituted. If there were but one hundred and ninety-six members present when he got one hundred and eighty-one and a half, he got two-thirds of the body, according to all our Parliamentary rules of construction. And if the Alabama and Louisiana delegates, who voted for him, be counted out, and after reducing his vote to one hundred and fifty-four, as is contended by some, the Convention having but one hundred and ninety-six in it, still he had two-thirds, according to the same rule or principle of construction which would authorize a bill to be passed over an Executive veto, or cause any change to be made in the fundamental law of our own State. I therefore consider him the regularly nominated candidate of the Democratic Party, and as such entitled to the support of his Party.

"No other rule of construction can be practically worked. How would it be with [John C.] Breckinridge and [Joseph] Lane, who are claimed to be the representatives of the National Democratic Party? In the Convention that nominated them, the same two-thirds rule, if I am not mistaken, was adopted—the old rule of the Party, I mean, and not the construction put upon it at Charleston, for with that construction they never could have made a nomination. Their Convention consisted of but one hundred and five Electoral votes—very little over one-third, all told, of the Electoral vote of the Union—so that if the same construction had been put upon it in that

Convention, which is insisted should be in the other, they never could have nominated anybody—if they had balloted until doomsday. Then let no man abandon his Party on the ground that the candidate was not regularly nominated. So much for this point. I pass to another objection.

"This, in the order, relates to the Platform. The Platform, it is said, is not sound—it is not National—it does not sustain the rights of the South. And what is the Platform adopted? I need not read it—it is known to you all. It is the well-known Platform of the Party based upon the doctrine of Non-Intervention by Congress with Slavery in the States or Territories, as set forth at Cincinnati in 1856, with an additional resolution, affirming the decision of the Supreme Court, in the Dred Scott case. Was not this all that our State Convention had asked? Was not this Platform, even without the additional resolution, sound enough in 1856? Was it not broad enough, and strong enough, for the Democracy of the whole Union then? And if so then, why not now? Do principles change so soon? Has anything occurred since, requiring any new tests? If so, when, and where, and what? Did not [our] Northern [Liberal] friends fail to adhere to it? Did they not rather renew their pledge to it, with the additional demand, as to the Dred Scott decision, made by our State Convention last December?

"If, then, this Platform of principles was sufficient to guard and protect our rights, and interest, and honor, in 1856, why is it not in 1860, especially with the additional guarantee given? This question I propound to all candid and reflecting minds. It is one that the country expects an answer to, by those who left the Convention because of the principles adopted, and whose secession has produced the strifes and divisions that now pervade the land. The only answer to it I have yet seen has been given by a Committee of the Seceding Delegation from this State. It is in their address, assigning the reasons for their course. It will be recollected that though they quit the Convention at Charleston, yet by great efforts made, were by urgent solicitation re-appointed to Baltimore, via Richmond. But they did not enter the Convention at Baltimore, after they got there, and for not doing so gave these reasons:

> 'That we are blameless in this matter, seems too plain to admit of a doubt. We could not enter a Convention, as a favor, at the sacrifice of principle, and of the honor and Sovereignty of our State. Nor have our demands been exorbitant or exacting. We have simply asked for protection for our property from the Government which demands our allegiance. These seem to us to be co-relative duties—allegiance to Government in return for protection to life, liberty, and property. It appears to us unnecessary to argue the question, for the absolute right of protection to property by the Government, in all its branches, is undenied by any man of any Party. But the application of this to

our slaves, in the Territories, is denied, and refused upon the untenable and fanatical ground that property is not recognized in slaves.'

"This is signed by three gentlemen who stand high in the estimation of the public. The statement seems to imply, if it means anything, that the Convention to which they had been sent had refused to recognize, a universally admitted principle of right, 'upon the untenable and fanatical ground that property is not recognized in slaves.' I have nothing to say against the character of these gentlemen. One of them is the Speaker of the House of Representatives of your State Legislature—another a gentleman of position in Savannah, and another an editor with high personal standing in Albany. But I do say that I think it would be a difficult task for them to sustain this statement by proof. What action of the Convention justifies it? What part of the Platform adopted declares that 'property is denied in slaves?' Nay, more, what member of the Convention, who refused their demand, holds any such 'untenable and fanatical' opinions? Not one, I venture to affirm. Then why was this statement made? They must answer who gave it as the best reason they had why they should be held blameless for the manner in which they performed the great public trust committed to their charge. Seeing no evidence of any such fanatical sentiment in the action of the Convention, or on the part of any member of it; having been satisfied with the Platform in 1856, and seeing no good reason to change my opinion in relation to it, I am therefore satisfied with it still. It was, in my judgment, good then, and good now, and will be good for all time to come. In its own language, it contains the only wise and safe solution of those sectional questions which have so often fearfully threatened the peace of the Union, and which may yet be its destruction, if the principles therein set forth be departed from. So much, therefore, for the objection to the Platform.

"I come now to the man. Here, I doubt not, lies the chief one of all the objections. We should have had no secession, no complaint about the want of a two-third vote, no objection to the Platform, had any other man been the decided choice of the Convention, but Mr. Douglas. The secession was not from principle; not from the manner of voting; but from the man whose strength, in the Convention, was far ahead of any of his competitors for the nomination.

"Let us, then, examine the objections to him. That he is a man of great ability, all admit. His integrity and purity of character none assail. That he was the favorite of the Convention, no one can deny. Whether he really had a majority, or not, as a first choice, no one will pretend but what he had at least three times as many, as a first choice, as any other man before the Convention. Then, what are the objections to him, which are sought to justify the rupture of the Party because of his nomination?

"The sum and substance of their objections, as I understand them, amount to this, and this only, that he refuses to declare it to be the duty of Congress to do what his assailants say they will not do themselves. They say it is the duty of Congress to protect Slavery in the Territories, and yet say that they will never discharge this duty by voting for any such law. He refuses to make any such declaration of duty never to be performed. This is about the whole difference between him and his assailants, for all practical purposes, so far as the question of protection is concerned, about which we hear so much. He says, he does not believe it to be his duty to do a certain thing, and therefore will not do it. They say they believe it to be their duty to do the same thing, but without a therefore or a wherefore say they will not do it.

"This seems to me, I repeat, to be the sum and substance of the objections to Mr. Douglas's peculiar views upon the Territorial policy of the country; for it is a matter of very little importance, none, practically, whatever, whether the people of a Territory have a right to protect or exclude slave property, or whether it is the duty of Congress to pass laws to protect it in the Territories, if their Legislatures refuse to protect or adopt unfriendly legislation, if this duty on the part of Congress is never to be performed—and that is my understanding of the position of the Protectionists.

"But it is said that Mr. Douglas entertains views and doctrines inconsistent with the equal rights of the South—that, according to his doctrine, slave property in the Territories does not stand upon the same fooling with other property. This is the substance of the objection, as I have met with it; and, if it be well founded, it is a good one. I should never advocate the election of any man to the Presidency, who denied the equality of States, and the equality of rights of the citizens of all the States, both as to person and property in the public Territories.

"My position on this subject is so well and fully set forth, in what is known as the Minority Report, at the last June Convention of the Democratic Party at Milledgeville, I will read two of those resolutions:

> Resolved, That we reaffirm the Cincinnati Platform, with the following additional propositions:
>
> 1st. That the citizens of the United States have an equal right to settle with their property, of any kind, in the organized Territories of the United States, and that under the decision of the Supreme Court of the United States, in the case of Dred Scott, which we recognize as the correct exposition of the Constitution in this particular, slave property stands upon the same footing as all other descriptions of property, and that neither the General Government, nor any Territorial Government can destroy or impair the right

to slave property in the common Territories, any more than the right to any other description of property; that property of all kinds, slaves as well as any other species of property, in the Territories, stands upon the same equal and broad Constitutional basis, and subject to like principles of recognition and protection in the Legislative, Judicial, and Executive Departments of the Government.

2nd. That we will support the man who may be nominated by the Baltimore Convention for the Presidency who holds the principles set forth in the foregoing proposition, and who will give them his indorsement; and that we will not hold ourselves bound to support any man who may be the nominee who entertains principles inconsistent with those set forth in the above propositions, or who denies that slave property in the Territories does stand on an equal footing and on the same Constitutional basis of other descriptions of property.

"These resolutions were offered in that Convention by Hon. Herschel V. Johnson, our candidate for the Vice Presidency. They, in my judgment, set forth true, correct, and sound doctrines, and upon them I stand to-night.

"To my amazement, I see the Executive Committee of the Seceding Convention at Baltimore have published these resolutions, with a view to show that Gov. Johnson, standing on them, could not support Mr. Douglas. They virtually admit that the principles set forth in them are right, and say, that according to the second resolution offered by Mr. Johnson, before the Georgia Convention, we stand pledged not to support, or vote for Mr. Douglas.

"Let us see whether they or I am mistaken. Let us see what Mr. Douglas's views upon this subject are. Let him speak for himself. He has spoken often, repeatedly. He is upon the record; and I shall now read his position from the record. Here is what he said in the Senate, on the 23rd February, 1859, in a discussion with Mr. [Albert G.] Brown, of Mississippi, on this very subject. I read from the Congressional Globe. Hear what Mr. Douglas himself says, as to his position:

> Mr, Douglas: 'We [that is, he and Senator Brown, who supports Congressional protection] agree that, under the decision of the Supreme Court of the United States, slaves are property, standing on an equal footing with all other property; and that, consequently, the owner of a slave has the same right to emigrate to a Territory and carry his slave property with him, as the owner of any other species of property has to move there and carry his property with him. . . . The right of transit to and from the Territories is the same for one species of property as it is for all others. Thus far, the Senator from Mississippi and myself agree that slave property in the Territories stands on an equal footing with every other species of property. Now, the question arises, to what extent is property, slaves included, subject to the local law of

the Territory? Whatever power the Territorial Legislature has over other species of property, extends, in my Judgment, to the same extent, and in like manner, to the slave property. The Territorial Legislature has the same power to legislate in respect to slaves that it has in regard to any other property to the same extent, and no further. If the Senator wishes to know what power it has over slaves in the Territories, I answer, let him tell me what power it has to legislate over every other species of property, either by encouragement or by taxation, or in any other mode, and he has my answer in regard to slave property.

'But the Senator says that there is something peculiar in slave property, requiring further protection than other species of property. If so, it is the misfortune of those who own that species of property. He tells us that if the Territorial Legislature fails to pass a slave-code for the Territories, fails to pass police regulations to protect slave property, the absence of such legislation practically excludes slave property, as effectually as a Constitutional prohibition would exclude it. I agree to that proposition. He says, furthermore, that it is competent for the Territorial Legislature, by the exercise of the taxing power, and other functions within the limits of the Constitution, to adopt unfriendly legislation, which practically drives slavery out of the Territories. I agree to that proposition. That is just what I said, and all I said, and just what I meant, by my Freeport speech, in Illinois, upon which there has been so much comment throughout the country.

'But, the Senator says that while non-action by the Territorial Legislature excludes Slavery; and while the Territorial Legislature may, within the limits of the Federal Constitution, adopt such a system of unfriendly legislation, as, in effect to exclude Slavery from its limits, yet it is wrong for the Legislature to pursue that policy; and, because the Territorial Legislature ought not to adopt that line of policy, he will not be content with such legislation, but will appeal to Congress and demand a Congressional code of laws protecting Slavery in the Territories, in opposition to the wishes of the people. Well, sir, his conclusion is a logical one, unless my position is right. All men must agree that non-action by the Territorial Legislature is practical exclusion. If the people of a Territory want Slavery, they will protect it by a Slave-code. If they do not want Slavery—if they believe it is not necessary—if they are of opinion that their interests do not require it, or will be prejudiced by it, they will not furnish the necessary remedies and police regulations, usually called a Slave-code for its protection.'

"From this, it clearly appears that Mr. Douglas does recognize property in slaves, and that, in his opinion, this species of property in the Territories stands upon the same broad Constitutional basis of right and equality as all other kinds of property—and, because it is property, he contends that it is, like all other kinds of property, a rightful subject of legislation by the law-making power in the Territory—no more and no less.

"But hear him further, in the same speech [in which he was asked: 'If a law, merely providing protection, is to be called a slave-code, then we ask, if larceny, in general terms, were punished by the Territorial law, and the Legislature should except the larceny of slaves, would he say he would submit to that, at the option of the Legislature?']:

> Mr Douglas: 'It is immaterial to me, whether you call this legislation a slave-code or by any other name. I will call it by any name the Senate chooses. I wish it to be understood, however, and to use such language as conveys the idea. I take the language of the Senator from Mississippi, if that is satisfactory. All I have to say, on the point presented by the Senator from Missouri, is this: While our Constitution does not provide remedies for stealing negroes, it does not provide remedies for stealing dry goods, or horses, or any other species of property. You cannot protect any property in the Territories, without laws furnishing remedies for its violation, and penalties for its abuse. Nobody pretends that you are going to pass laws of Congress making a criminal code for the Territories with reference to other species of property.
>
> 'The Congress of the United States never yet passed an Act creating a criminal code for any organized Territory. It simply organizes the Territory, and leaves its Legislature to make its own criminal code. Congress never passed a law to protect any species of property in the organized Territories; it leaves its protection in the Territorial Legislatures. The question is whether we shall make an exception as to Slavery. The Supreme Court makes no such distinction. It recognizes slaves as property. When they are taken to a Territory, they are on an equal footing with other property, and dependent upon the same system of legislation for protection as other property. While all other property is dependent on the Territorial legislation for protection, I hold that slave-property must look to the same authority for its protection.'

"And further on, in the same speech, he uses this language—in reply to another inquiry from Senator Brown:

> Mr. Douglas: 'I am ready to answer any inquiry of the Senator from Mississippi, whether, if I believe the Maine Liquor Law to be unconstitutional and wrong, and if a Territorial Legislature should pass it, I would vote here to annul? I tell him no.
>
> 'If the people of Kansas want a Maine Liquor Law, let them have it. If they do not want it, and any citizen thinks that law violates the Constitution, let him make a case, and appeal to the Supreme Court. If the Court sustains his objection, the law is void. If it overrules the objection, the decision must stand until the people, who alone are to be affected by it, may choose to repeal it. So I say with reference to Slavery. Let the Territorial Legislature pass just such laws in regard to Slavery as they think they have a right to enact

under the Constitution of the United States. If I do not like those laws, I will not vote to repeal them: but anybody aggrieved may appeal to the Supreme Court, and if they are constitutional, they must stand; and if they are unconstitutional, they are void. That was the doctrine of Non-Intervention, as it was understood at the time the Kansas-Nebraska bill was passed. That is the way it was explained and argued in the Senate and in the House of Representatives, and before the country. It was distinctly understood that Congress was never to intervene for or against Slavery, or for or against any other Institution in the Territories, but leave the Courts to decide all Constitutional questions as they might arise, and the President to carry the decrees of the Court into effect; and, in case of resistance to his authority in executing the judicial process, let him use, if necessary, the whole military force of the country, as provided by existing laws.'

"In these extracts is a full and clear exposition of those views of Mr. Douglas, which have been so fiercely denounced. I have read them to you at large, that you may judge for yourselves whether they put that kind of property upon any other basis in the Territories than all other kinds of property; whether all, in his view, does not stand on the same equal Constitutional footing. In these views you also have a clear exposition of Non-intervention or Non-Action, as Mr. [John C.] Calhoun called it, on the part of Congress. The whole subject of Slavery in the Territories was to be left to the people, subject to no limitation or restriction but the Constitution of the United States. If the Territorial Legislature passed any law infringing upon the rights of the slave-holder, or the rights of any person holding other kinds of property, either by taxation or any other kind of law, the subject was to be left to the Courts, with an appeal to the Supreme Court, but not to Congress. Property of all kinds was put upon the same footing. And so far from Mr. Douglas warring against the decision of the Supreme Court, as is alleged in the last extract read, it appears that he stands pledged to the execution of the judicial process, whatever it may be, in any case, with the whole military force of the country.

"The question I am now presenting is not what his opinions are as to the extent of the power of the Territorial Legislatures over slaves or other property, but that he puts all upon the same footing, and that they have no more power over rights to slaves than over other kinds of rights of person and property. Their powers over all rightful subjects of legislation, under the Constitution, are the same, and to be left to the Courts and not to Congress. If he ever uttered a sentiment different from those now presented on this subject, in the many speeches he has made upon it in the Senate, or on the stump, I have never met with it. The other day at Saratoga, in New York, he used this language:—

'I believe in the equality of the States, and in the equal rights of the citizens of all the States in the Territories of the United States. Whatever rights the citizens of any State may enjoy in the Territories pertain alike to the citizens of all the States, and on whatever terms the citizen of any State may move into the Territories with his property, the citizen of every other State may go and carry his property, and enjoy the same under the protection of the law.'

"If the Territorial Legislatures pass unconstitutional laws in relation to slave property, or any other kind of property, all alike are to be left to the Courts and not to Congress. In the Judicial, Executive, and Legislative Departments of a Territorial Government, slaves stand upon the same principles of recognition as other property under the Constitution of the United States, and entitled to protection on the same principles as other property.

"All rights of persons and property of every kind stand upon the same footing. When we advance a step further, and inquire how far a Territorial Legislature may constitutionally impair the right or usefulness of any kind of property, by any system of laws they may enact, a new question arises. On this I differ with Mr. Douglas. It is not, however, a point involving, in my judgment, either our equality in the Union, our honor as a people, or any principle essential to our security or future safety. It is a matter affecting alone the private rights of those who go into the Territories. This difference of opinion between him and those who take the same view of it as I do, it is agreed on both sides, are to be determined by the highest judicial tribunal in the land.

"By some it is contended that this point has already been decided by the Supreme Court in the Dred Scott case. If so, then there is an end of the question. For he has again and again indorsed every principle decided in that case; and all that is necessary is for the Executive to see that the decision is carried into effect by the whole military force of the country, if need be.

"But fellow-citizens, there is nothing that men, and even lawyers, and learned lawyers, differ more widely about than upon the principles embraced in a judicial question. So it is in this case. I am not going into an argument upon its merits; suffice it to say that, in my judgment, principles were decided in that case that would control those involved in a case arising under such a Territorial law. But until such a case does arise, it cannot be definitely and judicially settled. He and others who indorse every word of the Dred Scott decision believe, and I have no doubt, honestly believe, that the principle decided in that case would not control a case arising under a law that might be passed by a Territorial Legislature.

"I have been asked informally two questions, which I will here answer.

"The first is: How, differing from Mr. Douglas on this point, as I do, I can give him my support?

"I answer, because I look upon the matter as involving no principle of any vital importance.

"Practically, it amounts to nothing. With Mr. Douglas's view, Slavery will go wherever the people want it, and no law of Congress or a Territorial Legislature will ever carry it where they do not want it. Under the operation of his principles, whether right or wrong, our right of expansion to the utmost limit of capacity and population is complete; on the question, therefore, of the right or power of the people of an organized Territory through their Territorial Legislature, either directly or indirectly, to exclude Slavery while in a Territorial condition, and before they come to form a State Constitution, I stand where [Edmund] Burke, one of the greatest statesmen that England or any other country ever produced, stood upon the same question of the right or power of the British Parliament to tax the Colonies. That was a question upon which great and learned men differed, and so is this; and on this, I say to you to-night, what he said on the other in the House of Commons:

> 'Sir, I think you must perceive that I am resolved this day to have nothing to do with the question of the right of taxation. Some gentlemen startle, but it is true. I put it totally out of the question. It is less than nothing in my consideration. I do not wonder, nor will you, sir, in that gentleman of profound learning are fond of displaying it on this profound subject. But my consideration is narrow, confined, and wholly limited to the policy of the question. I do not examine whether the giving away a man's money be a power accepted and reserved out of the general trust of Government, and how far all mankind, in all forms of polity, are entitled to an exercise of that right by the charter of nature; or whether, on the contrary, a right of taxation is necessarily involved in the great principle of legislation, and inseparable from the ordinary supreme power. These are deep questions, where great names militate against each other, where reason is perplexed, and an appeal to authorities only quicken confusion. For high and revered authorities lift up their heads on both sides, and there is no sure footing in the middle. This point is the great "Serbonian bog betwixt Damatia [Dalmatia?] and Mount Cassius old, where armies whole have sunk."'

"Whether the people of a Territory have this right or not, under the Constitution, and whatever may be the decision of the Supreme Court on it, I am perfectly willing for them to exercise it. If they have not got it '*ex debito justitia*,' I would, if I could, give it to them '*ex gratia*.' If they have not got it as matter of right, being one of the essential principles of Self-government under our system, as many high authorities believe they have, I would, if I could, grant it to them as matter of favor. This is no new position with me; it is but a repetition of what I said in the House of Representatives on this subject on the

17th of January, 1856; that was before the decision of the Supreme Court. But my opinion as to the policy of the question in unchanged. Here is what I then said, and I feel no disposition to modify the sentiments now:—

> 'Now, sir, as I have stated, I voted for this bill leaving the whole matter to the people to settle for themselves, subject to no restriction or limitation but the Constitution. With this distinct understanding of its import and meaning, and with a determination that the existence of this power being disputed and doubted, it would be better and much more consistent with our old time Republican principles to let the people settle it than for Congress to do it. And, although my own opinion is that the people, under the limitations of the Constitution, have not the rightful power to exclude Slavery so long as they remain in a Territorial condition, yet I am willing that they may determine it for themselves, and when they please. I shall never negative any law they may pass, if it is the result of a fair legislative expression of the popular will. Never! I am willing that the Territorial Legislature may act upon the subject when and how they may think proper. We got the Congressional restriction taken off.
>
> 'The Territories were made open and free for immigration and settlement by the people of all the States alike, with their property alike. No odious and unjust discrimination or exclusion against any class or portion; and I am content that those who thus go there from all sections, shall do in this matter as they please under their organic law. I wanted the question taken out of the halls of Federal Legislation. It has done nothing but disturb the public peace for thirty-five years or more. So long as Congress undertakes to manage it, it will continue to do nothing but stir up agitation and sectional strife. The people can dispose of it better than we can. Why not then, by common consent, drop it at once and forever? Why not you, gentlemen, around me, give up your so-called and so-miscalled Republican ideas of restoring the Missouri Restriction, and let the people in the far off Territories of Kansas and Nebraska look after their own condition, present and future, in their own way.'

"So much, then, for the first question asked me. I see nothing dangerous in these doctrines of Mr. Douglas to our Institutions—nothing at war in the least with the great fundamental principles of popular rights upon which the whole fabric of Self-government rests. I am perfectly willing for the pioneers of civilization who quit the old States for new homes in the west, to form and regulate their own domestic Institutions in their own way, and make all other laws according to their liking. It was in this way our fathers settled this goodly land, and made the wilderness to blossom as the rose. They were all 'squatters,' in the popular slang of the day. When they wanted slaves of the African race, they had them, and I am perfectly willing that their descendants, with emigrants from all the other States who colonize and settle our broad Territories, shall exercise the same rights of Self-government that they did. If these opinions make a man a 'squatter sovereign,' then I am one. Nicknames will never drive me from the maintenance of sound principles.

"Having noticed the most prominent objections urged against supporting the National ticket, as I have seen them in the press, I come now, fellow-citizens, to some of the reasons why I give that ticket a warm and cordial support. The points wherein I differ from Mr. Douglas are small, compared with those wherein we agree. Upon all questions of Constitutional law he is a strict constructionist—of the straightest sect of the State Rights school. Upon our peculiar Institution, so far from being unsound, unsafe, or dangerous on all the essential principles upon which it rests, and its permanency depends, he is on the side of reason and truth. He holds that the Negro is of an inferior race [as Abraham Lincoln and most other Northerners also maintained]—that he is not and cannot be a citizen of the United States—that he was not intended to be embraced in the Declaration of Independence—that subordination to the White race is his natural and normal condition—that his status in society is a question, not of moral right, but one of political and social economy; and that every State and organized Community have the right to fix and settle this status for themselves.

"These are the, great principles and truths upon which our [American] system rests, and upon which it must depend on the fields of our battles with the public opinion of the world. On this arena we have got to meet our opponents sooner or later. We live in an age of discussion—all questions of science and arts, morals and governments, must pass this ordeal. The Institution of African slavery amongst us cannot escape it. If it does not stand upon the immutable principles of nature, as I believe it does, it must go down, and ought to go down. And in the vindication of these great fundamental truths, relating to Negro inequality and his natural subordinate position, which lie at the foundation of our social fabric, no man, North or South, or in the world, has displayed more boldness and power than this same much abused and grossly misrepresented Stephen A. Douglas.

"No man has ever uttered these, or any other truths, in this country, with more peril or hazard to himself. Whether in the Senate or on the hustings, whether at the South or the North—whether before party friends or Abolition mobs, he has never shrunk from their utterance from fear, favor, or affection. When duty required him to speak, he has never been silent. See him breasting the anathemas of the three thousand New England clergymen, hurled against him for the defence of your rights, under the Constitution. See him at Chicago, imperilling even life itself in vindication of the same cause—your rights under the Constitution—and say if it comes with a good grace, from a Southern man, to denounce him as an enemy to us or ours.

"Was there ever blacker ingratitude, since Adam's first great fall, than such demonstrations against such a man? Were I to remain silent while I hear them, and see him so unjustly slain, by those who know not what they do, I should feel myself to be as guilty of innocent blood as those who stood by and held [Saint] Stephen's clothes while he was stoned to death. Whatever may be his opinions of Popular Sovereignty, or Squatter Sovereignty, or the right of Self-government, on the part of all organized Communities—call it what you will—they are the same now that they have always been—the same that they were in 1856, when he was the favorite of the Georgia Democracy for the Presidency. I thought of his doctrine then just as I do now. If others have changed their opinions since, he has not. It is one of the qualities about him that increases my admiration, that he is no time-server—he does not change with the popular current—he bends to no storm—he maintains his fidelity and integrity to principle through woe as well as through weal.

"One of the most manly exhibitions of moral courage and nerve this country ever witnessed, was seen in his contest in Illinois in 1858. With the Abolition hosts in front, and all the forces of the Administration, so unnaturally and unjustly brought in the rear, he fought the battle single-handed and alone, achieving a victory unparalleled in the history of politics in this country. Why should not such a man receive our support? Not only Democratic, but Whig and American—a united Southern, as well as a national support? Are his principles not national, equal and just to all? Of his associate on the ticket, I need not speak here. Herschel V. Johnson needs no indorsement from any man in Georgia. No son of hers was ever more sensitively alive to all your great and most vital interests. He has been tried in the Senate, and the Executive Chair, in the highest and most responsible offices, proving himself to be equal to any and every occasion.

"Fellow-citizens, there is much more I wish to say—much upon the protection Platform of those who call themselves the true Democracy; but my strength has failed—I am completely exhausted. I can only add: Look at the questions in all their bearings, to your past records, to your present and future security, and as patriots, do your duty, trust the rest with God."

[An eyewitness: Here Mr. S., being unable longer to stand, took his seat. The audience remaining quiet, calls were made for Cumming, Wright, and others; but no one of the gentlemen called for appearing, Mr. Geo. W. Lamar arose on the steps, and announced that Mr. S. would be able to proceed in a few minutes. After some enlivening airs from the brass band, Mr. S. arose, with great physical weakness, and proceeded.]

"I do not feel, fellow-citizens, as if, in justice to myself, I ought to attempt to say more to-night; but there is no cause in which I would more willingly die than in the cause of my country; and I would just as soon fall here, at this time, in the advocacy of those principles upon which its past glory has been achieved, its present prosperity, and its future hopes depend, as anywhere else, or on any other occasion. I told you, at the outset, that the signs of the times portend evil. I gave you this as my deliberate judgment; the future must make its own disclosures. But you need not be surprised to see these States, now so peaceful, contented, prosperous, and happy, embroiled in war in less than twelve months. There are occasions too grave for excitement, or any appeal to the passions. Believe me, I mean all I say; the most terrific tornadoes, those which demolish cities, destroy whole fleets, and sweep everything before them, come most unexpectedly. So do the most violent revolutions amongst men. The human passions are the same everywhere. They are dangerous elements for public men, politicians, and Party leaders to deal with.

"The condition of the country threatens the most violent conflict of sectional feeling, antipathy, and animosity, at no distant day. Should an outbreak occur, where is the power that can control it? A ball may be put in motion by one who cannot stop it; a fire may be kindled by hands that cannot quench it. Those who begin revolutions seldom end them. I do not mean to say that the secession movement at Charleston and Baltimore was a Disunionist movement, or intended as such by all those who joined in it. I do not mean to say that Messrs. Breckinridge and Lane, who gave that movement their countenance, by accepting nominations under it, are Disunionists. I know both these gentlemen well, and doubt not their patriotism. Had either of them, or both, received the nominations from the regular Democratic Convention, I should have given them as warm a support as I do Messrs. Douglas and Johnson. Neither do I mean to say that the great mass of those who support the Seceders' ticket are Disunionists—no, far from it. But I do mean to say that the movement, whatever may have been the motive in which it originated, and by which it is countenanced and supported, whether by good men or bad, tends to disunion—to civil strife—may lead to it—and most probably will, unless arrested by the virtue, intelligence, and patriotism of the people. Is the cause assigned sufficient to put in hazard such even probable results? If it is, let the hazard be made; but if not, let us pause and consider. Much as I am attached to the Union, and as clearly convinced as I am that it is best for the interests and welfare of all sections, that it shall be preserved and maintained, if it can be, consistently with the rights, honor and security of all parts, yet I hold it subordinate to these great objects of its formation: life itself, dear as it must be held by all subordinate to essential rights and honor. This is true of individuals, and it is true of States and Nations. It was with these views and feelings, the ultimatum of our State was set forth in what is known as the Georgia Platform, in 1850. As I did then, so do I now, hold the Union subordinate to the objects therein set forth. On that Platform Georgia planted herself then, and on it I trust she will continue to stand. On the principles of that Platform I believe the Union ought to be maintained, and can be, if our Southern people are but true to themselves.

"Now, this Secession movement, if pushed to its legitimate consequences, is a departure from those principles. In politics, as in morals, the first false step is the dangerous step. It matters but little what men intend when they set out in error. One step leads the way to another. . . . Feelings, views, and objects change as they progress. Ideas that the mind would have revolted at, at first, are soon cordially embraced. The Scriptural character of Hazael is a striking illustration of human weakness in this particular. This Charleston Secession movement, I say, is founded upon a departure from principle. Not only a departure from the Georgia Platform, and from the long-established principles of the National Democratic [Conservative] Party, but upon an entire change of position of the entire South, of all Parties, not of all individuals, in relation to the power and jurisdiction of the Federal Government over the subject of African Slavery.

"I need not be reminded that this was not my position, and that of a few others. This I know, and if I had that personal vanity that could indulge individual gratification at the remotest hazard of the public welfare, I might now be claiming great credit for myself. All this I am aware of; but I have no such vanity. My position, however, was not that of the South on this question. It was overruled; I yielded to the demands of the South. A settlement of this question was made according to their demands; and with me, when a matter is settled, it is settled forever.

"What I affirm is, that the position of the South, for seventy years, has been a denial of the jurisdiction of Congress over the subject of Slavery in the States and Territories. It was upon this denial of jurisdiction that the South resisted the reception of Abolition petitions. This position is directly reversed at Charleston and Baltimore.

"If we go to Congress with a request, a petition, or demand, to pass a law to protect Slavery in the Territories, why may not, on the same principle, so far as jurisdiction of the question is concerned, the Anti-Slavery men of the North go before the same body with their request, petition or demand, and ask that such law shall not be passed, or that one of the contrary character shall be passed? The door of jurisdiction, which has been closed so long, will be clearly and fully opened by this Secession movement, if it is sustained by the people.

And I fear it will be like the opening of that great door on the confines of hell, 'grating harsh thunder' on its turning hinges, which permitted the escape from the bottomless pit of all the foul fiends with which this once heaven-like earth of ours has been cursed!

"I say I fear the most mischievous consequences from this change of position. What is to be gained by it? What is proposed to be gained by it? Do those who favor it ever expect to get a law passed by Congress carrying out the principles of their Platform? So far from it, the most prominent of their leaders openly assert that they will never vote for such a law themselves. Mr. Breckinridge, their candidate, has declared in his letter of acceptance just as fully against such a law, as Mr. Douglas ever did. Then what possible good can ever come of the movement, even if an election could be carried by it? But that, all must see, is utterly impossible. Then what is to come of it? What is to be the result? If no good can follow, may not great mischief? This, to me, appears a most palpable and inevitable result.

"It may secure the election of the Republican [Liberal] candidate. Whether it will succeed in this or not, time alone can disclose. But if it does, what then? Yes, what then? Let those answer who started the movement. To me, it seems clear, that the running of a Breckinridge and Lane ticket, at the South, can have no possible effect but to increase the chances of Mr. [Abraham] Lincoln, which were fearfully close before. With a united Democracy, North and South, on the old Platform of principled, I should not have permitted myself to doubt as to the result, under the lead of Mr. Douglas, or Mr. Breckinridge, Mr. [Howell] Cobb, Mr. [Robert M. T.] Hunter, or any other of the distinguished competitors for the nomination.

"But now the only hope is that Mr. Douglas may be able to carry enough Northern Electoral votes, over Mr. Breckinridge and Lincoln both, to save the country from the excitements and dangers of a Republican triumph. This may be done. The news from New York, Illinois, Indiana, and several other Northern States is such as to furnish grounds of hope, if not to inspire confidence. But it cannot be done by giving aid and comfort to this seceding movement. On the contrary, it will be done by an effort of patriotism rising superior to, and stronger than, the power of that movement. This is my judgment; I give it to you for what it is worth, consider of it as you think best. I do not give it to you as a partisan; I have no personal or partisan feelings on the subject. In all that I have said, I have been governed solely by considerations of the public good."

[Here Mr. Stephens, after returning thanks to the ladies who had honored the occasion with their presence, and addressing some remarks to them pertinent to the subject, and the influence of women in public affairs, though they took no active part in politics, and appealing to all classes, young and old, fathers, mothers, brothers, sisters, boys, and all, to exert whatever influence they possessed in the cause of their country in this hour of her great need; and expressing hope that, under Providence, the late bright prospect of a great future and high career for our young Republic, not yet having reached manhood, might not be cut off and blasted, but that it should continue, for ages to come, to bless untold millions, again took his seat amidst loud and prolonged applause.][93]

3

PUBLIC SPEECHES - PART 2
1861-1866

WE NOW COME TO THE bellum and postbellum span of Stephens' life, a period in which he gave countless numbers of speeches, many which have not survived—particularly those from the latter period. This chapter begins with examples of those he gave between 1861 and 1865, most of this time in which he was serving as vice president of the newly constitutionally formed Republic, the Confederate States of America, or C.S.A. Following these is a speech from 1866, shortly after the War, at which time he was drawn back into politics—returning to his seat as a Georgia state representative in the U.S. Congress. Though he had changed party affiliation numerous times antebellum, from this point on he was a staunch Democrat (a 19th-Century conservative), remaining a self-professed "states' rights man" for the rest of his life.

On January 16, 1861, Stephens attended Georgia's Secession Convention at Milledgeville. Here, the thoughtful statesman gave one of his more eloquent speeches, pleading for calm, reason, and patience in the face of the ever growing secessionist movement across the South. While he accurately predicted the horrors of the coming war with the North, the pro-Union sentiments he expressed only added to his already undeserved reputation (among Southerners) as being a "Southern Yankee."[94] His emotive address must have stirred many souls. But it did not change minds. Three days later, on January 19, Georgia left the Union, and a heartbroken Stephens went with it:

☛ "This step [of seceding from the Union] once taken, can never be recalled; and all the baleful and withering consequences that must follow will rest on the convention for all coming time. When we and our posterity shall see our lovely

South desolated by the demon of war, which this act of yours will inevitably invite and call forth; when our green fields of waving harvests shall be trodden down by the murderous soldiery and fiery car of war sweeping over our land; our temples of justice laid in ashes; all the horrors and desolation of war upon us; who but this convention will be held responsible for it? and who but him who shall have given his vote for this unwise and ill-timed measure, as I honestly think and believe, shall be held to strict account for this suicidal act by the present generation, and probably cursed and execrated by posterity for all coming time, for the wide and desolating ruin that will inevitably follow this act you now propose to perpetrate?

"Pause, I entreat you, and consider for a moment what reasons you can give that will even satisfy yourselves in calmer moments—what reasons you can give to your fellow-sufferers in the calamity that it will bring upon us. What reasons can you give to the nations of the earth to justify it? They will be the calm and deliberate judges in the case; and what cause or one overt act can you name or point on which to rest the plea of justification?

"What right has the North assailed? What interest of the South has been invaded? What justice has been denied? and what claim founded in justice and right has been withheld? Can either of you to-day name one governmental act of wrong, deliberately and purposely done by the Government of Washington, of which the South has a right to complain? I challenge the answer.

"While, on the other hand, let me show the facts (and believe me, gentlemen, I am not here the advocate of the North; but I am here the friend, the firm friend and lover of the South and her institutions, and for this reason I speak thus plainly and faithfully, for yours, mine, and every other man's interest, the words of truth and soberness), of which I wish you to judge, and I will only state facts which are clear and undeniable, and which now stand as records authentic in the history of our country. When we of the South demanded the slave-trade, or the importation of Africans for the cultivation of our lands, did they not yield the right for twenty years? When we asked a three-fifths representation in Congress for our slaves was it not granted? When we asked and demanded the return of any fugitive from justice, or the recovery of those persons owing labor or allegiance, was it not incorporated in the Constitution, and again ratified and strengthened in the Fugitive Slave Law of 1850?

"But do you reply that in many instances they have violated this compact and have not been faithful to their engagements? As individual and local communities they may have done so; but not by the sanction of Government; for that has always been true to Southern interests. Again, gentlemen, look at another fact, when we have asked that more territory should be added, that we might spread the institution of slavery, have they not yielded to our demands in giving us Louisiana, Florida, and Texas, out of which four States have been carved, and ample territory for four more may be added in due time if you by this unwise and impolitic act, do not destroy this hope, and perhaps by it lose all, and have your last slave wrenched from you by stern military rule, as South America and Mexico were, or by the vindictive decree of a universal emancipation, which may reasonably be expected to follow.

"But, again, gentlemen, what have we to gain by this proposed change of our relation to the general Government? We have always had the control of it, and can yet, if we remain in it and are as united as we have been. We have had a majority of the Presidents chosen from the South; as well as the control and management of most of those chosen from the North. We have had sixty years of Southern Presidents to their twenty-four, thus controlling the executive department. So of the judges of the Supreme Court, we have had eighteen from the South, and but eleven from the North; although nearly four-fifths of the judicial business has arisen in the Free States, yet a majority of the court has always been from the South. This we have required so as to guard against any interpretation of the Constitution unfavorable to us.

"In like manner we have been equally watchful to guard our interest in the legislative branch of Government. In choosing the presiding Presidents (*pro tem.*) of the Senate, we have had twenty-tour to their eleven. Speakers of the House we have had twenty-three, and they twelve. While the majority of the representatives, from their greater population, have always been from the North, yet we have so generally secured the Speaker, because he, to a greater extent, shapes and controls the legislation of the country. Nor have we had less control in every other department of the general Government. Attorney-Generals we have had fourteen, while the North have had but five. Foreign ministers we have had eighty-six and they but fifty-four. While three-fourths of the business which demands diplomatic agents abroad is clearly from the Free States, from their greater commercial interests, yet we have had the principal embassies, so as to secure the world's markets for our cotton, tobacco, and sugar on the best possible terms. We have had a vast majority of the higher offices of both army and navy, while a larger proportion of the soldiers and sailors were drawn from the North. Equally so of clerks, auditors, and comptrollers filling the executive department, the records show for the last fifty years that of the three thousand thus employed, we have had more than two-thirds of the same, while we have but one-third of the white population of the Republic.

"Again, look at another item, and one, be assured, in which we have a great and vital interest; it is that of revenue, or means of supporting Government.

From official documents we learn that a fraction over three-fourths of the revenue collected for the support of the Government has uniformly been raised from the North.

"Pause now, while you can, gentlemen, and contemplate carefully and candidly these important items. Leaving out of view, for the present, the countless millions of dollars you must expend in a war with the North; with tens of thousands of your sons and brothers slain in battle, and offered up as sacrifices upon the altar of your ambition—and for what? we ask again. Is it for the overthrow of the American Government, established by our common ancestry, cemented and built up by their sweat and blood, and founded on the broad principles of right, justice, and humanity? And, as such, I must declare here, as I have often done before, and which has been repeated by the greatest and wisest of statesmen and patriots in this and other lands, that it is the best and freest Government—the most equal in its rights, the most just in its decisions, the most lenient in its measures, and the most inspiring in its principles to elevate the race of men, that the sun of heaven ever shone upon.

"Now, for you to attempt to overthrow such a Government as this, under which we have lived for more than three-quarters of a century—in which we have gained our wealth, our standing as a nation, our domestic safety while the elements of peril are around us; with peace and tranquillity accompanied with unbounded prosperity and rights unassailed—is the height of madness, folly, and wickedness, to which I can neither lend my sanction nor my vote."[95]

What follows is arguably Stephens' most famous, or rather, infamous, address. Known as the "Cornerstone Speech," it was delivered at the Athenæum in Savannah, Georgia, on March 21, 1861. The beginning of the "Civil War" was only three weeks away. This address has been long and widely hailed by the anti-South movement as "proof" that the Old South was "inherently racist," that "slavery was the cause of the American Civil War," that Dixie's economic system was based "solely on slavery," and that the South's participation in that conflict was only to "preserve slavery." We in the South, of course, heartily disagree with this biased and uninformed assessment of Stephens' words.

It is true, at the time, that he believed blacks were ordained by God to be subordinate to whites (an idea he later rejected), and it is equally true that he here declares that slavery was the "cornerstone" of the South's economy. Yet, since less than 5 percent of the South owned slaves, it is obvious that the latter statement is impossibly incorrect. Why then did he make it?

With only a tiny minority of the South being interested in slavery, Stephens needed to say something that would get both his constituents' attention and their support in the terrible partisan political battles with the North. The most efficient way to accomplish this was to use the tried and true tactics of exaggeration, fear-mongering, and hyperbole, the same ones routinely used by politicians to this day.

We must also consider the bold fact that if slavery had been the "cause of the War," as pro-North advocates continue to maintain, then why did the conflict not end with Lincoln's Emancipation Proclamation on January 1, 1863? Instead, the War dragged on for another two years, proving once and for all that the North was only fighting to install an empire, and the South was only fighting to prevent it.[96]

Bear in mind that the Confederate States of America was officially just one month old. Here now are Stephens exact words. The call of the Confederacy's provisional vice president to the podium was greeted with "deafening rounds of applause":

☛ "Mr. Mayor, and Gentlemen of the Committee, and Fellow Citizens:—For this reception you will please accept my most profound and sincere thanks. The compliment is doubtless intended as much, or more, perhaps, in honor of the occasion, and my public position, in connection with the great events now crowding upon us, than to me personally and individually. It is however none the less appreciated by me on that account. We are in the midst of one of the greatest epochs in our history. The last ninety days will mark one of the most memorable eras in the history of modern civilization."

[At this point an uproar began from distant audience members, saying they could not hear Stephens.]

"When perfect quiet is restored, I shall proceed. I cannot speak so long as there is any noise or confusion. I shall take my time—I feel quite prepared to spend the night with you if necessary. [Loud applause.] I very much regret that every one who desires cannot hear what I have to say. Not that I have any display to make, or any thing very entertaining to present, but such views as I have to give, I wish all, not only in this city, but in this State, and throughout our Confederate Republic, could hear, who have a desire to hear them.

"I was remarking, that we are passing through one of the greatest revolutions in the annals of the world. Seven States have within the last three months thrown off an old government and formed a new [the C.S.A.]. This revolution has been signally marked, up to this time, by the fact of its having been accomplished without the loss of a single drop of blood. [Applause.] This new constitution [the C.S. Constitution], or form of government, constitutes the subject to which your attention will be partly invited. In reference to it, I make this first general remark. It amply secures all our ancient rights, franchises, and liberties. All the great principles of Magna Charta are retained in it. No citizen is deprived of life, liberty, or property, but by the judgment of his peers under the laws of the land. The great principle of religious liberty, which was the honor and pride of the old [U.S.] constitution, is still maintained and secured. All the essentials of the old constitution, which have endeared it to the hearts of the American people, have been preserved and perpetuated.

[Applause.] Some changes have been made. Of these I shall speak presently. Some of these I should have preferred not to have seen made; but these, perhaps, meet the cordial approbation of a majority of this audience, if not an overwhelming majority of the people of the Confederacy. Of them, therefore, I will not speak. But other important changes do meet my cordial approbation. They form great improvements upon the old constitution. So, taking the whole new constitution, I have no hesitancy in giving it as my judgment that it is decidedly better than the old. [Applause.]

"Allow me briefly to allude to some of these improvements. The question of building up class interests, or fostering one branch of industry to the prejudice of another under the exercise of the revenue power, which gave us so much trouble under the old constitution, is put at rest forever under the new. We allow the imposition of no duty with a view of giving advantage to one class of persons, in any trade or business, over those of another. All, under our system, stand upon the same broad principles of perfect equality. Honest labor and enterprise are left free and unrestricted in whatever pursuit they may be engaged. This subject came well nigh causing a rupture of the old Union, under the lead of the gallant Palmetto State, which lies on our border, in 1833. This old thorn of the tariff, which was the cause of so much irritation in the old body politic, is removed forever from the new. [Applause.]

"Again, the subject of internal improvements [known today as 'corporate welfare'], under the power of Congress to regulate commerce, is put at rest under our system. The power claimed by construction under the old constitution, was at least a doubtful one—it rested solely upon construction. We of the South, generally apart from considerations of constitutional principles, opposed its exercise upon grounds of its inexpediency and injustice. Notwithstanding this opposition, millions of money, from the common treasury had been drawn for such purposes. Our opposition sprang from no hostility to commerce, or all necessary aids for facilitating it. With us it was simply a question, upon whom the burden should fall. In Georgia, for instance, we have done as much for the cause of internal improvements as any other portion of the country according to population and means. We have stretched out lines of railroads from the seaboard to the mountains; dug down the hills, and filled up the valleys at a cost of not less than twenty-five millions of dollars. All this was done to open an outlet for our products of the interior, and those to the west of us, to reach the marts of the world. No State was in greater need of such facilities than Georgia, but we did not ask that these works should be made by appropriations out of the common treasury. The cost of the grading, the superstructure, and equipments of our roads, was borne by those who entered on the enterprise. Nay, more—not only the cost of the iron, no small item in the aggregate cost, was borne in the same way—but we were compelled to pay into the common treasury several millions of dollars for the privilege of importing the iron, after the price was paid for it abroad. What justice was there in taking this money, which our people paid into the common treasury on the importation of our iron, and applying it to the improvement of rivers and harbors elsewhere?

"The true principle is to subject the commerce of every locality, to whatever burdens may be necessary to facilitate it. If Charleston harbor needs improvement, let the commerce of Charleston bear the burden. If the mouth of the Savannah river has to be cleared out, let the sea-going navigation which is benefitted by it, bear the burden. So with the mouths of the Alabama and Mississippi river. Just as the products of the interior, our cotton, wheat, corn, and other articles, have to bear the necessary rates of freight over our railroads to reach the seas. This is again the broad principle of perfect equality and justice. [Applause.] And it is especially set forth and established in our new [Confederate] constitution.

"Another feature to which I will allude, is that the new constitution provides that cabinet ministers and heads of departments may have the privilege of seats upon the floor of the Senate and House of Representatives—may have the right to participate in the debates and discussions upon the various subjects of administration. I should have preferred that this provision should have gone further, and required the President to select his constitutional advisers from the Senate and House of Representatives. That would have conformed entirely to the practice in the British Parliament, which, in my judgment, is one of the wisest provisions in the British constitution. It is the only feature that saves that government. It is that which gives it stability in its facility to change its administration. Ours, as it is, is a great approximation to the right principle.

"Under the old [U.S.] constitution, a secretary of the treasury for instance, had no opportunity, save by his annual reports, of presenting any scheme or plan of finance or other matter. He had no opportunity of explaining, expounding, inforcing, or defending his views of policy; his only resort was through the medium of an organ. In the British parliament, the premier brings in his budget and stands before the nation responsible for its every item. If it is indefensible, he falls before the attacks upon it, as he ought to. This will now be the case to a limited extent under our system. In the new constitution, provision has been made by which our heads of departments can speak for themselves and the administration, in behalf of its entire policy, without resorting to the indirect and highly objectionable medium of a newspaper. It is to be greatly hoped that under our system we shall never have what is known as a government organ. [Rapturous applause.]

"*Another change in the constitution relates to the length of the tenure of the presidential office. In the new constitution it is six years instead of four, and the President rendered ineligible for a re-election. This is certainly a decidedly conservative change. It will remove from the incumbent all temptation to use his office or exert the powers confided to him for any objects of personal ambition. The only incentive to that higher ambition which should move and actuate one holding such high trusts in his hands, will be the good of the people, the advancement, prosperity, happiness, safety, honor, and true glory of the confederacy.* [Emphasis added, L.S.] [Applause.]

"But not to be tedious in enumerating the numerous changes for the better, allow me to allude to one other—though last, not least. The new constitution has put at rest, forever, all the agitating questions relating to our peculiar institution—African slavery as it exists amongst us—the proper status of the negro in our form of civilization. This was the immediate cause of the late rupture and present revolution. [Thomas] Jefferson in his forecast, had anticipated this, as the 'rock upon which the old Union would split.' He was right. What was conjecture with him, is now a realized fact. But whether he fully comprehended the great truth upon which that rock stood and stands, may be doubted. *The prevailing ideas entertained by him and most of the leading statesmen at the time of the formation of the old constitution, were that the enslavement of the African was in violation of the laws of nature; that it was wrong in principle, socially, morally, and politically.* It was an evil they knew not well how to deal with, but the general opinion of the men of that day was that, somehow or other in the order of Providence, the institution would be evanescent and pass away. This idea, though not incorporated in the constitution, was the prevailing idea at that time. The constitution, it is true, secured every essential guarantee to the institution while it should last, and hence no argument can be justly urged against the constitutional guarantees thus secured, because of the common sentiment of the day. Those ideas, however, were fundamentally wrong. They rested upon the assumption of the equality of races. This was an error. It was a sandy foundation, and the government built upon it fell when the 'storm came and the wind blew.' [Emphasis added, L.S.]

"Our new government is founded upon exactly the opposite idea; its foundations are laid, its corner-stone rests upon the great truth, that the negro is not equal to the white man; that slavery—subordination to the superior race—is his natural and normal condition. [Applause.]

"This, our new government, is the first, in the history of the world, based upon this great physical, philosophical, and moral truth. This truth has been slow in the process of its development, like all other truths in the various departments of science. It has been so even amongst us. Many who hear me, perhaps, can recollect well, that this truth was not generally admitted, even within their day. The errors of the past generation still clung to many as late as twenty years ago. Those at the North, who still cling to these errors, with a zeal above knowledge, we justly denominate fanatics. All fanaticism springs from an aberration of the mind—from a defect in reasoning. It is a species of insanity. One of the most striking characteristics of insanity, in many instances, is forming correct conclusions from fancied or erroneous premises; so with the anti-slavery fanatics; their conclusions are right if their premises were. They assume that the negro is equal, and hence conclude that he is entitled to equal privileges and rights with the white man. If their premises were correct, their conclusions would be logical and just—but their premise being wrong, their whole argument fails. I recollect once of having heard a gentleman from one of the northern States, of great power and ability, announce in the House of Representatives, with imposing effect, that we of the South would be compelled, ultimately, to yield upon this subject of slavery, that it was as impossible to war successfully against a principle in politics, as it was in physics or mechanics. That the principle would ultimately prevail. That we, in maintaining slavery as it exists with us, were warring against a principle, a principle founded in nature, the principle of the equality of men. The reply I made to him was, that upon his own grounds, we should, ultimately, succeed, and that he and his associates, in this crusade against our institutions, would ultimately fail. The truth announced, that it was as impossible to war successfully against a principle in politics as it was in physics and mechanics, I admitted; but told him that it was he, and those acting with him, who were warring against a principle. They were attempting to make things equal which the Creator [as is clearly evident in the Bible, according to Stephens] had made unequal.

"In the conflict thus far, success has been on our side, complete throughout the length and breadth of the Confederate States. It is upon this, as I have stated, our social fabric is firmly planted; and I cannot permit myself to doubt the ultimate success of a full recognition of this principle throughout the civilized and enlightened world.

"As I have stated, the truth of this principle may be slow in development, as all truths are and ever have been, in the various branches of science. It was so with the principles announced by Galileo—it was so with Adam Smith and his principles of political economy. It was so with [English physician William] Harvey, and his theory of the circulation of the blood. It is stated that not a single one of the medical profession, living at the time of the announcement of the truths made by him, admitted them. Now, they are universally acknowledged. May we not, therefore, look with confidence to the ultimate universal acknowledgment of the truths upon which our system rests? It is the first government ever instituted upon the principles in strict conformity to nature, and the ordination of Providence, in furnishing the materials of human society. Many governments have been founded upon the principle of the subordination and serfdom of certain classes of the same race; such were and are in violation of the laws of nature. Our system commits no such violation of nature's laws. With us, all of the white race, however high or low, rich or poor, are equal in the eye of the law. Not so with the negro. Subordination is his place. He, by nature, or by the curse against Canaan [modern Mormons continue to embrace and teach this concept], is fitted for that condition which he occupies in our system. The architect, in the construction of buildings, lays the foundation with the proper material—the granite; then comes the brick or the marble. The substratum of our society is made of the material fitted by nature for it, and by experience we know that it is best, not only for the superior, but for the inferior race, that it should be so. It is, indeed, in conformity with the ordinance of the Creator. It is not for us to inquire into the wisdom of his ordinances, or to question them. For his own purposes, he has made one race to differ from another, as he has made 'one star to differ from another star in glory.'

"The great objects of humanity are best attained when there is conformity to his laws and decrees, in the formation of governments as well as in all things else. Our confederacy is founded upon principles in strict conformity with these laws. This stone which was rejected by the first builders 'is become the chief of the corner'—the real 'corner-stone'—in our new edifice. [Applause.]

"I have been asked, what of the future? It has been apprehended by some that we would have arrayed against us the civilized world. I care not who or how many they may be against us, when we stand upon the eternal principles of truth, if we are true to ourselves and the principles for which we contend, we are obliged to, and must triumph. [Immense applause.]

"Thousands of people who begin to understand these truths are not yet completely out of the shell; they do not see them in their length and breadth. We hear much of the civilization and christianization of the barbarous tribes of Africa. In my judgment, those ends will never be attained, but by first teaching them the lesson taught to Adam, that 'in the sweat of his brow he should eat his bread,' [applause,] and teaching them to work, and feed, and clothe themselves.

"But to pass on: Some have propounded the inquiry whether it is practicable for us to go on with the confederacy without further accessions? Have we the means and ability to maintain nationality among the powers of the earth? On this point I would barely say, that as anxiously as we all have been, and are, for the border States [Delaware, Kentucky, Maryland, Missouri, and West Virginia], with institutions similar to ours to join us, still we are abundantly able to maintain our position, even if they should ultimately make up their minds not to cast their destiny with us. That they ultimately will join us—be compelled to do it—is my confident belief; but we can get on very well without them, even if they should not.

"We have all the essential elements of a high national career. The idea has been given out at the North, and even in the border States, that we are too small and too weak to maintain a separate nationality. This is a great mistake. In extent of territory we embrace five hundred and sixty-four thousand square miles and upward. This is upward of two hundred thousand square miles more than was included within the limits of the original thirteen States. It is an area of country more than double the territory of France or the Austrian empire. France, in round numbers, has but two hundred and twelve thousand square miles. Austria, in round numbers, has two hundred and forty-eight thousand square miles. Ours is greater than both combined. It is greater than all France, Spain, Portugal, and Great Britain, including England, Ireland, and Scotland, together. In population we have upward of five millions, according to the census of 1860; this includes white and black. The entire population, including white and black, of the original thirteen States, was less than four millions in 1790, and still less in 1776, when the independence of our fathers was achieved. If they, with a less population, dared maintain their independence against the greatest power on earth, shall we have any apprehension of maintaining ours now?

"In point of material wealth and resources, we are greatly in advance of them. The taxable property of the Confederate States cannot be less than twenty-two hundred millions of dollars! This, I think I venture but little in saying, may be considered as five times more than the colonies possessed at the time they achieved their independence. Georgia, alone, possessed last year, according to the report of our comptroller-general, six hundred and seventy-two millions of taxable property. The debts of the seven confederate States sum up in the aggregate less than eighteen millions, while the existing debts of the other of the late United States sum up in the aggregate the enormous amount of one hundred and seventy-four millions of dollars. This is without taking into the account the heavy city debts, corporation debts, and railroad debts, which press, and will continue to press, as a heavy incubus upon the resources of those States. These debts, added to others, make a sum total not much under five hundred millions of dollars. With such an area of territory as we have—with such an amount of population—with a climate and soil unsurpassed by any on the face of the earth—with such resources already at our command—with productions which control the commerce of the world—who can entertain any apprehensions as to our ability to succeed, whether others join us or not?

"It is true, I believe I state but the common sentiment, when I declare my earnest desire that the border States should join us. The differences of opinion that existed among us anterior to secession, related more to the policy in securing that result by co-operation than from any difference upon the ultimate security we all looked to in common.

"These differences of opinion were more in reference to policy than principle, and as Mr. [Thomas] Jefferson said in his inaugural, in 1801, after the heated contest preceding his election, there might be differences of opinion without differences on principle, and that all, to some extent, had been federalists and all republicans; so it may now be said of us, that whatever differences of opinion as to the best policy in having a co-operation with our border sister slave States, if the worst came to the worst, that as we were all co-operationists, we are now all for independence, whether they come or not. [Continued applause.]

"In this connection I take this occasion to state, that I was not without grave and serious apprehensions, that if the worst came to the worst, and cutting loose from the old government should be the only remedy for our safety and security, it would be attended with much more serious ills than it has been as yet. Thus far we have seen none of those incidents which usually attend revolutions. No such material as such convulsions usually throw up has been seen. Wisdom, prudence, and patriotism, have marked every step of our progress thus far. This augurs well for the future, and it is a matter of sincere gratification to me, that I am enabled to make the declaration. Of the men I met in the Congress at Montgomery, I may be pardoned for saying this, an abler, wiser, a more conservative, deliberate, determined, resolute, and patriotic body of men, I never met in my life. [Great applause.] Their works speak for them; the provisional government speaks for them; the constitution of the permanent government will be a lasting monument of their worth, merit, and statesmanship. [Applause.]

"But to return to the question of the future. What is to be the result of this revolution?

"Will everything, commenced so well, continue as it has begun? In reply to this anxious inquiry, I can only say it all depends upon ourselves. A young man starting out in life on his majority, with health, talent, and ability, under a favoring Providence, may be said to be the architect of his own fortunes. His destinies are in his own hands. He may make for himself a name, of honor or dishonor, according to his own acts. If he plants himself upon truth, integrity, honor and uprightness, with industry, patience and energy, he cannot fail of success. So it is with us. We are a young republic, just entering upon the arena of nations; we will be the architects of our own fortunes. Our destiny, under Providence, is in our own hands. With wisdom, prudence, and statesmanship on the part of our public men, and intelligence, virtue and patriotism on the part of the people, success, to the full measures of our most sanguine hopes, may be looked for. But if unwise counsels prevail—if we become divided—if schisms arise—if dissensions spring up—if factions are engendered—if party spirit, nourished by unholy personal ambition shall rear its hydra head, I have no good to prophesy for you. *Without intelligence, virtue, integrity, and patriotism on the part of the people, no republic or representative government can be durable or stable.* [Emphasis added, L.S.]

"We have intelligence, and virtue, and patriotism. All that is required is to cultivate and perpetuate these. Intelligence will not do without virtue. France was a nation of philosophers. These philosophers become Jacobins. They lacked that virtue, that devotion to moral principle, and that patriotism which is essential to good government. Organized upon principles of perfect justice and right—seeking amity and friendship with all other powers—I see no obstacle in the way of our upward and onward progress. Our growth, by accessions from other States, will depend greatly upon whether we present to the world, as I trust we shall, a better government than that to which neighboring States belong. If we do this, North Carolina, Tennessee, and Arkansas cannot hesitate long; neither can Virginia, Kentucky, and Missouri. They will necessarily gravitate to us by an imperious law. We made ample provision in our constitution for the admission of other States; it is more guarded, and wisely so, I think, than the old constitution on the same subject, but not too guarded to receive them as fast as it may be proper. Looking to the distant future, and, perhaps, not very far distant either, it is not beyond the range of possibility, and even probability, that all the great States of the north-west will gravitate this way, as well as Tennessee, Kentucky, Missouri, Arkansas, etc. Should they do so, our doors are wide enough to receive them, but not until they are ready to assimilate with us in principle.

"The process of disintegration in the old Union may be expected to go on with almost absolute certainty if we pursue the right course. We are now the nucleus of a growing power which, if we are true to ourselves, our destiny, and high mission, will become the controlling power on this continent. To what extent accessions will go on in the process of time, or where it will end, the future will determine. So far as it concerns States of the old Union, this process will be upon no such principles of reconstruction as now spoken of, but upon reorganization and new assimilation. [Loud applause.] Such are some of the glimpses of the future as I catch them.

"But at first we must necessarily meet with the inconveniences and difficulties and embarrassments incident to all changes of government. These will be felt in our postal affairs and changes in the channel of trade. These inconveniences, it is to be hoped, will be but temporary, and must be borne with patience and forbearance.

"As to whether we shall have war with our late confederates, or whether all matters of differences between us shall be amicably settled, I can only say that the prospect for a peaceful adjustment is better, so far as I am informed, than it has been.

"The prospect of war is, at least, not so threatening as it has been. The idea of coercion, shadowed forth in President [Abraham] Lincoln's inaugural, seems not to be followed up thus far so vigorously as was expected. Fort Sumter, it is believed, will soon be evacuated. What course will be pursued toward Fort Pickens, and the other forts on the gulf, is not so well understood. It is to be greatly desired that all of them should be surrendered. Our object is peace, not only with the North, but with the world. All matters relating to the public property, public liabilities of the Union when we were members of it, we are ready and willing to adjust and settle upon the principles of right, equity, and good faith. War can be of no more benefit to the North than to us. Whether the intention of evacuating Fort Sumter is to be received as an evidence of a desire for a peaceful solution of our difficulties with the United States, or the result of necessity, I will not undertake to say. I would fain hope the former. Rumors are afloat, however, that it is the result of necessity. All I can say to you, therefore, on that point is, keep your armor bright and your powder dry. [Enthusiastic cheering.]

"The surest way to secure peace, is to show your ability to maintain your rights. *The principles and position of the present administration of the United States—the republican [Liberal] party—present some puzzling questions. While it is a fixed principle with them never to allow the increase of a foot of slave territory, they seem to be equally determined not to part with an inch 'of the accursed soil.' Notwithstanding their clamor against the institution, they seemed to be equally opposed to getting more, or letting go what they have got. They were ready to fight on the accession of Texas, and are equally ready to fight now on her secession. Why is this? How can this strange paradox be accounted for? There seems to be but one rational solution—and that is, notwithstanding their professions of humanity, they are disinclined to give up the benefits they derive from slave labor. Their philanthropy yields to their interest. The idea of enforcing the laws, has but one object, and that is a collection of the taxes, raised by slave labor to swell the fund, necessary to meet their heavy appropriations. The spoils is what they are after—though they come from the labor of the slave.* [Emphasis added, L.S.] [Continued applause.]

[The original reporter's statement: Mr. Stephens reviewed at some length, the extravagance and profligacy of appropriations by the Congress of the United States for several years past, and in this connection took occasion to allude to another one of the great improvements in our new constitution, which is a clause prohibiting Congress from appropriating any money from the treasury, except by a two-third vote, unless it be for some object which the executive may say is necessary to carry on the government.]

"When it is thus asked for, and estimated for," Stephens continued, "the majority may appropriate. This was a new feature.

"Our fathers had guarded the assessment of taxes by insisting that representation and taxation should go together. This was inherited from the mother country, England. It was one of the principles upon which the revolution had been fought. Our fathers also provided in the old constitution, that all appropriation bills should originate in the representative branch of Congress, but our new constitution went a step further, and guarded not only the pockets of the people, but also the public money, after it was taken from their pockets."

[The original reporter's statement: Stephens then alluded to the difficulties and embarrassments which seemed to surround the question of a peaceful solution of the controversy with the old (U.S.) government. How can it be done? is perplexing many minds. The President (Lincoln) seems to think that he cannot recognize our independence, nor can he, with and by the advice of the Senate, do so. The (U.S.) constitution makes no such provision. A general convention of all the States has been suggested by some. Without proposing to solve the difficulty, Stephens barely made the following suggestion:]

"That as the admission of States by Congress under the [U.S.] constitution was an act of legislation, and in the nature of a contract or compact between the States admitted and the others admitting, why should not this contract or compact be regarded as of like character with all other civil contracts—liable to be rescinded by mutual agreement of both parties? The seceding States have rescinded it on their part, they have resumed their sovereignty. Why cannot the whole question be settled, if the north desire peace, simply by the [U.S.] Congress, in both branches, with the concurrence of the President, giving their consent to the separation, and a recognition of our independence?"

[The original reporter's statement: This Stephens merely offered as a suggestion, as one of the ways in which it might be done with much less violence by constructions to the constitution than many other acts of that government. The difficulty has to be solved in some way or other—this may be regarded as a fixed fact. Several other points were alluded to by Mr. Stephens, particularly as to the policy of the new government toward foreign nations, and our commercial relations with them. Free trade, as far as practicable, would be the policy of this government. No higher duties would be imposed on foreign importations than would be necessary to support the government upon the strictest economy. In olden times the olive branch was considered the emblem of peace; we will send to the nations of the earth another and far more potential emblem of the same, the cotton plant. The present duties were levied with a view of meeting the present necessities and exigencies, in preparation for war, if need be; but if we have peace, and he hoped we might, and trade should resume its proper course, a duty of ten per cent, upon foreign importations it was thought might be sufficient to meet the expenditures of the government. If some articles should be left on the free list, as they now are, such as breadstuffs, etc., then, of course, duties upon others would have to be higher—but in no event to an extent to embarrass trade and commerce. He concluded in an earnest appeal for union and harmony, on part of all the people in support of the common cause, in which we were all enlisted, and upon the issues of which such great consequences depend. "If," said he, "we are true to ourselves, true to our cause, true to our destiny, true to our high mission, in presenting to the world the highest type of civilization ever exhibited by man—there will be found in our lexicon no such word as fail."

[Mr. Stephens took his seat, amid a burst of enthusiasm and applause, such as the Athenæum has never had displayed within its walls, within 'the recollection of the oldest inhabitant.']

[A note by the original reporter: Your reporter begs to state that the above is not a perfect report, but only such a sketch of the address of Mr. Stephens as embraces, in his judgment, the most important points presented by the orator.][97]

On April 23, 1861, Stephens gave the following speech before the Virginia Secession Convention. The main topic was the recent vote by the state's delegates to withdraw from the Union, and whether or not this separation would ultimately be formalized. Four weeks later, on May 23, the people of Virginia would ratify their state's Ordinance of Secession, making the Old Dominion an official member of the Confederate States of America:

[A Reporter on the scene:] "President Jefferson Davis having again resumed the chair, said: 'Gentlemen Of The Convention:—I have the honor to introduce the Hon. Alexander H. Stephens, Vice-President of the Confederates States, who comes charged with a special mission from the Confederate States to the government of Virginia.'"

☞ "Mr. President And Gentlemen Of The Convention:—I appear before you on this occasion upon your own invitation, representing the government of the Confederate States. My mission was at your instance, in compliance with a resolution inviting that government to send a commissioner here. The powers by which I am accredited were, I presume, communicated to you by your executive yesterday; and I have simply in this interview, in accordance with your request, to state to you very freely, candidly, and frankly, what are the wishes and objects of our government in sending me here. I will premise by stating with equal candor and frankness that the communication from this convention to our government inviting this conference, was received with a great deal of gratification. I presume that no event since the separation of the more southern States from the late Union, has occurred to give such unbounded pleasure to the whole southern people, as the news that the Old Dominion [Virginia] had thrown her fortunes with ours.

"We had thought, from the beginning, that this result would ultimately be inevitable. Individually, you will allow me to say I had not the slightest doubt upon the subject, and I feel extremely gratified that my anticipations have been so early realized. When the communication was received that Virginia had seceded, and wished a conference with our government, there was not the slightest hesitation. The telegraph announced it at two o'clock, P.M., and by eight in the evening I was on my way here.

"It is true your resolution simply indicated a wish to form an alliance with the present Confederate States, in the present emergency, in the midst of the present perils which surround you and us alike. The condition of this body is not unknown to our government. The circumstances under which you are assembled, and the limitations of the powers under which you act, are very well known at Montgomery. We know the condition on which your ordinance of secession was necessarily passed—that it was, under the circumstances, properly subjected to the popular ratification of your people. Embarrassments, it was known, therefore, might attend any alliance that may be made; but the great question, looking to existing, present perils, and the dangers which instantly press upon you and us alike, was how best to meet these; how best to provide for to-day, leaving the troubles and embarrassments of future contingencies to be provided for as they may arise. An immediate alliance to the extent of your powers was by our government thought best. It was taken for granted that such, also, was your opinion. This seems to be too apparent to admit of doubt. The only question is as to details. Common dangers require common and united action. A war is upon us—upon you and the Confederate States alike. The extent of this war no human ken at this moment can foresee. Whether it be short or prolonged; whether it will be bloody and waged on the part of our enemies, with a view to subjugation and extermination, are matters of uncertainty. In this free conference I may be permitted to give you my individual opinion on these points, for what it is worth. We can lose nothing by looking dangers full in the face, however great; we may thereby be the better enabled to meet them. *My own opinion, then, is, that it is to be a war for our subjugation and the extermination, if possible, of the whole fabric of our civil and social institutions.* This is my view of its probable ultimate range; and that it will require all the resources of money and men of the southern people to maintain their cause successfully, unless, fortunately, by immediate and prompt action, such a decisive blow shall be given, on our part, as will turn the tide of victory in our favor at the outset, and show our full power to sustain independence. In this way it may be a war of short duration; but this is rather a hope than an expectation. [Emphasis added, L.S.]

"As to the ultimate result—whether long or short, whether waged on a small or extensive scale—I do not permit myself to entertain a doubt. We have the means—the men, and those resources which will command the money. All will be put forth, if necessary. Still the issue of this war, as of all wars, as well as the destinies of the nation, we should not forget, are in the hands of the Great Sovereign of the universe. In Him and the justice of our cause, and our own exertions, our trust and confidence of success should be placed. Our enemies may rely upon their superiority of numbers, but the race is not always to the swift nor the battle to the strong; but it is with God who gives the victory to the right. *The war has not been of our seeking. We have done all that we could to avoid it. We feel assured of the righteousness of our cause, and that 'thrice armed is he who hath his quarrel just.' We have committed no wrong on those who force the war on us; we have made no aggression on them or theirs; we have merely claimed and exercised the right of all free and independent States to govern ourselves as we please, and according to our own wishes, without interfering with or in any way molesting the other sovereign and independent States that formed the old Union. With those States we were united under a compact known as the constitution, that imposed obligations upon all the States. These obligations, on the part of the southern States, have been faithfully performed, while on the part of a large number of the northern States, they were openly and avowedly disregarded. The breach of faith was on their part. In the judgment of our people the only hope for safety was in a resumption of their delegated powers.* Having resumed the powers delegated to the general government—a right which Virginia distinctly reserved to herself in the adoption of the Federal [U.S.] constitution—there is no power on earth that can rightfully call in question our acts as free, sovereign, and independent States, so far as the old Union is concerned. Even in the opinion of Mr. [Daniel] Webster, the great northern expounder of the constitution, when the northern States refused to fulfill their obligations under the constitution, it was no longer binding upon the southern States. [Emphasis added, L.S.]

"But this is a digression. It was only intended to impress the rightfulness of our cause. The matter now before us is the formation of a new alliance that will better secure our rights and our safety—the first object of every State and community.

"The importance of a union or an alliance of some sort on the part of your commonwealth with the present Confederate States south, in this conflict for our common rights, I need not discuss before this intelligent body. Any one State, acting in its own capacity, without concert with other States, would be powerless, or at least could not exert its power efficiently. The cause of Virginia, and I will go further, the cause of Maryland, and even the cause of Delaware, and of all the States with institutions similar to ours, is the cause of the Confederate States—the cause of each, the interests of each, the safety of each is the same; and the destiny of each, if they could all but be brought to realize the dangers, would be the same. Therefore, where there is a common danger; where there is a common interest; where there is a common safety; where there is a common destiny, there ought to be a common and united effort.

"This is the view entertained by our government, and hence the invitation of the commonwealth of Virginia was responded to so promptly.

"There are various reasons that I might present to enforce the importance of such a policy, if I were aware of there being the slightest necessity for it; but I am not. Indeed, I am speaking without knowing any thing of the individual sentiments of the members of the convention; and it may be that what I am now stating to the convention as very important to them and to us, is a subject upon which there is no difference of opinion. The truth of the general propositions thus cursorily stated, seems to me to be so self-evident, that I feel it hardly necessary to argue them before you. I will, however, add a few things, briefly.

"First, as to the ends or objects of the alliance. To me it seems very important that your military should at least be in co-operation with, if not under the direction of the Confederate States government. We will necessarily have a large amount of forces in the field. When I left Montgomery there was 50,000 troops ordered out; 15,000 of them were then under arms, and most of them are perhaps under arms by this time. From information received from the Executive to-day, it appears that the President [Davis] of the Confederacy has ordered out thirteen more regiments since I left. That will be about 12,000 more troops. North Carolina may be considered as co-operating with us now, though this large force (72,000) does not embrace any from that State. Tennessee also has tendered 5000, with an assurance from distinguished gentlemen from that State to our government, on Tuesday of last week, that soon after the news of the bombardment of Fort Sumter, 15,000 had tendered their services, and that, if necessary, 50,000 would be forthcoming. So large a number, however, would not be called for from there.

"Kentucky, also, has a large body of men, who will be mustered into our service should the exigency arise. It may be that some of those troops may be discharged, and their places supplied by others; but 100,000 men will perhaps be in the field in less than three months. That is not counting Virginia. You, of course, will have a large force. All these forces should co-operate to be efficient; and while I don't claim to be a military man, it seems to me to be clear, on general rational principles, that all the forces—those of the Confederate States, those of Virginia, as well as those of the border States that are not yet out of the Union—should be under one head, as also all the military operations of the country directed to the same ends. It is generally admitted that, in the execution of laws, it is essential that there should be one head; but more important than in the usual execution of laws is it that military operations should be under one head. In physical economy all the parts and functions in each organism, to be efficient, are under the control of one head, one animating, moving spirit, with one sensorium, one mind, one directing will. In military matters, looking to the same ends and objects, there should be one head. It is probable Virginia will be the main theatre, to a great extent, of the pending conflict. Maryland may be, perhaps—we don't know; but the line of Virginia, your great waters on the North, necessarily make you, in this conflict, the theatre of large and extensive military operations, if not the scene of the bloodiest conflicts that this continent has ever yet witnessed. You will, necessarily, therefore, look to the southern confederacy immediately for aid, even whether you become a member of it or not. I will state here, however, before passing any further, that we are looking to this, your ultimate union with us, as a fixed fact; and the unanimous desire of every branch of our government is, that, just as speedily as possible, you will thus link your fortunes with ours. Your cause is ours, your future will be ours; and your destiny must be ours.

"But my mission relates to the intermediate time; to such alliance as may be necessary for the next twenty or forty days—before action can be taken by the people in their sovereign capacity at the ballot-box. In the meantime, between now and then, the *salus populi* [Latin: 'good of the people'] must be the rule of your action as the custodians of popular rights. Your duty to yourselves and your homes, is to look immediately to the pressing wants of your people, and, in the meantime, make such preparations as are necessary to meet this extraordinary exigency. Is it not essential that there should be concert and united action under one head? Now, what can Virginia do under a military organization distinct from that of the Confederate States? How can she act in concert with her allies, or those willing to help her without some compact or agreement? Troops from the South are already on the way here. Two regiments from South Carolina will, perhaps, be here within the next twenty-four hours. Forces have been ordered from Louisiana, and are coming immediately to your assistance. Ought there not to be some understanding as to how they shall be received and how directed? Would it not be better that these troops, as well as your whole military operations, should be under the control and supervision of our government? To me it seems essential for efficient action. These suggestions are thrown out for the consideration of the convention.

"There are other considerations which I might also present. I know the condition of your State in financial matters only to a limited extent. I know the vast resources of Virginia, and I know that her people, with the patriotism that has ever distinguished them, would never permit her cause to suffer for lack of means at any cost or sacrifice. But have you the means now at command? Arms must be had, munitions of war must be procured, men must be sent immediately to the field—these must be clothed and fed as well as armed. All this will require money. 'Money is the sinew of war.' Where money cannot be had, credit may answer. But money or credit, which will command it, is essential. On the financial point, so far as it relates to the Confederate States, I may state here, that our Congress authorized a loan of fifteen millions at its last session.

"The Secretary of the Treasury advertised for five millions. The loan was taken the day I left Montgomery. There were two days for its subscription. When I left, news had already reached by telegraph from the cities that seven millions of the loan of five that had been offered had been taken. The subscriptions in the interior towns had not been heard from, but it was believed that the whole amount would not fall far short of nine or ten millions—double the amount offered. This shows how our credit stands—the money thus raised is now at the disposal of our government; and it was believed that if an offer for the other five millions should be made, making the whole fifteen millions, it would be subscribed in ten days. Our people, from South Carolina to the Rio Grande, are in this movement heart and soul; and every dollar that can be raised will be used for the defence of the country in this emergency. No serious difficulty is apprehended as to our ability to raise the necessary means. In the State of Georgia, before we entered into an alliance with the other States, apprehensions were felt as to our available means. Georgia ordered a loan on her own account, of one million of dollars. This was promptly raised or provided for in our own State. What amount it will require to put your State in proper defence and to meet the invasion that may be looked for is a matter for your own considerate attention—and also whether the State at this time could, without a sacrifice of her credit, raise the requisite amount.

"An army of not less than 50,000 men will doubtless be required in your State. On this point your distinguished commander-in-chief [Robert E. Lee], just duly installed into office, can of course give better information than any conjecture of mine. But whether a small or large force shall be required, it may be considered as certain that many millions will be required to cover the expense. Whether you have the means to do this, is a matter for you to consider.

"Again: if you had the means, another question is, would it be right for Virginia, on her own account, to make this heavy expenditure in this enterprise? Because you stand on the border, it is not our desire that you should fight our battles. We don't wish you alone to fight these battles, or to bear yourself the expense of defending Virginia. I know that the intimation has been held out in other parts that we were not considering the peculiar circumstances of our brethren on the border States. I give you every assurance that our government feels thoroughly identified with you in interest, and we do not wish your great commonwealth to do more than bear her part in this contest. We know she is willing to do that. So far as the pecuniary matters are concerned then, I simply suggest whether it would not be wise and just and proper that all should share the burden equally—and whether we should not as our fathers did, in the first struggle for independence, look to each other, and bear equally the costs of a common cause? This I present, whether Virginia joins us ultimately or not. But to be entirely frank. I must say that we are looking to a speedy and early union of your State with our confederacy. Hence the greater importance for this immediate and temporary alliance. We want Virginia, the mother of States, as well as of statesmen, to be one of the States of our confederation. We want it because your people are our people—your interests are our interests; nay, more: because of the very prestige of the name of the old commonwealth. We want it, because of the memory of [Thomas] Jefferson, of [James] Madison, and [George] Washington, the father of his country—we want it for all the associations of the past—we want it because the principles in our constitution, both provisional and permanent, sprung from Virginia. They emanated from your statesmen—they are Virginian throughout—taught by your illustrious sages, and by their instrumentality mainly, were incorporated in the old constitution. That ancient and sacred instrument has no less of our regard and admiration now than it ever had. *We quit the Union, but not the constitution—this we have preserved. Secession from the old Union on the part of the Confederate States was founded upon the conviction that the time-honored constitution of our fathers was about to be utterly undermined and destroyed, and that if the present administration at Washington had been permitted to rule over us, in less than four years, perhaps, this inestimable inheritance of liberty, regulated and protected by fundamental law, would have been forever lost.* We believe that the movement with us has been the only course to save that great work of Virginia statesmen. [Emphasis added, L.S.]

"On this point indulge me a moment. *Under the latitudinarian construction of the constitution which prevails at the north, the general idea is maintained that the will of the majority is supreme; and as to constitutional checks or restraints, they have no just conception of them. The constitution was, at first, mainly the work of southern men, and Virginia men at that.* The government under it lasted only so long as it was kept in its proper sphere with due regard to its limitations, checks, and balances. *This, from the origin of the government, was effected mainly by southern statesmen.* It was only when all further effort seemed to be hopeless to keep the federal government within its proper sphere of delegated powers, that the [original American] Confederate States [1781-1789], each for itself, resumed those powers and looked out for new safeguards for their rights and domestic tranquillity. These are found not in abandoning the constitution, but in adhering only to those who will faithfully sustain it. [Emphasis added, L.S.]

"*We have rescued the constitution from utter annihilation. This is our conviction, and we believe history will so record the fact.* You have seen what we have done. Our [Confederate] constitution has been published. Perhaps most of you have read it. If not I have a copy here, which is at the service of any who may wish to examine it. It is the old constitution, with all its essentials and some changes, of which I may speak presently. [Emphasis added, L.S.]

"It is upon this basis we are looking to your union with us; first, by the adoption of the provisional constitution, and then of the permanent one, in such a way as you may consider best, under the limitations of your powers. This I may be pardoned for pressing upon the convention, and expressing the hope that they may do it, utterly ignoring all past differences of opinion.

"In all bodies of men differences of opinion may be expected; but the disagreements and differences with you, as was the case with us, will perhaps be found to relate more as to the mode of action, than to the propriety and necessity of action of some sort. As to differences in the past, on the subject of union and secession, let them be buried and forgotten forever. My position and views upon these questions in the past may be known to you. If not, it may be proper to state, and I feel no reluctance in declaring, in your presence here in the capitol of the old commonwealth of Virginia, that there never breathed a human spirit on the soil of America more strongly and devoutly attached to the Union of our fathers than I. I was, however, in favor of no Union that did not secure perfect equality and protection of all rights guaranteed under the constitution. I was not insensible of the fact that several of the northern States had openly repudiated their constitutional obligations, and that if the principles of the present dominant party should be carried out, ultimate separation was inevitable. But still, I did trust that there was wisdom and patriotism enough at the north, when aroused, to correct the evils, to right the wrongs and to do us justice. I trusted even to the last, for some hopeful reaction in the popular sentiment at the North.

"*I was attached to the Union, however, not on account of the Union per se, but I was attached to it for what was its soul, its vitality and spirit; these were the living embodiments of the great principles of self-government, springing from the great truth, that the just powers of all governments are derived from the consent of the governed, as it was transmitted to us by our fathers. This is the foundation on which alone all constitutional liberty is and must be based—and to these principles I am to-day attached just as ardently as I ever was before, and I now announce to you my solemn conviction that the only hope you have for the preservation of these principles, is by your alliance with those who have rescued, restored, and re-established them in the constitution of the Confederate States—there is no hope in the States north.* [Emphasis added, L.S.]

"The disagreements that existed in our State [Georgia] as to the course that we should pursue, before the last resort of secession was adopted, were more as to the mode and manner of redress, than as to the cause of the grievance or the existence of the grievance requiring redress. I take this occasion, in passing, to state to you, that in our convention there was considerable difference of opinion on this view of the subject. It may not be known to you that on that occasion, I disagreed with the majority on the course adopted. My vote was recorded against the secession ordinance in our State. I was for making one more effort, and for getting the whole South united if possible in that effort for redress.

"But when the State in her sovereign capacity determined otherwise, my judgment was yielded to hers. My allegiance was due to her. My fortunes were linked with hers; her cause was my cause; and her destiny was my destiny. A large minority in that convention voted as I did. But after secession was determined on by the majority, a resolution was drawn up to the effect, that whereas the lack of unanimity on the passage of the ordinance, was owing more to a disagreement as to the proper mode at the time for a redress of existing wrongs and threatened wrongs, than as to the fact of the existence of such wrongs as required redress; therefore, after the mode and manner was adopted by a majority of the convention, that all of us, as an evidence of our determination to maintain the State in her chosen remedy, should sign the ordinance; and with that determination under that resolution, every member of the convention, except six, signed it. Those six also declared upon record a like determination on their part. So our State became a unit upon the measure, when it was resolved upon. All anterior differences amongst us were dropped. The cause of Georgia was the cause of us all; and so I trust it will be in Virginia. Let all past differences be forgotten. Whether, if some other course had been adopted, our rights could have ultimately been secured in the old Union, is a problem now that can never be solved. *I am free to confess, as I frankly do, that the late indications afford strong evidence that the majority at the North were bent upon our destruction at every cost and every hazard.* At all events, we know that our only hope now is in our own strong arms and stout hearts, with unity among ourselves. Our course is adopted. We can take no steps backward. The time for compromise, if it ever existed, is past. Many entertained hopes from the 'Peace Congress'—that failed. Even an extension of the Missouri line, which was offered by prominent southern men, was sullenly rejected. *Every indication of northern sentiment on the part of the dominant party there, since the election last fall, shows that they were and are bent upon carrying out their aggressive and destructive policy against us. This they insidiously expected to succeed in, by relying upon the known strong Union sentiment in the border States. They evidently relied strongly on this in Virginia. Their policy being to divide and conquer.* In this, I think, however, they counted without their host. [Emphasis added, L.S.]

"*The people of Virginia may have been attached to the Union; but they are much more attached to their homes, their firesides and all that is dear to freemen—constitutional liberty.* [Emphasis added, L.S.]

"All hopes of preserving this in the old Union are gone forever. We must for the future look to ourselves. It is cheering to feel conscious that we are not without hope in that quarter. At first, I must confess, that I was not without serious apprehensions on that point. These apprehensions were allayed at Montgomery.

"The men who were sent there were not such materials as revolutions usually throw up. They seemed to understand thoroughly the position of affairs—the past, the present, and the future. They duly appreciated the magnitude of the responsibilities resting upon them, and proved themselves, I trust, not only determined to overthrow one government, but capable of building up another. Their work, as I have said, is before you. One leading idea runs through the whole—*the preservation of that time-honored constitutional liberty which they inherited from their fathers.* [Emphasis added, L.S.]

"The first thing was to organize a provisional government. This was done by the adoption of the provisional constitution. It is to last but one year, and conforms to our ancient usages as nearly as practicable. No changes in essential or fundamental principles. We have but one legislative body. This possesses the powers of the old Senate and House combined; but the rights of the States and the sovereign equality of each is fully recognized—more fully than under the old constitution, which was the basis of the action of the convention; for, during the provisional government, on all questions in Congress, each State has an equal vote. This provisional government was only a temporary arrangement to meet the exigencies until a permanent constitution could be formed and put into operation. This was really the great work before them.

"In this, as in the provisional government, the old constitution of our fathers—the constitution of Madison and Washington, was their model. I said I might say something touching its provisions. Time will not allow me to go much into details. You will please read and examine it minutely for yourselves. While the old constitution was the basis and model of its construction, you will find in it several changes and modifications. Some of them important. But of them all I make in passing this general remark—they are all of a *conservative* character. This is the most striking characteristic of our revolution or change of government thus far, that none of the changes introduced are of a radical or downward tendency.

"But all the changes—every one of them—are upon what is called the *conservative* side. Now, this I ask your special attention to. It is an important fact. I wish you specially to mark it, for I know that efforts has been made to create prejudice against our movement by telling the conservative men of the country that it sprung from some of the hot heads down South, and should not be relied on or trusted. But *take the [Confederate] constitution and read it, and you will find that every change in it from the old constitution is conservative. In many respects it is an improvement upon the constitution of our fathers. It has such improvements as the experience of seventy years showed were required. In this particular our revolution thus far is distinguished from popular revolutions in the history of the world. In it are settled many of the vexed questions which disturbed us in the old confederacy. A few of these may be mentioned—such as that no money shall be appropriated from the common treasury for internal improvements [corporate welfare]; leaving all such matters for the local and State authorities. The tariff question is also settled. The presidential term is extended [to six years], and no re-election allowed. This will relieve the country of those periodical agitations from which sprang so much mischief in the old government. If history shall record the truth in reference to our past system of government, it will be written of us that one of the greatest evils in the old government was the scramble for public offices—connected with the Presidential election. This evil is entirely obviated under the constitution which we have adopted.* [Emphasis added, L.S.]

"Many other improvements, as I think, could be mentioned, but it is unnecessary. I have barely alluded to the subject to show you that we do not invite you to any wild scheme of revolution. *We invite Virginia to join us in perpetuating the principles upon which she has ever stood—the only hope of constitutional liberty in the world, as I now seriously apprehend. If it fails with us, where else can we see hope? But for the South, what would have become of the principles of*

Jefferson, Madison, and Washington, as embodied in the old constitution long ago? Whatever the United States government has done in advancement of civilization, by solving the great principles of self-government by the people, through representatives clothed with delegated powers, is due mainly to the South. The achievement has been by southern statesmen. The honor and glory of the western republic, to which the eyes of the world has been directed for years, was the work mainly of southern men, and my judgment is, if you will pardon its expression, that just so soon as the South is entirely separated from the North, and the government at Washington has no longer the advice and counsel of your statesmen and the men of the South, they will go into confusion and anarchy speedily. It gives me no pleasure to think so. It would be to our advantage, as well as theirs, for them, as we can no longer live in safety and peace under the same constitution, to go on and be prosperous, and leave us to do the same. But my conviction is that they will not. They do not understand constitutional liberty. It is an exotic in their clime. It is a plant of southern growth. I have, however, no war to make on their institutions. They seem to think them better than ours, and, not satisfied with this, they war upon ours. Now, the true policy of both sides, should be to let each other alone. Let both try their systems, not in war, but in friendly rivalship. Hence it is from no unkind feelings toward them or their institutions, that I express the opinion I do. I believe that our institutions are by far the best. My judgment is that theirs will be a failure. I would give them every opportunity to try them thoroughly by themselves, and for themselves. I simply give my view of what I believe to be the prospect on both sides, as well as the true policy of both; but I seriously doubt whether the rivalry which I would fain indulge the hope of seeing carried out, will be engaged in. War is what they are bent on in the start. Where this will end, time alone can determine. What I have ventured to say of the probable future of the North, is founded upon the experience and associations of many years with their public men in Washington. They do not seem to understand the nature or workings of a federative [Confederate] system. They have but slender conceptions of limited powers. Their ideas run into consolidation. [Emphasis added, L.S.]

"Whilst I was in Congress I knew of but few men there from the North who ever made a constitutional argument on any question. They seemed to consider themselves as clothed with unlimited power. Mr. [Daniel] Webster was one of these distinguished few. Though he generally differed from southern men on points of constitutional power, yet he argued his side with great ability. Mr. [Stephen A.] Douglas is also another distinguished exception to the general remark. One or two others might be named as exceptions to the rule, but *the great majority, the almost entire representation from the North in Congress, both in the House and Senate, seemed really to have no correct idea of the nature of the government they were engaged in carrying on. They looked upon it simply as a government of majorities.* [Emphasis added, L.S.]

"They did not seem to understand that it was a government that bound majorities by constitutional restraints. Now, nothing is more fixed or certain than that constitutional liberty can be maintained only by a rigid adherence to fundamental principles. Government is a science—the northern mind seems disinclined to that sort of study. Excuse this digression. It may not, however, be altogether inappropriate to the occasion—all things being duly considered. It springs from no disposition on my part wantonly to disparage northern character. It is intended rather to show where our future safety and security lies. We have our destiny under Providence in our own hands, and we must work it out the best we can. *All we ask of our late confederates is to let us alone.* But, be this as it may, we shall, I trust, be equal to the future and our mission, whether they choose to pursue toward us a peace or a war policy. [Emphasis added, L.S.]

"With union, harmony, concert of action and patriotism, our ultimate success in establishing or rather perpetuating a stable and good government on our ancient republican model need not be feared.

"One good and wise feature in our new or revised constitution is, that we have put to rest the vexed question of slavery forever, so far as the confederate legislative halls are concerned. On this subject, from which sprung the immediate cause of our late troubles and threatened dangers, you will indulge me in a few remarks as not irrelevant to the occasion. The condition of the negro race amongst us presents a peculiar phase of republican civilization and constitutional liberty. To some, the problem seems hard to understand. The difficulty is in theory, not in practical demonstration; that works well enough—theories in government, as in all things else, must yield to facts. No truth is clearer than that the best form or system of government for any people or society is that which secures the greatest amount of happiness, not to the greatest number, but to all the constituent elements of that society, community or State. If our system does not accomplish this; if it is not the best for the negro as well as for the white man; for the inferior as well as the superior race, it is wrong in principle. But if it does, or is capable of doing this, then it is right, and can never be successfully assailed by reason or logic. That *the negroes with us, under masters who care for, provide for and protect them, are better off, and enjoy more of the blessings of good government than their race does in any other part of the world, statistics abundantly prove.* As a race, the African is inferior to the white man. Subordination to the white man is his normal condition. He is not his equal by nature, and cannot be made so by human laws or human institutions. Our system, therefore, so far as regards this inferior race, rests upon this great immutable law of nature. It is founded not upon wrong or injustice, but upon the eternal fitness of things. Hence, its harmonious working for the benefit and advantage of both. Why one race was made inferior to another, is not for us to inquire. The statesman and the Christian, as well as the philosopher, must take things as they find them, and do the best he can with them as he finds them.

[Emphasis added, L.S.]

"The great truth, I repeat, upon which our system rests, is the inferiority of the African. The enemies of our institutions ignore this truth. They set out with the assumption that the races are equal; that the negro is equal to the white man. If their premises were correct, their conclusions would be legitimate. But their premises being false, their conclusions are false also. Most of that fanatical spirit at the North on this subject, which in its zeal without knowledge, would upturn our society and lay waste our fair country, springs from this false reasoning. Hence so much misapplied sympathy for fancied wrongs and sufferings. These wrongs and sufferings exist only in their heated imaginations. There can be no wrong where there is no violation of nature's laws. We have heard much of the higher law. I believe myself in the higher law. We stand upon that higher law. I would defend and support no constitution that is against the higher law. I mean by that the law of nature and of God. Human constitutions and human laws that are made against the law of nature or of God, ought to be overturned; and if [Yankee William H.] Seward was right the constitution which he was sworn to support, and is now requiring others to swear to support, ought to have been overthrown long ago. It ought never to have been made. But in point of fact it is he and his [Northern] associates in this crusade against us, who are warring against the higher law—we stand upon the laws of the Creator, upon the highest of all laws. It is the fanatics of the North, who are warring against the decrees of God Almighty, in their attempts to make things equal which he made unequal. My assurance of ultimate success in this controversy is strong from the conviction, that we stand upon the right. Some years ago in the Hall of the House of Representatives, a very prominent gentleman from Ohio, announced with a great deal of effect, that we at the South would be obliged to yield upon this question of slavery, because we warred against a principle; and that it was as impossible to war successfully against principle in politics as it was in mechanics. The principle, said he, would ultimately prevail. He announced this with imposing effect, and endeavored to maintain that we were contending against the great principle of equality in holding our fellow men in the unnatural condition of bondage. In reply, I stated to him, that I admitted his proposition as he announced it, that it was impossible to war successfully against a principle in mechanics and the same was true in politics—the principle would certainly prevail—and from that stand point I had come to the conclusion that we of the South would ultimately succeed, and the North would be compelled to yield their ideas upon this subject. For it was they who were contending against a principle and not we. It was they who were trying to make the black man a white man, or his equal, which was nearly the same thing. The controlling laws of nature regulate the difference between them as absolutely as the laws of gravitation control whatever comes within their action—and until he could change the laws of gravitation, or any other law of nature, he could never make the negro a white man or his equal. No human efforts or human laws can change the leopard's spots or the Ethiopian's skin. These are the works of Providence—in whose hands are the fortunes of men as well as the destiny of nations and the distinctions of races.

"On this subject a change is evidently going on in the intellectual world—in the republic of thinkers. The British West India experiment has done much to produce this change. All theories on the problem of human society must in the end yield to facts—just as all theories and speculations in other departments of science must yield to the same sure and unerring test. The changes of sentiment upon the subject of negro subordination have been great already, for this is the proper term to designate his condition with us. That they will continue as truth progresses, there can be no doubt. All new truths progress slowly. With us this change of view and sentiment has been wonderful. There has been almost a complete revolution within the last half century. It was a question little understood by the eminent statesmen of the south seventy years ago. This is no disparagement to their wisdom or ability. They were occupied in the solution of other great new truths upon which rested the first great principles of self-government by the governing race. These principles they solved and established. They met and proved themselves equal to the exigencies of their day and generation—that was enough to fill the measure of their fame. Each generation in the eternal progress of all things connected with existence, must meet new questions, new problems, new phases of even old subjects, and it will be enough for the men of each generation, if they prove themselves equal to the requirement of the times in which they live. As our fathers were equal to all the questions of their day, so may their sons be at this and all succeeding times. This is the point to which our attention should be chiefly directed.

"In our constitution, provision is made for the admission of other States into the confederacy; but none can be admitted without first adopting our constitution, and, consequently, none can be admitted who does not first adopt the fundamental principles on which our social and domestic institutions rest—thereby removing forever from our public or confederate councils that question which gave rise to so much disturbance in the old government.

"I have, perhaps, detained you much longer than I ought to have done, and upon matters, perhaps, which you may consider not very pertinent to the object of my mission. This you will please excuse. As I said in the outset, I appeared before you upon your invitation and was rather at a loss what to say, until I knew more of your own objects and wishes—and without, therefore, trespassing further upon your time and patience, in conclusion, I will barely add, by way of recapitulation, the main object, then, I had in view in coming before you to-day, was simply to announce that our government hailed with joy the news of your secession from the old government, and a desire on your part to form an alliance with us. Our government is very desirous that your ancient commonwealth shall become a member of our confederacy. Your interests and ours are the same; your safety the same, and your ultimate destiny must be the same. We are looking to your union with us as a certainty. But, in the meantime—before that union can be perfected by the action of your people, we think a temporary alliance or convention of the highest importance to meet the exigencies of the day and the hour. The enemy is now on your border—almost at your door—he must be met. This can best be done by having your military operations under the common head at Montgomery—or it may be at Richmond. For, while I have no authority to speak on that subject, I feel at perfect liberty to say, that it is quite within the range of probability that, if such an alliance is made as seems to me ought to be made, the seat of our government will, within a few weeks, be moved to this place. There is no permanent location at Montgomery—and should Virginia become, as it probably will, the theatre of the war, the whole may be transferred here—then all your military operations with ours will be under a common head. Your distinguished commander-in-chief, (General Robert E. Lee,) will, doubtless, have such a position as his great military talents and merits deserve. Whether in the Confederate army proper, or in the State service, will, I doubt not, depend upon his own choice. The great object is to have perfect union, harmony, and co-operation under one head. We think also that it is better for you, in a financial point of view, to unite with us immediately. Besides this, we want your members at Montgomery. We want the voice of Virginia in our Confederate councils. On this point, I would suggest to you that this convention immediately, if you think you have got the power, appoint delegates to our provisional Congress. My opinion is you have got the power. You may have to refer back to your constituents whatever change you make in your federal relations and in your State constitution; but in all other matters you have plenary power. You certainly have full power to send delegates to the provisional Congress.

"Is it not expedient that you should send members immediately to the Congress that is to assemble at Montgomery next week? If you think it is necessary that this matter should be decided by the people, I would wait, even though perils threatened, before I would infringe upon the rights of the people. But at all events, I wish you to understand that we expect you to join us just as soon as you can. If you see fit to make an alliance offensive and defensive, we will have our military here just as soon after the alliance is concluded as possible. We want you to join us permanently by the adoption of the permanent constitution, which will go into operation next winter, and of course it will be important to you in regard to the elections, that you change your fundamental law so far as relates to the election of members to the southern Congress under that constitution. I must apologize to you for trespassing so long upon your patience. I have said so much in a desultory way that I have, I fear, overlooked or omitted some things that would have been more appropriate if I had known more of the temper and views of your body. But this is a time for free conference and consultation upon the general state of public affairs. It is from this conviction that I have addressed you as I have. You are now in possession of my views very fully and frankly. It may be that something may occur that may render it proper for me to appear before you again. In any discussions that may grow out of what I have submitted, I hold myself in readiness to confer with you; and if this body should decide to form any alliance or treaty that may be thought proper, such as I have intimated, I will be found ready to meet them or any number that may be appointed to negotiate with me on the subject. I am alone, and have no associate; but any number that may be thought best on your part to meet me can be appointed.

"If you desire to hear from me on any other point, most cheerfully I will be at your command."[98]

On November 1, 1862, Stephens gave the following (paraphrased) speech at Crawfordville, Georgia. This synopsis concerns "the proper use of cotton and other resources for carrying on the war, etc.":

☛ [In the words of reporter J. Henly Smith:] "On the present condition and prospect of our affairs, Mr. Stephens said he had nothing new to say, and nothing that was not known to all. From the past we had nothing to be discouraged for the future. We had met with some reverses, but of eighteen months' fighting, we had lost no great battle. We had gained many brilliant victories. The aggregate of advantage of the fight on land thus far had been decidedly on our side. This was no small consideration for hope and encouragement, looking at the odds against us. At the beginning, the enemy had all the army, all the navy, all the revenue, all the credit, as well as the prestige of the name of the old Government, on their side. We were few in number compared with them; without a regiment or a ship, without a dollar, and without credit, except such as the righteousness of our Cause, inspired in the breasts of our own people, secured. Thus we entered the contest, and thus we have maintained it. At first 75,000 men were thought sufficient to conquer us. This failing, 600,000 were called to the field. These, too, failing, 600,000 more have been added, with a view to crush us out with numbers. Judging from indications, the enemy seem determined to put forth all their power. This is the present prospect. We should be prepared to meet it to the best of our ability. No one should despair or even despond from this array of new forces to be brought against us. We may not be able to match them in numbers. We are not able to do it, and should not attempt it. It is not necessary to do it, to secure ultimate success, if we avail ourselves of our advantages, properly and wisely. Numbers is one advantage the enemy has, and had from the beginning. We have advantages on our side which we should avail ourselves of. Frederick of Prussia fought all the great neighboring Powers of Europe for seven years, and was successful in the end. The greatest number he could bring into the field was 200,000 against 600,000. With this disparity of three to one, they thought they could crush him, but they did not. It is true, his country was overrun, and his Capital, (Berlin,) was twice taken and sacked during the war. He, however, did not give it up. Richmond has not yet been taken, though three powerful onward movements have been made against it. If Richmond should yet fall, and twice fall, we should be no worse off than Prussia was in a like calamity; nor should we be less disposed than the great Frederick to give it up for a like cause.

"The war of our first Independence [the American Revolutionary War] lasted seven years. During that struggle, several of the States were overrun, occupied and held for long periods by the enemy [Great Britain]. The men of that 'day that tried men's souls' felt no inclination, on that account, to 'give it up.' Philadelphia, their Capital, was taken, but they did not 'give it up,' or think of giving up the Cause. They fought on, as we can, for the same principles and rights, until final success. Nor have our suffering or sacrifices, as great as they are, been anything like as severe as theirs were. If they suffered and bore with patience and fortitude all they did to acquire and establish principles so dear to them and to us, well may we, with equal patience and fortitude, bear all now upon us, and all that may hereafter await us, to maintain them.

"The ability of a people to support and wage war depends partly upon their resources, and partly upon the skill and economy with which they are wielded. We have resources—elements of power to wage war successfully, unknown to Frederick or the men of 1776. All necessaries of life, food and clothing, with the materials and munitions of war, can, with skill and forecast, be made and supplied within ourselves. This goodly land of ours is unequalled, or at least unsurpassed by any other part of the habitable globe, in the character and variety of its natural products, suited to man's needs and wants in every emergency. Its mineral resources are also inexhaustible. It is a land, besides its Institutions, well worth fighting for. Our means are sufficient; and they have only to be properly and skilfully developed and applied.

"But besides the products necessary to sustain ourselves, to support our armies, and carry on war, we have another element of tremendous power, if properly used and applied—a resource and power unknown in European wars, and unknown to our ancestors in the war of their Revolution. Mr. Stephens here said he alluded to our great staple, cotton; and he should not have said more upon it at this time, than barely to ask those present to call to their minds what he had said to most of them last year upon that subject, when he addressed them upon the Cotton Loan, but for some misconceptions that had got in the public mind from a paragraphic report of some remarks he made at a meeting lately in Sparta. Some, from that report, said Mr. Stephens, have taken the idea that I urged upon the planters there, to plant largely of cotton next year. Allow me in this connection to say, that nothing could be further from the fact. I urged upon the planters there, first, and above all, to grow grain and stock for home consumption, and to supply the army. What I said at Sparta upon the subject of cotton, many of you have often heard me say in private conversation, and most of you in the public speech last year, to which I alluded. Cotton, I have maintained, and do maintain, is one of the greatest elements of power, if not the greatest at our command, if it were but properly and efficiently used, as it might have been, and still might be. Samson's strength was in his locks. Our strength is in our locks—not of hair or wool, but in our locks of cotton. I believed from the beginning that the enemy would inflict upon us more serious injury by the blockade than by all other means combined. It was, in the judgment of all, a matter of the utmost, if not vital importance, to have it raised, removed or broken up. How was it to be done? That was, and is the question! It was thought by many that such was the demand for cotton in England, that she would disregard the blockade, as it was, and has been all along, not within the terms of the Paris agreement—that is, has not been at any time, entirely effectual, though close enough to do us great injury. I did not concur in this opinion, as most of you well know. I thought it would have to be done by ourselves, and could be done through the agency of cotton—not as a political, but as a commercial and financial power. I was in favor, as you know, of the Government's taking all the cotton that would be subscribed for eight per cent, bonds at a rate or price as high as ten cents a pound. Two millions of the last year's crop might have been counted upon as certain on this plan. This, at ten cents, with bags of the average commercial weight, would have cost the Government one hundred millions of bonds. With this amount of cotton in hand and pledged, any number, short of fifty, of the best iron-clad steamers could have been contracted for and built in Europe—steamers at the cost of two millions each, could be procured, every way equal to the [Union's first ironclad ship, the] *Monitor*. Thirty millions would have got fifteen of these, which might have been enough for our purpose. Five might have been ready by the first of January last to open some one of the ports blockaded on our coast. Three of these could have been left to keep the port open, and two could have convoyed the cotton across the water, if necessary. Thus, the debt could have been promptly paid with cotton at a much higher price than it cost, and a channel of trade kept open till others, and as many more as necessary, might have been built and paid for in the same way. At a cost of less than one month's present expenditure on our army, our coast might have been cleared. Besides this, at least two more millions of bales of the old crop on hand might have been counted on—this with the other making a debt in round numbers to the planters of $200,000,000. But this cotton, held in Europe until its price shall be fifty cents a pound, would constitute a fund of at least $1,000,000,000, which would not only have kept our finances in sound condition, but the clear profit of $800,000,000 would have met the entire expenses of the war for years to come.

"In this way cotton, as a great element of power at our command—such an element as no other people ever had—might have been used, not only in breaking up the blockade by our own means, without looking to foreign intervention, but in supplying the treasury with specie to pay interest on their bonds, thus giving a credit that no Government ever had before. The public credit is as essential as subsistence in war. Such, at least, was, and is my opinion. The Government, however, took a different view of the subject. Many thought it unconstitutional. Some looked upon it as a project to relieve the planters. Others thought it nothing short of a South-Sea speculation. I considered it, then and now, just as Constitutional as to give bonds for gunpowder, or to buy other munitions of war. It was not with a view to relieve the planter, though its incidental accommodation to them would not have been objectionable, but with the view of wielding effectually the element of the greatest power we could command, that I wished this course adopted. This resource, then,—this element of power, we still have—though not to the same extent. There is enough, however, to effect wonderful results, if properly used, as it can be. We may have lost a year or two, but we are far short of seven years' war yet. With our ports open many of the present evils and hardships of the war would be relieved. We would no longer have to give fifty dollars for a bushel of Liverpool salt, or ten dollars for the roughest sort of shoes. With ports open and this in hand, we should be much better able to make it a Peloponnesian struggle, if our enemy choose so to make it. This view, and one other idea, I presented to the people at Sparta, upon the subject of cotton, which I will repeat here.

"Many to be met with suppose that by abandoning the growth of cotton and burning what we have, we can force our recognition abroad. This, I told the people there, and tell you, is, in my judgment, a radical and fundamental error. England will never be controlled by such a policy. Our cotton should be treasured up, not sold—more precious is it than gold—for it is more powerful, as a sinew of war, than gold is. Like gold, and everything else of value, it should be destroyed, if need be, to prevent its falling into the hands of the enemy, but with no view to a foreign policy; nor should the production of cotton be abandoned, with such a view. You could not please [British Prime Minister and Confederate sympathizer] Lord Palmerston better than to let him know that there would not be grown a pound of cotton in the Southern Confederacy for twenty years. The power of cotton is well known to and felt by British statesmen. They know it is King in its proper sphere, and hence they want the scepter of this King for their own use.

"The great error of those who suppose that King cotton would compel the English ministry to recognize our Government and raise the blockade, and who will look for the same result from the total abandonment of its culture, consists in mistaking the nature of the kingdom of this potentate. His power is commercial and financial—not political. It has been one of the leading objects of Lord Palmerston, ever since he has been in office, to stimulate the production of cotton in his own dominions—or those of his Sovereign—so as not to be dependent upon us for a supply. This he cannot do to any extent, while his inexperienced producers have to compete with us. Cotton can be raised in their East India possessions, and those on the western coast of Africa, at eighteen or twenty cents a pound; but it cannot be raised there profitably, to any extent, in competition with us at eight or ten cents. If assured, however, of no competition from this quarter, they could, or it is believed would, after a while, get to producing it as cheaply as we can.

"Improvements in agriculture are slower in their progress than in any other department of life. No one can safely or wisely say how cheaply cotton may or may not be grown in those countries, with a few years' absolute control of the market, nor that the quality of the article may not be as good. No one can tell what may be effected by improvements in agriculture and the introduction of new varieties suitable to climate and soil. More money can be made here by growing cotton now at eight cents a pound, than could be made at eighteen cents forty years ago. The quality is also greatly superior to the old black seed. More persons can now pick three hundred pounds a day than could pick one hundred when I can first recollect; and one hand and horse or mule can cultivate twice as much land. It is a great mistake, I think, to suppose cotton cannot be grown as cheaply, and with as good a staple—fine a fibre—in other countries, as it can in this—not in all places where it is now grown, but in some.

"There is nothing within the bounds of human knowledge on which reliance can be placed with such certainty as to results, as upon the laws of nature. It is on these laws governing the races of men that our Institutions are based. And there is nothing better ascertained in the floral kingdom, than that on the same geological formation, within the same lines of temperature and climatic conditions, (either from altitude or latitude,) the same species and varieties of plants will grow, each producing its like under similar culture to as great perfection in one hemisphere as the other, and upon one continent as another. We have one advantage in the production of cotton which they have not in the British Provinces. This has no reference to climate, soil or varieties. It is our system of labor. On our advantage in this particular, and to this extent, (which is no inconsiderable item,) we may rely in looking at the prospect of competition in the future, with these countries, should they, by a continuation of our blockade, or our necessary abandonment of the culture for a time, have the market of the world to themselves.

"We should not, therefore, think of abandoning the production of cotton, with any idea of thereby advancing our interests—politically—abroad. This would be but playing into the hands of those Powers who are trying to break it down. We have had to curtail it, and shall have to curtail it while the war lasts—especially while the blockade continues. Duty and patriotism, as well as necessity, require this. The first great object of all now, should be to sustain our Cause; to feed, as well as clothe men in the field. To do this besides raising sufficient provisions for home consumption, will necessarily require larger grain crops. To have an abundance for home consumption, and for the army, should be the object of every one. This is dictated by the highest considerations of home policy, and not from any view of advancing our interests abroad. On the contrary, after sufficient provisions are made for home consumption and to supply the army, the more cotton that can be grown the better."[99]

Stephens gave the following speech March 16, 1864, before the Georgia legislature at Milledgeville, Georgia. The address, which records the Confederate vice president's criticisms of the Davis administration's new acts on taxes, conscription, and the writ of habeas corpus, was reported by A. E. Marshall and later revised by Stephens:

[Marshall's note: "At the hour of 7:30 P.M., the Hall had been filled to its utmost capacity by members of the legislature and citizens generally, and as the vast assemblage within saw the beloved form of Georgia's proud and noble son, every eye grew bright with joy, and a hearty and unanimous applause bid him welcome. Mr. Stephens ascended the Speaker's stand and spoke as follows."]

☞ "Gentlemen of the Senate and House of Representatives: In compliance with your request, or at least with that of a large portion of your respective bodies,

I appear before you tonight to speak of the state of public affairs. Never, perhaps, before, have I risen to address a public audience under circumstances of so much responsibility, and never did I feel more deeply impressed with the weight of it. Questions of the most momentous importance are pressing upon you for consideration and action. Upon these I am to address you. Would that my ability, physically, and in all other respects, were commensurate with the magnitude of the occasion. We are in the midst of dangers and perils. Dangers without and dangers within. Scylla on the one side and Charybdis on the other. *War is being waged against us by a strong, unscrupulous and vindictive foe; a war for our subjugation, degradation and extermination.* From this quarter threaten the perils without. Those within arise from questions of policy as to the best means, the wisest and safest, to repel the enemy, achieve our independence, to maintain and keep secure our rights and liberties. Upon the decision of these questions, looking to the proper development of our limited resources, wisely and patriotically, so that their entire efficiency may be exerted in our deliverance, with at the same time a watchful vigilance to the safety of the citadel itself, as much depends as upon the skill of our commanders and the valor of our citizen soldiers in the field. Every thing dear to us as freemen is at stake. An error in judgment, though springing from the most patriotic motives, whether in councils of war or councils of state, may be fatal. He, therefore, who rises under such circumstances to offer words of advice, not only assumes a position of great responsibility, but stands on dangerous ground. Impressed profoundly with such feelings and convictions, I should shrink from the undertaking you have called me to, but for the strong consciousness that where duty leads no one should ever fear to tread. Great as are the dangers that threaten us, perilous as is our situation—and I do not intend to overstate or understate, neither to awaken undue apprehension, or to excite hopes and expectations never to be realized—perilous, therefore, as our situation is, it is far, far from being desperate or hopeless, and I feel no hesitation in saying to you, in all frankness and candor, that if we are true to ourselves, and true to our cause, all may yet be well. [Emphasis added, L.S.]

"*In the progress of the war thus far, it is true there is much to be seen of suffering, of sacrifice and of desolation; much to sicken the heart and cause a blush for civilization and Christianity.* Cities have been taken, towns have been sacked, vast amounts of property have been burned, fields have been laid waste, records have been destroyed, churches have been desecrated, women and children have been driven from their homes, unarmed men have been put to death, States have been overrun and whole populations made to groan under the heel of despotism; all these things are seen and felt, but in them nothing is to be seen to cause dismay, much less despair; these deeds of ruin and savage barbarity have been perpetrated only on the outer borders, on the coast, and on the line of the rivers, where by the aid of their ships of war and gunboats the enemy has had the advantage; the great breadth of the interior—the heart of our country—has never yet been reached by them; they have as yet, after a struggle of nearly three years, with unlimited means, at a cost of not less than four thousand millions of dollars (how much more is unknown) and hundreds of thousands of lives, been able only to break the outter shell of the Confederacy. The only signal advantages they have as yet gained have been on the water, or where their land and naval forces were combined. That they should have gained advantages under such circumstances, is not a matter of much surprise. Nations in war, like individual men or animals, show their real power in combat when they stand upon the advantages that nature has given them, and fight on their own ground and in their own element. The lion, though king of the forest, cannot contend successfully with the shark in the water. In no conflict of arms away from gunboats, during the whole war, since the first battle of Manassas to that of Ocean Pond, have our gallant soldiers failed of victory when the numbers on each side were at all equal. The furthest advance into the interior from the base and protection of their gunboats, either on the coast or the rivers, that the enemy has been able to make for three years was the late movement from Vicksburg to Meridian, and the speedy turn of that movement shows nothing more clearly than the difficulties and disadvantages attending all such; these things should be noted and marked in considering our present situation and the prospects of the future. In all our losses up to this time, no vital blow has yet been given either to our cause or our energies. We still hold Richmond, after repeated efforts to take it, both by force and strategy. We still hold on the Gulf, Mobile, and, on the ocean front, Wilmington, Savannah and Charleston. These places have been, and are still held against the most formidable naval armament ever put afloat. At Charleston the enemy seem to direct all their power, land and naval, that can be brought to bear in combination—all their energy, rancor, and vengeance. '*Carthago delanda est*' ['Carthage must be destroyed'], is their vow as to this devoted city. Every means that money can command and ingenuity suggest, from the hugest engines of war never before known to the fiendish resort of Greek fire, have been and are being applied for its destruction. For nearly nine months the city, under the skill of our consummate commander, his subordinates, and the heroic virtues of our matchless braves in the ranks, still holds out against all the disadvantages of a defence without suitable naval aid. That she may continue to hold out, and her soil never be polluted by the unhallowed footprints of her vengeful besiegers, is, of course, the earnest wish of all. But even if so great a disaster should happen to us as the loss of Charleston, be not dismayed, indulge no sentiment akin to that of despair—Charleston is not a vital part. We may lose that place, Savannah, Mobile, Wilmington, and even Richmond, the seat of government, and still survive. We may lose all our strong places—the enemy may traverse our great interior as they have lately done in Mississippi, and we may still survive. We should, even under such calamities, be no worse off than our ancestors were in their struggle for independence. During the time that 'tried men's souls' with them every city on the coast, from Boston to Savannah, was taken by the enemy. Philadelphia was taken, and Congress driven away. South Carolina, North Carolina, portions of Georgia, Virginia, and other States, were overrun and occupied by the enemy as completely as Kentucky, Missouri, Louisiana and Tennessee are now. *Take courage from the example of your ancestors—disasters caused with them nothing like dismay or despair—they only aroused a spirit of renewed energy and fortitude. The principles they fought for, suffered and endured so much for, are the same for which we are now struggling—State rights, State sovereignty, the great principle set forth in the declaration of independence—the right of every State to govern itself as it pleases.* With the same wisdom, prudence, forecast and patriotism; the same or equal statesmanship on the part of our rulers in directing and wielding our resources, our material of war, that controlled public affairs at that time, in the camp and in the cabinet, and with the same spirit animating the breast of the people, devotion to liberty and right, hatred of tyranny and oppression, affection for the cause for the cause's sake; with the same sentiments and feelings on the part of rulers and people in these days as were in those, we might and may be overrun as they were; our interior may be penetrated by superior hostile armies, and our country laid waste as theirs was, but *we can never be conquered*, as they never could be. The issues of war depend quite as much upon statesmanship as generalship; quite as much upon what is done at the council board, as upon what is done in the field. Much the greater part of all wars, is business—plain practical every-day-life business; there is in it no art or mystery or special knowledge, except good, strong, common sense—this relates to the finances, the quartermaster's and commissary's departments, the ways and means proper—in a word to the resources of a country and its capacities for war. The number of men that can be spared from production, without weakening the aggregate strength—the prospect of supplies, subsistence, arms and munitions of all kinds. It is as necessary that men called out should be armed, clothed, shod and fed, as that they should be put in the field—subsistence is as essential as men. At present we have subsistence sufficient for the year, if it is taken care of and managed with economy. Upon a moderate estimate, one within reasonable bounds, the tithes [taxes] of wheat and corn for last year were not less, in the States east of the Mississippi, (to say nothing of the other side,) than eighteen million bushels. Kentucky and

Tennessee are not included in this estimate. This would bread an army of five hundred thousand men and one hundred thousand horses for twelve months, and leave a considerable margin for waste or loss. This we have without buying or impressing a bushel or pound. Nor need a bushel of it be lost on account of the want of transportation from points at a distance from railroads. At such places it could be fed to animals, put into beef and pork, and thus lessen the amount of these articles of food to be bought. Upon a like estimate the tithe [tax] of meat for the last year, will supply the army for at least six months—rendering the purchase of supplies of this article necessary for only half the year—the surplus in the country, over and above the tithes, is ample to meet the deficiency. All that is wanting is men of business capacity, honesty, integrity, economy and industry in the management and control of that department. There need be no fear of the want of subsistence this year, if our officials do their duty. But how it will be next year, if the policy adopted by Congress, at its late session, is carried out, no one can safely venture to say. [Emphasis added, L.S.]

"This brings me to the main objects of this address, a review of those acts of Congress to which your attention has been specially called by the governor [of Georgia, Joseph E. Brown], and on which your action is invoked—these are, the currency, the military, and the *habeas corpus* suspension acts. It is the beauty of our system of government, that all in authority are responsible to the people. It is, too, always more agreeable to approve than to disapprove what our agents have done. But in grave and important matters, however disagreeable or even painful it may be to express disapproval, yet sometimes the highest duty requires it. No exceptions should be taken to this when it is done in a proper spirit, and with a view solely for the public welfare. In free governments men will differ as to the best means of promoting the public good. Honest differences of opinion should never beget ill feelings, or personal alienations. The expressions of differences of opinion do no harm when truth alone is the object on both sides. Our opinions in all such discussions of public affairs, should be given as from friends to friends, as from brothers to brothers, in a common cause. We are all launched upon the same boat, and must ride the storm or go down together. Disagreements should never arise, except from one cause—a difference in judgment, as to the best means to be adopted, or course to be pursued, for the common safety. This is the spirit by which I am actuated in the comments I shall make upon these acts of [the Confederate] Congress.

"As to the first two of these measures, the Tax Act and Funding Act, known together as the financial and currency measures, I simply say, in my judgment, they are neither proper, wise or just. Whether in the midst of conflicting views, in such diversity of opinion and interests, any thing better could not be obtained, I know not—perhaps not. With that view we may be reconciled to what we do not approve. It is useless now to go into discussions of how better measures might have been obtained, or how bad ones might have been avoided—the whole is a striking illustration of the evils attending first departures from principle—the '*facilis descensus Averno*' [Latin: 'the decent to Hell is easy']. Error is ever the prolific source of error. Our present financial embarrassments had their origin in a blunder at the beginning, but we must deal with the present, not the past. These two acts make it necessary for you to change your legislation to save the State from loss. As to the course you should adopt to do this, I know of none better than that recommended by the governor [Brown]. His views and suggestions on this point seem to be proper and judicious.

"The military act by which conscription is extended so as to embrace all between the ages of seventeen and fifty, and by which the State is to be deprived of so much of its labor, and stripped of the most efficient portion of her enrolled militia, presents a much graver question. This whole system of conscription I have looked upon from the beginning as wrong, radically wrong in principle and in policy. Contrary opinions, however, prevailed. But whatever differences of opinion may have been entertained as to the constitutionality of the previous conscript acts, it seems clear to my mind that but little difference can exist as to the unconstitutionality of this late act. The act provides for the organizing of troops of an anomalous character—partly as militia and partly as a portion of the regular armies. But, in fact, they are to be organized neither as militia or part of the regular army. We have but two kinds of forces, the regular army and the militia—this is neither. The men are to be raised as conscripts for the regular forces, while their officers are to be appointed as if they were militia. If they were intended as militia, they should have been called out, through the governor, in their present organizations—if as regular forces, they cannot be officered as the act provides. It is most clearly unconstitutional. Who is to commission these officers? The governor [Brown] cannot, for they are taken from under his control; the President cannot constitutionally do it, for he can commission none except by and with the advice and consent of the Senate. It is for you to say whether you will turn over these forces, and allow them to be conscripted, as is provided, leaving the question of constitutionality for the courts, or whether you will hold them in view of agricultural and other interest, or for the execution of your laws, and to be called out for the public defence in case of emergency by the governor when he sees the necessity, or when they are called for as militia by the President. The act upon its face, in its provisions for details, seems to indicate that its object is not to put the whole of them in the field. Nothing could be more ruinous to our cause if such were the object and intention, and should it ever be carried into effect. For if all the white labor of the country, from seventeen to fifty—except the few exemptions stated—be called out and kept constantly in the field, we must fail, sooner or later, for want of subsistence and other essential supplies. To wage war successfully, men at home are as necessary as men in the field. Those in the field must be provided for, and their families at home must be provided for. In my judgment, no people can successfully carry on a long war, with more than a third of its arms-bearing population kept constantly in the field, especially if, cut off by blockade, they are thrown upon their own internal resources for all necessary supplies, subsistence and munitions of war. This is a question of arithmetic on well settled problems of political economy. But can we succeed against the hosts of the enemy unless all able to bear arms up to fifty years of age are called to and kept in the field? Yes, a thousand times yes, I answer, with proper and skilful management. If we cannot without such a call, we cannot with it, if the war last long. The success of Greece against the invasion by Persia—the success of the Netherlands against Philip [II of Spain]—the success of Frederick against the allied powers of Europe—the success of the colonies against Great Britain, all show that it can be done. If our only hope was in matching the enemy with equal numbers, then our cause would be desperate indeed. Superior numbers is one of the chief advantages of the enemy. We must avail ourselves of our advantages. We should not rely for success by playing into his hand. An invaded people have many advantages that may be resorted to, to counterbalance superiority of numbers. These should be studied, sought, and brought into active co-operation. To secure success, brains must do something as well as muskets.

"Of all the dangers that threaten our ultimate success, I consider none more imminent than the policy embodied in this act, if the object really be, as its broad terms declare, to put and keep in active service all between the ages of seventeen and fifty, except the exempts named. On that line we will most assuredly, sooner or later, do what the enemy never could do, conquer ourselves. And if such be not the object of the act—if it is only intended to conscript men not intended for service, not with a view to fill the army, but for the officials, to take charge of the general labor of the country and the various necessary vocations and pursuits of life, then the act is not only wrong in principle but exceedingly dangerous in its tendency.

"I come, now, to the last of these acts of [the Confederate] Congress. The suspension of the writ of *habeas corpus* in certain cases. This is the most exciting as it is by far the most important question before you. Upon this depends the question, whether the courts shall be permitted to decide upon the constitutionality of the late conscript act, should you submit that question to their decision, and upon it also depend other great essential rights enjoyed by us as freemen. This act upon its face, confers upon the President, secretary of war, and the general commanding in the trans-Mississippi department, (the two latter acting under the control and authority of the President,) the power to arrest and imprison any person who may be simply charged with certain acts, not all of them even crimes under any law; and this is to be done without any oath or affirmation alledging probable cause as to the guilt of the party. This is attempted to be done under that clause of the constitution, which authorizes Congress to suspend the privilege of the writ of *habeas corpus*, in certain cases.

"In my judgment this act is not only unwise, impolitic and unconstitutional, but exceedingly dangerous to public liberty. Its unconstitutionality does not rest upon the idea that Congress has not got the power to suspend the privilege of this writ, nor upon the idea that the power to suspend it is an implied one, or that clearly implied powers are weaker as a class and subordinate to others, positively and directly delegated.

"I do not understand the executive of this State to put his argument against this act upon any such grounds. He simply states a fact, as it most clearly is, that the power to suspend at all is an implied power. There is no positive, direct power delegated to do it. The power, however, is clear, and clear only by implication. The language of the constitution, that 'the privilege of the writ of *habeas corpus* shall not be suspended unless, when in cases of rebellion or invasion, the public safety may require it,' clearly expresses the intention that the power may be exercised in the cases stated; but it does so by implication only, just as if a mother should say to her daughter, you shall not go unless you ride. Here the permission and authority to go is clearly given, though by inference and implication only. It is not positively and directly given. This, and this only, I understand the governor [Brown] to mean when he speaks of the power being an implied one. He raises no question as to the existence of the power, or its validity when rightfully exercised, but he maintains, as I do, that its exercise must be controlled by all other restrictions in the constitution bearing upon its exercise. Two of these are to be found in the words accompanying the delegation. It can never be exercised except in rebellion or invasion. Other restrictions are to be found in other parts of the constitution—in the amendments to the constitution adopted after the ratification of the words as above quoted. These amendments were made, as is expressly declared in the preamble to them, to add 'further declaratory and restrictive clauses,' to prevent 'misconstruction or abuse of the powers' previously delegated. To understand all the restrictions, therefore, thrown around the exercise of this power in the constitution, these additional 'restrictive clauses' must be read in conjunction with the original grant, whether that was made positively and directly, or by implication only. These restrictions, among other things, declare, that 'no person shall be deprived of life, liberty, or property, without due process of law,' and that the right of the people to be secure in their persons, houses, papers and effects, against *unreasonable* searches and seizures, shall not be violated, and no warrants shall issue but upon probable cause, supported by oath or affirmation, and particularly describing the place to be searched, and the person or thing to be seized.

"All admit that under the clause as it stands in the original grant, with the restrictions there set forth, the power can be rightfully exercised only in cases of rebellion or invasion. With these additional clauses, put in as further restrictions to prevent the abuse of powers previously delegated, how is this clause conferring the power to suspend the privilege of the writ of *habeas corpus*, now to be read? In this way, and in this way only:

> The privilege of the writ of *habeas corpus* shall not be suspended, unless when in cases of rebellion or invasion the public safety may require it. [And no person] shall be deprived of life, liberty, or property, without due process of law. [And further.] The right of the people to be secure in their persons, houses, papers and effects against unreasonable searches and seizures, shall not be violated, and no warrants shall issue but upon probable cause, supported by oath or affirmation, and particularly describing the place to be searched, and the persons or things to be seized.

"The attempted exercise of the power to suspend the privilege of the writ of *habeas corpus* in this act, is in utter disregard in the very face and teeth of these restrictions, as much so, as a like attempt in time of profound peace would be in disregard of the restrictions to cases of rebellion and invasion, as the constitution was originally adopted. It attempts to provide for depriving persons 'of liberty, without due process of law.' It attempts to annul and set at naught the great constitutional 'right' of the people, to be secure in their persons against 'unreasonable seizures.' It attempts to destroy and annihilate the bulwark of personal liberty, secured in our great chart to the humblest as well as the highest, that 'no warrants shall issue but upon probable cause, supported by oath or affirmation,' and 'particularly describing the person to be seized.' Nay, more, it attempts to change and transform the distribution of powers in our system of government. It attempts to deprive the judiciary department of its appropriate and legitimate functions, and to confer them upon the President, the secretary of war, and the general officer commanding the trans-Mississippi department, or rather to confer them entirely upon the

President, for those subordinates named in the act hold their places at his will, and in arrests under this act are to be governed by his orders. This, by the constitution, never can be done. Ours is not only a government of limited powers, but each department, the legislative, executive and judicial, are separate and distinct. The issuing of warrants, which are nothing but orders for arrests, against civilians or persons in civil life, is a judicial function. The President, under the constitution, has not the power to issue any such. As commander-in-chief of the land and naval forces, and the militia when in actual service, he may order arrests for trials before courts-martial, according to the rules and articles of war. But he is clothed with no such power over those not in the military service and not subject to the rules and articles of war. This act attempts to clothe him with judicial functions, and in a judicial character to do what no judge, under the constitution, can do: issue orders or warrants for arrest, by which persons are to be deprived of their liberty, imprisoned, immured in dungeons, it may be without any oath or affirmation, even as to the probable guilt of the party accused or charged with any of the offences or acts stated. This, under the constitution, in my judgment, cannot be done. Congress can confer no such power upon our chief magistrate. There is no such thing known in this country as political warrants, or *'lettres de cachet'* [an arbitrary order issued by a king]. This act attempts to institute this new order of things so odious to our ancestors, and so inconsistent with constitutional liberty.

"This act, therefore, is unconstitutional, not because Congress has not power to suspend the privilege of the writ of *habeas corpus*, but because they have no power to do the thing aimed at in this attempted exercise of it. Congress can suspend the privilege of the writ—the power is clear and unquestioned—neither is the power, as it stands, objectionable. Georgia, in the convention, voted against the clause conferring it in the constitution as originally adopted—that, perhaps, was a wise and prudent vote. But, with the restrictions subsequently adopted there can be no well grounded objection to it. It is, under existing restrictions, a wise power. In time of war, in cases of rebellion or invasion, it may often be necessary to exercise it—the public safety may require it. I am not prepared to say that the public safety may not require it now. I am not informed of the reasons which induced the President [Jefferson Davis] to ask the suspension of the privilege of the writ at this time, or Congress to undertake its suspension as provided in this act. I, however, know of no reasons that require it and have heard of none. But in the exercise of an undisputed power, they have attempted to do just what cannot be done—to authorize illegal and unconstitutional arrests. There can be no suspension of the writ, under our system of government, against unconstitutional arrests—there can be no suspension allowing, or with a view to permit and authorize, the seizure of persons without warrant issued by a judicial officer upon probable cause, supported by oath or affirmation—the whole constitution must be read together, and so read and construed as that every part and clause shall stand and have its proper effect under the restrictions of other clauses.

"If any conflict arises between clauses in the original and the amendments subsequently made, the original must yield to the amendments—as a will previously made always yields to the modifications of a codicil. Such, of course, was the condition of the old [U.S.] constitution with its amendments, when the States of this confederacy adopted it—and it was adopted by these States with the meaning, force and effect it then had. In construing, therefore, those parts of the old constitution which we adopted, we stand just where we should have stood, under like circumstances, under it. With these views it will clearly appear that, under our constitution, courts cannot be deprived of their right or be relieved of their duty to inquire into the legality of all arrests except in cases arising in the land and naval forces or in the militia, when in actual service—for the government of which a different provision is made in the constitution. Under a constitutional suspension of the privilege of the writ, all the courts could do, would be to see that the party was legally arrested and held—upon proper warrant—upon probable cause, supported by oath or affirmation setting forth a crime or some violation of law. Literally and truly, then, the only effect of a constitutional exercise of this power over the writ of *habeas corpus* by Congress is to deprive a person, after being legally confined, of the privilege of a discharge before trial, by giving bail, or on account of insufficiency of proof as to probable cause or other like grounds. This privilege only can be suspended, and not the writ itself. The words of the constitution are aptly chosen to express the purpose and extent to which a suspension can go in this country. With this view the power is a wise one. It can work no serious injury to the citizen and it sufficiently guards the public safety. The party against whom a grave accusation is brought, supported by oath, or affirmation, founded upon probable cause, must be held for trial, and if found to be guilty is to be punished according to the nature of his offence. The monstrous consequences of any other view of the subject are apparent. The exercise of the power by Congress may be either general or limited to special cases, as in this instance. If it had been general, under any other view, what would have been the condition of every citizen in the land? The weaker would have been completely in the power of the stronger, without remedy or redress. Any one in the community might seize, for any motive or for any purpose, any other, and confine him most wrongfully and shamefully. Combinations of several against a few might be formed for a like purpose, and there would be no remedy or redress against this species of licensed lawlessness. The courts would be closed—all personal security and personal safety would be swept away. Instead of a land of laws, the whole country would be no better than a Whitefriars domain—a perfect Alsatia. This would be the inevitable effect of the exercise of the power, by a general suspension, with any other view of the subject, than this presented. The same effects as to outrages upon personal rights must issue under a limited suspension confined to any specified cases under any other view. No such huge and enormous wrongs can ever spring from our constitution if it be rightly administered. So that the conclusion of the whole matter is well stated by the governor [Brown] in his late message, in the brief, comprehensive, but exact terms:

> 'The only suspension of the privilege of the writ of *habeas corpus* known to our constitution and compatible with the provisions already quoted, goes to the simple extent of preventing the release, under it, of persons whose arrests have been ordered, under constitutional warrants from judicial authority.'

"On this subject much light is to be derived from English history. Our whole system of constitutional liberty rests upon principles established by our Anglo-Saxon ancestors. But between their system and ours, there are several differences that should be noted and marked—and none more striking and fundamental than the difference between the two upon this subject. With them the right of personal security against illegal arrests, was wrested from the crown by the parliament, and established by magna charta, the bill of rights, the abolition of star chamber, and the grant of the great right of the writ of *habeas corpus*, which is the means of redress against violations of law, and other wrongs against rights secured and acknowledged. In the abolition of the court of star chamber, the power was taken from the king, his heirs and successors forever, and every member of his privy council, to make any arrest of any person for any offence or alleged crime, except by due process of law. By this act, the power of the king to issue warrants or orders of arrest, unsupported by oath or affirmation, setting forth probable cause, which before had been claimed as a royal prerogative, was taken away from him and his successors forever . The ruling monarch, Charles I, gave his consent to the act, and yielded the power. He afterward broke his pledge. Civil commotions ensued from this and other causes. He lost his head upon the block. The subsequent history of that strife between the people and the crown of England, on this and other matters, is not now pertinent to the object before us. Suffice it to say that it ended in the settlement, as it is termed, between the parliament and their new sovereigns, [King] William [III] and [Queen] Mary [II]—in 1688, 1689. In this settlement, all the ancient rights and liberties of the English people, including the right of the writ of *habeas corpus*, were reaffirmed and secured. Such were the liberties, inherited as a birthright, that our British ancestors brought with them to this continent. The principles established in England, after centuries of struggle and blood, formed the basis upon which the great structure of American constitutional liberty was erected. But the striking difference between their system and ours, to which I have alluded, and which should never be lost sight of, is that, with them, all power originally belonged to the crown. All rights and liberties were grants from the crown to the parliament, and through them to the people, while with us all power originally belonged to the people—and, essentially, still resides with them. They have appointed agents to perform the functions of government in the different departments, executive, judicial, and legislative, under the form of government set forth in the constitution, clothed with the exercise of certain delegated, specific and limited powers. In England it is competent for the parliament at any time to return to the crown all the powers heretofore extorted from their kings. They are not restrained, as our Congress is, by a want of power to do so on their part. They can repeal, any day, magna charta, the *habeas corpus* act, and the whole bill of rights, and render their ruling monarch as absolute as either of the Tudors or Stuarts ever claimed or wished to be. The principles of magna charta as to personal liberty, and the rights of the writ of *habeas corpus* to secure those rights, are put in our fundamental law, and cannot be violated by Congress, for their powers are limited, and they are themselves bound by the constitution. That the British people would ever submit to a surrender of their rights by parliament, no one can for a moment believe. But parliament claims to be omnipotent, and could make the surrender, if they chose to run the risk. Hence analogies between this country and that on the suspension of the writ of *habeas corpus*, and the effect of such suspension, either generally or specially, should be closely scanned. Even in England, so great is the regard for liberty, suspensions have been rare since the settlement of 1688-89. The writ was suspended there in 1715 and in 1745—and in 1788 it was suspended in Ireland, with the power conferred on the lord-lieutenant to make arrest. Under the system of government in England, the parliament could confer this power upon the crown, or the lord-lieutenant, or upon any other person they saw fit. Not so with our Congress, under our constitution. In criticisms upon the governor's message, these suspensions have been alluded to against the positions of the message. They are not in conflict at all. What the governor [Brown] states is that he is not aware of any

> 'instance in which the British king has ordered the arrest of any person in civil

life in any other manner than by judicial warrant issued by the established courts of the nation, or in which he has suspended, or attempted to suspend, the privilege of the writ of *habeas corpus*, since the bill of rights and the act of settlement passed in 1689.'

"He did not say that parliament had not suspended it, or that our Congress could not suspend it, in a proper way, but that even in England, where parliament was unrestrained, they had not, since the settlement, conferred upon the crown the power to make arrests, so far as he was aware.

"At this point I will briefly refer to the suspension by our Congress, alluded to the other night by the distinguished gentleman (Hon. A. H. Kenan), who lately represented this district; a gentleman whose remarks I listened to with a great deal of interest, and whose personal friendship I esteem so highly. He referred to the act of the confederate Congress, passed October 13, 1862, and asked—Why were there no objections made to that? This act he read. I have it before me. It provides that the

> President, during the present invasion, shall have the power to suspend the privileges of the writ of *habeas corpus* in any city, town, or military district, whenever, in his judgment, the public safety may require it; but such suspension shall apply only to arrests made by the authorities of the confederate government, or for offences against the same, [and in section 2nd, that] the President shall cause proper officers to investigate the cases of all persons so arrested, in order that they may be discharged if improperly detained, unless they can be speedily tried in due course of law. [The 3rd section limits the act to thirty days after the meeting of the next Congress.]

"The answer to the inquiry, why there was no noise made about this act, while there is so much made about the one lately passed, is twofold. In the first place, this act applied 'only to arrests made by the authorities of the confederate government'—'for offences against the same.' The proper authorities for issuing warrants to arrest, are the courts, whose duty it is to issue warrants for arrests whenever offences or crimes are charged upon oath or affirmation, stating probable cause. The section directing the President to cause 'proper officers to investigate the cases, etc.,' in its immediate connection with the proceeding, had nothing in it calculated to awaken, alarm, or excite objection, for by 'proper officers' all naturally supposed judicial officers only could be meant—judges who would or might act in discharging under writs of *habeas corpus*, if that privilege had not been suspended. In this connection, these words seemed naturally enough to have a meaning far different from what they have when taken from their context and put into this late act, in which it is clear enough they are there intended to apply to other than judicial officers. There was not then, nor now, any objection, as far as I am aware of, to the suspension of the privilege of the writ of *habeas corpus* in any city, town, or district, or generally throughout the country, if Congress really has good reasons to believe the public safety requires it, and if the power to suspend be constitutionally exercised. The objection to the late act is that it attempts to do what cannot constitutionally be done.

"But in the second place, in answer to the inquiry, why no noise was made about the act of October, 1862, I need only say, that upon the bare statement of the real and substantial objections to that act, it was admitted to be unconstitutional and void, because it attempted to confer the power to suspend the writ upon the President, when, in his judgment, the public safety required it in the localities embraced in its terms. Congress alone, under the constitution, has the power to suspend the privileges of the writ. They cannot confer this power upon the President or anybody else. This is now conclusively admitted both by Congress and the President in the late act, for it is set forth in the preamble, 'whereas, the power of suspending the privilege of said writ is vested solely in the Congress,' etc. This is an admission on the record that the other act was unconstitutional and void. But, to my mind, it is just as clear that Congress cannot confer upon the President, or any other officer but a judicial one, the power to issue orders or warrants for the arrest of persons in civil life as it was then, and on the passage of a similar act previously that they could not confer the power upon the President to suspend the privilege of the writ of *habeas corpus*. The late act is just as void as the previous ones, and for a like reason. In it Congress has attempted to do what they had not power to do. The first act on the subject was assented to on the 27th February, 1862. That attempted to confer on the President the power not only to suspend the privilege of the writ of *habeas corpus* in certain cities, towns, military districts, etc., but to declare martial law, etc. This soon after was amended. But no one can say that during the progress of these events I was silent. My sentiments upon the subject of martial law, against the unconstitutional usurpations of power, were proclaimed throughout the confederacy, as they are now, and will be proclaimed against the dangerous departures from principle in this act. Martial law has been abandoned, and I trust the departures from principle in this act will be, too. I speak upon these as I wrote upon those. I have no inclination to arraign the motives of those who disagree with me. Great principles are at stake, and I feel impelled by a high sense of duty, when my opinions are sought, to give them fully, clearly and earnestly.

"A few thoughts more upon the subject in another view. These relate to the objects and workings of the act, if it be sustained and carried out. You have been told that it affects none but the disloyal, none but traitors, or those who are no better than traitors, spies, bridge-burners, and the like, and you have been appealed to and asked, if any such are entitled to your sympathies? I affirm, and shall maintain before the world that this act affects and may wrongfully oppress as loyal and as good citizens and as true to our cause as ever trod the soil or breathed the air of the South. This I shall make so plain to you that no man will ever venture to gainsay or deny it. This long list of offences, set forth in such array, in the thirteen specifications, are, as I view them, but rubbish and verbiage, which tend to cover and hide what in its workings will be found to be the whole gist of the act. Whether such was the real object and intention of its framers and advocates, I know not. Against their motives or patriotism I have nothing to say. I take the act as I find it. The real gist of the whole of it lies, so far as appears upon its face, covered up in the fifth specification near the middle of the act. It is embraced in these words—'and attempts to avoid military service!'

"Here is a plain indisputable attempt to deny every citizen in this broad land the right, if ordered into service, to have the question whether he is liable to military duty under the laws tried and adjudicated by the courts! Whether such was the real object and intention of those who voted for the bill, I know not, but such would be its undeniable effect if sustained and enforced. A man over fifty years of age, with half a dozen sons in the field, who has done every thing in his power for the cause from the beginning of the war, may, under instructions from the secretary of war, be arrested by the sub-enrolling officer and ordered to camp, upon the assumed ground that, in point of fact, he is under fifty. Under this law, if it be law, he would be without remedy or redress. A case to illustrate [this] by occurred within my own knowledge last fall. Orders were issued to examine the census returns of 1860, as to the ages of persons, and instructions given to sub-enrolling officers to be governed as to the age of parties by those returns. In the case alluded to by the census returns, the party was not forty-five at the time of arrest. He protested that he had not made the census returns himself—that the return was erroneous, it was not given in under oath—that he was able to prove by evidence entirely satisfactory, that he was over forty-five and not liable under the law as it then stood to military service. His privilege of the writ of *habeas corpus*—his right to have this question of fact and law settled by the courts—was not then suspended, and he was discharged. But what would be his situation, and that of all others in like circumstances, if this act be held to be law? It is said that the act affects none but the disloyal, and that no good law-abiding man can justly complain of it! As I view it, its main effect is to close the doors of justice against thousands of citizens, good and true, who may appeal to the courts for their legal rights. Take the case of those who availed themselves of the law to put in substitutes—some for one motive, and some for another—some, doubtless, for not only good but patriotic motives, believing that they could render the country more service at home than in the field. I know one who has put in two, one when the call was for those up to thirty-five years of age, the other when the call was to forty-five. One of these substitutes was an alien, whose services could not have been commanded by the government, and who is now at Charleston, and has been during the whole siege of that place. This man, who put in these two substitutes, remained at home most usefully employed in producing provisions for the army. All his surplus went that way, while he had two men, abler bodied than he was, fighting for him in the field. Who would say that such a man is disloyal to the cause, if, believing in his heart that he was not liable under his contract, as he supposed, with his government, he should appeal to the courts to decide the question whether he is liable under the law or not? As to the law allowing substitutes in the first instance, and then the law abrogating or annulling it, and calling the principals into the field, I have nothing to say. What I maintain is, that it is the great constitutional right of any and every party affected by the last of these acts on the subject, to have the question of his legal liability judicially determined if he chooses, and then as a good law-abiding citizen act accordingly.

"Take another illustration of the practical workings of the act. Congress by law exempted from conscription such State officers as the legislatures of the respective States might designate as proper to be retained for State purposes. At your last session you, by resolution, designated all the civil and militia officers of the State. A late order has been issued by [Confederate] General [Samuel] Cooper, as is seen in the papers, doubtless under order from the secretary of war, to enrol and send to camp a large number of these officers—amongst others, justices of the peace, tax receivers and collectors. This order is clearly against the law of Congress and your solemn resolution. It is in direct antagonism to the decision of the Supreme Court of this State, in the very case in which they sustained the power of Congress to raise troops by conscription, but in which they held that the power was limited, and that the civil officers of the States could not be constitutionally conscripted. I use the word *conscripted* purposely—I know there is no such word in the English language—neither is there any such word as *conscribe*, the one usually in vogue now a days. A new word had to be coined for a process or mode of raising armies, unheard of and undreamed of by our ancestors, and I choose to coin one which best expresses my idea of it. But under this order of General Cooper, is it not the right of these officers, is it not the right of the State, to have the question of their liability to conscription determined by the judiciary? Is it not the high duty of Congress to compel the secretary of war and General Cooper to abide by that decision and to obey their own laws, instead of attempting to close the doors of the courts against the adjudication of all such matters that come within the sphere of their constitutional duties.

"Again, Congress by the last section of the first conscript act, declared that all who were or should be subject to it might, previous to enrolment, volunteer in any companies then in the service. Notwithstanding this express law of Congress, securing the right of any person liable to conscription, to volunteer in any company then in the service previous to enrolment, General Cooper has issued an order, by direction of the secretary of war, doubtless, denying this right to volunteer in any company then in existence, unless the number in such company is less than sixty-four men. Under this illegal order a number of as brave, gallant, chivalrous, noble spirited youths, as ever went forth to battle for their country and peril their lives for constitutional liberty, will be deprived of their birthright—the right to have questions of law, affecting their liberty, determined by the courts—if this act, closing courts against them, shall be held to be valid! Tell me not that this act affects none but traitors, spies, and the disloyal. I heard not long since of a case in Albany; a father carried his son to the district enrolling officer; he had just arrived at the age when he was liable to conscription; he never wished him to go to the war as a conscript. His older brothers had gone before him, they went out early in the war as volunteers, and then formed part of that living wall of freemen which still stands between us and a ruthless foe. He told the enrolling officer, in substance, that he had brought his boy, the Benjamin of his heart, as another offering on the altar of his country. He was going as a volunteer under that clause of the act alluded to; he had selected the company to which his brothers belonged. He was told this could not be allowed. At this, the father was greatly surprised and mortified, as may be readily understood; he insisted upon the rights of his son. Great as his surprise was at first, however, greater was it still to be. The son was ordered to jail, to be sent to the camp of instruction, to be assigned to any company his officers might choose. The high spirited youth, scorning conscription, offering himself as a volunteer, asking nothing but his legal rights, instead of being sent on with cheers by the crowd, and a father's parting blessing, was sent to jail as a felon!

"Can any one say that this was not a most shameful outrage?

"It is, however, but one of a thousand cases like it that may occur, and probably will occur, should this law be held to be constitutional; and if the doors of the courts are to be closed against all who may be ordered to the military service, without any regard to law. I have here two letters which will further illustrate how this act will work. They are both addressed to the governor. One is from a Mr. Samuel H. Parker, written in Charleston jail."

[Reporter's note: "Here Mr. Stephens read the letter, stating that the writer was a native Georgian. That he lived in Whitfield county. That he was forty-seven years of age, as the record would show, then in Whitfield county. That he was at his home with his wife, (who was then sick,) with ten small children, on the 27th of February, of this year, when a party on horses came and arrested him, and carried him to Dalton. And from Dalton, he was carried to Atlanta. He protested that he was over age, and not liable to military duty; that he was forty-seven years old. He was told that that was the right age to make a soldier in South Carolina, and he was sent on to Charleston, where he was in jail. He appealed to the governor of his native State, and the State of his residence, to have justice done him."]

[Stephens continues:] "Of this Mr. Parker, I know nothing, except what is stated in this letter. It may be false, and yet it may be true. If true, justice ought to be done to a man so greatly outraged and wronged. But whether true or false, the courts ought never to be closed against an inquiry into the facts, and never will be, so long as personal security has any protection in this country.

"The other letter is from the Hon. John Oats, a member of this House, from the county of Murray. It is dated the 11th of this month, the day after the meeting of this session."

[Reporter's note: "Here Mr. Stephens read Mr. Oats' letter, stating that he was detained at Atlanta, under very painful circumstances. His oldest son, who had been in the army, was subject to epilepsy, and had been discharged in consequence. That afterward, he had been carried before a board of physicians, who pronounced his case incurable, and he was given a certificate of final discharge, on the grounds of permanent disability. That on the morning Mr. Oats left home for Milledgeville, the provost-guard at Dalton, went to his house at Spring Place, and carried his son off to Dalton. They carried him from there to Cartersville, to Captain Starr, the enrolling officer for the tenth Congressional district, and he, knowing all about his case, sent him back to Dalton, stating in writing on the order, that he was sent there under, that according to law, and his orders from the war department, he was not liable to conscription. That on his return to Dalton, they put him in irons, and assigned him to Charleston, to go into the fortifications, and that he expected him in Atlanta that evening. He was waiting with the best counsel he could get, to see if there was any virtue in the writ of *habeas corpus*. He asked that the governor would get some member to procure for him leave of absence from the House."]

[Stephens continues:] "Well for Mr. Oats and his afflicted son, there is some virtue yet in the writ of *habeas corpus*.

"But what virtue would be in it, if it is denied under this act, to all who attempt to avoid military service. Nothing could induce me to read such letters on such an occasion, but a sense of duty, to show you what will be the state of things all over the country, under the operation of such a law, when orders are issued for its enforcement, and to put you on your guard, against the flippant phrase that the act will effect none but traitors, spies, and disloyal people. Had it been in operation, had the courts regarded it, Mr. Oats' son, who had served his country faithfully, as long as he was able, might now have been beyond remedy, beyond redress, and beyond hope. Will you say, can you say, that the courts ought to be, or can be closed, against such monstrous wrongs? Will you not rather put upon the attempt to do it, the seal of your unqualified condemnation? Tell me not to put confidence in the President. That he will never abuse the power attempted to be lodged in his hands. The abuses may not be by the President. He will not execute the military orders that will be given. This will necessarily devolve upon subordinates, scattered all over the country, from the Potomac to the Rio Grande. He would have to possess two superhuman attributes, to prevent abuses—omniscience and omnipresence.

"These things our forefathers knew, and hence they threw around the personal security of the free citizens of this country a firmer, safer, surer protection than confidence in any man, against abuses of power, even when exercised under his own eye and by himself. That protection is the shield of the constitution. See to it that you do not in an evil hour tear this shield off and cast it away, or permit others to do it, lest in a day you wot [archaic: "know"] not of, you sorely repent it.

"Enough has been said, without dwelling longer upon this point, to show, without the possibility of a doubt, that the act does affect others, and large classes of others, than spies, traitors, bridge-burners, and disloyal persons—that the very gist of the act, whatever may have been the intent or the motive, will operate most wrongfully and oppressively on as loyal, as patriotic, and as true men as ever inherited a freeman's birthright under a southern sky. You have also seen that there is and can be no necessity for the passage of such an act, even if it were constitutional, in the case of spies, traitors, or conspirators. For, if there be a traitor in the confederacy—if such a monster exists—if any well grounded suspicion is entertained that any such exists, why not have him legally arrested, by judicial warrant, upon oath or affirmation, setting forth probable cause, and then he can be held under a constitutional suspension of the privileges of the writ—he can be tried, and if found guilty, punished. What more can the public safety by possibility require? Why dispense with the oath? Why dispense with judicial warrants? Why put it in the power of any man on earth to order the arrest of another on a simple charge, to which nobody will swear? Who is safe under such a law? Who knows, when he goes forth, when or whether he shall ever return? The President [Davis], according to this act, is to have power to arrest and imprison whoever he pleases, upon a bare charge, made, perhaps, by an enemy of disloyalty, the party making the charge not being required to swear to it! Who, I repeat, is safe, or would be, under such a law? What were the real objects of the act, in these clauses, as to treason, disloyalty, and the others, I do not know. To me it seems to be unreasonable to suppose that it was to reach real traitors and persons guilty of the offences stated. For that object could have been easily accomplished without any such extraordinary power. I was not at Richmond when the act passed. I heard none of the discussions, and knew none of the reasons assigned, either by the President in asking it, or the members or senators who voted for it. I was at home, prostrate with disease, from which I have not yet recovered, and by reason of which I address you with so much feebleness on this occasion. But I have heard that one object was to control certain elections and expected assemblages in North Carolina, to put a muzzle upon certain presses, and a bit in the mouth of certain speakers in that State. If this be so, I regard it the more dangerous to public liberty. I know nothing of the politics of North Carolina—nothing of the position of her leading public men. If there be traitors there, let them be constitutionally arrested, tried, and punished. No fears need be indulged of bare error there, or anywhere else, if reason is left free to combat it. The idea is incredible, that a majority of the people of that gallant and noble old State, which was foremost in the war of the revolution in her ever memorable Mecklenburg declaration of Independence can, if let alone, ever be induced to prove themselves so recreant to the principles of their fathers as to abandon our cause and espouse the despotism of the North. Her people, ahead of all the colonies, first flaunted in the breeze the flag of Independence and State sovereignty. She cannot be the first to abandon it—no, never! I cannot believe it! If her people were really so inclined, however, we could not prevent it by force—we could not, under the constitution, if we would, and we ought not if we could. Ours is a government founded upon the consent of sovereign States, and will be itself destroyed by the very act whenever it attempts to maintain or perpetuate its existence by force over its respective members. The surest way to check any inclination in North Carolina to quit our sisterhood, if any such really exist even to the most limited extent amongst her people, is to show them that the struggle is continued as it was begun, for the maintenance of constitutional liberty. If, with this great truth ever before them, a majority of her people should prefer despotism to liberty, I would say to her, as to a 'wayward sister, depart in peace.' I want to see no Maryland this side of the Potomac.

"Another serious objection to the measure, showing its impolicy, is the effect it will have upon our cause abroad. I have never looked to foreign intervention, or early recognition, and do not now. European governments have no sympathy with either side in this struggle. [Note: Stephens is partially in error here. Numerous European statesmen, as well as the upper classes of both England and France, and even Pope Pius IX at Rome, were all in great sympathy with Davis and the South. At the same time, the lower classes of Europe sided primarily with Lincoln and the North. L.S.] They are rejoiced to see professed republicans cutting each other's throats, and the failure, as they think, of the great experiment of self-government on this continent. They saw that the North went into despotism immediately on the separation of the South, and their fondest hopes and expectations are that the same destiny awaits us. This has usually been the fate of republics. This is the sentiment of all the governments in Europe. But we have friends there, as you heard last night, in the eloquent remarks of the gentleman [Lucius Q. C. Lamar] who addressed you on our foreign relations, and who has lately returned from those countries. Those friends are anxiously and hopefully watching the issue of the present conflict. In speeches, papers, and reviews they are defending our cause. No argument used by them heretofore has been more effectual than the contrast drawn between the federals [Liberals] and the confederates [Conservatives] upon the subject of the writ of *habeas corpus*. Here [in the American South], notwithstanding our dangers and perils, the military has always been kept subordinate to the civil authorities. Here all the landmarks of English liberty have been preserved and maintained, while at the North scarcely a vestige of them is left. There [in the North], instead of courts of justice with open doors, the country is dotted all over with prisons and bastiles. No better argument in behalf of a people struggling for constitutional liberty could have been presented to arouse sympathy in our favor. It showed that we were passing through a fiery furnace for a great cause, and passing through unscathed. It showed that whatever may be the state of things at the North, that at the South at least the great light of the principles of self-government, civil and religious liberty, established on this continent by our ancestors, which was looked to with encouragement and hope by the down-trodden of all nations, was not yet extinguished, but was still burning brightly in the hands of their southern sons, even burning the more brightly from the intensity of the heat of the conflict in which we are engaged. To us, in deed and in truth, is committed the hopes of the world as to the capacity and ability of man for self-government. Let us see to it that these hopes and expectations do not fail. Let us prove ourselves equal to the high mission before us.

"One other view only: that relates to the particularly dangerous tendency of this act in the present state of the country, and the policy indicated by Congress. Conscription has been extended to embrace all between seventeen and fifty years of age. It cannot be possible that the intention and object of that measure was really to call and keep in the field all between those ages. The folly and ruinous consequences of such a policy is too apparent. Details are to be made, and must be made, to a large extent. The effect and the object of this measure, therefore, was not to raise armies or procure soldiers, but to put all the population of the country between those ages under military law. Whatever the object was, the effect is to put much the larger portion of the labor of the country, both white and slave, under the complete control of the [Confederate] President. Under this system almost all the useful and necessary occupations of life will be completely under the control of one man. No one between the ages of seventeen and fifty can tan your leather, make your shoes, grind your grain, shoe your horse, lay your plough, make your wagon, repair your harness, superintend your farm, procure your salt, or perform any other of the necessary vocations of life, (except teachers, preachers, and physicians, and a very few others,) without permission from the President. This is certainly an extraordinary and a dangerous power. In this connection take in view this *habeas corpus* suspension act, by which it has been shown the attempt is made to confer upon him the power to order the arrest and imprisonment of any man, woman or child in the confederacy, on the bare charge, unsupported by oath, of any of the acts for which arrests are allowed to be made. Could the whole country be more completely under the power and control of one man, except as to life or limb? Could dictatorial powers be more complete? In this connection consider, also, the strong appeals that have been made for some time past, by leading journals, openly for a dictator. Coming events often cast their shadows before. Could art or ingenuity have devised a shorter or a surer cut to that end, for all practical purposes, than the whole policy adopted by the last Congress, and now before you for consideration? As to the objects, or motives, or patriotism of those who adopted that policy, that is not the question. The presentation of the case as it stands is what your attention is called to. Nor is the probability of the abuse of the power the question. Some, doubtless, think it for the best interests of the country to have a dictator. Such are not unfrequently to be met with whose intelligence, probity, and general good character in private life are not to be questioned, however much their wisdom, judgment, and principles may be deplored. In such times, when considering the facts as they exist, and looking at the policy indicated in all its bearings, the most ill-timed, delusive, and dangerous words that can be uttered are, can you not trust the President? Have you not confidence in him that he will not abuse the powers thus confided in him? To all such questions my answer is, without any reflection or imputation against our present chief magistrate, that the measure of my confidence in him, and all other public officers, is the constitution. To the question of whether I would not or cannot trust him with these high powers not conferred by the constitution, my answer is the same that I gave to one who submitted a plan for a dictatorship to me some months ago:

> '*I am utterly opposed to every thing looking to, or tending toward a dictatorship in this country. Language would fail to give utterance to my inexpressible repugnance at the bare suggestion of such a lamentable catastrophe. There is no man living, and not one of the illustrious dead, whom, if now living, I would so trust.*' [Emphasis added, L.S.]

"In any and every view, therefore, I look upon this *habeas corpus* suspension act as unwise, impolitic, unconstitutional, and dangerous to public liberty.

"But you have been asked what can you do? You can do much. If you believe the act to be unconstitutional, you can and ought so to declare your deliberate judgment to be. What can you do? What did Kentucky and Virginia do in 1798-99, under similar circumstances? What did [Thomas] Jefferson do, and what did [James] Madison do, and what did the legislators of those States then do?

"Though a war was then threatening with France—though armies were being raised—though [George] Washington was called from his retirement to take command as lieutenant-general—though it was said then as now, that all discussions of even obnoxious measures of Congress would be hurtful to the public cause, they did not hesitate, by solemn resolves by the legislatures, to declare the alien and sedition laws unconstitutional and utterly void. Those acts of Congress, in my judgment, were not more clearly unconstitutional, or more dangerous to liberty, than this act now under review. What can you do? You can invoke its repeal, and ask the government officials and the people in the meantime, to let the question of constitutionality be submitted to the courts, and both sides to abide by the decision. Some seem to be of the opinion, that those who oppose this act are for a counter-revolution. No such thing; I am for no counter-revolution. The object is to keep the present one, great in its aims and grand in its purposes, upon the right track—the one on which it was started, and that on which alone it can attain noble objects and majestic achievements. The surest way to prevent a counter-revolution, is for the State to speak out and declare her opinions upon this subject. For as certain as day succeeds night, the people of this confederacy will never live long in peace and quiet under any government with the principles of this act settled as its established policy, and held to be in conformity with the provisions of its fundamental law. The action of the Virginia legislature in 1799, saved the old government, beyond question, from a counter and a bloody revolution; kept it on the right track for sixty years afterward, in its unparelleled career of growth, prosperity, development, progress, happiness, and renown. *All our present troubles, North and South, sprang from violations of those great constitutional principles therein set forth.* [Emphasis added, L.S.]

"Let no one, therefore, be deterred from performing his duty on this occasion by the cry of counter-revolution, nor by the cry that it is the duty of all, in this hour of peril, to support the government. Our government is composed of executive, legislative and judicial departments, under the constitution. He most truly and faithfully supports the government who supports and defends the constitution. Be not misled by this cry, or that you must not say any thing against the administration, or you will injure the cause. This is the argument of the preacher, who insisted that his derelictions should not be exposed, because if they were, it would injure his usefulness as a minister. Derelict ministers are not the cause. Listen to no such cry. And let no one be influenced by that other cry, of the had effect such discussions and such action will have upon *our gallant citizen soldiers in the field. I know something of the feeling of these men. I have witnessed their hardships, their privations, and their discomforts in camp. I have witnessed and ministered to their wants and sufferings from disease and wounds, in hospitals. I know something of the sentiments that actuated the great majority of them, when they quit home, with all its endearments, and went out to this war*—not as mercenaries or human machines, but as intelligent, high-minded, noble-spirited gentlemen, who were proud of their birthright as freemen, and 'who knowing their rights,' dared maintain them, at any and every cost and sacrifice. The old Barons who extorted Magna Charta from their oppressor and wrongdoer by a resort to arms, did not present a grander spectacle for the admiration of the world when they went forth to their work, thoroughly imbued with a sense of the right for the right's sake, than this gallant band of patriots did when they went forth to this war [against Lincoln], inspired with no motive but a thorough devotion to and ardent attachment for constitutional liberty. To defend this and maintain it inviolate for themselves and those who should come after them, was their sole object. Their ancient rights, usages, institutions, and liberties were threatened by an insolent foe [liberal Yankees], who had trampled the constitution of our common [Southern] ancestors under foot. They and we all had quit the Union, when the rights of all of us were no longer respected under it, but *we had rescued the constitution—the ark of the covenant—and this is what they went forth to defend. These were the sentiments with which your armies were raised, as if by magic. These are the sentiments with which re-enlistments for the war have been made. These are the sentiments with which your ranks would have been filled to the last* man whose services can be relied upon in action if conscription had never been resorted to. You cannot, therefore, send these gallant defenders of constitutional liberty, a more cheering message than that, while they are battling for their rights and the common rights of all in the field, you are keeping sacred watch, and guard over the same in the public councils. They will enter the fight with renewed vigor, from the assurance that their toil, and sacrifice and blood will not be in vain, but that when the strife is over and independence is acknowledged, it will not be a bare name, a shadow and a mockery, but that with it they and their children after them shall enjoy that liberty for which they now peril all. Next to this, the most encouraging message you could send them is, that while all feel that the brunt of the fight must be borne by them, and the only sure hope of success is in the prowess of their arms, yet every possible and honorable effort will be made by the civil departments of the government to terminate the struggle by negotiation and adjustment upon the principles for which they entered the contest. [Emphasis added, L.S.]

"Gentlemen, I have addressed you longer than I expected to be able to do. My strength will not allow me to say more. I do not know that I shall ever address you again, or see you again. Great events have passed since, standing in this place, three years ago, I addressed your predecessors on a similar request, upon the questions then immediately preceding our present troubles. Many who were then with us have since passed away—some in the ordinary course of life, while many of them have fallen upon the battle-field, offering up their lives in the great cause in which we are engaged. Still greater events may be just ahead of us. What fate or fortune awaits you or me, in the contingencies of the times, is unknown to us all. We may meet again, or we may not. But as a parting remembrance, a lasting memento, to be engraven on your memories and your hearts, *I warn you against that most insidious enemy which approaches with her siren song, 'Independence first and liberty afterward.' It is a fatal delusion. Liberty is the animating spirit, the soul of our system of government, and like the soul of man, when once lost it is lost forever. There is for it, at least, no redemption, except through blood. Never for a moment permit yourselves to look upon liberty, that constitutional liberty which you inherited as a birthright, as subordinate to independence. The one was resorted to to secure the other. Let them ever be held and cherished as objects co-ordinate, co-existent, co-equal, co-eval, and forever inseparable. Let them stand together 'through weal and through woe,' and if such be our fate, let them and us all go down together in a common ruin. Without liberty, I would not turn upon my heel for independence. I scorn all independence which does not secure liberty. I warn you also against another fatal delusion, commonly dressed up in the fascinating language of, 'If we are to have a master, who would not prefer to have a southern one to a northern one?' Use no such language. Countenance none such. Evil communications are as corrupting in politics as in morals.* [Emphasis added, L.S.]

". . . *I would not turn upon my heel to choose between masters. I was not born to acknowledge a master from either the North or South. I shall never choose between candidates for that office. Shall never degrade the right of suffrage in such an election. I have no wish or desire to live after the degradation of my country, and have no intention to survive its liberties, if life be the necessary sacrifice of their maintenance to the utmost of my ability, to the bitter end. As for myself, give me liberty as secured in the constitution with all its guaranties, amongst which is the sovereignty of Georgia, or give me death. This is my motto while living, and I want no better epitaph when I am dead.* [Emphasis added, L.S.]

"Senators and representatives! the honor, the rights, the dignity, the glory of Georgia, are in your hands! See to it as faithful sentinels upon the watchtower, that no harm or detriment come to any of those high and sacred trusts, while committed to your charge." [Immense cheers and applause.][100]

Stephens gave the following speech before the General Assembly of the state of Georgia on February 22, 1866, George Washington's birthday. Against his own wishes he had been elected to the office of Georgia state senator by his friends and colleagues. Lincoln's War was now nearly a year in the past and the Yankees' vengeful, restrictive, punishing, and intentionally humiliating policy of "Reconstruction" was in full swing across the former Confederate states. Stephens used his address to console and encourage his fellow Southerners through an extremely trying time, one that would turn out to be a twelve year period (1865-1877) in which the South was stripped of her rights and placed under harsh military rule by the vindictive meddlesome North:

☛ "Gentlemen of the Senate and House of Representatives: I appear before you in answer to your call. This call, coming in the imposing form it does, and under the circumstances it does, requires a response from me. You have assigned to me a very high, a very honorable and responsible position. This position you know I did not seek. Most willingly would I have avoided it; and nothing but an extraordinary sense of duty could have induced me to yield my own disinclinations and aversions to your wishes and judgment in the matter. For this unusual manifestation of esteem and confidence, I return you my profoundest acknowledgments of gratitude. Of one thing only can I give you any assurance, and that is, if I shall be permitted to discharge the trusts thereby imposed, they will be discharged with a singleness of purpose to the public good.

"*The great object with me now, is to see a restoration, if possible, of peace, prosperity, and constitutional liberty in this once happy, but now disturbed, agitated, and distracted country. To this end, all my energies and efforts, to the extent of their powers, will be devoted.* [Emphasis added, L.S.]

"You ask my views on the existing state of affairs; our duties at the present, and the prospects of the future? This is a task from which, under other circumstances, I might very well shrink. He who ventures to speak, and to give counsel and advice in times of peril, or disaster, assumes no enviable position. Far be that rashness from me which sometimes prompts the forward to rush in where angels might fear to tread. In responding, therefore, briefly to your inquiries, I feel, I trust, the full weight and magnitude of the subject. It involves the welfare of millions now living, and that of many more millions who are to come after us. I am also fully impressed with the consciousness of the inconceivably small effect of what I shall say upon the momentous results involved in the subject itself.

"It is with these feelings I offer my mite of counsel at your request. And in the outset of the undertaking, limited as it is intended to be to a few general ideas only, well may I imitate an illustrious example in invoking aid from on high; 'that I may say nothing on this occasion which may compromit the rights, the honor, the dignity, or best interests of my country.' I mean specially the rights, honor, dignity, and best interests of the people of Georgia. With their sufferings, their losses, their misfortunes, their bereavements, and their present utter prostration, my heart is in deepest sympathy.

"We have reached that point in our affairs at which the great question before us is—'To be or not to be?'—and if to be—How? Hope, ever springing in the human breast, prompts, even under the greatest calamities and adversities, never to despair. Adversity is a severe school, a terrible crucible; both for individuals and communities. We are now in this school, this crucible, and should bear in mind that it is never negative in its action. It is always positive. It is ever decided in its effects, one way or the other. It either makes better or worse. It either brings out unknown vices, or arouses dormant virtues. In morals, its tendency is to make saints or reprobates—in politics to make heroes or desperadoes. The first indication of its working for good, to which hope looks anxiously, is the manifestation of a full consciousness of its nature and extent; and the most promising grounds of hope for possible good from our present troubles, or of things with us getting better instead of worse, is the evident general realization, on the part of our people, of their present situation: of the evils now upon them, and of the greater ones [under so-called 'Reconstruction'] still impending. These it is not my purpose to exaggerate if I could; that would be useless; nor to lessen or extenuate; that would be worse than useless. All fully understand and realize them. They feel them. It is well they do.

"Can these evils upon us—the absence of law; the want of protection and security of person and property, without which civilization cannot advance—be removed? or can those greater ones which threaten our very political existence, be averted? These are the questions.

"It is true we have not the control of all the remedies, even if these questions could be satisfactorily answered. Our fortunes and destiny are not entirely in our own hands. Yet there are some things that we may, and can, and ought, in my judgment, to do, from which no harm can come, and from which some good may follow, in bettering our present condition. States and communities, as well as individuals, when they have done the best they can in view of surrounding circumstances, with all the lights they have before them—let results be what they may—can at least enjoy the consolation—no small recompense that—of having performed their duty, and of having a conscience void of offence before God and man. This, if no more valuable result, will, I trust, attend the doing of what I propose.

"The first great duty, then, I would enjoin at this time, is the exercise of the simple, though difficult and trying, but nevertheless indispensable quality of patience. Patience requires of those afflicted to bear and to suffer with fortitude whatever ills may befall them. This is often, and especially is it the case with us now, essential for their ultimate removal by any instrumentalities whatever. We are in the condition of a man with a dislocated limb, or a broken leg, and a very bad compound fracture at that. How it became broken should not be with him a question of so much importance, as how it can be restored to health, vigor, and strength. This requires of him, as the highest duty to himself, to wait quietly and patiently in splints and bandages, until nature resumes her active powers—until the vital functions perform their office. The knitting of the bones and the granulation of the flesh require time; perfect quiet and repose, even under the severest pain, is necessary. It will not do to make too great haste to get well; an attempt to walk too soon will only make the matter worse. We must or ought now, therefore, in a similar manner to discipline ourselves to the same or like degree of patience. *I know the anxiety and restlessness of the popular mind to be fully on our feet again—to walk abroad as we once did—to enjoy once more the free outdoor air of heaven, with the perfect use of all our limbs. I know how trying it is to be denied representation in Congress, while we are paying our proportion of the taxes—how annoying it is to be even partially under military rule—and how injurious it is to the general interest and business of the country to be without post-offices and mail communications; to say nothing of divers other matters on the long list of our present inconveniences and privations. All these, however, we must patiently bear and endure for a season.* With quiet and repose we may get well—may get once more on our feet again. One thing is certain, that bad humor, ill-temper, exhibited either in restlessness or grumbling, will not hasten it. [Emphasis added, L.S.]

"Next to this, *another great duty we owe to ourselves is the exercise of a liberal spirit of forbearance amongst ourselves.* [Emphasis added, L.S.]

"The first step toward local or general harmony, is the banishment from our breasts of every feeling and sentiment calculated to stir the discords of the past. Nothing could be more injurious or mischievous to the future of this country, than the agitation, at present, of questions that divided the people anterior to, or during the existence of the late war. On no occasion, and especially in the bestowment of office, ought such differences of opinion in the past ever to be mentioned, either for or against any one, otherwise equally entitled to confidence. These ideas or sentiments of other times and circumstances are not the germs from which hopeful organizations can now arise. Let all differences of opinion, touching errors, or supposed errors, of the head or heart, on the part of any, in the past, growing out of these matters, be at once, in the deep ocean of oblivion forever buried. Let there be no criminations or recriminations on account of acts of other days. No canvassing of past conduct or motives. Great disasters are upon us and upon the whole country, and without inquiring how these originated, or at whose door the fault should be laid, let us now as common sharers of common misfortunes, on all occasions, consult only as to the best means, under the circumstances as we find them, to secure the best ends toward future amelioration. Good government is what we want. This should be the leading desire and the controlling object with all; and I need not assure you, if this can be obtained, that our desolated fields, our towns and villages, and cities now in ruins, will soon—like the Phoenix—rise again from their ashes; and all our waste places will again, at no distant day, blossom as the rose. [Emphasis added, L.S.]

"This view should also be borne in mind, that whatever differences of opinion existed before the late fury of the war, they sprung mainly from differences as to the best means to be used, and the best line of policy to be pursued, to secure the great controlling object of all—which was Good Government. Whatever may be said of the loyalty or disloyalty of any, in the late most lamentable conflict of arms, I think I may venture safely to say, that there was, on the part of the great mass of the people of Georgia, and of the entire South, no disloyalty to the principles of the constitution of the United States. To that system of representative government; of delegated and limited powers; that establishment in a new phase, on this continent, of all the essentials of England's Magna Charta, for the protection and security of life, liberty and property; with the additional recognition of the principle as a fundamental truth, that all political power resides in the people. With us it was simply a question as to where our allegiance was due in the maintenance of these principles—which authority was paramount in the last resort—State or federal. As for myself, I can affirm that no sentiment of disloyalty to these great principles of self-government, recognized and embodied in the constitution of the United States, ever beat or throbbed in breast or heart of mine. To their maintenance my whole soul was ever enlisted, and to this end my whole life has heretofore been devoted, and will continue to be the rest of my days—God willing. In devotion to these principles, I yield to no man living. This much I can say for myself; may I not say the same for you and for the great mass of the people of Georgia, and for the great mass of the people of the entire South? *Whatever differences existed amongst us, arose from differences as to the best and surest means of securing these great ends, which was the object of all. It was with this view and this purpose secession was tried. That has failed. Instead of bettering our condition, instead of establishing our liberties upon a surer foundation, we have, in the war that ensued, come well nigh losing the whole of the rich inheritance with which we set out.* [Emphasis added, L.S.]

"This is one of the sad realizations of the present. *In this, too, we are but illustrating the teachings of history. Wars, and civil wars especially, always menace liberty; they seldom advance it; while they usually end in its entire overthrow and destruction. Ours stopped just short of such a catastrophe. Our only alternative now is, either to give up all hope of constitutional liberty, or to retrace our steps, and to look for its vindication and maintenance in the forums of reason and justice, instead of on the arena of arms—in the courts and halls of legislation, instead of on the fields of battle.* [Emphasis added, L.S.]

"I am frank and candid in telling you right here, that our surest hopes, in my judgment, of these ends, are in the restoration policy of the President of the United States [Andrew Johnson]. I have little hope for liberty—little hope for the success of the great American experiment of self-government—but in the success of the present efforts for the restoration of the States to their former practical relations in a common government, under the constitution of the United States.

"We are not without an encouraging example on this line in the history of the mother country—in the history of our ancestors—from whom we derived, in great measure, the principles to which we are so much devoted. The truest friends of liberty in England once, in 1642, abandoned the forum of reason, and appealed, as we did, to the sword, as the surest means, in their judgment, of advancing their cause. This was after they had made great progress, under the lead of [Sir Edward] Coke, [John] Hampden, [Viscount] Falkland and others, in the advancement of liberal principles. Many usurpations had been checked; many of the prerogatives of the crown had been curtailed; the petition of right had been sanctioned; ship-money had been abandoned; courts-martial had been done away with; *habeas corpus* had been re-established; high courts of commission and star-chamber had been abolished; many other great abuses of power had been corrected, and other reforms established. But not satisfied with these, and not satisfied with the peaceful working of reason, to go on in its natural sphere, the denial of the sovereignty of the crown was pressed by the too ardent reformers upon Charles the First. All else he had yielded—this he would not. The sword was appealed to, to settle the question; a civil war was the result; great valor and courage were displayed on both sides; men of eminent virtue and patriotism fell in the sanguinary and fratricidal conflict; the king was deposed and executed; a commonwealth proclaimed. But the end [result] was the reduction of the people of England to a worse state of oppression than they had been in for centuries. They retraced their steps. After nearly twenty years of exhaustion and blood, and the loss of the greater portion of the liberties enjoyed by them before, they, by almost unanimous consent, called for restoration. The restoration came. Charles the Second ascended the throne, as unlimited a monarch as ever ruled the empire. Not a pledge was asked or a guarantee given, touching the concessions of the royal prerogative, that had been exacted and obtained from his father.

"The true friends of liberty, of reform and of progress in government, had become convinced that these were the offspring of peace and of enlightened reason, and not of passion nor of arms. The House of Commons and the House of Lords were henceforth the theatres of their operations, and not the fields of Newberry or Marston-Moor. The result was, that in less than thirty years, all their ancient rights and privileges, which had been lost in the civil war, with new securities, were re-established in the ever-memorable settlement of 1688; which, for all practical purposes, may be looked upon as a bloodless revolution. Since that time, England has made still further and more signal strides in reform and progress. But not one of these has been effected by resort to arms. Catholic emancipation was carried in parliament, after years of argument, against the most persistent opposition. Reason and justice ultimately prevailed. So with the removal of the disability of the Jews—so with the overthrow of the Rotten-Borough system—so with the extension of franchise—so with the modification of the corn-laws, and restrictions on commerce, opening the way to the establishment of the principles of free-trade—and so with all the other great reforms by parliament, which have so distinguished English history for the last half century.

"May we not indulge hope, even in the alternative before us now, from this great example of restoration, if we but do as the friends of liberty there did? This is my hope, my only hope. It is founded on the virtue, intelligence and patriotism of the American people. I have not lost my faith in the people, or in their capacity for self-government. But for these great essential qualities of human nature, to be brought into active and efficient exercise, for the fulfilment of patriotic hopes, it is essential that the passions of the day should subside; that the causes of these passions should not now be discussed; that the embers of the late strife shall not be stirred.

"Man by nature is ever prone to scan closely the errors and defects of his fellow man—ever ready to rail at the mote [sliver] in his brother's eye, without considering the beam [log] that is in his own. This should not be. We all have our motes or beams. We are all frail; perfection is the attribute of none. Prejudice or prejudgment should be indulged toward none. Prejudice! What wrongs, what injuries what mischiefs, what lamentable consequences, have resulted at all times from nothing but this perversity of the intellect! Of all the obstacles to the advancement of truth and human progress, in every department—in science, in art, in government, and in religion, in all ages and climes, not one on the list is more formidable, more difficult to overcome and subdue, than this horrible distortion of the moral as well as intellectual faculties. It is a host of evil within itself. I could enjoin no greater duty upon my countrymen now, North and South, than the exercise of that degree of forbearance which would enable them to conquer their prejudices. One of the highest exhibitions of the moral sublime the world ever witnessed, was that of Daniel Webster, when in an open barouche in the streets of Boston [Massachusetts], he proclaimed in substance, to a vast assembly of his constituents—unwilling hearers—that 'they had conquered an uncongenial clime; they had conquered a sterile soil; they had conquered the winds and currents of the ocean; they had conquered most of the elements of nature; but they must yet learn to conquer their prejudices!' I know of no more fitting incident or scene in the life of that wonderful man, '*Clarus et vir Fortissimus,*' for perpetuating the memory of the true greatness of his character, on canvas or in marble, than a representation of him as he then and there stood and spoke! It was an exhibition of moral grandeur surpassing that of Aristides when he said, 'Oh Athenians, what Themistocles recommends would be greatly to your interest, but it would be unjust'!

"I say to you, and if my voice could extend throughout this vast country, over hill and dale, over mountain and valley, to hovel, hamlet and mansion, village, town and city, I would say, among the first, looking to restoration of peace, prosperity and harmony in this land, is the great duty of exercising that degree of forbearance which will enable them to conquer their prejudices. Prejudices against communities as well as individuals.

"And next to that, the indulgence of a Christian spirit of charity. 'Judge not that ye be not judged,' especially in matters growing out of the late war. Most of the wars that have scourged the world, even in the Christian era, have arisen on points of conscience, or differences as to the surest way of salvation. A strange way that to heaven, is it not? How much disgrace to the church, and shame to mankind, would have been avoided, if the ejaculation of each breast had been, at all times, as it should have been,

> 'Let not this weak, unknowing hand,
> Presume Thy bolts to throw;
> And deal damnation round the land,

On him I deem Thy foe.'

"How equally proper is it now, when the spirit of peace seems to be hovering over our war-stricken land, that in canvassing the conduct or motives of others during the late conflict, this great truth should be impressed upon the minds of all,

> 'Who made the heart? Tis He alone
> Decidedly, can try us;
> He knows each chord, its various tone,
> Each spring, its various bias;
> Then at the balance, let's be mute,
> We never can adjust it;
> What's done, we partly may compute,
> But know not what's resisted.'

"Of all the heaven descended virtues, that elevate and ennoble human nature, the highest, the sublimest, and the divinest is charity. By all means, then, fail not to exercise and cultivate this soul-regenerating element of fallen nature. Let it be cultivated and exercised not only amongst ourselves and toward ourselves, on all questions of motive or conduct touching the late war, but toward all mankind. Even toward our enemies, if we have any, let the aspirations of our hearts be: 'Father, forgive them; they know not what they do.' The exercise of patience, forbearance, and charity, therefore, are the three first duties I would at this time enjoin—and of these three, 'the greatest is charity.'

"But to proceed. Another one of our present duties, is this: we should accept the issues of the war, and abide by them in good faith. This, I feel fully persuaded, it is your purpose to do, as well as that of your constituents. The people of Georgia have in convention revoked and annulled her ordinance of 1861, which was intended to sever her from the compact of Union of 1787. The constitution of the United States has been reordained as the organic law of our land. Whatever differences of opinion heretofore existed as to where our allegiance was due, during the late state of things, none for any practical purpose can exist now. Whether Georgia, by the action of her convention of 1861, was ever rightfully out of the Union or not, there can be no question that she is now in, so far as depends upon her will and deed. The whole United States, therefore, is now without question our country, to be cherished and defended as such, by all our hearts and by all our arms.

"The constitution of the United States, and the treaties and laws made in pursuance thereof, are now acknowledged to be the paramount law in this whole country. Whoever, therefore, is true to these principles as now recognized, is loyal as far as that term has any legitimate use or force under our institutions. This is the only kind of loyalty and the only test of loyalty the constitution itself requires. In any other view, every thing pertaining to restoration, so far as regards the great body of the people in at least eleven States of the Union, is but making a promise to the ear to be broken to the hope. All, therefore, who accept the issue of war in good faith, and come up to the test required by the constitution, are now loyal, however they may have heretofore been.

"But with this change comes a new order of things. One of the results of the war is a total change in our whole internal polity. Our former social fabric has been entirely subverted. Like those convulsions in nature which break up old incrustations, the war has wrought a new epoch in our political existence. *Old things have passed away, and all things among us in this respect are new. The relation heretofore, under our old system, existing between the African and European races, no longer exists. Slavery, as it was called, or the status of the black race, their subordination to the white, upon which all our institutions rested, is abolished forever, not only in Georgia, but throughout the limits of the United States. This change should be received and accepted as an irrevocable fact.* It is a bootless question now to discuss, whether the new system is better for both races than the old one was or not. That may be proper matter for the philosophic and philanthropic historian, at some future time to inquire into, after the new system shall have been fully and fairly tried. [Emphasis added, L.S.]

"All changes of systems or proposed reforms are but experiments and problems to be solved. Our system of self-government was an experiment at first. Perhaps as a problem it is not yet solved. Our present duty on this subject is not with the past or the future; it is with the present. The wisest and the best often err, in their judgments as to the probable workings of any new system. Let us therefore give this one a fair and just trial, without prejudice, and with that earnestness of purpose which always looks hopefully to success. It is an ethnological problem, on the solution of which depends, not only the best interests of both races, but it may be the existence of one or the other, if not both.

"*This duty of giving this new system a fair and just trial will require of you, as legislators of the land, great changes in our former laws in regard to this large class of population. Wise and humane provisions should be made for them. It is not for me to go into detail. Suffice it to say on this occasion, that ample and full protection should be secured to them [blacks], so that they may stand equal before the law, in the possession and enjoyment of all rights of person, liberty and property. Many considerations claim this at your hands. Among these may be stated their fidelity in times past.* They *cultivated your fields, ministered to your personal wants and comforts, nursed and reared your children; and even in the hour of danger and peril they were, in the main, true to you and yours. To them we owe a debt of gratitude, as well as acts of kindness. This should also be done because they are poor, untutored, uninformed; many of them helpless, liable to be imposed upon, and need it. Legislation should ever look to the protection of the weak against the strong.* Whatever may be said of the equality of races, or their natural capacity to become equal, no one can doubt that at this time this race among us is not [culturally] equal to the Caucasian. This inequality does not lessen the moral obligations on the part of the superior to the inferior, it rather increases them. From him who has much, more is required than from him who has little. The present generation of them, it is true, is far above their savage progenitors, who were at first introduced into this country, in general intelligence, virtue, and moral culture. This shows capacity for improvement. But in all the higher characteristics of mental development, they are still very far below the European type. What further advancement they may make, or to what standard they may attain, under a different system of laws every way suitable and wisely applicable to their changed condition, time alone can disclose. I speak of them as we now know them to be; having no longer the protection of a master, or legal guardian, *they now need all the protection which the shield of the law can give.* [Emphasis added, L.S.]

"But, above all, this protection should be secured, because it is right and just that it should be, upon general principles. All governments in their organic structure, as well as in their administration, should have this leading object in view; the good of the governed. *Protection and security to all under its jurisdiction, should be the chief end of every government. It is a melancholy truth that while this should be the chief end of all governments, most of them are used only as instruments of power, for the aggrandizement of the few, at the expense of, and by the oppression of, the many.* Such are not our ideas of government, never have been and never should be. Governments, according to our ideas, should look to the good of the whole, and not a part only. 'The greatest good to the greatest number,' is a favorite dogma with some. Some so defended our old system. But you know this was never my doctrine. The greatest good to all, without detriment or injury to any, is the true rule. Those governments only are founded upon correct principles, of reason and justice, which look to the greatest attainable advancement, improvement and progress, physically, intellectually and morally, of all classes and conditions within their rightful jurisdiction. If our old system was not the best, or could not have been made the best, for both races, in this respect and upon this basis, it ought to have been abolished. This was my view of that system while it lasted, and I repeat it now that it is no more. In legislation, therefore, under the new system, you should look to the best interest of all classes; their protection, security, advancement and improvement, physically, intellectually, and morally. *All obstacles, if there be any, should be removed, which can possibly hinder or retard, the improvement of the blacks to the extent of their capacity. All proper aid should be given to their own efforts. Channels of education should be opened up to them. Schools, and the usual means of moral and intellectual training, should be encouraged amongst them. This is the dictate, not only of what is right and proper, and just in itself, but it is also the promptings of the highest considerations of interest.* It is difficult to conceive a greater evil or curse, that could befall our country, stricken and distressed as it now is, than for so large a portion of its population, as this class will quite probably constitute amongst us, hereafter, to be reared in ignorance, depravity and vice. In view of such a state of things well might the prudent even now look to its abandonment. Let us not however indulge in such thoughts of the future, nor let us, without an effort, say the system cannot be worked. Let us not, standing still, hesitatingly ask, 'Can there any good thing come out of Nazareth?' but let us rather say as Gamaliel did, 'If this counsel or this work be of men, it will come to naught, but if it be of God ye cannot overthrow it, lest haply ye be found even to fight against God.' The most vexed questions of the age are social problems. These we have heretofore had but little to do with; we were relieved from them by our peculiar institution. *Emancipation of the blacks, with its consequences, was ever considered by me with much more interest as a social question, one relating to the proper status of the different elements of society, and their relations toward each other, looking to the best interest of all, than in any other light.* The pecuniary aspect of it, the considerations of labor and capital, in a politico-economic view, sunk into insignificance, in comparison with this. This problem, as one of the results of the war, is now upon us, presenting one of the most perplexing questions of the sort that any people ever had to deal with. Let us resolve to do the best we can with it, from all the lights we have, or can get from any quarter. With this view, and in this connection, I take the liberty of quoting for your consideration, some remarks even from the [Yankee abolitionist] Rev. Henry Ward Beecher. I met with them [i.e., Beecher's remarks] some months ago while pondering on this subject, and was as much struck as surprised, with the drift of their philosophy, coming from the source they did. I give them as I find them in the *New York Times* where they were reported. You may be as much surprised at hearing such ideas from Mr. Beecher, as I was. But however much we may differ from him on many questions, and on many questions connected with this subject, yet all must admit him to rank amongst the master spirits of the age. And no one perhaps has contributed more by the power of his pen and voice in bringing about the present state of things, than he has. Yet, nevertheless, I commend to your serious consideration, as pertinent to my present object, what he was reported to have said, as follows:

> 'In our land and time facts and questions are pressed upon us which demand Christian settlement—settlement on this ground and doctrine. We cannot escape the responsibility. Being strong and powerful, we must nurse, and help, and educate, and foster the weak, and poor, and ignorant. For my own part I cannot see how we shall escape the most terrible conflict of classes, by and by, unless we are educated into this doctrine of duty, on the part of the *superior to the inferior*. We are told by zealous and fanatical individuals, that all men are equal. We know better. *They are not equal. A common brotherhood teaches no such absurdity.* A theory of universal, physical likeness, is no more absurd than this. *Now, as in all times, the strong go to the top, the weak go to the bottom. Its natural, right and can't be helped.* All branches are not at the top of the tree, but the top does not despise the lower; nor do they all despise the limb or the parent trunk; and so with the body politic, there must be classes. *Some must be at the top and some must be at the bottom.* It is difficult to foresee, and estimate the development of the power of classes in America. They are simply inevitable. They are here now, and will be more. If they are friendly, living at peace, loving and respecting and helping one another, all will be well. But if they are selfish, unchristian; if the old heathen feeling is to reign, each extracting all he can from his neighbor, and caring nothing for him; society will be lined by classes as by seams—like batteries, each firing broadside after broadside, the one upon the other. If, on the other hand, the law of love prevails, there will be no ill-will, no envy, no disturbance. Does a child hate his father because he is chief, because he is strong and wise? On the contrary, he grows with his father's growth, and strengthens with his strength. And if in society there should be fifty grades or classes, all helping each other, there will be no trouble, but perfect satisfaction and content. This Christian doctrine carried into practice, will easily settle the most troublesome of all home present questions.' [Emphasis added, L.S.]

"What [Beecher] . . . here said of the state of things where he spoke in the State of New York, and the fearful antagonism of classes there, is much more applicable to us. Here, it is true, only two great classes exist, or are likely to exist, but these are deeply marked by distinctions bearing the impress of nature. The one is now beyond all question greatly superior to the other. These classes are as distinct as races of men can be. The one is of the highest type of humanity, the other of the lowest. *All that he says of the duty of the superior, to protect, to aid, to encourage, and to help the inferior, I fully and cordially indorse and commend to you as quite as applicable to us and our situation*, as it was to his auditors. Whether the doctrine, if carried out and practiced, will settle all these most troublesome home questions with us as easily as he seemed to think it would like home questions with those whom he was addressing, I will not undertake to say. I have no hesitancy, however, in saying that the general principles announced by him are good. Let them be adopted by us as far as practicable. No harm can come from it, much good may. Whether *the great barrier of races which the Creator has placed between this*, our inferior class and ourselves, shall prevent a success of the experiment now on trial, of a peaceful, happy, and prosperous community, composed of such elements and sustaining present relations toward each other, or even a further elevation on the part of the inferior, if they prove themselves fit for it, let the future, under the dispensations of Providence, decide. We have to deal with the present. [Emphasis added, L.S.] Let us do our duty now, leaving results and ultimate consequences to that

'Divinity which shapes our ends,
Rough hew them how we will.'

"In all things on this subject, as in all others, let our guide be the admirable motto of our State ['Wisdom, Justice, Moderation']. Let our counsels be governed by wisdom, our measures by moderation, and our principles by justice.

"So much for what I have to say on this occasion, touching our present duties on this absorbing subject, and some of our duties in reference to a restoration of peace, law and order; without which all must, sooner or later, end in utter confusion, anarchy and despotism. I have, as I said I should, only glanced at some general ideas.

"Now as to the future, and the prospect before us! On this branch of the subject I can add but little. You can form some ideas of my views of that from what has already been said. Would that I could say something cheerful; but that candor, which has marked all that I have said, compels me to say that to me the future is far from being bright. Nay, it is dark and impenetrable; thick gloom curtains and closes in the horizon all around us. Thus much I can say: my only hope is in the peaceful re-establishment of good government, and its peaceful maintenance afterward. And, further, the most hopeful prospect to this end now is the restoration of the old Union, and with it the speedy return of fraternal feeling throughout its length and breadth. These results depend upon the people themselves—upon the people of the North quite as much as the people of the South—upon their virtue, intelligence, and patriotism. I repeat, *I have faith in the American people, in their virtue, intelligence and patriotism. But for this I should long since have despaired. Dark and gloomy as the present hour is, I do not yet despair of free institutions. Let but the virtue, intelligence, and patriotism of the people throughout the whole country be properly appealed to, aroused and brought into action, and all may yet be well. The masses, everywhere, are alike equally interested in the great object. Let old issues, old questions, old differences, and old feuds, be regarded as fossils of another epoch. They belong to what may hereafter be considered, the Silurian period of our history. Great, new, living questions are before us. Let it not be said of us in this day, not yet passed, of our country's greatest trial and agony*, that, 'there was a party for [Julius] Caesar, a party for Pompey [the Great], and a party for [Marcus J.] Brutus [the Younger], but no party for Rome.'

"But let all patriots, by whatever distinctive name heretofore styled, rally, in all elections everywhere, to the support of him, be he who he may, who bears the standard with 'Constitutional Union' emblazoned on its folds. President [Andrew] Johnson is now, in my judgment, the chief great standard-bearer of these principles, and in his efforts at restoration should receive the cordial support of every well-wisher of his country.

"In this consists, on this rests, my only hope. Should he be sustained, and the government be restored to its former functions, all the States brought back to their practical relations under the constitution, our situation will be greatly changed from what it was before. A radical and fundamental change, as has been stated, has been made in that organic law. We shall have lost what was known as our 'peculiar institution' which was so intertwined with the whole framework of our State body politic. [Note: Since both the American slave trade and American slavery both got their start in Massachusetts, it would be far more accurate to call slavery the *North's* 'peculiar institution.' L.S.] We shall have lost nearly half the accumulated capital of a century. But we shall have still left all the essentials of free government, contained and embodied in the old constitution, untouched and unimpaired as they came from the hands of our fathers. With these, even if we had to begin entirely anew, the prospect before us would be much more encouraging than the prospect was before them, when they fled from the oppressions of the old world, and sought shelter and homes in this then wilderness land. The liberties we begin with, they had to achieve. With the same energies and virtues they displayed, we have much more to cheer us than they had. With a climate unrivalled in salubrity; with a soil unsurpassed in fertility; and with products unequalled in value in the markets of the world, to say nothing of our mineral resources, we shall have much still to wed us to the good old land. With good government, the matrix from which alone spring all great human achievements, we shall lack nothing but our own proper exertions, not only to recover our former prosperity, but to attain a much higher degree of development in every thing that characterizes a great, free, and happy people. At least I know of no other land that the sun shines upon, that offers better prospects under the contingencies stated.

"The old Union was based upon the assumption, that it was for the best interest of the people of all the States to be united as they were, each State faithfully performing to the people of the other States all their obligations under the common compact. I always thought this assumption was founded upon broad, correct, and statesman-like principles. I think so yet. It was only [after Lincoln's election] when it seemed to be impossible further to maintain it, without hazarding greater evils than would perhaps attend a separation, that I yielded my assent in obedience to the voice of Georgia, to try the experiment which has just resulted so disastrously to us. Indeed, during the whole lamentable conflict, it was my opinion that however the pending strife might terminate, so far as the appeal to the sword was concerned, yet after a while, when the passions and excitements of the day should pass away, an adjustment or arrangement would be made upon continental principles, upon the general basis of 'reciprocal advantage and mutual convenience,' on which the Union was first established. My earnest desire, however, throughout, was whatever might be done, might be peaceably done; might be the result of calm, dispassionate, and enlightened reason; looking to the permanent interests and welfare of all. And now, after the severe chastisement of war, if the general sense of the whole country shall come back to the acknowledgment of the original assumption, that it is for the best interests of all the States to be so united, as I trust it will; the States still being 'separate as the billows but one as the sea;' I can perceive no reason why, under such restoration, we as a whole, with 'peace, commerce, and honest friendship with all nations and entangling alliances with none,' may not enter upon a new career, exciting increased wonder in the old world, by grander achievements hereafter to be made, than any heretofore attained, by the peaceful and harmonious workings of our American institutions of self-government. All this is possible if the hearts of the people be right. It is my earnest wish to see it. Fondly would I indulge my fancy in gazing on such a picture of the future. With what rapture may we not suppose the spirits of our fathers would hail its opening scenes from their mansions above. Such are my hopes, resting on such contingencies. But if, instead of all this, the passions of the day shall continue to bear sway; if prejudice shall rule the hour; if a conflict of races shall arise; if ambition shall turn the scale; if the sword shall be thrown in the balance against patriotism; if the embers of the late war shall be kept a-glowing until with new fuel they shall flame up again, then our present gloom is but the shadow, the penumbra of that deeper and darker eclipse, which is to totally obscure this hemisphere and blight forever the anxious anticipations and expectations of mankind! Then, hereafter, by some bard it may be sung,

'The Star of Hope shone brightest in the West,

The hope of Liberty, the last, the best;
That, too, has set, upon her darkened shore,
And Hope and Freedom light up earth no more.'

"May we not all, on this occasion, on this anniversary of the birth day of [George] Washington, join in a fervent prayer to Heaven that the Great Ruler of events may avert from this land such a fall, such a fate, and such a requiem!"[101]

4

Recollections of Yankee Arrest & Imprisonment 1865

IN THE SPRING OF 1865 Stephens was illegally arrested at his Georgia home, "Liberty Hall" in Crawfordville, and shipped to Boston, Massachusetts, where he was imprisoned for five months. The following excerpts are from his journal from that period. I have focused mainly on the events surrounding his arrest, his transport to New England, and his first day of incarceration.

☛ "Liberty Hall, Georgia, Thursday, May 11, 1865.— This was a most beautiful and charming morning. After refreshing sleep, I arose early. Robert Hull, a youth, son of Henry Hull, of Athens, Ga., had spent the night at my house. I wrote some letters for the mail, my custom being to attend to such business soon as breakfast was over; and Robert and I were amusing ourselves at casino, when Tim [a negro servant] came running into the parlour saying: 'Master! more Yankees have come! a whole heap are in town, galloping all about with guns.' Suspecting what it meant, I rose, told Robert I expected they had come for me, and entered my bedroom to make arrangements for leaving, should my apprehensions prove true. Soon, I saw an officer with soldiers under arms approaching the house. The doors were all open. I met him in the library. He asked if my name was Stephens. I replied that it was. 'Alexander H. Stephens?' said he. I told him that was my name. He said he had orders to arrest me. I asked his name and to see his orders. He said he was Captain Saint of the 4th Iowa Cavalry, or mounted infantry, attached to General Nelson's command; he was then under General Upton: he showed me the order by General Upton, at Atlanta, directing my arrest and that of Robert Toombs; no charge was specified; he was instructed to go to Crawfordville, arrest me, proceed to Washington and arrest Mr. Toombs, and then carry both to General Upton's headquarters.

"I told him I had been looking for something of this kind; at least, for some weeks had thought it not improbable; and hence had not left home; General Upton need not have sent any force for me; had he simply notified me that he wished me at his headquarters, I should have gone. I asked how I was to travel. He said: 'On the cars.' I then learned that his party had come down on the train arriving just before Tim's announcement. I asked if I would be permitted to carry any clothing.

"He said, 'Yes.' I asked how long I might have for packing. He said: 'A few minutes—as long as necessary.' I set to packing. Harry [a servant] came in, evincing great surprise and regret, to pack for me. The Captain then said: 'You may take a servant with you if you wish.' I asked if he knew my destination. He said: 'First, Atlanta; then, Washington City.' I called in Anthony, a black boy from Richmond who had been waiting on me several years, and inquired if he wished to go; I told him I would send him from Washington to his mother in Richmond. He was willing, so I bade him be ready soon as possible.

"In the meantime, Mr. [William H.] Hidell [Stephen's secretary] had come in; he was living with me and had gone out after breakfast. None of my [half] brother John's family residing at the old homestead happened to be with me; however, Clarence [Stephens, John's son], who was going to school at the Academy, hearing of what had occurred (I suppose), came over with some friends from town. It was about 10 A.M. when Captain Saint arrived. In about fifteen minutes—not much over—we started for the depot, Anthony and I with the Captain and squad; friends, servants, and Clarence following, most of them crying. My own heart was full—too full for tears.

"While Anthony was getting ready, I had asked Captain Saint if I might write a letter or two to some friends, to my brother and to my sister-in-law's family. He said I might. My [half] brother [Linton Stephens] and his children had left me two days before, after a visit of nearly a week. I wrote him a note in about these words:

> 'Dear Brother: I have just been arrested by Captain Saint of the 4th Iowa Cavalry. The order embraces General Toombs. We are both to be carried to Atlanta, and thence to Washington City it seems. When I shall see you again, if ever, I don't know. May God enable you to be as well prepared for whatever fate may await me as I trust He will enable me to bear it. May His

blessings ever attend you and yours. My kindest regards to Cosby [Connel], [Richard M.] Dick Johnston, and all friends. I have not time to say more. My tenderest love to your dear little ones. Yours most affectionately, Alexander H. Stephens.'

"This I sealed and addressed to Linton and told Harry to send it over to Sparta immediately after I should leave. The Captain said he preferred that I should not send the note then; we should come back, and then I might send it. I told him it simply announced my arrest and destination; he might read it. I opened and handed it to him. He still objected, and I tore it up. Supposing similar objection would be made to my sending any other, I did not write to my sister-in-law's family. I knew that Mr. Hidell, Clarence, servants, and all present would give them full information. At the cars a great many people had assembled. All seemed deeply oppressed and grieved. Many wept bitterly. To me the parting was exceedingly sorrowful. Hidell was to leave for his home in Memphis on this day. He was all packed up and ready to start on the down train.

"When we left the depot, the train backed up several hundred yards and took on some soldiers who seemed to have been put out there as scouts. While we were standing, I saw Mr. Singleton Harris and, by the Captain's [Saint] permission, sent word to Hidell not to leave my house until he should hear from me. When all the soldiers were on the cars the train moved down the road again, not stopping until we reached Barnett; where we took another engine and started to Washington, Ga. About four miles from that town, the train slowed up at a shanty occupied by a track supervisor. Here, I was put off with about twenty soldiers to guard me. The Captain and the others went on to Washington. He said he expected to be back in an hour. He did not return until after dark. During his absence there was a heavy fall of rain, which was much needed as it had not rained for several weeks. The man of the house gave me dinner: fried meat and corn bread. He said it was the best he had. I was not hungry, but to show my gratitude for his hospitality, I shared his homely meal. Night came. The Captain had not returned. The good man asked me to partake of his supper; I accepted as before; his lady was kind, and apologized for having no better fare to offer.

"Soon after dark, the engine was heard. I was anxious to know the result of Captain Saint's trip. What we supposed was the train proved to be the engine only: the Captain was bringing his men commissary stores. He went back immediately, but not before I had asked the cause of the detention. What had occurred? was General Toombs at home? He answered evasively, and left me in doubt and perplexity. About nine the engine was heard again. It brought the train. I was put aboard, Anthony looking after the baggage. The ground was wet and I got my feet damp; this, with the chill of the night air gave me a sore throat with severe hoarseness. When the train was under way for Barnett, I asked the Captain if he had Mr. Toombs. 'No,' he replied, 'Mr. Toombs flanked us.' [Toombs was in his front door when Captain Saint entered his yard; he went out at the back and escaped to the woods.] This was said in a rather disappointed and irate tone, and I made no further inquires. Reaching Barnett about eleven, we remained for some time and then took the train for Atlanta. Some panes of glass were broken out of the car windows, and I was further chilled.

"Atlanta, Georgia, May 12.— This is one of the most eventful days of my life. Never before was I deprived of my liberty or under arrest. Reached Atlanta about eight-thirty. Quite unwell. Carried to General Upton's headquarters. The first person I saw that I knew was Felix, a coloured man who was a servant to Mr. Toombs and myself when we lived together in Washington City. He was very glad to see me and I gave him a hearty handshake. He was our cook in Washington, and a good cook he was. General Upton had gone to Macon but was expected back that night. Captain Gilpin, of his staff, received me and assigned me a room. Anthony made me a fire; Captain Gilpin ordered breakfast and Felix soon had it ready: fried ham and coffee. Walked about the city under guard. The desolation and havoc of war here are soul-rending. Several persons called to see me, Gip Grier [Stephens' cousin A. G. Grier] the first; my heart almost burst when I saw him, but I suppressed all show of emotion. [Confederate quartermaster] General Ira R. Foster was allowed to write me a note and I to answer it, but no interview was permitted. Colonel G. W. Lee was permitted to speak to me, but not to hold conversation. John W. Duncan was permitted to visit my room and remain as long as he pleased; so, too, was Gip Grier: both made me several visits during the day. Captain Saint called and said he would send the surgeon of his regiment to prescribe for my hoarseness. The surgeon came, and his remedies did me good. Major Cooper called and gave me a bottle of whisky.

"I started from home with about $590 in gold which had been laid up for a long time for such a contingency. I got Gip Grier to exchange $20 of it for greenbacks and small silver. I had first asked Captain Gilpin if this would be allowed and he made no objection. Gip offered me $100 additional in gold if I wished it. I declined it. Duncan offered any amount I might want. I told him I hoped I had enough. All this was in the presence of the officers. General Foster, in his note, offered any funds I might need. I informed him in my answer that I had plenty for present use and hoped I should need no more.

"May 13.— General Upton called early. I was so hoarse I could hardly talk. He informed me that he had removed all guards, that I was on my parole.

I told him I should not violate it. He was very courteous and agreeable; told me my destination was Washington. I learned from him that Mr. [Jefferson] Davis had been captured, that [Confederate Senator] Clement C. Clay had surrendered himself, and that Mr. Davis and party would be in Atlanta to-night on their way to Washington. He gave me choice of route: by Dalton and the lines of railroads northwest and north, or by sea from Savannah. I selected the sea route, but told him I did not wish to go with Mr. Davis. He said he would send me in a special train to-night to Augusta, but from there to Savannah I should have to travel on the boat with Mr. Davis and party; there was but one boat at Augusta. From Savannah to Hilton Head and on he would try to have me sent by separate packet if it could be done. I had frequent talks with General Upton during the day and was well pleased with him. Some friends called; Gip Grier and Duncan several times. Duncan gave me a bottle of Scotch ale which I put in my trunk. He told me of a banking-house in Europe in which he has funds, authorizing me to draw on his account for any amount I might need. I am truly grateful, but I trust I shall never be brought to the necessity of availing myself of his generous tender. He said he would write the house to cash any draft by me. Major Cooper called, Dr. Powell, Dr. Simmons and others; and some ladies, who wept in parting with me. Mrs. Powell sent refreshments; and Mrs. Thrasher the mattress and covers which form my comfortable bed.

"Felix [the servant] informs me that after he was cook for Mr. Toombs and myself in Washington, he was sold by Mr. Wallack to Senator Sebastian, of Arkansas, and was the Senator's cook until the war broke out. Senator Sebastian now lives in Memphis, has freed all his people, and Felix has been for some time the servant of Dr. Little, U.S.A. He inquired after Pierce, my servant boy who was with me in Washington. I told him I had let Pierce go where he pleased and do as he pleased for several years, and when last heard from, he was in Macon; if he would write Pierce there I thought the letter would reach Pierce, who would be glad to hear from him and much gladder to see him. They were very intimate in Washington. Anthony said Felix was going to try to go with me to Washington. I did not encourage this idea as I know Dr. Little would not like to have Felix quit him so suddenly, and then I am not certain of my ultimate destination.

". . . From my window, just before night, I took a bird's eye survey of the ruins of this place. I saw where the Trout House stood, where [Stephen A.] Douglas spoke in 1860—I thought of the scenes of that day, and my deep forebodings of all these troubles; and how sorely oppressed I was at heart, not much less so than now, in their full realization with myself among the victims. How strange it seems to me that I should thus suffer, I who did everything in the power of man to prevent them. I could but rest my eye for a time upon the ruins of the Atlanta Hotel, while the mind was crowded with associations brought to life in gazing upon it. There, on the fourth Sept., 1848, I was near losing my life for resenting the charge of being a traitor to the South: and now I am here, a prisoner under charge, I suppose, of being a traitor to the Union. In all, I have done nothing but what I thought was right. The result, be it what it may, I shall endeavour to meet with resignation.

"9 P.M.— General Upton informed me that my train starts at eleven; that I may stop at home, take breakfast, and get more clothing: the train carrying Mr. Davis and party leaves here two hours later than mine; I may remain home until it overtakes me. I immediately wrote Hidell. I hoped my brother might be in Crawfordville. I was anxious to see him and doubted not that word had been sent him of my arrest. Gip took the letter to the mail-train at ten-thirty, returned, and remained with me until near the hour for my departure, as did Duncan. I requested both to write Linton, giving him the particulars of my situation and destination as far as known.

"I told General Upton that there was another coloured boy at my house, Henry, Anthony's brother, whose mother is in Richmond and whom I should like, if there is no objection, to take to Fortress Monroe whence I could send him to her. He consented. Captain Gilpin requested my autograph, which I gave. A little past eleven, we were off.

"Crawfordville, May 14.— This is an ever memorable day to me. It is the anniversary of my stepmother's [Matilda Marbury Somerville Lindsay] death, the day on which was severed the last tie that kept the family circle around the hearthstone at the old homestead. My father [Andrew Baskins Stephens] died one week before, on the 7th, 1826. The date, to make this anniversary more impressive, falls now, as then, on Sunday.

"At eleven-thirty this morning, the cars reached Crawfordville. Hidell had gotten my letter. A large crowd was at the depot to see me. I hastened to my house as I had much to do and not much time to do it in. Church was just out, preaching over, and the congregation leaving. I could but give a parting shake of the hand to many whose eyes were filled with tears. Nearly all my servants from the homestead were at church, but none of my sister-in-law's family, except my nephew, Linton Andrew [Stephens]. Hidell had not had time to send them word I was coming. My nephew, John [Alexander Stephens], was gone to Washington, Ga. First, he had gone to Sparta and informed my brother Linton of my arrest. Hidell said John had reported Linton as ill. What a pang that struck to my heart!

"I ordered breakfast for myself, Captain Kennedy, and two others who had accompanied me on invitation. I had a hurried repacking of clothes into a larger trunk I borrowed from my true friend, Mr. Joseph Myers. Everything I could think of that I might need—that I had—was put in; besides clothing, two large bedblankets and one large afghan. Henry and Anthony were soon ready. Such hurried directions as I could give were given to the servants on the lot and to those from the homestead. Harry was told what to do in taking care of things; Fountain and George [two servants] were told how to manage the farm. I did not have as much talk with my nephew, Linton Andrew, as I wished, nor with Hidell. Leave-takings were hurried and confused. The servants all wept. My grief at leaving them and home was too burning, withering, scorching for tears. At the depot was an immense crowd, old friends, black and white, who came in great numbers and shook hands. That parting and that scene I can never forget. I could not stand it until the other train arrived, and I requested the Captain to move off. This he did.

"Augusta, Ga.— At Barnett, we waited for the other train. General Upton came in and suggested that I would be more comfortable in the car he had on that train. I told him, if he had no objection, I should prefer to remain where I was. He said he had none, and I remained. Mr. Davis and party were on the other train. In a short time we were under way again. Reached Augusta before sundown. General Upton had a carriage to take me to the boat, four or five miles down the river. The other train came up a half-hour behind us. Mr. and Mrs. Davis were put in a carriage, and some officer with them. Mr. and Mrs. Clay [wife of Clement C. Clay, Virginia (Tunstall) Clay] were in a carriage to themselves; as our vehicles passed, I, for the first time, saw them; they bowed to me and I to them. Mr. Davis did not see me until we reached the boat. Anthony rode in the carriage with me. Henry went with and took care of the baggage, consisting of Myers's trunk with my things in it, my trunk with Anthony's things, and Henry's box. My carpet-bag, shawl, greatcoat, umbrella, cane, and small overcoat I kept with me; Anthony kept his and Henry's carpet-bags. It was some time before all things were ready; all was under military arrangement. Mr. Davis's party, twelve in number, were placed foremost in vehicles that I could not see; then Mr. Davis's carriage, then Mr. Clay's; I brought up the rear. A [U.S.] major from Indiana was with me. Just before we started, Mrs. Davis's white nurse came and asked to ride in our carriage. The Major let her in. She had Mrs. Davis's [Varina Banks (Howell) Davis] infant [Varina Ann 'Winnie' Davis, later known as the 'Daughter of the Confederacy'] with her. Guards rode in front, at the sides, and in the rear, some on horse-back, some in wagons, all well armed. When the cortege, which looked much like a funeral procession, had gotten away from the depot, we found the streets lined on both sides with immense crowds. Occasionally I heard some one say, 'There goes Stephens'; but I recognized only one person, [editor] Morse of the *Chronicle and Sentinel*. I bowed to several who bowed to me, but whose faces I did not know. Everybody looked sad and depressed. We moved slowly. It was dark long before we reached the boat-landing. Outside the city, the Major requested Anthony to ride his horse, which some friend, who wished to return, had ridden to that point. Anthony acted the horseman better than I feared he could. After we reached the landing, it was a long time before we got the boat. The walk to the river-edge was rough; deep ravines without bridges had to be crossed. It was with great difficulty, even though assisted, that I was able to get along. The Major helped me. He was agreeable and cheerful in conversation, but I was suffering too much from headache to take interest in conversation. To board the boat, we had to walk a narrow plank, descending at that. This I could not do. Several helped me across. Here, we waited until the baggage was all aboard. I felt relieved when Anthony reported everything safe and Henry on board. The boat was a miserable affair, a river tug without cabin. There were a few berths which the ladies occupied; the rest of us were put on deck, except Mr. Davis, who staid in the part of the boat occupied by the ladies. A covering was overhead but the sides of the deck were open.

"We found [Confederate] General Joe [Joseph] Wheeler and four of his men on board. They had been captured near Athens some days before and had been sent down in advance of us. Our whole party now, Mr. Davis and those captured with him, Mr. and Mrs. Clay, myself, General Wheeler and his men, numbered over twenty. I don't know exactly how many were in Mr. Davis's party. I recognized [Texas] Governor [Francis R.] Lubbock and Colonel Johnston of his staff, Mr. Harrison, his private secretary, and Postmaster-General John H. Reagan. Mr. Davis had with him one man-servant, Bob, a woman, Ellen Bond, coloured, and a white woman, also a little mulatto boy [Jim Limber, a black orphan who the Davises had adopted during Lincoln's War]. His children, Jeff [Jefferson C. Davis], Maggie [Margaret H. Davis], and Willie [William H. Davis], I recognized, also Mrs. Davis [Varina Banks (Howell) Davis], her sister, Miss Howell, and her brother, Jefferson Davis Howell. A young Mr. Monroe, grandson of Judge Monroe, of Kentucky, was also with Mr. Davis, but I did not see him after the party got on the boat.

"Mrs. Davis and Mrs. Clay came on deck where we were. Our meeting was the first that the Davis party knew of my arrest. Mr. Clay had seen me at the depot and knew it from the fact of my situation, but had not heard of it before. General Wheeler had not heard of the arrest of any of us. Mr. Clay told me he had been on parole all the way, and had not come on in the procession with the rest of us, but had been permitted to drive with his wife about the city and visit some of her acquaintances. He gave me the particulars of his surrender.

"Before taking leave of me, General Upton turned me over to Colonel Pritchard of the 4th Michigan Cavalry, who had captured Mr. Davis and who now took charge of all the prisoners. The General told Colonel Pritchard that Mr. [Clement C.] Clay and I were on parole, and he allowed us the run of the boat. I asked him to grant me permission to write to my brother [Linton]. He said he supposed this privilege would not be denied whenever I got to a place where I could write.

"On the cars from Barnett to Augusta I had travelled with General Elzy [C.S.A.], who had been paroled, and had requested him to write John A. Stephens at Crawfordville that I wished him to remain with his mother until he should hear from me. I deeply regret that I did not meet John at home as I passed there.

"My feelings this night on this boat are past all description. We were all crowded together in a small space on the deck. The night was cool, the air on the water damp, and I was suffering, as I had been for hours, from a severe headache. No mention was made of supper, but I thought not of supper. I had taken breakfast at noon, and did not feel now as if I should ever want to eat again. Clay and I combined our cloaks, coats, shawls, etc.; General Wheeler sent us a blanket; Mrs. Davis sent us a mattress, and we made a joint bed in the open air on deck. I put the carpet-bags under our heads. Strange to say, I slept sweetly and soundly, and rose much refreshed next morning. The boat had raised steam and left the bluff, not the wharf, about nine that night. Reagan, Wheeler, and the rest, including Bob, Anthony, Henry, and the other servants, had stretched themselves on the open space the best way they could, all except one little boy, with covering of some sort. Just before I fell asleep, I witnessed this scene: A little black boy, ragged and woe-begone, lay in the passway. Whose he was or where going, I know not. An officer [U.S.] came along, gave him a shove and a push, and in harsh language ordered him to get away. The boy raised up, roused from his sleep, and replied plaintively: 'I have no lodging, sir.' That scene and that reply were vividly on my mind with all my personal cares when merciful slumber drowned them, as I was borne away from home and all dear to me, on the broad smooth bosom of the Savannah.

"May 15.— I awoke much refreshed. Morning beautiful. Got a rough soldier's breakfast. Mr. Davis came out on deck soon after I got up. It was our first meeting since our parting the night after my return from Hampton Roads Conference to Richmond. Much as I had disagreed with him and much as I deplored the ruin which, I think, his acts helped to bring upon the whole country, as well as on himself, I could but deeply sympathize with him in his present condition. His salutation was not unfriendly, but it was far from cordial. We passed but few words; these were commonplace. Talked to-day a good deal with Clay, Reagan, and Wheeler, but spent most of my time in lonely meditation on the side of the boat, looking out upon the willows along the margin of the sluggish, muddy, crooked stream. My thoughts were filled with home scenes and Sparta scenes and scenes of kindred association. Colonel Pritchard introduced to me Captain Hudson of his regiment, and a Mr. Stribling (I think the name is), a correspondent of the *New York Herald*. We talked a good deal on the state of the country, etc.

"Savannah to Hilton Head, May 16.— I omitted to note yesterday that we got dinner and tea at the usual hours: potatoes and beef stewed for dinner; at tea, a good cup of black tea that suited me well. There was hardtack, which some preferred, but I chose baker's bread. The table seated only four at once. It took some time for all to eat. We reached Savannah this morning at four; were transferred from the tug to a coast steamer, bound to Hilton Head. On it we got a good breakfast. Witnessed a scene at the breakfast table, in which Mr. Davis was chief actor, that I can never forget. About eleven A.M., we anchored in the harbour off Hilton Head and were transferred to the *Clyde*, a new steamer, bound for Fortress Monroe. There were several good berths in the cabin below and a number of staterooms on deck above. The ladies and most of the gentlemen selected staterooms. I preferred a berth below; which I found on the voyage an excellent choice. After we boarded, a number of officers and other persons came on the *Clyde*. They brought New York papers, *Harper's Weekly* and Frank Leslie's *Illustrated News*. It had been a long time since I had seen these prints. Here, for the first time, I heard of the Military Commission trying Mr. Lincoln's assassins.

"On the *Clyde*.— The officers came down in the cabin where I was and we talked for some time on the state of the country. They were all courteous and agreeable. Captain Kelly, who formerly knew me in Washington City, told me he was now in the quartermaster's department at Hilton Head. He was pleased to refer kindly to his recollection of me; alluded to my Milledgeville 'Union speech' of November, 1860; spoke highly of it and expressed regret that I had not adhered to it. I told him I had. In that speech I had, with all my ability, urged our people not to secede; the present consequences I then seriously apprehended; I told them that if, in solemn convention, the State should determine to resume her delegated powers and assert her sovereign and independent rights, I should be bound to go with her: to her I owed ultimate allegiance; her cause would be my cause, her destiny mine. I thought the step a wrong one—it might be fatal; and exerted my utmost power to prevent it; but when it was taken, even though against my judgment and counsel, I, as a good citizen, could but share the common fate, whatever it might be. I did, as a patriot, what I thought best before secession. I did the same after. Captain Kelly had not recollected that part of the speech acknowledging my ultimate allegiance as due to the State of Georgia.

"The whole conversation was quite friendly. He manifested a good deal of personal regard for me.

"About four, the *Clyde* put out to sea. Before leaving, Mrs. Davis addressed a note to [U.S.] General [Rufus] Saxton, who has charge of [black] colonization [i.e., deporting African-Americans out of the U.S.] in South Carolina, consigning to him the little mulatto boy [Jim Limber] she had with her. The parting of the boy with the family was quite a scene. He was about seven years old, and little Jeff's playfellow; they were always together; it was 'Jeff' and 'Jimmy' between them. When Jeff knew that Jimmy was to be left behind, he wailed, and so did Jimmy. Maggie cried and Billy cried, and the coloured woman (Ellen) cried. Mrs. Davis said the boy's mother had been dead a number of years and Ellen had been a mother to him. As the boat taking Jimmy moved off, he screamed. He had to be held to prevent his jumping overboard. He tried his best to get away from those holding him. At this, Jeff and Maggie and Billy screamed almost as loudly as Jimmy. Ellen wept aloud. Mrs. Davis shed tears. Mrs. Clay threw Jimmy some money but this had no effect. Some one on the deck of his boat picked it up and handed it to him; he paid no attention to it but kept on scuffling to get loose; he was wailing as long as he could be heard or seen by us.

"The sloop-of-war, *Tuscarora*, a steam propeller, put to sea soon after we left. We understood from Colonel Pritchard that she is bound to Fortress Monroe [Virginia]. The *Clyde* is long and narrow, and rolls very much. The purser, Mr. Moore, the captain's son, expressed some kind personal regard for me this evening; told me he was from Philadelphia; gave me a copy of *Harper's Weekly*: and said if I had any little thing that I could spare to give him as a memento, he would feel very much obliged. I was puzzled to think of anything I had that would answer his purpose. I chanced to have in my pocket a chess-piece of a set that was very prettily made. It was a bishop. I took it out, and asked him how that would do. He seemed highly pleased, and I was gratified that I was able to comply with his wishes.

"There was some misunderstanding about dinner. Nothing was said about it until we had left Hilton Head. It was getting late and several of our party expressed themselves as being hungry. I inquired about it of the steward, a coloured man from Washington City, who knew me. He said the captain had no provisions for us; our rations were on board but no arrangements had been made between Colonel Pritchard and the captain about cooking them. I gave him twenty-five cents in silver and told him to bring me some bread. This, with water, made my meal; I ate in the cabin below. The engineer, who in passing saw me, brought me some whisky. I knew from his manner and from what he said that, personally, he is a friend to me. I told the steward, Lucas, to give Anthony and Henry their dinners, and I would pay.

"Near night, a message came to me that dinner was ready. I went up on deck where I found a table set between two staterooms with several of our party, as many as could get at it, seated. It was a very good dinner. A remark by Mrs. Davis caused me to inquire about it afterward. She said we were indebted to her for it; she had ordered it. This led me to believe that we were each to pay for his meal, or that each ought to pay a ratable part. She did not say she had ordered it on private account. I inquired of the purser how it was. He said the captain, at the request of Mrs. Davis, had prepared dinner out of ship's stores and that it was furnished at seventy-five cents each. I paid him my part, and all the rest did likewise, I believe. Clear, beautiful night, but the vessel rolls very much.

"May 17.— Did not sleep much; not seasick, yet with symptoms strongly marked. This morning I told Anthony to come into the cabin with me. He was sick, seemingly almost unto death. I directed him to lie down, and remained with him. It seemed to do him good to have some one with him. He said Henry was forward and not sick much. Gave the steward fifty cents for breakfast, which I took myself in the cabin. Anthony could eat nothing. Saw Henry on deck. He seemed to be doing pretty well. Found General Wheeler on deck where he had spent the night; he was very seasick. Few of the party were out. Reagan had taken a berth in the lower cabin with me. He kept it closely. Mr. Clay was on deck; the sea never affects him, he told me. Mr. Davis was out. Did not seem to be much sick. He and Mr. Clay came into the lower cabin during the day, not together but separately. I had a long and friendly talk with each. Breakfast was served for the party at nine. I heard that a few were at table. The purser, during the morning, stripped bedclothes from all berths but mine in the cabin below. He indignantly said the occupants had gone to bed with their boots on. Reagan told me this was not the case with him. How it was with the others, I do not know. I had taken off my shoes but no other part of my clothing. The purser told me about one o'clock that Colonel Pritchard had arranged for our meals hereafter, and that they would be furnished without pay. About two [P.M.] dinner was announced. Mr. Davis, Mrs. Davis, Mr. Reagan, and myself were present, and some others. It was a good dinner for those who had appetites; I had none. The *Tuscarora* all day near us, sometimes in the rear, sometimes on the side, sometimes ahead. She spoke to our ship during the evening, giving the position at noon. Anthony continued very sick; I felt truly sorry for him.

"May 18.— Passed Cape Hatteras, the pilot told me, about one. Paid steward for cup of coffee and dry toast, which I took early. Anthony still very sick. Gave him some coffee and toast. He seemed to relish it but soon threw it up. Henry about on deck, not sick at all. General Wheeler still on deck, quite seasick. [Governor] Lubbock keeps close in his stateroom. So does Mrs. Clay. I called to see her with Mr. Clay. She seems to suffer severely. But no one seems so sick as Anthony. He can neither walk nor stand. Still in the cabin with me, where I can be with him.

"Dinner; present: Mr. Davis, Mr. Clay, Mr. Reagan and myself, with others. Mr. Davis's children, Jeff, Maggie, and Billy, do not appear to be seasick at all. Both nurses are ill. Mrs. Davis takes charge of the infant, relieved by Mr. Davis, Mr. Howell, her brother, and others. Jeff lost his hat somehow; it fell overboard; he wears General Wheeler's, as the General keeps stretched on deck in the shade and has no use for it. Grows cloudy toward night. Some entertain serious apprehensions that the *Clyde* could not weather a storm. She is too high and has too much exposure with her line of staterooms on deck.

"Tea at seven. Present: same as at dinner. Mr. Davis sits at the head of the table. All wait until he and Mrs. Davis are seated. He bows his head and asks a blessing, but not audibly. All wait until this is over; then the steward helps those seated, always beginning with Mr. Davis. About eight P.M. the *Tuscarora* came alongside and spoke to us, told the pilot our position and that we would enter Hampton Roads in the morning; to go about five knots an hour, no more.

"Hampton Roads, May 19.— On rising, was told by Lucas, that we were in sight of land. Cape Charles Lighthouse was quite visible when I went on deck. Breakfast for the party at nine. Mr. Davis looked quite well. Mrs. Davis well. Mrs. Clay now up. Governor Lubbock at the table, General Wheeler also. All the sick seem recovering except Miss Howell, whose illness is said to be more than seasickness. Anthony revives, walks out, gets his breakfast and seems all right again.

"Pilot boat meets us. We are asked where we wish to pilot to. 'To Washington' is the reply. A pilot comes aboard. The *Tuscarora* leads the way. Arrive at Hampton Roads. Colonel Pritchard goes to Fortress Monroe. Returns and says we must await orders from Washington. I had asked him to inquire if I might be permitted to telegraph or write home. He could bring no information on that point. We anchored in the harbour. *Tuscarora*, close by, anchored also. We see near us the iron steamer, *Atlanta*, captured at Savannah. Dinner at usual hour. All hands at table except Miss Howell, and all with good appetites except myself. My throat still sore, but much better than when I left Hilton Head; I had no cough last night. Sent for New York papers by the purser, who went ashore. He brought the *Richmond Enquirer*; said he could get no other paper.

"All anxious to know our destination; all desire to go to Washington.

"May 20.— Still at anchor in the Roads. Colonel Pritchard tells us that a telegram last night informed him that General [Henry W.] Halleck will be at the Fort at noon, and give him further orders. The day is dull; nothing to enliven it but the passing of steamboats and small sails. A British man-of-war and a French corvette lie near.

"Called Henry [the servant] into the cabin. Told him he would go from here to Richmond; sent my remembrance to his mother and Travis [a servant], gave him $10 and told him to be a good, industrious, honest and upright boy; not to gamble and never to bet. He promised to comply with my injunctions. Told him to tell Travis to come to see me if I should be sent to Washington. I told him Anthony would go with me for the present, if permitted.

"8 P.M.— Colonel Pritchard came to the cabin and told Judge Reagan and myself that some officers in the captain's room wished to see us there. We found [U.S.] Captain Frailey of the *Tuscarora* and [U.S.] Captain Parker of another war steamer. Captain Frailey received us courteously and told us he had orders to take Reagan and myself aboard the *Tuscarora* next day at ten; he had come to give notice that we might be prepared. 'What place is our destination, Captain?' I asked. 'Boston,' he replied. I knew then that Fort Warren was to be my place of imprisonment. I told him I feared the climate would be too cool and damp for me; I should greatly have preferred Washington if the authorities had so decided. I asked him how about Anthony's going with me. Told him the facts relating to Anthony. He could give no information but said he would inquire and let me know before ten in the morning. Before we left the captain's office, General Wheeler entered with his party. His conference was with Captain Parker. Captain Parker was to take them in his steamer to Fort Delaware. Reagan and I left Wheeler in the office. I sent for Captain Moody, now a fellow prisoner with Mr. Davis, and who had been a prisoner at Fort Warren, to learn something of regulations there. He spoke in favourable terms of them; said he had been in several prisons and had been better treated at Fort Warren than anywhere else. Being relieved of the suspense we had been in for several days, Reagan and I went to our berths at an early hour. I slept little. Thought of home, sweet home. Saw plainly that I was not to be permitted to communicate with any one there; this was the most crushing thought. Death, I felt, I could meet with resignation, if such was to be my fate, might I but communicate with Linton and other loved ones while life should last.

"Sunday.— Rose early. Took a towel bath, changed underclothes. Anthony rubbed me down for the last time. I told him I should leave him.

Gave him five dollars and the same advice and instructions I had given Henry. I added that I was going to Fort Warren. Told him to ask Mr. Baskerville to write this to Linton at Sparta and to John A. Stephens and George F. Bristow at Crawfordville, hoping that some one of them, if not all, might get the letters. Colonel Pritchard told me that all the coloured servants who should be left at this place, he would send to Richmond without charge. This I told Anthony, and bade him take care of his money, he might need it. I gave him my leather trunk that he had brought his clothes in.

"Saw Mrs. Clay and requested her to write Linton and Mrs. Dudley M. DuBose [Sallie Toombs, daughter of Robert A. Toombs] my destination and present condition. We do not know what is to be done with Mr. Clay, or where he is to be sent. After that shall be made known, it is Mrs. Clay's intention to go North if allowed; that is, if her husband shall be confined in prison. Yesterday we got New York papers. Saw the progress of the trial of the assassins [of Abraham Lincoln]. Mr. Clay expressed to me the fullest confidence that nothing could be brought out against him in such a crime; he spoke of the assassination in strongest terms of regret; said how deeply he deplored it; repeated his exclamation to that effect when he first heard the news. We had a long talk this morning.

"General Wheeler and those who went with him left at six A.M. I was up and took my leave of them. The parting all around was sad. At ten Captain Frailey came up in a tug, and boarded the *Clyde*. Reagan and I were ready. We took leave of all. Anthony and Henry looked very sad. Anthony stood by me to the last. Mrs. Davis asked Captain Frailey if Anthony might not go with me. He said he had inquired of the officer commanding the fleet and had been informed that his orders related to only two persons. This closed the matter just as I had anticipated. I bade Anthony goodbye the last one. Mr. and Mrs. Davis, Mr. and Mrs. Clay, and Mr. Harrison, I had taken leave of.

"On my taking leave of Mr. Davis, he seemed more affected than I had ever seen him. He said nothing but good-bye, and gave my hand a cordial squeeze; his tone evinced deep feeling and emotion. With assistance, I descended the rope-ladder to the tug's deck. All baggage being on, off we steamed to the *Tuscarora*. We stopped a short distance from her and took her lifeboat, as the tug could not well go alongside of her where the steps were let down for us to ascend by. The tide was running in fast, so that by the time we were in the oarboat and ready for the oarsmen, we had drifted farther from the *Tuscarora* than we were when we left the *Clyde*. The tide was coming right ahead of us at about six miles an hour and it was all that the stout seamen with their oars could do to make any head against it. Captain Frailey called twice, 'Send the tug!' but he was not heard on the *Tuscarora*. After a long while we reached the ship, but not without some wetting from splashing of waves over the sides of the lifeboat. Right glad was I when we reached the steps on the ship's side.

"On the *Tuscarora*.— On deck, we were introduced to several [U.S.] officers, Lieut. Blue, Purser Painter, and others. The captain showed us our quarters; we were to be in the cabin with him. There was but one berth or stateroom in it. This, he said, he would assign to me, and he and Reagan would sleep on the circular sofa which ran around the cabin. I declined depriving him of his room and bed. He said it was no deprivation, that he generally slept on the sofa or in a chair; that he resigned it to me 'in consideration of my age and past services to the country' [i.e., the U.S.]. These were his words. He was very polite and courteous.

"When boarding the *Clyde* that morning, he had brought some strawberries to Mrs. Davis, Mrs. Clay, and Mrs. Davis's children. He said he had known Mrs. Davis and Mrs. Clay before. The morning we entered Hampton Roads, he had come aboard to give orders to Colonel Pritchard. I did not see him then, but Mrs. Clay told me he had inquired for her; was very courteous to her, etc., and asked if there was any little delicacy he had that she needed, such as preserved or canned vegetables, etc. If so, he would take pleasure in sending her some. She declined; so the strawberries, I suppose, he thought would be acceptable. He had gotten them at Norfolk that morning.

"About eleven, anchor was weighed, and we were off. Our fellow prisoners on the *Clyde* stood on deck watching us. When we were fairly under way, we saw a white handkerchief waved toward us. This I felt was by Mrs. Clay, though we were too far off to see distinctly. Reagan and I waved handkerchiefs in return; thus bidding final adieu to them all, I went into the cabin below. Soon out of sight of land, with a clear sky over us, and nothing but the deep blue sea around. Took lunch with Captain Frailey: strawberries, cheese, etc. He lives to himself; the other officers mess to themselves. Dinner at three; soup, fish, roast beef, asparagus, etc. Tea at eight.

"May 22.— Last night I undressed and went to bed, as was my custom at home, for the first time since the night of the 10th, when I occupied my own bed for the last time. Slept sweetly and soundly. Breakfasted at eight; better appetite than for a week or more. Took a smoke in a room on upper deck. Met Lieut. Blue, Mr. Griffin, Mr. Painter, Mr. Mallard, officers of the ship and others. Spent a pleasant time in conversation with them. The captain joined us. The day passed off pleasantly. Lunch, dinner and tea as yesterday.

"May 23.— This morning thick fog. Captain made for Block Island [Rhode Island] to get a pilot. A signal gun was fired. Pilot came and took us to Newport [Rhode Island]. Reached there about twelve, and anchored in the harbour. The sun shone out. Lieut. Blue went ashore. Sent us papers.

Captain's son, in the naval school, came aboard and spent some time with his father. I passed the day, as yesterday, in the cabin and in the smoking-room above with officers. All courteous and agreeable.

"May 24.— Mr. Griffin knew Judge [Junius] Hillyer, of Georgia, and spoke kindly of him.

"We left Newport early this morning for Boston, with new pilot to take us through the sound, leaving Martha's Vineyard and Nantucket [Massachusetts] to the right. Lieut Blue told me that he met a lady, relative of [Lieutenant] Governor [William B.] Lawrence of Rhode Island, last evening, who expressed sentiments of personal kindness toward me. For this I felt profoundly grateful. It is a consolation to know and feel, as I do, that thousands in all sections of the earth sympathize with me, personally at least. We reached Boston Harbour at eleven P.M. and anchored just below Fort Warren.

"Fort Warren, May 25.— I rose early. Saw Boston in the distance; Fort Warren just ahead. We took our last breakfast with Captain Frailey. He informed us that General Dix was at the Fort and would come aboard to receive us at ten. The gunners got ready to fire a salute in the General's honour. Ten came. General Dix sent two officers, Colonel McMahon of his staff, to represent him, and Lieut. Ray, adjutant of the Post. They said they would take me first. A tug was brought alongside. Our steward, a Frenchman, and Isaac, the coloured cook who had attended to me well, had my baggage ready. I paid them for their attentions. I bade Judge Reagan good-bye in the cabin. Took my leave of all the boat's officers except the Captain, who accompanied the fort officers and myself. I expected we would go to General Dix, but was disappointed. Lieutenant Woodman, of the Fort, met us at the landing. To him I was turned over. Captain Frailey was with the officers who had brought me: before I was aware of it, we were separated, and I did not see him again; this I deeply regretted, inasmuch as I wished to say farewell and express again my sense of obligation for his many acts of kindness. Lieutenant Woodman brought me immediately inside the Fort; after going through the sally port and descending some steps, he stopped at the first room to the left, saying, 'This is your room,' or 'These are your quarters,' I forget which. I asked if I could not see Captain Frailey again. I asked if I could not see General Dix; I wished very much to see him about sending word to Linton and about my diet and conditions of prison life. He said 'No,' and left.

"I surveyed the room. A coal fire was burning; a table and chair were in the centre; a narrow, iron, bunk-like bedstead with mattress and covering was in a corner. The floor was stone—large square blocks. The door was locked. For the first time in my life I had the full realization of being a prisoner. I was alone."[102]

5

TESTIMONY BEFORE THE RECONSTRUCTION COMMITTEE 1866

LIKE MANY OTHER CONFEDERATE OFFICIALS and military officers, after Lincoln's War Stephens was dragged before the Yankees' farcical kangaroo court known as the "U.S. Reconstruction Committee." In fact, it was nothing more than a tribunal of retribution meant to further embarrass, terrorize, and persecute the already prostrate South. Stephens submitted to the ridiculous and unnecessary Nazi-style interrogation, proudly defending his conservative Southern principles to the end. Not only do we see clear evidence here of the Northern Liberal arrogance that both preceded and succeeded the War, but we gain insight into the condition of the Southern states, in particular Stephen's home state, Georgia, shortly following the conflict. The date is April 16, 1866. In this typical question and answer format, Stephens' words follow the "A."

[Alexander H. Stephens—Sworn and examined by Mr. Boutwell:]

Q. State your residence.

A. Crawfordville, Georgia.

Q. What means have you had since [Robert E.] Lee's surrender to ascertain the sentiments of the people of Georgia with regard to the Union?

A. I was at home, in Georgia, at the time of the surrender of General Lee, and remained there until the 11th of May, and during that time conferred very freely with the people in my immediate neighborhood, with the governor of the State, and with one or two other leading or prominent men in the State. From the 11th of May until my return to Georgia, which was the 25th of October, I had no means of knowing any thing of the public sentiment there, except through the public press and such letters as I received. From the time of my return until I left the State on my present visit here, I had very extensive intercourse with the people, visiting Augusta, visiting Milledgeville during the session of the legislature, first on their assembling, again in January upon their reassembling, and again in the latter part of February. While there, I conversed very freely and fully with all the prominent leading men, or most of them, in the legislature, and met a great many of the prominent, influential men of the State, not connected with the legislature; and by letters from and correspondence with men in the State whom I have not met. I believe that embraces a full answer to the question as to my means of ascertaining the sentiments of the people of that State upon the subject stated in the question.

Q. As the result of your observations, what is your opinion of the purpose of the people [of Georgia] with reference to the reconstruction of the government, and what are their desires and purposes concerning the maintenance of the government?

A. My opinion, and decided opinion, is that an overwhelming majority of the people of Georgia are exceedingly anxious for the restoration of the government, and for the State to take her former position in the Union, to have her senators and representatives admitted into Congress, and to enjoy all her rights and to discharge all her obligations as a State under the constitution of the United States as it stands amended.

Q. What are their present views concerning the justice of the rebellion? Do they at present believe that it was a reasonable and proper undertaking, or otherwise?

A. My opinion of the sentiment of the people of Georgia upon that subject is, that the exercise of the right of secession was resorted to by them from a desire to render their liberties and institutions more secure, and a belief on their part that this was absolutely necessary for that object. They were divided upon the question of the policy of the measure; there was, however, but very little division among them upon the question of the right of it. It is now their belief, in my opinion—and I give it merely as an opinion—that the surest, if not the only hope for their liberties is the restoration of the constitution of the United States and of the government of the United States under the constitution.

Q. Has there been any change of opinion as to the right of secession, as a right in the people or in the States?

A. I think there has been a very decided change of opinion, as to the policy, by those who favored it. I think the people generally are satisfied sufficiently with the experiment, never to resort to that measure of redress again, by force, whatever may be their own abstract ideas upon that subject. They have given up all idea of a maintenance of these opinions by a resort to force. They have come to the conclusion that it is better to appeal to the forums of reason and justice, to the halls of legislation and the courts, for the preservation of the principles of constitutional liberty, than to the arena of arms. It is my settled conviction that there is not any idea cherished at all in the public mind of Georgia, of ever resorting again to secession, or to the exercise of the right of secession by force. That whole policy for the maintenance of their rights, in my opinion, is at this time totally abandoned.

Q. But the opinion as to the right, as I understand, remains substantially the same?

A. I cannot answer as to that. Some may have changed their opinion in this respect. It would be an unusual thing, as well as a difficult matter, for a whole people to change their convictions upon abstract truths or principles. I have not heard this view of the subject debated or discussed recently, and I wish to be understood as giving my opinion only on that branch of the subject which is of practical character and importance.

Q. To what do you attribute the change of opinion as to the propriety of attempting to maintain their views by force?

A. Well, sir, my opinion about that—my individual opinion, derived from observation—is that this change of opinion arose mainly from the operation of the war among themselves, and the results of the conflict, from their own authorities on their individual rights of person and property—the general breaking down of constitutional barriers which usually attend all protracted wars.

Q. In 1861, when the ordinance of secession was adopted in your State, to what extent was it supported by the people?

A. After the proclamation of President Lincoln calling out seventy-five thousand militia, under the circumstances it was issued, and blockading the southern ports, and the suspension of the writ of *habeas corpus*, the southern cause, as it was termed, received the almost unanimous support of the people of Georgia. Before that they were very much divided on the question of the policy of secession. But afterward they supported the cause within the range of my knowledge, with very few exceptions, (there were some few exceptions, not exceeding half a dozen I think). The impression then prevailing was, that public liberty was endangered, and they supported the cause because of their zeal for constitutional rights. They still differed very much as to the ultimate object to be attained, and the means to be used, but these differences yielded to the emergency of the apprehended common danger.

Q. Was not the ordinance of secession adopted in Georgia, earlier in date than the proclamation for seventy-five thousand volunteers?

A. Yes, sir. I stated that the people were very much divided on the question of the ordinance of secession, but that after the proclamation the people became almost unanimous in their support of the cause. There were some few exceptions in the State—I think not more than half a dozen among my acquaintances. As I said, while they were thus almost unanimous in support of the cause, they differed also as to the end to be attained by sustaining it. Some looked to an adjustment or settlement of the controversy upon any basis that would secure their constitutional rights; others looked to a southern separate nationality as their only object and hope. These different views as to the ultimate objects did not interfere with the general active support of the cause.

Q. Was there a popular vote upon the ordinance of secession?

A. Only so far as in the election of delegates to the convention.

Q. There was no subsequent action?

A. No, sir; the ordinance of secession was not submitted to a popular vote afterward.

Q. Have you any opinion as to the vote it would have received, as compared with the whole, if it had been submitted to the free action of the people?

Witness [unnamed]. Do you mean after it was adopted by the convention?

Mr. Boutwell. Yes; after it was adopted by the convention, if it had been submitted forthwith, or within a reasonable time.

A. Taking the then state of things into consideration, South Carolina, Florida, and Mississippi, I think, having seceded, my opinion is that a majority of the people would have ratified it, and perhaps a decided or large majority. If, however, South Carolina and the other States had not adopted their ordinances of secession, I am very well satisfied that a majority of the people of Georgia, and perhaps a very decided majority, would have been against secession if the ordinance had been submitted to them. But as matters stood at the time if the ordinance had been submitted to a popular vote of the State, it would have been sustained. That is my opinion about that matter.

Q. What was the date of the Georgia ordinance?

A. The 18th or 19th; I think the 19th of January, 1861, though I am not certain.

Q. The question of secession was involved in the election of delegates to that convention, was it not?

A. Yes, sir.

Q. And was there on the part of candidates a pretty general avowal of opinions?

A. Very general.

Q. What was the result of the election as far as the convention expressed any opinion upon the question of secession?

A. I think the majority was about thirty in the convention in favor of secession. I do not recollect the exact vote.

Q. In a convention of how many?

A. In a convention based upon the number of senators and members of the House in the general assembly of the State. The exact number I do not recollect, but I think it was near three hundred, perhaps a few over or under.

Q. Was there any difference in different parts of the State in the strength of Union sentiment at that time?

A. In some of the mountain counties the Union sentiment was generally prevalent. The cities, towns, and villages were generally for secession throughout the State, I think, with some exceptions. The anti-secession sentiment was more general in the rural districts and in the mountain portions of the State; yet the people of some of the upper counties were very active and decided secessionists. There was nothing like a sectional division of the State at all. For instance, the delegation from Floyd county, in which the city of Rome is situated, in the upper portion of the State, was an able one, strong for secession, while the county of Jefferson, down in the interior of the cotton belt, sent one of the most prominent delegations for the Union. I could designate other particular counties in that way throughout the State, showing that there was not what might be termed a sectional or geographical division of the State on the question.

Q. In what particular did the people believe their constitutional liberties were assailed or endangered from the Union?

A. Mainly, I would say, in their internal social polity and their apprehension from the general consolidating tendencies of the doctrines and principles of that political party which had recently succeeded in the choice of a President and Vice-President of the United States. It was the serious apprehension that if the republican organization [the Republican Party in Stephens' day was identical to the Democratic Party of today], as then constituted, would succeed to power, it would lead ultimately to a virtual subversion of the constitution of the United States, and all essential guaranties of public liberty. I think that was the sincere and honest conviction in the minds of our people. Those who opposed secession did not apprehend that any such result would necessarily follow the elections which had taken place; they still thought that all their rights might be maintained in the Union and under the constitution, especially as there were majorities in both Houses of Congress who agreed with them on constitutional questions.

Q. To what feature of their internal social polity did they apprehend danger?

A. Principally the subordination of the African race as it existed under their laws and institutions.

Q. In what spirit is the emancipation of slaves received by the people?

A. Generally it is acquiesced in and accepted, I think, in perfect good faith, and with a disposition to do the best that can be done in the new order of things in this particular.

Q. What at present are the relations subsisting between the white people and black people, especially in the relation of employers and employed?

A. Quite as good, I think, as in any part of the world that ever I have been in, between like classes of employers and employees. The condition of things, in this respect, on my return last fall, was very different from what it was when I left home for my present visit to this city. During the fall and up to the close of the year, there was a general opinion prevailing among the colored people that at Christmas there would be a division of the lands, and a very general indisposition on their part to make any contracts at all for the present year. Indeed, there were very few contracts, I think, made throughout the State until after Christmas, or about the 1st of January. [U.S.] General [Davis] Tillson, who is at the head of the bureau in the State, and whose administration has given very general satisfaction to our people, I think, was very active in disabusing the minds of the colored people from their error in this particular. [Note: The Lincoln administration had lied to American blacks, stating that if the Union won the War, afterward Southern lands and plantations would be seized and divided up among them.] He visited quite a number of places in the State, and addressed large audiences of colored people, and when they became satisfied they were laboring under a mistake in anticipating a division of lands after Christmas and the 1st of January, they made contracts very readily generally, and since that time affairs have, in the main, moved on quite smoothly and quietly.

Q. Are the negroes generally at work?

A. Yes, sir; they are generally at work. There are some idlers; but this class constitutes but a small proportion.

Q. What upon the whole has been their conduct? Proper under the circumstances in which they have been placed, or otherwise?

A. As a whole, much better than the most hopeful looked for.

Q. As far as you know, what are the leading objects and desires of the negro population at the present time in reference to themselves?

A. It is to be protected in their rights of persons and of property—to be dealt by fairly and justly.

Q. What, if any thing, has been done by the legislature of your State for the accomplishment of these objects?

A. The legislature has passed an act of which the following is a copy:

> [No. 90.]
>
> AN ACT to define the term "persons of color," and to declare the rights of such persons.
>
> Sec. 1. Be it enacted, etc., That all negroes, mulattoes, mestizoes, and their descendants, having one eighth negro or African blood in their veins, shall be known in this State, as "persons of color."
>
> Sec. 2. Be it further enacted, That persons of color shall have the right to make and enforce contracts, to sue, be sued, to be parties and give evidence, to inherit, to purchase, and to have full and equal benefit of all laws and proceedings for the security of person and estate, and shall not be subjected to any other or different punishment, pain, or penalty for the commission of any act or offence than such as are prescribed for white persons committing like acts or offences.

"The third section of this act simply repeals all conflicting laws. It was approved by the governor on the 17th of March last.

Q. Does this act express the opinions of the people, and will it be sustained?

A. I think it will be sustained by the courts as well as by public sentiment. It was passed by the present legislature. As an evidence of the tone of the legislature of the State, as well as that of the people of the State upon this subject, I will refer you simply to a letter I wrote to [U.S.] Senator [William M.] Stewart upon the same subject. I submit to you a copy of that letter. It is as follows:

> 'Washington, D. C., April 4, 1866. Dear Sir: In answer to your inquiries touching the sentiments and feelings of the people of Georgia toward the freedmen, and the legal status of this class of population in the State, etc, allow me briefly to say that the address delivered by me on the 22nd of February last before the legislature (a copy of which I herewith hand you) expresses very fully and clearly my own opinions and feelings upon the subjects of your inquiry. This address was written and printed as you now see it, before its delivery. It was delivered verbatim as you now read it, that there might be no mistake about it. It was as it now stands unanimously indorsed by the Senate in a joint resolution, which was concurred in the House without dissent, and was ordered to be spread upon the journals of both Houses. This I refer you to as a better and more reliable index of the feelings and views of the people of the State on this subject than any bare individual opinion I might entertain or express. The legislature of the State,

it is to be presumed, is as correct an exponent of the general feelings and views of the State upon any political question as any that can be obtained from any quarter. In addition to this, the legislature subsequently evinced their principles by their works in passing an act, which I also inclose to you. This act speaks for itself. It is short, concise, pointed, as well as comprehensive. It secures to the colored race the right to contract and to enforce contracts, the right to sue and to be sued, the right to testify in the courts, subject to the same rules that govern the testimony of whites, and it subjects them to the same punishments for all offences as the whites. In these respects, embracing all essential civil rights, all classes in Georgia now stand equal before the law. There is no discrimination in these particulars on account of race or color. Please excuse this hasty note; I have no time to go more in detail. Yours, most respectfully, Alexander H. Stephens.'

Q. What, if any thing is being done in Georgia with regard to the education of the negroes, either children or adults?

A. Nothing by the public authorities as yet. Schools are being established in many portions of the State, under the auspices, I think, of the [U.S.] Freedmen's Bureau, and quite a number by the colored people themselves, encouraged by the whites.

Q. What disposition do the negroes manifest in regard to education?

A. There seems to be a very great desire on the part of the children and younger ones, and with their parents to have them educated.

Q. What is the present legal condition of those who have lived together as husband and wife? Do the laws recognize and sustain the relations and the legitimacy of their offspring?

A. Our State laws do. They recognize all those living as man and wife as legally man and wife. A good many of them took out licenses, and were married in the usual way. There is no difference in our laws in that respect. Licenses are issued for white and black alike, only they are prohibited from intermarrying with each other. The races are not permitted to intermarry [just as in the North before, during, and after the War].

Q. Were the amendments to the constitution of the State of Georgia, recently adopted, submitted to the people?

A. No, sir; they were not submitted. I have no hesitation, however, in expressing the opinion that nine tenths of the people would have voted for them if the constitution had been submitted. That is but an opinion. I heard no dissent at all in the State. I was there all the time. I got home before the convention adjourned. The State constitution, as made by the convention, would have been ratified almost without opposition. It would have been ratified *nem. con.* [an abbreviation of the Latin, *nemine contradicente*: "of one mind"; "without dissent"] if it had been submitted. This, at least, is my opinion.

Q. What was the voting population of your State in 1860?

A. Something upward of a hundred thousand.

Q. What is probably the present voting population?

A. The voting population of the State, under the present constitution, is perhaps eighty thousand. That is a mere estimate.

Q. Has there been any enumeration of the losses of Georgia in the field, in the military service?

A. No accurate estimate that I am aware of.

Q. What is it supposed to have been?

A. I am not able to answer the question with any thing like accuracy.

Q. What is the public sentiment of Georgia with regard to the extension of the right of voting to the negroes?

A. The general opinion in the State is very much averse to it [but only because most were still as yet quite uneducated].

Q. If a proposition were made to amend the constitution so as to have representation in Congress based upon voters substantially, would Georgia ratify such a proposed amendment, if it were made a condition precedent to the restoration of the State to political power in the government?

A. I do not think they would. The people of Georgia, in my judgment, as far as I can reflect or represent their opinions, feel that they are entitled under the constitution of the United States to representation without any further condition precedent. They would not object to entertain, discuss, and exchange views in the common councils of the country with the other States upon such a proposition, or any proposition to amend the constitution, or change it in any of its features, and they would abide by any such change if made as the constitution provides; but they feel that they are constitutionally entitled to be heard by their senators and members in the houses of Congress upon this or any other proposed amendment. I do not therefore think that they would ratify that amendment suggested as a condition precedent to her being admitted to representation in Congress. Such, at least, is my opinion.

Q. It is then your opinion that at present the people of Georgia would neither be willing to extend suffrage to the negroes, nor consent to the exclusion of the negroes from the basis of representation?

A. The people of Georgia, in my judgment, are perfectly willing to leave suffrage and the basis of representation where the constitution leaves it. They look upon the question of suffrage as one belonging exclusively to the States; one over which, under the constitution of the United States, Congress has no jurisdiction, power, or control, except in proposing amendments to the States, and not in exacting them from them, and I do not think, therefore, that the people of that State, while they are disposed, as I believe, earnestly, to deal fairly, justly, and generously with the freedmen, would be willing to consent to a change in the constitution that would give Congress jurisdiction over the question of suffrage. And especially would they be very much averse to Congress exercising any such jurisdiction, without their representatives in the Senate and House being heard in the public council upon this question that so vitally concerns their internal policy, as well as the internal policy of all the States.

Q. If the proposition were to be submitted to Georgia as one of the eleven States lately in rebellion, that she might be restored to political power in the government of the country upon the condition precedent that she should, on the one hand, extend suffrage to the negro, or, on the other, consent to their exclusion from the basis of representation, would she accept either proposition and take her place in the government of the country?

A. I can only give my opinion. I do not think she would accept either as a condition precedent presented by Congress, for they do not believe that Congress has the rightful power under the constitution to prescribe such a condition. If Georgia is a State in the Union, her people feel that she is entitled to representation without conditions imposed by Congress. And if she is not a State in the Union, then she could not be admitted as an equal with the others if her admission were trammelled with conditions that do not apply to all the rest alike. General universal suffrage amongst the colored people, *as they are now there* [i.e., still largely uneducated] would by our people be regarded as about as great a political evil as could befall them.

Q. If the proposition were to extend the right of suffrage to those who could read, and to those who had served in the Union armies, would that modification affect the action of the State?

A. I think the people of the State would be unwilling to do more than they have done for restoration. Restricted or limited suffrage would not be so objectionable as general or universal; but it is a matter that belongs to the State to regulate. The question of suffrage, whether universal or restricted, is one of State policy exclusively, as they believe. *Individually I should not be opposed to a proper system of restricted or limited suffrage to this class of our population* [i.e., educated blacks, which was Lincoln's view as well] but in my judgment it is a matter that belongs of constitutional right to the States to regulate exclusively, each for itself. But the people of that State, as I have said, would not willingly, I think, do more than they have done for restoration. *The only view in their opinion that could possibly justify the war which was carried on by the Federal [U.S.] government against them was the idea of the indissolubleness of the Union*—that those who held the administration for the time were bound to enforce the execution of the laws and the maintenance of the integrity of the country under the constitution; and since that was accomplished, since those who had assumed the contrary principle—the right of secession, and the reserved sovereignty of the States—had abandoned their cause, and the administration here was successful in maintaining the idea upon which war was proclaimed and waged, and the only view in which they supposed it could be justified at all—when that was accomplished, I say, the people of Georgia supposed their State was immediately entitled to all her rights under the constitution. That is my opinion of the sentiment of the people of Georgia, and I do not think they would be willing to do any thing further as a condition precedent to their being permitted to enjoy the full measure of their constitutional rights. I only give my opinion of the sentiment of the people at this time. They expected that as soon as the Confederate cause was abandoned, that immediately the States would be brought back into their practical relations with the government, as previously constituted. That is what they looked to. They expected that the State would immediately have their representatives in the Senate and in the House, and they expected in good faith, as loyal men, as the term is frequently used—I mean by it loyal to law, order, and the constitution—to support the government under the constitution. That was their feeling. *They [the Southern people] did what they did, believing it was best for the protection of constitutional liberty. Toward the constitution of the United States, as they construed it, the great mass of our people were as much devoted in their feelings as any people ever were toward any cause.* This is my opinion. As I remarked before, *they resorted to secession with a view of maintaining more securely these principles.* And when they found they were not successful in their object, in perfect good faith, as far as I can judge from meeting with them and conversing with them, looking to the future developments of their country in its material resources, as well as its moral and intellectual progress, their earnest desire and expectation was to allow the past struggle, lamentable as it was in its results, to pass by, and *to co-operate with the true friends of the constitution, with those of all sections who earnestly desire the preservation of constitutional liberty, and the perpetuation of the government in its purity.* They have been a little disappointed in this, and are so now. They are patiently waiting, however, and believing that when the passions of the hour have passed away, this delay in restoration will cease. They think they have done every thing that was essential and proper, and my judgment is that they would not be willing to do any thing further as a condition precedent. They would simply remain quiet and passive. [Emphasis added, L.S.]

Q. Does your own judgment approve the view you have given as the opinion of the people of the State?

A. My own judgment is very decided that the question of suffrage is one that belongs, under the constitution—and wisely so, too—to the States respectively and exclusively.

Q. Is it your opinion that neither of the alternatives suggested in the question ought to be accepted by the people of Georgia?

A. My own opinion is, that these terms ought not to be offered as conditions precedent. In other words, my opinion is, that it would be best for the peace, harmony, and prosperity of the whole country that there should be an immediate restoration—an immediate bringing back of the States into their original practical relations—and let all these questions then be discussed in common council. Then the representatives from the South could be heard, and you and all could judge much better of the tone and temper of the people than you could from the opinions given by any individuals. You may take my opinion, or the opinion of any individual, but they will not enable you to judge of the condition of the State of Georgia so well as for her own representatives to be heard in your public councils in her own behalf. My judgment, therefore, is very decided that it would have been better, as soon as the lamentable conflict was over, when the people of the South abandoned their cause and agreed to accept the issue—desiring, as they do, to resume their places for the future in the Union, and to look to the halls of Congress and the courts for the protection of their rights in the Union—it would have been better to have allowed that result to follow, under the policy adopted by the administration, than to delay it or hinder it by propositions to amend the constitution in respect to suffrage or any other new matter. I think the people of all the southern States would, in the halls of Congress, discuss these questions calmly and deliberately; and if they did not show that the views they entertained were just and proper, such as to control the judgment of the people of the other sections and States, they would quietly, patiently, and patriotically yield to whatever should be constitutionally determined in common council. But I think they feel very sensitively the offer to them of propositions to accept, while they are denied all voice in the common council of the Union under the constitution in the discussion of these propositions. I think they feel very sensitively that they are denied the right to be heard. And while, as I have said, they might differ among themselves in many points in regard to suffrage, they would not differ upon the question of doing any thing further as a condition precedent to restoration. And in respect to the alternate conditions to be so presented, I do not think they would accept the one or the other. My individual general views as to the proper course to be pursued in respect to the colored people are expressed in a speech made before the Georgia legislature, referred to in my letter to Senator Stewart, that was the proper forum, as I conceive, in which to discuss this subject. And I think a great deal depends in the advancement of civilization and progress, looking to the benefit of all classes, that these questions should be considered and kept before the proper forum.

Q. Suppose the States that are represented in Congress and Congress itself should be of the opinion that Georgia should not be permitted to take its place in the government of the country except upon its assent to one or the other of the two propositions suggested: is it then your opinion that under such circumstances Georgia ought to decline?

Witness [unnamed]. You mean the States now represented, and those only?

Mr. Boutwell. Yes.

Witness [unnamed]. You mean by Congress, Congress as it is now constituted, with the other eleven States excluded?

Mr. Boutwell. I do.

Witness [unnamed]. And you mean the same alternative proposition to be applied to all the eleven States as conditions precedent to their restoration?

Mr. Boutwell. I do.

A. *Then I think she ought to decline under the circumstances, and for the reasons stated; and so ought the whole eleven. Should such an offer be made and declined, and these States should thus continue to be excluded and kept out, a singular spectacle would be presented. A complete reversal of positions would be presented. In 1861 these States thought they could not remain safely in the Union without new guaranties, and now, when they agree to resume their former practical relations in the Union under the constitution as it is, the other States turn upon them and say they cannot permit them to do so, safely to their interest, without new guaranties on their part. The Southern States would thus present themselves as willing for immediate Union under the constitution, while it would be the Northern States opposed to it. The former disunionists would thereby become unionists, and the former unionists the practical disunionists.* [Emphasis added, L.S.]

[End of the first day of Stephens' testimony.]

[Second day of Stephens' testimony, under the questioning of Mr. Boutwell, resumes.]

Q. Do you mean to be understood in your last answer that there is no constitutional power in the government, as at present organized, to exact conditions precedent to the restoration to political power of the eleven States that have been in rebellion?

A. Yes, sir. That is my opinion.

Q. Do you entertain the same opinion in reference to the amendment to the constitution abolishing slavery?

A. I do. I think the States, however, abolished slavery in good faith, as one of the results of the war. Their ratification of the constitutional amendment followed as a consequence. I do not think there is any constitutional power on the part of the government to have exacted it as a condition precedent to their restoration under the constitution, or to the resumption of their places as members of the Union.

Q. What, in your opinion, is the legal value of the laws passed by Congress and approved by the President in the absence of senators and representatives from the eleven States?

A. I do not know what particular law you refer to; but my answer, generally, is, that the validity of all laws depends on their constitutionality. This is a question for the judiciary to determine. My own judgment, whatever it might be, would have to conform to the judicial determination of the question. It is a question for the courts to determine.

Q. Have you formed any opinion upon that question?

A. I cannot say that I have formed any matured opinion in reference to any particular act of Congress embraced in the question.

Q. Assume that Congress shall in this session, in the absence of senators and representatives from the eleven States, pass an act levying taxes upon all the people of the United States, including the eleven: is it your opinion that such an act would be constitutional?

A. I should doubt if it would be. It would certainly, in my opinion, be manifestly unjust, and against all ideas of American representative government. Its constitutionality would, however, be a question for the judiciary to decide, and I should be willing to abide by that decision, whatever it might be.

Q. If the eleven States have at present an immediate constitutional right to be represented in Congress on a footing with the States at present represented, has that been a continuous right from the formation of the government, or from the time of the admission of the new States respectively, or has it been interrupted by war?

A. *I think, as the Congress of the United States did not consent to the withdrawal of the seceding States, it was a continuous right under the constitution of the United States, to be exercised so soon as the seceding States respectively made known their readiness to resume their former practical relations with the federal government, under the constitution of the United States. As the general government denied the right of secession, I do not think any of the States attempting to exercise it thereby lost any of their rights under the constitution, as States, when their people abandoned that attempt.* [Emphasis added, L.S.]

Q. Is it or not your opinion that the legislatures and people of the eleven States, respectively, have at present such a right to elect senators and representatives to Congress; that it may be exercised without regard to the part which persons elected may have had in the rebellion?

A. I do not think they could exercise that right in the choice of their senators and members, so as to impair in the slightest degree the constitutional right of each House for itself to judge of the qualifications of those who might be chosen. The right of the constitutional electors of a State to choose, and the right of each House of Congress to judge, of the qualifications of those elected to their respective bodies, are very distinct and different questions. And in thus judging of qualifications, I am free to admit that in my opinion no one should be admitted as a member of either House of Congress who is not really and truly loyal to the constitution of the United States and to the government established by it.

Q. State whether from your observation the events of the war have produced any change in the public mind of the South upon the question of the reserved rights of the States under the constitution of the United States.

A. That question I answered in part yesterday. While I cannot state from personal knowledge to what extent the opinions of the southern States upon the abstract question of the reserved rights of the States may have changed, my decided opinion is that a very thorough change has taken place upon the practical policy of resorting to any such right.

Q. What events or experience of the war have contributed to this change?

A. First, the people are satisfied that a resort to the exercise of this right, while it is denied by the federal government, will lead to war, which many thought before the late attempted secession would not be the case; and civil wars they are also now very well satisfied are dangerous to liberty; and, moreover, their experience in the late war I think satisfied them that it greatly endangered their own. I allude especially to the suspension of the writ of *habeas corpus*, the military conscriptions, the proclamations of martial law in various places, general impressments, and the levying of forced contributions, as well as the very demoralizing effects of war generally.

Q. When were you last a member of the Congress of the United States?

A. I went out on the 4th of March, 1859.

Q. Will you state, if not indisposed to do so, the considerations or opinions which led you to identify yourself with the rebellion so far as to accept the office of Vice-President of the Confederate States of America, *so called*? [Emphasis added, L.S.]

A. I believed thoroughly in the reserved sovereignty of the several States of the Union under the compact of Union or constitution of 1787. I opposed secession, therefore, as a question of policy, and not one of right on the part of Georgia. When the State seceded against my judgment and vote, I thought my ultimate allegiance was due to her, and I preferred to cast my fortunes and destinies with hers and her people, rather than to take any other course, even though it might lead to my sacrifice and her ruin. *In accepting position under the new order of things, my sole object was to do all the good I could in preserving and perpetuating the principles of liberty, as established under the constitution of the United States. If the Union was to be abandoned either with or without force—which I thought a very impolitic measure—I wished, if possible, to rescue, preserve, and perpetuate the principles of the constitution. This, I was not without hope, might be done in the new confederacy of States formed.* When the conflict arose, my efforts were directed to as speedy and peaceful an adjustment of the questions as possible. This adjustment I always thought to be lasting, would have ultimately to be settled upon a continental basis, founded upon the principles of mutual convenience and reciprocal advantage on the part of the States, on which the constitution of the United States was originally formed. I was wedded to no particular plan of adjustment, except the recognition, as a basis, of the separate sovereignty of the several States. With this recognized as a principle, I thought all other questions of difference would soon adjust themselves, according to the best interests, peace, welfare, and prosperity of the whole country, as enlightened reason, calm judgment, and a sense of justice might direct. This doctrine of the sovereignty of the several States I regarded as a self-adjusting, self-regulating principle of our American system of State governments, extending, possibly, over the continent. [Emphasis added, L.S.]

Q. Have your opinions undergone any change since the opening of the rebellion in reference to the reserved rights of States under the constitution of the United States?

A. My convictions on the original abstract question have undergone no change, but I accept the issues of the war and the result as a practical settlement of that question. The sword was appealed to decide the question, and by the decision of the sword I am willing to abide.[103]

6

RESPONSE TO REVIEWERS 1872

Following the publication of his seminal two-volume work, *A Constitutional View of the Late War Between the States* in 1868 and 1870, Conservative Stephens was, of course, viciously attacked by Liberal Yankees. He received so many negative reviews, in fact, that by 1872 he felt it necessary to respond by coming out with a supplemental book entitled *The Reviewers Reviewed*, which contained a compilation of earlier replies to his critics.

Though criticism of the former Confederate vice president came from all corners of the North, covering every possible topic discussed in *A Constitutional View*, none encompassed the Victorian Yankee loathing and misunderstanding of Stephens and the South more than the review of his book by New England abolitionist-socialist Horace Greeley (owner and editor of the *New York Tribune*).

What follows is Stephens' "review" of Greeley's "review"—which, though undated, seems to have been originally published sometime in early to mid 1869. Stephens' August 17, 1869, response to Greeley was published in the Augusta, Georgia, paper, the *Constitutionalist*:

☞ "Liberty Hall, Crawfordville, Ga., August 17, 1869. Messrs. Editors of the *Constitutionalist*, Augusta, Ga.: Will you please allow me the use of your columns to reply to an article in a late number of the *New York Tribune*, written by the Hon. Horace Greeley, and which requires some notice from me.

"In this article, Mr. Greeley, after alluding to my work upon the 'War between the States,' and late letters in reply to Judge [S. S.] Nicholas upon the same subject, goes on to say:

'Mr. Stephens' theory is, that the Union was a mere league of Sovereign Powers; and, of course, dissoluble at the pleasure of those Powers respectively—of a minority, or, in fact, of anyone of them, so far as that one is concerned. And he quotes sundry conspicuous Republicans [Liberals]—among them, Abraham Lincoln, Benjamin F. Wade, and Horace Greeley—as having, at some time, favored this view.

'Mr. Stephens is utterly mistaken. Leaving others to speak for themselves, we can assure him that Horace Greeley never, at any moment of his life, imagined that a single State, or a dozen of States, could rightfully dissolve the Union. The doctrine of Horace Greeley, which Mr. Stephens has confounded with State Sovereignty, is that of Popular Sovereignty, or the right of a people to recast or modify their political institutions and relations—the right set forth by Thomas Jefferson in the Declaration of American Independence, as follows:

> "We hold these truths to be self-evident; that all men are created equal; that they are endowed by their Creator with certain inalienable rights; that among these are life, liberty, and the pursuit of happiness; that, to secure these rights, Governments are instituted among men, deriving their just powers from the consent of the governed; that, whenever any form of Government becomes destructive of these ends, it is the right of the people to alter or abolish it, and to institute a new Government, laying its foundation on such principles, and organizing its powers in such form as to them shall seem most likely to effect their safety and happiness."

'This doctrine of Jefferson's we have ever received; and we have held it precisely as it reads. The same is true, we presume, of Messrs. Lincoln, Wade, and other Republicans. Mr. Stephens may say it justifies the so-called Secession of the South; we think differently. We hold that Secession was the work of a violent, subversive, bullying, terrorizing minority, overawing and stifling the voice of a decided majority of the Southern people. The facts which justify this conclusion are embodied in *The American Conflict*, more especially in vol. I., chap. xxii. According to Mr. Stephens' conception, a majority of the people of Delaware, consisting of less than 100,000 persons, might lawfully dissolve the Union; but the whole population of New York south of the Highlands—at least 1,500,000 in number—could do nothing of the kind. Mr. Stephens' may possibly be the true doctrine, but it certainly never was ours, nor any Republican so far as we know. The right we affirm is not based on the Federal Constitution, but is before and above any and all Constitutions.'

"I quote him in full on the points to be commented on, that your readers and the public may thoroughly understand them, and be able to judge fairly and justly between us, and come to a correct conclusion as to whether I or he was or is mistaken in the premises.

"Now what is affirmed by me in the first volume of the 'Constitutional View of the Late War between the States,' and what Mr. Greeley, with other Republicans, is quoted therein to sustain, is this:

> 'Men of great ability of our own day—men who stand high in the Republican [Liberal] ranks at this time, who had and have no sympathy with the late Southern movement, are fully committed to the rightfulness of that movement. Mr. Lincoln himself was fully committed to it. Besides him, I refer you to but two others of this class, now prominent actors in public affairs. They are Senator Wade, of Ohio, at this time Vice President of the United States, and Mr. Greeley, of the *New York Tribune*, who is "a power behind the throne greater than the throne itself."'

"Then after quoting Senator Wade, with comments on his utterances, I go on to quote from the *New York Tribune*, of the 9th of November, 1860, an article which is acknowledged by Mr. Greeley to be his, and published in his history of the war, the 'American Conflict,' page 359, vol. I., as follows:

> 'The telegraph informs us that most of the Cotton States are meditating a withdrawal from the Union, because of Lincoln's election. Very well: they have a right to meditate, and meditation is a profitable employment of leisure. We have a chronic, invincible disbelief in Disunion as a remedy for either Northern or Southern grievances. We cannot see any necessary connection between the alleged disease and this ultra-heroic remedy; still, we say, if any one sees fit to meditate Disunion, let him do so unmolested. That was a base and hypocritic row that was once raised at Southern dictation, about the ears of John Quincy Adams, because he presented a petition for the dissolution of the Union. The petitioner had a right to make the request; it was the Member's duty to present it. And now, if the Cotton States consider the value of the Union debatable, we maintain their perfect right to discuss it. Nay: we hold with Jefferson, to the inalienable right of Communities to alter or abolish forms of Government that have become oppressive or injurious; and, *if the Cotton States shall decide that they can do better out of the Union than in it, we insist on letting them go in peace. The right to secede may be a revolutionary one, but it exists nevertheless; and we do not see how one party can have a right to do what another party has a right to prevent.* We must ever resist the asserted right of any State to remain in the Union, and nullify or defy the laws thereof; to withdraw from the Union is quite another matter. And, *whenever a considerable section of our Union shall deliberately resolve to go out, we shall resist all coercive measures designed to keep it in. We hope never to live in a Republic, whereof one section is pinned to the residue by bayonets.* [Emphasis added, L.S.]

'But, while we thus uphold the practical liberty, if not the abstract right of Secession, we must insist that the step be taken, if it ever shall be, with the deliberation and gravity befitting so momentous an issue. Let ample time be given for reflection; let the subject be fully canvassed before the people; and let a popular vote be taken in every case, before Secession is decreed. Let the people be told just why they are asked to break up the Confederation [an early name for the U.S., originally designed by the Founders to be a confederate republic]; let them have both sides of the question fully presented; let them reflect, deliberate, then vote; and let the act of Secession be the echo of an unmistakable popular fiat. A judgment thus rendered, a demand for Separation so backed, would either be acquiesced in without the effusion of blood, or those who rushed upon carnage to defy and defeat it, would place themselves clearly in the wrong.'

"I give above, this quotation [of Greeley's] in full, as I did in the book referred to, that no injustice may be done to him by partial extracts.

"What I quoted him to sustain, was, as clearly appears, the rightfulness of Secession in itself, and no particular theory of mine touching the principles upon which it was based. Does not the article from his own paper and book, above spread before your readers, fully sustain my affirmation for which the quotation was made? Was I 'utterly mistaken?' Or did I in any way confound State Sovereignty with Popular Sovereignty? What difference Mr. Greeley sees between State Sovereignty and Popular Sovereignty I know not. By State Sovereignty I understand the sovereignty of the people composing a State in an organized political body. But what I affirmed, and quoted him to sustain, rested upon no distinction between these phrases. It was simply as to the rightfulness of the act in itself, on the part of the people of a State, without reference to the source of the right. My comments on this question in the book, page 518, are as follows. I give them in full also, that it may be clearly seen that no injustice was done to him:

'What better argument could I make to show the rightfulness of Secession, if the Southern States, of their own good will and pleasure, chose to resort to it, even for no other cause than Mr. Lincoln's election, than is herein set forth in his own pointed, strong, and unmistakable language? It is true, he waives all questions of Compact between the States. He goes deeper into fundamental principles, and plants the right upon the eternal truths announced in the Declaration of Independence. That is bringing up principles, which I have not discussed, not because I do not endorse them as sound and correct, to the word and letter, but because it was not necessary for my purpose. Upon these immutable principles, the justifiableness of Georgia in her Secession Ordinance of the 19th of January, 1861, will stand clearly established for all time to come. For if, with less than one hundred thousand population, she was such a people in 1776 as had the unquestionable right to alter and change their form of Government as they pleased, how much more were they such a people, with more than ten times the number in 1861? The same principle applies to all the States which quit the old and joined the new Confederation. Mr. Greeley here speaks of the Union as a Confederation and not a Nation. This was, perhaps, the unconscious utterance of a great truth when the true spirit was moving him.

'The State of Georgia did not take this step, however, in withdrawing from the Confederation, without the most thorough discussion. It is true it was not a dispassionate discussion. Men seldom, if ever, enter into such discussions with perfect calmness, or even that degree of calmness with which all such subjects ought to be considered. But the subject was fully canvassed before the people. Both sides were strongly presented. In the very earnest remonstrance against this measure made by me, on the 14th of November, 1860, to which you have alluded, was an appeal equally earnest for just such a vote as he suggests, in order that the action of the State on the subject might be "the echo of an unmistakable popular fiat." On the same occasion I did say, in substance, just what he had so aptly said before, that the people of Geogia, in their Sovereign capacity, had the right to secede if they chose to do so, and that in this event of their so determining to do, upon a mature consideration of the question, that I should bow in submission to the majesty of their will so expressed!

'This, when so said by me, is what it seems was "the dead fly in the ointment" of that speech, so sadly "marring its general perfume." This was "the distinct avowal of the right of the State to overrule my personal convictions and plunge me," as he says, "into treason to the Nation."

'Was not the same "dead fly in the ointment" of his article of the 9th of November, only five days before? And if going with my State in what he declared she had a perfect right to do, plunged me into treason to the Nation, is he not clearly an accessory before the fact, by a rule of construction not more strained than that laid down in the trial of State cases by many judges not quite so notoriously infamous as Jeffreys? By a rule not more strained than that which would make out treason in the act itself! But I do not admit the rule in its application either to the accessory or the principal.'

"So much for the allegation that I was utterly mistaken!

"Now let me turn upon Mr. Greeley and ask, how it is with him in the premises? Was he not 'utterly mistaken' when he said so vauntingly for himself in the article now under review, 'Horace Greeley never at any moment of his life imagined that a single State or a dozen of States could rightly dissolve the Union!'

"Did he not expressly say, on the 9th of November, 1860, through the columns of the *Tribune*, that 'if the Cotton States shall decide that they can do better out of the Union than in it, we insist on letting them go in peace. The right to secede may be a revolutionary one, but it exists nevertheless; and we do not see how one party can have a right to do what another party has a right to prevent. We must ever resist the asserted right of any State to remain in the Union, and nullify or defy the laws thereof; to withdraw from the Union is quite another matter!'

"But, besides what I quoted him as saying, did he not, on the 17th day of December, 1860, three days before the Secession of South Carolina, in the *Tribune*, assert:

'If it [the Declaration of Independence] justified the Secession from the British Empire of three millions of colonists in 1776, we do not see why it would not justify the Secession office millions of Southrons from the Federal Union in 1861. If we are mistaken on this point, why does not some one attempt to show wherein and why?'

"Again: Did he not in the *Tribune*, on the 23rd day of February, 1861, five days after the inauguration of President Davis, at Montgomery, use this language:

'We have repeatedly said, and we once more insist, that the great principle embodied by Jefferson in the Declaration of American Independence, that Governments derive their just powers from the consent of the governed, is sound and just; and that if the Slave States, the Cotton States, or the Gulf States only, choose to form an Independent Nation, *they have a clear and moral right to do so.*'

"These quotations from the *Tribune* I see set forth by ex-President [James] Buchanan in his work entitled 'Buchanan's Administration,' page 97. I take it for granted they are correct. Then how, in the face of all these proofs, can the *Tribune* now say, that 'Horace Greeley never, at any moment of his life, imagined that a single State, or a dozen States, could rightfully dissolve the Union."

"Is not this a full and explicit acknowledgment of the right of a State to withdraw or secede? Did the Southern States ever attempt to dissolve the Union in any other way than by peaceably seceding or withdrawing from it? Mr. Greeley knows, and the world knows, that they did not.

"One other remark upon this editorial now under consideration. In it Mr. Greeley says:

'According to Mr. Stephens' conception, a majority of the people of Delaware, consisting of less than 100,000 persons, might lawfully dissolve the Union, but the whole population of New York, south of the Highlands—at least 1,500,000 in number—could do nothing of the kind. Mr. Stephens' may possibly be the true doctrine, but it certainly never was ours, nor of any Republican, so far as we know. The right, we affirm, is not based on the Federal Constitution, but is before and above any and all Constitutions.'

"Just so, let it be said to Mr. Greeley, with the doctrine advanced by me in the book referred to! It is not based on the Federal Constitution, but upon the authority that made that Compact. It is based upon principles existing 'before and above any and all Constitutions.' It is based upon the Paramount Authority (call it Popular Sovereignty or State Sovereignty, or by any other name) by which all organized States or Peoples can rightfully make or unmake State or Federal Constitutions at their pleasure; subject only to the great moral law, which regulates and governs the actions and conduct of nations!

"My conception, however, involves no such nonsense as that exhibited in his statement of it, touching the relative populations of the whole State of Delaware, and a portion only (being a large minority, however,) of the population of the State of New York. Populations in this respect must be looked to, and considered in their organized character. The doctrine advocated by me with all its corollaries rests upon the fact that Delaware, however small her population, is a perfectly organized State—is a Sovereign State—and as such is an integral Member of our Federal Republic, and that New York with her ever so many more people is no more. The doctrine is that ours is indeed a Federal Republic—constituted, not of one people in mass, as a single Republic is, but composed of a number of separate Republics.

"In this Federal Republic, the little Republic of Delaware by the Constitution of the United States, which sets forth the terms of the Compact between these several Republics composing the Union, has just as much political power in the enactment of all Federal laws, as the great Republic of New York has, without any regard to their relative, respective populations. In the Congress of States, which is provided for by the Constitution to take charge of all Federal matters entrusted to its control, Delaware, to-day, with her little over one hundred thousand population, stands perfectly equal in political power to New York with her nearly forty times that number! Congress under our system means the same now it ever meant. It means the meeting or assemblage of the States composing the Union by their accredited Representatives in Grand Council. In this Grand Council, or Congress of States, Delaware has as much political power as New York. It is true in one House of this Congress, her one member has but little showing against the thirty odd members of New York.

But her equality of power is maintained in the other. Here this perfect equality of political power between all the States is as distinctly retained under the second Articles of Union as it was under the first. No law can be passed by the Congress, if a majority of the States, through their 'Ambassadors' in the Senate, object.

"It is on this principle, that the six New England States with a fraction over three millions of population, under the census of 1860, have in the last resort in the Council Chambers of the Congress, six times as much power in determining all questions before them, as the State of New York, though New York alone has a population of over half a million more than all these other States together! It is upon this principle that these six States have as much power in the administration of the Government as the six States of New York, Pennsylvania, Virginia, Ohio, Indiana, and Illinois had with their aggregate population of thirteen and a half millions in 1860!

"These are facts which neither Mr. Greeley nor anybody else can successfully controvert.

"Ours, therefore, being a Federal Government, is and must be, as all other Federal Governments are, 'a Government of States, and for States,' with limited powers directed to specific objects; and not a Government in any sense or view for the masses of the people of the respective States in their internal and municipal affairs. This great Sovereign Power of Local Self-Government, for which Independence was declared and achieved, resides with the people of the respective States.

"A ready and sufficient answer to Mr. Greeley's distorted 'conception' about the political power of the comparative populations of Delaware and New York, may be given to him from his own doctrines. It is this: If a majority of the people of Delaware, after due deliberation and full consideration, have the same right, whether by virtue of State Sovereignty or Popular Sovereignty, to withdraw from the Union which they had to declare their Independence of Great Britain, which he admits they have, it does not therefore follow that less than half the population of the State of New York can, with equal right, carry that State out, against the will of the majority, though the minority in New York wishing to do so be five hundred or five thousand times greater in number than the majority in Delaware! He may, therefore, not be alarmed at any of the legitimate consequences of his own doctrines!

"What he says about Secession having been carried in the Southern States by 'a violent, subversive, bullying, terrorizing, minority, overawing and stifling' a majority of the people of these States, is nothing but bald and naked assertion, which cannot be maintained against the facts of history. The question was as thoroughly discussed as any ever was before the people. Conventions were regularly called by the duly constituted authorities of the States, and members duly elected thereto, according to law in all the States, which seceded before Mr. Lincoln's Proclamation of War. These elections were as orderly as elections usually are in any of the States on great occasions. In these Conventions, Ordinances of Secession were passed by decided majorities! It is true that a large minority in all these Conventions, save one, and in all these States, were opposed to Secession as a question of policy; very few in any of them questioned the Right, or doubted their Duty to go with the majority. But *after Mr. Lincoln's Proclamation of War—after his illegal and unconstitutional call for troops—after his suspension of the Writ of* Habeas Corpus, *no people on earth were ever more unanimous in any cause than were the people of the Southern States, in defence of what they deemed the great essential principles of American Free Institutions!* There was not one in ten thousand of the people, in at least ten of the Southern States, whose heart and soul were not thoroughly enlisted in the cause! Nor did any people on earth ever make greater or more heroic sacrifices for its success, during four long years of devastation, blood, and carnage! [Emphasis added, L.S.]

"A majority of the people overawed and terrorized by a minority! Indeed!

"If so, what became of this majority when the Confederate Armies, which stood between them and their deliverers, were overpowered? Where is this majority now, even with the sweeping disfranchisement which silences so many of the overawing tyrants? Why has it not been permitted to exercise the inalienable Right of Self-Government, even with the reinforcement of the enfranchised blacks? Why are so many of these States, till this day, held under military rule, with their whole populations 'pinned' to very bad Government by Federal [U.S.] bayonets, under the pretext of their continued 'disloyalty?' This assertion, as to the state of things in the beginning, is as utterly groundless in fact, as it is utterly inconsistent with the gratuitous assumptions on which the present pretext is based!

"Is it not amazing, Messrs. Editors, that Mr. Greeley in the face of the facts for the last four years, to say nothing of those of the war, when, according to his own showing, the Administration at Washington in rushing into it, were in 'the wrong'—I say, to omit all mention of the wrongs of the war, its immense sacrifices of blood and treasure, is it not amazing in the highest degree, that Mr. Greeley, in the face of the facts of the last four years only, should now repeat to us the Principles of American Independence as his creed? Have not the Constitutions of ten States, as made and adopted by the people thereof, 'founded on such principles and organized in such form as seemed to them most likely to effect their safety and happiness,' been swept from existence by military edict? Have not the people in these ten States, including the arbitrarily enfranchised blacks, been denied the right to form new Constitutions, laying their foundations on such principles and organizing its powers in such form as to them shall seem most likely to effect their safety and happiness? Have they not been required, and literally compelled, to form such Constitutions as seemed most likely to effect the safety and security of the dominant faction at Washington?

"Is this holding up to our gaze these immutable and ever-to-be-reverenced Principles of the Declaration of Independence, at this time and under the present circumstances, intended only as mockery added to insult, injury, and outrage? Yours, most respectfully, Alexander H. Stephens."[104]

7

EXCERPTS FROM STEPHENS' HISTORY OF THE U.S. 1874

IN 1874 STEPHENS PUBLISHED HIS *A Compendium of the History of the United States: From the Earliest Settlements to 1872*. According to its author the purpose of the work was "to give to the Youth of the country, as well as general readers, a condensed History of the United States of America; embracing all important facts connected with the discovery and early occupation of the country, within their limits, by immigrants from other lands; together with the facts attending the formation of their Governments, and the establishment of those free institutions which have so marked, as well as distinguished them, among the nations of the earth." What follows is a brief excerpt from Stephens' chapters on "The Administration of Lincoln."

☛ "The War Between the States: First Year.

"I. Abraham Lincoln, of Illinois, 16th President of the United States, was duly inaugurated at the usual place on the 4th of March, 1861, aged 52 years and 20 days. Borne in an open carriage, he was escorted and guarded from Willard's Hotel to the Capitol by an armed military force, under the direction of Gen. [Winfield] Scott, the General-in-chief of the Army of the United States. The oath of office was administered by Chief-Justice [Roger B.] Taney, in the presence of an audience estimated at 10,000. His Inaugural Address was read from a manuscript. It indicated no decisive policy, except the maintenance of the 'Union,' which he claimed to be 'older than the States,' and his purpose to collect the public revenues at the ports of the seceded States, as well as to 'hold, occupy, and possess' all the forts, arsenals, and other public property before held by the Federal authorities. . . .

"3. On the 12th of March the Confederate States Commissioners addressed a note to Mr. [William H.] Seward, Secretary of State, setting forth the character and object of their mission. In it they said:

> 'The undersigned are instructed to make to the Government of the United States overtures for the opening of negotiations, assuring the Government of the United States that the President, Congress, and people of the Confederate States earnestly desire a peaceful solution of these great questions; that it is neither their interest nor their wish to make any demand which is not founded in strictest justice, nor do any act to injure their late Confederates.'

". . . 4. From subsequent disclosures, it appears that it was the intention of Mr. Lincoln to withdraw the Federal forces from Fort Sumter at an early day, when the assurance to that effect was given; but when this intention became known in his party circles, the Governors of seven of the Northern States, which were under the control of the Agitators, assembled in Washington, and prevailed on him to change his policy. It was after this that the war preparations mentioned were secretly commenced and carried on; and 'faith as to Sumter' was only so far 'kept' as to give notice, on the 8th of April, not to the Confederate Commissioners, but to Gov. [Francis W.] Pickens, of S.C., of a change of the policy of the Administration in regard to the assurance given, and that a fleet was then on its way to reinforce the fort, as stated.

". . . 6. This was the beginning of a war between the States of the Federal Union, which has been truly characterized as 'one of the most tremendous conflicts on record.' The din of its clangor reached the remotest parts of the earth, and the people of all nations looked on, for four years and upwards, in wonder and amazement, as its gigantic proportions loomed forth, and its hideous engines of destruction of human life and everything of human structure were terribly displayed in its sanguinary progress and grievous duration.

"About this war—its origin, causes, conduct, guilt, crimes, consequences, and results, as well as its sufferings, sacrifices, and heroic exploits—many volumes have already been published, and many more will doubtless be published; but in reference to the whole, it may with reverence be
said, that if everything done in it, and 'every one' attending it deserving notice, should be duly recorded, 'even the world itself could not contain the books that should be written.'

". . . 7. The telegraphic announcement of the fall of Sumter enabled the Agitators to inflame the minds of the people of the Northern States under their influence to a higher pitch than ever, and to add to their ranks large accessions from the ranks of the Democratic [Conservative] and American parties. A cry was now raised by them for the maintenance of that Union which they had before denounced as 'a covenant with death, and an agreement with hell.' Upon the Confederates was charged the guilt of a desecration of the national flag, and with it the crime of treason. The beginning of the war with all its responsibilities was laid at their door. Mr. Lincoln, on the 15th of April, issued a Proclamation calling for 75,000 troops, and convening Congress to meet in Extra Session on the 4th of July. Thus stood the case on one side.

"On the other, the Confederates maintained that the silencing by them of the guns of Sumter was only an act of defence in anticipation of an approaching attack from a hostile fleet, as announced by the notification to Gov. Pickens of the intention of the Federal authorities to 'reinforce Fort Sumter, peaceably, if permitted; but forcibly, if necessary.' This they regarded as a declaration of war, already initiated by the Federals. They held that the war was in fact begun when this fleet put to sea for the purpose stated, and that it was formally declared by the notification given. They stood upon the well-established principle of public law, that 'the aggressor in a war' (that is, he who begins it) 'is not the first who uses force, but the first who renders force necessary.' They held, that under the Constitution of 1787, by which the previously existing Federal Union between the States had been strengthened and made 'more perfect,' the sovereignty of the several States was still reserved by the parties respectively, and with it the right of eminent domain was retained by each within its limits—that the Federal authorities had no rightful military jurisdiction over the soil upon which Fort Sumter was erected, except by the consent of the State of South Carolina. This was expressly stipulated in the Constitutional Compact, and when South Carolina had re-assumed her sovereign jurisdiction over her entire territory, the possession of this fort (erected by her consent, for the special protection of her own chief city, as well as the common defence of the other States) justly belonged to her. They maintained further that she and her new Confederates had the right legally and morally to claim and take possession of it; and that any attempt by force to resist the exercise of this right by any other Power, was an act of war upon her and them. Mr. Lincoln's call for troops, therefore, was met by the Government at Montgomery by a similar call for volunteers to repel aggressions. So matters stood on both sides.

". . . 12. The year of 1865 opened gloomily upon the Confederates. The greater part of their territory was occupied by the Federals, who had over a million of men now in the field; while they could muster under arms but little, if any, over 150,000. Their supply of subsistence was also nearly exhausted.

". . . The end was now rapidly approaching. [Yankee General William T.] Sherman commenced, about the 1st of February, his advance from Savannah through South Carolina, laying everything waste before him, as he had done in Georgia. Columbia was burnt by the Federals under him on the 17th of February. On the same day the small Confederate force which had continued to hold Charleston and Fort Sumter was withdrawn from that place. This, with the fragments of other shattered armies, amounting in all to about 35,000 men, constituted the entire force that could be brought to face Sherman's legions in their progress to join [Yankee General Ulysses S.] Grant in Virginia.

". . . 14. While Sherman was thus proceeding through the Carolinas, [Yankee General Philip H.] Sheridan, with a large cavalry force, was in motion in Virginia. He came down from the Shenandoah Valley, laying waste the country, and joined Grant near Petersburg, on the 26th of March. [Confederate General Robert E.] Lee, with less than 45,000 muskets, was now pressed in his trenches, extending thirty-five miles in length, in defence of the Confederate capital, by forces numbering over 200,000. On the 1st of April his right was turned, and the battle of Five Oaks was fought. On the 2nd, Grant, by a concentration of forces, succeeded in making a breach in the Confederate general line of defence, near Petersburg. Lee was now compelled to retire, and give up Richmond at last. Several sanguinary and heroic struggles ensued. The remaining thinned but resolute and undaunted columns of the Confederate chief, like the Spartan band at Thermopylae, were soon brought to their last death-grapple with the monster [U.S.] army of the Potomac. The tragic finale was at hand. On the 9th of April, at Appomattox Courthouse, the sword of Lee was surrendered, under liberal terms of capitulation. Not much else pertaining to the 'annihilated' army of Virginia was left to be passed under the formula of the general surrender then made. On this occasion Grant exhibited the greatest magnanimity. He declined to receive the sword of Lee, and in his capitulation paroled him and the less than 8,000 Confederates who then and there grounded their arms. Mr. [Jefferson] Davis and his Cabinet, with the other officials, had left Richmond on the night of the 2nd, after Lee's lines were broken, and thus made their escape. At Greensboro, N.C., the Confederate President, in consultation with Generals [Joseph E.] Johnston and [Pierre G. T.] Beauregard, and his Cabinet, authorized Johnston to make such terms as he might be able to do with Sherman, for a termination of the war, and general pacification. The result of this was what was known as the 'Sherman-Johnston Convention,' which was formally agreed to, and signed by them, on the 18th of April.

"15. While negotiations were going on between these Generals, and four days before the Convention was signed, on the night of the 14th of April, Mr. Lincoln was assassinated, at Ford's Theatre, in Washington City, by John

Wilkes Booth, an actor of note, and son of Junius Brutus Booth, the famous English tragedian. By the death of Mr. Lincoln the Presidency of the United States again devolved upon the Vice-President. Mr. Andrew Johnson, holding this position at the time, therefore immediately succeeded to the Federal Executive Chair. From the great excitement created by the horrible act by which Mr. Lincoln had been taken off, or from some other cause, the Sherman-Johnston Convention was disapproved by the newly-installed President. Upon being notified of this fact by Gen. Sherman, Gen. Johnston then, on the 26th of April, entered into a capitulation with him, by which he surrendered all the Confederate forces under his command, upon similar terms agreed upon between Lee and Grant. The course of Johnston was promptly followed by all the other Confederate commanders everywhere. The last surrender was that by Edmund Kirby Smith, in Texas, on the 26th of May. Three days after this, the 29th, President Johnson announced the facts by proclamation, with offer of amnesty, upon curtain conditions, to all who had participated in the conflict on the Confederate side, except fourteen designated classes. The whole number of Confederates thus surrendered, including Lee's and all, amounted to about 150,000 under arms. The whole number of Federals then in the field, and afterwards mustered out of service, as the records show, amounted, in round numbers, to 1,050,000.

"16. Thus ended the war between the States. It was waged by the Federals with the sole object, as they declared, of 'maintaining the Union under the Constitution;' while by the Confederates it was waged with the great object of maintaining the inestimable sovereign right of local self-government on the part of the Peoples of the several States. It was the most lamentable as well as the greatest of modern wars, if not the greatest in some respects 'known in the history of the human race.' It lasted four years and a little over, . . . with numerous sanguinary conflicts, and heroic exploits on both sides not chronicled in this Compendium; but many of which will live in memory, and be perpetuated as legends, and thus be treasured up as themes for story and song for ages to come.

"17. In conclusion, a few comments only will be added. One of the most striking features of the war was the great disparity between the numbers on the opposite sides. From its beginning to its end, near, if not quite, two millions more of Federals were brought into the field than the entire forces of the Confederates. The Federal records show that they had from first to last two million six hundred thousand men in the service; while the Confederates, all told, in like manner, had but little over six hundred thousand. The aggregate Federal population at its commencement was above twenty-two millions; that of the Confederates, was less than ten, near four millions of these being Negro slaves, and constituting no part of the arms-bearing portion of their population. [Note: Stephens is in error here. Modern research has determined that between 300,000 and 1 million armed Southern blacks fought both unofficially and officially for the Confederacy.] Of Federal prisoners during the war, the Confederates took in round numbers 270,000; while the whole number of Confederates captured and held in prisons by the Federals was in like round numbers 220,000. *In reference to the treatment of prisoners on the respective sides, about which much was said at the time, two facts are worthy of note: one is, that the*

Confederates were ever anxious for a speedy exchange, which the Federals would not agree to; the other is, that of the 270,000 Federal prisoners taken, 22,576 died in Confederate hands; and of the 220,000 Confederates taken by the Federals, 26,436 died in their hands: the mortuary tables thus exhibiting a large per cent, in favor of Confederate humanity. The entire loss on both sides, including those who were permanently disabled, as well as those killed in battle, and who died from wounds received and diseases contracted in the service, amounted upon a reasonable estimate 'to the stupendous aggregate of one million of men.' [When non-combatants of all races are added to these figures, modern Southern historians estimate that some 2 million Southerners died and 1 million Northerners died, making 3 million in total.] Both sides during the struggle relied for means to support it upon the issue of paper-money, and upon loans secured by bonds. An enormous public debt was thus created by each, and the aggregate of money thus expended on both sides, including the loss and sacrifice of property, could not have been less than eight thousand millions of dollars [or 110 billion dollars in today's currency]—a sum fully equal to three-fourths of the assessed value of the taxable property of all the States together when it commenced."[105] [Emphasis added, L.S.]

SECTION 2

EXCERPTS FROM
*A CONSTITUTIONAL VIEW OF THE
LATE WAR BETWEEN THE STATES*

1868-1870

8

LAYING THE FOUNDATION

STEPHENS WROTE HIS LIFEWORK, *A Constitutional View of the Late War Between the States*, over a period of several years. Volume One was published in 1868, just three years after the end of Lincoln's War; Volume Two came out in 1870. (The actual writing of the entire book seems to have taken place between the years 1865 and 1868, with possible polishing of the second volume occurring in 1869 and 1870.)

The book was hailed by Conservatives and strict constitutionalists as a brilliant vindication of the Southern Cause: the attempt to "rescue the Constitution" and preserve self government, personal liberty, and states' rights. However, it was severely denounced by Liberals, and by enemies of the South and the Constitution, who saw it as little more than unsubstantiated "poetry" and "philosophy," "broad, bold assertions" made by a "little jeering spirit," in a "logical but unhistorical" attempt to support a mere "idea": the inherent sovereignty of the states.

The battle over this "idea" continues to rage on into the present day, with largely the same foes facing one another across the same battlefield: Southern Conservatives on one side, Northern Liberals on the other. The musket may have been replaced by the computer keyboard, but the debate remains the same: was and is secession legal under the Constitution?

As Section Two reveals, Stephens' important tome, *A Constitutional View*, more than justifies this important states' right. As the U.S. Founding Fathers intended, it is set in stone for all time. Stephens himself says in the opening pages: "Times change, and men change with them, but principles never! These, like truths, are eternal, unchangeable and immutable!"[106]

Stephens, like every other Confederate statesmen, was clear as to the true cause of

Lincoln's War—and it was not slavery:

☛ "It is a postulate, with many writers of this day, that the late War was the result of two opposing ideas, or principles, upon the subject of African Slavery. Between these, according to their theory, sprung the 'irrepressible conflict,' in principle, which ended in the terrible conflict of arms. Those who assume this postulate, and so theorize upon it, are but superficial observers.

"That the War had its origin in opposing principles, which, in their action upon the conduct of men, produced the ultimate collision of arms, may be assumed as an unquestionable fact. But the opposing principles which produced these results in physical action were of a very different character from those assumed in the postulate. They lay in the organic Structure of the Government of the States. *The conflict in principle arose from different and opposing ideas as to the nature of what is known as the General [Central] Government. The contest was between those who held it to be strictly Federal [Confederate] in its character, and those who maintained that it was thoroughly National [Monarchical]. It was a strife between the principles of Federation [Confederation], on the one side, and Centralism, or Consolidation [Nationalism], on the other.* [Emphasis added, L.S.]

"*Slavery, so called, was but the question on which these antagonistic principles, which had been in conflict, from the beginning, on divers other questions, were finally brought into actual and active collision with each other on the field of battle.* [Emphasis added, L.S.]

"*Some of the strongest Anti-slavery men who ever lived were on the side of those who opposed the Centralizing principles which led to the War. Mr. [Thomas] Jefferson [of Virginia] was a striking illustration of this, and a prominent example of a very large class of both sections of the country [South and North], who were, most unfortunately, brought into hostile array against each other.* No more earnest or ardent devotee to the emancipation of the Black race, upon humane, rational and Constitutional principles, ever lived than he was. Not even [William] Wilberforce [leading British abolitionist] himself was more devoted to that cause than Mr. Jefferson was. And yet Mr. Jefferson, though in private life at the time, is well known to have been utterly opposed to the Centralizing principle, when first presented, on this question, in the attempt to impose conditions and restrictions on the State of Missouri, when she applied for admission into the Union, under the Constitution. He looked upon the movement as a political manœuvre to bring this delicate subject (and one that lay so near his heart) into the Federal Councils, with a view, by its agitation in a forum where it did not properly belong, to strengthen the Centralists [Liberals] in their efforts to revive their doctrines, which had been so signally defeated on so many other questions. The first sound of their movements on this question fell upon his ear as a "fire bell at night." The same is true of many others. *Several of the ablest opponents of that*

State Restriction, in Congress, were equally well known to be as decidedly in favor of emancipation as Mr. Jefferson was. Amongst these, may be named Mr. [William] Pinkney and Mr. [Henry] Clay, from the South, to say nothing of those men from the North, who opposed that measure with equal firmness and integrity. [Emphasis added, L.S.]

"It is the fashion of many writers of the day to class all who opposed the Consolidationists [Liberals] in this, their first step, as well as all who opposed them in all their subsequent steps, on this question, with what they style the Pro-Slavery Party. No greater injustice could be done any public men, and no greater violence be done to the truth of History, than such a classification. *Their opposition to that measure, or kindred subsequent ones, sprung from no attachment to Slavery; but, as Jefferson's, Pinkney's and Clay's, from their strong convictions that the Federal Government had no rightful or Constitutional control or jurisdiction over such questions; and that no such action, as that proposed upon them, could be taken by Congress without destroying the elementary and vital principles upon which the Government was founded.* [Emphasis added, L.S.]

"*By their acts, they did not identify themselves with the Pro-Slavery Party (for, in truth, no such Party had, at that time, or at any time in the History of the Country, any organized existence). They only identified themselves, or took position, with those who maintained the Federative [Confederate or Conservative] character of the General Government.* [Emphasis added, L.S.]

"In 1850, for instance, what greater injustice could be done any one, or what greater violence could be done the truth of History, than to charge [Lewis] Cass, [Stephen A.] Douglas, [Henry] Clay, [Daniel] Webster and [Millard] Fillmore, to say nothing of others, with being advocates of Slavery, or following in the lead of the [so-called] Pro-Slavery Party, because of their [conservative] support of what were called the adjustment measures of that year?

"Or later still, out of the million and a half, and more, of the votes cast, in the Northern States, in 1860, against Mr. [Abraham] Lincoln how many, could it, with truth, be said, were in favor of Slavery, or even that legal subordination of the Black race to the White, which existed in the Southern [and in the Northern] States?

"Perhaps, not one in ten thousand! It was a subject, with which, they were thoroughly convinced, they had nothing to do, and could have nothing to do, under the terms of the Union, by which the States were Confederated, except to carry out, and faithfully perform, all the obligations of the Constitutional Compact, in regard to it.

"*They simply arrayed themselves against that Party which had virtually hoisted the [liberal/socialist] banner of Consolidation. The contest, so commenced, which ended in the War, was, indeed, a contest between opposing principles; but not such as bore upon the policy or impolicy of African Subordination. They were principles deeply underlying all considerations of that sort. They involved the very nature and organic Structure of the*

Government itself. The conflict, on this question of Slavery, in the Federal Councils, from the beginning, was not a contest between the advocates or opponents of that peculiar Institution, but a contest, as stated before, between the supporters of a strictly Federative [Conservative] Government, on the one side, and a thoroughly National [Liberal] one, on the other."[107] [Emphasis added, L.S.]

To those, mainly uneducated Yankees, who frequently attacked Stephens (as they did all Southerners) for being a secessionist and allegedly "anti-Union," he gave this reply:

☛ "No stronger or more ardent Union man ever lived than I was. Not a man in the Convention which framed the Constitution of the United States, which sets forth the terms of "the Union," was or could have been more devoted to it than I was. But what Union? or the Union of what? Of course, the Union of the States under the Constitution. That was what I was so ardently devoted to. The Union is a phrase often used, I apprehend, without considering its correct import or meaning. By many it is used to signify the integrity of the country as it is called, or the unity of the whole people of the United States, in a geographical view, as one Nation. [Emphasis added, L.S.]

"[My liberal colleagues maintain that the original Union created by the Founding Fathers was national in character. To them] allow me . . . to say that there never was in this country any such union as [they] . . . speak of; there never was any political union between the people of the several States of the United States, except such as resulted indirectly from the terms of agreement or Compact entered into by separate and distinct political bodies. The first Union so formed, from which the present Union arose, was that of the [American] Colonies in 1774. They were thirteen in number. *These were distinct and separate political organizations or bodies.* After that the Union of States was formed under the Articles of Confederation, in 1777; and then, the modifications of the terms of this Union by the new Compact of 1787, known as the present Constitution [of the United States]. To this last Union, at first, only eleven of the original thirteen States became parties. Afterwards the other two (North Carolina and Rhode Island) also acceded and became members. The last of these (Rhode Island) rejoined her former associates in 1790. Subsequently, twenty new members were admitted into the association, on an equal footing with those first forming it. *Whatever intimate relationships, therefore, existed between the citizens of the respective thirty-three States constituting the Union in 1860, they) were created by, or sprung from, the terms of the Compact of 1787, by which the original States as States were united.* These terms were properly called the Constitution of the United States; not the Constitution of one people as one society or one nation, but the Constitution of a number of separate and distinct peoples, or political bodies, known as States. The absolute Sovereignty of these original States, respectively, *was never parted with by them in that or any other Compact of Union ever entered into by them.* This at least was my view of the subject. Georgia [Stephens' birthplace] was one of these States. My allegiance therefore was, as I considered it, not due to the United States, or to the people of the United States, but to Georgia in her Sovereign capacity. Georgia had never parted with her right to command the ultimate allegiance of her citizens. In that very speech this doctrine, or these principles, were clearly asserted and distinctly maintained. *However strongly opposed I was to the policy of Secession, or whatever views I gave against it as a policy, or wise measure . . . I declared my convictions to be, that if the people of Georgia, in their majesty, and in the exercise of their resumed full Sovereignty, should, in a regularly constituted Convention called for that purpose, withdraw from the Compact of Union, by which she was confederated, or united, with the other States under the Constitution, that it would be my duty to obey her high behest.* [My pro-Union Speech of 1860] . . . was made mainly, it is true, against the policy of Secession for then existing grievances complained of, but also against the unconstitutionality of measures proposed to be passed by the State Legislature, with a view of dissolving the Union. The Sovereign power of the people of the State, which alone could regulate its relations with the other States, was not vested in the Legislature. That resided with the people of the State. It had never been delegated either to the State authorities, or the authorities created by the Articles of Union. It could be exercised only by the people of the State in a regularly-constituted Convention, embodying the real Sovereignty of the State—just such Convention as had agreed to and adopted the Constitution of the United States. It required the same power to unmake as it had to make it. Hence, I said—'Let the sovereignty of the people of Georgia be first heard on this question of severing the bonds that united them with the other States;' and that, whatever decision the State might thus and then make, 'my fortunes would be cast with hers and her people.' [Emphasis added, L.S.]

"*I indulged a strong hope that when the Sovereignty of the people should be so invoked that it would take the same view I did of the policy of Secession or Disunion.* In this hope, however, I was disappointed. The Convention was called; it was regularly and legally assembled; the Sovereign will of the State, when expressed through its properly constituted organ, was for Secession, or a withdrawal of the State from the Union. The [Georgia Secession] Convention passed an Ordinance repealing and rescinding the State Ordinance of the second of January, 1788, by which Georgia became one of the United States under the constitutional Compact of 1787. I was in this Secession Convention, which assembled on the sixteenth day of January, 1861. The rescinding Ordinance passed that body on the nineteenth day of that month; I voted against that Ordinance. It was an Ordinance repealing and rescinding the Ordinance of a similar Sovereign Convention of the people of the State, passed the second day of January, 1788, as before stated, and placed Georgia just where she was, or would have been, if her Convention in 1788 had not passed the Ordinance by which she acceded to the Union under the Constitution of 1787. Such were my convictions. [Emphasis added, L.S.]

"*After the passage of this Ordinance by the State Convention on the nineteenth day of January, 1861, withdrawing from the Union, I obeyed the high and Sovereign behest of my State, as I felt bound in duty and patriotism to do, and as I had on all occasions declared that I should do. My position, in that Convention and after, was the same that it would have been if I had been in the State Convention of 1788. Had I been in that Convention, I should have been warmly in favor of Georgia's entering into the Union under the Constitution; but if she had decided otherwise, I should, as a good citizen, have felt myself bound to obey her Sovereign will.*"[108] [Emphasis added, L.S.]

When asked how he could support the secession of the Southern states when he had a responsibility to stay loyal to the central U.S. government, Stephens replied:

☞ "Allegiance, as we understand that term, is due to no Government. It is due the power that can rightfully make or change Governments. This is what is meant by the Paramount authority, or Sovereignty. Allegiance and Paramount authority do go together; we agree in that. But there is a great difference between the supreme law of the land and the Paramount authority, in our system of government, as well as in all others. Obedience is due to the one, while allegiance is due to the other. Obedience to law, while it is law, or the Constitution, which is an organic law for the time being, and allegiance to the Paramount authority, which can set aside all existing laws, fundamental laws, Constitutions, as well as any others, are very different things.

"[This question] . . . opens up the whole subject of the late war, its causes, nature, and character. It involves all the questions of right and wrong, in its beginning, conduct, and conclusion. This, too, necessarily involves an inquiry into and a correct understanding of the nature of the Government of the United States; the relations of the States to it; and the nature and character of that Union of which we have spoken, and about which we often hear so much. In a word, it involves a solution of the great question, where the Paramount authority or ultimate Sovereignty, under our system of Government, resides. If these matters had been properly discussed, and properly understood, and settled by reason, in accordance with truth and justice, before a resort to arms was had, our once happy and prosperous country would have been saved the widespread desolation that now broods over so large a section of it, and the far greater evils which I seriously apprehend still threaten the whole of it. The million of lives that were sacrificed in this fratricidal strife, and the billions of treasure that were expended in it, as well as the untold suffering which attended it, would have been saved.

"We have many Histories of this war, which, from the bench of the Supreme Court of the United States, has been pronounced to be 'the greatest civil war known in the history of the human race,' and 'the din of conflict' in which . . . 'was heard all over the world; and people of all nations were spectators of the scene!'

"Most of these Histories, that I have read, treat mainly of the current, or passing events, preceding and during its continuance. They are but the records and chronicles, and imperfect ones too, of the excited passions, imbittered prejudices, and extravagant utterances, of the public men, as well as of the masses of the people on both sides. Their most entertaining parts are chiefly devoted to a portrayal of the terrible conflict of arms, scenes of battlefields, the marshalling of hosts in hostile array, the skill of Generals, and deeds of valor and prowess on one or the other, or both sides, which excite the highest admiration with those who take pleasure in such descriptions; but none of them have taken any thing like an unimpassioned and Philosophical view of the real causes of this great scourge; or how it might have been and ought to have been prevented, or how like results and calamities, under like circumstances, may hereafter be avoided.

"[Indeed, most of my Northern friends completely misunderstand the true cause of Mr. Lincoln's War, wrongly attributing the main problem to slavery. Yankee abolitionist] Mr. [Horace] Greeley [for example], one of the ablest and fairest writers of the class I have alluded to, in his 'American Conflict,' treats the whole war as the culmination of a strife, for more than half a century, about 'Negro Slavery,' without scarcely giving a passing word upon the subject of the nature of the Government of the United States, or attempting to show that it had any rightful authority whatever over the subject matter of this strife. He writes as if it were conceded that the United States is one great Nation, one people, divided in sentiment upon the subject of African Slavery, or the legal status of the African race in some of the States. He traces and treats the discussion of this question just as a British historian might treat the discussions on the Corn Laws, or the extension of the franchise in his country. *All this manner of treatment of the subject is radically defective. It utterly ignores the true causes of the war, on which alone its Rightfulness depends. Slavery, so called, or that legal subordination of the black race to the white, which existed in all but one of the States, when the Union was formed, and in fifteen of them when the war began, was unquestionably the occasion of the war, the main exciting proximate cause on both sides, on the one as well as the other, but it was not the real cause, the 'Causa causans' of it. That was the assumption on the part of the Federal authorities, that the people of the several States were, as [Liberals] . . . say, citizens of the United States, and owed allegiance to the Federal Government, as the absolute Sovereign power over the whole country, consolidated into one Nation. The war sprung from the very idea [Liberals] . . . have expressed, and from the doctrine embraced in the question propounded to me. It grew out of different and directly opposite views as to the nature of the Government of the United States, and where, under our system, ultimate Sovereign power or Paramount authority properly resides.* [Emphasis added, L.S.]

"[Let us discuss the authentic reason the Southern states departed from the Union.] Considerations connected with the legal status of the Black race in the Southern States, and the position of several of the Northern States toward it, together with the known sentiments and principles of those just elected to the two highest offices of the Federal Government (Messrs. Lincoln and [Hannibal] Hamlin), as to the powers of that Government over this subject, and others which threatened, as was supposed, all their vital interests, prompted the Southern States to withdraw from the Union, for the very reason that had induced them at first to enter into it: that is, for their own better protection and security. Those [i.e., Northern Liberals] who had the control of the Administration of the Federal Government, denied this right to withdraw or secede. The war was inaugurated and waged by those at the head of the Federal Government, against these States, or the people of these States, to prevent their withdrawal from the Union. On the part of these States, which had allied themselves in a common cause, it was maintained and carried on purely in defence of this great Right, claimed by them, of State Sovereignty and Self-government, which they with their associates had achieved in their common struggle with Great Britain, under the Declaration of 1776, and which, in their judgment, lay at the foundation of the whole structure of American free Institutions.

"This is a succinct statement of the issue, and *when the calm and enlightened judgment of mankind, after the passions of the day shall have passed off, and shall be buried with the many gallant and noble-spirited men, who fell on both sides in the gigantic struggle which ensued, shall be pronounced, as it will be, upon the right or wrong of the mighty contest, it must be rendered in favor of the one side or the other, not according to results, but according to the right in the issue thus presented.* [Emphasis added, L.S.]

". . . if the History of this most lamentable and disastrous conflict, disastrous I fear to all the great principles of Self-government, established or attempted to be secured by the Constitution of the United States, shall ever be written, the Right and Justice of the cause will be found to be on the side [the South's] of those with whom my fortunes were cast, and with whom, in all their heroic struggles and unparalleled sacrifices, my feelings and sympathies were ever thoroughly enlisted, and my utmost exertions put forth for their success. *Whatever errors in policy they may have committed, either in the inception of the difficulties or in their subsequent management, the real object of those who resorted to Secession, as well as those who sustained it, was not to overthrow the Government of the United States; but to perpetuate the principles upon which it was founded. The object in quitting the Union was not to destroy, but to save the principles of the Constitution. The form of Government therein embodied, I did think, and do still think, the best the world ever saw, and I fear the world will never see its like again.*"[109] [Emphasis added, L.S.]

When a Northern Liberal asked Stephens if he thought he could change his mind concerning Lincoln's War, Stephens replied:
☛ "I did not mean to say that I thought that I could change your opinions on these subjects, but only that I could make it appear clearly to you, why I, with my convictions, acted as I did, under the circumstances. Our ideas of Truth, Justice and Right, in political as well as social matters, and all the relations of life, depend very much upon circumstances. This seems to be owing partly to the infirmities of human nature. *There ought, however, to be no difference between intelligent minds as to Truth, which rests simply and entirely upon matters of fact; but, in practical life, there are great and wide differences, even on this, owing to a disagreement or a different understanding as to the facts merely.* Justice and Right, depending on the Truth of the facts, must, of course, be the subjects of much wider differences in all cases where the facts are not first settled, or where the Truth is not admitted by both sides. *Men's convictions as to Truth, or what they receive as the Truth, depend entirely upon their understanding of facts. Convictions are always sincere.* There may be insincere professions of opinions, but there can be no insincere convictions, as to Truth, Justice, or Right, in any matter relating to human conduct. These depend upon laws of mind, over which volition has no control. . . . There is no such thing as convincing a man against his will. Galileo complied with the exactions of torture, by renouncing his belief in the rotatory motion of the earth; but his convictions of this great truth remained as firm as ever, notwithstanding. Belief and conviction are results with which the will has nothing to do, except in collecting and ascertaining the facts upon which depend the truth, or what is considered the truth, to which alone the mind yields its assent. Hence, the necessity of a very liberal charity in all discussions of this nature."[110] [Emphasis added, L.S.]

When asked how he, as a citizen of the United States, could reconcile with his sense of duty to go with his state against the Union, Stephens responded:
☛ ". . . allow me to premise, by making an observation or two on your remark about my being a citizen of the United States, and, as such, being bound by

allegiance, as a loyal citizen (to use a popular phrase, so current just now), to obey the acts of that Government, as the supreme law of the land.

"I agree . . . that allegiance and Paramount authority go together; that the first follows the latter. . . . But, first, as to citizenship. Is there any such thing as citizenship of the United States, apart from citizenship of a particular State or Territory of the United States? To me it seems most clearly that there is not. We are all citizens of particular States, Territories, or Districts of the United States, and thereby only, citizens of the United States. I was a citizen of Georgia; being a citizen of Georgia, I became, thereby, a citizen of the United States, only because Georgia was one of the United States under the Constitution, which was the bond, or compact, of the Union between the States thus united. Had Georgia never united with the other States, her people would never have been, in any sense of the word, citizens of the United States.

"[But, you ask, how would I classify naturalized foreigners, who are, by the laws, made citizens of the United States?] They are, as you and I are, citizens of the United States, because of their being, under the laws, admitted to citizenship of some one of the States or Territories of the United States. The only power Congress has, under the Constitution, on this subject, is to make uniform rules of naturalization. That is, to prescribe uniform rules, which are to be the same in all of the States, by which foreigners may be permitted to become citizens of the several States or Territories. Before this power was delegated to Congress, each State, as all other Sovereign, independent nations, had the uncontrolled right to admit foreigners to citizenship, upon such terms as each, for itself, saw fit. In order that the same terms or conditions might exist in all the States, each State, in the Constitution, agreed to delegate the power to Congress, to make the rules on the subject of naturalization uniform in all of the States. This is the view of all writers upon the subject.

"Mr. [William] Rawle, in his admirable treatise on the Constitution of the United States, has well said, on the subject of citizenship, generally: 'It cannot escape notice that no definition of the nature and rights of citizens appears in the Constitution.' And then, on the subject of naturalization, and the reason of giving power to Congress over the subject, he says:

> 'In the second section of the fourth article, it is provided that the citizens of each State shall be entitled to all the privileges and immunities of citizens in the several States; and the same rule had been ambiguously laid down in the Articles of Confederation. If this clause is retained, and its utility and propriety cannot be questioned, the consequence would be that, if each State retained the power of naturalization, it might impose on all other States such citizens as it might think proper. In one State, residence for a short time, with a slight declaration of allegiance, as was the case under the former

Constitution of Pennsylvania, might confer the rights of citizenship; in another, qualifications of greater importance might be required: an alien, desirous of eluding the latter, might, by complying with the requisites of the former, become a citizen of a State in opposition to its own regulations; and thus, in fact, the laws of one State become paramount to that of another. The evil could not be better remedied than by vesting the exclusive power in Congress.'

"That is, of making the rule for admission to citizenship in each State uniform in all the States. . . . When a foreigner, therefore, wishes to become a citizen of any one of the States or Territories, he has to file his petition to this effect, according to the uniform rules established by Congress; and the Courts, in the State or Territory, whether Federal or State, have to conform to these rules, in admitting to citizenship, where the application is made. He then becomes possessed of all the rights, privileges and immunities pertaining to citizenship which are possessed by native-born citizens in that State or Territory, and no more. He then and thereby only becomes a citizen of the United States as native-born citizens so become, and no more. He cannot enter suit, in any of the United States Courts, for a redress of any wrong within their jurisdiction, any more than a native-born citizen, without stating distinctly that he is a citizen of some one of the States, and of which one. He is, in every respect, after being naturalized in conformity to the uniform rules, as stated, on the same footing with native-born citizens. . . . This covers the whole question. There is no such thing as general citizenship of the United States under the Constitution.

". . . Secondly. Another observation now in the same way upon what you [Liberals] call the supreme law of the land. The Constitution does declare that 'this Constitution and the laws of the United States made in pursuance thereof, and all treaties made or which shall be made under the authority of the United States, shall be the supreme law of the land, and the Judges in every State shall be bound thereby, any thing in the Constitution or laws of any State to the contrary notwithstanding.'

"[There are those who would like to know whether or not U.S. citizens are bound to obey 'the supreme law of the land.' To this I reply most] certainly; so long as the Paramount authority over them shall so ordain and order, but no longer; so long as it is law, and no longer. There is a wide difference, as I stated at first, between the supreme law of the land and the Paramount authority. Obedience is due to the one as long as it is the law, and allegiance is due to the other when it declares, as it can, that the law no longer exists. In our Government, as in all Governments, there must be a supreme law-making power on the subjects within its jurisdiction; that is, the supreme power of making laws to be obeyed on these subjects must be lodged somewhere. It is not an absolute power in any Government founded upon the principles of ours. It is a power exercised in trust only. This supreme power, moreover, or the delegation of its exercise, emanates from Sovereignty or the Paramount authority, but it is not Sovereignty itself. All laws therefore passed in pursuance of the rules prescribed by the Sovereign or Paramount authority, are supreme, and to be obeyed so long as they remain of force by the continued authority of the Sovereign power. This is universally admitted; no one disputes it. *In this country it is equally admitted on all hands that Sovereignty, which is the Paramount authority, resides with the People. All government, according to our axioms and maxims, is but the exercise in trust of delegated powers. The exercise of supreme or Sovereign powers may be by delegation. In this country it is entirely by delegation; but whatever is delegated may be resumed by the authority delegating. No postulate in mathematics can be assumed less subject to question than this.* The exercise of supreme law-making power, even over the authority delegating it, may be legitimate so long as the delegated power is unresumed. Obedience to laws passed under such delegation of power, is, as I have said, a very different thing from allegiance which is due to the authority delegating the exercise of the supreme law-making power. *Whenever the delegated powers are resumed, allegiance must be due to the resuming Sovereign power; to that which can rightfully make and unmake Constitutions.* [Emphasis added, L.S.]

"The Government of the United States was created by the States. All its powers are held in trust by delegation from the States. These powers are specific and limited. They are supreme within the sphere of their limitations—supreme so long as the authorities delegating them continue the trust even over the authorities delegating them; but being held entirely by delegation, they exist no longer than the party or parties delegating see fit to continue the trust. In this sense alone is the authority of the General Government supreme, even over the subjects which lie within the sphere of the powers with which it was intrusted by delegation. The Paramount authority in this country, Sovereignty, that to which allegiance is due, is with the People somewhere. There is no Sovereignty either in the General Government or the State Governments. These are permitted to exercise certain Sovereign powers so long only as it shall suit the Sovereign will that they shall so do, and no longer. Sovereignty itself, from which emanates all political power, I repeat, remains and ever resides with the People somewhere. And with what People? Why, of necessity, it appears to me, with the same People who delegated whatever powers the General Government has ever been intrusted with; that is, the People of the several States; not the whole People of the United States as one mass, as can be most conclusively demonstrated.* [Emphasis added, L.S.]

"In addition to this, I remark that this clause of the Constitution contains no grant or delegation of power in itself. It only declares what would have been the effect of the previously delegated powers without it. All Treaties or Covenants between Sovereigns are the supreme law over their subjects, or citizens, so long as they last. Indeed, so far from containing any new or substantive power, upon its very face this clause shows that it was intended as a limitation of powers. So far from showing that absolute Sovereignty was thereby vested in the General Government, such Sovereignty as is entitled to the allegiance of anybody, it shows conclusively that even obedience is due to such laws, treaties, etc., only, as may be made in pursuance of the Constitution. *This, by itself, shows the Government to be one of limited powers—and so far from allegiance being due to it in any sense, that even obedience is due only to a limited extent.* [Emphasis added, L.S.]

"This was the opinion of Alexander Hamilton, who was one of the extremest of the Nationals [i.e., consolidating big government proponents] of his day, and who never failed to claim all acknowledged, as well as some doubtful, or questionable powers, which tended to strengthen the Federal Government. While the Constitution was before the several States, for their consideration before its adoption, he unequivocally declared, on several occasions, that this clause conveyed no grant of power, and was entitled to no such construction as that which would claim under it the allegiance of the citizens of the several States. Let us see what he wrote on the subject at that time. . .:

> 'But it is said that the laws of the Union are to be the supreme law of the land. But what inference is to be drawn from this, or what would they amount to, if they were not supreme? It is evident that they would amount to nothing. A law, by the very meaning of the term, includes supremacy. It is a rule which those, to whom it is prescribed, are bound to observe. If individuals enter a state of society, the laws of that society must be the supreme regulator of their conduct. If a number of political societies enter into a larger political society, the laws which the latter may enact, pursuant to the powers intrusted to it by its Constitution, must necessarily be supreme over those societies, and the individuals of whom they are composed.'

"And further in the same paper [Hamilton writes]:

> 'But it will not follow from this doctrine that acts of the larger societies, which are not pursuant to its constitutional powers, but which are invasions of the residuary authorities of the smaller societies, will become the supreme law of the land. These will be merely acts of usurpation, and will deserve to be treated as such. Hence we perceive that the clause which declares the supremacy of the laws of the Union, like the one we have just before considered, only declares a truth which flows immediately and necessarily

from the institution of a Federal government. It will not, I presume, have escaped observation, that it expressly confines this supremacy to the laws made pursuant to the Constitution, which I mentioned merely as an instance of caution in the Convention, since that limitation would have been to be understood, though it had not been expressed.'

"This shows conclusively that Mr. Hamilton, one of the extremest of the Nationals in his day—he who did wish a National government instituted instead of a Federal [Confederate] one, but who gave a cordial support to the Federal plan when the National one was abandoned . . . did not claim any delegation or grant of power from this clause of the Constitution, but expressly states that it was intended as a limitation, as its words fairly import, of other powers which had been delegated, and that this limitation had been inserted out of abundant caution on the part of the Convention. He maintained the same position in the State Convention of New York. This is quite enough I think to show in this place, by way of premise, that the allegiance of the citizens of the several States was never intended to be transferred to the United States, or to the Government of the United States, by this clause of the Constitution. And from what has been said, without going into a history of this clause, or explaining how it came to be introduced, which would strengthen the views given, it very clearly appears, as well as from the language of the clause itself, that *the Government of the United States is not, by virtue of it, supreme or Sovereign in the sense in which you [Liberals] use that term; and so far from being entitled thereby to claim the ultimate or any sort of allegiance of the citizens of the several States, it is not entitled even to claim their obedience to its laws except within the strict limit of its specifically-delegated powers.* Thus far, it appears clearly, that a thorough inquiry into and a full investigation of the nature of the Government of the United States, as well as the character and extent of its delegated powers, are essential to a correct understanding of the subject presented in the question propounded. Without this, there can be no correct knowledge or sound judgment as to the nature and character of the war, whether an Insurrection, a Rebellion, a Civil war, or a war of Aggression for unjust power and Dominion on one side—while one purely in defence of ancient and well-established Sovereign Rights on the other. Without this there can be no correct judgment as to whether I acted properly or improperly in the course I took, or as to the conduct or rectitude of any of the various actors therein, on one side or the other."[111] [Emphasis added, L.S.]

Stephens was well versed on the background of the U.S. Constitution's clause concerning the limited powers of the U.S. government (Article 1, Section 8):

☛ "The history of this clause of the Constitution is this. It is well known, or, at least, *it may be here stated, as it will be established without question, that, in the Convention that formed the Constitution, there was a party who were strongly in favor of doing away with the Federal [Confederate] system that existed before that time, and substituting, in its stead, a General National ['big'] Government over the whole people of all the States, as one body politic. This [Liberal] party wished to do away entirely with the Sovereignty of the several States. Their object was to give the Central National Government Paramount authority over the Sovereignty of the States. With this view, a proposition was brought forward, to give the National Government power 'to negative all laws, passed by the several States, contravening, in the opinion of the National Legislature, the articles of Union, or any treaties subsisting under the authority of the Union.' This proposition, if it had been adopted, would have greatly favored the object of the Nationals [i.e., the big government Liberals], but it was rejected by a decided vote.* Here is the journal of the Convention. Only three States voted for it, while seven voted against it. [Emphasis added, L.S.] It was then immediately afterwards that Luther Martin, of Maryland, the strongest States-Rights man, perhaps, in the Convention—one who would, under no circumstances, consent to any infringement upon the ultimate Sovereignty of the States, or agree to any thing tending to change the character of the Federal system, offered a proposition in these words:

'That the legislative acts of the United States, made by virtue and in pursuance of the articles of Union, and all treaties, made and ratified under the authority of the United States, shall be the supreme law of the respective States, as far as those acts or treaties shall relate to the said States, or their citizens and inhabitants; and that the Judiciaries of the several States shall be bound thereby in their decisions, any thing in the respective laws of the individual States to the contrary notwithstanding.'

"*This proposition expressly restricted the authority of the United States, in all cases within the sphere of its delegated powers.* It refused to confer upon the General Government the power or the right to judge of infractions upon the Articles of Union on the part of the States. It was a limitation against any construction by implication to that effect, and simply declared a truth, as Hamilton said of it. It simply asserted what would have been the result under fair construction without it; but it was offered from abundant caution, and was unanimously agreed to, as appears from the Journal on the same page. It was subsequently put in the form in which it is now found in the Constitution, by the committee on style and revision. There was no change in substance. And that it did not answer the purpose of the Nationals, as now contended for by many, appears conclusively, not only from the opinion of Hamilton cited; but from the action of the Nationals themselves in the Convention afterwards. For, *notwithstanding this clause was agreed to, as stated, on the 17th of July, yet we find that the very identical* *original proposition was again offered on the 23rd day of August afterwards, as appears on the Journal, page 260. It then met with no greater favor than it did at first. The Convention refused to entertain it, and it was withdrawn.* Moreover, I will here add, that no truth is better established than that the general view and understanding of the advocates of the adoption of the Constitution in that day, in reference to this clause, were in conformity with those given by Mr. Hamilton. That is, that no power was granted by the clause—that it simply declared a truth—that it was intended as a limitation of powers delegated, and only announced a principle that would have been recognized by the Courts, even if it had not been made, or in other words, that this clause did not in the least change the character of the former Government in this respect, and that *the acts of the General Government, under the present Constitution, are no more binding on the States, or the citizens of the States, by virtue of it, than they were under the Confederation.* This was the opinion of Mr. [James] Madison. Here, in a number of the Federalist, written by him (No. 37), he shows that 'treaties made by Congress, under the Articles of Confederation, had been declared by Congress, and recognized by most of the States, to be the supreme law of the land,' without any such declaration to that effect in the Articles of the Union. And further, if further argument be necessary to show the prevailing opinion at that time, I refer you to a decision of the Supreme Court of the United States, made in 1796. [Emphasis added, L.S.] In this case . . . Judge [Samuel] Chase says:

> 'It seems to me that treaties made by Congress, according to the Confederation, were superior to the laws of the States, because the Confederation made them obligatory in all of the States. They were so declared by Congress, on the 13th of April, 1787, were so declared by the Legislatures and Executives of most of the States, and were so decided by the judiciary of the General Government, and by the judiciaries of some of the State Governments.'

"So it appears conclusively from the language of the clause, from the opinions of Mr. Hamilton, and Mr. Madison, and Judge Chase of the Supreme Court of the United States, that the proposition offered by Mr. Martin, and incorporated substantially in the Constitution, conferred no more power under the new Constitution than existed without the declaration under the Confederation.

". . . That is my position [on the topic of the Constitution and state sovereignty], and I will add that Judge Chase, in the same opinion from which I have just read, and to which we may have occasion to refer again, held that under the Confederation the States severally were clothed with all the attributes of perfect sovereignty. And yet the Articles of Confederation were the

Supreme law of the land as much as the Constitution now is. All compacts between sovereigns are the supreme law over their subjects or citizens so long as they continue. This is the doctrine of [Swiss law expert Emerich de] Vattel. General [Charles C.] Pinckney, in the South Carolina Convention, when this clause of the Constitution was under discussion, after quoting Vattel to this effect, goes on:

> '[Swiss legal theorist Jean-Jacques] Burlamaqui, another writer of great reputation on political law, says, "that treaties are obligatory on the subjects of the powers who enter into treaties; they are obligatory as conventions between the contracting powers; but they have the force of law with respect to their subjects." These are his very words, "that two sovereigns, who enter into a treaty, impose, by such treaty, an obligation on their subjects to conform to it, and in no manner to contravene it."'

"Every treaty existing, to-day, between the United States and every other Government or Governments is the Supreme law over the subjects of such Government or Governments, as well as over the citizens of the several States of this Union. That is, every such treaty is a law, Superior to all other local laws in both countries, over which it operates. Their Courts are bound to so hold, and do so hold. This no more affects the allegiance of the subjects of those Governments than it does the allegiance of the citizens of these States. These treaties are Compacts between the Parties to them, and laws as to their subjects or citizens.

"This clause in the Constitution, therefore, settles nothing on the question of allegiance. The Constitution may be a bare convention or compact between the States as Sovereigns, and yet be the supreme law while it continues over their citizens, without affecting their ultimate allegiance in the slightest degree."[112]

THE CHARACTER OF THE FEDERAL GOVERNMENT

LIBERALS HAVE ALWAYS CONSIDERED THE Federal government a body that is meant to tend toward centralization and even empire, and the Constitution an instrument by which to help to consolidate power and grow that empire. As Stephens shows in the following excerpts from his book *A Constitutional View of the Late War Between the States*, such ideas could not be further from the truth. A Confederate Founding Father with a scholarly background in *authentic* American history, Stephens cites the original American Founding Fathers—most of whom were Southerners—in support of his views.

Stephens on the true purpose of creating the U.S. Constitution:
☛ "The present [Constitution] is not the first Constitution of the United States. 'The Union' existed under an old [i.e., earlier] Constitution [known as the Articles of Confederation]. The main object of the present Constitution, as appears in its preamble, was to make 'the Union' then existing more perfect. It was not to make a new one, or to change the fundamental character of the one then existing; no such purpose at least is declared on the face of the instrument; it was only to make the previous 'Union' more perfect, or better adapted to secure the great objects for which it had been originally formed."[113]

Nineteenth-Century Liberals often argued that the Articles of Confederation were not a true Constitution, and that therefore the U.S. Constitution could not be and was not based upon them. They would then cite Northern statesman Daniel Webster: "If there is one word in the English language that the people of the United States understand, it is the word Constitution. It means the fundamental law." To this nonsensical argument

Stephens replied:

☛ "Mr. Webster did say something like what you quote him as saying. I remember it well. . . . But were not the Articles of Confederation a Constitution even according to his own definition? Did they not constitute the fundamental law of the Union of the States under the Confederation of which you speak? Being the fundamental law for their government for the time being, is it not perfectly proper to style them a Constitution upon the authority of Mr. Webster himself? In so styling them, I use the same term that has been applied to them by the highest authority, not only of that day, but since. As you question its propriety, however, we had better settle all points of difference as we go along, especially as a great deal often depends upon words barely, which are frequently, as Mr. Webster says, much more than sounds, being real things within themselves. Let me therefore just here refer to some authorities which I think clearly justify the use of the term as made by me. Mr. [George T.] Curtis, in his *History of the Constitution of the United States* . . . says these Articles of Confederation were 'the first written Constitution of the United States.' . . . In . . . [George] Washington's letter to the Governors of the several States, dated 8th of June, 1783, . . . he speaks of the Articles of the then existing Confederation as '*the Constitution*' of the States. [Also, in an April 18, 1783, letter] from the then Congress to the several States, . . . these words occur: 'The last object recommended is a Constitutional change of the rule by which a partition of the common burthens is to be made.' This shows that the men of that day understood the Articles of 'the Union' then existing to be a Constitution. Changes in these Articles they characterized as Constitutional changes. . . . In [George Washington's letters from 1788 he] called this instrument, as I did, the *new Constitution*. Here is a letter written on the 23rd of February, 1789, to Mr. [James] Monroe, in which Washington says: 'I received, by last night's mail, your letter dated the fifteenth of this month, with your printed observations on the *new Constitution*,' etc. Here is another letter written by Washington to Henry Lee [III], under date 22nd September, 1788, in which he also calls it the *new Constitution*. Another to Benjamin Lincoln, on the 26th of October, 1788, in which he uses the same language. These letters (and I refer to but few of them) show, beyond cavil, that Washington considered the old Articles of 'Union,' as much as the new, a *Constitution*. Besides this, the writers in the Federalist usually designated the paper then before the States for their consideration as the *new Constitution* in contradistinction to the old or the Articles of Confederation. . . . Moreover, two of the States at least, Massachusetts and New Hampshire, in their Ordinances adopting and ratifying the present Constitution, expressly style it a *new Constitution*. Is more authority needed on this point to justify my use of the term Constitution in applying it as

I did to the Articles of Confederation, as well as to the Articles of the present 'Union,' whatever they may be. The first was a fundamental law as long as it lasted as much as the other.

". . . Well, then, if the old Articles of Union [i.e., the Articles of Confederation] were a Constitution, the new Constitution is but new Articles of Union between the same parties; unless the new Constitution changes fundamentally the character of 'the Union' then existing between them. The bare change of name, of course, does not affect any change of substance.

". . . Thirteen of those bodies now known as States of 'the Union,' were originally, or before the date of our common history, Colonies of Great Britain. Some of them were known as Provincial Colonies, some Proprietary, and some Charter Colonies, but all Colonies of Great Britain. These thirteen Colonies were New Hampshire, Massachusetts, Connecticut, Rhode Island, New York, New Jersey, Delaware, Pennsylvania, Maryland, Virginia, North Carolina, South Carolina, and Georgia. These were all distinct political organizations, having no connection whatever between each other, except that the inhabitants of all were common subjects of the Government of Great Britain. They were all planted at different times, and had different forms of government; that is, the Constitutions or Charters of no two of them were alike, though all were founded upon the representative principle. They were all free Democratic Governments. The Charter of the Virginia Government was the oldest; it dates back to 1606. The charter of the last of these Colonies was that of Georgia; it was granted in 1732. These Colonies, as stated, were all separate and distinct political bodies, without any direct permanent political connection between them until 1774. It is true, in 1643, a Convention or Union of some sort for their own mutual protection, was formed between two or more of the New England Colonies, a name given to all those lying East of New York, which lasted until 1683-1684, when it was dissolved by the abrogation of their original charters by the British Government. No farther notice, therefore, . . . need be taken of that 'Union' or its character. Subsequently, in 1754 and 1765, attempts were made by certain Colonies to form some sort of a general Union or Confederation of all these Colonies for their better protection, in combined efforts against the Indians, as well as for joint consultation between themselves on questions of policy adopted by the mother country touching their common interests. These efforts failed. No Union of any sort resulted from them. The last and successful effort was made in 1774. This was at the instance of Virginia. This was after what is known as the Boston Port Bill passed the British Parliament, and after the act of Parliament again changing the Charter of the Massachusetts Colonial Government, and against her consent. These measures awakened a profound sensation in all the Colonies, though the blow was aimed directly at one of them only, yet they all saw that the principle involved the rights and liberties of each severally. Virginia appealed to all to send up delegates to a General Convention or Congress, for joint consultation and concert of action. Mr. [Daniel] Webster once said that the American Revolution was fought on a Preamble—on the Preamble of the act of Parliament, which, while it reduced the tax on tea to a nominal amount, yet declared the right of the British Parliament to tax the Colonies in all cases whatsoever. This statement has in it much more of the exuberance of a figure of rhetoric than the exact accuracy of historical statement. The first moving cause which aroused all the Colonies to that concert of action which ended in the Revolution, was the direct assault of the British Government upon the chartered Rights of Massachusetts. This, and not the tax on tea, or what was contained in the Preamble to that act, is what caused the Colonial Legislature of Virginia to pass an order appointing a day for fasting, humiliation and prayer, to implore the Divine interposition for averting the heavy calamity which threatened their civil rights, and which caused them, when dissolved on account of this Resolution by their Royal Governor, to call for a Congress of all the Colonies.

"It was then that the cry went up, from the St. Croix to the Altamaha, 'the cause of Boston is the cause of all.' The violation of the chartered rights of Massachusetts, prompted the call for a general Congress. This was the moving cause. This appeal, made by Virginia, was responded to by the Colonies generally. The result was the assemblage of deputies from twelve Colonies, which met at Philadelphia on the fifth of September, 1774. This is the first Convention or Congress of the Colonies from which the present 'Union' sprung. The first thing settled in this Congress was the nature of its own character and organization. It was determined to be a Congress of separate, distinct political bodies. In all its deliberations each Colony was to be considered as equal, and each was to have an equal vote and voice upon all questions coming before it, without reference to the number of delegates sent up by the respective Colonies; for the object of all was the defence and preservation of what was claimed to be the inalienable right of each. This Congress, so organized and so constituted, after making a declaration of the indefeasible Rights of all the Colonies, made several recommendations to the Governments of the Colonies respectively, as to the course which should be adopted by them in common, for a redress of the wrongs of each in particular. After this action, this body was dissolved, with a recommendation to the Colonies to meet in Congress again by deputies, on the tenth of May, 1775. The Colonies did accordingly send up deputies to another Congress as recommended, which assembled on the tenth of May, 1775, as recommended.

All the thirteen Colonies, above stated, were represented by delegates in this Assemblage. This is the Congress by which the first permanent 'Union' between the Colonies was formed. At first, as [did] their predecessor, they adopted various measures and recommendations for the relief of grievances, which failing, they came to the conclusion finally, on the fourth day of July, 1776, that the only hope for the inalienable as well as chartered liberties of each was for all to throw off their allegiance to the British Crown and to declare their separate Independence of it. This is the Congress, or body of men, that formed the Articles of Confederation to which you referred, and which Mr. [George T.] Curtis styles, as I have shown, the first written Constitution of the United States. This was the first 'Union.' And after this brief historical review, with these further preliminaries settled, I proceed to assert, as a matter of history, that the former 'Union,' or 'the Union' under the Articles of Confederation, the first Constitution, was a 'Union' of separate, distinct, Sovereign and Independent States. In other words, that the thirteen States, formerly British Colonies, after they asserted their Independence as Sovereign States, entered into 'a Union' as separate Sovereignties, and that it was a Union of States, as States. This 'Union' was formed in 1777, during the common struggle of all the States for the separate and several Independence and Sovereignty of each. Eleven States, to wit: New Hampshire, Massachusetts, Rhode Island, Connecticut, New York, Pennsylvania, New Jersey, Virginia, North Carolina, South Carolina, and Georgia, ratified that 'Union' in the year 1778. Delaware entered it in February 1779, and Maryland in March 1781. Each of these States entering into it did so as a distinct, separate, Sovereign political body. This was 'the Union' of the Confederation, as you [Liberals] styled it. Mr. Curtis, in his *History of the Constitution of the United States*, to which I have just referred, in speaking of 'this Union,' says: 'the Parties to this instrument (the Articles of Confederation) were free, Sovereign, political Communities—each possessing within itself all the powers of Legislation and Government over its own citizens, which any political Society can possess.'

"This, I assume, then, as an unquestionable truth or fact in our History . . . "[114]

Did the Declaration of Independence make the entire population of the United States one people, one political society, bound together under one National Government, one nation, as Liberals have long maintained? This is an important question, because if it is true, the idea of the constitutional legality of secession is thrown into question. Stephens responded to it this way:

☛ "The Declaration [of Independence] . . . was made by the people of each Colony, for each Colony, through representatives acting by the Paramount authority of each Colony, *separately and respectively. The Declaration of Independence was, in this way, a joint act of all the Colonies, for the benefit of each severally, as well as for the whole. The Congress that made it was a Congress of States.* The deputies or delegates from no State assumed to vote for it until specially instructed and empowered so to do. Massachusetts had instructed and empowered her delegation so to act as early as January before; South Carolina in March; Georgia in April; North Carolina in April; Rhode Island in May; Virginia in May; New Hampshire in June; Connecticut in June; New Jersey in June; Maryland in June; Pennsylvania and New York were the last. The powers and instructions from these States did not arrive until after the 1st day of July, which caused a postponement of final action of the Congress on the Declaration until the 4th day of that month, when, full powers being received from all the States, it was then, after being voted upon by States and carried by States, unanimously proclaimed by all the States, so in Congress assembled. *The Declaration of Independence was, be it remembered, voted upon and carried by States, and proclaimed by and in the name of States.* [Emphasis added, L.S.]

"This is the true history of the matter.

". . . That these men did look forward hopefully for a continued Union of the States, under a Compact to be formed securing the Independence and Sovereignty of each, I do not doubt; but that they did not then consider each as an Independent Sovereign power, is wholly at variance with all the attending facts. The very Declaration itself shows this conclusively without going farther into a detail of these facts. The very title shows how it was made. Here it is: 'In Congress, July 4th, 1776, the unanimous Declaration of the thirteen United States of America.' *It was the Declaration of States in Congress assembled, by their deputies, empowered by the Paramount authority of each, to make it. The Declaration was not that they were to be one State, as New Hampshire had instructed her representatives to make it, but, in their own language, 'thirteen free, Sovereign and Independent States.'* This was in strict accordance with the instructions of their constituents. The people of the several Colonies would not consent for a Declaration to be made in any other way. This appears from the instructions of all the Colonies or States except New Hampshire. In their several instructions and powers for *the Declaration of Independence*, were instructions and powers for forming *a Confederation of Independent States*. So universal was this sentiment, that Richard Henry Lee's [the first cousin of Confederate General Robert E. Lee] first motion for the Declaration of Independence, early in June, was not only for Independence, but farther—for '*a plan of Confederation*, to be prepared and transmitted to the respective Colonies for their consideration and approbation.' [Emphasis added, L.S.]

"The plan for a Confederation of separate Independent Sovereign States, was moved in the very resolution which proposed the Declaration of their Independence. And subsequently, on the 24th of June, 1776, the Congress declared, by resolution, that

> all persons abiding within any of the United Colonies and deriving protection from the laws of the same, owed allegiance to the said laws, and were members of such Colony; and that all persons passing through, or making a temporary stay in any of the Colonies being entitled to the protection of the laws, during the time of such passage, visitation, or temporary stay, owed, during the same, allegiance thereto.

"Hence, with these views and objects, after enumerating the causes which induced the people of each Colony, as a separate political body, or one people, to take the course they did, this unanimous Declaration of the thirteen United States, was in these words:

> We, therefore, the Representatives of the United States of America in General Congress assembled (that is of the States thus united in Congress assembled), appealing to the Supreme Judge of all the world for the rectitude of our intentions, do, in the name and by the authority of the good people of these Colonies, solemnly publish and declare, that *these United Colonies are, and of right ought to be, free and independent States*; that they are absolved from all allegiance to the British Crown, and that all political connection between them and the State of Great Britain is, and ought to be, totally dissolved; and that, *as free and independent States, they have full power to levy war, conclude peace, contract alliances, establish commerce, and to do all other acts and things which independent States may of right do. And for the support of this declaration, with a firm reliance on the protection of Divine Providence, we mutually pledge to each other our lives, our fortunes, and our sacred honor.* [Emphasis added, L.S.]

"The Declaration was then signed by the delegates from each Colony or State, separately, each delegation acting in behalf and by the Paramount authority of each State severally and respectively. [Emphasis added, L.S.]

". . . The Delegates themselves say, in the paper signed by them, that it [the Declaration of Independence] was done in the name, and by the authority, of the People of the Colonies. That is, the Sovereign authority of the People of each Colony, respectively. For not one of them had any authority to speak for the People of any Colony, except the one he was delegated to represent; nor did any one assume or presume to speak for his own Colony, until empowered to do so. The object of [my Liberal friends] . . . seems to have been to produce the impression, without positively stating the fact so in truth to be, that the Declaration of Independence was a National act. That it was not made by the States, as States, but by an assembly of men, assuming to speak for the

American Colonists as one People or Nation; and that, too, without any authority whatever, except their own assumed powers. [Emphasis added, L.S.]

"[My Liberal friends must be] . . . hard pressed, indeed, [in their] . . . efforts to prove that the whole People of the United States now constitute one Nation, when [they are] . . . compelled to resort to such logic, to establish so great and so important an historical fact! . . . But nothing is easier to be done, than to show that [their conclusions], . . . so drawn, from premises of the imagination entirely, has not a solitary fact to stand upon. *Our history at this period rests not upon legends or fables. That Congress itself did not regard their act as the result of assumed, or unauthorized powers, their acts at the time abundantly show. That they did not consider the Declaration of Independence as a National act, or put any such construction upon it, as [Liberals have so often]* . . . *done, appears clearly from what they were then doing. At the very time the Declaration of Independence was made, a Committee, consisting of one delegate from each State, was organized to prepare articles of Confederation between the States, as separate, distinct Sovereign political Communities.* [Emphasis added, L.S.] That Committee, which was appointed on the 11th of June, even before the Declaration of Independence was agreed to, and in anticipation of it, reported the Articles of Confederation, before referred to, which, Mr. [George T.] Curtis says, was the first written Constitution of the United States. The title of these Articles speaks for itself. It is in these words:

> Articles of Confederation and perpetual Union between the States of New Hampshire, Massachusetts-Bay, Rhode Island and Providence Plantations, Connecticut, New York, New Jersey, Pennsylvania, Delaware, Maryland, Virginia, North Carolina, South Carolina, and Georgia.

"After stating the style of the Confederacy to be 'The United States of America,' the very first clause in these Articles of Union is in these words:

> *Each State retains its Sovereignty, freedom and independence, and every power, Jurisdiction and right, which is not by this Confederacy expressly delegated to the United States, in Congress assembled.* [Emphasis added, L.S.]

"These Articles were reported on 12th day of July, eight days after the Declaration. Moreover, this argument and conclusion of [Liberals] . . . are utterly inconsistent with the facts acknowledged and set forth in the treaty of Peace with Great Britain, in 1783 [in which each state is listed separately, as individual nation-states]. The very first article of that treaty is in these words:

> [From Great Britain:] His Britannic Majesty acknowledges the said United States, viz.: New Hampshire, Massachusetts-Bay, Rhode Island and

Providence Plantations, Connecticut, New York, New Jersey, Pennsylvania, Delaware, Maryland, Virginia, North Carolina, South Carolina, and Georgia, to be free, Sovereign and Independent States; that he treats with them as such; and for himself, his heirs, and successors, relinquishes all claim to the Government, propriety, and territorial rights of the same, and every part thereof.

"The fifth article of the treaty clearly shows how the States, the other party to it, understood it. This is in these words:

[From the United States of America:] It is agreed that the Congress shall earnestly recommend it to the Legislatures of the respective States, to provide for the restitution of all estates, rights and properties, which have been confiscated, belonging to real British subjects, and also of the estates, rights and properties of persons resident in Districts in possession of his Majesty's arms, and who have not borne arms against the said United States. And that persons of any other description shall have free liberty to go to any part or parts of any of the thirteen United States, and therein to remain twelve months, unmolested in their endeavors to obtain the restitution of such of their estates, rights and properties, as may have been confiscated; and that Congress shall also earnestly recommend to the several States a reconsideration and revision of all acts or laws regarding the premises, so as to render the said laws or acts perfectly consistent, not only with justice and equity, but with that spirit of conciliation, which on the return of the blessings of peace should universally prevail. And that Congress shall also earnestly recommend to the several States, that the estates, rights and properties of such last mentioned persons, shall be restored to them, they refunding to any persons who may be now in possession, the *bona fide* price (where any has been given) which such persons may have paid on purchasing any of the said lands, rights or properties, since the confiscation. And it is agreed, that all persons who have any interest in confiscated lands, either by debts, marriage settlements, or otherwise, shall meet with no lawful impediment in the prosecution of their just rights.

"*So far from the Federal Government assuming a national character at that time, it would not presume to bind the States or enter into an obligation upon matters that related to their own separate Sovereign Jurisdiction. That Government only engaged to use its influence in recommending to the Sovereign States respectively certain stipulations. This statement of [my Liberal friends, that the Founding Fathers did not consider the original thirteen colonies to be separate and independent states] . . . is the more remarkable, because it is in direct conflict with numerous decisions of the Supreme Court of the United States.* [Emphasis added, L.S.]

"This Court, in the case of *McIlvaine* vs. *Coxe*, . . . in 1805, held that, 'on the 4th of October, 1776, the State of New Jersey was completely a Sovereign, Independent State, and had a right to compel the inhabitants of the State to become citizens thereof.' In delivering the opinion of the Court in this case, Mr. Cushing says:

> 'The Court deems it unnecessary to declare an opinion upon a point which was much debated in this case, whether a real British subject, born before the 4th of July, 1776, who never from the time of his birth resided within any of the American Colonies or States, can upon the principles of the common law take lands by descent in the United States; because Daniel Coxe, under whom the lessor of the plaintiff claims, was born in the Province of New Jersey, long before the Declaration of Independence, and resided there until some time in the year 1777, when he joined the British forces.
>
> 'Neither does this case produce the necessity of discriminating very nicely the precise point of time, when Daniel Coxe lost his right of election to abandon the American cause and adhere to his allegiance to the King of Great Britain; because he remained in the State of New Jersey, not only after she declared herself a Sovereign State, but after she had passed laws by which she pronounced him to be a member of, and in allegiance to the new Government. The Court entertains no doubt, that after the 4th of October, 1776, he became a member of the new Society, entitled to the protection of its Government, and bound to that Government by the ties of allegiance.'

"One of the points in this case was citizenship, and to what power allegiance was due; or in other words, where Sovereignty or Paramount authority under our system then resided—that is, under the Confederation. These, as we settled in the beginning, belong to Sovereignty and follow it. In this case the Supreme Court of the United States decided that both citizenship and allegiance, in 1776, after the Declaration of Independence, belonged to the States severally and respectively. Further on, in the same case, the Court says:

> 'If then, at the period of the treaty of peace, the laws of New Jersey, which made Daniel Coxe a subject of that State, were in full force, and were not repealed, or in any manner affected by that instrument—if, by force of these laws, he was incapable of throwing off his allegiance to the State, and derived no right to do so by virtue of the treaty, it follows that he still retains the capacity he possessed before the treaty,' etc.

"That capacity was the right to claim citizenship of the State of New Jersey, with all its privileges and immunities, with their accompanying obligations, amongst which was allegiance to her Sovereignty, which he could not throw off. In another case decided by the same Court, in February, 1796, nine years before *Ware*, etc., vs. *Hylton*, etc., [the Justice], in delivering his opinion, says:

'The first point raised by the counsel for the plaintiff in error was, that the Legislature of Virginia had no right to make the law of the 20th of October, 1777, above in part recited. If this objection is established, the judgment of the Circuit Court must be reversed, because it destroys the defendant's plea in bar, and leaves him without defence to the plaintiff's action. I would also remark, that the law of Virginia was made after the Declaration of Independence by Virginia, and also by Congress, and several years before the Confederation of the United States, which, although agreed to by Congress on the 15th of November, 1777, and assented to by ten States in 1778, was only finally completed and ratified on the first of March, 1781. I am of opinion that the exclusive right of confiscating, during the war, all and every species of British property, within the territorial limits of Virginia, resides only in the Legislature of that Commonwealth. It is worthy of remembrance, that delegates and representatives were elected by the people of the several counties and corporations of Virginia, to meet in general Convention, for the purpose of framing a new Government, by the authority of the people only; and that the said Convention met on the sixth of May, and continued in session until the fifth of July, 1776; and, in virtue of their delegated power, established a Constitution or form of Government, to regulate and determine by whom, and in what manner, the authority of the people of Virginia was thereafter to be executed. As *the people of that country were the genuine source and fountain of all power that could be rightfully exercised within its limits*, they had therefore an unquestionable right to grant it to whom they pleased, and under what restrictions or limitations they thought proper. The people of Virginia, by their Constitution or fundamental law, granted and delegated all their supreme civil power to a Legislature, an Executive, and a Judiciary; the first to make; the second to execute; and the last to declare or expound the laws of the Commonwealth. This abolition of the old Government, and this establishment of a new one, was the highest act of power that any people can exercise. From the moment the people of Virginia exercised this power, all dependence on, and connection with, Great Britain, absolutely and forever ceased; and no formal Declaration of Independence was necessary, although a decent respect for the opinions of mankind required a Declaration of the causes which impelled the separation, and was proper to give notice of the event to the nations of Europe. I hold it as unquestionable, that the Legislature of Virginia, established as I have stated by the authority of the people, was forever thereafter invested with the supreme and Sovereign power of the State, and with authority to make any laws in their discretion, to affect the lives, liberties, and property of all the citizens of that Commonwealth. The Legislative power of every nation can only be restrained by its own Constitution; and it is the duty of its Courts of Justice not to question the validity of any law made in pursuance of the Constitution.

There is no question but the act of the Virginia Legislature (of the 20th of October, 1777), was within the authority granted to them by the people of that country; and this being admitted, it is a necessary result that the law is obligatory on the Courts of Virginia, and, in my opinion, on the Courts of the United States. If Virginia, as a Sovereign State, violated the ancient or modern law of nations in making the law of the 20th of October, 1777, she was answerable in her political capacity to the British nation, whose subjects have been injured inconsequence of that law. In June, 1776, the Convention of Virginia was a free, Sovereign, and Independent State; and on the fourth of July, 1776, following, the United States, in Congress assembled, declared the thirteen United Colonies free and Independent States; and that, as such, they had full power to levy war, conclude peace, etc. *I consider this as a Declaration, not that the United Colonies Jointly, in a collective capacity, were Independent States, etc., but that each of them was a Sovereign and Independent State; that is, that each of them had a right to govern itself by its own authority and its own laws, without any control from any other power upon earth!*' [Emphasis added, L.S.]

"Is authority clearer, stronger, or higher, needed to show the utter groundlessness of [the Liberal's] . . . argument? If so let us turn to what Chief Justice [John] Marshall said, in delivering the decision of the Supreme Court of the United States, in the great case of *Gibbons* vs. *Ogden*, in 1824. Here it is:

'As preliminary to the very able discussion of the Constitution which we have heard from the bar, and as having some influence on its construction, reference has been made to the political situation of these States anterior to its formation. *It has been said that they were Sovereign, were completely Independent, and were connected with each other only by a league. This is true!*' [Emphasis added, L.S.]

"*Judge Marshall here distinctly affirms, judicially affirms, from the Bench of the Supreme Court of the United States, that the States were separate and distinct Sovereignties when the Articles of Confederation were entered into, and that these articles were but a league between Sovereign Powers.* [As for my historical sources, they are] strong! Why, . . . there is no answer to them. [The Liberals'] . . . account of the matter, and [their] whole argument built upon it, has not a single fact to rest upon; and unless something can be offered in reply, not to me, but to these authorities, I shall take up no more time in establishing the correctness of the assumption with which I set out, that is, that the States, in forming their first political Union, from which the present sprung, entered into it, as free, Sovereign, Independent Powers, or, in other words, in the further prosecution of our inquiry, we may now take it as an established fact, that Mr. [George T.]

Curtis was right, in saying that

> 'the Parties to this instrument (the Articles of Confederation) were free, Sovereign, political Communities, each possessing within itself powers of Legislation and Government over its own citizens, which any political society can possess.' [Emphasis added, L.S.]

"This is equivalent to saying, that the first Constitution was a Compact between Sovereign States, and that the ultimate Paramount authority or Sovereignty under that union remained and resided with the States severally."[115] [Emphasis added, L.S.]

10

America's First Two Constitutions

IN THIS CHAPTER STEPHENS CONTINUES his discussion on the "old" Articles of Confederation and the "new" Constitution of the United States, with special emphasis on the nature of the compact between the states, the sovereignty of the states, and the delegation of powers concerning the states and the central government. He also covers the reasons why the Articles of Confederation were replaced by the U.S. Constitution at the Philadelphia Convention in 1787, and provides the actual responses of the states to the call for a meeting "to remedy the evils complained of."

To those who challenged Stephens' views on the history of the Union, he replied in this manner:

☛ "[I have easily] historically and judicially established that the thirteen States, as separate and distinct Sovereign Powers, declared their Independence, and as such entered into their first Union under the Articles of Confederation of 1777 or 1781, according as we may consider the date of the agreement to the terms of the Union by their deputies in Congress, or the time when these terms were acceded to and ratified by all the States; it being further established that citizenship and allegiance were within and under the control of each State under that Confederation as with all other nations; and that *each of the States severally, at this period in our history, had full power to confiscate and do what all other Sovereign States by the laws of nations may of right do; and that the right of Eminent Domain which ever accompanies and distinguishes Sovereignty in its fullest extent, was possessed by them severally as separate, distinct States*. . . . If Sovereignty, beyond question, resided with the States severally at that time, has it ever been changed or parted with by them since? . . . *Sovereignty cannot pass by implication. If the States were Sovereign when they entered into the Articles of Confederation, they must still remain so, unless they parted with that Sovereignty in those articles, or in the new articles*—the new Constitution, as it was called—of 1787, which are the basis of the present Union. Now, in this instrument, the new Constitution of 1787, did the States surrender the Sovereignty which they undeniably and beyond all question possessed in 1783? In this instrument have they parted with their control over the citizenship and allegiance of their citizens respectively? This is the great question. In investigating it, . . . I . . . look not only into the instrument itself, but into the old Constitution, to understand correctly the evils arising under its operation and the remedies applied. [Emphasis added, L.S.]

". . . I premise by assuming an unquestionable position, and that is, that all grants by Sovereignty are to be strictly construed. Nothing can pass by inference or implication against Sovereignty. It is a fundamental maxim of public law that in construing grants from the Sovereign power, nothing is to be taken by implication against the power granting; nothing will pass to the grantee but by clear and express words. This is true of all grants, even of private rights, from the Sovereign power, and much more stringently is the rule to be adhered to in grants, purporting to surrender Sovereign powers themselves. It is likewise a universal principle and maxim of political law, that *Sovereign States cannot be deprived of any of their rights by implication; nor in any manner whatever but by their own voluntary consent or by submission to a conqueror.* [Emphasis added, L.S.]

"[Examining] the Articles of Confederation, as they were styled, . . . [it is plain to see] the nature and extent of the powers delegated by them. The stipulations entered into by these Articles, as appear from their face, may be divided into two classes:

"First, mutual Covenants between the parties, which, at that time, we have seen, were beyond question separate, distinct, Sovereign States.

"Secondly, delegations of power by the several Parties to the Compact to all the States, to be exercised by them jointly, in a general Congress of the States.

"The mutual Covenants between the States, upon analysis, may be stated as follows:

1st. The style of the Confederacy was to be 'The United States of America.'

"2nd. *Each State retained its Sovereignty, freedom and Independence, and every power and right which is not expressly delegated to the United States.* [Emphasis added, L.S.]

"3rd. *The object of the Confederation was for their mutual defence, the security of their liberties and their mutual and general welfare, binding themselves to assist each other against all force offered to or attacks made upon them, or any of them, on account of religion, Sovereignty, trade, or any other pretence whatever.* [Emphasis added, L.S.]

"4th. In determining all questions in Congress each State was to have one vote.

"5th. Each State was to maintain its own Delegates.

"6th. The free inhabitants of each State, Paupers, Vagabonds and Fugitives from Justice excepted, were to be entitled to all privileges and immunities of free citizens in the several States.

"7th. All Fugitives from Justice from one State into another were to be delivered up on demand.

"8th. Full faith and credit were to be given to the records of each State in all the others.

"9th. Congress was to grant no title of nobility.

"10th. No person holding any office was to receive a present from a foreign power.

"11th. No State was to form any agreement or alliance with a foreign power without the consent of the States in Congress assembled.

"12th. No two or more States were to form any alliance between themselves, without the like consent of the States in Congress assembled.

"13th. No State, without the like consent of Congress, was to keep war ships or an army in time of peace, but each was to keep a well organized and disciplined militia with munitions of war.

"14th. No State was to lay any duty upon foreign imports which would interfere with any treaty made by Congress.

"15th. No State was to issue letters of marque or to engage in war without the consent of the Congress, unless actually invaded or menaced with invasion.

"16th. When land forces were raised, each State was to raise the quota required by Congress, arm and equip them, at the expense of all the States, and to appoint all officers of and under the rank of colonel.

"17th. Each State was to levy and raise the quota of tax required by Congress.

"18th. The faith of all the States was pledged to pay all the bills of credit emitted, or money borrowed, on their joint account, by the Congress.

"19th. It was agreed and covenanted that Canada might accede to the Union, so formed, if she chose to do so.

"20th (and lastly). Each State was to abide by the determination of all the States, in Congress assembled, on all questions which, by the Confederation, were submitted to them. The Articles of Confederation were to be inviolably observed by every State, and the Union was to be perpetual. No article of the Confederation was to be altered without the consent of every State.

"So much for the mutual covenants.

"Secondly. The Delegations of power by each of the States to all the States, in general Congress assembled, upon a like analysis, may be stated as follows:—

"1st. The sole and exclusive power to determine on war and peace, except in case a State should be invaded or menaced with invasion.

"2nd. To send and receive Ambassadors.

"3rd. To make Treaties, with a Proviso, etc.

"4th. To establish rules for Captures.

"5th. To grant Letters of Marque and Reprisal.

"6th. To appoint Courts for Trial of Piracies and other crimes, specified.

"7th. To decide Questions of Dispute, between two or more States, in a prescribed manner.

"8th. The sole and exclusive power to coin Money, and regulate the value.

"9th. To fix the standard of Weights and Measures.

"10th. To regulate trade with the Indian Tribes.

"11th. To establish Post-Offices.

"12th. To appoint all officers of land forces, except Regimental.

"13th. To appoint all officers of the Naval Forces.

"14th. To make rules and regulations for the Government of Land and Naval Forces.

"15th. To appropriate and apply public money for public expenses, the common defence and general welfare.

"16th. To borrow money and emit bills of credit.

"17th. To build and equip a navy.

"18th. To agree upon the number of land forces, and make requisitions upon the States, for their quotas, in proportion to the number of white inhabitants in each State.

"The foregoing powers were delegated, with this limitation—the war power, the treaty power, the power to coin money, the power to regulate the value thereof, the power of fixing the quotas of money to be raised by the States, the power to emit bills of credit, the power to borrow money, the power to appropriate money, the power to regulate the number of land and naval forces, the power to appoint a commander-in-chief for the army or navy, were never to be exercised, unless nine of the States were assenting to the same.

"These are the general provisions of the Articles of Confederation of 1777-1781."[116]

If the Articles of Confederation were so perfectly created, why did the Founding Fathers feel it necessary to design a second Constitution, the one that became the Constitution of the United States of America? Stephens explains that there were only two real "defects" in our first Constitution:

☛ "One was the want of power on the part of the States in Congress assembled, to regulate trade with foreign nations, and between the States, as well as with the Indian Tribes; and the other was the want of a like power to lay taxes directly upon the people of the several States, or to raise revenue by levying duties upon imports, without resorting to requisitions, or quotas, upon the States, in their organized political capacity. This is abundantly clear from the history of the times, and the action of the States in Congress assembled, under the Articles of Confederation. The first movement for additional power, or a change of the Constitution, in any respect, was in Congress, on the 3rd of February, 1781. This was an adoption by the States, in Congress, assembled of the following resolution:

> Resolved, That it be recommended to the several States, as indispensably necessary, that they vest a power in Congress to levy, for the use of the United States, a duty of five per cent. *ad valorem*, at the time and place of importation, upon all goods, wares, and merchandise, of foreign growth or manufacture, which may be imported into any of the said States, from any foreign port, island, or plantation, after the 1st day of May, 1781; except arms, ammunition, clothing, and other articles imported on account of the United States, or any of them; and except wool cards, and cotton cards, and wire for making them; and, also, except salt, during the war.
> Also, a like duty of five per cent. on all prizes and prize goods, condemned in the court of admiralty of any of these States, as lawful prize.
> That the moneys arising from said duties be appropriated to the discharge of the principal and interest of the debts already contracted, or which may be contracted, on the faith of the United States, for supporting the present war.
> That the said duties be continued until the said debts shall be fully and finally discharged.

"This proposition was not concurred in by the States, and it is useless to trace its history and final rejection.

"The second effort at amendment was in 1783, after the [American Revolutionary] war was over, and the independence of the States acknowledged. On the 18th of April, 1783, Congress adopted the following resolution:

> Resolved, by nine States, that it be recommended to the several States as indispensably necessary to the restoration of public credit, and to the punctual and honorable discharge of the public debts, to invest the United States, in Congress assembled, with the power to levy, for the use of the United States,

the following duties upon goods imported into the said States from any foreign port, island, or plantation [etc.].

"Then follows a long list of articles on which it was asked to vest the United States, in Congress assembled, with the power to levy duties upon, and the rate of duty proposed.

"This request of Congress for additional powers, though accompanied by an able and strong letter from Congress to the States, asking them to make 'the constitutional change' proposed, was never acceded to by the States, and no farther notice of it is necessary here.

"On the 30th of April, 1784, Congress again 'recommended to the Legislatures of the several States to vest the United States, in Congress assembled, for the term of fifteen years,' etc., with certain specified powers over commerce with foreign nations. This proposition was also rejected by the States. Several States agreed to it, but it lacked the necessary number to carry it into effect.

"The next movement to effect a change in the Articles of Confederation was by Mr. [James] Monroe, in Congress, July, 1785. His proposition was for the States to vest in the United States, in Congress assembled, 'the power of regulating trade.' Congress never acted upon this proposition. 'It was deemed, in the language of the day, that any proposition for perfecting the Articles of Confederation should originate with the State Legislatures.' Accordingly, Mr. [James] Madison went into the Legislature of Virginia, and under his auspices a movement was made in that body, in December, 1785, with a view to vest in the United States, in Congress assembled, the powers that had been previously proposed by the Congress. This first movement in the Virginia Legislature failed; but subsequently, on the 21st of January, 1786, that body passed the following resolution:

> Resolved, That Edmund Randolph, James Madison, Jr., Walter Jones, St. George Tucker, Meriwether Smith, David Ross, William Ronald, and George Mason, Esquires, be appointed Commissioners, who, or any five of whom, shall meet such Commissioners as may be appointed by the other States in the Union, at a time and place to be agreed on, to take into consideration the trade of the United States; to examine the relative situation and trade of the said States; to consider how far a uniform system in their commercial regulations may be necessary to their common interest and their permanent harmony; and to report to the several States such an act relative to this great object as when unanimously ratified by them, will enable the United States, in Congress assembled, to provide for the same; That the said Commissioners shall immediately transmit to the several States copies of the preceding resolution, with a circular letter requesting their concurrence therein, and

proposing a time and place for the meeting aforesaid.

"Four other States responded to this resolution of the Virginia Legislature, to wit: New York, New Jersey, Pennsylvania, and Delaware. They all appointed Commissioners, as suggested by Virginia. These Commissioners met in convention at Annapolis, in Maryland, 11th September, 1786. They did nothing, however, but make a report to the Legislatures appointing them and recommending the calling of a General Convention of all the States, to meet at Philadelphia on the second Monday in May, 1787,

> 'to take into consideration the situation of the United States; to devise such further provisions as shall appear to them necessary to render the Constitution of the Federal Government adequate to the exigencies of the Union; and to report such an Act for that purpose to the United States, in Congress assembled, as when agreed to by them, and afterwards confirmed by the Legislatures of every State, will effectually provide for the same.'

"As a reason for this course, they say

> 'they are the more naturally led to this conclusion, as, in the course of their reflections on the subject, they have been induced to think that the power of regulating trade is of such comprehensive extent, and will enter so far into the general system of the Federal Government, that, to give it efficacy, and to obviate questions and doubts concerning its precise nature and limits, may require a correspondent adjustment of other parts of the Federal system.'

"This communication was addressed to the States from whom the parties held their commissions, and copies of it were likewise sent to the United States, in Congress assembled, and to the Executives of all the States. The Congress took up the subject on the 21st of February, 1787, and came to the following resolution upon it:

> Resolved, That, in the opinion of Congress, it is expedient that, on the second Monday in May next, a Convention of Delegates, who shall have been appointed by the several States, be held at Philadelphia, for the sole and express purpose of revising the Articles of Confederation, and reporting to Congress and the several Legislatures, such alterations and provisions therein as shall, when agreed to in Congress, and confirmed by the States, render the Federal Constitution adequate to the exigencies of Government, and the preservation of the Union.

"It was under this resolution of Congress that the ever-memorable Federal [or Philadelphia] Convention of 1787 was called and met. The initiative step to this movement was the resolution of the 21st of January, 1786, of the Virginia Legislature. Mr. Madison was the author of that resolution, though it was offered by Mr. [John] Tyler [Sr.], father of the late Ex-President [John] Tyler. Mr. Madison's agency in first starting this movement is what has given him the title of father of the present Constitution. *In none of these proceedings, either in Congress, or in the Virginia Legislature, or in the communication of the Commissioners at Annapolis, is there any intimation of a wish or desire to change the nature of the Government, then existing, in any of its essential Federative [Confederative] features.* It does, however, very clearly appear, from the letter of the Commissioners, that, in granting additional powers to the United States, in Congress assembled, it might and would be, in their opinion, proper to make 'a correspondent adjustment of other parts of the Federal system.' This, doubtless, referred to a division of the powers vested in the States, jointly, under the then Constitution. These were mostly, as we have seen, committed to one body—to the Congress of the States. [Emphasis added, L.S.]

"Already, the idea had begun to develop itself, of introducing a new feature in the Federal plan—that of dividing the powers delegated, into Legislative and Executive departments, each distinct from the Judicial; and also dividing the Legislative department into two branches, or houses; and, further still, of allowing the Federal machinery to act directly upon the citizens of the States in special cases, and not on the States in their corporate capacity, as had been in all former Confederacies. This idea, at first, was not fully developed. All new truths are slow of development. Mankind, generally, at first, see new truths indistinctly; as the man we read of in the Scriptures, who, having been born blind, when his eyes were opened, at first, 'saw men, as trees, walking.' This new feature, or new features, in the Federal plan is but dimly shadowed forth in the letter of the Commissioners, wherein they speak of some necessary correspondent adjustment of the Federal system. Mr. [Thomas] Jefferson, soon after, gives the idea more form and substance, in a letter to Mr. Madison, written at Paris, 16th of December, 1786. Here is his letter:—

> 'I find, by the public papers, that your Commercial Convention failed in point of Representation. If it should produce a full meeting in May, and a broader reformation, it will still be well. To make us one nation, as to foreign concerns, and keep us distinct in domestic ones, gives the outline of the proper division of powers between the general and particular Governments. But, to enable the Federal head to exercise the powers, given it, to best advantage, it should be organized, as the particular ones are, into Legislative, Executive and Judiciary. The first and last are already separated. The second should be. When last with Congress, I often proposed to members to do this,

by making of the Committee of the States an Executive Committee, during the recess of Congress; and, during its session, to appoint a committee to receive and despatch all Executive business, so that Congress itself should meddle only with what should be Legislative. But I question if any Congress (much less all successively) can have self-denial enough to go through with this distribution. The distribution, then, should be imposed on them.'

"This, as far as I have been able to discover, after no inconsiderable research, is the first embodied conception of the general outline of those proper changes of the old Constitution or Articles of Confederation, which were subsequently, as we shall see, actually and in fact, ingrafted on the old system of Confederations; and which makes the most marked difference between ours, and all other like systems. Of all the Statesmen in this country, none ever excelled Mr. Jefferson in grasp of political ideas, and a thorough understanding of the principles of human Government.

"This is a brief, but unquestionable, history of the complaints under the old system. The great leading object, at the time, with Congress, was to get additional power to regulate trade, and to raise revenue directly by law, operating on the individual citizens of the States, and not on the States in their corporate character. Under the Articles of Union, as they then were, Congress could regulate trade, as we have seen, with the Indian tribes, but not between the States respectively, or with foreign nations; nor could they raise revenue, as we have seen, except by requisitions upon the States. The main and leading objects were to get the Federal Constitution amended in these particulars. Could these new ideas and new principles be incorporated in a system strictly Federal [Confederal]? This was the great problem of that day. Congress gave consent to the calling of a Convention of the States, as desired, for the sole and express purpose of revising the Articles of Confederation, to the attainment, if possible, of these ends and objects. *No intimation was given, in any of the proceedings that led to the call of this [Philadelphia] Convention, of any wish, much less a desire, to change the character of the Federal system, or to transform it from a Confederate Republic, as it was then acknowledged to be, into a consolidated nation.* It is important to pay strict attention to the proceedings at this time. *The Convention was called, not to change the nature of the General Government, but to delegate to it some few additional powers, and to adjust its machinery, in accordance with these additional powers. It was with this view, and for this purpose, with this 'sole and express purpose,' that the States, in Congress, gave the movement their sanction.* Now, then, how did this matter proceed? How did the States, in their Sovereign capacities, respond to this call for a Convention, to change the Articles of their Confederation, so as to remedy the evils complained of? *Each of the States, be it remembered, at that time, was a perfect State, clothed with all the attributes of*

Sovereignty. In our inquiries into the nature and extent of the changes in the fundamental law, especially so far as they trenched upon the Sovereign powers of the States, proposed by that Convention, it is of the utmost importance to know what the States did, both anterior to the call of the Convention, and subsequently. [Emphasis added, L.S.]

"Let us, then, direct our special attention to the responses of each of the States to the call itself. Here are the responses of all of them. We will take them up singly and separately.

FIRST, GEORGIA.

"The response of my own State is seen in the following ordinance:

> An ordinance for the appointment of deputies from this State for the purpose of revising the Federal Constitution.
>
> Be it ordained, by the Representatives of the State of Georgia, in General Assembly met, and by authority of the same, that William Few, Abraham Baldwin, William Pierce, George Walton, William Houston, and Nathaniel Pendleton, Esqrs., be, and they are hereby, appointed Commissioners, who, or any two or more of them, are hereby authorized, as deputies from this State, to meet such deputies as may be appointed and authorized by other States, to assemble in Convention at Philadelphia, and to join with them in devising and discussing all such alterations and further provisions as may be necessary to render the Federal Constitution adequate to the exigencies of the Union, and in reporting such an Act for that purpose to the United States in Congress assembled, as, when agreed to by them, and duly confirmed by the several States, will effectually provide for the same. In case of the death of any of the said Deputies, or of their declining their appointments, the Executive is hereby authorized to supply such vacancies.

"By virtue of this ordinance, the Governor of the State issued commissions, or credentials, to the several Delegates thus appointed. I read one of these. The others are exactly similar to it.

> 'The State of Georgia, by the grace of God, free, Sovereign, and Independent:
>
> 'To the Hon. William Few, Esqr.:
>
> 'Whereas, you, the said William Few, are, in and by an Ordinance of the General Assembly of our said State, nominated and appointed a Deputy to represent the same in a Convention of the United States, to be assembled at Philadelphia, for the purposes of devising and discussing all such alterations and further provisions as may be necessary to render the Federal Constitution adequate to the exigencies of the Union—
>
> 'You are, therefore, hereby commissioned to proceed on the duties

required of you in virtue of the said ordinance.

'Witness our trusty and well-beloved George Matthews, Esq., our Captain-General, Governor, Commander-in-chief, under his hand and our great seal, this 17th day of April, in the year of our Lord 1787, and of our Sovereignty and Independence the eleventh.'

"Signed by the Governor and countersigned by his Secretary.

"From this it clearly appears that Georgia responded to the call for a Convention of her Co-Sovereign States, with the sole view of discussing and making such alterations in their then Federal Constitution as might be deemed proper and necessary for the better providing for the exigencies of 'the Union.' That is, *the continued Union of Sovereign Confederated States. Nothing could have been further from the intention of Georgia, or the Congress, than a dissolution of that Union by a general merger of all the people of the United States in one Nation. The object was to preserve the Union as it existed, and not to destroy it.* [Emphasis added, L.S.]

"How utterly demolishing this record is to the reported statement of Mr. [Charles C.] Pinckney, quoted by Judge [Joseph] Story, 'that no one of the distinguished band of patriots of that day ever thought of the separate independence of the several States.' The commission of Governor [John] Mathews shows beyond cavil that at least one of those distinguished patriots, and at least one of those States, not only thought of such an idea, but acted upon it, as a known, fixed, and acknowledged fact. This fact was set forth in the credentials by which the Delegates from Georgia were received by their associates from all the other States. *They were received into the Federal Convention, as Delegates from a State claiming at least to be Free, Sovereign, and Independent; and, being so received, all the other parties which so received them should be held to be forever estopped from denying the character of the powers or authority under which they were received and acted.* This commission shows, too, that this claim of Sovereignty and Independence was from the date that her Delegates in Congress, in her name, and by her Paramount authority, had joined the Delegates from all the other States in proclaiming the great fact in their general Declaration on the ever memorable 4th of July, 1776. [Emphasis added, L.S.]

"'The 17th of April,' says Governor Mathews, 'in the year of our Lord, 1787, and of our Sovereignty and Independence the eleventh.'

"The responses of all the States which did respond (and all did respond except Rhode Island), are no less significant than that of Georgia. It is quite a labor to go through with them all, but the important bearing they have upon the great questions we are now considering, requires not only that we should look into them, but examine them thoroughly, and scan them closely. These establish very essential facts, to which we should look in our inquiry. They are the deep footprints of truth, impressed upon our earlier history, which assertion can never obliterate, argument cannot remove, sophistry cannot obscure, time cannot erase, and which even wars can never destroy! However upheaved the foundations of society may be by political convulsions, these will stick to the very fragments of the rocks of our primitive formation, bearing their unerring testimony to the ages to come!

"The responses of all the States show conclusively the great indisputable fact that they all, at that time, claimed to be Sovereign and Independent, and that their sole object in going into Convention at that time was barely to provide for such changes as could be made in their then Constitution, as experience had shown to be proper, and not to change its Federal character. [Emphasis added, L.S.] Let us examine each of them closely."

SECOND, MASSACHUSETTS.

"The response of [this] State . . . appears from the following commission to her Delegates:

> By his excellency, James Bowdoin, Esq., Governor of the Commonwealth of Massachusetts.
>
> To the Hon. Francis Dana, Elbridge Gerry, Nathaniel Gorham, Rufus King, and Caleb Strong, Esqrs., greeting:
>
> Whereas, Congress did, on the 21st day of February, A.D., 1787, Resolve, 'That, in the opinion of Congress, it is expedient that, on the second Monday in May next, a Convention of Delegates, who shall have been appointed by the several States, be held at Philadelphia, for the sole and express purpose of revising the Articles of Confederation, and reporting to Congress and the several Legislatures such alterations and provisions therein as shall, when agreed to in Congress, and confirmed by the States, render the Federal Constitution adequate to the exigencies of government and the preservation of the Union:'
>
> And whereas, the General Court have constituted and appointed you their Delegates, to attend and represent this Commonwealth in the said proposed Convention, and have, by a resolution of theirs of the 10th of March last, requested me to commission you for that purpose:
>
> Now, therefore, know ye, That, in pursuance of the resolutions aforesaid, I do, by these presents, commission you, the said Francis Dana, Elbridge Gerry, Nathaniel Gorham, Rufus King, and Caleb Strong, Esqrs., or any three of you, to meet such Delegates as may be appointed by the other, or any of the other States in the Union, to meet in Convention at Philadelphia, at the time and for the purposes aforesaid.
>
> In testimony whereof, I have caused the public seal of the Commonwealth aforesaid to be hereunto affixed.
>
> Given at the Council Chamber, in Boston, the ninth day of April, A.D., 1787, and in the eleventh year of the Independence of the United States of

America.

THIRD, CONNECTICUT.

"The response of [this] State . . . is seen in the following act of its General Assembly of the second Thursday of May, 1787:

> An Act for appointing Delegates to meet in Convention of the States to be held at Philadelphia, on the second Monday of May instant.
> Whereas, the Congress of the United States, by their Act of the 21st February, 1787, have recommended that, on the second Monday of May instant, a Convention of Delegates, who shall have been appointed by the several States, be held at Philadelphia, for the sole and express purpose of revising the Articles of Confederation:
> Be it enacted by the Governor, Council, and Representatives, in General Court assembled, and by the authority of the same, That the Hon. William Samuel Johnson, Roger Sherman, and Oliver Ellsworth, Esqrs., be, and they hereby are, appointed Delegates to attend the said Convention, and are requested to proceed to the City of Philadelphia, for that purpose, without delay; and the said Delegates, and, in case of sickness or accident, such one or more of them as shall attend the said Convention, is, and are hereby authorized and empowered to represent this State therein, and to confer with such Delegates appointed by the several States, for the purposes mentioned in the said Act of Congress, that may be present and duly empowered to sit in said Convention, and to discuss upon such alterations and provisions, agreeably to the general principles of Republican [Confederate] Government, as they shall think proper to render the Federal Constitution adequate to the exigencies of government and the preservation of the Union; and they are further directed, pursuant to the said Act of Congress, to report such alterations and provisions as may be agreed to by a majority of the United States represented in Convention, to the Congress of the United States, and to the General Assembly of this State.

FOURTH, NEW YORK.

"The State of New York, by a joint resolution of her Legislature, passed the 6th of March, 1787, responded as follows:

> Resolved, That the Hon. Robert Yates, John Lansing, Jr., and Alexander Hamilton, Esqrs., be, and they are hereby declared duly nominated and appointed Delegates, on the part of this State, to meet such Delegates as may be appointed on the part of the other States, respectively, on the second Monday in May next, at Philadelphia, for the sole and express purpose of revising the Articles of Confederation, and reporting to Congress, and to the several Legislatures, such alterations and provisions therein as shall, when

agreed to in Congress, and confirmed by the several States, render the Federal Constitution adequate to the exigencies of government and the preservation of the Union.

"To these proceedings Governor [George] Clinton, Governor of the State, officially certified in the following words:

'In testimony whereof I have caused the privy seal of the said State to be hereunto affixed this ninth day of May, in the eleventh year of the Independence of the said State.'

FIFTH, NEW JERSEY.

"The State of New Jersey responded as follows:

To the Hon. David Brearley, William Churchill Houston, William Paterson, and John Neilson, Esqrs., greeting:

The Council and Assembly, reposing especial trust and confidence in your integrity, prudence, and ability, have, at a joint meeting, appointed you, the said David Brearley, William Churchill Houston, William Patterson, and John Neilson, Esqrs., or any three of you, Commissioners, to meet such Commissioners as have been, or may be, appointed by the other States in the Union, at the City of Philadelphia, in the Commonwealth of Pennsylvania, on the second Monday in May next, for the purpose of taking into consideration the state of the Union as to trade and other important objects, and of devising such other provisions as shall appear to be necessary to render the Constitution of the Federal Government adequate to the exigencies thereof.

In testimony whereof, the great seal of the State is hereunto affixed. Witness, William Livingston, Esq., Governor, Captain-General, and Commander-in-chief, in and over the State of New Jersey, and territories thereunto belonging, Chancellor and Ordinary in the same, at Trenton, the 23rd day of November, in the year of our Lord, 1786, and of our Sovereignty and Independence the eleventh.

SIXTH, PENNSYLVANIA.

"The State of Pennsylvania responded as follows:

An Act appointing Deputies to the Convention, intended to be held in the City of Philadelphia, for the Purpose of revising the Federal Constitution.

Sec. 1. Whereas, the General Assembly of this Commonwealth, taking into their serious consideration, the representations heretofore made to the Legislatures of the several States in the Union, by the United States in Congress assembled, and also weighing the difficulties under which the Confederated States now labor, are fully convinced of the necessity of revising the Federal Constitution, for the purpose of making such alterations and amendments as the exigencies of our public affairs require: And, whereas, the Legislature of the State of Virginia have already passed an Act of that Commonwealth, empowering certain Commissioners to meet at the City of Philadelphia, in May next, a Convention of Commissioners or Deputies from the different States; and the Legislature of this State are fully sensible of the important advantages which may be derived to the United States, and every of them, from co-operating with the Commonwealth of Virginia, and the other States to the Confederation, in the said design.

Sec. 2. Be it enacted, and it is hereby enacted, by the Representatives of the freemen of the Commonwealth of Pennsylvania, in General Assembly met, and by the authority of the same, That Thomas Mifflin, Robert Morris, George Clymer, Jared Ingersoll, Thomas Fitzsimons, James Wilson, and Gouverneur Morris, Esqrs., are hereby appointed Deputies from this State, to meet in the Convention of the Deputies of the respective States of North America, to be held at the City of Philadelphia, on the 2nd day in the month of May next; and the said Thomas Mifflin, Robert Morris, George Clymer, Jared Ingersoll, Thomas Fitzsimons, James Wilson, and Gouverneur Morris, Esqrs., or any four of them, are hereby constituted and appointed Deputies from this State, with powers to meet such Deputies as may be appointed and authorized by the other States, to assemble in the said Convention, at the city aforesaid, and join with them in devising, deliberating on, and discussing, all such alterations and further provisions as may be necessary to render the Federal Constitution fully adequate to the exigencies of the Union, and in reporting such act or acts, for that purpose, to the United States in Congress assembled, as, when agreed to by them, and duly confirmed by the several States, will effectually provide for the same.

Sec. 3. And be it further enacted by the authority aforesaid, That, in case any of the said Deputies hereby nominated shall happen to die, or to resign his or their said appointment or appointments, the supreme executive council shall be, and hereby are, empowered and required to nominate and appoint other person or persons, in lieu of him or them so deceased, or who has or have so resigned, which person or persons, from and after such nomination and appointment, shall be, and hereby are, declared to be vested with the same powers respectively as any of the Deputies nominated and appointed by this Act is vested with by the same; provided always, that the council are not hereby authorized, nor shall they make any such nomination or appointment, except in vacation and during the recess of the General Assembly of the State.

"This Act passed December 30th, 1786. By a supplemental Act passed the 28th day of March, 1787, Dr. [Benjamin] Franklin was appointed as an additional Delegate.

SEVENTH, DELAWARE.

"The State of Delaware responded as follows:

His Excellency, Thomas Collins, Esqr., President, Captain-General, and Commander-in-chief, of the Delaware State.

To all to whom these presents shall come, Greeting: Know ye, that, among the laws of the said State, passed by the General Assembly of the same, on the 3rd day of February, in the year of our Lord, 1787, it is thus enrolled:—In the eleventh year of the Independence of the Delaware State.

An Act appointing Deputies from this State to the Convention proposed to be held in the City of Philadelphia, for the Purpose of revising the Federal Constitution.

Whereas, the General Assembly of this State are fully convinced of the necessity of revising the Federal Constitution, and adding thereto such further provisions as may render the same more adequate to the exigencies of the Union; and, whereas, the Legislature of Virginia have already passed an Act of that Commonwealth, appointing and authorizing certain Commissioners to meet, at the City of Philadelphia, in May next, a Convention of Commissioners or Deputies from the different States; and this State being willing and desirous of cooperating with the Commonwealth of Virginia, and the other States in the Confederation, in so useful a design:—

Be it, therefore, enacted by the General Assembly of Delaware, that George Read, Gunning Bedford [Jr.], John Dickinson, Richard Basset, and Jacob Broom, Esqrs., are hereby appointed Deputies from this State, to meet in the Convention of the Deputies of other States, to be held at the City of Philadelphia, on the 2nd day of May next; and the said George Read, Gunning Bedford, John Dickinson, Richard Basset, and Jacob Broom, Esqrs., or any three of them, are hereby constituted and appointed Deputies from this State, with powers to meet such Deputies as may be appointed and authorized by the other States to assemble in the said Convention at the city aforesaid, and to join with them in devising, deliberating on, and discussing, such alterations and further provisions as may be necessary to render the Federal Constitution adequate to the exigencies of the Union; and in reporting such Act or Acts, for that purpose, to the United States in Congress assembled, as, when agreed to by them, and duly confirmed by the several States, may effectually provide for the same. So always and provided, that such alterations or further provisions, or any of them, do not extend to that part of the 5th Article of the Confederation of the said State, finally ratified on the 1st day of March, in the year 1781, which declares that, "In determining questions in the United States in Congress assembled, each State shall have one vote." And be it enacted, That in case any of the said Deputies hereby nominated shall happen to die, or resign his or their appointment, the President or Commander-in-chief, with the advice of the privy council, in the recess of the General Assembly, is hereby authorized to supply such vacancies.

In testimony whereof, I have hereunto subscribed my name, and caused the great seal of the said State to be affixed to these presents, at New Castle, the 2nd day of April, in the year of our Lord, 1787, and in the 11th year of the Independence of the United States of America.

EIGHTH, MARYLAND.
"The State of Maryland responded as follows:

An Act for the Appointment of, and conferring Powers on, Deputies from this State to the Federal Convention.

Be it enacted by the General Assembly of Maryland, That the Hon. James McHenry, Daniel of St. Thomas Jenifer, Daniel Carroll, John Francis Mercer, and Luther Martin, Esqrs., be appointed and authorized, on behalf of this State, to meet such Deputies as may be appointed and authorized, by any other of the United States, to assemble in Convention at Philadelphia, for the purpose of revising the Federal system, and to join with them in considering such alterations and further provisions as may be necessary to render the Federal Constitution adequate to the exigencies of the Union; and in reporting such an Act for that purpose, to the United States in Congress assembled, as, when agreed to by them, and duly confirmed by the several States, will effectually provide for the same; and the said Deputies, or such of them as shall attend the said Convention, shall have full power to represent this State for the purposes aforesaid; and the said Deputies are hereby directed to report the proceedings of the said Convention, and any Act agreed to therein, to the next Session of the General Assembly of this State.

NINTH, VIRGINIA.
"The State of Virginia responded as follows:

An Act for appointing Deputies from this Commonwealth to a Convention proposed to be held in the City of Philadelphia, in May next, for the purpose of revising the Federal Constitution.

Whereas, the Commissioners who assembled at Annapolis, on the 14th day of September last, for the purpose of devising and reporting the means of enabling Congress to provide effectively for the Commercial interests of the United States, have represented the necessity of extending the revision of the Federal system to all its defects, and have recommended that Deputies, for that purpose, be appointed by the several Legislatures, to meet in Convention, in the City of Philadelphia, on the 2nd day of May next,—a provision which was preferable to a discussion of the subject in Congress, where it might be too much interrupted by the ordinary business before them, and where it would, besides, be deprived of the valuable counsels of sundry individuals who are disqualified by the Constitution or laws of particular States, or restrained by peculiar circumstances from a seat in that Assembly: and whereas the General Assembly of this Commonwealth, taking into view the actual situation of the Confederacy, as well as reflecting on the alarming representations made, from time to time, by the United States in Congress, particularly in their Act of the 15th day of February last, can no longer doubt that the crisis is arrived at which the good people of America are to decide the solemn question—whether they will, by wise and magnanimous efforts, reap the just fruits of that independence which they have so gloriously acquired, and of that Union which they have cemented with so much of their common blood—or whether, by giving way to unmanly jealousies and prejudices, or to partial and transitory interests, they will renounce the auspicious blessings prepared for them by the Revolution, and furnish to its enemies an eventful triumph over those by whose virtues and valor it has been accomplished: And whereas the same noble and extended policy, and the same fraternal and affectionate sentiments, which originally determined the Citizens of this Commonwealth to unite with their brethren of the other States in establishing a Federal Government, cannot but be felt with equal force now as motives to lay aside every inferior consideration, and to concur in such further concessions and provisions as may be necessary to secure the great objects for which that Government was instituted, and to render the United States as happy in peace as they have been glorious in war:—

Be it, therefore, enacted by the General Assembly of the Commonwealth of Virginia, That Seven Commissioners be appointed, by joint ballot of both Houses of Assembly, who, or any three of them, are hereby authorized, as Deputies from this Commonwealth, to meet such Deputies as may be appointed and authorized by other States, to assemble in Convention at Philadelphia, as above recommended, and to join with them in devising and discussing all such alterations and further provisions as may be necessary to render the Federal Constitution adequate to the exigencies of the Union; and in reporting such an Act, for that purpose, to the United States in Congress, as, when agreed to by them, and duly confirmed by the several States, will effectually provide for the same.

And be it further enacted, That, in case of the death of any of the said Deputies, or of their declining their appointments, the Executive is hereby authorized to supply such vacancies; and the Governor is requested to transmit forthwith a copy of this Act to the United States in Congress, and to the Executives of each of the States in the Union.

"Under this Act, Deputies were appointed, as provided; at the head of the list of whom was placed George Washington.

TENTH, NORTH CAROLINA.

"The State of North Carolina responded, as appears from the following Commission to her Deputies given by the Governor:

To the Hon. Alexander Martin, Esq., greeting:

Whereas, our General Assembly, in their late session, holden [held] at Fayetteville, by adjournment, in the month of January last, did, by joint ballot of the Senate and House of Commons, elect Richard Caswell, Alexander Martin, William Richardson Davie, Richard Dobbs Spaight, and Willie Jones, Esqrs., Deputies to attend a Convention of Delegates from the several United States of America, proposed to be held at the City of Philadelphia, in May next, for the purpose of revising the Federal Constitution:

We do, therefore, by these presents, nominate, commissionate, and appoint you, the said Alexander Martin, one of the Deputies for and in behalf, to meet with our other Deputies at Philadelphia on the 1st of May next, and with them, or any two of them, to confer with such Deputies as may have been, or shall be appointed by the other States, for the purpose aforesaid: To hold, exercise, and enjoy the appointment aforesaid, with all powers, authorities, and emoluments, to the same belonging, or in any wise appertaining, you conforming in every instance to the Act of our said Assembly, under which you are appointed.

Witness, Richard Caswell, Esq., our Governor, Captain-General, and Commander-in-Chief, under his hand and our seal, at Kinston, the 24th day of February, in the eleventh year of our independence, A.D. 1787.

"Similar Commissions were given to each of the other Delegates appointed.

ELEVENTH, SOUTH CAROLINA.

"The State of South Carolina responded as follows:

By his Excellency, Thomas Pinckney, Esq., Governor and Commander-in-Chief, in and over the State aforesaid:

To the Hon. John Rutledge, Esq., greeting:

By virtue of the power and authority invested by the Legislature of this State, in their Act passed the 8th day of March last, I do hereby commission you, the said John Rutledge, as one of the Deputies appointed from this State, to meet such Deputies or Commissioners as may be appointed and authorized by other of the United States to assemble in Convention, at the City of Philadelphia, in the month of May next, or as soon thereafter as may be, and to join with such Deputies or Commissioners (they being duly authorized and empowered) in devising and discussing all such alterations, clauses, articles, and provisions, as may be thought necessary to render the Federal Constitution entirely adequate to the actual situation and future good government of the Confederated States; and that you, together with the said Deputies or Commissioners, or a majority of them, who shall be present (provided the State be not represented by less than two), do join in reporting such an act to the United States, in Congress assembled, as, when approved and agreed to by them, and duly ratified and confirmed by the several States, will effectually provide for the exigencies of the Union.

Given under my hand and the Great Seal of the State, in the City of Charleston, this 10th day of April, in the year of our Lord 1787, and of the Sovereignty and Independence of the United States of America, the eleventh.

"Signed by the Governor, and countersigned by the Secretary.

TWELFTH, NEW HAMPSHIRE.

"The State of New Hampshire responded, in the language of the following Act of her Legislature:

An Act for appointing Deputies from this State to the Convention proposed to be holden in the City of Philadelphia in May, 1787, for the purpose of revising the Federal Constitution.

Whereas, in the formation of the Federal Compact, which frames the bond of union of the American States, it was not possible, in the infant state of our Republic, to devise a system which, in the course of time and experience, would not manifest imperfections that it would be necessary to reform:

And whereas, the limited powers, which, by the Articles of Confederation, are vested in the Congress of the United States, have been found far inadequate to the enlarged purposes which they were intended to produce; and whereas, Congress hath, by repeated and most urgent representations, endeavored to awaken this, and other States of the Union, to a sense of the truly critical and alarming situation in which they may inevitably be involved, unless timely measures be taken to enlarge the powers of Congress, that they may thereby be enabled to avert the dangers which threaten our existence as a free and independent people; and whereas, this State hath been ever desirous to act upon the liberal system of the general good of the United States, without circumscribing its views to the narrow and selfish objects of partial convenience; and has been at all times ready to make every concession, to the safety and happiness of the whole, which justice and sound policy could vindicate:

Be it therefore enacted, by the Senate and House of Representatives in General Court convened, that John Langdon, John Pickering, Nicholas Oilman, and Benjamin West, Esqrs., be, and hereby are, appointed Commissioners; they, or any two of them, are hereby authorized and empowered, as Deputies from this State, to meet at Philadelphia said Convention, or any other place to which the Convention may be adjourned, for the purposes aforesaid, there to confer with such Deputies as are, or may be, appointed by the other States for similar purposes, and with them to discuss and to procure and decide upon the most effectual means to remedy the defects of our Federal Union, and to procure and secure the enlarged purposes which it was intended to effect, and to report such an Act to the United States in Congress, as, when agreed to by them, and duly confirmed by the several States, will effectually provide for the same.

"*From all these responses of the States, to the call for a Convention of the States, it clearly appears that the sole object of all was to change and modify the Articles of Confederation, so as better to provide for the wants and exigencies of 'the Union,' which must have meant the Union then existing, and which we have seen was a Union of Sovereign States. The object was not to change the Federative character of that Union. This is an important point to be kept constantly in view, and never lost sight of. The Convention was called with this sole view, and the call was responded to by every State with this sole view.* [Emphasis added, L.S.]

"Under the call and appointment of Delegates, as we have seen, the Convention did meet in Philadelphia, on the second Monday in May (14th of that month), 1787. [George] Washington, a Deputy or Delegate from the State of Virginia, was chosen the President of the Convention. The Convention remained in session until the 17th of September thereafter—four months and three days. *It was assembled as a Convention of the States. The Delegates represented distinct, separate, and acknowledged Sovereign powers.* The vote upon all questions was taken by States, without respect to the number of Delegates from the several States respectively. Here is the Journal of their proceedings from the day of their meeting to their adjournment. The result of their deliberations and actions was such changes in the Federal Constitution as were set forth in the paper which they presented to the States. This paper is what has ever since been known as the present Constitution of the United States."[117] [Emphasis added, L.S.]

11

THE NATURE OF THE U.S. GOVERNMENT

LIBERALS IN STEPHENS' DAY OFTEN charged that the "new U.S. Constitution," which replaced the old Articles of Confederation, overturned the original concept of the Union (as a "Confederacy of Sovereign States"), thereby stripping the states of their "paramount authority" as small independent nations with the right to accede or secede from that Union.

If true, this means the Founding Fathers intended to establish a purely national government rather than a confederated one. It would also mean that secession was rendered unconstitutional at the time, and that the Southern states were guilty of treason for departing from the Union in 1860 and 1861. Finally, this would fully justify Lincoln's invasion of the South and the deaths of some 3 million Americans.[118]

In the following excerpts from *A Constitutional View of the Late War Between the States*, Stephens meets these false notions head-on during his discussion on the nature of the United States government.

☞ "Now, what grounds has this argument or consideration of the subject to rest upon? These and these only: The first Resolution passed by the [Philadelphia] Convention was . . . not the first acted upon. It was the last of a series of three. The Convention was in committee of the whole, having under consideration a plan of Government, submitted by Governor [Edmund] Randolph, of Virginia. The [last of these] series of Resolutions . . . was offered by Gouverneur Morris, of Pennsylvania, to be substituted in lieu of the first Resolution in the plan offered by Governor Randolph. Here are these Resolutions constituting this series:

> 1. Resolved, That a Union of the States, merely Federal, will not accomplish the objects proposed by the Articles of Confederation, namely, common defence, security of liberty, and general welfare.
> 2. Resolved, That no treaty or treaties among any of the States, as Sovereign, will accomplish or secure their common defence, liberty, or welfare.
> 3. Resolved, That a National Government ought to be established, consisting of a supreme Judicial, Legislative, and Executive.

"The first two of these resolutions were not agreed to. It was said, that if the first of this series of resolutions was agreed to, the business of the Convention was at an end. The first two, therefore, were dropped. The last was taken up and adopted—but how adopted or in what sense, very clearly appears from Mr. [Edward] Yates's account of it. 'This last Resolve,' he says, 'had also its difficulties; the term supreme required explanation. It was asked, whether it was intended to annihilate State Governments? It was answered, only so far, as the powers intended to be granted to the new Government, should clash with the States, when the latter were to yield.'

"The resolution, with this explanation and understanding, then passed in Committee, eight States only being present. But the refusal of the Committee to agree to the other two, or, rather, their abandonment without a division, shows very clearly, to all fair and right-thinking minds, that *it was not the intention of the Convention, by the adoption of this third resolution in Committee, to abandon the Federal system, and institute a National Government, as Judge Story argues; and that the Convention did not intend or indicate any purpose, thereby, to travel out of, or beyond their powers, which confined them, in the main, to the sole purpose of revising and amending the terms of their Union, on the basis of a Confederation of Sovereign States*. Now, when these first two resolutions, which contained the gist of the whole question, had been abandoned without a count, it is easy to conceive that any one might have supposed that the object of this resolution, after the explanation given, was barely to declare that such changes in the Articles of Confederation were intended by it, as Mr. [Thomas] Jefferson had foreshadowed—that is, that, in the changes to be made, there should be a division, in the powers delegated, into Legislative, Judicial and Executive, without any departure from the Federal basis of the Union. This is, also, strengthened by the fact that Delaware voted for the resolution. It is well known that that State never would have voted for the resolution, with the construction put upon its words [as a newly nationalized government].... The introduction of the word *National* may not have struck the minds of the

Delegates from Delaware and others, as bearing, or being intended to bear, the import now sought to be given to it, or which, upon close scrutiny, legitimately belongs to it. National was a word often loosely used in application to the Government under the Confederation, and even by the strictest adherents to the Sovereignty of the States. *In the letter read yesterday from Mr. Jefferson, he spoke of the Government being so modelled as to make us one Nation as to all foreign powers, and yet separate and distinct Nations, as to ourselves. This Unity, or Nationality, as to foreign powers, was to be founded upon a Federal basis or Compact between the internal Nationalities* [i.e., individual states]. *It is no strain of presumption, therefore, to suppose that this word was understood in this sense by many who voted for that resolution.* [Emphasis added, L.S.]

"But the great controlling fact in the case, one that removes every particle of ground upon which [Liberals build their] . . . entire theory of the Government, is, that subsequently, on the 20th of June, when the report of the Committee of the Whole was before the Convention, for consideration; after the whole plan, submitted by Governor [Edmund] Randolph, had been gone through with; after the ideas and objects of the members, generally, had been developed; and after the bearing of this word National, or the sense in which some used it, had been fully disclosed, and when eleven States were present, it was moved, by Mr. [Oliver] Ellsworth, of Connecticut, to strike out this resolution, that had been previously agreed to, as before stated, and to insert the following:—

> Resolved, That the Government of the United States ought to consist of a Supreme Legislative, Judiciary and Executive.

"*This resolution was agreed to; and, after this action of the Convention upon this resolution, the word 'National,' wherever it occurred, throughout Governor Randolph's whole plan, was stricken out, and the 'Government of the United States,' or its equivalent, inserted. So, the 'fundamental proposition' upon which* [Liberals build their] *. . . whole superstructure, is completely knocked from under* [them]. *. . . The grounds, upon which it temporarily rested for the short space of twenty-one days, were completely removed by the Convention itself.* The truth is, the debates between the 30th of May and the 20th of June, had disclosed the fact that there were quite a number of Delegates in the Convention, who were in favor of [nationalizing the government]. . . . They were, as clearly appears from Gouverneur Morris's first resolution, for doing away with the Federal [Confederate] system entirely, and for establishing one great National Government; or, in other words, they were for abandoning the whole idea of a Federal [Confederate] Union, and incorporating the several State Sovereignties into one National Sovereignty.

"Among these, none were more prominent or zealous than Governor [Edmund] Randolph and Mr. [James] Madison, of Virginia, Mr. [Gouverneur] Morris and Mr. [James] Wilson, of Pennsylvania, Mr. [Rufus] King, of Massachusetts, and Mr. [Alexander] Hamilton, of New York. These differed widely amongst themselves, as to the form of Government which should be instituted upon this National basis. Governor Randolph and Mr. Wilson seemed to have been for a Consolidated Democratic Republic, with two Houses for Legislation, and an Elective Executive. In this view, Mr. Madison concurred. Mr. Hamilton and Mr. Morris were also for one single National Republic, but based upon different principles. Some thought their scheme looked toward Monarchy, but justice requires it to be stated, that nothing that fell from them, or either of them, in the debates, authorizes such a conclusion. They were all, however,—Randolph, Madison, Morris, Hamilton, Wilson and King—for a great National Republic, with a total departure from the Federal [conservative confederated] system. While the Nationals in the Convention were so divided, an overwhelming majority of the Delegates, as well as a majority of the States, were utterly opposed to either of their systems. Nothing could induce them to depart from the Federal [Confederate] system, or cause them to yield the equality of the States, as Sovereigns, in the Union, and the equality of their votes in all measures that might be passed upon by the new Government, as it was in the old. *It was after this disclosure that the States agreed to the resolution of Mr. Ellsworth, to strike out 'National Government,' wherever it occurred in Governor Randolph's plan, and substitute for it, 'Government of the United States.' It was thus settled by the Convention, in their final action upon this very first resolution, that the work of their hands, whatever might be its details, was to be a plan, or organization, or Constitution, or Articles of Compact, call you it what you may, of a Government of States, of Sovereign States, formed and instituted by States and for States.*"[119] [Emphasis added, L.S.]

Early Liberals believed, and still do, that the U.S. Constitution ordered a national government, and that the individual states were meant to be subject to it. To this notion Stephens replied:

☛ "[Our government] . . . is a Government instituted by States and for States, and . . . all the functions it possesses, even in its direct action on the individual citizens of the several States, spring from and depend upon a Compact between the States constituting it. *It is, therefore, a Government of States and for States.* The final action upon the very first resolution . . . shows that the object of the Convention was to form a Government of States. 'The Government of the United States' ought to consist, they declared, 'of a Supreme Legislature, Judiciary and Executive.' This is the same as if they had declared 'the

Government of the States United, ought to consist,' etc. The first Constitution, we have seen, was *a Government of States*. The States in Congress assembled passed all laws, made all treaties, and exercised all powers vested in them jointly. No measure could be passed without the equal voice of each State, however small. Delaware had the same influence as New York, Massachusetts, or Virginia, and in this respect I maintain there is no essential change in the new Constitution. Examine it! Sift it, and dissect it as you may, and you will find it to be nothing but *a Government of States*, as much so, in principle, as the old Confederation. The powers to be exercised by the States jointly, Legislatively, Judicially, and Executively, have been enlarged, and it does not require so many States now to determine many questions as before; but under the present Constitution no measure can be passed, no law can be enacted, if a majority of the States oppose it."[120] [Emphasis added, L.S.]

When asked to prove that the Founders intended for the U.S. government to be a "government of states for states," Stephens answered:

☛ ". . . [Is] it not undeniably true? Has not each State an equal vote in the Senate? Can any law be passed if a majority of the States in the Senate withhold their sanction? The Senators, two to each State, are selected by the States, severally, in their corporate and Sovereign capacity. Can any treaty be made, if any more than a bare third of the States in the Senate refuse to agree to it? Can any man be appointed to any office of dignity or profit, if a majority of the States in the Senate vote against it? If the Electoral Colleges fail to choose a President, does not the election devolve upon the House of Representatives, where the election is by States, each State casting one vote only? If they fail to elect a Vice President does not the election devolve on the Senate, where no one can be chosen if a majority of the States vote against him? Can the Government be worked at all if a majority of the States in the Senate refuse their co-operation? If a majority of the States were to refuse to elect Senators would not the Government, of necessity, cease to exist? The Supreme Court of the United States has so held. Chief Justice [John] Marshall, delivering the opinion, in the case of *Cohens* vs. *Virginia*, uses this language:

> 'It is true, that if all the States, or a majority of them, refuse to elect Senators, the Legislative powers of the Union will be suspended!'

"[Alexander] Hamilton, in the Convention from New York, when the Constitution was before that body for approval or disapproval, in reply to arguments going to show that the State authorities would be endangered by the powers conferred on the General Government, declared that 'the Union is dependent on the will of the State Governments for its Chief Magistrate and for its Senate.' 'The States,' said Mr. Hamilton, 'can never lose their powers till the whole people of America are robbed of their liberties.' His great mind never gave utterance to a mightier truth!

"Is it not entirely proper and correct, therefore, to say, of a Government that cannot be carried on rightfully at all against the will of a majority of the States, that it is a Government of States, and nothing but a Government of States?"[121]

Big government Liberals countered Stephens' view by stating that the House of Representatives is elected by population, in which the larger states dominate the smaller ones, while in the Senate the vote is taken per capita, not by states. With each senator voting as he pleases, they argued, "a law may pass without a majority of the States voting for it, and a treaty may be ratified without a majority of two thirds of the States voting for it." Stephens had a handy retort:

☛ "[While this may be true,] . . . it does not interfere in the least with what I have said, and maintain, that no law or measure can be passed if a majority of the States, through their Senators who represent their Sovereignty, vote against it. Under the system the power is with the States. If the Senators of a State be divided, the voice of that State is simply not heard on the question, exactly as it was under the Confederation, and in the Convention that formed the Constitution. It is in such case as if the State voluntarily absented herself from the vote, and let the other States decide it. In this there is no change in the new system from the old. Under the Articles of Confederation, when the Delegation from a State was equally divided on any question, the vote of that State was not counted. It had no effect. The States, in forming the new Constitution, did make one concession, and that was that a House of Representatives, to be elected by the people in the several States, in proportion to population, on a certain basis, known ever as the Federal basis, might join in Legislation. But they never did yield their right to an equal vote in the Senate, or, that it might by possibility be without their power as States, to defeat any measure that the popular branch might adopt or pass. In this particular, relating only to the machinery and operation of the system, there is a change in the new Constitution from the old, but none in the principle. The equal voice of all the States, as States, on all questions coming before the Congress of States, now as before, though divided into two Houses, is still retained in the Senate. The right and power of holding a complete and absolute veto in the hands of a majority of the States, over the House, or the popular branch of the Congress, was, and is, retained in the States. This was the great point on which the Convention, that framed the Constitution, came near breaking up without agreeing to any thing. The Nationals, as they were called, insisted upon changing the principle of an equality of votes, on the part of the States, in the Senate. The Federals were willing to yield a change, as to the votes in the House, but would never yield their right to an equal voice in one, or the other of the branches of the Congress. They were determined to maintain an equality of political power in the States severally, in whatever form of Constitution might be adopted. It was at this stage of the proceedings that Dr. [Benjamin] Franklin moved for prayers. On the first test vote on the motion to allow each State an equal vote in the Senate, the States stood five for it, and five against it, with one divided. Eleven States only were present. New Hampshire was absent. It was at this stage of the proceedings, that Mr. [Gunning] Bedford [Jr.], from Delaware, declared

> 'That all the States at present are equally Sovereign and Independent, has been asserted from every quarter in this House. Our deliberations here are a confirmation of the position, and I may add to it that each of them acts from interested, and many from ambitious motives. The small States never can agree to the Virginia plan, and why, then, is it still urged? Let us then do what is in our power—amend and enlarge the Confederation, but not alter the Federal [Confederate] system.'

"The Virginia plan was Governor Randolph's National plan. It was after this dead lock, at which the Convention had come, between the Nationals [Liberals] and the State Sovereignty advocates, or Federals [Conservatives], as they were then called—between those [Liberals] who were in favor of what was called a National Government proper, and those [Conservatives] in favor of the continued Union of the several States on a Federal basis—a Government National for external purposes, but leaving ultimate Sovereignty with the several States—after this speech of Mr. [Gunning] Bedford and like speeches of others—after it was seen that nothing could be done on the National line, that a Grand Committee was raised, consisting of one Member from each State, to see if any Compromise could be effected. The Committee consisted of Mr. [Elbridge T.] Gerry, of Massachusetts, Mr. [Oliver] Ellsworth, of Connecticut, Mr. [Edward] Yates, of New York, Mr. [William] Paterson, of New Jersey, Dr. [Benjamin] Franklin, of Pennsylvania, Mr. [Gunning] Bedford, of Delaware, Mr. [Luther] Martin, of Maryland, Mr. [William R.] Davie, of North Carolina, Mr. [Edward] Rutledge, of South Carolina, and Mr. [Abraham] Baldwin, of Georgia.

"Mr. Yates has given an exceedingly interesting account of the proceedings of this Grand Committee.

'The Grand Committee met July 3rd. Mr. Gerry was chosen Chairman. The Committee proceeded to consider in what manner they should discharge the business with which they were intrusted. By the proceedings in the Convention, they were so equally divided on the important question of representation in the two branches, that the idea of a conciliatory adjustment must have been in contemplation of the House in the appointment of this Committee. But still, how to effect this salutary purpose was the question. Many of the members, impressed with the utility of a General Government, connected with it the indispensable necessity of a representation from the States according to their numbers and wealth; while others, equally tenacious of the rights of the States, would admit of no representation but such as was strictly Federal [Confederate], or, in other words, equality of suffrage. This brought on a discussion of the principles on which the House had divided, and a lengthy recapitulation of the arguments advanced in the House in support of these opposite propositions. As I had not openly explained my sentiments on any former occasion on this question, but constantly, in giving my vote, showed my attachment to the National Government on Federal principles, I took this occasion to explain my motives.

'These remarks gave rise to a motion of Dr. Franklin, which, after some modification, was agreed to, and made the basis of the following report of the Committee:'

The Committee to whom was referred the eighth resolution reported from the Committee of the whole House, and so much of the seventh as had not been decided on, submit the following report:

That the subsequent propositions be recommended to the Convention, on condition that both shall be generally adopted.

That in the first branch of the Legislature, each of the States now in the Union be allowed one member for every forty thousand inhabitants of the description reported in the seventh resolution of the Committee of the whole House. That each State, not containing that number, shall be allowed one member.

That bills for raising or apportioning money, and for fixing salaries of the officers of Government of the United States, shall originate in the first branch of the Legislature, and shall not be altered or amended by the second branch; and that no money shall be drawn from the public treasury but in pursuance of appropriations to be originated in the first branch.

That in the second branch of the Legislature, each State shall have an equal vote.

[Stephens continues:] "This report was the basis of the great compromise, as it was called, between the two distinct parties in the Convention—the Nationals [Liberals] and the Federals [Conservatives]. It discloses the nature and the extent of the contest. At first it would seem that it was a fair adjustment of the question—not so thought the vigilant sentinels and guardians of the Sovereignty of the States; for it conceded the absolute power of the popular branch of the Congress over the States in the Senate on one class of measures. That a majority of the States would not yield. The right of the States to hold an absolute negative in their own hands, in all cases, they would not give up. The first part of this report, after being discussed, and after it was ascertained that it could never receive the sanction of a majority of the States, was recommitted to a committee of five. Their report was also discussed, and likewise failed to receive the sanction of a majority of the States. The subject was then recommitted to another Grand Committee, consisting of one from each State, whose final report was agreed to. That fixed the number of members to which each State should be entitled in the first House of Representatives, and provided for future apportionments according to population, etc., as it stands in the Constitution. The clause in the first report, that gave the House of Representatives absolute power over money, bills, etc., was abandoned. The latter part of the first report, securing to the States severally an equal vote in the Senate, was not touched afterwards. It stood as first reported, that in the Senate, or second branch of the Congress, each State should have an equal vote. This, however, was not finally adopted without another struggle. Before the question was taken on agreeing to it, it was moved that instead of an equality of votes, the States should be represented in the second branch as follows: New Hampshire, by two members; Massachusetts, four; Rhode Island, one; Connecticut, three; New York, three; New Jersey, two; Pennsylvania, four; Delaware, one; Maryland, three; Virginia, five; North Carolina, three; South Carolina, three; Georgia, two; making, in the whole, thirty-six.

"This, by several, was thought to be a fair settlement of the dispute, allowing the Sovereign States still to be represented as such, but not equally. Mr. [James] Wilson, Mr. [James] Madison, and the Nationals [Liberals] generally, favored it as a last hope of getting as near what they desired as possible. Some of the Federals [Conservatives] were not disinclined to accede to it as a compromise; amongst these was Mr. Gerry, of Massachusetts; but not so the unyielding advocates of State Sovereignty [i.e., those tending toward Libertarianism].

". . . So the final report of the Second Grand Committee on this subject was adopted, which retained to the States an equal vote in the Senate, the same equality under the new Constitution which they had under the former Articles of Confederation. It was well ascertained that without this security the smaller States would not confederate further upon any basis; and that all attempts at remodelling the Confederation would inevitably fail unless all views of getting them to surrender this right were abandoned. They were so abandoned. The complete negative of a majority of the States in the Senate was retained. So the bond of this 'more perfect Union' was written. In this, as in the old, each State, as a State, has an equal vote in the last resort upon all measures.

Mr. [George T.] Curtis, in his *History of the Constitution* speaking of this feature in the Constitution, says:

> 'It is a part of the Constitution which it is vain to try by any standard of theory; for it was the result of a mere compromise of opposite theories and conflicting interests.'

"It was, without question, a compromise between the contending parties in the Convention, to the extent that the unyielding advocates of a strictly Federal system did, by it, consent to a Popular Representation from the several States, in the House, but with the full reservation, on the part of the States, of a complete and absolute negative, in the Senate, on all the acts of the popular Branch thus conceded; and it is utterly vain to attempt, by any bare theory or speculation, to make any thing else of it. This feature, itself, conclusively establishes the Federal [Confederate] character of the Government—not upon any theory, but by the 'inexorable logic' of the fact itself. It, moreover, totally annihilates all bare theories or speculations, however ingeniously put forth, in whatever speciousness of garb or rhetoric, going to show that the Government of the United States is a Government of the People of the Whole Country, as one community or Nation.

"Upon such a theory, what a caricature of a National Representative Government it would be! Just consider its structure a moment under such a theory! The six New England States, Maine, New Hampshire, Massachusetts, Rhode Island, Connecticut and Vermont, according to the census of 1860, had a population, all together, of three millions one hundred and thirty-five thousand three hundred and eighty-three. New York, alone, by the same census, had a population of three millions eight hundred and eighty thousand seven hundred and thirty-five! This single State had over a half a million more population than the other six, all together! And yet, under the Constitution, the three millions of people in these six States have six times the power in the Government that the three millions and a half have who are in New York. Or take another view. This little over three millions of people, in these six New England States, have just as much power in the Administration of the Government as the thirteen and a half millions have who constitute the aggregate population of the six States of New York, Pennsylvania, Virginia, Ohio, Indiana and Illinois. That is, they have just as much power in passing or defeating any measure whatever.

"All this is perfectly consistent with the fact of its being a strictly Federal [Confederate] Government, limited, in its action, to strictly Federal [Confederal] objects. But, upon the supposition, idea, or theory, that it is a Government of the entire population of the United States, as one community or Nation, with control over internal State affairs, the whole matchless framework of our ancestors—the Constitution—which, as it was made, deserves the just admiration of the world—would become, in its practical workings, nothing but a frightful political monstrosity! Well might the New England States, looking to no higher motives than their interest and power, be satisfied to have such a theory established, so long as they could hold on to the present structure, if that theory, however, should, unfortunately for Public Liberty, ever be established, a Reconstruction, of a very different character from that we now hear so much about, will, sooner or later, be inevitable!

"But, no . . . *this is not a Government of the People of this Country as one Nation.* [Emphasis added, L.S.]

"*It is still, under the Constitution, as it was under the Articles of Confederation, a Government of States, and for States. It was so agreed to in the Convention. It was so nominated in the bond. It was so submitted to the States for their approval and ratification, and not to the people of the whole country, in the aggregate, as . . . [Liberals] . . . maintain; but it was so submitted to the States, in their political organizations, and by them, as States, it was so agreed to and ratified. Each State retained the absolute power to govern its own people in its own way, in all their domestic relations, without any interference by the people of the other States, or the Federal Government, except in the specified cases set forth in the Constitution.*"[122] [Emphasis added, L.S.]

In attacking the case for small government, states' rights, and secession, big government Liberals point to the Preamble to the Constitution, which says: "We, the people of the United States." Their claim is that this demonstrates that the Constitution "was submitted to the whole people, and by them [it was] acted upon, ratified and adopted, and not by the States, as States." Here is Stephens' reply to this falsity:

☛ "[The Preamble] . . . shows no such thing; and it is a wonder to me how any one should ever have entertained such an idea. . . . what is the meaning of 'We, the people of the United States,' as they here stand? The meaning and sense of words must always be understood from the connection in which they are found. We have abundant and conclusive evidence that they could not have been intended to mean, in the connection where they here stand, what [Liberals] . . . would have them imply. Because, the very authority of the Delegates—their credentials—which, we have seen, stated that what they should do, should be referred back to the States, should be submitted to them, and should not be binding, unless approved by them, severally and respectively. [Emphasis added, L.S.] And, besides, we know that this preamble, as it unanimously passed the Convention, on the 7th of August, 1787, was in these words:—

> We, the people of the States of New Hampshire, Massachusetts, Rhode Island and Providence Plantations, Connecticut, New York, New Jersey, Pennsylvania, Delaware, Maryland, Virginia, North Carolina, South Carolina, and Georgia, do ordain, declare, and establish the following Constitution . . .

"*This shows what was the meaning of the Convention. It was we the people of each State. The change in the phraseology was made by a sub-committee on style, not by the Convention, except in their agreement to the Report of said committee. Why was it made? For a very obvious reason. It was not known which of the States would ratify it. Hence it was exceedingly inappropriate to set forth in advance the States by name. By the terms of the Constitution, Article VII, it was to go into operation between such of the States as might ratify it, if as many as nine or more should do so. The committee on style readily perceived that it would be exceedingly out of place, to have, in the preamble to the organic law, terms embracing a people, or States, who might not put themselves under it. For instance, Rhode Island and North Carolina did not ratify the Constitution for some time. During this period they were entirely out of the Union. They might have remained out until now. Suppose they had. How oddly would this preamble to the Constitution have read: 'We the people of New Hampshire, Rhode Island, North Carolina, etc., in order to form a more perfect Union,' etc., when the people of Rhode Island and North Carolina had done no such thing. To preserve symmetry in their work, and retain the same idea was what the Committee did in their change of phraseology. As they put it, it would embrace the people of such States only as should adopt it. They would then be the people of the States, respectively, which would thereby be United. States United and United States mean the same thing.* Upon a close scrutiny of the change of language in the Preamble, as it was at first adopted by the Convention, and as it was reported by the committee on style, some exceedingly interesting views are suggested, but these are far from favoring the inference usually drawn from it. [Emphasis added, L.S.] Let me call your special attention to them, for they have a direct and important bearing upon the point. . . . The words, as agreed to at first, in Convention, as we have seen, were:

> We, the people of the States of New Hampshire, Massachusetts, Rhode Island and Providence Plantations, Connecticut, New York, New Jersey, Pennsylvania, Delaware, Maryland, Virginia, North Carolina, South Carolina, and Georgia, do ordain, declare, and establish the following Constitution for the government of ourselves and our posterity.

"Now look closely to the words substituted, and weigh nicely the import of the words left out, as well as those inserted. As the clause was changed by the committee on style, and afterwards unanimously adopted in the Convention, it reads as follows:

> We, the people of the United States, in order to form a more perfect Union, establish justice, insure domestic tranquillity, provide for the common defence, promote the general welfare, and secure the blessings of liberty to ourselves and our posterity, do ordain and establish this Constitution for the United States of America.

"*The most striking difference in phraseology between the two, is that which sets forth the object in forming 'a more perfect Union,' etc., to be, to 'ordain and establish this Constitution,' not for the people in any sense, but for States as political societies. As the words originally stood, the inference might have been drawn from the bare words themselves, that the object was to form a government for the people in the aggregate. 'We, the people of the States of New Hampshire, Massachusetts, etc., do ordain and establish the following Constitution for the government of ourselves and our posterity.' From these words, I say, the inference might have been drawn that the object was to form a government for the people in the aggregate, but this inference is completely rebutted by the change of phraseology. As it stands, the instrument 'is ordained and established' as a Constitution for States—for the United States. The same as if it read 'for the States of this Union.'* [Emphasis added, L.S.]

"The change, in this particular, is very important, and the very Preamble, which is so often alluded to, for a directly opposite purpose, conclusively shows that the Government was intended to be, and is a Government States, and for States, as I said. In the change of phraseology the introduction of the word Union has a wonderful significance of itself. The new Constitution was proposed 'in order to form a more perfect Union,' that is, it was to make more perfect 'the Union' then existing. That, we have seen, was a Union of States under the Articles of Confederation. It was to revise these Articles, to enlarge the powers under them, or, in other words, to perfect that Union, that the Convention was called; and that was the object aimed at in all their labors to the conclusion of their work as set forth in this Preamble. So much for the evidence furnished by the Preamble. [Emphasis added, L.S.]

"But to put the matter beyond all cavil the last clause of the Constitution settles that question. That clause is in these words:

> The ratification of the Conventions of nine States shall be sufficient for the establishment of this Constitution between the States so ratifying the same.

"The word, *between*, was put in on special motion, which shows how closely words were watched, weighed, and guarded at the time. This shows, beyond all doubt or cavil, that *it was to be acted upon by States as States, and not by the people of all the States in one aggregate mass.* That, you will permit me, most respectfully and good-humoredly, to say, as it seems to me, is one of the most preposterous ideas that ever entered into the head of a sensible man. [Emphasis added, L.S.]

"Why the very last act of the Convention, in giving a finishing touch to the Constitution, and thereby impressing upon it forever their understanding of their own work, that it was a Union of States, is in these words:

> Done in Convention, by the unanimous consent of the States present, the 17th day of September, in the year of our Lord, 1787, and of the Independence of the United States of America the twelfth. In witness whereof we have hereunto subscribed our names.

"The Delegates signing their names by States.

"The Constitution was then sent, with a letter, to the States in Congress assembled, requesting that it should be submitted by them to the several State Legislatures, for them to provide for its submission to Conventions in the several States, to be acted on by them, and to go into effect *between* such States as should ratify it, if so many as nine or more should so ratify it.

"Congress, immediately upon the receipt of the report of the Convention, passed the following resolution:

> *Resolved unanimously*, That the said report, with the resolutions and letter accompanying the same, be transmitted to the several Legislatures, in order to be submitted to a Convention of Delegates in each State, by the people thereof, in conformity to the resolves of the Convention made and provided in that case.

"These are facts about which there can be no dispute or doubt. What then, becomes of [the Liberal's] . . . statement that

> 'the Constitution was not drawn up by the States! It was not promulgated in the name of the States! It was not ratified by the States! The States never acceded to it! It was "ordained and established" over the States by the people of the whole land in their aggregate capacity, acting through Conventions of Delegates expressly chosen for the purpose within each State, independently of the State Governments after the project had been framed!'

"Was a grave statement of historical facts ever more reckless or more directly in conflict with indisputable public records? By whose authority did the Convention meet that framed the Constitution but that of the several States?

Whose work was the Constitution so framed but that of the States themselves through their appointed Deputies or Delegates, as the Constitution declares on its very face? By whose authority were the State Conventions called to act upon it in their Sovereign capacity but the authority of the State Governments, the State Legislatures? How can it be said that the Constitution was established over the States by a power superior to the States, when the paper itself declares it to be a Constitution 'for the United States,' that is, for the States that were to be united by it, and to be established, not *over*, but *'between the States so ratifying'* it? Yes, *'between* the *States so ratifying'* it? The States, as States, through Conventions of their people, embodying the Sovereignty of each State severally, were to ratify it, before it could have any binding force or effect upon any one of them or their people.

"Yes, I repeat, *between* the States so ratifying it! That is the language of the Constitution itself, and there it will stand as an everlasting refutation of the assertion of [big government Liberals] . . . and all others of like character, by whomsoever made, without further comment by me!"[123]

National government proponents found it difficult to accept such reasoning, claiming that the Constitution's Preamble clearly shows "that it was expected and intended, that the whole people should act on it through their State Conventions. Was it not, therefore, virtually submitted to them for their approval and adoption? Why was it not simply referred back to the State Legislatures?," they asked. To these questions Stephens gave this answer:

☛ "For the clearest reason in the world. It was because ultimate, absolute Sovereignty resided with the people of each State respectively. The additional Sovereign powers, which were proposed to be delegated to the States jointly under the Constitution, such as the taxing power, and the power to regulate trade, with the right to pass laws acting directly upon the citizens of the Sovereign States, etc., could only be delegated by the people in their Sovereign capacity. This delegation could be made only by a Convention of the people for that purpose. These powers, by their then existing Constitutions, were vested in their State Legislatures. The Legislatures of the several States, at that time, had the sole power to tax, to regulate trade, etc. These powers had to be resumed by the people of each State separately, and taken by them from that set of agents and delegated to another set of agents. No power short of the Sovereignty itself, in each State, could do this; or in other words, as ultimate Sovereignty resided in the people of the States respectively, all new delegations of power, as well as all changes of agents in whom the delegated powers were to be intrusted, could only be made by the people themselves of each state in their Sovereign capacity. This is the whole of it in a nutshell. [Emphasis added, L.S.]

"The Legislatures of the States were not competent to make this delegation of additional powers to the United States, because they were acting under delegated powers themselves. They were possessed of no power, except such as the people of the States, in their Sovereign capacity, had delegated to them, and amongst those delegated powers, with which they were clothed, none had been granted, empowering them to make this new delegation of powers to the General Government. It was for this reason, amongst others, that Mr. [Alexander] Hamilton, in the twenty-second number of the *Federalist*, showed why the Constitution should be submitted to *Conventions* in the several States, instead of to the *Legislatures*. This is why he said its foundation ought to be deeper than 'the mere sanction of delegated authority,' why the fabric 'ought to rest on the solid basis of the consent of the people.' All political power, said he, 'ought to flow, immediately, from that pure original fountain of all legitimate authority.'

"Among the advocates in the Convention for submitting the Constitution to the people of the States, or rather to Conventions in the States, representing the people directly upon this question, none was more zealous or conspicuous, than Mr. [George] Mason, of Virginia, one of the strongest State Sovereignty men in the body. [According to one historical source:]

> '[Mason] considered a reference of the plan, to the authority of the people, as one of the most important and essential of the resolutions. The Legislatures have no power to ratify it. They are the mere creatures of the State Constitutions, and cannot be greater than their Creators. And he knew of no power in any of the Constitutions—he knew there was no power in some of them—that could be competent to this object. Whither, then, must we resort? To the people, with whom all power remains, etc. It was of great moment, he observed, that this doctrine should be cherished, as the basis of free Government.'

"Mr. Curtis, in his *History of the Constitution*, gives, somewhat, more elaborate reasons, but all based upon the same principle. He says:

> 'The States, in their corporate capacities, and through the agency of their respective Governments, were parties to a Federal system, which they had stipulated with each other, should be changed only by unanimous consent. The Constitution, which was now in the process of formation, was a system, designed for the acceptance of the people of all the States, if the assent of all could be obtained; but it was also designed for the acceptance of a less number than the whole of the States, in case of a refusal of some of them; and it was at this time highly probable that at least two of them would not adopt it. Rhode Island had never been represented in the Convention; and the

whole course of her past history, with reference to enlargements of the powers of the Union, made it quite improbable, that she would ratify such a plan of Government, as was now to be presented to her. The State of New York had, through her Delegates, taken part in the proceedings, until the final decision, which introduced into the Government a system of popular representation; but two of those Delegates, entirely dissatisfied with that decision, had withdrawn from the Convention, and had gone home to prepare the State for the rejection of the scheme. The previous conduct of the State had made it not at all unlikely that their efforts would be successful. Nor were there wanting other indications of the most serious dissatisfaction, on the part of men of great influence in some of the other States. Unanimity had already become hopeless, if not impracticable; and it was necessary, therefore, to look forward to the event of an adoption of the system by a less number than the whole of the States, and to make it practicable for a less number to form the new Union for which it provided. This could only be done by presenting it for ratification to the people of each State, who possessed authority to withdraw the State Government from the Confederation, and to enter into new relations with the people of such other States as might, also, withdraw from the old and accept the new system.'

"The whole of this view rests upon the acknowledged principle, that Sovereignty, under our system, or that Paramount authority, which can rightfully make and unmake Constitutions, and which has the uncontrolled right to resume and re-invest, by delegation, the exercise of Sovereign Powers at will, subject only to the laws of Nations, resided at that time with the several States. It suggests a very pertinent inquiry, and that is, if any number of States, by virtue of this ultimate, absolute Sovereignty, had the undoubted right, as [Mr. Curtis] . . . clearly admits they had, to withdraw at that time from the old Union, which was declared upon its face to be perpetual, why could not a like number, or any number, of the same States, by virtue of the same ultimate, absolute Sovereignty, in like manner, in 1861, withdraw from the new Union, wherein no such pledge for perpetuity was given or required?"[124] [Emphasis added, L.S.]

To such words 19th-Century Nationalists offered a letter by George Washington, in which he says that "the great object with the [Philadelphia] Convention was to consolidate the Union." Does this not show that Washington considered that the sovereignty of all the States was then merged in the Union under the new Constitution? How do you respond?, they asked Stephens. He answered:

☛ "Why I show from that the same principles I show from all the facts of our history. That shows that the object of the Convention had been to perfect the terms of the Union, which was the sole object for which the Convention had been called. [Note: The object was most definitely not the Consolidation of the

Union, nor did Washington consider the Sovereignty of all the States merged in the Union under the Constitution.] By no means. So far from it, it shows most clearly directly the contrary. That letter, you must recollect, was not prepared by Washington, but by the Convention that framed the Constitution. It was prepared and reported with the Constitution. It was taken up and adopted, paragraph by paragraph, the same day, and immediately after the adoption of the seventh Article of the Constitution, which I have just read. It was contemporaneous action with it, and by the same body of men, and cannot, therefore, be presumed to have any thing in it intended to be inconsistent with that Article of the Constitution. The letter was one from the Convention that had just finished its labors, which they authorized Washington to send to the States, in Congress assembled, for the purpose of presenting them with the result of their work. It is in these words.

> 'We have now the honor to submit to the consideration of the United States, in Congress assembled, that Constitution which has appeared to us the most advisable.
>
> 'The friends of our country have long seen and desired that the power of making war, peace, and treaties; that of levying money and regulating commerce; and the correspondent executive and judicial authorities, shall be fully and effectually vested in the General Government of the Union. But the impropriety of delegating such extensive trust to one body of men is evident. Thence results the necessity of a different organization. It is obviously impracticable, in the Federal Government of these States, to secure all rights of Independent Sovereignty to each, and yet provide for the interest and safety of all. Individuals entering into society must give up a share of liberty to preserve the rest. The magnitude of the sacrifice must depend as well on situation and circumstances as on the object to be obtained. It is at all times difficult to draw with precision the line between those rights which must be surrendered, and those which may be reserved. And, on the present occasion, this difficulty was increased by a difference, among the several States, as to their situation, extent, habits, and particular interests.
>
> 'In all our deliberations on this subject, we kept steadily in our view that which appeared to us the greatest interest of every true American—the consolidation of the Union, in which is involved our prosperity, felicity, safety—perhaps our National existence. This important consideration, seriously and deeply impressed on our minds, led each State in the Convention to be less rigid in points of inferior magnitude, than might have been otherwise expected. And thus the Constitution which we now present is the result of a spirit of amity, and of that mutual deference and concession which the peculiarity of our political situation rendered indispensable.
>
> 'That it will meet the full and entire approbation of every State is not, perhaps, to be expected. But each will doubtless consider that, had her

interest alone been consulted, the consequences might have been particularly disagreeable and injurious to others. That it is liable to as few exceptions as could reasonably have been expected, we hope and believe; that it may promote the lasting welfare of that country so dear to us all, and secure her freedom and happiness, is our most ardent wish.'

"Washington signed this letter as President of the Convention, and addressed it to the United States, in Congress assembled. Who were these States thus addressed? Thirteen Sovereignties, as [I have shown,] between whom there was a well-known Union existing, founded upon Articles of Confederation. These States thus addressed were then in Congress assembled, under the terms of that Union. The body of men addressing them was a Convention of Delegates from each of these States, which had met in pursuance of a resolution of that Congress, as we have seen, for the sole and express purpose of revising the Articles of the Union which then existed between them as separate and distinct Sovereign Powers. This letter simply informed the States thus assembled what they had done in the premises, and that they thought that the work of their hands, so sent them in accordance with their instructions, was the best that could be done with the great business intrusted to their charge. They say, and say truly, that the great object with them in their deliberations was the consolidation of the Union. This, of course, was not its abrogation and dissolution, or the formation of a new and different one. *The object was to strengthen the Union of States. That was the only Union existing, and the only Union to which they could have referred. The object was to strengthen or consolidate the bonds of that Union, and not to weaken them, much less to sever and utterly destroy them, as would be the import of the word according to* [the Nationalist's] *. . . construction. The object was to render the Union of States more perfect or better calculated to accomplish the ends for which it was at first formed.* Is not this perfectly clear and true beyond all question? Could any thing be more preposterous or absurd than to suppose that such a body of men, so called together, would, in giving an account of their labors to the body calling them, have stated that the great object with them had been to do the very reverse of what they had been called to do? Can any one believe that Washington could ever have been induced to sign a letter with such design and intention? If the Federal [Confederate] character of the Government had been intended to be abandoned in the plan they proposed, would not these very words have been necessarily left out? *Do not the words of themselves, in their connection with their contemporaneous action, under all the circumstances and surroundings, most conclusively rebut the inference that you and others draw from them, and establish beyond the shadow of doubt that the object was not to merge the Sovereignty of all the States into one, and to abandon the Union of Sovereign States by the establishment of a great National Government?* [Emphasis added, L.S.]

"Look, also, to other words in the same letter. 'It is obviously impracticable in the Federal Government of these States to secure all rights of Independent Sovereignty to each,' etc. Many Sovereign powers had been delegated under the Articles of Confederation. More were now proposed to be delegated in the same way. This required 'a different organization.' That is, a division of the departments into which all the powers were to be intrusted. *A change of machinery in operating the system, and not a change of the basis of the system.* The difficulty attending these changes 'was increased by a difference among the States.' 'This important consideration, etc., led each State in the Convention,' etc. Does not the whole of this paper most clearly show that the Convention meant by it simply to say that their great object was to strengthen and make more perfect the bonds of the Federal Union then existing? and that they thought that object would be accomplished by the States adopting the plan proposed. 'That it will meet the full and entire approbation of every State,' they say, ' is not perhaps to be expected.' [Emphasis added, L.S.]

"In what respect, in tone or sentiment, touching the character of the Union to be consolidated, does this letter differ from a similar one sent to the States by Congress with the first Articles of Union, in 1777? In that, amongst other things, Congress said,

> that to form a permanent Union, accommodated to the opinions and wishes of the Delegates of so many States, differing in habits, produce, commerce, and internal police, was found to be a work which nothing but time and reflection, conspiring with a disposition to conciliate, could mature and accomplish. Hardly is it to be expected that any plan, in the variety of provisions essential to our Union, should exactly correspond with the maxima and political views of every particular State. Let it be remarked, that after the most careful inquiry and the fullest information, this is proposed as the best which could be adapted to the circumstances of all, and as that alone which affords any tolerable prospect of general ratification. Permit us, then, earnestly to recommend these Articles to the immediate and dispassionate attention of the Legislatures of the respective States. Let them be candidly reviewed under a sense of the difficulty of combining, in one general system, the various sentiments and interests of a continent, *divided into so many Sovereign and Independent communities*, under a conviction of the absolute necessity of uniting all our councils, and all our strength, to maintain and defend our common liberties. [Emphasis added, L.S.]

"Does the letter of the Convention look any more to the abrogation of State Sovereignties than the letter of Congress to the States in 1777?

"Here is also a letter from Roger Sherman and Oliver Ellsworth, two very distinguished Delegates to the Convention from Connecticut, written on the

26th of September, 1787, and addressed to the Governor of their State, making a report to him of the action of the Convention, and the result of their labors. This shows clearly that their understanding of the letter of the Convention to Congress was in accordance with the views now presented.

> 'We have the honor to transmit to your Excellency, a printed copy of the Constitution formed by the Federal Convention, to be laid before the Legislature of the State.
>
> 'The general principles which governed the Convention, in their deliberations on the subject, are stated in their address to Congress.
>
> 'We think it may be of use to make some further observations on particular parts of the Constitution.
>
> 'The Congress is differently organized; yet the whole number of members, and this State's proportion of suffrage, remain the same as before.
>
> 'The equal representation of the States in the Senate, and the voice of that branch in the appointment to offices, will secure the rights of the lesser as well as of the greater States.
>
> 'Some additional powers are vested in Congress, which was a principal object that the States had in view in appointing the Convention. Those powers extend only to matters respecting the common interests of the Union, and are specially defined, so that *the particular States retain their Sovereignty in all other matters*.
>
> 'The objects for which Congress may apply moneys are the same mentioned in the eighth article of the Confederation, viz.: for the common defence and general welfare, and for payment of the debts incurred for those purposes. It is probable that the principal branch of revenue will be duties on imports. What may be necessary to be raised by direct taxation is to be apportioned on the several States, according to the number of their inhabitants; and although Congress may raise the money by their own authority, if necessary, yet that authority need not be exercised, if each State will furnish its quota.
>
> 'The restraint on the Legislatures of the several States respecting emitting bills of credit, making any thing but money a tender in payment of debts, or impairing the obligation of contracts by *ex post facto* laws, was thought necessary as a security to commerce, in which the interest of foreigners, as well as of the citizens of different States, may be affected.
>
> '*The Convention endeavored to provide for the energy of Government on the one hand, and suitable checks on the other hand, to secure the rights of the particular States, and the liberties and properties of the citizens*. We wish it may meet the approbation of the several States, and be a means of securing their rights and lengthening out their tranquillity. With great respect, we are, Sir, your Excellency's obedient, humble servants.' [Emphasis added, L.S.]

"Could any thing be more pertinent or conclusive, upon these points, than this letter?

"But we have numerous contemporaneous letters from [George] Washington to divers persons, which throw a flood of light upon the subject, and show clearly his understanding of that letter of Congress to have been in accordance with the views I have presented. These letters also show what little weight is to be given to [the Liberal's] . . . assertion that the States never acceded to the Constitution as a Compact between them. On this point we have in these letters authority higher than that of [the Liberal] . . . . What the States did do, [I shall show]. . . . Whether their action can be properly termed accession or not, has been a matter on which men have differed. [The Nationalist] . . . is on one side, while General Washington, Mr. Jefferson, Governor Randolph, Judge Marshall, Mr. Madison, and a host of others, are on the other side.

"In a letter of General Washington to Bushrod Washington, on the 10th of November, 1787, while the Constitution was before the States for consideration, he says:

> 'Let the opponents of the proposed Constitution in this State be asked—and it is a question they certainly ought to have asked themselves—what line of conduct they would advise it to adopt, if nine other States, of which I think there is little doubt, should accede to the Constitution?'

"In [another] . . . letter from General Washington to Mr. Madison, dated the 10th of January, 1788, . . . he says:

> 'But of all the arguments that may be used at the Convention which is to be held, the most prevailing one I expect will be that nine States at least will have acceded to it.'

"Here is a letter from Washington to Charles C. Pinckney, dated the 28th of June, 1788, in which he says:

> 'No sooner had the citizens of Alexandria, [Virginia,] who are Federal [Conservative] to a man, received the intelligence by the mail last night, than they determined to devote this day to festivity. But their exhilaration was greatly increased, and a much keener zest given to their enjoyment, by the arrival of an Express, two hours before day, with the news that the Convention of New Hampshire had, on the 21st instant, acceded to the new Confederacy by a majority of eleven voices—that is to say, fifty-seven to forty-six. From the local situation, as well as the other circumstances of North Carolina, I should be truly astonished if that State should withdraw itself from the Union. On the contrary, I flatter myself with a confident

expectation that more salutary counsels will certainly prevail. At present there is more doubt how the question will be immediately disposed of in New York; for it seems to be understood that there is a majority in the Convention opposed to the adoption of the new Federal system.'

"In General Washington's Speech to Congress, on the 8th of January, 1790, he spoke of the adoption of the Constitution by North Carolina, as 'the recent accession of that State to the Constitution.' The Senate, in their reply to his Speech, use the same word.

"But why continue these extracts? Are they not quite sufficient to show that General Washington—he who stood at the head of that band of patriots who framed the Constitution for a more perfect Union between the States—entertained different ideas of the nature of the action of the States upon it from those of [our present day Nationalists, Liberals, and Consolidationists] . . . ? He says the States acceded to it. [Liberals say] . . . they did not. There the matter may rest, upon that point. But *these letters also throw quite a flood of light, as I said, upon the true meaning of the words, 'a Consolidation of the Union,' which we have just been speaking of. They show that Washington clearly understood the new system to be a Federal system [i.e. a Confederacy], as the old one was [under the Articles of Confederation]. That there was no change of the locus of ultimate absolute Sovereignty under it. That the Union, which was perfected and consolidated, was to be still a Union of States, each Sovereign as before, and not a Union of the entire people of the whole country, as [Liberals contend]. . . . Washington emphatically styles it, 'the new Confederacy'*—'the new Federal System.' [Liberals say] that the present Government is no Confederacy, that 'we had already enough of a Confederacy.' Here again, [they are] . . . directly at issue with Washington. Washington speaks of the new system, as of the old, and styles it 'the new Confederacy.' Here, again, I will leave the issue between [the Liberals] . . . and General Washington."¹²⁵ [Emphasis added, L.S.]

Nineteenth-Century Liberals believed that the so-called "consolidation of the Union," mentioned in the letter of the Convention to Congress, merged the sovereignty of all the states into one, and that it was for this reason that such men as Edward Yates, John Lansing Jr., Luther Martin, Edmund Randolph, George Mason, and Patrick Henry all took issue with it. To this Stephens replied:

☛ "There was [indeed] . . . strong opposition to the Constitution upon [this ground]. Mr. Lansing and Mr. Yates, from New York, did quit the Convention because of their dissatisfaction with its proceedings. So did Luther Martin. Mr. Mason, of Virginia, and Governor Randolph, of Virginia, both refused to vote for it, and both refused to sign it; as also did Mr. [Elbridge T.] Gerry, from Massachusetts. But they all acted from different motives, and assigned different reasons for their conduct.

"Lansing and Yates quit the Convention because they were for an equality of votes on the part of the States in both Houses of Congress. Yates had agreed to the adjustment proposed by the first grand Committee of Conference. . . . That report met with so little favor, was so violently denounced by Mr. [James] Madison and others, that he immediately left, supposing it would not be adopted. His colleague left with him.

"Other equally strong State Sovereignty and State Rights men remained; and, by the final action of the Convention, an equality of votes in the Senate was secured to the States. . . . They were perfectly satisfied that the Federal [Confederate] system was still retained by this adjustment.

"Luther Martin was unyielding upon the point of equality of suffrage on the part of the States in both Houses of Congress. Indeed, he was unalterably opposed to many of the new and additional powers delegated by the Constitution. He was opposed to the Executive and Judiciary Departments, as constituted, and to the prohibitions on the States against emitting Bills of Credit or passing laws impairing the obligations of contracts. He thought the Government, notwithstanding the opinion of its friends to the contrary, would end in despotism, and so warned his countrymen, in eloquence of the highest order.

"Mr. Mason and Mr. Gerry opposed several features in the new plan and thought it departed too far from a strictly Federal [Confederate] alliance.

"Governor [Edmund] Randolph, on the other hand, opposed the new plan and refused to sign it, because, in his judgment, it did not depart from the Federal [Confederate] system.

"[One historian has said] . . . that Governor Randolph thought the Constitution was 'a system containing far greater restraints upon the powers of the States than he believed expedient or safe,' etc. This is certainly a mistake. Just the contrary is the fact. Governor Randolph, in assigning his reasons for not voting for the Constitution and withholding his signature from it, in a letter to the Speaker of the House of Representatives of Virginia, says, amongst other things:

> 'It follows, too, that the General Government ought to be the supreme arbiter for adjusting every contention among the States. In all their connections, therefore, with each other, and particularly in commerce, which will probably create the greatest discord, it ought to hold the reins.'

"Governor Randolph was opposed to many features of the Constitution, such as the Executive department. The whole was summed up in this.

'But, now, sir, permit me to declare, that in my humble judgment, the powers by which alone the blessings of a General Government can be accomplished, cannot be interwoven in the Confederation, without a change in its very essence, or, in other words, that the Confederation must be thrown aside.'

"This shows that Governor Randolph did not consider that there was a general merger of the Sovereignty of all the States in the Union, which the Convention had consolidated. . . . It clearly shows that, in his opinion, the Federative [Confederative] system was still retained in the new Constitution, as it existed under the old. He had put forth the utmost of his strength in the Convention, for what he called a National Government. One based upon the abandonment of the Federal [Confederate] system. His views were embodied in his plan of Government, and in his Resolution, which proposed to give the power to the General Government to judge as between it and the States of infractions of the Constitution, which, [I have shown,] . . . was negatived, and Martin's Resolution agreed to instead. The essence of Confederation was abandoned in his plan; but his plan, in this particular, was not adopted. The new Constitution continued upon the same Federative [Confederative] basis, and simply sought to make the Union upon that basis more perfect. At this Governor Randolph was disappointed and chagrined—hence his lamentations and opposition. He was elected to the Convention, in Virginia, to which the Constitution was submitted, pledged to go against its ratification, mainly for this very reason; but when he found that there was no hope, whatever, of getting Virginia and the other States to adopt such a National Government as he wanted, or to depart in the slightest degree from the essence of the Federative [Confederative] system, he then ceased his opposition to the Constitution, as it was, and voted for its ratification.

"But still there was a very general and strong opposition, throughout all the States, upon the grounds [that Liberals] . . . state. It was urged by many, 'That the Union, upon the Federal [Confederate] basis, was proposed to be abandoned, and a new Union to be formed by a consolidation of the separate Sovereignties of the States.' In the glowing language of the day it was asserted:

'That a Government, so organized, and absorbing all the powers of the States, would produce from their ruins one consolidated Government, founded upon the destruction of the several Governments of the States. . . . The powers of Congress, under the Constitution, are complete and unlimited over the purse and the sword, and are perfectly independent of and supreme over the State Governments, whose intervention, on these great points, is utterly destroyed. By virtue of the power of taxation Congress may command the whole or any part of the properties of the people. They may impose what imposts upon Commerce, they may impose what land taxes, and taxes, excises, and duties on all instruments, etc., to any extent they please. When the spirit of the people shall be gradually broken, when the National Government shall be firmly established, and when a numerous standing army shall render opposition vain, the Congress may complete the system of Despotism in renouncing all dependence on the people by continuing themselves, [and successors in power forever].'

"Patrick Henry did head this opposition with all his might in the Convention of Virginia. His grounds were various. He saw but little in any of its features that he liked. The Executive Department, in his judgment, 'squinted towards Monarchy.' His chief objection to it, however, was the want of a Bill of Rights, and because it was not expressly stated on the face of the Constitution that the Sovereignty of the States was retained or reserved, as it had been in the Articles of Confederation. It was in vain that he was told, by many as strongly in favor of State Sovereignty as he could be, that the whole system, upon its face, was one of delegated powers, and that none could be claimed, or exercised, except those delegated. That, as a matter of course, all which were not delegated were retained and reserved,—that Sovereignty, not being expressly parted with, still remained with the States. He, however, thought that what had been aimed at, and so assiduously attempted by the Nationals in the Convention, would be ultimately attained by them by implication and construction, if the Constitution should be adopted and put in operation without numerous amendments which he proposed. With these amendments he declared his willingness to agree to the Constitution, notwithstanding his strong objections to various other features in the new organization. The principles of most of these amendments, proposed by him, were afterwards adopted. He was, then, far advanced in years, and though his opposition to the Constitution, after the adoption of the amendments, 'abated in a measure, yet he remained fearful, to the end of his life, that the final result would be the destruction of the rights of the Sovereignty of the States.'

"With unsurpassed eloquence, Patrick Henry possessed one of those wonderful minds which, by a sort of instinct or supernatural faculty, scents the approaches of power, even in the distance. This instinct, or far-seeing superhuman endowment, prompted him to sound the alarm when the Constitution was at first presented to him.

"This is all true, but it is also true that his opposition, and that of all others at the time, sprung rather from apprehensions of evils that would result from constructions that would be put upon the Constitution, than from anything that appeared upon its face, or from powers under it claimed by its framers or advocates. Power, it was said by the opponents of the Constitution, was ever insidious in its approaches, and the lines between the Sovereign powers delegated in the Constitution to the States jointly, to be exercised by them jointly, and those retained to the several States, were not drawn with sufficient clearness and distinctness. The whole opposition was argumentative. The reply, on all hands, even by those who had contended in the Convention for an abandonment of the Federal system, was that this system had not been abandoned in the plan proposed—that enlarged powers had been delegated and new machinery for the exercise of those powers had been introduced, but no change in the nature or character of the Government. This, we have just seen, was Washington's position. His name was a host in itself. It was also the position of [Alexander] Hamilton, of [Rufus] King, of [James] Wilson, of [James] Madison, of [Gouverneur] Morris, of [Edmund] Randolph, and all the Nationals of the Convention. . . . What was argued would be the legitimate tendency and ultimate results of a Government so organized was strenuously denied by the friends and advocates of the Constitution. This is abundantly clear from the history of the times. Not a supporter or defender of the Constitution advocated it upon the grounds that the Sovereignty of the States was parted with under it. *So thoroughly Federal was the Constitution admitted to be by its advocates everywhere that they universally took to themselves the name of Federalists [identical to Confederalists or Confederates]*. Washington . . . said that the people of Alexandria 'were Federal [Confederate] to a man;' that is they were all for the Constitution, believing and understanding it to be Federal [Confederate] in its nature and character. That series of Articles, eighty-five in number, which have become historic, written by Hamilton, Madison, and [John] Jay (all national [liberal] before), urging upon the people reasons for adopting the Constitution, were styled 'the Federalist' [i.e., 'the Confederalist']. The Constitution was universally called the 'Federal Constitution' [i.e., the 'Confederate Constitution']. The seat of Government was to be known as 'The Federal City' [i.e., 'The Confederate City']. So strongly and deeply impressed was this idea and understanding upon the minds of the people that it assumed solid embodiment in outward forms, representations, and symbols. In Boston, after the ratification of the Constitution by Massachusetts, 'there issued from the gates of Faneuil Hall an imposing procession of five thousand citizens, embracing all the trades of the town and its neighborhood, each with its appropriate decorations, emblems and mottoes. In the centre of this long pageant, to mark the relation of every thing around it to maritime commerce, and the relation of all to the new Government, was borne the Ship *Federal Constitution* [i.e., the ship *Confederate Constitution*] with full colors flying and attended by the merchants, captains and seamen of the Port.' [According to historians:] 'This was the first of a series of similar pageants which took place in the other principal cities of the Union in favor of the ratification of the Constitution.'

"In Baltimore they had a ball, an illumination, and a grand procession of trades. In this procession was borne a miniature ship, *The Federalist* [i.e., *The Confederate*]. [Again, historians tell us that:]

> 'The ratification of Virginia took place on the 25th of June. The news of this event was received in Philadelphia on the 2nd of July. The press of the city was at once filled with rejoicings over the action of Virginia. She was the tenth pillar in the Temple of Liberty. She was Virginia—the oldest and foremost of the States—land of statesmen, whose Revolutionary services were household words in all America—birthplace and home of Washington! We need not wonder, when she had come so tardily, so cautiously into the support of the Constitution, that men should have hailed her accession with enthusiasm! The people of Philadelphia had been some time preparing a public demonstration in honor of the adoption of the Constitution by nine States. Now that Virginia was added to the number, they determined that all possible magnificence and splendor should be given to this celebration, and they chose for it the anniversary of the National Independence.
>
> 'A taste for allegory appears to have been quite prevalent among the people of the United States at this period. Accordingly, the Philadelphia Procession of July 4, 1788, was filled with elaborate and emblematical representations. It was a long pageant of banners of trades and devices. A decorated car bore the Constitution, framed as a banner and hung upon a staff. Then another decorated car carried the American Flag. Then followed the Judges, in their robes, and all the public bodies, preceding a grand Federal [Confederate] Edifice, which was carried by a carriage drawn by ten horses. On the floor of this edifice were in chairs ten gentlemen representing the citizens of the United States at large, to whom the Federal Constitution had been committed before its ratification. When it arrived at "Union Green," they gave up their seats to ten others, representing ten States, which had ratified the instrument.'

"What force was there, in this stage representation, to the popular mind of the process through which the Constitution passed in its ratification? The first ten gentlemen, representing the citizens of all the ten States at large, each acting for themselves, in their several Sovereign capacities, after having given it their several sanction, then turning it over to ten others, representing the ten States for whom it had been so ordained and established, for them to hold, keep, preserve, and maintain, *not over them, but between them, and over the Government instituted by it!* [Emphasis added, L.S.]

"These demonstrations, devices, mottoes, and symbols, clearly show how the great mass of the people, in all the States, understood the new Constitution. It was nothing but a more perfect bond of Union between States. Federal [i.e., Confederal or Confederate] was the watchword of the day in Boston, New York, Philadelphia, Baltimore, Richmond, and Charleston. It was the grand symbolized idea throughout the whole length and breadth of the land. There can be no doubt that the people thought they were adopting a Federal [Confederate] Constitution—forming a Federal [Confederate] Union.

"Now, then, what is the meaning of this word Federal, which entered so deeply into the thoughts, the hearts, and understandings of the people at that day. Here words are things! Dr. [Samuel] Johnson, the highest authority of that day, in his *Dictionary*, thus defines the word:—Federal—(*Fœdus*, Lat.) relating to a League or Contract. Federate, he defines (*Federatus*, Lat.) [meaning] leagued, joined in a Confederacy.

"The great American lexicographer, Noah Webster, says of this word '*Federal*,' that it is derived from the Latin word '*Fœdus*,' which means a League. A League he defines to be 'an Alliance or Confederacy between Princes or States for their mutual aid or defence.' And, in defining the meaning of the word Federal, he uses this language:

> 'Consisting in a Compact between States or Nations; founded on alliance by contract or mutual agreement; as, a Federal Government, such as that of the United States.'

"Dr. [Joseph E.] Worcester, in his new *Dictionary*, another standard work with philologers of the first rank, says, of this word '*Federal*' that it is from the Latin '*Fœdus*,' 'a Compact.' He defines it thus:

> '1. Relating to a League or Compact. 2. Relating to, or joined in, a Confederacy, as Communities or States; Confederate;—particularly, belonging to the Union, or the United States.'

"[The word] Federal, from its very origin and derivation, therefore, has no meaning, and can have none, dissociated from Compact or Agreement of some sort, and it is seldom ever used to qualify any Compacts or Agreements except those between States or Nations. So that *Federal and Confederate mean substantially the same thing*. When applied to States they both imply and import a Compact between States. *Washington, in one of his letters, which I have just read, spoke of the new Government as 'a Confederacy.' In another, to Sir Edward Newenham, dated the 20th July, 1788, he speaks of the new Government then ratified by enough States to carry it into effect as a 'Confederated Government.' In his response to the reply of the Senate to his first speech to Congress after the new Government was organized, in*

1789, he expressed his happiness in the conviction that 'the Senate would at all times co-operate in every measure which may tend to promote the welfare of this Confederated Republic.' These are the terms by which he characterized 'the Union,' after the present Constitution was formed and after it was in operation. There is no difference between the words Federal and Confederated as thus used and applied. We see that Washington used them both, at different times, to signify the same thing, that is, the Union of the American States under the Constitution. [Emphasis added, L.S.]

"It being universally admitted, then, by the advocates of the Constitution at the time of its adoption, that it was Federal [Confederate] in its character, and that the Government under it would be a Confederated or Federal Republic, which means the same thing, [I would like to discuss] . . . what is the nature and very essence of all such Governments. Dropping Dictionaries, let us go to writers upon the Laws of Nations. Here is [Baron de] Montesquieu [the French philosopher]. In Book ix, chap. 1, he speaks first of Republics generally. These may exist either under Democratic or Aristocratic Constitutions.

> 'If a Republic is small, it is destroyed by a foreign force; if it be large, it is ruined by an internal imperfection.
>
> 'It is, therefore, very probable, that mankind would have been at length obliged to live constantly under the Government of a single person, had they not contrived a kind of Constitution that has all the internal advantages of a Republican, together with the external force of a Monarchical Government. I mean a *Confederate Republic.* [Emphasis added, L.S.]
>
> 'This form of Government is a Convention, by which several small States agree to become members of a larger one which they intend to form. It is a kind of assemblage of societies, that constitute a new one, capable of increasing by means of new associations, till they arrive to such a degree of power, as to be able to provide for the security of the united body.
>
> '*The State (that is the State formed by the Confederation) may be destroyed on one side, and not on the other; the Confederacy may be dissolved, and the Confederates preserve their Sovereignty.* [Emphasis added, L.S.]
>
> 'As *this Government is composed of petty Republics*, it enjoys the internal happiness of each; and with respect to its external situation, it is possessed, by means of the association, of all the advantages of large monarchies.' [Emphasis added, L.S.]

"This, by the highest authority, is the form and nature of all Federal or Confederated Republics. The Government of the United States, in the judgment of [President George] Washington, belongs to that class. *All the States of the Union were small Republics [i.e., tiny nation-states] within themselves. By entering the Union for foreign and inter-State purposes, they did not, therefore, according to Montesquieu, forfeit or part with their separate sovereignty.* [Emphasis added, L.S.]

On the same subject, [Emerich de] Vattel, another writer, universally admitted to be authority of high order, says:

> 'Several Sovereign and Independent States may unite themselves together by a perpetual Confederacy, without ceasing to be, each individually, a perfect State. They will together constitute a Federal Republic; their joint deliberations will not impair the Sovereignty of each member, though they may, in certain respects, put some restraint on the exercise of it in virtue of voluntary engagements.'

"That, I maintain, was exactly what the States of our Union did, by the adoption of the Constitution. . . . This, I think, is quite enough to satisfy [the Liberals] . . . that whatever apprehensions were indulged in by many as to results from abuse of powers, yet *it was universally admitted by the advocates of the Constitution that a Federal Republic [i.e., a Confederacy] was to be established by it, and not a National Consolidation.*"[126] [Emphasis added, L.S.]

12

A Study of the U.S. Constitution

IN THIS CHAPTER WE REVIEW excerpts from *A Constitutional View* in which Stephens used his analysis of the U.S. Constitution to show further proof that the original government was intended by the Founding Generation to be a Confederate Republic, or a "Confederacy"—as the United States of America was officially known from 1781 to 1789 under the Articles of Confederation.

☞ "Let us now look into the Constitution itself, and see the nature of the Government instituted by it, so far as appears from the words, and the terms used in it;—keeping closely in mind all the antecedent facts—these are mainly—the separate Sovereignty of the States, by whose Delegates it was framed—the old law—the articles of Confederation—the evils complained of under them, and the remedies proposed. Keep in mind the purpose for which the [Philadelphia] Convention [of 1787] was called, the instructions and powers, under which the Delegation from each State acted, as well as what the Convention said of their work, after it was done, in transmitting it to the States, then in Congress assembled. Recollect, also, what [Oliver] Ellsworth and [Roger] Sherman said of it, and what [George] Washington, in his own name, said of it. All these matters should be kept constantly in view in our examination of the terms of the Constitution. With these facts, then, thoroughly impressed upon the mind, let us enter upon an examination of the Instrument itself.

"Upon an analysis of the entire provisions of the Constitution, from the beginning to the end, similar to the analysis made of the Articles of

Confederation, we see that the whole may be divided and arranged:

"First, into mutual Covenants and Agreements between the States, and

"Secondly, the delegation of specific powers, by the States severally, to the States jointly, to be exercised by them jointly, in the mode and manner specifically set forth in the mutual Covenants, as stated.

"The mutual Covenants relate partly to the new organization, and the general division of the exercise of the powers granted or delegated to the different departments; and partly to restrictions upon the several States, and duties or obligations assumed by them, just as under the former, or old Constitution.

"The Covenants of the First Class, for a clearer understanding, by proper analysis, may be further subdivided under appropriate heads, and in classification arranged accordingly. Those relating to the new organization and division of powers being placed by themselves, in order, and those relating to the restraints upon the several States and the duties and obligations assumed by them as States, being, also, arranged by themselves, in like order. . . .

". . . Now, *after scanning the whole, taken together, what section, clause, phrase or word, on the face of the Constitution itself, shows any intention, on the part of the framers, to merge the separate Sovereignty of all the States into one, under it; and, by its adoption, to establish a National Government, instead of perfecting and continuing, under a new organization, with enlarged powers, the Federal Union, then existing between the States, and for the remedying of which, the Convention was called? It was made, we see, by States. It was to be established,* we see, *not over, but between, the States ratifying it.* [Emphasis added, L.S.]

"[For those familiar with the U.S. Constitution, is] *. . . not the leading idea, throughout the whole instrument, that the new Government was to be a Compact between States, as the old one was? States pervade the whole instrument.* The Senators are to be elected by the Legislatures of the several States. The House of Representatives is to be composed of members, chosen by the people of the several States; and to be chosen by electors, possessing such qualifications as each State, for itself, may prescribe for the electors of the most numerous branch of its own State Legislature. [Emphasis added, L.S.] Thus providing that every member of the Legislative body should be chosen, in the one branch, directly by the States, as such, and in the other branch, by constituencies, to be formed and controlled absolutely by the States, severally.

> [Stephens paraphrasing the Constitution:] Representatives and taxation shall be apportioned among the *several States. Each State* shall have, at least, one Representative. When vacancies happen in *any State,* etc.
>
> The Congress shall have power to regulate commerce with foreign nations, and among the *several States.* The migration and importation of such persons

as any of the *States*, etc.

No preference shall be given, etc., to the ports of *one State* over those of another, etc. Nor shall vessels, bound to or from *one State*, be obliged to enter, clear, or pay duties in another.

No *State* shall enter into any treaty, etc.

No *State* shall, without the consent of *the Congress*, lay any imposts, etc.

No *State* shall, without the like consent of the Congress, lay any duty of tonnage, keep troops or ships of war in time of peace, enter into any agreement or compact with another *State*, or with a foreign Power, or engage in war, unless actually invaded, etc.

"Nothing appears more prominent in the whole instrument than *States*. The very first Article in the Constitution declares that all Legislative powers under it shall be vested in '*a Congress of the United States.*' The term 'Congress of the United States' was familiar to all at that day. It was well known to mean 'The United States in Congress assembled.' Congress means a meeting or an assemblage. A Congress of States means a Meeting or Assemblage of States. The title of Congress, under the Confederation, had been 'The United States of America in Congress assembled.' The same title is still retained. To this very day, the enacting clause of every law, passed by 'the Congress,' under the Constitution, is in these words:—

> Be it enacted by the Senate and House of Representatives of the United States of America in Congress assembled.

"*Every law that has been passed, from the beginning, under this Constitution, as under the Articles of Confederation, derives its sole authority, as its face shows, from States in Congress assembled!* [Emphasis added, L.S.]

"*The whole operation of the Government, from its first starting, depended upon the action of the States. The election of President and Vice President, from the first to the last, depended entirely upon the States, as States, and, also, the election of Senators. Nor can there be a House of Representatives in the Congress without the co-operation of the States! The General Government, created by the instrument, has no authority, as appears from its face, to enter any State, or take jurisdiction over a foot of her soil, even for the erection of forts and arsenals, etc., except by her consent, first had and obtained by contract or purchase. This shows that the Right of Eminent Domain, the indisputable attribute and accompaniment of Sovereignty, remained with the States, severally, even over such places as might thus pass, in fee, from them, or their citizens, to the United States, as in like purchases, in all cases whatsoever.* [Emphasis added, L.S.]

"What is there, then, in this whole instrument, that looks towards such a consolidation of the whole people of this country into one community or

Nation, as [Liberals and Nationalists contend]?"[127]

Civil War Liberals (at that time the Republicans) believed that the constitutional clause concerning treason indicated that the U.S. was meant to be a country consolidated into one nation. To this Stephens countered:

☛ "[This assumption is false] . . . if it be true that the Constitution was a Compact between Sovereign States. That is the point in issue. All such inferences . . . depend upon this primary and essential fact, touching the nature and character of the Government. Nothing is clearer than that Sovereign States may agree, by Compact, between themselves, that certain acts of the citizens of each, against all jointly, shall be deemed and held to be criminal against them jointly, and punished by their joint authority. Such is the case, in this Constitution, as to counterfeiting the current coin and securities of the United States, and divers other offences. The granting of power to punish such offences against the joint authority of all, while the Compact lasts, does not, in the least, in itself, compromit the Sovereignty of each, or change the allegiance of her citizens; which, independently of the Compact, must, by acknowledgment, be admitted to be due to her Paramount authority. The Articles of Confederation delegated the power to punish piracy.

"So, it is perfectly consistent with the reserved Sovereignty of each party to such a Compact, to agree among themselves that levying war upon all of them, or adhering to their enemies, giving them aid and comfort, by the citizens of any one of them, shall be considered Treason against all; inasmuch as such an act would, unquestionably, be Treason against the State, of which such persons are citizens, in the breach, which it would necessarily involve, of their allegiance, due to the Paramount authority of the State, in entering into such a Compact, which, by its very nature, is to be binding upon each State, and all her citizens, as the Supreme law, so long as it may last. It is perfectly competent for Sovereign States to make such an agreement, or compact, as this, without compromitting their Sovereignty, or changing, in the least degree, the ultimate, absolute allegiance of all their citizens, which, by the laws of Nations, is due to their Paramount authority. This is just what the Constitution did on that subject, if it be a Compact between Sovereign States, and that is the point of our inquiry.

"In further illustration of the view I was presenting, to show that it is such a Compact, and that no such inference, as you would draw from the words about treason, is at all maintainable, I call your special attention to the fact that there is, in the Constitution, no Covenant, or Delegation of power to the Congress, to define, or punish treason, generally, as all Sovereigns, without doubt, have power to do. That is left with the States, severally, and a solemn

Compact entered into, that all persons, charged with treason against any one of the States, fleeing into another State, shall, upon demand, etc., be given up, etc. This shows, clearly, that the general allegiance of the citizens of the several States was not intended to be transferred, by this clause of the Constitution, to the United States. Indeed, there is not a word about allegiance in the whole of it.

"Moreover, all that is said upon the subject, in this clause, is only an enlargement in one sense, and a restriction in another, of powers under the Articles of Confederation. There is no change of principle in the nature of the Government, in this particular, in the new Constitution, from the old.

"Under the Articles of Confederation, the States, in Congress assembled, had power, as we have seen, to make 'Rules for the Government of the land and naval forces,' etc. By virtue of this clause they had power not only to punish, but to define what acts should constitute treason against the joint authority of all the States, when committed by any one in the land or naval forces. It was under this clause, doubtless, or under the Rules and Articles of War, established by virtue of it, that [Benedict] Arnold would have been executed, if he had not made his escape. But no one thought that, because Arnold, a citizen of the State of Connecticut, was held and deemed to be guilty of treason against the United States, that, therefore, his allegiance, and the allegiance of all the people of Connecticut, and the allegiance of all the people of all the States, was necessarily, thereby, under the Confederation, transferred from the States, severally, to the United States. . . . [T]he Supreme Court of the United States has decided the very reverse, or, that the allegiance of the citizens of the States, severally, during the Confederation, was due to their States respectively. Hence it follows that it was perfectly consistent, with a full reservation of power to the States, severally, over the allegiance of their citizens, to enter into just such a Compact, as I maintain this to be. This part of the Constitution, as I have said, is but an enlargement, in one sense, and a restriction, in another, of powers delegated under the Articles of Confederation. It is enlarged, so as to embrace all citizens of the States, respectively, whether in the land or naval forces or not; and restricted in this, that the offence, defined in the Constitution to be Treason against the United States, shall consist, only, in levying war against them, or in adhering to their enemies, giving them aid and comfort, with a limitation as to the extent of the punishment. A farther restriction is that a person charged with treason, now, cannot be tried by Military Courts. The trial, in all cases, must be by the Civil Courts. The crime can only exist, when the act is committed by the citizens of any State, not only against her, but against all the other States with which she stands united by a solemn Compact.

"The Paramount Sovereignty of each State to command the allegiance of her citizens, in case she should exercise it—in severing, as in making, the Compact—cannot be transferred by inference or implication. This, as we have seen, can pass, only, by express terms of surrender. There is no such express surrender in the Constitution, nor can any intention to make such be inferred, even upon taking the whole Constitution together. None, at least, from this clause of the Constitution. Is there any other that even looks that way?

". . . [As further proof, consider the clause which declares that this Constitution, and the laws of the United States, which shall be made in pursuance thereof, and all treaties made, or which shall be made, under the authority of the United States, shall be the supreme law of the land, etc.] . . . [It] contains no delegation of power,—makes no acknowledgment of a surrender of any. It simply declares a fact, or truth, which results from the nature of the Compact. The same fact, here declared, was admitted to exist under the Articles of the Confederation. They were equally the supreme law of the land, while they lasted, as the Constitution now is. They were just as obligatory, upon the States, as the Constitution is. So said Mr. [Alexander] Hamilton and Mr. [James] Madison, and so held Mr. Justice [Samuel] Chase, on the Supreme Court Bench, as we have seen. This clause, as Mr. Hamilton said, is only a limitation inserted out of abundant caution. That limitation was to rebut the very [erroneous] inference that [Liberals and Nationalists] . . . would draw. It was inserted to make it clear that not only was the allegiance of the citizens of the several States not transferred, by virtue of any thing in the Constitution, to the United States, but that even obedience to their laws, etc., could be enjoined, only so far as these laws were made in pursuance of the Constitution!

"The great difference between this clause, offered in substance by Luther Martin, and the one offered by the Nationals, and for which Martin's was substituted, was, that theirs gave to the United States the power or right to judge as between them and the States severally upon Constitutional infractions, while his refused to delegate this power, leaving it, therefore, with the States, where it was before."[128]

Why then, Liberals asked, were the members of the several state legislatures, and all Executive and Judicial officers of the states, required to take an oath to support the Constitution? Did this not indicate the nationalization of the central government? Stephens replied:

☞ "This [question] can be easily . . . [answered], and in no more pertinent language, perhaps, than Mr. [James] Madison used in answering the same question, when asked, while the Constitution was before the people for their consideration. In the forty-third number of the *Federalist*, he says:

'It has been asked why it was thought necessary that the State magistracy should be bound to support the Federal Constitution, and unnecessary that a like oath should be imposed on the officers of the United States in favor of the State Constitutions. Several reasons might be assigned for the distinction. I content myself with one which is obvious and conclusive. The members of the Federal Government will have no agency in carrying the State Constitutions into effect. The members of the State Governments, on the contrary, will have an essential agency in giving effect to the Federal Constitution. The election of the President and Senate will depend, in all cases, on the Legislatures of the several States.'

"This is the reason Mr. Madison assigned for it. Whether it was a conclusive reason for the propriety of putting this clause in or not, yet his giving it, when he did, and as he did, is conclusive proof that no inference can be drawn from the clause, as it stands in the Constitution, that it was intended, by virtue of it, any more than by virtue of the other clause just before it, to transfer the allegiance of the citizens of the several States to the United States; and, thereby, form a National Government instead of a Federal one. Mr. Madison, recollect, was one of the extremest in the Convention for a National Government, and not a Federal [Confederate] one; but here, in speaking of the nature of the Government which was finally agreed upon, he calls it 'the Federal [Confederate] Government' and the Constitution he styles 'the Federal [Confederate] Constitution.'

"This oath was opposed by Mr. [James] Wilson, one of the leading Nationals [Liberals] in the Convention. . . . [A]lso quite pertinent in further answer to [the] . . . question, I refer to what Mr. Madison said, in the next number of the *Federalist*, upon the general nature of the powers delegated under the Constitution, from which it clearly appears that he did not consider the nature of the new Government essentially changed, in any particular, from what it was under the Confederation.

'If the new Constitution be examined with accuracy and candor, it will be found that the change which it proposes consists much less in the addition of New Powers to the Union, than in the invigoration of its Original Powers. The regulation of commerce, it is true, is a new power; but that seems to be an addition which few oppose, and from which no apprehensions are entertained. The powers relating to war and peace, armies and fleets, treaties and finances, with the other more considerable powers, are all vested in the existing Congress by the Articles of Confederation. The proposed change does not enlarge these powers; it only substitutes a more effectual mode of administering them. The change relating to taxation may be regarded as the most important; and yet the present Congress have as complete authority to

Require of the States indefinite supplies of money for the common defence and general welfare, as the future Congress will have to require them of individual citizens; and the latter will be no more bound than the States themselves have been, to pay the quotas respectively taxed on them.'

"From both these extracts from the *Federalist*, it clearly appears that Mr. Madison, who is styled the father of the Constitution, did not consider that the Federative [Confederative] nature and character of the previously existing Union between the States was essentially changed in any particular by the new Constitution, framed with the view of perfecting that Union.

"'The change,' says he, 'consists much less in the addition of new powers to the Union than in the invigoration of its original powers!' Words of what import are these, coming from the source they did? And how true we shall find them to be upon examining closely the analysis of the various provisions of the two instruments, the Articles of Confederation and the Constitution which we have made? What are the new powers delegated in the Constitution?

"These, upon examining the analysis in each case and comparing them, will be found to be

"1st. The power to raise revenue by duties upon imposts and taxes directly upon the people without resort to requisitions upon the States.

"2nd. The power to make the rules for aliens to be admitted to citizenship in the several States, uniform in all the States, and like uniform rules regulating bankruptcy.

"3rd. The power to promote the progress of science and useful arts by securing, for limited times, to authors and inventors, the exclusive right to their writings and discoveries.

"4th. The power to regulate commerce with Foreign Nations, among the several States, and with the Indian Tribes.

"This, Mr. Madison puts amongst the new powers. Though, in fact, it was but an enlargement of a previously existing power in the Congress. By the Articles of the Confederation, the Congress had power to regulate trade with the Indian Tribes. This power in the Constitution was only enlarged by extending it to Foreign Nations and among the several States as well as the Indian Tribes. It is in principle not a new power, but an old one, extended and enlarged.

"Besides these four there is hardly a new power delegated in the new Constitution of sufficient importance to need special notice.

"The Covenants between the States, imposing restraints and assuming obligations, run almost in the same language throughout both instruments.

"Amongst the new restraints the most important are

"1st. That no State shall emit bills of credit or make any thing but gold and silver a legal tender in the payment of debts; pass any bill of attainder; or *ex post facto* law, or law impairing the obligation of contracts, or grant any title of nobility.

"2nd. No State shall, without the consent of Congress, lay any imposts or duty upon imports, exports, etc.

"The prohibitions against any of the States forming alliances, etc., making war, etc., are nearly the same in both.

"One striking feature in the new Constitution is that the States under it have entire control over their *militia*.

"The Congress, under the Constitution, has no power over them, except to provide by law for organizing, arming, disciplining them; and for calling them out for specific purposes and governing them when in the service of the United States. But the States have retained to themselves severally the power of training and officering and sending them forth upon any call made for them.

"By the Articles of Confederation the Congress had the appointment of all the officers of the militia when in service, from the regimental officers up. By the Constitution the power is reserved to the States to appoint all the officers of the militia, whether in service or not, from the lowest to the highest.

"Great stress, by many, has been put upon the Judicial Department in the new system. This, however, is no new feature. Under the Articles of Confederation there was a Judiciary provided. It is enlarged in the new Constitution, that is all. There is no change in principle in this particular.

"Of all the new obligations assumed by the States, the most important, and one without which, it was universally admitted, the Constitution could not be formed, is that which provides for the rendition of fugitives from service from one State to another. . . . It was, however, only an enlargement of the principle in the Articles of Confederation on which fugitives from justice were to be delivered up. And Mr. Madison truly said, after his enumeration, that all the other *more considerable powers* under the Constitution were vested in the Congress under the Articles of Confederation. If the States then, under the Confederation, retained their Sovereignty severally, why do they not under this Constitution?

"Did their people, by adopting this Constitution, understand that, thereby, they were surrendering the separate Sovereignty of the States? That, for which the war of the [American] Revolution had been fought, and for the maintenance of which the Confederation had been formed? Did they understand that, thereafter, there were to be no more States United by a Compact of Union between them, but that all the people of the whole land, by the ratification of this Constitution, were to be merged into one body-politic, into one Community, one Nation under a social Compact? Does the Constitution, on its face, taken altogether or in any part, admit any such construction? Does not the clause next to the last, which provides for future changes or amendments in it, utterly refute and negative forever every such idea or supposition; or rather every such gross heresy?

"In this it is expressly stipulated, that upon all future changes, or amendments, the States, as States, shall act, and that it shall require the concurrence of three fourths of all the States, in their State organization, and by their State Governments, to make any alteration or amendment. *It is especially stipulated, that no amendment shall ever be made, which shall deprive the States of their equal suffrage in the Senate! Does not this clearly show where ultimate Sovereign power rests under this system? That is, that it remains with the States severally, now, just as it did under the Confederation.* [Emphasis added, L.S.]

"Can this clause of the Constitution admit of any other version or reading without the grossest violation of the plainest import of language? Was not that the understanding of it by its authors and framers? If not, what mockery is there in the last of the mutual Covenants in our classification? That is in these words:

> The United States shall guarantee to every State in this Union a Republican [Confederate] form of Government, and shall protect each of them against invasion, and on application of the Legislature, or of the Executive (when the Legislature cannot be convened) against domestic violence.

"Is not this the language of Confederation? The language of Compact? The language of Alliance between Sovereign States? Alliance for mutual safety and protection against foes without, as well as foes within? Do not all the States United, under this Compact, by this clause, guarantee its own Institutions to each State in the Alliance thus formed? Not that the clause confers any power on the States jointly to interfere in any manner or form, or in any contingency, in changing, modelling, moulding, or shaping the Institutions of any State according to their joint will or pleasure! No more palpable, or gross a perversion of the meaning of words could be made, than such a construction as that. But does it not clearly set forth a solemn obligation on the part of her Confederates to maintain, sustain and secure, by their joint authority and means, to each State, such Republican [Confederate] Institutions as each State, for itself, in its own Sovereign will, may adopt?

". . . [W]hat is a State? Did not the framers of this instrument understand the meaning of the words they used? Is it not a body-politic—a Community organized with all the functions and powers of Government within itself?

"Vattel says:

> 'Nations, or States, are bodies-politic. Societies of men, united together for

the purpose of their mutual safety and advantage by the efforts of their combined strength. Such society has her affairs and her interests; she deliberates and takes resolutions in common, thus becoming a moral person, who possesses an understanding and a will peculiar to herself and is susceptible of obligations and rights.'

"Were not the States for which this Constitution was framed, and by which it was adopted as a bond of Union, such bodies politic? Such 'several Sovereign and independent States,' as, according to the same author previously quoted, 'may unite themselves together by a perpetual Confederacy, without ceasing to be, each, a *perfect State*' and without any impairment, as he says, of 'the Sovereignty of each.'

"Were they not just such States as, Montesquieu says, may form 'a Confederate Republic,' in which case 'the Confederacy may be dissolved, and the Confederates preserve their Sovereignty?' Were they not such States as, [the ancient Roman statesman Marcus Tullius] Cicero says, ought to possess within themselves principles of indestructibility? 'A State,' says he, 'should be so constituted as to live forever! For a Commonwealth there is no natural dissolution, as there is for a man to whom death not only becomes necessary, but often desirable.' When 'a State,' however, 'is put an end to, it is destroyed, extinguished,' annihilated!

"There is nothing, says this profound philosopher, in another place, 'in which human virtue can more closely resemble the Divine Powers, than in establishing new States, or in preserving those already established!'

"*Were States ever more Providentially, yea, Divinely, established, than these had been? Under their whole superstructure, in their Declaration of Independence, lie the great truths, announced by political bodies for the first time in the history of the world, of the capacity and right of man to self-government. That all Governments 'derive their just powers from the consent of the governed,' and that, 'whenever any Government becomes destructive of the ends' for which it is established, 'it is the right of the people to alter or abolish it, and to institute a new Government, laying its foundation on such principles, and organizing its powers in such forms, as to them may seem most likely to effect their safety and happiness.' This is asserted to be the inalienable right of all Peoples and all States! On these immutable principles, the Governments of these States had been established, separately, and severally. Were States ever established that so well deserved to live forever?* [Emphasis added, L.S.]

"Was there ever a grander exhibition of this highest of all bare human virtues, according to Cicero, than was presented by the Patriot Fathers of 1787, in forming this Constitution? Was not their main, chief, and leading object throughout, and the object of the Union under it, to preserve, and to perpetuate, as far as possible by human agency, these separate and several States so established? Is not this apparent from the whole work? Is it not apparent from the face of the instrument, from its Alpha to its Omega [i.e., beginning to end]? In other words, is not the Constitution, upon its face, as made, without looking into the subsequent amendments, Federal [Confederate] in its every feature, from beginning to end?"[129]

13

How the States Understood the Constitution & the Union

IN HIS EFFORT TO SHOW evidence of state sovereignty and states' rights in the Constitution, as well as the logically resulting right of secession, Stephens often discussed, as he does in the following excepts from *A Constitutional View*, the action of the states upon the Constitution.

Though, as the vice president himself admits, it may be tedious to peruse these old records, they are nothing short of "the title-deeds of our political inheritance of Constitutional Liberty." Thus, this exercise is vital to a true understanding of authentic American history, rather than the false one presented by pro-North writers and anti-South historians.

Stephens begins by covering each state in order of their ratification of the U.S. Constitution in 1787 and 1788. Here again the reader can see clearly the Confederate character intended by the Founding Fathers of the United States of America—a Republic which, from 1781 to 1789, was officially known as the "Confederacy."

☞ "[Let us take the individual states] . . . in their order of ratification. In each case, looking first into the action of the State, and, secondly, into the debates, where any have been preserved, as part of the *res gestæ* [Latin: 'things done'], showing the understanding of the States, in their ratification, as appears from the record.

FIRST, DELAWARE

"The Legislature of the State of Delaware called a Convention of her people to consider the Constitution, and take action upon it, according to the request of Congress. In the Convention of this State, there seems to have been no division and no discussion. At least, none of the debates in that body, if any were had, have been preserved. Here is the action of the Convention.

> We, the Deputies of the People of the Delaware State, in Convention met, having taken into our serious consideration the Federal [Confederate] Constitution, proposed and agreed upon by the Deputies of the United States, in a General Convention, held at the City of Philadelphia, on the seventeenth day of September, in the year of our Lord one thousand seven hundred and eighty-seven, have approved, assented to, ratified, and confirmed, and by these presents do, in virtue of the power and authority to us given, for and in behalf of ourselves and our constituents, fully, freely, and entirely approve of, assent to, ratify, and confirm, the said Constitution.
> Done in Convention, at Dover, this seventh day of December, in the year aforesaid, and in the year of the Independence of the United States of America, the twelfth.

"In this very act of ratification, we see it styled, by the Sovereign people of Delaware, 'The Federal Constitution.' Indeed, no one can doubt, for a moment, from the Course of her Delegates, in the Philadelphia Convention, that the People of Delaware understood the Constitution, as they here style it, to be Federal [Confederate] in its character, and that the Sovereignty of the State was still retained.

SECOND, PENNSYLVANIA

"The next State in order was Pennsylvania. In this, as in the case of Delaware, let us look first into the action of the State and then into the debates, as far as we have them, to see what light they throw upon this action. First, then, the action of the Convention is in these words.

> In the Name of the People of Pennsylvania. Be it known unto all men, that we, the Delegates of the people of the Commonwealth of Pennsylvania, in General Convention assembled, have assented to and ratified, and by these presents do, in the name and by the authority of the same people, and for ourselves, assent to and ratify the foregoing Constitution for the United States of America. Done in Convention at Philadelphia, the twelfth day of December, in the year of our Lord one thousand seven hundred and eighty-seven, and of the independence of the United States of America the twelfth. In witness whereof, we have hereunto subscribed our names.

"No allusion in this is made to the [Confederate] character of the instrument or of the understanding of the members of the Convention of it, farther than their styling it a 'Constitution *for the United States* of America.' That is a Constitution *for States* United, and not for the whole mass of the people of these States in the aggregate. This of itself is quite enough to show that they considered it Federal or Federative [Confederate] in its character!

"But we are not left in doubt or to inference on this point. The debates in the Convention of Pennsylvania have been in part preserved. The speeches of Mr. [James] Wilson, at least, who had been in the Federal Convention that framed the Constitution, and who was also in the State Convention that ratified it, we have. These, it is true, are all of these debates that we have, but they throw much light upon the subject.

"Mr. Wilson, recollect, was one of the ablest and most zealous of the Nationals [big government Liberals] in the Federal Convention. But when their plan failed, he, as [Alexander] Hamilton, [Gouverneur] Morris, [Rufus] King, and [James] Madison, gave the Constitution agreed upon, his warm support. What he said, therefore, in the State Convention, touching the character, or nature of the Constitution, which was finally agreed upon, is entitled to great weight, and particularly all his disclaimers, as to its being a Consolidation of the whole people of the country into one single grand National Republic. Let us, then, in the second place, see what was his judgment of it, as given to the Pennsylvania Convention. In opening the deliberations of that body, he [James Wilson] said:

> 'The system proposed, by the late Convention, for the Government of the United States, is now before you. Of that Convention, I had the honor to be a member. As I am the only member of that body, who has the honor to be also a member of this, it may be expected that I should prepare the way for the deliberations of this Assembly, by unfolding the difficulties, which the late Convention was obliged to encounter; by pointing out the end which they proposed to accomplish; and by tracing the general principles which they have adopted for the accomplishment of that end.
>
> 'A very important difficulty arose from comparing the extent of the country to be governed, with the kind of Government, which it would be proper to establish in it. It has been an opinion, countenanced by high authority [Montesquieu],
>
>> "that the natural property of small States is to be governed as a Republic; of middling ones, to be subject to a monarchy; and of large empires, to be swayed by a despotic prince;—and that the consequence is, that, in order to preserve the principles of the established Government, the State must be supported in the extent it has acquired; and that the spirit of the State will alter in proportion as it extends or contracts its limits."

'This opinion seems to be supported, rather than contradicted, by the history of the Governments in the old world. Here, then, the difficulty appeared in full view. On one hand, the United States contain an immense extent of Territory; and, according to the foregoing opinion, a despotic Government is best adapted to that extent. On the other hand, it was well known, that, however the citizens of the United States might with pleasure submit to the legitimate restraints of a Republican Constitution, they would reject with indignation the fetters of despotism. What, then, was to be done? The idea of a Confederate Republic presented itself. This kind of Constitution has been thought to have [as Montesquieu said] "all the internal advantages of a Republican, together with the external force of a monarchical Government."

'Its description is [as Montesquieu stated] "a Convention, by which several States agree to become members of a larger one, which they intend to establish. It is a kind of assemblage of societies that constitute a new one, capable of increasing by means of further association." The expanding quality of such Government is peculiarly fitted for the United States, the greatest part of whose territory is yet uncultivated.

'But while this form of Government enables us to surmount the difficulty last mentioned, it conducted us to another of which I am now to take notice. It left us almost without precedent or guide, and, consequently, without the benefit of that instruction which, in many cases, may be derived from the Constitution, and history, and experience, of other nations. Several associations have frequently been called by the name of Confederate States, which have not, in propriety of language, deserved it. The Swiss Cantons are connected only by alliances. The United Netherlands are, indeed, an assemblage of societies; but this assemblage constitutes no new one, and, therefore, it does not correspond with the full definition of a Confederate Republic. The Germanic body is composed of such disproportioned and discordant materials, and its structure is so intricate and complex, that little useful knowledge can be drawn from it. Ancient history discloses, and barely discloses, to our view, some Confederate Republics—the Achæan League, the Lycian Confederacy, and the Amphictyonic Council. But the facts recorded concerning their Constitutions are so few and general, and their histories are so unmarked and defective, that no satisfactory information can be collected from them, concerning many particular circumstances, from an accurate discernment and comparison of which, alone, legitimate and practical inferences can be made, from one Constitution to another. Besides, the situation and dimension of those Confederacies, and the state of society, manners, and habits, in them, were so different from those of the United States, that the most correct descriptions could have supplied but a very small fund of applicable remark. Thus, in forming this system, we were deprived of many advantages, which the history and experience of other ages and other countries would, in other cases, have afforded us.

'To be left without guide or precedent was not the only difficulty in which the Convention was involved, by proposing to their constituents a plan of a *Confederated Republic.* They found themselves embarrassed with another, of peculiar delicacy and importance. I mean, that of drawing a proper line between the National Government and the Governments of the several States. It was easy to discover a proper and satisfactory principle on the subject. Whatever object of Government is confined, in its operation and effects, within the bounds of a particular State, should be considered as belonging to the Government of that State; whatever object of Government extends, in its operation or effects, beyond the bounds of a particular State, should be considered as belonging to the Government of the United States. But though this principle be sound and satisfactory, its application to particular cases would be accompanied with much difficulty, because, in its application, room must be allowed for great discretionary latitude of construction of the principle. In order to lessen or remove the difficulty arising from discretionary construction on this subject, an enumeration of particular instances, in which the application of the principle ought to take place, has been attempted with much industry and care. It is only in mathematical science that a line can be described with mathematical precision. But I flatter myself, that, upon the strictest investigation, the enumeration will be found to be safe and unexceptionable, and accurate, too, in as great a degree as accuracy can be expected in a subject of this nature. Particulars under this head will be more properly explained, when we descend to the minute view of the enumeration, which is made in the proposed Constitution.

'After all, it will be necessary that, on a subject so peculiarly delicate as this, much prudence, much candor, much moderation, and much liberality should be exercised and displayed, both by the Federal Government, and by the Governments of the several States. It is to be hoped that those virtues of Government will be exercised and displayed, when we consider that the powers of the Federal Government, and those of the State Governments, are drawn from sources equally pure.

'The United States may adopt any one of four different systems. They may become consolidated into one Government, in which the separate existence of the States shall be entirely absolved. They may reject any plan of Union or association, and act as separate and unconnected States. They may form two or more Confederacies. They may unite in one Federal [Confederate] Republic. Which of these systems ought to have been formed by the Convention?'

"After giving his opinion against the first three, he [James Wilson] concludes thus:

'The remaining system which the *American States* may adopt, is a *Union of them* under one *Confederate Republic.* It will not be necessary to employ much time, or many arguments, to show that this is the most eligible system that can be proposed. By adopting this system, the vigor and decision of a wide spreading monarchy, may be joined to the freedom and beneficence of a contracted Republic. The extent of territory, the diversity of climate and soil, the number, and greatness, and connection, of lakes and rivers, with which the United States are intersected, and almost surrounded,—all indicate an enlarged Government to be fit and advantageous for them. If those opinions and wishes are as well founded as they have been general, the late Convention were justified in proposing to their constituents *one Confederate Republic*, as the best system of a National Government for the United States.'

"In another speech, on 1st December, 1787, as the discussion progressed, [Wilson] . . . said:

'We have heard much about a consolidated Government. I wish the honorable gentleman would condescend to give us a definition of what he meant by it. I think this the more necessary, because I apprehend that the term, in the numerous times it has been used, has not always been used in the same sense. It may be said, and I believe it has been said, that a consolidated Government is such as will absorb and destroy the Governments of the several States. If it is taken in this view, the plan before us is not a consolidated Government, as I showed on a former day, and may, if necessary, show further on some future occasion. On the other hand, if it is meant that the General Government will take from the State Governments their power in some particulars, it is confessed, and evident, that this will be its operation and effect.'

"Again, on the 4th of December, [Wilson] . . . said:

'The very manner of introducing this Constitution, by the recognition of the authority of the people, is said to change the principles of the present Confederation, and to introduce a Consolidating and absorbing Government.

'In this Confederated Republic, the Sovereignty of the States, it is said, is not preserved. We are told that there cannot be two Sovereign powers, and that a subordinate Sovereignty is no Sovereignty.

'It will be worth while, Mr. President, to consider this objection at large. When I had the honor of speaking formerly on this subject, I stated, in as concise a manner as possible, the leading ideas that occurred to me, to ascertain where the Supreme and Sovereign power resides. It has not been, nor, I presume, will it be denied, that somewhere there is, and of necessity must be, a Supreme, absolute, and uncontrollable authority. This, I believe, may justly be termed the Sovereign power; for, from that gentleman's (Mr. [William] Findley) account of the matter, it cannot be Sovereign unless it is Supreme; for, says he, a subordinate Sovereignty is no Sovereignty at all. I had the honor of observing, that, if the question was asked, where the

Supreme power resided, different answers would be given by different writers. I mentioned that [Sir William] Blackstone would tell you that, in Britain, it is lodged in the British Parliament; and I believe there is no writer, on this subject, on the other side of the Atlantic, but supposed it to be vested in that body. I stated, further, that, if the question was asked of some politician, who had not considered the subject with sufficient accuracy, where the Supreme power resided in our Government, he would answer, that it was vested in the State Constitutions. This opinion approaches near the truth, but does not reach it; for the truth is, that the Supreme, absolute, and uncontrollable authority remains with the people. I mentioned, also, that the practical recognition of this truth was reserved for the honor of this country. I recollect no Constitution founded on this principle; but we have witnessed the improvement, and enjoy the happiness of seeing it carried into practice. The great and penetrating mind of [English philosopher John] Locke seems to be the only one that pointed towards even the theory of this great truth.

'When I made the observation that some politicians would say the Supreme power was lodged in our State Constitutions, I did not suspect that the honorable gentleman from Westmoreland (Mr. Findley) was included in that description; but I find myself disappointed; for I imagined his opposition would arise from another consideration. His position is, that the Supreme power resides in the States, as Governments; and mine is, that it resides in the people, as the fountain of Government; that the people have not—that the people meant not—and that the people ought not—to part with it to any Government whatsoever. In their hands it remains secure. They can delegate it in such proportions, to such bodies, on such terms, and under such limitations, as they think proper. I agree with the members in opposition, that there cannot be two Sovereign powers on the same subject. This, I say, is the inherent and unalienable right of the people; and as an illustration of it, I beg to read a few words from the Declaration of Independence, made by the Representatives of the United States, and recognised by the whole Union.

> We hold these truths to be self-evident, that all men are created equal; that they are endowed by their Creator with certain inalienable rights; that among these are life, liberty, and the pursuit of happiness; that, to secure these rights, Governments are instituted among men, deriving their just powers from the consent of the governed; that, whenever any form of Government becomes destructive of these ends, it is the right of the people to alter, or abolish it, and institute a new Government, laying its foundation on such principles, and organizing its powers in such forms, as to them shall seem most likely to effect their safety and happiness.

'This is the broad basis on which our Independence was placed: on the same certain and solid foundation this system is erected.

'It is mentioned that this Federal Government will annihilate and absorb all the State Governments. I wish to save, as much as possible, the time of the house; I shall not, therefore, recapitulate what I had the honor of saying last week on this subject. I hope it was then shown that, instead of being abolished (as insinuated), from the very nature of things, and from the organization of the system itself, the State Governments must exist, or the General Government must fall amidst their ruins. Indeed, so far as to the forms, it is admitted they may remain; but the gentlemen seem to think their power will be gone.

'I shall have occasion to take notice of this power hereafter; and, I believe, if it was necessary, it could be shown that the State Governments, as States, will enjoy as much power, and more dignity, happiness, and security, than they have hitherto done.

'I say, Sir, that it was the design of this system to take some power from the State Governments, and to place it in the General Government. It was also the design that the people should be admitted to the exercise of some powers, which they did not exercise under the present Federation [Confederation]. It was thought proper that the citizens, as well as the States, should be represented. How far the representation in the Senate is a representation of States, we shall see by and by, when we come to consider that branch of the Federal Government.

'This system, it is said, unhinges and eradicates the State Governments, and was systematically intended so to do. To establish the intention, an argument is drawn from Article 1st, Section 4th, on the subject of elections. I have already had occasion to remark upon this, and shall, therefore, pass on to the next objection.

'That the last clause of the 8th Section of the 1st Article, gives the power of Self-preservation to the General Government, independent of the States; for, in case of their abolition, it will be alleged, in behalf of the General Government, that Self-preservation is the first law, and necessary to the exercise of all other powers.

'Now, let us see what this objection amounts to. Who are to have this Self-preserving power? The Congress. Who are Congress? It is a body that will consist of a Senate and a House of Representatives. Who compose this Senate? Those who are elected by the Legislature of the different States. Who are the electors of the House of Representatives? Those who are qualified to vote for the most numerous branch of the Legislature in the separate States. Suppose the State Legislatures annihilated; where is the criterion to ascertain the qualification of electors? and unless this be ascertained, they cannot be admitted to vote; if a State Legislature is not elected, there can be no Senate, because the Senators are to be chosen by the Legislatures only.

'This is a plain and simple deduction from the Constitution; and yet the objection is stated as conclusive, upon an agreement expressly drawn from the last clause of this section.

'It is repeated, with confidence, "that this is not a Federal [Confederate]

Government, but a complete one, with Legislative, Executive, and Judicial powers; it is a Consolidating Government." I have already mentioned the misuse of the term; I wish the gentleman would indulge us with his definition of the word. If, when he says it is a consolidation, he means so far as relates to the general objects of the Union; so far it was intended to be a consolidation, and on such a consolidation, perhaps, our very existence, as a nation, depends. If, on the other hand (as something, which has been said, seems to indicate), he (Mr. [William] Findley) means that it will absorb the Governments of the individual States,—so far is this position from being admitted, that it is unanswerably controverted.

'Sir, I think there is another subject with regard to which this Constitution deserves approbation. I mean the accuracy with which the line is drawn between the powers of the General Government and those of the particular State Governments. We have heard some general observations, on this subject, from the gentlemen who conduct the opposition. They have asserted that these powers are unlimited and undefined. These words are as easily pronounced as limited and defined. They have already been answered by my honorable colleague (Mr. M'Kean), therefore I shall not enter into an explanation. But it is not pretended that the line is drawn with mathematical precision; the inaccuracy of language must, to a certain degree, prevent the accomplishment of such a desire. Whoever views the matter in a true light, will see that the powers are as minutely enumerated and defined as was possible, and will also discover that the general clause, against which so much exception is taken, is nothing more than what was necessary to render effectual the particular powers that are granted.

'But let us suppose—and this supposition is very easy in the minds of the gentlemen on the other side,—that there is some difficulty in ascertaining where the true line lies. Are we, therefore, thrown into despair? Are disputes between the General Government and the State Governments to be necessarily the consequence of inaccuracy? I hope, sir, they will not be the enemies of each other, or resemble comets in conflicting orbits, mutually operating destruction; but that their motion will be better represented by that of the planetary system, where each part moves harmoniously within its proper sphere, and no injury arises by interference or opposition. Every part, I trust, will be considered as a part of the United States. Can any cause of distrust arise here? Is there any increase of risk? Or, rather, *are not the enumerated powers as well defined here, as in the present Articles of Confederation?*'

"Again, on the 11th December, 1787, . . . [James Wilson] said:

'It is objected to this system, that under it there is no Sovereignty left in the State Governments. I have had occasion to reply to this already; but I should be glad to know at what period the State Governments became possessed of the Supreme power. On the principle on which I found my arguments,—and that is the principle of this Constitution,—the Supreme power resides in the people.

'We are next told, by the honorable gentlemen in opposition (as, indeed, we have been from the beginning of the debates in this Convention, to the conclusion of their speeches, yesterday), that this is a Consolidated Government, and will abolish the State Governments.

'Definitions of a Consolidated Government have been called for; the gentlemen gave us what they termed definitions, but it does not seem, to me, at least, that they have, as yet, expressed clear ideas upon that subject. I will endeavor to state their different ideas upon this point. The gentleman from Westmoreland (Mr. Findley), when speaking on this subject, says, that he means, by a consolidation, "that Government which puts the thirteen States into one."

'The honorable gentleman from Fayette (Mr. Smilie), gives you this definition: "What I mean, by a Consolidated Government, is one that will transfer the Sovereignty from the State Governments to the General Government."

'The honorable member from Cumberland (Mr. Whitehill), instead of giving you a definition, sir, tells you again, that "it is a Consolidated Government, and we have proved it so."

'These, I think, sir, are the different descriptions given to us of a Consolidated Government. As to the first, that it is a Consolidated Government, that puts the thirteen United States into one,—if it is meant that the General Government will destroy the Governments of the States, I will admit that such a Government would not suit the people of America. It would be improper for this Country, because it could not be proportioned to its extent, on the principles of freedom. But that description does not apply to the system before you. This, instead of placing the State Governments in jeopardy, is founded on their existence. On this principle its organization depends; it must stand or fall, as the State Governments are secured or ruined! Therefore, though this may be a very proper description of a Consolidated Government, yet it must be disregarded, as inapplicable to the proposed Constitution. It is not treated with decency when such insinuations are offered against it.'

"So much for the debates in the Pennsylvania Convention. It is to be regretted that no part of these debates has been preserved but the speeches of Mr. Wilson, from which these extracts have been read. From these, however, it abundantly appears that the nature and character of the Government to be instituted under the Constitution of the United States was thoroughly discussed. It appears clearly, that there was strong opposition to many of its features, but, what is of very great importance in our investigation, it is equally clear that Mr. Wilson, and the majority who acted with him in that Convention, held the

Constitution to be strictly Federal [Confederate], and that the Government instituted by it was a Federal [Confederate] Government, or Confederated Republic. Whatever may have been his original views as to a consolidation of the States into one National Republic, he distinctly and frankly avowed that the Constitution which had been agreed upon did not effect that result. He declared further, that according to his understanding of the Constitution, the State Governments, as States under it, would enjoy as much power, and more dignity, happiness, and security, than they had done before. He insisted that no cause of distrust should arise from apprehensions on that score; for the powers of the Federal Government, said he, with emphasis, were as well defined in the Constitution as under the Articles of Confederation. His whole powers seem to have been put forth to demonstrate that it was not a Consolidated Government, as the opponents of it argued that it would be construed to be. He declared that it was not treating the Constitution with decency, to make such insinuations against it. These speeches of Mr. Wilson, without doubt, controlled the majority of the Pennsylvania Convention, who gave the Constitution their sanction. They show clearly what must have been the understanding of the friends and advocates of the Constitution as to its nature, and as to the nature of the Union thereby established, when they styled it, in their ordinance of ratification, 'a Constitution for States.' These speeches of Mr. Wilson were also extensively published in the newspapers of the day. They were widely circulated in other States, and, Mr. [George T.] Curtis says, had great influence on the action of other State Conventions. Let us, however, proceed with the other States. The next in order is New Jersey.

THIRD, NEW JERSEY

"The Legislature of this State called a Convention of her people, to which the Constitution was referred. That Convention came to the following Resolutions and Ordinance.

In Convention of the State of New Jersey, (18 December, 1787.)

Whereas, A Convention of Delegates from the following States, viz.: New Hampshire, Massachusetts, Connecticut, New York, New Jersey, Pennsylvania, Delaware, Maryland, Virginia, North Carolina, South Carolina and Georgia, met at Philadelphia, for the purpose of deliberating on, and forming, a Constitution for the United States of America,—finished their session on the 17th day of September last, and reported to Congress the form which they had agreed upon, in the words following, viz.:

And whereas, Congress, on the 28th day of September last, unanimously did resolve, 'That the said report, with the Resolutions and letter accompanying the same, be transmitted to the several Legislatures, in order to be submitted to a Convention of Delegates, chosen in each State by the people thereof, in conformity to the resolves of the Convention made and provided in that case;'

And whereas, The Legislature of this State did, on the 29th day of October last, resolve in the words following, viz.:

Resolved, unanimously, That it be recommended to such of the inhabitants of this State as are entitled to vote for Representatives in General Assembly, to meet in their respective counties on the fourth Tuesday in November next, at the several places fixed by law for holding the annual elections, to choose three suitable persons to serve as delegates from each county in a State Convention, for the purposes hereinbefore mentioned, and that the same be conducted agreeably to the mode, and conformably with the rules and regulations, prescribed for conducting such elections;—

Resolved, unanimously, That the persons so selected to serve in State Convention, do assemble and meet together on the second Tuesday in December next, at Trenton, in the county of Hunterdon, then and there to take into consideration the aforesaid Constitution, and if approved of by them, finally to ratify the same in behalf and on the part of this State, and make report thereof to the United States in Congress assembled, in conformity with the resolutions thereto annexed.

Resolved, That the sheriffs of the respective counties of this State shall be, and they are hereby, required to give as timely notice as may be, by advertisements, to the people of their counties, of the time, place and purpose of holding elections, as aforesaid.

And whereas, The Legislature of this State did also, on the 1st day of November last, make and pass the following act, viz.:

An Act to authorize the people of this State to meet in Convention, deliberate upon, agree to, and ratify, the Constitution of the United States proposed by the late General Convention,—Be it enacted by the Council and General Assembly of this State, and it is hereby enacted by the authority of the same, That it shall and may be lawful for the people thereof, by their Delegates, to meet in Convention to deliberate upon, and, if approved of by them, to ratify, the Constitution for the United States proposed by the General Convention held at Philadelphia, and every act, matter and clause, therein contained, conformably to the resolutions of the Legislature passed the 29th day of October, 1787,—any law, usage, or custom, to the contrary in any wise notwithstanding;

Now be it known, That we, the Delegates of the State of New Jersey, chosen by the people thereof, for the purposes aforesaid, having maturely deliberated on and considered the aforesaid proposed Constitution, do hereby, for and on the behalf of the people of the said State of New Jersey, agree to, ratify, and confirm, the same and every part thereof.

Done in Convention, by the unanimous consent of the members present, this 18th day of December, in the year of our Lord 1787, and of the independence of the United States of America, the twelfth.

"There was no opposition to the Constitution in the Convention of New Jersey. It was unanimously adopted. But the action of the Convention shows how they understood it. They agreed to and ratified it as 'a Constitution for the United States of America.'

FOURTH, GEORGIA

"The next State in order is Georgia. Here is her action, embodied in the Ordinance of 2nd January, 1788, referred to before.

> In Convention, Wednesday, January 2nd, 1788. To all to whom these presents shall come, greeting:
> Whereas, the form of a Constitution for the Government of the United States of America, was, on the 17th day of September, 1787, agreed upon and reported to Congress, by the Deputies of the said United States, convened in Philadelphia, which said Constitution is written in the words following, to wit:
> And whereas, the United States in Congress assembled did, on the 28th day of September, 1787, Resolve, unanimously, 'That the said report, with the resolutions and letter accompanying the same, be transmitted to the several Legislatures, in order to be submitted to a Convention of Delegates chosen in each State by the people thereof, in conformity to the resolves of the Convention made and provided in that case;'—
> And whereas, the Legislature of the State of Georgia did, on the 26th day of October, 1787, in pursuance of the above-recited resolution of Congress, Resolve, That a Convention be elected on the day of the next general election, and in the same manner that representatives are elected; and that the said Convention consist of not more than three members from each county; and that the said Convention should meet at Augusta, on the fourth Tuesday in December then next, and as soon thereafter as convenient, proceed to consider the said report and resolutions, and to adopt or reject any part or the whole thereof;
> Now know ye, that we, the Delegates of the people of the State of Georgia, in Convention met, pursuant to the resolutions of the Legislature aforesaid, having taken into our serious consideration the said Constitution, have assented to, ratified, and adopted, and by these presents do, in virtue of the powers and authority to us given by the people of the said State for that purpose, for and in behalf of ourselves and our constituents, fully and entirely assent to, ratify, and adopt the said Constitution.
> Done in Convention, at Augusta, in the said State, on the 2nd day of January, in the year of our Lord, 1788, and of the Independence of the United States the twelfth.

"In the Georgia Convention there was no opposing voice. The Constitution was unanimously assented to, ratified, and adopted as 'a Constitution for the Government of the United States of America.' A Government of States. A Federal [Confederate] Republic.

FIFTH, CONNECTICUT

"We come now . . . [to Connecticut]. First, we will look at the words of her ratification. These are as follows:

> In the name of the People of the State of Connecticut. We, the Delegates of the people of said State, in General Convention assembled, pursuant to an Act of the Legislature in October last, have assented to, and ratified, and by these presents do assent to, ratify, and adopt the Constitution reported by the Convention of Delegates in Philadelphia, on the 17th day of September, A.D., 1787, for the United States of America.
>
> Done in Convention, at Hartford, this 9th day of January, A.D., 1788. In witness whereof, we have hereunto set our hands.

"Connecticut ratified the Constitution as a form of Government for States. This shows the understanding of the Convention so far as these words, used in the ratification, go. But we are not left to bare inference or argument from them. We have seen what Roger Sherman and Oliver Ellsworth, two of the Delegates from this State, had said of the Constitution in their letter to the Governor of the State, on the adjournment of the Federal Convention. In that they stated distinctly, that the Sovereignty of the States was retained. But besides this we have the debates in the ratifying Convention.

"Let us look into these, then, in the second place. There were several men of great ability in this Convention. Amongst whom no one was more prominent than Mr. Ellsworth himself. He was afterwards Chief Justice of the Supreme Court of the United States. On him, as a member of the Philadelphia Convention, devolved the part of opening the discussion in the body then assembled, to consider the Constitution. His opening words were as follows:

> 'Mr. President:—It is observable that there is no preface to the proposed Constitution, but it evidently presupposes two things; one is the necessity of a Federal [Confederate] Government; the other is the inefficiency of the old Articles of Confederation.'

"After going through with a detail of the structure of the Government proposed, he concluded by saying:

> 'The Constitution before us is a complete system of Legislative, Judicial, and Executive power. It was designed to supply the defects of the former system;

and I believe, upon a full discussion, it will be found to answer the purposes for which it was designed.'

"[Many Nationals and Liberals assume that in one of his speeches Judge Ellsworth declared that the Constitution was not a Federal (Confederate) Compact between the States, but that it established a complete National Government over the whole people of the United States.] But no such idea . . . was intended to be conveyed by the speech, and none such appears in it taken, altogether. Here is that speech. It was in reply to objections that the powers delegated by the Constitution were of themselves inconsistent with the nature of a Federal Government. He combated that idea, and maintained that States, by compact, might delegate power to act directly upon their citizens. Here is . . . [Ellsworth's] speech on that subject.

> 'But, says the honorable objector, if Congress levies money, they must legislate. I admit it. Two legislative powers, says he, cannot legislate on the same subject in the same place. I ask, why can they not? It is not enough to say they cannot. I wish for some reason, grant that both cannot legislate upon the same object at the same time, and carry into effect laws which are contrary to each other. But the Constitution excludes every thing of this kind. Each Legislature has its province; their limits may be distinguished. . . . Two several Legislatures have in fact existed, and acted at the same time, and in the same territory. It is in vain to say they cannot exist, when they actually have done it. In the time of the war, we had an army. Who made the laws for the army? By whose authority were offenders tried and executed? Congress. By their authority a man was taken, tried, condemned, and hanged, in this very city. He belonged to the army; he was a proper subject of military law; he deserted to the enemy; he deserved his fate.'

"In this way . . . [Ellsworth] maintained that there would be no change in principle in the operation of laws passed by the Congress, under the Constitution, in levying taxes directly upon the people, from laws that had been passed by the Congress, under the Confederation, in other cases. The great benefit that would flow from the extension, in the Constitution, of this principle, that had been acted on to a limited extent, under the Confederation, he proceeded to explain with great force, and showed its perfect practicability under a Federal [Confederate] system. The point was the collection of revenues by levies on the people, instead of requisitions on the States. Afterwards comes the part from which the extract [that Liberals] . . . refer to is taken. Here is the whole of it.

> 'Hence, we see how necessary, for the Union, is a coercive principle. No

man pretends the contrary; we all see and feel this necessity. The only question is, shall it be a coercion of law, or a coercion of arms? There is no other possible alternative. Where will those who oppose a coercion of law come out? Where will they end? A necessary consequence of their principles is a war of the States, one against the other. I am for coercion by law—that coercion which acts only upon delinquent individuals. This Constitution does not attempt to coerce Sovereign bodies, States, in their political capacity. No coercion is applicable to such bodies, but that of an armed force. If we should attempt to execute the laws of the Union by sending an armed force against a delinquent State, it would involve the good and bad, the innocent and guilty, in the same calamity. But this legal coercion singles out the guilty individual, and punishes him for breaking the laws of the Union.'

". . . [Ellsworth] was speaking [here] of the great advantage that would result from delegating to the Congress power to pass laws that would operate directly upon the people, and not upon the States in their corporate capacities. This, he maintained, would be a great improvement in the Federal system, especially in the collection of taxes. And he contended further, that it really involved no new principle; that the Congress had, by virtue of the Articles of Confederation, acted upon the same principle, so far as persons in the land and naval forces were concerned. Nothing in this speech is inconsistent with his and Mr. [Roger] Sherman's joint letter to Governor Huntingdon [i.e., Samuel Huntington] touching the reserved Sovereignty of the States. Indeed, in this very speech, he says the Constitution does not attempt to coerce Sovereign bodies, States, in their political capacity. There is no trace, in the debates in the Connecticut Convention, of a contrary opinion being entertained. The general doctrine of all the friends of the Constitution in this Convention was, not only that it established a Federal Government, but that the rights of the States were amply secured by it. This was the judgment of Governor Huntingdon [i.e., Samuel Huntington], who was a member of the Convention. It was the judgment of Richard Law, who said:

> 'Consider that this General Government rests upon the State Governments for its support. It is like a vast and magnificent bridge, built upon thirteen strong and stately pillars. Now, the rulers, who occupy the bridge, cannot be so beside themselves as to knock away the pillars which support the whole fabric.'

"Oliver Wolcott, he who was afterwards Secretary of the Treasury, and the devoted political friend of Mr. [Alexander] Hamilton, said:

> 'The Constitution effectually secures the States in their several rights. It must

secure them, for its own sake; for they are the pillars which uphold the general system. The Senate, a constituent branch of the general Legislature, without whose assent no public act can be made, are appointed by the States, and will secure the rights of the several States. . . . So well guarded is this Constitution throughout, that it seems impossible that the rights either of the States or of the people should be destroyed.'

"This is quite enough to show what the Convention of Connecticut thought of the Constitution, and hence we see in their ratification they use the same words; they adopt it as a Constitution for the United States of America.

SIXTH, MASSACHUSETTS

"We now come [to Massachusetts] . . . . It is tedious to go through with all these dry, musty records. But it is essential to our investigation; they are the title-deeds of our political inheritance of Constitutional Liberty. From them alone can we arrive at the truth touching the object of our inquiry. I call your special attention . . . to the action of [the] . . . State in the premises. No better or more conclusive proof could be adduced to establish the fact that Massachusetts, at the time, considered the Union perfected by the Constitution to be a Federal [Confederate] one between States, than her own action on the adoption of it furnishes.

"First, the ratification itself. It is in these words:—

Commonwealth of Massachusetts. The Convention having impartially discussed, and fully considered, the Constitution for the United States of America, reported to Congress by the Convention of Delegates from the United States of America, and submitted to us by a resolution of the General Court of the said Commonwealth, passed the 25th day of October, last past,—and acknowledging, with grateful hearts, the goodness of the Supreme Ruler of the Universe in affording the people of the United States, in the course of his providence, an opportunity, deliberately and peaceably, without fraud or surprise, of entering into an explicit and solemn compact with each other, by assenting to and ratifying a *new Constitution* in order to form a more perfect Union, establish justice, insure domestic tranquillity, provide for the common defence, promote the general welfare, and secure the blessings of liberty to themselves and their posterity,—do, in the name and in behalf of the people of the Commonwealth of Massachusetts, assent to and ratify the said Constitution for the United States of America. [Emphasis added, L.S.]

And as it is the opinion of this Convention, that certain amendments and alterations in the said Constitution would remove the fears, and quiet the apprehensions, of many of the good people of this Commonwealth, and more effectually guard against an undue administration of the Federal [Confederate] Government,—the Convention do therefore recommend that the following alterations and provisions be introduced into the said Constitution:—

I. That it explicitly declare that all powers not expressly delegated by the aforesaid Constitution are reserved to the several States, to be by them exercised.

II. That there shall be one representative to every thirty thousand persons, according to the census mentioned in the Constitution, until the whole number of the representatives amounts to two hundred.

III. That Congress do not exercise the powers vested in them by the 4th Section of the 1st Article, but in cases where a State shall neglect or refuse to make the regulations therein mentioned, or shall make regulations subversive of the rights of the people to a free and equal representation in Congress, agreeably to the Constitution.

IV. That Congress do not lay direct taxes but when the moneys arising from the impost and excise are insufficient for the public exigencies, nor then until Congress shall have first made a requisition upon the States to assess, levy, and pay, their respective proportions of such requisition, agreeably to the census fixed in the said Constitution, in such way and manner as the Legislatures of the States shall think best; and in such case, if any State shall neglect or refuse to pay its proportion, pursuant to such requisition, then Congress may assess and levy such State's proportion, together with interest thereon at the rate of six per cent. per annum, from the time of payment prescribed in such requisition.

V. That Congress erect no company of merchants with exclusive advantages of commerce.

VI. That no person shall be tried for any crime by which he may incur an infamous punishment, or loss of life, until he be first indicted by a grand jury, except in such cases as may arise in the government and regulation of the land and naval forces.

VII. The Supreme Judicial Federal Court shall have no jurisdiction of causes between citizens of different States, unless the matter in dispute, whether it concerns the realty or personalty, be of the value of three thousand dollars at the least; nor shall the Federal Judicial powers extend to any actions between citizens of different States, where the matter in dispute, whether it concerns the realty or personalty, is not of the value of fifteen hundred dollars at least.

VIII. In civil actions between citizens of different States, every issue of fact, arising in actions at common law, shall be tried by a jury, if the parties, or either of them, request it.

IX. Congress shall at no time consent that any person, holding an office of trust or profit under the United States, shall accept of a title of nobility, or any other title or office, from any king, prince, or foreign State.

And the Convention do, in the name and in behalf of the people of this Commonwealth, enjoin it upon their representatives in Congress, at all times, until the alterations and provisions aforesaid have been considered, agreeably to the fifth article of the said Constitution, to exert all their influence, and use all reasonable and legal methods, to obtain a ratification of the said alterations and provisions, in such manner as is provided in the said article.

And that the United States, in Congress assembled, may have due notice of the assent and ratification of the said Constitution by this Convention, it is Resolved, That the assent and ratification aforesaid be engrossed on parchment, together with the recommendation and injunction aforesaid, and with this resolution; and that his Excellency, John Hancock, Esqr., President, and the Hon. William Cushing, Esqr., Vice President of the Convention, transmit the same, countersigned by the Secretary of the Convention, under their hands and seals, to the United States in Congress assembled.

"Here we see potent words! The instrument is recognized as a new Constitution! New in contradistinction to the old one! That was the Articles of Confederation. It is distinctly declared to be a Compact to form a more perfect Union—a more perfect Union, of course, between the same parties. Those parties were the several States, or the people of the several States, in their Sovereign character. We see it was adopted as 'a Constitution for the United States of America'—not, as I have often said, for the whole American people, but for the American States united by the Compact. The Government, we see, was to be Federal [Confederate]. The Supreme Court of the United States is styled 'the Supreme Judicial Federal [Confederate] Court.' The whole proceedings, from beginning to end, show upon their face Federal [Confederate] action and Federal [Confederate] engagements. The instrument, ratified, was directed to be sent 'to the United States in Congress assembled.' But this is not all. The Constitution did not pass the Convention of Massachusetts without violent opposition. What was said pro and con is upon record. These sayings, at the time, constitute a part of the *res gestæ* [facts which spring from the main fact and serve to illustrate it], and are to be taken with it, if necessary, for a clearer explanation of the understanding of the Resolutions they came to. [Emphasis added, L.S.]

"There were great men in that Convention. Men who were the lights of the age in which they lived. Samuel Adams, Fisher Ames, Rufus King, Theophilus Parsons, James Bowdoin, and John Hancock, were there. The questions involved were deemed of the most momentous character. None of greater importance had engaged the attention of Massachusetts' statesmen, since the ever-memorable struggles over their Charter, in 1685 and 1774, and which finally ended in the war of the [American] Revolution, and establishment of the complete Independence and Sovereignty of the Commonwealth. By many it was thought, that this Sovereignty would be endangered by the adoption of this new Constitution. At the head of this class was the renowned Samuel Adams. With him, stood conspicuously, [Amos] Singletary, [William] Bodman, [William] Widgery, [John] Taylor, [Samuel] Nason, and [John] Choate.

"They doubtless had in mind the insidious encroachments upon their ancient rights, by the crown of Great Britain, through the instrumentality of a

[John] Randolph [father of Edmund Randolph] and Andrews, in 1683-1685. The reply of the Deputies of Massachusetts, to the proposition of the crown at that time, was not forgotten.

> 'The civil liberties of New England are part of the inheritance of their fathers; and shall we give that inheritance away? Is it objected that we shall be exposed to greater sufferings? Better suffer than sin. It is better to trust the God of our fathers, than to put confidence in Princes! If we suffer, because we dare not comply with the wills of men against the will of God, we suffer in a good cause, and shall be accounted Martyrs in the next generation, and at the great day! The Deputies consent not, but adhere to their former Bills!'

"They did not lose sight of the fact, that these fathers did become Martyrs, and that their self-sacrifice was amply vindicated in the Revolution of 1688 [the overthrow of King James II], and in the re-establishment of their charter. It was also fresh in their minds, how like attempts to despoil them of their Liberties had been made in their own times by George III, in 1774, and how gloriously their resistance to his encroachments had resulted.

"We can easily account, therefore, for the apprehensions awakened in the breasts of such men upon the presentation of this new Constitution. On its face it did not reserve expressly the Sovereignty of the States, severally, as the old one had done. At first a very large majority of the Convention were decidedly opposed to its adoption. The session lasted for a month lacking two days. The debates have been published by order of the State Legislature and make a volume of themselves.

"Secondly, then, let us sample these debates to see the prevailing sentiments on both sides.

"Mr. Shurtliff: 'The Convention says, they aimed at a consolidation of the Union.'

"Mr. [Theophilus] Parsons: 'The distinction is between a consolidation of the States and a consolidation of the Union.'

"Mr. Jones, of Boston: 'The word consolidation has different ideas—as different metals melted into one mass, two twigs tied into one bundle.'

"Mr. [Fisher] Ames: *The Senators will represent the Sovereignty of the States. The Representatives are to represent the people.*' [Emphasis added, L.S.]

"Mr. Gore. 'The Senate represents the Sovereignty of the States,' etc.

"Mr. Ames again observed,

> 'that an objection was made against the Constitution, because the Senators are to be chosen for six years. It has been said, that they will be removed too far from the control of the people, and that, to keep them in proper dependence,

they should be chosen annually. It is necessary to premise, that no argument against the new plan has made a deeper impression than this, that it will produce a consolidation of the States. This is an effect which all good men will deprecate. For it is obvious, that, if the State powers are to be destroyed, the representation is too small. The trust, in that case, would be too great to be confided to so few persons. The objects of Legislation would be so multiplied and complicated, that the Government would be unwieldy and impracticable. The State Governments are essential parts of the system, and the defence of this article is drawn from its tendency to their preservation. The Senators represent the Sovereignty of the States; in the other House, individuals are represented. The Senate may not originate bills. It need not be said that they are principally to direct the affairs of wars and treaties. They are in the quality of ambassadors of the States, and it will not be denied that some permanency in their office is necessary to a discharge of their duty. Now, if they were chosen yearly, how could they perform their trust? If they would be brought by that means more immediately under the influence of the people, then they will represent the State Legislatures less, and become the representatives of individuals. This belongs to the other House. The absurdity of this, and its repugnancy to the Federal principles of the Constitution, will appear more fully, by supposing that they are to be chosen by the people at large. If there is any force in the objection to this article, this would be proper. But whom, in that case, would they represent?—Not the Legislatures of the States, but the people. This would totally obliterate the Federal [Confederate] features of the Constitution. What would become of the State Governments, and on whom would devolve the duty of defending them against the encroachments of the Federal Government? A consolidation of the States would ensue, which, it is conceded, would subvert the *new Constitution*, and against which this very article, so much condemned, is our best security. *Too much provision cannot be made against a consolidation. The State Governments represent the wishes, and feelings, and local interests, of the people. They are the safeguard and ornament of the Constitution; they will protract the period of our liberties; they will afford a shelter against the abuse of power, and will be the natural avengers of our violated rights.* [Emphasis added, L.S.]

'A very effectual check upon the power of the Senate is provided. A third part is to retire from office every two years. By this means, while the Senators are seated for six years, they are admonished of their responsibility to the State Legislatures. If one third new members are introduced, who feel the sentiments of their States, they will awe that third whose term will be near expiring. This article seems to be an excellence of the Constitution;, and affords just ground to believe that it will be, in practice as in theory, a Federal [Confederate] Republic.'

"Mr. [William] Bodman (in speaking of the clause conferring the general powers of the Congress in levying and collecting taxes, etc.,) remarked, 'It had been said that the Sovereignty of the States remains with them. He thought this section endangered that Sovereignty, and the powers in that section ought to have been more clearly defined, as to the right or power of the Government to use force in collecting the taxes, etc.'

"Mr. [Amos] Singletary 'Thought that no more power could be given to a despot than to give up the purse strings of the people.'

"Mr. [John] Choate: 'Gentlemen say this section (8th, giving general powers to Congress) is as clear as the sun, and that all power is retained that is not given. But where is the Bill of Rights, which shall check the power of Congress; which shall say, thus far shall ye come, and no farther.'

"Mr. Porter asked 'If a better rule of yielding power could be shown than in the Constitution; for what we do not give,' said he, 'we retain.'

"Mr. [Charles] Sumner:

'But some gentlemen object further and say the delegation of these great powers will destroy the State Legislatures; but, I trust, this never can take place, for the General Government depends on the State Legislatures for its very existence. The President is to be chosen by Electors, under the Regulations of the State Legislatures. The Senate is to be chosen by the State Legislatures, and the Representative body by the people, under like Regulations of the Legislative body in the different States. If gentlemen consider this, they will, I presume, alter their opinion; for nothing is clearer than that the existence of the Legislatures in the different States, is essential to the very being of the General Government. I hope, sir, we shall all see the necessity of a Federal Government, and not make objections unless they appear to us to be of some weight.'

"Mr. Parsons, after speaking of the several kinds of Government, said,

'The Federal Constitution establishes a Government of the last description, and, in this case, the people divest themselves of nothing! The Government, and the powers which the Congress can administer, are the mere result of a Compact, etc. . . .

'But if gentlemen will still insist that these powers are a grant from the people, and, consequently, improper, let it be observed that it is now too late to impede the grant. It is already completed. The Congress, under the [U.S.] Confederation [1781-1789], are already invested with it by solemn Compact. They have power to demand what moneys and forces they judge necessary, for the common defence, and general welfare. Powers as extensive as those proposed in this Constitution. . . .

'It has been objected that we have no Bill of Rights. If gentlemen, who make this objection, would consider what are the supposed inconveniences resulting from a want of a declaration of rights, I think they would soon satisfy themselves that the objection has no weight. Is there a single natural right that we enjoy uncontrolled by our own Legislature, that Congress can infringe? Not one! Is there a single political right secured to us, by our Constitution, against the attempts of our own Legislature, which we are deprived of in this Constitution? Not one that I can recollect.'

"Mr. Rufus King (who had been in the Philadelphia Convention and who was, while the question was open, for a National Government proper instead of a Federal [Confederate] one) said:

'To conclude, sir, if we mean to support an efficient Federal Government, which, under the old Confederation, can never be the case, the proposed Constitution is, in my opinion, the only one that can be substituted.'

"It was on the 30th of January, after the [Philadelphia] Convention had been in session for three weeks, and after it was well ascertained that the Constitution could not get the approval of a majority of that body without some declaration accompanying it setting forth the understanding with which it was adopted, that John Hancock, the President, left the chair and offered his proposition, which was, in substance, for its adoption in the form in which it stands.

"After this proposition was so brought forward, the venerable Samuel Adams, and quite a number with him, yielded their former opposition. He expressed himself thus:—

'As your Excellency was pleased yesterday to offer, for the consideration of this Convention, certain propositions intended to accompany the ratification of the Constitution before us, I did myself the honor to bring them forward by a regular motion, not only from the respect due your Excellency, but from a clear conviction, in my own mind, that they would tend to effect the salutary and important purposes which you had in view—"the removing the fears and quieting the apprehensions of many of the good people of this Commonwealth, and the more effectually guarding against an undue administration of the Federal Government."

'I beg leave, sir, more particularly to consider those propositions, and, in a very few words, to express my own opinion, that they must have a strong tendency to ease the minds of gentlemen who wish for the immediate operation of some essential parts of the proposed Constitution, as well as the most speedy and effectual means of obtaining alterations in some other parts of it, which they are solicitous should be made. I will not repeat the reasons I offered when the motion was made, which convinced me that the measure now under consideration will have a more speedy, as well as a more certain influence, in effecting the purpose last mentioned, than the measure proposed in the Constitution before us.

'Your Excellency's first proposition is, "that it be explicitly declared, that all powers not expressly delegated to Congress are reserved to the several States, to be by them exercised." This appears, to my mind, to be a summary of a bill of rights, which gentlemen are anxious to obtain. It removes a doubt which many have entertained respecting the matter, and gives assurance that, if any law made by the Federal Government shall be extended beyond the power granted by the proposed Constitution and inconsistent with the Constitution of this State, it will be an error, and adjudged by the courts of law to be void. It is consonant with the second article in the *present Confederation* that each state retains its Sovereignty, freedom, and independence, and every power, jurisdiction, and right, which is not, by this Confederation, expressly delegated to the United States in Congress assembled. *I have long considered the watchfulness of the people over the conduct of their rulers the strongest guard against the encroachments of power; and I hope the people of this country will always be thus watchful.*' [Emphasis added, L.S.]

"Amongst others, Fisher Ames followed, in a speech of some length, in which he said:

'There was not any Government, which he knew to subsist, or which he had ever heard of, that would bear a comparison with the new Constitution. Considered merely as a literary performance, it was an honor to our country: Legislators have at length condescended to speak the language of philosophy; and, if we adopt it, we shall demonstrate to the sneering world, who deride liberty, because they have lost it, that the principles of our Government are as free as the spirit of our people.

'I repeat it, our debates have been profitable, because, upon every leading point, we are at last agreed. Very few among us now deny that a Federal Government is necessary to save us from ruin; that the Confederation is not that Government; and that the proposed Constitution, connected with the amendments, is worthy of being adopted. The question recurs, Will the amendments prevail, and become part of the system? In order to obtain such a system, as the Constitution and the amendments, there are but three ways of proceeding—to reject the whole, and begin anew; to adopt this plan, upon condition that the amendments be inserted into it; or to adopt his Excellency's proposition.'

"President Hancock concluded the debate. 'I give my assent,' said he, 'to the Constitution, in full confidence that the amendments proposed will soon become a part of the system. These amendments, being no wise local, but calculated to give security and ease alike to all the States, I think that all will agree to them.'

"The Constitution was then ratified, as we have seen, by only nineteen majority. The whole number of the Convention was three hundred and fifty-five.

"Governor Hancock, in his message to the Legislature, 27th February, 1788, communicating the action of the Convention, said:

> 'The objects of the proposed Constitution are, defence against external enemies, and the promotion of tranquillity and happiness amongst the States.
> . . .
> 'The amendments proposed by the Convention are intended to obtain a Constitutional security of the principles to which they refer themselves, and must meet the wishes of all the States. I feel myself assured, that they will very early become a part of the Constitution, and when they shall be added to the proposed plan, I shall consider it the most perfect system of Government, as to the objects it embraces, that has been known amongst mankind.'

"With this record in hand, who can doubt as to how Massachusetts understood what she was doing? Is it not clear, beyond question, that she ratified the new Constitution in place of the old? That she considered it a Compact, between States, as much as the Articles of Confederation? Was there a single supporter or advocate of it in the Convention, who did not hold it to be strictly Federal [Confederate] in its character? Did they not all understand its great object to be, as Governor Hancock said, defence against foreign enemies, and the promotion of tranquillity and happiness amongst States? Were not all their apprehensions quieted by the early adoption of their first great amendment, and nearly all the rest? Can there be a reasonable doubt on the question?

"But we will proceed to the next State in order.

SEVENTH, MARYLAND

"The action of the State of Maryland is recorded in these words:

> In Convention of the Delegates, of the people of the State of Maryland, April 28, 1788. We, the Delegates of the people of the State of Maryland, having fully considered the Constitution of the United States of America, reported to Congress, by the Convention of Deputies, from the United States of America, held in Philadelphia, on the 17th day of September, in the year 1787, of which the annexed is a copy, and submitted to us by a resolution of the General Assembly of Maryland, in November Session, 1787, do, for ourselves, and in the name, and on behalf of the people of this State, assent to, and ratify the said Constitution. In witness whereof, we have hereunto subscribed our names.

"In this State there was no material division of sentiment. There was little or no discussion. The vote on it was sixty-three to eleven. It was simply assented to, and ratified as the 'Constitution of the United States of America.' The Convention of Maryland styled it a Constitution of States.

EIGHTH, SOUTH CAROLINA

"The next State, in order, is South Carolina. First, as to the action of her Convention. That is set forth in these words:

> In Convention of the people of the State of South Carolina, by their representatives, held in the City of Charleston, on Monday, the 12th day of May, and continued by divers adjournments to Friday, the 23rd day of May, *Anno Domini*, 1788, and in the twelfth year of the Independence of the United States of America.
>
> The Convention, having maturely considered the Constitution, or form of Government, reported to Congress by the Convention of Delegates from the United States of America, and submitted to them by a resolution of the Legislature of this State, passed the 17th and 18th days of February last, in order to form a more perfect Union, establish justice, insure domestic tranquillity, provide for the common defence, promote the general welfare, and secure the blessings of liberty to the people of the said United States, and their posterity,—Do, in the name and behalf of the people of this State, hereby assent to and ratify the said Constitution.
>
> Done in Convention, the 23rd day of May, in the year of our Lord, 1788, and of the Independence of the United States of America the twelfth.
>
> And whereas, it is essential to the preservation of the rights reserved to the several States, and the freedom of the people, under the operations of a General Government, that the right of prescribing the manner, time, and places of holding the elections to the Federal Legislature, should be forever inseparably annexed to the Sovereignty of the several States,—This Convention doth declare, that the same ought to remain, to all posterity, a perpetual and fundamental right in the local, exclusive of the interference of the General Government, except in cases where the Legislatures of the States shall refuse or neglect to perform and fulfil the same, according to the tenure of the said Constitution. This Convention doth also declare, that no section or paragraph of the said Constitution warrants a construction, that the States do not retain every power not expressly relinquished by them, and vested in the General Government of the Union.
>
> Resolved, That the General Government of the United States ought never to impose direct taxes, but where the moneys arising from the duties, imposts, and excise, are insufficient for the public exigencies, nor then until Congress shall have made a requisition upon the States to assess, levy, and pay, their respective proportions of such requisitions; and in case any State shall neglect or refuse to pay its proportion, pursuant to such requisition, then

Congress may assess and levy such State's proportion, together with interest thereon, at the rate of six *per centum per annum*, from the time of payment prescribed by such requisition.

Resolved, That the third section of the sixth article ought to be amended by inserting the word 'other' between the words 'no' and 'religious.'

Resolved, That it be a standing instruction to all such Delegates as may hereafter be elected to represent this State in the General Government, to exert their utmost abilities and influence to effect an alteration of the Constitution, conformably to the aforegoing resolutions.

Done in Convention, the 23rd day of May, in the year of our Lord, 1788, and of the Independence of the United States of America the twelfth.

"In these proceedings we see, clearly, that the under standing was that the Constitution was Federal [Confederate] in its character. The Congress is styled 'The Federal Legislature,' and, in the accompanying paper, proposing amendments, the reserved Sovereignty of the several States is mentioned as a matter understood, and an express declaration that the Constitution had been assented to and ratified, with the understanding that no section or paragraph of the Constitution warranted a construction that the States did not retain every power not expressly relinquished by them. This was in the nature of a Protocol, which went up with the paper, forever fixing the understanding of the State, with which she had entered into the Compact, and the understanding with which her ratification was accepted by the other States.

"Secondly, let us look into the debates. Very few speeches, made in this Convention, have been preserved. No one disputed the character of the Government. The speeches related, mostly, to particular powers delegated. From one of them we perceive, however, that there was spirited opposition made by a respectable minority. This was headed by Patrick Dollard, of Prince Fredericks. He said,

> 'My constituents are highly alarmed at the large and rapid strides which this new Government has taken towards despotism. They say it is big with political mischiefs, and pregnant with a greater variety of impending woes to the good people of the Southern States, especially South Carolina, than all the plagues supposed to issue from the poisonous box of Pandora!'

"On the question of ratification, the vote stood 149 to 73.

"The most important debate in South Carolina, on the Constitution, was in the Legislature, on the proposition to call a Convention to take it into consideration. In this body, as in the Convention, there was a respectable and spirited minority against the Constitution, though the call for a Convention was unanimous. In the debate on that question, Hon. Rawlins Lowndes concluded his speech by saying

> 'I wish for no other epitaph, than to have inscribed on my tomb: "*Here lies the man that opposed the Constitution, because it was ruinous to the liberty of America!*"'

"These apprehensions and forebodings were, doubtless, awakened by the utterance of such sentiments as those which fell from General [Charles C.] Pinckney, in this discussion.... He did maintain that the States, severally, were never Sovereign, but in this position he was not sustained, either by the Legislature, or the Convention, as we have seen by the Protocol of the latter.

NINTH, NEW HAMPSHIRE

"The next State, in order, is New Hampshire. Her action is set forth in the following words:

> In Convention of the Delegates of the People of the State of New Hampshire, June the 21st, 1788.
>
> The Convention, having impartially discussed and fully considered the Constitution for the United States of America, reported to Congress by the Convention of Delegates from the United States of America, and submitted to us by a resolution of the General Court of said State, passed the 14th day of December last past, and acknowledging, with grateful hearts, the goodness of the Supreme Ruler of the Universe in affording the people of the United States, in the course of His providence, an opportunity, deliberately and peaceably, without fraud or surprise, of entering into an explicit and solemn compact with each other, by assenting to and ratifying a *new Constitution* [emphasis added, L.S.] in order to form a more perfect Union, establish Justice, insure domestic tranquillity, provide for the common defence, promote the general welfare, and secure the blessings of liberty to themselves and their posterity,—Do, in the name and behalf of the people of the State of New Hampshire, assent to and ratify the said Constitution for the United States of America. And as it is the opinion of this Convention, that certain amendments and alterations, in the said Constitution would remove the fears and quiet the apprehensions of many of the good people of this State, and more effectually guard against an undue administration of the Federal Government,—The Convention do, therefore, recommend that the following alterations and provisions be introduced in the said Constitution:—
>
> I. That it be explicitly declared that all powers not expressly and particularly delegated by the aforesaid Constitution, are reserved to the several States, to be by them exercised.
>
> II. That there shall be one representative to every thirty thousand persons, according to the census mentioned in the Constitution, until the whole number of representatives amount to two hundred.

III. That Congress do not exercise the powers vested in them, by the fourth section of the first article, but in cases when a State shall neglect or refuse to make the regulations therein mentioned, or shall make regulations subversive of the rights of the people to a free and equal representation in Congress; nor shall Congress in any case make regulations contrary to a free and equal representation.

IV. That Congress do not lay direct taxes, but when the moneys arising from impost, excise, and their other resources, are insufficient for the public exigencies; nor then, until Congress shall have first made a requisition upon the States to assess, levy, and pay, their respective proportions of such requisition, agreeably to the census fixed in the said Constitution, in such way and manner as the Legislature of the State shall think best; and in such case, if any State shall neglect, then Congress may assess and levy such State's proportion, together with the interest thereon, at the rate of six *per cent. per annum*, from the time of payment prescribed in such requisition.

V. That Congress shall erect no company of merchants with exclusive advantages of commerce.

VI. That no person shall be tried for any crime, by which he may incur an infamous punishment, or loss of life, until he first be indicted by a grand jury, except in such cases as may arise in the Government and regulation of the land and naval forces.

VII. All common-law cases, between citizens of different States, shall be commenced in the common law courts of the respective States; and no appeal shall be allowed to the Federal court, in such cases, unless the sum or value of the thing in controversy amount to three thousand dollars.

VIII. In civil actions, between citizens of different States, every issue of fact, arising in actions at common-law, shall be tried by jury, if the parties, or either of them, request it.

IX. Congress shall at no time consent that any person, holding an office of trust or profit under the United States, shall accept any title of nobility, or any other title or office, from any king, prince, or foreign State.

X. That no standing army shall be kept up in time of peace, unless with the consent of three fourths of the members of each branch of Congress; nor shall soldiers, in time of peace, be quartered upon private houses, without the consent of the owners.

XI. Congress shall make no laws touching religion, or to infringe the rights of conscience.

XII. Congress shall never disarm any citizen, unless such as are or have been in actual rebellion.

And the Convention do, in the name and in behalf of the people of this State, enjoin it upon their representatives in Congress, at all times, until the alterations and provisions aforesaid have been considered, agreeably to the fifth article of the said Constitution, to exert all their influence, and use all reasonable and legal methods, to obtain a ratification of the said alterations and provisions, in such manner as is provided in the article.

And that the United States, in Congress assembled, may have due notice of the assent and ratification of the said Constitution by this Convention, it is Resolved, That the assent and ratification aforesaid be engrossed on parchment, together with the recommendation and injunction aforesaid, and with this resolution; and that John Sullivan, Esqr., President of the Convention, and John Langdon, Esqr., President of the State, transmit the same, countersigned by the Secretary of Convention, and the Secretary of State, under their hands and seals, to the United States in Congress assembled.

"New Hampshire followed the precedent of Massachusetts, and adopted her form of proceedings throughout, in almost the same words. No farther comment is necessary on these. What has just been said on the Massachusetts ratification is applicable with all its force to that of New Hampshire. But one speech, made in the Convention of this State, has been preserved, and that throws no light upon the object of our inquiry. The action of the Convention, however, abundantly shows that the new Constitution was understood to be Federal [Confederate] in its character as the old one was.

TENTH, VIRGINIA

"We come now to Virginia, the mother of States, as she has properly been called.

"First, we will look into her action, then into the debates. The words of her ratification are as follows:—

We, the Delegates of the people of Virginia, duly elected in pursuance of a recommendation from the General Assembly, and now met in Convention, having fully and freely investigated and discussed the proceedings of the Federal Convention, and being prepared as well as the most mature deliberation hath enabled us, to decide thereon,—Do, in the name and in behalf of the people of Virginia, declare and make known, that the powers granted under the Constitution, being derived from the people of the United States, may be resumed by them, whensoever the same shall be perverted to their injury or oppression, and that every power not granted thereby remains with them, and at their will; that, therefore, no right, of any denomination, can be cancelled, abridged, restrained, or modified, by the Congress, by the Senate or House of Representatives, acting in any capacity, by the President, or any department or officer of the United States, except in those instances in which power is given by the Constitution for those purposes; and that, among other essential rights, the liberty of conscience, and of the press, cannot be cancelled, abridged, restrained, or modified, by any authority of the United States. With these impressions, with a solemn appeal to the Searcher of all hearts for the purity of our intentions, and under the conviction that whatsoever imperfections may exist in the Constitution ought rather to be examined in the mode prescribed therein, than to bring the Union into danger by a delay with a hope of obtaining amendments previous to the ratifications,—We, the said Delegates, in the name and in behalf of the people of Virginia, do, by these presents, assent to and ratify the Constitution recommended, on the 17th day of September, 1787, by the Federal Convention, for the Government of the United States, hereby announcing to all those whom it may concern, that the said Constitution is binding upon the said people, according to an authentic copy hereto annexed, in the words following.

Done in Convention, this 26th day of June, 1788.

"The language here used by the Convention of Virginia, in her adoption of the Constitution, styles the instrument a Constitution 'for the Government of the United States.' The form of expression is the same as that used by Georgia. The meaning is the same in both. It was to be a Constitution for the Government of States in their foreign and inter State affairs. *It is to be noted that in it they expressly declare and make known that the powers granted under it may be resumed by them whensoever they may be perverted to their injury.* [Emphasis added, L.S.]

"[It is clear then that the people of Virginia understood that, because the powers granted under the Constitution are derived from the people of the United States, that they could resume these powers by themselves. To clarify, let me explain in more depth.] The meaning of the people of the United States here, is, the people of the States severally. This is clear. The delegation of the powers was by the States severally. Whoever delegates can resume. The right to resume or recall attends all delegations of all sorts. Where there is a separate or several delegation there cannot be a joint resumption. The resumption must be by the party making the delegation. But the debates in the Convention remove all doubts as to their understanding upon this point. These are the *res gestæ* that fully explain it.

"Secondly, then, let us look into the debates.

"In Virginia, as in Massachusetts, the Constitution underwent a thorough discussion. The Convention was in session nearly a month. Many of the ablest men of the State were members of it. Men who had first put the ball of the Revolution in motion. Patrick Henry was there. George Mason, Bushrod Washington, Henry Lee of Westmoreland, George Nicholas, Edmund Pendleton, Edmund Randolph, James Monroe, James Madison, and John Marshall. A brighter galaxy of talent, statesmanship and oratory was never assembled in the Old Dominion. The debates fill a large volume by themselves. Here it is. Let us glean from these discussions the leading ideas of the advocates as well as the opponents of the Constitution on the main point of our inquiry, that is, the nature and character of the Government instituted by it. As in Massachusetts, so in Virginia, the opposition was able and formidable. The greatest orator of the age headed it, Patrick Henry:

> '*This proposal of altering our Federal Government is of a most alarming nature! Make the best of this new Government—say it is composed by any thing but inspiration—you ought to be extremely cautious, watchful, jealous of your liberty; for, instead of securing your rights, you may lose them forever*. . . . [Emphasis added, L.S.]
>
> '*I have the highest veneration for those gentlemen; but, sir, give me leave to demand, What right had they to say, 'We, the people?' My political curiosity, exclusive of my anxious solicitude for the public welfare, leads me to ask, who authorized them to speak the language of, 'We, the people,' instead of, 'We, the States?' States are the characteristics and the soul of a Confederation! If the States be not the agents of this Compact, it must be one great, consolidated, National Government, of all the States!*' [Emphasis added, L.S.]

"Edmund Pendleton, President of the Convention, answered:

> "'We, the people,' possessing all power, form a Government, such as we think will secure happiness: and suppose, in adopting this plan, we should be mistaken in the end; where is the cause of alarm on that quarter? In the same plan we point out an easy and quiet method of reforming what may be found amiss. No, but, say gentlemen, we have put the introduction of that method in the hands of our servants, who will interrupt it from motives of self-interest. What then? We will resist, did my friend say? conveying an idea of force. Who shall dare to resist the people? No, we will assemble in Convention; wholly recall our delegated powers, or reform them so as to prevent such abuse. . . .
>
> 'This is the only Government founded in real Compact. There is no quarrel between Government and liberty; the former is the shield and protector of the latter.'

[Patrick Henry later replied:]

> '*This Constitution is said to have beautiful features, but, when I come to examine these features, sir, they appear to me horribly frightful! Among other deformities, it has an awful squinting; it squints towards monarchy; and does not this raise indignation in the breast of every true American?* [Emphasis added, L.S.]
>
> 'We are told that this Government, collectively taken, is without an example; that it is National in this part, and Federal [Confederate] in that part, etc. We may be amused, if we please, by a treatise of political anatomy. In the brain it is National; the stamina are Federal; some limbs are Federal,

others National. The Senators are voted for by the State Legislatures; so far it is Federal. Individuals choose the Members of the first branch; here it is National. It is Federal in conferring general powers, but National in retaining them. It is not to be supported by the States; the pockets of individuals are to be searched for its maintenance. What signifies it to me that you have the most curious anatomical description of it in its creation? To all the common purposes of legislation, it is a great Consolidation of Government. You are not to have the right to legislate in any but trivial cases; you are not to touch private contracts; you are not to have the right of having arms in your own defence; you cannot be trusted with dealing out justice between man and man. What shall the States have to do? Take care of the poor, repair and make highways, erect bridges, and so on, and so on? Abolish the State Legislatures at once. What purposes should they be continued for? Our Legislature will, indeed, be a ludicrous spectacle—one hundred and eighty men marching in solemn, farcical procession, exhibiting a mournful proof of the lost liberty of their country, without the power of restoring it. But, sir, we have the consolation that it is a mixed Government; that is, it may work sorely on your neck, but you will have some comfort by saying, that it was a Federal Government in its origin.

'*I beg gentlemen to consider: lay aside your prejudices. Is this a Federal [Confederate] Government? Is it not a consolidated [National] Government for almost every purpose? Is the Government of Virginia a State Government after this Government is adopted? I grant that it is a republican Government, but for what purposes? For such trivial domestic considerations as render it unworthy the name of a Legislature. I shall take leave of this political anatomy, by observing that it is the most extraordinary that ever entered into the imagination of man. If our political diseases demand a cure, this is an unheard-of medicine. The honorable member, I am convinced, wanted a name for it. Were your health in danger, would you take new medicine? I need not make use of these exclamations; for every member in this committee must be alarmed at making new and unusual experiments in Government.*' [Emphasis added, L.S.]

"Mr. [Henry] Lee answered:

'But, sir, this is a Consolidated Government, he tells us; and most feelingly does he dwell on the imaginary dangers of this pretended Consolidation. I did suppose that an honorable gentleman, whom I do not now see (Mr. James Madison), had placed this in such a clear light that every man would have been satisfied with it.

'If this were a consolidated Government, ought it not to be ratified by a majority of the people as individuals, and not as States? Suppose Virginia, Connecticut, Massachusetts, and Pennsylvania, had ratified it; these four States, being a majority of the people of America, would, by their adoption, have made it binding on all the States, had this been a Consolidated

Government. But it is only the Governments of those seven States who have adopted it. If the honorable gentleman will attend to this, we shall hear no more of Consolidation. . . .

'I say, that this new system shows, in stronger terms than words could declare, that the liberties of the people are secure. It goes on the principle that all power is in the people, and that rulers have no powers but what are enumerated in that paper. When a question arises with respect to the legality of any power, exercised or assumed by Congress, it is plain on the side of the governed: Is it enumerated in the Constitution? If it be, it is legal and just. It is otherwise arbitrary and unconstitutional. Candor must confess that it is infinitely more attentive to the liberties of the people than any State Government.'

[Stephens' note:] "(Mr. Lee then said, that, under the State Governments, the people reserved to themselves certain enumerated rights, and that the rest were vested in their rulers; that, consequently, the powers reserved to the people were but an inconsiderable exception from what were given to their rulers; but that, in the Federal Government, the rulers of the people were vested with certain defined powers, and that what were not delegated to those rulers were retained by the people. The consequence of this, he said, was, that the limited powers were only an exception to those which rested in the people, and that they knew what they had given up, and could be in no danger. He exemplified the proposition in a familiar manner. He observed, that, if a man delegated certain powers to an agent, it would be an insult upon common sense to suppose that the agent could legally transact any business for his principal which was not contained in the commission whereby the powers were delegated; but that if a man empowered his representative or agent to transact all his business except certain enumerated parts, the clear result was, that the agent could lawfully transact every possible part of his principal's business, except the enumerated parts; and added, that these plain propositions were sufficient to demonstrate the inutility and folly—were he permitted to use the expression—of bills of rights.)

"Governor Randolph, who had favored a National Government in the Convention, replied as follows:

'The liberty of the press is supposed to be in danger. If this were the case, it would produce extreme repugnancy in my mind. If it ever will be suppressed in this country, the liberty of the people will not be far from being sacrificed. Where is the danger of it? He says that every power is given to the General Government that is not reserved to the States. Pardon me if I say the reverse of the proposition is true. I defy any one to prove the contrary. Every power not given it by this system is left with the States.'

"John Marshall (afterwards Chief Justice), in reply to Mr. Henry, said:

> 'We are threatened with the loss of our liberties by the possible abuse of power, notwithstanding the maxim, that those who give may take away. It is the people that give power, and can take it back. What shall restrain them? They are the masters who give it, and of whom their servants hold it.' [Emphasis added, L.S.]

"George Nicholas said:

> 'But it is objected to for want of a bill of rights. It is a principle universally agreed upon, that all powers not given are retained. Where, by the Constitution, the General Government has general powers for any purpose, its powers are absolute. Where it has powers with some exceptions, they are absolute only as to those exceptions. In either case, the people retain what is not conferred on the General Government, as it is by their positive grant that it has any of its powers. In England, in all disputes between the king and people, recurrence is had to the enumerated rights of the people, to determine. Are the rights in dispute secured? Are they included in Magna Charta, Bill of Rights, etc.? If not, they are, generally speaking, within the king's prerogative. In disputes between the Congress and the people, the reverse of the proposition holds. Is the disputed right enumerated? If not, Congress cannot meddle with it.'

"Mr. [James] Madison said:

> 'The powers of the General Government relate to external objects, and are but few. But the powers in the States relate to those great objects which immediately concern the prosperity of the people. Let us observe, also, that *the powers in the General Government are those which will be exercised mostly in time of war, while those of the State Governments will be exercised in time of peace.* I should not complete the view which ought to be taken of this subject, without making this additional remark,—that the powers vested in the proposed Government are not so much an augmentation of powers in the General Government, as a change rendered necessary for the purpose of giving efficacy to those which were vested in it before. It cannot escape any gentleman, that this power, in theory, exists in the Confederation as fully as in this Constitution. The only difference is this—that now they tax States, and by this plan they will tax individuals. There is no theoretic difference between the two. But in practice there will be an infinite difference between them. The one is an ineffectual power; the other is adequate to the purpose for which it is given. This change was necessary for the public safety. [Emphasis added, L.S.]
>
> 'Let us suppose, for a moment, that the acts of Congress, requiring money from the States, had been as effectual as the paper on the table; suppose all the

laws of Congress had complete compliance; will any gentleman say that, as far as we can judge from past experience, the State Governments would have been debased, and all consolidated and incorporated into one system? My imagination cannot reach it. I conceive that had those acts that effect, which all laws ought to have, the States would have retained their Sovereignty.'

"George Mason (in opposition) said:

> 'The objection was, that too much power was given to Congress—*power that would finally destroy the State Governments more effectually by insidious, underhanded means, than such as could be openly practiced*.' [Emphasis added, L.S.]

"Mr. Marshall replied:

> 'When the Government is drawn from the people, and depending on the people for its continuance, oppressive measures will not be attempted, as they will certainly draw on their authors the resentment of those on whom they depend. On this Government, thus depending on ourselves for its existence, I will rest my safety, notwithstanding the danger depicted by the honorable gentleman. I cannot help being surprised that the worthy member thought this power so dangerous.'

"[Marshall] . . . then concluded by observing, that

> 'the power of governing the militia was not vested in the States, by implication, because, being possessed of it antecedent to the adoption of the Government, and not being divested of it by any grant or restriction in the Constitution, they must necessarily be as fully possessed of it as ever they had been. And it could not be said that any of the States derived any powers from that system, but retained them, though not acknowledged in any part of it.'

"Mr. Henry again spoke, as follows:

> 'A bill of rights may be summed up in a few words. What do they tell us? That our rights are reserved. Why not say so? Is it because it will consume too much paper? Gentlemen's reasoning against a bill of rights does not satisfy me—without saying which has the right side, it remains doubtful. A bill of rights is a favorite thing with the Virginians, and the people of the other States, likewise. It may be their prejudice, but the Government ought to suit their geniuses; otherwise, its operation will be unhappy. A bill of rights, even if its necessity be doubtful, will exclude the possibility of dispute; and, with great submission, I think the best way is to have no dispute. In the present Constitution, they are restrained from issuing general warrants to search suspected places, or seize persons not named, without evidence of the commission of a

fact, etc. There was certainly some celestial influence governing those who deliberated on that Constitution; for they have, with the most cautious and enlightened circumspection, guarded those indefeasible rights which ought ever to be held sacred!' [Emphasis added, L.S.]

"Mr. George Nicholas, in answer, said:

'That, though there was a declaration of rights in the Government of Virginia, it was no conclusive reason that there should be one in this Constitution; for, if it was unnecessary in the former, its omission in the latter could be no defect. They ought, therefore, to prove that it was essentially necessary to be inserted in the Constitution of Virginia. There were five or six States in the Union which had no bill of rights, separately and distinctly as such; but they annexed the substance of a bill of rights to their respective Constitutions. These States . . . were as free as this State, and their liberties as secure as ours. If so, gentlemen's arguments from the precedent were not good. In Virginia, all powers were given to the Government without any exception. It was different in the General Government, to which certain special powers were delegated for certain purposes. He asked which was the more safe. Was it safer to grant general powers than certain limited powers?

'. . . A bill of rights is only an acknowledgment of the pre-existing claim to rights in the people. They belong to us as much as if they had been inserted in the Constitution. But it is said that, if it be doubtful, the possibility of dispute ought to be precluded. Admitting it was proper for the Convention to have inserted a bill of rights, it is not proper here to propose it as the condition of our accession to the Union. Would you reject this Government for its omission, dissolve the Union, and bring miseries on yourselves and posterity? I hope the gentleman does not oppose it on this ground solely. Is there another reason? He said that it is not only the general wish of this State, but all the States, to have a bill of rights. If it be so, where is the difficulty of having this done by way of subsequent amendment? We shall find the other States willing to accord with their own favorite wish. The gentleman last up says that the power of legislation includes every thing. A general power of legislation does. But this is a special power of legislation. Therefore, it does not contain that plenitude of power which he imagines. They cannot legislate in any case but those particularly enumerated. No gentleman, who is a friend to the Government, ought to withhold his assent from it for this reason.'

"Mr. Henry continued his strenuous opposition in the following language:

'The Honorable gentleman (Gov. Randolph), who was up some time ago, exhorts us not to fall into a repetition of the defects of the Confederation. He said, we ought not to declare that each State retains every power, jurisdiction, and right, which is not expressly delegated, because experience has proved the insertion of such a restriction to be destructive, and mentioned an instance to prove it. That case, Mr. Chairman, appears to me to militate against himself. . . . They can exercise power, by implication, in one instance as well as in another. Thus, by the gentleman's own argument, they can exercise the power, though it be not delegated. . . . We have nothing local to ask. We ask rights which concern the general happiness. Must not justice bring them into the concession of these? The honorable gentleman was pleased to say that the new Government, in this policy, will be equal to what the present is. If so, that amendment will not injure that part. . . .

'He speaks of war and bloodshed. Whence do this war and bloodshed come? I fear it, but not from the source he speaks of. I fear it, sir, from the operation and friends of the Federal Government. He speaks with contempt of this amendment. But whoever will advert to the use made, repeatedly, in England, of the prerogative of the king, and the frequent attacks on the privileges of the people, notwithstanding many Legislative acts to secure them, will see the necessity of excluding implications. Nations who have trusted to logical deductions have lost their liberty! . . .

'The worthy member who proposed to ratify has also proposed that what amendments may be deemed necessary should be recommended to Congress, and that a committee should be appointed to consider what amendments were necessary. But what does it all come to at last? That it is a vain project, and that it is indecent and improper! I will not argue unfairly, but I will ask him if amendments are not unattainable? Will gentlemen, then, lay their hands on their hearts, and say that they can adopt it in this shape? When we demand this security of our privileges, the language of Virginia is not that of respect! Give me leave to deny! She only asks amendments previous to her adoption of the Constitution. . . .

'He tells you of the important blessings which, he imagines, will result to us and mankind in general from the adoption of this system [a bill of rights]. I see the awful immensity of the dangers with which it is pregnant! I see it! I feel it! I see beings of a higher order anxious concerning our decision! When I see beyond the horizon that bounds human eyes, and look at the final consummation of all human things, and see those intelligent beings which inhabit the ethereal mansions, reviewing the political decisions and revolutions which, in the progress of time, will happen in America, and the consequent happiness or misery of mankind, I am led to believe that much of the account, on one side or the other, will depend on what we now decide! Our own happiness alone is not affected by the event! All nations are interested in the determination! We have it in our power to secure the happiness of one half of the human race! Its adoption may involve the misery of the other hemisphere!'

"Just at this point in Mr. Henry's speech, the heavens blackened with a gathering tempest [a violent rain storm], which burst with so terrible a fury as to put the whole House in such disorder that he could proceed no farther! It was the last speech that Patrick Henry made in that Convention!

"Did he possess a superhuman vision, or had he caught something of the spirit of the ancient prophets, which enabled him to see farther into the future, and understand better the workings of political systems controlled by human passion, than any of his many great and equally patriotic colleagues, in that renowned body of sages and statesmen? Did he see farther in the future than [Edmund] Pendleton, [James] Madison, or [John] Marshall, when he said, 'I see it! I feel it!' Did he get glimpses of the terrible scenes of the last seven years [1861-1868]? or, of the still more horrible ones yet ahead of us? [The horrors of so-called "Reconstruction" indeed were to last another nine years, until 1877.]

"Mr. [George] Nicholas replied, by urging

> 'that the language of the proposed ratification would secure every thing which gentlemen desired, as it declared that all powers vested in the Constitution were derived from the people, and might be resumed by them whensoever they should be perverted to their injury and oppression; and that every power not granted thereby remained at their will. No danger whatever could arise; for, says he, these expressions will become a part of the contract. The Constitution cannot be binding on Virginia, but with these conditions. If thirteen individuals are about to make a contract, and one agrees to it, but at the same time declares that he understands its meaning, signification, and intent, to be (what the words of the contract plainly and obviously denote), that it is not to be construed so as to impose any supplementary condition upon him, and that he is to be exonerated from it whensoever any such imposition shall be attempted,—I ask whether, in this case, these conditions, on which he has assented to it, would not be binding on the other twelve? In like manner these conditions will be binding on Congress. They can exercise no power that is not expressly granted them.'

"On the question of ratification, the vote stood 89 to 79, being only ten majority in its favor.

"Immediately afterwards the amendments, which had been agreed upon to be proposed, were taken up and adopted, without opposition. They were twenty in number. Very similar, in many respects, to those incorporated by Massachusetts in her ratification. The first, and most important, was in these words:

> 1st. That each State in the Union shall, respectively, retain every power, jurisdiction, and right, which is not by this Constitution delegated to the Congress of the United States, or to the departments of the Federal

Government.

"These proceedings conclusively show how the Convention of Virginia understood the Constitution. That is, that it was Federal [Confederate] in its character, and that the Government under it was to be a Federal [Confederate] Government, one founded upon Compact between Sovereign States. Not a member of the Convention advocated the Constitution upon any other principles. The opposition of Patrick Henry, George Mason, and others, was altogether argumentative, and sprung mainly from apprehensions that the Constitution would not be construed as its friends maintained that it would be, and that powers not delegated would be assumed, by construction and implication. These proceedings also show clearly, that Virginia understood by the declaration, in her ratification, that her people had the right to resume the powers that they had delegated, in case these powers, in their judgment, should be perverted to their injury.

ELEVENTH, NEW YORK

"The next State, in order, is New York. First we will see what was done by her Convention. Here is her ratification.

> We, the Delegates of the people of the State of New York, duly elected, and met in Convention, having maturely considered the Constitution for the United States of America, agreed to on the 17th day of September, in the year 1787, by the Convention then assembled at Philadelphia, in the Commonwealth of Pennsylvania (a copy whereof precedes these presents), and having, also, seriously and deliberately considered the present situation of the United States,—Do declare and make known,—
>
> That all power is originally vested in, and consequently derived from the people, and that Government is instituted by them for their common interest, protection, and security.
>
> That the enjoyment of life, liberty, and the pursuit of happiness, are essential rights, which every Government ought to respect and preserve.
>
> That the powers of Government may be re-assumed by the people, whensoever it shall become necessary to their happiness; that every power, jurisdiction, and right, which is not by the said Constitution clearly delegated to the Congress of the United States, or the departments of the Government thereof, remains to the people of the several States, or to their respective State Governments, to whom they may have granted the same; and that those clauses, in the said Constitution, which declare that Congress shall not have or exercise certain powers, do not imply that Congress is entitled to any powers not given by the said Constitution; but such clauses are to be construed either as exceptions to certain specified powers, or as inserted merely for greater caution.

That the people have an equal, natural, and unalienable right, freely and peaceably, to exercise their religion, according to the dictates of conscience; and that no religious sect, or society, ought to be favored or established by law in preference to others.

That the people have a right to keep and bear arms; that a well regulated militia, including the body of the people capable of bearing arms, is the proper, natural, and safe defence of a free State.

That the militia should not be subject to martial law, except in time of war, rebellion or insurrection.

That standing armies, in time of peace, are dangerous to liberty, and ought not to be kept up, except in cases of necessity, and that at all times the military should be under strict subordination to the civil power.

That, in time of peace, no soldier ought to be quartered in any house without the consent of the owner, and in time of war only by the civil magistrate, in such manner as the laws may direct.

That no person ought to be taken, imprisoned, or disseized of his freehold, or be exiled, or deprived of his privileges, franchises, life, liberty, or property, but by due process of law.

That no person ought to be put twice in jeopardy of life or limb, for one and the same offence; nor, unless in case of impeachment, be punished more than once for the same offence. That every person restrained of his liberty is entitled to an inquiry into the lawfulness of such restraint, and to a removal thereof if unlawful; and that such inquiry, or removal, ought not to be denied or delayed, except when, on account of public danger, the Congress shall suspend the privilege of the writ of *Habeas Corpus*. That excessive bail ought not to be required, nor excessive fines imposed, nor cruel or unusual punishments inflicted.

That (except in the government of the land and naval forces, and of the militia, when in actual service, and in cases of impeachment) a presentment, or indictment, by a grand jury, ought to be observed, as a necessary preliminary to the trial of all crimes cognizable by the judiciary of the United States; and such trial should be speedy, public, and by an impartial jury of the county where the crime was committed; and that no person can be found guilty without the unanimous consent of such jury. But in cases of crimes not committed within any county of any of the United States, and in cases of crimes not committed within any county in which a general insurrection may prevail, or which may be in the possession of a foreign enemy, the inquiry and trial may be in such county as the Congress shall by law direct; which county, in the two cases last mentioned, should be as near as conveniently may be to that county in which the crime may have been committed;—and that, in all criminal prosecutions, the accused ought to be informed of the cause and nature of his accusation, to be confronted with his accusers and the witnesses against him, to have the means of producing his witnesses, and the assistance of counsel for his defence; and should not be compelled to give evidence against himself.

That the trial by jury, in the extent that it obtains by the common law of England, is one of the greatest securities to the rights of a free people, and ought to remain inviolate.

That every freeman has a right to be secure from all unreasonable searches and seizures of his person, his papers, or his property; and, therefore, that all warrants to search suspected places, or seize any freeman, his papers, or property, without information upon oath, or affirmation of sufficient cause, are grievous and oppressive; and that all general warrants (or such in which the place or person suspected are not particularly designated) are dangerous, and ought not to be granted.

That the people have a right peaceably to assemble together, to consult for their common good, or to instruct their representatives, and that every person has a right to petition, or apply to the Legislature, for redress of grievances.

That the freedom of the press ought not to be violated, or restrained.

That there should be, once in four years, an election of the President and Vice President, so that no officer, who may be appointed by the Congress, to act as President, in case of the removal, death, resignation, or inability, of the President and Vice President, can in any case continue to act beyond the termination of the period for which the last President and Vice President were elected.

That nothing contained in the said Constitution is to be construed to prevent the Legislature of any State from passing laws at its discretion, from time to time, to divide such State into convenient districts, and to apportion its Representatives to and amongst such districts.

That the prohibition contained in the said Constitution, against *ex post facto* laws, extends only to laws concerning crimes.

That all appeals in causes determinable according to the course of the common law, ought to be by writ of error, and not otherwise.

That the judicial power of the United States, in cases in which a State may be a party, does not extend to criminal prosecutions, or to authorize any suit by any person against a State.

That the judicial power of the United States, as to controversies between citizens of the same State, claiming lands under grants from different States, is not to be construed to extend to any other controversies between them, except those which relate to such lands, so claimed, under grants of different States.

That the jurisdiction of the Supreme Court of the United States, or of any other Court to be instituted by the Congress, is not in any case to be increased, enlarged, or extended, by any faction, collusion, or mere suggestion; and that no treaty is to be construed so to operate as to alter the Constitution of any State.

Under these impressions, and declaring that the rights aforesaid cannot be abridged, or violated, and that the explanations aforesaid, are consistent with the said Constitution, and in confidence that the amendments, which shall have been proposed to the said Constitution, will receive an early and mature consideration. We, the said delegates, in the name and in the behalf of the people of the State of New York, do, by these presents, assent to, and ratify the said Constitution. In full confidence, nevertheless, that, until a Convention shall be called and convened, for proposing amendments to the said Constitution, the militia of this State will not be continued in service out of this State for a longer term than six weeks, without the consent of the Legislature thereof; that the Congress will not make or alter any regulation in this State, respecting the times, places, and manner, of holding elections for Senators or Representatives, unless the Legislature of this State shall neglect or refuse to make laws or regulations for the purpose, or from any circumstance, be incapable of making the same; and that in those cases, such power will only be exercised until the Legislature of this State shall make provision in the premises; that no excise will be imposed on any article of the growth, production, or manufacture of the United States, or any of them, within this State, ardent spirits [strong alcoholic liquors] excepted; and that Congress will not lay direct taxes within this State, but when the moneys arising from the impost and excise shall be insufficient for the public exigencies, nor then, until Congress shall first have made a requisition upon this State, to assess, levy, and pay, the amount of such requisition, made agreeably to the census fixed in the said Constitution, in such way and manner as the Legislature of this State shall judge best; but that, in such case, if the State shall neglect or refuse to pay its proportion, pursuant to such requisition, then the Congress may assess and levy this State's proportion, together with interest, at the rate of six *per centum per annum*, from the time at which the same was required to be paid.

Done, in Convention, at Poughkeepsie, in the county of Duchess, in the State of New York, the 26th day of July, in the year of our Lord 1788.

"A careful perusal of these proceedings leaves no doubt as to how the Convention of New York understood the Constitution. They recognized it as a Constitution for States. As Virginia, New York accompanied her ratification with the express declaration that the powers of Government may be resumed by the people whensoever it shall become necessary to their happiness, etc. 'Under these impressions, and declaring that the rights aforesaid (after the enumeration of many, especially the reserved rights of the people of the several States as States) cannot be abridged or violated,' a majority of the members of the Convention gave it their assent and ratification. So much for what was done.

"Secondly, let us examine the *res gestæ*—the debates.

"In New York the opposition was stronger in numbers, comparatively, than in Virginia. On the final vote on the ratification there was but three majority in its favor. Some of the ablest men of the State were in the Convention. At the head of the list may be placed the venerable Robert R. Livingston, the Chancellor of the State. Next to him stood Alexander Hamilton, who had been in the Philadelphia Convention.

"Now let us, as in the other State Conventions, sample the debates in this. The Constitution here, as in Massachusetts and Virginia, was thoroughly discussed. How was it understood by its advocates?

"Chancellor Livingston opened the discussion. After some general remarks 'he next adverted to the form of the Federal Government. He said that, though justified when considered as a mere diplomatic body, making engagements for its respective States, which they were to carry into effect, yet, if it was to enjoy legislative, judicial, and executive powers, an attention as well to the facility of doing business as to the principles of freedom, called for a division of those powers.'

"In another speech afterwards, he says:

'The gentleman from Duchess [County] appears to have misapprehended some of the ideas which dropped from me. My argument was, that a Republic might very properly be formed by a league of States, but that the laws of the general Legislature must act, and be enforced upon individuals. I am contending for this species of Government. The gentlemen who have spoken in opposition to me have either misunderstood or perverted my meaning; but, sir, I flatter myself, it has not been misunderstood by the Convention at large.

'If we examine the history of the Federal Republics, whose legislative powers were exercised only in States, in their collective capacity, we shall find in their fundamental principles the seeds of domestic violence and consequent annihilation. This was the principal reason why I thought the old Confederation would be forever impracticable.' [Stephens' note:] (Livingston was for a Government founded on a Compact or League of States, with authority to act on the individual citizens of each State, and maintained that such was the form of Government then presented.)

'... Let us take a view of the present Congress. The gentleman is satisfied with our present Federal Government, on the score of corruption. Here he has confidence. Though each State may delegate seven, they generally sent no more than three; consequently thirty-nine men may transact any business under the old Government; while the new Legislature, which will be, in all probability, constantly full, will consist of ninety-one. But, says the gentleman, our present Congress have not the same powers. I answer, they have the very same. Congress have the power of making war and peace, of levying money and raising men; they may involve us in a war at their pleasure; they may negotiate loans to any extent, and make unlimited demands upon the States. Here the gentleman comes forward, and says, that the States are to carry these powers into execution; and they have the power of non-compliance. But is not every State bound to comply? What power have they to control Congress in the exercise of those rights which they have pledged themselves to support? It is true they have broken, in numerous instances, the compact by which they were obligated; and they may do it again; but will the gentleman draw an argument of security from the facility of violating their faith? Suppose there should be a majority of creditor States, under the present Government; might they not combine, and compel us to observe the covenants by which we had bound ourselves?

'We are told that this Constitution gives Congress the power over the purse and the sword. Sir, have not all good Governments this power? Nay, does any one doubt that, under the old Confederation, Congress holds the purse and the sword? How many loans did they procure, which we are bound to pay! How many men did they raise, whom we are bound to maintain! How will gentlemen say, that that body, which is indeed extremely small, can be more safely trusted than a much larger body possessed of the same authority? What is the ground of such entire confidence in the one—what the cause of so much jealousy of the other?'

"Mr. Williams, in opposition, spoke as follows:

'Sir, I yesterday expressed my fears that this clause would tend to annihilate the State Governments. I also observed, that the powers granted by it were indefinite, since the Congress are authorized to provide for the common defence and general welfare, and to pass all laws necessary for the attainment of these important objects. The Legislature is the highest power in a Government. Whatever they judge necessary for the proper administration of the powers lodged in them, they may execute without any check or impediment. Now, if the Congress should judge it a proper provision, for the common defence and general welfare, that the State Governments should be essentially destroyed, what, in the name of common sense, will prevent them? Are they not Constitutionally authorized to pass such laws? Are not the terms, common defence and general welfare, indefinite, indefinable terms? What checks have the State Governments against such encroachments? Why, they appoint the Senators once in six years. So do the electors of Germany appoint their Emperor. And what restraint have they against tyranny in their head? Do they rely upon any thing but arms, the *ultima ratio* [the "final argument"]? And to this most undesirable point must the States recur in order to secure their rights.'

"Mr. [Alexander] Hamilton, on the other side, said:

'Sir, the most powerful obstacle to the members of Congress betraying the interest of their constituents, is the State Legislatures themselves, who will be standing bodies of observation, possessing the confidence of the people, jealous of Federal encroachments, and armed with every power to check the first essays of treachery. They will institute regular modes of inquiry. The complicated domestic attachments, which subsist between the State Legislators and their electors, will ever make them vigilant guardians of the people's rights. Possessed of the means and the disposition of resistance, the spirit of opposition will be easily communicated to the people, and, under the conduct of an organized body of leaders, will act with weight and system. Thus, it appears that the very structure of the Confederacy affords the surest preventions from error, and the most powerful checks to misconduct.

'. . . The gentlemen are afraid that the State Governments will be abolished. But, sir, their existence does not depend upon the laws of the United States. Congress can no more abolish the State Governments, than they can dissolve the Union. The whole Constitution is repugnant to it, and yet the gentleman would introduce an additional useless provision against it.'

"Mr. [John] Lansing, doubting, expressed himself as follows:

'I know not that history furnishes an example of a Confederated Republic coercing the States composing it, by the mild influence of laws operating on the individuals of those States. This, therefore, I suppose to be a new experiment in politics; and, as we cannot always accurately ascertain the results of political measures, and, as reasoning on them has been frequently found fallacious, we should not too confidently predict those to be produced by the new system.'

"Mr. Hamilton, in a general exposition of the Constitution, said:

'We contend that the radical vice in the old Confederation is, that the laws of the Union apply only to States in their corporate capacity. Has not every man, who has been in our Legislature, experienced the truth of this position? It is inseparable from the disposition of bodies, who have a Constitutional power of resistance, to examine the merits of a law. This has ever been the case with the Federal requisitions. In this examination, not being furnished with those lights which directed the deliberations of the general Government, and incapable of embracing the general interests of the Union, the States have almost uniformly weighed the requisitions by their own local interests, and have only executed them so far as answered their particular convenience or advantage.

'. . . It has been observed, to coerce the States is one of the maddest projects that was ever devised. A failure of compliance will never be confined to a single State. This being the case, can we suppose it wise to hazard a civil war? Suppose Massachusetts, or any large State, should refuse, and Congress should attempt to compel them, would they not have influence to procure assistance, especially from those States which are in the same situation as themselves? What picture does this idea present to our view? A *complying State at war with a non-complying State; Congress marching the troops of one State into the bosom of another; this State collecting auxiliaries, and forming, perhaps, a majority against its Federal head. Here is a nation at war with itself. Can any reasonable man be well disposed towards a Government which makes war and carnage the only means of supporting itself—a Government that can exist only by the sword? Every such war must involve the innocent with the guilty. This single consideration should be sufficient to dispose every peaceable citizen against such a Government. But can we believe that one State will ever suffer itself to be used as an instrument of coercion? The thing is a dream; it is impossible.* Then we are brought to this dilemma—either a Federal standing army is to enforce the requisitions, or the Federal treasury is left without supplies, and the Government without support. What, sir, is the cure for this great evil? Nothing, but to enable the national laws to operate on individuals, in the same manner as those of the States do. This is the true reasoning upon the subject, sir. The gentlemen appear to acknowledge its force; and yet, while they yield to the principle, they seem to fear its application to the Government. [Emphasis added, L.S.]

'. . . The State Governments possess inherent advantages, which will ever give them an influence and ascendancy over the National Government, and will forever preclude the possibility of Federal encroachments. That their liberties, indeed, can be subverted by the Federal head, is repugnant to every rule of political calculation. Is not this arrangement, then, sir, a most wise and prudent one? Is not the present representation fully adequate to our present exigencies, and sufficient to answer all the purposes of the Union? I am persuaded than an examination of the objects of the Federal Government will afford a conclusive answer.'

"Mr. [John] Jay, afterwards Chief Justice of the United States, said:

'Sir, it seems to be, on all sides, agreed that a strong, energetic, Federal Government is necessary for the United States. It has given me pleasure to hear such declarations come from all parts of the House. If gentlemen are of this opinion, they give us to understand that such a Government is the favorite of their desire; and also, that it can be instituted; that, indeed, it is both necessary and practicable; or why do they advocate it.'

"Mr. R. Morris said:

'I am happy, Mr. Chairman, to perceive that it is a principle on all sides conceded, and adopted by this committee, that an energetic Federal Government is essential to the preservation of our Union; and that a Constitution for these States ought to unite firmness and vigor in the National operations, with the full securities of our rights and liberties.'

"Mr. Hamilton, again, said:

'I insist that it never can be the interest or desire of the National Legislature to destroy the State Governments. It can derive no advantage from such an event; but, on the contrary, would lose an indispensable support, a necessary aid in executing the laws, and conveying the influence of Government to the doors of the people. The Union is dependent on the will of the State Governments for its Chief Magistrate, and for its Senate. The blow aimed at the members must give a fatal wound to the head; and the destruction of the States must be at once a political suicide.

'. . . The States can never lose their powers till the whole people of America are robbed of their liberties. These must go together; they must support each other, or meet one common fate.

'With regard to the jurisdiction of the two Governments, I shall certainly admit that the Constitution ought to be so formed as not to prevent the States from providing for their own existence; and I maintain that it is so formed, and that their power of providing for themselves is sufficiently established. This is conceded by one gentleman, and in the next breath the concession is retracted. He says, Congress have but one exclusive right in taxation—that of duties on imports; certainly, then, their other powers are only concurrent. But, to take off the force of this obvious conclusion, he immediately says, that the laws of the United States are supreme; and that where there is one supreme, there cannot be concurrent authority; and further, that where the laws of the Union are supreme, those of the States must be subordinate, because there cannot be two supremes. This is curious sophistry. That two supremes cannot act together, is false. They are inconsistent only when they are aimed at each other, or at one indivisible object. The laws of the United States are supreme, as to all their proper, constitutional objects; the laws of the States are supreme in the same way. These supreme laws may act on different objects without clashing, or they may operate on different parts of the same object, with perfect harmony. Suppose both Governments should lay a tax, of a penny on a certain article: had not each an independent and uncontrollable power to collect its own tax? The meaning of the maxim, there cannot be two supremes, is simply this—two powers cannot be supreme over each other. This meaning is entirely perverted by the gentleman. But it is said disputes between collectors are to be referred to the Federal courts. This is again wandering in the field of conjecture. But suppose the fact certain: is it not to be presumed that they will express the true meaning of the Constitution and the laws? Will they not be bound to consider the concurrent jurisdiction; to declare that both the taxes shall have equal operation; that both the powers, in that respect, are Sovereign and co-extensive? If they transgress their duty, we are to hope that they will be punished. Sir, we can reason from probabilities alone. When we leave common sense, and give ourselves up to conjecture, there can be no certainty, no security in our reasonings.

'I imagine, I have stated to the committee abundant reasons to prove the entire safety of the State Governments and of the people.'

"This is quite sample enough of the debates in New York Convention, (which lasted for more than a month) to show how the leading advocates of the Constitution in that State understood it, and especially how Mr. Hamilton understood it. His own copious and elaborate speeches abundantly show that he considered the plan, finally adopted by the Philadelphia Convention, to be a Federal [Confederate] Constitution. And his greatest efforts were put forth against those who argued that a different construction might be put upon it. In all of the speeches I have read, he speaks of the Government as Federal [Confederate], and in one he styles it a Confederacy. As such, he gave it his zealous support, though it was not such a one as he wished to see organized. Nor was it one in which he had much real confidence. The idea on which it was based was not his own; failing in his own, he patriotically took the plan adopted, and threw his whole soul in its support as an experiment.

TWELFTH, NORTH CAROLINA

"The next State in order is North Carolina. She remained out of the Union for some time. As in the other cases we will look first into her action, and then the debates. Her ratification is in these words:

> Whereas, the General Convention, which met in Philadelphia, in pursuance of a recommendation of Congress, did recommend to the citizens of the United States a Constitution, or form of Government, in the following words, namely: Resolved, That this Convention, in behalf of the freemen, citizens, and inhabitants of the State of North Carolina, do adopt and ratify the said Constitution and form of Government.
>
> Done, in Convention, this twenty-first day of November, one thousand seven hundred and eighty-nine.

"The proceedings in North Carolina are short. Upon their face there is nothing that would indicate the understanding of the members of the Convention as to the nature and character of the Government instituted by the Constitution they adopted. In the debates, the points discussed related mostly to the details of the Constitution. But quite enough, however, appears in them to show the general understanding.

"Secondly, let us look into the debates in this Convention, as we have in those of the other States.

"Mr. [William R.] Davie, who was in the Philadelphia Convention, opened the discussion, and amongst other things, said:

'Another radical vice in the old system which was necessary to be corrected, and which will be understood without a long deduction of reasoning, was, that it legislated on States, instead of individuals; and that its powers could not be executed but by fire or by the sword—by military force, and not by the intervention of the civil magistrate. Every one who is acquainted with the relative situation of the States, and the genius of our citizens, must acknowledge that, if the Government was to be carried into effect by military force, the most dreadful consequences would ensue. It would render the citizens of America the most implacable enemies to one another. If it could be carried into effect against the small States, yet it could not be put in force against the larger and more powerful States. It was, therefore, abundantly necessary that the influence of the magistrate should be introduced, and that the laws should be carried home to individuals themselves.

'In the formation of this system, many difficulties presented themselves to the Convention.

'Every member saw that the existing system would ever be ineffectual, unless its laws operated on individuals, as military coercion was neither eligible nor practicable.

'. . . Mutual concessions were necessary to come to any concurrence. A plan that would promote the exclusive interests of a few States would be injurious to others. Had each State obstinately insisted on the security of its particular local advantages, we should never have come to a conclusion. Each, therefore, amicably and wisely relinquished its particular views. The Federal Convention have told you, that the Constitution, which they formed, 'was the result of a spirit of amity, and of that mutual deference and concession which the peculiarity of their political situation rendered indispensable.' I hope the same laudable spirit will govern this Convention in their decision on this important question.

'The business of the Convention was to amend the Confederation, by giving it additional powers. The present form of Congress being a single body, it was thought unsafe to augment its powers, without altering its organization. The act of the Convention is but a mere proposal, similar to the production of a private pen. I think it a Government which, if adopted, will cherish and protect the happiness and liberty of America; but I hold my mind open to conviction. I am ready to recede from my opinion, if it be proved to be ill-founded. I trust that every man here is equally ready to change an opinion he may have improperly formed. The weakness and inefficiency of the old Confederation produced the necessity of calling the Federal Convention. Their plan is now before you; and, I hope, on a deliberate consideration, every man will see the necessity of such a system. It has been the subject of much jealousy and censure out of doors. I hope gentlemen will now come forward with their objections, and that they will be thrown out and answered with candor and moderation.

'. . . A consolidation of the States is said by some gentlemen to have been intended. They insinuate that this was the cause of their giving this power of elections. If there were any seeds in this Constitution which might, one day, produce a consolidation, it would, sir, with me, be an insuperable objection, I am so perfectly convinced that so extensive a country as this, can never be managed by one consolidated Government. The Federal Convention were as well convinced as the members of this House, that the State Governments were absolutely necessary to the existence of the Federal Government. They considered them as the great massy pillars on which this political fabric was to be extended and supported; and were fully persuaded that, when they were removed, or should moulder down by time, the General Government must tumble into ruin. A very little reflection will show that no department of it can exist without the State Governments.

'Let us begin with the House of Representatives. Who are to vote for the Federal Representatives? Those who vote for the State Representatives. If the State Government vanishes, the General Government must vanish also. This is the foundation on which this Government was raised, and without which it cannot possibly exist.

'The next department is the Senate. How is it formed? By the States themselves. Do they not choose them? Are they not created by them? And will they not have the interest of the States particularly at heart? The States, sir, can put a final period to the Government, as was observed by a gentleman who thought this power over elections unnecessary. If the State Legislatures think proper, they may refuse to choose Senators, and the Government must be destroyed.'

"Besides this act of ratification and the speeches of Mr. Davie, we have a set of Resolutions which were passed by the Convention, recommending six amendments to the Constitution, which fully explain their understanding of the Constitution.

"The first of these is as follows:

1. Each State in the Union shall respectively retain every power, jurisdiction, and right, which is not by this Constitution delegated to the Congress of the United States, or to the departments of the General Government; nor shall the said Congress, nor any department of the said Government, exercise any act of authority over any individual in any of the said States, but such as can be justified under some power particularly given in this Constitution; but the said Constitution shall be considered at all times a solemn instrument, defining the extent of their authority, and the limits of which they cannot rightfully in any instance exceed.

"This is quite sufficient to show that the people of North Carolina understood the Constitution they adopted to be Federal [Confederate] in its character. That is the object of our inquiry.

THIRTEENTH, RHODE ISLAND

"We come now to Rhode Island, the last of the States which acted upon the Constitution. Her proceedings are very voluminous. Nothing but the importance of the question at issue could induce me to ask you to attend to their reading. Their very length, however, shows how completely Federal [Confederate] they were, and guarding against every possible danger to their Sovereignty.

"Here is the Document by which she became a member of the United States, under their present Union:

> We, the Delegates of the people of the State of Rhode Island and Providence Plantations, duly elected, and met in Convention, having maturely considered the Constitution for the United States of America, agreed to on the seventeenth day of September, in the year one thousand seven hundred and eighty-seven, by the Convention then assembled at Philadelphia, in the Commonwealth of Pennsylvania (a copy whereof precedes these presents), and having also seriously and deliberately considered the present situation of this State, do declare and make known,—
>
> I. That there are certain natural rights of which men, when they form a social Compact, cannot deprive or divest their posterity,—among which are the enjoyment of life and liberty, with the means of acquiring, possessing, and protecting property, and pursuing and obtaining happiness and safety.
>
> II. That all power is naturally vested in, and consequently derived from, the people; that magistrates, therefore, are their trustees and agents, and at all times amenable to them.
>
> III. That the powers of Government may be resumed by the people whensoever it shall become necessary to their happiness. That the rights of the States respectively to nominate and appoint all State officers, and every other power, jurisdiction, and right, which is not by the said Constitution clearly delegated to the Congress of the United States, or to the Departments of Government thereof, remain to the people of the several States, or their respective State Governments, to whom they may have granted the same; and that those clauses in the Constitution which declare that Congress shall not have or exercise certain powers, do not imply that Congress is entitled to any powers not given by the said Constitution; but such clauses are to be construed as exceptions to certain specified powers, or as inserted merely for greater caution.
>
> IV. That religion or the duty which we owe to our Creator, and the manner of discharging it, can be directed only by reason and conviction, and not by force and violence; and, therefore, all men have a natural, equal, and

unalienable right to the exercise of religion according to the dictates of conscience; and that no particular religious Sect, or Society, ought to be favored or established by law, in preference to others.

V. That the legislative, executive, and judiciary powers of Government should be separate and distinct; and; that the members of the two first may be restrained from oppression, by feeling and participating the public burdens, they should, at fixed periods, be reduced to a private station, returned into the mass of the people, and the vacancies be supplied by certain and regular elections, in which all, or any part of the former members to be eligible, or ineligible, as the rules of the Constitution of Government and the laws shall direct.

VI. That elections of representatives in Legislature ought to be free and frequent: and all men having sufficient evidence of permanent common interest with, and attachment to, the community, ought to have the right of suffrage; and no aid, charge, tax, or fee, can be set, rated, or levied, upon the people, without their own consent, or that of their representatives so elected, nor can they be bound by any law to which they have not in like manner consented for the public good.

VII. That all power of suspending laws, or the execution of laws, by any authority, without the consent of the representatives of the people in the Legislature, is injurious to their rights, and ought not to be exercised.

VIII. That, in all capital and criminal prosecutions, a man hath the right to demand the cause and nature of his accusation, to be confronted with the accusers and witnesses, to call for evidence, and be allowed counsel in his favor, and to a fair and speedy trial by an impartial jury in his vicinage [vicinity], without whose unanimous consent he cannot be found guilty, (except in the government of the land and naval forces,) nor can he be compelled to give evidence against himself.

IX. That no freeman ought to be taken, imprisoned, or disseized of his freehold, liberties, privileges, or franchises, or outlawed, or exiled, or in any manner destroyed, or deprived of his life, liberty, or property, but by the trial by jury, or by the laws of the land.

X. That every freeman, restrained of his liberty, is entitled to a remedy, to inquire into the lawfulness thereof, and to remove the same if unlawful, and that such remedy ought not to be denied or delayed.

XI. That in controversies respecting property, and in suits between man and man, the ancient trial by jury, as hath been exercised by us and our ancestors, from the time whereof the memory of man is not to the contrary, is one of the greatest securities to the rights of the people, and ought to remain sacred and inviolable.

XII. That every freeman ought to obtain right and justice, freely and without sale, completely and without denial, promptly and without delay; and that all establishments, or regulations contravening these rights are oppressive and unjust.

XIII. That excessive bail ought not to be required, nor excessive fines imposed, nor cruel or unusual punishments inflicted.

XIV. That every person has a right to be secure from all unreasonable searches and seizures of his person, his papers, or his property; and, therefore, that all warrants to search suspected places, to seize any person, his papers, or his property, without information upon oath or affirmation of sufficient cause, are grievous and oppressive; and that all general warrants (or such in which the place or person suspected are not particularly designated) are dangerous, and ought not to be granted.

XV. That the people have a right peaceably to assemble together, to consult for their common good, or to instruct their representatives; and that every person has a right to petition or apply to the Legislature for redress of grievances.

XVI. That the people have a right to freedom of speech, and of writing, and publishing their sentiments. That freedom of the press is one of the greatest bulwarks of liberty, and ought not to be violated.

XVII. That the people have a right to keep and bear arms; that a well regulated militia, including the body of the people capable of bearing arms, is the proper, natural, and safe defence of a free State; that the militia shall not be subject to martial law, except in time of war, rebellion, or insurrection; that standing armies, in time of peace, are dangerous to liberty, and ought not to be kept up, except in cases of necessity; and that, at all times, the military should be under strict subordination to the civil power; that, in time of peace, no soldier ought to be quartered in any house without the consent of the owner, and in time of war only by the civil magistrates, in such manner as the law directs.

XVIII. That any person religiously scrupulous of bearing arms ought to be exempted upon the payment of an equivalent to employ another to bear arms in his stead.

Under these impressions, and declaring that the right aforesaid cannot be abridged or violated, and that the explanations aforesaid are consistent with the said Constitution, and in confidence that the amendments hereafter mentioned will receive an early and mature consideration, and, conformably to the fifth article of said Constitution, speedily become a part thereof,—We, the said Delegates, in the name and in the behalf of the people of the State of Rhode Island and Providence Plantations, do, by these presents, assent to and ratify the said Constitution. In full confidence, nevertheless, that, until the amendments hereafter proposed and undermentioned shall be agreed to and ratified, pursuant to the aforesaid fifth article, the militia will not be continued in service out of this State, for a longer term than six weeks, without the consent of the Legislature thereof; that the Congress will not make or alter any regulation in this State respecting the times, places, and manner of holding elections for Senators or Representatives, unless the Legislature of this State shall neglect or refuse to make laws or regulations for the purpose, or from any circumstance, be incapable of making the same; and that, in those cases, such power will only be exercised until the Legislature of this State shall make provision in the premises; that the Congress will not lay direct taxes within this State, but when the moneys arising from impost, tonnage, and excise, shall be insufficient for the public exigencies, nor until the Congress shall have first made a requisition upon this State to assess, levy, and pay, the amount of such requisition made, agreeably to the census fixed in the said Constitution, in such way and manner as the Legislature of this State shall judge best; and that Congress will not lay any capitation or poll tax.

Done in Convention, at Newport, in the County of Newport, in the State of Rhode Island and Providence Plantations, the twenty-ninth day of May, in the year of our Lord one thousand seven hundred and ninety, and in the fourteenth year of the Independence of the United States of America.

"We have now gone through with the action of all the States upon the Constitution. We have examined the records themselves, and not mere assertions touching them. This concludes that sketch of the history of the Union, as it is called, which I proposed. In it we see, that it was first formed by separate and distinct Colonies for the common maintenance of the chartered rights of each. When this failed, it became a Union of separate, distinct States, by Articles of Confederation, for the support and maintenance of the Independence and Sovereignty of each. The absolute right of local Self Government, or State Sovereignty, was the primal and leading idea throughout. We have seen that these States, as Sovereign, responded to a call of a General Federal Convention, to revise the first Articles of Confederation. The present Constitution was the result of their labors. We have seen that it was submitted to the Legislatures of each State, in their separate State organizations, to be referred by them to a Convention, in each State, of the people thereof, that they, in their Sovereign majesty, might approve or reject each, separately, for themselves, as States, and that it was to be established between such States only as should ratify it, and then only in case as many as nine should ratify it.

"We have seen that the State Conventions did so act upon it separately and severally, and adopt it as a Constitution for the States, so to be united thereby, each believing it to be a Federal [Confederate] Constitution, and that all powers not delegated were reserved to the States; but, to quiet apprehensions on this point, a majority of them, in their acts of ratification, demanded an amendment which should make this express declaration, and it was in confidence that this should be done, that they assented to it. Which we shall see was immediately afterwards done.

"We have further gone into the debates in the several State Conventions, and seen what were the leading ideas of both friends and opponents as to the nature and character of the Constitution. While many apprehended danger to the Sovereignty of the separate States from constructions and implications, yet on all hands it was universally admitted that it purported to be a Federal [Confederate] Constitution; and it was with this avowed understanding of its nature, by every advocate and supporter it had in every State in the Union, even by Hamilton, Morris, Wilson, King, Madison, and Randolph, who had favored a National Government proper, in the Federal Convention, instead of the plan embodied in the Constitution. *The leading idea in all the Conventions was that a Confederate Republic was to be established by it upon the model set forth in Montesquieu. According to that model an artificial State is created for Foreign or National, as well as inter State purposes, and these only, by several small Republics, thus Confederating, for their common defence and happiness; each retaining its separate Sovereignty, and the artificial State so created by them being, at all times, subject to their will and power. That this artificial State so created may be dissolved, and yet the separate Republic survive, retaining, at all times, their State organization and Sovereignty. This model of a Confederate Republic, by Montesquieu, was the leading idea with the advocates of the system, as appears from their debates, in every State where we have access to them.* [Emphasis added, L.S.]

"Now, then, after this review, *is it not clear that the United States are, or constitute, a Confederated Republic (as Washington styled it), bound together by the solemn Compact of Union, entered into by the several members thereof, under the Constitution?* . . . Is not the Constitution, as appears not only from the history of its formation thus given, but from its face, a Compact between Sovereign States?"[130] [Emphasis added, L.S.]

14

WEBSTER & CALHOUN ON THE U.S. CONSTITUTION

ONE OF THE REASONS NORTHERNERS did not believe that the South had a constitutional right to secede in 1860 and 1861 was a speech given by the famed New England Liberal Daniel Webster before the U.S. Senate on February 16, 1833. In it he argued vociferously against the ideas that the Constitution was a Confederate Compact, that the U.S. government was a Confederate government, and that the U.S. herself was a Confederacy.

Though Webster was, of course, wrong on all of these points, his words had a major impact on how Yankees later perceived the Constitution and the War for Southern Independence—which explains, in part, why so many Northerners supported U.S. President Abraham Lincoln in his quest to destroy states' rights in the constitutionally formed Southern Confederacy.

In this chapter of excerpts from *A Constitutional View*, Stephens begins by providing a few samples from Webster's 1833 speech. These are followed by Stephens himself, whose discourse includes a powerful rebuttal by noted Southern Conservative John C. Calhoun. First, a very brief selection from the original lengthy speech of anti-South, anti-Confederate statesman Daniel Webster.

["What follows are excerpts from Mr. Daniel Webster of Massachusetts:]

"I maintain:—

"1. That the Constitution of the United States is not a League, Confederacy or Compact, between the people of the several States in their Sovereign capacities; but a Government proper, founded on the adoption of the people, and creating direct relations between itself and individuals.

"2. That no State authority has power to dissolve these relations; that nothing can dissolve them but revolution; and that, consequently, there can be no such thing as Secession without revolution.

"3. That there is a supreme law, consisting of the Constitution of the United States, and Acts of Congress, passed in pursuance of it, and treaties; and that, in cases not capable of assuming the character of a suit in law or equity, Congress must judge of, and, finally, interpret, the supreme law, so often as it has occasion to pass acts of legislation; and, in cases capable of assuming, and actually assuming, the character of a suit, the Supreme Court of the United States is the final interpreter.

"4. That an attempt by a State to abrogate, annul, or nullify an Act of Congress, or to arrest its operation within her limits, on the ground that, in her opinion, such law is unconstitutional, is a direct usurpation on the just powers of the General Government, and on the equal rights of other States; a plain violation of the Constitution, and a proceeding essentially Revolutionary in its character and tendency.

"Whether the Constitution be a Compact between States in their Sovereign capacities, is a question which must be mainly argued from what is contained in the instrument itself. We all agree that it is an instrument which has in some way been clothed with power. We all admit that it speaks with authority. The first question then is, what does it say of itself? What does it purport to be? Does it style itself a League, Confederacy, or Compact between Sovereign States? It is to be remembered, sir, that the Constitution began to speak only after its adoption. Until it was ratified by nine States, it was but a proposal, the mere draught of an instrument. It was like a deed drawn, but not executed. The Convention had framed it; sent it to Congress, then sitting under the Confederation; Congress had transmitted it to the State Legislatures; and by these last it was laid before Conventions of the people in the several States. All this while it was inoperative paper. It had received no stamp of authority, no sanction; it spoke no language. But when ratified by the people in their respective Conventions, then it had a voice, and spoke authentically. Every word in it had then received the sanction of the popular will, and was to be received as the expression of that will. What the Constitution says of itself, therefore, is as conclusive as what it says on any other point. Does it call itself a 'Compact?' Certainly not. It uses the word Compact but once, and that is when it declares that the States shall enter into no Compact. Does it call itself a 'League,' a 'Confederacy,' a 'subsisting Treaty between the States?' Certainly not. There is not a particle of such language in all its pages. But it declares itself a Constitution. What is a Constitution? Certainly not a League, Compact, or Confederacy, but a fundamental law. That fundamental regulation which determines the manner in which the public authority is to be executed, is what forms the Constitution of a State. Those primary rules which concern the body itself, and the very being of the political society, the form of Government, and the manner in which power is to be exercised,—all, in a word, which form together the Constitution of a State, these are the fundamental laws. This, sir, is the language of the public writers. But do we need to be informed, in this country, what a Constitution is? Is it not an idea perfectly familiar, definite, and well settled? We are at no loss to understand what is meant by the Constitution of one of the States; and the Constitution of the United States speaks of itself as being an instrument of the same nature. It says, this Constitution shall be the law of the land, any thing in any State Constitution to the contrary, notwithstanding. And it speaks of itself, too, in plain contradistinction from a Confederation; for it says that all debts contracted, and all engagements entered into, by the United States, shall be as valid under this Constitution as under the Confederation. It does not say, as valid under this Compact, or this League, or this Confederation, as under the former Confederation, but as valid under this Constitution.

"This, then, sir, is declared to be a Constitution. A Constitution is the fundamental law of the State; and this is expressly declared to be the supreme law. It is as if the people had said, 'We prescribe this fundamental law,' or 'this supreme law,' for they do say that they establish this Constitution, and that it shall be the supreme law. They say that they ordain and establish it. Now, sir, what is the common application of these words? We do not speak of ordaining Leagues and Compacts. If this was intended to be a Compact or League, and the States to be parties to it, why was it not so said? Why is there found no one expression, in the whole instrument, indicating such intent? The old Confederation was expressly called a League; and into this League it was declared that the States, as States, severally entered. Why was not similar language used in the Constitution, if a similar intention had existed? Why was it not said, 'the States enter into this new League,' 'the States form this new Confederation,' or 'the States agree to this new Compact?' Or why was it not said, in the language of the gentleman's Resolution, that the people of the several States acceded to this Compact in their Sovereign capacities? What reason is there for supposing that the framers of the Constitution rejected expressions appropriate to their own meaning, and adopted others wholly at war with that meaning?

"Again, sir, the Constitution speaks of that political system which is established as 'the Government of the United States.' Is it not doing a strange violence to language to call a League or a Compact between Sovereign powers a Government? The Government of a State is that organization in which the political power resides. It is the political being created by the Constitution or fundamental law. The broad and clear difference between a Government and a League or Compact is, that a Government is a body politic; it has a will of its own; and it possesses powers and faculties to execute its own purposes. Every Compact looks to some power to enforce its stipulations. Even in a Compact between Sovereign communities, there always exists this ultimate reference to a power to insure its execution; although, in such case, this power is but the force of one party against the force of another; that is to say, the power of war. But a Government executes its decisions by its own supreme authority. Its use of force in compelling obedience to its own enactments is not war. It contemplates no opposing party having a right of resistance. It rests on its power to enforce its own will; and when it ceases to possess this power, it is no longer a Government. . . ."[131]

☞ [Stephens response to Webster's speech:] "Yes, I remember that contest well; and it is true that I ever regarded Mr. Webster as one of the ablest of our statesmen: this the bust and the picture in the hall fully attest. In many respects I considered him the first man in this country, and, indeed, the first man of the age in which he lived. In mental power, in grasp of thought, and in that force and manner of expression which constitute eloquence, he had no superior. Intellectually he was a man of huge proportions, and his patriotism was of the loftiest and purest character. Such was and is my estimation of him. I was exceedingly anxious to see him President, and what a President he would have made! [Liberals do] . . . well, therefore, in selecting his argument on this subject. It is the embodiment of all that can be said upon your side of the question. It was the characteristic of Mr. Webster to leave nothing unsaid, on his side of any subject he spoke on, that could be said to strengthen it, and all that could be said, he always said better than any body else. Hence, whether at the bar, on the hustings, or in the Senate, his speeches were always the best that were made on his side. It used to be a remark, often made by our Chief Justice [Joseph H.] Lumpkin, who was a man himself of wonderful genius, profound learning, and the first of orators in this State, that Webster was always foremost amongst those with whom he acted on any question, and that even in books of selected pieces, whenever selections were made from Webster, those were the best in the book. This, I think, was not too great a eulogium upon his transcendent powers and varied abilities. But it is not the lot of any man to be perfect. I am far from believing Mr. Webster free from political errors. And this speech of his, which, by many (his biographer included, I believe), is considered the greatest of his life, you will allow me to say, contains more errors of this sort than any he ever made. His premises being erroneous, his conclusions must be of the same character. The superstructure is grand. It is the work of a master genius. But the foundations are not solid. It was this speech, by the by, which gave him the appellation of the 'Great Expounder of the Constitution,' with the Consolidationists [Liberals] of that day. In it he did throw all the might of his Gigantic and Titan powers. But the subject was an overmatch for him; the undertaking was too great for even him. Facts were too stubborn. His whole soul was in the subject, and he strove to establish what he wished rather than what actually existed. His effort was to make facts bend to theory. This could not be done. This speech, I readily admit, is the best and ablest that ever was made upon that side of the question. It stands as a monument of genius and eloquence. As such it may well take its place by the side of the great argument of Hume in defence of the Prerogatives of the Crown, claimed by the Stuarts, or of Sir Robert Filmer's famous productions in favor of the Divine Right of Kings, or Sir George McKenzie's '*Jus Regium*.'

"Much of the answer to this speech, you perceive, has been anticipated. For instance, what is said about 'we, the people,' etc., near the conclusion, has been sufficiently explained in our investigations. The broad assertion that all parties agreed that the Convention had formed a National Government and had not continued the Federal system, doubtless made a deep impression at the time upon those not conversant with the history of the facts, but it can have no effect upon us who have travelled so carefully through the records of those days. Equally unimpressively falls upon us the declaration that in 'none of the productions and publications of those days did any one intimate that the new Constitution was but another Compact between States.' We have seen that such was the opinion of Washington, Madison, Hamilton, Rufus King, Ellsworth, Morris, and Randolph; that is, they all held that the Government established by it was Federal [Confederal]. This implies Compact; and we have seen that it was the opinion of all the advocates of the Constitution in every one of the Conventions of the States that ratified it, that the Federative [Confederative] character of the Union was preserved! No advocate of the Constitution in any State admitted that the Federal [Confederate] System was abandoned in it, and no writer in the *Federalist* admitted it!

"What is said in this speech about Mr. [William] Paterson's proposition in the Convention that formed the Constitution for continuing the Articles of Confederation, which was offered on the 15th of June and rejected on the 19th of the same month, needs this explanation, and this only. Mr. Paterson's proposition was for continuing requisitions on the States as States, and for leaving all Legislative powers in the Congress composed of but one body as before.

"His proposition ignored the division of the Legislative body into two Houses, which was a leading object of a large majority of the States in the new organization. His proposition was rejected, not because it proposed to continue the Federal System, but because it did not propose to continue it under a proper organization. That the Convention, by the rejection of his plan, did not intend to abandon the Federal [Confederate] system, has been conclusively shown by the vote on the 20th of June. That vote ordered the word 'National' to be stricken out of Governor Randolph's plan and 'the Government of the United States' to be inserted in lieu of it. It is also worthy of note in this connection, that this plan of Mr. Paterson, which Mr. Webster admits was nothing but a continuation of the Articles of Confederation, had in it these clauses:

> 6. Resolved, That the Legislative, Executive and Judicial powers within the several States ought to be bound by oath to support the Articles of Union.
> 7. Resolved, That all Acts of the United States, in Congress assembled, made by virtue and in pursuance of the powers hereby vested in them and by the Articles of Confederation, and all treaties made and ratified under the authority of the United States, shall be the supreme law of the respective States, as far as those acts or treaties shall relate to the said States or their citizens; and that the judiciaries of the several States shall be bound thereby in their decisions every thing in the respective laws of the individual States to the contrary notwithstanding.

"This . . . is the substance of the clause in the present Constitution which was afterwards offered by Mr. [Luther] Martin, as has been seen, and upon which Mr. Webster relies so much in his argument to show that a National Government and not a Federal [Confederate] one was instituted by the Constitution. This fact I wish you to bear in mind at this point in connection with what has been before said on that subject, as it clearly shows that no person in the Convention put such construction upon these words as Mr. Webster puts upon them. This clause was not thought by Mr. Paterson or Mr. Martin, or any body else in the Convention, to be at all inconsistent with a continuation of the former Articles of Union, which Mr. Webster admits was but a bare League or Compact between States. We have seen that Mr. [Alexander] Hamilton and Mr. [James] Madison, and Judge [Samuel] Chase, were of the same opinion. This much I say in passing.

"Now, in full answer to the main points in this truly great argument of Mr. Webster, . . . I will read the reply to it by Mr. [John C.] Calhoun. Great as Mr. Webster's was in my judgment, this speech of Mr. Calhoun was a complete refutation of its principles and a clear vindication of the correctness of his Resolutions that Mr. Webster made such powerful assault upon.

"Before taking it up, however, allow me to say, that I think Mr. Calhoun was greatly misunderstood in his day and time. He was generally regarded as an enemy to the Union. This was certainly a great mistake. He was, in my judgment, as ardent a friend of the Union as Mr. Webster was. Both were as true patriots as ever lived. They only differed as to the nature of the Union, and the principles upon which it should be maintained. Mr. Calhoun held that it could be maintained and perpetuated consistently with the preservation of Constitutional liberty only on the principle of the recognition of the ultimate Sovereign rights of the States. These doctrines he advocated with an earnestness which showed the profound convictions of his judgment as well as his fearful apprehensions from the ascendancy of opposite principles. By many he was regarded as an alarmist. Sergeant S. Prentiss is reported to have said of him that 'he claims our confidence by his very fears, and like the needle he trembles into place.' Whether Prentiss ever made the remark or not, the figure is no less characteristic of the reported author than of him to whom it is said to have been applied. Amongst the many great men with whom he was associated, Mr. Calhoun was by far the most philosophical statesman of them all. Indeed, with the exception of Mr. [Thomas] Jefferson, it may be questioned if in this respect the United States has ever produced his superior. Government he considered a science, and in its study his whole soul was absorbed. His Treatise on the Constitution of the United States is the best that was ever penned upon that subject, and his Disquisition on Government generally, is one of the few books of this age, that will outlive the language in which it was written. He studied the controlling principles of all systems, their organic laws, and the inevitable results of their action. Webster, [Henry] Clay, and [Andrew] Jackson, all his rivals to some extent, were much more practical in their ideas as well as actions. He was regarded as too much of an abstractionist, dealing in incomprehensible metaphysical distinctions. But no better reply to this charge and no better introduction to the speech I propose to read can be made, than the reply he made himself, to this charge, a few days before, in the Senate. [Said Calhoun, February 26, 1833:]

> 'The Senator from Massachusetts [Daniel Webster] in his argument against the Resolutions, directed his attack almost exclusively against the first; on the ground, I suppose, that it was the basis of the other two, and that, unless the first could be demolished, the others would follow of course. In this he was right. As plain and as simple as the facts contained in the first are, they cannot be admitted to be true without admitting the doctrines for which I, and the State I represent, contend. He commenced his attack with a verbal criticism on the Resolution, in the course of which he objected strongly to two words, "Constitutional" and "accede." To the former, on the ground that the word, as used (Constitutional Compact), was obscure—that it conveyed no definite meaning—and that Constitution was a noun-substantive, and not an adjective. I regret that I have exposed myself to the criticism of the Senator. I certainly did not intend to use any expression of doubtful sense, and if I have done so, the Senator must attribute it to the poverty of my language, and not to design I trust, however, that the Senator will excuse me, when he comes to hear my apology. In matters of criticism, authority is of the highest importance, and I have an authority of so high a character, in this case, for using the expression which he considers so obscure and so unconstitutional, as will justify me even in his eyes. It is no less than the authority of the

Senator himself—given on a solemn occasion (the discussion on Mr. [Henry S.] Foote's Resolution), and doubtless with great deliberation, after having duly weighed the force of the expression. [Stephens' note: Here Mr. Calhoun read from Mr. Webster's speech, in the debate on the Foote Resolutions, in 1830:]

" Nevertheless, I do not complain, nor would I countenance any movement to alter this arrangement of representation. It is the original bargain—the Compact—let it stand—let the advantage of it be fully enjoyed. The Union itself is too full of benefits to be hazarded in propositions for changing its original basis. I go for the Constitution, as it is, and for the Union, as it is. But I am resolved not to submit, in silence, to accusations, either against myself, individually, or against the North, wholly unfounded and unjust—accusations which impute to us a disposition to evade the Constitutional Compact, and to extend the power of the Government over the internal laws and domestic condition of the States."

[Calhoun continues:] 'It will be seen by this extract that the Senator not only used the phrase "Constitutional Compact," which he now so much condemns, but, what is still more important, he calls the Constitution a Compact—a bargain—which contains important admissions, having a direct and powerful bearing on the main issue, involved in the discussion, as will appear in the sequel. But, strong as his objection is to the word "Constitutional," it is still stronger to the word "accede," which, he thinks, has been introduced into the Resolution with some deep design, as I suppose, to entrap the Senate into an admission of the doctrine of State Rights [i.e., states' rights]. Here, again, I must shelter myself under authority. But I suspect the Senator, by a sort of instinct (for our instincts often strangely run before our knowledge), had a prescience, which would account for his aversion for the word, that this authority was no less than Thomas Jefferson himself, the great apostle of the doctrines of State Rights. The word was borrowed from him. It was taken from the Kentucky Resolution, as well as the substance of the resolution itself. But I trust I may neutralize whatever aversion the authorship of this word may have excited in the mind of the Senator, by the introduction of another authority—that of Washington, himself—who, in his speech to Congress, speaking of the admission of North Carolina into the Union, uses this very term, which was repeated by the Senate in their reply. Yet, in order to narrow the ground between the Senator and myself as much as possible, I will accommodate myself to his strange antipathy against the two unfortunate words, by striking them out of the Resolution, and substituting, in their place, those very words which the Senator himself has designated as Constitutional phrases. In the place of that abhorred adjective "Constitutional," I will insert the very noun substantive "Constitution;" and, in the place of the word "accede," I will insert the word "ratify," which he designates as the proper term to be used.

'As proposed to be amended, the Resolution would read:—

Resolved, That the people of the several States composing these United States are united as parties to a Compact, under the title of the Constitution of the United States, which the people of each State ratified as a separate and Sovereign community, each binding itself by its own particular ratification; and that the Union of which the said Compact is the bond, is a Union between the States ratifying the same.

'Where, sir, I ask, is that plain case of revolution? Where that hiatus, as wide as the globe, between the premises and the conclusion, which the Senator proclaimed would be apparent, if the Resolution was reduced into Constitutional language? For my part, with my poor powers of conception, I cannot perceive the slightest difference between the Resolution, as first introduced, and as it is proposed to be amended in conformity to the views of the Senator. And, instead of that hiatus between the premises and conclusion, which seems to startle the imagination of the Senator, I can perceive nothing but a continuous and solid surface, sufficient to sustain the magnificent superstructure of State Rights. Indeed, it seems to me that the Senator's vision is distorted by the medium through which he views every thing connected with the subject; and that the same distortion which has presented to his imagination this hiatus, as wide as the globe, where not even a fissure exists, also presented that beautiful and classical image of a strong man struggling in a bog, without the power of extricating himself, and incapable of being aided by any friendly hand; while, instead of struggling in a bog, he stands on the everlasting rock of truth.

'Having now noticed the criticisms of the Senator, I shall proceed to meet and repel the main assault on the Resolution. He directed his attack against the strong point, the very horn of the citadel of State Rights. The Senator clearly perceived that, if the Constitution be a Compact, it was impossible to deny the assertions contained in the Resolutions, or to resist the consequences which I had drawn from them, and, accordingly, directed his whole fire against that point; but, after so vast an expenditure of ammunition, not the slightest impression, so far as I can perceive, has been made. But to drop the simile, after a careful examination of the notes which I took of what the Senator said, I am now at a loss to know whether, in the opinion of the Senator, our Constitution is a Compact or not, though the almost entire argument of the Senator was directed to that point. At one time he would seem to deny directly and positively that it was a Compact, while at another he would appear, in language not less strong, to admit that it was.

'I have collated all that the Senator [Webster] has said upon this point; and, that what I have stated may not appear exaggerated, I will read his remarks in juxtaposition. He said that:

"The Constitution means a Government, not a Compact. Not a Constitutional Compact, but a Government. If Compact, it rests on plighted faith, and the mode of redress would be to declare the whole void. States may secede, if a League or Compact."

'I thank the Senator for these admissions, which I intend to use hereafter:

[Calhoun quoting Webster:] "The States agreed that each should participate in the Sovereignty of the other."

'Certainly, a very correct conception of the Constitution; but where did they make that agreement but by the Constitution, and how could they agree but by Compact?

[Calhoun quoting Webster:] "The system, not a Compact between States in their Sovereign capacity, but a Government proper, founded on the adoption of the people, and creating individual relations between itself and the citizens."

'This, the Senator lays down as a leading, fundamental principle to sustain his doctrine, and, I must say, with strange confusion and uncertainty of language; not, certainly, to be explained by any want of command of the most appropriate words on his part.

[Calhoun quoting Webster:] "It does not call itself a Compact, but a Constitution. The Constitution rests on Compact, but it is no longer a Compact."

'I would ask, to what Compact does the Senator refer, as that on which the Constitution rests? Before the adoption of the present Constitution, the States had formed but one Compact, and that was the old Confederation; and, certainly, the gentleman does not intend to assert that the present Constitution rests upon that. What, then, is his meaning? What can it be, but that the Constitution itself is a Compact? And how will his language read, when fairly interpreted, but that the Constitution was a Compact, but is no longer a Compact? It had, by some means or another, changed its nature, or become defunct.
'He next states that—

[Calhoun quoting Webster:] "A man is almost untrue to his country who calls the Constitution a Compact."

'I fear the Senator, in calling it a "Compact, a bargain," has called down this heavy denunciation on his own head. He finally states that—

[Calhoun quoting Webster:] "It is founded on Compact, but not a Compact. It is the result of a Compact."

'To what are we to attribute this strange confusion of words? The Senator has a mind of high order, and perfectly trained to the most exact use of language. No man knows better the precise import of the words he uses. The difficulty is not in him, but in his subject. He who undertakes to prove that this Constitution is not a Compact, undertakes a task which, be his strength ever so great, must oppress him by its weight. Taking the whole of the argument of the Senator together, I would say that it is his impression that the Constitution is not a Compact, and will now proceed to consider the reason which he has assigned for this opinion.

'He thinks there is an incompatibility between Constitution and Compact. To prove this, he adduces the words "ordain and establish," contained in the preamble of the Constitution. I confess I am not capable of perceiving in what manner these words are incompatible with the idea that the Constitution is a Compact. The Senator will admit that a single State may ordain a Constitution; and where is the difficulty, where the incompatibility, of two States concurring in ordaining and establishing a Constitution? As between the States themselves, the instrument would be a Compact; but in reference to the Government, and those on whom it operates, it would be ordained and established—ordained and established by the joint authority of two, instead of the single authority of one.

'The next argument which the Senator advances to show that the language of the Constitution is irreconcilable with the idea of its being a Compact, is taken from that portion of the instrument which imposes prohibitions on the authority of the States. He said that the language used, in imposing the prohibitions, is the language of a superior to an inferior; and that, therefore, it was not the language of a Compact, which implies the equality of the parties. As a proof, the Senator cited several clauses of the Constitution which provide that no State shall enter into treaties of alliance and confederation, lay imposts, etc., without the assent of Congress. If he had turned to the Articles of the old Confederation, which he acknowledges to have been a Compact, he would have found that those very prohibitory Articles of the Constitution were borrowed from that instrument; that the language, which he now considers as implying superiority, was taken verbatim from it. If he had extended his researches still further, he would have found that it is the habitual language used in treaties, whenever a stipulation is made against the performance of any act. Among many instances, which I could cite, if it were necessary, I refer the Senator to the celebrated treaty negotiated by Mr. [John] Jay with Great Britain, in 1793, in which the very language used in the Constitution is employed.

'To prove that the Constitution is not a Compact, the Senator next observes that it stipulates nothing, and asks, with an air of triumph, "Where are the evidences of the stipulations between the States?" I must express my surprise at this interrogatory, coming from so intelligent a source. Has the Senator never seen the ratifications of the Constitution by the several States? Did he not cite them on this very occasion? Do they contain no evidence of stipulations on the part of the States? Nor is the assertion less strange that the Constitution contains no stipulations.

'So far from regarding it in the light in which the Senator regards it, I consider the whole instrument but a mass of stipulations. What is that but a stipulation to which the Senator refers when he states, in the course of his argument, that each State had agreed to participate in the Sovereignty of the others.

'But the principal argument on which the Senator relied to show that the Constitution is not a Compact, rests on the provision, in that instrument, which declares that "this Constitution, and laws made in pursuance thereof, and treaties made under their authority, are the supreme laws of the land." He asked, with marked emphasis, "Can a Compact be the supreme law of the land?" His argument, in fact, as conclusively proves that treaties are not Compacts as that the Constitution is not a Compact. I might rest the issue on this decisive answer; but, as I desire to leave not a shadow of doubt on this important point, I shall follow the gentleman in the course of his reasoning.

'He defines a Constitution to be a fundamental law, which organizes the Government, and points out the mode of its action. I will not object to the definition, though, in my opinion, a more appropriate one, or, at least, one better adapted to American ideas, could be given. My objection is not to the definition, but to the attempt to prove that the fundamental laws of a State cannot be a Compact, as the Senator seems to suppose. I hold the very reverse to be the case; and that, according to the most approved writers on the subject of Government, these very fundamental laws which are now stated not only not to be Compacts, but inconsistent with the very idea of Compacts, are held invariably to be Compacts; and, in that character, are distinguished from the ordinary laws of the country. I will cite a single authority, which is full and explicit on this point, from a writer of the highest repute. [Swiss legal theorist Jean-Jacques] Burlamaqui says:

> "It entirely depends upon a free people to invest the Sovereigns, whom they place over their heads, with an authority either absolute or limited by certain laws. These regulations, by which the supreme authority is kept within bounds, are called the fundamental laws of the State. The fundamental laws of a State, taken in their full extent, are not only the decrees by which the entire body of the nation determine the form of Government, and the manner of succeeding to the Crown, but are likewise covenants between the people and the person on whom they confer the Sovereignty, which regulate the manner of governing, and by which the supreme authority is limited.
>
> "These regulations are called fundamental laws, because they are the basis, as it were, and foundation of the State on which the structure of

the Government is raised, and, because the people look upon these regulations as their principal strength and support.

"The name of laws, however, has been given to these regulations in an improper and figurative sense, for, properly speaking, they are real covenants. But as these covenants are obligatory between the contracting parties, they have the force of laws themselves."

"[In the same volume Burlamaqui says:]

"The whole body of the nation, in whom the supreme power originally resides, may regulate the Government by a fundamental law, in such manner, as to commit the exercise of the different parts of the supreme power to different persons or bodies, who may act independently of each other in regard to the rights committed to them, but still subordinate to the laws from which those rights are derived.

"And these fundamental laws are real covenants, or what the civilians call *pacta conventa* [Latin: "the conditions agreed upon"] between the different orders of the republic, by which they stipulate that each shall have a particular part of the Sovereignty, and that this shall establish the form of Government. It is evident that, by these means, each of the contracting parties acquires a right, not only of exercising the power granted to it, but also of preserving that original right."

'A reference to the Constitution of Great Britain, with which we are better acquainted than with that of any other European Government, will show that that is a Compact. Magna Charta may certainly be reckoned among the fundamental laws of that kingdom. Now, although it did not assume, originally, the form of a Compact, yet, before the breaking up of the meeting of the Barons which imposed it on King John, it was reduced into the form of a covenant, and duly signed by Robert Fitzwater and others, on the one part, and the King on the other.

'But we have a more decisive proof that the Constitution of England is a Compact, in the resolution of the Lords and Commons, in 1688, which declared:

"King James the Second, having endeavored to subvert the Constitution of the kingdom, by breaking the original contract between the King and people, and having, by the advice of Jesuits and other wicked persons, violated the fundamental law, and withdrawn himself out of the kingdom, hath abdicated the Government, and that the throne is thereby become vacant."

'But why should I refer to writers upon the subject of Government, or inquire into the Constitution of foreign States, when there are such decisive proofs that our Constitution is a Compact? On this point the Senator is estopped. I borrow from the gentleman, and thank him for the word. His adopted State, which he so ably represents on this floor, and his native State, the States of Massachusetts and New Hampshire, both declared, in their ratification of the Constitution, that it was a Compact. The ratification of Massachusetts is in the following words: [Stephens' note: Here Mr. Calhoun called special attention to the ratification of the State of Massachusetts, in which the Constitution is spoken of as a "Solemn Compact"]:

"The ratification of New Hampshire is taken from that of Massachusetts, and almost in the same words. But proof, if possible, still more decisive, may be found in the celebrated resolutions of Virginia on the alien and sedition law, in 1798, and the responses of Massachusetts and the other States. These resolutions expressly assert that the Constitution is a Compact between the States, in the following language:

"That this Assembly doth explicitly and peremptorily declare, that it views the powers of the Federal Government, as resulting from the compact, to which the States are parties, as limited by the plain sense and intention of the instrument constituting that Compact, as no farther valid than they are authorized by the grants enumerated in that Compact; and that in case of a deliberate, palpable, and dangerous exercise of other powers not granted by the said Compact, the states who are parties thereto have the right, and are in duty bound, to interpose for arresting the progress of the evil, and for maintaining within their respective limits the authorities, rights, and liberties appertaining to them.

"That the General Assembly doth also express its deep regret that a spirit has, in sundry instances, been manifested by the Federal Government to enlarge its powers by forced constructions of the Constitutional Charter, which defines them; and that indications have appeared of a design to expound certain general phrases (which, having been copied from the very limited grant of powers in the former Articles of Confederation, were the less liable to be misconstrued), so as to destroy the meaning and effect of the particular enumeration which necessarily explains and limits the general phrases, and so as to consolidate the States, by degrees, into one sovereignty, the obvious tendency and inevitable result of which would be, to transform the present republican system of the United States into an absolute, or, at best, a mixed monarchy!"

'They were sent to the several States. We have the replies of Delaware, New York, Connecticut, New Hampshire, Vermont, and Massachusetts, not one of which contradicts this important assertion on the part of Virginia; and, by their silence, they all acquiesce in its truth. The case is still stronger against Massachusetts, which expressly recognizes the fact that the Constitution is a Compact. [Stephens' note: Here Mr. Calhoun read from the answer of Massachusetts, in which the Constitution is called a solemn Compact.]

'Now, I ask the Senator [Webster] himself—I put it to his candor to say, if South Carolina be estopped on the subject of the protective system, because Mr. Burke and Mr. Smith proposed a moderate duty on hemp, or some other article, I know not what, nor do I care, with a view of encouraging its production (of which motion, I venture to say, not one individual in a hundred in the State ever heard), whether he and Massachusetts, after this clear, full, and solemn recognition that the Constitution is a Compact (both on his part and that of his State), be not forever estopped on this important point?

'There remains one more of the Senator's arguments, to prove that the Constitution is not a Compact, to be considered. He says it is not a Compact, because it is a Government; which he defines to be an organized body, possessed of the will and power to execute its purposes by its own proper authority; and which, he says, bears not the slightest resemblance to a Compact. But I would ask the Senator, Whoever considered a Government, when spoken of as the agent to execute the powers of the Constitution, and distinct from the Constitution itself, as a Compact? In that light it would be a perfect absurdity. It is true that, in general and loose language, it is often said that the Government is a Compact, meaning the Constitution which created it, and vested it with authority to execute the powers contained in the instrument; but when the distinction is drawn between the Constitution and the Government, as the Senator has done, it would be as ridiculous to call the Government a Compact, as to call an individual, appointed to execute the provisions of a contract, a contract; and not less so to suppose that there could be the slightest resemblance between them. In connection with this point, the Senator, to prove that the Constitution is not a Compact, asserts that it is wholly independent of the State, and pointedly declares that the States have not a right to touch a hair of its head; and this, with that provision in the Constitution that three-fourths of the States have a right to alter, change, amend, or even to abolish it, staring him in the face.

'I have examined all of the arguments of the Senator intended to prove that the Constitution is not a Compact; and I trust I have shown, by the clearest demonstration, that his arguments are perfectly inconclusive, and that his assertion is against the clearest and most solemn evidence—evidence of record, and of such a character that it ought to close his lips forever.

'I turn now to consider the other, and, apparently, contradictory aspect in which the Senator presented this part of the subject: I mean that in which he states that the Government is founded in Compact, but is no longer a Compact. I have already remarked, that no other interpretation could be given to this assertion, except that the Constitution was once a Compact, but is no longer so. There was a vagueness and indistinctness in this part of the Senator's argument, which left me altogether uncertain as to its real meaning. If he meant, as I presume he did, that the Compact is an executed, and not an executory one—that its object was to create a Government, and to invest it with proper authority—and that, having executed this office, it had performed its functions, and, with it, had ceased to exist, then we have the extraordinary avowal that the Constitution is a dead letter—that it had ceased to have any binding effect, or any practical influence or operation.

'It has, indeed, often been charged that the Constitution has become a dead letter; that it is continually violated, and has lost all its control over the Government; but no one has ever before been bold enough to advance a theory on the avowed basis that it was an executed, and, therefore, an extinct instrument. I will not seriously attempt to refute an argument, which, to me, appears so extravagant. I had thought that the Constitution was to endure forever; and that, so far from its being an executed contract, it contained great trust powers for the benefit of those who created it, and of all future generations,—which never could be finally executed during the existence of the world, if our Government should so long endure.

'I will now return to the first Resolution, to see how the issue stands between the Senator from Massachusetts [Webster] and myself. It contains three propositions. First, that the Constitution is a Compact; second, that it was formed by the States, constituting distinct communities; and, lastly, that it is a subsisting and binding Compact between the States. How do these three propositions now stand? The first, I trust, has been satisfactorily established; the second, the Senator has admitted, faintly, indeed, but still he has admitted it to be true. This admission is something. It is so much gained by discussion. Three years ago even this was a contested point. But I cannot say that I thank him for the admission; we owe it to the force of truth. The fact that these States were declared to be free and independent States at the time of their independence; that they were acknowledged to be so by Great Britain in the treaty which terminated the war of the [American] Revolution, and secured their independence; that they were recognized in the same character in the old Articles of the Confederation; and, finally, that the present Constitution was formed by a Convention of the several States; afterwards submitted to them for their respective ratifications, and was ratified by them separately, each for itself, and each, by its own act, binding its citizens,—formed a body of facts too clear to be denied, and too strong to be resisted.

'It now remains to consider the third and last proposition contained in the Resolution,—that it is a binding and a subsisting Compact between the States. The Senator was not explicit on this point. I understood him, however, as asserting that, though formed by the States, the Constitution was not binding between the States as distinct communities, but between the American people in the aggregate; who, in consequence of the adoption of the Constitution, according to the opinion of the Senator, became one people, at least to the extent of the delegated powers. This would, indeed, be a great change. All acknowledge that, previous to the adoption of the Constitution, the States constituted distinct and independent communities, in full possession of their

Sovereignty; and, surely, if the adoption of the Constitution was intended to effect the great and important change in their condition which the theory of the Senator supposes, some evidence of it ought to be found in the instrument itself. It professes to be a careful and full enumeration of all the powers which the States delegated, and of every modification of their political condition. The Senator said that he looked to the Constitution in order to ascertain its real character; and, surely, he ought to look to the same instrument in order to ascertain what changes were, in fact, made in the political condition of the States and the country. But, with the exception of "we, the people of the United States," in the preamble, he has not pointed out a single indication in the Constitution, of the great change which as he conceives, has been effected in this respect.

'Now, sir, I intend to prove, that the only argument on which the gentleman relies on this point, must utterly fail him. I do not intend to go into a critical examination of the expression of the preamble to which I have referred. I do not deem it necessary. But if it were, it might be easily shown that it is at least as applicable to my view of the Constitution as to that of the Senator; and that the whole of his argument on this point rests on the ambiguity of the term thirteen United States; which may mean certain territorial limits, comprehending within them the whole of the States and Territories of the Union. In this sense, the people of the United States may mean all the people living within these limits, without reference to the States or Territories in which they may reside, or of which they may be citizens; and it is in this sense only, that the expression gives the least countenance to the argument of the Senator.

'But it may also mean, *the States united*, which inversion alone, without further explanation, removes the ambiguity to which I have referred. The expression in this sense, obviously means no more than to speak of the people of the several States in their united and confederated capacity; and, if it were requisite, it might be shown that it is only in this sense that the expression is used in the Constitution. But it is not necessary. A single argument will forever settle this point. Whatever may be the true meaning of the expression, it is not applicable to the condition of the States as they exist under the Constitution, but as it was under the old Confederation, before its adoption. The Constitution had not yet been adopted, and the States, in ordaining it, could only speak of themselves in the condition in which they then existed, and not in that in which they would exist under the Constitution. So that, if the argument of the Senator proves any thing, it proves, not (as he supposes) that the Constitution forms the American people into an aggregate mass of individuals, but that such was their political condition before its adoption, under the old Confederation, directly contrary to his argument in the previous part of this discussion.

'But I intend not to leave this important point, the last refuge of those who advocate consolidation, even on this conclusive argument. I have shown that the Constitution affords not the least evidence of the mighty change of the political condition of the States and the country, which the Senator supposed it effected; and I intend now, by the most decisive proof, drawn from the instrument itself, to show that no such change was intended, and that the people of the States are united under it as States, and not as individuals. On this point there is a very important part of the Constitution entirely and strangely overlooked by the Senator in this debate, as it is expressed in the first Resolution, which furnishes conclusive evidence not only that the Constitution is a Compact, but a subsisting Compact, binding between the States. I allude to the seventh Article, which provides that the ratification of the Conventions of nine States shall be sufficient for the establishment of this Constitution "between the States so ratifying the same." Yes, "between the States." These little words mean a volume. Compacts, not laws, bind between States; and it here binds, not as between individuals, but between the States: the States ratifying; implying, as strong as language can make it, that the Constitution is what I have asserted it to be—a Compact, ratified by the States, and a subsisting Compact, binding the States ratifying it.

'But, sir, I will not leave this point, all-important in establishing the true theory of our Government, on this argument alone, as demonstrative and conclusive as I hold it to be. Another, not much less powerful, but of a different character, may be drawn from the tenth amended Article [i.e., the Tenth Amendment], which provides that the powers not delegated to the United States by the Constitution, nor prohibited by it to the States, are reserved to the States respectively or to the people. The Article of Ratification, which I have just cited, informs us that the Constitution, which delegates powers, was ratified by the States, and is binding between them. This informs us to whom the powers are delegated,—a most important fact in determining the point immediately at issue between the Senator and myself. According to his views, the Constitution created a union between individuals, if the solecism may be allowed, and that it formed, at least to the extent of the powers delegated, one people, and not a Federal Union of the States, as I contend; or, to express the same idea differently, that the delegation of powers was to the American people in the aggregate (for it is only by such delegation that they could be constituted one people), and not to the United States,—directly contrary to the Article just cited, which declares that the powers are delegated to the United States. And here it is worthy of notice, that the Senator cannot shelter himself under the ambiguous phrase, "to the people of the United States," under which he would certainly have taken refuge, had the Constitution so expressed it; but fortunately for the cause of truth and the great principles of Constitutional liberty for which I am contending, "people," is omitted: thus making the delegation of power clear and unequivocal to the United States, as distinct political communities, and conclusively proving that all the powers delegated are reciprocally delegated by the States to each other, as distinct political communities.

'So much for the delegated powers. Now, as all admit, and as it is expressly provided for in the Constitution, the reserved powers are reserved "to the States respectively, or to the people." None will pretend that, as far as they are concerned, we are one people, though the argument to prove it, however absurd, would be far more plausible than that which goes to show that we are one people to the extent of the delegated powers. This reservation "to the people" might, in the hands of subtle and trained logicians, be a peg to hang a doubt upon; and had the expression "to the people" been connected, as fortunately it is not, with the delegated instead of the reserved powers, we should not have heard of this in the present discussion.

'I have now established, I hope, beyond the power of controversy, every allegation contained in the first Resolution—that the Constitution is a Compact formed by the people of the several States, as distinct political communities, and subsisting and binding between the States in the same character; which brings me to the consideration of the consequences which may be fairly deduced, in reference to the character of our political system, from these established facts.

'The first and most important is, they conclusively establish that ours is a Federal [Confederate] system—a system of States arranged in a Federal [Confederate] Union, each retaining its distinct existence and Sovereignty. Ours has every attribute which belongs to a Federative [Confederative] System. It is founded on Compact; it is formed by Sovereign communities, and is binding between them in their Sovereign capacity. I might appeal, in confirmation of this assertion, to all elementary writers on the subject of Government, but will content myself with citing one only. Burlamaqui, quoted with approbation by Judge [St. George] Tucker, in his Commentary on [Sir William] Blackstone, himself a high authority, says:

> [Calhoun quoting Tucker's Blackstone:] "Political bodies, whether great or small, if they are constituted by a people formerly independent, and under no civil subjection, or by those who justly claim independence from any civil power they were formerly subject to, have the civil supremacy in themselves, and are in a State of equal right and liberty with respect to all other States, whether great or small. No regard is to be had in this matter to names, whether the body-politic be called a kingdom, an empire, a principality, a dukedom, a country, a republic, or free town. If it can exercise justly all the essential parts of civil power within itself, independently of any other person or body-politic,—and no other has any right to rescind or annul its acts,—it has the civil supremacy, how small soever its territory may be, or the number of its people, and has all the rights of an independent State.
>
> "This independence of States, and their being distinct political bodies from each other, is not obstructed by any alliance or confederacies whatsoever, about exercising jointly any parts of the supreme powers, such as those of peace and war, in league offensive and defensive. Two States, notwithstanding such treaties, are separate bodies, and independent.

"These are, then, only deemed politically united, when some one person or council is constituted with a right to exercise some essential powers for both, and to hinder either from exercising them separately. If any person or council is empowered to exercise all these essential powers for both, they are then one State: such is the State of England and Scotland, since the Act of Union made at the beginning of the eighteenth century, whereby the two kingdoms were incorporated into one, all parts of the supreme power of both kingdoms being thenceforward united, and vested in the three Estates of the realm of Great Britain; by which entire coalition, though both kingdoms retain their ancient laws and usages in many respects, they are as effectually united and incorporated, as the several petty kingdoms, which composed the heptarchy, were before that period.

"But when only a portion of the supreme civil power is vested in one person or council for both, such as that of peace and war, or of deciding controversies between different States, or their subjects, while each, within itself, exercises other parts of the supreme power, independently of all the others—in this case they are called Systems of States, which Burlamaqui defines to be an assemblage of perfect Governments, strictly united by some common bond, so that they seem to make but a single body with respect to those affairs which interest them in common, though each preserves its Sovereignty, full and entire, independently of all others. And in this case, he adds, the Confederate States engage to each other only to exercise, with common consent, certain parts of the Sovereignty, especially that which relates to their mutual defence against foreign enemies. But each of the Confederates retains an entire liberty of exercising, as it thinks proper, those parts of the Sovereignty which are not mentioned in the treaty of Union, as parts that ought to be exercised in common. And of this nature is the American Confederacy, in which each State has resigned the exercise of certain parts of the supreme civil power which they possessed before (except in common with the other States included in the Confederacy), reserving to themselves all their former powers, which are not delegated to the United States by the common bond of Union.

"A visible distinction, and not less important than obvious, occurs to our observation, in comparing these different kinds of Union. The kingdoms of England and Scotland are united into one kingdom; and the two contracting States, by such an incorporate Union, are, in the opinion of Judge Blackstone, totally annihilated, without any power of revival; and a third arises from their conjunction, in which all the rights of Sovereignty, and particularly that of Legislation, are vested. From whence he expresses a doubt, whether any infringements of the fundamental and essential conditions of the Union would, of itself, dissolve the Union of those kingdoms; though he readily admits that, in the case of a Federate [Confederate] alliance, such an infringement would certainly rescind the Compact between the Confederated States. In the United States of America, on the contrary, each State retains its own antecedent form of Government; its own laws, subject to the alteration and control of its own Legislature only; its own executive officers and council of State; its own courts of Judicature, its own judges, its own magistrates, civil officers, and officers of the militia; and, in short, its own civil State, or body politic, in every respect whatsoever. And by the express declaration of the 12th [i.e., the 10th] article of the amendments to the Constitution, the powers not delegated to the United States by the Constitution, nor prohibited by it to the States, are reserved to the States respectively, or to the people. In Great Britain, a new civil State is created by the annihilation of two antecedent civil States; in the American States, a general Federal council and administration is provided, for the joint exercise of such of their several powers as can be more conveniently exercised in that mode than any other, leaving their civil State unaltered; and all the other powers, which the States antecedently possessed, to be exercised by them respectively, as if no Union or connection were established between them.

"The ancient Achaia seems to have been a Confederacy founded upon a similar plan; each of those little States had its distinct possessions, territories, and boundaries; each had its Senate or Assembly, its magistrates and judges; and every State sent Deputies to the General Convention, and had equal weight in all determinations. And most of the neighboring States which, moved by fear of danger, acceded to this Confederacy, had reason to felicitate themselves.

"These Confederacies, by which several States are united together by a perpetual league of alliance, are chiefly founded upon this circumstance, that each particular people choose to remain their own masters, and yet are not strong enough to make head against a common enemy. The purport of such an agreement usually is, that they shall not exercise some part of the Sovereignty, there specified, without the general consent of each other. For the leagues, to which these systems of States owe their rise, seem distinguished from others (so frequent among different States), chiefly by this consideration, that, in the latter, each confederate people determine themselves, by their own judgment, to certain mutual performances; yet so that, in all other respects, they design not, in the least, to make the exercise of that part of the Sovereignty, whence these performances proceed, dependent on the consent of their allies, or to retrench any thing from their full and unlimited power of governing their own States. Thus, we see that ordinary treaties propose, for the most part, as their aim, only some particular advantage of the States thus transacting—their interests happening, at present, to fall in with each other—but do not produce any lasting union as to the chief management of affairs. Such was the treaty of alliance between America and France, in the year 1778, by which, among other articles, it was agreed that neither of the two parties should conclude either truce or peace with Great Britain, without the formal consent of the other, first obtained, and whereby they mutually engaged not to lay down their arms until the independence of the United States should be formally or tacitly assured by the treaty or treaties which should terminate the war. Whereas, in these confederacies of which we are now speaking, the contrary is observable, they being established with this design, that the several States shall forever link their safety, one with another; and, in order to their mutual defence, shall engage themselves not to exercise certain parts of their Sovereign power, otherwise than by a common agreement and approbation. Such were the stipulations, among others, contained in the Articles of Confederation and perpetual Union between American States, by which it was agreed that no State should, without the consent of the United States, in Congress assembled, send any embassy to, or receive any embassy from, or enter into any conference, agreement, alliance or treaty with, any king, prince or State; nor keep up any vessels of war, or body of forces, in time of peace; nor engage in any war, without the consent of the United States in Congress assembled, unless actually invaded; nor grant commissions to any ships of war, or letters of marque and reprisal, except after a declaration of war by the United States in Congress assembled, with several others; yet each State, respectively, retains its Sovereignty, freedom and independence, and every power, jurisdiction and right which is not expressly delegated to the United States in Congress assembled. The promises made in these two cases, here compared, run very differently; in the former, thus: I will join you, in this particular war, as a confederate, and the manner of our attacking the enemy shall be concerted by our common advice; nor will we desist from war, till the particular end thereof, the establishment of the independence of the United States, be obtained. In the latter, thus: None of us who have entered into this alliance, will make use of our right as to the affairs of war and peace, except by the general consent of the whole confederacy. We observed before that these Unions submit only some certain parts of the Sovereignty to mutual direction; for it seems hardly possible that the affairs of different States should have so close a connection, as that all and each of them should look on it as their interest to have no part of the chief Government exercised without the general concurrence. The most convenient method, therefore, seems to be, that the particular States reserve to themselves all those branches of the supreme authority, the management of which can have little or no influence in the affairs of the rest."

[Calhoun continues:] 'If we compare our present system with the old Confederation, which all acknowledge to have been Federal [Confederate] in its character, we shall find that it possesses all the attributes which belong to that form of Government as fully and completely as that did. In fact, in this particular, there is but a single difference, and that not essential, as regards the point immediately under consideration, though very important in other respects. The Confederation was the act of the State Governments, and formed a union of Governments. The present Constitution is the act of the States themselves, or, which is the same thing, of the people of the several States, and forms a union of them as Sovereign communities. The States, previous to the adoption of the Constitution, were as separate and distinct political bodies as the Governments which represent them, and there is nothing in the nature of things to prevent them from uniting under a Compact, in a Federal Union, without being blended in one mass, any more than uniting the Governments themselves, in like manner, without merging them in a single Government. To illustrate what I have stated by reference to ordinary transactions, the Confederation was a contract between agents—the present Constitution a contract between the principals themselves; or, to take a more analogous case, one is a League made by ambassadors; the other, a League made by Sovereigns—the latter no more tending to unite the parties into a single Sovereignty than the former. The only difference is in the solemnity of the act and the force of the obligation.

'We will now proceed to consider some of the conclusions which necessarily follow from the facts and positions already established. They enable us to decide a question of vital importance under our system: Where does Sovereignty reside? If I have succeeded in establishing the fact that ours is a Federal [Confederate] system, as I conceive I conclusively have, that fact of itself determines the question which I have proposed. It is of the very essence of such a system, that the Sovereignty is in the parts, and not in the whole; or, to use the language of Mr. [Sir Francis] Palgrave, "The parts are the units in such a system, and the whole the multiple; and not the whole the unit and the parts the fractions." Ours, then, is a Government of twenty-four Sovereignties, united by a Constitutional Compact, for the purpose of exercising certain powers through a common Government as their joint agent, and not a Union of the twenty-four Sovereignties into one, which, according to the language of the Virginia Resolutions, already cited, would form a Consolidation. And here I must express my surprise that the Senator from Virginia should avow himself the advocate of these very Resolutions, when he distinctly maintains the idea of a Union of the States in one Sovereignty, which is expressly condemned by these Resolutions as the essence of a Consolidated Government.

'Another consequence is equally clear, that, whatever modifications were made in the condition of the States under the present Constitution, they extended only to the exercise of their powers by Compact, and not to the Sovereignty itself, and are such as Sovereigns are competent to make: it being a conceded point, that it is competent to them to stipulate to exercise their powers in a particular manner, or to abstain altogether from their exercise, or to delegate them to agents, without in any degree impairing Sovereignty itself. The plain state of the facts, as regards our Government, is, that these States have agreed by Compact to exercise their Sovereign powers jointly, as already stated; and that, for this purpose, they have ratified the Compact in their Sovereign capacity, thereby making it the Constitution of each State, in nowise distinguished from their own separate Constitutions, but in the super-added obligation of Compact—of faith mutually pledged to each other. In this Compact, they have stipulated, among other things, that it may be amended by three fourths of the States: that is, they have conceded to each other by Compact the right to add new powers or to subtract old, by the consent of that proportion of the States, without requiring, as otherwise would have been the case, the consent of all: a modification no more inconsistent, as has been supposed, with their Sovereignty, than any other contained in the Compact. In fact, the provision to which I allude furnishes strong evidence that the Sovereignty is, as I contend, in the States severally, as the amendments are effected, not by any one three fourths, but by any three fourths of the States, indicating that the Sovereignty is in each of the States.

'If these views be correct, it follows, as a matter of course, that the allegiance of the people is to their several States, and that treason consists in resistance to the joint authority of the States united, not, as has been absurdly contended, in resistance to the Government of the United States, which, by the provision of the Constitution, has only the right of punishing.

'Having now said what I intended in relation to my first Resolution, both in reply to the Senator from Massachusetts [Webster], and in vindication of its correctness, I will now proceed to consider the conclusions drawn from it in the second Resolution—that the General Government is not the exclusive and final judge of the extent of the powers delegated to it, but that the States, as parties to the Compact, have a right to judge, in the last resort, of the infractions of the Compact, and of the mode and measure of redress.

'It can scarcely be necessary, before so enlightened a body, to premise that our system comprehends two distinct Governments—the General and State Governments, which, properly considered, form but one—the former representing the joint authority of the States in their Confederate capacity, and the latter that of each State separately. I have premised this fact simply with a view of presenting distinctly the answer to the argument offered by the Senator from Massachusetts to prove that the General Government has a final and exclusive right to judge, not only of delegated powers, but also of those reserved to the States. That gentleman relies for his main argument on the assertion that a Government, which he defines to be an organized body, endowed with both will, and power, and authority in *proprio vigore* [Latin: "by its own force"] to execute its purpose, has a right inherently to judge of its powers. It is not my intention to comment upon the definition of the Senator, though it would not be difficult to show that his ideas of Government are not very American. My object is to deal with the conclusion, and not the definition. Admit then, that the Government has the right of judging of its powers, for which he contends. How, then, will he withhold, upon his own principle, the right of judging from the State Governments, which he has attributed to the General Government? If it belongs to one, on his principle, it belongs to both; and if to both, when they differ, the veto, so abhorred by the Senator, is the necessary result: as neither, if the right be possessed by both, can control the other.

'The Senator felt the force of this argument, and, in order to sustain his main position, he fell back on that clause of the Constitution which provides that "this Constitution, and the laws made in pursuance thereof, shall be the supreme law of the land."

'This is admitted; no one has ever denied that the Constitution, and the laws made in pursuance of it, are of Paramount authority. But it is equally undeniable that laws not made in pursuance are not only not of Paramount authority, but are of no authority whatever, being of themselves null and void; which presents the question, who are to judge whether the laws be or be not pursuant to the Constitution? and thus the difficulty, instead of being taken away, is removed but one step further back. This the Senator also felt, and has attempted to overcome, by setting up, on the part of Congress and the judiciary, the final and exclusive right of judging, both for the Federal Government and the States, as to the extent of their respective powers. That I may do full justice to the gentleman, I will give his doctrine in his own words. He states,—

[Calhoun quoting Webster:] "That there is a supreme law, composed of the Constitution, the laws passed in pursuance of it, and the treaties; but in cases coming before Congress, not assuming the shape of cases in law and equity, so as to be subjects of judicial discussion, Congress must interpret the Constitution so often as it has occasion to pass laws; and in cases capable of assuming a judicial shape, the Supreme Court must be the final interpreter."

'Now, passing over this vague and loose phraseology, I would ask the Senator upon what principle can he concede this extensive power to the Legislative and Judicial departments, and withhold it entirely from the Executive? If one has the right it cannot be withheld from the other. I would also ask him on what principle—if the departments of the General Government are to possess the right of judging, finally and conclusively, of their respective powers—on what principle can the same right be withheld from the State Governments, which, as well as the General Government, properly considered, are but departments of the same general system, and form together, properly speaking, but one Government? This was a favorite idea of Mr. Macon, for whose wisdom I have a respect increasing with my experience, and who I have frequently heard say, that most of the misconceptions and errors in relation to our system, originated in forgetting that they were but parts of the same system. I would further tell the Senator, that, if this right be withheld from the State Governments; if this restraining influence, by which the General Government is confined to its proper sphere, be withdrawn, then that department of the Government from which he has withheld the right of judging of its own powers (the Executive), will, so far from being excluded, become the sole interpreter of the powers of the Government. It is the armed interpreter, with powers to execute its own construction, and with out the aid of which the construction of the other departments will be impotent.

'But I contend that the States have a far clearer right to the sole construction of their powers than any of the departments of the Federal Government can have. This power is expressly reserved, as I have stated on another occasion, not only against the several departments of the General Government, but against the United States themselves. I will not repeat the arguments which I then offered on this point, and which remain unanswered, but I must be permitted to offer strong additional proof of the views then taken, and which, if I am not mistaken, are conclusive on this point. It is drawn from the ratification of the Constitution by Virginia, and is in the following words:

> We, the Delegates of the people of Virginia, duly elected in pursuance of a recommendation from the General Assembly, and now met in Convention, having fully and freely investigated and discussed the proceedings of the Federal Convention, and being prepared, as well as the most mature deliberation hath enabled us, to decide thereon, do, in the name and in behalf of the people of Virginia, declare and make known that the powers granted under the Constitution, being derived from the people of the United States, may be resumed by them, whensoever the same shall be perverted to their injury or oppression, and that every power not granted thereby remains with them, and at their will; that, therefore, no right, of any denomination, can be cancelled, abridged, restrained, or modified, by the Congress, by the Senate or House of Representatives, acting in any capacity, by the President, or any department or officer of the United States, except in those instances in which power is given by the Constitution for those purposes; and that, among other essential rights, the liberty of conscience, and of the press, cannot be cancelled, abridged, restrained, or modified by any authority of the United States. With these impressions, with a solemn appeal to the Searcher of all hearts for the purity of our intentions, and under the conviction that whatsoever imperfections may exist in the Constitution ought rather to be examined in the mode prescribed therein, than to bring the Union in danger by a delay, with the hope of obtaining amendments previous to the ratifications,—We, the said Delegates, in the name and in the behalf of the people of Virginia, do, by these presents, assent to and ratify the Constitution recommended, on the 17th day of September, 1787, by the

Federal Convention for the Government of the United States, hereby announcing to all those whom it may concern, that the said Constitution is binding upon the said people, according to an authentic copy hereto annexed, in the words following . . . etc.

'It thus appears that this sagacious State (I fear, however, that her sagacity is not so sharp-sighted now as formerly) ratified the Constitution, with an explanation as to her reserved powers; that they were powers subject to her own will, and reserved against every department of the General Government—Legislative, Executive, and Judicial—as if she had a prophetic knowledge of the attempts now made to impair and destroy them: which explanation can be considered in no other light than as containing a condition on which she ratified, and, in fact, making part of the Constitution of the United States—extending as well to the other States as herself. I am no lawyer, and it may appear to be presumption in me to lay down the rule of law which governs in such cases, in a controversy with so distinguished an advocate as the Senator from Massachusetts. But I shall venture to lay it down as a rule in such cases, which I have no fear that the gentleman will contradict, that, in case of a contract between several partners, if the entrance of one on condition be admitted, the condition enures to the benefit of all the partners. But I do not rest the argument simply upon this view Virginia proposed the tenth amended article, the one in question, and her ratification must be at least received as the highest evidence of its true meaning and interpretation.

'If these views be correct—and I do not see how they can be resisted—the rights of the States to judge of the extent of their reserved powers stands on the most solid foundation, and is good against every department of the General Government; and the judiciary is as much excluded from an interference with the reserved powers as the Legislative or Executive departments. To establish the opposite, the Senator relies upon the authority of Mr. [James] Madison, in the *Federalist*, to prove that it was intended to invest the Court with the power in question. In reply, I will meet Mr. Madison with his own opinion, given on a most solemn occasion, and backed by the sagacious Commonwealth of Virginia. The opinion to which I allude will be found in the celebrated Report of 1799, of which Mr. Madison was the author. It says:

> [Calhoun quoting Madison:] "But it is objected, that the Judicial Authority is to be regarded as the sole expositor of the Constitution in the last resort; and it may be asked for what reason the declaration by the General Assembly, supposing it to be theoretically true, could be required at the present day, and in so solemn a manner.
> "On this objection it might be observed, first, that there may be instances of usurped power, which the forms of the Constitution would never draw within the control of the Judicial department; secondly, that, if the decision of the judiciary be raised above the authority of the

Sovereign parties to the Constitution, the decisions of the other departments, not carried by the forms of the Constitution before the judiciary, must be equally authoritative and final as the decisions of this department. But the proper answer to this objection is, that the Resolution of the General Assembly relates to those great and extraordinary cases in which all the forms of the Constitution may prove ineffectual against infractions dangerous to the essential rights of the parties to it. The Resolution supposes that dangerous powers, not delegated, may not only be usurped and executed by the other departments, but that the Judicial department, also, may exercise or sanction dangerous powers beyond the grant of the Constitution; and, consequently, that the ultimate right of the parties to the Constitution to judge whether the Compact was dangerously violated, must extend to violations by one delegated authority as well as by another; by the judiciary as well as by the executive or the Legislature.

"But why should I waste words in reply to these or any other authorities, when it has been so clearly established that the rights of the States are reserved against each and every department of the Government, and no authority in opposition can possibly shake a position so well established? Nor do I think it necessary to repeat the argument which I offered when the bill was under discussion, to show that the clause in the Constitution which provides that the judicial power shall extend to all cases in law or equity arising under this Constitution, and to the laws and treaties made under its authority, has no bearing on the point in controversy; and that even the boasted power of the Supreme Court to decide a law to be unconstitutional, so far from being derived from this or any other portion of the Constitution, results from the necessity of the case—where two rules of unequal authority come in conflict—and is a power belonging to all courts, superior and inferior, State and General, Domestic, and Foreign."

[Calhoun continues:] 'I have now, I trust, shown satisfactorily, that there is no provision in the Constitution to authorize the General Government, through any of its departments, to control the action of a State within the sphere of its reserved powers; and that, of course, according to the principle laid down by the Senator from Massachusetts [Webster] himself, the Government of the States, as well as the General Government, has the right to determine the extent of their respective powers, without the right on the part of either to control the other. The necessary result is the veto, to which he so much objects; and to get clear of which, he informed us, was the object for which the present Constitution was formed. I know not whence he has derived his information, but my impression is very different, as to the immediate motives which led to the formation of that instrument. I have always understood that the principle was, to give to Congress the power to regulate commerce, to lay impost duties, and to raise a revenue for the payment of the public debt and the expenses of the Government; and to subject the action of the citizens, individually, to the operation of the laws, as a substitute for force. If the object had been to get clear of the veto of the States, as the Senator states, the Convention, certainly, performed their work in a most bungling manner. There was, unquestionably, a large party in that body, headed by men of distinguished talents and influence, who commenced early and worked earnestly to the last, to deprive the States—not directly, for that would have been too bold an attempt, but indirectly—of the veto. The good sense of the Convention, however put down every effort, however disguised and perseveringly made. I do not deem it necessary to give, from the journals, the history of these various and unsuccessful attempts—though it would afford a very instructive lesson. It is sufficient to say that it was attempted, by proposing to give to Congress power to annul the acts of the States which they might deem inconsistent with the Constitution; to give to the President the power of appointing the Governors of the States, with a view of vetoing State laws through his authority; and, finally, to give the judiciary the power to decide controversies between the States and the General Government; all of which failed—fortunately for the liberty of the country—utterly and entirely failed; and in this failure we have the strongest evidence, that it was not the intention of the Convention to deprive the States of the veto power. Had the attempt to deprive them of this power been directly made, and failed, every one would have seen and felt, that it would furnish conclusive evidence in favor of its existence. Now, I would ask, what possible difference can it make in what form this attempt was made? Whether by attempting to confer on the General Government a power incompatible with the exercise of the veto on the part of the States, or by attempting directly to deprive them of the right to exercise it? We have thus direct and strong proof that, in the opinion of the Convention, the States, unless deprived of it, possess the veto power—or, what is another name for the same thing, the right of Nullification. I know that there is a diversity of opinion among the friends of State Rights in regard to this power, which I regret, as I cannot but consider it as a power essential to the protection of the minor and local interests of the community, and the liberty and the Union of the country. It is the very shield of State Rights, and the only power by which that system of injustice against which we have contended for more than thirteen years can be arrested: a system of hostile Legislation—of plundering by law, which must necessarily lead to a conflict of arms, if not prevented.

'But I rest the right of a State to judge of the extent of its reserved powers, in the last resort, on higher grounds—that the Constitution is a Compact, to which the States are parties in their Sovereign capacity; and that, as in all other cases of Compact between parties having no common umpire, each has a right to judge for itself. To the truth of this proposition, the Senator from Massachusetts has himself assented, if the Constitution itself be a Compact—and that it is, I have shown, I trust, beyond the possibility of a doubt. Having established this point, I now claim, as stated I would do, in the course of the discussion, the admissions of the Senator, and, among them, the right of Secession and Nullification, which he conceded would necessarily follow if the Constitution be, indeed, a Compact.

'I have now replied to the arguments of the Senator from Massachusetts so far as they directly apply to the Resolutions, and will, in conclusion, notice some of his general and detached remarks. To prove that ours is a consolidated Government, and that there is an immediate connection between the Government and the citizen, he relies on the fact that the laws act directly on individuals. That such is the case I will not deny; but I am very far from conceding the point that it affords the decisive proof, or even any proof at all, of the position which the Senator wishes to maintain. I hold it to be perfectly within the competency of two or more States to subject their citizens, in certain cases, to the direct action of each other, without surrendering or impairing their Sovereignty. I recollect, while I was a member of Mr. [James] Monroe's cabinet, a proposition was submitted by the British Government to permit a mutual right of search and seizure, on the part of each Government, of the citizens of the other, on board of vessels engaged in the slave-trade, and to establish a joint tribunal for their trial and punishment. The proposition was declined, not because it would impair the Sovereignty of either, but on the ground of general expediency, and because it would be incompatible with the provisions of the Constitution which establish the judicial power, and which provisions require the judges to be appointed by the President and Senate. If I am not mistaken, propositions of the same kind were made and acceded to by some of the Continental powers.

'With the same view the Senator cited the suability of the States as evidence of their want of Sovereignty; at which I must express my surprise, coming from the quarter it does. No one knows better than the Senator that it is perfectly within the competency of a Sovereign State to permit itself to be sued. We have on the Statute-book a standing law, under which the United States may be sued in certain land cases. If the provision in the Constitution on this point proves any thing, it proves, by the extreme jealousy with which the right of suing a State is permitted, the very reverse of that for which the Senator contends.

'Among other objections to the views of the Constitution for which I contend, it is said that they are novel. I hold this to be a great mistake. The novelty is not on my side, but on that of the Senator from Massachusetts. The doctrine of Consolidation which he maintains is of recent growth. It is not the doctrine of [Alexander] Hamilton, [Fisher] Ames, or any of the distinguished Federalists of the period, all of whom strenuously maintained the Federative [Confederate] character of the Constitution, though they were accused of supporting a system of policy which would necessarily lead to Consolidation. The first disclosure of that doctrine was in the case of M'Culloch; in which the Supreme Court held the doctrine, though wrapped up in language somewhat indistinct and ambiguous. The next, and more open avowal, was by the Senator of Massachusetts himself, about three years ago, in the debate on Foote's resolution. The first official annunciation of the doctrine was in the recent proclamation of the President, of which the bill that has recently passed this body is the bitter fruit.

'It is further objected by the Senator from Massachusetts, and others, against the doctrine of State Rights, as maintained in this debate, that, if it should prevail, the peace of the country would be destroyed. But what if it should not prevail? Would there be peace? Yes, the peace of despotism: that peace which is enforced by the bayonet and the sword; the peace of death, where all the vital functions of liberty have ceased. It is this peace which the doctrine of State Sovereignty may disturb by that conflict, which, in every free State, if properly organized, necessarily exists between liberty and power; but which, if restrained within proper limits, gives a salutary exercise to our moral and intellectual faculties. In the case of Carolina, which has caused all this discussion, who does not see, if the effusion of blood be prevented, that the excitement, the agitation, and the inquiry which it has caused, will be followed by the most beneficial consequences? The country had sunk into avarice, intrigue, and electioneering—from which nothing but some such event could rouse it, or restore those honest and patriotic feelings which had almost disappeared under their baneful influence. What Government has ever attained power and distinction without such conflicts? Look at the degraded state of all those nations where they have been put down by the iron arm of the Government.

'I, for my part, have no fear of any dangerous conflict, under the fullest acknowledgment of State Sovereignty: the very fact that the States may interpose will produce moderation and justice. The General Government will abstain from the exercise of any power in which they may suppose three fourths of the States will not sustain them; while, on the other hand, the States will not interpose but on the conviction that they will be supported by one fourth of their co-States. Moderation and justice will produce confidence, attachment and patriotism; and these, in turn, will offer most powerful barriers against the excess of conflicts between the States and the General Government.

'But we are told that, should the doctrine prevail, the present system would be as bad, if not worse, than the old Confederation. I regard the assertion only as evidence of that extravagance of declaration in which, from excitement of feeling, we so often indulge. Admit the power, and still the present system would be as far removed from the weakness of the old Confederation as it would be from the lawless and despotic violence of consolidation. So far from being the same, the difference between the Confederation and the present Constitution would still be most strongly marked. If there were no other distinction, the fact that the former required the concurrence of the States to execute its acts, and the latter, the act of a State to arrest them, would make a distinction as broad as the ocean. In the former, the *vis inertia* [Latin: the "power of inactivity"] of our nature is in opposition to the action of the system. Not to act was to defeat. In the latter the same principle is on the opposite side—action is required to defeat. He who understands human nature will see, in this fact alone, the difference between a feeble and illy-contrived Confederation, and the restrained energy of a Federal system. Of the same character is the objection that the doctrine will be the source of weakness. If we look to mere organization and physical power as the only source of strength, without taking into the estimate the operation of moral causes, such would appear to be the fact; but if we take into the estimate the latter, we shall find that those Governments have the greatest strength in which power has been most efficiently checked. The Government of Rome furnishes a memorable example. There, two independent and distinct powers existed—the people acting by Tribes, in which the Plebeians prevailed, and by Centuries, in which the Patricians ruled. The Tribunes were the appointed representatives of the one power, and the Senate of the other; each possessed of the authority of checking and overruling one another, not as departments of the Government, as supposed by the Senator from Massachusetts, but as independent powers,—as much so as the State and General Governments. A shallow observer would perceive, in such an organization, nothing but the perpetual source of anarchy, discord, and weakness; and yet experience has proved that it was the most powerful Government that ever existed; and reason teaches that this power was derived from the very circumstances which hasty reflection would consider the cause of weakness. I will venture an assertion, which may be considered extravagant, but in which history will fully bear me out, that we have no knowledge of any people where the power of arresting the improper acts of the Government, or what may be called the negative power of Government, was too strong,—except Poland, where every freeman possessed a veto. But even there, although it existed in so extravagant a form, it was the source of the highest and most lofty attachment to liberty, and the most heroic courage: qualities that more than once saved Europe from the domination of the crescent and cimeter. It is worthy of remark, that the fate of Poland is not to be attributed so much to the excess of this negative power of itself, as to the facility which it afforded to foreign influence in controlling its political movements.

'I am not surprised that, with the idea of a perfect Government which the Senator from Massachusetts has formed—a Government of an absolute majority, unchecked and unrestrained, operating through a representative body—he should be so much shocked with what he is pleased to call the absurdity of the State veto. But let me tell him that his scheme of a perfect Government, as beautiful as he conceives it to be, though often tried, has invariably failed,—has always run, whenever tried, through the same uniform process of faction, corruption, anarchy, and despotism. He considers the representative principle as the great modern improvement in legislation, and of itself sufficient to secure liberty. I cannot regard it in the light in which he does. Instead of modern, it is of remote origin, and has existed, in greater or less perfection, in every free State, from the remotest antiquity. Nor do I consider it as of itself sufficient to secure liberty, though I regard it as one of the indispensable means—the means of securing the people against the tyranny and oppression of their rulers. To secure liberty, another means is still necessary—the means of securing the different portions of society against the injustice and oppressions of each other, which can only be effected by veto, interposition, or Nullification, or by whatever name the restraining or negative power of Government may be called.'

"This is quite enough of Mr. Calhoun's reply [to Webster]. I have read all of it that bears directly upon the main points in issue between them. On these points never was a man more completely answered than Mr. Webster was. The argument is a crusher, an extinguisher, an annihilator!

"[Webster never offered an official rejoinder to Calhoun. . . .] He followed with a few remarks only, disavowing any personal unkind feelings to Mr.

Calhoun, explaining how he had used the term 'Constitutional Compact,' in 1830; and attempting to parry one or two of the blows, but he never made any regular set reply or rejoinder. He never came back at his opponent at all on the real questions at issue. Mr. Calhoun stood master of the arena. This speech of his was not answered then, it has not been answered since, and in my judgment never will be, or can be answered while truth has its legitimate influence, and reason controls the judgment of men!

"The power and force of this speech must have been felt by Mr. Webster himself. He was a man of too much reason and logic not to have felt it. This opinion I am the more inclined to from the fact, that he not only did not attempt a general reply to it at the time, but from the further fact, that in after life he certainly, to say the least of it, greatly modified the opinions held by him in that debate.

". . . I refer specially to a speech made by him before the Supreme Court of the United States, in 1839, and to his speech at Capon Springs, in Virginia, in 1851, as well as some other matters."[132]

15

WEBSTER, CALHOUN, & DAVIS ON THE U.S. CONSTITUTION

STEPHENS' POLITICAL FOES, THE LIBERALS, Nationalists, Centralists, Consolidationists, and South-haters of the day, refused to accept that the Declaration of Independence, the Articles of Confederation, and the U.S. Constitution were intended by the Founding Fathers to forever establish the United States of America as a Confederacy, with the states having full sovereignty and all the other rights of independent nations. One of the "proofs" they offered for their erroneous view was that the law of international comity obtained between the States of our Union is the same doctrine held by the British Courts between Scotland and England. "And yet no one there," they claimed, "holds that Scotland is separately Sovereign from England, or that Scotland could dissolve the Compact of their Union." In this chapter excerpting portions of Stephens' *A Constitutional View*, the former Confederate vice president replies to his Liberal opponents on this topic.

☛ "The cases are totally different. There is no analogy between them. The decision was not made on any such view. The Sovereignties of England and Scotland are not united by Compact at all. The separate Sovereignties of these countries became united by a union of the Crowns of both, by regular descent in the person of James VI, of Scotland, who became James I, of England, upon the death of [Queen] Elizabeth [I]. The declaratory Act of the Parliaments of both, setting forth the fact of the Union thus resulting, and the respective rights of each, under it, distinctly states that the two Kingdoms thereafter shall be created into one Kingdom by the name of Great Britain. This was but the declaration of a unity of Sovereignty, which had occurred by the union of

Crowns by descent, and not one of Compact at all. This distinction is clearly drawn by [Sir William] Blackstone in his Commentaries. That was what he called an 'Incorporate Union' which was very different from a 'Federate alliance.'

"But the difference between the Union of the Sovereignties of England and Scotland and the Federal Union of these States, is fully set forth by Judge [Bushrod] Washington, of the Supreme Court of the United States, in the Circuit Court of the Eastern District of Pennsylvania, in the case of *Lonsdale* vs. *Brown*. This decision was made in 1821. In delivering the opinion the judge says,

> 'The Union between England and Scotland is, politically speaking, as intimate as between England and Wales, or between the different counties of either. They form one Kingdom; are subject to the same Government; and are represented in the same legislative body; and although the laws and customs of Scotland in force at the time of the Union were suffered to continue, yet they are alterable by the Parliament of Great Britain, even as they relate to private rights; if the alteration should be deemed for the evident utility of the people of Scotland.
>
> 'How different is the Union of these States? They are, in their separate political capacities, Sovereign and independent of each other, except so far as they have united for their common defence and for National purposes. They have each a Constitution and form of Government, with all the attributes of Sovereignty. As to matters of National concern they form one Government, are subject to the same laws, and may emphatically be denominated one people. In all other respects, they are as distinct as different forms of Government and different laws can render them. It is true, that the citizens of each State are entitled to all the privileges and immunities of citizens in every other State; that the Sovereignty of the States in relation to fugitives from justice, and from service, is limited; and that each State is bound to give full faith and credit to the public acts, records and judicial proceedings of her sister States. But these privileges and disabilities are mere creatures of the Constitution; and it is quite fair to argue that the framers of that instrument deemed it necessary to secure them by express provisions.
>
> 'In the case of *Warder* vs. *Arrell* . . . the question, in part, was, whether the tender laws of Pennsylvania, where the contract was made, ought to be regarded by the Courts of Virginia, where the suit was brought? and throughout the opinions delivered by the judges, Pennsylvania was treated as a foreign country. The president of the Court is express upon this point. He observes that, in cases of contracts, the laws of a foreign country where the contract is made must govern. The same principle applies, though with no greater force, to the different States of America; for though they form a Confederated Government, yet the several States retain their individual Sovereignties, and with respect to their municipal laws, are to each other

foreign.'

"But in further proof of the modification of the views of Mr. [Daniel] Webster on the subject, I refer to his celebrated letter to the Barings, in London, written the same year. Here it is. In it he uses this language:

'Your first inquiry is, "whether the Legislature of one of the States has legal and Constitutional power to contract loans at home and abroad?"

'To this I answer, that the Legislature of a State has such power; and how any doubt could have arisen on this point it is difficult for me to conceive. Every State is an independent, Sovereign, political community, except in so far as certain powers, which it might otherwise have exercised, have been conferred on a General Government, established under a written Constitution, and exerting its authority over the people of all the States. This General Government is a limited Government. Its powers are specific and enumerated. All powers not conferred upon it still remain with the States and with the people. The State Legislatures, on the other hand, possess all usual and extraordinary powers of Government, subject to any limitations which may be imposed by their own Constitutions, and, with the exception, as I have said, of the operation on those powers of the Constitution of the United States. The powers conferred on the General Government cannot of course be exercised by any individual State; nor can any State pass any law which is prohibited by the Constitution of the United States. . . .

'The security for State loans is the plighted faith of the State, as a political Community. It rests on the same basis as other contracts with established Governments—the same basis, for example, as loans made in the United States under the authority of Congress; that is to say, the good faith of the Government making the loan, and its ability to fulfil its engagements. . . .

'It has been said that the States cannot be sued on these bonds. But neither could the United States be sued, nor, as I suppose, the Crown of England, in a like case. Nor would the power of suing, probably, give the creditor any substantial additional security. The solemn obligation of a Government, arising on its own acknowledged bond, would not be enhanced by a judgment rendered on such bond. If it either could not, or would not, make provision for paying the bond, it is not probable that it could or would make provision for satisfying the judgment.'

"He here distinctly states that every State is an Independent, Sovereign, political Community, except in so far as certain powers, which it might otherwise have exercised, have been conferred on a General Government by a written Constitution, containing certain specified powers. This language is substantially identical with the language of the first Article of the old Confederation.

"An important fact in this connection, to be borne in mind, is that there was no vote taken on Mr. [John C.] Calhoun's Resolutions, in the Senate, in 1833. The matter rested there with the discussion. The controversy that gave rise to it was amicably adjusted . . . [as I shall show]. The subject of the discussion, however, was taken up by the press, by public speakers, by the State Legislatures, and by the people generally. The great discussions of 1798, 1799 and 1800, were revived. Old landmarks of principles were traced. The rapid strides of the Federal Government towards consolidation were again stopped.

"Mr. Calhoun had, on the 28th of December, 1837, renewed the subject in the Senate. He then brought forward another set of Resolutions on the same subject, covering the same ground, embodying the same principles, and pressed them to a vote. These Resolutions are as follows:

> I. Resolved, That in the adoption of the Federal Constitution, the States adopting the same acted, severally, as free, independent, and Sovereign States; and that each, for itself, by its own voluntary assent, entered the Union with the view to its increased security against all dangers, domestic as well as foreign, and the more perfect and secure enjoyment of its advantages, natural, political, and social.
>
> II. Resolved, That, in delegating a portion of their powers to be exercised by the Federal Government, the States retained, severally, the exclusive and sole right over their own domestic institutions and police, to the full extent to which those powers were not thus delegated, and are alone responsible for them; and that any intermeddling of any one or more States, or a combination of their citizens, with the domestic institutions and police of the others, on any ground, political, moral, or religious, or under any pretext whatever, with the view to their alteration or subversion, is not warranted by the Constitution, tending to endanger the domestic peace and tranquillity of the States interfered with, subversive of the objects for which the Constitution was formed, and, by necessary consequence, tending to weaken and destroy the Union itself.
>
> III. Resolved, That this Government was instituted and adopted by the several States of this Union as a common agent, in order to carry into effect the powers which they had delegated by the Constitution for their mutual security and prosperity; and that in fulfilment of this high and sacred trust, this Government is bound so to exercise its powers, as not to interfere with the stability and security of the domestic institutions of the States that compose this Union; and that it is the solemn duty of the Government to resist, to the extent of its Constitutional power, all attempts by one portion of the Union to use it as an instrument to attack the domestic institutions of another, or to weaken or destroy such institutions.
>
> IV. Resolved, That domestic slavery, as it exists in the Southern and Western States of this Union, composes an important part of their domestic

institutions, inherited from their ancestors, and existing at the adoption of the Constitution, by which it is recognized as constituting an important element in the apportionment of powers among the States, and that no change of opinion or feeling, on the part of the other States of the Union in relation to it, can justify them or their citizens in open and systematic attacks thereon, with the view to its overthrow; and that all such attacks are in manifest violation of the mutual and solemn pledge to protect and defend each other, given by the States respectively, on entering into the Constitutional Compact which formed the Union, and as such are a manifest breach of faith, and a violation of the most solemn obligations.

V. Resolved, That the interference by the citizens of any of the States, with the view to the abolition of slavery in this District, is endangering the rights and security of the people of the District; and that any act or measure of Congress designed to abolish slavery in this District, would be a violation of the faith implied in the cessions by the States of Virginia and Maryland, a just cause of alarm to the people of the slaveholding States, and have a direct and inevitable tendency to disturb and endanger the Union.

And resolved, That any attempt of Congress to abolish slavery in any Territory of the United States in which it exists, would create serious alarm, and just apprehension, in the States sustaining that domestic institution; would be a violation of good faith towards the inhabitants of any such territory who have been permitted to settle with, and hold slaves therein, because the people of any such Territory have not asked for the abolition of slavery therein; and because when any such Territory shall be admitted into the Union as a State, the people thereof will be entitled to decide that question exclusively for themselves.

[Editor's note: John C. Calhoun's views on slavery have been greatly misunderstood, and worse, perverted from their original meaning by anti-South partisans. Though he was one of the few Southerners who accepted slavery, he did not push his views on the North, nor did he expect *all* Southerners to embrace the institution. He merely wanted the individual states to maintain the right to choose to practice slavery or not, as promised in the U.S. Constitution at the time. Northern abolitionists (and Yankee Liberals in general), such as William Lloyd Garrison, however, *did* push their views on everyone else, and rigidly expected both Northerners *and* Southerners to embrace them. Calhoun, along with most other Southerners, desired only that the legality of slavery in the Constitution be honored, and that the individual states retain their full sovereignty and rights as laid down in the Ninth and Tenth Amendments. Today's uneducated South-haters continue to claim that in 1861 the South went to war with the North to "preserve slavery." In reality, the South fought to preserve exactly what Calhoun preached: the preservation of the Constitutional rights as set forth by the Founding Fathers; not just regarding slavery, but every other aspect of human life. In short, the South, understandably, wanted to be able to make its own mind up, and not be told by the North how to think, live, and behave. L.S.][133]

[Stephens continues:] "The first of these Resolutions, which distinctly affirms the great truth set forth in the first of . . . [Calhoun's] series in 1833, passed the Senate by the large majority of thirty-two to thirteen, on the third of January, 1838. . . . This was certainly the highest authoritative exposition of the subject that could be given. It was the amplest vindication of the merits of Mr. Calhoun's argument in 1833. His argument and Mr. Webster's had gone to the country, and this was the verdict of the States upon the issue presented by them. *More than two to one of the Senate of the United States affirmed most positively and solemnly that the Union of the States was Federal [Confederate], and that in entering into it under the Constitution, the States did so severally as free, independent, Sovereign Powers. That the Union was one of States, formed by States, and not by the people in the aggregate as one nation.* [Emphasis added, L.S.]

"But upon an analysis of the vote upon this Resolution, and the others of the series, this authoritative exposition derives increased importance. For if we look at the vote by States, it will be seen that eighteen States voted for this Resolution, while only six voted against it. One was divided, and one did not vote. More than two thirds of the States give this construction to the character of the Government in 1838. It is true, Mr. Webster was then in the Senate, and did not vote for it. But he did not take up the gauntlet thrown down by Calhoun for another contest in debate on the principles thus re-announced. Mr. [Henry] Clay, however, voted for it, which shows his understanding of the nature of the Government.

"On the second of these Resolutions, the vote stood thirty-one to nine on the per capita vote. By States the vote was twenty States for it, only four against it, one divided, and one not voting.

"Three fourths of the States voted for this Resolution, enough to have amended the Constitution according to its provision, if they had been in Convention for that purpose.

"The vote on the third Resolution was thirty-one to eleven. By States the vote was sixteen in favor and only four against it; three were divided, and three not voting. A large majority of the States thus expressly affirmed that the Federal Government was nothing but a common agent of the States, and held all its powers by delegation and in trust.

"On the fourth Resolution, the vote stood thirty-four for it, and only five against it. By States the vote was eighteen for it, and only two against it, while two were divided, and four not voting.

"On the fifth Resolution, the vote was thirty-six to eight. This Resolution was slightly amended, on motion of Mr. Clay, from what it was when at first introduced. On the second clause of it, the vote by States was nineteen for it, three only against it; three divided, and one not voting.

"These votes all show conclusively how the Constitution was then understood by the 'ambassadors of the States,' as Mr. [Fisher] Ames, in the Massachusetts Convention, had styled the Senators. This is the construction of it they put on perpetual record. Could any man desire an ampler vindication of the correctness of his position than Mr. Calhoun had of the truth of his principles, of 1833, thus declared by two thirds of the States themselves, through their ambassadors in the Senate, five years afterwards.

"It was after these Resolutions had been passed, after the discussions that had ensued between 1833 and 1838, after the revival of the principles of 1798-1799-1800, which had slumbered so long on these subjects, that Mr. Webster, in 1839, made the speech he did, before the Supreme Court of the United States, and wrote the letter he did to the Baring Brothers & Co., touching the nature of the Government, in both of which he fully admits that the States are Sovereign, except in so far as they have delegated specific Sovereign powers. But 'Sovereignty' itself, as he says, not being mentioned in the Constitution, must, as a necessary result, remain with the States, or the people thereof.

"But besides all this, as a further proof of Mr. Webster's change of views as to the Constitution being a Compact between the States, I cite you to a later speech made by him at Capon Springs, in Virginia, on the 28th June, 1851. Here it is. In this he says:

> [Stephens quoting Webster:] 'The leading sentiment in the toast from the Chair is the Union of the States. The Union Of The States! What mind can comprehend the consequences of that Union, past, present, and to come? The Union of these States is the all-absorbing topic of the day; on it all men write, speak, think, and dilate, from the rising of the sun to the going down thereof. And yet, gentlemen, I fear its importance has been but insufficiently appreciated. . . . How absurd it is to suppose that when different parties enter into a Compact for certain purposes, either can disregard any one provision, and expect, nevertheless, the other to observe the rest! I intend, for one, to regard, and maintain, and carry out, to the fullest extent, the Constitution of the United States, which I have sworn to support in all its parts and all its provisions. It [the Fugitive Slave Clause] is written in the Constitution:
>
>> No person held to service or labor in one state, under the laws thereof, escaping into another, shall, in consequence of any law or regulation therein, be discharged from such service or labor, but shall be delivered up on claim of the party to whom such service or labor may be due.

'That is as much a part of the Constitution as any other, and as equally binding and obligatory as any other on all men, public or private. And who denies this? None but the abolitionists of the North. And pray what is it they will not deny? They have but the one idea; and it would seem that these fanatics at the North and the secessionists at the South, are putting their heads together to derive means to defeat the good designs of honest and patriotic men. They act to the same end and the same object, and the Constitution has to take the fire from both sides.

'I have not hesitated to say, and I repeat, that if the Northern States refuse, wilfully and deliberately, to carry into effect that part of the Constitution which respects the restoration of fugitive slaves, and Congress provide no remedy, the South would no longer be bound to observe the Compact. A bargain cannot be broken on one side and still bind the other side. I say to you, gentlemen, in Virginia, as I said on the shores of Lake Erie and in the city of Boston, as I may say again, in that city or elsewhere in the North, that you of the South have as much right to receive your fugitive slaves, as the North has to any of its rights and privileges of navigation and commerce. . . . I am as ready to fight and to fall for the Constitutional rights of Virginia, as I am for those of Massachusetts.'

"In this speech Mr. Webster distinctly held that the Union was a Union of States. That the Union was founded upon Compact. And that a Compact broken on one side could not continue to bind the other.

"That this speech shows a modification of the opinions expressed in his speech of 1833, must be admitted by all. He had grown older and wiser. The speech of 1851, was in his maturer years, after the nature of the Government had been more fully discussed by the men of his own generation than it had been in 1830 and 1833. He was too great a man and had too great an intellect not to see the truth when it was presented, and he was too honest and too patriotic a man, not to proclaim a truth when he saw it, even to an unwilling people. In this quality of moral greatness I often thought Mr. Webster had the advantage of his great contemporaries, Messrs. Clay and Calhoun. Not that I would be understood as saying that they were not men of great moral courage, for both of them showed this high quality in many instances, but that they never gave the world such striking exhibitions of it as he did. It was the glory of his life that his was put to a test, in this particular, that theirs never was. On no occasion that I am aware of did Mr. Clay ever take a position which he did not know that he would be sustained in by the people of Kentucky. So with Mr. Calhoun, as to South Carolina. I do not say that they might not have done it if a sense of duty had required it, but they were either so fortunate or so unfortunate as never to have that issue presented to them.

"Webster, on the contrary, often passed this ordeal, and that he passed it with unflinching firmness is one of the grandest features in the general grandeur of his character. Even his detractors have been constrained to render him unwilling homage in this respect.

"Theodore Parker, in his tirade on his character, after his death, is an illustration of this. He graphically described, if you recollect, his position, in Faneuil Hall, when he returned to give an account of his stewardship to his constituents, in 1842. Webster, you know, had remained in President [John] Tyler's cabinet after Mr. Tyler had come to an open breach with the Whig party. This was exceedingly displeasing to the Whigs of Massachusetts. His object in so remaining, however, was to preserve peace with England by effecting a settlement of the North Eastern Boundary question. This he saw a prospect of accomplishing, and this, by remaining, he had accomplished. But even this great act could not atone for his disregard of the wishes of his party. They were in the main disaffected, displeased, and indignant. The opposition had assumed a hostile attitude. The crisis in his affairs was gloomy enough. The political elements were gathering against him from every point. The storm had been brewing for some time. Denunciations opened from every quarter. All this Parker vividly described, on the occasion alluded to, and then said (I quote from memory):

'The clouds had thickened into blackness all around, and over him, and hurled their thunders fearfully upon his devoted head! But there he stood in Faneuil Hall and thundered back again! It was the ground lightning from his Olympian brain!'

"This figure was not too exaggerated for the occasion. It gave a truthful representation of the majesty of the man whom he was endeavoring to depreciate, disparage, and defame. In rendering this homage he was but reenacting the part of the Prophet of Aram, who went out to curse, but was constrained to honor instead.

"This was not the only instance in which Mr. Webster exhibited this highest quality of human nature.

"On this point you will excuse me for repeating what I said on another occasion: One of the highest exhibitions of the moral sublime the world ever witnessed, was that of Daniel Webster, when, in an open barouche in the streets of Boston, he proclaimed, in substance, to a vast assembly of his constituents—unwilling hearers—that 'they had conquered an uncongenial clime; they had conquered a sterile soil; they had conquered the winds and currents of the Ocean; they had conquered most of the elements of nature; but they must yet learn to conquer their prejudices!' I know of no more fitting incident or scene in the life of that wonderful man, *Glarus et vir Fortissimus*, for perpetuating the memory of the true greatness of his character, on canvas or in marble, than a representation of him as he then and there stood and spoke! It was an exhibition of moral grandeur surpassing that of Aristides when he said, 'O! Athenians, what Themistocles recommends would be greatly to your interests, but it would be unjust!'

"Such exhibitions of moral courage his great rivals never gave—never had occasion, perhaps, to give. But you see the estimation in which I hold Mr. Webster. I did entertain for him the highest esteem and admiration. I did not agree with him in his exposition of the Constitution in 1833, but I did fully and cordially agree with him in his exposition in 1839, and 1851. According to that the Constitution was and is a Compact between the States.

"But to return from this digression. Whether Mr. Webster ever did or did not modify the opinions expressed in the speech you have read is not the question before us, that is what is the true construction of the Constitution on the point under immediate consideration. We have seen the exposition of the Supreme Court of the United States, which Mr. Webster maintained was the final arbiter, and we have seen the exposition of the United States Senate, that is the exposition of the States themselves by their ambassadors in 1839. Now, in addition to this, I wish to call your special attention to a like exposition by the same high authority, as late as 1860, not twelve months before the war began.

"Mr. Jefferson Davis . . . submitted to the Senate, on the 29th of February, a series of resolutions, declaratory of the principles of the Government on the very subjects out of which the war sprung. He was then Senator from Mississippi. These Resolutions passed the Senate May 24, 1860. Here they are. I call your special attention to the first and second of these.

> 1. Resolved, That, in the adoption of the Federal Constitution, the States adopting the same, acted severally as free and independent Sovereignties, delegating a portion of their powers to be exercised by the Federal Government for the increased security of each against dangers, domestic as well as foreign; and that any intermeddling by any one or more States, or by a combination of their citizens, with the domestic institutions of the others, on any pretext whatever, political, moral, or religious, with a view to their disturbance or subversion, is in violation of the Constitution, insulting to the States so interfered with, endangers their domestic peace and tranquillity—objects for which the Constitution was formed—and, by necessary consequence, tends to weaken and destroy the Union itself.
>
> 2. Resolved. That negro Slavery, as it exists in fifteen States of this Union, composes an important portion of their domestic institution, inherited from their ancestors, and existing at the adoption of the Constitution, by which it is recognized as constituting an important element in the apportionment of powers among the States, and that no change of opinion or feeling on the part

of the non-slaveholding States of the Union, in relation to this institution, can justify them or their citizens in open or covert attacks thereon, with a view to its overthrow; and that all such attacks are in manifest violation of the mutual and solemn pledge to protect and defend each other, given by the States respectively on entering into the Constitutional Compact which formed the Union, and are a manifest breach of faith, and a violation of the most solemn obligations.

3. Resolved, That the Union of these States rests on the equality of rights and privileges among its members; and that it is especially the duty of the Senate, which represents the States in their Sovereign capacity, to resist all attempts to discriminate either in relation to persons or property in the Territories, which are the common possessions of the United States, so as to give advantages to the citizens of one State which are not equally assured to those of every other State.

4. Resolved, That neither Congress nor a Territorial Legislature, whether by direct legislation or legislation of an indirect and unfriendly character, possesses power to annul or impair the Constitutional right of any citizen of the United States, to take his slave property into the common Territories, and there hold and enjoy the same while the territorial condition remains.

5. Resolved, That, if experience should at any time prove that the Judicial and Executive authority do not possess means to insure adequate protection to Constitutional rights in a Territory, and if the Territorial Government should fail or refuse to provide the necessary remedies for that purpose, it will be the duty of Congress to supply such deficiency.

6. Resolved, That the inhabitants of a Territory of the United States, when they rightfully form a Constitution to be admitted as a State into the Union, may, then, for the first time, like the people of a State, when forming a new Constitution, decide for themselves whether slavery, as a domestic institution, shall be maintained or prohibited within their jurisdiction; and "they shall be admitted into the Union, with or without slavery, as their Constitution may prescribe at the time of their admission."

7. Resolved, That the provision of the Constitution for the rendition of fugitives from service or labor, without the adoption of which the Union could not have been formed, and the laws of 1793 and 1850, which were enacted to secure its execution, and the main features of which, being similar, bear the impress of nearly seventy years of sanction by the highest judicial authority, should be honestly and faithfully observed and maintained by all who enjoy the benefits of our Compact of Union, and that all acts of individuals or of State Legislatures to defeat the purpose or nullify the requirements of that provision, and the laws made in pursuance of it, are hostile in character, subversive of the Constitution, and revolutionary in their effect.

"These Resolutions decidedly affirmed that the Constitution was formed by

States—independent Sovereignties—that the Government established by it is a Federal Government—one founded on Compact, and that any interference, openly or covertly, directly or indirectly, by any of the States or their citizens, with the black population in any other of the States, or with the domestic institutions of any of the States against their own internal policy, would be a manifest breach of plighted faith—and, further, that all acts of the individual citizens of any of the States, as well as of the Legislatures of any of the States, intended to defeat or nullify that clause of the Constitution requiring the rendition of fugitives from service, were hostile to and subversive of the Constitution itself.

"[To those Northern Liberals who maintain that this was merely Mr. Davis' way of introducing the idea of the secession of the Southern states, I say that] I think all accusations of this kind were exceedingly unjust to him, and so, I think in this case . . . do great injustice to Mr. Davis.

"[The Liberals] . . . are mistaken in saying that the vote upon these Resolutions was a strict party vote [with all Conservatives voting for it and all Liberals voting against it]. Here is the vote. There were thirty-six Senators in favor of the first Resolution and only nineteen against it; nearly two to one on the per capita vote. Among the yeas I see James A. Pearce, John P. Kennedy and John J. Crittenden. When were they ever considered or looked upon as Democrats [the Conservatives of the day] in the sense in which you use that term? They certainly did not belong to the same political organization with Mr. Davis at that time, and had no sympathy with its bare party objects. While the per capita vote is so striking, if we look at it by States it will appear even more so. From a view of it, in this respect, it appears that nineteen States voted for the first Resolution, only ten voted against it, while two were divided, and two did not vote. Had the two absent States, Delaware and Illinois, been present, the vote would have been twenty for it, ten against is, and three divided; for [Stephen A.] Douglas, of Illinois, would have voted for it, and [Lyman] Trumbull of the same State would have voted against it. Would it not have been a strange spectacle to see twenty of the thirty-three States in Senatorial Council, taking the initiative step for a dismemberment of the Union? Is such a supposition reasonable? Can any one suppose that these States, acting through their Senators, could have had any such design? Does not the object of these Resolutions clearly appear to have been just the reverse? Was not this simply but earnestly to declare the nature of the Government, and the only way in which the Union, under it, could be preserved? The vote on the seventh Resolution, looking to the per capita vote, or the vote by States, is equally striking. On the per capita the yeas were thirty-six, and nays six. By States the vote was twenty for the Resolution, and only four against it. One State divided, and eight not voting.

"An important fact, in connection with these Resolutions, should ever be borne in mind. That is that every one of these ten States, whose Senators voted against them, had, by their State Legislatures . . . openly and intentionally disregarded their obligations, under that clause of the Constitution, which required the rendition of fugitives from service, and which acts, on their part, a large majority of the States thus by their resolves declared to be a breach of their plighted faith. Indeed, all these ten States were then under the influence of those who held that the Constitution was but 'a Covenant with Death and an agreement with Hell.' Is it just or fair to Mr. Davis to say that he was meditating or planning Secession at that time, any more than it was the design of the nineteen States which actually agreed with him in the sentiments of the Resolutions?

"Is it not more in accordance with strict justice, to say nothing of that charity which should ever be exercised in investigations of this sort, to suppose that his object was to preserve the Union by having all the members to conform their action to its plain and unmistakable provisions? If there were any dis-union sentiments then existing to whom should they be rightly attributed? Should they be attributed to those States and those Senators who were for maintaining the Union on the principles upon which it was formed, or those who were for maintaining a Government, barely, upon totally different principles? Three of these Resolutions of the series offered by Mr. Davis, and which passed the Senate, I am frank to say, I thought, at the time, though not then in public life, and still think, ought not to have been brought forward [i.e., the Fourth, Fifth, and Sixth Resolutions—also known a the 'doctrine of Popular or Squatter Sovereignty.']

". . . My objections [to these three Resolutions are] related solely to the policy of introducing them. They presented questions which tended to divide and thus weaken the Constitutional Party—the State Rights, State Sovereignty Party—the great party throughout the country, everywhere, whatever cognomen its various subdivisions bore, which was for maintaining the Constitution, and the Union under it, as it was made and handed down to them from their ancestors. It seemed to me to be exceedingly inexpedient and impolitic as a matter of statesmanship to divide those thus cordially united on the more essential and vital principles of the Government, upon questions of so little practical importance, especially at such a crisis as that was in public affairs. The [Liberals'] new Anti-Constitutional Party, as it might in my view very properly be styled, was then thoroughly organized under the old but misapplied name of Republican, and it should have been a matter of the utmost importance with the real friends of the Constitution, and Union under it, not to divide their ranks upon such questions as those embraced in these three Resolutions. This, in short, was my view of that subject. The only hope of the new party was in a division of its opponents. In case this division should become complete and irreconcilable I saw that a rupture of that party was an inevitable result, and with its rupture a rupture of the Union, upon the principles upon which it was formed, seemed to me to be equally inevitable. I am equally frank in stating that there were some amongst us who meant to use this question for no purpose whatever, but to produce such a rupture both of the party and of the Union. I did not, however, then or now, think that Mr. Davis belonged to that class. No man, in my opinion, which I give you candidly, is less understood at the North, and perhaps to a great extent, at the South, too, than Mr. Davis, on this question. I may be wrong, but I assure you I never regarded him as a Secessionist, properly speaking; that is, I always regarded him as a strong Union man in sentiment, so long as the Union was maintained on the principles upon which it was founded. He was, without doubt, a thorough State Rights, State Sovereignty man. He believed in the right of Secession; but what I mean to say is, that in my opinion, he was an ardent supporter of the Union on the principles, as he understood them, upon which, and for which, the Union was formed. There were, as I have said, many public men amongst us who after these Resolutions passed the Senate, and after the Presidential canvass was opened upon them, and the various issues presented in the Party platforms of the day, as we shall see, who were openly for Secession in case [the anti-Constitution, big government Liberal] Mr. [Abraham] Lincoln should be elected upon the principles on which he was nominated. But Mr. Davis, as far as I know or believe, did not belong even to this class. If he was in favor of Secession barely upon the grounds of Mr. Lincoln's election, I am not aware of it. He certainly made no speech or wrote any letter for the public during that canvass that indicated such views or purposes. I never saw a word from him recommending Secession as the proper remedy against threatening dangers until he joined in the general letter of the Southern Senators and Representatives in Congress to their States, advising them to take that course.

"This was in December, 1860, and not until after it was ascertained in the Committee of the Senate, on Mr. [John J.] Crittenden's proposition for quieting the apprehensions and alarm of the Southern States from the accession of Mr. Lincoln to power, that the Republicans [Liberals of the day], his supporters, would not agree to that measure. It is well known that he and Mr. [Robert A.] Toombs both declared their willingness to accept the adoption of Mr. Crittenden's measure as a final settlement of the controversy between the States and sections, if the party coming into power would agree to it in the same spirit and with the same assurance. It was after it was known that this party would not enter into any such settlement, or give any assurance for the future, that Mr. Davis joined other Southern Senators and Representatives advising the Southern States to secede, as the proper remedy for what he and they considered impending dangers to their rights, security, and future welfare. There is nothing in Mr. Davis's life, or public conduct, that I am aware of, that affords just grounds for believing that he ever desired a separation of the States, if the principles of the Union, under the Constitution, had been faithfully adhered to by all the Parties to it. These were the sentiments of all his speeches, in Congress and out of it, as far as I have ever seen, even down to his last most touching leave-taking address to the Senate!

"But all this is digressing from the matter before us. . . . The point we are now considering is not the object or motive of Mr. Davis in offering these Resolutions. It is the exposition actually made by the Senate of the United States, nineteen States to ten States, of the real nature and character of the Government. Mr. Davis was but the instrument, the draftsman, through whom this overwhelming majority of the States announced for themselves the nature of the bonds of their Union! This exposition was as late as 1860, and substantially the same that had been given by the same August Body of ambassadors representing their Sovereignty in 1838, twenty-two years before! That exposition was that the Constitution is a Compact between Sovereign States. So . . . we finally return to the same place at which we had arrived before taking up Mr. Webster's speech. We now stand just where we did then. We have gone through with his great argument and Mr. Calhoun's reply, to which no rejoinder was ever made. We have seen that the Senate, by a nearly three fourths vote of the States, in 1838, and by a vote of nearly two to one, in 1860, sustained that construction of the Constitution which was set forth in the first of Mr. Calhoun's Resolutions in 1833, and which I maintain. The decisions of the Supreme Court referred to, sustain the same view also. We have seen further, that Mr. Webster himself, in his riper years, held that the Union was 'a Union of States.' That it was founded upon 'Compact,' and that 'a bargain cannot be broken on one side and still bind the other side.'

"Does it not, therefore, clearly appear from these high authorities, and even upon the authority of Mr. Webster himself, that the Government of the United States is a Federal Government, or as [George] Washington styled it, a Confederated Republic? What further, if any thing, have [the Liberals] . . . to say against this as an indisputably established conclusion?"[134]

16

ANDREW JACKSON ON THE U.S. CONSTITUTION

TO DEFEND THEIR SKEWED VIEW of the Constitution, 19th-Century Liberals often went to any length, even making up anti-states' rights theories, which they tried to pass off as legitimate. They also attempted to use historical figures to reinforce their opinions. One of these was the venerable Southern Conservative Andrew Jackson, who, in his famous proclamation, Liberals so believed, denounced nullification (the right of states to veto Federal laws) and the whole theory of the Government as proposed by John C. Calhoun and other Southern states' rights advocates. In the following excerpts from *A Constitutional View*, Stephens corrects these errors.

☞ "Before looking into [Jackson's] . . . Proclamation I must set [the Liberals] . . . right on some matters of fact, [in particular concerning the idea that] General Jackson put down Nullification and silenced Mr. Calhoun. . . .

"Nullification [a doctrine upholding the right of a U.S. state to declare an act of the Federal government null and void] in South Carolina, whether it be considered as an incipient Rebellion, or as a proper and peaceable mode of obtaining a redress of grievances as its advocates contended, was never put down or quelled by General Jackson or any body else. Its further prosecution was abandoned by those who initiated it as a mode of redress, when the wrongs and grievances complained of were redressed by Congress, and not till then.

"It is not my purpose to defend the doctrine of Nullification, or to say how far General Jackson as President was right in issuing a Proclamation declaring his purpose to execute the laws in that instance. It is proper, however, to state that *the primary and leading object of its advocates was not Secession or Disunion. It was just the contrary*. But so subtle were the principles upon which it was founded, that it was never understood by the country. South Carolina, as well as a number of the other States, held, that the power to levy duties upon imports, not with a view to revenue, but to protect and aid particular classes, was not delegated to the Congress. Nullification, without Secession, was a remedy she resorted to, to defeat the operation of protective laws passed by the Congress. Many who believed in the perfect right of Secession, and looked upon that as the proper remedy in such cases of abuse of power as South Carolina complained of, were utterly opposed to Nullification. How a State could remain in the Union, with Senators and Representatives in Congress, and yet refuse obedience to the laws of Congress not set aside by the Judiciary as unconstitutional, was, to this class, utterly incomprehensible! But the merits of this doctrine are not now before us. Suffice it to say I was never an advocate of it. And all I mean now to say on this point is, that whether right or wrong in principle, it was never abandoned until the protective policy, which it was resorted to change, was abandoned by the Government. The Proclamation did not either put it down or silence its advocates or defenders. Mr. [John C.] Calhoun's speech, which we have read, was made after that. The giving way was on the part of the Federal Government and not the State Government. [Emphasis added, L.S.]

"A brief statement of the matter is this. The Nullification Ordinance of South Carolina, which was to test the question, was passed the latter part of November, 1832, to go into effect on the 1st of February, 1833. The Proclamation was issued on the 11th of December, 1832. Congress was in session: on the 21st of January, 1833, a Bill was introduced to meet the provisions of the Nullification Ordinance of the State, by counteracting Legislation and clothing the President with the necessary power to execute it, putting at his disposal the whole of the land and naval forces. This was called the Force Bill. The Constitutionality of the provisions of this Bill was denied by many who did not hold to the doctrine of Nullification. Unusual excitement prevailed. A great debate sprung up—the greatest since the formation of the Government, for then principles were discussed. The speeches of Mr. Webster and Mr. Calhoun constitute part of this debate. Mr. Calhoun offered his Resolutions the day after the Force Bill was introduced. Serious fears were entertained that if the Bill should pass, and become a law, while South Carolina held the position she did, that a collision would take place between the United States forces and the forces of the State; and that war would ensue. For, though South Carolina did not, in her Ordinance, contemplate the use of any force in the *modus operandi* of her chosen remedy, yet she declared her intention to be, to repel force by force, in case the United States should resort to force.

"We can get some glimpses as to the position of the parties from the debates in the Senate at this time. Here is the opening of the discussion by Mr. [William] Wilkins, who introduced the Force Bill.

[Wilkins] 'All have agreed that on the first of next month, this solemn epoch will arrive. The ordinance of the State of South Carolina—the test law—that unprecedented law called the Replevin Act—and the law for the protection of the citizens of South Carolina—all looking to one object; all go into operation on that day. He had said all these pointed to one object. To what object did they point? The answer was simple. To nullification of existing laws: To violent resistance to the United States.'

[Calhoun] 'I cannot sit silent and permit such erroneous constructions to go forth. South Carolina had never contemplated violent resistance to the laws of the United States.'

[Wilkins] 'I was at a loss to understand how any man could read the various acts of the State of South Carolina, and not say that they must lead, necessarily lead, in their consequences, to violent measures. I understand the Senator from South Carolina (Mr. Calhoun) the other day as acknowledging that there was military array in South Carolina, but contending that it followed and did not precede the array of force by the United States.'

[Calhoun] 'I admit that there was military preparation, not array.'

[Wilkins] 'If we examine the measures taken by the Administration, in reference to the present crisis, it would be found that they were not at all of that military character to justify the measures of South Carolina which it was alleged had followed them.'

[Calhoun] 'South Carolina was undoubtedly preparing to resist force by force. But let the United States withdraw her forces from its borders, and lay this Bill upon the table, and her preparations would cease.'

[Wilkins] 'That is, sir, if we do not oppose any of her movements all will be right. If we fold our arms and exhibit a perfect indifference whether the laws of the Union are obeyed or not, all will be quiet!'

[Calhoun] 'Who relies upon force in this controversy? I have insisted upon it that South Carolina relied altogether upon civil process, and that, if the General Government resorts to force, then only will South Carolina rely upon force. If force be introduced by either party, upon that party will fall the responsibility.'

[Wilkins] 'The General Government will not appeal, in the first instance, to force. It will appeal to the patriotism of South Carolina—to that magnanimity of which she boasts so much.'

[Calhoun] 'I am sorry that South Carolina cannot appeal to the sense of justice of the General Government.'

[Wilkins] 'The Government will appeal to that political sense which exhorts obedience to the laws of the country, as the first duty of the citizen. It will appeal to the moral force in the community. If that appeal be in vain, it will appeal to the judiciary. If the mild arm of the judiciary be not sufficient to execute the laws, it will call out the civil force to sustain the laws. If that be insufficient, God save and protect us from the last resort. But if the evil does come upon the country, who is responsible for it? If force be brought in to the aid of law, who, I ask of gentlemen, is responsible for it to the people of the United States? That is the question. Talk of it as you please, mystify matters as you will, theorize as you may, pile up abstract propositions to any extent, at last the question resolves itself into one of obedience or resistance of the laws—in other words, of Union or dis-Union.'

[Felix Grundy of Tennessee] 'The true question before the Senate is, shall the State of South Carolina be permitted to put down the revenue laws of the Union, prevent their execution within her limits, and no effort be made by this Government to maintain the majesty of the laws, and to counteract the measures adopted by that State to defeat and evade them.'

"The debate so commenced became exceedingly interesting as it progressed. It furnishes a rich mine for exploration at this time. Let us dig a little further into it, and sample some other fragments of its strata.

"In the [official Senate] Register . . . we have the following specimens, from Judge [George M.] Bibb, of Kentucky:

[Bibb] 'It seems to me that a false issue was presented. The question of war against South Carolina is presented as the only alternative. The issue is false. The first question is between justice and injustice. Shall we do justice to the States who have united with South Carolina in complaint and remonstrance against the injustice and oppression of the tariff? Shall we cancel the obligations of justice to five other States, because of the impetuosity and impatience of South Carolina under wrong and oppression? The question ought not to be whether we have the physical power to crush South Carolina, but whether it is not our duty to heal her discontents, to conciliate a member of the Union, to give peace and happiness to the adjoining States which have made common cause with South Carolina so far as complaint and remonstrance go. Are we to rush into a war with South Carolina to compel her to remain in the Union? Shall we keep her in the Union by force of arms, for the purpose of compelling her submission to the tariff laws of which she complains? How shall we do this? By the naval and military force of the United States, combined with the militia? Where will the militia come from? Will Virginia, will North Carolina, will Georgia, Mississippi, or Alabama, assist to enforce submission to the tariff laws, the justice and Constitutionality of which they have, by resolutions on your files, denied over and over again? Will those States assist to forge chains by which they themselves are to be bound? Is this to be expected, in the ordinary course of chance and probability? . . .

'My creed is that, by the Declaration of Independence, the States were declared to be free and independent States, thirteen in number, not one Nation—that the old Articles of Confederation united them as distinct States, not as one people:—that the treaty of peace, of 1783, acknowledged their independence as States, not as a single Nation; that the Federal Constitution was framed by States, submitted to the States, and adopted by the States, as distinct Nations or States, not as a single Nation or people.

'By canvassing these conflicting opinions, we shall the better understand how far South Carolina has transcended her reserved powers as a Sovereign State—how far we can lawfully make war upon her—and whether we, or South Carolina, are likely to transcend the barriers provided in the Constitution of the United States.

'I do not wish to be misunderstood. In these times of political excitement, whatever is spoken or reported, may be misrepresented. I wish it to be understood, that I do not approve of the doctrines of Carolina, in their full extent. But, if we make war upon her, to put down her principles, we must be sure that those principles are bad and dangerous.

'What are her principles? That she has a right to judge, in the last resort, in all questions concerning her rights; or, to put it in still stronger language—if Congress attempts to enforce the revenue laws, she will resume her independence and Sovereignty. I do not approve of this course on the part of South Carolina, under all the circumstances. Still, I would like to know when and where South Carolina surrendered the right to secede from the Union, in case of a dangerous invasion of her rights by the Federal Government. In the solemn declaration of principles with which some of the States accompanied the adoption of the Constitution, this right it declared to be inalienable. There was too much truth in the axiom contained in many State Constitutions, that "a frequent recurrence to first principles is necessary to the maintenance of liberty." [I read here from the Declaration of Independence:]

> We hold these truths to be self-evident, that all men are created equal, that they are endowed by their Creator with certain unalienable rights; that among these are life, liberty, and the pursuit oi happiness.

'Now, if South Carolina has mistaken her injury and her remedy, shall we make war upon her, and put down the principles asserted by the Declaration of Independence. The ratification, by the several States, of the Constitution, adopted the same principles; and they were accepted as forming a part of the Constitution.

[Stephens' note: "Bibb is referring here to the declaration accompanying the ratification of the Constitution by the State of New York—that 'all power was derived from the people, and could be resumed by the people whenever it became necessary for their happiness; . . . under these impressions, and declaring that the rights aforesaid cannot be abridged or violated, and that the explanations aforesaid are consistent with the said Constitution; and in confidence, that the amendments which shall have been proposed to the said Constitution, will receive an early and mature consideration, we, the said Delegates, in the name and in the behalf of the people of the State of New York, do, by these presents, assent to, and ratify the said Constitution,' etc."]

'The Articles of the old Confederation declared the Union should be perpetual, and that no alteration should be made in the Articles, but by consent of Congress, and of the Legislatures of each State of the Union. Here the Compact was declared to be perpetual, and yet we undertook to arrest it without the consent of any State. The Constitution provides that when nine States have ratified the Constitution, it shall go into operation. Why were the fundamental Articles of the old Confederation violated? How could nine States be supposed to combine, and throw the other four out of the Union? They claimed the right, under the principles adopted in the Declaration of Independence, to alter, reform, and amend their form of Government as much and as often as such change was necessary, in their opinion, to the right ends of Government, the interests of the people. The people have an unalienable, indefeasible right to make a Government which shall be adequate to their ends. Upon this principle it was that the old Compact was destroyed, and a new one made.

'We are now about to make war upon a State, which formed a part of the old Confederation, and became a party to the new Constitution, with an express reservation of powers not expressly delegated by her.

'Is it possible that the people of the States, in adopting this Constitution, could have intended to surrender absolutely and forever the right which they had obtained by a Revolution? So well did they understand the difficulty of shaking off the powers which once enchained us, and so jealous were they of their newly acquired freedom, that they took care to say in the Constitution, that the powers not delegated by them, were reserved to themselves.

'It stood on record, that one of the Roman provinces rebelled against the Government, again and again. The leaders were subdued, and many of the Senators of this party, and many of the people were taken or killed. The conquered province sent ambassadors to Rome, and when these ambassadors appeared, the consul asked of them, "what punishment did they deserve?" The answer of the ambassador was, "such punishment as he deserves who contends for liberty." It was demanded of them by the Senate, "whether, if terms of peace were granted them, they would abide faithfully by them?" They replied emphatically, that "if the terms were good and just, they would faithfully abide by them, and the peace should be perpetual; but if they were unjust, the peace could barely last until they could return to their homes to tell the people what they were." The Roman Senate were pleased with the spirit which was thus exhibited, declared that "they who thus contended for freedom, were worthy to be Roman citizens," and gave them all which they demanded.'

[Note of the reporter of the official Senate Register:] 'Bibb wished then an American Senate to imitate their noble example. It was a cause worthy of imitation. He invoked the Senate to sift the complaints of South Carolina, for they alone were worthy to be American citizens who contended zealously for the principles of civil liberty, and are not fit subjects to be denounced and accursed.'

"This is enough of the general debates to show the temper of the times, the contrariety of sentiments existing in various quarters, and the grounds for the apprehensions so universally prevailing that a collision might ensue and the peace of the country be disturbed.

"Meantime hopes were entertained that Congress would abandon the protective policy, and strong efforts were made to get South Carolina to postpone the day of final action on her Ordinance, to give time for Congress to grant the relief sought. Mr. [Gulian C.] Verplanck, of New York, had introduced a Bill in the House of Representatives reducing the duties. This was on the 28th December, 1832. The State of Virginia, who sympathized thoroughly with South Carolina in her complaints against the injustice of the Tariff laws, but who did not agree with her as to the remedy she had adopted to get rid of them by, sent one of her most distinguished statesmen, Benjamin Watkins Leigh, as a Commissioner to intercede, and to urge South Carolina to rescind her Ordinance, or at least to postpone action on it until the close of the first session of the next Congress. Mr. Leigh's high mission was successful in part. South Carolina agreed, in view of the prospect of Congress reducing the duties to a revenue standard, to postpone action on her Ordinance until the close of that session of Congress, which was on the 4th of March.

"It was at this stage of affairs that Mr. [Henry] Clay, who was the author of the [big government] protective policy known as 'the American system,' brought forward his celebrated compromise of 1833, upon the subject of the Tariff laws. He gave notice of his intention to ask leave to introduce such a Bill on the 11th of February, and did bring it forward on the next day, the 12th.

"His object was two-fold, as stated by him. One was to preserve the manufacturing interest from that ruin which would attend an immediate repeal of the protective duties; the other was by yielding the principle of protection to prevent that collision between the Federal and State Governments which was then so seriously apprehended.

"[Clay] . . . said, on introducing it:

> 'I yesterday, sir, gave notice that I should ask leave to introduce a bill to modify the various acts imposing duties on imports. I, at the same time, added, that I should, with the permission of the Senate, offer an explanation of the principle on which that bill is founded. I owe, sir, an apology to the Senate for this course of action, because, although strictly parliamentary, it is, nevertheless, out of the usual practice of this body; but it is a course which I trust that the Senate will deem to be justified by the interesting nature of the subject. I rise, sir, on this occasion, actuated by no motive of a private nature, by no personal feelings, and for no personal objects; but exclusively in obedience to a sense of the duty which I owe to my country. I trust, therefore, that no one will anticipate on my part any ambitious display of such humble powers as I may possess. It is sincerely my purpose to present a plain, unadorned, and naked statement of facts connected with the measure which I shall have the honor to propose, and with the condition of the country. . . . In presenting the modification of the Tariff laws, which I am now about to submit, I have two great objects in view. My first object looks to the Tariff. I am compelled to express the opinion, formed after the most deliberate reflection, and on full survey of the whole country, that, whether rightfully or wrongfully, the Tariff stands in imminent danger. If it should even be preserved during this session, it must fall at the next session. By what circumstances, and through what cause, has arisen the necessity for this change in the policy of our country, I will not pretend now to elucidate. Others there are who may differ from the impressions which my mind has received upon this point. Owing, however, to a variety of concurrent causes, the Tariff, as it now exists, is in imminent danger, and if the system can be preserved beyond the next session, it must be by some means not now within the reach of human sagacity. The fall of that policy, sir, would be productive of consequences calamitous indeed. When I look to the variety of interests which are involved, to the number of individuals interested, the amount of capital invested, the value of the buildings erected, and the whole arrangement of the business for the prosecution of the various branches of the manufacturing art which have sprung up under the fostering care of this Government, I cannot contemplate any evil equal to the sudden overthrow of all those interests. History can produce no parallel to the extent of the mischief which would be produced by such a disaster. The repeal of the Edict of Nantes itself was nothing in comparison with it. That condemned to exile, and brought to ruin a great number of persons. The most respectable portion of the population of France were condemned to exile and ruin by that measure. But, in my opinion, sir, the sudden repeal of the Tariff policy

would bring ruin and destruction on the whole people of this country. There is no evil, in my opinion, equal to the consequences which would result from such a catastrophe.

'What, sir, are the complaints which unhappily divide the people of this great country? On the one hand, it is said by those who are opposed to the Tariff, that it unjustly taxes a portion of the people and paralyzes their industry; that it is to be a perpetual operation; that there is to be no end to the system; which, right or wrong, is to be urged to their inevitable ruin. And what is the just complaint, on the other hand, of those who support the Tariff? It is, that the policy of the Government is vacillating and uncertain, and that there is no stability in our legislation. Before one set of books are fairly opened, it becomes necessary to close them, and to open a new set. Before a law can be tested by experiment, another is passed. Before the present law has gone into operation, before it is yet nine months old, passed as it was under circumstances of extraordinary deliberation, the fruit of nine months' labor, before we know any thing of its experimental effects, and even before it commences its operations, we are required to repeal it. On one side we are urged to repeal a system which is fraught with ruin: on the other side, the check now imposed on enterprise, and the state of alarm in which the public mind has been thrown, renders all prudent men desirous, looking ahead a little way, to adopt a state of things, on the stability of which they may have reason to count. Such is the state of feeling on the one side and on the other. I am anxious to find out some principle of mutual accommodation, to satisfy, as far as practicable, both parties—to increase the stability of our legislation; and at some distant day—but not too distant, when we take into view the magnitude of the interests which are involved—to bring down the rate of duties to that revenue standard for which our opponents have so long contended. The basis on which I wish to found this modification, is one of time; and the several parts of the Bill to which I am about to call the attention of the Senate, are founded on this basis. I propose to give protection to our manufactured articles, adequate protection, for a length of time, which, compared with the length of human life, is very long, but which is short, in proportion to the legitimate discretion of every wise and parental system of Government—securing the stability of legislation, and allowing time for a gradual reduction, on one side; and, on the other, proposing to reduce the duties to that revenue standard for which the opponents of the system have so long contended. I will now proceed to lay the provisions of this bill before the Senate, with a view to draw their attention to the true character of the bill.'

"[Henry Clay's] bill proposed a gradual reduction of the duties on all articles on which they were then over twenty per cent. for ten years, so that at the end of ten years no duties should be above twenty per cent., which was assumed to be about the revenue standard. After explaining the bill and stating his second object in offering it, [Clay] . . . said:

> 'If there be any who want civil war—who want to see the blood of any portion of our countrymen spilt, I am not one of them—I wish to see war of no kind; but above all, I do not desire to see a civil war. When war begins, whether civil or foreign, no human sight is competent to foresee when, or how, or where, it is to terminate. But when a civil war shall be lighted up in the bosom of our own happy land, and armies are marching, and commanders winning their victories, and fleets are in motion on our coasts—tell me, if you can, tell me if any human being can tell its duration? God alone knows where such a war will end. In what state will be left our institutions? In what state our liberties? I want no war; above all no war at home.
>
> 'Sir, I repeat, that I think South Carolina has been rash, intemperate, and greatly in the wrong; but I do not want to disgrace her, nor any other member of this Union. No: I do not desire to see the lustre of one single star dimmed of that *glorious Confederacy*, which constitutes our political sun; still less do I wish to see it blotted out, and its light obliterated forever. Has not the State of South Carolina been one of the members of this Union "in days that tried men's souls?" Have not her ancestors fought alongside our ancestors? Have we not, conjointly, won together many a glorious battle? If we had to go into a civil war with such a State, how would it terminate? Whenever it should have terminated, what would be her condition? If she should ever return to the Union, what would be the condition of her feelings and affections—what the state of the heart of her people? She has been with us before, when her ancestors mingled in the throng of battle, and as I hope our posterity will mingle with hers for ages and centuries to come in the united defence of liberty, and for the honor and glory of the Union. I do not wish to see her degraded or defaced as a member of this Confederacy.
>
> 'In conclusion, allow me to entreat and implore each individual member of this body to bring into the consideration of this measure, which I have the honor of proposing, the same love of country which, if I know myself, has actuated me; and the same desire of restoring harmony to the Union, which has prompted this effort. If we can forget for a moment—but that would be asking too much of human nature—if we could suffer, for one moment, party feelings and party causes—and as I stand here, before my God, I declare I have looked beyond those considerations, and regarded only the vast interests of this united people—I should hope that, under such feelings and with such dispositions, we may advantageously proceed to the consideration of this bill, and heal, before they are yet bleeding, the wounds of our distracted country.'

"The introduction of this bill, by Mr. Clay, caused great sensation. It was, perhaps, the most trying period of his life. Public meetings had been held in various places, in the manufacturing States, denouncing any modification of the protective system, and charging a disposition to such legislation to intimidation from the threats of South Carolina. The Legislatures of Massachusetts, Rhode Island, Vermont, New Jersey and Pennsylvania, had passed resolutions strongly opposed to any such legislation. Mr. Clay, on this occasion, had to break with his old political friends, while he was offering up the darling system of his heart upon the altar of his country.

"Whatever else may be said of him, no one can deny that Henry Clay was a patriot—every inch of him—a patriot of the highest standard. It is said, that when he was importuned not to take the course he had resolved upon, for the reason amongst others, that it would lessen his chances for the Presidency, his reply was, 'I would rather be right than be President.' This showed the material he was made of. It was worthy a Marcellus or Cato.

"Just so soon as he got through with the speech announcing the introduction of the bill, Mr. [John C.] Calhoun immediately arose. The scene was intensely interesting as described by those who witnessed it. It was just such a scene as occurred in the same hall on the 17th day of June, 1850, seventeen years afterwards, when Mr. Webster arose to speak on the turning question of the great adjustment of that year. . . . All eyes were instantly fixed upon the Senator of South Carolina, as he addressed the Chair. The galleries and lobbies and aisles of the Chamber were crowded. The record of what occurred is thus put up. [According to an observer:]

> 'Mr. Calhoun rose and said, he would make but one or two observations. Entirely approving of the object for which this bill was introduced, he should give his vote in favor of the motion for leave to introduce it. He who loved the Union must desire to see this agitating question brought to a termination. Until it should be terminated, we could not expect the restoration of peace or harmony, or a sound condition of things, throughout the country. He believed that to the unhappy divisions which had kept the Northern and Southern States apart from each other, the present entirely degraded condition of the country (for entirely degraded he believed it to be) was solely attributable. The general principles of this bill received his approbation. He believed that if the present difficulties were to be adjusted, they must be adjusted on the principles embraced in the bill, of fixing *ad valorem* duties, except in the few cases in the bill to which specific duties were assigned.
>
> 'He said that it had been his fate to occupy a position as hostile as any one could, in reference to the protecting policy; but, if it depended on his will, he would not give his vote for the prostration of the manufacturing interest. A very large capital had been invested in manufactures, which had been of great service to the country; and he would never give his vote to suddenly withdraw all those duties by which that capital was sustained in the channel into which it had been directed. But he would only vote for the *ad valorem* system of duties, which he deemed the most beneficial and the most

equitable. At this time, he did not rise to go into a consideration of any of the details of this bill, as such a course would be premature, and contrary to the practice of the Senate. There were some of the provisions which had his entire approbation, and there were some to which he objected. But he looked upon these minor points of difference as points in the settlement of which no difficulty would occur, when gentlemen meet together in that spirit of mutual compromise which, he doubted not, would be brought into their deliberations, without at all yielding the constitutional question as to the right of protection.' [Here there was a tumultuous approbation in the galleries, which induced the Chair to order the galleries to be cleared.]

"This . . . was the end of Nullification! The Euthanasia of what was looked upon by so many as another Polyphemus, a real *'Monstrum horrendum, informe, ingens, cui lumen ademptum!'* [Latin: 'a monster frightful, formless, immense, with sight removed']. It was neither put down or up, nor was the theory of the Government, on which the doctrine was founded, ever put down or up. It simply was never put to a practical test. There were then no steam cars, much less telegraphic wires, to send the glad news of this adjustment, which was received by shouts at the Capital, throughout the country. Not on the wings of lightning, but as fast as it could be borne by lumbering stages, and puffing steamboats, it was received with rejoicing everywhere by the mass of the people, and by it new energy, new life, and new hope were inspired. At this result no one felt more relieved, or rejoiced, perhaps, than General [Andrew] Jackson himself.

"Mr. Clay's bill became a law on the 2nd of March, 1833. South Carolina soon after repealed her ordinance. In this way was peace preserved, harmony restored, the Union saved, and the Constitution maintained for further progress in that career of greatness on which the States under it had so gloriously entered. So much on that point.

"[Another point I would like to make concerns Thomas Jefferson. Does not his every political act prove that the original United States was intended to be a Confederacy? If so,] then [Liberals] will have to give it up as an indisputably established truth, I think, that the Constitution of the United States is a Compact between Sovereignties, because Mr. Jefferson was elected upon this very issue.

"*The administration of John Adams, who succeeded Washington in the Presidency, in 1797, bearing the popular name of Federal [an abbreviation of the word Confederal; thus identical to the word Confederacy], had endeavored, as was believed and charged, by construction and implication, to give that effect to the Constitution which Patrick Henry thought would be done in its practical workings. The party still bearing this name, during Mr. Adams's term of office, claimed virtually, it was said, for the Federal*

[Confederate] Government, general, absolute power, and maintained that the Supreme Court was the only arbiter between the General Government and State Governments, or the people, on all questions arising from the action of the General Government. They passed the Alien and Sedition laws, and acted generally upon the principle that the Federal Government was a consolidated Union of the people of all the States in one single, great Republic. They still kept the Party name of Federal [Confederate], because it was popular. This Party name, however, with their avowed principles, was nothing but a mask. It was but 'the livery of Heaven,' stolen 'to serve the Devil in.' [In other words, the Federalists of this period were actually anti-Confederalists, big government Liberals who wanted to consolidate all power in Washington and nationalize the central government. Adding to the confusion, after this, conservatives—originally called "Federalists"—became known as "Anti-Federalists." L.S.] [Emphasis added, L.S.]

"It was then that the true friends of a real Federal [Confederate] Government, and not a consolidated [National] one, were aroused from one end of the Union to the other. Mr. Jefferson's opinions were well known. As early as 1798, he had drawn up a set of Resolutions for the Kentucky Legislature, setting forth the true nature of the Government. The first of these Resolutions is in these words:

> Resolved, That the several States composing the United States of America, are not united on the principle of unlimited submission to their General Government; but that by Compact under the style and title of a Constitution for the United States, and of amendments thereto, they constituted a General Government for special purposes, delegated to that Government certain definite powers, reserving, each State to itself, the residuary mass of right to their own Self-government; and, that whensoever the General Government assumes undelegated powers, its acts are unauthoritative, void, and of no force; that to this Compact each State acceded as a State; and is an integral party, its co-States forming as to itself the other party; that this Government, created by this Compact, was not made the exclusive or final judge of the extent of the powers delegated to itself; since that would have made its discretion, and not the Constitution, the measure of its powers; but, that as in all other cases of Compact, among parties having no common judge, each party has an equal right to judge for itself, as well of infractions as of the mode and measure of redress.

"This Resolution, and a whole series on the same subject drawn up by him [Thomas Jefferson], passed the Legislature of Kentucky, with some slight modifications.

"Virginia also took her stand, not less decisive or unmistakable. She passed the Resolutions which we have seen quoted in Mr. Calhoun's speech. These

Resolutions were sent to all the States. The party in most of the States, claiming to be Federal [they were actually anti-Confederate consolidationists], replied to them, joining issue with the doctrines set forth in these Resolutions. Virginia, in 1799, took up the subject again and gave it a grave reconsideration. She re-affirmed her Resolutions of the year before with an elaborate report, drawn by Mr. [James] Madison. These Resolutions, and this report of Mr. Madison, contain an exceedingly clear and able exposition of the nature of the Government which no student in our history ought to fail to read and study. It was upon these that the great contest, fierce it was, . . . was waged between the [Liberal] so-called Federalists [pro-Centralists, anti-Confederacy, anti-states' rights] and the [Conservative] Jeffersonian Party [anti-Centralists, pro-Confederacy, pro-states' rights], in 1800. Mr. Jefferson, as the acknowledged leader of the State Sovereignty Party was chosen as the standard bearer of the principles set forth in his own Resolutions. The Party name assumed by the Anti-Centralists, under the lead of Mr. Jefferson, was generally that of Republican; but [contributing to the verbal anarchy] in some places it was Democratic. But the issue in every State was squarely made upon the issue presented in the Kentucky and Virginia Resolutions, and Mr. Madison's Report of 1799. That was the most memorable epoch in our history, from the adoption of the Constitution down to the breaking out of the war, in 1861. The question as to a proper construction of the Constitution was submitted to the people of the several States, and by them it was decided in favor of Mr. Jefferson's construction, and by that decision it was held to be settled, for more than half a century, that the Government of the United States is a Compact between States. Upon these principles and construction of the Constitution, Mr. Jefferson was re-elected [as U.S. president] in 1805. Upon them Mr. Madison was elected in 1809, and 1813. Upon them Mr. [James] Monroe was elected in 1817, and in 1821. Upon them Mr. John Quincy Adams (who had renounced the party which had made such a departure from principle during the Presidency of his father) was elected, in 1825. Upon these principles General [Andrew] Jackson was elected in 1829, and re-elected in 1833. Upon them Mr. [Martin] Van Buren was elected in 1837. Indeed no President was elected, from Mr.[Thomas] Jefferson to Mr. [Abraham] Lincoln, who denied these principles. It is true that, in the [presidential] election of General [William H.] Harrison, other questions entered into the contest, but on these principles he was a Republican [at the time, the Conservative Party] of the Jeffersonian school. . . . I mean to say that he was a Jeffersonian Republican—that he believed in the principles of the Kentucky and Virginia Resolutions of 1798-99. And I mean to say, that no man was elected President of the United States, from 1800 to 1860, from Mr. Jefferson to Mr. Lincoln, who did not.

"Here is . . . [President Harrison's] inaugural [address, given March 4, 1841]. From that I read as follows:

'Our Confederacy, fellow-citizens, can only be preserved by the same forbearance. Our citizens must be content with the exercise of the powers with which the Constitution clothes them. The attempt of those of one State to control the domestic institutions of another, can only result in feelings of distrust and jealousy, and are certain harbingers of disunion, violence, civil war, and the ultimate destruction of our free institutions. Our Confederacy is perfectly illustrated by the terms and principles governing a common co-partnership. There a fund of power is to be exercised under the direction of the joint counsels of the allied members, but that which has been reserved by the individuals is intangible by the common Government, or the individual members composing it. To attempt it finds no support in the principles of our Constitution. It should be our constant and earnest endeavor mutually to cultivate a spirit of concord and harmony among the various parts of our Confederacy. Experience has abundantly taught us that the agitation by citizens of one part of the Union of a subject not confided to the General Government, but exclusively under the guardianship of the local authorities, is productive of no other consequences than bitterness, alienation, discord, and injury to the very cause which is intended to be advanced. Of all the great interests which appertain to our country, that of Union—cordial, confiding, fraternal, Union—is by far the most important, since it is the only true and sure guarantee of all others.'

"Do [my Liberal friends] . . . want more pointed or conclusive testimony than this?

"Mr. [Daniel] Webster, I will here remark, was General Harrison's Secretary of State, and the presumption is that he must have approved, at that time (1841), the general principles of this inaugural, to whatever extent its doctrines may imply a modification of his views expressed in 1833. But I said, and maintain, that no man, from Mr. Jefferson to Mr. Lincoln, was elected to the Presidency, who held contrary principles.

"The opinions of Mr. Van Buren, Mr. [James K.] Polk, Mr. [Franklin] Pierce, and Mr. [James] Buchanan, are well known. General [John] Taylor, as General [William H.] Harrison, was elected on other issues. No public expression of opinion on these principles was ever made by him, that I am aware of, except that in the construction of the Constitution he should be governed 'by the practice of the earlier Presidents, who had so large a share in its formation.' [George] Washington, [Thomas] Jefferson, [James] Madison, and [James] Monroe must have been alluded to. He was well known, however, in early life, to have belonged to the Jefferson [limited government] school of politics. Indeed, the very name of Federalist [i.e., big government proponent] had become so odious to the popular mind throughout the United States, by the abuse of the word by those who applied it to themselves during the administration of the elder Adams [John], that no man openly professing the principles of that party could ever have been chosen President, from 1800 to 1860. This, I think, may be asserted as an incontrovertible truth. Not only Mr. Jefferson, but every President elected, from him to Mr. Lincoln, held the Constitution to be a Compact between the States! On this point there can be no doubt or question. [Actually, Stephens was wrong concerning Lincoln's beliefs on this topic.]

"Under this construction the Union, or Federal Republic formed by it, grew and flourished as no nation ever did before. Under this construction the States, in number, had increased from thirteen to thirty-three! The territory had been enlarged from less than a million of square miles to nearly three millions! The population had increased from less than four millions to over thirty-one millions! The exports had increased from less than forty millions to upwards of three hundred and sixty millions of dollars *per annum*! The great mass of internal productions and developments had grown in an increased ratio!

"Under this construction South Carolina had acted in 1832. Under this construction the peace of the country was then maintained and our unsurpassed progress was not only not checked or impeded by it, but received new impetus, and moved on with greatly increased momentum and brilliancy.

"Under the principles of free trade then established, to go into full operation in 1843, the manufacturing interests were not crippled. The industry of the country in none of its departments was paralyzed. New life and new energy sprung up everywhere. The exports of domestic manufactures from 1843 to 1860 increased from about eleven to upwards of thirty millions of dollars *per annum*! The tonnage of shipping increased from a little over two millions to upwards of five millions! The miles of railroad, a system of internal improvement just commenced about the time of Nullification, increased from about five thousand to upwards of twenty-five thousand! The exports of domestic products, staples, etc., increased from less than one hundred to upwards of three hundred millions! The production of cotton alone increased from less than sixty millions to upwards of one hundred and sixty millions of dollars *per annum*!

"More than twelve hundred thousand square miles of territory were acquired during this period, between 1843 and 1860, and seven new States, more than half the original number, were admitted into the Union! Within the same period, the genius of [Samuel F. B.] Morse had seized the idea of the magnetic telegraph, and had brought that wonderful discovery into practical operation by extending these iron nerves throughout the length and breadth of the country, connecting the most distant points and uniting all together, as if under the influence of a common *sensorium*! Was the material progress, to say nothing of the moral and intellectual, of any nation in the world, greater, in the same space of time than was that of this Confederated Republic, from 1843 to 1860? Under this construction of the Constitution all this prosperity and progress, anterior to and subsequent to Nullification, were achieved; and, I maintain, might have gone on, under the same construction, with like common prosperity and joint happiness, until the system covered the entire continent, to the wonder and amazement of all other peoples and nations of the earth! It was only when this great fundamental law of our political existence was violated, in 1860, by a different construction, the anti-Jeffersonian construction, that disorder, confusion, war, and all its disastrous results ensued. The vital laws of every organism must be obeyed and conformed to, if its health, vigor, and development, are preserved. The whole of our late troubles [i.e., Lincoln's War] came from a violation of this essential and vital law of our political existence.

"But this is anticipatory. I only meant to say . . . that if [a Liberal holds] . . . to the doctrines of Mr. Jefferson, [he] . . . must admit that the Constitution is a Compact between States, and that the Government under it is strictly Federal [Confederate] in its character.

"We will now take up the Proclamation of General Jackson . . . and see how it squares with the doctrine of Mr. Jefferson.

> [As cited by a Liberal:] 'In his proclamation, President Andrew Jackson distinctly affirms . . . "the people of the United States formed the Constitution." That they constitute "one people," "one nation." That the allegiance of the people of the several States was, by it, transferred to the Government of the United States, and that they thereby became American citizens. That no State has any right to nullify a law of Congress, or to secede from the Union. That the Supreme Court of the United States had been instituted as an arbiter to decide in the last resort upon all Constitutional questions touching either the powers of the General Government or the reserved rights of the States; that States, as well as individuals, must be bound by the adjudications of that tribunal, and that any forcible resistance to the execution of the laws of Congress, thus expounded, would be treason. . . . These words seem to . . . be utterly inconsistent . . . with the principles of Mr. Jefferson, embodied in the Kentucky resolution.'

"[In response,] I have several things to say [on this topic].

"In the first place, what General Jackson said in this Proclamation, should be considered in connection with the exact state of public affairs at the time it was issued. South Carolina had not [yet] attempted to secede. Her policy was based upon the idea of remaining in the Union, and yet defeating [via Nullification] the execution of the Federal laws upon the tariff within her limits. This was the state of thing which called forth the Proclamation. A prominent feature in the Proclamation, which must be borne in mind, in construing all its parts, is this:

> [Stephens quoting Jackson:] 'The Ordinance (that is South Carolina's Ordinance of Nullification) is founded, not on the indefeasible right of resisting acts which are plainly unconstitutional, and too oppressive to be endured; but on the strange position that any one State may not only declare an act of Congress void, but prohibit its execution; that they may do this consistently with the Constitution; that the true construction of that instrument permits a State to retain its place in the Union, and yet be bound by no other of its laws than those it may choose to consider as Constitutional.'

"This was the statement by him of the case which prompted the Proclamation, and nothing in the Proclamation should be received as the authoritative exposition of the principles of General Jackson touching the nature of the Government, except such as bear directly upon the case then before him, and as stated by himself. Judges never hold themselves bound by any expressions that fall from them in delivering their opinions upon any matter, except those which bear directly upon the case at bar. These only are authoritative. All else are *'obiter dicta'* [Latin: "a casual comment made in passing"].

"Applying this rule to [Jackson's] . . . Proclamation, there is in it much of that character. It was evidently hastily penned, and it has in it many not well guarded expressions. Under this character may be considered what was said on the subject of citizenship and allegiance, for we have seen what the Supreme Court, the very tribunal to which he refers as the final arbiter in the last resort, had held upon these subjects. That it would have been treason in any of the individual citizens of South Carolina, or any number of them, in their private character, to forcibly resist the laws of the United States, while the State was a member of the Union with her Sovereign powers unresumed, no one ever denied. South Carolina did not deny it. She did not contemplate any forcible resistance to these laws. There is nothing in that statement against my position. Upon reading this entire Proclamation by itself, however, I frankly admit that a disciple of the Jefferson school may well say of it as Peter said of some of Paul's epistles, that is, that there 'are some things' in it 'hard to be understood, which they that are unlearned and unstable wrest, as they do also the other scriptures, unto their own destruction.' But that General Jackson himself did not mean what some suppose his words in particular passages imply, will be made clearly to appear before I get through. Just now, in reply to the view given in the Proclamation, as [Liberals] . . . seem to understand it, but as General Jackson did not, touching the powers of the Supreme Court to decide between the States and the General Government, upon questions involving their respective powers, the answer of Madison, in his report referred to, is conclusive. This was quoted, as we have seen, by Mr. [John C.] Calhoun. But, in addition to this, the answer of Judge [George M.] Bibb, of Kentucky, in the Senate at the time, was so much fuller and so perfectly exhaustive of the subject, you will pardon me for reading extensively from it. . . . Here it is. And in it [Bibb] . . . says:

> 'That there are powers, authorities, and liberties, appertaining to the States, which belonged to them as States, and which they have not surrendered, but reserved, is undeniable. The general principle is clear, that in all Compacts, Leagues, Conventions, and Treaties between Sovereign States, Powers, and Potentates, each party has the right to judge whether a breach has been committed by the other party; and in case of a wilful, deliberate breach, to take such measures for redress as prudence and the discretion of the injured party shall dictate.
>
> 'Is the Compact between these States an exception to this general rule? If it is, then the States must, by some action of theirs, have surrendered this portion of their Sovereignty. What part of the Constitution declares such a surrender? There is no such express declaration of surrender. In the various enumerations of powers prohibited to the States, and agreed not to be exercised by them, there is no declaration that they shall not exercise the right, appertaining to them as parties to the Compact, to judge of an excessive, alarming, and dangerous stretch of power by the Federal Government. The abridgment of the powers of the States in this particular not being expressed, cannot be made out by implication, or by construction. The powers not delegated by the States to the United States, nor prohibited to the States by the Constitution, are reserved to the States. So says the Constitution. What clause in the Constitution delegates to the Federal Government the sole power of deciding the extent of the grant of powers to itself, as well as the extent of the powers reserved to the States?
>
> 'It is said that this power is vested by the Constitution in the Supreme Court of the United States. The provisions are:
>
> > The Judicial power shall extend to all cases in law and equity, arising under this Constitution, the laws of the United States, and treaties made, or which shall be made, under their authority.
> >
> > This Constitution, and the laws of the United States which shall be made in pursuance thereof, and all treaties made, or which shall be

made, under the authority of the United States, shall be the supreme law of the land, and the Judges in every State shall be bound thereby, any thing in the Constitution or laws of any State to the contrary, notwithstanding.

'These are the two provisions of the Constitution which are referred to as delegating the power to the Supreme Court, to be the sole judge of the extent of the powers granted, and of the powers reserved; and as denying to the States the Sovereign power of protecting themselves against the usurpation of their reserved powers, authorities, and privileges. If the delegation to the Supreme Court, and prohibition to the States, are not contained in these two clauses, then they are not to be found in the Federal Constitution.

'The latter clause cannot touch the question in debate; for that only declares the supremacy of the Constitution, and the treaties "and laws made in pursuance thereof." Powers exercised contrary to the Constitution, acts done contrary to the Constitution, by the exercise of authorities not under, but in violation of the Constitution, and by usurpation of State rights, State authorities, and State privileges, are the subjects under consideration.

'Let us examine the former clause:

The Judicial power shall extend to all cases, in law and equity, arising under this Constitution.

'The case must be of "Judicial power;" it must be a case, "in law or equity," arising under the Constitution. The expression is not to all cases arising under the Constitution, treaties, and laws of the United States, but it is "to all cases in law and equity."

Use is the law and rule of speech.

'By this law and this rule we must examine the language of the Constitution.

'A judicial power is one subject,—a political power is another and a different subject. A case in law, or a case in equity is one subject,—a political case is another and a different subject.

'Judicial cases in law and equity, arising under the regular exercise of Constitutional powers, by laws and treaties made by authority, are different from political questions of usurpation, surmounting the Constitution, and involving the high prerogatives, authorities, and privileges of the Sovereign parties who made the Constitution.

'In judicial cases arising under a treaty, the Court may construe the treaty, and administer the rights arising under it, to the parties who submit themselves to the jurisdiction of the Court in that case. But the Court must confine itself within the pale of judicial authority. It cannot rightfully exercise the political power of the Government, in declaring the treaty null because the one or the other party to the treaty has broken this or that article; and, therefore, that the whole treaty is abrogated. To judge of the breach of the articles of the treaty, by the Sovereign contracting parties, and in case of breach to dissolve that treaty, and to declare it no longer obligatory, is a political power belonging not to the judiciary. It belongs to other departments of the Government, who will judge of the extent of the injury resulting from the violation, and whether the reparation shall be sought by amicable negotiation, or whether the treaty shall be declared no longer obligatory on the Government and the people of the injured party. Yet, by the law of Nations, the wilful and deliberate breach of one article is a breach of all the articles, each being the consideration of the others; and the injured party has the right so to treat it.

'By the Act approved on the 7th of July, 1798, the Congress of the United States declared themselves of right freed and exonerated from the stipulations of the treaties, and of the Consular Convention theretofore concluded between the United States and France, and that they should not thenceforth be regarded as legally obligatory on the Government or citizens of the United States—because of the repeated violations on the part of the French Government, etc.

'Before this declaration, the Supreme Court of the United States was bound, in cases of judicial cognizance coming before them, to take the treaties as obligatory, and to administer the rights growing out of the treaties between France and the United States. After that declaration, the Court was bound to consider the treaties as abrogated. The Courts had no power, before the Act of July, 1798, to inquire into violations, and, therefore, to declare the treaties not obligatory. After that act they had no power to demand evidence of the violations recited and revise the political decision of the Government.

'To declare these treaties no longer obligatory was a political power, not a judicial power. Yet, the violations of these, committed under the authority of the French Government, and the consequent injuries to the citizens and Government of the United States, and the rights of the United States consequent therefrom, before the Act of July, 1798, were "cases arising under the Constitution," and treaties of the United States. But the judicial power did not extend to those cases of violation, so as to declare the treaties no longer obligatory. The question whether those violations should or should not abrogate the treaties, did not make a case in law or equity, for the decision of a judicial tribunal. Yet they were cases arising under the Constitution. The power to decide them belonged to the Government of the United States as a political Sovereign; but the judicial power did not extend to them; those cases belonged to the political powers, not to the judicial powers of the Government.

'The British Courts of Admiralty executed upon the commerce of the United States the British orders in council, disclaiming the power to decide whether those orders in council were conformable to the general law of Nations, which every nation is bound to respect and observe. In like manner, the French Courts of Admiralty executed upon the commerce of the United

States the Berlin and Milan decrees.

'The British and French Courts had not cognizance to judge the Sovereign powers of the Nations, and to declare those orders and decrees contrary to the law of Nations—that was not a judicial power. So the Courts of the United States, even the Supreme Court, had not the power to declare the treaties between the United States and France, and Great Britain, no longer obligatory upon the citizens and Government of the United States, because of the multiplied wrongs and injuries committed upon the citizens of the United States, under color of those orders in council, and decrees, infracting the laws of Nations, and treaties, and hostile to the rights of the Government of the United States. Those cases, in their effects upon the treaties and amicable relations between the United States and those Governments, did not fall within the judicial power of the Courts of the United States. Those questions did not fall within the description of 'cases in law and equity,' as used in the Constitution of the United States, in conferring, vesting, and defining the powers of the judicial department. Those political powers belong to other departments of the Government. According to the law and rule of speech established by use, such powers are classed under the denomination of political powers, prerogative powers, not under the head of judicial powers.

'Before I proceed to illustrate, by other examples, the distinctions which I have taken, between political powers and judicial powers, between political questions and cases and judicial questions or cases, I will refer to the declaration of one, whose opinions on Constitutional questions I know will command respect; a man to whose opinions I willingly yield my respect, without, however, submitting with that implicit faith which belongs to fools. On the resolution of Mr. [Edward] Livingston, touching the conduct of President Adams, in causing Thomas Nash, alias Jonathan Bobbins, to be arrested and delivered over to a British naval officer, without any accusation, or trial, or investigation in a Court of Justice, Mr. [John] Marshall, then a Representative of Virginia, now Chief Justice of the United States, in defending the conduct of the President, thus delivered his opinion in that debate:

[Bibb quoting Marshall:] "This being established, the inquiry was, to what department was the power in question allotted?

"The gentleman from New York had relied on the second section of the third article of the Constitution, which enumerates the cases to which the judicial power of the United States extends, as expressly including that now under consideration. Before he examined that section, it would not be improper to notice a very material mis-statement of it, made in the Resolutions offered by the gentleman from New York. By the Constitution, the judicial power of the United States is extended to all cases in law and equity, arising under the Constitution, Laws, and Treaties of the United States; but the

Resolutions declare that judicial power to extend to all questions arising under the Constitution, treaties, and laws of the United States. The difference between the Constitution and the Resolutions was material and apparent. A case in law or equity was a term well understood, and of limited signification. It was a controversy between parties, which had taken a shape for judicial decision. If the judicial power extended to every question under the Constitution, it would involve almost every subject proper for Legislative discussion and decision; if to every question under the laws and treaties of the United States, it would involve almost every subject on which the Executive could act. The division of power, which the gentleman had stated, could exist no longer, and the other departments would be swallowed up by the Judiciary. But it was apparent that the Resolutions had essentially misrepresented the Constitution. He did not charge the gentleman from New York with intentional misrepresentation; he would not attribute to him such an artifice in any case, much less in a case where detection was so easy and so certain. Yet this substantial departure from the Constitution, in Resolutions affecting substantially to unite it, was not less worthy of remark for being unintentional. It manifested the course of reasoning by which the gentleman had himself been misled, and his judgment betrayed into the opinions those Resolutions expressed. By extending the judicial power to all cases in law and equity, the Constitution had never been understood to confer on that department any political power whatever. To come within this description, a question must assume a legal form for forensic litigation and judicial decision. There must be parties to come into Court, who can be reached by its process, and bound by its power; whose rights admit of ultimate decision by a tribunal to which they are bound to submit.

"A case in law or equity, proper for judicial decision, may arise under a treaty, where the rights of individuals, acquired or secured by a treaty, are to be asserted or defended in Court. As under the fourth or sixth article of the Treaty of Peace with Great Britain, or under those articles of our late treaties with France, Prussia, and other nations, which secure to the subjects of those nations their property within the United States; or, as would be an article, which, instead of stipulating to deliver up an offender, should stipulate his punishment, provided the case was punishable by the laws and in the Courts of the United States. But the judicial power cannot extend to political compacts; as the establishment of the boundary line between the American and British dominions; the case of the late guarantee in our treaty with France, or the case of the delivery of a murderer under the twenty-seventh article of our present treaty with Britain."

[Bibb continues:] 'This distinction between a political power and a judicial power, is recognized and acted upon by the Supreme Court of the United

States, in the case of *Williams* vs. *Armroyd*.

'Again, in the case of *Marbury* vs. *Madison*, this distinction between the political powers of Government and the judicial power, is most explicitly avowed and recognized by the Supreme Court.

'The supremacy of that is a judicial supremacy only. It is supreme in reference to the other Courts in questions of a judicial character, brought within the sphere of judicial cognizance by controversies which shall have assumed a legal form for forensic litigation and judicial decision. There must be parties amenable to its process, bound by its power, whose rights admit of ultimate decision by a tribunal to which they are bound to submit. "Questions in their nature political, or which are by the Constitution and laws submitted to the Executive, can never be made in this Court."

'The decision of the Executive, upon political questions submitted to its discretion, is as supreme as the decision of the Court within its jurisdiction. Neither department ought to invade the jurisdiction of the other,—so said the Supreme Court of the United States, in *Marbury* vs. *Madison*. . . .

'The twelfth amendment to the Constitution takes away the jurisdiction which had been given to the Supreme Court to hold jurisdiction of a suit against one of the United States by a citizen of another State, or by citizens or subjects of any foreign State; but leaves the jurisdiction conferred over controversies between two or more States. If two States, therefore, have a controversy, which, in its character, makes a case in law or equity proper for judicial cognizance, it may be brought before the Supreme Court. Controversies between two or more States, about territory or limits, may be litigated before the Supreme Court of the United States. But then each State must have an opportunity, as a party, to prosecute or defend her right before the decision can bind her. Those are questions of *meum et tuum* [Latin: "mine and thine"] rights of property which one State claims to the exclusion of the other; not political rights belonging to all the States respectively, where the rights and powers of one State does not exclude but establishes the rights of each and every other. Such rights claimed for all, as belonging equally to each and every of the States respectively, cannot make a controversy in law or equity between two States.

'Political powers not delegated to the Federal Government; political powers reserved to the States, constitute the subjects of the propositions which are affirmed on the one side and denied on the other. The propositions affirmed are, that the powers of the Federal Government result from the Compact to which the States are parties, that these powers are limited by the plain sense and intention of the instrument constituting that Compact, and no farther valid than they are authorized by the grants enumerated in that Compact; "and that, in case of a deliberate, palpable, and dangerous exercise of other powers, not granted by the said Compact, the States, who are parties thereto, have the right, and are in duty bound, to interpose for arresting the progress of the evil, and for maintaining, within their respective limits, the authorities, rights, and liberties appertaining to them."'

[Stephens resumes:] "This argument of Judge [George M.] Bibb, in the United States Senate, I have read so copiously from, was the overwhelming answer given at the time, to what were then supposed to be the doctrines of the Proclamation upon the powers and jurisdiction of the Supreme Court, as an arbiter in the last resort between the General Government and the States as States. It is not only conclusive on these points, but it is completely exhaustive of the whole question of the general powers and jurisdiction of this Court, on which so much has been said and written. With it I conclude what I have to say, as I remarked, on [Jackson's] . . . Proclamation in the first place.

"Now, in the second place, I will let General Jackson's own authoritative explanation of those parts [Liberals] . . . particularly refer to speak for itself. General Jackson had been elected as a Jeffersonian Republican. Many parts of this Proclamation were not understood by his most devoted political friends. It was thought to contain doctrines inconsistent with the teachings of the Fathers of that school. Many who agreed with him thoroughly in his position on Nullification thought that there were principles in that paper, not bearing directly on that question, however, which were inconsistent with the true principles of State Rights and State Sovereignty, and which savored much of the doctrines of the Consolidationists of the elder Adams' times. This called forth from him, through the *Washington Globe* newspaper, an explanation. The explanation was editorial—published not long after the great debate on his Proclamation and Force Bill. It was published, as stated, by authority. Now in this explanation will be found the best answer to [the Liberals'] . . . question, for it came from General Jackson himself. Here it is:

From the *Washington Globe*
THE PRESIDENT'S PROCLAMATION.
'The editors of the *Richmond Enquirer* and of the *Petersburg Intelligencer*, in appealing to the fearless, honest, disinterested patriotism, which dictated the Proclamation, for an interpretation of those points in which it has suffered misconstruction, evinces the just estimation in which they hold the character of the President. Oracular silence and mystery with regard to his official documents, or Executive acts, form no part of General Jackson's policy. As Chief Magistrate, he does not entertain a thought which he would hide from the American people. He, who, from youth to age, has borne his life in his hand, ready to offer it up at any moment in defence of his country, now carries his heart as openly towards those, in whose service it is, and has ever been, so affectionately devoted. With him, dignity of station is nothing. He does not allow the ceremonies of office—the outworks which are everywhere thrown round the Chief Magistracy—to separate him from his fellow-citizens. With a wise man of another age, he thinks that "plain and round dealing is the Honor of man's nature"—and the charm of existence to

him is the consciousness of doing his duty—and the highest distinction is only valued, as it evinces the public confidence and a proper appreciation of his motives. Nothing, therefore, gives him more pain than the misconstruction to which the opinions expressed in his Proclamation have been subjected, and nothing, we are sure, will give him more pleasure, than to find, when properly understood, that they meet the approbation of the enlightened Republicans [at this time Conservatives], the friends of the Union and State Rights, upon whose principles he has uniformly acted, throughout his public life.

'With these preparatory remarks, we proceed to the reply, which we are authorized to give, to the inquiries of the editors of the *Richmond Enquirer* and *Petersburg Intelligencer*.

'The impression that the President had given evidence of a "dereliction from his principles" in "those passages which relate to the great question of the origin and character of our Federal Compact," would he fully sustained, if those passages warranted the interpretation given by Dr. Cocke in the Resolution submitted by him to the Senate of Virginia. That Resolution assumed that it was "set forth in the late Proclamation of the President of the United States, that the Federal Constitution results from the people in the aggregate, and not from the States," etc., and from this assumption, the Resolution goes on to infer, that "this theory of our Government would tend, in practice, to the most disastrous consequences, giving a minority of States, having a majority of population, the control over the other States," etc. This is the interpretation of the expression of the President's Proclamation, and the implication of consequences, which has given the alarm to many of the sincere friends of State Rights, who have considered the doctrine thus promulgated, as the [Conservative] doctrine of the old Federal [limited government] Party. If the interpretation were true, we would not hesitate to admit the justice of the censure. But we assert, authoritatively, that the inferences made by Mr. Cocke are totally repugnant to the opinions of the President, and the views he meant to inculcate by the passage in the Proclamation, from which they are drawn; and these deductions were repelled, in this print, under the direction of the President, the instant he was apprized they had assumed the shape of a Resolution in the Senate of Virginia. The difficulty in the minds of the editors of the *Richmond Enquirer* and *Petersburg Intelligencer*, arises from the same passage in the Proclamation. We have, therefore, we hope, only to recur to them and give the sense in which they were intended by the President, to give perfect satisfaction in relation to the principles he entertains.

'The first passage, to which we are referred in the articles we quote from the *Richmond Enquirer* and *Petersburg Intelligencer*, is as follows:

"The people of the United States formed the Constitution, acting through the State Legislatures in making the Compact, to meet and discuss its provisions, and acting in separate Conventions, where they ratified those provisions; but the terms used in its construction, show it to be a Government in which the people of all the States collectively are represented."

'This is not theory, it is simple history,—but the phraseology, like that of the Constitution itself, which it copies *verbatim* in the leading member of the sentence, has been subjected to various interpretations. But the President, in saying that "The people of the United States formed the Constitution," although he used the very language of the Constitution itself, did not leave it open to the construction, which the latitudinarian party have put upon its terms. He followed up the general declaration, by particularizing, that the Constitution originated in a Compact, that the Compact was the offspring of the people of the several States, acting through their respective State Legislatures, and further, that the Constitution or Government, founded in this Compart, received its sanction from the people of the several States, acting through independent separate State Conventions, to ratify its provisions. With such precise definite and positive ascription of the Constitution, in its origin, to a Compact among the several States, as the organized agents of several communities of people, and again making the obligatory sanction of the instrument, as derived from the same independent communities, depend on its ratification in separate Conventions, it would seem that the idea of its being the work of the whole people, in "the aggregate" or united in one body, was absolutely precluded. Indeed, as we said before, in commenting on Dr. Cocke's Resolution, the simple language of the Constitution in proclaiming its origin in its first words, "We, the People of the United States," "do ordain and establish this Constitution for the United States of America," does, of itself, imply, what is so precisely specified in the added explanation of the Proclamation. It excludes, by its terms, the idea of a people embodied in a Consolidated Government, by describing them as composing different "States," and by speaking of the "States" as "united," it repels the idea that the Union intended, is that of "the people in the aggregate," but of States as forming separate communities. The close of the preamble to the Constitution (which we have quoted above, in connection with its first words) preserve the same idea. The Constitution is declared to be established, not for an aggregate people, but "for the United States of America."

'The interpretation, forced by the Resolutions, to which we have referred, on the Proclamation, in spite of its explanations, is precisely that which the friends of a Consolidated Government have attempted to force on the Constitution itself. If this were admitted, the conclusion drawn from it, that it would give "to a minority of States, having a majority of the population, a control over the other States," would inevitably follow. . . . While the Proclamation thus recognizes the Constitution as the creature of the people of the States severally, and as only susceptible of change, through the agency of "two thirds of the States," in proposing amendments to be effectuated only by the ratification of three fourths of the States, it is difficult to conceive how any one could infer, from its doctrines, that it concedes to "a minority of States having the majority of population," absolute sway over the Constitution and Government.

'The only other difficulty to which we are referred as requiring explanation, by our friends of the *Richmond Enquirer* and *Petersburg Intelligencer*, will be found in the close of the following passage, which speaks of "the unity of our political character. . . ." It would be sufficient here, again, to observe, that it is history which speaks in this passage, and not the President. The facts are indubitably as he states them. And it is only by confounding the unity, which is derived from a Confederacy among the States (making them, to a certain extent, "one Nation"), with the idea of a consolidation of all power in the Federal Government, that an objection is created. "The unity of our political character," here spoken of, it is expressly said, is not intended to denote "an undivided Sovereignty," or authority in the General Government. On the contrary, the text shows that it only refers to that special delegated authority which is vested in the Constitution out of the powers belonging to the several State communities, united in one common Government for the purpose of establishing a National character, and National relations with the other Nations of the world. And as it was especially the scope of the Constitution, to give unity to our political character in its exterior aspect, and to confer upon the Government all the attributes of Nationality, in regard to Foreign powers, it is strange that jealousy should be excited by the use of terms pointing out this design, or by references to various periods of our history, to prove that, in this respect, a connection has always existed among the independent communities composing the Confederacy. . . . We were a Nation under the Articles of Confederation, however feeble the means of the National authority then to bring the energies of the several States to act in unison—and we are, surely, not less a Nation, now that Government has been established to form a more perfect Union, endowed with all the faculties which can constitute us a Nation in our relations with Foreign powers. . . . The Proclamation, then, in the passage objected to, has merely spoken the facts of history—the language of the Constitution, and of the Declaration of Independence. There is no speculative opinion advanced—no theory proposed. And we have endeavored to show, that nothing in these generalities tended, in the slightest degree, to justify the inferences drawn from them, and which have been substituted as the principles of the Proclamation. But we are authorized to be more explicit, and to say positively, that no part of [President Jackson's] . . . Proclamation was meant to countenance principles which have been ascribed to it. On the contrary, its doctrines, if construed in the sense they were intended, and carried out, inculcate that the Constitution of the United States is founded on Compact—that this Compact derives its obligation from the agreement, entered into by the people of each of the States, in their political capacity, with the people of the other States—that the Constitution, which is the offspring of this Compact, has its sanction in the ratification of the people of the several States, acting in the capacity of separate communities—that the majority of the people of the United States, in the aggregate, have no power to alter the Constitution of the General Government, but that change, or amendment can only be proposed in the mode pointed out in the Constitution, and can never become obligatory unless ratified by the people of three fourths of the States through their respective Legislatures or State Conventions. . . . That in the case of a violation of the Constitution of the United States, and the usurpation of powers not granted by it on the part of the functionaries of the General Government, the State Governments have the right to interpose and arrest the evil, upon the principles which were set forth in the Virginia Resolutions of 1798, against the Alien and Sedition Laws—and finally, that in extreme cases of oppression (every mode of Constitutional redress having been sought in vain), the right resides with the people of the several States to organize resistance against such oppression, confiding in a good cause, the favor of heaven, and the spirit of freemen, to vindicate the right.

'We beg leave here to submit, in aid of our own, an exposition which touches the points involved in the controverted passages of the Proclamation, and which received the sanction of the President, at the threshold of the controversy that led to the promulgation of that paper. During the progress of the debate on Foote's Resolutions, the editor of this print (who was then connected with a press in Kentucky, which sustained the principles of the Republican party), received from the Postmaster General the speech delivered by Mr. [Edward] Livingston, accompanied by a letter, saying, that the views contained in it were sanctioned by the President; and might be considered as exhibiting the light in which his administration considered the subject under debate. The following extracts from that speech will serve in illustrating the principles on which the President then took his stand, to explain the more condensed view given of them in his Proclamation.'

"Reference is made in this explanation to certain extracts from the speech of Mr. [Edward] Livingston, in the Senate, in the debate on Foote's Resolutions, in 1830. The extracts, published by the *Globe*, I have never seen. The explanation I have read is a republication from the *Globe*, in the *Augusta Constitutionalist*, 11th Oct., 1833. The doctrines of that whole speech, however, it was said, met the approval of General Jackson, at the time it was delivered. Here is that speech . . . I call your special attention to these portions of it.

[Stephens quoting Livingston:] 'I now approach a graver subject; one, on the true understanding of which the Union, and of course the happiness of our country, depends. The question presented is that of the true sense of that Constitution which it is made our first duty to preserve in its purity. Its true construction is put in doubt—not on a question of power, between its several departments, but on the very basis upon which the whole rests; and which, if erroneously decided, must topple down the fabric, raised with so much pain, framed with so much wisdom, established with so much persevering labor, and for more than forty years the shelter and protection of our liberties, the proud monument of the patriotism and talent of those who devised it, and which, we fondly hoped, would remain to after ages as a model for the imitation of every nation that wished to be free. Is that, sir, to be its destiny? The answer to that question may be influenced by this debate. How strong the motive, then, to conduct it calmly; when the mind is not heated by opposition, depressed by defeat, or elate with fancied victory; to discuss it with a sincere desire, not to obtain a paltry triumph in argument, to gain applause by a tart reply, to carry away the victory by addressing the passions, or gain proselytes by specious fallacies, but, with a mind open to conviction, seriously to search after truth, earnestly, when found, to impress it on others. What we say on this subject will remain; it is not an every day question; it will remain for good or for evil. As our views are correct or erroneous; as they tend to promote the lasting welfare, or accelerate the dissolution of our Union; so will our opinions be cited, as those which placed the Constitution on a firm basis, when it was shaken; or deprecated, if they should have formed doctrines which led to its destruction. . . . The States existed before the Constitution; they parted only with such powers as are specified in that instrument; they continue still to exist, with all the powers they have not ceded, and the present Government, itself, would never have gone into operation, had not the States, in their political capacity, consented. That consent is a Compact of each one with the whole, not (as has been argued in order to throw a kind of ridicule on this convincing part of the argument of my friend from South Carolina), with the Government which was made by such Compact. It is difficult, therefore, it would appear, with all these characters of a Federative nature, to deny to the present Government the description of one founded on Compact, to which each State was a party; and a conclusive proof, if any more were wanted, would be in the fact, that the States adopted the Constitution at different times, and many of them on conditions which were afterwards complied with by amendments. If it were strictly a popular Government, in the sense that is contended for, the moment a majority of the people of the United States had consented, it would have bound the rest; and yet, after all the others, except one, had adopted the Constitution, the smallest still held out, and if Rhode Island had not consented to enter into the [U.S.] Confederacy, she would, perhaps, at this time, have been unconnected with us. . . . I place little reliance on the argument, which has been mostly depended on, to show that this is a popular Government. I mean the preamble; which begins with the words, "We, the people." It proves nothing more than the fact, that the people of the several States had been consulted, and had given their consent to the instrument. To give these words any other construction, would be to make them an assertion directly contrary to the fact. We know—and it has never been imagined, or asserted, that the people of the United States, collectively, as a whole people, gave their assent, or were consulted in that capacity—the people of each State were consulted to know whether that State would form a part of the United States, under the Articles of the Constitution, and to that they gave their assent, simply as citizens of that State.

'It is a Compact, by which the people of each State have consented to take from their own Legislatures some of the powers they had conferred upon them, and to transfer them, with other enumerated powers, to the Government of the United States, created by that Compact. . . .

'Although, in my opinion, in every case which can lawfully be brought within the jurisdiction of the Supreme Court, that tribunal must judge of the Constitutionality of laws on which the question before them depends, and its decrees must be final, whether they affect State rights or not; and, as a necessary consequence, that no State has any right to impede or prevent the execution of such sentence; yet, I am far from thinking that this Court is created an umpire to judge between the General and State Governments. I do not see it recorded in the instrument, but I see it recorded that every right not given is retained. In an extreme case that has been put, of the United States declaring that a particular State should have but one Senator, or should be deprived of its representation, I see nothing to oblige the State to submit this case to the Supreme Court; on the contrary, I see, by the enumeration of the cases and persons which may be brought within their jurisdiction, that this is not included; in this, the injured State would have a right at once to declare that it would no longer be bound by a Compact which had been thus grossly violated.'

"The authoritative explanation, by General Jackson, of the doctrines of his Proclamation . . . and these parts of the speech of Mr. Livingston, which, it was asserted, as we have seen, met his entire approval, clearly and beyond doubt show that General Jackson held the Constitution to be a Compact between States, and that he adhered to the old Republican creed of 1798-99. He was express in his injunction that it should be made known that he held to the right of State interposition in certain cases, upon the principles of the Virginia Resolutions of 1799.

"From this speech of Mr. Livingston it also appears that General Jackson did not mean, by any thing he said in the Proclamation about the Supreme Court of the United States, to be understood as holding, that that Court had any Constitutional jurisdiction over political questions, or such as involved the reserved rights of the States. Mr. Livingston is explicit on this point. He says that the Supreme Court is not an umpire between the States and General Government. In this, he agrees entirely with Judge Bibb. General Jackson, in his Proclamation on this subject, must have meant nothing more, therefore, than that the United States Judiciary was clothed with power to decide the

Constitutionality of the Tariff laws, as between citizens, in cases made, so long as the State was a member of the Union. That was the case he was addressing the country upon. But Mr. Livingston expressly says, that, in case of a gross violation of the Constitution, where the matter cannot be brought before that Court, that the State would no longer be bound by the Compact. His position, in this respect, was the same as that of Mr. Webster, at Capon Springs, when he said, "a bargain cannot be broken on one side and still bind the other side."

"Neither General Jackson, therefore, nor any thing in his Proclamation, can be brought up as authority against what I claimed as an indisputably established conclusion. That was, that the Government of the United States is founded upon Compact between States, and is therefore strictly Federal in its character, or, in other words, that it is what [George] Washington styled it, a Confederated Republic.

"No better or stronger proof need have been adduced to establish this conclusion than the Proclamation itself, with the explanation that was given afterwards. If with this alone more had been called for, so far as General Jackson's authority goes, the material could be easily and abundantly supplied. His whole administration furnishes it. His numerous vetoes, and the principles upon which he put them, show him to have been a Republican of the old [Conservative] school. His almost every message, from his inaugural to his Farewell Address, abounds with arguments to prove, if it were necessary, that this Government, in his opinion, is a Confederated Republic [i.e., a Confederacy]. In the very second paragraph of his first inaugural, he speaks of the Constitution as 'the Federal Constitution.' Further on in the same, [Andrew Jackson] . . . says:

> 'In such measures as I may be called on to pursue, in regard to the rights of the separate States, I hope to be animated by a proper respect for those Sovereign members of our Union; taking care not to confound the powers they have reserved to themselves, with those they have granted to the [U.S.] Confederacy.'

"The same sentiments pervade all his messages for the eight years of his ever memorable administration [1829-1837], and in his Farewell Address [given March 4, 1837] he is no less distinct and emphatic. Listen to General Jackson's parting words to the people of the United States:

> '. . . It is well known that there have always been those among us, who wish to enlarge the powers of the General Government; and experience would seem to indicate that there is a tendency on the part of this Government to over-step the boundaries marked out for it by the Constitution. Its legitimate

authority is abundantly sufficient for all the purposes for which it was created; and its powers being expressly enumerated, there can be no justification for claiming any thing beyond them. Every attempt to exercise power beyond these limits should be promptly and firmly opposed. For one evil example will lead to other measures still more mischievous; and if the principle of constructive powers, or supposed advantages, or temporary circumstances, shall ever be permitted to justify the assumption of a power not given by the Constitution, the General Government will, before long, absorb all the powers of Legislation, and you will have, in effect, but one Consolidated Government. From the extent of our country, its diversified interests, different pursuits, and different habits, it is too obvious for argument, that a single Consolidated Government would be wholly inadequate to watch over and protect its interests; and every friend of our free institutions should be always prepared to maintain unimpaired, and in full vigor, the rights and Sovereignty of the States, and to confine the action of the General Government strictly to the sphere of its appropriate duties.'

"How wise, patriotic, and even prophetic, were these admonitions of the Hero of New Orleans, and the Sage of the Hermitage! He was, indeed, both hero and sage! In him was presented the rare combination of both military and civic attainments of a very high order. Highest in eminence above all others of this class in the annals of the world stands [George] Washington! Jackson approached as near this great unapproachable model of the general and statesman combined, as perhaps any ever will or can. He left the impress of his ideas deeply fixed upon the times in which he lived. And no more important admonition did he ever give his countrymen than that in the closing part of the extract from his Farewell Address I have just read. This, with all the solemnity of dying declarations, may be received as the strongest evidence of his opinions that *ours is a Confederacy of Sovereign States, and that our liberties, as well as the preservation of the Union, which was so dear to him, depend upon their preservation as such!* His last parting words to his countrymen were, to be prepared to maintain unimpaired, and in full vigor, the Sovereignty of the States! [Emphasis added, L.S.]

"May I not, then, upon his authority, again ask if the conclusion, before stated, that the Constitution is a Compact between Sovereign States, is not indisputably established?"[135]

17

THE NATURE OF THE COMPACT OF OUR UNION

IN THIS CHAPTER OF EXCERPTS from Stephens' *A Constitutional View*, he provides more evidence that the Union formed by the Founding Generation was intended to be a social compact between separate sovereign nation-states.

☛ "[It is obvious then] . . . that *the Constitution of the United States was formed by separate, distinct, and Sovereign States. This is the conclusion to which we are all, however willingly or reluctantly, compelled to come at last, not only by the testimony of witnesses of the highest order, and by the decisions of the judicial tribunal of the highest authority, the Supreme Court of the United States, Chief Justice [John] Marshall at its head, but by the everlasting records themselves, by all the great facts of our history, which can never be obliterated or effaced.* [Emphasis added, L.S.]

"We have seen that the Union existing between these States, anterior to the formation of the new Constitution, was a Compact, or as Judge Marshall expressed it, nothing but 'a league' between Sovereign States.

"We have seen that *in remodelling the Articles of the old Confederation, it was not the object, or design of any of the parties, to change the nature or character of that Union; but only to make it more perfect, by an enlargement of the delegation of powers conferred upon the Government thereby established with such changes in its organic structure, touching the mode and manner of exercising them, as might be thought best to attain the object of their delegation.* [Emphasis added, L.S.]

"We have also seen, both by the instrument itself, and by the understanding of all the parties at the time; that this was what was done by the adoption of the present Constitution, and nothing more. In other words we have seen, and come to the conclusion from a review of all the facts, that the Constitution, as the Articles of Confederation, is a Compact between 'the Sovereign members of the Union' under it, as General Jackson styles the States.

"With these essential points first settled, beyond dispute or question, we are now prepared to go a step further and approach the end of our immediate and important inquiry, touching the nature and character of the Government, so formed and constituted, and to see clearly where, under it, Paramount or ultimate Sovereignty necessarily resides.

"*That the Government of the United States is a Confederated Republic, or Confederacy, of some sort, and not a Consolidated Government, is now no longer a matter of investigation or question. Whatever other characteristics, peculiar or anomalous, it possesses, it is beyond doubt, cavil, or dispute, Federal [Confederate] in its nature and character.* [Emphasis added, L.S.]

"That it presents, in its structure, several new features, wholly unknown in all former Confederacies of which the world's history furnishes examples, all admit. This was well understood at the time of its formation, as well as ever since. No exactly similar model is to be found amongst all the nations of the earth, or in the annals of mankind, in the past or present. But *we have seen the model which was in the minds of its authors at the time it was framed, and which formed the basis of their conceptions and designs. That was the model of a Confederated Republic given by Montesquieu. This model was not only in the minds of the Convention which framed the Constitution, but in the minds of all the Conventions of the States which adopted it. This has been shown from the proceedings of those bodies. That model exhibited several small Republics so united into a larger one, for foreign and inter State purposes, as to present themselves in joint Combination to the world, as one Nation, while as between themselves each one retained unimpaired its own inherent, innate Sovereignty and Nationality. This was the ideal before all the States of this Union, at the time of the formation of the Constitution. According to this model, which was as far as the wisdom of men then had gone in forming Governments for the preservation of free institutions, and to prevent the principle of universal Monarchical Rule, the action of the larger and conventional State or Nation so, formed for external or foreign purposes, was confined in its internal operations exclusively to the integral members of the Union or Confederation. No power was conferred upon this joint agent of all to interfere, in any way or under any circumstances, with the individual citizens of the separate Republics.* [Emphasis added, L.S.]

"But a new idea had for sometime been in embryo. It was then struggling into birth. [Thomas] Jefferson's brain had first felt the impulse of its quickening life. The framers of the Constitution saw its star, as the wise men of the East saw the star of Bethlehem. They did homage to it, even in the manger, where it then lay in its swaddlings, as *the political Messiah just born for the regeneration of the down trodden Peoples of the Earth*. That idea was to apply a new principle to the model before them, to improve upon it by a division of its Powers, and by extending its operations, without changing the basis upon which it was formed. It was simply for these separate Republics to empower their joint agent, the artificial or conventional Nation of their own creation, to act, in the discharge of its limited functions, directly upon their citizens respectively, and to organize these functions into separate departments, Executive, Judicial and Legislative, as their own separate systems were organized. This, it is true, was a new and a grand development in the progress of the science of Government, which, of all sciences, unfortunately for mankind, is the slowest in progress. [Emphasis added, L.S.]

"But this was the idea—this the design, and this was just what was done.

"The great object was to obviate the difficulties and the evils, so often arising in all former Federal Republics, of resorting to force against separate members, when derelict in the discharge of their obligations under the terms and covenants of their Union. Difficulties of this sort had already been felt under their own Confederation, which they were convened to remedy. Some States had failed to meet the requisitions upon them for their quota of taxes to pay the common expenses, and to sustain the common public credit. By the laws of Nations, the Confederates of States thus derelict, had the clear right to compel a fulfilment of their solemn obligations, though the very act of doing it would necessarily have put an end to the Confederation. The question of coercion in the collection of unpaid requisitions, on the part of some of the States, had been raised during the old Confederation. Jefferson saw that this would be necessary if that system could not be amended. All, however, saw that a resort to force, in such cases, would result in war which might become general, and the loss of the liberties of all might, perhaps, ensue. This newly born idea presented an easy solution of the whole vexed question. It was adopted, by the Parties agreeing in the Compact itself, that in the collection of the taxes for the common defence and general welfare, and in some other cases, this common agent of all the members of the Confederacy, should act directly upon the individual citizens of each, within the sphere of its specific and limited powers, and with a complete machinery of functions, for this purpose, similar to their own. This is the whole of it.

"It is this exceedingly simple, but entirely new feature, in Confederated Republics, which has so puzzled and bewildered so many in this as in other countries, as to the nature and character of the United States Government. It is this feature, in the American plan, which struck the learned and philosophic [French historian Alexis] de Tocqueville, who, of all foreigners, seems most deeply to have studied our institutions, and to have become most thoroughly imbued with their spirit and principles.

"On this point [Tocqueville] . . . says:

> 'This Constitution, which may at first be confounded with the Federal Constitutions which have preceded it, rests, in truth, upon a wholly novel theory, which may be considered as a great discovery in modern political science. In all the Confederations which preceded the American Constitution of 1789, the allied States, for a common object, agreed to obey the injunctions of a Federal Government; but they reserved to themselves the right of ordaining and enforcing the execution of the laws of the Union. The American States, which combined, in 1789, agreed, that the Federal Government should not only dictate, but should execute its own enactments. In both cases, the right is the same, but the exercise of the right is different; and this difference produced the most momentous consequences.'

"In all this he is perfectly right. The principle thus introduced was a new one. It was unknown to the old world. Unknown to Plato, Aristotle, Cicero, [Hugo] Grotius, [Samuel von] Pufendorf, or Montesquieu. It was, indeed, a grand discovery. The honor, the glory of this discovery, was reserved for this Continent, and for those who had first proclaimed the great truth that all 'Governments derive their just powers from the consent of the governed.' From this simple discovery, did, indeed, follow the most momentous consequences. From it sprang that unparalleled career of prosperity and greatness which marked our history under its beneficent operations for nearly three quarters of a century!

"These momentous consequences in rapid growth and development, and the unsurpassed happiness and prosperity, resulted from this simple, but wonderful improvement made by the Fathers, in 1787, upon Montesquieu's model of a Confederated Republic. This new feature, however, in the workmanship of their master-hands has been what has caused so much confusion in the minds of many as to the nature and character of the Government. They do not seem to understand how this new feature is consistent with a strictly Federal [Confederate] System. The difficulty with them seems to arise entirely from the fact, that none such ever existed before. They have no specific name for this new development or discovery in the science of Government. Hence the great variety of sentiments in the several State Conventions, some calling it a consolidated Government, and some of its friends styling it a mixed Government—partly Federal [Confederate] and partly National—Federal [Confederate] in its formation and National in its operation. Of this class was Mr. [James] Madison. And hence, also, some in later times have styled it a Compositive Government.

"A little analysis and generalization may enable us to bring order out of this confusion. In one sense it is a National Government. In this, however, there is nothing new or peculiar in the Government established by the New Constitution. In the same sense in which it is National, and none other, was the old Confederation National. The United States, under that, we have seen was called and properly called a Nation, for certain purposes. For the same purposes, and in the same sense, and none other, may they now properly be called a Nation. Their present Government is National in the same sense in which the Governments of all Confederated Republics are National, and none other. *The very object in forming all Confederated Republics is to create a new and an entirely artificial or conventional State or Nation, which springs from their joint Sovereignties, and which has no existence apart from them, and which is but the Corporate Agent of all those Sovereignties creating it, and through which alone they are to be known to Foreign Powers, during the continuance of the Confederation. This Conventional Nation is but a Political Corporation. It has no original or inherent powers whatever. All its powers are derived—all are specific—all are limited—all are delegated—all may be resumed—all may be forfeited by misuser, as well as non-user. It is created by the separate Republics forming it. They are the Creators. It is but their Creature—subject to their will and control. They barely delegate the exercise of certain Sovereign powers to their common agent, retaining to themselves, separately, all that absolute, ultimate Sovereignty, by which this common agent, with all its delegated powers, is created. This is the basis, and these are the principles, upon which all Confederated Republics are constructed. The new Conventional State or Nation thus formed is brought into being by the will of the several States or Nations forming it, and by the same will it may cease to exist, as to any or all of them, while the separate Sovereignties of its Creators may survive, and live on forever.* [Emphasis added, L.S.]

"A Government so constructed, being itself founded on Compact between distinct Sovereign States, is necessarily Federal [Confederate] in its nature, while it at the same time gives one national character and position amongst the other Powers of the world, to all the Parties constituting it! In this sense, all Confederated Governments are both Federal and National. The Government of the United States is no exception to the rule. In this sense, *Washington, Jefferson, and Jackson, spoke of the United States under the Constitution as a Nation*, as well as a *Confederated Republic. In this sense, it is properly styled by all a Nation*. This was the idea symbolized in the motto, 'E pluribus unum.' *One from many.* That is, one State or Nation—one Federal [Confederate] Republic—from many Republics, States, or Nations. This is what is meant by the Nation when properly applied to the United States. It is not the whole people, in the aggregate constituting one body united on the principles of a social Compact, but that conventional State which springs from and is dependent upon the several State Sovereignties creating it, as in all other cases of Confederated Republics. The bare fact that it operates on the individual citizens of the several States, in specified cases, and has in its organization the requisite functions for this purpose, does not change, in the least, the nature of the Government, if this arrangement is agreed upon in the Compact between the Sovereign Parties to it. That depends entirely upon the great fact which we were so long in establishing, that the Government itself, with all its powers as well as machinery, was founded upon Compact between separate and distinct Sovereign States. If this be so, as has been conclusively established, then the Government, so constructed, must of necessity be Federal [Confederate], and purely Federal [Confederate], in its character. This character is not changed by the adoption of any machinery, for its practical workings, which may be thus agreed upon. For it is perfectly competent for independent and Sovereign Nations, by treaty or compact, to make any agreement they please touching the enforcement of such treaties, or the terms of such compacts, over the irrespective citizens or subjects, and by such agencies as they may please jointly to agree upon, without the least impairment whatever of their respective Sovereignties. [Emphasis added, L.S.]

"The great question, therefore, in this investigation was, is the Constitution a Compact between Sovereignties? If so, the Government established by it is purely, entirely, and thoroughly Federal in its nature, and no more National in any sense than all former Federal Republics. All those features in its operations directly upon individuals, instead of upon States, which give rise to ideas of Nationality, or of its being of a mixed nature, spring themselves from the Federal Compact. *Ours, therefore, is a pure Confederated Republic, upon the model of Montesquieu, with the new principle referred to incorporated into the system, without changing, in the least, the basis of its organization—at least, so thought the Fathers by whom it was established.* It is true we have as yet no apt distinctive word in political nomenclature, by which to characterize this specific distinctive improvement in the purely Federal system. This only shows the barrenness of language. Actualities often precede nomenclature. And, hence, De Tocqueville, perceiving this in our system, said of it, that 'the new word, which ought to express this novel thing, does not yet exist.' 'The human understanding,' says he, 'more easily invents new things than new words, and we are hence constrained to employ many improper and inadequate expressions.' No truer remark was ever made about the Government of the United States. *All the difficulty or confusion on the subject, however, relates only to the name. It is one of nomenclature, and not substance. That stands out perfectly distinct in all its features, however unlanguaged it, with these features, may yet be. This want of a suitable name applies, also, only to its specific character, that name which will perfectly characterize its specific difference from other Confederacies, ancient or modern.*

There is no difficulty as to the proper generic term applicable to it. That is unquestionably Federal [Confederate]. Its genus, with all the incidents of the class, is a Federal or Confederated Republic. That is fixed by the fact that it is founded upon Compact—Confederation between distinct Sovereign Powers. [Emphasis added, L.S.]

"What makes any Government Federal [Confederate], but the fact that it springs, with all its powers and functions, of whatever character, from covenants and agreements between the Sovereign contracting parties creating it? And is it not as competent for a Sovereign State to agree, that the Federal agent or Government shall act upon her citizens, in specified cases, as it is for her to agree, that the same agent or Government may act upon herself? may pass edicts of equal force and obligation upon her, which she is equally bound by the Compact to execute by her own machinery of laws? Where is the difference? What makes the Union between any States Federal [Confederate] is not the manner of its action, but the *Fœdus*, the Covenant, the Convention, the Compact upon which it is founded!

"So much for the nature of the Government of the United States, and the terms by which it may be characterized.

"Where, under the system so constituted, does Sovereignty reside? This is now the great and last question. It must reside somewhere. It must reside, as all admit, with the people somewhere. Does it reside with the whole people in mass of all the States together, or with the people of the several States separately? That is the only question. The whole subject is narrowed down to this: *Where, in this country, resides that Paramount authority that can rightfully make and unmake Constitutions? In all Confederated Republics, according to Montesquieu, Vattel, and Burlamaqui, it remains with the Sovereign States so Confederated.* Is our Confederated Republic an exception to this rule? If so, how does it appear? Is there any thing in its history, anterior to the present Compact of Union, that shows it to be an exception? Certainly not; for the Sovereignty of each State was expressly retained in the first Articles of Union. Is there then any thing in the present Compact itself that shows that it was surrendered by them in that? If so, where is the clause bearing that import? None can be found! Again: if it was thereby surrendered, to whom was it surrendered? to whom did it pass? Did it pass to all the people of the United States? Of course not; for not one particle of power of any sort, much less Sovereignty, is delegated in the Constitution to the people of the United States. All powers therein delegated are to the States in their Sovereign character, under the designation of United States. Is it then surrendered to the United States jointly? Certainly not, for one of the main objects in forming the Compact, as before stated, and as clearly appears from the instrument itself, was, to preserve and perpetuate separate State existence. The guarantee to this effect, from the very words used, implies their Sovereignty. *There can be no such thing as a perfect State without Sovereignty.* It certainly is not parted with by any express terms in that instrument. If it be surrendered thereby it must be by implication only. But how can it be implied from any words or phrases in that instrument? If carried by implication, it must be on the strange assumption that it is an incident only of some one or all of those specific and specially enumerated powers expressly delegated. This cannot be, as that would be making the incident greater than the object, the shadow more solid than the substance. For *Sovereignty is the highest and greatest of all political powers. It is itself the source as well as embodiment of all political powers, both great and small. All proceed and emanate from it. All the great powers specifically and expressly delegated in the Constitution, such as the power to declare war and make peace; to raise and support armies, to tax and lay excise duties, etc., are themselves but the incidents of Sovereignty.* If this great embodiment of all powers was parted with, why were any minor specifications made? Why any enumeration? Was not such specification or enumeration both useless and absurd? [Emphasis added, L.S.]

"All the implications are the other way. The bare fact that all the powers parted with by the States were delegated only, as all admit, necessarily implies that the greater power delegating still continued to exist.

"If, then, this ultimate absolute Sovereignty did reside with the several States separately, as without question it did, up to the formation of the Constitution, and if, in the Constitution, Sovereignty is not parted with by the States in express terms, if, as Mr. Webster said, in 1839, there is not a word about Sovereignty in it, and if, further, this greatest of all political powers cannot justly be claimed as an incident to lesser ones, and thereby carried by implication, then, of course, was it not, most clearly, still retained and reserved to the people of the several States in that mass of residuary rights, in the language of Mr. Jefferson, which was expressly reserved in the Constitution itself?

"It is true it [state sovereignty] was not so expressly reserved in the Constitution at first, because it was deemed, as the debates in the Federal Convention, as well as the State Conventions, clearly show, wholly unnecessary; so general was the understanding that it could not go, by inference or implication, from any thing in the Constitution; or in other words, that it could not be surrendered without express terms to that effect. The general understanding was the universally acknowledged principle in public law, that nothing is held good against Sovereignty by implication. But to quiet the apprehensions of Patrick Henry, Samuel Adams, and the Conventions of a majority of the States, this reservation of Sovereignty was soon after put in the Constitution amongst other amendments, in plain and unequivocal language.

So cautious and guarded were the men of that day that the Government had hardly commenced operations before all inferences that had been drawn against the reserved Sovereignty of the States, from the silence of the Constitution, in this particular and some others, were fully rebutted by several amendments, proposed by the States, in Congress assembled, at their first session. These amendments were preceded by a preamble, which shows that they were both declaratory and restrictive in their object. Here is what was done:—

> The Conventions of a number of the States; having, at the time of their adopting the Constitution, expressed a desire, in order to prevent misconstruction or abuse of its powers, that further declaratory and restrictive clauses should be added: And as extending the ground of public confidence in the Government, will best insure the beneficent ends of its institution;
>
> Resolved, by the Senate and Home of Representatives of the United States of America, in Congress assembled, two thirds of both Houses concurring, That the following Articles be proposed to the Legislatures of the several States, as amendments to the Constitution of the United States, all, or any of which Articles, when ratified by three fourths of the said Legislatures, to be valid to all intents and purposes, as part of the said Constitution.

"The language of one of the amendments then proposed, on the subject we are now upon, is as follows:

> The powers not delegated to the United States by the Constitution, nor prohibited by it to the States, are reserved to the States, respectively, or to the people.

"This amendment [the Tenth], which was promptly agreed to by the States unanimously, declares that all powers not delegated were reserved to the States respectively; this, of course, includes, in the reservation, Sovereignty, which is the source of all powers, those delegated as well as those reserved. This reservation Mr. Samuel Adams said, we have seen in the Massachusetts Convention, was consonant with the like reservation in the first Articles of Confederation. And such was the universal understanding at the time. Most of the other amendments, then proposed, were likewise agreed to by the States, but not unanimously.

"Can any proposition within the domain of reason be clearer, from all these facts, than that the Sovereignty of the States, that great Paramount authority which can rightfully make and unmake Constitutions, resides still with the States? Does not this declaratory amendment, added to the original covenant in the Constitution, which provides for its own amendment, show this beyond all doubt or question? Why were further amendments to it to be submitted to the States for their ratification before they could be binding, but upon the indisputable principle or postulate that Sovereignty, which alone has control of all such matters, still resides with the States severally? There is . . . no answer [from the Liberals] to this.

"The Government of the United States, however new some of its features are in the machinery of its operation, is no exception to the general rule, applicable to all Federal [Confederate] Republics, as to *where the ultimate absolute Sovereign or Paramount authority resides. According to that rule, in all of them, it is retained by the Parties to the Compact. Such was the case in the model of Montesquieu. Such is the case in all Confederacies of this character, according to Vattel, as we have seen. Such is, necessarily, the case in our system, built upon these models. All unions of separate States, under Compacts of this sort, are founded upon the same essential basis. Sovereignty, with us, therefore, upon these fixed and indisputable principles, now resides, as I said before, just where it did in 1776—just where it did in 1778—and just where it did in 1787: that is, with the people of the several States of the Federal Union. This Sovereignty, so residing with them, is the Paramount authority to which allegiance is due.* Allegiance, a word brought from the Old World, of Latin origin, from *ligo*, to bind, means the obligation which every one owes to that Power in the State, to which he is indebted for the protection of his rights of person and property. Allegiance and Sovereignty, as we have seen, are reciprocal. 'To whatever Power a citizen owes allegiance, that Power is his Sovereign.' *To what Power are the citizens of the several States indebted for protection of person and property, in all the relations of life, for the regulation of which Governments are instituted? Certainly not to the Federal Government. That Government, in its operations, has no right to interfere, in any way whatever, with the citizens of the several States*, but in a few exceptional cases; and then, not for protection, but in the enforcement of laws, which the State would have been bound, by her plighted faith, to execute herself, had not this new feature been introduced into the Federal system. The Government of the United States, in its internal polity, is known to the citizens of the several States only by its requisitions upon individuals, instead of States, except in a very few specified cases. In its National character, it gives ample protection abroad. This was one of its main objects. In its postal arrangements, it furnishes many conveniences, for which it is duly paid. In these particulars, there is no difference between the Constitution and the first Articles of Confederation. But it was no part of the objects of either to afford protection to the citizens of the States, respectively, in all those relations of life which mark the internal polity of different States and Nations. These, now, as before, all depend upon the Sovereign will of the States. This Sovereign will fixes the status of the various elements of Society, as well as their rights. In the States, severally, remains the great right of Eminent Domain, which reserves to them complete jurisdiction and control over the rights of person and property of their entire population. With them remains, untrammelled, the power to establish codes of laws—civil, military, and criminal. They may punish for what crimes they please, and as they please, and the Government of the United States cannot interfere. To their own Legislatures, their own Judiciaries, their own Executives, their own laws, established by their own Paramount authority, do all the citizens of all the States look for whatever protection and security they receive, possess, or enjoy, in all the civil relations of life. In all such matters as require that protection to which allegiance is due, the Government of the United States is unknown to them. [Emphasis added, L.S.]

"It is true that the States did covenant, in the Constitution, that no State should 'pass any law, making any thing but gold and silver coin a legal tender in the payment of debts; pass any bill of attainder, or *ex post facto* law, or law impairing the obligation of contracts;' but this, in no wise, changes the principle. Those provisions were put in by each State, to protect the rights of her citizens against the unjust legislation of other States, and not against her own legislation. By the Constitution, the citizens of each State have all the privileges and immunities of all the citizens of the several States, in their intercourse with each other. Hence, the propriety and wisdom of these provisions. It is, in itself, only a negative protection, and such as each State provided, in the Compact, for the protection of her own citizens, in other States, against the acts of the other States, and not against their own. It was inserted from no such view as that the citizens of the several States were to look to the Federal Government for that protection, in any sense, which is the foundation of all allegiance. The guarantee of rights, in the amendments to the Constitution, such as the right to bear arms, freedom from arrest, etc., apply, exclusively, to the Federal [Confederate] Government. They were but bulwarks, thrown around the citadel of State Rights, to protect the citizens of the respective States from the exercise of unjust powers over them by the General Government. They were not inserted with any view of protecting the citizens of the respective States from the action of their own State Governments.

"On the several State authorities, therefore, are all the citizens, of all the States, under our system, entirely dependent for the protection of all those civil rights and franchises, for which, mainly, human societies are organized, and for which, mainly, Governments are instituted by men. To this several State authority, when properly expressed, is the allegiance proper of every citizen due. This is his Sovereign.

"These things being so, I think I have made it very clearly appear, why I acted as I did, in going with my State [when she seceded from the Union in

1861], and obeying her high behest, when she resumed the Sovereign Powers she had delegated to the United States, by entering into a Compact of Union with them in 1788, and asserted her right to be a free and independent State, which she was acknowledged to be by George the Third of England, in the treaty of peace, in 1783.

"The rightfulness of this act, on the part of the State, is not now the question. . . . But the question now is, was it not the duty of all her citizens to go with her in her solemn Resolve? Was not every one bound to do so, or become guilty of incivism, the highest of all political offences against the society of which one is a member? Would not every one, refusing to obey the mandate of the State, in such case have subjected himself to her laws against treason to her Sovereignty? In that case, could the United States, either *de jure* ['by right'] or *de facto* ['in fact'] have saved him or afforded him any protection whatever against the prescribed penalty? By the very terms of the Compact, if that was still in force, if he had escaped, and gone into another State, he would, necessarily, upon demand, have been delivered up to the State for trial and punishment! But in point of fact, the United States had not an officer, civil or military, within the State. All had retired, either voluntarily or by compulsion. Not an emblem even of their authority was to be found within her borders. To whose authority then could any citizen look for any sort of protection, but the authority of the State? Was not obedience both proper and due to that authority which alone could afford proper protection, both *de jure* and *de facto*?

"Now as to the rightfulness of the State's thus resuming her Sovereign powers! In doing it she *seceded* from that Union, to which, in the language of Mr. [Thomas] Jefferson, as well as General Washington, she had *acceded* as a Sovereign State. She repealed her ordinance by which she ratified and agreed to the Constitution and became a party to the Compact under it. She declared herself no longer bound by that Compact, and dissolved her alliance with the other parties to it. The Constitution of the United States, and the laws passed in pursuance of it, were no longer the supreme law of the people of Georgia, any more than the treaty with France was the supreme law of both countries, after its abrogation, in 1798, by the same rightful authority which had made it in the beginning. [Emphasis added, L.S.]

"In answer to [the Liberals'] . . . question, whether she could do this without a breach of her solemn obligations, under the Compact, I give this full and direct answer: she had a perfect right so to do, subject to no authority, but the great moral law which governs the intercourse between Independent Sovereign Powers, Peoples, or Nations. Her action was subject to the authority of that law and none other. *It is the inherent right of Nations, subject to this law alone, to disregard the obligations of Compacts of all sorts, by declaring themselves no* longer bound in any way by them. This, by universal consent, may be rightfully done, when there has been a breach of the Compact by the other party or parties. It was on this principle, that the United States abrogated their treaty with France, in 1798. The justifiableness of the act depends, in every instance, upon the circumstances of the case. The general rule is, if all the other States—the Parties to the Confederation—faithfully comply with their obligations, under the Compact of Union, no State would be morally justified in withdrawing from a Union so formed, unless it were necessary for her own preservation. Self-preservation is the first law of nature, with States or Nations, as it is with individuals. [Emphasis added, L.S.]

"But in this case the breach of plighted faith was not on the part of Georgia, or those States which withdrew or attempted to withdraw from the Union. Thirteen of their Confederates had openly and avowedly disregarded their obligations under that clause of the Constitution which covenanted for the rendition of fugitives from service, to say nothing of the acts of several of them, in a like open and palpable breach of faith, in the matter of the rendition of fugitives from justice. These are facts about which there can be no dispute. Then, by universal law, as recognized by all Nations, savage as well as civilized, the Compact, thus broken by some of the Parties, was no longer binding upon the others. The breach was not made by the seceding States. Under the circumstances, and the facts of this case, therefore, the legal as well as moral right, on the part of Georgia, according to the laws of Nations and nature, to declare herself no longer bound by the Compact, and to withdraw from the Union under it, was perfect and complete. These principles are too incontestably established to be questioned, much less denied, in the forum of reason and justice. [Emphasis added, L.S.]

"Hence the broad and unqualified admission of Mr. [Daniel] Webster, that, if the Constitution was a Compact between Sovereign States, the right to secede followed as a matter of course. This right comes not from any thing in the Constitution, but from the great law of Nations, governing all Compacts between Sovereigns. [Emphasis added, L.S.] His language, you recollect, was:

> 'Where Sovereign communities are parties, there is no essential difference between a Compact, a Confederation, and a League. They all equally rest on the plighted faith of the Sovereign party. A League, or Confederacy, is but a subsisting or continuing treaty. . . . If, in the opinion of either party it be violated, such party may say that he will no longer fulfil its obligations on his part, but will consider the whole League or Compact at an end, although it might be one of its stipulations that it should be perpetual.'

"The right of a State to secede from the Union upon this principle of the laws of Nations was fully admitted by Mr. Webster, if it be true that the Constitution is a Compact between States; and that too when, even in the opinion of any Party to it, the Compact had been broken on the other side. But in this case there is no question as to the fact of the breach on the other side.

"Judge [Joseph] Story, who strove so hard to establish the position that the Government of the United States is a National Government, proper and not Federal [Confederate], is equally explicit in his admission as to the right of Secession, if it be true that the Constitution is a Compact between States. On this point there is no disagreement between him and Mr. Webster. Judge Story first states the position of Judge [St. George] Tucker, in his Commentaries on the Constitution, as follows:—

> *'It is a Federal Compact. Several Sovereign and independent States may unite themselves together by a perpetual Confederation, without each ceasing to be a perfect State. They will, together, form a Federal Republic. The deliberations in common will offer no violence to each member, though they may in certain respects put some constraint on the exercise of it in virtue of voluntary engagements. The extent, modifications, and objects of the Federal authority are mere matters of discretion. So long as the separate organization of the members remains, and, from the nature of the Compact, must continue to exist, both for local and domestic, and for Federal purposes, the Union is, in fact as well as in theory, an association of States, or a Confederacy.'* [Emphasis added, L.S.]

"This is Story's statement of Tucker's position. It is substantially correct. He afterwards comments on it, as follows:—

> *'The obvious deductions, which may be, and indeed have been drawn, from considering the Constitution as a Compact between the States, are, that it operates as a mere treaty, or convention between them, and has an obligatory force upon each State no longer than it suits its pleasure, or its consent continues; that each State has a right to judge for itself in relation to the nature, extent, and obligations of the instrument, without being at all bound by the interpretation of the Federal Government, or by that of any other State; and that each retains the power to withdraw from the Confederacy, and to dissolve the connection, when such shall be its choice; and may suspend the operations of the Federal Government, and nullify its acts within its own territorial limits, whenever, in its own opinion, the exigency of the case may require. These conclusions may not always be avowed; but they flow naturally from the doctrines which we have under consideration. They go to the extent of reducing the Government to a mere Confederacy during pleasure; and of thus presenting the extraordinary spectacle of a nation existing only at the will of each of its constituent parts.'* [Emphasis added, L.S.]

"In this, Judge Story fully admits the right of a State to withdraw or secede from the Union, if the Constitution be a Compact between the States as States, even without an open breach of the Compact by the Confederates. He says, it is an obvious deduction from the fact of its being a Government founded on

Compact; too clear and logical to give room for doubt or question. He was too thoroughly versed in the laws of nations to raise a point even on this conclusion, if the premises as to the Constitution being a Compact between States be correct. Hence his labored argument in assault upon the premises. Hence his utmost efforts were put forth, with what success we have seen, to show that the States were never Sovereign, and that the Constitution is not a Compact between States, but that it is a social Compact between all the people of the United States in mass as one nation. *However extraordinary, in the opinion of Judge Story, would be the spectacle of a nation existing only at the will of each of its constituent parts, yet just such a nation ours is, according to his own frank admission, if it be true that the Constitution is founded upon Compact between Sovereign States, (and this, by common consent between us, is a question now no longer open for consideration.)* [Emphasis added, L.S.]

"Our 'Nation,' such as it is, is indeed a most extraordinary and wonderful spectacle! This we have abundantly seen in the course of our present investigation; and if Judge Story had more profoundly studied its nature and character, he might have been much more profoundly struck with many even more extraordinary features in it than that one to which he here specially refers.

"That one has nothing in it more extraordinary than every other Federal [Confederate] Republic that ever existed. Montesquieu saw in such systems nothing more extraordinary than that under them the world had been saved from universal monarchical rule.

"*This right of a State to consider herself no longer bound by a Compact which, in her judgment, has been broken by her Confederates, and to secede from a Union, formed as ours was, has nothing about it, either new or novel. It is incident to all Federal Republics. It is not derived from the Compact itself. It does not spring from it at all. It is derived from the same source that the right is derived to abrogate a treaty by either or any of the parties to it. That is seldom set forth in the treaty itself, and yet it exists, whether it be set forth or not. So, in any Federal Compact whatever, the parties may or may not expressly provide for breaches of it. But where no such provision is made, the right exists by the same laws of Nations which govern in all matters of treaties or conventions between Sovereigns. The admission of the right of Secession, under this law, on the part of the several States of our Union, by Mr. Webster and Judge Story, if it be true that the Constitution is a Compact between the States, might be considered ample authority, in answer to [the Liberals'] . . . question on that point; since the conclusion, to which we arrived, that it is such a Compact.* [Emphasis added, L.S.]

"But I do not mean to let it rest barely on this.

"I maintain that such was the general understanding of the parties to the Constitution at the time it was adopted, as well as that such is its true exposition.

"'*Contemporanea Expositio est optima et fortissimo, in Lege.*' (Latin: 'The best and surest mode of expounding an instrument is by referring to the time when, and the circumstances under which, it was made.']

"First, then, I maintain that it is a necessary incident of that Sovereignty which was believed to be reserved to the States severally, in the original Constitution, but which reservation, to quiet the apprehensions of the more cautious, was immediately after inserted in express terms, by way of amendment [Ninth and Tenth]. It was expressly reserved in the ratifications of Virginia, New York, and Rhode Island. These ratifications were received by the other States, which fixes the construction of all at the time. Moreover, the Government was formed, or to be formed, according to the very terms of the Constitution, by the Secession of nine States at least from their former Union, which was declared to be perpetual, and to which their faith was plighted in the most solemn manner, that no changes in the Articles of their Union should ever be made without the unanimous consent of its thirteen members. What is there in the history of the times or in the acts of the parties, which goes to show that the same general opinion, as to the Sovereign right to secede, did not continue to exist in reference to the present Constitution, which required no pledge as to its perpetuity? [Emphasis added, L.S.]

"Secondly. It is very clear that Mr. [Thomas] Jefferson believed in this right. This, the Kentucky Resolutions fully establish. The large majority by which he was elected, after the fierce contest of 1800, shows that the same opinion must have been then very generally entertained. Even Mr. [Alexander] Hamilton must have believed that this right was incident to the system; for in his urgent appeals to Mr. Jefferson, as early as 1790, for his influence with members of Congress, in aid of the bill for the assumption of the State debts, he presented the strong reason, that if that measure should not pass, there was great danger of a Secession of the members from the creditor States, which would end in 'a separation of the States.' He was then connected with the Government. He was Secretary of the Treasury. Would he have urged such an argument if he had not believed that those States had a right to withdraw? Moreover, his letter to Mr. Gouverneur Morris, of the 27th of February, 1802, shows very clearly, taken in connection with his whole career, that he did not believe that the Government of the United States had any inherent Sovereign power whatever. He looked upon the system as radically defective in this particular. 'Perhaps,' says he in this letter, 'no man in the United States has sacrificed or done more for the present Constitution than myself; and contrary to all my anticipations of its fate, as you know from the very beginning. I am still laboring to prop the frail and worthless fabric. Yet I have the murmurs of its friends no less than the curses of its foes, for my reward.' The worthlessness of the fabric, in his opinion, consisted, as we know, in the want of the energy of a consolidation of the Sovereignties of the several States in one single grand Republic, which he had at first insisted upon in the Federal Convention of 1787. When that failed, he did give the Federal plan agreed upon a zealous and patriotic support. He contributed greatly to its adoption by the States. But he never had confidence in its durability. He thought it would go to pieces by State disintegration. His belief and conviction of the want of power on the part of the General Government, as formed to prevent such disintegration, is shown from all that he said in the New York State Convention, when the Constitution was before that body, and what he wrote on the same subject in the *Federalist* afterwards. [Emphasis added, L.S.]

"But, thirdly. One of the earliest, if not the earliest, commentators on the Constitution, not as a politician, but as a jurist and publicist, was Judge [St. George] Tucker, Professor of Law in the University of William and Mary, in Virginia. In his edition of [Sir William] Blackstone's Commentaries, there is an appendix by him to the first volume, of considerable length, devoted to the consideration of Governments generally, and particularly the Constitution of the United States. He wrote in 1803. He held, as we have seen, that the Constitution was a Federal Compact between States. And while no more devoted friend to the Union under the Constitution perhaps ever lived, he yet was forced, from this indisputable fact, to what Story said was an obvious deduction—that is, that *the right of Secession, on the part of any one or more of the States, was a necessary incident from the very nature of the system.* [Emphasis added, L.S.] His language is this:

> '*The Constitution of the United States, then, being that instrument by which the Federal Government hath been created, its powers defined and limited, and the duties and functions of its several departments prescribed, the Government, thus established, may be pronounced to be a Confederate Republic, composed of several Independent and Sovereign Democratic States, united for their common defence and security against foreign Nations, and for the purposes of harmony and mutual intercourse between each other; each State retaining an entire liberty of exercising, as it thinks proper, all those parts of its Sovereignty which are not mentioned in the Constitution, or Act of Union, as parts that ought to be exercised in common.* [Emphasis added, L.S.]
>
> '*In becoming a member of the Federal Alliance, established between the American States by the Articles of Confederation, she expressly retained her Sovereignty and Independence. The constraints, put upon the exercise of that Sovereignty by those Articles, did not destroy its existence.* . . . [Emphasis added, L.S.]
>
> '*The Federal Government, then, appears to be the organ through which the united Republics communicate with foreign Nations, and with each other. Their submission to its operation is voluntary; its councils, its engagements, its authority, are theirs, modified and united. Its Sovereignty is an emanation from theirs, not a flame, in which they have been consumed, nor a vortex, in which they are swallowed up. Each is still a perfect State, still Sovereign, still independent, and still capable, should the occasion require, to resume the exercise of its functions, as such, in the most unlimited extent.* . . . [Emphasis added, L.S.]

'But, until the time shall arrive, when the occasion requires a resumption of the rights of Sovereignty by the several States (and far be that period removed, when it shall happen), the exercise of the rights of Sovereignty by the States, individually, is wholly suspended or discontinued in the cases before mentioned; nor can that suspension ever be removed, so long as the present Constitution remains unchanged, but by the dissolution of the bonds of union; an event which no good citizen can wish, and which no good or wise administration will ever hazard.' [Emphasis added, L.S.]

"A clearer or truer exposition of this feature of the Constitution of the United States was never made in fewer words. This exposition went to the country with the sanction of his high authority, and was not gainsayed or controverted by any writer of distinction, that I am aware of, until Chancellor [James] Kent's Commentaries appeared in 1826, and Story's, in 1833. I do not mean to say that no one of that class of politicians, barely, who figured during the Administration of the elder Adams [John], denied this right; but that no jurist or publicist of eminence denied it up to that time. Chancellor Kent goes into no argument. He barely deals, as Mr. [John L.] Motley does, in assertion. This, we have seen, will not do. But, meanwhile, Mr. [William] Rawle, an eminent jurist of Pennsylvania, wrote an elaborate work upon the Constitution [*A View of the Constitution of the United States of America*], which was published in 1825. He was United States District Attorney under [George] Washington, and had been offered, by him, the Attorney-Generalship of the United States. He was, also, a firm supporter of the Administration of the elder Adams. This shows the character of the man, and the authority with which his opinions should be received. His investigations brought him to the same conclusion to which Judge Tucker had come. That conclusion is expressed by him in the following language:—

[Stephens quoting Rawle:] 'Having thus endeavored to delineate the general features of this peculiar and invaluable form of Government, we shall conclude with adverting to the principles of its cohesion, and to the provisions it contains for its own duration and extension.

'The subject cannot, perhaps, be better introduced than by presenting, in its own words, an emphatical clause in the Constitution:—

The United States shall guarantee, to every State in the Union, a Republican [Confederate] form of Government; shall protect each of them against invasion; and, on application of the Legislature, or of the Executive, when the Legislature cannot be convened, against domestic violence.

'The Union is an association of the people of Republics; its preservation is calculated to depend on the preservation of those Republics. The principle of representation, although, certainly, the wisest and best, is not essential to the being of a Republic; but, to continue a member of the Union, it must be preserved; and, therefore, the guarantee must be so construed. It depends on the State itself, to retain or abolish the principle of representation; because it depends on itself, whether it will continue a member of the Union. To deny this right, would be inconsistent with the principles on which all our political systems are founded; which is, that the people have, in all cases, a right to determine how they will be governed.

'*This right must be considered as an ingredient in the original composition of the General Government, which, though not expressed, was mutually understood*; and the doctrine, heretofore presented to the reader, in regard to the indefeasible nature of personal allegiance, is so far qualified, in respect to allegiance to the United States. It was observed that it was competent for a State to make a Compact with its citizens, that the reciprocal obligations of protection and allegiance might cease on certain events; and it was further observed that allegiance would necessarily cease on the dissolution of the society to which it was due. . . . [Emphasis added, L.S.]

'The Secession of a State from the Union depends on the will of the people of such State. The people, alone, as we have already seen, hold the power to alter their Constitution. The Constitution of the United States is, to a certain extent, incorporated into the Constitutions of the several States, by the act of the people. The State Legislatures have only to perform certain organical operations in respect to it. To withdraw from the Union, comes not within the general scope of their delegated authority. There must be an express provision to that effect inserted in the State Constitutions. This is not, at present, the case with any of them, and it would, perhaps, be impolitic to confide it to them. A matter, so momentous, ought not to be intrusted to those who would have it in their power to exercise it lightly and precipitately, upon sudden dissatisfaction or causeless jealousy, perhaps against the interests and the wishes of a majority of their constituents.

'But in any manner by which a Secession is to take place, nothing is more certain than that the act should be deliberate, clear, and unequivocal. The perspicuity and solemnity of the original obligation require correspondent qualities in its dissolution. The powers of the General Government cannot be defeated or impaired by an ambiguous or implied Secession on the part of the State, although a Secession may, perhaps, be conditional. The people of the State may have some reasons to complain in respect to acts of the General Government; they may, in such cases, invest some of their own officers with the power of negotiation, and may declare an absolute Secession in case of their failure. Still, however, the Secession must in such case be distinctly and peremptorily declared to take place on that event, and in such case—as *in the case of an unconditional Secession—the previous ligament with the Union would be legitimately and fairly destroyed*. But, in either case, the people is the only moving power. . . . [Emphasis added, L.S.]

'Under the Articles of Confederation the concurrence of nine States was requisite for many purposes. If five States had withdrawn from that Union, it would have been dissolved. In the present Constitution there is no specification of numbers after the first formation. It was foreseen that there would be a natural tendency to increase the number of States with the increase of population then anticipated, and now so fully verified. *It was also known, though it was not avowed, that a State might withdraw itself.* The number would therefore be variable. . . . [Emphasis added, L.S.]

'To withdraw from the Union is a solemn, serious act. Whenever it may appear expedient to the people of a State, it must be manifested in a direct and unequivocal manner. If it is ever done indirectly, the people must refuse to elect Representatives, as well as to suffer their Legislature to re-appoint Senators. The Senator whose time had not yet expired, must be forbidden to continue in the exercise of his functions.

'But without plain, decisive measures of this nature, proceeding from the only legitimate source, the people, the United States cannot consider their Legislative powers over such States suspended, nor their Executive or Judicial powers any way impaired, and they would not be obliged to desist from the collection of revenue, within such State.

'As to the remaining States, among themselves, there is no opening for a doubt.

'Secessions may reduce the number to the smallest integer admitting combination. They would remain united under the same principles and regulations, among themselves, that now apply to the whole. For a State cannot be compelled by other States to withdraw from the Union, and, therefore, if two or more determine to remain united, although all the others desert them, *nothing can be discovered in the Constitution to prevent it.* [Emphasis added, L.S.]

'The consequences of an absolute Secession cannot be mistaken, and they would be serious and afflicting.

'The Seceding State, whatever might be its relative magnitude, would speedily and distinctly feel the loss of the aid and countenance of the Union. The Union, losing a proportion of the National revenue, would be entitled to demand from it a proportion of the National debt. *It would be entitled to treat the inhabitants and the commerce of the separated State, as appertaining to a foreign country.* In public treaties already made, whether commercial or political, it could claim no participation, while foreign powers would unwillingly calculate, and slowly transfer to it, any portion of the respect and confidence borne towards the United States.' [Emphasis added, L.S.]

"Mr. Rawle came to the same logical conclusion upon the subject of Secession that Judge Tucker had come to. He also distinctly asserts that it was known at the time, though not avowed, that a State might withdraw itself. 'It was mutually understood,' he says. He was a living actor in the scenes.

"Fourthly. *It is upon the grounds or assumption that this was the general understanding of the nature of the Government at the time, that we can account for the triumphant success of Mr. Jefferson, in 1800, on the principles of the Virginia and Kentucky Resolutions of 1798-1799, and Mr. Madison's Report, referred to before. It is in accordance with this general understanding that we can account for Mr. Hamilton's strong reason for Mr. Jefferson's co-operation in the matter just stated.* [Emphasis added, L.S.]

"It is in accordance with the same general understanding that we can account for what I have seen it stated was the action of the Massachusetts Legislature in 1803, on the acquisition of Louisiana. That State, it is said, then declared, by solemn resolve,

> That the annexation of Louisiana to the Union, transcends the Constitutional power of the Government of the United States. It formed a new Confederacy to which the States united by the former Compact are not bound to adhere.

"Whether this Resolution ever was, in fact, passed by the Massachusetts Legislature, or not, I have not been able to ascertain with absolute certainty. . . . Well, be that as it may, the Legislature of Massachusetts, in 1844, did, without question, pass a series of Resolutions upon the annexation of Texas, of which the following is a part:

> Resolved, That the project of the annexation of Texas, unless arrested on the threshold, may drive these States into a dissolution of the Union.

"On the same subject, on the 22nd of February, 1845, the same body adopted another series of Resolutions, in which the following occurs:

> Resolved, and as the powers of Legislation granted in the Constitution of the United States to Congress, do not embrace the case of the admission of a foreign State, or foreign territory, by Legislation, into the Union, such an act of admission would have no binding force whatever on the people of Massachusetts.

". . . [These Resolutions] . . . are not at all inconsistent with those said to have been passed on a similar subject in 1803. *These Resolutions show clearly the understanding of Massachusetts as late as 1844-1845, of the nature of the Compact of our Union. Though she did not see fit to exercise her right to secede or withdraw, she nevertheless unmistakably asserted her right to do so under circumstances then existing, by asserting that she would not be bound by the anticipated action of the General Government in the matter of the annexation of Texas.* [Emphasis added, L.S.]

"Moreover, it is in strict accordance with this general understanding that several of the Eastern States, upon the call of Massachusetts assembled by their deputies in the well-known New England or *Hartford Convention*, in December, 1814 [to consider seceding from the Union, and forming what would be called the 'New England Confederacy']. These States, it is well known, were greatly disaffected towards the Federal Administration. It was during our last war with Great Britain. They conceived their interest to be improperly sacrificed by the policy pursued in the conduct of the war. The Convention was called to devise some course to be taken by these States for a redress of their common grievances. They did nothing, however, but issue an address setting forth their grievances, and appoint a delegation to present them, with their views, to the Federal authorities at Washington; and provide for another Convention to take further action in the premises. This address went into a very full review of the nature of the Government. In it the following principles are set forth:

> It is as much the duty of the State authorities to watch over the rights reserved, as of the United States to exercise the powers which are delegated.
> . . . But in cases of deliberate, dangerous and palpable infractions of the Constitution, affecting the Sovereignty of a State and liberties of the people, it is not only the right, but the duty of such a State to interpose its authority for their protection in the manner best calculated to secure that end. When emergencies occur which are either beyond the reach of the judicial tribunals, or too pressing to admit of the delay incident to their forms, States which have no common umpire must be their own judges, and execute their own decisions.

"To this document are signed, amongst others, the venerable names of Nathan Dane, George Cabot, Zephenia Swift, James Hillhouse, and Harrison G. Otis. Dane was the founder of the Professorship of Law in the Cambridge University, and was the author of the *Abridgment of American Law*, so often quoted by Judge [Joseph] Story, as well as the author of the celebrated ordinance for the government of the North-western Territory, in 1787. That these States did intend to secede and withdraw from the Union [and form a new and separate country to be called the 'New England Confederacy'], unless their grievances complained of were redressed, there can be no doubt, and that these eminent jurists thought then that they had a right to do so, is equally clear.

"The news, however, of the treaty of peace which had been signed at Ghent, on the 24th day of December, 1814, was soon after received in this country, and put an end to all other proceedings under this [secession] movement of these States.

"But what is remarkable in the history of that controversy is, that in no debate in

Congress were the fundamental [secession] doctrines of this address called in question, so far as I have been able to discover. Mr. [James] Madison, then President, made no allusion, in his message to Congress, to this movement. *Niles's Register* contains six able leading editorial articles against this Convention and its proceedings, but in none of them is the right of the States to withdraw from the Union, if they choose to do so, questioned. It is true, the Convention was generally odious, at the time, to the people of a large majority of the States, and has been ever since. This was from the fact that the threatened Secession was in time of war, and a war which had been undertaken mainly, at the instance of these States, in defence of their shipping and navigating interests. It is also true, that some journalists and partisans of the day did charge the movement to be treasonable. But what have not partisan journalists and public speakers, in times of excitement, charged to be treasonable! Almost every matter in the administration of Government, that does not suit their own peculiar views and notions. This charge was not made by any of the officials of the Government, that I am aware of, and what I mean to say is, that *the right of a State to withdraw from the Union was never denied or questioned, that I am aware of, by any jurist, publicist, or statesman of character and standing, until Kent's Commentaries appeared, in 1826, nearly forty years after the Government had gone into operation!* From the weight of evidence, therefore, the conclusion follows, that in the opinion of the [Founding] fathers generally, as well as of the great mass of the people throughout the country, the right existed. It has been stated by high authority [U.S. President James Buchanan], that '*the right of Secession is not a plant of Southern origin—it first sprung up in the North.*' A more accurate statement would be that it was not sectional but continental in its origin. It was generally recognized in all parts of the Union during the earlier days of the Republic. [Emphasis added, L.S.]

"Fifthly and lastly, this right, so apparent to all clear and unbiassed minds from all the facts connected with the history and nature of the Government, is fully and clearly recognized by all foreign writers and publicists who have made our institutions their study. Prominent in this class stands [French historian Alexis] De Tocqueville, before alluded to. On this point he says:—

> 'However strong a Government may be, it cannot easily escape from the consequences of a principle which it has once admitted as the foundation of its Constitution. The Union was formed by the voluntary agreement of the States; and these, in uniting together, have not forfeited their Nationality, nor have they been reduced to the condition of one and the same people. If one of the States chose to withdraw its name from the contract, it would be difficult to disprove its right of doing so, and the Federal Government would have no means of maintaining its claims directly, either by force or by right.'

"To the name of De Tocqueville, the names of many of the most eminent writers in Europe, upon our institutions, might be added. Why, however, multiply authorities of this sort to show either the unprejudiced judgment of foreign writers upon the subject, or the general understanding of all parties in this country, during the earlier and better days of the Republic? Men of great ability of our own day—men, who stand high in the Republican [Liberal] ranks at this time, who had and have no sympathy with the late Southern movement, are fully committed to the rightfulness of that movement. Mr. [Abraham] Lincoln himself was fully committed to it [though only *before* he initiated his war on the South and the Constitution]. Besides him, I refer you to but two others of this class, now prominent actors in public affairs. They are Senator [Benjamin F.] Wade, of Ohio, at this time the Vice President of the United States, and Mr. [Horace] Greeley, of the *New York Tribune*, who is 'a power behind the throne greater than the throne itself.'

"Mr. Wade, in the Senate of the United States, on the 23rd of February, 1855, used the following language:

> 'Who is to be judge, in the last resort, of the violation of the Constitution of the United States by the enactment of a law? Who is the final arbiter? The General Government, or the States in their Sovereignty? Why, sir, to yield that point, is to yield up all the rights of the States to protect their own citizens, and to consolidate this Government into a miserable despotism. I tell you, sir, whatever you may think of it, if this bill pass, collisions will arise between the Federal and State jurisdictions—conflicts more dangerous than all the wordy wars which are got up in Congress—conflicts in which the States will never yield; for the more you undertake to load them with acts like this, the greater will be their resistance.
>
> '. . . I said there were States in this Union whose highest tribunals had adjudged that bill to be unconstitutional, and that I was one of those who believed it unconstitutional; that my State believed it unconstitutional; and that, under the old Resolutions of 1798 and 1799, a State must not only be the judge of that, but of the remedy in such a case.'

"This is enough to show that he put himself at that time squarely upon the old States' Rights State Sovereignty Jeffersonian platform of 1798 and 1799. Judge Story has told us what the obvious deductions from these principles are.

"Let us now see what Mr. Greeley . . . [said on November 9, 1860]:

> 'The telegraph informs us that most of the Cotton States are meditating a withdrawal from the Union, because of Lincoln's election. Very well: they have a right to meditate, and meditation is a profitable employment of leisure. We have a chronic, invincible disbelief in Disunion as a remedy for either

Northern or Southern grievances. We cannot see any necessary connection between the alleged disease and this ultra-heroic remedy; still, we say, *if any one sees fit to meditate Disunion, let him do so unmolested.* That was a base and hypocritic row that was once raised at Southern dictation, about the ears of John Quincy Adams, because he presented a petition for the dissolution of the Union. The petitioner had a right to make the request; it was the Member's duty to present it. And now, *if the Cotton States consider the value of the Union debatable, we maintain their perfect right to discuss it.* Nay: we hold, with Jefferson, *to the unalienable right of communities to alter or abolish forms of government that have become oppressive or injurious; and, if the Cotton States shall decide that they can do better out of the Union than in it, we insist on letting them go in peace. The right to secede may be a revolutionary one, but it exists nevertheless; and we do not see how one party can have a right to do what another party has a right to prevent. We must ever resist the asserted right of any State to remain in the Union, and nullify or defy the laws thereof; to withdraw from the Union is quite another matter. And, whenever a considerable section of our Union shall deliberately resolve to go out, we shall resist all coercive measures designed to keep it in. We hope never to live in a Republic, whereof one section is pinned to the residue by bayonets.* [Emphasis added, L.S.]

'But, while we thus uphold the practical liberty, if not the abstract right, of Secession, we must insist that the step be taken, if it ever shall be, with the deliberation and gravity befitting so momentous an issue. Let ample time be given for reflection; let the subject be fully canvassed before the people; and let a popular vote be taken in every case, before Secession is decreed. Let the people be told just why they are asked to break up *the Confederation*; let them have both sides of the question fully presented; let them reflect, deliberate, then vote; and let the act of Recession be the echo of an unmistakable popular fiat. A judgment thus rendered, a demand for separation so backed, would either be acquiesced in without the effusion of blood, or those who rushed upon carnage to defy and defeat it, would place themselves clearly in the wrong.' [Emphasis added, L.S.]

"What better argument could I make to show the rightfulness of Secession, if the Southern States of their own goodwill and pleasure chose to resort to it, even for no other cause than Mr. Lincoln's election, than is herein set forth in [Greeley's] . . . own pointed, strong, and unmistakable language? It is true, he waives all questions of Compact between the States. He goes deeper into fundamental principles and plants the right upon the eternal truths announced in the Declaration of Independence. That is bringing up principles which I have not discussed, not because I do not indorse them as sound and correct, to the word and letter, but because it was not necessary for my purpose. *Upon these immutable principles the justifiableness of Georgia in her Secession Ordinance of the 19th of January, 1861, will stand clearly established for all time to come. For if, with less than one hundred thousand population, she was such a people in 1776 as had the* unquestionable right to alter and change their form of Government as they pleased, how much more were they such a people, with more than ten times the number, in 1861? The same principle applies to all the States which quit the old and joined the new Confederation. Mr. Greeley here speaks of the Union as a Confederation, and not a Nation. This was, perhaps, the unconscious utterance of a great truth when the true spirit was moving him. [Emphasis added, L.S.]

"The State of Georgia did not take this step, however, in withdrawing from the Confederation, without the most thorough discussion. It is true it was not a dispassionate discussion. Men seldom, if ever, enter into such discussions with perfect calmness, or even that degree of calmness with which all such subjects ought to be considered. But the subject was fully canvassed before the people. Both sides were strongly presented. In the very earnest remonstrance against this measure made by me, on the 14th of November, 1860, . . . was an appeal equally earnest for just such a vote as he suggests in order that the action of the State on the subject might be 'the echo of an unmistakable, popular fiat.' On the same occasion I did say, in substance, just what he had so aptly said before, that *the people of Georgia, in their Sovereign capacity, had the right to secede if they chose to do so*, and that in this event of their so determining to do, upon a mature consideration of the question, that I should bow in submission to the majesty of their will so expressed! [Emphasis added, L.S.]

"This, when so said by me, is what it seems was 'the dead fly in the ointment' of that speech; so sadly 'marring its general perfume.' This was 'the distinct avowal of the right of the State to overrule my personal convictions and plunge me,' as he says, 'into treason to the Nation!'

"Was not the same 'dead fly in the ointment' of his article of the 9th of November, only five days before? And if going with my State, in what he declared she had a perfect right to do, plunged me into treason to the Nation, is he not clearly an accessory before the fact by a rule of construction not more strained than that laid down in the trial of State cases by many judges not quite so notoriously infamous as Jeffreys? By a rule not more strained than that which would make out treason in the act itself! But I do not admit the rule in its application either to the accessory or the principal.

"Now in relation to Mr. Lincoln. He himself, in 1848, announced the same general principles as above announced by Mr. Greeley in 1860. On the 12th day of January, 1848, Mr. Lincoln, in the House of Representatives, made a speech which I heard. Here is that speech. In it [Lincoln] . . . used this language.

> 'Any people any where, being inclined and having the power, have the right to rise up and shake off the existing Government, and form a new one that suits them better. This is a most valuable, a sacred right—a right which, we hope and believe, is to liberate the world. Nor is this right confined to cases

in which the whole people of an existing Government may choose to exercise it. Any portion of such people that can, may revolutionize, and make their own of so much of the territory as they inhabit. More than this, a majority of any portion of such people may revolutionize, putting down a minority, intermingled with, or near about them, who may oppose their movements. Such minority was precisely the case of the Tories of our own Revolution. It is a quality of revolutions not to go by old lines, or old laws; but to break up both, and make new ones.'

[Stephens neglects to mention the bold fact that by the time South Carolina seceded in December 1860, just twelve years later, Lincoln's belief in the legal right of secession had completely evaporated. In March 1861, for example, Dishonest Abe called secession "the essence of anarchy," while in July 1861 he referred to it as an "ingenious sophistry."][136]

"Even if Secession was but a revolutionary right, and did not spring at all from the nature of the Compact between the States, Mr. Lincoln here distinctly admits the right,—a 'most valuable and sacred right'—as one of a revolutionary character. If this be a sacred right, even in this view, how in the language of Mr. Greeley, can there exist any legal or moral right anywhere else to prevent its exercise? There cannot be two antagonistic rights! Rights, like truths, always fit as between themselves! They never jar, impinge, or collide!

"Thus the moral and political worlds, when rightly administered, present the same beauty and symmetry which pervade the physical in all its parts, extending throughout creation; and in the practical workings of all their parts, produce a perfect concord and harmony, not unlike that symphony of the spheres in the material universe which has gone forth from the time the most distant stars raised the grand chorus in the morning of their birth!

"You thus have, gentlemen, a very full review of the grounds upon which my convictions of duty, in regard to the right of Secession, were founded. They arose from my understanding of the nature of the Government of the United States, and where, under the system, that Paramount authority resides, to which ultimate allegiance is due. *The conclusion to which I came was, that this ultimate Paramount authority had never been parted with by the States—that, from the nature of the Federal Government, and from the very terms of the Compact between the States, this Sovereign power was reserved to them, severally. If I erred in that conclusion, you see I erred with many of the brightest intellects, ablest statesmen, and purest patriots of this as well as other countries.* [Emphasis added, L.S.]

"But even if I erred with them on this point, we see it fully and clearly admitted, by very high authority in the ranks of modern [i.e., Victorian] Republicanism [Liberalism], that it does nevertheless still there reside, according to the great fundamental principles of the American Revolution! In either view, was I not fully justified in the course I took?

"[To all of you big government Liberals, Centralists, Consolidationists, and Socialists,] I will not ask your judgment upon the matter, how ever clearly I may think that this exposition of my course shows that I acted rightly and patriotically. I know full well that you have been too thoroughly schooled in different opinions for any one reasonably to expect so radical a change of them in so short a time. Men's opinions or convictions upon such questions do not so readily or easily change. Truths of this character do not bring forth their fruits in a day. They must have time to germinate, grow, and develop, first.

"It is better, therefore, to leave these questions for the verdict of posterity—for the enlightened and unimpassioned judgment of mankind. By this, we or our memories must all abide. All that any of us can do in the premises is, to see to it that all the facts, as well as a true account of our actions, shall be transmitted to that August tribunal. This is the work of history. The only anxiety I have on the matter is, that this work shall be faithfully performed—that the record shall be rightly put up. This being done, I entertain no apprehensions as to the verdict and judgment upon it hereafter to be rendered. *From these opposing and conflicting principles, however, as I said in the beginning, the war sprung. These were the latent but real causes.*"[137] [Emphasis added, L.S.]

18

THE BEST GOVERNMENT THE WORLD EVER SAW

NATURALLY, 19TH-CENTURY LIBERALS, JUST AS they do today, did not agree with Stephens, that the original Confederate Republic known as the United States of America is "the best the world ever saw." Always strong supporters of big government and socialistic policies, they felt that such

> "an association of States, bound by nothing stronger than their own will and pleasure, would be no Government at all. It would have no adhesive quality between its parts or members. It would have no stability, no durability, no strength; the bonds of union would be no better than a rope of sand. A Government, to be worth any thing, must be strong; it must be held together by force. It must be clothed with power, not only to pass laws, but to command obedience. What would become of the public faith, of the public credit, of the public property? What Nation would put any confidence in such a Government, if its nature and organic structure were so understood abroad? Who would treat with such a country, or enter into any agreements, or conventions, with a Government so constructed, upon any matters of trade, commerce, finance, or any thing else? It would be virtually treating with an ideal power that had no real existence! The solemn agreements entered into one day, by what [Conservatives] . . . call the bare agent of a number of separate Sovereignties, might be annulled the next, by any one of these Sovereigns. Such a Government, so far from being entitled to the respect even, of any one, would deserve and receive nothing but the contempt of mankind!"[138]

Stephens was well prepared for this type of uninformed, anti-American sentiment, as he reveals in the following excerpts from his book *A Constitutional*

View.

☞ "Just such Governments, founded upon just such principles, have existed, and have received, . . . not the contempt but the admiration of mankind! What think you [Liberals] of the Confederations of Greece? They were just such Governments. To whom is the world so much indebted for European civilization at this time, as to the little Republics upon the Archipelago, held together by no other bonds than their own consent? By whom were the battles of Marathon, and Salamis, and Platæa, fought? By whom was the progress of Asiatic Empire stayed in its westward march, but by States so united? What people on earth have left more enduring monuments of their greatness in the defence and maintenance of liberty, or the development of art, science, eloquence, or song, than these same small Hellenic States, confederated upon precisely the principles which [Liberals] . . . consider of so little worth? When did their greatness and glory depart? Not until these principles were departed from.

"What think you of the United Netherlands? In maintaining successfully, as they did, the great principles of civil and religious liberty, in the dawn of modern political reformation, did they deserve nothing but the contempt of mankind? On the contrary, will not their glorious achievements live in history amongst the grandest of any age or country? These States were united by no bonds but their own voluntary consent. *Passing over many other instances, what think you of our own old Confederation? Did it not carry these States, then thus united, successfully through the War of Independence? A war against one of the greatest powers then existing? A war of seven years' duration? A war jointly waged to establish this very principle? Did not France, Sweden and Prussia, treat with them? Did not England treat with them upon boundary, upon trade, upon commerce, upon matters of public right, upon all matters of public faith, when she knew that the sanction and co-operation of each State was necessary to give absolute validity to some articles of the treaty?* Though the public credit was not so well sustained under the machinery of that Confederation as it has been under the new one, yet was it not sufficient to carry them through the most perilous struggle that any States ever passed successfully through? Have we, or mankind, no feelings towards that Confederacy, so constituted, which effected such grand results, but contempt? [Emphasis added, L.S.]

"Now all these Governments, the Grecian, the Germanic, as well as our own first Confederation, were founded . . . upon just such a principle. . . . The principle of voluntary consent. This is the principle upon which are founded all Confederations. Just such Governments are all Confederated Republics. And these are the only kinds of

Governments, as Montesquieu informs us, which have saved the human race from universal monarchical rule. Low as [the Liberal's] . . . estimate of them may be, they are the only escape yet discovered by man for free institutions, among bordering States or Nations. Governments which have done so much for mankind certainly do not deserve, nor have they received from them, such sentiments as you imagine. [Emphasis added, L.S.]

"But *we have seen that our present system is a great improvement upon all former models of this kind of Confederation. While it is founded upon the same basis of consent and voluntary agreement, as I hope I have clearly shown, yet it has several new and important features in its organization, unknown before, and to which we are mainly indebted for its unparalleled success in the past. It is because of these new features, all resting upon the same basis as all other Confederations, placing it far above all other systems, that I considered it the best Government the world ever saw.* [Emphasis added, L.S.]

"*The same view was entertained by John Hancock, when, in his message to the Legislature of Massachusetts, as we have seen, he said, that if the proposed amendments, which he had himself offered in the State Convention, should be adopted, the chief one of which was the expressly declared reservation of the Sovereignty of the States, he should 'consider it the most perfect system of Government as to the objects it embraces that has been known amongst mankind.'* [Emphasis added, L.S.]

"A Government, to be worth any thing, . . . must be strong. Its parts and members must be held together by force of some sort. This I cordially admit. We do not differ as to the force or its extent; we differ only as to its nature and character. Should it be a physical or moral force? *In my judgment, the strongest force that can hold the parts or constituent elements of any Government together is the affection of the people towards it.* The Universe is held together by force—the greatest of all forces, by Omnipotence itself! This force in the material world, which binds and holds together in indissoluble union all its parts in their respective and most distant orbits throughout the illimitable regions of space, is *the simple law of attraction!* So should it be with all Governments, especially with those formed by distinct States United or Confederated upon any sort of Compact, Agreement, or Constitution, as ours was, with a view, and a sole view, to their mutual convenience and reciprocal advantage. [Emphasis added, L.S.]

"These, also, evidently, were the views of Mr. John Quincy Adams. In his celebrated address before the Historical Society of New York, in 1839, in speaking of the Union of these States, he says:

> 'With these qualifications we may admit the same right as vested in the people of every State in the Union, with reference to the General Government, which was exercised by the people of the United Colonies with reference to

the supreme head of the British Empire, of which they formed apart; and *under these limitations have the people of each State in the Union a right to secede from the Confederated Union itself.* Here stands the right! But the indissoluble union between the several States of this Confederated Nation is, after all, not in the right, but in the heart! *If the day should ever come (may Heaven avert it), when the affections of the people of these States shall be alienated from each other; when the fraternal spirit shall give way to cold indifference, or collision of interest shall fester into hatred, the bands of political asseveration will not long hold together parties no longer attached by the magnetism of conciliated interests and kindly sympathies; and far better will it be for the people of the dis-United States, to part in friendship from each other, than to be held together by constraint;* then will be the time for reverting to the precedents which occurred at the formation and adoption of the Constitution, to form again a more perfect Union by dissolving that which could no longer bind, and to leave the separated parts to be re-united by the law of political gravitation to the centre!' [Emphasis added, L.S.]

"The strength of the Union, in the opinion of Mr. Adams, was not in the right to hold it together by physical force, but in the moral power which springs from the heart of the people, and which prompts them to sustain it by their own voluntary action. This was also doubtless the opinion of Mr. [Thomas] Jefferson, when he declared the Government of the United States in his judgment, to be the strongest in the world. In his first inaugural, soon after his election, upon the principles of his own Resolutions touching the nature of the Government and the principles upon which it was founded, he said:

'I know, indeed, that some honest men fear that a Republican Government cannot be strong; that This Government is not strong enough. But would the honest patriot, in the full tide of successful experiment, abandon a Government which has so far kept us free and firm, on the theoretic and visionary fear that this Government, the World's best hope, may by possibility want energy to preserve itself? I trust not. *I believe this, on the contrary, the strongest Government on the Earth!'* [Emphasis added, L.S.]

"Its strength, in his opinion, lay not in physical force, but in moral power, in the hearts and affections of its constituent elements. He fully believed in the right of any State to withdraw when the terms of the Compact were broken by the other parties to it, and he believed in the perfect and absolute right of each party for itself to judge as well of infractions of the Compact as the mode and measure of redress.

"Indeed, this is the self-adjusting principle of the system. It is the only principle upon which the safety, security and existence even of the separate members can be maintained and preserved, which is the chief object of all

Federal [Confederate] Republics. "[The arguments of the Liberals] . . . are but a repetition of the views expressed by the advocates of one great consolidated Government, when the new Constitution was under consideration in the Philadelphia Convention [in 1787]. The same that caused [Alexander] Hamilton to look upon the new Constitution which continued the Federal [Confederate] System as 'a frail and worthless fabric,' though he gave this plan, when he could not get his own, a zealous and patriotic support as an experiment. It was indeed an experiment, a wonderful experiment, and most wonderfully was it performing its high mission, to his utter astonishment as well as that of all others of his class, so long as the primary law of its existence was recognized in its administration. In illustration of my views of the normal action of the system in its practical workings, with its new features differing . . . from all former Federal [Confederate] Republics, you will excuse me for calling your attention to what I said on this subject in the House of Representatives on the 12th day of February, 1859. The views then expressed I still entertain. They were given in a speech made on the admission of Oregon. In that speech, after going at some length into those agitating questions which were then culminating in that crisis which ended in the war [for Southern Independence] which we are now considering, and after speaking of the nature of the Government and urging 'a strict conformity to the laws of its existence,' as essential not only 'for the safety and prosperity of all its members,' but for its own preservation, I went on further to speak not only of what it had accomplished, but of the still greater results that might be expected, if it should continue to be administered upon the principles and for the objects upon which and for which it was formed. Here is what was then added:—

> [Stephens quoting himself:] 'Such is the machinery of our theory of self-government by the people. This is the great novelty of our peculiar system, involving a principle unknown to the ancients, an idea never dreamed of by Aristotle or Plato. The union of several distinct, independent communities upon this basis (the Federal machinery acting directly upon the citizens of the several States within the sphere of its limited powers), is a new principle in human Governments. It is now a problem in experiment for the people of the nineteenth century, upon this continent, to solve. As I behold its workings in the past and at the present, while I am not sanguine, yet I am hopeful of its successful solution. The most joyous feeling of my heart is the earnest hope that it will, for the future, move on as peacefully, prosperously, and brilliantly, as it has in the past. If so, then we shall exhibit a moral and political spectacle to the world something like the prophetic vision of Ezekiel, when he saw a number of distinct beings or living creatures, each with a separate and distinct organism, having the functions of life within itself, all of one external likeness, and all, at the same time, mysteriously connected, with

one common animating spirit pervading the whole, so that when the common spirit moved they all moved; their appearance and their work being, as it were, a wheel in the middle of a wheel; and whithersoever the common spirit went, thither the others went, all going together; and when they went, he heard the noise of their motion like the noise of great waters, as the voice of the Almighty! Should our experiment succeed, such will be our exhibition—a machinery of Government so intricate, so complicated, with so many separate and distinct parts, so many independent States, each perfect in the attributes and functions of Sovereignty, within its own jurisdiction, all, nevertheless, united under the control of a common directing power for external objects and purposes, may naturally enough seem novel, strange, and inexplicable to the philosophers and crowned heads of the world!

'It is for us, and those who shall come after us, to determine whether this grand experimental problem shall be worked out; not by quarrelling amongst ourselves; not by doing injustice to any; not by keeping out any particular class of States; but by each State remaining a separate and distinct political organism within itself—all bound together, for general objects, under a common Federal [Confederate] head; as it were, a wheel within a wheel. Then the number may be multiplied without limit; and then, indeed, may the nations of the earth look on in wonder at our career; and when they hear the noise of the wheels of our progress in achievement, in development, in expansion, in glory, and renown, it may well appear to them not unlike the noise of great waters; the very voice of the Almighty—*Vox populi! Vox Dei!*' [Latin: "The voice of the people! The voice of God!"]

"Such was the spectacle presented to my mind by the harmonious workings of our 'glorious institutions,' (as Mr. Webster styled them, in 1839,) under the Constitution of the United States, as I understood its nature and character! That Constitution which sets forth the terms of Union between Free, Sovereign, and Independent States—each retaining its separate Sovereignty, and only delegating such powers to all the rest as are most conducive, by their joint exercise, to its own safety, security, happiness, and prosperity, as well as most conducive to the like safety, security, happiness and prosperity of all the other members of the great American Federal Republic—the work of their own voluntary creation!

"The chief strength of the system, in its proper administration, lay, according to my view, in that moral power which brought the several members into Confederation. It lay in the hearts of the people of the several States, and in no right or power of keeping them together by coercion. The right of any member to withdraw, which [Liberals] . . . consider an element of weakness, was really, in my judgment, one of the greatest elements of strength, looking in its practical workings to the attainment of the objects for which the Union was formed. This right is not only the basis upon which all Confederated

Republics must necessarily be formed, but without it there is, and can be, in such systems, no check, no real barrier, nothing, indeed, that can be successfully relied upon to prevent their running, sooner or later, into centralized despotic Empire, to escape from which, the Federative principle was resorted to in the institution of Governments for neighboring States. This right is essential to avoid that final and inevitable result which, without it, must necessarily ensue. Its full recognition, as I have said, becomes the self-adjusting principle of the system by which all its temporary perturbations and irregularities of motion will correct and rectify themselves. No system of Government, as yet discovered, is perfect. All have their defects, their irregularities, their eccentricities of action. The Federate principle resorted to is only an approximation to the hitherto unattained standard. But it is the nearest approximation, up to this time, reached by the wisdom of man. Ours was a long stride nearer the desired goal, by an improvement on this principle, than any that ever existed before.

"All Governments of this character are formed upon the assumption that it is for the best interest of all the members of the Confederation to be united on such terms as may be agreed upon, each faithfully performing all its duties and obligations under the Compact. Ours was, certainly, formed on this assumption, and in this belief.

"No State, therefore, would withdraw, or be inclined to withdraw, without a real or supposed breach of faith, on the part of her Confederates, or some of them. If the complaint were real, the derelict States would right the wrong, rather than incur the loss attending the failure to do so. For the maintenance of the Union, so long as the objects for which it was formed alone are looked to, is of equal interest to all. If the complaint were imaginary, and a State should withdraw, without a real and substantial cause, the withdrawal would be but for a very brief period of time. It would be but a temporary aberration. For such State would soon find that she had lost more than she had gained in her new position. New burthens [burdens] would devolve on her. New responsibilities, as well as her just proportion of those resting on her in common with her former Confederates, would have to be assumed; or, in a word, all the disadvantages of isolation, which impelled the Union at first, would be encountered. Under these circumstances and necessary consequences, no Federal Union would remain long dissevered, where this principle was left to its full normal action, which was really for the benefit and interest of all its members. It is true that none would stand long that was inherently and permanently injurious to any, and none such ought to stand. For it would be in opposition to the very principles and objects upon which, and for which, all such unions are formed.

"In what [Liberals] . . . consider, then, the weakness of our Government, according to my idea of its nature, I repeat, its chief strength, its great beauty, its complete symmetry, its ultimate harmony, and, indeed, its very perfection, mainly consist; certainly, so long as the objects aimed at in its formation are the objects aimed at in its administration. And, *on this principle, on the full recognition of the absolute ultimate Sovereignty of the several States, I did consider it the best, and the strongest, and the grandest Government on earth! My whole heart and soul were devoted to the Constitution, and the Union under it, with this understanding of its nature, character, objects, and functions!* [Emphasis added, L.S.]

"When, therefore, the State of Georgia seceded, against my judgment, viewing the measure in the light of policy, only, and not of right (for the causes, as we have seen, and shall see more fully, hereafter, were more than ample to justify the act, as a matter of right), *I felt it to be my duty to go with her, not only from a sense of the obligations of allegiance, but from other high considerations of patriotism of not much less weight and influence. These considerations pressed upon the mind the importance of maintaining this principle [the right of secession], which lies at the foundation of all Federal systems; and to which we were mainly indebted, in ours, for all the great achievements of the past. It was under this construction of the nature of our system, that all these achievements had been attained. This was the essential and vital principle of the system, to which I was so thoroughly devoted. It was that which secured all the advantages of Confederation, without the risk of Centralism and Absolutism; and on its preservation depended, not only the safety and welfare, and even existence, of my own State, but the safety, welfare, and ultimate existence of all the other States of the Union! The States were older than the Union! They made it! It was but their own creation! Their preservation was of infinitely more importance than its continuance! The Union might cease to exist, and yet the States continue to exist, as before! Not so with the Union, in case of the destruction or annihilation of the States! With their extinction, the Union necessarily becomes extinct also! They may survive it, and form another, more perfect, if the lapse of time and changes of events show it to be necessary, for the same objects had in view when it was formed; but it can never survive them! What may be called a Union may spring from the common ruins, but it would not be the Union of the Constitution!—the Union of States! By whatever name it might be called, whether Union, Nation, Kingdom, or any thing else, according to the taste of its dupes or its devotees, it would, in reality, be nothing but that deformed and hideous Monster which rises from the decomposing elements of dead States, the world over, and which is well known by the friends of Constitutional Liberty, everywhere, as the Demon of Centralism, Absolutism, Despotism! This is the necessary reality of that result, whether the Imperial Powers be seized and wielded by the hands of many, of few, or of one!* [Emphasis added, L.S.]

"The question, therefore, with me, assumed a magnitude and importance far above the welfare and destiny of my own State, it embraced the welfare and ultimate destiny of all the States, North as well as South; nay, more, it embraced, in its range, the general interest of mankind, so far, at least, as the oppressed of all other lands and climes were looking to this country, not only for a present asylum against the evils of misrule in their own, but were anxiously and earnestly looking forward to the Federative [Confederative] principles here established, as 'the World's best hope,' in the great future, for the regeneration, the renaissance, of the Nations of the Earth! Such, in my judgment, were the scope and bearing of the question and the principles involved.

"*Had this foundation principle of the system then been generally acknowledged—had no military force been called out to prevent the exercise of this right of withdrawal on the part of the seceding States—had no war been waged against Georgia and the other States, for their assertion and maintenance of this right, had not this primary law of our entire system of Government been violated in the war so waged, I cannot permit myself to entertain the shadow of a doubt, that the whole controversy, between the States and Sections, would, at no distant day, have been satisfactorily and harmoniously adjusted, under the peaceful and beneficent operation of this very law itself. Just as all perturbations and irregularities are adjusted in the solar system, by the simple law of gravitation, from which alone it sprung in the beginning, and on which alone its continuance, with its wonderfully harmonious workings, depends!* [Emphasis added, L.S.]

"A brief illustration will more clearly unfold this view. Had the right of withdrawal [i.e., secession] not been denied or resisted, those [Northern] States, which had openly, confessedly, and avowedly disregarded their obligations, under the Compact, in the matter of the rendition of fugitives from service, and fugitives from justice, appealing, as they did, to 'a higher Law' than the Constitution, would have reconsidered their acts, and renewed their covenants under the bonds of Union, and the Federal administration would have abandoned its policy of taking charge of subjects not within the limits of its delegated powers. The first aberrations in the system; that is the disregard of plighted faith, which had caused the second, that is the secession movement, would themselves have been rectified by that very movement! This rectification on the one side would have been attended by a corresponding rectification on the other. This would have been a necessary and inevitable result, whatever parties, under the influence of passion at the time, may have thought of the nature and permanency of the separation. That is, it would necessarily and inevitably have been the result, if the assumption on which the Union was founded be correct, namely, that it was for the best interest of all the States to be united upon the terms set forth in the Constitution—each State faithfully performing all its obligations, and the Federal [Confederate] Head confining its action strictly to the subjects with which it was charged. On this point, that the Union was best for all, my own convictions were strong and thorough for many reasons, that may be given hereafter. If this postulate was correct, then the ultimate result of this action and re-action in the operation of the system in bringing about a re-adjustment of the parts to their original places, would have been as inevitable as the continued harmonious re-adjustment of continual disturbances in the material world is being produced by like action and counter-action continually going on throughout its entire organization, and the whole resulting from the same all-pervading and all-controlling law, the same law continuing the organization which brought it at first into existence

"But if, on the contrary, the whole assumption on which the Union was formed was wrong,—if it were not for the true and best interests of all the States, constituted as they were, to be so united,—if it were true, as asserted by the controlling [Liberal] spirits of the derelict [Northern] States, that *the Constitution itself as to them, was but a 'covenant with death and an agreement with Hell,'*—then, of course, the re-adjustment would not have taken place, and ought not to have taken place. But I did not believe that the masses of the people in these States entertained any such sentiments towards the work of their Fathers! [Emphasis added, L.S.]

"*My opinion was, that it only required those masses to see, feel, and appreciate the great advantages of that Union to them; and to realize the fact that a Compact, broken by them, could no longer be binding upon others, as Mr. [Daniel] Webster had said, to cause them to compel their officials to comply with the terms of an engagement, which, upon the whole, was of so great importance to their best interests. My convictions were equally strong that, when this was done, the masses of the people at the South, influenced by like considerations, would have controlled all opposition to their cheerful and cordial return to their proper places.* [Emphasis added, L.S.]

"*There would have been no war, no bloodshed, no sacking of towns and cities, no desolation, no billions of treasure expended, on either side, and no million of lives sacrificed in the unnatural and fratricidal strife; there would have been none of the present troubles about restoration, or reconstruction; but, instead of these lamentable scenes, a new spectacle of wonder would have been presented for the guide and instruction of the astonished Nations of the earth, greater than that exhibited after the Nullification pacification, of the matchless workings of our American Institutions of Self-Government by the people!* [Emphasis added, L.S.]

"*You readily perceive, therefore, how thoroughly, looking to the grand results, my entire feelings, heart, and soul, with every energy of mind and body, became enlisted in the success of this cause, when force was invoked, when war was waged to put it down. It was the cause, not only of the Seceding States, but the cause of all the States, and in this view it became, to a great extent, the cause of Constitutional Liberty everywhere. It was the cause of the Federative [Confederative] principle of Government, against the principle of Empire!* The cause of the Grecian type of Civilization against the Asiatic! So, at least, I viewed it, with all the earnestness of the profoundest convictions. *The matter of Slavery, so-called, which was the proximate cause of these irregular movements on both sides, and which ended in the general collision of war, as we have seen, was of infinitely less importance to the Seceding States, than the recognition of this great principle. I say Slavery, so-called, because there was with us no such thing as Slavery in the full and proper sense of that word. No people ever lived more devoted to the principles of liberty, secured by free democratic institutions, than were the people of the South. None had ever given stronger proofs of this than they had done, from the day that Virginia moved in behalf of the assailed rights of Massachusetts, in 1774, to the firing of the first gun in Charleston Harbor, in 1861. What was called Slavery amongst us, was but a legal subordination of the African to the Caucasian race. This relation was so regulated by law as to promote, according to the intent and design of the system, the best interests of both races, the Black as well as the White, the Inferior, as well as the Superior. Both had rights secured, and both had duties imposed. It was a system of reciprocal service, and mutual bonds. But even the two thousand million dollars invested in the relation thus established, between private capital and the labor of this class of population, under the system, was but as the dust in the balance, compared with the vital attributes of the rights of Independence and Sovereignty on the part of the several States. For with these whatever changes and modifications, or improvements in this domestic institution, founded itself upon laws of nature, time, and experience, might have shown to be proper in the advancing progress of civilization, for the promotion of the great ends of society in all good Governments—that is the best interest of all classes, without wrong or injury to any—could, and would have been made by the superior race in these States, under the guidance of that reason, justice, philanthropy, and statesmanship, which had ever marked their course, without the violent disruption of the entire social fabric, with all its attendant ills, and inconceivable wrongs, mischiefs, and sufferings; and especially without those terrible evils and consequences which must almost necessarily result from such disruptions and reorganizations as make a sudden and complete transfer of political power from the hands of the superior to the inferior race, in their present condition, intellectually and morally, in at least six States of the Union!* [Emphasis added, L.S.]

"The [Southern] system, as it existed, it is true, was not perfect. All admit this. No human systems are perfect. But great changes had been made in it, as this class of persons [African-Americans] were gradually rising from their original barbarism, in their subordinate sphere, under the operation of the system, and from their contact, in this way, with the civilization of the superior race. Other changes would certainly have been made, even to the extinction of the system, if time, with its changes, and the progress of attainments on the part of these people had shown it to be proper—that is, best for both races. For if the system, as designed, was not really the best, or could not have been made the best for both races, or whenever it should have ceased to be so, it could and would have been thoroughly and radically changed, in due time, by the only proper and competent authority to act in the premises. [Emphasis added, L.S.]

"The erroneous dogma of the greatest good to the greatest number, was not the basis on which this Institution [i.e., slavery] rested. Much less was it founded upon the dogma of principle of the sole interest or benefit of the white race to the exclusion of considerations embracing the interests and welfare of the other. It was erected upon no such idea as that might, barely, gives right, but it was organized and defended upon the immutable principles of justice to all, which is the foundation of all good Governments. This requires that society be so organized as to secure the greatest good possible, morally, intellectually, and politically, to all classes of persons within their jurisdictional control, without necessary wrong or detriment to any. This was the foundation principle on which this institution in these States was established and defended. [Emphasis added, L.S.]

"These questions are not now, however, before us. We are at present considering the workings of the Federal [Confederate] system, and not the wisdom or policy of the social systems of the several States, or the propriety of the status of their constituent elements respectively.

"This whole question of Slavery, so-called, was but one relating to the proper tatus of the African as an element of a society composed of the Caucasian and African races, and the status which was best, not for the one race or the other, but best, upon the whole, for both. [Emphasis added, L.S.]

"Over these questions, the Federal Government had no rightful control whatever. They were expressly excluded, in the Compact of Union, from its jurisdiction or authority. Any such assumed control was a palpable violation of the Compact, which released all the parties to the Compact, affected by such action, from their obligations under the Compact. On this point there can be no shadow of doubt. [Emphasis added, L.S.]

"Waiving these questions, therefore, for the present, I repeat that this whole subject of Slavery, so-called, in any and every view of it, was, to the Seceding States, but a drop in the ocean compared with those other considerations involved in the issue. Hence, during the whole war, being thoroughly enlisted in it from these other and higher considerations, but being, at the same time, ever an earnest advocate for its speediest termination by an appeal from the arena of arms to the forum of reason, justice, and right, I was wedded to no idea as a basis of peace, but that of the recognition of the ultimate absolute Sovereignty of all the States as the essential basis of any permanent union between them, or any of them, consistent with the preservation of their ultimate existence and liberties. And I wanted, at no time, any recognition of Independence on the part of the Confederate States, but that of George III, of England. That is, the recognition of the Sovereignty and Independence of each, by name. [Emphasis added,

L.S.]

"*The Confederate States [of 1860-1861] had made common cause for this great principle [state sovereignty], as the original thirteen States had done in 1776. The recognition of this I regarded as essential to the future well-being, happiness, and prosperity of all the States, in existence and to be formed, as well as the countless millions of people who are hereafter to inhabit this half of the Western Hemisphere.*

"With this simple recognition I saw no formidable difficulty likely to arise in the future, from controversies between States or Sections. Whenever the passions of the day passed off, whatever Union or Unions were, or might be, really beneficial to all the States, would have resulted sooner or later, as inevitably as natural laws produce their natural effects. This they do in the moral and political world, if left to their proper and legitimate action, with as much certainty as they do in the material.

"With this principle [state sovereignty] recognized, I looked upon it hereafter, and at no distant day, to become, by the natural law of political affinity—'mutual convenience and reciprocal advantage'—the great Continental Regulator of the Grand Federal Republic of 'the United States of America,' to whatever limits their boundaries might go, or to whatever extent their number might swell."[139]

19

GOVERNMENT, SLAVERY, & THE START OF LINCOLN'S WAR

IN THIS CHAPTER OF SELECTIONS from Stephens' *A Constitutional View*, he takes on three of the most significant subjects pertaining to American history: the authentic nature of the U.S. government, the facts about so-called Southern "slavery," and the true instigator of the "Civil War."

In this passage Stephens gives a brief review of his elucidation thus far:
☛ "[I have shown, through] historical review, . . . a correct understanding of the nature and character of the Government of the United States, from a violation of the organic principles of which, as I stated in the outset, the [American Civil] war had its origin. We have seen from this review that ours is a Federal [Confederate] Government. In other words, we have seen that it is a Government formed by a Convention, a *Fœdus*, or Compact between distinct, separate, and Sovereign States. We have seen that this Federal or Conventional Government, so formed, possesses inherently no power whatever. All its powers are held by delegation only, and by delegation from separate States. These powers are all enumerated and all limited to specific objects in the Constitution. Even the highest Sovereign Power it is permitted to exercise—the war power, for instance—is held by it by delegation only. Sovereignty itself—the great source of all political power—under the system, still resides where it did before the Compact was entered into, that is, in the States severally, or with the people of the several States respectively. By the Compact, the Sovereign Powers to be exercised by the Federal Head were not surrendered by the States—were not alienated or parted with by them. They were delegated only. The States by voluntary engagements, agreed only to

abstain from their exercise themselves, and to confer this exercise by delegation upon common agents under the Convention, for the better security of the great objects aimed at by the formation of the Compact, which was the regulation of their external and inter-State affairs."[140]

What type of government does the U.S. possess? Stephens notes that this question is not easily answered:
☛ "Our system, taken altogether, we have seen, is a peculiar one. The world never saw its like before. It has no prototype in any of all the previous Confederations, or Federal Republics, of which we have any account. It is neither a 'Staaten-bund' [a Confederation of states] exactly, nor a 'Bundesstaat' [a Federal state], according to the classification of Federal Republics by the German Publicists. It differs from their 'Staatenbund' in this, that the powers to be exercised by the Federal Head are divided into three departments, the Legislative, Judicial, and Executive, with a perfectly organized machinery for the execution of these powers within its limited sphere, and for the specific objects named, upon citizens of the several States without the intermediate act or sanction of the several States. In the 'Staaten-bund,' or 'States' Confederation,' according to their classification, the Federal Government can enact no laws which will operate upon the citizens of the several States composing it, until the States severally give them their sanction. Such was our Federal [Confederate] Union under the first Articles [of Confederation]. But our present system, as we have seen, went a step further, and introduced a new principle in Confederations. While, therefore, our system differs specifically in this particular from their 'Staatenbund,' or 'States' Confederation,' yet it agrees entirely with it in its essential Generic difference from their Bundesstaat, in this, that the States collectively constitute an international unit as regards third parties, but do not cease to be international units as regards each other."[141]

Stephens explains how the United States of America came to be described by the Founding Fathers as a "Confederate Republic":
☛ "[Our nation] differs . . . generically from . . . [the Germans'] 'Bundesstaat,' or 'Federative State,' or what may properly be called 'an incorporate Union,' in this, that no Sovereign Power whatever, under our system, is surrendered or alienated by the several States; it is only delegated. The difference between our system and their 'Staaten-bund,' is, however, only specific, as we see. It is not Generic. They are both essentially the same. Ours is a newly developed species of Government of their Genus 'Staaten-bund.' This specific difference is what struck [Alexis] De Tocqueville as 'a wholly novel theory, which may be considered as a great discovery in modern political science,' and for which there

was as yet no specific name. His language [as I have noted], . . . is:

> 'This Constitution, which may at first be confounded with the Federal Constitutions which have preceded it, rests, in truth, upon a wholly novel theory, which may be considered as a great discovery in modern political science. In all the Confederations which preceded the American Constitution of 1789, the allied States, for a common object, agreed to obey the injunctions of a Federal Government; but they reserved to themselves the right of ordaining and enforcing the execution of the laws of the Union. The American States, which combined in 1789, agreed, that the Federal Government should not only dictate, but should execute its own enactments. In both cases, the right is the same, but the exercise of the right is different; and this difference produced the most momentous consequences. . . . The new word, which ought to express this novel thing, does not yet exist. The human understanding more easily invents new things than new words, and we are hence constrained to employ many improper and inadequate expressions.'

"This new principle of so constituting a Federal [Confederate] Republic as to make us 'one nation as to Foreign concerns, and to keep us distinct as to domestic ones,' with a division of the delegated powers into Legislative, Judiciary, and Executive Departments, and with an organization and machinery in the Conventional Government, thus formed, for the full exercise of all its delegated and limited powers, similar to those of the separate States creating it, . . . was indicated as early as December 1786, by Mr. [Thomas] Jefferson in a letter to Mr. [James] Madison. This was the grand principle finally carried out. It was a grand step in progress in the science of Government. This was what so signalized our career for sixty years, and this is the peculiar specific difference between our Federal Republic and all others of similar general type, to which Lord [Henry] Brougham alludes when he says:

> 'It is not at all a refinement that a Federal Union should be formed; this is the natural result of men's joint operations in a very rude state of society. But the regulation of such a Union upon pre-established principles, the formation of a system of Government and legislation in which the different subjects shall be not individuals but States, the application of legislative principles to such a body of States, and the devising means for keeping its integrity as a federacy [Confederacy], while the rights and powers of the individual States are maintained entire, is the very, greatest refinement in social policy to which any state of circumstances has ever given rise, or to which any age has ever given birth.'

"From this exposition, we see clearly the proper solution of the vexed question, whether the United States constitute a Nation or not. We see clearly not only that they do constitute a Nation, but also what sort of a Nation it is. *It is not a Nation of individuals, blended in a common mass, with a consolidated Sovereignty over the whole; but a Nation the constituent elements, or members of which, are separate and distinct political organizations, States, or Sovereignties.* It is a 'Confederated Republic,' as Washington styled our present Union. This is the same as if he had styled it a Confederated Nation. It is, in truth, a Confederated Nation [i.e., a Confederacy]. That is, it is a Nation of States, or in other words, a Nation of Nations. In this sense, these States, thus united, do constitute a Nation, and a Nation of the highest and grandest type the world ever saw!"¹⁴² [Emphasis added, L.S.]

How did Stephens define the terms sovereignty, ultimate sovereignty, and paramount authority? Here is his answer:

☛ "[The word sovereignty] . . . involves the idea of a divisibility of Sovereignty itself. It is essential that [one] . . . shall first clearly understand the real import of this word in its proper political sense. I will therefore answer . . . first, by stating as distinctly as I can, what I mean by Sovereignty in this connection. . . . It is true, we have no very clear or accurate definition of it, by any political writer or publicist, that I have seen. Most of them have given their ideas of it by explanations and descriptions.

"By Sovereignty and Paramount authority I mean the same thing. If I were to undertake to express my ideas of it in regular formula, I should say that *Sovereignty or Paramount authority, in a proper political sense, is that inherent, absolute power of self-determination, in every distinct political body, existing by virtue of its own social forces, which, in pursuit of the well-being of its own organism, within the limitations of natural justice, cannot be rightfully interfered with by any other similar body, without its consent.* With this explanation . . . I have only to add, that Sovereignty, as I understand it, is that innate attribute of the Political Body so possessing it, which corresponds with the will and power of self action in the personal body, and by its very nature is indivisible; just as much so as the Mind is in the individual organism.

"This is the doctrine clearly taught by all writers of note on the subject, in both ancient and modern times. Hence, no Political Body can be absolutely Sovereign for any purpose, and not Sovereign for all purposes which lie within the domain of Sovereignty itself. Bodies-Politic may, by delegation, exercise certain Sovereign powers for some purposes and not for all. This is the case with all Conventional States. *We must, moreover, discriminate between the powers of Sovereignty and Sovereignty itself. Sovereign powers are divisible. The exercise of them in all good Governments has been and is entrusted by delegation to different hands; such as the Executive Power, the Legislative Power, the Judicial Power. These are all high Sovereign powers committed to separate and distinct hands. Sovereignty itself, however, from which they all emanate, remains meanwhile the same indivisible unit. This is the Trinity in Unity exhibited in all properly constituted Representative Governments.* Nor is the delegation to another of the right to exercise a power of any kind, whether Sovereign or not, an alienation of it. The fact of its being delegated, shows that the source from which the delegation proceeds continues to exist."[143] [Emphasis added, L.S.]

☛ "In our system, or united systems, Sovereign powers are not only divided into the three great branches, as I have stated, both in the Federal Government and in the several State Governments; but they are also divided in like manner between these two systems of Governments. Some of the Sovereign powers are delegated to all the States to be exercised jointly by them in Congress assembled, as well as by special officers of the Federal Government; and some of them are delegated to the various officers of the several State Governments. Those delegated to each, being delegated by the Sovereign power of the people of the several States separately; and divided similarly in each case. There is no alienation of any portion of Sovereignty itself in either case. This continues to reside with the people of the several States as separate, integral units. I have only further to add in answer to [the Liberals] . . . inquiry, that *by ultimate Sovereignty in this argument, I mean that original, inherent, innate and continually existing rightful Power, or Will of the several Bodies-Politic, or States of our Union—that source and fountain of all political power—which is unimpaired by voluntarily assumed obligations; and which at any time, within the terms stated, can rightfully resume all its delegated powers—those to the Federal Government as well as those to the several State Governments.*

"These great and essential truths of our history [are now] thus forever established beyond question or doubt . . ."[144] [Emphasis added, L.S.]

Stephens now moves on to an important discussion concerning the South's institution of black "slavery" (as distinct from white, red, yellow, and brown slavery—which have also been quite popular throughout world history)[145] and the War for Southern Independence:
☛ "[I will now proceed to] the immediate and exciting question, which brought the organic principles of the Government into such terrible physical conflict in the inauguration of the war. This was, as stated in the outset, the question of *negro Slavery, or more properly speaking that political and legal subordination of the black race to the white race*, which existed in the Seceding States. [Emphasis added, L.S.]

"I thus speak of Slavery as it existed with us, purposely. For, it is to be remembered in all our discussions on this subject, that *what was called Slavery with us, was not Slavery in the usual sense of that word, as generally used and understood* by the ancients, and as generally used and understood in many countries in the present age. It was with us a political Institution. It was, indeed, nothing but that *legal subordination of an Inferior race to a Superior one* [Note: Stephens is referring here to what he believed was the cultural, social, moral, and religious superiority of Anglo-Saxon society, just as the African has long considered his society culturally, socially, morally, and religiously superior to that of the European; L.S.] *which was thought to be the best in the organization of society for the welfare politically, socially, morally and intellectually of both races.* The slave, so-called, was not in law regarded entirely as a chattel, as has been erroneously represented. He was by no means subject to the absolute dominion of his master. He had important personal rights, secured by law. His service due according to law, it is true, was considered property, and so in all countries is considered the service of all persons, who according to law are bound to another or others for a term, however long or short. So is the legal right of parents to the service of their minor children in all the States now considered as property. *A right or property that may be assigned, transferred or sold.* [Emphasis added, L.S.] [Alexander] Hamilton expressed the idea of this peculiar Institution, as it existed with us, clearly, when he said:

> 'The Federal Constitution, therefore, decides with great propriety on the case of our slaves, when it views them in the mixed character of persons and of property. This is in fact their true character. It is the character bestowed on them by the laws under which they live.'

"*They [Southern black 'slaves'] were so viewed and regarded by the Constitutions and laws of all the States. The relation of master and slave under the Institution, as before said, was but one of 'reciprocal service and mutual bonds.' The view of them as property related to their services due according to law.*"[146] [Emphasis added, L.S.]

☛ "This matter of negro subordination, I repeat, was the exciting question in 1860. There were, it is true, many other questions involving the same principles of the Government, which had agitated the public mind almost from the time it went into operation, still exciting the public mind to a greater or less degree: but this question of the status of the Black race in the Southern States, was by far the most exciting and all-absorbing one, at that time, on both sides, and was the main proximate cause which brought those principles of the Government into active play, resulting in the conflict of arms. *This relation of political and legal subordination of the Inferior to the Superior race, as it existed in 1860, in all the Seceding States, had at one time, be it constantly kept in mind, existed in all the States of the Union, and did so exist in all, save one, in 1787, when the present Articles of Union were entered into.* [Emphasis added, L.S.]

"By these Articles this relation was fully recognized, as appears from the solemn covenant therein made, that fugitives from service, under this system, as it then thus existed, escaping from one State into another, should, upon claim, be delivered up to the party to whom the service was due. This was one of the stipulations of the Compact upon which the Union was formed, as we have seen, and of which Judge [Joseph] Story said, on an important occasion, in delivering an opinion from the Bench of the Supreme Court of the United States, 'it cannot be doubted that it constituted a fundamental article, without the adoption of which the Union could not have been formed.'

"These are all great facts never to be lost sight of in this investigation of the rightfulness of this most terrible war, and in determining correctly and justly upon which side the huge responsibility of its inauguration, and of the enormous wrongs, and most disastrous consequences attending its subsequent conduct, must, in the judgment of mankind, forever rest."[147]

☛ "It is not at all germane to [my] . . . purpose in this investigation, at this time, to inquire into the Right, or Wrong of the Institution of Slavery itself, as it thus existed in what were then [incorrectly and unfairly] known as the Slave States. Neither is it in the line of my argument now, to treat of the defects, or abuses of the system. Nor is it at all necessary, or pertinent to my present object, to trace from its inception to its culmination, the history or progress of that movement against it, which was organized for the purpose of bringing the questions it involved into the arena of Federal Councils, and within the range of Federal action. *Suffice it here barely to say, and assume as a fact what is known to us all so well, that, in 1860, a majority of the Northern States, having long previously of their own accord abolished this Institution, within their own limits respectively, had, also, by the action of their Legislatures, openly and avowedly violated that clause in the Constitution of the United States [i.e., the Fugitive Slave Clause], which provided for the rendition of fugitives of this class from service.* [Emphasis added, L.S.]

"To give a history of that movement to which I allude, to trace its progress from its origin, would require a volume of itself. A volume both interesting and instructive, might be devoted to it. This is what is known as the Abolition movement in this country, and this is what Mr. [Horace] Greeley is pleased to style the 'American Conflict.' But from entering into an investigation of that sort, I now forbear. It is in no way pertinent or essential to my purpose. Whoever feels an interest in the subject, will see it treated fully, truthfully, and ably by the master hand of Mr. George Lunt, of Boston, in his history of the '*Origin of the War*.'"[148]

Stephens next lays out the Truth about so-called Southern "slavery" and the real cause of the War for Southern Independence:

☛ "Suffice it, therefore, for me, at present, on this subject, only to say, generally, that such a movement was started, such a conflict was begun at an early day after our present system of Government went into operation. As early as the 12th day of February, 1790, within twelve months after [George] Washington was inaugurated as President, a petition invoking the Federal authorities to take jurisdiction of this subject, with a view to the ultimate abolition of this Institution in the States respectively, was sent to Congress, headed by Dr. [Benjamin] Franklin. This movement, in its first step thus taken so early, was partially checked by the Resolution to which the house of Representatives came, after the most mature consideration of the petition and its objects. That Resolution declared:

> That Congress have no authority to interfere in the emancipation of slaves, or in the treatment of them within any of the States; it remaining with the several States alone to provide any regulations therein, which humanity and true policy may require.

"This clear exposition of the nature of the Federal Government, and its utter want of power to take any action upon the subject, as sought for by the petitioners, checked, I say, for a time, this movement, or conflict so started and commenced. *The conflict, however, was only partially checked; it went on until in 1860, when those who so entered into this movement standing forth as the Abolition or Anti-Slavery Party under the [erroneous] name of Republican, but which in truth was the [Liberal] party of Centralism and Consolidation, organized upon the principle of bringing the Federal Powers to bear upon this Institution in a way to secure its ultimate Abolition in all the States, succeeded in the election of the two highest officers of the Government [Liberal President Abraham Lincoln and Liberal Vice President Hannibal Hamlin], pledged to carry out their principles, and to carry them out in open disregard of the decision of the Supreme Court, which highest Judicial Tribunal under the Constitution, had by solemn adjudication denied the power of the Federal Government to take such action as this Party and its two highest officers stood pledged to carry out.* With all these questions, I repeat, I have nothing now to do, except to say that *the conflict from its rise to its culmination, was not a conflict between the advocates and opponents of the Institution itself.* It seems to have been Mr. [Horace] Greeley's leading object, throughout his work, to give this idea of the nature of the conflict, as I stated in the beginning. *This, however, was in no sense the fact of the case. The [slavery] conflict, fierce and bitter as it was for seventy years, was a conflict between those who were for maintaining the Federal [Confederate] character of the Government, and those who were for centralizing all power in the Federal Head [in Washington, D.C.].* This was the conflict. *It was a conflict between the true [Conservative] supporters of the Federal [Confederate] Union of States established by the Constitution, and those [Liberals] whose object was to overthrow this Union of States, and by usurpations to erect a National Consolidation in its stead.*"¹⁴⁹ [Emphasis added, L.S.]

☛ "The same conflict arose upon divers other questions, also, at an early day. It exhibited itself in the discussions of the first Judiciary Act. In the financial measures submitted by Mr. [Alexander] Hamilton, the then Secretary of the Treasury. In the assumption of the State debts. In the first Apportionment Bill, which was vetoed on these grounds by [George] Washington, in 1792, and much more formidably it exhibited itself in the passage of the Alien and Sedition Acts, in 1798, under the elder Adams [John]. *This [big government Liberal] Party, as we have seen, then [wrongly] assumed the popular name of Federal, as it [wrongly] assumed the popular name of Republican in 1800. These latter measures of 1798 came near stirring up civil war, and would most probably have resulted in such a catastrophe, if the Party, so organized with such principles and objects, had not been utterly overthrown, and driven from power by the advocates of our true Federal [Confederate] system of Government, under the lead of [the Confederacy advocate] Mr. [Thomas] Jefferson, in 1800. It was after this complete defeat on these other questions, that the Centralists rallied upon this question of the Status of the Black race in the States, where it continued to exist, as the most promising one for them to agitate and unite the people of the Northern States upon, for the accomplishment of their sinister objects of National Centralization or Consolidation.*"¹⁵⁰ [Emphasis added, L.S.]

Stephens comments on the underhanded ploys instigated by big government Northern liberals, who used slavery as a false issue to try and push through their agenda:
☛ "On this question, Mr. Greeley and other writers speak of only two Parties during the entire conflict. The *Pro-Slavery party*, and the *Anti-Slavery* or *Liberty party*. The truth is there never was in the United States, or in any one of them, an organized Pro-Slavery party. No such antagonism, as he represents, ever existed in the Federal Councils. The antagonism on this question, which was clearly exhibited in the beginning, as appears from the Resolution of the House of Representatives referred to, was an antagonism growing out of Constitutional principles, and not any sort of antagonism growing out of the principles involved in the right or wrong of negro Slavery, as it then existed in the several States of the Union. It was an antagonism growing out of principles lying at the foundation of the common Government of the States. Of those men, for instance, who voted for the Resolution referred to, in 1790 [which proposed that the central government be prohibited from interfering with the institution of slavery in the individual states], how many can be supposed to have been Pro-Slavery in their sentiments, or in favor of the Institution? Let us look into it. Here is the record of the vote. Amongst the prominent supporters of the Resolution, and on the list of those who voted for it, is the name of Roger

Sherman, of Connecticut. Here is Benjamin Huntington, also of the same State. From Massachusetts, we see the names of Theodore Sedgwick, Elbridge Gerry, and Benjamin Goodhue. From New Hampshire, we see the name of Nicholas Oilman. From New Jersey, Elias Boudinot and Lambert Cadwallader. From Pennsylvania, Frederick A. Muhlenberg, Thomas Hartley, and Daniel Heister. These were all prominent men in the formation of the Constitution. *All from the Northern States. The vote shows, that not only a majority of the members from the Northern States voted for the Resolution, but that a majority of those who did vote for it, were from the Northern States.* Those from the South who voted against it, the debate shows so voted, because they did not think the petition should be considered, or acted upon at all, as it related to subjects not within their Constitutional jurisdiction. But how many of this majority of the Northern members who voted for it, can be reasonably supposed to have been Pro-Slavery in sentiment? In their action in entertaining the petition, they intended only to show what they considered a due regard to the right of petition, and at the same time prove themselves true to the Constitution of their country. This the debate conclusively shows. So in all after times up to the election in 1860. *Those who resisted the action of the Abolitionists did so, because it was based upon revolutionary principles—principles utterly at war with those upon which the Union was established. As a striking illustration of this, Mr. [Thomas] Jefferson himself is well-known to have been as much opposed to the Institution of Slavery, as it then existed in the United States, as any man in either of them; and yet he headed the great party in opposition to this mode of effecting the object of those who desired its Abolition, as he had led the same party to success over the Centralists on other questions, in 1800. He utterly denied that the Federal Government could rightfully exercise any power with the view to the change of any of the Institutions of the States respectively.* [Emphasis added, L.S.]

"The same is true of all the prominent leaders of this party, as well as the great mass of the people composing it, from the days of Jefferson to those of General [Lewis] Cass and Mr. [Stephen A.] Douglas. Mr. [William] Pinkney and Mr. [Henry] Clay, *though Southern men as Mr. Jefferson was, were decidedly Anti-Slavery in their sentiments, and yet they ever acted with the party of Mr. Jefferson upon this question.* General Cass and Mr. Douglas were Northern men with sentiments equally averse to Slavery, and for the same reasons opposed the Abolition movement in the Federal Councils. Even Chief Justice [Roger B.] Taney, who delivered the opinion of the Supreme Court in the case referred to, was by no means individually Pro-Slavery in his sentiments. His views upon the Institution are understood to have been very similar to those of Mr. Pinkney and Mr. Clay. Out of the million and half, and more, of men in the Northern States who voted against Mr. [Abraham] Lincoln, in 1860, perhaps not ten thousand could be said, with truth, to be in favor of the Institution, or would have lived in a State where it existed. It was a subject with which they were thoroughly convinced they had nothing to do, and could have nothing to do under the terms of the Union by which the States were confederated, except to carry out and faithfully perform all the obligations of the Constitutional Compact in regard to it. In opposing the 'Liberty Party,' so-called, they enlisted under no banner of Slavery of any sort, but only arrayed themselves against that [Liberal] organization, which had virtually hoisted the banner of Consolidation. *The struggle or conflict, therefore, from its rise to its culmination, was between those who in whatever State they lived, were for maintaining our Federal [Confederate] system as it was established, and those who were for a consolidation of power in the Central Head.*"[151] [Emphasis added, L.S.]

☛ ". . . the great fact now to be considered in this investigation, is, that this Anti-Constitutional Party [i.e., the Republicans, the Liberals of the day], in 1860, came into power upon this question in the Executive branch of the Federal Government. [Emphasis added, L.S.]

"This is the state of things which produced so much excitement and apprehension in the popular mind of the Southern States at that time. This Anti-Slavery Party had not only succeeded in getting a majority of the Northern States to openly violate their Constitutional faith in the avowed breach of the Compact, as stated; but had succeeded in electing a President and Vice President pledged to principles which were not only at war with the domestic Institutions of the States of the South, but which must inevitably, if carried out, ultimately lead to the absorption of all power in the Central Government, and end sooner or later in Absolutism or Despotism. These were the principles then brought into conflict, which, as stated, resulted in the conflict of arms. [Emphasis added, L.S.]

"The Seceding States feeling no longer bound by a Compact which had been so openly violated, and a majority of their people being deeply impressed with the conviction that the whole frame-work of the Constitution would be overthrown by this Party which would soon have control of the Executive Department of the Government, determined to withdraw from the Union, for the very reasons which had induced them to enter it in the beginning. Seven of these States, South Carolina, Georgia, Florida, Alabama, Mississippi, Louisiana, and Texas, did withdraw. Conventions of their people, regularly called by the proper authorities in each of these States respectively—Conventions representing the Sovereignty of the States similar in all respects to those which by Ordinances had ratified the Constitution of the United States—passed Ordinances resuming the Sovereign Powers therein delegated. These were the Secession Ordinances. . . . These Conventions also appointed Delegates, to meet in Montgomery, Alabama, on the 4th of February, 1861, with a view to form a new Confederation among themselves, upon the same essential basis of the Constitution of the United States. [Emphasis added, L.S.]

"It was not in opposition to the principles of that Government that they withdrew from it. They quit the Union to save the principles of the Constitution, and to perpetuate, on this Continent, the liberties which it was intended to secure and establish. Mr. [James] Buchanan was then President of the United States. He held that the Federal Government had no power to coerce a Seceding State to remain in the Union, but, strangely enough, at the same time held, that no State could rightfully withdraw from the Union. Mr. Lincoln came into power on the 4th of March, 1861. He held that the Federal Government did possess the Constitutional Power to maintain the Union of States by force, and it was in the maintenance of these views, the war was inaugurated by him."[152] [Emphasis added, L.S.]

Anti-South proponents, pro-North writers, and Liberals in general have long put forth the notion that the South started the American "Civil War." "Did not Confederate General Pierre G. T. Beauregard in command of the Confederate forces, so-called, at Charleston, South Carolina, fire upon Fort Sumter in that Harbor?" they ask. "Did he not compel Union Major Robert Anderson, the United States officer in command of that Fort, to capitulate and surrender? Was it not this outrage upon the American flag that caused such deep and universal excitement and indignation throughout the entire North? Was it not this that caused the great meetings in New York, Boston and every Northern city? How can one maintain in the face of these notorious facts, that the war was begun by Mr. Lincoln, or the Federal authorities? Is it not as plain as day that the Insurgents, or Confederates launched this war?" Stephens knew the truth:

☛ "My whole argument is based upon facts, and upon facts that can never be erased or obliterated. It is a fact that the first gun was fired by the Confederates. It is a fact that General Beauregard did, on the 12th of April, 1861, bombard Fort Sumter, before any blow had actually been struck by the Federal authorities. That is not disputed at all. That is a fact which I have no disposition to erase or obliterate in any way. That is a great truth which will live forever. But did the firing of the first gun, or the reduction of Fort Sumter inaugurate or begin the war? That is a question to be first solved, before we can be agreed upon the fact as to who inaugurated the war; and in solving this question, you must allow me to say that in personal or national conflicts, it is not he who strikes the first blow, or fires the first gun that inaugurates or begins the conflict. [English historian Henry] Hallam has well said that 'the aggressor in a war (that is, he who begins it,) is not the first who uses force, but the first who renders force necessary.' [Emphasis added, L.S.]

"Which side, according to this high authority, (that only announces the common sentiments of mankind,) was the aggressor in this instance? Which side was it that provoked and rendered the first blow necessary? The true answer to that question will settle the fact as to which side began the war.

"*I maintain that it was inaugurated and begun, though no blow had been struck, when the hostile [U.S.] fleet, styled the 'Relief Squadron,' with eleven ships, carrying two hundred and eighty-five guns and two thousand four hundred men, was sent out from New York and Norfolk, with orders from the authorities at Washington, to reenforce Fort Sumter peaceably, if permitted—'but forcibly if they must.'* [Emphasis added, L.S.]

"*The war was then and there inaugurated and begun by the authorities at Washington. General Beauregard did not open fire upon Fort Sumter until this fleet was, to his knowledge, very near the harbor of Charleston, and until he had inquired of Major Anderson, in command of the Fort, whether he would engage to take no part in the expected blow, then coming down upon him from the approaching fleet. Francis W. Pickens, Governor of South Carolina, and General Beauregard, had both been notified that the fleet was coming, and of its objects, by a messenger from the authorities at Washington. This notice, however, was not given until it was near its destination. When Major Anderson, therefore, would make no such promise, it became necessary for General Beauregard to strike the first blow, as he did; otherwise the forces under his command might have been exposed to two fires at the same time—one in front, and the other in the rear.*"[153] [Emphasis added, L.S.]

☛ "To understand this fully, let us see how matters stood in Charleston Harbor at the time.

"The Confederate States, then seven in number, had, as stated, all passed Ordinances of Secession. All of them, in regularly constituted Conventions, had withdrawn all their Sovereign powers previously delegated to the United States. They had formed a new Confederation, with a regularly constituted Government, at Montgomery, Alabama, *as they had a perfect right to do*, if our past conclusions were correct, and these [no truthful person can] . . . assail. This new Confederation had sent a [peace] commission to the [Yankee] authorities at Washington . . . to settle all matters amicably and peacefully. *War was by no means the wish or desire of the [Confederate] authorities at Montgomery*. Very few of the public men in the Seceding States even expected war. All of them, it is true, held themselves in readiness for it, if it should be forced upon them against their wishes and most earnest protestations. This is abundantly and conclusively apparent from the speeches and addresses of their leading public men at the time. It is apparent from the resolutions of the State Legislatures, and the State Conventions, before, and in their acts of Secession. It is apparent and manifest from their acts in their new Confederation at Montgomery. It is apparent from the inaugural address of [Confederate] President [Jefferson] Davis. *It is apparent from the appointment of commissioners to settle all matters involved in the separation from their former Confederates honorably, peaceably, amicably, and justly. It is apparent and manifest from every act that truly indicates the objects and motives of men, or from which their real aims can be justly arrived at. Peace not only with the States from which they had separated, but peace with all the world, was the strong desire of the Confederate States.* [Emphasis added, L.S.]

"It was under these circumstances, that the Confederate commissioners were given to understand, that Fort Sumter would be peacefully evacuated. An assurance to this effect was given, though in an informal manner, by Mr. [William H.] Seward, the Secretary of State under Mr. Lincoln. *This pledge was most strangely violated by sending the armed squadron, as stated, to re-enforce and provision the Fort.* The information that this fleet had put to sea with such orders, reached General Beauregard, when it was already near the offing, as I have stated. He immediately communicated the fact, by telegraph, to the [Confederate] authorities at Montgomery [Alabama]. In reply, he received this order from the Secretary of War of the Confederate States Government [Leroy P. Walker]:

> 'If you have no doubt of the authorized character of the agent who communicated to you the intention of the Washington Government to supply Fort Sumter by force, you will at once demand its evacuation; and if this is refused, proceed in such manner as you may determine, to reduce it.'

"Accordingly, on the 11th of April, [Confederate] General Beauregard made a demand on [U.S.] Major [Robert] Anderson, in command of the Fort, for its evacuation.

"In reply Major Anderson stated:

> 'I have the honor to acknowledge the receipt of your communication demanding the evacuation of this Fort, and to say in reply thereto, that it is a demand with which I regret that my sense of honor and my obligation to my Government prevent my compliance.'

"To this he added, verbally, to the messenger: 'I will await the first shot, and, if you do not batter us to pieces, we will be starved out in a few days.'

"This written reply, as well as the verbal remark, were forthwith sent by General Beauregard to the [C.S.] Secretary of War [Walker] at Montgomery, who immediately returned the following response:

> 'Do not desire needlessly to bombard Fort Sumter. If Major Anderson will state the time at which, as indicated by himself, he will evacuate, and agree that, in the meantime, he will not use his guns against us, unless ours should be employed against Fort Sumter, you are authorized thus to avoid the effusion of blood. If this or its equivalent be refused, reduce the Fort, as your

judgment decides most practicable.'

"This was communicated to [U.S.] Major Anderson. He refused to comply with the terms. He would not consent to any such arrangement.

"Whereupon, [C.S.] General Beauregard opened fire on the Fort at 4:30, on the morning of the 12th of April. The fire was returned. The bombardment lasted for thirty-two hours, when Major Anderson agreed to capitulate. General Beauregard exhibited no less of the magnanimity of the true soldier in the terms of capitulation, than he had of high military skill and genius in forming his plans, and in their execution for the reduction of the Fort. The entire [U.S.] garrison numbering eighty in all, officers and men, was permitted to be marched out with their colors and music. They were permitted to salute their flag with fifty guns. All private as well as company property was also allowed to be taken by those to whom it belonged. These were the same terms that General Beauregard had offered on the 11th, before he opened fire. As Providence ordered it, not a life was lost in this most memorable and frightful combat. The firing on both sides, at some times, particularly at night, was represented by those who witnessed it, as both 'grand and terrific.'

"*This was the first blow. It is true, the first gun was fired on the Confederate side. That is fully admitted. But all the facts show that, if force was thus first used by them, it was so first used only, because it was rendered necessary in self-defence on the part of those thus using it, and so rendered necessary by the opposite side. This first use of force, therefore, under the circumstances, cannot, in fact, be properly and justly considered as the beginning of the war.* [Emphasis added, L.S.]

"What has been stated, also, shows how earnestly the [Confederate] authorities at Montgomery, had in every possible way, consistent with honor and safety, endeavored to avoid a collision of forces. *The whole question of the right or wrong, therefore, in striking this first blow, as well as the right or wrong of the war, depends upon the Constitutional points we have been discussing. If the Seceding States were right on these points, then this first blow was perfectly justifiable, even if it had not been given, as it was, to avert one then impending over them.*"[154] [Emphasis added, L.S.]

Stephens' liberal friends were quick to respond to the South's view concerning the start of Lincoln's War. "Did the Fort not belong to the United States?" they responded. "Was it not the property of the United States? Were not the officers and men in it attached to the service of the United States? What right, therefore, had Confederate General Beauregard, or any body else, to attempt to prevent the United States Government from provisioning the garrison then holding it, and reenforcing it, if they thought proper? Was it not the duty of Mr. Lincoln to do it, as well as, his right?" Stephens was ready with his usual well informed reply:

☛ "Not if South Carolina had the Sovereign right to demand the possession of the Fort. Rights, whether civil, moral, or political, never conflict. If South Carolina had this Sovereign right to demand the possession of the place, which was within her jurisdiction, then Mr. Lincoln could have had no right to continue to hold it against this demand; nor was it his duty, in any sense, to attempt, even, to provision it by force, under the circumstances. [Emphasis added, L.S.]

"The Fort was within the jurisdiction of South Carolina. It was built specially for her protection, and belonged to her in part as well as to the other States jointly. On the 11th of January, Governor [Francis W.] Pickens, in behalf of the Sovereign Rights of the State, demanded its possession of Major Anderson for the use of the State. On his refusal to deliver it up, the Governor immediately sent I. W. Hayne, the Attorney General of the State, to Washington, and made a like demand for its possession of Mr. [James] Buchanan, the [U.S.] President, alleging that the possession of this Fort was necessary for the safety of the State for whose protection it had been erected. In this letter, Governor Pickens also stated, that a full valuation of the property would be accounted for, on settlement of the relations of South Carolina with the United States. [Emphasis added, L.S.]

"This whole question, relating to the right in this matter, and the side on which the right existed, depends, as I have said, upon the correctness of our conclusions on the points discussed. *If South Carolina, after the resumption of her delegated powers, was a separate, Sovereign State (which is one of our established truths), then, of course, she had a perfect right to demand the possession of any landed property whatever, lying within the limits of her jurisdiction, if she deemed it of importance for her public use and benefit.* This perfect right so to do, was subject to but one limitation, and that was the moral obligation to pay a fair and just compensation for the property so demanded for public use. There can be no question of the correctness of this principle. It is the foundation of the great right of Eminent domain, which ever accompanies Sovereignty. We have seen that this right of Eminent domain was never parted with by her, even under the Constitution. *South Carolina, then, even before Secession, and while she held herself to be bound by the Constitution, had a perfect right to demand of the United States Government the possession of this identical property, on paying a just compensation for it, if she had deemed it essential for her public interests.* This Fort never could have been erected on her soil without her consent. . . . The title, therefore, of the United States to the land on which Fort Sumter was built, was in no essential respect different from the title of any other land-holder in the State. The tenure by which the United States claimed and held this property, differed in no essential respect from the tenure by which every other land-owner held similar property in the State; nor was this property of the United States, so purchased and held under grant from South Carolina, any less subject to the right of Eminent domain on the part of the State, than any other lands lying within her limits. If this was so even before Secession, (and no one can successfully assail the position,) then how much more clearly this right (by virtue of the principle of Eminent domain,) to demand the possession of this property for public use, for her own protection, appears after she had expressly resumed the exercise of all of her Sovereign powers? *This right to demand the possession of this Fort, therefore, being unquestionably perfect in her as a Sovereign State after Secession, whether it was before or not, she had transferred to the Confederate States. Hence, their right to demand the evacuation of Fort Sumter, was perfect, viewed either morally, or politically.*"[155] [Emphasis added, L.S.]

☛ "The Confederate States had offered to come to a fair and just settlement with the United States, as to the value of this property, as well as all other public property belonging to all the States in common, at the time of their separation. This Fort, as well as all else that belonged to the United States, belonged in part to these seven Seceded States. They constituted seven of the United States, to which all this joint property belonged. All the Forts which lay within the limits of the Seceded States, had been turned over by these States, respectively, to the Confederacy. . . . *The Confederate States, therefore, through their authorities, had a right to demand, and take possession of all of these Forts, so lying within their limits, for their own public use, upon paying a just compensation for them to their former associates of the United States, who still adhered to that Union.* These principles cannot be assailed. *The offer so to pay whatever should be found to be due upon a general and just account, had been made. Mr. Lincoln, therefore, had no right under the circumstances, to hold any of these Forts by force, after the demand for the possession had been made; much less was it his duty either morally, or politically, when it was known that the attempt would inevitably lead to a war between the States. This is my answer to [the Liberals'] . . . property view.*"[156] [Emphasis added, L.S.]

☛ ". . . I do stand upon facts, and these are the incontestable facts of this case, which will forever perpetuate the truth of my assertion, that *upon the head of the Federal Government will forever rest the inauguration of this most terrible war which did ensue.* [Emphasis added, L.S.]

"No part of its responsibility rests upon the Southern States. They were the aggressors in no instance. They were ever true to their plighted faith under the Constitution. No instance of a breach of its mutual covenants can be ever laid to their charge. The open and palpable breach was committed by a number of their Northern Confederates [i.e., Yankee comrades]. No one can deny this. Those States at the North, which were untrue to their Constitutional engagements, claimed powers not delegated, and *elected a Chief Magistrate pledged to carry out principles openly in defiance of the decision of the highest Judicial Tribunal known to the Constitution.* [Emphasis added, L.S.]

"Their policy tended inevitably to a Centralized Despotism. It was under these circumstances that Secession was resorted to, as before stated; and, then, the war was begun and waged by the North to prevent the exercise of this Right. All that the Southern States did, was in defence, even in their firing the first gun."[157] [Emphasis added, L.S.]

☛ "[Here is how the Northern States repudiated, and thus violated, their constitutional obligations.] *They did what I say by passing State laws—'Personal Liberty Bills,' so-called—which effectively prevented the execution of that clause of the Constitution which provided for the rendition of fugitives from service.* Several of these States also refused to deliver fugitives from justice, when the crime charged was that of stealing or enticing away any person owing service to another. For, besides their personal liberty acts, which nullified, in the language of Mr. [Daniel] Webster, that provision of the Constitution for the rendition of slaves, the Governors of Maine, New York, and Ohio, had refused to deliver up fugitives from justice, who had been charged with a breach of the laws of the Southern States, in matters relating to the status of the Black race. [Emphasis added, L.S.]

". . . as to [this] . . . fact, there can be no doubt. Here, for instance, is the law of Vermont upon the subject.

> Every person who may have been held as a slave, who shall come or who may be brought into this State, with the consent of his or her alleged master or mistress, or who shall come or be brought, or shall be in this State, shall be free.
>
> Every person who shall hold, or attempt to hold, in this State, in slavery, as a slave, any free person, in any form or for any time, however short, under the pretence that such person is or has been a slave, shall, on conviction thereof, be imprisoned in the State prison for a term not less than five years, nor more than twenty, and be fined not less than one thousand dollars, nor more than ten thousand dollars.

"From this it clearly appears, that that State utterly refused to comply with her Constitutional obligations. She did more. She made it penal for any person to attempt to carry out this provision within her limits.

"The acts of Massachusetts were not dissimilar. . . . But it is useless to go through with them. I have a document here which renders all that unnecessary. It is the speech of Judge [Salmon P.] Chase before the Peace Congress, so-called, in February, 1861.

"So anxious were the people of the South to continue the Union under the Constitution, so desirous were they to stand by and perpetuate the principles of the Constitution, that even after South Carolina seceded, Virginia, the mother of States and Statesmen, she that took the lead in the separation from Great Britain and in the formation of our Federal Republic, as we have seen, made a great and strong effort still to save the Union by calling an informal Congress of the States to deliberate and see if no scheme could be devised to save the country from impending dangers and feuds. A number of States sent deputies to this Congress. Amongst these deputies was Judge Chase, then a distinguished leader of the [Liberal] Anti-Slavery Party, so-called, subsequently Mr. Lincoln's Secretary of Treasury, and now Chief Justice of the United States. *In that Peace Congress, so assembled, Judge Chase, on the 6th of February, 1861, in all the candor of his nature, declared most emphatically to the Southern members, that the Northern States never would fulfil that part of their Constitutional obligations.* [Emphasis added, L.S.] His whole speech is exceedingly interesting as one of the 'footprints' of the momentous events of that day. Let me call your special attention to these parts:

'The result of the national canvass which recently terminated in the election of Mr. Lincoln, has been spoken of by some as the effect of a sudden impulse, or of some irregular excitement of the popular mind; and it has been somewhat confidently asserted that, upon reflection and consideration, the hastily formed opinions which brought about that election will be changed. It has been said, also, that subordinate questions of local and temporary character have augmented the Republican vote, and secured a majority which could not have been obtained upon the national questions involved in the respective platforms of the parties which divide the country.

'I cannot take this view of the result of the Presidential election. I believe, and the belief amounts to absolute conviction, that the election must be regarded as a triumph of principles cherished in the hearts of the people of the Free States. These principles, it is true, were originally asserted by a small party only. But, after years of discussion, they have, by their own value, their own intrinsic soundness, obtained the deliberate and unalterable sanction of the people's judgment.

'*Chief among these principles is the Restriction of Slavery within State limits; not war upon Slavery within those limits, but fixed opposition to its extension beyond them. Mr. Lincoln was the candidate of the people opposed to the extension of Slavery.* We have elected him. *After many years of earnest advocacy and of severe trial, we have achieved the triumph of that principle.* By a fair and unquestionable majority, we have secured that triumph. Do you think we, who represent this majority, will throw it away? Do you think the people would sustain us if we undertook to throw it away? I must speak to you plainly, gentlemen of the South. It is not in my heart to deceive you. I therefore tell you explicitly, that if we of the North and West would consent to throw away all that has been gamed in the recent triumph of our principles, the people would not sustain us, and so the consent would avail you nothing. And I must tell you further, that *under no inducements, whatever, will we consent to surrender a principle which we believe to be so sound and so important as that of restricting Slavery within State limits.*' [Emphasis added, L.S.]

"This part of the speech was in reference to the claim of power on the part of the Federal Government to prevent the people of the Southern States from going into the common Territories with their slaves, and which power the Supreme Court had decided the General Government had no right to exercise. [Judge Chase] . . . here deliberately asserted, that the Party which elected Mr. Lincoln would not regard this decision of the Supreme Court. But then he goes on to say:

> 'Aside from the Territorial question—the question of Slavery outside of Slave States—I know of but one serious difficulty. I refer to the question concerning fugitives from service. The clause in the Constitution concerning this class of persons is regarded by almost all men, North and South, as a stipulation for the surrender to their masters of slaves escaping into Free States. The people of the Free States, however, who believe that Slave-holding is wrong, cannot and will not aid in the reclamation, and the stipulation becomes, therefore, a dead letter. You complain of bad faith, and the complaint is retorted by denunciations of the cruelty which would drag back to bondage the poor slave who has escaped from it. You, thinking Slavery right, claim the fulfilment of the stipulation; we, thinking Slavery wrong, cannot fulfil the stipulation without consciousness of participation in wrong. Here is a real difficulty, but it seems to me not insuperable. It will not do for us to say to you, in justification of non-performance, "the stipulation is immoral, and therefore we cannot execute it;" for you deny the immorality, and we cannot assume to judge for you. On the other hand, you ought not to exact from us the literal performance of the stipulation when you know that we cannot perform it without conscious culpability. A true solution of the difficulty seems to be attainable by regarding it as a simple case where a contract, from changed circumstances, cannot be fulfilled exactly as made. A court of equity in such a case decrees execution as near as may be. It requires the party who cannot perform to make compensation for non-performance. Why cannot the same principle be applied to the rendition of fugitives from service? We cannot surrender—but we can compensate. Why not then avoid all difficulties on all sides and show respectively good faith and good-will by providing and accepting compensation where masters reclaim escaping servants and prove their right of reclamation under the Constitution? Instead of a judgment for rendition, let there be a judgment for compensation, determined by the true value of the services, and let the same

judgment assure freedom to the fugitive. The cost to the National Treasury would be as nothing in comparison with the evils of discord and strife. All parties would be gainers.'

"Whatever may be thought of this as a proposed compromise to induce the Parties to remain in the Union, *no one can doubt its unequivocal declaration that the Non-Slave-holding States would not comply with their acknowledged obligations under the Constitution. It was a confession of one high in authority that that part of the Constitution was a dead letter, and, of course, if the Southern States would not agree to his offer, they were absolved from all further obligation to the Compact.* This is conclusive upon well settled principles of public law."[158] [Emphasis added, L.S.]

☛ "This declaration that the Northern States would not comply with their Constitutional obligations, bear in mind, was made by the Chancellor of the Exchequer, under Mr. Lincoln. He spoke for the President and his Party. He spoke for that [Liberal Northern] Party which, after the Southern States had seceded, in the House, passed this Resolution:

> Resolved, That as our country, and the very existence of the best government ever instituted by man, are imperilled by the most causeless and wicked rebellion that the world has seen, and believing, as we do, that the only hope of saving this country and preserving this Government is by the power of the sword, we are for the most vigorous prosecution of the war until the Constitution and laws shall be enforced and obeyed in all parts of the United States; and to that end we oppose any armistice, or intervention, or mediation, or proposition for peace from any quarter, so long as there shall be found a Rebel in arms against the Government; and we ignore all party names, lines, and issues, and recognize but two parties in this war—patriots and traitors.

"This Resolution passed the [U.S.] House, December 17, 1863, by a vote of ninety-four to sixty-five. The ninety-four votes all belonged to that [Liberal] party for which Judge [Salmon P.] Chase spoke.

"*Was there ever an instance in the history of the world of such inconsistency, or—no! I will withhold the word I was about to utter. But let me ask, if the Federal arms had been directed against those who resisted the enforcement of the Constitution and the laws of the United States, with the real purpose of preserving 'the best Government ever instituted by man,' was there a single one of those who voted for this Resolution, who would not justly have been the first subjects of slaughter? These are the men who still talk of 'loyal States!' Who still have so much to say of 'loyal men!' Was ever noble word, when properly applied, so prostituted, as this is in its present use by this class of boasting patriots?*"[159] [Emphasis added, L.S.]

☛ "*The Southern States were ever loyal and true to the Constitution. This I maintain as a great truth for history. The only true loyalty in this country is fidelity to the principles of the Constitution!* The openly 'disloyal,' or those avowedly untrue to the Constitution, were those [Liberals in the North] who instigated, inaugurated, and waged this most unrighteous war against their Confederate neighbors! If I express myself with too much fervor on this point, you will please excuse me. I do, however, but express the thorough convictions of my judgment."[160] [Emphasis added, L.S.]

Stephens never backed down from a debate over the Constitution, states' rights, slavery, secession, or the causes of Lincoln's War, and for good reason:

☛ "... there is nothing that [a Liberal] ... can say on any of these subjects, in accordance with truth and fact, which can ruffle me in the least. It is truth when told to one's disadvantage which generally ruffles temper the quickest. . . .

"In this case, I know there is no truth, that can hurt, and as for bare epithets, or declamation, after I have heard with perfect equanimity all that [Northern Liberals] Mr. [Joshua R.] Giddings, Mr. [Owen] Lovejoy, and Mr. [Charles] Sumner have said about 'Slavery,' 'the Slave Power,' the 'Slavery Oligarchy,' the 'Slave Driver,' etc., I can promise you, in advance, that nothing that [the Liberals] ... can say upon these subjects, or any other within the range of [these topics] ... will ruffle me in the least."[161]

20

THE TRUTH ABOUT AMERICAN SLAVERY

NINETEENTH-CENTURY LIBERALS HAD A LONG list of grievances against the South, nearly all of them based on faulty information that itself was derived from fictional anti-South wartime propaganda, or just as often, a simple misunderstanding of the facts. Victorian progressives were particularly bothered by an incident that occurred in 1844 in South Carolina, in which "colored Northern seamen" (i.e., free black sailors from Massachusetts) were imprisoned, and Yankee abolitionist-attorney Samuel Hoar (who traveled to South Carolina to contest the state's laws and "stir up ill blood") was prevented from investigating the matter. In this chapter Stephens examines and dispatches a number of these myths one by one, in particular the many fictions surrounding so-called Southern "slavery."

☛ ". . . first and foremost, let it be remembered that [even the most incorrigible big government Liberals and Centralists admit] . . . that Northern States did openly and avowedly disregard their obligations under the Constitution in the matter stated [earlier] by me. This we will, therefore, consider as an established fact. [Still, they] . . . admit its truth, but attempt to justify. We will now see how far the facts sustain [them] . . . in this attempt.

"The act of South Carolina referred to, which [they] . . . seem to think so clearly violated the Constitution of the United States, was not passed 'in the year 1835,' as Mr. [Horace] Greeley says, but on the 21st December, 1822. At least an act containing all [they] . . . complain of, was then passed by that State. It had, however, no such purpose or intent as [the Liberals] . . . seem to think. This was not its professed object, nor was it at all in violation of the

Constitution, according to a decision of the Supreme Court of the United States. . . . It was passed soon after an attempted insurrection by the Blacks in Charleston [South Carolina]. This attempted insurrection was in June 1822. It was supposed to have been instigated by that class of persons against whom the law was enacted; and it was only intended to secure the domestic peace and tranquillity of the State against the future schemes and mischievous operations of such foreign emissaries, not from the Northern States exclusively, but from all other countries, against the safety and welfare of the State. This, the State had a perfect right to do under the Constitution, as I shall clearly show.

"Here is the section of the act complained of. It is the third section of an act passed 21st December, 1822, entitled 'An Act for the better regulation and government of free negroes and persons of color, and for other purposes,' and is in these words:

> And be it further enacted by the authority aforesaid, That if any vessel shall come into any port or harbor of this State, from any other State or foreign port, having on board any free negroes, or persons of color, as cooks, stewards, mariners, or in any other employment on board said vessel, such free negroes, or persons of color shall be liable to be seized and confined in jail, until said vessel shall clear out and depart from this State; and that when said vessel is ready to sail, the captain of said vessel shall be bound to carry away the said free negro or person of color, and pay the expenses of his detention; and in case of his neglect or refusal so to do, he shall be liable to be indicted, and, on conviction thereof, shall be fined a sum not less than one thousand dollars, and imprisoned not less than two months; and such free negroes or persons of color shall be deemed and taken as absolute slaves, and sold in conformity to the provisions of the act passed on the twentieth day of December, one thousand eight hundred and twenty, aforesaid.

". . . I do not think that [this act] . . . violated the Constitution at all, nor did the Legislature of South Carolina so think. It is true, there were differences of opinion upon the subject, at the time, by eminent jurists both in and out of the State. The only way to settle the point was by judicial decision. In this way it was settled by the courts in South Carolina. Suits were brought by persons coming under its operation, and the Constitutionality of the act was sustained. But I do not rest, what I affirm of its Constitutionality, solely upon that adjudication. After that decision, the subject was brought to the attention of the Federal authorities at Washington [D.C.], both by a memorial from the commanders of American vessels, complaining of wrongs suffered by seamen under their charge, and by the British Minister, in behalf of like wrongs suffered by colored seamen, subjects of his Majesty, the King of England [George IV]. Let me [quote] . . . the letter of the British Minister to the Secretary of State

[George Canning] upon the subject. Here it is, dated Washington, February 15th, 1823. In it he says:

> 'It is my duty to bring under your notice an act lately passed by the Legislature of South Carolina, which cannot remain in force without exposing the vessels of his Majesty's subjects, entering the ports of that State, in prosecution of their lawful commerce, more especially such as are engaged in the colonial trade, to the treatment of the most grievous and extraordinary description.
>
> 'The accompanying transcript of the third section of the act, to which I refer, will make you acquainted with the particular nature of the grievance attendant on the enforcement of the law in question. I am confident that a mere perusal of the enactment will suffice to engage your interference for the purpose of securing his Majesty's subjects, when trading with this country, from the effects of its execution.
>
> 'One vessel, under the British flag, has already experienced a most reprehensible act of authority under the operation of this law; and if I abstain, for the present, from laying before you the particulars of the transaction, it is only in the persuasion that ample redress has, by this time, been obtained on the spot, at the requisition of his Majesty's consul, at Charleston, and that the interference of the General Government, in compliance with the representation which I have now the honor to address to you, will be so effectual as to prevent the recurrence of any such outrage in future.'

"Let us now go on with the subject and see how it ended.

"This letter of Mr. Canning, the British Minister, was submitted to the consideration of the [U.S.] Attorney-General by the Secretary of State, under instructions from the President. Mr. [William] Wirt, who, at that time, was the Attorney-General, gave it as his opinion that the act in question was in violation of the Constitution of the United States, but not upon the grounds [the Liberals] . . . maintain. That clause of the Constitution, to which [they] . . . refer, has no bearing upon the subject whatever, as we shall see. Mr. Wirt, however, held that it did violate that clause which gives Congress the power to regulate commerce as well as the clause relating to the Treaty power. His letter to the [U.S.] Secretary of State, giving this opinion, is dated the 8th of May, 1824, and in it he uses this language:

> 'All foreign and domestic vessels, complying with the requisitions prescribed by Congress, have a right to enter any port of the United States, and a right to remain there unmolested, in vessel and crew, for the peaceful purposes of commerce. No State can interdict a vessel which is about to enter her ports, in conformity with the laws of the United States, nor impose any restraint or embarrassment on such vessel in consequence of her having entered in

conformity with those laws. It seems very clear to me, that this section of the law of South Carolina is incompatible with the National Constitution, and the laws passed under it, and is therefore void. All nations in amity with the United States, have a right to enter the ports of the Union for the purpose of commerce, so long as, by the laws of the Union, commerce is permitted, and so far as it is permitted; and inasmuch as this section of the law of South Carolina is a restriction upon this commerce, it is incompatible with the rights of all nations which are in amity with the United States.

'There is another view of this subject. By the National Constitution, the power of making treaties with Foreign Nations, is given to the General Government, and the same Constitution declares that the treaties so made shall constitute a part of the Supreme Law of the land. The National Government has exercised this power, also, of making treaties. We have treaties subsisting with various nations, by which the commerce of such nations, with the United States, is expressly authorized, without any restriction as to the color of the crews by which it shall be carried on. We have such a treaty with Great Britain, as to which nation this question has arisen. This act of South Carolina forbids, or what is the same thing, punishes, what this treaty authorizes.

'I am of the opinion, that the section of the law under consideration is void, for being against the Constitution, treaties and laws of the United States, and incompatible with the rights of all nations in amity with the United States.'

"This opinion of the Attorney-General, under the direction of the President of the United States [James Monroe], was communicated by the Secretary of State to the Governor of South Carolina [John L. Wilson], under date the 6th of July, 1824, with the expression of a hope, on the part of the President, that 'the inconvenience complained of, would be remedied by the Legislature of the State of South Carolina itself.'

"The whole matter was subsequently submitted by the Governor to the Legislature, in a message, in which he put the right upon the grounds of 'police regulations,' and claimed that, 'under the Constitution, South Carolina had the right to interdict the entrance of such persons into her ports, whose organization of mind, habits, and associations rendered them peculiarly calculated to disturb the peace and tranquillity of the State, in the same manner as she could prohibit those afflicted with infectious disease to touch her shores.' 'The necessity of self-preservation,' said he, 'was alone to be determined by the power to be preserved; it, therefore, rested with those whose rights were to be affected to judge how long such laws should exist, as were enacted for the peace and security of the community.'

"The Legislature sustained the position of the Governor. This presented a new view of the subject; and so the matter rested for a time. If the British

Government took any further action on the subject, I am not aware of it. No case was carried to the Supreme Court of the United States under this act. But a case involving the same principle, arising under a law of the State of New York, passed in 1824, was carried up to that court, and the decision in it fully sustained the position of the Governor and Legislature of South Carolina upon this subject. This is the decision to which I refer as settling the question, and from which I now read. [According to the judge who delivered the opinion of the court:]

> 'This case comes before this court upon a certificate of division of the Circuit Court of the United States for the Southern District of New York.
> 'It was an action of debt brought in that court by the plaintiff, to recover of the defendant, as consignee of the ship called the *Emily*, the amount of certain penalties imposed by a statute of New York, passed February 11th, 1824; entitled, "An act concerning passengers in vessels coming to the port of New York."
> 'The statute, amongst other things, enacts, that every master or commander of any ship, or other vessel, arriving at the port of New York, from any country out of the United States, or from any other of the United States than the State of New York, shall, within twenty-four hours after the arrival of such ship or vessel in the said port, make a report in writing, on oath or affirmation, to the major of the city of New York, or, in case of his sickness, or absence, to the recorder of said city, of the name, place of birth, and last legal settlement, age and occupation, of every person who shall have been brought as a passenger in such ship or vessel, on her last voyage from any country out of the United States into the port of New York, or any of the United States, and from any of the United States other than the State of New York, to the city of New York, and of all passengers who shall have lauded, or been suffered or permitted to land, from such ship, or vessel, at any place, during such her last voyage, or have been put on board, or suffered, or permitted to go on board of any other ship or vessel, with the intention of proceeding to the said city, under the penalty on such master or commander, and the owner or owners, consignee or consignees of such ship or vessel, severally and respectively, of seventy-five dollars for every person neglected to be reported as aforesaid, and for every person whose name, place of birth, and last legal settlement, age, and occupation, or either or any of such particulars, shall be falsely reported as aforesaid, to be sued for and recovered as therein provided.'

"From this statement of the case by the court, it clearly appears that the principle involved in the New York law was identical with the principle involved in the South Carolina law, so far as concerned the Constitutional power to pass it, and that is the point we are now upon. On this point, and in direct reply to Mr. Wirt's view, the court say:

> 'We shall not enter into any examination of the question, whether the power to regulate commerce, be or be not exclusive of the States, because the opinion which we have formed renders it unnecessary: in other words, we are of opinion that the act is not a regulation of commerce, but of police; and that being thus considered, it was passed in the exercise of a power which rightfully belonged to the States.
>
> 'That the State of New York possessed power to pass this law before the adoption of the Constitution of the United States, might probably be taken as a truism, without the necessity of proof. But as it may tend to present it in a clearer point of view, we will quote a few passages from a standard writer upon public law, showing the origin and character of this power.
>
>> "The Sovereign may forbid the entrance of his Territory, either to foreigners in general, or in particular cases, or to certain persons, or for certain particular purposes, according as he may think it advantageous to the State.
>>
>> "Since the lord of the Territory may, whenever he thinks proper, forbid its being entered, he has, no doubt, a power to annex what conditions he pleases, to the permission to enter.'"

"We have seen that this Right of Eminent Domain here referred to still resides in the States under the Constitution. But to proceed with the decision:

> 'The power then of New York to pass this law having undeniably existed at the formation of the Constitution, the simple inquiry is, whether by that instrument it was taken from the States, and granted to Congress; for if it were not, it yet remains with them.
>
> 'If, as we think, it be a regulation, not of commerce, but police; then it is not taken from the States. To decide this, let us examine its purpose, the end to be attained, and the means of its attainment.
>
> 'It is apparent, from the whole scope of the law, that the object of the Legislature was, to prevent New York from being burdened by an influx of persons brought thither in ships, either from foreign countries, or from any other of the States; and for that purpose a report was required of the names, places of birth, etc., of all passengers, that the necessary steps might be taken by the city authorities, to prevent them from becoming chargeable as paupers.
>
> 'Now, we hold that both the end and the means here used, are within the competency of the States, etc. . . . The *Federalist*, in the 45th number, speaking of this subject, says:
>
>> "the powers reserved to the several States, will extend to all the objects, which in the ordinary course of affairs, concern the lives, liberties, and

properties of the people; and the internal order, improvement, and prosperity of the State."

'And this Court, in the case of *Gibbons* vs. *Ogden*, . . . which will hereafter be more particularly noticed, in speaking of the inspection laws of the States, say: they form a portion of that immense mass of legislation which embraces everything within the Territory of a State, not surrendered to the General Government, all which can be most advantageously exercised by the States themselves. Inspection laws, quarantine laws, health laws of every description, as well as laws for regulating the internal commerce of a State, etc.

'Now, if the act in question be tried by reference to the delineation of power laid down in the preceding quotations, it seems to us that we are necessarily brought to the conclusion, that it falls within its limits. There is no aspect in which it can be viewed in which it transcends them. If we look at the place of its operation, we find it to be within the territory, and, therefore, within the jurisdiction of New York. If we look at the person on whom it operates, he is found within the same Territory and jurisdiction. If we look at the persons for whose benefit it was passed, they are the people of New York, for whose protection and welfare the Legislature of that State are authorized and in duty bound to provide.

'If we turn our attention to the purpose to be attained, it is to secure that very protection, and to provide for that very welfare. If we examine the means by which these ends are proposed to be accomplished, they bear a just, natural, and appropriate relation to those ends.

'. . . There is, then, no collision between the law in question, and the acts of Congress just commented on; and, therefore, if the State law were to be considered as partaking of the nature of a commercial regulation; it would stand the test of the most rigid scrutiny, if tried by the standard laid down in the reasoning of the court, quoted from the case of Gibbons against Ogden.

'But we do not place our opinion on this ground. We choose rather to plant ourselves on what we consider impregnable positions. They are these: That *a State has the same undeniable and unlimited jurisdiction over all persons and things, within its territorial limits, as any foreign nation; where that jurisdiction is not surrendered or restrained by the Constitution of the United States. That, by virtue of this, it is not only the right, but the bounden and solemn duty of a State, to advance the safety, happiness and prosperity of its people, and to provide for its general welfare, by any and every act of legislation, which it may deem to be conducive to these ends; where the power over the particular subject, or the manner of its exercise is not surrendered or restrained, in the manner just stated. That all those powers which relate to merely municipal legislation, or what may, perhaps, more properly be called internal police, are not thus surrendered or restrained; and that, consequently, in relation to these, the authority of a State is complete, unqualified, and exclusive.* [Emphasis added, L.S.]

'We are aware, that it is at all times difficult to define any subject with proper precision and accuracy; if this be so in general, it is emphatically so in relation to a subject so diversified and multifarious as the one which we are now considering.

'If we were to attempt it, we should say, that every law came within this description which concerned the welfare of the whole people of a State, or any individual within it; whether it related to their rights, or their duties; whether it respected them as men, or as citizens of the State; whether in their public or private relations; whether it related to the rights of persons, or of property, of the whole people of a State, or of any individual within it; and whose operation was within the territorial limits of the State, and upon the persons and things within its jurisdiction. But we will endeavor to illustrate our meaning rather by exemplification, than by definition. No one will deny, that a State has a right to punish any individual found within its jurisdiction, who shall have committed an offence within its jurisdiction, against its criminal laws. We speak not here of foreign ambassadors, as to whom the doctrines of public law apply. We suppose it to be equally clear, that a State has as much right to guard, by anticipation, against the commission of an offence against its laws, as to inflict punishment upon the offender after it shall have been committed. The right to punish or to prevent crime, does in no degree depend upon the citizenship of the party who is obnoxious to the law. The alien who shall just have set his foot upon the soil of the State, is just as subject to the operation of the law, as one who is a native citizen. In this very case, if either the master, or one of the crew of the [ship] *Emily*, or one of the passengers who were landed, had, the next hour after they came on shore, committed an offence, or indicated a disposition to do so; he would have been subject to the criminal law of New York, either by punishment for the offence committed, or by prevention from its commission where good ground for apprehension was shown, by being required to enter into a recognizance with surety, either to keep the peace, or be of good behavior, as the case might be; and if he failed to give it, by liability to be imprisoned in the discretion of the competent authority.

'. . . We think it as competent and as necessary for a State to provide precautionary measures against the moral pestilence of paupers, vagabonds, and possibly convicts; as it is to guard against the physical pestilence, which may arise from unsound and infectious articles imported, or from a ship, the crew of which may be laboring under an infectious disease.'

"This decision of the Supreme Court covered every principle of Constitutional power involved in the act of South Carolina as a police regulation of the State, and so fully and clearly sustained the position of the Governor and Legislature of that State in that view of it, that nothing further was done by the Federal Authorities upon the subject. You see it fully meets and completely answers your views as to the rights of the citizens of Massachusetts in South Carolina, under the Constitution. When they are in South Carolina, they are upon the same footing as the citizens of that State, so far as concerns the criminal law of the State; and that imprisonment may be as rightfully resorted to, to prevent the commission of crime, as to punish it after its commission.

"But besides this, I refer [the Liberals] . . . to what Justice [John] McLean, who was well known to be no sympathizer with Slavery, said, in his separate opinion delivered from the Bench of the Supreme Court of the United States, in the case of *Groves* vs. *Slaughter*, as late as 1841. In that opinion, this eminent jurist said:

> 'Each State has a right—to guard its citizens against the inconvenience and dangers of a slave population. The right to exercise this power by a State is higher and deeper than the Constitution. The evil involves the prosperity, and may endanger the existence of a State. Its power to guard against, or to remedy the evil, rests upon the law of self-preservation; a law vital to every community, and especially to every Sovereign State.'

"It very clearly appears from these decisions of the Supreme Court of the United States, that South Carolina acted strictly within her Constitutional rights, in the passage of the law in question. There was no violation of the Constitution by it, either intentionally or otherwise. This is not pretended to be the case in reference to those acts of the Legislatures of the Northern States to which I have referred. [My Liberal friends] . . . admit that those States did intentionally and avowedly violate their obligations under the Constitution; while South Carolina not only did not avow, nor intend any such thing, but stands perfectly justified in all she did in this matter by the judgment of the highest judicial Tribunal of the land!

"What becomes, now, of [the Liberals'] . . . plea of justification, so far as concerns this act of South Carolina? Not being sustained by the facts, it cannot be permitted to go with the confession of guilty, on the part of the Northern States referred to, even in mitigation of the great wrong established by that confession. Moreover, South Carolina did not object to a judicial judgment upon her acts. *The mission of Mr. [Samuel] Hoar was not intended for the purpose of obtaining an adjudication by the Supreme Court of the United States on this law. He went down to South Carolina on a mission really of strife. It was to stir up ill blood.* If any persons aggrieved under the operation of this act, or any other law of South Carolina, had been disposed to seek redress by suits at law, actions could have been brought, either in the State Courts or the Federal Courts, as well without his mission as with it. By the terms of this law, as appears in another part of it, a public registry was required to be made of all persons so put in custody or imprisoned, which was open to the inspection of any and every person. [Emphasis added, L.S.]

"Whether the action of the people of Charleston towards Mr. Hoar (which, by-the-by, was nothing but an urgent request by some of the most respectable citizens for him to leave, lest his presence on such a mission might excite a mob,) was politic or not, is not the question. The question we have in hand is, whether the act of the Legislature alluded to was, or was not Constitutional? We have seen that it was; and that the plighted faith of South Carolina was in no way sullied or tarnished by its adoption. So [the Liberals] . . . will have to present some other, and very different instance, before [they] . . . can make good [their] . . . assault upon my position, that no State of the South was ever untrue to her plighted faith under the Constitution. I repeat, no instance of the kind can be named."[162]

Stephens here takes aim at the rank hypocrisy of the Northern states:
☛ "The proverb, about casting stones, is a very good one, when properly applied. In this instance, however, the whole force of its logic, as well as its rhetoric, recoils with damaging effect upon him who uses it. *These Northern States referred to, were the dwellers in glass houses, who charged the Southern States with violating the Constitution when they were the only violators of it themselves.* [Emphasis added, L.S.]

"But [my Liberal friends from the North ask] . . . if Judge [Salmon P.] Chase's proposition was not a fair and just one for the admitted breach of the Compact on their part; and even [assume] . . . to think that I could not but have so considered it, as well as all other fair-minded men everywhere. To this, it would be enough for me to say, that there was no obligation on the part of the Southern States to accept it, even if they had thought it fair and just. It was not in accordance with the provisions of the Compact. It could in effect be considered in no other light than a proposition to amend the Constitution in this particular. In this view, it was certainly a matter of discretion entirely with them, whether they would agree to it or not. In the exercise of this discretion, they did not agree to it. How far they were influenced by the consideration that a people, who would not stand to the terms of one Compact, might not stand to those of another, I do not know. It is quite sufficient that they did not agree to it, and they had a perfect right to refuse so to do.

"How then stood the political as well as moral aspect of the question? *Politically, this failure to perform their obligations under the existing Compact, as it was, on the part of the Northern States, according to the universal principles of public law, totally absolved their Southern Confederates from any further obligations under it.* This principle of public law cannot be denied. If that [Liberal] Party, then controlling these derelict [Northern] States, from an enlightenment of their consciences, had been brought to see that this Compact of their Fathers was founded in sin, or, in other words, if they had come to see that the Constitution, as it was made, and as it then stood, was but '*a Covenant with Death and an Agreement with Hell,*' as many of the leading men of this party declared, and as nearly all really believed, not excepting even the Judge himself, (as we may legitimately infer from his remarks,) what, then, was their proper course as a truly moral and upright people? Was it not peacefully to withdraw from an alliance founded upon such '*a summation of all iniquity,*' or at least to permit those peacefully to withdraw with whom they were bound in stipulations, which they confessed they could not in conscience perform? Ought they not to have agreed to separate in peace? If the Compact was in truth so founded in sin, in violation of the laws of God, it was utterly void from the beginning. No rights or obligations could arise under it on either side. The parties were remitted to their original positions. They stood towards each other just as they did before it was made. I fully agree to the doctrine of a higher law—that Supreme law of right, ordained by the Most High, which governs the moral universe, and to which all human laws, as well as Compacts, must conform. [Emphasis added, L.S.]

"*But what sort of Christian consciences must an intelligent world think those people possessed, who could and did swear to support and defend a Compact at the same time they held it to be so great a sin in the sight of men and of God? Who refused to perform an acknowledged obligation, and yet in the face of this refusal, insisted upon holding on to all the advantages of the Compact, to them, even at the point of the bayonet? This seems to me to be a strange enlightenment of conscience! Such an enlightenment it seems to me could not have come from studying the precepts of Him [Jesus] who said, 'as ye would that men should do to you, do ye also to them likewise.*' This does not imply, much less enjoin, that there should be no distinctions in society, and no differences between the relations of the various members of it towards each other. It clearly means that all, of every class and condition in life, at all times and under all circumstances, should do unto others as they would have others do unto them, on a reversal of relative positions. In this sense, it is equally applicable to the high and the low, the rich and the poor, the judge and the convict, the ruler and the ruled, the parent and the child, the guardian and the ward, the teacher and the pupil, the employer and the laborer, the master and the slave!

"This is the whole of it, and upon this view of this precept, however unholy the war with Mexico may have been, in the estimation [of the Liberals], . . . or any one else, he must permit me to say that this war, so waged under the circumstances as stated by himself, must, by all right-minded men, ever be considered infinitely more wicked, and much more horribly sinful, if the doctrines of Christ are to be taken as the standard.

"But, besides this, I say to him that I did not consider Judge Chase's proposition either fair or just. There was no such change of circumstances, as he stated. The relations of the Parties to the Compact remained just as they were left when it was made; nor did he propose an equitable equivalent for its breach. The penalty for a failure to perform, was under his proposition, not to fall exclusively upon the delinquents. The money equivalent was to come out of the common Treasury, and to be equally contributed by the faithful and the faithless. It was, therefore, not just [fair] either to the Southern States, or those Northern States who were true to their engagements."[163]

Stephens was often called upon, by the uninformed, to defend and explain so-called "slavery" as it existed in the Old South:

☛ "One digression I am here compelled to make here [concerns various anti-South remarks made by my Liberal friends regarding Slavery]. . . . [They speak] . . . of Slavery as it existed with us, as a 'sin in the sight of men and in the sight of God'—as the 'summation of all iniquity!' I stated in the outset that the right or wrong of this Institution did not legitimately come within the purview of our present discussion. That related exclusively to the rightful powers of the Federal Government over it, to interfere with it in any way, except as is expressly provided in the Compact. But these remarks of [the Liberals] . . . demand notice. They require a reply. In replying briefly as possible, but pointedly, [concerning Slavery] I have to say I know of but one sure standard in determining what is, and what is not sin or sinful. That standard is the written law of God as prescribed in the Old and the New Testament. By that standard the relation of master and slave, even in a much more abject condition than existed with us, is not founded in sin. *Abram, afterwards called Abraham, the father of the faithful, with whom the Divine Covenant was made for man's salvation and the redemption of the world from the dominion of sin, was a slave-holder.* He was enjoined to impart the seal of this everlasting covenant not only to those who were born in his house; but to those who were 'bought with his money.' It was into his bosom, in Heaven, that the poor man, who died at the rich man's gate, was borne by angels, according to the Parable of the Saviour. *Job certainly was one of the best men we read of in the Bible. He was a large slave-holder. So, too, were Isaac and Jacob and all the Patriarchs. The great moral law which defines sin, the Ten Commandments given to Moses on Mount Sinai, written on stone by the finger of God himself, expressly recognizes Slavery, and enjoins certain duties of masters towards their slaves. The chosen people of God, by the Levitical Law, proclaimed under divine sanction, were authorized to hold slaves—not of their own race—(of these they were to hold bondmen for a term of years)—but of the Heathen around them—of these they were authorized to buy slaves 'bondmen and bondwomen,' for life, who were to be to them 'an inheritance' and 'possession forever.'* [Emphasis added, L.S.]

"Slavery existed when the gospel was preached by Christ and his Apostles, and where they preached it was all around them. And though the Scribes and Pharisees were denounced by Christ for their hypocrisy and robbing widows' houses and divers other sins, yet not a word did he utter, as far as we are informed, against slaveholding. On the contrary, he said he had not found so great faith in all Israel, as in the slave-holding Centurion! Was he truckling to [i.e., flattering] a Slavery Oligarchy when he made this declaration? *In no place in the New Testament is the relation of master and slave spoken of as sinful.* Several of the Apostles alluded to it; but none of them, not one of them, condemned it as sinful in itself, or as violative of the laws of God, or even of Christian duty. *They enjoin the relative duties of both masters and slaves.* Paul sent a fugitive slave, Onesimus, back to Philemon his master. He did not consider it any violence to his conscience to do this, even when he was under no stipulated obligation to do it. [Emphasis added, L.S.]

"*He frequently alludes to Slavery in his letters to the Churches, but in no case speaks of it as sinful.* What he says in one of these epistles, I must read to you. It is the first five verses of chapter vi. of the First Epistle to Timothy:

    1. 'Let as many servants [slaves] as are under the yoke count their own masters worthy of all honor, that the name of God and his doctrine be not blasphemed.
    2. 'And they that have believing masters,' (according to the [Liberal's] . . . idea, there could be no such thing as a Slave-holding believer, but so did not think Paul,) 'let them not despise them, because they are brethren; but rather do them service, because they are faithful and beloved, partakers of the benefit. These things teach and exhort.
    3. 'If any man teach otherwise, and consent not to wholesome words, even the words of our Lord Jesus Christ, and to the doctrine which is according to godliness;
    4. 'He is proud, knowing nothing, but doting about questions and strifes of words, whereof cometh envy, strife, railings, evil surmisings,
    5. 'Perverse disputings of men of corrupt minds, and destitute of the truth, supposing that gain is godliness: from such withdraw thyself.'

"Can we suppose that Paul would have so written, if he had considered that there was anything morally wrong in the relation of master and slave, much less if he had looked upon it as the 'summation of all iniquity;' and if our Ministers of the Gospel did continue to teach the same doctrine, to enjoin the same duties upon master and slave, can it be justly said that they thereby 'desecrated the Temples of the Living God?' If they withdrew themselves from those who taught otherwise, and whose doctrines brought 'envy, strife, railings,' and finally war, did they not follow the advice of the great Apostle of the Gentiles, and likewise the words, as he affirms, of our Lord Jesus Christ, 'that the name of God and his doctrine be not blasphemed?'

"It is not, as I have said, within the purview of this discussion, to speak of the right or wrong of Slavery morally, or the evils of the Institution politically, arising from an abuse of power under it, any more than it is to speak of the institution of marriage, or the relation of parent and child, as it is regulated in any State. These are matters which under the Federal [Confederate] system belong exclusively to the several States. What I have here said in reply to [the accusations of the Liberals] . . . is therefore a digression. From this I will now return, with but one single additional remark upon what [the Liberals have] . . . said on this point; and that is this: To maintain that Slavery is in itself sinful, in the face of all that is said and written in the Bible upon the subject, with so many sanctions of the relation by the Deity himself, does seem to me to be little short of blasphemous! *It is a direct imputation upon the wisdom and justice, as well as the declared ordinances of God, as they are written in the inspired oracles, to say nothing of their manifestation in the universe around us.* [Emphasis added, L.S.]

"James H. Hammond, of South Carolina, one of the most intellectual men this country ever produced, when Governor of his State, in 1844, in reply to a communication he received from the Free Church of Glasgow, Scotland, upon the subject of Slavery, amongst other things, said:

> 'Your memorial, like all that have been sent to me, denounces Slavery in the severest terms; as 'traversing every law of nature, and violating the most sacred domestic relations, and the primary rights of man.' You and your Presbytery are Christians. You profess to believe, and no doubt do believe, that the laws laid down in the Old and New Testaments for the government of man, in his moral, social and political relations, were all the direct revelation of God himself. *Does it never occur to you, that in anathematizing Slavery, you deny this divine sanction of those laws, and repudiate both Christ and Moses; or charge God with downright crime, in regulating and perpetuating Slavery in the Old Testament, and the most criminal neglect, in not only not abolishing, but not even reprehending it, in the New? If these Testaments came from God, it is impossible that Slavery can 'traverse the laws of nature, or violate the primary rights of man.'* What those laws and rights really are, mankind have not agreed. But they are clear to God; and it is blasphemous for any of His creatures to set up their notions of them in opposition to His immediate and acknowledged Revelation. Nor does our system of Slavery outrage the most sacred domestic relations. Husbands and wives, parents and children, among our Slaves, are seldom separated, except from necessity or crime. The same reasons induce much more frequent separations among the white population in this, and, I imagine, in almost every other country.' [Emphasis added, L.S.]

"To return, then, to other points presented by [my Liberal friends]."[164]

Stephens continues with his discussion on black servitude in the American South, including an explanation of his infamous "Cornerstone Speech." He begins by demolishing the long held Northern myth that the South possessed a great "Slavery Dynasty":

☛ "In [only] one thing [have the Liberals] . . . done me full justice, and that was in [their] . . . assumption, that I had no sympathy with any conspirators or conspiracy aiming at the overthrow of the Constitution of the United States, with the view of establishing a '*Slavery Dynasty*' in its stead. If any such body of men existed in the country, they certainly had no sympathy from me. Nay, more, if any such body was organized in Washington or elsewhere, or had any existence anywhere, it was wholly unknown to me. *I think it had existence, if [my Liberal friends] . . . will allow me respectfully to say so, only in [their] . . . imagination[s], and that of others who have written fictions called histories. The only real conspiracy against the Constitution organized in Washington, as I understand it, was that of the seven Governors, from seven Northern States, who assembled there, and by their mischievous machinations caused Mr. [Abraham] Lincoln to change his purpose as to the evacuation of Fort Sumter. Caused him to fail to 'keep faith as to Fort Sumter.' This was the conspiracy which inaugurated the war. It was a conspiracy well typified by the Seven Headed monster Beast in the Apocalypse!* The analogy I will not stop to trace, striking as it is, but will follow the [Liberals]. . . . [Emphasis added, L.S.]

"[They quote] . . . from my speech on the annexation of Texas. [They] . . . did not, however, quote fully. In that speech I said, and said truly, that I was '*no defender of Slavery in the abstract.*' I was speaking of it politically and not morally, and of Slavery in the general sense of that term applied to men of the same race, and not as it existed in the States of this Union. This was true then, and now, and always with me. I said also on that occasion, in the next sentence, and now repeat, that

> 'Liberty always had charms for me, and I would rejoice to see all the sons of Adam's family, in every land and clime, in the enjoyment of those rights which are set forth in our Declaration of Independence as 'natural and inalienable,' if a stern necessity, bearing the marks and impress of the hand of the Creator himself, did not, in some cases, interpose and prevent. Such is the case with the States where Slavery now exists.'

"Here is that speech. [The Liberals were] . . . as much at fault in [their] . . . memory in regard to it, as [they were] . . . in regard to the Union speech of 1860.

"There is, moreover, nothing in the 'Corner-Stone' speech, as [they call it] . . . , inconsistent with the sentiments delivered in the Texas speech. Here is the 'Corner-Stone' speech, also. In it I said:

'Many Governments have been founded upon the principle of the subordination and serfdom of certain classes of the same race; such were, and are in violation of the laws of nature. Our system commits no such violation of nature's laws. With us, all of the white race, however high or low, rich or poor, are equal in the eye of the law. Not so with the negro. Subordination is his place. He, by nature, or *by the curse against Canaan*, is fitted for that condition which he occupies in our system. The architect, in the construction of buildings, lays the foundation with the proper material—the granite; then comes the brick or the marble. The substratum of our society is made of the material fitted by nature for it, and by experience we know that it is lest, not only for the Superior, but for the Inferior race, that it should be so. *It is, indeed, in conformity with the ordinance of the Creator. It is not for us to inquire into the wisdom of his ordinances, or to question them. For his own purposes, he has made one race to differ from another, as he has made "one star to differ from another star in glory."* [Emphasis added, L.S.]

'The great objects of humanity are best attained when there is conformity to his laws and decrees, in the formation of Governments as well as in all things else. Our Confederacy is founded upon principles in strict conformity with these laws. This stone which was rejected by the first builders "is become the chief of the corner"—the real "corner-stone"—in our new edifice.'

"In the corner-stone metaphor, I did but repeat what Judge [Henry] Baldwin of the Supreme Court of the United States, had said of the Federal Government itself, in the case of *Johnson* vs. *Tompkins*. In that case he declared that 'the foundations of this Government are laid, and rest on the rights of property in slaves, and the whole fabric must fall by disturbing the corner-stone.'

"It was disturbed, as we have seen, and the only intended difference between the old 'edifice' and the 'new,' in this respect, was to fix this corner-stone more firmly in its proper place in the latter, than it had been in the former. This is the substance of that speech; and there is no conflict between the sentiments expressed in both upon the same subject matter.

"So much for all these points, irrelevant as all of them, and *ad hominem* as some of them are, which have been presented by the [Liberals]. . . . I assure [them], . . . none of them announced any truth which hurts in the least. . . . But what bearing have they upon the matter under immediate consideration?

"How stands the issue between us as to the character of the conflict about Slavery? My position was that in the Federal Councils and before Federal Authorities it was not a conflict between the advocates of the system of Slavery, as it existed, and its opponents, as Mr. [Horace] Greeley has treated it throughout; but that it was in all its stages and phases so far as Federal Politics were concerned, a conflict between those who claimed, and those who denied, that the Federal Authorities had any rightful power, under the Constitution, to take any action whatever upon it, with a view to its immediate or ultimate extinction, or its regulation in any way in contravention of the Rights of the States.

"By [the Liberals'] . . . reference to the Congress of the Colonies and what occurred upon drawing up the Declaration of their Independence, or subsequently, [have they] . . . stated a single fact to unsettle or even jostle that position? *Why was the Declaration finally made without any allusion to the subject? Was it not because it was a matter over which each Sovereign State was to exercise its own discretion as it ought to? Was not Mr. [Thomas] Jefferson, the draftsman of that instrument, as much opposed to Slavery as Mr. [John] Adams, or Dr. [Benjamin] Franklin, or Roger Sherman, or Robert R. Livingston, his colleagues on the committee, and all of whom, except himself, were Northern men?* Did he who penned that soul-stirring defiance to British power 'truckle' [i.e., bow down] to the 'insolent' demands of any miserable 'Slavery Oligarchy' or did John Adams, Dr. Franklin, Roger Sherman, or Robert R. Livingston, to say nothing of John Hancock, and others who voted for it, as it stands, so 'truckle'? Did the Supreme Court so truckle in declaring the Constitution to be as they did, in the case I have read? Especially did Justice [John] McLean, well known to have been an opponent of Slavery, as I have said, so truckle in delivering the opinion cited from him? [Emphasis added, L.S.]

"In a word, . . . [have my Liberal friends] . . . ventured to deny a single fact, stated by me . . . in relation to the nature of this conflict, and the position of the great names mentioned upon it, from the time of its first introduction in Congress down to the election of Mr. Lincoln? [They have] . . . not, and I am sure [they] . . . will not. *We are bound, therefore, to take it as a fact, admitted by silence, at least, that the conflict on this subject in the Federal Councils and before Federal Authorities, was not one between the 'principles of human rights and human bondage' at all; but that it was a conflict between the advocates and supporters of a Federal [Confederate] Government, with limited and specific powers, on the one side, and those who favored Centralism and Consolidation on the other.* [Emphasis added, L.S.]

"*The States South were all on the side of the Constitution. They never invoked any stretch of Federal power to aid or protect that peculiar Institution, either in the States or Territories. Their position from the beginning to the end, upon the Territorial question, was 'non-intervention,' by Congress, either for or against the Institution. All they asked of Congress, in this particular, was simply not to be denied equal rights in settling and colonizing the common public domain, and that the people in these inchoate States might be permitted to act as they pleased upon the subject of the status of the Negro race amongst them, as upon all other subjects of internal policy, when they came to form their*

Constitutions for admission into the Union, as perfect States upon an equal footing with the original Parties, without dictation or control from the Federal Authorities, one way or the other. They claimed the same Sovereign Right of local Self-government on the part of these new States which was the moving cause of the Declaration of Independence, and was the basis upon which our whole system of Government rested. This was their position on the admission of Missouri, and their position throughout. They never asked the Federal Government to extend, or strengthen their particular interest in any such way, as stated. No case of the kind can be named."[165] [Emphasis added, L.S.]

Despite such facts, Stephens' anti-South colleagues believed that the acquisition of Louisiana and Florida, as well as the annexation of Texas, was brought about by the Southern states for the sole purpose of extending Dixie's alleged "Slave Power." Here is Stephens' response to this particular Northern myth:

☛ "Louisiana cannot be said to have been acquired by the Southern States. It is true, that Mr. [Thomas] Jefferson, a Southern man, was the President under whose auspices the treaty for it was negotiated; and it is true, he doubted whether he was fully authorized, under the treaty-making power to enter into such a negotiation. The acquisition, however, was of so much importance, in his opinion, not for the advancement of the interest of the 'Slave Power,' however, but for the benefit and welfare of the great Northwest, as well as the Union generally, that he thought it best not to permit the occasion for its acquisition to pass, preferring to submit the question to Congress for an amendment of the Constitution, after the acquisition, if it should be thought to be necessary, than to let the then favorable opportunity pass, which might never again recur, without securing, when he could, the great public advantages of the acquisition. But the overwhelming opinion North and South, was that the treaty-making power was sufficient, that there was no violation of the Constitution in the acquisition, and this view of the case was afterwards fully sustained, by the Supreme Court, in the case of *The American Insurance Company* vs. *Canter*, and subsequently re-affirmed in a great many cases.

"So there was no breach of the Constitution in that matter, and especially none that can be properly laid to the charge of the Southern States, or the 'Slave Power' *so-called*. For Mr. Jefferson under whose auspices, as President, the treaty was negotiated, was as much opposed to the Institution of Slavery, as it existed in the United States, as any man in the whole country; and, moreover, Northern States joined in carrying out the treaty and approved it as heartily as the Southern States did. So in the acquisition of Florida. The treaty with Spain by which that Territory was secured was negotiated by Mr. John Quincy Adams, who cannot be supposed to have been actuated by any undue desire to pander to the 'Slave Power' in doing it, or to strengthen in any way the particular interests of the Southern States. This view of [my Liberal friends] . . . about the acquisition of Louisiana, Florida and Texas, I cannot answer more pointedly than I did when the same view was presented in the House of Representatives by Mr. [Lewis D.] Campbell, of Ohio, in 1855. The answer then given him, I then thought, and still think, was conclusive upon the subject. What I then said to Mr. Campbell, I now repeat . . . on that point:

'To this I say, it was not the South alone that secured the acquisition of Louisiana. Nor was it alone for the benefit of the South. There were but twenty-three votes in this House against that acquisition. It was a national acquisition. Sustained by national men from all sections, there was hardly a show of opposition to it from any quarter. I should suppose that Ohio would be the last State in this Union to raise her voice against that measure, or hold that it was exclusively for the benefit of the South. What would have become of her trade and commerce if Louisiana and the mouth of the Mississippi were still in the hands of Spain or France? If the fifteen millions of money, which we paid, be the grounds of the gentleman's objection, all that has been more than refunded by the sale of public lands embraced within the limits of that acquisition. These sales, up to this time, have amounted to $25,928,732.23, besides what is yet to be realized from the hundreds of thousands of square miles yet to be sold. So the fifteen millions was no bonus to the South, even if the South had carried the measure for their own benefit.

'Again, was the acquisition of that territory made to extend the southern area of the country? Let us examine this view of the subject. What extent of territory was comprised within the limits of Louisiana? It extended not only far up the Mississippi river, to Iowa and Minnesota, but westward to the Rocky Mountains, even, without now mooting the question whether Oregon was not then acquired. Grant, for the sake of this argument, that Oregon was not then acquired. The Territory of Louisiana stretched from the extreme south on the Gulf to the extreme north on parallel 49° of north latitude. All that immense domain, including Kansas and Nebraska, was part of it. Was all this Southern territory? *The object of the gentleman from Ohio in alluding to this subject seemed to be to intimate that all this acquisition was for the South. But how is the fact? Let us look at it. By this acquisition, taking all the Indian Territory into account, the South acquired only 231,960 square miles, while the North got by it 667,599 square miles! Is this the way the South is to be taunted? When the very acquisition, held up as the taunt, brought more than double the extent of territory to the North than it did to the South!* [Emphasis added, L.S.]

'Again, in the acquisition of Florida, the gentleman from Ohio says, that the South carried that measure at a cost of $5,000,000. This is the tenor of his argument. Sir, this measure was not carried by the South, nor for the South exclusively. There was not even a division in this House on the question. As to the extent of the acquisition, if we did not get Oregon when we acquired Louisiana, we certainly acquired it when we purchased Florida.

It was by the treaty then made that we got Spain's relinquishment to Oregon. The North, by this measure, got 308,052 square miles of territory, including the Territories of Oregon and Washington, while the South got only the State of Florida, 59,268 square miles. If the South carried this question by her votes, I ask, were those who gave the votes sectional in their policy? Did not the South, if that be the gentleman's argument, gain quite as much, nay, more, nay, double, nay, more than five tunes as much territory for the North in that acquisition, as she obtained for herself? Again, in the acquisition of Texas, considering the Mexican war as part of that proceeding, as the gentleman does, the South only secured 237,504 square miles, while the North secured 632,157 square miles, including California, New Mexico, and Utah.'

"In another part of the same speech I also said, what may here be very properly repeated; for it is true, that *the Southern States never did appeal to the Federal Government for any aid or protection, or legislation which did not lie clearly within the stipulations of the Articles of Union. They not only did not violate any of these stipulations, but never looked to that Government for the exercise of any power with a view to the advancement of their material interests.* [Emphasis added, L.S.] What I then said upon that subject, and now repeat, is in these words:

'The gentleman says, in his speech, "we are told that the South gets nothing, that the South asks nothing." Now, sir, in my reply to the gentleman from Indiana, [Daniel Mace,] I spoke of the great fact, well known, living, and "fixed fact," that the industrial pursuits of *the South do not, in the main, look for the protection or fostering care of the Government, and that the general industrial pursuits of the North do.* I did not say that the South gets nothing, or that the South asks nothing. I said that *the South asks but few favors*; and I repeat it, sir. Nor am I to be answered by being told that General [Andrew] Jackson and Mr. [Henry] Clay—Southern men—were in favor of fostering, as far as they could by proper legislation, the interests of the North. That does not disprove the fact which I uttered, that *the South does not generally look to the Government for protection, and that the North does.* Sir, it rather proves the opposite, and confirms my statement. Because I stated that the industrial pursuits of the North look to the Government for protection, is that statement disproved by the fact that Southern men, or even myself, have voted to favor those interests, as far as was consistent with public duty? So far from disproving, it tends rather to establish it. What I stated on this point was in reply to the gentleman from Indiana, whose tone of argument was, that the South carried measures promotive of their interest by bluster.' [Emphasis added, L.S.]

"The truth is they asked nothing of the sort, except the performance, in good faith, of the clearly stipulated covenants of the Constitution by all the Parties to it. I was in Congress sixteen years, and never, during that whole period, asked the passage of any law for the particular interests of my constituents, except the establishment of Post Roads, and the making of the city of Augusta a Port of Delivery. I do not mean to say that the Legislatures of the Southern States never passed any acts which were in violation of some of the provisions of the Constitution. Far from that. Many such acts were passed by them, as by Northern States, which were set aside and declared void by the Courts, either State or Federal. But what I do mean to affirm is, that no Southern State ever did, intentionally or otherwise, fail to perform her obligations to her Confederates [i.e., fellow states] under the Constitution, according to the letter and spirit of its stipulated covenants, and that they never asked of Congress any action, or invoked their powers upon any subject, which did not lie clearly within the provisions of the Articles of Union.

"This . . . I think is quite enough to satisfy [my Liberal friends] . . . upon cool reflection, that there was no breach of the Constitution in the acquisition of Louisiana, Florida, or Texas, and if there was, the breach cannot properly be laid at the door of the Southern States, and, above all, that it was not made with a view of advancing *their* interests exclusively—much less was it carried by the undue power of the 'three-fifths representation,' to which [they allude]. . . .

"On this point of the 'three-fifths' representation clause of the Constitution, I should have been amazed at what [my Liberal friends say] . . . if I had not so often heard the same thing stated by others of equally high position and equally distinguished for general intelligence: but [they] . . . will allow me to say, most respectfully, that it is utterly without foundation, in fact. *There is no clause [i.e., the Three-Fifths Clause] in the Constitution, the history or effects of which seem to be so little understood by men of note and high standing, both at the North and South, as this. It is not among the compromises, so-called, of the Constitution at all. It was not carried by any bluster, insolence, or dictation, or even demand of Southern members in the Convention. It did not emanate in that body from the Slavery interest, so-called, or any one connected with it, and its effects whether so designed or not, have been greatly to weaken and lessen the just powers in the Federal Government of these States, in which Slavery existed, instead of strengthening and enlarging them.*"[166] [Emphasis added, L.S.]

Liberals have long enjoyed haughtily lecturing the South on the evils of slavery—despite the fact that both the American slave trade and American slavery both began in the North! In particular Northerners seemed obsessed with the "sinfulness" of the relation of master and slave, declaring that "many great sins grew out of it, or might have been traced to it, as their immediate cause." To this Stephens answered simply:

☛ "The same may be said of every other relation of life."[167]

Another point on which the North has long berated the South is the "Three-Fifths Clause" in the Constitution (Article 1, Section 2, Clause 3), which allowed slave owners to count each servant as three-fifths of a person so that those states with heavy slave populations would be more fairly represented in Congress (as the number of representatives allowed from each state is based on the state's population). Stephens dissembles this particular fiction piece by piece, beginning with the fact that the idea was proposed by a Northerner, James Wilson:

☛ "The proposition in the Convention came from James Wilson, the distinguished member from Pennsylvania. It was offered at an early day in their proceedings, on the 11th of June. . . . It was offered in this way:

"Mr. Rufus King, of Massachusetts, had submitted a Resolution that the vote in the House of Representatives ought not to be as it was under the Articles of Union as they then were: that is, that each State ought not, in that Branch of the Congress about to be established, to be entitled to an equal vote without regard to population, but that the votes in that Branch of the Congress ought to be according to some equitable ratio of Representation.

"Whereupon, Mr. Wilson offered an amendment in these words:

'In proportion to the whole number of white and other free citizens and inhabitants, of every age, sex, and condition, including those bound to servitude for a term of years, and three-fifths of all other persons not comprehended in the foregoing description, except Indians not paying taxes, in each State.'

"This was intended to include only 'three-fifths' of the Negro population of the States, who were bound to service, not for a term, but for life; in other words, it was intended that five negro slaves should be counted as only three, in fixing a basis of popular representation in the lower House of the Congress. His amendment was immediately adopted, and it thus stands in the Constitution. Every State in the Convention voted for it, North and South, except New Jersey and Delaware. Here is the record of the vote. It was not carried by any bluster, insolence, threats, or menaces on the part of Southern members, or any truckling on the part of Northern members.

"To understand how this came about as it did, why the amendment was so offered as it was, and so readily and generally accepted as it was, and thus became engrafted in the Constitution, we shall have to go back to the proceedings of the Congress in forming the first Articles of Union, and their proceedings under those Articles.

"This examination will make the whole matter perfectly clear, and utterly refute what the [Liberals] . . . and others have said about this clause in our present Compact of Union.

"Bear in mind, then, if you please, that the same committee which was raised by Richard Henry Lee's resolution to draw up a Declaration of the Independence of the States, in June, 1776, were instructed also to report Articles of Union and Confederation between them.

"Bear in mind, also, that this committee did report Articles of Union between the States on the 12th of July, 1776.

"These Articles, then reported, contained this, amongst other clauses. I read from the Record made by Mr. [Thomas] Jefferson:

> Art. XI. All charges of war, and all other expenses that shall be incurred for the common defence, or general welfare, and allowed by the United States assembled, shall be defrayed out of a common treasury, which shall be supplied by the several colonies, in proportion to the number of inhabitants of every age, sex, and quality, except Indians not paying taxes, in each colony—a true account of which, distinguishing the white inhabitants, shall be triennially taken, and transmitted to the Assembly of the United States.

"This proposition for levying the quotas of taxes, for the Federal Treasury, which each State was to bear in equal and just proportion, rested upon the then generally received opinion that population was the best and most reliable standard that could be resorted to in estimating the capacity of a people, community or State, to raise money for taxes. It was thought that the productive capacity of a people, in the accumulation of wealth, which was the proper subject of taxation, could be more nearly arrived at by estimating their numbers than in any other way. Hence numbers, or the relative entire population of the States respectively, was thought to be the best criterion for the levy of the quotas to be contributed by each for the common defence.

"This is apparent from the discussion on this Article.

"There were, then, not over two-thirds of the slaves in all the States at the South, if General Bloomfield's estimate furnished the Convention in 1787, as it appears on their Journal, was at all correct. Two objections, however, were raised to the Article as reported. These objections were not confined to members from the Southern States. The first was that negro slaves were property, and as population, and not property, was to be the basis of taxation, this species of property should not enter at all in the count of numbers. The other was much better founded in reason and justice. That was, that the value of the labor of negroes was not equal to the value of the labor of white men. That the capacity of the negro to produce wealth, was greatly inferior to that of the white man; and hence in the count the negro element, in the population of the several States, should not be rated equal to the white element. Some contended that the ratio, in this respect, should be one white person to two negro Slaves. Mr. John Adams fully answers the first objection, and insisted that there was no merit in the second. Here is what he said on both:

> 'Mr. John Adams observed, that the numbers of people are taken, by this article, as an index of the wealth of the State, and not as subjects of taxation; that, as to this matter, it was of no consequence by what name you called your people, whether by that of freemen or of slaves; that, *in some countries, the laboring poor are called freemen, in others they were called slaves; but that the difference as to the State was imaginary only.* What matters it whether a landlord, employing ten laborers on his farm, give them annually as much money as will buy them the necessaries of life, or give them those necessaries at short hand? The ten laborers add as much wealth to the State, increase its exports as much, in the one case as the other. Certainly five hundred freemen produce no more profits, no greater surplus for the payment of taxes, than five hundred slaves. Therefore *the State in which the laborers are called freemen should be taxed no more than that in which are those called slaves.* Suppose, by an extraordinary operation of nature or of law, one half the laborers of a State could, in the course of one night, be transformed into slaves; would the State be made the poorer, or the less able to pay taxes? That *the condition of the laboring poor in most countries—that of the fishermen, particularly, of the Northern States—is as abject as that of slaves.* It is the number of laborers which produces the surplus for taxation; and numbers, therefore, indiscriminately, are the fair index to wealth; that it is the use of the word "property" here, and its application to some of the people of the State, which produce the fallacy. [Emphasis added, L.S.]
> '*That a slave may, indeed, from the custom of speech, be more properly called the wealth of his master, than the free laborer might be called the wealth of his employer; but as to the State, both were equally its wealth*, and should therefore equally add to the quota of its tax.' [Emphasis added, L.S.]

"The objection on the 'property' view, after the conclusive speech of Mr. Adams on that point, seems to have been given up, but from a failure to agree upon the proper ratio between the relative capacities of the Negroes and Whites to produce wealth, the basis of population, as a standard for levying quotas on the States, in the first Articles of Union, was abandoned, and the value of lands in the several States was adopted in lieu, as we have seen.

"But that was not found to work well. The subject was again revived in the Congress, and a proposition was made by that body on the 18th April, 1783, to amend the Constitution in this particular, and to go back upon population as the proper basis. It was then that this 'three-fifths' clause was agreed upon as the proper ratio in this respect. The matter underwent a very full discussion. It was not characterized by Sectional lines, as we see from Mr. [James] Madison's report. The whole debate was upon the isolated point, as to how the negroes should be rated in the count in reference exclusively to the efficiency of their labor, or their relative capacity to produce wealth. Here is what he says of the position of members upon it:

'Mr. [Oliver] Wolcott was for rating them as four to three.
'Mr. [Daniel] Carroll as four to one.
'Mr. [Hugh] Williamson said, he was principled against Slavery; and that he thought slaves an encumbrance to society, instead of increasing its ability to pay taxes.
'Mr. [Stephen] Higginson, as four to three.
'Mr. [John] Rutledge said, for the sake of the object, he would agree to rate slaves as two to one, but he sincerely thought three to one would be a juster proportion.
'Mr. [Samuel] Holten, as four to three.
'Mr. [Samuel] Osgood said, he did not go beyond four to three.'

"Now, in this discussion, we see Mr. Wolcott, from Connecticut, was for rating them as four to three. Mr. Higginson, the same. Mr. Holten and Mr. Osgood, from Massachusetts, the same. Mr. Rutledge, from South Carolina, contended that three to one was a proper basis, but he would agree to two to one. While Mr. Williamson, from North Carolina, stated that 'he was principled against Slavery,' and looked upon the Blacks as 'an encumbrance to society, instead of increasing its ability to pay taxes.'

"The first vote was taken: on rating the slaves at three to two. On this the States were equally divided—ten only voting. It was then that Mr. [James] Madison (well known to have been himself against Slavery), said 'that in order to give proof of the sincerity of his professions, of liberality, he would propose that slaves should be rated as five to three.' This was accepted by Mr. [James] Wilson, and agreed to by a decided majority of the States—two only voting against it—Rhode Island and Connecticut. Massachusetts was divided on the question.

"The debates on it, when and where it originated, and when it was agreed to by the States, show that *there was nothing sectional in it*. When agreed to it had no reference whatever to *representation*, nor any rule or ratio of representation in Congress, of either *persons* or *property*. The States all, then, had an *equal vote* in the Congress, without regard to the number or character of their respective populations. But this counting of five negro slaves as equal to three white persons, was agreed upon after mature consideration, and a thorough investigation of the subject for years, as a proper basis of direct taxation, when population was resorted to as the proper standard of fixing the quotas of the States respectively.

"It was offered by Mr. Wilson in the Convention that framed the Constitution, and was adopted by that body, as we have seen, unquestionably upon the then universally admitted doctrine, that representation in Legislative Bodies and direct taxation should go together. It was with this view, and upon this principle solely, and with no view to a property representation at all, that it was incorporated, as it is, in the Constitution. The counterpart of this provision, which followed, as a matter of course, from the principle on which it was adopted, is the 4th Clause of the 9th Section of the 1st Article of the Constitution, which declares that,

> No Capitation, or other direct, Tax shall be laid, unless in proportion to the Census or Enumeration hereinbefore directed to be taken.

"And, as I have stated, whatever may have been the design when it was offered, the effect of this 'three-fifths' clause was greatly to weaken instead of strengthening the political power of the States in which Slavery existed. For very soon, the number of slaves in the Southern States was considerably increased by accessions from the Northern States. The acts of these Northern States, to which the [Liberals have] . . . referred, abolishing the Institution within their limits, were generally prospective in their character. Under the operation of these acts, humane as they were, in his estimation, *the slaves in these [Northern] States, were to some extent, to what is not and never will be exactly known, brought South, and sold before the period fixed for their final emancipation. Less than half, it is believed by some, in point of fact, ever became free under these acts*, however philanthropic, and however inspired by the 'Christian principles of the age,' they may be considered by him to have been. *This is the way in which many of them [slaves], at least, found a resting-place in the more Southern States.* [Emphasis added, L.S.]

"But besides this, and mainly, it must be borne in mind, that the system of direct taxation, which was looked to at the time, as the chief mode of raising the ordinary revenues of the Federal Government, was soon virtually abandoned; and *the Southern States, in which the slaves had almost entirely 'found a resting-place,' under the Northern system of Abolition*, lost their full and just popular representation under it, without the compensating advantages contemplated at the time of its adoption, in the matter of the assessment of the taxes. The taxes were raised in another way, and by this clause these States were deprived of their equal and just voice in their imposition, though they had to pay their full part of them. Under the operation of other clauses of the Constitution, by construction, the principle intended to be carried out by the adoption of this clause, was not only ignored, but reversed. Taxation and Representation did not go together. For under the indirect mode of raising the revenues of the Federal Government, there is no reason in justice, or right, or any principles of political or moral equity, whatever, why the entire population of the Southern States, should not have been taken in the estimate for a basis of popular representation in the House of Representatives, as well as the entire population in the Northern States. Instead of counting only 'three-fifths' of the Negro portion of their laboring population, the whole five-fifths should have been counted. The fact that they were called 'property,' made no difference in principle, whatever, as Mr. Adams clearly showed in the speech quoted from him. The 'property' in them consisted in nothing but the *legal right* to their services for life. [Emphasis added, L.S.]

"*This legal right, on the part of the owner, was truly called 'property,' but it in no respect differed in kind or species of property from the legal right of every employer, to the service of those who, by contract or law, are bound to service for any time shorter than that of life. This legal right to services so due for a term ever so short, is as much 'property' in the one case as the other. It is a 'property' that is maintained in all Courts, without reference to the length of the term for which it is due. On this view, therefore, which is just and correct, there is no reason why all those persons in the Southern States, who were bound to service for life, 'should not have been counted in a census for a basis of popular representation, as well as all minors, apprentices, or others,' bound to service for a shorter term in all the States. The owner of five slaves at the South, therefore, was not endowed, under this clause of the Constitution, with as much political power as three white men at the North. The owner of five, or a hundred, or a thousand, was endowed with no political power under it. No more than the employer of five, or a hundred, or a thousand of operatives at the North.*"[168] [Emphasis added, L.S.]

When Stephens was asked to elaborate on the true difference in the relation of a free laborer of the North towards his employer, and that of a slave at the South towards his owner, he replied:

☞ "I did not say that there was no difference, whatever, between these relations. *What I maintained is, that there was no difference in the 'property' view of them so far as relates to this clause of the Constitution. The right to the service, or labor of the one, under contract, whether, for a short or long term, was as much 'property' as the right to the service of the other, under law, though it was for life. The only difference, in this respect, (and that is what we are considering,) is that the labor of the one, was for a term only, and that of the other, was for life* [though Southern "slaves" could purchase their freedom at any time]. *The laborers in each case were equally recognized by the laws, North and South, as persons; and they were so equally recognized in the Constitution. In this respect there was no difference; and in this respect there is no* reason why there should have been any difference in the count for arriving at an equal basis of popular representation. [Emphasis added, L.S.]

"The slave-owner was endowed with no political power by this clause, no more than the employer of other kinds of labor at the North. This was, and is, my position; and from all this it clearly appears, I think, that this 'three-fifths' clause of the Constitution, was no 'Slavery Oligarchical,' or 'aristocratic provision' of the Constitution, carried at the dictation of the Southern States, and for their especial benefit. On the contrary, it was a curtailment of their just powers, as the Government has been administered. But for it, the Southern States would have had six more members than they had under the first census. But for it, and the consequent want of her full and just power in Congress, at the time, the Alien and Sedition laws, might not, and, most probably, would not have been passed; and the other centralizing acts of the Government, passed during that decade, which have since been claimed as precedents might, and, most probably, never would have had existence. But for it, in 1820, the Southern States would have had twelve more members in the House of Representatives, than they then had, and the Missouri Restriction of that year, which [Liberals] . . . call a Solemn Compact, would not have been carried as it was. Here I might properly reply to the points made on that subject, and show that *the conflict on that measure, however portentous, was not a conflict, as I have before said, between the advocates and opponents of the Institution of Slavery, as it existed in the States, but a conflict, as all others of a like character, between those who defended the Federal [Confederate] principles of the Government, and those who were endeavoring to centralize its powers. It can be easily shown that, for these political ends, this subject of Slavery was then seized upon, by leaders defeated on other questions, as one which would be most likely to enlist the general sympathy of the people, and one on which, from conscientious scruples, they might more easily be led to disregard the obligations of Compacts.*"[169] [Emphasis added, L.S.]

Nineteenth-Century Northerners frequently attacked the Confederacy, and in particular the state of South Carolina, for attempting to create a "secession conspiracy," "overthrow the Federal Government," and establish a "Slavery Oligarchy." To this nonsense Stephens responded:

☛ ". . . I wish to notice one or two other points presented by the [Liberals]. . . . These relate to the position of South Carolina on Secession, and the manner in which the 'Conspiracy,' as [they call] . . . it, was concocted by a 'Slavery Oligarchy,' and carried throughout the South by impositions and usurpations.

"Now, first, as to whether South Carolina 'cared a button' for the breach of faith on the part of Northern States, or not; let us see what she said of her own act, and upon what grounds she put her withdrawal from the Union. Whether Mr. [Robert B.] Rhett, or Mr. [Laurence M.] Keitt, or others, made the speeches you [Liberals] refer to or not, I do not know. But South Carolina is by far the best and most authoritative exponent of her own acts. Here is her Ordinance of Secession, and the Declaration of her people in Convention, giving to the world their reasons for it. This Convention was no 'secret Junto' of Conspirators. It was a Convention legally called and legally elected, according to law, by the regularly constituted authorities of the State—chosen to consider and determine upon the Federal relations of the State. Here is what this body of men, so selected and so chosen, said of their own action and of their reasons for it. In this paper, after giving a history of the Union, and the nature of the Federal Government, netting forth, specifically, the two mutual Covenants of the States providing for the rendition of fugitives from service, and fugitives from crime, they based their acts solely and exclusively upon breaches of faith on the part of their Northern Confederates [i.e., the Northern people]. Of these and other articles of the Constitution they say:

> We maintain that in every Compact between two or more parties, the obligation is mutual; that the failure of one of the contracting parties to perform a material part of the agreement, entirely releases the obligation of the other; and that where no arbiter is provided, each party is remitted to his own judgment to determine the fact of failure, with all its consequences.
> . . . The General Government, as the common agent, passed laws to carry into effect these stipulations of the States. For many years these laws were executed. But an increasing hostility on the part of the non-Slaveholding States to the Institution of Slavery has led to a disregard of their obligations, and the laws of the General Government have ceased to effect the objects of the Constitution. The States of Maine, New Hampshire, Vermont, Massachusetts, Connecticut, Rhode Island, New York, Pennsylvania, Illinois, Indiana, Michigan, Wisconsin and Iowa, have enacted laws which either nullify the acts of Congress or render useless any attempt to execute them. In many of these States the fugitive is discharged from the service or labor claimed, and in none of them has the State Government complied with the stipulation made in the Constitution. The State of New Jersey, at an early day, passed a law in conformity with her Constitutional obligation; but the current of Anti-Slavery feeling has led her more recently to enact laws which render inoperative the remedies provided by her own law and by the laws of Congress. In the State of New York, even the right of transit for a Slave has been denied by her tribunals; and the States of Ohio and Iowa have refused to surrender to justice fugitives charged with murder, and with inciting servile insurrection in the State of Virginia. Thus *the Constitutional Compact has been deliberately broken and disregarded by these non-Slaveholding States, and the consequence follows that South Carolina is released from her obligation.* [Emphasis added, L.S.]

"This is quite enough to show the grounds upon which South Carolina based her action in her Ordinance of Secession. That was entitled, *An Ordinance to dissolve the Union between the State of South Carolina and other States, united with her under the Compact, entitled, 'The Constitution of the United States of America,'* and is in these words:

> We, the People of the State of South Carolina, in Convention assembled, do declare and ordain, and it is hereby declared and ordained,
>
> That the Ordinance adopted by us, in Convention, on the twenty-third day of May, in the year of our Lord one thousand seven hundred and eighty-eight, whereby the Constitution of the United States of America was ratified, and also, all Acts and parts of Acts of the General Assembly of this State, ratifying Amendments of the said Constitution, are hereby repealed; and that the Union now subsisting between South Carolina and other States, under the name of "The United States of America," is hereby dissolved.

"Now, as further evidence of the reasons and motives by which the extremest men of the South were governed, in advising the people of their States, respectively, to secede, I call your special attention to the speech made by Mr. [Robert A.] Toombs, of Georgia, in the Senate of the United States, on the 7th of January, 1861, more than two weeks after South Carolina had passed her Ordinance, and two days after, you [Liberals] say, the conspiracy, of which he was a prominent member, was organized in Washington, with a view to overthrow the Federal Government, and to establish, in its stead, a Slavery Oligarchy. Let us look into this speech. I will read such portions only as present its substance upon the points we have under immediate consideration. In speaking of the action of the people of South Carolina, and the Secessionists of the South generally, in this assemblage of the Ambassadors of the States, on that occasion, he said:

> 'Inasmuch, sir, as I have labored earnestly, honestly, sincerely with these men to avert this necessity, so long as I deemed it possible, and inasmuch as I heartily approve their present conduct of resistance, I deem it my duty to state their case to the Senate, to the country, and to the civilized world.
>
> '*Senators, my countrymen have demanded no new Government, they have demanded no new Constitution. Look to their records at home and here, from the beginning of this strife until its consummation in the disruption of the Union, and they have not demanded a single thing, except that you shall abide by the Constitution of the United States; that Constitutional rights shalt be respected, and that justice shall be done. Sirs, they have stood by your Constitution; they have stood by all its requirements; they have performed all of its duties unselfishly, uncalculatingly, disinterestedly, until a Party sprang up in this Country which endangered their social system—a Party which they arraign, and which they charge before the American people and all mankind with having made proclamation of outlawry against thousands of millions of their property*

in the Territories of the United States; with having aided and abetted insurrection from within and invasion from without, with the view of subverting their Institutions, and desolating their homes and their firesides. I shall proceed to vindicate the justice of their demands, the patriotism of their conduct. I will show the injustice which they suffer, and the rightfulness of their resistance. [Emphasis added, L.S.]

'*The discontented [Southern] States of this Union have demanded nothing but clear, distinct, unequivocal, well-acknowledged Constitutional rights—rights affirmed by the highest judicial Tribunals of their Country; rights older than the Constitution; rights which are planted upon the immutable principles of natural justice; rights which have been affirmed by the good and the wise of all countries and of all centuries. We demand no power to injure any man. We demand no right to injure our Confederate [Northern] States. We demand no right to interfere with their Institutions, either by word or deed. We have no right to disturb their peace, their tranquillity, their security. We have demanded of them simply, solely—nothing else—to give us equality, security, and tranquillity. Give us these, and peace restores itself.* [Emphasis added, L.S.]

'I will now read my own demands, acting under my own convictions. They are considered the demands of an extremist. I believe that is the appellation these [Yankee] traitors employ. I accept their reproach rather than their principles. *Accepting their designation of treason and rebellion, there stands before them as good a traitor and as good a rebel as ever descended from Revolutionary lotus.* [Emphasis added, L.S.]

'What do these Rebels [of South Carolina] demand?

'First. "*That the people of the United States shall have an equal right to emigrate and settle in the present, or any future acquired Territories, with whatever property they may possess, (including slaves,) and be securely protected in its peaceable enjoyment until such Territory may be admitted as a State into the Union, with or without Slavery, as she may determine, on an equality with all existing States.*" That is our territorial demand. We have fought for this Territory when blood was its price. We have paid for it when gold was its price. *We have not proposed to exclude you, though you have contributed very little of either blood or money. I refer especially to New England. We demand only to go into those Territories upon terms of equality with you, as equals in this great Confederacy, to enjoy the common property of the whole Union, and receive the protection of the common Government until the Territory is capable of coming into the Union as a Sovereign State, when it may fix its own institutions to suit itself.* [Emphasis added, L.S.]

'The second proposition is: "that property in slaves shall be entitled to the same protection from the Government of the United States, in all of its department, everywhere, which the Constitution confers the power upon it to extend to any other property, provided nothing herein contained shall be construed to limit or restrain the right now belonging to every State to prohibit, abolish, or establish and protect slavery within its limits." *We demand of the common government to use its granted powers to protect our property as well as yours. For this protection we pay as much as you do. This very property [i.e.,* slaves] is subject to taxation. It has been taxed by you and sold by you for taxes.* [Emphasis added, L.S.]

'The title to thousands and tens of thousands of slaves is derived from the United States. We claim that the government, while the Constitution recognizes our property for the purposes of taxation, shall give it the same protection that it gives yours.

'Ought it not to be so? You say no. Every one of you upon the committee said no. Your senators say no. Your House of Representatives says no. Throughout the length and breadth of *your conspiracy against the Constitution* there is but one shout of no! *This recognition of this right is the price of my allegiance. Withhold it, and you do not get my obedience.* This is the philosophy of the armed men who have sprung up in this country. *Do you ask me to support a government that will tax my property; that will plunder me; that will demand my blood, and will not protect me? I would rather see the population of my native State laid six feet beneath her sod than they should support for one hour such a government. Protection is the price of obedience everywhere, in all countries. It is the only thing that makes government respectable. Deny it and you can not have free subjects or citizens; you may have slaves.* [Emphasis added, L.S.]

'We demand, in the next place, "that persons committing crimes against slave property in one State, and fleeing to another, shall be delivered up in the same manner as persons committing crimes against other property, and that the laws of the State from which such persons flee shall be the test of criminality." That is another one of the demands of an extremist and a rebel.

'But the nonslaveholding [Northern] States, treacherous to their oaths and compacts, have steadily refused, if the criminal only stole a negro and that negro was a slave, to deliver him up. It was refused twice on the requisition of my own State as long as twenty-two years ago. It was refused by [Edward] Kent and by [John] Fairfield, governors of Maine, and representing, I believe, each of the then federal parties. [Kent was a Whig and Fairfield was a Democrat.] We appealed then to fraternity, but we submitted; and this constitutional right has been practically a dead letter from that day to this. *The next case came up between us and the State of New York, when the present senior senator [William H. Seward] was the governor of that State; and he refused it. Why? He said it was not against the laws of New York to steal a negro, and therefore he would not comply with the demand. He made a similar refusal to Virginia. Yet these are our confederates; these are our sister States! There is the bargain; there is the compact. You have sworn to it. Both these governors swore to it. The senator from New York swore to it. The governor of Ohio swore to it when he was inaugurated. You can not bind them by oaths. Yet they talk to us of treason; and I suppose they expect to whip freemen into loving such brethren! They will have a good time in doing it!* [Emphasis added, L.S.]

'It is natural we should want this provision of the Constitution carried out. The Constitution says slaves are property; the Supreme Court says so; the Constitution says so. The theft of slaves is a crime; they are a subject-matter of felonious asportation. By the text and letter of the Constitution you agreed to give them up. You have sworn to do it, and you have broken your oaths. Of course, those who have done so look out for pretexts. Nobody expected them to do otherwise. I do not think I ever saw a perjurer, however bald and naked, who could not invent some pretext to palliate his crime, or who could not, for fifteen shillings, hire an Old Bailey lawyer to invent some for him. Yet this requirement of the Constitution is another one of the extreme demands of an extremist and a rebel.

'The next stipulation is that fugitive slaves shall be surrendered under the provisions of the Fugitive Slave Act of 1850, without being entitled either to a writ of *habeas corpus*, or trial by jury, or other similar obstructions of legislation, in the State to which he may flee. Here is the Constitution:

> No person held to service or labor in one State, under the laws thereof, escaping into another, shall, in consequence of any law or regulation therein, be discharged from such service or labor, but shall be delivered up on claim of the party to whom such service or labor may be due.

'This language is plain, and everybody understood it the same way for the first forty years of your government. In 1793, in [George] Washington's time, an act was passed to carry out this provision. It was adopted unanimously in the Senate of the United States, and nearly so in the House of Representatives. Nobody then had invented pretexts to show that the Constitution did not mean a negro slave. It was clear; it was plain. Not only the federal courts, but all the local courts in all the States, decided that this was a constitutional obligation.

'How is it now? I have heretofore shown that *this plain Constitutional provision has been violated by specific acts in thirteen of these States*. [Emphasis added, L.S.]

'The next demand made on behalf of the South is, "that Congress shall pass efficient laws for the punishment of all persons, in any of the States, who shall, in any manner, aid and abet invasion or insurrection in any other State, or commit any other act against the laws of nations tending to disturb the tranquillity of the people or Government of any other State."

'That is a very plain principle. The Constitution of the United States now requires, and gives Congress express power, to define and punish piracies and felonies committed on the high seas, and offences against the laws of nations. *When the honorable and distinguished Senator from Illinois [Stephen A. Douglas], last year, introduced a bill for the purpose of punishing people thus offending under that clause of the Constitution, Mr. [Abraham] Lincoln, in his speech at New York, which I have before me, declared that it was a "Sedition Bill;" his press and party hooted at it. So far from recognizing the bill as intended to carry out the Constitution of the United States, it received their jeers and gibes. The Republicans [Liberals] of Massachusetts elected the admirer and eulogist of [Yankee abolitionist] John Brown's courage, as their Governor, and we may suppose he will throw no impediments in the way of John Brown's successors.* [Emphasis added, L.S.]

'We demand these five propositions. Are they not right? Are they not just? Take them in detail, and show that they are not warranted by the Constitution, by the safety of our people, by the principles of eternal justice. We will pause, and consider them; but mark me, *we will not let you decide the questions for us*. [Emphasis added, L.S.]

'But we are told by well meaning but simple minded people that admit your wrongs, your remedies are not justifiable. Senators, I have little care to dispute remedies with you, unless you propose to redress my wrongs. If you propose that in good faith, I will listen with respectful deference; but when the objectors to my remedies propose no adequate ones of their own, I know what they mean by the objection. They mean *Submission*. But, still, I will as yet argue it with them. [Emphasis added, L.S.]

'These thirteen Colonies originally had no Bond of Union whatever—no more than Jamaica and Australia have to-day. *They were wholly separate Communities, independent of each other, and dependent on the Crown of Great Britain. All the Union between them that was ever made is in writing.* They made two written Compacts. One was known as the *Articles of Confederation*, which declared that the Union thereby formed should be perpetual—an argument very much relied upon by "the friends of the Union," now. Those Articles of Confederation, in terms, declared that they should be perpetual. I believe that expression is used in our last treaty with Billy Bowlegs, the Chief of the Seminoles. I know it is a phrase used in treaties with all nations, civilized and savage. Those that are not declared eternal are the exceptions; but usually treaties profess to be for "perpetual friendship and amity," according to their terms. So was that treaty between the States. After awhile, though, the politicians said it did not work well. It carried us through the [American] Revolution. *The difficulty was, that after the war there were troubles about the regulation of commerce, about navigation, but above all, about financial matters. The Government had no means of getting at the pockets of the people; and but for that one difficulty, this present Government would never have been made.* The country is deluded with the nonsense that this Bond of Union was cemented by the blood of brave men in the Revolution. Sir, it is false. It never cost a drop of blood. A large portion of the best men of the Revolution voted against it. It was carried in the Convention of Virginia by but ten majority, and among its opponents were [James] Monroe and [Patrick] Henry, and other men who had fought the war, who recorded their judgment that it was not a good Bond; and I am satisfied to-day that they were the wiser men. Some of the bravest, and the boldest and the best men of the Revolution, who fought from its beginning to its end, were opposed to the plan of Union. Are we to be deterred by the cry that we are laying our unhallowed hands on this holy altar? Sir, *I have no hesitation in saying that a very large portion of the people of Georgia, whom I represent, prefer to remain in this Union with their Constitutional rights—I would say ninety per cent, of them—believing it to be a good Government.* I think it had but little to do with their prosperity beyond securing their peace with other nations, and that boon has been paid for at a price that no freeman ought to submit to. These are my opinions; they have been announced to my constituents, and I announce them here. *Had I lived in that day, I should have voted with the minority in Virginia, with Monroe, Henry, and the illustrious patriots who composed the seventy-nine votes [in the Virginia Convention] against the adoption of the present plan of government. In my opinion, if they had prevailed, to-day the men of the South would have the greatest and most powerful nation of the earth. Let this judgment stand for future ages.* [Emphasis added, L.S.]

'Senators, the Constitution is a Compact. It contains all our obligations and duties of the Federal Government. I am content, and have ever been content, to sustain it. While I doubt its perfection; while I do not believe it was a good Compact; and while I never saw the day that I would have voted for it as a proposition *de novo* [Latin: "a second time"]; I have given to it, and intend to give to it, unfaltering support and allegiance; but I choose to put that allegiance on the true ground, not on the false idea that anybody's blood was shed for it. I say, that the Constitution is the whole Compact. All the obligations, all the chains that fetter the limbs of my people, are nominated in the Bond, and they wisely excluded any conclusion against them, by declaring that *the powers not delegated by the Constitution to the United States, or forbidden by it to the States, belonged to the States respectively or the people.* Now I will try it by that standard; I will subject it to that test. The law of nature, the law of justice would say—and it is so expounded by the publicists—that equal rights in the common property shall be enjoyed. Even in a monarchy, the King cannot prevent the subjects from enjoying equality in the disposition of the public property. Even in a despotic Government this principle is recognized. It was the blood and the money of the whole people (says the learned [Dutch jurist Hugo] Grotius, and say all the publicists) which acquired the public property, and therefore it is not the property of the Sovereign. This right of equality being, then, according to justice and natural equity, a right belonging to all States, when did we give it up? You say Congress has a right to pass rules and regulations concerning the Territory and other property of the United States. Very well. Does that exclude those whose blood and money paid for it? Does "dispose of" mean to rob the rightful owners?

'But, you say, try the right. I agree. But how? By our judgment? No; not until the last resort. What then; by yours? No; not until the same time. How then try it? The South has always said by the Supreme Court. But that is in our favor, and Lincoln says he will not stand that judgment. Then each must judge for himself of the mode and manner of redress. But you deny us that privilege, and finally reduce us to accepting your judgment. We decline it. You say you will enforce it by executing laws; that means, your judgment of what the laws ought to be. The Senator from Kentucky comes to your aid, and says he can find no Constitutional Right of Secession. Perhaps not; but *the Constitution is not the place to look for State Rights. If that right belongs to independent States, and they did not cede it to the Federal Government, it is reserved to the States, or to the people.* Ask your new Commentator where he gets your right to judge for us. Is it in the Bond? [Emphasis added, L.S.]

'The Supreme Court has decided that, by the Constitution, we have a right to go to the Territories, and be protected there, with our property. You say, we cannot decide the Compact for ourselves. Well, can the Supreme Court decide it for us? Mr. Lincoln says he does not care what the Supreme Court decides, he will turn us out anyhow. He says this in his debate with the honorable Senator from Illinois (Mr. [Stephen A.] Douglas). I have it before me. He said he would vote against the decision of the Supreme Court. Then you do not accept that arbiter. You will not take my construction; you will not take the Supreme Court as an arbiter; you will not take the practice of the Government; you will not take the treaties under [Thomas] Jefferson and [James] Madison; you will not take the opinion of Madison upon the very question of prohibition, in 1820. What, then, will you take? You will take nothing but your own judgment; that is, you will not only judge for yourselves, not only discard the Court, discard our construction, discard the practice of the Government, but *you will drive us out, simply because you will it. Your party says that you will not take the decision of the Supreme Court. You said so at Chicago; you said so in committee; every man of you in both Houses says so. What are you going to do? You say we shall submit to your construction. We shall do it, if you can make us; but not otherwise, or in any other manner.* That is settled. [Emphasis added, L.S.]

'You have no warrant in the Constitution for this declaration of outlawry. The Court says you have no right to make it. The treaty says you shall not do it. The Treaty of 1803 declares that the property of the people shall be protected by the Government until they are admitted into the Union as a State. That treaty covers Kansas and Nebraska. The law passed in 1804, or 1805, under Mr. Jefferson, protects property in slaves in that very Territory. *In 1820, when the question of Prohibition came up, Mr. Madison declared it was not warranted by the Constitution, and Jefferson denounced its abettors as enemies of the human race.* Here is the Court; here are our fathers; here is contemporaneous exposition for fifty years, all asserting our right. The Republican [then the Liberal] Party says, "We care not for your precedents, or practices; we have progressive [liberal] Politics as well as a progressive Religion." [Emphasis added, L.S.]

'But, *no matter what may be our grievances, the honorable Senator from Kentucky [John J. Crittenden], says we cannot secede. Well, what can we do? We cannot revolutionize; he will say that is treason. What can we do? Submit? They say they are the strongest, and they will hang us. Very well, I suppose we are to be thankful for that boon. We will take that risk. We will stand by the right; we will take the Constitution; we will defend it by the sword with the halter around our necks! Will that satisfy the honorable Senator from Kentucky? You cannot intimidate my constituents by talking to them about treason. They are ready to fight for the right with the rope around their necks!* [Emphasis added, L.S.]

'But, although I insist upon this perfect equality in the Territories, yet, when it was proposed, as I understand the Senator from Kentucky now proposes, that the line of 36° 30' shall be extended, acknowledging and protecting our property on the south side of that line, for the sake of peace—permanent peace—I said to the Committee of Thirteen, and I say here, that with other satisfactory provisions, I would accept it.

'Yet, not only did your committee refuse that, but my distinguished friend from Mississippi [Jefferson Davis],—another moderate gentleman like myself—proposed simply to get a recognition that we had the right to our own: that man could have property in man; and it met with the unanimous refusal even of the most moderate, Union-saving, compromising portion of the Republican [Liberal] Party. They do not intend to acknowledge it.

'Very well; you not only want to break down our Constitutional Rights; you not only want to upturn our social system; your people not only steal our slaves and make them freemen to vote against us; but you seek to bring an Inferior race in a condition of equality, socially and politically, with our own people. Well, sir, t*he question of Slavery moves not the people of Georgia, one-half as much as the fact that you insult their rights as a Community. You Abolitionists are right when you say, that there are thousands and tens of thousands of men in Georgia, and all over the South, who do not own slaves. A very large portion of the people of Georgia own none of them. In the mountains, there are comparatively but few of them; but no part of our people are more loyal to their race and country, than our bold and brave mountain population; and every flash of the electric wires brings me cheering news from our mountain tops, and our valleys, that these Sons of Georgia are excelled by none of their countrymen in loyalty to the rights, the honor, and the glory of the Commonwealth. They say . . . and as one man, they would meet you upon the border with the sword in one hand, and the torch in the other. We [Southerners] will tell you [Northerners] when we choose to abolish this thing [slavery]; it must be done under our direction, and according to our will; our own, our native land, shall determine this question, and not the Abolitionists of the North. That is the spirit of our freemen.* [Emphasis added, L.S.]

'I have already adverted to the proposition in regard to giving up criminals who are charged with stealing Negroes, and I have referred to the cases of Maine, New York, and Ohio. I come now to the last specification—the requirement that laws should be passed punishing all who aid and abet insurrection. These are offences recognized by the laws of Nations, as inimical to all society; and I will read the opinions of an eminent Publicist, when I get to that point. I said that you had aided and abetted insurrection. John Brown certainly invaded Virginia. John Brown's sympathizers, I presume, are not Democrats [the Conservatives of the day]. Two of the accomplices of John Brown fled—one to Ohio, one to Iowa. The Governors of both States refused to give up the fugitives from justice. The Party maintained them. I am aware that, in both cases, pretexts were gotten up, to cover the shame of the transaction. I am going to show you that their pretexts were hollow, unsubstantial, not only against Constitutional law, but against the law of Nations. I will show you that it was their duty to seize them under the law of Nations, and bring them to their Confederate States, or even to a friendly State. The first authority I will read, is [the Swiss legal authority Emerich de] Vattel on the Law of Nations. If there had been any well-founded ground, if the papers had been defective, if the case had been defectively stated, what was the general duty of a friendly State without any Constitutional obligations? This general principle is, that one State is bound to restrain its citizens from doing anything tending to create disturbance in another State; to ferment disorders; to corrupt its citizens, or to alienate its allies.

'Vattel says:

"And since the latter (the Sovereign) ought not to suffer his subjects to molest the subjects of another State, or to do them an injury, much less to give open, audacious offence to Foreign powers, he ought to compel the transgressors to make reparation for the damage or injury, if possible, or to inflict on him an exemplary punishment; or finally, according to the nature and circumstances of the case, to deliver him up to the offended State, to be there brought to justice. This is pretty generally observed with respect to great crimes, which are equally contrary to the laws and safety of all Nations. Assassins, incendiaries, and robbers, are seized everywhere at the desire of the Sovereign in whose Territories the crime was committed, and are delivered up to his justice. The matter is carried still further in States that are more closely connected by friendship and good neighborhood. Even in cases of ordinary transgressions, which are only subjects of civil prosecution, either with a view to the recovery of damages, or the infliction of a slight civil punishment, the subjects of two neighboring States are reciprocally obliged to appear before the magistrate of the place where they are accused of having failed in their duty. Upon a requisition of that magistrate, called letter rogatory, they are summoned in due form by their own magistrates, and obliged to appear. An admirable institution, by means of which many neighboring States live together in peace, and seem to form only one Republic! This is in force through all Switzerland. As soon as the letters rogatory are issued in form, the superior of the accused is bound to enforce them. It belongs not to him to examine whether the accusation be true or false; he is to presume on the justice of his neighbor, and not to suffer any doubts on his own part to impair an Institution so well calculated to preserve harmony and good understanding between the States."

'That is the law of nations, as declared by one of its ablest expounders; but, besides, we have this principle embodied in the Constitution. We have there the obligation to deliver up fugitives from justice; and though it is in the Constitution: though it is sanctioned, as I said, by all ages and all centuries, by the wise and the good everywhere, our Confederate States are seeking false pretexts to evade a plain, social duty, in which are involved the peace and security of all society. If we had no Constitution, this obligation would devolve upon friendly States. If there were no Constitution, we ought to demand it. But, instead of giving us this protection, we are met with reproaches, reviling, tricks, and treachery, to conceal and protect incendiaries and murderers.

'This man, Brown, and his accomplices, had sympathizers. Who were they? One of them, as I have before said, who was, according to his public speeches, a defender and laudator of John Brown, is Governor of Massachusetts. Other officials of that State applauded Brown's heroism, magnified his courage, and, no doubt, lamented his ill success. Throughout the whole North, public meetings, immense gatherings, triumphal processions, the honors of the hero and conqueror, were awarded to this incendiary and assassin. They did not condemn the traitor; think you, they abhorred the treason?

'Yet, I repeat, when a distinguished Senator from a non-Slaveholding State (Mr. Douglas) proposed to punish such attempts at invasion and insurrection, Lincoln and his [Liberal Republican] Party come before the world and say, "Here is a Sedition Law." To carry out the Constitution, to protect States from invasion, and suppress insurrection, to comply with the laws of the United States, is a "Sedition Law," and the Chief of this Party treats it with contempt; yet, under the very same clause of the Constitution which warranted this important bill, you derive your power to punish offences against the laws of nations. Under this warrant you have tried and punished our citizens for meditating the invasion of foreign States; you have stopped illegal expeditions; you have denounced our citizens as pirates, and commended them to the bloody vengeance of a merciless enemy.

'Under this principle alone you protect our weaker neighbors of Cuba, Honduras, and Nicaragua. By this alone are we empowered and bound to prevent our people from conspiring together, giving aid, giving money, or arms, to fit out expeditions against any foreign nation. Foreign nations get the benefit of this protection; but *we are worse off in the Union than if we were out of it. Out of it, we should have the protection of the Neutrality laws. Now you can come among us; raids may be made; you may put the incendiary's torch to our dwellings, as you did last summer, for hundreds of miles on the frontiers of Texas; you may do what John Brown did, and when the miscreants escape to your States you will not punish them; you will not deliver them up. Therefore, we stand defenceless. We must cut loose from the accursed "body of this death," even to get the benefit of the law of nations.* [Emphasis added, L.S.]

'You will not regard Confederate obligations; you will not regard Constitutional obligations; you will not regard your oaths. What, then, am I to do? Am I a freeman? Is my State a free State? We are freemen. We have rights; I have stated them. We have wrongs; I have recounted them. *I have demonstrated that the [Liberal Republican] party now coming into power has declared us outlaws, and is determined to exclude thousands of millions of our property from the common Territories; that it has declared us under the ban of the Union, and out of the protection of the laws of the United States everywhere. They have refused to protect us from invasion and insurrection by the Federal Power, and the Constitution denies to us in the Union the right either to raise fleets or armies for our defence. All these charges I have proven by the record; and I put them before the civilized world, and demand the judgment of to-day, of to-morrow, of distant ages, and of Heaven itself, upon the justice of these causes. I am content, whatever it be, to peril all in so noble, so holy a cause. We have appealed, time and time again, for these Constitutional rights. You have refused them. We appeal again. Restore us these rights as we had them, as your Court adjudges them to be, just as our people have said they are; redress these flagrant wrongs, seen of all men, and it will restore fraternity, and peace, and unity, to all of us. Refuse them, and what then? We shall then ask you, "Let us depart in peace." Refuse that, and you present us war. We accept it; and, inscribing upon our banners the glorious words, "Liberty and Equality," we will trust to the blood of the brave, and the God of Battles, for security and tranquillity.'*[170] [Emphasis added, L.S.]

"[In my opinion Senator Toombs' speech] . . . will take a place, side by side, with that of Pericles addressed to the Athenian Council, just before the outbreak of the Peloponnesian War, though not analogous, so far as concerns the parties addressed. Its greatest power, however, consisted in the unquestionable facts, upon which it rested.

". . . *[It is plain to see that Toombs' object, as well as that of his coadjutors,] . . . was the perpetuation of that liberty and equality which was established by the Constitution of the United States. This [even my Liberal friends] . . . must admit. It was the same liberty and equality that the men of 1776 had perilled their lives, their honor, and all that they held sacred, to establish. The speech shows clearly who were the real conspirators against our form of Government, as established by the Fathers. It shows that the 'naked question' presented by him and the other leading men from the South at Washington [D.C.], at that time, was not, as [the Northern Liberals] . . . maintained, to overthrow that Government and to establish a 'Slavery Oligarchy' in its stead. On the contrary, it puts beyond all question the fact, that the leading men of the South, whom you styled conspirators, even the extremest of them, for no man was more extreme, as all will readily grant, not even Mr. [William L.] Yancey, of Alabama, or Mr. [Robert B.] Rhett, of South Carolina, than Mr. Toombs was, aimed at nothing, and desired nothing, but the maintenance, in good faith, of the Constitution, with all its guarantees as they stood! They wanted and desired nothing but that Constitutional liberty and equality which the Fathers had established! They wanted no new Constitution, nor any new 'Slavery Dynasty!'* That is the question! [Emphasis added L.S.]

"In this speech, Mr. Toombs said, and said truly, that ninety out of every hundred of the people of Georgia, were devoted to the Union, under the Constitution, as it then stood! Though he thought it not a good one, yet they did, and he was willing, in good faith, to stand to it, if the other Parties to it would. He said then, after South Carolina had seceded, that if the Northern

States would comply with their obligations under the Constitution, that it would restore Fraternity and Unity! He said, truly, that the non-slaveholders of Georgia were as much opposed to the policy of the Abolition Party, to carry out their designs of Negro equality as the slaveholders were. They were as truly 'loyal' to the Constitution, as it stood in this particular, as any class in the Commonwealth, and were as ready to defend the principles of that Constitution, by defending the Sovereign Right of Secession, even 'with the rope around their necks,' as their slaveholding neighbors. Indeed, I think he might have gone further, and have said, with truth, that they were even readier; for, in this State, I believe a majority of the slaveholders were against the policy of Secession, at the time. They were generally what were called Conservatives, and a large portion of them, if not a majority, voted the Bell-Everett ticket in the Presidential election [i.e., John Bell and Edward Everett's Constitution Union Party]. My opinion is, that a majority of them, in this State, voted against Secession Delegates to the Convention which was called in this State. How this matter really was, there is no way to determine, that is, on which side a majority of this class was on that question; but it is well known that a large portion of the most active opponents of that measure, were amongst the largest slaveholders of the State. This I state in reply to the [Liberals'] . . . idea, that it was a movement gotten up by what [they call] . . . a Slavery Oligarchy, at the South. *The truth is, no such Oligarchy existed.* [Emphasis added L.S.]

"But mark you, when and where this speech was made.

"*It was on the 7th of January, 1861, in the Senate of the United States, two days after, you [Liberals] say, the conspirators aiming at the overthrow of the Government had organized in secret junto at Washington! Is anything wanting more thoroughly to refute that idea than this speech? It clearly shows that on the 7th January, 1861, after South Carolina had seceded, as we have seen—after the conspiracy had entered into a regular organization, with a usurpation of all power over Southern public affairs, according to this fabulous account of it, that Mr. Toombs, and even Mr. [Jefferson] Davis, who was the selected chief, were willing to settle the whole controversy, if any assurance would be given by the leading men of the Party coming into power on the 4th of the ensuing March, that the clearly stipulated guarantees of the Constitution would be carried out in good faith by them? This assurance it is well known was not given. It was refused to be given. This is a correct version of that matter. The whole story of any such conspiracy, and the election of Mr. Davis as President of a new Dynasty, is altogether fabulous.* [Emphasis added L.S.]

"After this refusal, if the Senators—the Ambassadors of the Southern States at Washington—did assemble together in that city, and did resolve jointly upon such action as they thought best for the people of their States, respectively, to adopt in their State Conventions, then called by the regularly constituted authorities, in this emergency; and if after this meeting and consultation, Mr. Toombs, one of them, did go into the Senate, and there deliver this manifesto, and make another appeal for the Union, even after the advice was given, who can justly maintain that they, in the performance of this high duty, were a set of secret conspirators or anything like it? It is notorious that they did so meet, so consult, and so advise. But their meeting was no secret. Nothing was more generally known in Washington. It was announced in the newspapers of the day.

"But it is utterly untrue, as I am informed, and have good reasons to believe, that there was any usurpation of power by them, or any attempt or object on their part, to do anything but advise such course as they thought best for the people of the Southern States, in which Conventions were then called, to pursue in the crisis then impending, if no assurance should be given, that the Constitution would be maintained. There was no such thing as an election of a Chief Commander of any military forces, or any usurpation of power, whatever. The Sovereign people of these States were left to their own free will to adopt the policy they advised, or reject it as they pleased. The sum and substance of the advice was embodied in this speech. Their wrongs demanded redress, and if it were not granted, that they should 'depart in peace,' and form a new Confederation amongst themselves. The redress was not given, and these States did depart in peace. They all passed Ordinances of Secession as South Carolina had done, and in Convention at Montgomery [Alabama], formed a new Confederation. *This is a correct version of the matter.*"[171] [Emphasis added L.S.]

21

THE MISSOURI COMPROMISE OF 1820

IN THE FOLLOWING EXCERPTS FROM Stephens' *A Constitutional View*, he carefully examines the Missouri Compromise of 1820, in which the expansion of slavery into the new Western Territories was strictly regulated.

☛ "[I] . . . will now take up the Missouri Compromise, and see how far [the Liberals'] . . . position, on that subject . . . is sustained by the facts of the case: in other words, we will see whether there was any 'breach of faith,' or of 'Compact,' on the part of the South, in regard to that measure, or in regard to the Compromise Measures of 1850, which [they speak] . . . of in the same connection; and in regard to which [they] . . . also alleged breach of faith on the part of the [South's] 'Slave Power,' so-called. I shall consider both these matters together; for the subjects are both intimately connected, and there can be no correct understanding of the latter, without a clear and full understanding of the former.

". . . I was very much struck, as well as greatly surprised, at what the Ex-President [James Buchanan] wrote upon both of these measures [in his work *Buchanan's Administration*]. I read, first, . . . where he speaks of the Compromise of 1850:

> 'The Compromise of 1850 ought never to have been disturbed by Congress. After long years of agitation and alarm, the country, under its influence, had enjoyed a season of comparative repose, inspiring the people with bright hopes for the future.
>
> 'But how short-lived and delusive was this calm! The very Congress which had commenced so auspiciously, by repealing the Missouri Compromise before the end of its first session, re-opened the floodgates of sectional strife, which, it was fondly imagined, had been closed forever. This has ever since

gone on increasing in violence and malignity, until it has involved the country in the greatest and most sanguinary civil war recorded in history.'

"Then after speaking of what [Mr. Buchanan] . . . calls the repeal of the Missouri Compromise in 1854, which he maintains reopened the floodgates of sectional strife that had been closed by the Compromise of 1850, he uses this language . . .:

> 'After a careful review of the history of the AntiSlavery Party, from its origin, the candid inquirer must admit that up till this period [i.e., 1854], it had acted on the aggressive against the South. From the beginning it had kept the citizens of the slaveholding States in constant irritation, as well as serious apprehension for their domestic peace and security. They were the assailed Party, and had been far more sinned against than sinning. It is true, they had denounced their assailants with extreme rancor and many threats; but had done nothing more. In sustaining the repeal of the Missouri Compromise, however, the Senators and Representatives of the Southern States became the aggressors themselves, and thereby placed the country in an alarming and dangerous condition from which it has never since been rescued!'

"Upon the Missouri Compromise itself, he speaks thus . . .:

> 'The Missouri Compromise finally passed Congress by large majorities. On a test question in the Senate on the 2nd March, 1820, the vote in its favor was against fifteen; and in the House, on the same day, it was one hundred and thirty-four against forty-two. Its wisdom and policy were recognized by Congress, a quarter of a century afterwards, in March, 1845, when Texas, being a Slave [optional] State, was annexed to the Union. Acting on the presumption that several new States might be formed out of her territory, one of the express conditions of her annexation was, that in such of these States as might lie north of the Missouri Compromise line, Slavery shall be prohibited.
>
> 'The Missouri Compromise had remained inviolate for more than thirty-four years before its repeal. It was a Covenant of peace between the free [i.e., slavery prohibited states] and the slaveholding [i.e., the slavery optional] States. Its authors were the wise and conservative statesmen of a former generation. Although it had not silenced Anti-Slavery discussion in other forms, yet it soon tranquillized the excitement which for some months previous to its passage had convulsed the country in regard to Slavery in the Territories. It is true that the power of a future Congress to repeal any of the Acts of its predecessors, under which no private rights had been vested, cannot be denied, still the Missouri Compromise, being in the nature of a Solemn Compact between conflicting parties, whose object was to ward off great dangers from the Union, ought never to have been repealed by

Congress.

'The question of its Constitutionality ought to have been left to the decision of the Supreme Court, without any legislative intervention. Had this been done, and the Court had decided it to be a violation of the Constitution, in a case arising before them in the regular course of judicial proceedings, the decision would have passed off in comparative silence, and produced no dangerous excitement among the people.'

"I have said I was surprised at what Mr. Buchanan wrote on the subject. I repeat, I am exceedingly surprised at it, not only because it is so utterly unsustained by the facts, but so directly inconsistent with what he affirmed in his letter, accepting the nomination of the Democratic Party, for the Presidency, in 1856. Here is that letter, dated June 16, 1856; and in it he used this language in reference to the action of Congress in 1854, which, as he says, repealed the Missouri Compromise, and opened afresh the agitation of the Slavery question, and in which the South was, for the first time, the aggressor. Hear what he said on this subject in 1856:

'The agitation of the question of domestic Slavery has too long distracted and divided the people of this Union, and alienated their affections from each other. This agitation has assumed many forms since its commencement, but it now seems to be directed chiefly to the [Western] Territories; and judging from its present character, I think we may safely anticipate that it is rapidly approaching a "finality." The recent legislation of Congress respecting domestic Slavery, derived, as it has been, from the original and pure fountain of legitimate political power, the will of the majority, promises, ere long, to allay the dangerous excitement. This legislation is founded upon principles as ancient as free Government itself, and in accordance with them, has simply declared that the people of a Territory, like those of a State, shall decide for themselves, whether Slavery shall or shall not exist within their limits.'

"This was the truth of the case . . . and I cannot well see how he could have expressed himself, as he did in his book, in 1865, on the same subject, without a total forgetfulness, not only of the real facts of the case, but of what he had himself expressly stated, when he was before the people of the States, as a candidate for the Presidency. But let that pass.

"I shall now first take up the Missouri Compromise [of 1820], so-called, and then the Compromise of 1850; and show that if there was anything like a 'Solemn Compact,' or 'covenant' of any sort, between the States, in either, that there was no breach of faith on the part of the Southern States, in relation to either."[172]

Stephens begins his explanation of the compromises that helped lead to Lincoln's War in April 1861:

☛ "The history of the first of these measures, so little understood, and so greatly misrepresented, briefly stated, is this:

"In 1818, at the Second Session of the Fifteenth Congress, an application was made by the people of the Territory of Missouri to be admitted into the Union as a State. The Territory of Missouri, as is well known, was embraced in the Louisiana cession by France, in 1803. In Article III, of the Treaty by which that whole acquisition was made, it was stipulated in behalf of the inhabitants then residing within its limits, that,

> The inhabitants of the ceded Territory shall be incorporated in the Union of the United States, and admitted as soon as possible, according to the principles of the Federal Constitution, to the enjoyment of all the rights, advantages, and immunities of citizens of the United States; and in the meantime they shall be maintained and protected in the free enjoyment of their liberty, property, and the religion which they profess.

"Negro slaves were then held as property in this Territory, and were embraced in the Treaty as other property.

"Now, in pursuance of this stipulation, as well as in pursuance of the general principles and authority of the Constitution of the United States, the application of the people of Missouri for admission into the Union as a State, was made in the usual way in 1818, as I have remarked. The bill for this purpose came up for action in the House of Representatives on the 13th day of February, 1819. To that bill Mr. [James] Tallmadge, of New York, moved an amendment in these words:

> And provided, That the further introduction of Slavery or involuntary servitude be prohibited, except for the punishment of crimes, whereof the party shall have been fully convicted; and that all children born within the said State, after the admission thereof into the Union, shall be free at the age of twenty-five years.

"This amendment presented an issue, mark you, not between the advocates and opponents of Slavery, as it then existed in the States, but an issue between the advocates and opponents of principles lying at the foundation of the Federal system. It presented the question of the power of the Federal Government to impose the restriction, as well as the question of the power of Congress to violate a treaty stipulation: the debate and votes upon it show that the members of the House, North and South, took their position upon it, in this view of the subject.

"The vote in committee on agreeing to it, was seventy-nine for, and sixty-seven against it. On the report of the Committee in the House, the question was divided. On the first branch, the vote, by ayes and noes, was eighty-seven for it, seventy-six against it. On the second branch, the vote was eighty-two for it, and seventy-eight against it!

"Mr. [Henry R.] Storrs, of New York, who was opposed to the restriction, but no advocate of Slavery, then moved to amend the bill, by striking out so much as says, 'that the new State shall be admitted on an equal footing with the original States;' for the very clear reason, that if the bill should pass, and the State be admitted under the restriction, she would not be a State in the Union on an 'equal footing' with the original States. This motion, however, did not prevail, and the bill passed the House with this restriction.

"When it went to the Senate, the first branch of the restriction was stricken out, by a vote of twenty-two to strike it out, against sixteen to retain it; and on the second branch of the restriction, the vote to strike it out was thirty-one, while only seven voted to retain it.

"The House adhered to the restriction, and the Senate would not recede from their action upon it; so Missouri failed to be admitted at that session of Congress.

"The application was renewed on the 9th of December, 1819, on the opening of the First Session of the Sixteenth Congress. A bill, in the usual form, for the admission of the State of Missouri on an equal footing with the original States, was again reported.

"To this bill the same restriction, in effect, though not in the same words, was renewed by Mr. [John W.] Taylor, of New York. *This gave rise to a renewal of the conflict of the session before, with increased spirit and vigor. Never had a discussion so thoroughly shaken the very foundations of the Government, from its beginning, as this did! The conflict, fierce and angry as it was, was a conflict, however, between principles. It was one growing out of the different views of members and Senators, as to the legitimate power of the Federal Government over the subject matter of debate. The South, to a man, held, without any regard to the right or wrong of Slavery, or the policy, or impolicy, of the Institution, that Congress had no power to interfere with it, in the manner sought, either one way or the other. Several gentlemen of the North took the same ground.* It would be interesting to review these debates, as from these alone we can thoroughly understand the true nature of the conflict. I can only glance at them, and thus present a few samples, which will sufficiently characterize the whole for present purposes. [Emphasis added, L.S.]

"First, then, let [us hear] . . . what Mr. [John] Holmes, from [Massachusetts] . . . said upon this occasion:

'Mr. Chairman, when a man is fallen into distress, his neighbors surround him to offer relief. Some, by an attempt at condolence, increase the grief which they would assuage; others, by administering remedies, inflame the disorder; while others, affecting all the solicitude of both, actually wish him dead. It is so with Liberty. Always in danger—often in distress—she not only suffers from open and secret foes, but officious and unskilful friends. And among the thousands and millions that throng her Temples, from curiosity, fashion, or policy, how few—very few—there are, who are her sincere, faithful, and intelligent worshippers!

'Among these few, I trust, are to be found all the advocates for restriction in this House. And I readily admit, that most of those out of doors, whose zeal is excited on this occasion, are of the same description. But, is it not probable that there are some jugglers behind the screen, who are playing a deeper game—who are combining to rally under this standard, as the last resort, the forlorn hope of an expiring party?

'But, while we admit this in behalf of the respectable gentlemen who advocate the restriction of Slavery in Missouri, we ask, may we demand of them the same liberality? We are not the advocates or the abettors of Slavery. For one, sir, I would rejoice if there was not a slave on earth. Liberty is the object of my love—my adoration. I would extend its blessings to every human being. But, though my feelings are strong for the abolition of Slavery, they are yet stronger for the Constitution of my country. And, if I am reduced to the sad alternative, to tolerate the holding of Slaves in Missouri, or violate the Constitution of my country, I will not admit a doubt to cloud my choice. Sir, of what benefit would be Abolition, if at a sacrifice of your Constitution? Where would be the guaranty of the Liberty which you grant? Liberty has a temple here, and it is the only one which remains. Destroy this, and she must flee—she must retire among the brutes of the wilderness—to mourn and lament the misery and folly of man.

'Let us then proceed, with that candor and caution which the subject demands, to examine the nature of this power, and ascertain whether it is given in the Constitution of the United States.

'The extraordinary doctrines which have been advanced, on this subject, in and out of doors, render it necessary to be exceedingly particular, and carefully to examine the ground as we advance. An American politician would scarcely have deemed it necessary to prove, at this day, that to regulate the relation between the different members of a community, is an attribute of Sovereign Power. That I may not be mistaken, I will inform the Committee what I intend by Sovereign Power, and the sense in which I purpose to use it in this discussion. It is the power of making and executing laws, to regulate the conduct and condition of men. It is, more or less, absolute, as it is limited and defined, or, unlimited and undefined. In the origin of Government, if we can conceive such a period, the rights vested in the Sovereign, by the community, necessarily included the power to determine the mutual dependence of the several members. The community had a right to control and establish it themselves, or delegate it to the Sovereign. In either way they could establish a difference of dependence of one man upon another. The nearer equal this dependence, however, the more perfect the Government. Yet, Sovereign Power can establish such a dependence as that of the slave on his master. . . .

'Then, did the [American] Revolution alter the relation? We have been made to understand, from very respectable authority, that the Declaration of Independence proclaimed freedom to every slave in the United States! It seems, then, that all the slaves have been free, in fact, for more than forty years, and they do not know it. And we are gravely legislating to perform that which was most effectually performed in 1776. Why attempt to do what is already done? Why create all this excitement if we have no slaves? Humanity might, perhaps, require that we should pass a Declaratory Act, to give notice to two millions of people, that, by applying to the Supreme Court, they can be relieved from their thraldom. . . .

'Mr. Chairman, I should not have noticed this strange and ridiculous vision, that the Declaration of Independence was a decree of universal emancipation, had it not issued, from respectable sources, and been seriously enforced upon the credulity of the public. . . .

'At the [American] Revolution, the rights of the Crown vested in the States, and they succeeded to all the Sovereign Power, which, until then, belonged to the Provinces and the Mother Country [Great Britain]. There was no suspension or death of political power. Property was retained by the owner, laws continued to have force, and Sovereign Power was transferred to the States and vested temporarily in their Legislatures, until a more permanent Government could be established, originating from, and effected by this temporary power. The doctrine that the Revolution is not the origin, but the perfection of the State Governments, and that the States are the successors, as well, of the [British] Crown, as the Colonies, has been so long and so well established, that it is considered the foundation, not only of Political Power, but of private right. This Political Power existing, and having been exercised up to the Revolution, was not thereby extinguished. This, also, agrees with fact. Those States which were disposed to liberate their slaves, did not consider it as already effected by the Revolution, but found it necessary to do it by some Constitutional or Legislative Act. Consequently, this Political or Sovereign Power, existed after the Revolution. And, as there was no diminution of Sovereign Power, from that time, up to the adoption of the Federal Constitution, it existed up to that time. Did the Constitution of itself take it from the States? There is no such prohibition upon the States, either express, or implied. Moreover, the Constitution recognizes and confirms the right. The third Section, of the fourth Article, inhibits a State from protecting or liberating fugitive slaves from other States, and compels it to deliver them up. The Constitution, so far from destroying, establishes this power in a State.'

"I wish I could read more of this very able and truly patriotic speech. But what I have read shows the nature of the conflict, fully and clearly: and it also shows that there was no truckling [kowtowing] to the 'Slave Power' on the part of Northern members who opposed the restriction; but a stern devotion to the Constitution of their country. Mr. [Henry] Baldwin, of Pennsylvania, and Mr. [Henry] Meigs, of New York, took the same position as that taken by Mr. Holmes, though their speeches are not reported in full.

"Now, then, let us sample Southern sentiment in the same debate. Here, in passing, I see the speech of Mr. [Robert E.] Reid, of Georgia. In it, upon the subject of Slavery, he said:

> 'I would hail that day as the most glorious in its dawning, which should behold, with safety to themselves and our citizens, the Black population of the United States placed upon the high eminence of equal rights, and clothed in the privileges and immunities of American citizens! But this is a dream of philanthropy which can never be fulfilled; and whoever shall act in this country upon such wild theories, shall cease to be a benefactor, and become a destroyer of the human family.'

"He opposed the restriction, however, as others did, mainly upon Constitutional grounds. This his speech abundantly shows.

"Here are a few sentences from the speech of Mr. [Philip P.] Barbour, of Virginia, which may be taken as a fair specimen of the tenor of the whole of what he said:

> 'Are we now called to decide, as an abstract question, whether Slavery is or is not justifiable? No, sir, that question had been long settled, before the formation of our Constitution: Slavery existed in many of the States at that period; its existence and its continuance were recognized by that Instrument; the States surrendered to the Federal Government no power over the subject, except after a given period, to prohibit the importation of Slaves from abroad. I tell gentlemen, then, that this is neither the time nor the occasion for the discussion of the abstract justice or injustice of Slavery. If we were called upon in our respective State Legislatures to decide upon its continuance or abolition; or if we were now in Convention for the purpose of forming a new Federal Constitution—in either of these cases their arguments of that kind would have some application. But who are we, and what are our functions? We are the creatures of the Constitution, not its creators; we are called here to execute, not to make one. Let gentlemen, then remember that it is not sufficient for them to show that Slavery cannot be justified in itself; that it is, if you please, a moral and political evil; they will yet fail to maintain their ground, unless they can also show that the Constitution gives us power over it.'

"Mr. [Alexander] Smyth, of Virginia, used the following language:

'By treaty we are bound to admit Missouri in the Union; . . . to guaranty to her a Republican [i.e., Confederate] form of Government, (that is, a government by and for the people themselves, not a government imposed on them, nor a Patrimonial Government;) and to leave her all power not delegated by the Constitution to the United States, nor prohibited by it to the States. Treaties are in part the Supreme law of the land, and paramount to the Constitution of any State; yet you propose to violate the treaty with France by the means of a State Constitution, which is of inferior obligation to a treaty. . . .

'Will you be unjust, false, and perfidious, because you are powerful? Would it be honorable to violate a treaty because those who claim the benefits of its provisions are our own citizens? . . . By your Constitution, a treaty is the Supreme law of the land, and paramount to the Constitution which you propose to force Missouri to adopt. You may, indeed, repeal the treaty by an Act of Congress; but the effect of a measure of that kind should be well considered. And you must repeal the treaty directly or by implication before the proposed measure can have the desired effect; for the treaty, until it is repealed, is paramount to the imposed Constitution; and the Judges would sustain it.'

"This is enough from the House speeches. I ask attention to one specimen only from the Senate. That is from the speech of the great William Pinkney, of Maryland, who was well known to have been against Slavery:

'"New States may be admitted by the Congress into this Union?" It is objected that the word "may" imports power, not obligation—a right to decide—a discretion to grant or refuse.

'To this it might be answered that power is duty, on many occasions. But let it be conceded that it is discretionary. What consequence follows? A power to refuse, in a case like this, does not necessarily involve a power to exact terms. You must look to the result, which is the declared object of the power. Whether you will arrive at it or not may depend on your will; but you cannot compromise with the result intended and professed.

'What, then, is the professed result? To admit a State into this Union.

'*What is that Union? A Confederation of States equal in Sovereignty, capable of everything which the Constitution does not forbid, or authorize Congress to forbid. It is an equal Union between parties equally Sovereign. They were Sovereign, independently of the Union. The object of the Union was common protection for the exercise of already existing Sovereignty.* . . . *By acceding to it, the new State is placed on the same footing with the original States. It accedes for the same purpose, that is, protection for its unsurrendered Sovereignty. If it comes in shorn of its beams—crippled and disparaged beyond the original States, it is* not into the original Union that it comes. For it is a different sort of Union. The first was Union *inter pares* [Latin: "first among equals"]: This is a Union between disparates, between giants and a dwarf, between power and feebleness, between full proportioned Sovereignties, and a miserable image of power—a thing which that very Union has shrunk and shrivelled from its just size, instead of preserving it in its true dimensions. [Emphasis added, L.S.]

'It is into "this Union," that is, the Union of the Federal [Confederate] Constitution, that you are to admit, or refuse to admit. You can admit into no other. You cannot make the Union, as to the new State, what it is not as to the old; for then it is not this Union that you open for the entrance of a new Party.'

"So much for samples of the speeches in the debate on the question."[173]

☛ "As additional strong proof on the same line, establishing beyond doubt the nature of the conflict, as well as the objects of the leaders of the Restrictionists, who had espoused this question with so much apparent zeal, I will ask your indulgence while I read something Mr. [Thomas] Jefferson said of both. Here is a letter he wrote to Mr. [William] Pinkney, from whose speech I have just read. In this letter, Mr. Jefferson said:

> 'The Missouri question is a mere party trick. The leaders of Federalism—(he here uses Federalism in the sense in which it was used in 1798 and 1799 [i.e., to mean a Confederate governmental system])—defeated in their schemes of obtaining power by rallying partisans to the principle of Monarchism, a principle of personal, not of local division, have changed their tack, and thrown out another barrel to the whale. They are taking advantage of the virtuous feelings of the people to effect a division of parties by a geographical line; they expect that this will ensure them, on local principles, the majority they could never obtain on principles of Federalism [Confederatism]; but they are still putting their shoulder to the wrong wheel; they are wasting *jeremiades* [French: "whining" or "moaning"] on the miseries of Slavery, as if we were advocates for it.'

"Here is another letter Mr. Jefferson wrote to Mr. Holmes, from whose speech I also read. [Concerning slavery, in] . . . this he says:

> 'I thank you, dear sir, for the copy you have been so kind as to send me of the letter to your constituents on the Missouri question. It is a perfect justification to them. I had for a long time ceased to read newspapers, or pay any attention to public affairs, confident they were in good hands, and content to be a passenger in our bark to the shore from which I am not distant. But

this momentous question [on what to do about slavery], like a fire bell in the night, awakened me and filled me with terror. I considered it at once as the [death] knell of the Union. It is hushed, indeed, for the moment. But this is a reprieve only, not a final sentence. A geographical line, coinciding with a marked principle, moral and political, once conceived and held up to the angry passions of men, will never be obliterated; and every new irritation will mark it deeper and deeper. I can say, with conscious truth, that there is not a man on earth who would sacrifice more than I would to relieve us from this heavy reproach, in any practicable way. The cession of that kind of property, for so it is misnamed, is a bagatelle which would not cost me a second thought, if, in that way, a general emancipation and expatriation [i.e., the colonization of American blacks in foreign lands] could be effected; and, gradually, and with due sacrifices, I think it might be. But as it is, *we have the wolf by the ears, and we can neither hold him, nor safely let him go*. Justice is in one scale, and self-preservation in the other. Of one thing I am certain, that as the passage of slaves from one State to another, would not make a slave of a single human being who would not be so without it, so their diffusion over a greater surface would make them individually happier, and proportionally facilitate the accomplishment of their emancipation, by dividing the burthen [burden] on a greater number of coadjutors. An abstinence, too, from this act of power, would remove the jealousy excited by the undertaking of Congress to regulate the condition of the different descriptions of men composing a State. This certainly is the exclusive right of every State, which nothing in the Constitution has taken from them and given to the General Government. Could Congress, for example, say, that the non-freemen of Connecticut shall be freemen, or that they shall not emigrate into any other State? [Emphasis added, L.S.]

'*I regret that I am now to die in the belief, that the useless sacrifice of themselves by the generation of 1776, to acquire self-government and happiness to their country, is to be thrown away by the unwise and unworthy passions of their sons, and that my only consolation is to be, that I live not to weep over it. If they would but dispassionately weigh the blessings they will throw away, against an abstract principle, more likely to be effected by Union than by scission, they would pause before they would perpetrate this act of suicide on themselves, and of treason against the hopes of the world.* To yourself, as the faithful advocate of the Union, I tender the offering of my high esteem and respect.' [Emphasis added, L.S.]

"Then, here is another letter [Jefferson] . . . wrote to Mr. [James] Madison, in which he says:

'I am indebted to you for your two letters of February 7th and 19th. The Missouri question, by a geographical line of division, is the most portentous one I ever contemplated. . . . [Mr. So-and-so] is ready to risk the Union for any chance of restoring his party to power, and wriggling himself to the head of it; nor is [he] without his hopes, nor scrupulous as to the means of fulfilling them.'

"These evidences, without resorting to more, show fully and conclusively, that *the conflict in this Missouri Controversy, was not one between the advocates and opponents of Slavery, but between the advocates and opponents of our true Federal [Confederate] system under the Constitution.*"[174] [Emphasis added, L.S.]

☛ "But I must proceed with the narrative. On the 18th of February, the House received from the Senate the bill for the admission of the State of Maine, which the House had passed on the 3rd of January previous. When this House Bill was before the Senate, a motion was made, and carried in that body, to tack on to it a bill for the like admission of Missouri. To this proposition Mr. [Jesse B.] Thomas, of Illinois, moved the following amendment:

> And be it further enacted, That in all that Territory ceded by France to the United States, under the name of Louisiana, which lies North of thirty-six degrees and thirty minutes north latitude, excepting only such part thereof as is included within the limits of the State contemplated by this act, Slavery and involuntary servitude, otherwise than in the punishment of Crimes whereof the party shall have been duly convicted, shall be, and is hereby forever prohibited: Provided always, That any person escaping into the same, from whom labor or service is lawfully claimed in any State or Territory of the United States, such fugitive may be lawfully reclaimed, and conveyed to the person claiming his or her labor or service, as aforesaid.

"This was the Missouri Compromise, so-called. *It did not come from the South. It was not moved by any member, or Senator from the South. Even Mr. [Henry] Clay [of Kentucky], whose name has been so erroneously connected with it, had nothing to do with its origination. It was proposed, as I have stated, by Mr. [Jesse B.] Thomas, a Senator from Illinois, as an additional section to the bill providing for the admission of Maine and Missouri, without any restriction on either, as all the other new States had been admitted. It related to matter entirely extraneous to the bill, and passed the Senate the 17th day of February, by a vote of thirty-four to ten. Of the ten noes, every one was from the South, except two. [James] Noble and [Waller] Taylor, Senators from Indiana, voted against it.*"[175] [Emphasis added, L.S.]

☛ "Now, let us see what reception it met with in the House, where, on a test question, Mr. [James] Buchanan says it passed by one hundred and thirty-four against forty-two! A greater historical error on an important matter was hardly ever committed. This House Bill for the admission of Maine, which had passed that body on the 3rd of January, and which, as stated, was sent back to them with these Senate amendments, (first, the admission of Missouri, and secondly, the Slavery restriction outside of the State,) was taken up in the House on the 19th day of February, and its consideration was then postponed until a future day. Meantime, the House went on discussing their own separate bill for the admission of Missouri. Before coming to any final vote upon that, they again, on the 22nd of February, resumed the consideration of the Maine Bill, with the Senate amendments, and disagreed to both of them by separate votes: to this Thomas Provision, they disagreed by a vote of one hundred and fifty-nine to eighteen! They then took up and went on with their own bill for the admission of Missouri, with the Restriction on the State in it. On the 28th of February, the House received a message from the Senate, that they insisted on their amendments to the Maine Bill. The message was taken up, and after insisting on their disagreement to this Thomas Provision by a vote of one hundred and sixty to fourteen, the House went on, still, with their own separate bill as to Missouri.

"The Senate asked a Committee of Conference on the disagreeing votes of the two Houses on the Maine Bill. This was granted by the House, 29th February, and Messrs. Holmes, of Massachusetts, [John W.] Taylor, of New York, [William] Lowndes, of South Carolina, [James] Parker, of Massachusetts, and [Charles] Kinsey, of New Jersey, were appointed as the House Committee, every man of them from the Northern States except Mr. Lowndes. After this, the House still went on with their own Missouri Bill, and on the same day adopted the Restriction of Mr. Taylor, by a vote of ninety-four to eighty-six; and with this Restriction the Bill passed the House the next day, March 1st, by the vote of ninety-one to eighty-two! It so went to the Senate. On the 2nd of March, Mr. Holmes, from the Conference Committee on the part of the House, on the Maine Bill, reported. The Report was, that the Senate should recede from its Amendments to the Maine Bill, and that both Houses should pass the House Bill for the admission of Missouri, by striking out the House Restriction of Slavery on the State, and substituting, in lieu of it, the Thomas Provision, imposing a restriction on territory outside of the State, as we have seen. This was the Compromise, so-called. A similar report was made to the Senate, on the 3rd of March, and was agreed to without a count. But, in the House, on agreeing to this Report, the question was first taken on striking out the Slavery Restriction on the State, as it then stood in the House Bill, for the admission of Missouri. This was the test vote in that body, and on this vote the ayes and noes, as they appear upon the record now open for inspection, stand, for it, ninety, and against it, eighty-seven. This is far from being as Mr. Buchanan says—one hundred and thirty-four in favor of the Compromise, with only forty-two against it! Of the ninety votes in favor of striking out the

Restriction on the State, only fourteen were from the non-slaveholding [i.e., slavery-prohibited] States. These are Messrs. [Mark L.] Hill, [John] Holmes, [Jonathan] Mason, and [Henry] Shaw, of Massachusetts; [Samuel] Foot and [James] Stevens, of Connecticut; [Samuel] Eddy, of Rhode Island; [Henry] Meigs and [Henry R.] Storrs, of New York; [Henry] Baldwin and [David] Fullerton, of Pennsylvania; [Joseph] Bloomfield, [Charles] Kinsey, and [Bernard] Smith, of New Jersey. The question, then, came up on concurring with the Senate in the insertion of the Thomas Amendment, which provided for the exclusion of Slavery from all the Louisiana Cession outside of Missouri, and north of 36° 30' north latitude.

"This is the question on which the vote stood one hundred and thirty-four to forty-two. It is readily understood. Nearly all those who could not get the Restriction on the State, very willingly took this Territorial Restriction, as the next best thing for the accomplishment of their general objects, without the slightest abandonment of their most determined purpose to accomplish these objects, whenever a case should again arise in which they could effect them. This vote of one hundred and thirty-four to forty-two was, in no sense, a test vote upon the admission of Missouri without the State Restriction, in consideration of the Territorial Restriction. If the question could then have come up for the admission of Missouri, under the bill, as it then stood amended, the vote would very certainly have been just as it was upon the motion to strike out the Restriction upon the State; for all knew perfectly well what would be the result of that vote. There was, however, no vote, and could be none, under the Rules, on the direct question of the admission of the State, by the Bill as it was then amended. It passed from the control of the House, and became a law, so far as they were concerned, by the vote agreeing to the amendment. The real test vote, therefore, was on striking out the State Restriction.

"Nearly all the forty-two noes against concurring with the Senate amendment, as to this Territorial Restriction, were from the South. They voted against it, because they believed it to be equally as unconstitutional as the restriction attempted to be put upon the State. They believed that Congress had no more power to control this Institution in the Territories, than they had to control it in the States. It is true, that a large number of Southern members, a small majority of them, did vote for it as a settlement of the Territorial controversy, upon the principle of a division of the public domain between the Sections. In this view they accepted it, agreed to it, and voted for it, under the circumstances, as a compromise on that question. This very clearly appears from the speech of Mr. [Charles] Kinsey, of New Jersey, one of the House Committee of Conference. In this, addressing himself to the northern side of the House, he said:

'Do our Southern brethren demand an equal division of this wide-spread, fertile region; this common property, purchased with the common funds of the Nation? No; they have agreed to fix an irrevocable boundary, beyond which Slavery shall never pass; thereby surrendering to the claims of humanity and the non-slaveholding States, to the enterprising agriculturist of the North, the Middle and Eastern States, nine-tenths of the country in question. In rejecting so reasonable a proposition, we must have strong and powerful reasons to justify our refusal; and notwithstanding you may plead your conscientious scruples, be it remembered, you must shortly account to that August and stern tribunal—impartial history and the strict scrutiny of public opinion. Can you plead conscience in bar to such a Compromise? If so, how reconcile votes you have, on similar questions, already given? When Mississippi, at the last Session, was received into the Union, your votes made Slavery interminable.

'. . . I much fear, notwithstanding all your solemn asseverations, a scrutinizing public will assign other views, other motives; and what more probable than that unhallowed one of political ascendency? And it is to be feared that a lurking ambition, the bane of all government, has had too great an influence in this debate. If so, it is time now to pause before we pass the Rubicon: to hesitate before it is too late to retract. In persisting in our Restriction on Missouri, are we dealing to our brethren of the South, the same measures we would be willing they should mete to us? When, with magnanimity unparalleled, they have conceded to us nine-tenths of this great common property, can we wish to deprive them of the remainder? And whilst gentlemen, on the part of the majority, arrogate to themselves a greater portion of moral refinement, it would be highly honorable to exhibit greater manifestations; of liberality in sentiment.'

"With this view, looking to it as a division of the public domain between the Sections, these members did regard this settlement so made as a compromise on the question."[176]

☛ "I am now upon what was the understanding of the nature and effect of the Compromise, at the time, and what I wish to impress upon [the Liberal mind], . . . at this point, is, that the only conceivable parties to this understanding, agreement, or compact, or covenant, in relation to this division of the public domain, between the Sections, viewed in that light, were the Restrictionist, or Centralist [Liberal] Party, on the one side, and the State Rights, or State Sovereignty [Conservative] Party on the other. Did, then, the Restrictionist Party so regard it at that time, or ever afterwards? I affirm that they did not! These Annals of Congress, from which I have just read, show that they utterly ignored and repudiated it, at the very next Session of Congress. Missouri was denied Representation in the Senate, and in the House, as a State in the Union, under the provisions of this bill, so passed, based upon this agreement and understanding. Her vote for President and Vice President, which had been cast at the election, held in the following fall, was not allowed to be counted.

"[My] . . . views on this question will be seen in the following extract from a debate in the House of Representatives, 17th of January, 1856:

> 'Mr. [Felix K.] Zollicoffer. If Congress has the power to exclude Slavery from one half of the Territory, has it not power to exclude it from all the Territory?
>
> 'Mr. Stephens. No, sir. That is the point. It would be unjust; and for that very reason no such power of general exclusion could be properly exercised. The Government of the United States, under the operation of the Revenue Laws, and not within the purview or contemplation of any of the delegated powers of the Government, acquired a surplus revenue. It was never contemplated, by the Constitution, that such a fund should be amassed. A distribution of the fund fairly and justly between all the States, I hold, was perfectly Constitutional. But suppose the North had said, "Here is a case outside of the Constitution. There is not a word in that instrument on the subject. The fund has been unexpectedly acquired under the operation of the Government; but it shall not be divided among all the States equally; it shall be taken exclusively by those where Slavery does not exist; that no slaveholding State shall touch a dollar of it." Would that have been Constitutional?
>
> 'This is an apt case in point of illustration, for the Constitution is silent on the subject. It was never contemplated, by that Instrument, that a surplus fund should be accumulated; but such a fund did accumulate, and may again. The power of distribution was a resulting power, and, when fairly and justly exercised, was Constitutional. I do not now discuss the expediency of the distribution, but the Constitutionality of it. I do not doubt that it was Constitutional if the distribution was fair and just, but it would have been nothing short of usurpation for the North to have taken the whole of it. That is my answer, and so with the Territories. Here was an acquisition of public domain, which the Constitution never looked to or provided for, made by the common treasure, by the common blood of Northern men and Southern men—men from all sections contributed in acquiring it. In some States Slavery existed, in others it did not; and was it not right that the people of all the States should have an equal enjoyment of, or a just and fair participation in, this public domain? Just as in the case of the surplus fund; when that fund came to be divided, it would have been monstrous, and unjust, and violative of the Constitution—of its spirit, if not of its letter—if the distribution had not been an equal and a fair one.'

"On the resolution of Mr. [William] Lowndes, of South Carolina, offered in the House, on the 13th of December, 1820, recognizing Missouri as a State in the Union, under her Constitution, adopted in pursuance of the Act of Congress, so passed at the Session before, the vote was seventy-nine for it and ninety-three against it! Here is the record. Of these ninety-three votes against it, seventy-two are the identical men who voted against striking out the State Restriction on the test vote in the House, as before stated, on the recommendation of the Committee of Conference, on the 2nd of March, at the last Session; and sixty-seven of them are the identical men who voted, immediately afterward, (2nd of March, 1820,) for the insertion of the Territorial Restriction, which was carried by one hundred and thirty-four to forty-two, which Mr. Buchanan has styled, a Test Vote on the Missouri Compromise! If they had entered into any such covenant, as he says, that Missouri should be admitted without the State Restriction, in consideration of the Territorial Restriction adopted in lieu of it, why did they not abide by it? If there was any breach of 'Compact' in this case, who made it? Was the Compromise of 2nd of March, 1820, held inviolate by the Restrictionists for twelve months much less for thirty years? If so, why was not Missouri recognized as a member of the Union under it? The pretext of this refusal so to recognize her, was, that the Constitution of Missouri, as formed, directed the Legislature to pass laws to prevent free negroes and mulattoes from going to or settling in the State. It was pretended, that this was in violation of the Constitution of the United States. It was, however, nothing but a pretext; for if the State Constitution contained anything inconsistent with the Constitution of the United States, it was, of course, inoperative, void, and of no effect. This, therefore, was a proper matter for the Courts to determine. But the same [Liberal] Party persistently refused to acknowledge Missouri as a State in the Union. She was, in point of fact, never admitted at all under the Missouri Compromise, so-called.

"The conflict was even fiercer at this Session than at the last. It was, at this stage of the proceedings, that Mr. [Henry] Clay threw himself in the breach, and exerted his transcendent powers in efforts of conciliation and harmony. He moved, on the 2nd of February, that a Committee of thirteen be appointed to report such action as was proper to be taken in view of the situation. The Committee consisted of himself as Chairman, Messrs. [William] Eustis, of Massachusetts, [William] Smith, of Maryland, [John] Seargeant, of Pennsylvania, [William] Lowndes, of South Carolina, [William D.] Ford, of New York, [William S.] Archer, of Virginia, [Aaron] Hackley, of New York, [Samuel] Moore, of Pennsylvania, [Thomas W.] Cobb, of Georgia, [Gideon] Tomlinson, of Connecticut, [Josiah] Butler, of New York, and [John W.] Campbell, of Ohio.

"Mr. Clay, as Chairman of this Committee, reported on the 10th of February. Here is the report and the vote upon it. The report, in substance, was, that Missouri should be recognized as a State, in the Union, upon the 'fundamental condition,' that her Legislature should pass no law in violation of the rights of citizens of other States, and that the Legislature should, also, by proper act, give its assent to this 'fundamental condition' before the fourth Monday in November, next ensuing; and that the President of the United States [James Monroe], upon the receipt of this assent of the Legislature, should announce the fact by proclamation, and then the State was to be considered in the Union. In other words, this Committee reported that Missouri should be admitted into the Union on an equal footing with the original States, upon the 'fundamental condition,' that the State Government, in all its Departments, should be subject to the Constitution of the United States, as all the other State Governments were! What more could the other 'Conflicting Party' have asked, if they had agreed to the Compromise on the question of Congressional Restriction. This Resolution was rejected by a vote of eighty for it, and eighty-three against it. This shows what was the real objection to the admission of Missouri, at that time, and that the Restrictionists had not agreed to the Compromise, and did not intend to abide by it.

"The parties, in the main, continued to stand as they stood in the beginning, and as they stood at the Session before. The passions on both sides waxed warmer as the conflict was prolonged. The excitement became intense, as the debates show. The strife was really between Centralism [Liberalism] and Confederation [Conservatism]. The rejection of Mr. Clay's resolution was reconsidered the next day; but, when it was again put on its passage, it was again lost, by a vote of eighty-two to eighty-eight. Discordant opinions now prevailed as to what was the real status of the people of Missouri in their relations to the Federal [Confederate] Government. Some held that they were still in a Territorial condition, subject to Federal authority, while others maintained that they constituted an independent State out of the Union.

"Mr. Clay, undaunted by his previous failure, again came to the rescue. On the 22nd of February, he moved that a grand joint Committee, consisting of members of the House and Senate, should be raised, to propose suitable action for the alarming crisis. The Committee, on the part of the House, was to consist of twenty-three members. These were to be elected by the House. This was agreed to. The Senate concurred. The Committee was raised.

"Mr. Clay was Chairman of the Grand Committee on the part of the House, and made the Report from it on the 26th of February. It was a Joint Resolution, substantially the same as that reported by him before, from the Committee of Thirteen. Here it is:

Resolved, by the Senate and House of Representatives of the United States of America in Congress assembled, That Missouri shall be admitted into this Union on an equal footing with the Original States, in all respects whatever, upon the fundamental condition, that the fourth clause of the twenty-sixth section of the third Article of the Constitution, submitted on the part of said State to Congress, shall never be construed to authorize the passage of any law, and that no law shall be passed, in conformity thereto, by which any citizen of either of the States in this Union shall be excluded from the enjoyment of any of the privileges and immunities to which such citizen is entitled under the Constitution of the United States: Provided, That the Legislature of the said State, by a solemn public act, shall declare the assent of the said State to the said fundamental condition, and shall transmit to the President of the United States, on or before the fourth Monday in November next, an authentic copy of the said Act; upon the receipt whereof, the President, by proclamation, shall announce the fact: whereupon, and without any further proceeding on the part of Congress, the admission of the said State into this Union shall be considered as complete.

"This Resolution passed the House the same day, by a vote of eighty-seven to eighty-one. It was sent to the Senate, and passed that body the next day, by a vote of twenty-six to fifteen; and was approved by the President [James Monroe] on the 2nd of March, 1821. The Legislature of Missouri readily passed the indicated Act on the 26th of June thereafter, and on the tenth day of August, 1821, the President issued his Proclamation accordingly, declaring the admission of Missouri into the Union is being complete.

"This is the real [Missouri] Compromise [of 1820], if it can be considered in that light at all, under which Missouri entered the Union as a State. It was on the fundamental condition that as a member of the Union, she should be subject to the Constitution as all the other States were. This is the substance of it, and this is the only Compromise, on the subject, in which Mr. Clay took any prominent part. It has no direct connection whatever with the exclusion of Slavery from any portion of the public domain. Of the eighty-seven votes for this Resolution, every one was from the Southern States, except seventeen. These seventeen were Messrs. [Mark L.] Hill and [Henry] Shaw, of Massachusetts; [Samuel] Eddy, of Rhode Island; [James] Stevens, of Connecticut; [William D.] Ford, [James] Guyon, [Aaron] Hackley, [Henry] Meigs, and [Henry R.] Storrs, of New York; [Henry] Baldwin, [Samuel] Moore, [Thomas J.] Rogers, and [Daniel] Udree, of Pennsylvania; [Ephraim] Bateman, [Joseph] Bloomfield, [Bernard] Smith and [Henry] Southard, of New Jersey; only three more in all from the entire North than had voted against the State Restriction on the 2nd of March the year before.

"This is a correct account of the Missouri Compromise [of 1820], so-called, up to the recognition of that State as a member of the Union. We see that it was utterly repudiated by a large majority of the members of the House from every Northern State, except Rhode Island and New Jersey, even before the consummation of that admission. What weight has Mr. [James] Buchanan's bare assertion 'that its wisdom and policy' had been 'recognized by Congress,' and had 'remained inviolate' for more than thirty years, against the unassailable and enduring facts of history here presented? Did the adoption of the Thomas Provision for the exclusion of Slavery from all the Louisiana Cession outside of Missouri, and north of 36° 30' north latitude, on the 2nd of March, 1820, and the passage of the Act for the admission of Missouri with that provision in it, quiet, or tranquillize the agitation of the Slavery question in Congress, for a day or a moment, much less for thirty years? Was not the conflict over the recognition of Missouri as a State in the Union, with a Constitution tolerating Slavery, just as fierce in 1821, as it had been in 1820, if not fiercer, notwithstanding the Act of Congress providing for her admission, with this extra territorial exclusion in it, instead of the State Restriction, which had been passed, as we have seen? Most assuredly it was!

"'A Solemn Compact between the conflicting Parties,' Mr. Buchanan calls it! When and where did the Restrictionists or Centralists [Liberals]—they certainly were one of the conflicting Parties, in his view—ever so regard it? Besides the votes of their Senators and Members in the House, as we have seen, did not a number of the Northern States, in which this Party had got into power, by their leaders seizing upon this question, immediately in their character as States, enter their most solemn protest against any such construction of the Act of Congress referred to? Here are the Resolutions of the Legislatures of two of these States, New York and Vermont, to say nothing of others, sent up to the very next Session of Congress, in direct renunciation of any such agreement or Compact. Is any fact in our history more notorious than that the Restrictionists and Centralists [Liberals] resorted to every epithet in the vocabulary of detraction and abuse, in their attempts to bring odium upon the names and memories of the fourteen men of the North, who voted to strike out the State Restriction, on the 2nd of March, 1820; and the seventeen who voted in favor of Mr. Clay's Resolution, in 1821, for their action on these measures, from the day the votes were given down to the proposed legislation referred to by Mr. Buchanan, in 1854? This brings me to the consideration of that measure, but before taking it up, I must trace further the history of this 'Missouri line,' and the Compromise of 1850. In the subsequent history of this question is to be found not only the reason, but the complete justification of the legislation of 1854, as I shall show. From this it will clearly appear, that this legislation was founded upon no breach of faith or 'of Compact,' on the part of the Southern States, but, as Mr. Buchanan himself said, in his letter of acceptance referred to, 'upon principles as ancient as free Government itself!' "Then, let us proceed with the narrative."[177]

☞ "The next time this question arose in Congress, was on the admission of Arkansas into the Union, in 1836. This State was formed out of a part of the Louisiana purchase, south of 36° 30' north latitude. By the terms of the Missouri Compromise, or Compact, as it has been called, she was to come in as a slave State, if her people in their Constitution so provided. Did the North then so recognize and act upon these terms? Did Northern members then raise no objection to the admission of Arkansas, because of her Constitution tolerating Slavery? Was this Compact then recognized, or adhered to, by that Party which had so persistently resisted the admission of Missouri for the same reason? In the House of Representatives, on the 13th of June, 1836, when the bill for the admission of Arkansas was before that body, Mr. John Quincy Adams, who was then the leader of the Abolition agitators in Congress, and who had, for years, presented there, the question of Slavery generally, as it existed in the District of Columbia and in the States, by petition, and in every conceivable form, for the purpose of excitement and irritation, offered the following amendment:

> And nothing in this act shall be construed as an assent by Congress, to the article in the Constitution of the said State, in relation to Slavery, or the emancipation of slaves,' etc.

"This amendment was cut off by the previous question, so that no direct vote was taken upon it, but when he presented it in Committee of the Whole, [Adams] . . . said he wished it to be inserted in the bill in italics, which showed the spirit with which it was proposed, and that he did not look upon the division of the public domain between the sections on the line of 36° 30' as a 'Compact' binding upon him or his Party. The same is shown by his vote, and that of every other Abolitionist in the House, against the admission of Arkansas as a slave State; though she was south of the Missouri Compromise line. If Arkansas came into the Union, therefore, without any restriction as to Slavery, it was not because the Abolition agitators recognized and acquiesced in the obligation of this Compact, but because of the very large majority of the Jefferson State Sovereignty Party [Conservatives] then in Congress.

"So of Texas in 1845. The same Party was then largely in the majority, and this line was extended by the members of it, to this new acquisition; but not with the consent, or agreement of 'the other conflicting Party [the Liberals].' They resisted it with strong and bitter opposition, as the debates conclusively show. In the settlement of the question as to Texas, it was provided that Slavery should be forever excluded north of 36° 30', and that *south of that line, the people forming Constitutions for new States, might tolerate Slavery, as it existed in other States, or not, as they pleased. The South did not ask for anything more, than that the people of the new States might regulate their domestic affairs in this particular, and all others, as they might in Sovereign Conventions determine for themselves, without any dictation or control from Congress, one way or the other.* [Emphasis added, L.S.]

"Soon after this, on the 12th of May, 1846, the country became involved in the Mexican war. It was apparent, at an early day, that the administration of Mr. [James K.] Polk, who was the [U.S.] President, looked to a large acquisition of additional Territory as one of the results of that war. This gave new and increased interest to the question of Slavery in the public domain, and on the admission of new States into the Union. On the 8th of August, 1846, Mr. David Wilmot, of Pennsylvania, offered in the House his celebrated 'Proviso,' for the exclusion of Slavery from all the public domain, which might be thus acquired without any recognition of the principle of division. Mr. Wilmot had, before this time, acted with the Anti-Restrictionists, or State Sovereignty Party [Conservatives], on this question. He had voted with them in the Texas settlement; and his 'Proviso,' coming from the quarter it did, struck the House, especially the Southern members of it, with very great surprise; but not greater than the result of the vote which was taken upon it. A very large majority of both of the then nominal Political Parties at the North, Whig and Democratic, voted for it. This measure, or Proviso, failed that Session, in the Senate, but the vote referred to, and the discussion in and out of Congress, upon the subject, awakened serious apprehensions and disquietude throughout the entire Southern States. Early, at the next Session, on the 15th of January, when the bill for organizing a Territorial Government for Oregon was up for consideration in the House, Mr. [Armistead] Burt, of South Carolina, deemed it a proper occasion to test the sentiments of Northern members, upon the principle of a division of the public domain, on the line designated in the Act of March, 1820. He therefore moved an amendment to that clause of the Oregon Bill, which excluded Slavery from that Territory, in the following words:

> Inasmuch as the whole of said Territory, lies north of 36° 30' north latitude, known as the line of the Missouri Compromise.

"The object of this amendment was to put a direct test to the Representatives of the Northern States, whether they intended to recognize the principle upon which the controversy on the subject of Slavery, in the public domain, was disposed of in 1820, or not. Northern members understood the object of the mover, as well as the question involved in the amendment, clearly;

and they met it promptly. Their response was that they did not. Here is the vote upon this question. There were in the House then, eighty-two votes for Mr. Burt's amendment, and one hundred and thirteen against it. Of these noes every man was from the North. Every Southern man in the House voted for it. And of the eighty-two who voted to adhere to the principle of the adjustment made in 1820, there were but six from the entire North. They were Clinton L. Hastings, of Iowa; Francis A. Cunningham and Isaac Parrish, of Ohio; Charles J. Ingersoll, of Pennsylvania; and Robert Smith and Stephen A. Douglas, of Illinois. This bill for the organization of a Territorial Government, for Oregon, failed that Session in the Senate.

"Mr. [John C.] Calhoun had in the meantime, 19th February, 1847, introduced a series of Resolutions in the Senate upon this subject, which were denounced at the time as factious abstractions and firebrands, intended to inflame sectional excitement, and to produce disunion. They, however, set forth with great clearness and power what was the general view of the people of the Southern States, in relation to the matter embraced in them. No action was had on them, then or afterwards; but they deserve special notice in this connection, and were in these words:

> Resolved, That the Territories of the United States belong to the several States composing this Union, and are held by them as their joint and common property.
>
> Resolved, That Congress, as the joint agent and representative of the States of this Union, has no right to make any law, or do any act whatever, that shall directly, or by its effects, make any discrimination between the States of this Union, by which any of them shall be deprived of its full and equal right in any territory of the United States, acquired or to be acquired.
>
> Resolved, That the enactment of any Law which should directly, or by its effects, deprive the citizens of any of the States of this Union from emigrating, with their property, into any of the Territories of the United States, will make such discrimination, and would, therefore, be a violation of the Constitution, and the rights of the States from which such citizens emigrated, and in derogation of that perfect equality which belongs to them as members of this Union, and would tend directly to subvert the Union itself.
>
> Resolved, That it is a fundamental principle in our political creed, that a people, in forming a Constitution, have the unconditional right to form and adopt the Government which they may think best calculated to secure their liberty, prosperity, and happiness; and that, in conformity thereto, no other condition is imposed by the Federal Constitution on a State, in order to be admitted into this Union, except that its Constitution shall be Republican [Confederate]; and that the imposition of any other by Congress would not only be in violation of the Constitution, but in direct conflict with the principle on which our political system rests.

"So this subject remained until the first of March, 1847, when a bill appropriating three million of dollars, to enable the President [James K. Polk] to effect such treaty with Mexico as he wished, came up before the Senate for consideration. Mr. [William] Upham, of Vermont, then moved to amend the bill by the insertion of what had become well known as the 'Wilmot Proviso.' That is,

> That there shall be neither Slavery nor involuntary servitude in any Territory which shall hereafter be acquired or be annexed to the United States, otherwise than in the punishment of crimes whereof the party shall have been duly convicted: Provided always, That any person escaping into the same from whom labor or service is lawfully claimed in any one of the United States, such fugitive may be lawfully reclaimed and conveyed out of said Territory, to the person claiming his or her labor or service.

"On agreeing to this amendment, the vote was twenty-one for it, and thirty-one against it. Every one of the yeas was from the non-slaveholding States, except John M. Clayton, of Delaware; and every one of the nays was from the slaveholding States, except Sidney Breese of Illinois, Jesse D. Bright and Edward A. Hannegan of Indiana, Lewis Cass of Michigan, and Daniel S. Dickinson of New York.

"This proposition re-opened in the Senate, as Mr. Wilmot's motion did in the House the year before, the Missouri question, so far as it related to the public domain, in its totality, and as it was presented in the beginning. We see from the vote that there were then in the Senate but five votes from the entire North who were in favor of abiding by the settlement of that question as made in 1820. These live votes from the North, with the Southern votes, defeated the amendment, and the Three Million Bill went from the Senate to the House without the restriction. When it came up for consideration before that body, on the 3rd of March, Mr. Wilmot moved his Proviso in the same words, substantially, as it had been presented to the Senate by Mr. Upham. To this Mr. [William A.] Graham, of North Carolina, moved a substitute, as follows:

> Provided, That if any Territory be acquired by the United States, from Mexico, the Missouri Compromise Line of 36° 30' shall be extended direct to the Pacific Ocean; that is, Slavery shall be prohibited north of that line, and allowed south of it.

"Mr. Graham's substitute was rejected, and the 'Wilmot Proviso' was incorporated in the bill, by ayes ninety, noes eighty, while the house was in Committee of the Whole. When the bill was reported to the House from the

Committee of the Whole, the question came up on agreeing to this amendment. Upon this direct question of agreeing to this 'Proviso' as it stood, the ayes were ninety-seven, and the noes one hundred and two! The 'Proviso' was therefore lost by a majority of five only. Every one of the ninety-seven votes for it were from the Northern States, except John W. Houston, of Delaware. And of the one hundred and two against it, every one was from the Southern States, except thirteen. These were Stephen A. Douglas and Robert Smith, of Illinois; James Black, Richard Brodhead, Charles J. Ingersoll, and Jacob Erdman, of Pennsylvania; Francis A. Cunningham, Isaac Parrish, and William Sawyer, of Ohio; Robert Dale Owen, and William W. Wick, of Indiana; Joseph Russell, of New York; Joseph E. Edsall, of New Jersey. Here is the record.

"*A most insuperable obstacle it is, too, in the way of those who undertake to maintain that the South was the offending Party, in her want of fidelity in adhering to the Missouri Line of Compromise, between the sections, as agreed upon in 1820! It was, as we have seen, literally forced upon the Southern States at first. If they had had their just representation in the House—the twelve more members which they would have had, but for the three-fifths clause of the Constitution—it never would have been forced upon them as it was. A bare majority of her Representatives accepted it under the circumstances, reluctantly then, as an alternative of two evils; but their entire people, nearly, were willing ever afterwards to abide by it in good faith. Up to this time, March, 1847, it had been preserved only, however, by a united South, aided by a comparatively very small number from the entire North, as this history of it clearly shows. From this last vote, the people of the Southern States still hoped that it might continue to be so preserved for all time to come. This hope, however, soon proved to be utterly delusive.* [Emphasis added, L.S.]

"It is proper to state here, that a goodly number of the members of Congress from the South, in the House, with Mr. [John C.] Calhoun in the Senate, had disapproved of the policy which led to the war; and did not favor the acquisition of Territory as one of the objects for which it should be prosecuted. This great South Carolina Statesman had, in language almost prophetic, characterized Mexican Territory in this view as 'the forbidden fruit' to the United States. In this sentiment I fully concurred, and, hence, in every possible way opposed the acquisition, even as a cession by purchase, unless the Slavery question should be first settled in regard to it; and under no circumstances was I in favor of it, as the spoils of conquest. Mr. [Robert A.] Toombs, my colleague, then in the House, occupied in the main a similar position. But the great majority of the South, however, both in the Senate and House, under the delusive hope, perhaps, inspired by the final vote on the Three Million Bill, sustained the Administration throughout, and thus secured the acquisition without any previous settlement of this question.

"This vote so given in both Houses, on the Three Million Bill, as stated, was the last, by which this line of 36° 30' was ever even indirectly recognized by the joint action of both Houses of Congress on any measure whatever."[178]

☛ "We now approach the end—its final and total abandonment in the Senate, as well as the House, not by the Southern States, but by the Northern States! It was on another bill for the organization of a Territorial Government for Oregon, which came up in the House of Representatives, on the 2nd of August, 1848, after the treaty of peace had been negotiated with Mexico, and the acquisition of an immense area of unsettled public domain, including the Territories of California, Utah, and New Mexico, amounting in all, to several hundred thousand square miles, to which the Southern States had contributed as liberally, in blood and treasure, as their Northern Confederates.

"In this new bill for organizing a Territorial Government for Oregon, no provision was made touching the new acquisitions. The bill came up and was passed in the House with a general Slavery Restriction in it, on the 2nd of August, 1848. An effort was made to strike this restriction out, but on the motion, the vote was eighty-eight to one hundred and fourteen. It was sent to the Senate with the Restriction. In that body, on the 10th of August, Mr. [Stephen A.] Douglas, then a Senator, moved to strike out the restriction as it stood in the bill, and to insert in lieu the following:

> That the line of thirty-six degrees thirty minutes of north latitude, known as the Missouri Compromise line, as defined by the eighth section of an Act entitled 'An act to authorize the people of the Missouri Territory to form a Constitution and State Government, and for the admission of such State into the Union on an equal footing with the original States, and to prohibit Slavery in certain Territories,' approved March 6th, 1820, be, and the same is hereby, declared to extend to the Pacific Ocean; and the said eighth section, together with the Compromise therein effected, is hereby revived and declared to be in full force and binding for the future organization of the Territories of the United States, in the same sense and with the same understanding with which it was originally adopted.

"His object appears clearly from the proposition itself. It evidently was, that now, after these large additional acquisitions had been made by the common blood and treasure of all the States, to settle this Territorial question throughout the whole, by the recognition of this line of division known as the Missouri Compromise. His amendment was carried in the Senate by a vote of thirty-three to twenty-one. But, when the bill went back, the House refused to concur by a vote of eighty-two to one hundred and twenty-one. The House continued persistently to refuse. The Senate, finally, on the 12th of August, gave way! They on that day receded from their amendment and passed the House bill, with an unconditional Territorial Restriction in it, by a vote of twenty-nine to twenty-five! *This was a complete and total abandonment of the Missouri Compromise, so-called, by both Houses of Congress. It met its final doom on the 12th of August, 1848. On that day it fell, and was buried in the Senate, where it had originated twenty-eight years before, but had never quieted the Abolitionists a day! It fell too, not by Southern, but by Northern hands. The very State to which it owed its paternity struck the last decisive blow!*"[179] [Emphasis added, L.S.]

☛ "A few more words in relation to these last votes in both Houses in the last stages of this memorable Compact, so-called, in the Federal Halls of Legislation. On the vote in the House, on the 2nd of August, of the eighty-eight in favor of still standing by this division as a Compromise, every one was from the South, except ten; and of the one hundred and fourteen against it, every one was from the North, except two. Of the thirty-three votes in the Senate on the 10th of August, in favor of Mr. [Stephen A.] Douglas's Amendment, twenty-six were from the South, and seven only were from the entire North. These seven were [Jesse D.] Bright and [Edward A.] Hannegan, of Indiana; [Stephen A.] Douglas, of Illinois; [Daniel S.] Dickinson, of New York, [Thomas] Fitzgerald, of Michigan; and [Simon] Cameron and [Daniel] Sturgeon, of Pennsylvania. Every Southern Senator present voted for it. Of the twenty-one votes against it, every one was from the North.

"An analysis of this vote, by States, presents the following results. There were sixteen States in favor of abiding by the line of 36° 30', nine against it, three divided, and two not voting. There were then thirty States in the Union. Of the sixteen yeas, fourteen were Southern States, to wit, Delaware, Maryland, Virginia, North Carolina, South Carolina, Georgia, Alabama, Mississippi, Louisiana, Tennessee, Kentucky, Missouri, Arkansas, and Texas, while only two were Northern States, to wit, Indiana and Pennsylvania. Of the nine nays, every one was a Northern State, to wit, Maine, New Hampshire, Massachusetts, Rhode Island, Connecticut, Vermont, New Jersey, Ohio, and Wisconsin. The three divided States were Northern, to wit, New York, Michigan, and Illinois. The two not voting, were Iowa, and Florida; one a Northern State, and the other a Southern State. When this amendment was before the House, on the 11th of August, of the eighty-two votes for it, every one of them was from the South, except four. These were Ausburn Birdsall, of New York, Charles Brown, Charles J. Ingersoll and Richard Brodhead, of Pennsylvania. Of the one hundred and twenty-one against it, every one was from the North, except one, John W. Houston, of Delaware.

On the final vote, in the Senate, on receding, when the yeas were twenty-nine, and nays twenty-five, every Northern Senator voted with the yeas, and every Southern Senator with the nays, except Mr. [Thomas H.] Benton, of Missouri. His vote would not have changed the result. So that every Northern State, both in the Senate and in the House, abandoned this principle of division, on the 12th of August, 1848. The vote by States on this question presented for the last time in the Senate, stands thirteen yeas for the Missouri Compromise line, to wit, Delaware, Maryland, Virginia, North Carolina, South Carolina, Georgia, Alabama, Mississippi, Arkansas, Tennessee, Kentucky, Louisiana, and Texas—all Southern States; and fourteen nays against it, to wit, Maine, Massachusetts, Connecticut, Rhode Island, New Hampshire, Vermont, New York, New 'Jersey, Pennsylvania, Ohio, Indiana, Illinois, Michigan, and Wisconsin, all Northern States. Missouri, a Southern State, was divided. Iowa and Florida failed to vote in this case as before.

"Now in the face of all the facts of these Records, which no one can gainsay or deny, with any regard for truth, who can justly charge upon the South, or the Southern States, the abandonment of the Missouri Compromise, so-called, or a violation of this sacred Compact, so-called? If there was any breach of faith in this matter, to whose door is it to be laid? . . . Well, then, I repeat, if there was any 'breach of faith' on this subject, to which side is it justly to be charged? With what renewed force does [the Liberals'] . . . proverb react?"[180]

22

The Missouri Compromise of 1850
Part One

Having discussed the Missouri Compromise of 1820, in the following excerpts from *A Constitutional View* Stephens turns to the Missouri Compromise of 1850, a five-bill package that included the controversial Fugitive Slave Act—in which runaway slaves, both in the North and in the South, were ordered to be returned to their owners.

☞ "We come now to the Compromise of 1850. How far the measures of that year are entitled to that appellation, the facts will show. The general ideas in relation to them are quite as erroneous, as in relation to the one we have just gone through with. For a correct understanding of the subject then, this must be borne distinctly in mind, that *the old principle of a division of the public domain between the sections having been presented by the North, and reluctantly accepted by the South, and then entirely rejected by the North*, as we have seen, the whole Territorial controversy on this question came up before the Thirty-first Congress, which assembled in December, 1849, just as it did before the Fifteenth Congress, as to the then unsettled public lands [in the West]. California, New Mexico, and Utah, were still undisposed of, in any way. . . . It is true, two other attempts, besides those noticed, had been made to settle the controversy as to these new acquisitions, which had both failed. One was known as the 'Clayton Compromise' in 1848; and the other as the 'Walker Amendment,' in 1849. As neither of these measures, however, had any direct bearing on the point, which we now have in hand, they may both be passed by at this time, without any inquiry into their respective merits or demerits.

"The whole question, therefore, came up in 1849, as it did in the beginning in 1818. A new Administration [under Whig President Zachary Taylor] had, in the meantime, come into power. The Democratic Party, under whose auspices these acquisitions of Territory had been made, had lost, not only the Presidential election in 1848, but had also lost their majority in the House of Representatives. Never had any Congress convened under so much excitement, or under so great responsibility as did the one on which then devolved the disposition of this question, under all the circumstances attending it. The embarrassments of the period were increased from the fact that, for the first time, Southern Senators and Members were greatly divided, as to the proper course to pursue, in view of the question with all its bearings. Some believed the time had come for a separation of the States, and that everything should be done with a view to effect that result. Others believed that the Union might still be preserved upon Constitutional principles, and that the object was worth the most earnest and patriotic efforts. This class believed, however, that the time had come for a total abandonment of all old Party associations, and that the united South should act in Party organization with those [Conservatives] of the North only, who would maintain the Federal [Confederate] system, as it was established by the Constitution.

"The principle of division having been abandoned by the North, from which side it had originally been proposed, this class maintained that the South should now firmly and unitedly occupy their original position against the Restrictionists [Liberals] from the beginning of the Government, and present the distinct question to the North of a continued Union under the Constitution, or an immediate separation. They believed that on this issue, squarely presented, a majority of the North would stand by the Constitution. The entire South, with few exceptions, were resolved not to submit to the 'Wilmot Proviso,' or, what was the same thing, a total exclusion from the public domain. Nearly all of the Southern States, if not every one, had passed Resolutions to this effect.

"But the particular class in Congress, so mentioned, who were then of opinion that the best policy for the South was thus to make a united effort, through a reorganization of Parties, to bring the administration of the government back to original principles, with hopes thus to preserve the Union, and the equality of the States, was confined at first, almost exclusively, to those known as Southern Whigs. They set the ball in motion by refusing to act further with the Whig organization, as it was then constituted, when the Party met in caucus to nominate a candidate for Speaker of the House. A Resolution, previously prepared, was submitted to this meeting, which in substance was, that Congress ought not to put any restriction upon any State Institution in the [Western] Territories, and ought not to abolish Slavery as it then existed in the District of Columbia [i.e., Washington, D.C.]. Upon the refusal of this Caucus even to entertain this proposition, this class retired from the meeting and would not act with the Whigs in the organization of the House. If all the Southern Members had then occupied the same position, with the view to an entire reorganization of Parties, as stated, it would, I doubt not, have been much better for the country. But no Southern Democrat [Conservative] favored the movement, while a majority of the Southern Whigs refused to sanction it. Howell Cobb, of Georgia, was the Democratic [Conservative] nominee for the Speaker's Chair, and Robert C. Winthrop, of Massachusetts, was put in nomination for the same by the Whigs. But neither of these two great Parties, then so called, as matters stood at the tune, had a majority in the House. Besides the Southern Whigs, who had thus separated themselves from their former Party organization, there were fourteen extreme Restrictionists [Liberals] from the North, composed partly of Whigs and partly of Democrats, who refused to support either of these nominees. In this way the election of a Speaker was prevented for nearly a month, and would have been prevented from ever taking place, on old Party lines, if the entire South had united with this separate Southern organization in their purpose, or if the Rules of the House had not been violated by the passage of a Resolution declaring that a bare plurality of votes cast for any one, instead of a majority of the whole, should constitute an election. This, subsequent events clearly proved. The position and views of these Southern Whigs, as well as the temper of the times, can best be known from a sample of the debates in the House, on the question of the election of a Speaker.

"My colleague, Mr. [Robert A.] Toombs, took the lead in this matter, in behalf of his associates. He it was who presented the Resolution in the Whig caucus referred to. I now call your attention to what he said in the midst of the confusion and excitement attending the organization of the House. It was on the 13th of December, after nine days had been consumed in unsuccessful ballotings for Speaker. But before taking up this speech, it is proper to add to what has been said, a few words more in further explanation. The Democrats, having become satisfied that in no event could they concentrate a majority of votes upon their regular candidate, [Mr. Cobb,] had informally taken his name down, and run up that of Mr. William J. Brown, of Indiana. On the 12th of December, after Mr. Brown had received a full majority of all the votes in the House, but before the result was announced, a very discreditable arrangement between him and certain members belonging to the extreme Restrictionists referred to, then known as 'Free-Soilers,' by which he had pledged himself to constitute three important committees in such way as they had required, was exposed, when Southern Democrats immediately withdrew their votes, and he failed of an election. Mr. Albert G. Brown, of Mississippi, then introduced a

Resolution declaring Mr. Cobb the Speaker.

"It was amidst the confusion growing out of this state of things that Mr. [William] Duer, of New York, next day, addressed the House at some length. Amongst other things, he said:

> 'The gentleman from Mississippi [Mr. Brown] had introduced a proposition, declaring the gentleman from Georgia [Mr. Cobb] to be the Speaker of this House; in other words, a proposition calling upon his (Mr. Duer's) side of the House (the Whig side) to make an unconditional surrender. It appeared to him that this was asking altogether too much; for his own part, so anxious was he that an organization should be effected, that he was willing to organize in almost any way, by electing to the Speaker's chair either a Whig or a Democrat, or a Free-Soiler—any one, in short, except a Dis-unionist. He never would give his vote for any man whom he believed to be inimical to the Union.
>
> 'Mr. [Thomas H.] Bayly (interposing) said: There are no Disunionists in this House.
>
> 'Mr. Duer. I wish I could think so, but I fear there are.'

"In this speech, Mr. Duer made no special mention of the Southern Whigs, who thus stood aloof, and did all in their power, to prevent an organization, under circumstances then existing; but he evidently referred to them, in his remarks about not voting for a Dis-unionist; for, the position of these Whigs was well known at the time to be for a separation of the States, or the abandonment by Congress of the general Territorial Restriction.

"It was now that Mr. Toombs, in his own behalf, as well as in behalf of these Southern Whigs, who, up to this time, had been silent, rose, and in his bold, dashing, impromptu, Mirabeau strain, delivered himself in these words:

> 'The difficulties in the way of the organization of this House, are apparent and well understood here, and should be understood by the country. A great sectional question lies at the foundation of all these troubles. The disgraceful events of yesterday, and the explanations consequent upon their exposure, prove conclusively that the Democratic Party and the Free-Soilers were both acting in reference to it. The Southern Democrats were satisfied, from the public course and private assurances both of the member whom they supported and his friends, that he was worthy of trust upon these important sectional issues. The disclosures which were made proved that they were mistaken; and, with a promptness honorable to them, they instantly withdrew their support, and left the discredit to fall where it properly belonged. The *Free-Soilers*, who were engaged in the discreditable conspiracy, secretly and dishonorably sought to acquire advantages in the organization of the House by private pledges, concealed and intended to be concealed from the great

majority of those whose votes were necessary to elect the person for whom they voted. They sought, by a discreditable trick, to secure those advantages in the organization which they had not the courage or the boldness openly to demand. They affected to rely on a written pledge which they knew was given in fraud and treachery. I leave the morality and honesty of this Party to be tested by the simple fact of this transaction, with the single remark, that *these are the men whose consciences have no rest on account of what they call the sin of Slavery*. The Whig party presented their nominee, who has received the support of the great majority of that Party. No pledges were asked by the Northern members of that Party, for the very sufficient reason that, being in a majority of nearly three to one, they were very abundantly able to take care of themselves. I did not act with them, because, the events of the past, of the present, and the prospect of the future, force the conviction on my mind that *the interests of my section [i.e., the South] of the Union are in danger*, and I am therefore unwilling to surrender the great power of the Speaker's Chair without obtaining security for the future.

'We have just listened to strong appeals upon the necessity of organizing the House. I confess I do not feel that necessity. From the best lights before me, I cannot see that my constituents have anything to hope from your legislation, but every thing to fear. We are not impatient to have the doors of your Treasury thrown open, and forty millions of the common taxes of the whole nation thrown into the lap of one half of it. We ask for none of it; we expect none of it; therefore gentlemen must pardon my want of sympathy for their impatience. By giving you the control of the Treasury, we increase your ability to oppress. I want grievances redressed, and security against their further perpetration, before I am willing to give you power over the supplies. Sir, I do not regret this state of things in the House. It is time we understood one another; that we should speak out, and carry our principles in our foreheads.

'It seems, from the remarks of the gentleman from New York, that we are to be intimidated by eulogies upon the Union, and denunciations of those who are not ready to sacrifice national honor, essential interests, and Constitutional rights, upon its altar. Sir, I have as much attachment to the Union of these States, under the Constitution of our Fathers, as any freeman ought to have. I am ready to concede and sacrifice for it whatever a just and honorable man ought to sacrifice. I will do no more. I have not heeded the aspersions of those who did not understand, or desired to misrepresent, my conduct or opinions in relation to these questions, which, in my judgment, so vitally affect it. The time has come when I shall not only utter them, but make them the basis of my political action here. *I do not, then, hesitate to avow before this House and the country, and in the presence of the living God, that if by your legislation you seek to drive us from the Territories of California and New Mexico, purchased by the common blood and treasure of the whole people, and to abolish Slavery in the District, thereby attempting to fix a national degradation upon half the States of this Confederacy, I am for disunion; and if my physical courage be equal to the maintenance of my convictions of right and duty, I will devote all I am and all I have on earth to its consummation.* [Emphasis added, L.S.]

'From 1787 to this hour, the people of the South have asked nothing but justice—nothing but the maintenance of the principles and the spirit which controlled our Fathers in the formation of the Constitution. Unless we are unworthy of our ancestors, we will never accept less as a condition of Union. A great Constitutional right which was declared by a distinguished Northern Justice of the Supreme Court (Judge [Henry] Baldwin) to be the cornerstone of the Union, and without which he avers, in a judicial decision, it would never have been formed, has already practically been abrogated in all of the non-slaveholding States. I mean the right to reclaim fugitives from labor. I ask any and every Northern man on this floor, to answer me, now, if this is not true—if this great right, indispensable to the formation of the Union, is any longer, for any practicable purpose, a living principle? There are none to deny it. You admit you have not performed your Constitutional duty; that you withhold from us a right which was one of our main inducements to the Union; yet you wonder that we look upon your eulogies of a Union whose most sacred principles you have thus trampled under foot as nothing better than mercenary, hypocritical cant. This District [of Columbia, i.e., Washington, D.C.] was ceded immediately after the Constitution was formed. It was the gift of Maryland [and Virginia] to [their] . . . sister States for the location of their common Government. Its municipal law maintained and protected domestic Slavery. You accepted it. Your honor was pledged for its maintenance as a National Capital. Your faith was pledged to the maintenance of the rights of the people who were thus placed under your care. Your fathers accepted the trust, protected the slaveholder and all other citizens in their rights, and in all respects faithfully and honestly executed the trust; but they have been gathered to their fathers, and it was left to their degenerate sons [in the North] to break their faith with us, and insolently to attempt to play the master where they were admitted as brethren. I trust, sir, if the representatives of the North prove themselves unworthy of their ancestors, we shall not prove ourselves unworthy of ours; that we have the courage to defend what they had the valor to win. [Emphasis added, L.S.]

'The [unformed Western] Territories are the common property of the people of the United States, purchased by their common blood and treasure. You are their common agents; it is your duty, while they are in a Territorial state, to remove all impediments to their free enjoyment by all sections and people of the Union, the slaveholder and the non-slaveholder. You have given the strongest indications that you will not perform this trust—that you will appropriate to yourselves all of this Territory, perpetrate all these wrongs which I have enumerated; yet, with these declarations on your lips, when Southern men refused to act in Party caucuses with you, in which you have a controlling majority—when we ask the simplest guarantee for the future—we are denounced out of doors as recusants and factionists, and in doors we are met with the cry of "Union, Union."

'Sir, we have passed that point. It is too late. I have used all my energies, from the beginning of this question, to save the country from this convulsion. I have resisted what I deemed *unnecessary and hurtful agitation*. I hoped against hope, that a sense of justice and patriotism would induce the North to settle these questions upon principles honorable and safe to both sections of the Union. I have planted myself upon a National platform, resisting extremes at home and abroad, willingly subjecting myself to the aspersions of enemies, and, far worse than that, the misconstruction of friends, determined to struggle for, and accept any fair and honorable adjustment of these questions. I have almost despaired of any such, at least from this House. We must arouse and appeal to the Nation. We must tell them, boldly and frankly, that *we prefer any calamities to submission*, to such degradation and injury as they would entail upon us; that we hold that to be the consummation of all evil. I have stated my positions. I have not argued them. I reserve that for a future occasion. These are the principles upon which I act here. Give me securities that the power of the Organization which you seek will not be used to the injury of my constituents, then you can have my co-operation; but not till then. Grant them, and you prevent the recurrence of the disgraceful scenes of the last twenty-four hours, and restore tranquillity to the country. Refuse them, and, as far as I am concerned, "let discord reign forever!"' [Emphasis added, L.S.]

[Several times during the delivery of these remarks, Mr. Toombs was interrupted by loud bursts of applause.]

"This speech produced a profound sensation in the House, and in the country. It received rounds of applause from the floor and the galleries. It did not, however, assuage, in the slightest degree, either the bitterness, or the determination of the Restrictionists [Liberals]. This is apparent from the fact that, the next day, a Resolution was passed prohibiting all further debate, and also from another specimen of the proceedings, on the 22nd of December, which deserves special notice. But before referring to this specimen, it is proper to state that after the disclosure of the arrangement which Mr. [Albert G.] Brown had entered into, his name was immediately withdrawn by the Democrats, and that of Mr. [Howell] Cobb again put up; but no election had taken place, and it was evident that none could take place under the Rules without an abandonment of the then Party organizations. The Whigs and the Democrats, in order to get over the difficulty, and to elect a Speaker without coming to the terms of these Southern Whigs, as stated, had come to a joint resolution, which was presented to the House by Mr. [Fred P.] Stanton, of Tennessee, from the Democratic side of the Conference Committee between the two great Parties, on the 22nd of December, and which declared in substance that that person should be speaker who should receive the largest number of votes, barely, on a certain ballot; provided the number so received should be a majority of a quorum, though it fell short of a majority of the House. This was the Plurality Resolution under which the House was organized as before referred to, in direct violation of its Rules. The scenes which occurred when it was presented, constitute the specimen of the proceedings on that day to which I refer, and in which Mr. Toombs again figured in the style we shall see. It is unnecessary to read the whole. A sample of the most striking points in the general prevailing disorder will suffice. The parts omitted have no material bearing upon those here reproduced:

'Mr. [Fred P.] Stanton, of Tennessee, rose and said, that he desired to present a proposition to the House. He presumed that, under the rule which had been adopted, it would not be in order to debate it. He would, however, be permitted to say, that it was a proposition known to have been presented on the part of the committee appointed by the Whig caucus, to confer with a similar committee appointed by the Democratic caucus.

'Mr. Toombs inquired of the gentleman from Tennessee [Mr. Stanton] if he yielded the floor?

'Mr. Stanton. I do, if it is understood that I am to have the floor, as soon as the question is decided.

'Mr. Toombs, (still remaining upon the floor,) said: I desire to be heard, to show this House, that they have no right to pass such an order, as they adopted on the 14th instant; that, according to the Constitution, and the act of Congress of 1789, this House [in its present condition,] has not the right to pass that or any other Rule.

'Mr. [William] Duer. I am willing to hear the gentleman from Georgia, and I propose that the unanimous consent be given, to allow that gentleman, and all other gentlemen, to discuss the point.

'Mr. [Edward D.] Baker. I move that by unanimous consent the gentleman from Georgia be allowed to debate this question.

'Mr. [Samuel W.] Inge called attention to the fact, that the motion of the gentleman from Illinois [Mr. Baker] could not be received, as there was already a question pending upon his motion, to rescind the Resolution of the 14th instant.

'The clerk, (to Mr. Toombs). Will the gentleman from Georgia allow me to put the question upon the motion to rescind the Rule?

'Mr. Toombs. No. I have the floor. I deny the Constitutional right of this House, to pass that Resolution, or any other rule or Resolution. It is an unauthorized infringement of the great right of freedom of speech. The Constitution and the law of 1789—

[Loud cries to order.]

'Mr. Toombs. You may cry order, gentlemen, till the heavens fall; you cannot take this place from me. I have the right to protest against this transaction. It is not with you to say whether this right shall be yielded, and when it shall be yielded. I desire, then, gentlemen of the House, to show that you are without rules, and that no orders can—

[Cries to order—"Sit down; you have no right to debate."]

'Mr. Toombs, (continuing.) I am attempting to show to you, that no man can rise to order—

[Calls to order.]

'Mr. [Thaddeus] Stevens, of Pennsylvania. I call the gentleman to order.

'Mr. Toombs, (continuing.) I say that, by the law of 1789, this House, until a Speaker is elected, and gentlemen have taken the oath of office, has no right to adopt any rules, whatsoever.

[Loud cries of order!]

'Mr. Toombs. Gentlemen may amuse themselves by crying order—

[Calls to order.]

'Mr. Toombs. But I have the right, and I intend to maintain the right to—

'Mr. [John] Van Dyke. I call upon the clerk to put the question, and let us see whether the gentleman will disregard the order of this House.

'Mr. Toombs. I have the floor, and the clerk cannot put the question. I submit that—

[Calls to order.]

'Mr. Toombs, (continuing.) The clerk has not the right to put the question of order.

[Order! Order!]

'Mr. Toombs, (continuing.) That it cannot be done. The House has no right. Gentlemen may cry "order," and interrupt me. It is mere brute force, attempting, by the power of lungs, to put down a gentleman in the exercise of his right.

[Cries to order.]

'Mr. Toombs, (continuing.) But gentlemen cannot deprive me of my rights. I shall insist upon them to the last extremity.

'Mr. Van Dyke. It is for the House to decide, whether the gentleman is in order or not.

'The Clerk. The gentlemen from New Jersey rises to a question of order. The question submitted to the House is—

'Mr. Toombs. I deny the right of the clerk, to put the question. I am upon the floor, and it is my right to—

[Calls for the yeas and nays, from various parts of the House.]

'The Clerk, (Mr. Toombs still upon the floor.) The yeas and nays are demanded upon the motion of the gentleman from Alabama, [Mr. Inge.] Gentlemen, you, who are in favor of agreeing to the motion, will, when your names are called, say "aye;" those of a contrary opinion will say "no." The clerk will call the roll.

'Mr. Toombs, (continuing.) I deny the right of these gentlemen to—

[Cries of order!—call the roll!]

'Mr. Toombs. I shall debate the question, whether you call the roll or not.

[Great confusion.]

'Mr. [Daniel] Breck. I move that this House do now adjourn.

'Mr. Toombs (continuing.) I keep upon the floor. Shall the clerk deprive me of my Constitutional rights? [Order, order.] Shall members, by crying "order," deprive me of those rights? I desire to show my rights under the Constitution. You do well to call the roll, and to cry "order:" [loud calls to order]—but I deny the right of any and every man to interrupt me.

[Cries of "Go it, Toombs"—"call the roll"—"order"—and great confusion.] In the midst of this, and while Mr. Toombs was still addressing the House, the Clerk commenced to take the yeas and nays, on the motion of Mr. Inge.

Mr. Toombs continued to speak.

[Great confusion prevailed.]

'Toombs said: If you seek, by violating the common law of Parliament, the laws of the land, and the Constitution of the United States, to put me down, [order, order,—"call the roll,"] you will find it a vain and futile attempt. [Order, order.] I am sure I am indebted to the ignorance of my character of those who are thus disgracing themselves, [order, order,] if they suppose any such efforts as they are now making, will succeed in driving me from the position I have assumed. [Order, order.] It is too strongly planted in the very foundations of public liberty. [Order, order.] I stand upon the Constitution of my country, upon the liberty of speech, [order, order,] which you have treacherously violated, and upon the rights of my constituents, and your fiendish yells may be well raised to drown an argument which you tremble to hear. You claim and have exercised the power to prevent all debate upon any and every subject; [order, order,] yet you have not even as yet, shown your right to sit here at all. I will not presume that you have any such right—[order, order.] I will not suppose that the American people have selected such agents to represent them; and I therefore demand that they shall comply with the act of 1789, before I shall be bound to submit to their authority. [Loud cries of order, order.] The second section of that act is [in] these words:

> That at the first Session of Congress after every general election of Representatives, the oath or affirmation aforesaid shall be administered by any one member of the House of Representatives to the speaker, and by him to all the members present, and to the clerk, previous to entering on any other business.

'This you have not done. [Order, order.] Your power to make rules for your own Government does not belong to you in your unorganized condition. [Cries of order.] You must first be sworn to obey the Constitution, before you can bind me, or yourselves, or any other citizen, by your rules. [Loud cries of "order, order."]

'You refuse to hear either the Constitution or the law, or the comments upon it. Perhaps you do well to listen to neither; they all speak a voice of condemnation to your reckless proceedings. But if you will not hear them, the country will. Every freeman, from the Atlantic to the Pacific shore, shall hear them, and every honest man will consider them. They are the securities for his rights as well as mine. You cannot stifle the voice that shall reach their ears. The electric shock shall proclaim to the freemen of this Republic, [order, order,] that *an American Congress, having conceived the purpose to violate the Constitution and the laws, to conceal those enormities, have disgraced the Record of their proceedings by placing upon it a resolution that their Representatives shall not be heard in their defence; and finding this illegal resolution inadequate to secure so vile an end, have resorted to brutish yells and cries, to stifle the words of those whom they cannot intimidate.* [Order, order.] The law is clear, plain, and conclusive. You cannot answer it. It has been solemnly affirmed by an American Congress, in 1839. [Order, order.] I read from the Congressional Globe, page 56: On motion of Mr. [George C.] Dromgoole, of Virginia, to adopt the standing rules and orders of the (then) last House of Representatives, as the rules and orders of that House, it was moved by Mr. Louis Williams to lay the resolution on the table. Mr. W. C. Johnson here made a point of order, that by the act of 1789, to which I have referred, the House had no power to adopt rules until they were sworn. The speaker (Mr. R. M. T. Hunter,) suggested that the better way of deciding the question would be on the motion (of Mr. Williams) to lay it on the table. The yeas and nays were called, and the Resolution was laid upon the table by the casting vote of the speaker: Congress thus deciding that, even after a more advanced stage of the proceedings, after a speaker was elected, the House could not, before its members were sworn, even adopt rules for their own government. [Emphasis added, L.S.]

[The clerk still continued to call the roll, a few members were answering, others inquiring what was the question, others demanding that their names should be called, and great confusion; during all of which, Mr. Toombs held on in his remarks.]

'I ask (said Mr. Toombs) by what authority that man (pointing to the clerk's desk) stands there and calls those names? By what authority does he interfere with the rights of a member of this House? [The clerk continued to call.] He is an intruder, and how dares he to interrupt members in the exercise of their Constitutional rights? Gentlemen, has the sense of shame departed with your sense of right, that you permit a creature, an interloper, in no wise connected with you, to stand at that desk and interrupt your order. [Order, order.]

'I have shown you that the House of Representatives decided this question in 1839, pending the New Jersey contested election. At the head of the names affirming it, stands that of John Q. Adams—a gentleman, distinguished at least for his vast and varied knowledge of Constitutional law and the science of government. The members of the House whose seats were not contested, having decided (before they were sworn or organized,) that the votes of certain members of New Jersey should not be counted, and the validity of that decision being insisted upon, Mr. Adams said,

"That decision was illegal, unconstitutional, null and void, on the ground, also, that the House, in its then unorganized State, had no power under the Constitution to decide any question."

'The history of that whole controversy shows such to have been the general opinion of the House, as I am prepared to show from the debates now before me; but as the House seems to be a little more patient, I will not inflict further quotations upon them. The House continued, without making any new rules, for days, until it was finally organized, and the members were sworn; then rules were adopted for its government.

'If, then, the House, before its organization, could decide no question, how can it enact a law, binding upon its members, abridging the liberty of speech? I venture to say that no such rule was ever before adopted in any deliberative assembly. It is without a precedent in the annals of civilization. Even the Revolutionary tribunals of France, during the Reign of Terror, did not soil their blood-stained records with an order denying the liberty of speech. This deed was reserved for you, Representatives of a free people. [Order! order!] What, then, is your condition?—what your rights, and what your duties, in your present condition? Under the Constitution you have the right "to choose your speaker and other officers." This must be done in conformity to existing laws, for you cannot now make a new law. The general Parliamentary law, the common law of Parliament, as far as it is not inconsistent with your Constitution and Statute law, is your law. By it you are bound, until you are in a condition to make others. It is amply sufficient for all legitimate purposes of organization. Thirty Congresses have met and been organized under it, and no such tyrannical proceeding as that which you have adopted has ever been deemed necessary. But you find yourselves trammelled by your Party ties. Your plain duty is to break these ties, and perform your Constitutional duty; but you prefer to break the Constitution of your country. Therefore, you will this day, do what you have already determined in caucus to do—you will delegate that power which the Constitution vests in the House of Representatives to a minority of that House, and you will permit that minority to exercise your Constitutional duty to choose a Speaker. A power delegated to the House must be used by a majority of the House. In [Thomas] Jefferson's Manual, we find the true and correct doctrine laid down, page 183:

"The voice of the majority decides; for the *lex majoris partis* [Latin: 'majority rule'] is the law of all councils, elections, etc., where not otherwise expressly provided."

'It is not otherwise provided in the Constitution, nor laws, nor rules of Parliament, nor in any rule of any preceding Congress. They, one and all, where the question is referred to, sustain the majority rule. It is the basis of our whole system. The will of any assembly can only be known by a majority. Therefore, whether every member of Congress is present, or but a majority of one, it is but a "House," and a majority must declare its will. I therefore, demand of you, before the country, in the name of the Constitution and of the people, to repeal your illegal rule, reject the one on your table, and proceed to the discharge of the high duties which the people have confided to you, according to the unvarying precedents of your predecessors and the law of the land.

[During the latter part of Mr. Toombs' speech, the House was more tranquil.]'

"This whole stenographic picture, from which I have extracted the most prominent parts, by Henry W. Wheeler, then reporter for the *Congressional Globe*, is one of the best of the kind ever put upon paper. The concluding note, however, hardly does full justice to the effect of the speech. The statement that the House was more tranquil, falls short of conveying an exact idea of its real condition. Members, it is true, were still out of their seats, and standing in the aisles; but the clerk had stopped calling the roll, all noise and interruptions had ceased, and every eye was staringly fixed upon the speaker.

"This speech of Mr. Toombs, as well as the other one cited, in tone and manner, was deemed by some as bullying, menacing, and insolent; but the former seemed to me, then and now, to be justly obnoxious to no such censure, while the latter, I thought, should rather be considered in the light of a wonderful exhibition of physical as well as intellectual prowess—in this, that a single man should have been able, thus successfully, to speak down a tumultuous crowd, and by declamatory denunciations, combined with solid argument, silence an infuriated assemblage. The House at that time was little else. Mr. [Stephen A.] Douglas tried a similar experiment some months afterwards, at Chicago, but failed in it.

"The Resolution, which had been agreed upon by the Representatives of the two nominal Parties, Whig and Democratic, was immediately adopted by the House. Under this Resolution, Mr. [Howell] Cobb received one hundred and two votes, and Mr. [Robert C.] Winthrop ninety-nine. The whole number of votes cast was two hundred and twenty-one. So Mr. Cobb was declared to be the Speaker, though he fell short by nine votes of receiving a majority of the whole, as required by law. These samples must suffice for the phase of things as presented in the House [of Representatives]."[181]

☛ "[Concerning the Missouri Compromise of 1850 we] . . . will now turn to the Senate. Mr. [Henry] Clay had just been returned again after being in retirement for several years. He had been defeated for the Presidency by Mr. [James K.] Polk, in 1844. He was in politics a disciple of the Jefferson school, and had lost his election for the Presidency by a defection at the North from the Party then running him, because of their violent opposition to the incorporation of Texas into the Union. He had expressed himself in favor of that measure in a letter, which was published not long before the election. He had stood amongst the most prominent of the Anti-Restrictionists upon the Missouri question, though he was known to be opposed to Slavery. [Clay's] . . . position on this question, in 1821, and on the Tariff question, in 1832, had secured to him the appellation of 'The Great Pacificator.' Coming back to the Senate, therefore, now, in this even more alarming crisis than either of the former ones, all friends of the Constitution, and Union under it, looked to him with more interest than ever before, and with more hope than to any other man then living. He was approaching the sunset of life; and, personally, it was a brilliant one to him. The clouds and tempests of the morning, noon, and evening of his day, had passed away. All party and personal bitterness had ceased. He had the respect and the confidence of the entire country. He, therefore, took the lead in the Senate, where he again met Mr. [John C.] Calhoun and Mr. [Daniel] Webster, the other two of the illustrious trio of their day. This body never before presented a greater array of talent than it did at the beginning of this Session of Congress.

"Besides Mr. Clay, Mr. Calhoun and Mr. Webster, there were, at this time, in the Senate of the older class, connecting and lapping the outgoing with the incoming generation of Statesmen, quite a number who had gained great distinction, and who will ever hereafter occupy a high place on the Roll of the men who made their mark upon the history of the country, during the period in which they lived.

"Amongst these, without invidious distinction, may be named Lewis Cass, Thomas H. Benton, John McPherson Berrien, William R. King, John Bell, Willie P. Mangum, James Alfred Pearce, Samuel S. Phelps, and Samuel Houston.

"Then of the younger class, just rising to note on that August arena, may be, in like manner, named Stephen A. Douglas, Jefferson Davis, Salmon P. Chase, William H. Seward, Robert M. T. Hunter, James M. Mason, Moses Norris, George E. Badger, John P. Hale, and Henry S. Foote.

"These, to say nothing of others, all added more or less lustre, by vigor of thought or brilliancy of wit, to that grandest intellectual constellation—moral qualities and all considered—which was ever beheld in the Political firmament of this or any other country.

"The crowning halo was imparted by Millard Fillmore, who presided over the whole as Vice President of the United States. He was of most imperturbable temper, and of a personal appearance, in every respect, exceedingly impressive. There was a dignity in this Head of the Ambassadors of the States in Grand Council assembled, which fully accorded with all the surroundings. Order and decorum, with all the proprieties which should govern high debate, were stamped upon his brow. Of him, taken altogether, it might be said with as much truth as of any other public character I ever met with: There, 'indeed,' is a man 'in whom is no guile!'

"On the 29th of January, 1850, Mr. Clay introduced his celebrated series of Resolutions covering, as was supposed, all the questions involving sectional controversy, agitation and alienation. It was known for several days previous, that, on this day, he would address the Senate, and present to their consideration propositions for the adjustment of all these questions. The announcement of this fact, which had gone to the country, had brought an immense crowd of strangers to the city. At an early hour in the morning, long before the hour for the meeting of the Senate, the chamber, in every aisle, nook and corner, was jammed to hear the words which, on this occasion, would fall from the lips of the 'Sage of Ashland.' Thousands were disappointed from inability to reach even within ear-shot of the speaker. On the conclusion of this speech, one of the most eloquent of his life, which was continued to the next day, he formally submitted the Resolutions referred to, which were the basis of what is known as the Compromise of that year.

"They, however, did not contain the main provision upon which the final legislation of that year depended and turned. To understand the bearing of his Resolutions, and the difference between them and the final acts of Congress upon the subjects embraced by them, it is proper to state that before the meeting of this Session of Congress, and without any authority from Congress, the people of California had, during the Summer of 1849, under a proclamation of General [B.] Riley, of the United States Army, then in command of that Military District, called a Convention, which had framed a Constitution, with an exclusion of Slavery, and asked to be admitted as a State into the Union under it. This was understood to have been done in pursuance of the policy of General [Zachary] Taylor's Administration, which was to get rid of the vexed question, by stimulating the people of the Territories to form State Constitutions, with the exclusion of Slavery in them, and for them thus to apply for admission into the Union without any previous authority from Congress. This policy met the approval of very few of any Party. To say nothing of other considerations, the people of Utah and New Mexico were in no condition to become States.

"Mr. Clay's Compromise proposed to admit California under the Constitution so formed—to organize Territorial Governments for Utah and New Mexico, without any restriction as to Slavery—to settle the question of boundary between New Mexico and Texas by negotiation with that State—to pass an efficient act for the rendition of fugitive slaves, and to abolish the slave trade, as it was called, in the District of Columbia. These propositions, taken together, like the Administration plan, satisfied very few members, either of the Senate or the House. The great majority of the North were utterly unwilling to abandon the Restriction of Slavery in the Territories. A formidable minority of the same section was equally as unwilling to comply with that clause of the Constitution requiring the rendition of fugitive slaves. This latter class, also, were not satisfied with the bare suppression of the slave trade in the District of Columbia, but insisted upon a total abolition.

"On the Southern side an overwhelming majority were opposed to the admission of California as a State, under the Constitution so formed, irregularly and without the authority of law. *The class of Southern Whigs referred to were willing to admit California under her Constitution; but required that in the organization of the Territorial Governments for Utah and New Mexico, the people from the South, settling and colonizing these Territories, should be permitted to carry their slaves with them, if they chose; and that the whole people, then, should be permitted to frame such Constitutions as they might please in reference to African Slavery; and upon their application for admission into the Union, they should he received as States without any Congressional Restriction upon that subject.* So matters stood in both Houses. The debates in each were continued with great bitterness. No active demonstration of forces was made in either until the 18th of February. [Emphasis added, L.S.]

"On that day, Monday, which was the day of the week under the Rules when Resolutions were in order from the States, Mr. James D. Doty, of Wisconsin, offered, in the House, a resolution instructing the committee on Territories, to report a bill for the admission of California under her Constitution, and called the previous question upon it. This was a nigh cut to get California in without any settlement of the other questions. A large majority of the House was in favor of the admission of California; but there were some of this majority, to wit, the Southern Whigs referred to, who were opposed to her admission, until the Territorial question should be adjusted. They therefore resisted the passage of Mr. Doty's resolution. They could resist it successfully, in one way only—that was by making dilatory motions; for, under the operation of the previous question, if the call for that had been allowed to be sustained, the resolution of instruction would have immediately passed by a large majority. The only possible way, therefore, to defeat this result, and the admission of California without the adjustment of the other question, was to prevent the vote being taken. This was done by repeated motions to adjourn, for calls of the House, to go into Committee of the Whole, etc., and the consumption of time in taking the yeas and nays upon these various motions. In this movement, Southern members generally joined zealously. One-fifth of the members present, under the Constitution, could require the yeas and nays to be taken upon any motion or question. Forty-one members constituted a fifth of the House. More than that number pledged themselves so to resist the question and prevent its ever coming to a vote under such circumstances. I made the list, saw the members, and secured the pledges. The whole of the day, and the early hours of night, were consumed in this way. *The vote finally became almost exclusively sectional. Nearly all, if not every one, on the one side, were from the North; while nearly all, if not every one, on the other, were from the South. The passions on both sides became highly excited. Very little intercourse took place between the members of either of the great Parties from the two sections, even on the same sides of the House.* [Emphasis added, L.S.]

"In this condition of affairs, Mr. John A. McClernand, of Illinois, a gentleman whose general courtesy and urbanity of manner secured him the personal respect of all, came round to the seats occupied by Mr. Toombs and myself, and inquired if there was no possible way by which the contest then going on in the House could be ended. We stated to him our positions fully. We did not object to the admission of California, if the Territorial question could be first satisfactorily adjusted. On this we insisted, not only that there should be no Congressional exclusion of Slavery from the public domain, but that, in organizing Territorial Governments, the people under each should be distinctly empowered so to legislate as to allow the introduction of slaves, and to frame their Constitutions in respect to African Slavery, as they pleased, and when admitted as States into the Union, should be received without any Congressional Restriction upon the subject. We stated that we never would permit California to be admitted, if we could possibly prevent it, until these Territorial principles were first settled. The propositions were briefly set forth in writing. I have given their substance only. He read them, and stated that he thought a compromise might be effected on the basis therein set forth, and he would return to his side of the House and endeavor to get enough members to agree to an adjournment, to see what could be done in the premises. No adjournment, however, was effected until the hour of twelve arrived, when the speaker ruled that the Legislative day had ceased, that the motion of Mr. Doty was no longer in order for consideration, as the resolution he had offered under the Rules could only be entertained or considered on Mondays. The House acquiescing in this decision then adjourned. Mr. McClernand came round to our seats again, and we agreed to meet him at the Speaker's house, the next night, with such friends as he might bring with him, from the North, to see if the terms we had proposed could be agreed upon and put in proper language.

"The meeting accordingly took place the next night at Mr. [Howell] Cobb's house. There were present Mr. Cobb, Mr. Toombs, Mr. Linn Boyd, of Kentucky, and myself, from the South; Mr. John A. McClernand, and Mr. William A. Richardson, of Illinois, and Mr. John K. Miller, of Ohio, from the North. Some one or two more, perhaps, were present whose names or where from, I do not now recollect. Mr. McClernand stated that Mr. [Stephen A.] Douglas, of the Senate, with whom he had consulted, would act in concert with him in anything he might agree to on the subject, and had declined being present simply because it was a meeting of members of the House. Mr. Douglas was Chairman of the Committee on Territories of the Senate, and Mr. McClernand was Chairman of the like Committee of the House. They conferred freely together and understood each other thoroughly.

"At this meeting it was agreed that California should be admitted, and the Territorial Governments should be organized as stated, and that all our joint efforts should be united to effect these results, as well as the defeat of any attempt to abolish Slavery, in the District of Columbia. The words of the Territorial Bills, which in our judgment would effect our objects, were reduced to writing. Mr. McClernand and Mr. Douglas therefore prepared bills on this basis for their respective Committees. Mr. Douglas reported his in the Senate on the 25th of March. Mr. McClernand announced to the House the substance of his bills, as he had had no opportunity to report them, on the 3rd of April. In the meantime, on the 27th of February, Mr. Doty introduced into the House, in the regular way, a bill for the admission of California, which was referred to the Committee of the Whole. On the same day, Mr. Toombs addressed the House, at great length, upon the whole subject. I cannot ask you to go through with the entire speech which I have here, but a short extract will suffice to show its tenor. Addressing himself to the North, he said:

> 'We had our Institutions when you sought our alliance. We were content with them then, and we are content with them now. We have not sought to thrust them upon you, nor to interfere with yours. If you believe what you say, that yours are so much the best to promote the happiness and good government of society, why do you fear our equal competition with you in the [Western] Territories? *We only ask that our common Government shall protect us both, equally, until the Territories shall be ready to be admitted as States, into the Union, then to leave their citizens free to adopt any domestic policy in reference to this subject, which, in their judgment, may best promote their interest and their happiness. The demand is just. Grant it, and you place your prosperity and ours upon a solid foundation; you perpetuate the Union, so necessary to your prosperity; you solve the true problem of Republican Government; you vindicate the power of Constitutional guarantees.* . . . The fact cannot longer be concealed—the declaration of members here proves it, the action of this House is daily demonstrating it—that *we are in the midst of a legislative revolution, the object of which is to*

trample under foot the Constitution and the laws, and to make the will of the majority the supreme law of the land. In this emergency our duty is clear—it is to stand by the Constitution and laws, to observe in good faith all its requirements, until the wrong is consummated, until the act of exclusion is put upon the statute book. It will then be demonstrated that the Constitution is powerless for our protection; it will then be not only the right, but the duty of the slaveholding States to [secede in order to] resume the powers which they have conferred upon this Government, and to seek new safeguards for their future security.' [Emphasis added, L.S.]

"On the next day, February the 28th, Mr. John Bell, of Tennessee, introduced into the Senate a series of Resolutions, setting forth in substance what was then considered a modified form of the Executive policy for a proper adjustment, which he supported in a speech of great length, and with all the powers he could command.

"On the 4th of March, Mr. [John C.] Calhoun's sentiments on the crisis were delivered in the Senate. He was too feeble to speak, but he was present, and Mr. [James M.] Mason, of Virginia, read what Mr. Calhoun had written for the occasion. In this speech he manifested strong attachment to the Union under the Constitution, but maintained that *all the dangers which then threatened its continuance arose from the Centralizing tendency of the Government. This had, by its Tariffs, and by several other measures specified by him, given a preponderance to the population of the non-slaveholding [Northern] States, and the tendency was towards Consolidation.* [Emphasis added, L.S.] He said:

'What was once a Constitutional Federal Republic [i.e., a Confederacy], is now converted, in reality, into one as absolute as that of the Autocrat of Russia, and as despotic in its tendency as any absolute government that ever existed.'

"He alluded to the ligaments of the Union from the beginning. They were chiefly ecclesiastical, social and political. The two former had already been broken. Most of the churches North and South had separated.

[Calhoun continues:] 'The political ties only remained, and these too, as the tendency was, must soon be broken, except the sections were held together by force. Force might keep them connected, but the combination would partake more of the character of subjugation on the part of the weaker to the stronger than the Union of free, independent, sovereign States in one Confederation, as they stood in the early days of the Government, and which only is worthy the name of Union. There was only one way in which the Union could be preserved, and that was by adopting such measures as would satisfy the States belonging to the Southern section, that they could remain in the Union consistently with their honor and safety.

'. . . [The Union] cannot, then, be saved by eulogies on the Union, however splendid or numerous. The cry of "Union, Union, the glorious Union!" can no more prevent disunion than the cry of "Health, health, glorious health!" on the part of the physician can save a patient lying dangerously ill. So long as the Union, instead of being regarded as a protector, is regarded in the opposite character, by not much less than a majority of the States, it will be in vain to attempt to conciliate them by pronouncing eulogies on it.

'Besides, this cry of Union comes commonly from those whom we cannot believe to be sincere. It usually comes from our assailants [in the North]. But we cannot believe them to be sincere; for, *if they loved the Union, they would necessarily be devoted to the Constitution. It made the Union, and to destroy the Constitution would be to destroy the Union. But the only reliable and certain evidence of devotion to the Constitution is to abstain, on the one hand, from violating it, and to repel, on the other, all attempts to violate it. It is only by faithfully performing these high duties that the Constitution can be preserved, and with it the Union.* [Emphasis added, L.S.]

'But how stands the profession of devotion to the Union by our assailants, when brought to this test? Have they abstained from violating the Constitution? Let the many acts passed by the Northern States to set aside and annul the clause of the Constitution, providing for the delivery up of fugitive slaves, answer. I cite this, not that it is the only instance, (for there are many others,) but because the violation in this particular is too notorious and palpable to be denied. Again, have they stood forth faithfully to repel violations of the Constitution? Let their course in reference to the agitation of the Slavery question, which was commenced and has been carried on for fifteen years, avowedly for the purpose of abolishing Slavery in the States—an object all acknowledged to be unconstitutional, answer. Let them show a single instance, during this long period, in which they have denounced the agitators or their attempts to effect what is admitted to be unconstitutional, or a single measure which they have brought forward for that purpose. How can we, with all these facts before us, believe that they are sincere in their profession of devotion to the Union, or avoid believing their profession is but intended to increase the vigor of their assaults, and to weaken the force of our resistance!

'Nor can we regard the profession of devotion to the Union, on the part of those who are not our assailants, as sincere, when they pronounce eulogies upon the Union, evidently with the intent of charging us with disunion, without uttering one word of denunciation against our assailants. If friends of the Union, their course should be to unite with us in repelling these assaults, and denouncing the authors as enemies of the Union. Why they avoid this, and pursue the course they do, it is for them to explain.

'Nor can the Union be saved by invoking the name of the illustrious

Southerner [George Washington], whose mortal remains repose on the Western bank of the Potomac. He was one of us—a slaveholder and a planter. We have studied his history, and find nothing in it to justify submission to wrong. On the contrary, *his great fame rests on the solid foundation that, while he was careful to avoid doing wrong to others, he was prompt and decided in repelling wrong.* I trust that, in this respect, we profited by his example. [Emphasis added, L.S.]

'*Nor can we find anything in his history to deter us from seceding from the Union, should it fail to fulfil the objects for which it was instituted, by being permanently and hopelessly converted into the means of oppressing, instead of protecting us. On the contrary, we find much in his example to encourage us, should we be forced to the extremity of deciding between submission and disunion.* [Emphasis added, L.S.]

'. . . Having now shown what cannot save the Union, I return to the question with which I commenced, How can the Union be saved? There is but one way by which it can, with any certainty; and that is, by a full and final settlement, on the principle of justice, of all the questions at issue between the two sections. The South asks for justice, simple justice, and less she ought not to take. She has no Compromise to offer but the Constitution, and no concession or surrender to make. She has already surrendered so much, that she has little left to surrender. Such a settlement would go to the root of the evil, and remove all cause of discontent, by satisfying the South she could remain honorably and safely in the Union; and thereby restore the harmony and fraternal feelings between the sections which existed anterior to the Missouri agitation. Nothing else can, with any certainty, finally and forever settle the questions at issue, terminate agitation, and save the Union. [Emphasis added, L.S.]

'It is time, Senators, that there should be an open and manly avowal on all sides, as to what is intended to be done. If the question is not now settled, it is uncertain whether it ever can hereafter be; and we, as the Representatives of the States of this Union, regarded as Governments, should come to a distinct understanding, as to our respective views, in order to ascertain whether the great questions at issue can be settled or not. If you, who represent the stronger portion, cannot agree to settle them on the broad principle of justice and duty, say so; and let the States we both represent, agree to separate and part in peace. If you are unwilling we should part in peace, tell us so, and we shall know what to do, when you reduce the question to submission or resistance. If you remain silent, you will compel us to infer by your acts what you intend. In that case, California will become the test question.

'. . . I have now, Senators, done my duty in expressing my opinions fully, freely, and candidly, on this solemn occasion. In doing so, I have been governed by the motives which have governed me in all the stages of the agitation of the Slavery question, since its commencement. I have exerted myself, during the whole period, to arrest it, with the intention of saving the Union, if it could be done; and, if it could not, to save the section where it has pleased Providence to cast my lot, and which I sincerely believe has justice and the Constitution on its side. Having faithfully done my duty to the best of my ability, both to the Union and my section, throughout this agitation, I shall have the consolation, let what will come, that I am free from all responsibility.'

"In this speech Mr. Calhoun also suggested, as a further security for the permanency as well as the strength of the Union, for the future, in case the then questions should be settled upon right principles, *a Constitutional amendment providing for a dual Executive [i.e., U.S. president]*. The idea was barely presented, not elaborated. But it was that the Executive office should be filled with two instead of one. One of these two to be selected by the slaveholding States, and the other by the non-slaveholding States, who, upon all sectional questions, should have the same check upon each other as that which existed in the amended Constitution of Rome between the Consuls and the Tribunes. This he thought would be necessary for harmony, which he considered as essential for strength, after the equality then existing between the number of slaveholding [slavery optional] and non-Slaveholding [slavery prohibited] States would be destroyed by the admission of California. But he lived to see the end of none of these measures. He died twenty-five days afterwards, on the 31st of March [1850]. In his death passed away one of the ablest, truest and most patriotic public men this country ever produced. He was a close reasoner, a clear and profound thinker. A model of sobriety, temperance and morals in every respect. The science of Government was his favorite study; and, in his day, he had few equals and no superior in all the elements of real Statesmanship. The two survivors [Henry Clay and Daniel Webster] of the illustrious trio referred to, both did honor to themselves, in their feeling tributes to his memory on the occasion of his funeral obsequies."[182]

☛ "[I will now] . . . proceed with a rapid glance at facts, with their dates, during this stormy, as well as momentous Session. On the 7th of March, three days after Mr. [John C.] Calhoun's speech, Mr. [Daniel] Webster addressed the Senate. What he then said has become famous as his 7th of March Speech, or 'Union Speech.' In it he took, for the first time, decided ground against Congressional Restriction in the Territories. The speech made a profounder sensation upon the public mind throughout the Union, than any one ever delivered by him before. The friends of the Union, under the Constitution, were strengthened in their hopes, and inspired with renewed energies by its high and lofty sentiments.

"Mr. [Stephen A.] Douglas addressed the Senate on the 13th of March, on the same line, and with great power and eloquence. On the 18th of April, a resolution, previously offered by Mr. Henry S. Foote, of Mississippi, an active and zealous co-operator with Mr. [Henry] Clay in his general objects, was passed in the Senate, to raise a select committee of thirteen, to whom the Resolutions of Mr. Clay and Mr. [John] Bell were referred. This Committee was chosen by that body the next day. The Chairmanship of it was, by almost unanimous consent, awarded to Mr. Clay. The other members of the Committee consisted of Gen. [Lewis] Cass, of Michigan, Mr. [Daniel S.] Dickinson, of New York, Mr. [Jesse D.] Bright, of Indiana, Mr. [Daniel] Webster, of Massachusetts, Mr. [Samuel S.] Phelps, of Vermont, Mr. [James] Cooper, of Pennsylvania, Mr. [William R.] King, of Alabama, Mr. [James M.] Mason, of Virginia, Mr. [Solomon W.] Downs, of Louisiana, Mr. [Willie P.] Mangum, of North Carolina, Mr. [John] Bell, of Tennessee, and Mr. [John M.] Berrien, of Georgia.

"On the 8th of May, Mr. Clay, as Chairman of this Committee, reported to the Senate one bill, (which afterwards was known as the '*Omnibus*,') covering all the matters embraced in his Resolutions on the 29th of January before: that is, for the admission of California, Territorial Governments for Utah and New Mexico, the settlement of the question of boundary with Texas, the rendition of fugitive slaves, and the abolition of what was called the slave trade in the District of Columbia. Those portions of the bill providing Territorial Governments for Utah and New Mexico were identical with the separate bills on the same subjects introduced by Mr. Douglas, in the Senate, on the 25th of March, as before stated, except in one particular; that is, after the words in his bills declaring that the Territorial Legislatures should pass 'no law interfering with the primary disposal of the soil,' the Committee had added, 'nor in respect to African Slavery.'

"This amendment, in the opinion of many Southern men, was tantamount in legal effect to a positive Congressional exclusion of the South; for, by the law of Mexico, Slavery was prohibited in these Territories at the time of their acquisition, and if the Legislative power there were restrained by Congress from ever changing this law, then in force there, no Southern man could ever colonize any of this portion of the public domain with his slaves. Mr. Clay said this amendment had been put in by a majority of the Committee, against his wishes; but he did not regard it as an insuperable objection to the bill, as it was not, in his opinion, a positive Congressional Restriction. He said Slavery was abolished by Mexican Law in these Territories at the time of their acquisition, and he never would vote to change it.

"Mr. Jefferson Davis, of Mississippi, on the 16th of May, moved an amendment to the words added by the Committee, which he afterwards, on the 27th of May, mollified so as to read as follows:

That nothing herein contained shall be construed so as to prevent said Territorial Legislature from passing such laws as may be necessary for the protection of the rights of property of every kind, which may have been, or may be hereafter, conformably to the Constitution and laws of the United States, held in or introduced into said Territory.

"The object of this amendment, as [Mr. Davis] . . understood its legal effect, was evidently to declare this Territory open alike for settlement and colonization by citizens of all the States, with their property, of every kind, while in a Territorial condition, without any restriction or discrimination, one way or the other. His amendment, however, was rejected on the 5th of June, by a vote of twenty-five to thirty. Mr. [Stephen A.] Douglas then moved to strike out the Select Committee's amendment to his original bill, which left the Territorial Legislature free to pass all laws consistent with the Constitution of the United States, and the provisions of the Act. His motion, too, was lost, but the same motion was renewed by Mr. [Moses] Norris, of New Hampshire, on the 31st of July, when it was adopted—which accomplished, in the opinion of the Southern Whigs referred to, all that Mr. Davis's amendment would have done."[183]

☛ "We turn now to the House again. In that body, on the 11th of June, Mr. [James D.] Doty's bill, regularly introduced on the 27th of February, as stated, came up for action in that body, and was discussed, from day to day, in Committee of the Whole. Mr. [James S.] Green, of Missouri, moved as an amendment, the recognition of the Missouri line through all the newly-acquired territory. This was rejected by a large majority. Mr. [Fred P.] Stanton, of Tennessee, on the 13th of June, offered the following amendment:

> Provided, however, that it shall be no objection to the admission into the Union, of any State which may be hereafter formed out of the territory lying south of the parallel of latitude of 36° 30', that the Constitution of said State may authorize or establish African Slavery therein.

"This proposition was rejected upon a count by tellers—yeas seventy-eight, nays eighty-nine. This was almost exclusively a sectional vote. The debates grew warmer and more excited. Speeches on the question, under an order of the House, were now limited to five minutes. The 14th of June was consumed in the same way. On the 15th of June, the question was put, in debate, to the ultra Northern advocates, of the admission of California, if they would ever, under any circumstances, vote for the admission of a Slave State into the Union. They refused to say that they would. It was in this condition of affairs that Mr.

Toombs took the floor and spoke as follows [as quoted by a reporter]:

'Mr. Toombs renewed the amendment, and said the gentleman from Ohio had just charged that the opposition to California with her present Constitution, by the South, was founded upon the Anti-Slavery Clause in her Constitution, and therefore, in the denial of this right of a people forming a State Constitution, to admit or exclude Slavery. Mr. T. denied the fact, and demanded proof. On the contrary, he asserted that the South had uniformly held and maintained this right. That in 1820, on the Missouri question, the North denied it, but the South unanimously affirmed it. From that day till this, the South, through all her authorized exponents of her opinions, has affirmed this doctrine; her Legislatures, her Governors of States, her Members upon this floor, and even her primary assemblies, have all affirmed it, and the gentleman from Ohio cannot point to a single particle of evidence to support his unfounded charge. The South can proudly point to her whole political history for its reputation. *But how stands the case with the North? She denied the truth of this great principle of Constitutional right in 1820, acquiesced in the Compromise then made as long as it was to her interest, and then repudiated the Compromise and re-asserted her right to dictate Constitutions to Territories seeking admission into the Union. She put her Anti-Slavery proviso upon Oregon, and at the last session of Congress, when the present Secretary of the Navy introduced a bill to authorize California to form a State government and come into the Union, leaving her free to act as she pleased upon the question of Slavery, the North put the Anti-Slavery proviso upon this State bill.* I know of no Northern Whig who voted against that proviso. A few gentlemen of the Democratic Party from the North-west, and my friend from Illinois among them, [William A. Richardson] boldly and honestly struck for the right, and opposed it; but they were powerless against the torrent of Northern opposition. The evidence is complete; the North repudiated this principle—and while, for sinister and temporary purposes, they may pretend to favor the President's plan, which affirms it, they will not sustain it. They will not find a right place to affirm it until they get California into the Union, and then they will throw off the mask and trample it under foot. I intend to drag off the mask before the consummation of that act. We do not oppose California on account of the Anti-Slavery clause in her Constitution. It was her right, and I am not even prepared to say that she acted unwisely in its exercise—that is her business; but I stand upon the great principle that the South has right to an equal participation in the [Western] Territories of the United States. I claim the right for her to enter them all with her property and securely to enjoy it. She will divide with you, if you wish it; but the right to enter all, or divide, I shall never surrender. In my judgment, this right, involving, as it does, political equality, is worth a thousand such Unions as we have, even if they each were a thousand times more valuable than this. I speak not for others, but for myself. Deprive us of this right and appropriate this common property to yourselves, it is then your Government, not mine. Then I am its enemy, and I will then, if I can, bring my children and my constituents to the altar of liberty, and like Hamilcar [the famed Carthaginian general and statesman], I would swear them to eternal hostility to your foul domination. *Give us our just rights, and we are ready, as ever heretofore, to stand by the Union, every part of it, and its every interest. Refuse it, and for one, I will strike for Independence!*' [Emphasis added, L.S.]

"*In sampling these debates with the view to present the tone and temper of the times, I purposely select the speeches made by Mr. Calhoun and Mr. Toombs, because they have been generally regarded as the extremest of the Ultras on that side, and have both been very greatly misrepresented on this subject. No man was ever more so than Mr. Toombs. It has been the object of many to hold him up as the embodiment of Slavery Propagandism. Even histories have been written in which the statement is made that he had declared that he would yet call the roll of his slaves on Bunker Hill. This has been done, too, without a particle of proof, and after the most positive denial by him of his ever having made such a declaration.*"[184] [Emphasis added, L.S.]

☛ "But to proceed. This speech of Mr. Toombs delivered on the 15th of June, produced the greatest sensation in the House that I ever witnessed by any speech in that body during my Congressional course. It created a perfect commotion. Several Southern Whigs who had not before sympathized with the class first alluded to, now openly took sides with them. The House adjourned without coming to any further vote. The excitement in the House increased that in the Senate. It extended to the city, and the subjects discussed in the House became the topics of heated conversations on the streets and at the hotels. This was Saturday. Monday, Mr. [James D.] Doty made another effort to get a resolution passed, requiring the Committee of the Whole to report his bill. The effort failed. In the Senate, on the same day, the excitement was no less than it was in the House. It was at this stage of the proceedings, that Mr. [Pierre] Soulé, of Louisiana, offered to Mr. Clay's Compromise Bill an amendment to the first section which related to the Territorial Government of Utah in these words:

> And when the said Territory, or any portion of the same, shall be admitted as a State, it shall be received into the Union with or without Slavery, as their Constitution may prescribe at the time of their admission.

"This presented to that body the issue squarely, as it had been presented by Mr. Toombs in the House, on Saturday, and covered one of the essential points made by the Southern Whigs referred to in the beginning. When the Missouri line was thus, for the last time, voted down in the House, the South fell back in almost solid column to their original position. They now maintained that there should be no Congressional Restriction of Slavery, either North or South of 36° 30'. On this principle alone would they now settle. This amendment, therefore, of Mr. Soulé was the turning point, and upon its adoption everything depended, so far as concerned Mr. Clay's proposed Compromise. In this connection, allow me to read what I said on a former occasion, in reference to the action of the Senate, that day, on this amendment:

> 'I well recollect the intensity of interest felt upon the fate of that proposition in the Senate. Upon its rejection, in the then state of the public mind, depended consequences, which no human forecast could see, or estimate. The interest was enhanced from the great uncertainty and doubt as to the result of the vote. Several Northern Senators, who had before yielded the question of positive restriction—that is, the 'Wilmot Proviso'—had given no indication of how they would act upon this clear declaration, that the people of the Territories might, in the formation of their State Constitutions, determine this question for themselves. Among these was Mr. Webster. Just before the question was put, and while anxiety was producing its most torturing effects, this most renowned Statesman from New England arose to address the Senate. An immense crowd was in attendance. The lobby was full, as well as the galleries. All eyes were instantly turned toward him, and all ears eager to catch every word that should fall from his lips upon this, the most important question, perhaps, which had ever been decided by an American Senate. His own vote, even, might turn the scale. That speech I now have before me. In it he declared himself for the amendment. His conclusion was in these words:
>
>> [Stephens quoting Webster:] "Sir, my object is peace—my object is reconciliation. My purpose is not to make up a case for the North, or to make up a case for the South. My object is not to continue useless and irritating controversies. I am against agitators North and South; I am against local ideas North and South, and against all narrow and local contests. I am an American, and I know no locality in America. That is my country. My heart, my sentiments, my judgment, demand of me that I should pursue such a course as shall promote the good, and the harmony, and the union of the whole country. This I shall do, God willing, to the end of the chapter."
>
> [The honorable Senator resumed his seat amidst the general applause from the gallery.]
>
> [Stephens continues:] 'Yes, sir; he did. I was there and witnessed the scene; and no one, I fancy, who was there, can ever forget that scene. Every heart beat easier. The friends of the measure felt that it was safe. The vote

was taken—the amendment was adopted. The result was soon communicated from the galleries, and, finding its way through every passage and outlet to the rotunda, was received with exultation by the crowd there; with quick steps it was borne through the city; and in less than five minutes, perhaps, the electric [telegraph] wires were trembling with the gladsome news to the remotest parts of the country. It was news well calculated to make a nation leap with joy, as it did, because it was the first decisive step taken towards the establishment of that great principle upon which this Territorial question was disposed of, adjusted, and settled in 1850.'

"The *per capita* vote on this amendment, thus establishing the new principle of no Congressional intervention anywhere in the Territories in lieu of the former principle of a division of the public domain, and thus bringing the Government back to the original position of the South upon the whole question, was thirty-eight yeas to twelve nays. The twelve nays against it were, Messrs. [Roger S.] Baldwin, of Connecticut; [Salmon P.] Chase, of Ohio; [John H.] Clark, of Rhode Island; [John] Davis, of Massachusetts; [William L.] Dayton, of New Jersey; [Henry] Dodge, of Wisconsin; [Albert C.] Green, of Rhode Island; [John P.] Hale, of New Hampshire; [Jacob W.] Miller, of New Jersey; [Truman] Smith, of Connecticut; [William] Upham, of Vermont; and [Isaac P.] Walker, of Wisconsin.

"By States, the vote for and against the new principle was twenty yeas; six nays; two divided, and two not voting. The yeas were Pennsylvania, Indiana, Illinois, Michigan, Iowa, Delaware, Maryland, Virginia, North Carolina, South Carolina, Georgia, Alabama, Florida, Mississippi, Tennessee, Kentucky, Missouri, Arkansas, Louisiana and Texas. The six nays were, Connecticut, Rhode Island, New Jersey, Ohio, Vermont and Wisconsin. The two States divided, were New Hampshire and Massachusetts. The two not voting were Maine and New York. Mr. [William H.] Seward, of New York, was within convenient distance, but voted neither one way nor the other. Thus two-thirds of the States in 1850, did affirm the original position of the South upon the Territorial question. This was the gist of that Compromise."[185]

☞ "We have now to follow the progress of this principle, thus established by the Senate on the 17th of June, to its final consummation. On the 9th of July, President [Zachary] Taylor died. Vice President [Millard] Fillmore immediately assumed the duties of the Executive chair. He was known to be in full sympathy with Mr. [Henry] Clay in his objects. Mr. [Daniel] Webster was transferred from the Senate to the Cabinet. He became Secretary of State in the new Administration. Mr. [James D.] Doty's bill for the admission of California was not again taken up in the House.

"Mr. Clay's bill continued the subject matter of angry discussion in the Senate until the 31st of July, when it was so amended by striking out first one part and then another, until nothing of it was left but that portion providing a Government for the Territory of Utah, with the select Committee's amendment stricken out, and the Soulé amendment of the 17th of June incorporated in it, as stated. This bill so passed the Senate the 1st of August and went down to the House. In this way Mr. Clay's 'Omnibus Bill,' as it was called, went to pieces on the 31st of July; but the Senate immediately took up the separate parts, embodied them in separate bills, passed them, and sent them down to the House in like manner, where they took their regular place on the Speaker's table. In that body on the 28th of August, the Senate Utah Bill was reached. It was referred to the Committee of the Whole without debate. The next one of the Senate Bills reached, the same day, was the one for the settlement of the boundary between Texas and New Mexico. When this came up Mr. [Linn] Boyd, of Kentucky, offered an amendment providing for a Territorial Government for New Mexico with the Soulé amendment in it. This amendment so offered by Mr. Boyd, in other respects, was substantially the same bill prepared for New Mexico by Mr. Douglas and Mr. McClernand, as before stated. On this the great Sectional Contest was now fought in the House as it had been in the Senate. It may not be uninteresting to notice in detail the various phases of the conflict as it progressed. We will, therefore, rapidly review some of the scenes. Civic conflicts have their interest as well as conflicts of arms. Though bloodless and less exciting, yet the lessons they teach, in a historic view, are quite as instructive.

"On the 4th of September, then, when this Senate bill with Mr. Boyd's proposed amendment to it, and also an amendment to the amendment proposed by Mr. [Thomas L.] Clingman, of North Carolina, providing another Territorial Government for a portion of the country which he designated as 'Colorado,' came up for consideration under a special order, a motion was made to refer the bill with the pending amendments to the Committee of the Whole on the state of the Union. The previous question was seconded, and the main question on this reference was ordered by a vote of yeas one hundred and thirty-three to nays sixty-eight.

"On the question of reference, the vote was one hundred and one to ninety-nine. So the motion to refer was carried.

"Mr. [Hiram] Walden, of New York, moved to reconsider the vote by which the bill and amendments had been referred.

"Mr. [Joseph M.] Root, of Ohio, moved to lay that motion on the table.

"The vote to lay the motion to reconsider on the table was one hundred and three to one hundred and two. The Speaker, Mr. [Howell] Cobb, voted in the negative. So the vote stood one hundred and three to one hundred and three, and the motion to lay on the table the motion to reconsider was not carried.

"The question to reconsider then recurred. Upon it the yeas were one hundred and four, the nays ninety-eight, so the vote by which the bill had been referred was reconsidered.

"The question, then, again recurred upon the reference of the bill with amendments. The vote now stood one hundred and one to one hundred and three. So the House refused to refer the bill with amendments to the Committee of the Whole.

"The first question, then, was on Mr. Clingman's amendment to Boyd's amendment. The vote on this was sixty-nine to one hundred and thirty. So his amendment was lost.

"Mr. [Jacob] Thompson, of Mississippi, said that as no amendment under the previous question was now in order, he moved as a test vote to lay the whole thing on the table.

"Mr. [Thomas H.] Bayly, of Virginia, protested against its being considered a test vote.

"Mr. [Samuel F.] Vinton, of Ohio, wished to know if the motion to lay on the table was in order after the previous question was ordered.

"The Speaker said that it was.

"Mr. [John] Wentworth, of Illinois, wished to know if there was any amendment pending.

"The Speaker said there was.

"Mr. Wentworth wanted to know if the 'Wilmot Proviso' was in it. He was informed that it was not—the amendment pending was Mr. Boyd's, which did not contain it.

"Mr. [Jacob] Thompson, of Mississippi, withdrew his motion to lay on the table.

"Mr. [William] Ashe, of North Carolina, renewed it.

"Mr. [John A.] McClernand, of Illinois, asked the yeas and nays: when four or five members had answered to their names on the call of the roll, the confusion in the Hall became so great, the Clerk could not proceed. The call was suspended.

"Mr. [David T.] Disney, of Ohio, rose to a question of order.

"The Speaker decided it was too late, as several members had answered to their names on the call. The call of the roll was then resumed and completed, when the vote stood sixty-one for laying on the table, to one hundred and forty-one against it—so the bill was not laid on the table.

"The question then came on Boyd's amendment.

"Mr. [Daniel] Gott, of New York, demanded the yeas and nays. The vote stood ninety-eight to one hundred and six; so the amendment was rejected.

"Mr. [Robert C.] Schenck, of Ohio, moved to reconsider the vote, by which Boyd's amendment had been rejected, and to lay that motion on the table.

"Mr. [F. E.] McLean, of Kentucky, called for the yeas and nays.

"Mr. [David A.] Bokee, of New York, called for a division of the question. It then came up, first, to lay on the table the motion to reconsider.

"Mr. Schenck withdrew his motion to reconsider.

"Mr. [David K.] Cartter, of Ohio, renewed it.

"Mr. [Joseph M.] Root moved to lay Mr. Cartter's motion to reconsider on the table.

"Mr. Boyd moved that the House adjourn. On this question the vote stood seventy-one to one hundred and twenty-eight.

"Mr. Cartter then withdrew his motion to reconsider.

"The question came then on ordering the bill to be engrossed without the Boyd amendment. On this the vote stood yeas eighty, nays one hundred and twenty-six. So the bill was not ordered to be engrossed, and passed to a third reading, which was in effect its defeat. Great confusion prevailed in the Hall. Many members addressed the Speaker at the same time. Mr. Boyd, of Kentucky, was recognized. He moved to reconsider the vote, by which the engrossment of the bill had been rejected.

"Mr. [Armistead] Burt, of South Carolina, moved to lay Mr. Boyd's motion to reconsider on the table.

"Mr. [Thomas L.] Harris, of Illinois, moved that the House adjourn, which motion prevailed.

"In this position of affairs night closed upon the parties. So ended the first day's action."[186]

☛ "The next day, September the 5th, the motion to lay Mr. Boyd's motion to reconsider on the table, was the first question in order. On this the vote stood seventy-one to one hundred and thirty-five. So the motion to reconsider was not laid on the table. The previous question was seconded on Mr. Boyd's motion to reconsider—the main question was ordered.

"Mr. [Ransom] Halloway, of New York, inquired of the Speaker if the vote should be reconsidered, whether the bill would then be open for amendment.

"The Speaker said it would.

"The vote on Mr. Boyd's motion to reconsider the vote, by which the engrossment of the bill had been rejected, was then taken, and stood one hundred and thirty-one in law, and seventy-five against it. So the motion prevailed.

"Mr. [Joseph] Grinnell, of Massachusetts, then moved to reconsider the vote, by which Mr. Boyd's amendment had been rejected the day before, and called the previous question, which was seconded.

"Mr. [Lewis D.] Campbell, of Ohio, moved to lay the motion to reconsider on the table. The vote stood ninety-six to one hundred and eight. The question then came up on Mr. Grinnell's motion to reconsider. The vote stood, yeas one hundred and six, nays ninety-nine. So the rejection of Mr. Boyd's amendment was reconsidered. Many members now again addressed the Chair at the same time. Mr. Boyd was recognized. He called the previous question. Strong appeals were made to him to withdraw it. Cries came from all sides of the House, 'question!' 'question!'

"Mr. [Richard K.] Meade, of Virginia, inquired if it was then in order to move to refer the whole matter to the Committee of the Whole on the state of the Union.

"The Speaker said it was not, pending the demand for the previous question.

"Mr. Preston King, of New York, asked if it was in order to move an amendment to the bill?

"The Speaker said not pending the motion for the previous question.

"Mr. King asked if the Chair had not decided that it would be open for amendment, if it was reconsidered?

"The Speaker said he had, and it would be now, but for the demand for the previous question; if the demand for the previous question was voted down, the subject matter would lie open for amendment.

"On the demand for the previous question, the vote was in favor of sustaining it, eighty-eight, and against it, ninety-nine. So the previous question was not ordered.

"Mr. [Robert A.] Toombs, of Georgia, obtained the floor, and moved an additional section, in these words:

> And be it further enacted, That no citizen of the United States shall be deprived of his life, liberty, or property in said Territory, except by the judgment of his peers and the laws of the land; and that the Constitution of the United States, and such Statutes thereof as may not be locally inapplicable, and the common law as it existed in the British Colonies of America, until the 4th day of July, 1776, shall be the exclusive laws of said Territory, upon the subject of African Slavery, until altered by the proper authority.

"Mr. Toombs said he had no desire to debate the question or to close debate on it, and would not move the previous question. Several members addressed the Chair. Mr. [John] Wentworth was recognized. He inquired whether it would be in order to move a substitute for Mr. Toombs' amendment.

"The Speaker said it would not be, as that was an amendment to an amendment already pending.

"Mr. Wentworth inquired if it was in order to move to commit.

"The Speaker said it was.

"Mr. Wentworth. Is it in order to move to commit with instructions?

"The Speaker said that it was.

"Mr. Wentworth then moved to commit the bill with the following instructions:

> So to amend the amendment as to exclude Slavery From all the territory acquired from Mexico by the treaty of Guadalupe Hidalgo eastward of California.

"Several members addressed the Chair. Mr. Wentworth, holding the floor, inquired of the Speaker whether he could adopt other instructions that might be suggested to him, and after his demand for the previous question whether separate votes could be taken on the different sets of instructions?

"The Speaker said the motion to commit with instructions, was indivisible; but upon the instructions a separate vote could be called, so as to leave with the motion to commit a separate and distinct proposition. Mr. Wentworth then accepted from Mr. [Volney E.] Howard, of Texas, certain instructions relating to boundary and the settlement proposed to be made between the United States and Texas, and moved the previous question; but yielded the floor to Mr. [W. S.] Featherstone, who wished an additional instruction, to wit, strike out all of the original bill after the enacting clause, and insert as follows:

> That the boundaries of the State of Texas, as defined and established by the act of the Texas Congress, passed December 19, 1836, for that purpose; are hereby recognized by the Government of the United States.

"He renewed Mr. Wentworth's call for the previous question. Great confusion prevailed. Many inquiries were addressed to the Chair, as to what would be the effect of ordering the previous question, and what would be the order of voting, if the previous question should be sustained. In answer the Speaker said:

> 'The Chair will state the question. If the previous question should be sustained, and the main question ordered, the question will be first on the amendment to the instructions offered by the gentleman from Mississippi,

[Mr. Featherstone]. Secondly, on the motion to commit with instructions, (amended or not, as the case may be.) If the House should refuse to commit with instructions, the question then recurs on the amendment of the gentleman from Georgia, [Mr. Toombs,] and then on the amendment of the gentleman from Kentucky, [Mr. Boyd,] amended or not, as the House may determine, and then on ordering the bill to a third reading. After the vote shall have been taken on the last-mentioned proposition, and not before, the previous question will be exhausted.

"The call for the previous question was sustained by a vote of one hundred and two to forty.

"The question on Mr. Featherstone's instruction was then decided by a vote of seventy-one yeas to one hundred and twenty-eight nays.

"The question then to commit with Mr. Wentworth's instructions coupled with Mr. Howard's, was decided by a vote of eighty yeas to one hundred and twenty-one nays. So the motion to commit with instructions failed. The question then recurred upon Mr. Toombs' amendment. On this a division was called. The first branch of his amendment was agreed to without a count. The second branch was rejected by a vote of sixty-four yeas to one hundred and twenty-one nays.

"The question then came up for a second time upon agreeing to the amendment of Mr. Boyd.

"Mr. [Thaddeus] Stevens, of Pennsylvania, moved a division of the question.

"The Speaker held it to be indivisible. The question on Mr. Boyd's amendment was then decided by one hundred and six yeas to ninety-nine nays. So Mr. Boyd's amendment, as amended, was agreed to; and the question recurred on ordering the bill, as it stood amended, to be engrossed for a third reading. Mr. [Daniel] Gott called for the yeas and nays. Mr. [Samuel W.] Inge moved that the House adjourn. The House refused to adjourn.

"Mr. Inge moved to lay the whole subject on the table. The House decided against the motion without division.

"The question then recurred on ordering the bill as amended to be engrossed for a third reading. The roll was called. Intense excitement prevailed. The Speaker arose and very slowly was about to announce the result. Cries of 'report! report! report!' came up from all sides of the Hall.

"Mr. [James] McDowell, of Virginia [the editor's cousin, L.S.], rose and said he desired to know of the Speaker, in the event of the bill being lost by the present vote, if it would be open to reconsideration. Cries of 'order! order!' The Speaker made no reply.

"Mr. McDowell still remained on the floor.

"The Speaker inquired if the gentleman of Virginia desired to vote. Mr. McDowell said he had voted. Cries from all sides, 'report, report,' etc.

"The Speaker commenced his announcement by saying, 'upon ordering the bill to be engrossed, the vote is ninety-seven—'

"Mr. [Edward C.] Cabell, of Florida, rose and said he desired to have his name called. The Speaker inquired if he was within the bar of the House when his name was called on the roll. He said he was. His name was then again called, and he responded 'aye.' Demands were again made upon the Speaker to report.

"Mr. [Emory D.] Potter, of Ohio, rose and asked that his name be called. The inquiry was made if he was within the bar of the House when his name had been called. He answered he was. His name was again called, and be also voted aye.

"Mr. [F. E.] McLean insisted that order should be restored in the Hall before the result was announced. The area was then cleared and order restored.

"The Speaker arose and announced the vote. Yeas ninety-nine, nays one hundred and seven. So the engrossment of the bill was again lost!

"Mr. Howard, of Texas, moved a reconsideration of the vote.

"Mr. Inge moved to lay that motion on the table.

"The Speaker decided that the motion to reconsider was not in order—as a motion to reconsider the vote on the third reading of the bill, had been once reconsidered.

"Mr. Howard appealed from the decision. The question was, Shall the decision of the Chair stand as the judgment of the House? Pending this question, on motion of Mr. McClernand, an adjournment took place.

"So closed the second day upon the scenes of strife."[187]

☛ "On the 6th of September, the question recurring upon the appeal from the decision of the Chair, Mr. Duer moved to lay the appeal on the table. On this question the yeas were seventy-seven, and the nays one hundred and twenty-three. So the appeal was not laid on the table.

"The question then was, 'Shall the decision of the Chair stand as the judgment of the House?' On this the yeas were eighty-three, and the nays one hundred and twenty-three. So Mr. Speaker Cobb's decision was overruled.

"The question now was, Shall the vote by which the House refused to order the bill as amended to be engrossed for a third reading, be reconsidered? The vote was yeas one hundred and twenty-two, nays eighty-four. So the rejection of the engrossment of the bill, was again reconsidered. The question then recurred, Shall the bill as amended be ordered to be engrossed for a third reading? Mr. Howard demanded the previous question. On ordering it, there were yeas one hundred and fifteen, nays ninety-one—and upon the engrossment of the bill for a third reading, the yeas now were one hundred and eight, nays ninety-eight. So Boyd's amendment was thus finally adopted! The Anti-Restrictionists [Conservatives] had won the day at last! The Hall was in a general uproar!

"Mr. Burt moved to lay the bill on the table. The vote was, yeas ninety-seven, nays one hundred and eight. The bill as it then stood amended, was put upon its passage, and was carried by a vote of one hundred and eight yeas to nays ninety-seven.

"Such are some of the scenes and struggles through which this new principle, established in the Senate on the 17th of June, passed before its final consummation in the House on the 6th of September, 1850. This was the Compromise of that year. The other associated measures all depended upon it. The Senate concurred in the House amendments thus made to their bill. The other measures were all soon afterwards taken up and passed—the Utah bill; the bill for the admission of California; the fugitive slave bill; and the bill forbidding slaves to be introduced into the District of Columbia, for the purpose of offering them in public market for sale."[188]

☛ "It is proper here to state that the Utah Bill thus passed, embraced within the boundaries of that Territory a portion of the Louisiana cession to which the old Missouri Restriction applied. It embraced that portion of this cession lying on the head-waters of the Colorado River, known as the Middle Park, 'so glowingly described by Colonel [John C.] Frémont;' while the New Mexico Bill embraced a degree and a-half of latitude, and nearly four degrees of longitude, of that portion of Territory north of 36° 30', which was covered by the Congressional exclusion of Slavery, as provided by the Resolutions under which Texas became incorporated as a State into the Union. This is seen by a perusal of these acts. The new principle now established, removed these old Restrictions so far as they came within the range of its action, at the time, and the establishment of this new Territorial principle, was the real and only Compromise of 1850. The other measures, except the District Slave-trade Bill, were but cognate accompaniments.

"In procuring the establishment of this new principle there was no other threat, menace, or bluster, on the part of Southern Senators and Members, except the firm and determined declaration that their States would not remain in the Union, when it became a fixed fact that the principle of a division of the public domain between the opposing Sections had been forever repudiated, unless Territorial Restriction by Congress should be totally abandoned, and unless the principles of the Federal Constitution should be adhered to in good faith on this question on the part of their Northern Confederates [i.e., the Northern people]. The Compromise was an agreement on the part of the slaveholding States to continue in the Union, in consideration of these renewed pledges on the part of the non-slaveholding States, through their Members and Senators, to abide by the Constitution. It is true, Southern Members and Senators were far from being unanimous in favor of this Compromise. A protest against the admission of California was presented to the Senate, the 14th of August, signed by Messrs. [Robert M. T.] Hunter and [James M.] Mason, Senators of Virginia; Messrs. [A. P.] Butler and [Robert W.] Barnwell, of South Carolina; and Mr. Davis, of Mississippi, and some others: while thirty Members in the House, from the South, voted against the bill, which we have just traced through its perils to its final passage, and which embraced the principle of the Compromise, as we have seen.

"An analysis of this vote in the House, close as it was, presents some interesting facts, when made either by States or per capita. Analyzed by States, it shows that, in that body, the votes stood fifteen States for it, thirteen States against it, with two divided. The States voting for it were New Hampshire, Pennsylvania, Illinois, Iowa, Delaware, Maryland, Virginia, North Carolina, Georgia, Florida, Tennessee, Kentucky, Missouri, Texas, Indiana—five Northern and ten Southern. The States voting against it were Massachusetts, Connecticut, Vermont, New York, New Jersey, Ohio, Michigan, Wisconsin, South Carolina, Alabama, Mississippi, Arkansas, and Louisiana—eight Northern and five Southern. The two States divided, were Maine and Rhode Island, both Northern.

"The per capita view of the vote is interesting only as it exhibits the position of the two great nominal Parties upon the then living issues of the day—North as well as South. The one hundred and eight votes by which the Compromise was carried, were composed of fifty-nine Democrats and forty-nine Whigs. Of these Democrats, thirty-two were from non-slaveholding [i.e., slavery-prohibited] States, and twenty-seven from slaveholding [i.e., slavery-optional] States. Of the forty-nine Whigs, twenty-four were from the non-slaveholding States, and twenty-five from slaveholding States. Of the ninety-seven votes against the Compromise, forty-six were Democrats, and fifty-one Whigs. Of the forty-six Democrats, seventeen were from non-slaveholding States, and twenty-nine from slaveholding States. Of the fifty-one Whigs, fifty were from non-slaveholding States, and one from a slaveholding State.

"This exhibition of itself is quite enough to show that those Southern Whigs to whom I have alluded, were right in their opinion at the beginning of the Session, that the time had come for a reorganization of Parties. This was the conclusion to which Mr. Clay and Mr. Cobb, and many other distinguished opposing Party leaders, came when the struggle was over. This appears from a paper drawn up and signed by them with over forty others and published as a manifesto to the country, that they would in the future support no man for office either State or Federal, who would not agree to stand by and support the principles established by these measures. The effect of this paper, together with the action of the Georgia State Convention in December, 1850, and the elections in this State and Mississippi, in 1851, which were carried by overwhelming majorities under a new Party organization styled the Constitutional Union Party, showed clearly to the two old Parties that their days were numbered, unless they in their Conventions should proclaim their determination to abide by the settlement so made. The Sovereign Convention of this State had, in December, 1850, as stated, set forth her position on all these questions in a series of Resolutions which became famous as the Georgia Platform, and gave to her the appellation of the Union State as well as the Empire State of the South. Upon the principles announced in this Platform, Mr. Howell Cobb was triumphantly elected Governor, in 1851, over Mr. Charles J. McDonald, who had been twice Governor before, and who was thought to be, personally, the most popular man at that time in the State. On the same principles, Mr. Henry S. Foote was elected Governor of Mississippi the same year, over Mr. Jefferson Davis. McDonald and Davis were run by those of all Parties who were opposed to the Compromise Measures. The truth is an overwhelming majority of the people, North as well as South, were in favor of maintaining the principles affirmed by the Measures of 1850. This is apparent from the action of both the two great nominal Parties, Whig and Democratic, when they met in their respective Conventions to nominate candidates for President in 1852. The Democratic Convention assembled in Baltimore, on the 1st of June of that year, and endorsed these measures by Resolutions in the following words:

> Resolved, That Congress has no power under the Constitution, to interfere with, or control the domestic Institutions of the several States, and that such States are the sole and proper judges of everything appertaining to their own affairs, not prohibited by the Constitution; that *all efforts of the Abolitionists, or others, made to induce Congress to interfere with questions of Slavery, or to take incipient steps in relation thereto, are calculated to lead to the most alarming and dangerous consequences; and that all such efforts have an inevitable tendency to diminish the happiness of the people, and endanger the stability and permanency of the Union, and ought not to be countenanced by any friend of our political institutions.* [Emphasis added, L.S.]
>
> Resolved, That the foregoing proposition covers, and was intended to embrace, the whole subject of Slavery agitation in Congress; and, therefore,

the Democratic Party of the Union, standing on this National Platform, will abide by, and adhere to a faithful execution of the Acts known as the Compromise Measures, settled by the last Congress—'the Act for reclaiming fugitives from service or labor,' included; which Act being designed to carry out an express provision of the Constitution, cannot, with fidelity, thereto, be repealed, nor so changed as to destroy or impair its efficiency.

"The Whig Convention, which met at the same place, on the 16th of June, gave them an endorsement, in words, even more pointed and explicit. The language used by that body, is as follows:

1. That the Government of the United States is of a limited character, and it is confined to the exercise of powers expressly granted by the Constitution, and such as may be necessary and proper for carrying the granted powers into full execution; and that all powers not thus granted, or necessarily implied, are expressly reserved to the States respectively, or to the people. . . .

7. That the Federal and State Governments are parts of one system, alike, necessary for the common prosperity, peace, and security, and ought to be regarded alike, with a cordial, habitual, and immovable attachment. Respect for the authority of each, and the acquiescence in just Constitutional measures of each, are duties required by the plainest considerations of National, of State, and of individual welfare.

8. That the series of acts of the 31st Congress, known as the Compromise Measures of 1850—the act known as the Fugitive Slave Law included—are received and acquiesced in by the Whig Party of the United States as a settlement, in principle and substance, of the dangerous and exciting questions which they embrace; and so far as they are concerned, we will maintain them, and insist on their strict enforcement, until time and experience shall demonstrate the necessity of further legislation, to guard against the evasion of the laws on the one hand, and the abuse of their powers on the other—not meaning their present efficiency; and we deprecate all further agitation of the questions thus settled, as dangerous to our peace, and will discountenance all efforts to continue or renew such agitation, whenever, wherever, or however the attempt may be made; and we will maintain this system as essential to the nationality of the Whig Party and the integrity of the Union.

"These Resolutions, Mr. [Horace] Greeley styles the 'Southern Platform,' and speaks of it as having been 'imposed' upon the Convention by the 'Southern Delegates.' According to his idea, it was but another dictation of the 'Slave Power.' This is certainly a very great mistake. My opinion is, that it was drawn up by Northern delegates, or Northern men, at least. All that I know about it is, that Mr. [Rufus] Choate, of Massachusetts, a delegate to the Convention, was with Mr. [Daniel] Webster a few days before its meeting. Mr. Webster called over to my quarters, while Mr. Choate was still with him (we lived in adjacent houses), and submitted to me a series of Resolutions prepared to be offered to the Convention. They were substantially the Resolutions which were adopted. The eighth one in particular, I think, is just as it then was, with one exception. The words 'in principle and substance' were not then in it. Having been struck with the point and force of these words, which he had used in a letter published some time before, and the great appropriateness of the same words in Mr. [Millard] Fillmore's message, in December 1851, I suggested to him to put them in this Resolution after the word 'settlement.' He instantly assented, and interlined them himself on my table. I saw them afterwards in the report of the Committee of the Convention on Resolutions as they now stand. Mr. George Ashmun, of Massachusetts, was Chairman of that Committee. My opinion then was, and now is, that these Resolutions were prepared by the Northern friends of Mr. Webster, at his house, and met with his full concurrence. Southern friends were doubtless consulted, but they did nothing in relation to them which could be justly styled as imposing them upon the Convention. Mr. Ashmun, Chairman of the Committee on Resolutions, in his speech on reporting the whole series, stated that they had been agreed to by the Committee by an almost unanimous vote. Mr. [William L.] Dayton, of New Jersey, who in his place in the Senate, had been a most decided and earnest advocate of Territorial Restriction, while that question was open, now as member of this Convention, gave this Resolution his emphatic endorsement. The published proceedings show these striking facts. On the adoption of the whole platform, with this Resolution in it, the per capita vote stood two hundred and twenty-seven yeas to sixty-five nays. By States the vote in Convention stood twenty-seven States for the platform, three States only against it, and one State divided. The three States against it, were New York, Ohio, and Michigan. The State equally divided—four delegates for—and four against it—was Maine. Every other State of the Union, by their delegates in that Convention, affirmed and endorsed it.

"How in the face of these facts Mr. Greeley could have stated, as a historic truth, that the Platform was imposed upon the Convention by Southern Delegates, I cannot well perceive. Another equally singular error is made by him in stating that General [Winfield] Scott, who was nominated, 'made haste to plant himself unequivocally and thoroughly on the platform thus erected.' The truth is, General Scott refused to express any direct approval of the platform, when he knew that the support of a large class of persons at the South, including Mr. Toombs and myself, and other Members of Congress, who had before 1850, acted with the Whig Party, depended upon his giving an unequivocal endorsement of that portion of it relating to the Compromise. He acted, as was supposed, under the advisement of Mr. [William H.] Seward, then in the Senate, from New York, who was on intimate terms with him—was one of his most active friends in procuring his nomination, and who was known to be very much opposed to the platform. To this refusal of General Scott 'to plant himself unequivocally and thoroughly on the platform thus erected,' in my judgment, his great defeat was mainly owing. Mr. [Franklin] Pierce, who received the Democratic nomination, gave these measures his cordial approval, as well as another Resolution of the Democratic Convention, reaffirming the Kentucky and Virginia Resolutions of 1798-1799. He it is known carried every State in the Union except four.

"Was there ever a more general and decided popular approval of any measure, than that given by the people and States of this Union, in that election, to the establishment of this new principle on the Territorial question? So much, then, for the Compromise of 1850, and its bearing upon the question of Slavery in the public domain."[189]

23

THE MISSOURI COMPROMISE OF 1850
PART TWO

HAVING DISCUSSED THE HISTORY OF the Missouri Compromise of 1850, in this chapter of excerpts from *A Constitutional View* Stephens investigates the finer points of the agreement.

☛ "We now come to the last point under consideration. That is, the legislation of 1854, in which Mr. [James] Buchanan says the South, for the first time, was the aggressor. We will soon see how little weight this assertion, however high the authority from which it comes, has against the indisputable facts of history. These facts will show that the legislation of this year, was in strict conformity with the Territorial principle established in 1850.

"What then are these facts? In the first place, what was the principle settled, in 1850, upon the Territorial question which had for so long a time caused so great and fearful agitation, both in and out of Congress? This we have just seen. To repeat for the purpose of keeping it distinctly in mind, it was clearly this, that after the principle of division had been abandoned and repudiated by the North, in the organization of all Territorial Governments, the principle of Congressional Restriction should be totally abandoned also, and that all new States, whether North or South of 36° 30', should be admitted into the Union, 'either with or without Slavery, as their Constitutions might prescribe,' at the time of their admission. This was, unquestionably, the principle established in 1850 on this subject.

"Well, then, in 1854, certain portions of the public domain embraced in the Louisiana cession, not included in Utah, lying outside of Missouri, and north of 36° 30', known as Nebraska and Kansas, became sufficiently populated to require local Governments. Two delegates to Congress were chosen, and petitions presented for the organization of Governments for them by Congress. Early in this Session, on the 4th of December, 1853, Mr. [Augustus C.] Dodge, of Iowa, introduced into the Senate a bill for the organization of a Territorial Government for Nebraska. This was referred to the Committee on Territories.

"At this time the Senate was changed in its personal composition very materially from what it was four years before. Several of the great lights then in it had departed. Some had gone down never more to shed their splendor upon subjects of earthly investigation. Mr. [Henry] Clay survived his last great efforts in restoring peace and harmony between the Sections only two years. He sank to rest from all mortal cares in Washington, on the 29th of June, 1852. Mr. [Daniel] Webster followed him within a few months. He closed his earthly existence the 24th of October, the same year. William R. King, of Alabama, who had been elected Vice President on the [Franklin] Pierce ticket, was also no more.

"Others who added lustre to the Senatorial galaxy in 1850, were now filling other posts of honor and trust. Mr. [Jefferson] Davis, of Mississippi, was Secretary of War. Mr. [Thomas H.] Benton who had been beaten for the Senate in Missouri, mainly on account of his vote to recede on the disagreeing vote between the two Houses on the Oregon Bill, in 1848, was now a member of the House of Representatives. Mr. [John M.] Berrien was in private life. General [Lewis] Cass, General [Samuel] Houston, of Texas, and Mr. [John] Bell, of Tennessee, of all the most distinguished characters of the former generation of statesmen who were in the Senate in 1850, were the only ones who at this time still continued to occupy their seats in that body. Of the younger members, however, a goodly number were still there. Amongst these may be mentioned Mr.[Stephen A.] Douglas, of Illinois, who had in the meantime added greatly to his fame. For mental vigor and power of debate, he had already received the general appellation of 'The Little Giant.' Messrs. [Robert M. T.] Hunter and [James M.] Mason, of Virginia, Mr. [William H.] Seward, of New York, Mr. [Salmon P.] Chase, of Ohio, Mr. [James A.] Pearce, of Maryland, Mr. [George E.] Badger, of North Carolina, who were all men of great ability, were also still there. Besides these, and others who might be named, the vacated seats had been filled by men of a very high order of genius and eloquence. Amongst the latter class may be mentioned Mr. [Robert A.] Toombs, of Georgia, Mr. [Charles] Sumner, of Massachusetts, Mr. [A. P.] Butler, of South Carolina, Mr. [Clement C.] Clay, of Alabama, and Mr. [Isaac] Toucey, of Connecticut. So the Senate of the United States was still, notwithstanding the changes, a most August body—not inferior to that of Rome in her palmiest days. This is but a glance at the general character of that

Assembly at the time we are now to enter upon an examination of their proceedings. Nor is this notice at all out of place considering the grave charge which has been brought against their acts. To go on then with the narrative."[190]

☛ "Mr. Douglas, of Illinois, was still Chairman of the Committee on [the still unformed Western] Territories. On the 4th of January, 1854, he reported back Mr. [Augustus C.] Dodge's Bill with amendments so changing its language as to make it accord with the language of the Utah and New Mexico Bills of 1850, on the question of Slavery, and accompanied his amendments with an elaborate report stating fully the reasons which had induced the Committee to change its phraseology in these particulars. The sole object was to carry out the principle established in 1850. In speaking of this report [Douglas] . . . said in the Senate:

> 'We were aware that from 1820 to 1850, the Abolition doctrine of Congressional interference with Slavery in the Territories and new States had so far prevailed as to keep up an incessant Slavery agitation in Congress, and throughout the country, whenever any new territory was to be acquired or organized. We were also aware that, in 1850, the right of the people to decide this question for themselves, subject only to the Constitution, was substituted for the doctrine of Congressional intervention. The first question, therefore, which the Committee were called upon to decide, and, indeed, the only question of any material importance in framing this bill, was this: Shall we adhere to and carry out the principle recognized by the Compromise measures of 1850, or shall we go back to the old exploded doctrine of Congressional interference, as established in 1820, in a large portion of the country, and which it was the object of the Wilmot Proviso, to give a universal application, not only, to all the territory which we then possessed, but all which we might hereafter acquire? There were no other alternatives. We were compelled to frame the bill upon the one or the other of these two principles. The doctrine of 1820, or the doctrine of 1850, must prevail. In the discharge of the duty imposed upon us by the Senate, the Committee could not hesitate upon this point, whether we consulted our individual opinions and principles, or those which were known to be entertained and boldly avowed by a large majority of the Senate. The two great political Parties of the country stood solemnly pledged before the world, to adhere to the Compromise Measures of 1850, 'in principle and substance.' A large majority of the Senate, indeed every member of the body, I believe, except the two avowed Abolitionists, [Mr. Salmon P. Chase and Mr. Charles Sumner] profess to belong to the one or the other of these Parties, and hence was supposed to be under a high moral obligation to carry out the 'principle and substance' of those measures in all new territorial organizations. The report of the Committee was in accordance with this obligation.'

"[Douglas] . . . then read from that portion of the report in which the Committee had laid down the principle by which they proposed to be governed:

'In the judgment of your Committee, those measures [Compromise of 1850] were intended to have a far more comprehensive and enduring effect than the mere adjustment of the difficulties arising out of the recent acquisition of Mexican territory. They were designed to establish certain great principles, which would not only furnish adequate remedies for existing evils, but, in all time to come, avoid the perils of a similar agitation, by withdrawing the question of Slavery from the Halls of Congress and the political arena, and committing it to the arbitrament of those who were immediately interested in, and alone responsible for its consequences.

'. . . The substitute for the bill which your Committee have prepared, and which is commended to the favorable action of the Senate, proposes to carry these propositions and principles into practical operation, in the precise language of the Compromise Measures of 1850.

'. . . But my accusers attempt to raise up a false issue, and thereby divert public attention from the real one, by the cry that the Missouri Compromise is to be repealed or violated by the passage of this bill. Well, if the eighth section of the Missouri Act, which attempted to fix the destinies of future generations in those Territories, for all time to come, in utter disregard of the rights and wishes of the people when they should be received into the Union as States, be inconsistent with the great principle of self-government and the Constitution of the United States, it ought to be abrogated. The legislation of 1850 abrogated the Missouri Compromise, so far as the country embraced within the limits of Utah and New Mexico was covered by the Slavery Restriction. It is true, that those Acts did not in terms, and by name, repeal the Act of 1820, as originally adopted, or as extended by the resolutions annexing Texas in 1845, any more than the report of the Committee on Territories proposes to repeal the same Acts this Session. But the Acts of 1850 did authorize the people of those Territories to exercise "all rightful powers of legislation consistent with the Constitution," not excepting the question of Slavery; and did provide that, when those Territories should be admitted into the Union, they should be received with, or without Slavery, as the people thereof might determine at the date of their admission. These provisions were in direct conflict with a clause in any former enactment, declaring that Slavery should be forever prohibited in any portion of said Territories, and hence rendered such clause inoperative and void to the extent of such conflict. This was an inevitable consequence, resulting from the provisions in those Acts, which gave the people the right to decide the Slavery question for themselves, in conformity with the Constitution. It was not necessary to go further and declare that certain previous enactments, which were incompatible with the exercise of the powers conferred in the bills, "are hereby repealed." The very act of granting those powers and rights have the legal effect of removing all obstructions to the exercise of them, by the people, as prescribed in those Territorial bills. Following that example, the Committee on Territories did not consider it necessary to declare the eighth section of the Missouri Act repealed. We were content to organize Nebraska in the precise language of the Utah and New Mexican Bills. Our object was to leave the people entirely free to form and regulate their domestic Institutions and internal concerns in their own way, under the Constitution; and we deemed it wise to accomplish that object in the exact terms in which the same thing had been done, in Utah and New Mexico, by the Acts of 1850.'

"Thus stood the Nebraska Bill with these words in it, 'that the legislative power of the Territory shall extend to all rightful subjects of legislation consistent with the Constitution of the United States and the provisions of this act,' and 'the said Territory, or any portion of the same, shall be received into the Union with or without Slavery, as their Constitution may prescribe at the time of their admission,' which were transcribed literally from the Utah and New Mexican Bills of 1850; when on the 17th of January, Mr. Sumner, of Massachusetts, introduced into the Senate a memorial against Slavery generally, and also gave notice, that when the bill to organize Nebraska Territory should come up for consideration, he should offer an amendment reaffirming the old Congressional Restriction of 1820. His amendment was presented informally and ordered to be printed. This opened the whole Territorial question settled in 1850 *de novo* [Latin: 'a second time']. If this was Pandora's box, as has been stated, who opened it? If there was a renewal of the agitation of the sectional controversy, settled as we have seen, who made it? Was it made by the friends of the Compromise or by its open and avowed enemies?

"It was then that the Restrictionists [Liberals] again raised their clamor. A manifesto was issued from Washington on the 19th of January, signed by Mr. Sumner and Mr. Chase, and a few others, calling their clans and hosts to action everywhere. In this they spoke of the old Missouri line of division as a 'sacred pledge' which was never to be violated. This old line of division all at once came to be considered by them and their allies as a 'Solemn Compact.' Three thousand New England clergymen, assuming to speak in the name of Almighty God, joined in the chorus. But when did these men, or any of their class, singly or collectively, ever before acknowledge any binding obligation of this now so-called 'Solemn Compact?' Was it, when Missouri was denied admission by them under it? Was it, when the admission of Arkansas was opposed by them? Was it, when provision was made for the admission of Texas? Was it, when a Government for Oregon was organized? Was it, when this line was voted down for the last time in the House on the 13th of June, 1850? Was it, when the proposition was then distinctly made to them that the South would still abide by this line of division with the exclusion of Slavery north of it, and leaving the people South of it to do as they pleased upon the subject, accompanied with the declaration, that if this was rejected, then there should be no exclusion anywhere, but that the people everywhere, in all parts of the public domain, should be permitted to do as they pleased on this subject, and that all new States should come into the Union either with or without Slavery, as their State Constitutions should determine?

"We have seen from the facts in the history of this controversy that, in all these stages of the conflict, the leaders of this Party utterly repudiated the idea of its being in any sense whatever 'a Compact' binding upon them. In this view of the case, the supporters of the settlement of 1850 had but one course to pursue in 1854; and that was to adhere strictly to their own principles, leaving the consequences of all agitation which might be gotten up by the enemies of these principles, to be properly charged to those who renewed the agitation. A few days after Mr. Sumner's notice of his intended movement, the Committee on Territories, looking to the extent of the country, as well as the fact that two separate organizations had been formed in it, and that two delegates had been sent to Congress asking two separate Territorial Governments, thought it expedient to divide the country into two Territories, and to provide Governments for each separately—one for Nebraska, and the other for Kansas. A substitute, therefore, for the first bill was reported to the Senate by Mr. Douglas, from the Committee on Territories, on the 23rd of January. This bill provided for organizing two Territorial Governments instead of one—one for Kansas, as well as Nebraska. The language in each upon the subject of Slavery, was identical with that in the first Nebraska bill, with an addition of some words which we will now notice. Here they are:

> . . . except the eighth section of the act preparatory to the admission of Missouri into the Union, approved March 6th, 1820, which being inconsistent with the principle of non-intervention by Congress, with Slavery in the States and Territories, as recognized by the legislation of 1850, commonly called the Compromise Measures, is hereby declared inoperative and void; it being the true intent and meaning of this act, not to legislate Slavery into any Territory or State, nor to exclude it therefrom, but to leave the people thereof perfectly free to form and regulate their domestic Institutions in their own way, subject only to the Constitution of the United States.

"These words made no change in the legal effect of those already in the bill, as we have seen. They were deemed necessary, however, by quite a number of Senators to preserve a perfect symmetry in the bill. In section thirty-two, in that portion of the bill providing a Government for Kansas, these words had been copied from section seventeen of the New Mexico Bill of 1850, 'that the Constitution and laws of the United States which are not locally inapplicable, shall have the same force and effect within the said Territory of Kansas as elsewhere within the United States.'

"Now, as the eighth section of the act of the 6th of March, 1820, did have a local application to this country by its terms, it was thought that a general affirmance of all laws locally applicable might be construed by some as a re-enactment of this old exclusion of Slavery, especially after the intimated movement of Mr. Sumner, notwithstanding the entire inconsistency of such a construction with the other explicit provisions of the bill upon the subject of Slavery, copied from the measures of 1850, as I have shown. Hence it was thought both expedient and proper to add the excepting words stated, to put the matter beyond all cavil or question as to the true meaning and intent of Congress in the premises. That was, to adhere strictly to the principles established in 1850. It was to prevent an erroneous construction by implication.

"The same words, in the same connection, were added to the Nebraska Bill. All the strife which ensued in 1854, upon this bill, as it thus stood, known as the Kansas-Nebraska Bill, arose therefore, was gotten up and waged by the enemies of the Compromise of 1850. It was, indeed, a fierce and bitter contest. The most exciting appeals were made to the passions of the people, and the heaviest denunciations were hurled against those who stood by the Constitution and maintained, in this instance, as they did in all others, their plighted faith to support, stand to, and abide by the settlement of 1850, on this subject, both 'in principle and substance.' As a sample of the ragings of the Restrictionists at this period, Mr. [Horace] Greeley, of the [New York] Tribune, said, in one of his leaders, while the measure was before Congress:

> 'We urge, therefore, unbending determination on the part of the Northern members hostile to this intolerable outrage, and demand of them, in behalf of freedom—in behalf of justice and humanity—resistance to the last. Better that confusion should ensue—better that discord should reign in the National councils—better that Congress should break up in wild disorder—nay, better that the Capitol itself should blaze by the torch of the incendiary, or fall and bury all its inmates beneath its crumbling ruins, than this perfidy and wrong should be finally accomplished.'

"But this, and all others of like character, had no effect upon those who had passed through the perilous struggle of 1850, in procuring the establishment of the new principle on the Territorial question. They remained firm almost to a man in both the Senate and the House. This bill, so worded upon this subject, with one or two other slight amendments, not varying the sense or effect of the language given, passed the Senate on the 3rd of March, by a vote of thirty-seven yeas to fourteen nays. By a majority of more than two to one on the per capita vote. By States, the vote stood twenty-one yeas, seven nays, and three divided. Two-thirds of the States, therefore, gave this legislation in the Senate their emphatic endorsement. The yeas were New Hampshire, New Jersey, Pennsylvania, Illinois, Indiana, Michigan, Iowa, Delaware, Maryland, Virginia, North Carolina, South Carolina, Georgia, Florida, Mississippi, Missouri, Arkansas, Kentucky, Alabama, Louisiana, and California. The nays were Maine, Massachusetts, Rhode Island, Vermont, New York, Ohio, and Wisconsin. The States divided were Connecticut, Tennessee, and Texas.

"The same bill passed the House with one or two other slight amendments, not changing the substance on the main points in the slightest particular, on the 20th of May, by a vote of one hundred and thirteen yeas to one hundred nays. The majority in this branch of Congress, on the per capita vote, was greater for this confirmation of the Compromise of 1850, than it had been for the establishment of the principle upon which it was based in that year. By States, this vote in the House stood eighteen yeas to thirteen nays. There were then thirty-one States in the Union.

"*Thus we see that the legislation of 1854 did nothing but carry out, in good faith, the Territorial principle established in 1850. There was no aggression in it on the part of the South. There was no 'perfidy,' or 'breach of Compact,' or 'wrong,' perpetrated by anybody in securing its accomplishment. Apart from its being the fulfilment of a pledge to maintain the principle of 1850, was it not perfectly just and right in itself? What wrong did the Act contain? Wrong to whom? Was it wrong to the people of the South, one large section of the Union, to permit them to enjoy an equal and fair participation of the public domain, purchased by the common blood and common treasure of all? Was it wrong to the people of the North to permit those of them who might emigrate to these Territories, to be as free there, as they were in their native homes? Was it wrong and unjust to allow all, from all the States, who might be disposed to quit their father-land and to seek to better their fortunes in these rich and fertile plains, to enjoy the same rights which their fathers did in the early formation of their State Constitutions and Governments? Whom did the bill wrong? To whom did it deal any injustice? Was it the slave—the African—whom a Southern master might take there? How could it be unjust, even to him? Was not his condition as much bettered by new lands and virgin soils, as that of his master? Was not expansion of that portion of Southern population quite as necessary for their comfort and well-being, as it was for the whites? Was it either just, right, or humane to keep them hemmed in within their then limits, until by failure of subsistence they should be reduced to starvation, even in the Slavery view of the subject?*

[Emphasis added, L.S.] Allow me to call your attention to what I said in the House, when it was under consideration there. Upon the subject of the Missouri Compromise, which had then assumed, for the first time, such a sacred form in the opinion of the opponents of the measure, I said:

> 'The principle upon which it was based has been abandoned—totally abandoned—as I have shown by those who now contend for it, and superseded by another, a later, a better, and a much more national and republican one. We do not propose to repeal any "Compact" or to violate faith in any sense—we only invoke you to stand upon the Territorial principle established by what is known as the Compromise of 1850. That has already received the sanction of an overwhelming majority of the American people, as I doubt not it always will receive when fairly presented. It has been suggested that if a proposition should be made to extend the provisions of this bill to the guarantee to the South in the Texas Annexation Resolutions for the admission of Slave States from Texas, south of 36° 30', that such proposition would certainly defeat it. By no means, sir; those who reason thus show nothing so clearly as how little they understand the real merits of the question. *That guarantee secured in the Texas Resolutions, so far as the character of the Institutions of such States hereafter to be formed, is concerned—that is, whether they be slave or free—is, itself, in perfect accordance with the present provisions of this bill. That guarantee was not that those new States should be Slave States, but the people there might do as they pleased upon the subject. The reason that the guarantee was important, at the time, was, because the policy of Congressional Restriction had not then been abandoned. The South never asked any discrimination in her favor from your hands. All that the South secured by those resolutions, so far as the character of the States is concerned, was, simply, that they should be admitted at a proper time, "either with or without Slavery," as the people may determine.* As to the number of States, that is a different question. So that if you should repeal that so-called guarantee for Slave States, by extending; the provisions of this bill to that country, you would only erase to fill again with the same words. We ask no discrimination in our favor. All we ask of you of the North, is that you make none in your own. And why should you wish to? Why should you even have the desire to do it? Why should you not be willing to remove this question forever from Congress, and leave it to the people of the Territories, according to the Compromise of 1850? You have greatly the advantage of us in population. The White population of the United States is now over twenty millions. Of this number the Northern States have more than two to one, compared with the Southern States. There are only a little over three millions of Blacks. If immigration into the Territories, then, should be assumed to go on in the ratio of population, we must suppose that there would be near seven White persons to one slave at least; and of these seven, two from the free States to one from the South. This is without taking into the estimation the immense foreign immigration. With such an advantage are you afraid to trust

this question to your own people? To those reared under the influence of your own boasted *superior Institutions*? With all the prejudices of birth and education against us, are you afraid to let them judge for themselves? [Emphasis added, L.S.]

'. . . *Do you consider it Democratic to exercise the high prerogative of stifling the voice of the adventurous pioneer, and restricting his suffrage in a matter concerning his own interest, happiness and government, which he is much more capable of deciding than you are? As for myself and the friends of the Nebraska Bill, we think that our fellow citizens who go to the frontier, penetrate the wilderness, cut down the forests, till the soil, erect school-houses and churches, extend civilization, and lay the foundation of future States, do not lose by their change of place, in hope of bettering their condition, either their capacity for self-government, or their just rights to exercise it conformably to the Constitution of the United States. We of the South are willing that they should exercise it upon the subject of the condition of the African race amongst them, as well as upon other questions of domestic policy. If they see fit to let them hold the same relation to the White race which they do in the Southern States, from the conviction that it is better for both races that they should, let them do it. If they see fit to place them on the same footing they occupy in the Northern States, that is, without the rights of a citizen, or the protection of a master, outcasts from society, in a worse condition than that of Cain, who, though sent forth as a vagabond, yet had a mark upon him that no man should hurt him*—*I say, if they choose to put this unfortunate race on that footing, let them do it. That is a matter that we believe the people there can determine for themselves better than we can for them. We do not ask you to force Southern Institutions, or our form of civil polity upon them; but to let free emigrants to our vast public domain, in every part and parcel of it, settle this question for themselves, with all the experience, intelligence, virtue and patriotism they may carry with them. This, sir, is our position. It is, as I have said, the original position of the South. It is the position she was thrown back upon in June 1850.*' [Emphasis added, L.S.]

"Similar views were presented by the advocates of the Kansas-Nebraska Bill from all sections of the Union. It was with these views and upon these principles it triumphantly passed both Houses of Congress, notwithstanding the clamor and excitement raised by its opponents. It was with these views and upon these principles that it received an emphatic endorsement by the Democratic Convention in Cincinnati, in 1856, which nominated Mr. [James] Buchanan for the Presidency. In accepting that nomination so expressly endorsing this legislation, and making the principle upon which it was based a part of the Democratic creed, declaring it to be in strict conformity with the Compromise Measures of 1850, Mr. Buchanan himself, as we have seen, in express words announced that 'this legislation is founded upon principles as ancient as free government itself.' Under that announcement and by this emphatic endorsement of this very legislation, he was triumphantly elected

President of the United States, over the most powerful efforts ever before made by the agitators and Restrictionists to defeat him. He carried the Electoral Colleges in nineteen States of the Union, while the Restrictionists who voted for Col. [John C.] Frémont carried eleven only—one State, Maryland, voted for Mr. [Millard] Fillmore. The entire popular vote which the Restrictionists could command for their candidate, with all their 'bluster' about 'breach of compact,' 'perfidy,' etc., was 1,341,264; while the entire popular vote throughout the Union against them, given partly for Mr. Buchanan, and partly for Mr. Fillmore, was 2,802,703. But Mr. Buchanan's majority over both his competitors in the Electoral Colleges was sixty.

"This election was another most signal condemnation of the principles as well as policy of the Restrictionists by the people and States of the Union. It was the more so from the fact that after their utter defeat in the Halls of Congress, on the principles of the legislation of 1854, they had openly resorted to the policy of stirring up bloody strife in the Territories. *Large amounts of money were raised for what were called 'Emigrant Aid Societies.' The object of these was to send to these Territories as many as possible of the most daring characters to drive Southern settlers from the Territories by force. Arms were bought and put in the hands of these desperadoes, thus sent out as warriors and not as peaceful colonists. This was done, too, by many who styled themselves Ministers of the Gospel! The result, for a time, was what during this Presidential campaign, was called the 'Civil War in Kansas,' which was charged by them and their allies upon the Legislation of 1854, while in truth the whole strife was instigated and gotten up by the avowed enemies of that legislation, enraged by their defeat, and with the view to kindle a general war in the States, for the total abolition of Slavery.* It was in these Kansas scenes of blood in 1856, that the noted John Brown first figured, who afterwards closed his career by his most infatuated 'raid' on the United States Armory at Harper's Ferry, in 1859. All these wild, reckless and revolutionary measures, so instigated and controlled by these mischievous malcontents, did not prevent the general condemnation stated, in 1856. There can be no question that there was then a very large majority of the people of the United States, South as well as North, devotedly attached to the Union under the Constitution and who were resolved to maintain, if possible, the Federal [Confederate] system against all [the Liberals'] attempts, whether covert or open, at Centralism or Consolidation. [Emphasis added, L.S.]

"Allow me to say, further, that my opinion then was, and now is, if Mr. Buchanan had adhered to the principles on which he was so triumphantly elected, in 1856, he, or whoever else might have been nominated on the same platform at Charleston, on which he had been nominated at Cincinnati, would have been even more triumphantly elected in 1860. *For, by the Kansas policy of the Restrictionists, and from their avowed sympathy for John Brown in his desperate undertaking in getting up civil war in Virginia, the supporters of the Constitution and Union, everywhere, saw that revolution was their real object*, and were ready to give them a sterner rebuke than ever before. But Mr. Buchanan did not adhere to the principles on which he had been elected. He insisted upon another plank being introduced into the Party Platform, which, however right it might have been on principle, as an original question, was, nevertheless, a distinct departure from the doctrine of strict Non-intervention on the part of Congress, with Slavery in the Territories in any way, either for or against, which had been agreed upon as the basis of the final settlement in 1850. This we shall have occasion, perhaps, to look into hereafter. The result of his policy, which may be here stated, was the rupture of the Party by which he had been elected, and the success of Mr. [Abraham] Lincoln, the [Liberal] candidate of the Restrictionists, by a popular vote of only 1,857,610, against the combined vote of 2,787,780, cast for the other three candidates voted for, even with the distractions and bitter feelings growing out of the rupture. This shows how easily the Restrictionists and Centralists could have been again defeated, if, by wiser statesmanship, the supporters of the Union, under the Constitution, on the basis of the Compromise of 1850, and as carried out by the legislation of 1854, had been brought, as they might have been, to act in concert in that election [instead of dividing up the vote among Lincoln's opponents]. [Emphasis added, L.S.]

"I have now gone through with what Mr. [James] Buchanan was pleased to say in his book on the Missouri Compromise, the Compromise of 1850, and the legislation of 1854. I cannot quit the subject, however, without one other remark, upon another statement by him, in the extract which I read; and to express my very great surprise, that it should have been made by him. I allude to what he says about the Constitutionality of the old Missouri Restriction, and his assertion that, if 'this question had been decided by the Supreme Court of the United States, to be in violation of the Constitution, in a case arising before them, in the regular course of judicial proceedings, the decision would have passed off in comparative silence, and produced no dangerous excitement among the people.' Now, it is well known that the Supreme Court did decide this question in the very way and manner spoken of by him, and that they did decide it to be in violation of the Constitution, and, therefore, void from the beginning; yet, nothing that Congress had ever done so much excited the Restrictionists, as this regular and solemn adjudication did. By resolves and denunciations in every form and shape, this entire class of agitators expressed their fixed determination never to be bound by it, and resorted to all the epithets of abuse they could command to cast odium upon the learned Judges who made it; especially did they exhaust their vocabulary of defamation in their attempts to blacken the name of Chief Justice [Roger B.] Taney, who delivered the judgment of the Court. This eminent jurist, who thus became the marked object of their vituperations, was no less distinguished for his public than his private virtues. In all the qualities which characterize a good citizen, as well as an able statesman, he had no superior in the country. By his legal and judicial acquirements, he had added new lustre to that Bench to which [John] Marshall, whom he succeeded, had already given so much distinction and renown, not only in this, but in foreign countries. Enough, however, on this subject."[191]

☛ "The facts adduced show that there was no 'breach of Compact' or of 'faith,' and that there was no 'aggression' on the part of the South in the legislation of 1854. Whatever excitement followed that legislation was gotten up by the Restrictionists, who would be bound by no Compact in the premises, not even by the Constitution itself, which they were sworn to support. These are the enduring facts of history. So after all these three last long talks, in which we have gone over extensive new grounds, we come back to the point at which we had arrived before, in relation to *the open, palpable, and avowed violation of the Constitution by the Centralists and Restrictionists in the matter of the rendition of fugitives from service. We have seen, conclusively, that in that matter the wrong, the aggression, the acknowledged 'breach of faith,' was on the side of the non-slaveholding* [i.e., Northern] *States alluded to, and that in no instance pointed out by* [my Liberal friends,] . . . *as an excuse or palliation, was there any aggression or breach of faith by the Southern States. They were ever true to their Constitutional obligations, and resorted to a withdrawal from the Union only when it became the thorough conviction of their leading men, that it was the object of the Centralists* [i.e., the Northern Liberals]*, by using this question, to accomplish their purpose of effecting a Consolidated Empire instead of continuing the Federal* [Confederate] *Republic. We have seen that by public law they had a perfect right to withdraw. In denial of this right to withdraw, the war was inaugurated, as we have seen. The cry, on the part of those* [i.e., the Republicans, the Liberal party of the day] *controlling the Federal Government at the time, of saving the Union, was but a pretext to cover their design of overthrowing the Principles of the Constitution. It remains, then, for us now to proceed . . . to consider the conduct of the war thus inaugurated; and, after that, to take some notice of the results of this conflict of principles, so brought into physical play on both sides.*"[192] [Emphasis added, L.S.]

24

THE MYTH OF THE "IRREPRESSIBLE CONFLICT"

AFTER LINCOLN'S WAR, NORTHERN LIBERALS had many questions for C.S. Vice President Alexander Hamilton Stephens of Georgia. Why, as a pro-Union man, did he leave the Union with his state? And what about his correspondence with Abraham Lincoln shortly after his election to U.S. president? What did they discuss, and was any progress made by either party toward avoiding war? In this chapter of excerpts from *A Constitutional View*, Stephens addresses these and a host of other questions about the South and the War for Southern Independence.

☛ "[The question as to why I eventually chose secession] . . . entirely reverses the order of our proceedings, and will require for the present, at least, a change of front.

[My Liberal friends] . . . put me on my defence for yielding obedience to the Ordinance of Secession of my State after it was passed, and [they] . . . now put me on a like defence for not supporting and advocating it in the first instance. My answer to [them] . . . has been fully given; and the reasons which induced me to oppose its passage, I intended to give when I came to speak of that Ordinance itself: but as [they] . . . have propounded the question [they] . . . have, I may as well give them now as hereafter. They were perfectly satisfactory to me at the time, and are still so; though I very much question if they will, in the judgment of mankind, be considered as complete a vindication and justification of my opposition to that measure, as those given in answer to [the Liberals] . . . will be deemed a justification of my course after its adoption. Especially in view of subsequent events. It must, however, be recollected that when one line of policy is adopted instead of another, either in civil or military affairs, or even in the ordinary business of life, it is impossible ever afterwards to form any very satisfactory conclusion as to what would or might have been the results of that other line which was rejected.

"In illustration of what I mean, let me say that if the views of Nicias instead of those of Alcibiades [both of ancient Greece] had prevailed at Athens, when war against Syracuse was resolved upon, no one can now, with any assurance, venture to assert what would have been the difference in the results upon the well-being of that Commonwealth. So in this instance. What would or might have been the result of the line of policy I advocated, can never be positively known. It can only be considered or appreciated upon the principle of probabilities. Its merits must ever remain a matter of speculation only. The reasons, however, by which I was influenced in the premises, whatever weight they were entitled to then, at present, or hereafter, I will now proceed to state.

"My opposition to the measure, it must be borne in mind, was not to the right or power of the State to secede, or to any want of conviction that she had ample cause to justify her in doing it, but solely to the expediency of the policy of resorting to that measure at the time, and under all the circumstances, then attending the questions involved."[193]

☞ "[My Liberal friends would like to know about my correspondence with Mr. Lincoln, after his election, upon this subject. They are also interested to know about Lincoln's offer to place me in his cabinet. It is true that there] . . . was a correspondence between us after his election, but not directly upon this subject, nor in any manner, whatever, connected with the subject of his Cabinet. That rumor, to whatever extent it prevailed, was utterly groundless; or if he ever addressed any communication to me on that subject, it never reached me. His correspondence with me was in reference to my Union speech on the 14th of November, 1860, to which [my Liberal friends] alluded at first: and as the reasons for my course upon this subject, which I was about to state, appear to a considerable extent in that speech, perhaps the better way would be to answer both [of these] . . . questions together, first, by exhibiting that correspondence, and then the speech to which it refers.

"Here, then, is the correspondence about which [my progressive friends] . . . inquired. It was given to the public for the first time in Mr. [Henry] Cleveland's book . . . [*Alexander H. Stephens: in Public and Private*].

"Mr. Lincoln's injunction in his second letter (which I considered as applicable to the whole correspondence,) was strictly observed until the close of the war. No 'eye' had ever seen his letters except my Private Secretaries' into whose hands they fell. Nor did I ever allude to the subject of any such correspondence between us, except to Messrs. [Robert M. T.] Hunter and [John A.] Campbell, as we were on our way to the famous Hampton Roads Conference. I mentioned it to them at that time, that they might be fully apprized of the personal relations existing between Mr. Lincoln and myself. He and I had been in Congress together. We had both opposed the policy of the Mexican war, and had both cordially co-operated together in the nomination and election of General [Zachary] Taylor to the Presidency in 1848, as the surest means of arresting a consummation of that policy. We succeeded in the election, but not in the object. Neither Mr. Hunter nor Mr. Campbell knew much of Mr. Lincoln, except from his public acts, after his elevation to the Presidency. Personally, I knew him well, and esteemed him highly; and to them mentioned this correspondence as evidence of our kind relations, individually, anterior to the war.

"With this explanation, I show you the letters. First, his autograph letter to me, and the copy I kept of my reply to him; then his second letter to me, and my reply to that . . . [Stephens shows the actual letters between he and Lincoln to his Liberal friends.]

[Lincoln's initial letter to Stephens reads:]

'Springfield, Ill., November 30, 1860.
'Hon. A. H. Stephens
'My dear Sir, I have read, in the newspapers, your speech recently delivered (I think) before the Georgia Legislature or its assembled members. If you have revised it, as is probable, I shall be much obliged if you will send me a copy—Yours very truly, A. Lincoln'

[Stephens replied to Lincoln's note on December 14, 1860, after which Lincoln responded as follows:]

'For your eyes only; Springfield, Ill. Dec. 22, 1860
'Hon. A. H. Stephens—
'My dear Sir, Your obliging answer to my short note is just received, and for which please accept my thanks—I fully appreciate the present peril the country is in, and the weight of responsibility on me.
'Do the people of the South really entertain fears that a Republican [Liberal] administration would, directly or indirectly, interfere with their slaves, or with them, about their slaves?
'If they do I wish to assure you, as once a friend, and still I hope, not an enemy, that there is no cause for such fears. The South would be in no more danger in this respect, than it was in the days of [George] Washington. I suppose, however, this does not meet the case. *You think slavery is right, and ought to be extended; while we think it is wrong and ought to be restricted. That I*

suppose is the rub. It certainly is the only substantial difference between us. Your very truly, A. Lincoln [Emphasis added, L.S.]

[Stephens continues on with his narrative:]
". . . The copy retained of my second letter to [Mr. Lincoln] . . . of the 30th [December 1860], after the usual heading and address, is in these words:

'Yours of the 22nd instant was received two days ago. I hold it and appreciate it as you intended. Personally I am not your enemy—far from it—and however widely we may differ politically, yet *I trust we both have an earnest desire to preserve and maintain the Union of the States, if it can be done upon the principles and in furtherance of the objects for which it was formed.* It was with such feelings on my part, that I suggested to you in my former note the heavy responsibility now resting on you, and with the same feelings I will now take the liberty of saying in all frankness and earnestness, that *this great object can never be attained by force.* This is my settled conviction. Consider the opinion, weigh it, and pass upon it for yourself. An error on this point may lead to the most disastrous consequences. I will also add, that in my judgment the people of the South do not entertain any fears that a Republican Administration [the Liberal Party of the day], or at least the one about to be inaugurated [in March 1861], would attempt to interfere directly and immediately with Slavery in the States. Their apprehension and disquietude do not spring from that source. They do not arise from the fact of the known Anti-Slavery opinions of the President elect. [George] Washington, [Thomas] Jefferson, and other presidents are generally admitted to have been Anti-Slavery in sentiment. But in those days Anti-Slavery did not enter as an element into Party organizations. [Emphasis added, L.S.]

'Questions of other kinds, relating to the foreign and domestic policy—commerce, finance, and other legitimate objects of the General Government—were the basis of such associations in their day. The private opinions of individuals upon the subject of African Slavery, or the state of the Negro with us, were not looked to in the choice of Federal officers, any more than their views upon matters of religion, or any other subject over which the Government under the Constitution had no control. But now this subject, which is confessedly on all sides outside of the Constitutional action of the Government so far as the States are concerned, is made the 'central idea' in the Platform of principles announced by the triumphant Party. The leading object seems to be simply, and wantonly, if you please, to put the Institutions of nearly half the States under the ban of public opinion and national condemnation. This, upon general principles, is quite enough of itself to arouse a spirit not only of general indignation, but of revolt on the part of the proscribed. Let me illustrate. It is generally conceded, by the Republicans [Liberals] even, that Congress cannot interfere with Slavery in the States. It is equally conceded that Congress cannot establish any form of religious worship. Now, suppose that any one of the present Christian Churches or Sects prevailed in all the Southern States, but had no existence in any one of the Northern States—under such circumstances suppose the people of the Northern States should organize a political Party—not upon a foreign or domestic policy, but with one leading idea of condemnation of the doctrines and tenets of that particular Church, and with the avowed object of preventing its extension into the common Territories, even after the highest judicial tribunal of the land had decided they had no such Constitutional power! And suppose that a Party so organized should carry a Presidential election! Is it not apparent that a general feeling of resistance to the success, aims, and objects of such a Party would necessarily and rightfully ensue? Would it not be the inevitable consequence? And the more so, if possible, from the admitted fact that it was a matter beyond their control, and one that they ought not in the spirit of comity between co-States to attempt to meddle with. I submit these thoughts to you for your calm reflection. We at the South do think African Slavery, as it exists with us, both morally and politically right. This opinion is founded upon the [cultural] inferiority of the Black race. You, however, and perhaps a majority of the North, think it wrong. Admit the difference of opinion. The same difference of opinion existed to a more general extent amongst those who formed the Constitution, when it was made and adopted. The changes have been mainly to our side. As Parties were not formed on this difference of opinion then, why should they be now? The same difference would of course exist in the supposed case of religion. When Parties or combinations of men, therefore, so form themselves, must it not be assumed to arise not from reason or any sense of justice, but from *Fanaticism*? The motive can spring from no other source, and when men come under the influence of fanaticism, there is no telling where their impulses or passions may drive them. *This is what creates our discontent and apprehension.* You will also allow me to say, that it is neither unnatural nor unreasonable, especially when we see the extent to which this reckless spirit has already gone. Such, for instance, as the avowed disregard and breach of the Constitution, in the passage of the statutes in a number of the Northern States against the rendition of fugitives from service, and such exhibitions of madness as the John Brown raid into Virginia, which has received so much sympathy from many, and no open condemnation from any of the leading men of the present dominant Party. For a very clear statement of the prevailing sentiment of the most moderate men of the South upon them, I refer you to the speech of Senator [A. O. P.] Nicholson, of Tennessee, which I inclose to you. Upon a review of the whole, who can say that the general discontent and apprehension prevailing is not well founded? [Emphasis added, L.S.]

'In addressing you thus, I would have you understand me as being not a personal enemy, but as one who would have you to do what you can to save our common country. A word "fitly spoken" by you now, would indeed be "like apples of gold, in pictures of silver." I entreat you be not deceived as to the nature and extent of the danger, or as to the remedy. *Conciliation and harmony, in my judgment, can never be established by force. Nor can the Union, under the Constitution, be maintained by force. The Union was formed by the consent of Independent Sovereign States. Ultimate Sovereignty still resides with them separately, which can be resumed, and will be, if their safety, tranquillity and security in their judgment require it. Under our system, as I view it, there is no rightful power in the General Government to coerce a State, in case any one of them should throw herself upon her reserved rights, and resume the full exercise of her Sovereign Powers. Force may perpetuate a Union. That depends upon the contingencies of war. But such a Union would not be the Union of the Constitution. It would be nothing short of a Consolidated Despotism.* Excuse me for giving you these views. Excuse the strong language used. Nothing but the deep interest I feel in prospect of the most alarming dangers now threatening our common country, could induce me to do it. Consider well what I write, and let it have such weight with you, as in your judgment, under all the responsibility resting upon you, it merits.' [Emphasis added, L.S.]

"This is the whole of the correspondence [with Lincoln] the [Liberals] . . . inquired about. It had no influence whatever with me, in the course I took upon the Ordinance of Secession. The general views I entertained upon that subject, at the time, are to be found in the speech referred to by Mr. Lincoln, as well as in a substitute that was offered for the Secession Ordinance, in the State Convention, on the 19th of January, 1861, and in the speech I made in this Convention on the Ordinance and the substitute. To each of these I will presently call . . . attention in their order. But, before doing so, it is proper here to state, that these views were all based upon a firm conviction, on my part, that *Mr. Lincoln's election was not, in any proper sense, an endorsement of the principles of his Party by a majority of the people of the non-slaveholding States. I did not think it was to be considered as anything like a fair exponent of the fixed sentiments of a majority of even all those States which had cast their Electoral votes, as they had, for Mr. Lincoln. I considered it as nothing but the result of the unfortunate rupture of the Democratic Party, at Charleston, in 1860 [in which the Southern conservatives unwisely split up their votes, allowing Lincoln to win]. This rupture I also attributed directly to the very injudicious and unwise policy of Mr. [James] Buchanan, before referred to, in insisting upon a new article in the creed of the Democratic Party, or a new plank in the Platform, as it was called.* A few additional facts must be borne in mind for a right understanding of the due import of the Presidential election, in 1860, as I viewed it, and upon which my convictions were founded."[194] [Emphasis added, L.S.]

☛ "Be it borne in mind, then, that the new article, so insisted to be inserted in the Democratic creed, was substantially embraced in a resolution proposed to the regular Convention of that Party, assembled at Charleston, on the 23rd of April, 1860, for the purpose of nominating candidates for the offices of President and Vice President. The Resolution was in the following words:

> That the Government of a Territory, organized by an act of Congress, is provisional and temporary; and during its existence, all citizens of the United States have an equal right to settle with their property in the Territory, without their rights, either of person or property, being destroyed or impaired by Congressional or Territorial Legislation.

"This Resolution it will be seen contains, in substance, the fourth and fifth of the series offered by Mr. [Jefferson] Davis in the Senate, on the 29th of February before, and about which I gave my opinion, when we had them under consideration. For my views, more at large, however, on this subject, and the merits of this particular Resolution, as well as upon its effects on the Presidential election of that year, I must refer . . . to two letters, and a speech made by me, as the events transpired. . . . [However,] I must waive their reading at present, and go on with the brief rehearsal of facts.

"The only new principle proposed to be incorporated by this Resolution into the Cincinnati Platform as it stood, and which, in other respects, met the general approbation of the Convention at Charleston, was covered by the two words, 'Territorial Legislation,' as they appear in their connection. The object of it evidently was, to make an issue with a large class of Democrats, who had ever been firm against Congressional Restriction, on the subject of Slavery in the Territories, but who, nevertheless, entertained the opinion that the Territorial Legislatures could Constitutionally regulate the subject of Slavery, or property in slaves in the Territories, as well as property of any other kind or character. It was, without doubt, aimed chiefly at the doctrine of Mr. [Stephen A.] Douglas, who, it was well known, held that the people of an organized Territory, through their Legislature, could Constitutionally regulate this subject, as rightfully as the people of a State. In other words, that this was as rightful a subject of local legislation, as any other committed to the Territorial Legislatures, upon the principle established in 1850. This doctrine of his, upon the rights and powers of the Territorial Legislatures, in this respect, was what was at that time called 'Squatter Sovereignty.' He also, it was known, was the favorite candidate of a large majority of the Convention, for the office of President, while a minority were unwilling to support him under any circumstances. When this Resolution, therefore, was rejected, quite a number of the delegates, as is well known, withdrew from the Convention, and after organizing themselves into a separate body, called another Convention, to meet on the second Monday in June, at Richmond, Virginia, for the purpose of nominating candidates on a Platform more to their liking, than that adopted in 1856, at Cincinnati. The remaining delegates, constituting a large majority of the Convention as organized, then resolved without doing any further business, to adjourn, to meet again on the 18th of June, in the city of Baltimore, with a request to the Democratic Party of the several States, to supply the vacancies in their respective delegations, occasioned by the withdrawal of their delegates. The Convention did so reassemble at the time stated. After the adjournment from Charleston, Conventions were held in several of the States to fill the vacancies as requested. But, in the meantime, the Convention which had been called at Richmond, was postponed and adjourned to the same time and place, as that of the regular organization. Upon the reassembling of the regular Convention at Baltimore, on the 18th of June, another withdrawal took place, headed by Mr. Caleb Gushing, the President, and Mr. Benjamin F. Butler, of Massachusetts. A majority of the original body, however, still remained. Those who then withdrew, immediately joined the new organization, which had assembled in another part of the city.

"The rupture of the Democratic Party was, therefore, now complete. Both wings of it put forth their candidates upon their respective Platforms. The regular organization, after adopting the Cincinnati Platform, and giving a pledge to maintain the principles of the decision of the Supreme Court of the United States, in the Dred Scott case, put in nomination Mr. Douglas, for the Presidency, and Mr. Benjamin Fitzpatrick, of Alabama, for the Vice Presidency. The other organization, calling itself the Democratic [Conservative] Party of the United States, after adopting the same Cincinnati Platform, with the additional plank respecting the powers of a Territorial Legislature, with some other less material matters, put in nomination Mr. John C. Breckinridge, of Kentucky, for the office of President, and Mr. Joseph Lane, of Oregon, for that of Vice President. Mr. Breckinridge was, at that time, Vice President of the United States, having been elected to that office, on the ticket with Mr. [James] Buchanan, in 1856. He was a man of a high order of talents, of most fascinating manners, and of great popularity. Very few contributed more than he did in the House, to the Kansas-Nebraska legislation of 1854. Mr. Lane was, at the time, Senator from Oregon. He had been a Brigadier General in the Mexican war, where he acquired distinction, and was justly regarded in civil affairs as a statesman of high order, having ever been an able defender of the Constitution, according to the [conservative/libertarian] principles of the Jeffersonian school.

"In the meantime, then, while these distractions were going on in the Democratic [Liberal] Party, another portion of the people strongly opposed to the principles and objects of the Party which supported Messrs. Lincoln and [Hannibal] Hamlin, had met at Baltimore, some time in May, and had presented the names of Mr. John Bell, of Tennessee, and Mr. Edward Everett, of Massachusetts, for the same offices. Mr. Lincoln and Mr. Hamlin were nominated by a Convention of their Party, on the 18th of the same month, at Chicago. Mr. Fitzpatrick, of Alabama, having declined to accept the nomination tendered him, the same position was assigned Mr. Herschel V. Johnson, of Georgia, who did accept it. Thus the campaign of 1860 was opened, and continued during the canvass with four full tickets in the field. That headed by Mr. Breckinridge claimed to be the regular Democratic ticket, and was understood to be the favorite of every member of the Administration; while the ticket headed by Mr. Douglas claimed, also, and with more right, as it seemed to me, to be the regular Democratic ticket. The result was not different from what might reasonably have been expected. The Restrictionists [i.e., the Republicans or Liberals, headed by Lincoln and Hamlin] carried the election, as we have seen, by a minority vote, owing to this division of their opponents.

"It has been supposed by some that this state of things was brought about intentionally by those who favored the policy which led to the rupture of the Democratic organization, with a view to effect the very result which ensued, in order to avail themselves of it in their ulterior purpose of dis-union. This, in my judgement, is a great mistake, at least so far as relates to the action of Mr. Buchanan, the members of his Cabinet, Mr. Breckinridge, Mr. Lane, Mr. Davis, and an overwhelming majority of those who advocated that policy. They anticipated no such results, and were in the main as much disappointed, I think, at what occurred, as men ever were at the consequences of their own acts. They really hoped and expected the final result to be the election of Mr. Breckinridge. They thought he would carry the entire South, and might get enough Electoral votes at the North to secure this end, through the Electoral Colleges. But failing in that, they felt quite assured that he would receive enough Electoral votes at the North and South together, to carry his name in the House of Representatives, where, in case no one of the four candidates should receive a majority of the votes cast by the Electoral Colleges, the election, under the Constitution, was to be determined by the States. And as the majority of the Representatives in the House, from a majority of the States, was Democratic, but opposed to Mr. Douglas, they considered Mr. Breckinridge's election as certain, if it should in the end have to be determined by that body.

"But again, even failing in the election of Mr. Breckinridge in this way, by any factious movement on the part of the House of Representatives in staving off the election, (as the per capita majority in that body was against him,) then they looked with confidence to the election of Mr. Lane as Vice President, either by the Electoral Colleges, or by the Senate, (which was Democratic,) in case of the [Electoral] Colleges failing to make a choice of Vice President, upon whom, after being so elected Vice President by the Senate, would devolve the office of President, under the Constitution, if no choice for President should be made by the Electoral Colleges, nor by the House of Representatives, before the 4th of March, 1861. They, therefore, felt quite assured that the final result would be the election to the Presidency, of one or the other of the nominees on their ticket—if not Mr. Breckinridge, then Mr. Lane.

"These were their views and expectations, as I understood them. They were founded in too little regard, if not too much contempt of the forces of the Restrictionists, as well as upon too little regard for the effects upon the Northern mind, of the party warfare that had been made upon Mr. Douglas. *When the candidates entered the field in June, not a man of this class, perhaps, thought it to be within the range of probability even, that Mr. Lincoln and Mr. Hamlin would receive a majority of the Electoral votes, as they did.* This policy, therefore, which brought about this state of things, with its results, viewed in the light of true statesmanship, appeared to me then, neither prudent nor sagacious. It so appears still. It risked and perilled, by too many chances, matters involving too great and even momentous consequences, upon differences on points comparatively of entirely too little importance. [Emphasis added, L.S.]

"The final result was not generally looked for at all in the beginning of the canvass. When I stated in the speech, [the one I gave at Augusta, Georgia, on the 1st of September,] that the people need not be surprised to see the States involved in war, in less than six months, it was said by many, that 'the weakness of my body was extending to my head;' or in other words, it was said, I was becoming 'crazy.' As the day of election approached, however, especially after the State elections at the North, in October, apprehensions as to the result became serious, and many of the leading men and presses supporting the ticket headed by Mr. Breckinridge, not only in Georgia, but in the States of the South generally, declared openly for Secession, in case this result should occur. When it did come, it struck the masses of the people with general consternation.

"These facts have required more time in giving them in detail, than I expected; but they are important outside of this connection, and must be borne specially in mind, in considering the grounds upon which my convictions were founded, and on which my action was based. Hence, while *I regarded the success of the Centralists and Restrictionists [Liberals] in the election of Mr. Lincoln, as a great public calamity*; yet I did not think that all further maintenance of Constitutional principles was hopelessly lost by it. The Centralists had, by a minority of the people only, gotten possession of one branch of the Government only. A majority of the Senate was still true to the Constitution. The House of Representatives elected to go into office, on the same day with Mr. Lincoln, had also a large majority in it still true to the Constitution, and the principles established in 1850. The changes in this House, at the very same election in the Northern States, were upon the whole against the Restrictionists. The Supreme Court was still, also, unfaltering in their firm maintenance of the Constitution on all these subjects. Hence, I saw no immediate serious danger from the triumph of the Centralists in the election of Mr. Lincoln, under the circumstances. He was powerless to effect much mischief before the people of the several States could, under wiser counsels, and better statesmanship, be brought to act more harmoniously upon sound principles, on which, in the main, an overwhelming majority of them in the aggregate were agreed. Having stated so much by way of premise, I now present the views on this subject as expressed in the speech to which Mr. Lincoln referred in his first letter to me. This speech, as appears from the correspondence, was delivered before the Georgia Legislature, on the 14th of November, 1860 [just eight days after Lincoln's election]. It was entirely extemporaneous, and was not thoroughly revised by me before publication. In reading such parts as are pertinent to the matters we now have under consideration, [please] . . . bear in mind that I read from the newspaper report with the correction of a few verbal mistakes only, omitting some parts not pertinent to our present purpose, and which in the report break the close connection of those parts which are thus pertinent. It was addressed to that body on the subject of Secession, in view of the then condition of public affairs; and in reply, in part, to the idea entertained by some, at the time, that the Legislature could resume the delegated Sovereign powers of the State. Here is what I then said upon these subjects, with the interruptions and responses of the audience as given by the reporter. These phonographed [photographed?] 'foot-prints,' small matters as they are, possess within themselves a special interest, in throwing light upon the temper and spirit of the times:

> 'Fellow Citizens: I appear before you to-night at the request of Members of the Legislature and others, to speak of matters of the deepest interest that can possibly concern us all, of an earthly character. There is nothing, no question or subject connected with this life, that concerns a free people so intimately as that of the Government under which they live. *We are now, indeed, surrounded by evils. Never since I entered upon the public stage, has the country been so environed with difficulties and dangers that threatened the public peace and the very existence of our Institutions as now.* I do not appear before you at my own instance. It is not to gratify any desire of my own that I am here. Had I consulted my personal ease and pleasure, I should not be before you; but believing that it is the duty of every good citizen, when called on, to give his counsels and views whenever the country is in danger, as to the best policy to be pursued, I am here. For these reasons, and these only, do I bespeak a

calm, patient, and attentive hearing. [Emphasis added, L.S.]

'My object is not to stir up strife, but to allay it; not to appeal to your passions, but to your reason. Let us therefore, reason together. It is not my purpose to say aught to wound the feelings of any individual who may be present; and if in the ardency with which I shall express my opinions, I shall say anything which may be deemed too strong, let it be set down to the zeal with which I advocate my own convictions. There is with me no intention to irritate or offend.

'I do not, on this occasion, intend to enter into the history of the reasons or causes of the embarrassments which press so heavily upon us all at this time. In justice to myself, however, I must barely state upon this point that I do think much of it depended upon ourselves. *The consternation that has come upon the people is the result of a sectional election of a President [Lincoln] of the United States, one whose opinions and avowed principles are in antagonism to our interests and rights, and we believe, if carried out, would subvert the Constitution under which we now live.* But are we entirely blameless in this matter, my countrymen? I give it to you as my opinion, that *but for the policy the Southern people pursued, this fearful result [i.e., Lincoln's election] would not have occurred.* [Emphasis added, L.S.]

'The first question that presents itself is, shall the people of Georgia secede from the Union in consequence of the election of Mr. Lincoln to the Presidency of the United States? My countrymen, I tell you frankly, candidly, and earnestly, that I do not think that they ought. In my judgment, the election of no man, constitutionally chosen to that high office, is sufficient cause to justify any State to separate from the Union. It ought to stand by and aid still in maintaining the Constitution of the country. To make a point of resistance to the Government, to withdraw from it because any man has been elected, would put us in the wrong. We are pledged to maintain the Constitution. Many of us have sworn to support it. Can we, therefore, for the mere election of any man to the Presidency, and that, too, in accordance with the prescribed forms of the Constitution, make a point of resistance to the Government, without becoming the breakers of that sacred instrument ourselves, by withdrawing ourselves from it? Would we not be in the wrong? *Whatever fate is to befall this country, let it never be laid to the charge of the people of the South, and especially to the people of Georgia, that we were untrue to our national engagements. Let the fault and the wrong rest upon others. If all our hopes are to be blasted, if the Republic is to go down, let us be found to the last moment standing on the deck with the Constitution of the United States waving over our heads.* [Applause.] Let the fanatics of the North break the Constitution, if such is their fell purpose. Let the responsibility be upon them. I shall speak presently more of their acts; but let not the South, let us not be the ones to commit the aggression. We went into the election with this people [the Yankees]. The result was different from what we wished; but the election has been constitutionally held. Were we to make a point of resistance to the Government and go out of the Union merely on that account, the record would be made up hereafter against us.

[Emphasis added, L.S.]

'But it is said Mr. Lincoln's policy and principles are against the Constitution, and that, if he carries them out, it will be destructive of our rights. Let us not anticipate a threatened evil. If he violates the Constitution, then will come our time to act. Do not let us break it because, forsooth, he may. If he does, that is the time for us to act. [Applause.] I think it would be injudicious and unwise to do this sooner. I do not anticipate that Mr. Lincoln will do anything, to jeopard our safety or security, whatever maybe his spirit to do it; for he is bound by the Constitutional checks which are thrown around him, which at this time render him powerless to do any great mischief. This shows the wisdom of our system. The President of the United States is no Emperor, no Dictator—he is clothed with no absolute power. He can do nothing, unless he is backed by power in Congress. The House of Representatives is largely in a majority against him. In the very face and teeth of the majority of the Electoral votes, which he has obtained in the Northern States, there have been large gains in the House of Representatives, to the Conservative Constitutional Party of the country, which I here will call the National Democratic Party, because that is the cognomen it has at the [liberal] North. There are twelve of this Party elected from New York, to the next Congress, I believe. In the present House, there are but four, I think. In Pennsylvania, New Jersey, Ohio, and Indiana, there have been gains. In the present Congress, there were one hundred and thirteen Republicans, when it takes one hundred and seventeen to make a majority. The gains in the Democratic [Conservative] Party in Pennsylvania, Ohio, New Jersey, New York, Indiana, and other States, notwithstanding its distractions, have been enough to make a majority of near thirty, in the next House, against Mr. Lincoln. Even in Boston, Mr. [Anson] Burlingame, one of the noted leaders of the [Liberal] fanatics of that section, has been defeated, and a Conservative man returned in his stead. Is this the time, then, to apprehend that Mr. Lincoln, with this large majority in the House of Representatives against him, can carry out any of his unconstitutional principles in that body?

'In the Senate he will also be powerless. There will be a majority of four against him. This, after the loss of Bigler, Fitch, and others, by the unfortunate dissensions of the National Democratic Party in their States. Mr. Lincoln cannot appoint an officer without the consent of the Senate—he cannot form a Cabinet without the same consent. He will be in the condition of George the Third (the embodiment of Toryism), who had to ask the Whigs to appoint his ministers, and was compelled to receive a Cabinet utterly opposed to his views; and so Mr. Lincoln will be compelled to ask of the Senate to choose for him a Cabinet, if the Democracy or that Party choose to put him on such terms. He will be compelled to do this, or let the Government stop, if the National Democratic Senators (for that is their name at the North), the Conservative men in the Senate, should so determine. Then how can Mr. Lincoln obtain a Cabinet which would aid him, or allow him to violate the Constitution? Why then, I say, should we disrupt the ties of this Union, when his hands are tied—when he can do nothing against us?

'I have heard it mooted, that no man in the State of Georgia, who is true to her interests, could hold office under Mr. Lincoln. But I ask, who appoints to office? Not the President alone; the Senate has to concur. No man can be appointed without the consent of the Senate. Should any man, then, refuse to hold office that was given him by a Democratic Senate?

'[Robert A. Toombs interrupts:] If the Senate was Democratic, it was for Breckinridge.

'[Mr. Stephens:] Well, then, I apprehend that no man could be justly considered untrue to the interests of Georgia, or incur any disgrace, if the interests of Georgia required it, to hold an office which a Breckinridge Senate had given him, even though Mr. Lincoln should be President. [Prolonged applause, mingled with interruptions.]

I trust, my countrymen, you will be still and silent. I am addressing your good sense. I am giving you my views, in a calm and dispassionate manner, and if any of you differ with me, you can on some other occasion give your views, as I am doing now, and let reason and true patriotism decide between us. In my judgment, I say, under such circumstances, there would be no possible disgrace for a Southern man to hold office. No man will be suffered to be appointed, I have no doubt, who is not true to the Constitution, if Southern Senators are true to their trusts, as I cannot permit myself to doubt that they will be.

'My honorable friend who addressed you last night (Mr. Toombs), and to whom I listened with the profoundest attention, asks if we would submit to Black Republican [Liberal Northern] rule? I say to you and to him, as a Georgian, I never would submit to any Black Republican aggression upon our Constitutional rights.

'*I will never consent myself, as much as I admire this Union, for the glories of the past or the blessings of the present; as much as it has done for civilization; as much as the hopes of the world hang upon it; I would never submit to aggression upon my rights to maintain it longer; and if they cannot be maintained in the Union standing on the Georgia Platform, where I have stood from the time of its adoption, I would be in favor of disrupting every tie which binds the States together. I will have equality for Georgia, and for the citizens of Georgia, in this Union, or I will look for new safeguards elsewhere. This is my position.* The only question now is, can this be secured in the Union? That is what I am counselling with you to-night about. Can it be secured? In my judgment it may be, yet it may not be; but let us do all we can, so that in the future, if the worst comes, it may never be said we were negligent in doing our duty to the last. [Emphasis added, L.S.]

'My countrymen, I am not of those who believe this Union has been a curse up to this time. True men, men of integrity, entertain different views from me on this subject. I do not question their right to do so; I would not impugn their motives in so doing. Nor will I undertake to say that this Government of our Fathers is perfect. There is nothing perfect in this world of human origin; nothing connected with human nature, from man himself to any of his works. You may select the wisest and best men for your Judges, and yet how many defects are there in the administration of justice? You may select the wisest and best men for your Legislators, and yet how many defects are apparent in your laws? And it is so in our Government. But that *this Government of our Fathers, with all its defects, comes nearer the objects of all good Governments than any other on the face of the earth*, is my settled conviction. Contrast it now with any on the face of the earth? [Emphasis added, L.S.]

'[Mr. Toombs:] England.

'[Mr. Stephens:] England, my friend says. Well, that is the next best, I grant; but I think we have improved upon England. Statesmen tried their apprentice hand on the Government of England, and then ours was made. Ours sprung from that, avoiding many of its defects, taking most of the good, and leaving out many of its errors, and from the whole our Fathers constructed and built up this model Republic—the best which the history of the world gives any account of. Compare, my friends, this Government with that of France, Spain, Mexico, the South American Republics, Germany, Ireland—(are there any sons of that down-trodden nation here to-night?)—Prussia; or if you travel further east, to Turkey, or China? Where will you go, following the sun in its circuit round our globe, to find a Government that better protects the liberties of its people, and secures to them the blessings we enjoy? [Applause.] *I think that one of the evils that beset us is a surfeit of liberty, and exuberance of the priceless blessings for which we are ungrateful.* We listened to my honorable friend who addressed you last night [Mr. Toombs] as he recounted the evils of this Government. The first was the Fishing Bounties paid mostly to the sailors of New England. Our friend stated that forty-eight years of our Government was under the administration of Southern Presidents. Well, these fishing bounties began under the rule of a Southern President, I believe. No one of them during the whole forty-eight years ever set his administration against the principle or policy of them. It is not for me to say whether it was a wise policy in the beginning; it probably was not, and I have nothing to say in its defence. But the reason given for it was to encourage our young men to go to sea, and learn to manage ships. We had at the time but a small navy. It was thought best to encourage a class of our people to become acquainted with seafaring life; to become sailors, to man our naval ships. It requires practice to walk the deck of a ship, to pull the ropes, to furl the sails, to go aloft, to climb the mast; and it was thought by offering this bounty, a nursery might be formed, in which young men would become perfected in these arts, and it applied to one section of the country as well as to any other. The result of this was, that in the war of 1812, our sailors, many of whom came from this nursery, were equal to any that England brought against us. At any rate, no small part of the glories of that war were gained by the veteran tars of America, and the object of these bounties was to foster that branch of the national defence. My opinion is, that whatever may have been the reason at first, this bounty ought to be discontinued—the reason for it at first no longer exists. A bill for this object did pass the Senate the last Congress I was in, to which my honorable friend [Toombs] contributed greatly, but it was not reached in the House of Representatives. I trust that he will yet see that he may with honor continue his connection with the Government, and that his eloquence unrivalled in the Senate, may hereafter, as heretofore, be displayed in having this bounty, so obnoxious to him, repealed and wiped off from the statute book. [Emphasis added, L.S.]

'The next evil that my friend complained of, was the Tariff. Well, let us look at that for a moment. About the time I commenced noticing public matters, this question was agitating the country almost as fearfully as the Slave question now is. In 1832, when I was in college, South Carolina was ready to nullify or secede from the Union on this account. And what have we seen? The tariff no longer distracts the public councils. Reason has triumphed! The present tariff was voted for by Massachusetts and South Carolina. The lion and the lamb lay down together—every man in the Senate and House from Massachusetts and South Carolina, I think, voted for it, as did my honorable friend himself. And if it be true, to use the figure of speech of my honorable friend, that every man in the North, that works in iron and brass and wood, has his muscle strengthened by the protection of the government, that stimulant was given by his vote, and I believe every other Southern man. So we ought not to complain of that.

'[Mr. Toombs:] That tariff lessened the duties.

'[Mr. Stephens:] Yes, and Massachusetts, with unanimity, voted with the South to lessen them, and they were made just as low as Southern men asked them to be, and those are the rates they are now at. If reason and argument, with experience, produced such changes in the sentiments of Massachusetts from 1832 to 1857, on the subject of the tariff, may not like changes be effected there by the same means, reason and argument, and appeals to patriotism on the present vexed question! and who can say that by 1875 or 1890, Massachusetts may not vote with South Carolina and Georgia upon all those questions that now distract the country and threaten its peace and existence? *I believe in the power and efficiency of truth, in the omnipotence of truth, and its ultimate triumph when properly wielded.* [Applause.] [Emphasis added, L.S.]

'Another matter of grievance alluded to by my honorable friend, was the Navigation Laws. This policy was also commenced under the administration of one of these Southern Presidents, who ruled so well, and has been continued through all of them since. The gentleman's views of the policy of these laws and my own do not disagree. We occupied the same ground in relation to them in Congress. It is not my purpose to defend them now. But it is proper to state some matters connected with their origin.

'One of the objects was to build up a commercial American marine by giving American bottoms [cargo ships] the exclusive carrying trade between our own ports. This is a great arm of national power. This object was accomplished. We have now an amount of shipping not only coast-wise but to foreign countries which puts us in the front rank of the nations of the world. England can no longer be styled the mistress of the seas. What American is not proud of the result? Whether those laws should be continued is another question. But one thing is certain, no President, Northern or Southern, has ever yet recommended their repeal. And my friend's effort to get them repealed has met with but little favor North or South.

'These were three of the grievances or grounds of complaint against the general system of our Government and its workings; I mean the administration of the Federal Government. As to the acts of several of the States, I shall speak presently, but these three were the main ones urged against the common Head. Now suppose it be admitted that all of these are evils in the system; do they overbalance and outweigh the advantages and great good which this same Government affords in a thousand innumerable ways that cannot be estimated? Have we not at the South, as well as the North, grown great, prosperous and happy under its operation? Has any part of the world ever shown such rapid progress in the development of wealth, and all the material resources of national power and greatness, as the Southern States have under the General Government, notwithstanding all its defects?

'[Mr. Toombs:] In spite of it!

'[Mr. Stephens:] My honorable friend says we have, in spite of the General Government; that without it I suppose he thinks we might have done as well, or perhaps better than we have done. This grand result is in spite of the Government! That may be, and it may not be; but the great fact that we have grown great and powerful under the Government, as it exists, is admitted. There is no conjecture or speculation about that; it stands out bold, high, and prominent, like your Stone Mountain, to which the gentleman alluded, in illustrating home facts, in his record—this great fact of our unrivalled prosperity in the Union as it is, is admitted—whether all this is in spite of the Government—whether we of the South would have been better off without the Government, is, to say the least, problematical. On the one side we can only put the fact against speculation and conjecture on the other. But even as a question of speculation, I differ from my distinguished friend. What we would have lost in border wars without the Union, or what we have gained, simply by the peace it has secured, is not within our power to estimate. Our foreign trade, which is the foundation of all our prosperity, has the protection of the navy which drove the pirates from the waters near our coast, where they had been buccaneering for centuries before, and might have been still, had it not been for the American navy, under the command of such a spirit as Commodore [David] Porter. Now, that the coast is clear, that our commerce flows freely, outwardly and inwardly, we cannot well estimate how it would have been, under other circumstances. The influence of the Government on us, is like that of the atmosphere around us. Its benefits are so silent and unseen, that they are seldom thought of or appreciated.

'We seldom think of the single element of oxygen, in the air we breathe, and yet, let this simple, unseen, and unfelt agent be withdrawn, this life-giving element be taken away from this all-pervading fluid around us, and what instant and appalling changes would take place, in all organic creation!

'It may be, that we are all that we are, in spite of the General Government, but it may be that without it, we should have been far different from what we are now. It is true, there is no equal part of the earth with natural resources superior, perhaps, to ours. That portion of this country known as the Southern States, stretching from the Chesapeake to the Rio Grande, is fully equal to the picture drawn by the honorable and eloquent Senator [Toombs], last night, in all natural capacities. But how many ages, centuries, passed before these capacities were developed to reach this advanced stage of civilization? There, these same hills, rich in ore, same rivers, same valleys and plains, are, as they have been since they came from the hand of the Creator. Uneducated and uncivilized, man roamed over them, for how long no history informs us.

'It was only under our Institutions as they are, that they were developed. Their development is the result of the enterprise of our people under operations of the Government and Institutions under which we have lived. Even our people, without these, never would have done it. The organization of society has much to do with the development of the natural resources of any country on any land. The Institutions of a people, political and moral, are the matrix in which the germ of their organic structure quickens into life, takes root, and develops in form, nature, and character. Our Institutions constitute the basis, the matrix from which spring all our characteristics of development and greatness. Look at Greece! There is the same fertile soil, the same blue sky, the same inlets and harbors, the same Ægean, the same Olympus—there is the same land where Homer sung, where Pericles spoke—it is, in nature, the same old Greece; but it is 'living Greece no more!' [Applause.]

'Descendants of the same people inhabit the country [of Greece]; yet what is the reason of this mighty difference? In the midst of present degradation we see the glorious fragments of ancient works of art—temples with ornaments and inscriptions that excite wonder and admiration, the remains of a once high order of civilization, which have outlived the language they spoke. Upon them all, Ichabod is written—their glory has departed. Why is this so? I answer this, their Institutions have been destroyed. These were but the fruits of their forms of Government, the matrix from which their grand development sprung; and when once the Institutions of our people shall have been destroyed, there is no earthly power that can bring back the Promethean spark to kindle them here again, any more than in that ancient land of eloquence, poetry, and song! [Applause.] The same may be said of Italy. Where is Rome, once the mistress of the world? There are the same seven hills now, the same soil, the same natural resources; nature is the same; but what a ruin of human greatness meets the eye of the traveller throughout the length and breadth of that most down-trodden land! Why have not the people of that heaven-favored clime, the spirit that animated their fathers? Why this sad difference? It is the destruction of her Institutions that has caused it. And, my countrymen, if we shall, in an evil hour, rashly pull down and destroy those Institutions, which the patriotic hand of our Fathers labored so long and so hard to build up, and which have done so much for us, and for the world; who can venture the prediction that similar results will not ensue? Let us avoid them if we can. I trust the spirit is amongst us that will enable us to do it. Let us not rashly try the experiment of change, of pulling down and destroying; for, as in Greece and Italy, and the South American Republics, and in every other place, whenever our liberty is once lost, it may never be restored to us again. [Applause.]

'There are defects in our Government, errors in our administration, and short-comings of many kinds, but in spite of these defects and errors, Georgia has grown to be a great State. Let us pause here a moment. In 1850 there was a great crisis, but not so fearful as this, for of all I have ever passed through, this is the most perilous, and requires to be met with the greatest calmness and deliberation.

'There were many amongst us in 1850 zealous to go at once out of the Union—to disrupt every tie that binds us together. Now do you believe, had that policy been carried out at that time, we would have been the same great people that we are to-day? It may be that we would, but have you any assurance of that fact? Would we have made the same advancement, improvement, and progress, in all that constitutes material wealth and prosperity, that we have?

'I notice in the Comptroller-General's report, that the taxable property of Georgia is six hundred and seventy million dollars, and upwards—an amount not far from double what it was in 1850. I think I may venture to say that for the last ten years the material wealth of the people of Georgia has been nearly if not quite doubled. The same may be said of our advance in education, and everything that marks our civilization. Have we any assurance that had we regarded the earnest but misguided patriotic advice, as I think, of some of that day, and disrupted the ties which bind us to the Union, we would have advanced as we have? I think not. Well, then, let us be careful now, before we attempt any rash experiment of this sort. I know that there are friends whose patriotism I do not intend to question, who think this Union a curse, and that we would be better off without it. I do not so think; if we can bring about a correction of these evils which threaten—and I am not without hope that this may yet be done. This appeal to go out with all the promises for good that accompany it, I look upon as a great, and I fear, a fatal temptation.

'When I look around and see our prosperity in everything—agriculture, commerce, art, science, and every department of progress, physical, mental, and moral—certainly, in the face of such an exhibition, if we can, without the loss of power, or any essential right or interest, remain in the Union, it is our duty to ourselves and to posterity to do so. Let us not unwisely yield to this temptation. Our first parents [Adam and Eve], the great progenitors of the human race, were not without a like temptation when in the garden of Eden. They were led to believe that their condition would be bettered—that their eyes would be opened—and that they would become as Gods. They, in an evil hour, yielded—instead of becoming Gods, they only saw their own nakedness!

'*I look upon this country with our Institutions as the Eden of the world, the Paradise of the Universe*. It may be that out of it we may become greater and more prosperous, but I am candid and sincere in telling you that I fear if we yield to passion, and without sufficient cause shall take that step, that instead of becoming greater or more peaceful, prosperous, and happy—instead of becoming Gods, we will become demons, and at no distant day commence cutting one another's throats. This is my apprehension. Let us, therefore, whatever we do, meet these difficulties, great as they are, like wise and sensible men, and consider them in the light of all the consequences which may attend our action. Let us see first, clearly, where the path of duty leads, and then we may not fear to tread therein. [Emphasis added, L.S.]

'Now, upon another point, and that the most difficult, and deserving your most serious consideration, I will speak. That is, the course which this State should pursue toward those Northern States which, by their legislative acts, have attempted to nullify the Fugitive Slave Law.

'Northern States, on entering into the Federal Compact, pledged themselves to surrender such fugitives; and it is in disregard of their Constitutional obligations that they have passed laws which even tend to hinder or inhibit the fulfilment of that obligation. They have violated their plighted faith. What ought we to do in view of this? That is the question. What is to be done? By the law of nations, you would have a right to demand the carrying out of this article of agreement, and I do not see that it should be otherwise with respect to the States of this Union; and in case it be not done, we would, by these principles, have the right to commit acts of reprisal on these faithless Governments, and seize upon their property, or that of their citizens, wherever found. The States of this Union stand upon the same footing with foreign Nations in this respect.

'Suppose it were Great Britain that had violated some Compact of agreement with the General Government—what would be first done? In that case our Ministers would be directed, in the first instance, to bring the matter to the attention of that Government, or a commissioner be sent to that country to open negotiations with her, ask for redress, and it would only be after argument and reason had been exhausted in vain that we would take the last resort of nations. That would be the course toward a foreign Government, and toward a member of this Confederacy [i.e., the United States of America], I would recommend the same course. Let us not, therefore, act hastily, or ill-temperedly in this matter. Let your Committee on the state of the Republic make out a bill of grievances; let it be sent by the Governor to those faithless States; and if reason and argument shall be tried in vain—if all shall fail to induce them to return to their Constitutional obligations, I would be for retaliatory measures, such as the Governor has suggested to you. This mode of resistance in the Union is in our power.

'Now, then, my recommendation to you would be this: In view of all these questions of difficulty, let a Convention of the people of Georgia be called, to which they may be all referred. Let the Sovereignty of the people speak. Some think that the election of Mr. Lincoln is cause sufficient to dissolve the Union. Some think those other grievances are sufficient to justify the same; and that the Legislature has the power thus to act, and ought thus to act. I have no hesitancy in saying that the Legislature is not the proper body to sever our Federal relations, if that necessity should arise.

'I say to you, you have no power so to act. You must refer this question to the people, and you must wait to hear from the men at the cross-roads, and even the groceries; for the people of this country, whether at the cross-roads or groceries, whether in cottages or palaces, are all equal, and they are the Sovereigns in this country. *Sovereignty is not in the Legislature. We, the People, are Sovereign! I am one of them, and have a right to be heard; and so has every other citizen of the State. You Legislators—I speak it respectfully—are but our servants. You are the servants of the people, and not their masters. Power resides with the people in this country. The great difference between our country and most others, is, that here there is popular Sovereignty, while there Sovereignty is exercised by kings or favored classes. This principle of popular Sovereignty, however much derided lately, is the foundation of our Institutions. Constitutions are but the channels through which the popular will may be expressed. Our Constitutions, State and Federal, came from the people. They made both, and they alone can rightfully unmake either.* [Emphasis added, L.S.]

'Should Georgia determine to go out of the Union, I speak for one, though my views might not agree with them, whatever the result may be, I shall bow to the will of her people. Their cause is my cause, and their destiny is my destiny; and I trust this will be the ultimate course of all. *The greatest curse that can befall a free people, is civil war.* [Emphasis added, L.S.]

'As to the other matter, I think we have a right to pass retaliatory measures, provided they be in accordance with the Constitution of the United States; and I think they can be made so. But whether it would be wise for this Legislature to do this now, is a question. To the Convention, in my judgment, this matter ought to be referred. Before making reprisals, we should exhaust every means of bringing about a peaceful settlement of the controversy. Thus did General [Andrew] Jackson in the case of the French. He did not recommend reprisals until he had treated with France and got her to promise to make indemnifications, and it was only on her refusal to pay the money which she had promised, that he recommended reprisals. It was after negotiation had failed. I do think, therefore, that it would be best before going to extreme measures with our Confederate [Northern] States, to make the presentation of our demands, to appeal to their reason and judgment to give us our rights. Then if reason should not triumph, it will be time enough to make reprisals, and we should be justified in the eyes of a civilized world.

At least, let these offending and derelict [Northern] States know what your grievances are, and if they refuse, as I said, to give us our rights under the Constitution, I should be willing, as a last resort, to sever the ties of our Union with them. [Applause.]

'My own opinion is, that if this course be pursued, and they are informed of the consequences of refusal, these States will recede, will repeal their nullifying acts; but if they should not, then let the consequences be with them, and the responsibility of the consequences rest upon them. Another thing I would have that Convention to do. Re-affirm the Georgia Platform with an additional plank in it. Let that plank be the fulfilment of these Constitutional obligations on the part of those States—their repeal of these obnoxious laws as the condition of our remaining in the Union. Give them time to consider it, and I would ask all States South to do the same thing.

'I am for exhausting all that patriotism demands, before taking the last step. I would invite, therefore, South Carolina to a conference. I would ask the same of all the other Southern States, so that if the evil has got beyond our control, which God in his mercy grant may not be the case, we may not be divided among ourselves; [cheers,] but if possible, secure the united co-operation of all the Southern States, and then, in the face of the civilized world, we may justify our action, and, with the wrong all on the other side, we can appeal to the God of Battles, if it comes to that, to aid us in our cause. [Loud applause.] But do nothing, in which any portion of our people, may charge you with rash or hasty action. It is certainly a matter of great importance, to tear this Government asunder. You were not sent here for that purpose. I would wish the whole South to be united, if this is to be done; and I believe if we pursue the policy which I have indicated, this can be effected.

'In this way, our sister Southern States can be induced to act with us; and I have but little doubt, that the States of New York, and Pennsylvania, and Ohio, and the other Western States, will compel their Legislatures to recede from their hostile attitude, if the others do not. Then, with these we would go on without New England, if she chose to stay out.

'[A voice in the assembly:] "We will kick them out."

'[Mr. Stephens:] No: I would not kick them out. But if they chose to stay out, they might. I think, moreover, that these Northern States, being principally engaged in manufactures, would find that they had as much interest in the Union, under the Constitution, as we, and that they would return to their Constitutional duty—this would be my hope. If they should not, and if the Middle States and Western States do not join us, we should, at least, have an undivided South. I am, as you clearly perceive, for maintaining the Union as it is, if possible. I will exhaust every means, thus, to maintain it with an equality in it. *My position, then, in conclusion, is for the maintenance of the honor, the rights, the equality, the security, and the glory of my native State in the Union, if possible; but if these cannot be maintained in the Union, then I am for their maintenance, at all hazards, out of it.* Next to the honor and glory of Georgia, the land of my birth, I hold the honor and glory of our common country. In Savannah, I was made to say by the reporters, who very often make me say things which I never did, that I was first for the glory of the whole country, and next for that of Georgia. I said the exact reverse of this. I am proud of Georgia, of her history, of her present standing. I am proud even of her motto, which I would have duly respected, at the present time, by all her sons—'Wisdom, Justice, and Moderation.' I would have her rights, and those of the Southern States maintained now upon these principles. Her position now is just what it was in 1850, with respect to the Southern States. Her Platform, then established, was subsequently adopted by most, if not all the other Southern States. Now I would add but one additional plank to that Platform, which I have stated, and one which time has shown to be necessary, and if that shall likewise be adopted in substance by all the Southern States, all may yet be well. But, if all this fails, we shall at least have the satisfaction of knowing that we have done our duty, and all that patriotism could require. [Emphasis added, L.S.]

'Mr. Stephens then took his seat, amidst great applause.'

"This speech shows how earnestly devoted I was to the Sovereignty of the several States, as well as to the Union of the States, based upon that Sovereignty. It shows how profoundly I was impressed with the belief, that the happiness and prosperity of all the States depended greatly upon the continued maintenance of the Federal Union, upon the principles upon which it was founded; and that I did not then despair of so maintaining it, if the real and true friends of the Union, on these principles, everywhere, could but be brought to unite their energies and patriotic efforts to that object. It shows also that I then did not despair of the prospect of bringing about such united effort.

"So much, therefore, for the views presented in the speech of the 14th of November, 1860."[195]

☞ "I come now to the substitute offered for the Secession Ordinance in the Georgia Convention, to which I referred, as a further presentation of the reasons of my course. I shall read only such parts of it in this connection, as clearly set forth that line of policy which I thought the best for the State to pursue. This paper was drawn up by Mr. Herschel V. Johnson. Of him I may here be permitted to say a few words. His eminent ability is well known. As an orator, he is logical and brilliant. As a jurist, he stands high in the estimation of the legal profession. He was in the Senate of the United States a short time, where he acquired considerable reputation amongst the distinguished men of that body in 1848, and was afterwards Governor of the State twice, in which office he added to that reputation, and gained the distinction in the public mind of a statesman of high order. In the Presidential election, just over, he had been supported for the office of Vice President of the United States, on the same ticket which bore the name of Stephen A. Douglas for President. He was a delegate from his county in the Secession Convention, and after consultation with myself, and other delegates entertaining similar general opinions, he prepared this paper as an embodiment of our joint views on the subjects, as the right policy for the State to adopt under the circumstances. So much in advance by way of explanation. Now, let us look into those parts of this paper to which I have referred:

'The State of Georgia is attached to the Union, and desires to preserve it, if it can be done consistently with her rights and safety; but existing circumstances admonish her of danger: that danger arises from the assaults that are made upon the Institution of domestic Slavery, and is common to all the Southern States. From time to time, within the last forty years, Congress has attempted to pass laws in violation of our rights, and dangerous to our welfare and safety; but they have been restrained by the united opposition of the South and the true men of the North, and thus far the country has prospered, and the South has felt comparatively secure. Recently, however, events have assumed a more threatening aspect, *several of the non-slaveholding States refuse to surrender fugitive slaves, and have passed laws, the most oppressive, to hinder, obstruct, and prevent it, in palpable violation of their Constitutional obligations.* The Executive Department of the Government is about to pass into the hands of a sectional, political [Liberal] Party [under big government proponent Abraham Lincoln], pledged to principles and a policy which we regard as repugnant to the Constitution. These considerations, of themselves, beget a feeling of insecurity which could not fail to alarm a people jealous of their rights. By the regular course of events, the South is in a minority in the Federal Congress, and the future presents no hope of a restoration of the equilibrium between the sections, in either House thereof. Hence the Southern States are in imminent peril. This peril is greatly augmented by the recent secession of South Carolina, Florida, Alabama, and Mississippi, from the Union, by which the Southern States are deprived of the benefit of their co-operation, and left in a still more hopeless minority in the Federal Congress. Therefore, whilst the State of Georgia will not and cannot, compatibly with her safety, abide permanently in the Union, without new and ample security, for future safety, still she is not disposed to sever her connection with it precipitately, nor without respectful consultation with her Southern Confederates. She invokes the aid of their counsel and co-operation, to secure our rights, in the Union, if possible, or to protect them out of the Union, if necessary. [Emphasis added, L.S.] Therefore,

'First. *Be it ordained by the State of Georgia in Sovereign Convention assembled*, That Delaware, Maryland, Virginia, Kentucky, North Carolina, Louisiana, Texas, Arkansas, Tennessee, and Missouri be, and they are hereby respectfully invited to meet with this State, by delegates, in a Congress, at

Atlanta, Georgia, on the 16th of February, 1861, to take into consideration the whole subject of their relations to the Federal Government, and to devise such a course of action as their interest, equality, and safety may require.

'*Be it further ordained, &c.*, That the Independent Republics of South Carolina, Florida, Alabama, and Mississippi, be, and they are hereby cordially invited to send Commissioners to said Congress.

'*Be it further ordained, &c.*, That refraining from any formal demand upon those non-slaveholding [Northern] States which have passed them, of the repeal of the Personal Liberty, and other Acts, in any wise militating against the rendition of fugitive slaves, or fugitives from justice, yet the State of Georgia, hereby announces her unalterable determination not to remain permanently in confederation with those States, unless they shall purge their statute books of all such Acts.

'*Be it further ordained, &c.*, That if, between now and the time of final action upon the question of her continuance in the Union, the General Government should attempt to coerce any one of the States that have recently withdrawn, or shall hereafter withdraw therefrom, the State of Georgia will make common cause with such States, and hereby pledges all her resources for their protection and defence.

'*Be it further ordained, &c.*, That a Commissioner be appointed by this Convention to each of the slaveholding States, now members of the Federal Union, to inform them of the action of Georgia, and to urge their conformity to the policy herein indicated, and that in response to the request of Alabama, this Convention will also appoint a Commissioner to the Convention, which she has invited at Montgomery, on the 4th of February next, who is hereby instructed to urge upon that Convention so to shape their action, as to conform to, and co-operate with, that of the proposed Congress at Atlanta, on the 16th day of the same month.

'*Be it further ordained, &c.*, That, if all effort fail to secure the rights of the State of Georgia, in the Union, and she is reluctantly compelled to resume her separate Independence, she will promptly and cordially unite with the other Southern States, similarly situated, in the formation of a Southern Confederacy, upon the basis of the present Constitution of the United States.

'*Be it further ordained*, That this Convention will adjourn, to meet again on the twenty-fifth day of February next, to take such action in the premises as may be required by the proceedings of the Congress, at Atlanta, and the development of intervening events, keeping steadfastly in view the rights, equality, and safety of Georgia, and her unalterable determination to maintain them at all hazards, and to the last extremity.'

"This paper was drawn up as stated, and moved by Mr. Johnson, at first, on the 18th of January, as a substitute for two Resolutions, on that day submitted by Mr. Eugenius A. Nisbet. . . . The first of Mr. Nisbet's Resolutions declared, that the State had a right to secede, and ought to secede. The second proposed the appointment of a Committee for the purpose of reporting an Ordinance to that effect. It was in lieu of these Resolutions, [that] Mr. Johnson offered his as a substitute, and moved to refer both sets of Resolutions to a Committee of twenty-one. It was afterwards moved as a substitute for the Secession Ordinance . . . but it was when it was first offered, at this stage of the proceedings, that I said what I now submit to your consideration, as a further and last presentation of the reasons and views, as given to the public, while these events were transpiring, by which my action in opposing and voting against Secession was governed.

'Mr. President: It is well known that my judgment is against Secession for existing causes. I have not lost hope of securing our rights in the Union and under the Constitution. My judgment on this point is as unshaken as it was when the Convention was called. I do not now intend to go into any arguments on the subject. No good could be effected by it. That was fully considered in the late canvass, and I doubt not every delegate's mind is made up on the question. I have thought, and still think, that we should not take this extreme step before some positive aggression upon our rights by the General Government, which may never occur; or until we fail, after effort made, to get a faithful performance of their Constitutional obligations, on the part of those Confederate [Northern] States which now stand so derelict in their plighted faith. I have been, and am still opposed to Secession as a remedy against anticipated aggressions on the part of the Federal Executive, or Congress. I have held, and do now hold, that the point of resistance should be the point of aggression.

'Pardon me, Mr. President, for trespassing on your time but for a moment longer. I have ever believed, and do now believe, that it is to the interest of all the States to be and remain united under the Constitution of the United States, with a faithful performance by each of all its Constitutional obligations. If the Union could be maintained on this basis, and on these principles, I think it would be the best for the security, the liberty, happiness, and common prosperity of all. I do further feel confident, if Georgia would now stand firm, and unite with the Border States, as they are called, in an effort to obtain a redress of these grievances on the part of some of their Northern Confederates, whereof they have such just cause to complain, that complete success would attend their efforts; our just and reasonable demands would be granted. In this opinion I may be mistaken, but I feel almost as confident of it as I do of my existence. Hence, if upon this test vote, which I trust will be made upon the motion now pending, to refer both the propositions before us to a committee of twenty-one, a majority shall vote to commit them, then I shall do all I can to perfect the plan of united Southern co-operation, submitted by the honorable delegate from Jefferson, and put it in such a, shape as will, in the opinion of the Convention, best secure its object. That object, as I understand it, does not look to Secession by the 16th of February, or the 4th of March, if redress should not be obtained by that time. In my opinion, it cannot be obtained by the 16th of February, or even the 4th of March. But by the 16th of February we can see whether the Border States and other non-seceding Southern States will respond to our call for the proposed Congress or Convention at Atlanta. If they do, as I trust they may, then that body, so composed of representatives, or delegates, or commissioners as contemplated, from the whole of the slaveholding States, could, and would I doubt not, adopt either our plan or some other, which would fully secure our rights with ample guarantees, and thus preserve and maintain the ultimate peace and Union of the States. Whatever plan of peaceful adjustment might be adopted by such a Congress, I feel confident would be acceded to by the people of every Northern State. This would not be done in a month, or two months, or perhaps short of twelve months, or even longer. Time would necessarily have to be allowed for a consideration of the question submitted to the people of the Northern States, and for their deliberate action on them in view of all their interests, present and future. How long a time should be allowed, would be a proper question for that Congress to determine. Meanwhile, this Convention could continue its existence, by adjourning over to hear and decide upon the ultimate result of this patriotic effort.

'My judgment, as is well known, is against the policy of immediate Secession for any existing causes. It cannot receive the sanction of my vote; but if the judgment of a majority of this Convention, embodying as it does the Sovereignty of Georgia, be against mine; if a majority of the delegates in this Convention shall, by their votes, dissolve the Compact of Union which has connected her so long with her Confederate States, and to which I have been so ardently attached, and have made such efforts to continue and perpetuate upon the principles on which, it was founded, I shall bow in submission to that decision.'

"[My Liberal friends now] . . . have a very full exposition of the views, motives, and reasons by which I was governed in my opposition to Secession at the time, and under the circumstances then existing. I will add that I did not attach any serious importance to the fact that the equality which had so long been maintained in the number of the non-slaveholding and slaveholding States no longer existed. It is true the loss of that equilibrium, or balance of power, as it was called, caused many at the time to come to the conclusion that the slaveholding States could not, with safety to themselves, remain longer in the Union without some additional guarantee. This we have seen was the belief of Mr. [John C.] Calhoun. In this view I did not concur. *The only true equilibrium, or balance of power, in my opinion, under our system, which it was essential to maintain, was the recognized Sovereignty of the several States. This was the all powerful check against aggression upon the rights of any State. This was the complete Regulator of the entire system.* This was my view on the admission of California as it was on the admission of Oregon. The result showed, that so far from the admission of those States working injuriously to the interests of the slaveholding States, by the loss of this balance of power, so-called, California and Oregon became their allies on all these great Constitutional questions. California and Oregon were as strongly opposed to the doctrines of the Centralists [Liberals] as the Southern States were. The Party which supported Mr. Breckinridge in the election of 1860, looked chiefly to Oregon in the last resort for the success of their candidate. The Southern States had been in a minority in the House of Representatives, under the three-fifths clause of the Constitution, from the beginning, yet they, by uniting with the Anti-Centralists [Conservatives] of the Northern States, had controlled the action of the General Government, in the main, for sixty years out of the seventy two of its existence; not by bluster, but by prudent and wise statesmanship. [Emphasis added, L.S.]

"In this way they had united in the election, and sustained most of the leading measures of the administration of Washington for eight years, that of [Thomas] Jefferson for eight, [James] Madison for eight, [James] Monroe for eight, [Andrew] Jackson for eight, [Martin] Van Buren for four, [John] Tyler for four, [James K.] Polk for four, [Millard] Fillmore for four, [Franklin] Pierce for four, and [James] Buchanan for four; and with the same wise statesmanship, I saw no reason why they might not thus preserve the Federal system for as many more years to come, or for all time to come, by this continued concert of action between the true friends of this system, in opposition to the Consolidationists [Liberals]. *The doctrine of the 'Irrepressible Conflict' between the Institutions of the several States, was, in my view, itself the embodiment of Centralism. The Federal Government, in my judgment, so far from being weakened, was strengthened by the heterogeneous interests of the several States. Nothing tends more to Centralization of power, even in a separate State or Nation, than homogeneousness of interests on the part of its constituent elements. All progress in Governments, as well as progressive developments in everything else, is marked by successive steps from the 'simplex to the complex,' from the homogeneous to the heterogeneous. This is the true law of progress in all things. In nature, in art, and in science in all their departments. The chief safe-guards of liberty, in every political organization, owe their origin to a diversity of pursuits and a conflict of interests between its various members.* [Emphasis added, L.S.]

"But I forbear on the present occasion to enlarge upon this idea. What I have said is all that I have to give you in answer to your inquiry. With this I submit the question: Whether I was right, or whether my reasons were sufficient to justify my course, at the time, in the judgment of mankind, I will leave without any reflections upon the course of those who differed from me on these subjects, for you and others to determine."[196]

25

SECESSION & THE FORMATION OF THE C.S.A.

STEPHENS HAS PROVEN THAT SECESSION was and is legal. In this chapter of selections from *A Constitutional View*, he details the actual secession of the Southern states beginning in 1860—along with the formation of the Confederate States of America, or C.S.A. This he does through the lenses of the U.S. Constitution and contemporary politics.

☞ "... [Having gone over the acknowledged dereliction and breach of faith of several of the non-slaveholding states, I] will now again return to the point at which [I] ... had [first] ... arrived, and proceed in our consideration of the grand drama of the war—that 'physical conflict' inaugurated, [as we will see, by Abraham Lincoln]; and which grew out of that 'conflict of principles,' which we have so fully discussed and are now through with.

"This war or terrible 'conflict' of physical forces is the greatest of the kind, in many respects, which has disturbed the peace of the world since the Christian era. Its general conduct, in a political and Constitutional view, is the next object of our inquiry. The exciting scenes and stirring events of the battle-fields which marked its progress do not come within the limits of the special objects of our investigation. These have been quite graphically described by many writers, but by none, so far as I have seen, with greater ability or more impartiality than by Mr. William Swinton in his two works: the one entitled '*The Army of the Potomac*;' and the other, '*The Twelve Decisive Battles of the War.*' It is true, *he was attached to the Federal side, and therefore not without bias*, but in his general account he has not shown himself to be incapable, as several others have, of doing justice to the merits of an opposing and gallant foe—'to that body of incomparable infantry'—that array of 'tattered uniforms and bright muskets,' which for four years, under [Confederate General Robert E.] Lee, carried the 'revolt' as he terms it, 'on its bayonets, opposing a stout front to the mighty concentration of power brought against it; which receiving terrible blows, did not fail to give the like; and which, vital in all its parts, died only with its annihilation!'

"I do not intend, by any means, to say that either of his works alluded to, are faultless, or even without some grave errors, which, perhaps, were owing to a want of access to correct information on matters which belonged to the Confederate side; but, I mean simply to state, that upon the whole, I regard these two works from his pen, as the best and most accurate chronicle of the military operations, which he undertook to describe, that I have met with from any quarter. [Note: In the opinion of the editor, Edward A. Pollard's *Southern History of the War*, having been written from the South's point of view, is far more accurate, detailed, and factual than Swinton's work. L.S.]

"With these ever so interesting and thrilling scenes, however, it is not our purpose to deal so directly, as with the principles, aims, and motives, which gave impulse to these most wonderful and heroic exploits on both sides while it raged; and then to take a survey of the ultimate results, of the intermediate vicissitudes of victory and defeat, and the final fortunes of this uncertain arbitrament of arms. In pursuit of these, our main objects, a slight retrospect is necessary to understand clearly the position of both Parties politically as well as physically, or in other words, the principles in the maintenance of which each was enlisted—the organizations under them, and the material resources of each for maintaining their principles at the fall of Fort Sumter. . . . To this point in our investigation of these subject, we will now return."[197]

☛ "After the secession of South Carolina [December 20, 1860] , then, . . . let it be borne in mind, that the other six States, before named, followed, by passing similar Ordinances of Secession. Mississippi, on the 9th of January, 1861; Alabama on the 11th; Florida on the 10th; Georgia on the 19th; Louisiana on the 26th; and Texas on the 1st of February. It is unnecessary to examine all these. One other only, that of Georgia, I call your attention to. An examination of the action of this State on this subject must suffice with the general remark, that the action of the other six States in the premises was of like import in principle and in substance.

"The Convention of Georgia had been called by an Act of the Legislature, in the month of November, 1860, soon after the speech made by me before that body, which I have read. The election of delegates took place, on the first Monday in January, 1861. The representation of the counties in this

Convention was, by the Act referred to, equal to their Senators and Members of the House, in the Legislature. The election was held in conformity to the laws regulating all public elections in the State as far as applicable. I was chosen as one of the delegates to which this county was entitled. The Convention met at Milledgeville, the Seat of Government, on the 16th day of January, 1861. The whole number of delegates was three hundred and one.

"George W. Crawford, Ex-Governor of the State, and Ex-Secretary of War under General [Zachary] Taylor's Administration, was chosen President of the Convention by acclamation, and Albert R. Lamar, a journalist of considerable repute, was chosen Secretary.

"On the 18th of January, Mr. [Eugenius A.] Nisbet, as stated [earlier] . . . offered his two resolutions; the first declaring that the State had a right to secede and ought to secede, and the second authorizing the appointment of a committee to report an ordinance to that effect. It was as a substitute for these resolutions that the paper prepared by Mr. [Herschel V.] Johnson, before alluded to, was offered. A vote on this paper, at that stage of the proceedings, was cut off under the operation of the previous question, and Mr. Nisbet's resolutions were adopted. This Committee, of which he was Chairman, consisted of seventeen.

"Mr. Nisbet was himself a gentleman of great distinction in the State. He had been brought up in the [conservative] Jeffersonian States' Rights' school of politics. He had, however, opposed the doctrine of Mr. [John C.] Calhoun upon Nullification. He was a member of the Congress of the United States, from 1839 to 1843. He supported the election of Mr. [Henry] Clay for the Presidency in 1844, with great zeal and ability; and was among the most prominent actors in procuring his nomination to that office by the Whig Party, as then constituted in this State. He had occupied for a number of years a seat upon the Bench of our Supreme Court, where he had acquired the well-earned reputation of an eminent jurist. He was a warm supporter of the position assumed by Georgia upon the Compromise Measures of 1850. He was afterward a prominent leader in what was known as the American Party, and gave his support to Mr. [Millard] Fillmore in 1856. In religion and politics, from the time he entered public life, he had been regarded as the embodiment of Conservatism. For all those virtues and excellencies which constitute what is recognized as real worth in private character, no man was esteemed higher. Such is but a glimpse at the antecedents distinguishing the head and heart of the mover of the Ordinance of Secession in Georgia. On the 19th of January, he, as Chairman of the Committee of Seventeen, reported that measure in these words:

An Ordinance to dissolve the Union between the State of Georgia and other States united with her under a Compact of Government, entitled 'the Constitution of the United States of America.'

We, the people of the State of Georgia, in Convention assembled, do declare and ordain, and it is hereby declared and ordained:

That the Ordinance adopted by the people of the State of Georgia, in Convention, on the second day of January, in the year of our Lord, seventeen hundred and eighty-eight, whereby the Constitution of the United States of America was assented to, ratified and adopted; and also all acts and parts of acts of the General Assembly of this State ratifying and adopting amendments of the said Constitution, are hereby repealed, rescinded and abrogated.

We do further declare and ordain, That the Union now subsisting between the State of Georgia and other States, under the name of the 'United States of America,' is hereby dissolved, and that the State of Georgia is in the full possession and exercise of all those rights of Sovereignty which belong and appertain to a Free and Independent State.

"It was, now, when this Ordinance of Secession was before the Convention, that Mr. Benjamin H. Hill renewed the motion that the paper offered the day before by Ex-Governor [Herschel V.] Johnson be adopted in lieu of the proposed measure. The object was to get a test vote between the advocates of the two respective lines of policy. It was still a matter of doubt or uncertainty how the majority really stood. On agreeing to Mr. Hill's motion the vote was one hundred and thirty-three yeas to one hundred and sixty-four nays. This showed a decided majority of thirty-one in favor of the Ordinance for immediate Secession; and upon the direct vote on the passage of the Ordinance, taken immediately afterwards, there were two hundred and eight yeas for its adoption, to eighty-nine nays against it. Whereupon the President said it was his privilege and pleasure to declare that the State of Georgia was Free, Sovereign and Independent. My name was amongst the nays, as well as that of Ex-Governor Johnson and a large majority of those who agreed with us, in the main, on the line of policy indicated in those parts of his paper which I have read. After this a motion was made for all the delegates to sign the Ordinance. Before the question was put on this motion, Mr. Linton Stephens, my brother and junior by eleven years, who was a delegate from the county of Hancock, and a prominent actor in all these events, and who had voted against the Ordinance of Secession, drew up and submitted to me a preamble and resolution which he deemed proper to be passed before the question should be taken on the motion for the signatures of the delegates to the Ordinance, or rather as a substitute for it. It met my full concurrence, and upon my suggestion that it had better come from Mr. Nisbet, if it met his like approval, it was so submitted to him, and being highly approved, was presented by him to the Convention, in lieu of that other motion. This Preamble and Resolution were in these words:

> Whereas, The lack of unanimity in the action of this Convention, in the passage of the Ordinance of Secession, indicates a difference of opinion amongst the members of the Convention, not so much as to the rights which Georgia claims, or the wrongs of which she complains, as to the remedy and its application before a resort to other means of redress:
> And whereas, It is desirable to give expression to that intention which really exists among all the members of this Convention, to sustain the State in the course of action which she has pronounced to be proper for the occasion, therefore:
> Resolved, That all members of this Convention, including those who voted against the said Ordinance, as well as those who voted for it, will sign the same as a pledge of the unanimous determination of this Convention to sustain and defend the State, in this her chosen remedy, with all its responsibilities and consequences, without regard to individual approval or disapproval of its adoption.

"This Preamble and Resolution met with general favor, and was carried without a count. The Ordinance was accordingly signed by every delegate present except six. These six entered upon the journal a statement wherein they declared their purpose to 'yield to the will of the majority of the people of the State as expressed by their Representatives' and 'pledged their lives, their fortunes, and their sacred honor to the defence of Georgia,' etc. The names of these six are James P. Simmons, of Gwinnett, James Simmons, of Pickens, Thomas M. McRae, F. H. Latimer, Davis Whelchel, and P. M. Byrd.

"Thus the Convention became unanimously committed to the maintenance of the Sovereignty of Georgia, however much they had disagreed upon the policy or expediency of her thus resuming the full exercise of her Sovereign powers under the circumstances."[198]

☛ "As a portion of the history of the times, and for the purpose of throwing additional light upon the general objects of Mr. Linton Stephens, as well as my own, aimed at by the Preamble and Resolution drawn up by him, and which the Convention adopted with so much unanimity, and for the purpose also of throwing additional light upon what were the prevailing sentiments and views of the Union Party of the State, who were then styled Co-operationists, in contradistinction to Secessionists, it may not be out of place here to present a letter which he wrote during the canvass for delegates to this Convention. It was addressed to Hon. Eli H. Baxter, a distinguished citizen of his county, who belonged to what was then called the American Party, and who had supported the [John] Bell and [Edward] Everett ticket in the Presidential election then just over. The letter was written on the 29th of November, 1860, and after usual caption and address, is in these words:

[Stephens quoting his half-brother Linton:] 'With a view to the nomination of a ticket, on next Tuesday, to be run in this county for the approaching State Convention, allow me to interchange views with you in relation to the proper policy to be pursued by that Convention. The greatness of the occasion, and the incalculable mischief of divided counsels, call, in an eminent degree, for unanimity among the people of Georgia, and among the people of the South, in whatever policy may be adopted. Distraction among ourselves is the worst possible calamity that can befall us. Perfect unanimity I know to be unattainable, but the concurrence of our people can be attained with the exception of a few extreme Union men on the one hand, and a few extreme Disunion men on the other. I have an abiding faith that the great bulk of Georgia and of the South, can be united upon a policy which lies between the two extremes, and which for that very reason commends itself to men of "Wisdom, Justice, and Moderation" [Georgia's state motto]. Neither a majority of the Southern States nor a majority of the people of Georgia, can unite upon any line of policy, unless there shall prevail a spirit of concession—a willingness on the part of each man to sacrifice somewhat of his own chosen policy in order that a common policy may be adopted on which all can stand. The true wisdom in all emergencies, whether in private life or in statesmanship, is to strive for that which, is the best attainable; and not for that which, while it appears absolutely the best, if it could be achieved, yet is plainly unattainable. And especially should an effort for the unattainable be avoided, when that effort must result, as in this case, in the defeat of the good that is attainable.

'A very few men, perhaps, may be found who think it best to do nothing. That policy is out of the question, and those who hold to it ought to abandon it for something that can be accomplished. Another large class think that retaliatory laws would be the best remedy. It is possible that Georgia would be content to try this remedy, and my own opinion is, that she would be so, if herself alone were concerned. The tendency of a large majority of Georgia is to Conservatism. But then she has got to act, not only so as to satisfy herself, but also, (if possible,) to reconcile her sister Southern States to the policy she may adopt. She must either tender them such a lead as her more fiery sisters will accept, or she must accept an extreme lead from them—or there must inevitably be division and confusion and discord in the Southern Sisterhood. I think the only remedy which will be acceptable to some two or three of our Sisters is Secession; and for the very reason that none other will suffice them. I believe that Georgia will and ought to tender that remedy for their acceptance. They desire to apply it immediately. Georgia will not consent, I think; and surely Virginia, North Carolina, Maryland, Kentucky, and Tennessee will not consent to apply it, except as an ultimatum. If Georgia should declare Secession to be her remedy, but that she will not apply it, until a fair opportunity shall have first been given to the Northern States to recede from the obnoxious laws which now blacken the faith of some of them, and should pledge herself to apply it, after such an opportunity given and rejected, and should earnestly urge all of her Southern Sisters to cooperate with her on that line of policy. I have strong faith that the more extreme [Southern] States would fall one step back, and the more Conservative [Southern] States would come one step forward, and thus all would stand united upon ground which would preserve our honor and preserve our rights, and which would certainly be maintained, because it would be defended by a United South. If this policy should result in our continuance in the Union, we would remain under a flag which would then be purified from stain, and would afford protection alike to all over whom it might wave. If it should result in our going out of the Union, we would go in solid column, go peacefully and without let or hindrance, to make for ourselves the best new destiny of which we are capable. I will frankly say, that I do not consider the policy thus indicated to be the best for the emergency, but I do firmly believe it to be the best that is attainable. Therefore, I go for it, heart and soul. I think it will be about the policy adopted by the Convention, and that it is acceptable to a very large majority of the people of Hancock, without regard to any former Party divisions. Those of us who concur in it have called a meeting for next Tuesday, to nominate a ticket which will represent a policy that will be substantially such as I have sketched.

'Now, the question is, who shall compose that ticket? To avoid all occasion for exciting any Party jealousy, it is deemed best to have one [John] Bell man, one [Stephen A.] Douglas man, and one [John C.] Breckinridge man, if a man of each class can be had, who will be a fit representative of the county on so great an occasion, and who will be a faithful adherent to the general line of policy indicated in our call, and more fully explained in this letter.

'Your name [Eli H. Baxter] has been suggested as one of the ticket. I need not assure you, that your personal qualifications are entirely acceptable to me, and to all those who know you, and it will give me great pleasure to learn that your views are such as to justify me in using my efforts to have you put on the ticket. This letter is written without consultation with anybody except Mr. [Andrew J.] Lane. He was absent when the call for a meeting was signed, but he heartily approves of it. It was he who suggested your name. I enclose you a copy of the call as it has appeared in the newspapers. Please let me hear from you by Saturday's mail.'

"I read this letter, though hastily written by [Linton] . . . at the time, and not at all intended for the public in any way, as one of the best and most reliable *indicia* [indicators] of the general views and sentiments of the Union or

Co-operation Party of this State, during the very heated canvass for delegates to the Convention, and the views and sentiments by which they were governed in that body, after the Ordinance of Secession was adopted. They were earnest, zealous, and unremitting in their efforts in support of what they deemed the best course of policy for the State and the Southern States to pursue, so long as that was an open question. But a great object with them, throughout, was harmony after that question was settled, and a perfect concert of action by a thoroughly united people, in the vindication and maintenance of the chosen remedy of the State, when that was determined upon by her Representatives in Sovereign Convention assembled.

"The truth is, in my judgment, the wavering scale in Georgia was turned by a sentiment, the key-note to which was given in the words—'*We can make better terms out of the Union than in it.*' It was Mr. Thomas R. R. Cobb who gave utterance to this key-note, in his speech before the Legislature, two days anterior to my address before the same body. This one idea did more, in my opinion, in carrying the State out, than all the arguments and eloquence of all others combined. Two-thirds, at least, of those who voted for the Ordinance of Secession, did so, I have but little doubt, with a view to a more certain Re-formation of the Union, on the general principles of its Rectification, as set forth in the paper of Mr. Johnson. In other words, they acted under the impression and belief that the whole object, on that line of policy, could better be accomplished by the States being out of the Union, than in it. So much upon that point."[199]

☛ "We will now proceed with some further action of the Convention. Another Ordinance, to which there was very little, if any opposition, was passed in these words:

> An Ordinance to resume jurisdiction over those places within the limits of Georgia, over which jurisdiction has been heretofore ceded to the late United States of America, and to provide for compensation to the said United States for the improvements erected thereon.
> The people of Georgia in Convention assembled do hereby declare and ordain,
> That the cessions heretofore made by the General Assembly of this State, granting jurisdiction to the United States of America, over specified portions of the territory within the present limits of the State of Georgia, be, and the same are hereby revoked and withdrawn, and the full jurisdiction and sovereignty over the same, are hereby resumed by said State.
> Be it further ordained, That the buildings, machinery, fortifications, or other improvements erected on the land so heretofore ceded to the said United States, or other property found therein belonging to the United States,

shall be held by this State, subject to be accounted for in any future adjustment of the claims between this State and the said United States.

"On the 23rd of January, a Resolution was passed for the election, by the Convention, of ten delegates to represent the State of Georgia in the proposed Congress of such States as might secede from the Union, to be held at Montgomery, in the State of Alabama, on the 4th of February ensuing. The number of delegates, so determined to be sent, was equal to the number of the Senators and Members of the House to which the State was then entitled in the old Congress. It was under this Resolution, very much to my surprise I may state, that I was unanimously elected a delegate to the Montgomery Congress. It was a matter of several days' serious reflection with me, whether I would accept the trust or not. My final determination was not made until after the Convention on the 28th of January, with great unanimity, adopted the following Resolutions which I had drawn up and offered for their consideration on that day.

> Resolved, That the delegates sent from this State, by this Convention, to the proposed Congress to assemble at Montgomery, Alabama, on the 4th day of February next, be fully authorized and empowered, upon free conference and consultation with delegates that may be sent from other Seceding States, to said Congress, to unite with them in forming and putting into immediate operation, a temporary or Provisional [Confederate] Government, for the common safety and defence of all the [Southern] States represented in said Congress. Such temporary or Provisional Government not to extend beyond the period of twelve months from the time it goes into operation, and to be modelled as nearly as practicable on the basis and principles of the Government of the United States of America. The powers of the delegates so appointed by this Convention, in this particular, being hereby declared to be full and plenary.
> Be it further Resolved, That said delegates be likewise authorized, upon like conference and consultation with the delegates from the other States in said Congress, to agree upon a plan of permanent Government for said States, upon the principles and basis of the Constitution of the United States of America, which said plan or Constitution of permanent Government shall not be binding or obligatory upon the people of Georgia, unless submitted to, approved, and ratified by this Convention.

"The conclusion I finally came to was, that it was my duty to do all I could to preserve and perpetuate the principles of our model Federal [Confederate] system.

"The Convention also sent Commissioners to Virginia, North Carolina,

Maryland, Delaware, Tennessee, Kentucky, Missouri, Arkansas, Louisiana, and Texas to make known to the Governors and Legislatures of these States the position of Georgia, and to invoke their co-operation with her. The Commissioners so sent to these States, respectively, and in the order in which they are named, were Henry L. Benning, Samuel Hall, Ambrose R. Wright, D. C. Campbell, H. P. Bell, William C. Daniel, Luther J. Glenn, D. P. Hill, W. J. Vason, and John W. A. Sanford. Mr. Henry R. Jackson was first appointed to Kentucky; but upon his resignation, William C. Daniel was appointed in his place. So much for the action of the Georgia Secession Convention at present."[200]

☛ "The Senators from this State, and Members of the House, immediately severed their connection with the Congress of the United States upon being informed of the passage of her Ordinance of Secession. The same is true of the Senators and Members of all the other States named, respectively, with a single exception. Mr. John E. Bouligney, of Louisiana, continued to hold his seat in the House of Representatives, notwithstanding the Ordinance of Secession of his State. His case is the only exception. We will now turn our attention to events elsewhere."[201]

☛ "The Congress of Seceded States, called at the instance of South Carolina, as we have seen, met accordingly, at the time and place stated. The first day of its session, six of the States only were present. The delegates from Texas had not arrived, and did not arrive until after the organization of a Provisional Government. They came in soon afterwards, however, and here is a list of the seven States which, in compliance with the call so made, did so meet in Congress, with the names of the delegates by whom they were represented:

"Alabama:—Richard W. Walker, Robert. H. Smith, Colin J. McRae, Jno. Gill Shorter, William Parish Chilton, Stephen F. Hale, David P. Lewis, Thomas Fearn, and Jabez L. M. Curry.

"Florida:—Jackson Morton, James B. Owens, and J. Patton Anderson.

"Georgia:—Robert Toombs, Francis S. Bartow, Martin J. Crawford, Eugenius A. Nisbet, Benjamin H. Hill, Howell Cobb, Augustus R. Wright, Thomas R. R. Cobb, Augustus H. Kenan, and Alexander H. Stephens.

"Louisiana:—John Perkins, Jr., Alexander de Clouét, Charles M. Conrad, Duncan F. Kenner, Edward Sparrow, and Henry Marshall.

"Mississippi:—W. P. Harris, Alexander M. Clayton, W. S. Wilson, James T. Harrison, Walker Brooke, William S. Barry, and J. A. P. Campbell.

"South Carolina:—R. Barnwell Rhett, R. W. Barnwell, Laurence M. Keitt, James Chesnut, Jr., Charles G. Memminger, W. Porchér Miles, Thomas J. Withers, and William W. Boyce.

"Texas:—Thomas M. Waul, Williamson S. Oldham, John Gregg, John H. Reagan, W. B. Ochiltree, John Hemphill, and Louis T. Wigfall.

"Of the personnel of this body of men, I may be excused for saying, in passing, that, taken collectively, I never was associated with an abler one. There was in it no one who, in ability, was not above the average of the members of the House of Representatives of any one of the sixteen Congresses I had been in at Washington; while there were several who may be justly ranked, for intellectual vigor, as well as acumen of thought and oratorical powers, amongst the first men of the Continent at that time.

"They were not such men as revolutions or civil commotions usually bring to the surface. They were men of substance, as well as of solid character—men of education, of reading, of refinement, and well versed in the principles of Government. They came emphatically within the class styled by [Thomas] Carlyle, 'earnest men.' Their object was not to tear down, so much as it was to build up with the greater security and permanency. The debates were usually characterized by brevity, point, clearness, and force."[202]

☛ "On assembling [the Provisional Confederate Congress], Howell Cobb, of Georgia, who had filled the Speaker's chair in the Thirty-first Congress with such rare ability, was chosen the presiding officer of the body, and J. J. Hooper, of Alabama, who had acquired an extensive reputation from his connection with the press and literary publications, was elected Secretary.

"The first subject which engaged attention, after organization, was the rules by which the body should be governed, and, especially, the manner of voting on all questions which should come before it. The number of delegates which each State had sent was, as in the case of Georgia, a number equal to the Senators and Members to which each State had been entitled in the Congress of the United States, according to the then Federal ratio of representation. The question was, how should the votes be taken? Per capita, or by States? A Committee was appointed to report upon this point, as well as upon the subject of the general rules for the government of the body in its deliberations. The Chairmanship of this Committee was assigned to me. The report was that, as it was a Congress or Convention of States, the vote should, upon all questions, be taken and decided by States, without regard to the number of delegates from the States respectively. The Rules for the government of the body also introduced a new feature in Parliamentary law, which deserves special attention. It is that one which does away with the Previous Question; but substitutes another one for it, which effects all the good of the Previous Question, and obviates numerous objections to it. This new Rule established what was styled 'The Question,' in lieu of the Previous Question. Under general Parliamentary law, the Previous Question, when called and sustained, not only stops debate, but cuts off all amendments, and brings the House to a direct vote on the main or first proposition. By the modification of this principle of the general Parliamentary law, as made by the Rules of the House of Representatives of the United States, when the call for the Previous Question is sustained by a majority of the House, the effect is to stop all debate and bring the House to a vote, first, upon the pending amendments, and, then, upon the main or first proposition, as it may, or may not be amended by the votes thus taken. In this way, its operation is to cut off all amendments, except those pending at the time the call is sustained. Great inconvenience often results from this. But by the new Rule referred to, no such effect follows. Under its operation, when the House is not inclined to hear further debate on any pending motion, any member may call for 'The Question,' on which the sense of the House must be immediately taken without debate, and if the call is sustained by a majority of the House, the vote is then taken without further debate on the pending question, whatever it may be. In this way, the majority of the House can secure a vote upon any matter they please, in the speediest manner. This Rule worked well in all the deliberations of this Montgomery Convention, and aided greatly in the expedition with which its business was transacted. The Rules thus reported were unanimously adopted."[203]

☛ "The next subject which engaged the attention of the body was the formation of a Temporary or Provisional Government for the States thus assembled. This matter was referred to a Committee of which Mr. Charles G. Memminger, of South Carolina, was constituted Chairman. I was a member of this Committee. The result of their labors was the draft of a Constitution for the Provisional Government of these States, to be known as *The Confederate States of America*.

The original draft of this Constitution, so reported, is substantially the same as that which was finally adopted. A few changes only in the report was made by the House. As it now stands it received the unanimous sanction of the States on the 8th of February."204

☛ "The next step was the election of officers under that Provisional Government. The Provisional Constitution was adopted at a late hour on Friday night the 8th. A motion was then made to go immediately into the election of officers, but upon suggestion that it would be better to allow each of the State delegations time to confer among themselves, it was resolved to defer the election until next day, Saturday the 9th. On that day, as is known, Mr. Jefferson Davis, of Mississippi, received the unanimous vote of the six States then present, for the office of President; and in like manner I was elected to the office of Vice President. Mr. Davis was not at Montgomery. He was in Mississippi. It was generally understood from statements made by the Mississippi delegation, as well as from others who knew his personal views upon the subject, that *he did not desire the office of President.* He preferred a military position, and the one he desired above all others was the chief command of the Army, which the States might deem it necessary to organize."205 [Emphasis added, L.S.]

When asked how Davis and Stephens, both pro-Union men, came to be elected president and vice president of the Confederate States of America, Stephens replied:
☛ "I have no objection to giving . . . my opinion on the subject, as to how Mr. Davis came to be chosen under the circumstances. It is, however, only an opinion. I was somewhat surprised myself at both results as they occurred, but as I took only a very small part in the elections any way, I cannot speak of my own knowledge as to but few facts connected with either. The conclusion I came to, from all the facts I learned from others before and afterwards, was that the selection of Mr. Davis grew out of a misapprehension on the part of some of the delegates of one, or, perhaps, two or three of the States, in their consultations of the night before, as to the man that the Georgia delegation had determined to present. A majority of the States, as I understood, and afterwards learned, were looking to Georgia for the President. . . . Mr. [Robert A.] Toombs was the man whom they then unanimously agreed to present; at least there was perfect unanimity on the subject, with all the delegates in attendance. Two, Mr. [Benjamin H.] Hill and Mr. [Augustus R.] Wright, were absent. I now speak of my own knowledge. I was at this meeting of the Georgia delegation, and therein was acted the only part I took in the matter. That was by making the motion for Mr. Toombs's nomination to the

Convention, supposing that it would be unanimously acceptable to that body; but in this meeting, it was stated after my motion was made, that two or three of the States in their consultations, which had been held the night before, had determined to present the name of Mr. Davis. The fact only, without any reason for it, was stated. It was stated also, only as something which had been heard, but not positively known. On this announcement, a committee of our delegation, of which Mr. [Martin J.] Crawford was chairman, or perhaps he alone, (I am not certain whether any or how many more were united with him), was appointed, to ascertain if what had been heard in relation to the action of the delegations of the other States referred to, was true; and if it was, it was understood, at the instance of Mr. Toombs, that his name was not to be presented by Georgia, and that our delegation would vote for Mr. Davis, and have no contest on the subject.

"In this meeting of our delegation, after the announcement alluded to had been made, and the course in reference to it had been resolved upon, Mr. [Augustus H.] Kenan moved, that in case what had been stated as rumor should be found to be true, and the name of Mr. Toombs should not be presented for the first office, then mine should be for the second. This motion was cordially seconded by Mr. Nisbet, and was unanimously agreed to, after a distinct understanding arrived at, by what I said in reference to it, which was, that in no event was my name to be presented, unless it was first ascertained positively, that Mr. Davis's name was to go before the Convention, and not that of Mr. Toombs, and further, that my name would be unanimously acceptable to the States and their respective delegations. These points the committee of our delegation was instructed speedily to inquire into and report upon, to the delegation at the Capitol, before the hour of the meeting of the Convention. Soon after the adjournment of our delegation, Mr. Crawford reported to me, that upon inquiry, what had been stated in our meeting was found to be true, and that Mr. Toombs had forbidden the presentation of his name, and further that my name was acceptable to all the States, and to every member of the Convention, as far as he could ascertain, and he believed it to be acceptable to every one. Being thus informed of these facts, I did not that day go to the Convention. The election, however, as is known, was made by ballot. On the call of each State, the chairman of the delegation presented the vote of the State for each officer to be chosen, and upon counting out the votes, the result was as before stated.

"What I learned afterwards from others, upon which I have expressed the opinion I have, was that some members of the delegations from South Carolina and Florida, and I believe Alabama too, had heard that Georgia intended to present the name of Mr. Howell Cobb, whom these members, from old feelings of some sort, produced in some way in past Party conflicts, were unwilling to support. The same objections did not apply to Mr. Toombs. They were perfectly willing to vote for him. As all these members were willing, however, to harmonize upon Mr. Davis, it was thought best and determined by these delegations, therefore, to present his name, notwithstanding his known preference for another position.

"I will here state that Mr. Cobb is a man of very marked and positive character. There is nothing negative about him. His convictions are always strong, and his action is governed by them. When he determines upon any line of policy, he pursues it with all his energies, openly and boldly, without regard to opposition, and with very little inclination to win by conciliation those who differ from him, whether in or out of his own Party. His joining the Constitutional Union organization in 1850-1851, and other like acts, had caused strong personal opposition to him in the Democratic Party, even when there was no disagreement upon a common line of policy. This kind of opposition existed not only in this State, but in the adjoining States. From his general course and characteristics stated, there was generally more opposition to him, on bare personal considerations, in the ranks of his own Party than out of it. But for him and his influence, I think the Georgia Platform would not have been adopted in 1850; and, but for him and his influence, I also think that Secession would not have been carried in Georgia, in 1861. Apart from his own active agency in this latter matter, his influence I have no doubt controlled the action of his brother Thomas R. R. Cobb, and brought to bear upon this question his tremendous agency, to which I have alluded. He and I have been on the kindest personal relations all our lives, ever since our college days at least. We have often been thrown in concert of action politically, and often in opposition. We have often discussed questions during the most exciting times before the people, occupying opposite sides, but never did a word pass from the lips of either, on such occasions, to interrupt even for a moment our personal kind feelings. In all our differences, I considered him a truly honorable and magnanimous opponent, and not only esteemed him personally very highly, but regarded him as one of the ablest men in the United States. His election as President of the Confederate States would have received my cordial approval, as did that of Mr. Davis. But of all the men in the Confederate States, I thought Mr. Toombs was by far the best fitted for that position, looking to all the qualifications necessary to meet its full requirements.

"Whether what I learned about the matter in reference to this indisposition on the part of some of the delegates to support Mr. Cobb, which thus induced the presentation of the name of Mr. Davis, was really true or not, I do not know. I did not inquire specially into it, but from what I heard and the sources from which I heard it, I believed it to be true, at the time, and hence the opinion I have given.... There was, however, no canvassing or electioneering in the usual sense of these words, I think, by any one. Of this, indeed, I feel quite confident. General harmony next to the obtainment of a competent man was the object of all. By all Mr. Davis was regarded as eminently a Conservative man.

"This embraces substantially all the facts I know about the election of both President and Vice President, and how in each case it came to be made as it was."[206]

☞ "Returning from this digression, therefore, we will proceed. Mr. Davis was immediately sent for by a special messenger, Mr. William M. Browne, former editor of the *Constitution* newspaper in Washington. Meanwhile the Convention went to work on the second great object before them—the formation of a Constitution for a Permanent Government. Mr. R. Barnwell Rhett, of South Carolina, was constituted Chairman of the Committee appointed for this purpose. This Committee consisted of two from each State. The members from Georgia, on this Committee, were Mr. Toombs and Mr. Thomas R. R. Cobb. This remarkable man deserves special notice. He was a brother of Howell Cobb, and his junior by several years, but in natural ability and intellectual culture was his inferior in no respect. He had never taken any active part in politics until after Mr. Lincoln's election. Before that he had confined himself exclusively to business connected with his profession—that of the law—with the exception of such portions of his time as he devoted to ecclesiastical matters and to the duties of a Professorship in the Lumpkin Law School, which he held at the time. He was by nature profoundly religious. He was an elder in the Presbyterian Church, and was a most devout worshipper, according to the creed of the Old School General Assembly. At the law, he had acquired a considerable estate, and was in the full tide of successful practice. Very few men were capable of performing the amount of physical labor he did. He had done more in the way of book-making than any man of his age in the Southern States. This is seen in the Reports of our Supreme Court, in his Digest of the laws of Georgia, and in his part of the Georgia Code, besides a very learned work he had published on the Law of Slavery. So much as a brief outline of his general character.

"Politics, as I have said, [Thomas R. R. Cobb] . . . eschewed until Mr. Lincoln's election, but hardly had the news of this result reached the State, before he became thoroughly changed in this respect. A new spirit and life seemed to enter into him. He then, all at once, became enlisted, soul and body, in the cause of Secession. He was seized with a sort of religious enthusiasm upon the subject, as much so, almost, as Peter the Hermit was for the rescue of the Holy Sepulchre. Through the press and on the hustings, he was unremitting in his efforts. He canvassed various parts of the State, and aroused the people by the most stirring appeals. It was he who gave the key-note to the sentiment that really carried immediate Secession in Georgia, as I have stated. He was a prominent actor in the Convention at Milledgeville, and also in the Convention at Montgomery. *In the formation of the Permanent Government, its Constitution and laws, however, four leading ideas seemed to be his favorites. One was the name of the new Confederacy, another was the recognition of the Providence of God in the fundamental law, another was the suppression of the foreign African Slave Trade, and the other was the prohibition of carrying the mails on Sunday. He failed in his first object, after many earnest and eloquent appeals. His wish was that the Confederate States should be known as 'The Republic of Washington.' In his second and third objects, he was entirely successful, greatly to his gratification; and he came exceedingly near the accomplishment of his fourth intensely cherished wish. His motion to prohibit Sunday mails was at one time lost by a tie vote only.*"[207] [Emphasis added, L.S.]

☛ "[Concerning the new Constitution of the Confederate States of America,] . . . let us proceed to examine this instrument. Here is the Constitution for the Permanent Government as finally unanimously adopted by the seven States. It is, as will be seen, based on the general principles of the Federal Constitution, framed by the Philadelphia Convention, in 1787, with the amendments thereafter adopted. Several changes in the details appear. Some of the more prominent of these may very properly be specially noted.

"*The first is in the Preamble. In this, the words 'each State acting in its Sovereign and Independent character' were introduced to put at rest forever the argument of the Centralists [big government Liberals], drawn from the Preamble of the old Constitution, that it had been made by the people of all the States collectively, or in mass, and not by the States in their several Sovereign character.* [Emphasis added, L.S.]

"*The official term of the [C.S.] President was extended, in the new Constitution, to six years instead of four, with a disqualification for re-election.* [Emphasis added, L.S.]

"The question of the 'Protective Policy,' as it was called, under the old Constitution, was put to rest under the new, by the express declaration that no duties or taxes on importations from foreign nations should be laid to promote or foster any branch of industry. Under the new Constitution, Export duties were allowed to be levied with the concurrence of two-thirds of both Houses of Congress.

"In passing acts of Bankruptcy, it was expressly declared that no law of Congress should discharge any debt contracted before the passage of the same. Considerable controversy had existed on this point under the old Constitution.

"The [C.S.] President, under the new Constitution, was empowered to approve any appropriation, and disapprove any other appropriation in the same bill, returning to the House those portions disapproved as in other like cases of veto.

"The impeachment of any judicial, or other Federal officer, resident and acting solely within the limits of any State, was allowed by a vote of two-thirds of both branches of the Legislature thereof, as well as by the House of Representatives of Congress. The Senate of the Confederate States, however, still having the sole power to try all such impeachments.

"No general appropriation of money was allowed, unless asked and estimated for by some one of the Heads of Departments, except by a two-thirds vote in both branches of Congress. The object of this was to make, as far as possible, each Administration responsible for the public expenditures.

"All extra pay or extra allowance to any public contractor, officer, agent, or servant, was positively prohibited as well as all bounties. Great abuses had grown up under the old system in this particular.

"Internal improvements [today known as 'corporate welfare'] by Congress, another subject which had given rise to great controversy under the old, were prohibited by the new Constitution, but Congress was empowered to lay local duties, to support lights, beacons, buoys, and for the improvement of harbors, the expenses to be borne by the navigation facilitated thereby.

"The general power of the [C.S.] President to remove from office was restricted to the extent that he could remove for special cause only, and in all cases of removal, he was required to report the same to the Senate, with his reasons, except in the case of the principal officer in each of the Executive Departments, and all persons connected with the Diplomatic service. These, and these only, he could remove at pleasure, and without assigning any reasons therefor.

"Citizens of the several States, under the new Constitution, were not permitted to sue each other in the Federal Courts, as they are under the old Constitution. They were left to their actions in the State Courts.

"The right of any citizen of one State to pass through or sojourn in, another with his slaves or other property, without molestation, was expressly guaranteed.

"The admission of other States into the Confederacy required a vote of two-thirds of the whole House of Representatives, and two-thirds of the Senate, the Senate voting by States, instead of a bare majority in each.

"A Convention of the States to consider proposed amendments of the Constitution was to be assembled for that purpose upon the call of any three States legally assembled in their several Conventions; and if a Convention so called should agree to the proposed amendments, the vote on them being taken by States, and the same should afterwards be ratified by the Legislatures of two-thirds of the several States, or by Conventions in them, then the proposed amendments were to form a part of the Constitution.

"Congress was authorized by law to grant to the principal officer in each of the Executive Departments a seat upon the floor of either House, with the privilege of discussing any measures appertaining to his Department.

"And, lastly, the power of Congress over the Territories was settled, in express language, in opposition both to the doctrine of the Centralists and the doctrine of 'Squatter Sovereignty,' so called.

"These are the more prominent of the changes made. Several others will be seen upon a close examination. Some of them, however, verbal merely. Most of the prominent ones noticed emanated from Mr. Rhett, the Chairman. A few of them from Mr. Toombs. Those proposed by Mr. Toombs were the ones prohibiting bounties, extra allowances, and internal improvements, with some others of less importance. The leading changes proposed by Mr. Rhett, were the ones in relation to the Protective policy, the Presidential term, the modification upon the subject of removal from office, and the mode provided for future amendments. The clause in relation to the admission of new States occupied the special attention of Mr. [John] Perkins [Jr.], of Louisiana. The change in the old Constitution, which authorized Congress to pass a law to allow Cabinet Ministers to occupy seats in either House of Congress, and to participate in debates on subjects relating to their respective Departments, was the one in which I took most interest. The clause, as it stands, did not go so far as I wished. I wanted the [C.S.] President to be required to appoint his Cabinet Ministers from Members of one or the other Houses of [the C.S.] Congress. This feature in the British Constitution, I always regarded as one of the most salutary principles in it. But enough on this subject."[208]

☞ "All of these amendments were decidedly of a conservative character. It is true, I did not approve of all of them. They were all, however, such as in the judgment of a majority of these States, the experience of seventy years had shown were proper and necessary for the harmonious working of the system. *The whole document utterly negatives the idea which so many have been active in endeavoring to put in the enduring form of history, that the Convention at Montgomery was nothing but a set of 'Conspirators,' whose object was the overthrow of the principles of the Constitution of the United States, and the erection of a great 'Slavery Oligarchy,' instead of the free Institutions thereby secured and guaranteed. This work of the Montgomery Convention, with that of the Constitution for a Provisional Government, will ever remain not only as a monument of the wisdom, forecast and statesmanship of the men* who constituted it, but an everlasting refutation of the charges which have been brought against them. These works together show clearly that their only leading object was to sustain, uphold, and perpetuate the fundamental principles of the Constitution of the United States. [Emphasis added, L.S.]

"The Constitution for the Permanent Government was adopted unanimously by the seven States represented, on the 11th of March, 1861. In the meantime, however, and while the Convention was going on with their work, Mr. Davis, the President elect under the Provisional Government, had arrived. He reached Montgomery on Saturday evening, the 16th of February, and was regularly inaugurated on Monday, the 18th. In his inaugural, he used this language, which shows the feelings and sentiments with which he assumed the high trust confided to him:

> 'Gentlemen of the Congress of the Confederate States of America; Friends and Fellow-Citizens:
>
> 'Called to the difficult and responsible station of Chief Executive of the Provisional [Confederate] Government which you have instituted, I approach the discharge of the duties assigned to me, with an humble distrust of my abilities, but with a sustaining confidence in the wisdom of those who are to guide and aid me in the administration of public affairs, and an abiding faith in the virtue and patriotism of the people.
>
> '*Looking forward to the speedy establishment of a Permanent Government to take the place of this, and which, by its greater moral and physical power, will be better able to combat with the many difficulties which arise from the conflicting interests of separate Nations, I enter upon the duties of the office, to which I have been chosen, with the hope that the beginning of our career, as a Confederacy, may not be obstructed by hostile opposition to our enjoyment of the separate existence and independence which we have asserted, and, with the blessing of Providence, intend to maintain. Our present condition, achieved in a manner unprecedented in the history of Nations, illustrates the American idea that Governments rest upon the consent of the governed, and that it is the right of the people to alter or abolish Governments whenever they become destructive of the ends for which they were established.* [Emphasis added, L.S.]
>
> 'The declared purpose of the Compact of Union from which we have withdrawn, was to "establish justice, insure domestic tranquillity, provide for the common defence, promote the general welfare, and secure the blessings of liberty to ourselves and posterity;" and when, in the judgment of the Sovereign States now composing this Confederacy, it had been perverted from the purpose for which it was ordained, and had ceased to answer the ends for which it was established, a peaceful appeal to the ballot-box declared that, so far as they were concerned, the Government created by that Compact should cease to exist. In this, they merely asserted a right which the Declaration of Independence of 1776, had defined to be inalienable. Of the time and occasion for its exercise, they, as Sovereigns, were the final judges, each for itself. The impartial and enlightened verdict of mankind will vindicate the rectitude of our

conduct, and He who knows the hearts of men, will judge of the sincerity with which we labored to preserve the Government of our Fathers in its spirit. The right, solemnly proclaimed at the birth of the States, and which has been affirmed and re-affirmed in the Bills of Rights of States subsequently admitted into the Union of 1789, undeniably recognizes in the people the power to resume the authority delegated for the purposes of Government. Thus the Sovereign States, here represented, proceeded to form this Confederacy, and it is by abuse of language that their act has been denominated a Revolution. They formed a new alliance, but within each State its Government has remained, and the rights of persons and property have not been disturbed. The agent, through whom they communicated with foreign nations, is changed; but this does not necessarily interrupt their international relations. [Emphasis added, L.S.]

'Sustained by the consciousness that the transition from the former Union to the present Confederacy, has not proceeded from a disregard on our part of just obligations, or any failure to perform any Constitutional duty; moved by no interest or passion to invade the rights of others; anxious to cultivate peace and commerce with all nations, if we may not hope to avoid war, we may at least expect that posterity will acquit us of having needlessly engaged in it. Doubly justified by the absence of wrong on our part, and by wanton aggression on the part of others, there can be no cause to doubt that the courage and patriotism of the people of the Confederate States, will be found equal to any measures of defence which honor and security may require. [Emphasis added, L.S.]

'An agricultural people, whose chief interest is the export of a commodity required in every manufacturing country, our true policy is peace and the freest trade which our necessities will permit. It is alike our interest, and that of all those to whom we would sell and from whom we would buy, that there should be the fewest practicable restrictions upon the interchange of commodities. There can be but little rivalry between ours and any manufacturing or navigating community, such as the Northeastern States of the American Union. It must follow, therefore, that a mutual interest would invite good will and kind offices. If, however, passion or the lust of dominion should cloud the judgment or inflame the ambition of those States, we must prepare to meet the emergency, and to maintain, by the final arbitrament of the sword, the position which we have assumed among the Nations of the earth. We have entered upon the career of Independence, and it must be inflexibly pursued. Through many years of controversy with our late associates, the Northern States, we have vainly endeavored to secure tranquillity, and to obtain respect for the rights to which we were entitled. As a necessity, not a choice, we have resorted to the remedy of separation; and henceforth our energies must be directed to the conduct of our own affairs, and the perpetuity of the Confederacy which we have formed. If a just perception of mutual interest shall permit us peaceably to pursue our separate political career, my most earnest desire will have been fulfilled; but if this be denied to us, and the integrity of our territory and jurisdiction be assailed, it will but remain for us, with firm resolve, to appeal to arms, and invoke the blessings of Providence on a just cause. [Emphasis added, L.S.]

'With a Constitution differing only from that of our Fathers, in so far as it is explanatory of their well-known intent, freed from the sectional conflicts which have interfered with the pursuit of the general welfare, it is not unreasonable to expect, that States from which we have recently parted may seek to unite their fortunes with ours, under the Government which we have instituted. For this, your Constitution makes adequate provision; but beyond this, if I mistake not the judgment and will of the people, *a re-union with the [Northern] States from which we have separated is neither practicable nor desirable.* [Emphasis added, L.S.]

'*Should reason guide the action of the Government from which we have separated, a policy so detrimental to the civilized world, the Northern States included, could not be dictated by even the strongest desire to inflict injury upon us; but if otherwise, a terrible responsibility will rest upon it, and the suffering of millions will bear testimony to the folly and wickedness of our aggressors.* [Emphasis added, L.S.]

'*We have changed the constituent parts, but not the system of our Government. The Constitution formed by our Fathers is that of these Confederate States, in their exposition of it; and, in the judicial construction it has received, we have a light which reveals its true meaning.* [Emphasis added, L.S.]

'Thus instructed as to the just interpretation of the instrument, and ever remembering that all offices are but trusts held for the people, and that delegated powers are to be strictly construed, I will hope, by due diligence in the performance of my duties, though I may disappoint your expectations, yet to retain, when retiring, something of the good-will and confidence which welcomed my entrance into office.'

"*This address affords additional evidence, if any were wanting, to show the objects aimed at by the Confederate States in their separation from their former associates. It clearly shows, as the Acts of the Convention show, that these States had quit the Union only to preserve for themselves, at least, the principles of the Constitution. It shows, also, that there was no purpose, wish, design, or intention, on the part of Mr. Davis, to make war, commit aggression, or do any wrong to those States, or the people of those States which remained in the old Union, or to interfere improperly in any way, with the Government of their choice.*"[209] [Emphasis added, L.S.]

☛ "At an early day Mr. Davis organized his Cabinet.

"The Department of State was filled by Mr. Toombs, of Georgia.

"The Department of War by Mr. Leroy P. Walker, of Alabama.

"The Treasury Department by Mr. Charles G. Memminger, of South Carolina.

"The Post-Office Department by Mr. John H. Reagan, of Texas.

"The Navy Department by Mr. Stephen R. Mallory, of Florida.

"The Department of Justice [a new Department which Congress had created, and which was quite an improvement on the Washington organization,] was filled by Mr. Judah P. Benjamin, of Louisiana, under the title of

Attorney-General.

"On the 15th of February, before the arrival of Mr. Davis, Congress had passed a Resolution declaring its sense,

> that a Commission of three persons be appointed by the President elect, as early as may be convenient after his inauguration, and sent to the Government of the United States of America, for the purpose of negotiating friendly relations between that Government and the Confederate States of America, and for the settlement of all questions of disagreement between the two Governments, upon principles of right, justice, equity, and good faith.

"In pursuance of this Resolution, three Commissioners were appointed and sent to Washington [D.C.] very soon after the inauguration of Mr. Davis. This Commission was constituted of the very best material to accomplish the object, if it could be done. It consisted of Mr. John Forsyth [Jr.], of Alabama, Mr. Martin J. Crawford, of Georgia, and Mr. A. B. Roman, of Louisiana. Mr. Forsyth was the son of the renowned Georgian of the same name [John Forsyth Sr.], who had at one time been Envoy and Minister Plenipotentiary to Spain, and had afterwards won such distinction as the leader of General [Andrew] Jackson's Administration in the Senate of the United States, in 1834 and 1835, against the combined assaults of the great trio, Mr. [Henry] Clay, Mr. [John C.] Calhoun, and Mr. [Daniel] Webster. This Commissioner had also, himself, been in the Diplomatic service of the United States, as Minister to Mexico. Mr. Crawford was a member of the Provisional Congress from this State. He had served several years in the old Congress with marked ability and distinction. Mr. Roman was Ex-Governor of Louisiana, and was a gentleman of fortune, of education, and most agreeable manners. These Commissioners were clothed with plenary powers to open negotiations for the settlement of all matters of joint property, Forts, Arsenals, arms, or property of any other kind within the limits of the Confederate States, and all joint liabilities with their former associates, upon principles of right, justice, equity, and good faith. Mr. Forsyth and Mr. Crawford reached Washington just upon the eve of Mr. [James] Buchanan's retirement from office. As soon after the inauguration of Mr. [Abraham] Lincoln, and the organization of his Cabinet, as convenient, they addressed a communication to Mr. William H. Seward, the newly appointed [U.S.] Secretary of State, upon the subject of their mission. Here is that communication and the whole correspondence connected with their mission. It deserves special notice, as it must ever be regarded as one of the most interesting portions of the history of the times. *The whole conduct of the [Confederate Peace] Commissioners was marked with perfect frankness and integrity of purpose, while they were met with an equivocation, a duplicity, a craft, and deceit,* which, taken altogether, is without a parallel in modern times! It was to this correspondence I alluded before, and to see that the remarks then and now made about it are justified by the facts, we have only to examine the papers themselves. [Emphasis added, L.S.] In their first note the [Confederate] Commissioners amongst other things say:

> 'Seven [Southern] States of the late Federal Union, having, in the exercise of the inherent right of every free people to change or reform their political Institutions, and through Conventions of their people, withdrawn from the United States, and resumed the attributes of Sovereign Power delegated to it, have formed a Government of their own.
>
> 'With a view to a speedy adjustment of all questions growing out of this political separation, upon such terms of amity and good-will as the respective interests, geographical contiguity, and future welfare of the two nations may render necessary, the undersigned are instructed to make to the Government of the United States overtures for the opening of negotiations, assuring the Government of the United States that the President, Congress, and people of the Confederate States earnestly desire a peaceful solution of these great questions; that *it is neither their interest nor their wish to make any demand which is not founded in strictest justice, nor do any act to injure their late [Northern] Confederates.*' [Emphasis added, L.S.]

"No direct answer was received to this communication by the Commissioners, until the 8th of April, *twenty-three days after it was delivered to the Secretary of State.* But an indirect and informal answer was given in this way. Two days after Secretary Seward had received the note from the Commissioners, and while he was being pressed for a reply by Mr. John T. Pickett, their Secretary, Mr. Justice Nelson, of the Supreme Court of the United States, a personal friend of the Secretary of State, called upon Mr. Justice John A. Campbell, of the same Court, and informed him of Mr. Seward's 'strong disposition in favor of peace, and that he was greatly oppressed with a demand of the Commissioners of the Confederate States for a reply to their letter, and that he desired to avoid making any at that time, if possible.' Upon this intimation, Judge Campbell immediately had a personal interview with Mr. Seward, hoping he might be useful as an intermediate, in bringing about a peaceful adjustment of the questions at issue, as he was a citizen of Alabama and on terms of personal friendship with the Commissioners. This interview with Mr. Seward, which was evidently sought by him, in the way stated, was had without any conference on the part of Judge Campbell with the Commissioners. On the evening of the same day, after the interview was had, Judge Campbell gave to the Commissioners in writing, the following statement:

'I feel entire confidence that Fort Sumter will be evacuated in the next ten days. And this measure is felt as imposing great responsibility on the Administration. I feel entire confidence that no measure changing the existing status, prejudiciously to the Southern Confederate States, is at present contemplated. I feel an entire confidence that an immediate demand for an answer to the communication of the Commissioners will be productive of evil, and not of good. I do not believe that it ought at this time to be pressed.'

"Mr. Seward was immediately informed by Judge Campbell of what he had communicated to the Commissioners. On this assurance the Commissioners relied, and ceased to urge a formal reply to their communication. Mr. Seward in his interview with Judge Campbell used stronger language than that employed by him in his written statement to the Commissioners. *The assurance given to Judge Campbell, supposing it would be given by him to the Commissioners, was, that there was no design to re-enforce Fort Sumter, and that it would be evacuated in less than ten days, even before a letter could go from Washington to Montgomery. It was in this way, the Commissioners were given to understand that the United States forces at Fort Sumter would be peacefully withdrawn in a few days; and hence they did not press their demand for an immediate answer to their note, but communicated the information they had received to President Davis, and the substance of it was communicated by him to General [Pierre G. T.] Beauregard.* [Emphasis added, L.S.]

"After a sufficient time had elapsed, General Beauregard telegraphed to the Commissioners at Washington, that Fort Sumter was not evacuated, but that [U.S.] Major [Robert] Anderson was at work making repairs. On receipt of this, Judge Campbell had another interview with Mr. Seward, and was assured by him 'that the failure to evacuate Sumter was not the result of bad faith, but was attributable to causes consistent with the intention to fulfil the engagement, and that as regarded Fort Pickens, in Florida, notice would be given of any design to alter the existing status there.' This renewed assurance was immediately communicated to the Commissioners, and by them communicated to President Davis, and by him to General Beauregard.

"On the 7th of April, after the movement of the Relief Squadron from New York had caused a general alarm, Judge Campbell addressed a letter to Mr. Seward, and 'asked if the assurances he had given, were well or ill founded?' The reply he received was, '*Faith as to Sumter fully kept—wait and see.*' This was after the Fleet had put to sea, and when it was near the harbor of Charleston, for the purpose of provisioning and reinforcing Fort Sumter 'peaceably,' if permitted; 'otherwise by force.' *The way faith was kept as to Sumter, was by notifying the Governor of South Carolina, Francis W. Pickens, of the intention to reinforce the Fort, after the Fleet had set out for Charleston!* [Emphasis added, L.S.]

"The actual state of things was not known to the [Confederate] Commissioners, until the 8th of April. They had been most 'atrociously' imposed upon and deceived! [Emphasis added, L.S.] On the 9th of April they addressed to Mr. Seward another communication in which, besides giving a recapitulation of the facts at which I have glanced, they used the following language:

>'Your Government has not chosen to meet the undersigned, in the conciliatory and peaceful spirit in which they are commissioned. Persistently wedded to those fatal theories of construction of the Federal Constitution, always rejected by the Statesmen of the South, and adhered to by those of the Administration School, until they have produced their natural and often predicted result of the destruction of the Union, under which we might have continued to live happily and gloriously together, had the spirit of the ancestry who framed the common Constitution animated the hearts of all their sons. . . . Had you met these issues with the frankness and manliness with which the undersigned were instructed to present them to you and treat them, the undersigned had not now the melancholy duty to return home and tell their Government and their countrymen, that their earnest and ceaseless efforts in behalf of peace had been futile, and that the Government of the United States meant to subjugate them by force of arms. Whatever may be the result, impartial history will record the innocence of the Government of the Confederate States, and place the responsibility of the blood and mourning that may ensue, upon those who have denied the great fundamental doctrine of American Liberty, that "Governments derive their just powers from the consent of the governed," and who have set naval and land armaments in motion, to subject the people of one portion of the land to the will of another portion. [Emphasis added, L.S.]
>
>'Your refusal to entertain these overtures for a peaceful solution, the active Naval and Military preparations of this Government, and a formal notice to the Commanding General of the Confederate forces in the harbor of Charleston, that the [U.S.] President [Lincoln] intends to provision Fort Sumter by forcible means, if necessary, are viewed by the undersigned, and can only be received by the world, as a declaration of war against the Confederate States,' etc.' [Emphasis added, L.S.]

"It was indeed more than a mere declaration of war. It was an act of war itself!"[210]

☛ "Whatever change of views may have taken place in the mind of Mr. Lincoln, as to the line of policy he intended to pursue in relation to Fort Sumter and the other United States Forts within the Confederate States, after the assurance given, can in no way excuse or palliate the duplicity and fraud practiced afterwards on the Confederate Commissioners. My own opinion from all the facts, as they have been subsequently disclosed, is, that Mr. Lincoln did change his policy on this subject, and that at the time the assurance was given to the Commissioners, he did intend in good faith to withdraw the troops from Fort Sumter at an early day. How far he may have been aware of the extent of the assurance given to the Commissioners, I have no means of knowing; but it is known that this policy of withdrawing the troops was recommended by General Winfield Scott, then in chief command of the Army of the United States. He thought it the best under the circumstances. In his opinion the proper course for the Federal Government to take, that indicated by true wisdom and statesmanship, was, in his own language, to 'let the wayward sisters [the Confederate States] depart in peace.' [Emphasis added, L.S.]

"Moreover, the Senate, which was convened in extra session on Executive business, had taken up the subject and given it serious discussion. In this body every Democrat or Anti-Centralist [i.e., Conservative] was understood to be in favor of the withdrawal of the United States troops from all these Forts, except those at Key West and Tortugas. Mr. [Stephen A.] Douglas [of Illinois] himself offered a Resolution to that effect, on the 15th of March. In support of it, he said:

'We certainly cannot justify the holding of Forts there, much less the re-capturing of those which have been taken, unless we intend to reduce those States, themselves, into subjection. I take it for granted no man will deny the proposition that whoever permanently holds Charleston and South Carolina, is entitled to the possession of Fort Sumter. Whoever permanently holds Pensacola and Florida, is entitled to the possession of Fort Pickens. Whoever holds the States in whose limits those Forts are placed, are entitled to the Forts themselves, unless there is something peculiar in the location of some particular Fort that makes it important for us to hold it for the general defence of the whole country, its commerce and interests, instead of being useful only for the defence of a particular city or locality. It is true that Forts Taylor and Jefferson, at Key West and Tortugas, are so situated as to be essentially national, and therefore important to us without reference, to our relations with the seceded States. Not so with Moultrie, Johnson, Castle Pinckney, and Sumter, in Charleston Harbor; not so with Pulaski, on the Savannah River; not so with Morgan, and other Forts in Alabama; not so with those other Forts that were intended to guard the entrance of a particular harbor for local defence.

'[Mr. James R. Doolittle:] Will the Senator allow me to ask a question? How is it with the Forts at the mouth of the Mississippi River?

'[Mr. Douglas:] Well, sir, I will say that those do not form an exception to my remark, for this reason; we have no use for the Forts at the mouth of the Mississippi River, if we allow the Southern Confederacy to hold the State of Louisiana and command both sides of the River. . . . We cannot deny that there is a Southern Confederacy, *de facto*, in existence, with its Capital at Montgomery. We may regret it. I regret it most profoundly; but I cannot deny the truth of the fact, painful and mortifying as it is. . . . I proclaim boldly the policy of those with whom I act. We are for peace. There is no concealment on this side. . . . . I repeat, it is time that the line of policy was adopted and that the country knew it. In my opinion, we must, choose, and that promptly, between one of three lines of policy:

'1. The restoration and preservation of the Union, by such amendments to the Constitution as will insure the domestic tranquillity, safety, and equality of all the States, and thus restore peace, unity, and fraternity to the whole country.

'2. A peaceful dissolution of the Union, by recognizing the Independence of such States as refuse to remain in the Union without such Constitutional amendments, and the establishment of a liberal system of commercial and social intercourse with them, by treaties of commerce and amity.

'3. War, with a view to the subjugation and military occupation of those States which have seceded, or may secede from the Union.

'I repeat that, in my opinion, you must adopt and pursue one of these three lines of policy. The sooner you choose between them and proclaim your choice to the country, the better for you, the better for us, the better for every friend of Liberty and Constitutional Government throughout the world. In my opinion, the first proposition is the best, and the last the worst. Why cannot we arrive at some amicable adjustment of the questions in dispute?'

"His Resolution was laid upon the table by a vote of twenty-three to eleven, as the Senate was left in possession of the Centralists [Northern big government Liberals], on the retirement therefrom of the fourteen Senators from the Confederate States. Besides this Resolution of Mr. Douglas, other resolutions were offered, one by Mr. Thomas L. Clingman, then a Senator from North Carolina, and another by Mr. John C. Breckinridge, who took his seat as Senator-elect from Kentucky, on the expiration of his term of office as Vice President, on the 4th of March, recommending and advising the withdrawal of the United States troops, from the limits of the Confederate States. Neither of these Resolutions was acted upon before the adjournment of this special Executive Session of the Senate, which took place on the 28th of March. But the understanding in the city, at the time of Mr. Douglas's speech, and the time the assurance was given, was that Fort Sumter was to be immediately evacuated. This intelligence was telegraphed throughout the country on the 14th of March, the second day after the date of the Commissioners' letter to Mr. Secretary Seward, and the day before the first interview he had with Judge Campbell. I have but little doubt, therefore, that, at that time, Mr. Lincoln had determined to withdraw all United States forces from the limits of the Confederate States."[211] [Note: Stephens is here giving Lincoln the benefit of the doubt, which, from today's perspective, as well as the sure knowledge of the U.S. president's many subsequent nefarious actions, was overly generous in the editor's opinion. L.S.]

☛ "It was at this juncture, however, when this news reached the North, that the seven [radical anti-South] Governors from the seven Northern States referred to, hastened to Washington, and then and there organized their 'Conspiracy,' and by appeals to Mr. Lincoln, and tendering to him their organized military forces, caused him to change his policy, and to adopt theirs, which aimed at an entire overthrow of the Constitution of the United States, and the Federative principles of Government on which it was based. This conspiracy is the Seven Headed Monster, or 'Apocalyptic Beast,' to which I have alluded before. It was by and through its active agency Mr. Lincoln's policy was changed. *This change, however, was not communicated to the [Confederate] Commissioners. They were still kept uninformed and left to rest upon the assurances given, while the most energetic measures and active preparations for war and subjugation were being concocted and executed*. The sequel, so far as relates to the striking of the first blow and the fall of Port Sumter, we have seen. [Emphasis added, L.S.]

"It is, perhaps, needless to speak of the effect of this great event, either at the North or South. I will here only say that, within my observation, the first general feeling produced by it, was one of surprise, accompanied with deep regret. *The duplicity of the Washington authorities* was, it is true, the cause of general indignation; for the informal assurance on the subject of the early evacuation of that Fort, was extensively known to the intelligent in all parts of the country. President Davis immediately summoned an extra session of Congress, at Montgomery. This body, after having gotten through with their labors on the Constitution for the Permanent Government, on the 11th of March, and having adopted such general measures as they thought proper and sufficient, in view of the peaceful prospect before them, had, on the 16th, adjourned, subject to the call of the [C.S.] President, in case of need, to report their action to their respective State Conventions. The Sovereign State Conventions all promptly, and with great unanimity, ratified the Constitution proposed for their Permanent Government. Alabama ratified it, on the 13th of March, by a vote of eighty-seven yeas to five nays; Georgia, on the 16th of March, without a dissentient voice—two hundred and seventy-six voted for the ratification, and not one against it; Louisiana, on the 21st of March, by one hundred and one yeas to seven nays; Texas, on the 25th of March, by sixty-eight yeas to two nays; Mississippi, on the 30th of March, by a vote of seventy-eight yeas to seven nays. The exact vote in South Carolina and Florida I do not know, but the action of both these States on the ratification, was not less decisive. The call for the extra session was made on the fall of Fort Sumter; but hardly had that summons reached the country by the telegraphic wires, before these mystic messengers, with the wings of lightning, brought Mr. Lincoln's celebrated Proclamation of the 15th of April [declaring war on the South and calling for

75,000 U.S. troops]. [Emphasis added, L.S.]

"The effect of this upon the public mind of the Southern States cannot be described or even estimated. The shock was not unlike that produced by great convulsions of nature—the upheavings and rocking of the earth itself! It was not that of fright. Far from it! But a profound feeling of wonder and astonishment! Up to this time, a majority, I think, of even those who had favored the policy of Secession, had done so under the belief and conviction that it was the surest way of securing a redress of grievances, and of bringing the Federal Government back to Constitutional principles. Many of them indulged hopes that a Re-formation, or a Re-construction of the Union would soon take place on the basis of the new Montgomery Constitution, and that the Union, under this, would be continued and strengthened, or made more perfect, as it had been in 1789, after the withdrawal of nine States from the first Union, and the adoption of the Constitution of 1787. This proclamation [of Lincoln's] dispelled all such hopes. *It showed that the [Liberal Northern] Party [the Republicans] in power intended nothing short of complete Centralization. There was no longer any division amongst the people of the Confederate States.* . . . What I have said clearly shows the political position of both Parties to the war, at the time of its inauguration and the fall of Fort Sumter, so far as concerns the principles on which they acted. *The principles actuating the Washington authorities were those aiming at Consolidated Power; while the principles controlling the action of the Montgomery authorities were those which enlisted devotion and attachment to the Federative [Confederate] system as established by the [Founding] Fathers in 1778 and in 1787. The [Liberals'] object on the one side—the aggressive side—the Federal side, so miscalled—was to overthrow the very principles upon which every Federal system is based; while, on the other, it was to defend and maintain those principles. In short, the cause of the Confederates was State Sovereignty, or the Sovereign Right of local Self-Government on the part of the States severally. It was the same cause, to maintain which all the Colonies at first, and all the States afterwards, united, in the ever memorable conflict with the Mother Country [Great Britain], in 1776; and on the success of which, in that contest, depended the whole fabric of American Free Institutions. The cause of their assailants involved the overthrow of this entire fabric, and the erection of a Centralized Empire in its stead! This is the issue, in a Constitutional point of view, fairly presented.*"[212] [Emphasis added, L.S.]

When asked if he thought that "the United States, by putting down Secession, became a Centralized Empire?", Stephens replied:

☛ "No. I do not maintain that they have as yet reached that point; but I do mean to maintain that the principles upon which they [the Northern Liberals] waged the war, involved that final result, and will, unless abandoned, necessarily and inevitably lead to that ultimate result."²¹³

☛ "The present object [of my discussion is] to present these organic principles clearly, and the position of the Parties towards them in the beginning, as well as the comparative physical ability, or material resources of each to sustain and maintain its side. What has been said is sufficient on the first of these points; before proceeding further on the main line, however, it is not only proper, but necessary, to examine somewhat in detail Mr. Lincoln's [war] Proclamation referred to, of the 15th of April, and the effect it produced upon the public mind throughout all the Southern States. This [I] . . . will postpone to another occasion. But before suspending just now, it may be proper to add, that amongst the general measures adopted by the Confederate Congress before its adjournment, was the full assumption of jurisdiction over and control of the Forts, Arsenals, and all other joint property of the United States, in each of the Confederate States, which had by them, severally, been transferred to the Confederate States. All the existing Federal laws, so far as applicable, were adopted, and everything was done that was necessary for the complete organization of the Confederate States Government, under the Provisional Constitution, in its Judicial and Military Departments, as well as in its Legislative and Executive. The whole machinery of a regularly organized Government was put into complete and practical operation in all its functions. Ways and means for raising funds for present and prospective needs were provided.

"*The navigation of the Mississippi River had also been declared to be open and free.* [In other words, the Confederacy did not attempt to prevent the Union from using the Mississippi River, more proof that the C.S.A. was *not* trying to hurt the U.S.] Besides the Commission sent to Washington, another very able one had been sent to Europe to present the Confederate cause and position to England and France, with the view of opening negotiations with those Powers. At the head of this latter Commission was placed, Mr. William L. Yancey, of Alabama, a man of brilliant genius, with many eminent qualities of natural as well as acquired ability. He it was, who took the lead on the policy of Mr. [James] Buchanan, in the Charleston Convention, which, in 1860, led to the rupture of that body [which allowed Lincoln to win the election that year]. He was amongst the ablest men of the South who zealously espoused the cause of Secession at an early day, and no one felt a deeper interest in its success. With him were associated in this, Commission, Mr. Ambrose D. Mann, of Virginia, and Mr. Pierre A. Rost, of Louisiana. Mr. Mann had already become distinguished in the Diplomatic service of the United States."²¹⁴

26

THE WAR FOR
SOUTHERN INDEPENDENCE
PART ONE

TO THIS DAY MOST AMERICANS have a greatly distorted view of the "Civil War," no doubt because they have gleaned their American history from pro-North books—which brim with false anti-South propaganda, junk research, and outright intellectual fraud.[215] Here, from *A Constitutional View*, Stephens offers the Southern perspective on Lincoln's War, taking the opportunity to shatter numerous ridiculous Northern fictions, defamations, disinformation, and Yankee fairy tales in the process.

Despite Stephens' factual argument to the contrary, Liberals in his day continued to hold that the War, on the part of the Lincoln administration, was a constitutional "resort to force to maintain lawful authority," while "on the part of the Confederates, under all the circumstances, looked at in any light, must be considered a Rebellion." Stephens was ready with a reply:

☞ "Well, we can only agree to disagree on this point. . . . We are, I believe, fully agreed upon all the essential facts. The point of disagreement is only one of conclusion, or the logical sequence which properly follows from undisputed facts. If all the great facts of our history be as I have set them forth, and which [the Liberals] . . . have not been able successfully to assail, then the conclusion which I draw from these facts, it seems to me, according to all correct principles of reasoning, is not only legitimate, but irresistible! This conclusion, on my part, on the point of our disagreement, is, that *the Sovereign Right of each State, within the limitations mentioned, to withdraw from a Union formed as ours is admitted to have been, was perfect, considered either morally or politically. On the same principles, too, the Sovereign Right of all the States so withdrawing, to enter into a new Confederation, as they had done, was equally perfect. Where any party has a perfect right to perform an act, no other party can have a right, either legal or moral, to prevent the doing of it. This seems to me to be a perfectly rational conclusion. In the domain of reason, moreover, the conclusions of logic are inexorable!* [Emphasis added, L.S.]

"The whole question, whether the acts of the people of the Seceding States are to be considered a Rebellion, depends upon the fact of whether the United States was a Federal [Confederate] Republic or not. In other words, it depends upon the true answer to the question, where under the system does ultimate Sovereignty reside? Is it lodged in the General Government, or has it passed to the whole people of the United States as one aggregate mass, or does it still remain unimpaired with the people of the several States as distinct political organizations, just where and as it did when the Constitution was formed? This question, I think, has been clearly and fully answered and settled by the facts established, and, according to these principles, *I do maintain there was no rebellion, no resistance to lawful authority in the action of the Confederates in what occurred at Fort Sumter, but, on the contrary, I maintain that their resistance there was a resistance to open and palpable usurpations of power by the [Liberal Republican] authorities at Washington, and in the maintenance of that rightful authority to which both their obedience and allegiance were due.* [Emphasis added, L.S.]

"This point, however, as the one relating to the justifiableness of my course in the premises, we, not being able to agree upon it, will leave to the impartial judgment of mankind. With the understanding that we do thus agree to disagree on this point, I will proceed now to the consideration of the subject postponed to this occasion. That was the [War] Proclamation of Mr. Lincoln, of the 15th of April [1861], and the effect it produced on the other Southern States not then embraced in the new Confederacy, with the events which immediately followed.

"Let it be borne in mind then, that in all these States, movements of some sort had been made after the election of Mr. Lincoln, to take the sense of the people in Sovereign Conventions, respectively, upon the question of Secession, as had been taken in the States which did secede, and at about the same time. These movements it is proper to notice, and to these we will now direct our attention in a brief review."[216]

☛ "On the 16th of January, 1861, the Legislature of Arkansas passed an Act submitting to the people of that State the question whether there should be a Sovereign Convention assembled or not. The vote on this question was ordered to be taken on the 18th of February. The vote for the Convention on that day was 27,412 in favor, and 15,826 against it. The majority for the Convention was 11,586. A Convention, regularly elected, accordingly assembled on the 4th of March. In this, an Ordinance for Secession was defeated by a vote of thirty-five yeas in favor of it, and thirty-nine nays against it. On the 17th of March, the question was disposed of by the unanimous adoption, by the Convention, of a measure providing that the question of 'Secession' or 'Co-operation' with the Border States should be submitted to the people, to be decided by a vote to be taken on the first Monday in August thereafter, and providing for the appointment of delegates to a Convention of the Border States, which was to be held in the meantime, and also that the Convention when it adjourned, should re-assemble on the 17th of August thereafter. This was the state of things in Arkansas.

"The Legislature of Missouri met 31st December, 1860. Early in January 1861, both Houses were addressed in the Hall of the Representatives by Mr. D. R. Russell, a Commissioner from the State of Mississippi. On the 16th of January, an Act was passed calling a Convention of the people to be assembled the 28th of February, with a provision that the action of this Convention was to be submitted to a popular vote, for its ratification or rejection. The Convention met. A large majority was against Secession. Mr. Luther J. Glenn, who had been sent as a Commissioner from Georgia to that State, was respectfully heard by the Convention, and a respectful answer given to the views presented by him, stating the reasons why the Convention did not concur with him in the policy of immediate Secession. Mr. Hamilton R. Gamble was Chairman of the Committee on Federal Relations, in this Convention. The final action of this body, on the general subject, was the adoption of Resolutions expressing an earnest desire for the perpetuation of the Union, and the peaceful adjustment of all the difficulties of the crisis—approving the Crittenden proposition in the Senate—advocating the call of a National Convention of the States; and expressing the opinion that civil war might be avoided, by withdrawing Federal troops from Forts in the Seceded States, and recommending this policy. The last Resolution, recommending this policy, passed by a vote of eighty-nine yeas to six nays. This was on the 19th of March. This Convention also sent delegates to the proposed Convention of the Border States, as well as to the Peace Congress. So matters stood in this State.

"In Kentucky, the Governor, Beriah Magoffin, recommended to the Legislature then in session, the calling of a Convention of the people of the State, to whom their Federal relations should be submitted. He advised the policy of uniting with the Border States, in a Convention to be held by them early in February, at Baltimore. The action of the Seceded States was disapproved by him, in very decided language, but in language equally decided, he protested against the Constitutional power or policy of coercing them. The Legislature did not agree to the proposition for the call of a State Convention, but on the 22nd of January, passed Resolutions asking the other States to unite in calling for a Convention of all the States to amend the Constitution, and afterwards passed another Resolution pledging the people of Kentucky 'to unite with their brethren of the South, in resisting an invasion of their soil at all hazards, and to the last extremity.' They also sent delegates to the Peace Congress at Washington, which had been called by Virginia. . . . So matters stood in Kentucky.

"In Tennessee, Governor Isham G. Harris called an extra Session of the Legislature, which assembled the 7th of January, 1861. This body passed an act submitting to the people of the State the question whether there should be a State Convention or not; the election to be held on the 9th of February, and the Convention to be assembled on the 25th of February, in case a majority of the voters should be in favor of the call. The vote was 24,749 in favor of calling the Convention, and 91,803 against it. The popular majority against the Convention was 67,054. So matters stood in Tennessee.

"In North Carolina, the Legislature being in regular session passed an Act on the 24th of January, providing for an election of delegates to a State Convention. This act directed that voters at the same election should express their wish for or against the meeting of the Convention. If a majority should be in favor of the Convention, then the Governor was by proclamation to assemble the delegates on a day to be designated; and if a majority should be against it, then the Convention was not to be assembled. The vote in favor of the Convention was 46,672, and against it 47,323. The majority against the Convention was 651, and it therefore was not convened. So matters stood in North Carolina.

"In Virginia an extra Session of the Legislature was convened on the 7th of January. This body, deeply impressed with the perils of the crisis, went earnestly to work to preserve, if possible, the Union of the States and the Sovereignty of the States upon the principles on which the Constitution was based. On the 19th, Resolutions were passed asking all the States to send delegates to meet in Washington, on the 4th of February, to devise, if possible, some plan for general harmony and pacification. This was the Peace Congress to which twenty States sent delegates in response to this call of Virginia, and which did so assemble. The States which were represented in this Congress, or Conference, as it has been called, were Maine, New Hampshire, Vermont, Massachusetts, Rhode Island, Connecticut, New York, New Jersey, Pennsylvania, Ohio, Indiana, Illinois, Iowa, Delaware, Maryland, Virginia, North Carolina, Kentucky, Tennessee and Missouri. It was in this Congress that Mr. [Salmon P.] Chase, as a delegate from the State of Ohio, made the speech to which I have referred. To this Peace Congress Virginia sent as Delegates, or Commissioners, Ex-President John Tyler, William C. Rives, John W. Brockenbrough, George W. Summers, and James A. Seddon. John Tyler was chosen President of this body.

"The Legislature of Virginia also passed an Act calling a State Convention to express the Sovereign will of the people of the State upon their Federal relations. By the Act, the election of delegates was to be on the 4th of February, and the Convention to meet on the 13th."[217]

☛ "The Convention met at the time appointed. The whole number of delegates was one hundred and fifty-two. John Janney, of Loudon, a man of renown in the 'Old Dominion,' and distinguished as much for his devotion to the Union as for anything else, was chosen President. In his address he said, that 'Virginia would insist on her own construction of her rights as a condition of her remaining in the present Union.' This Convention watched with the deepest interest the proceedings of the Peace Congress, which had assembled at the instance of the State. After that body adjourned, and its action was known, Mr. Jeremiah Morton, on the 28th of February, made a speech in favor of immediate Secession, viewing, as he did, the result of the Peace Congress as a failure. On the 1st of March, Mr. [John] Goode [Jr.], of Bedford, offered a Resolution on the line of policy indicated by Mr. Morton, which was referred for consideration. After the inaugural address of Mr. Lincoln, on the 4th of March, reached Richmond, the excitement in the Convention became more intense. A delegation was sent from that body to Washington, to confer with Mr. Lincoln, and to ascertain from him what line of policy he intended to pursue, and to urge upon him the importance of not attempting to coerce the Seceding States. This delegation consisted of William Ballard Preston, Alexander H. H. Stuart, and George W. Randolph. In the Senate of the Legislature, a Resolution had, in the meantime, unanimously passed, declaring 'that if all efforts to reconcile the unhappy differences between sections of our country shall prove abortive, then every consideration of honor and interest demands that Virginia shall unite her destinies with her Sister Slave-holding States.' *To the delegation sent by the Convention to confer with Mr. Lincoln, no satisfactory reply was given by him.* So stood matters in Virginia when news reached the Convention of the occurrences at Fort Sumter. [Emphasis added, L.S.]

"In Maryland, the general popular excitement of the times was not much less intense than in the more Southern States. In the late Presidential election, the vote of this State had been cast for the [John C.] Breckinridge ticket. Mr. Lincoln, however, received of the popular vote 2,294, which really tended to increase the excitement in that State. The aggregate vote for the three other candidates was upwards of 90,000. The Legislature not being in session, urgent appeals were made to Thomas H. Hicks, the Governor, to convene an extra session, to consider the questions involved in the crisis. This he persistently refused to do, from apprehensions that measures would be immediately adopted looking to a withdrawal of this State from the Union. Mr. A. H. Handy had been appointed a Commissioner by the Legislature of Mississippi, to present the views of that State to the Legislature of Maryland. He addressed Governor Hicks upon the subject of his mission. To this communication the Governor made a reply on the 19th of December. In this reply he declared his purpose to be 'to act in full concert with the other Border States,' and said he did 'not doubt that the people of Maryland were ready to go with the people of those States for weal or woe.' He fully agreed in 'the opinion as to the necessity for protection to the rights of the Southern States, and while his sympathies were with the gallant people of Mississippi, he hoped they would act with prudence as well as with courage.' In February, he received Mr. [Ambrose R.] Wright, the Commissioner from Georgia, and expressed to him similar sentiments, while he still refused to convene the Legislature. Governor Hicks had also responded to the call of Virginia for the Peace Congress, and gave that movement his cordial approval.

"An irregular State Convention was held at Baltimore during the latter part of February, in which most of the counties were represented, and by several of the ablest men in the State. Among these were Ezekiel F. Chambers, the President; Thomas G. Pratt, E. Louis Lowe, Robert M. McLane, T. Parker Scott, William P. Whyte, S. Teackle Wallis, R. B. Carmichael, I. D. Jones, and John E. Franklin. The object of this Convention was to take into consideration the position of Maryland in her Federal [Confederate] relations. Its final action was the adoption of an address and a series of resolutions strongly Southern in their character. They justified the secession of the seven States of the Confederacy, and maintained that it was caused by aggressions upon their rights. They looked hopefully to the result of the Peace Congress then in session, and declared that if no satisfactory settlement was made by it, then, in the opinion of the Convention, the Governor should call a regular Sovereign Convention of the State to determine on the state of public affairs, as it was understood the Governor intended to do. It was further resolved that in case the State of Virginia should determine to secede, the Convention was to be immediately re-assembled at the call of its President; and if the Governor should decline to call a Sovereign Convention, on the contingency stated, previous to the 12th of March, then this body declared its intention to recommend to the people to proceed of their own accord to the election of delegates to a Sovereign Convention of the State. This irregular Convention then adjourned to the 12th of March, on which day they re-assembled. The Governor had not acted—Virginia had not seceded. They thereupon did nothing further than to adopt Resolutions favoring a Convention of the Border States, and sent a deputation to visit the Virginia Convention upon the subject. Resolutions were also submitted, but not acted upon, declaring that 'all attempts upon the part of the Federal Government to re-occupy, repossess, or retake any Forts, or other property, within the limits of the Seceded States, would be acts of war, and that such acts would absolve Maryland and the Border States from all connection with the United States.' So matters stood in the State of Maryland.

"In Delaware, the Legislature assembled on the second of January. The next day, Mr. Henry Dickinson, Commissioner from the State of Mississippi, was permitted to address both Houses, in the Representative Chamber, upon the general state of public affairs, with an earnest desire that the State of Delaware would join her Southern Sister States in withdrawing from the Union. After the address, the House passed a Resolution, in which the Senate concurred, stating that, 'having extended the Hon. H. Dickinson, the Commissioner of Mississippi, the courtesy due him, as the Representative of a Sovereign State of the Confederacy, as well as to the State he represents, we deem it proper, and due to ourselves and the people of Delaware, to express our unqualified disapproval of the remedy for existing difficulties suggested by the Resolutions of the Legislature of Mississippi.' Mr. [D. C.] Campbell, the Commissioner from Georgia, was received by Governor [William] Burton, who gave him a respectful audience, and expressed the opinion that no action would be taken by that State until Virginia moved; that his State would go with Maryland and Virginia. So matters stood in Delaware."[218]

☛ "This brief sketch presents very clear indications of the prevailing sentiments on the exciting subject in all the slaveholding States which had not seceded on the 15th of April, when Mr. Lincoln's [War] Proclamation of that date made its appearance. And after this brief but necessary survey, we will now look into that paper itself. Here it is:

> [Stephens quoting Lincoln:] 'Whereas, The laws of the United States have been for some time past and are now opposed, and the execution thereof obstructed, in the States of South Carolina, Georgia, Alabama, Florida, Mississippi, Louisiana, and Texas, by combinations too powerful to be suppressed by the ordinary course of judicial proceedings, or by the powers vested in the Marshals by law:
>
> 'Now, therefore, I, Abraham Lincoln, President of the United States, in

virtue of the power in me vested by the Constitution and the laws, have thought fit to call forth, and hereby do call forth, the militia of the several States of the Union, to the aggregate number of seventy-five thousand, in order to suppress said combinations, and to cause the laws to be duly executed.

'The details for this object will be immediately communicated to the State authorities through the War Department.

'I appeal to all loyal citizens to favor, facilitate and aid this effort to maintain the honor, the integrity, and the existence of our National Union, and the perpetuity of popular Government, and to redress wrongs already long enough endured.

'I deem it proper to say that the first service assigned to the forces called forth will probably be to re-possess the forts, places, and property which have been seized from the Union; and in every event the utmost care will be observed, consistently with the objects aforesaid, to avoid any devastation, any destruction of or interference with property, or any disturbance of peaceful citizens in any part of the country.

'And I hereby command the persons composing the combinations aforesaid to disperse and retire peaceably to their respective abodes within twenty days from this date.

'Deeming that the present condition of public affairs presents an extraordinary occasion, I do hereby, in virtue of the power in me vested by the Constitution, convene both Houses of Congress.

'Senators and Representatives are therefore summoned to assemble at their respective Chambers, at 12 o'clock, noon, on Thursday, the fourth day of July next, then and there to consider and determine such measures as, in their wisdom, the public safety and interest may seem to demand.

'In witness whereof, I have hereunto set my hand and caused the seal of the United States to be affixed. Done at the city of Washington, this fifteenth day of April, in the year of our Lord one thousand eight hundred and sixty-one, and of the Independence of the United States the eighty-fifth. Abraham Lincoln.

'By The President: William H. Seward, Secretary of State.'

"The effect of this extraordinary paper upon the people of the Seceded States, I have already mentioned. It united them almost to a man, while the effect upon the people of the other Southern States which had not seceded, was not much less significant. This is what we are now to look to. First, as a sample of the general feeling produced by it, we need but take a glance at the responses of the Governors of these States to the call made on them [by Lincoln] for their respective quotas of military force. These quotas were as follows: Delaware was to furnish 780 men; Maryland, 3123; Virginia, 2340; North Carolina, 1560; Kentucky, 3123; Missouri, 3123; and Arkansas, 780.

"In reply to the requisition for the quota of Delaware, Governor William

Burton responded in substance, that he had no lawful authority for raising the troops.

"Governor [Thomas H.] Hicks, of Maryland, made no direct response for some days, but indirectly urged upon Mr. Lincoln not to have troops sent through the city of Baltimore, as the excitement there produced by the call was so great that violence would be almost inevitable. On the 18th of April, he issued a Proclamation to the people of Maryland, in which he said, he would not 'send any troops in obedience to the call, except to defend the National Capital.' On the fourth day after the Proclamation was issued, the 6th Massachusetts Regiment, in its passage through the city of Baltimore, was stopped by barricades in the streets, and was attacked with stones and other missiles by an infuriated mob. This gave rise to a great riot, in which several lives were lost on the part of the troops as well as the citizens. Every effort was made by George W. Brown, Mayor of the city, and George P. Kane, Marshal of Police, to prevent the outbreak, and to restore quiet to the excited multitude. After the Mayor had succeeded in suppressing actual violence, and had got the troops through the city, by going himself in front at the head of the column, he addressed the people publicly in Monument Square, where they had assembled. He there assured them, that he had conferred with Governor Hicks, who had united with him in telegraphing to Washington, that no more Northern troops should be sent through Maryland, and that Governor Hicks concurred with him in opinion against the policy of coercing the Seceded States. Governor Hicks was sent for, and made his appearance in this meeting, and is reported to have said:

> 'I coincide in the sentiment of your worthy Mayor. After three conferences we have agreed, and I bow in submission to the people. I am a Marylander; I love my State, and I love the Union; but I will suffer my right arm to be torn from my body, before I will raise it to strike a sister State.'

"This gave great satisfaction to the excited crowd, which thereupon dispersed. Mayor Brown also sent three persons of high character and the greatest respectability, to wit, H. L. Bond, J. C. Brune, and George W. Dobbin, as special messengers to Mr. Lincoln, with a dispatch in these words:

> 'The people are exasperated to the highest degree by the passage of troops, and the citizens are unusually decided in the opinion that no more troops should be ordered to come. The authorities of the city did their best to-day to protect both strangers and citizens, and to prevent a collision, but in vain; and but for their great efforts, a fearful slaughter would have occurred. Under these circumstances, it is my solemn duty to inform you, that it is not

possible for more soldiers to pass through Baltimore, unless they fight their way at every step. I, therefore, hope and trust, and most earnestly request, that no more troops be permitted or ordered by the Government to pass through the city. If they should attempt it, the responsibility for the bloodshed will not rest upon me.'

"The very able and distinguished President of the Baltimore and Ohio Railroad, J. W. Garrett, fully concurred in this policy. He declined to transport any more troops over his road, in the then state of excitement.

"The Messengers of the Mayor sent to Washington, telegraphed back the next day that Mr. Lincoln had given them a letter to the Mayor of the city and the Governor of the State, that no more troops would be brought through Baltimore, if, in a military point of view, they could be marched around the city without opposition. So much for the effect of the proclamation upon Maryland.

"*In reply to the call for the quota of Virginia, Governor [John] Letcher stated that it 'would not be furnished for any such purpose'—'an object' which, in his judgment, 'was not within the purview of the Constitution or the laws.' 'You have,' said he, 'chosen to inaugurate civil war.'* [Emphasis added, L.S.]

Governor [John W.] Ellis, of North Carolina, replied that he 'regarded the levy of troops made for the purpose of subjugating the States of the South, as in violation of the Constitution, and a usurpation of power; and that he could be no party to the wicked violation of the laws of the country, and to this war upon the liberties of a free people.' [Emphasis added, L.S.]

"*Governor [Beriah] Magoffin, of Kentucky, replied: 'Kentucky will furnish no troops for the wicked purpose of subduing her sister Southern States.'* [Emphasis added, L.S.]

"*Governor [Isham G.] Harris, of Tennessee, replied: 'Tennessee will not furnish a man for purposes of coercion, but 50,000, if necessary, for the defence of our rights, and those of our Southern brothers.'* [Emphasis added, L.S.]

"*Governor Henry M. Rector, of Arkansas, replied: 'No troops from Arkansas will be furnished to subjugate the Southern States. The demand is only adding insult to injury.'* [Emphasis added, L.S.]

"*Governor Claiborne F. Jackson, the recently inaugurated Governor of Missouri, replied: 'The requisition is illegal, unconstitutional, revolutionary, inhuman, diabolical, and cannot be complied with.'* [Emphasis added, L.S.]

"I give but the substance of these replies. They clearly indicate the tone and temper of the times, and the impression the proclamation made upon the public mind in what were then styled the Border States. The effect upon the North was far different. The 'seven Governors' seem to have been ready with troops already organized to send forward in obedience to the call promptly, which they were perhaps daily expecting. Several companies from Pennsylvania reached Washington on the 16th, and reported for duty the day after the call was made.

The 6th Massachusetts Regiment left Boston on the evening of the 17th, and left another all but ready to follow. It was this regiment which reached Baltimore about noon on the 19th, and which was the occasion of the riot."²¹⁹

☛ "But to return to the effect upon the Border States. Virginia now took the lead. Her Convention, still in session, two days after this proclamation, passed an Ordinance of Secession. The vote in favor of it was eighty-eight, and against it fifty-five. In it she set forth the fact, that in her Ordinance ratifying the Constitution of the United States, in 1788, she had reserved the right to resume the powers therein delegated, whensoever the same should be perverted to the injury of her people. The Convention also submitted the Ordinance to a popular vote of the State. If the people should reject it, then it was to be of no force; but if they ratified it, then it was to be considered as complete and binding upon all parties. This action of the State was immediately communicated by Governor Letcher to Mr. [Jefferson] Davis, at Montgomery, with a request at the instance of the Convention, that a Commissioner should be sent by the Confederate States Government to negotiate an alliance with that Commonwealth. This position was assigned to me by Mr. Davis. I reached Richmond on the 22nd of April. In the meantime another most extraordinary proclamation by Mr. Lincoln made its appearance, which should be noticed in this connection. It was in these words:

> 'Whereas an insurrection against the Government of the United States has broken out in the States of South Carolina, Georgia, Alabama, Florida, Mississippi, Louisiana, and Texas, and the laws of the United States for the collection of the revenue cannot be efficiently executed therein conformably to that provision of the Constitution which requires duties to be uniform throughout the United States:
>
> 'And whereas, a combination of persons engaged in such insurrection, have threatened to grant pretended Letters of Marque, to authorize the bearers thereof to commit assaults on the lives, vessels, and property of good citizens of the country lawfully engaged in commerce on the high seas, and in waters of the United States:
>
> 'And whereas, an Executive Proclamation has been already issued, requiring the persons engaged in these disorderly proceedings to desist therefrom, calling out a militia force for the purpose of repressing the same, and convening Congress in extraordinary session to deliberate and determine thereon:
>
> 'Now, therefore, I, Abraham Lincoln, President of the United States, with a view to the same purposes before mentioned, and to the protection of the public peace, and the lives and property of quiet and orderly citizens pursuing their lawful occupations, until Congress shall have assembled and deliberated

on the said unlawful proceedings, or until the same shall have ceased, have further deemed it advisable to set on foot a blockade of the ports within the States aforesaid, in pursuance of the laws of the United States and of the laws of nations in such cases provided. For this purpose a competent force will be posted so as to prevent entrance and exit of vessels from the ports aforesaid. If, therefore, with a view to violate such blockade, a vessel shall approach, or shall attempt to leave any of the said ports, she will be duly warned by the Commander of one of the blockading vessels, who will endorse on her register the fact and date of such warning; and if the same vessel shall again attempt to enter or leave the blockaded port, she will be captured and sent to the nearest convenient port for such proceedings against her and her cargo as prize, as may be deemed advisable.

'And I hereby proclaim and declare, that if any person, under the pretended authority of said States, or under any other pretence, shall molest a vessel of the United States, or the persons or cargo on board of her, such person will be held amenable to the laws of the United States for the prevention and punishment of piracy.

'In witness whereof, I have hereunto set my hand, and caused the seal of the United States to be affixed. Done at the City of Washington, this nineteenth day of April, in the year of our Lord one thousand eight hundred and sixty-one, and of the Independence of the United States the eighty-fifth.'

"This was signed and countersigned as the other. These two papers had rendered the Convention of Virginia, and the people of all parts of the State, except the extreme northwestern counties, almost as thoroughly united against the dangerous principles and doctrines they enunciated, as the people in the more southern States were. A Committee of the Convention, consisting of Ex-President John Tyler, William Ballard Preston, Samuel M. Moore, James P. Holcombe, James C. Bruce, and Lewis E. Harvie, was appointed to confer with me on the subject of the proposed alliance. This Conference resulted in our agreeing, on the 24th to the following Articles, entitled:

CONTENTION BETWEEN THE COMMONWEALTH OF VIRGINIA AND THE CONFEDERATE STATES OF AMERICA.

The Commonwealth of Virginia, looking to a speedy union of said Commonwealth, and the other slave States, with the Confederate States of America, according to the provisions of the Constitution for the Provisional Government of said States, enters into the following temporary Convention and Agreement with said States, for the purpose of meeting pressing exigencies affecting the common rights, interests, and safety of said Commonwealth and said Confederacy.

1st. Until the union of said Commonwealth with said Confederacy shall be perfected, and said Commonwealth shall become a member of said

Confederacy, according to the Constitutions of both Powers, the whole military force, and military operations, offensive and defensive, of said Commonwealth, in the impending conflict with the United States, shall be under the chief control and direction of the President of said Confederate States, upon the same principles, basis, and footing, as if said Commonwealth were now, and during the interval, a member of said Confederacy.

2nd. The Commonwealth of Virginia will, after the consummation of the union contemplated in this Convention, and her adoption of the Constitution for a Permanent Government of the said Confederate States, and she shall become a member of said Confederacy under said permanent Constitution, if the same occur, turn over to the said Confederate States all the public property, naval stores, and munitions of war, etc., she may then be in possession of, acquired from the United States, on the same terms and in like manner as the other States of said Confederacy have done in like cases.

3rd. Whatever expenditures of money, if any, said Commonwealth of Virginia shall make before the union, under the Provisional Government, as above contemplated, shall be consummated, shall be met and provided for by said Confederate States.

This Convention entered into and agreed to in the City of Richmond, Virginia, on the 24th day of April, 1861, by Alexander H. Stephens, the duly authorized Commissioner to act in the matter for the said Confederate States, and John Tyler, William Ballard Preston, Samuel M. Moore, James P. Holcombe, James C. Bruce, and Lewis E. Harvie, parties duly authorized to act in like manner for the said Commonwealth of Virginia—the whole subject to the approval and ratification of the proper authorities of both Governments respectively.

In testimony whereof, the parties aforesaid have hereto set their hands and seals, the day and year aforesaid, and at the place aforesaid, in duplicate originals.

"These Articles were ratified by the Convention the next day."[220]

☛ "While speaking of this mission and its results, I may here, by way of a short digression, state that it was in connection with it, I for the first time became personally acquainted with Robert E. Lee. The incidents attending this first acquaintance with this distinguished personage, are not without historic interest in themselves, but it is not so much with that view, as for the purpose of illustrating the character of the man, I give them. They very fully exhibited to me, at the time, the distinguishing qualities of the heart as well as of the head of the man who had already won a very honorable distinction in this country, and whose justly merited fame now extends to the limits of the civilized world. . . . He was . . . then temporarily in Washington City, and considering his ultimate allegiance due to his State [Virginia], after she had resumed the full exercise of her Sovereign Powers, he had promptly, though not without deep regret at the causes which impelled him to do it, resigned his commission [as commander of the 2nd United States Cavalry Regiment, stationed in Texas], and cast his fortunes with those of the people of his own State. He accompanied his resignation with a letter to [U.S.] General [Winfield] Scott, which is a model of its kind, and fully characteristic of the man. He was specially devoted to the Commander-in-Chief of the Army of the United States, and I believe it is generally conceded, that the feelings of personal attachment were reciprocal between the chief and his subaltern.

"My becoming acquainted with him occurred in this way: The Legislature of Virginia, in view of the great dangers threatening from the position of Mr. Lincoln, had provided by law for raising ten or twenty thousand men to defend the State, and had authorized the Governor to appoint a Commander-in-Chief of all the military forces of the State, with the rank of Major-General. The Governor had appointed him to this position, and the Convention had, with great unanimity, ratified the appointment the day on which I had reached Richmond. The ceremony of General Lee's installation to this high and responsible office, was to take place in the Convention the day after. This came off according to the programme, in a very imposing form.

"General Lee was escorted into the Hall of the House of Representatives, in which the members of the Convention were assembled, where I was also by invitation, and, upon being presented to that body, Mr. John Janney, the President, rose and addressed him in a speech of some length, which produced a profound sensation. I will read such parts of it as are pertinent to present purposes. These are as follows:

> 'Major-General Lee, in the name of the people of your native State here represented, I bid you a cordial and heartfelt welcome to this hall, in which we may almost yet hear the echo of the voices of the statesmen, the soldiers, and sages of by-gone days, who have borne your name, and whose blood now flows in your veins.
>
> 'We met in the month of February last, charged with the solemn duty of protecting the rights, the honor, and the interests of the people of this Commonwealth. We differed for a time as to the best means for accomplishing that object; but there never was, at any moment, a shade of difference among us as to the great object itself.
>
> 'When the necessity became apparent of having a leader for our forces, all hearts and eyes, by the impulse of an instinct which is a surer guide than reason itself, turned to the old county of Westmoreland. We knew how prolific she had been in other days, of heroes and statesmen. We knew she had given birth to the Father of his Country, to Richard Henry Lee, to [James] Monroe, and last, though not least, to your own gallant father [Henry Lee III];

and we knew well by your deeds, that her productive power was not yet exhausted.

'Sir, we watched with the most profound and intense interest the triumphal march of the army led by General Scott, to which you were attached, from Vera Cruz to the Capital of Mexico. We read of the sanguinary conflicts, and the blood-stained fields, in all of which victory perched upon our own banners. We knew of the unfading lustre that was shed upon the American name by that campaign, and we knew, also, what your modesty has always disclaimed, that no small share of the glory of those achievements was due to your valor and your military genius.

'Sir, one of the proudest recollections of my life will be to the honor that I yesterday had of submitting to this body, confirmation of the nomination made by the Governor of this State, of you as Commander-in-chief of the military and naval forces of this Commonwealth. I rose to put the question, and when I asked if this body should advise and consent to that appointment, there rushed from the hearts to the tongues of all the Members, an affirmative response, told with an emphasis that could leave no doubt of the feeling whence it emanated. I put the negative of the question for form's sake, but there was an unbroken silence.

'Sir, we have by this unanimous vote, expressed our convictions that you are at this day among the living citizens of Virginia, "first in war." We pray to God most fervently that you may so conduct the operations committed to your charge, that it will soon be said of you, that you are "first in peace;" and when that time comes, you will have earned the still prouder distinction of being "first in the hearts of your countrymen."'

"At the close of this address, General Lee in a clear, distinct, full volumed, as well as melodious voice, replied as follows:

'Mr. President, and Gentlemen of the Convention:— Profoundly impressed with the solemnity of the occasion for which, I must say, I was not prepared, I accept the position assigned me by your partiality. I would have much preferred your choice had fallen upon an abler man. Trusting in Almighty God, an approving conscience, and the aid of my fellow-citizens, I devote myself to the service of my native State, in whose behalf alone will I ever again draw my sword.'

"All the force which personal appearance could add to the power and impressiveness of the words, as well as sentiments uttered by him, was imparted by his manly form, and the great dignity as well as grace in his every action and movement. All these, combined, sent home to the breast of every one the full conviction that he was thoroughly impressed himself with the full consciousness of the immense responsibility he had assumed. A more deeply interesting or solemn scene of the character I never witnessed.

"So much for this ceremony by way of premise, and what occurred at my first sight of General Lee. This is not that first acquaintance with the man of which I spoke. That occurred on the evening of this memorable day, and at my quarters in the Ballard House, and requires something further still by way of premise.

"On my arrival at Richmond, and hearing what had been done by the Governor and the Convention, in relation to the rank of General Lee, I knew full well that every thing pertaining to the success of the mission depended mainly upon this man. For no practical alliance, as matters then stood, could be formed between the Confederate States and the Commonwealth of Virginia, which would not in effect, or might not in effect, *razee* [French: 'shaved close'] to some extent the high official position and rank just conferred upon him. This I felt quite certain the Convention would be exceedingly reluctant to agree to, and would not agree to unless the members became perfectly satisfied that the measure, having even by possibility this effect, met with his full and cordial approval. If Virginia came into an alliance with the Confederate States, her Commander-in-Chief, by virtue of the State commission, would necessarily have to be subordinate to officers of lower grade or rank in the Confederate Army in certain contingencies. The highest grade in the Confederate Army, at that time, was that of Brigadier-General.

"Of the man personally I knew nothing, but feeling assured that all depended in a great degree upon him, my first object was to see how the land lay in that quarter. Upon invitation, [Lee] . . . met me at my quarters in a private conference that evening. It was at this conference I first became acquainted with the man. I unfolded to him, with perfect candor, the object of my mission, the nature of the alliance I should propose, and particularly the effect it might have upon his official rank and position. There was on his part equal candor and frankness—no reserve whatever. He understood the situation fully. With a clear understanding of its bearing upon himself individually, he expressed himself as perfectly satisfied, and as being very desirous to have the alliance formed. He stated, in words which produced thorough conviction in my mind of their perfect sincerity, that he did not wish anything connected with himself individually, or his official rank or personal position, to interfere in the slightest degree with the immediate consummation of that measure, which he regarded as one of the utmost importance in every possible view of public considerations. From what occurred, I felt quite assured that there was no danger in the quarter from which I had apprehended that there might probably be the most.

"The omission in the Articles to make special provision for General Lee's official rank, was soon discovered in the Convention. The Commissioners on the part of the State were urged to get a change made in this particular. I was appealed to by a number of the members on the subject. Knowing that no such change could be made, and feeling the deepest solicitude in the result, I barely referred all parties approaching me in relation to it, to General Lee himself. I advised them to consult him, and to submit the whole matter to him, as he was the party immediately interested, and assured them that I believed he would cordially approve what had been done; and if he did, I thought the Convention ought to be satisfied. He was thoroughly sounded by several of his most devoted friends in the Convention, who left him feeling as fully assured as I did that he was perfectly satisfied with the Articles as they stood, and that there was no bare affectation on his part in this matter. The truth is, a look, or an intonation of voice even, at this time, which would have indicated that his professed satisfaction was not the real and unaffected feeling of his heart, would have defeated that measure. This I knew; but the result was as I believed it would be from the time of our first interview.

"General Lee on this occasion, as well as on the occasion of the resignation of his commission in the United States Army, after Mr. Lincoln had made the most tempting offers to him [i.e., full command of the U.S. army], as has been stated by high authority, showed a personal disinterestedness, and an unselfish devotion to principles and country, rarely to be met with in this world. These are the facts in relation to him, which I have thought not inappropriate to state in this connection. It was on this occasion and in this way, when put to the test in this severe crucible, he exhibited those sterling inner qualities of the man which greatly exalted him in my estimation on our first acquaintance, and which have contributed in no small degree, to the brilliant lustre that crowns his public character throughout his great career, even under the most adverse fortunes of war. But to return from this digression."[221]

☞ "The Convention being fully assured, that General Lee was perfectly satisfied with the Articles as they stood, immediately ratified them with an additional Ordinance in these words:

> An Ordinance for the adoption of the Constitution of the Provisional Government of the Confederate States of America.
> We, the Delegates of the people of Virginia, in Convention assembled, solemnly impressed by the perils which surround the Commonwealth, and appealing to the Searcher of hearts for the rectitude of our intentions in assuming the grave responsibility of this act, do by this Ordinance adopt and ratify the Constitution of the Provisional Government of the Confederate States of America, ordained and established at Montgomery, Alabama, on the

8th day of February, eighteen hundred and sixty-one: Provided, that this Ordinance shall cease to have any legal operation or effect, if the people of this Commonwealth, upon the vote directed to be taken on the Ordinance of Secession passed by this Convention, on the 17th day of April, eighteen hundred and sixty-one, shall reject the same.

"They also elected a delegation to represent the State in the Provisional Congress at Montgomery. This delegation consisted of William C. Rives, Robert M. T. Hunter, John W. Brockenbrough, and Waller R. Staples.

"In this connection it is also proper to state, before leaving Virginia, that the popular vote on the ratification of the Ordinance of Secession, which was taken on the fourth Thursday in May, as provided for in the Ordinance itself, resulted in 125,950 being cast in favor of the ratification, and 20,373 against it. This opposition minority was mostly in the Northwestern counties. The Eastern and Southwestern portions of Virginia were almost unanimous in favor of it. In the central portion of the State, there were very few against it, and even in Alexandria, one of the strongest Union populations in the State before this, there were only 106 votes against the Ordinance, while there were 900 in favor of it. The impression attempted to be made, that this election was carried by the soldiery, or by threats or intimidation, is utterly without foundation in fact. The true solution of it is to be found in such appeals as that put forth by Alexander H. H. Stuart, a Union Delegate to the State Convention, who had opposed Secession to the last. In an address made to the people through the press, amongst other things, he said:

> 'In my judgment, it is the duty of all good citizens to stand by the action of the State. It is no time for crimination or recrimination. We cannot stop now to inquire who brought the troubles upon us, or why. It is enough to know that they are upon us; and we must meet them like men. We must stand shoulder to shoulder. Our State is threatened with invasion, and we must repel it as best we can.'

"John B. Baldwin, another man of eminent ability who occupied a similar position to that of Mr. Stuart, came out with equal decision and earnestness. William C. Rives, formerly United States Senator, twice Minister to France, who stood by the Union as long as there was hope, now went with the State heart and soul. Many more of this class might be named. The feelings and views of the most devoted friends of the Union in Virginia, were in the main not unlike those of the same class in Georgia. But the masses of the people were really ahead of their leaders on this subject in both these States. So much for the general state of things in Virginia for the present."[222]

☞ "We will now turn our attention to the progress of events in the other Border States. In North Carolina, Governor John W. Ellis, two days after his reply to the call for troops under Mr. Lincoln's [War] Proclamation, as we have seen, convened the Legislature to meet the 1st of May. He also issued an order for the enlistment of 30,000 men to march at a day's notice. The Legislature, immediately on assembling, passed an Act providing for the election of delegates to another Sovereign Convention of the State. At this election the Delegates were to be clothed with plenary powers. The election was directed to take place on the 13th of May, and the Convention to meet on the 20th of May. This Convention on the day of its meeting, which was the eighty-sixth anniversary of the Mecklenburg Declaration of Independence, passed an Ordinance of Secession with great unanimity. They sent Thomas L. Clingman as special Commissioner to Montgomery, and afterwards elected a full delegation to the Confederate Provisional Congress.

"In Tennessee, Governor [Isham G.] Harris, also, immediately after his reply to the call for troops under Mr. Lincoln's proclamation, summoned an extra session of the Legislature to meet on the 25th of April. In no State perhaps did this Proclamation of the 15th of April, by Mr. Lincoln, produce a greater effect than it did in Tennessee. Many of the strongest Union men in the State, up to this time, then declared themselves thoroughly for Secession. Amongst these was Felix K. Zollicoffer. When the Legislature assembled on the 25th of April, a large majority were found to be in favor of immediate Secession. About this time Neil S. Brown, formerly Governor of the State, who had theretofore strenuously opposed Secession, appeared before the public in a letter, in which he said:

'I have hoped obstinately against such an alternative; but the conviction is forced upon my mind, that it is the settled policy of the Administration, and, so far as I can see, of the whole North, to wage a war of extermination against the South.'

"Mr. Zollicoffer also appeared in a letter, in which he said:

'We are involved in war, and no mistake, waged for the purpose of humbling the Southern States. It cannot be done. But we must have unity, energy, and action, to save ourselves. Let us drop Party, and Party names. Let us emulate the glorious example of our fathers in arms. We must not, can not, stand neutral, and see our Southern brothers butchered.' [Emphasis added, L.S.]

"On the 30th of April, Henry W. Hilliard, of Alabama, a man of high character, who had been connected with the Diplomatic service of the United

States, as *Charge d'Affaires* at Belgium, under President [John] Tyler's Administration, appeared before the Legislature as a Commissioner from the Confederate States, and addressed that body upon the subject of forming an alliance with the State of Tennessee.

"On the 1st of May, the Legislature, by Joint Resolution, directed the Governor to enter into such an alliance. The Governor immediately appointed Gustavus A. Henry, Archibald O. W. Totten, and Washington Barrow, as Commissioners, on the part of the State, for that purpose. On the 7th of May, an alliance, or convention, was entered into between the respective parties in the same language, names and dates being changed, as that which had been entered into by Virginia, which was immediately communicated to the Legislature by the Governor. It was ratified in both Houses. In the Senate, on its adoption, the vote was fourteen in favor to six against it. In the House the vote was forty-two in favor to fifteen against it.

On the day previous, the 6th of May, the Legislature had passed an Ordinance entitled: 'An Act to submit to the vote of the people a Declaration of Independence, and for other purposes.' This Ordinance, or Act, provided that the Governor should order the respective officers in each county to hold the polls open in their several precincts on the 8th day of June ensuing, and that a certain Declaration therein specifically set forth should be submitted to a vote of the qualified voters of the State for their ratification or rejection. This was an Ordinance of Secession. The Act further provided that the vote should be by ballot, and that those voting for the Declaration, or Ordinance, should have on their ballots the word, 'Separation,' and those voting against it should have on their ballots the words, 'No Separation.' The returns were to be made to the Secretary of State by the 24th of June, and if a majority of the votes were given for Separation, the Governor was required immediately to issue his Proclamation, declaring all connection by the State of Tennessee with the Federal Union dissolved, and that Tennessee is a Free, Independent Government, free from all obligations to, or connection with, the Federal Government [of Lincoln and the U.S.].

"The Act further set forth specifically, an Ordinance for the adoption of the Constitution of the Provisional Government of the Confederate States, and directed that all voters in favor of that measure, looking to a representation in the Confederate Congress, should have written on their ballots the word 'Representation,' and those opposed to it should have written on their ballots 'No Representation.' The Act also provided for an election of delegates to the Confederate Congress, in case the Provisional Constitution should be adopted by the popular vote, so directed to be taken.

"This Act, so submitting the question of Secession, and the adoption of the

Provisional Constitution of the Confederate States, passed the Senate by a vote of twenty yeas to four nays; and passed the House by a vote of forty-six yeas to twenty-one nays. On the questions so submitted to the people for their decision on the 8th of June, the majority in favor of the adoption of both the Ordinances, so set forth in this Act of the Legislature, was over 57,000. A full delegation was also chosen at this election, to represent the State in the Confederate Congress.

"In Arkansas, the President of the State Convention, upon the publication of Mr. Lincoln's [War] Proclamation of the 15th of April, immediately issued a call for the reassembling of that Convention on the 6th of May. On that day the Convention met agreeably to the call, and immediately passed an Ordinance of Secession, with only one dissenting vote. On the adoption of the Ordinance, there were sixty-nine votes in the affirmative, and one in the negative. Immediate steps were also taken by the Convention to unite with the Confederate States. They elected a delegation to represent Arkansas in the Confederate Congress. This delegation consisted of Robert W. Johnson, Albert Rust, Augustus H. Garland, W. H. Watkins, and W. F. Thomason.

"In Missouri, Governor [Claiborne F.] Jackson, after his reply to the call for troops under the Proclamation, convened the State Legislature, but

> 'declared his policy to be in favor of peace, saying that he convened the Legislature only for the purpose of more perfectly organizing the militia, and putting the State in a proper attitude of defence. He urged the President of the State Convention not to call that body together for the passage of a Secession Ordinance; he was in favor of retaining the present status of the State, leaving it to time and circumstances, as they might arise, to determine the best course for Missouri to pursue. He thought the President [Lincoln], in calling out troops to subdue the Seceded States, threatened civil war, and he pronounced the act unconstitutional, and as tending towards the establishment of a consolidated Despotism. He recommended ample preparations against aggressions by all assailants. He appealed to the Legislature to do nothing imprudently or precipitately, but endeavor to unite all for the preservation of the honor of the State, the security of property, and the performance of the high duties imposed by their obligations to their country and to their God.'

"No further immediate steps were taken for a union of the fortunes of Missouri with those of the Confederate States. The object of Governor Jackson seems to have been to hold Missouri in a position of neutrality. In this, however, his efforts failed. The State was soon plunged into all the horrors of civil war."[223]

☛ "In Kentucky, Governor [Beriah] Magoffin, after his reply to the Federal call for troops, convened an extra session of the Legislature, which met on the 6th of May. In the House of Representatives, a series of Resolutions was passed approving the refusal of the Governor to furnish troops to the Federal Government, and 'declaring that Kentucky should maintain a strict neutrality during the present contest.' Their object in reference to Kentucky was similar to that of Governor Jackson in reference to Missouri. In this policy some of the strongest Union men of the State concurred. An address to the people of Kentucky, on the condition of the country, was made by a Committee of what was called the Union Party of the State, declaring it to be the duty of the State to maintain neutrality, and to take no part either with the Government or the Confederates. [They said:]

> 'Kentucky could not comply with the appeal of the [U.S.] Government without outraging her solemn convictions of duty, and without trampling upon that natural sympathy with the Seceding States, which neither their contempt for her interests, nor their disloyalty to the Union, had sufficed to extinguish. The present duty of Kentucky was to maintain her present independent position, taking sides not with the Government, and not with the Seceding States, but with the Union, against them both; declaring her soil to be sacred from the hostile tread of either, and, if necessary, making the declaration good with her strong right arm. And to the end that she might be fully prepared for this last contingency, and all other possible contingencies, they would have her arm herself thoroughly, at the earliest practicable moment.'

"On the 19th of April, Mr. James Guthrie, one of the most distinguished men of the State, who had been Secretary of the Treasury under Mr. [Franklin] Pierce, and who had taken the most prominent lead in the Peace Congress, addressed a Union meeting at Louisville. He opposed the call of the [U.S.] President for troops, and asserted that Kentucky would not take part with either the Federal or Confederate side in the pending contest. He declared her soil sacred against the hostile foot of either. So matters continued to stand in Kentucky for some time."[224]

☛ "From this rapid glance at these almost simultaneous as well as most eventful movements, it appears that the effect of these Proclamations of Mr. Lincoln was, in less than thirty days, to drive the inner tier of the four Border States, so-called, from the old into the new Confederacy. Before the 15th of May, Virginia, Tennessee, North Carolina, and Arkansas, were fully united, not only in heart, but in energy and fortunes, politically, with the Confederate States. This accession, besides its moral effect, was of great importance to them in view of the material advantages attending it. These States brought an aggregate increase, in area of territory, of 204,150 square miles; a like aggregate increase of population of 4,134,191; and a like aggregate increase of real and personal taxable property, of the value of $1,260,770,445. Swelling the grand aggregate, in these particulars, of the eleven Confederate States as now organized, to 727,448 square miles of territory—and 9,103,333 of population, White and Black—and $3,441, 596,607 of taxable property.

"The territory within the actual limits of the other twenty-two States [Northern], in January, 1861, covered an area, in the aggregate, of 941,149 square miles. There was, at the same time, outside of the limits of the organized States, 1,294,949 square miles of public domain, to which the Seceded States were jointly entitled with the other States. These other twenty-two [Northern] States, after the eleven had withdrawn, had an aggregate population, White and Black, of 22,030,159. Their taxable property, real and personal, according to assessment, was of the value of $6,822,493,901."[225]

☛ "[These figures, of course, do not include the South's black servants.] The $3,441,596,607 representing the assessed value of real and personal property in the eleven Confederate States, is over and above the estimated value of their slaves. That amounted nearly to two thousand million of dollars itself! This, however, is digressing from the point in hand. My object was simply to show, at this stage of our investigation, the effect of these two proclamations of Mr. Lincoln upon the public mind, in the then Border States, and the accessions it secured from them to the Confederate States."[226]

Stephens' Liberal opponents maintained that they could "see nothing in either of Lincoln's Proclamations which was not required of him in the faithful discharge of his duties, under his oath of office." To this the Confederate vice president responded:
☛ "There again is where we shall, perhaps, have to agree to disagree, I suppose; for this not being a matter involving a question of fact, so much as the proper conclusion which should be drawn from admitted facts, will, as other like points, have to be left to the judgment of mankind. For myself, I can only say that, so far from his oath of office requiring him to do anything of the sort, its requirements were just the other way. [Abraham Lincoln] . . . was sworn to 'preserve, protect and defend the Constitution,' and 'faithfully to execute the office of President of the United States.' This oath imposed a solemn obligation on him not to violate the Constitution, or to exercise, under color of his office, any power not conferred upon him by that instrument. He was required to see to the faithful execution of the laws of the United States, us passed by the Congress of States, and as construed by Judiciary. He said in the first of these Proclamations be made the call for the militia 'in virtue of the

vested in him by the Constitution and the laws.' But no such power was vested in him by the Constitution, nor was there any law of the United States authorizing to call out the militia for any such purposes as those for which he made this call, nor was there any law authorizing him 'to set on foot' the Blockade he did in Second of these Proclamations. It is true, he said he did it in pursuance of law, but there was no such law. As these two papers did produce such an effect, they deserve special notice. We will, therefore, take them up in order. In reference to the first, I have this to say, that Congress alone has power, under the Constitution, to declare war and to raise armies. Congress alone has power to provide by law for calling out the militia of the several States. This Congress had done, but had not provided for calling them out under any such state of things as existed when this Proclamation was issued by Mr. Lincoln."[227] [Emphasis added, L.S.]

But did Lincoln not have the power to "call out the militia to suppress an insurrection in a State?" the Liberals asked Stephens:
☛ "Not at all! The President under the Constitution has no power to call out the militia to suppress an insurrection in a State, except 'on application of the Legislature' of a State, 'or of the Executive, when the Legislature cannot be convened.' This is one of the provisions of the Constitution, which Mr. Lincoln swore to 'preserve, protect and defend.' That clause of the Constitution is amongst the mutual covenants between the States guaranteeing to each a 'Republican Form of Government' and 'protection against invasion and domestic violence.' It contemplated and authorized no interference whatever, on the part of the Federal authorities, with the internal affairs of the several States, unless called upon for that purpose, either by the Legislature of a State, or by the Governor, when the Legislature could not be assembled. Congress had by law, passed in 1795, provided how this guarantee should be made good, and had directed how the President should act in making it good, when so called upon by the State authorities. He had no authority to take any action in the suppression of an insurrection in a State, except in conformity to this provision of the Constitution and the laws which had been passed by Congress for carrying it out. But no application had been made to him by the Legislature of South Carolina, nor any other State. Neither had the Governor of South Carolina, nor any other of the Seceded States, applied to him for aid in this respect, under that clause of the Constitution.

"If by insurrection [my Liberal colleagues] . . . mean an armed resistance to the execution of the Federal laws, or against the Federal authorities in any particular State, then it is equally clear that he was not authorized either by the Constitution or laws of the United States, to use military force of any kind, except as 'a *posse comitatus*' [Latin: '(man) power of the county'] in aid of the civil authorities. This was provided for by the Act of 1807. In this way, and in this way only, could the President, under his oath, use the military forces at his command in the execution of Federal laws.

"On this point, Mr.[Stephen A.] Douglas [of Illinois], in his speech on the 15th of March, in the Senate, from which I have read before, in relation to the policy of withdrawing the Federal troops from the Forts in the Seceded States, was so clear, conclusive, and unanswerable, that I will here read a portion of it in further reply to your view. In this speech, on this point, Mr. Douglas said:

> 'But we are told that the President [Lincoln] is going to enforce the laws in the Seceded States. How? By calling out the militia and using the Army and Navy! These terms are used as freely and as flippantly as if we were in a Military Government where martial law was the only rule of action, and the will of the Monarch was the only law to the subject. Sir, the President cannot use the Army, or the Navy, or the militia, for any purpose not authorized by law; and then he must do it in the manner, and only in the manner, prescribed by law. What is that? If there be an insurrection in any State against the laws and authorities thereof, the President can use the military to put it down only when called upon by the State Legislature, if it be in session, or, if it cannot be convened, by the Governor. He cannot interfere except when requested. If, on the contrary, the insurrection be against the laws of the United States instead of a State, then the President can use the military only as a *posse comitatus* in aid of the marshal in such cases as are so extreme that judicial authority and the powers of the Marshal cannot put down the obstruction. The military cannot be used in any case whatever, except in aid of civil process to assist the marshal to execute a writ. I shall not quote the laws upon this subject; but if gentlemen will refer to the Acts of 1795, and 1807, they will find that under the Act of 1795, the militia only could be called out to aid in the enforcement of the laws when resisted to such an extent that the marshal could not overcome the obstruction. By the Act of 1807, the President is authorized to use the Army and Navy to aid in enforcing the laws in all cases where it was before lawful to use the militia. Hence the military power, no matter whether Navy, regulars, volunteers, or militia, can be used only in aid of the civil authorities.
>
> 'Now, Sir, how are you going to create a case in one of these Seceded States, where the President would be authorized to call out the military? You must first procure a writ from the Judge describing the crime; you must place that in the hands of a Marshal, and he must meet such obstructions as render it impossible for him to execute it; and then, and not till then, can you call upon the military. Where is your Judge in the Seceded States? Where is your Marshal? You have no civil authorities there, and the President, in his inaugural, tells you he does not intend to appoint any. He said he intended to use the power confided to him, to hold, occupy, and possess the Forts, and collect the revenue; but beyond this he did not intend to go. You are told,

therefore, in the inaugural, that he is going to appoint no Judges, no Marshals, no civil officers, in the Seceded States, that can execute the law; and hence, we are told that he does not intend to use the Army, the Navy, or the Militia, for any such purpose. Then, Sir, what cause is there for apprehension, that the President of the United States is going to pursue a war policy, unless he shall call Congress for the purpose of conferring the power and providing the means? I presume no Senator will pretend that he has any authority, under the existing law, to do anything in the premises except what I have stated, and in the manner I have stated. If I am mistaken in regard to these laws, I shall be obliged to any Senator who will correct me. I have examined them carefully, and I think I have stated them accurately; but if not, I should like to be corrected.

'But it may be said that the President of the United States ought to have the power to collect the revenue on ship-board, to blockade the ports, to use the military to enforce the law. I say, it may be said he ought to have that power. Be that as it may, the President of the United States has not asked for that power. He knew that he did not possess it under the existing laws—for we are bound to presume that he is familiar with the laws which he took an oath to execute. We are bound to presume that [President Lincoln] . . . knew, when he spoke of collecting revenue, that he had no power to collect it on shipboard, or elsewhere than at the ports. We are bound to presume that, when he said he would use the power confided to him to hold, occupy, and possess the Forts and other property of the United States, he knew he could not call out the militia for any such purpose, under the existing law. We are bound to presume that he knew of this total absence of power on all these questions.'

"In this speech Mr. Douglas was no less accurate in his facts, than he was correct in his position upon the laws and the Constitution. There was not, at the time, a civil officer of the [U.S.] Federal Government of any kind, in any of the Seceded States [C.S.]. There was no Federal Collector, or Federal Judge, or Federal Solicitor, or Federal Marshal throughout the limits of the Confederate States, to be resisted or interfered with in any way, by combinations of any sort, either 'powerful' or weak! Those in office had all resigned, and no new ones had been appointed. There was, of course, no judicial process to be resisted or obstructed in any way. There were no civil authorities to be aided in the execution of Federal laws. *This call for troops, therefore, was neither in aid of the execution of any law, nor in pursuance of the provisions of any law. It was nothing short of a clear and palpable usurpation of power, under color of office!* This is enough for the present, in reference to the first of these Proclamations."[228] [Emphasis added, L.S.]

☛ "We will now briefly examine the second of these extraordinary edicts—the one 'setting on foot' a Blockade of the Ports of the Confederate States. This is extraordinary, not only for its clear usurpations of power, but for the strange inconsistencies with itself, which so glaringly appear upon its very face.

"First. *If the Ordinances of Secession were void, upon which assumption the Proclamation was based, then the Seceded States were still in the Union with all their Ports, and under the Constitution no discrimination could be made between them and other ports of the United States, either by Congress or the President, without a violation of this solemn Compact of Union.* This provision of the Constitution, Mr. Lincoln's oath of office required him to 'preserve, protect, and defend;' and yet in this Proclamation, without any regard to the requirement of his oath in this particular, he openly, and avowedly, put under blockade the ports of seven States, which he claimed as still members of the Union! This too, he said he did in pursuance of law! What law? Did Congress ever pass any law for the blockading of our own Ports? Never! [Emphasis added, L.S.]

"But, on the other hand, secondly: *If the Secession Ordinances were valid, and the Confederate States were, as they claimed to be, a foreign power, so far as concerned their relations to the United States, then this Proclamation was equally a palpable violation of the Constitution, because it was an act of war, which the President had no right to resort to, unless first authorized and empowered by Congress.* [Emphasis added, L.S.]

"*Viewed in either light, therefore, it was unquestionably a most flagrant usurpation of power!* The Blockade was in no sense a measure to aid the civil authorities in the collection of revenues at Charleston, or elsewhere. It was in effect, as well as design, a war measure! Its purpose was to weaken an acknowledged Belligerent. If a blockade had been necessary or proper, either to suppress a rebellion or to weaken a neighboring foreign inimical Power, Congress alone had authority, under the Constitution, to 'set it on foot.' [Emphasis added, L.S.]

"Then, again, *the Proclamation was itself most strangely utterly inconsistent with the assumption on which it was based. The act of blockading the ports of the Confederate States, by the very laws of nations to which he refers, was an acknowledgment of Public War*—*not an Insurrection or Rebellion; which acknowledgment carried upon its very face a concession to the Confederate States of all the rights of Belligerents, in a Public War, under the laws of nations.* This was the necessary effect and legitimate consequence of the measure itself. But this most extraordinary paper, after thus conceding, as it did, by its very terms, all the rights of Belligerents, under the laws of nations, went on to declare a purpose to consider and punish as pirates any persons who might engage, under 'letters of marque' on the high seas, on the opposite side, in this Public War, so recognized by him! By the laws of nations, Privateers are not pirates, as Mr. Lincoln himself afterwards admitted, at least by his acts. [Emphasis added, L.S.] As very pertinent to this subject, so far as relates to Mr. Lincoln's authority to issue this Proclamation, I will read another portion of the same speech of Mr. [Stephen A.] Douglas.

Here is what he said in reference to a Blockade of Southern Ports under the circumstances:

> 'But we are told the country is to be precipitated into war by blockading all the Southern ports; blockading ports within the United States; blockading our own ports, with our own Army and Navy! Where is the authority for that? What law authorizes the President of the United States to blockade Federal ports at discretion? He has no more authority to blockade New Orleans or Charleston than he has to blockade New York or Boston; and no more legal right to blockade Mobile than Chicago. Sir, I cannot consent that the President of the United States may, at his discretion, blockade the ports of the United States or of any other country. *He can do only what the Constitution and Laws authorize him to do.* He dare not attempt to obstruct commerce at the mouth of the Mississippi river, or at Mobile, or at any other port in the Seceded States, or even those that have remained loyal to the Constitution and to the Union. *The intimation that he is to do this, implies a want of respect for the integrity of the President, or an ignorance of the laws of the land on the part of 'those who are disturbing the harmony and quiet of the country by threats of illegal violence.'* [Emphasis added, L.S.]

"In this connection, I will also call your attention to what even Mr. [Daniel] Webster said on the same subject, in 1832, in the days of Nullification. He was addressing a Massachusetts audience—a Convention of his Party at Worcester. What I propose to read is as follows:

> 'Now, sir, I think it exceedingly probable that the President [Andrew Jackson] may come to an open rupture with that portion of his original Party which now constitutes what is called the Nullification Party. I think it likely he will oppose the proceedings of that Party, if they shall adopt measures coming directly in conflict with the laws of the United States. But how will he oppose? What will be his course of remedy? Sir, I wish to call the attention of the Convention, and of the people, earnestly to this question—How will the President attempt to put down Nullification, if he shall attempt it at all?
>
> 'Sir, for one, I protest in advance against such remedies as I have heard hinted. The Administration itself keeps a profound silence, but its friends have spoken for it. We are told, sir, that the President will immediately employ the military force, and at once blockade Charleston! A military remedy, a remedy by direct belligerent operation, has been thus suggested, and nothing else has been suggested, as the intended means of preserving the Union. Sir, there is no little reason to think, that this suggestion is true. We cannot be altogether unmindful of the past, and, therefore, we cannot be altogether unapprehensive for the future. *For one, Sir, I raise my voice beforehand against the unauthorized employment of military power, and against*

superseding the authority of the laws, by an armed force, under pretence of putting down Nullification. The President has no authority to blockade Charleston; the President has no authority to employ military force, till he shall be duly required so to do by law, and by the civil authorities. His duty is to cause the laws to be executed. His duty is to support the civil authority. His duty is, if the laws be resisted, to employ the military force of the country, if necessary, for their support and execution; but to do all this in compliance only with law, and with decisions of the tribunals.' [Emphasis added, L.S.]

"It is useless to multiply arguments or authorities on this point. It seems to me there ought to be, and can be no rational controversy upon the subject. *In the forum of reason, these Proclamations of Mr. Lincoln must be considered as gross violations of the Constitution, and most unscrupulous usurpations of power. The people of the Southern States were too well versed in Constitutional doctrines, and too thoroughly wedded to the principles of Liberty derived from their ancestors, not to be thoroughly aroused by the dangers thus portentously threatened against the very foundations of Free Institutions.* They looked upon these Proclamations, and rightly too, as I think, as their English ancestors looked upon the royal edicts of Charles I, for ship money, and other equal outrages upon their well established Rights. Even the strongest Union men, as Mr. Zollicoffer, Neil S. Brown, and John Bell, of Tennessee, John Janney, Robert E. Scott, and William C. Rives, of Virginia, to say nothing of others of the same class in that State, and thousands of others of the same class in other States, who resisted Secession to the last, now saw that this claim of Executive power unless checked, sooner or later, would lead inevitably to a centralized Despotism. These are the considerations which produced the wonderful effect of these most extraordinary papers. And to show that these apprehensions were right, that they were well founded, and that *the Administration at Washington was aiming at a complete overthrow of the Institutions of the country*, I may, as well here as elsewhere, call attention to three other Presidential Proclamations, which followed each other in quick succession, and all on the same line of progress towards Despotic Power. First, the one of the 27th of April extending the Blockade to Virginia and North Carolina, after they had taken steps to ally themselves with the Confederate States. [Emphasis added, L.S.] Then the one of the 3rd of May, which is in these words:

[Lincoln's proclamation:] 'Whereas, existing exigencies demand immediate and adequate measures for the protection of the national Constitution and the preservation of the national Union, by the suppression of the insurrectionary combinations now existing in several States for opposing the laws of the Union, and obstructing the execution thereof, to which end a military force in addition to that called forth by my Proclamation of the fifteenth day of April, in the present year, appears to be indispensably necessary, now, therefore, I, Abraham Lincoln, President of the United States, and Commander-in-Chief of the Army and Navy thereof, and of the militia of the several States, when called into actual service, do hereby call into the service of the United States forty-two thousand and thirty-four volunteers, to serve for a period of three years, unless sooner discharged, and to be mustered into service as infantry and cavalry. The proportions of each arm, and the details of enrolment and organization, will be made known through the Department of War; and I also direct that the regular army of the United States be increased by the addition of eight regiments of infantry, one regiment of cavalry, and one regiment of artillery, making altogether a maximum aggregate increase of 22,714 officers and enlisted men, the details of which increase will also be made known through the Department of War; and I further direct the enlistment, for not less than one nor more than three years, of 18,000 seamen, in addition to the present force, for the naval service of the United States. The details of the enlistment and organization will be made known through the Department of the Navy. The call for volunteers, hereby made, and the direction of the increase of the regular army, and for the enlistment of seamen hereby given, together with the plan of organization adopted for the volunteers and for the regular forces hereby authorized, will be submitted to Congress as soon as assembled.

'In the meantime, I earnestly invoke the co-operation of all good citizens in the measures hereby adopted for the effectual suppression of unlawful violence, for the impartial enforcement of constitutional laws, and for the speediest possible restoration of peace and order, and with those of happiness and prosperity throughout our country.

'In testimony whereof, I have hereunto set my hand, and caused the seal of the United States to be affixed. Done at the City of Washington, this third day of May, in the year of our Lord one thousand eight hundred and sixty one, and of the Independence of the United States the eighty fifth.'

"He still speaks of 'insurrectionary combinations' in the Seceded States to 'oppose' and 'obstruct' the Federal officers in the execution of the laws, as if there was a single Federal civil officer to execute any law within their entire limits, for whose aid the force was to be used. It was under the pretence that there were such officers that the force was called out, but really for very different purposes. *In this Proclamation, moreover, Mr. Lincoln actually increased the Army 64,748 men, and the Navy 18,000 men, by his own act, without the shadow of lawful or Constitutional authority. No ukase [czarist order] of the Autocrat of Russia was ever more imperial or absolute in its character!*"[229] [Emphasis added, L.S.]

☛ "Even before this, as early as the 27th of April, [Lincoln] . . . had, by an order to the Commanding General of the Army, authorized him to suspend the Privilege of the Writ of *Habeas Corpus* in certain localities, but it was not until the 10th of May that the *initiative Proclamation* for the general suspension of the privilege of this Writ made its appearance. This seems to have been a feeler to test public sentiment in the 'loyal States,' so-called. It was evidently experimental in its character; and as an experiment, it was tried first on the Islands, on the coast of Florida. Seeing by this experiment thus made, that he might, with impunity, proceed further in the same direction, this initiative step was not long afterwards followed by the bolder one of a virtual general suspension of the privilege of this Writ throughout the United States, by like orders to commanding [U.S.] Generals. *By these acts successively, the most direct blows were struck at the very vitals of civil liberty as secured by England's Great Charter, and which was the priceless heritage of the people of all these States!* [Emphasis added, L.S.]

"It was in the full exercise of this despotic power that Mr. Seward boasted, in conversation with Lord Lyons, that he could do what her Majesty, Queen Victoria, could not do. In this conversation with the British Minister, Mr. Lincoln's Secretary of State [Seward] is reported to have said:

> '*I can touch a bell on my right hand and order the arrest of a citizen of Ohio. I can touch the bell again and order the arrest of a citizen of New York. Can Queen Victoria do as much?*' [Emphasis added, L.S.]

"He well knew that she could not, and that no Crowned Head in Europe, not even the Czar of Russia, could do more!"[230]

☛ "This Proclamation of the 10th of May, being, as it was, the initiative public step to the more general assumptions of power which followed subsequently on the same line, deserves special notice at this time. Here it is:

> [Lincoln's proclamation:] 'Whereas, An insurrection exists in the State of Florida, by which the lives, liberty, and property of loyal citizens of the United States are endangered:
> 'And whereas, It is deemed proper that all needful measures should be taken for the protection of such citizens, and all officers of the United States in the discharge of their public duties in the State aforesaid:
> 'Now, therefore, be it known, that I, Abraham Lincoln, President of the United States, do hereby direct the Commander of the forces of the United States on the Florida coast, to permit no person to exercise any office or authority upon the Islands of Key West, the Tortugas, and Santa Rosa, which may be inconsistent with the laws and Constitution of the United States, authorizing him at the same time, if he shall find it necessary, to suspend there the writ of *Habeas Corpus*, and to remove from the vicinity of the United States fortresses all dangerous or suspected persons.

'In witness whereof, I have hereunto set my hand, and caused the seal of the United States to be affixed. Done at the City of Washington, this tenth day of May, in the year of our Lord one thousand eight hundred and sixty-one, and of the Independence of the United States the eighty-fifth.'

"In this, as in his previous orders referred to, he not only assumed publicly the power to suspend the privilege of the writ of *Habeas Corpus*, but assumed to confer that power upon a commanding General of the Army!"[231]

Stephens' friends on the Liberal side of the aisle believed Lincoln was fully justified in issuing such edicts, despite their obvious unconstitutionality. In an attempt to buttress their argument they declared: "If it was an extraordinary exercise of power, it was completely justified by the necessity of the occasion. . . . 'Necessity has no law,' is an old and time-honored maxim. . . . 'To consult the safety of the people, is the first great law,' is also a maxim with all statesmen. It is much older than the Constitution. In all such cases, the public safety is the supreme law, and all Constitutions, as well as all laws, must yield to it. Upon these principles, it was necessary for Mr. Lincoln to exercise the powers he did, to save the life of the Nation; and it was upon these principles, he was both justified and sustained in what he did." To this Stephens replied:

☛ *"Necessity is always the usurper's, as well as the tyrant's plea. It is never tolerated for an instant, by those who are jealous and watchful of their rights and liberties. The 'solus populi,' or 'safety of the people,' in all free governments, is to be 'consulted' by those entrusted with delegated powers, by a strict observance of those barriers and safeguards which the people have themselves erected for their own protection and safety. The well-being of every Body-Politic, like the well-being of every physical organism, is to be consulted by a rigid conformity with the laws of its existence. These laws in the Body-Politic are to be found in its Constitution. The object of all written Constitutions established for the security of the ultimate safety of the people is, as Mr. [Thomas] Jefferson says, 'to bind down their rulers' 'with the chains' of the fundamental law, 'to prevent them from doing mischief' in the exercise of their individual judgment, upon what concerns the safety of the people. Of this, the people themselves are the only proper judges in the last resort.* [Emphasis added, L.S.]

"The maxims [my Liberal friends] . . . quote, I admit, are older than the Constitution. So is Tyranny! The latter sprung from the former. The object of written Constitutions is to put an end to both. No Statesman should ever be trusted in this country in the exercise of any power under the 'plea of necessity' or who 'consults' the 'safety of the people,' or attempts 'to preserve the life of the Nation' upon any maxims outside of the Constitution. *The life of the Nation is the Constitution!* From this springs all the life our wonderful Nation, constituted as it is, ever had. In it alone this Conventional Nation, as we have seen it is, lives, and moves, and has its being! It is this alone which gave it existence, and it is this alone which can give it immortality! Of all the absurdities, (you will please excuse the expression,) I ever heard uttered, the strangest to me is that set forth in the proposition, that the preservation of the life of anything can be effected by its destruction or extinguishment! *I know nothing approximating it, unless it be that other most preposterous notion from which all these proceedings sprung, that a voluntary Union of separate Independent States could be preserved and maintained by coercion! The life of the Nation can only be preserved, as the life of anything else, by maintaining the principles of its organic law!*"232 [Emphasis added, L.S.]

☛ "Let us examine the practical workings of the maxims you quote in their preservation of the 'life of the Nation.' Under these acts, suspending the privilege of the writ of *Habeas Corpus*, Northern prisons were soon filled with hundreds, if not thousands, of the best and truest citizens of the country, for no reason except that of raising their voice against these utterly indefensible assumptions of Executive power which Mr. Douglas, and even Mr. Webster, had clearly stated would be crimes for which an impeachment should be made. Fort McHenry, Fort La Fayette, and Fort Warren were turned into Bastiles! Strange means these to preserve the liberties of the people, except upon the maxim, that the best way to preserve Liberty, as well as life, is to destroy it!

"*The Members of the Legislature of Maryland were prevented from assembling for the performance of their public duties by arrests and imprisonments under military orders issued in pursuance of these Executive edicts. The Mayor and Marshal, and most, if not all the civil officers of Baltimore, besides many other of the most respectable and worthy citizens of that State and other States, were seized and immured in prison without any charge of crime or violation of law against them. Not only was the freedom of speech denied, but the liberty of the press was openly assailed and effectually suspended throughout all the Northern States. Here is a list of a hundred and seventy-five of some of the best citizens in this country, who were thus seized and imprisoned in Fort La Fayette alone, in less than one hundred days, without any charge of crime against them, and in open violation of an express clause of the Constitution! Maryland, of all the States, however, suffered most from these arbitrary and tyrannical proceedings.* [Emphasis added, L.S.]

"The order for these arrests was in these words to [U.S.] General [Nathaniel P.] Banks:

'U.S. War Department, Sept. 11, 1601
'General Banks:—The passage of an Act of Secession by the Legislature of Maryland must be prevented. If necessary, all or any part of the members must be arrested. Exercise your own judgment as to the time and manner,

but do the work effectually.
'Very respectfully, your obedient servant,
'Simon Cameron, Secretary of War.'

" The general sympathy and feeling of the people of the Southern States for this 'down-trodden' sister, at the time, found expression in the stirring poetic utterances of James R. Randall, one of her 'exiled' sons, in the ever memorable stanzas beginning: 'The despot's heel is on thy shore, Maryland!' These stanzas were set to music, and became one of the most popular songs of the period in all classes of society. The tender voices of young maidens were often united with the full tones of hardy warriors in giving increased effect to the soul-inspiring chorus. 'The despot's heel,' however, pressed none the lighter!

"It was in vain, that the venerable [Roger B.] Taney at the head of the Judiciary was appealed to. All that he could do, during this *reign of terror*, was to proclaim to the world, and enter on the Records of his Court, his judicial condemnation of these monstrous outrages upon the liberties of his country. In this he evinced a firmness and integrity, in resisting the encroachments of Executive power at this crisis in our history, not surpassed by Sir Edward Coke, in the days of the Stuarts in England! I wish I had time to read this decision in the case of John Merryman. I can now barely refer to it, with a special commendation of it to [my colleagues'] . . . careful perusal hereafter. In it [they] . . . will find what should put to blush every one in authority in this country, whether in high or low position, who assumes, either under the plea of necessity, or what he may consider the 'maxims of statesmen,' 'to consult' the safety of the people, by tearing down those barriers, and removing those guards which the people themselves have established in their organic laws, for their own protection and safety. In it, also, will be found those vital principles of our Federal Compact—made for War as well as for Peace—which should ever be the guide of all in authority, whether in the civil or military service; and which will remain forever to be studied and cherished by every true friend of Constitutional Liberty in this country, in whatever position, or so long, at least, as an enlightened votary shall live to do homage at its hallowed shrine!"[233] [Emphasis added, L.S.]

Upon hearing Stephens' words, a Liberal friend made the following comments to the conservative Confederate vice president: "Well, pray tell us what Mr. Lincoln was to do under the circumstances? Was he to do nothing but to remain still and let the Government go to pieces, and even to permit himself to be driven from Washington, when the purpose of the Confederate Government was officially announced, on the day Fort Sumter was fired upon, by Mr. Leroy P. Walker, the Secretary of War, to be to overthrow the United States Government, and to plant the Confederate States flag 'over the dome of the old Capitol at Washington before the first of May,' and 'eventually over Faneuil Hall [in Boston, Massachusetts] itself?' Was Mr. Lincoln to sit still and take no action to prevent the consummation of this openly declared purpose?

"What you have read from Mr. Douglas's speech, and from Mr. Webster's, all sounds well enough in peaceful times; but you should recollect that Mr. Douglas virtually took back all that he said in this speech, when the hour of real danger came—when the National Capital and the very existence of the Government was thus boastingly threatened. Notwithstanding his political differences, he then cordially united with Mr. Lincoln, in support of these measures which you have commented on with so much severity, and have even quoted him as authority to sustain you in the comments you have made."

Stephens gave this reply:

☛ "How this is, we shall see. Your remarks open a wide field, and require several distinct replies. These I will make in as regular order, and as briefly, as the subject admits. First, in reply to your inquiry as to what Mr. Lincoln ought to have done, I have a two-fold answer. I will, in the first place, state what, in my opinion, he ought not to have done; and in the second place, what he ought to have done. *He ought not, then, to have ordered the forcible supply of the troops at Fort Sumter. He ought to have withdrawn those troops, as advised by Mr. Douglas, General [Winfield] Scott, and all the leading real friends of the Union, under the Constitution, in all parts of the country. In other words, he ought not to have inaugurated the war as he did. If he really believed that the Union of the States under the Constitution was such as could and ought to be maintained by force, then he ought to have convened the Congress of the Non-Seceding States, and asked that body by law to put at his command the military force necessary to meet the exigencies of the crisis. He ought not to have assumed the exercise of this power himself, for it is clear the Constitution vested no such power in him. This is what he ought not to have done, as well as what he ought to have done, in that view of the powers of the Federal Government.* [Emphasis added, L.S.]

"But, in my view of the powers of the Federal Government, I will say that, on the withdrawal of the Seceding States, when there was not a Federal officer left in any of them to be aided by the military in the execution of the laws, he ought to have convened the Congress and taken their judgment upon the proper course to be pursued, in a case which was clearly not within any of the provisions of the Compact of Union. This was clearly a '*casus non fœderis*' [Latin: 'case outside the compact']; and he should have left it to the Congress to determine the proper action to be taken in relation to it. So much for what he ought not to have done, as well as what [Lincoln] . . . ought to have done under the circumstances, in both views of the question, in my opinion."[234]

☛ "I will now go further, and tell you what I think the Congress of States ought to have done under the circumstances, if they had been so convened by him. *They should have called a Convention of all the States, with a view to a readjustment of their relations. If the Seceded States had responded to that call, well and good. In that event, I have but little doubt that the result would have been a peaceful adjustment of all matters in controversy, by the derelict States heretofore referred to—those which had openly and avowedly refused to perform their obligations under the Constitution—receding from their position . . . , and that upon this redress of grievances and righting of the wrong complained of, the Seceded States would have returned to their positions; and the whole Federal machinery, at no distant day, would have been restored to its normal and harmonious action in all its parts, as peacefully and joyously as when it first went into operation.* [Emphasis added, L.S.]

"But in the event that the Seceded States had not responded to the call, or in the event that the derelict States had refused to renew their pledges of fidelity in the matter complained of, from conscientious scruples or other considerations, then in either of these alternatives the fact would have been demonstrated, that we had arrived at that period in our history spoken of by Mr. John Quincy Adams. In either of these contingencies it would have appeared that the different States of the Union were 'no longer attached by the magnetism of conciliated interests and kindly sympathies.' With this fact demonstrated, this Convention of States should have come to the same conclusion in reference to it that Mr. Adams did. He said that if that day in our history should ever arrive, it would be far better for the people of the several States 'to part in friendship from each other, than to be held together by constraint,' and 'to leave the separated parts to be re-united by the law of political gravitation' to their respective centres. This is the wise and patriotic conclusion to which that Convention should have come, if it had been called under the circumstances, and the fact of irreconcilable difference between the States had been thus demonstrated. The result whichever way it might have been, whether a restoration of the Union of all the States as before, each State faithfully performing all its obligations under the Constitution, or a peaceful separation, would have been in strict conformity with the great principles upon which our entire system of Free Institutions is based. *There would have been no war, nor any of those outrages upon public liberty to which I have alluded, and which have brought so much reproach upon our Institutions of Self-government throughout the world, and which have but one inevitable end, if not abandoned, and that is absolute Despotism!* [Emphasis added, L.S.]

"*My own opinion, as I have said, is, that if Mr. Lincoln had pursued the course which I think he ought to have done, there would have been a speedy restoration of the Union, by all the States returning to their duties and obligations under the Constitution, and the Federal Government would have entered upon a new and a grander career of greatness.*"²³⁵ [Emphasis added, L.S.]

Stephens continues on with his response to his Liberal friend's comments:
☞ ". . . Now, a few words in reply to what you say of Mr. Douglas, and what you style the official announcement of the purpose of the authorities at Montgomery. Either you are greatly mistaken, or I am, if you suppose Mr. Douglas ever took back or modified, in the slightest degree, a single phrase or word in the speech from which I have quoted. It is true, as I understand, that, under the influence or impression produced by the telegram to which you refer, purporting to give the substance of what Mr. [Leroy P.] Walker said, on the occasion alluded to, Mr. Douglas did advise Mr. Lincoln to convene Congress, and did approve of all proper steps being taken for the defence of the Capital against, what he considered, a threatened attack upon the Government of the United States, and a war of invasion. He did not, however, as far as I have ever seen, utter a word in modification of what he had said, as to the powers or duties of the President, under the circumstances.

"[Douglas] . . . certainly did not give these measures I have been commenting upon, or the general policy of Mr. Lincoln, either before or after the events at Fort Sumter, his cordial endorsement or support; for, on his return to Illinois, a few days afterward, he assured his political friends that he did not know what Mr. Lincoln's policy was. He was soon stricken with disease, attended with delirium, and died on the 3rd of June. The last intelligent words uttered by [Douglas] . . ., as reported, conveyed a message to his sons, Robert and Stephen, then at college, 'to obey the laws and support the Constitution of the United States.' In this dying declaration there was no taking back, but a reaffirmance of the sentiments and principles of the speech which I have quoted.

"[Douglas] . . . never could have held that Mr. Lincoln was obeying either the laws or the Constitution, in these usurpations of power to which I have referred. He may have held, for aught I know, with you and many eminent men in the country, what seems to me to be so irrational a position, that the Federal Government did possess the abstract rightful power to maintain the Union by force, but I never saw anything from him which warrants the belief that he endorsed or approved the policy of exercising the power, even though, in his judgment, it existed, in case any of the States should see fit peaceably to withdraw without any aggression upon the rights and interests of the others. In October, 1860, he did most emphatically endorse the Georgia Platform of 1850, before at least twenty thousand freemen at Atlanta!

"This Platform distinctly claimed the right, in the contingency of a breach of faith of the other Confederates, to sever, in the last resort, every tie that bound her to the Union. This right he fully recognized. Whether he considered it a revolutionary right, as did Mr. Webster, is immaterial for all practical purposes. If the right existed, it is immaterial therefore from what source it sprung. There could be no opposing right to prevent its peaceful exercise. He certainly never did utter a sentiment, so far as I have seen, advocating the power of the President to do, without the authority of Congress, what Mr. Lincoln did in the matters I have referred to. My opinion is, that his position on this subject was very similar to that of Mr. Adams.

"Mr. Douglas was no changeling in principles or opinions. Of all the men I ever knew, he was about the last who might have been expected to take back anything he had said. I knew him well for sixteen years. We went into Congress together, in December, 1843, and a more unyielding and inflexible man in his positions and matured opinions I never met with. His death, at the time, I regarded as one of the greatest calamities, under the dispensations of Providence, which befell this country in the beginning of these troubles. So much for Mr. Douglas's position.[236]

☛ "Now a word or two in reply to that portion of your remarks which relates to the telegram from Montgomery. Whether Mr. [Leroy P.] Walker really did make such a speech, as reported by that telegram, or not, I do not know; for I was not there: but I do know that many things were reported by telegraph to have been said by parties, which were never said by them, and I cannot believe it possible that Mr. Walker could have made a speech justly admitting the construction which you and others put upon the words of the telegram referred to. For, if there is anything I do know, it is that such were not the views of the Cabinet, or of the people generally of the Confederate States, nor do the words of the telegram require that construction which you and others put upon them. Another and a very different construction is perfectly consistent with them.

"With this view, I will add that it is not at all improbable that Mr. Walker, in speaking on that occasion of the war, inaugurated as this was, and of *the acts of Mr. Lincoln in bringing it on in such open and palpable violation of the fundamental principles of the Government*, may have indulged in the expression of the hope that the people of all the States would be so aroused by its alarming tendency to Centralism and Despotic Power, that the cry might go forth, the 'cause of Charleston is the cause of us all'—and that Maryland, as well as Virginia and the other Border States, would now certainly join her sisters of the South, as Virginia, North Carolina, Tennessee, and Arkansas actually did subsequently. With these views, and animated with such sentiments as these, it is not improbable that he may have indulged in the belief, and expressed the opinion, that 'before the 1st of May,' the flag under which he then spoke might wave 'over the dome of the old Capitol at Washington,' planted there, not by a conquering army, but by the willing hands of a free people, holding the great truth that 'all Governments derive their just powers from the consent of the governed,' just as the same flag had been planted where he was then speaking. In the same vein and in the indulgence of the same sentiments, it is not improbable that he may have expressed the opinion and hope, that 'eventually' the final result of that conflict of principles which we have been tracing, and of that physical conflict growing out of them, that day begun, would be the planting of the same flag—the symbol of the Sovereign Right of local Self-government—the emblem of *Federation [i.e., Confederation] against Centralism*—over Faneuil Hall itself—the Cradle of American Liberty; but planted there in the same way by the voluntary hands of a free people! [Emphasis added, L.S.]

"That a speech, embodying these sentiments, may have been made by him, is not at all improbable, nor would it have been inconsistent with the words of the telegram itself. But I do not think that [Walker] . . . could have made a speech declaring a design or purpose, on the part of the Authorities at Montgomery, to wage a war, as you suppose, with a view to overthrow the Government of the United States, or by conquest to plant their flag anywhere; for *war, if it could possibly be avoided, was not the object, wish, desire, or intention of the Confederate States—much less conquest. Peace was their object.* This their every act shows. This, Mr. Walker's telegram to [Confederate] General Beauregard, before the fire upon Fort Sumter was opened, clearly shows."[237] [Emphasis added, L.S.]

☛ "These remarks bring me to the point I was coming to in the course of what I proposed for this occasion. After the very rapid glance which we have taken at the movements elsewhere, the very next subject, on the line I was pursuing, was a notice of the progress of events in the meantime at Montgomery. To this, therefore, we will now turn our attention.

"The Confederate Congress, as stated before, had been summoned by Mr. [Jefferson] Davis, immediately after the occurrences at Fort Sumter, to re-assemble on the 29th of April. On their re-assembling, in giving them his views upon the situation, after recounting all his efforts at peace, and the duplicity which had been practised upon the Commissioners sent to Washington, and urging upon them the most energetic measures to repel the invasion, and to defend themselves and their Institutions against the most formidable array of military power which was threatened to be brought against them, Mr. Davis used the following language in conclusion—to which I wish to call . . . special attention. . . . Here is what he said:

'We feel that our cause is just and holy, and protest solemnly, in the face of mankind, that we desire peace at any sacrifice save that of Honor and Independence. We seek no conquest, no aggrandizement, no concessions from the Free States. All we ask is to be let alone—that none shall attempt our subjugation by arms. This we will, and must resist, to the direst extremity. The moment this pretension is abandoned, the sword will drop from our hands, and we shall be ready to enter into treaties of amity and commerce mutually beneficial. So long as this pretension is maintained, with firm reliance on that Divine Power which covers with its protection the just cause, we will continue to struggle for our inherent right to freedom, independence, and self-government.'

"This is the official announcement of the purpose and policy of the Authorities at Montgomery in regard to the war. In it Mr. Davis expressed the unanimous views and sentiments of his Cabinet, Mr. Walker included; and in it he announced the feelings, views, and sentiments of an overwhelming majority of the people of the Confederate States. *It was, on their part, a war entirely in defence of what they considered the inherent, sovereign, and inalienable Right of Self-government.*"[238] [Emphasis added, L.S.]

27

THE WAR FOR SOUTHERN INDEPENDENCE PART TWO

IN THIS CHAPTER OF EXCERPTS from *A Constitutional View*, Stephens provides more details on Abraham Lincoln's developing assault on the South, the U.S. Constitution, and states' rights.

☞ "The war now, on both sides, began to assume gigantic proportions. It was no Insurrection or Rebellion, or even Civil War in any proper sense of these terms. A Rebellion or Insurrection is resistance to the Sovereign Power of any Society, Commonwealth, or State by those owing it allegiance, and may be justified or not, according to the facts of the case. A Civil War is but another name for the same sort of resistance, where it assumes so formidable a magnitude as to divide the members of the same Society or Commonwealth into two great Parties, between which ultimate supremacy becomes a matter of uncertainty and doubt. Vattel has well and truly said, that 'custom appropriates the term of "civil war" to every war between the members of one and the same Political Society.' [Emphasis added, L.S.] Further on he says, where such a

> 'war breaks the bands of society and Government, or, at least, suspends their force and effect, [it produces] two independent parties, who consider each other as enemies, and acknowledge no common judge. These two parties, therefore, must necessarily be considered as thenceforward constituting, at least for a time, two separate Bodies, two distinct Societies.'

"But this war, properly and truly considered, was not of this character at all. For, if the facts of our history be, as they appear incontestably to be from the review which we have made of them, *the people of the United States never did form or constitute one Political Society, or Body-Politic. The Union of the States was a Union of distinct and separate Political Societies or Bodies-Politic. The States held no such relation to the Union as Departments or Provinces do to an Empire, or as Counties and Districts do to a State, as maintained by Mr. Lincoln. The citizens of each State owed allegiance, as we have seen, to their own separate States.* [Emphasis added, L.S.]

"The war, therefore, was a war between States regularly organized into two separate Federal Republics. Eleven States on the one side, under the name and style of 'The Confederate States of America' [or C.S.A.], and twenty-two States on the other side, under the like name and style of 'The United States of America' [or U.S.A.]. In our further notice of the conduct of this war, we may properly enough, therefore, designate the Parties to it by the terms 'Confederates' and 'Federals,' though the latter term will by no means correctly represent the principles of those thus designated. *In the beginning, and throughout the contest, the object of the 'Confederates' was to maintain the separate Sovereignty of each State, and the right of Self-government, which that necessarily carries with it. The object of the 'Federals,' on the contrary, was to maintain a Centralized Sovereignty over all the States, on both sides. This was the fundamental principle involved in the Conflict,' which must be kept constantly in mind.*"[239] [Emphasis added, L.S.]

☛ "The Congress of the Confederate States . . . was in session. The Federal [U.S.] Congress was summoned to meet on the 4th of July. But in advance of this, Mr. Lincoln, by his Proclamation, as we have seen, had ordered an increase to the Regular Federal Army of 64,748 men, and an increase to the Navy of 18,000 men. The Regular Federal Army, besides the volunteer forces called out, before this increase, consisted of about 16,000 men. The new force added by Presidential edict swelled the number of the Regular Army to about 80,748 men. The Federal Navy, before the increase so ordered, consisted of about 10,000 men, exclusive of officers and marines. The total number of vessels of all classes belonging to this Navy was ninety, carrying or designed to carry, about 2,415 guns. The increase of men under the Presidential edict run [ran] the aggregate of seamen in service up to nearly 30,000.

"The Confederates, on their assembling in Congress, on the 29th of April, as stated, went to work the best way they could to meet this formidable array of power against them. By Act of Congress they simply recognized the existence of the war so inaugurated against them, excluding from their Act the States of Missouri, Kentucky, Maryland, and Delaware. These they did not recognize as Parties to the war. With this recognition of the war so forced upon them, [the Confederate states] . . . resorted to all the means at their command to repel it. At their first organization, less than three months before, they were without an Exchequer, an Army, or a Navy of any sort, and without any munitions of war, except those which had fallen into the hands of the several States in the Federal Forts, and which had been turned over to them, to be used in the common cause. The State of Alabama, on the first assembling of the Convention, at Montgomery, had tendered them, for temporary use, a half million of dollars, and, before the affair at Sumter, the Congress had provided, by law, for making a loan of $15,000,000, to repay Alabama's advance, and to meet other necessary emergencies. But now further means became necessary. To meet the forces arrayed against them a large army was necessary. To raise and equip this required much larger expenditures of money than the amounts at their command. Another loan was authorized to the amount of $50,000,000. This was to be effected by the sale of Confederate States Bonds, redeemable at the expiration of twenty years from their date, bearing an interest of eight *per cent. per annum*. The same act authorized the issuance of twenty millions of Treasury notes, in lieu of a like amount of bonds to answer the same purposes, if the Secretary of the Treasury and the President should deem it better to issue the Treasury notes instead of making a sale of the bonds. Besides this, another measure was adopted, known as the Produce Loan. By this, invitations were given for contributions of cotton, tobacco, corn, wheat, flour, meat, and army subsistence generally, in the way of a loan. By the terms of the act, the articles so contributed were to be sold, and the proceeds to be turned over to the Secretary of the Treasury, who was to issue eight per cent, bonds for the same. These were the extraordinary methods adopted for raising means, besides the other regular modes of providing revenue without resorting to direct taxation. So much for the financial measures of the Confederates, at present.

"In view of the exigency for an immediate military force in the field, the [Confederate] Congress looked almost exclusively to the volunteer spirit of the people. By Act, they authorized the President to accept the services of one hundred thousand volunteers, either as cavalry, mounted riflemen, artillery, or infantry, in such proportions of these several arms as he might deem expedient, to serve for and during the war, unless sooner discharged. The Congress also provided for the appointment of five General officers, to have the rank of 'General,' instead of 'Brigadier-General' as previously provided. This was to be the highest military grade known in the Confederate States service.

"In lieu of a Regular Navy, their only resort was the enlistment of armed ships under *Letters of Marque*. Very soon quite a number of small vessels were thus put in commission, and reached the high seas by running the Blockade. Amongst these may be named the *Calhoun*, the *Petrel*, the *Spray*, the *Ivy*, the

Webb, the *Dixey*, the *Jeff Davis*, the *Bonita*, the *Gordon*, the *Coffee*, the *York*, the *McRae*, the *Savannah*, the *Nina*, the *Jackson*, the *Tuscarora*—besides others. In less than a month, more than twenty prizes were taken and run into Southern Ports. The steamers *Sumter* and *Nashville*, fitted out by the Government, and under the command of Naval officers, went to sea at a later date. The *Sumter* ran the Blockade at the mouth of the Mississippi, on the 30th of June, in charge of Commander Raphael Semmes, a gallant officer who had resigned his position in the Navy of the United States, and who thus entered upon that brilliant career in the Confederate Service which has secured to him a lasting fame and renown. The *Nashville* was put in command of Captain Robert B. Pegram, another resigned officer of the U.S. Navy, of experience, skill, and distinction. It was several months later, before Captain Pegram got his vessel out of the Port of Charleston.

"This 'militia upon the high seas' captured many millions of the enemy's property, and produced a great sensation throughout the Northern States. As many as twenty prizes, and several prisoners, were taken by those which first got to sea, before the end of May. The [Confederate] Congress at Montgomery, by law, immediately provided for their proper treatment, which was in strict accordance with the usage and humanity of the most civilized nations. The Act directed that they should be treated 'as prisoners of war,' and 'furnished with rations in quantity and quality as those furnished to enlisted men in the Army of the Confederacy.'[240]

☞ "After these measures on the Finances, the Army, and the Navy, the [C.S.] Congress adjourned on the 21st of May, to meet again on the 20th of July, in the City of Richmond, Virginia, which was settled upon as the future Seat of [the Confederate] Government.

"In the meantime, the call which had been made for volunteers had been most enthusiastically responded to. Before the re-assembling of the [C.S.] Congress in Richmond, more than a hundred thousand men had pressed the tender of their services in the cause, and more than fifty thousand were under arms organized into battalions and regiments, and ready for duty in one part of the country or another. The largest number were collected in different places in Virginia, where the first blow from the enemy was expected. Meantime the Privateer *Savannah*, under command of T. Harrison Baker, with a crew of twenty men had been captured, on the 3rd of June, off Charleston, by the U.S. Brig *Perry*. Her crew had been placed in irons and sent to New York, where they were to be tried for piracy, under Mr. Lincoln's Proclamation. It was now that the question about prisoners arose, for the first time, between the Parties Belligerent, which, from the importance this question assumed in the subsequent conduct of the war, deserves special notice here. News of the treatment of these prisoners taken on the Privateer *Savannah*, having reached Richmond through the public press, Mr. Davis immediately addressed a communication to Mr. Lincoln, and committed it to the hands of a special messenger, Col. [Thomas] Taylor, an officer of the Confederate Army, with directions to obtain, if possible, a passage by flag of truce through the Federal lines, and to deliver it in person. In this communication, dated Richmond, July 6th, 1861, [Davis] . . . said to Mr. Lincoln:

> 'Having learned that the Schooner *Savannah*, a private armed vessel in the service, and sailing under a commission issued by authority of the Confederate States of America, had been captured by one of the vessels forming the blockading squadron off Charleston harbor, I directed a proposition to be made to the officer commanding that squadron, for an exchange of the officers and crew of the *Savannah*, for prisoners of war held by this Government, "according to number and rank." To this proposition, made on the 19th ultimo, [U.S.] Captain Mercer, the officer in command of the blockading squadron, made answer, on the same day, that "the prisoners (referred to) are not on board of any of the vessels under my command."
>
> 'It now appears, by statements made, without contradiction, in newspapers published in New York, that the prisoners above mentioned were conveyed to that city, and have been treated, not as prisoners of war, but as criminals; that they have been put in irons, confined in jail, brought before the Courts of Justice on charges of piracy and treason; and it is even rumored that they have been actually convicted of the offences charged, for no other reason than that they bore arms in defence of the rights of this Government, and under the authority of its commission.
>
> 'I could not, without grave discourtesy, have made the newspaper statements above referred to the subject of this communication, if the threat of treating as pirates the citizens of this Confederacy, armed for its service on the high seas, had not been contained in your proclamation of the 19th of April last; that proclamation, however, seems to afford a sufficient justification for considering these published statements as not devoid of probability.
>
> 'It is the desire of this Government so to conduct the war now existing as to mitigate its horrors, as far as may be possible; and, with this intent, its treatment of the prisoners captured by its forces has been marked by the greatest humanity and leniency consistent with public obligation. Some have been permitted to return home on parole, others to remain at large, under similar conditions, within this Confederacy, and all have been furnished with rations for their subsistence, such as are allowed to our own troops. It is only since the news has been received of the treatment of the prisoners taken on the *Savannah*, that I have been compelled to withdraw these indulgences, and to hold the prisoners taken by us in strict confinement.
>
> 'A just regard to humanity and to the honor of this Government, now

requires me to state explicitly, that painful as will be the necessity, this Government will deal out to the prisoners held by it, the same treatment and the same fate as shall be experienced by those captured on the *Savannah*; and if driven to the terrible necessity of retaliation, by your execution of any of the officers or crew of the *Savannah*, that retaliation will be extended, so far as shall be requisite to secure the abandonment of a practice unknown to the warfare of civilized man, and so barbarous, as to disgrace the nation which shall be guilty of inaugurating it.

'With this view, and because it may not have reached you, I now renew the proposition made to the Commander of the Blockading Squadron, to exchange for the prisoners taken on the *Savannah*, an equal number of those now held by us, according to rank.'

"This overture of Mr. Davis was so far respected as to let Col. Taylor, the bearer of it, pass the enemy's lines, and to go to Washington, but a personal interview with Mr. Lincoln was denied. He was permitted to return the next day, with a verbal reply from General [Winfield] Scott, that the communication had been delivered to Mr. Lincoln, and that he would answer it in writing as soon as possible. *No answer in writing, or in any other way, however, was ever made by Mr. Lincoln to the communication.* The only resort left to Mr. Davis, therefore, was the extreme one of retaliation, recognized by the most civilized nations. A number of Northern prisoners was selected by lot, to meet whatever fate should be measured out to these, and other privateers taken on the high seas. Amongst the Federal prisoners thus selected for retaliation, were Colonels [Michael] Corcoran, Lee, [Milton] Cogswell, [Oliver B.] Wilcox, Woodruff, and [A. M.] Wood; Majors Potter, Revere, and Vogdes; Captains Rockwood, Bowman, and Keffer. Bowman and Keffer were substituted in like manner, by lot, in lieu of Captains Rickett and McQuade who were wounded, and who, in consequence, were exempted from the lot which fell on them in the first instance. [Emphasis added L.S.]

"The end of this whole matter, so revolting to the common sentiment of the age, in all enlightened countries, was a desistance by Mr. Lincoln, from the position and doctrines assumed in his Proclamation. These prisoners on both sides, were all subsequently duly exchanged. Whether the authorities at Washington were induced to change their policy and purpose in this particular, by a recognition of the laws of war, or from a sense of humanity, or from fears excited in another quarter, will, perhaps, be left forever to conjecture; for no explanation of it has ever been given to the public, as far as I am aware.

"No further reply was ever made to Mr. Davis's communication referred to. Judging, therefore, from the subsequent course of the Federal authorities upon the subject of prisoners generally, about which so much has been said and written, especially about the thousands of Federal prisoners, who were permitted by these authorities to suffer and die in Southern stockades, from wounds and diseases incident to the climate, (to which the men were not accustomed,) rather than to agree upon just terms of exchange, . . . it is not outside of a legitimate presumption to come to the conclusion that the desistance in this case was induced from no considerations of the sufferings or impending fate of the gallant officers of their army thus held as hostages. The change of policy evidently came more from fear than from any sense of humanity, or the acknowledgment of the universally recognized principles of civilized warfare. That fear was excited by the position of England on the subject. This was made known by what occurred in the House of Lords of the British Parliament, on the 16th of May, soon after Mr. Lincoln's most extraordinary Proclamation of the 19th of April reached that country. On this day, in that body, the Earl of Derby said:

> 'He apprehended that if one thing was dearer than another, it was that privateering was not piracy, and that no law could make that piracy, as regarded the subjects of one Nation, which was not piracy by the law of Nations. Consequently the United States must not be allowed to entertain the doctrine, and to call upon her Majesty's Government not to interfere. He knew it was said that the United States treated the Confederate States of the South as mere Rebels, and that as Rebels these expeditions were liable to all the penalties of high treason. That was not the doctrine of this country, because we have declared that they are entitled to all the rights of Belligerents. The Northern States could not claim the rights of Belligerents for themselves, and, on the other hand, deal with other parties not as Belligerents, but as Rebels.'

"Lord Brougham said that 'it was clear that privateering was not piracy by the law of Nations.'

"Lord Kingsdown took the same view. 'What was to be the operation of the Presidential Proclamation upon this subject was a matter for the consideration of the United States.' But he expressed the opinion that *the enforcement of the doctrine of that Proclamation 'would be an act of barbarity, which would produce an outcry throughout the civilized world.'* [Emphasis added L.S.]

"It is no strain of presumption to assign this change of policy in reference to the privateersmen on the part of the Federal Authorities to apprehensions and fears awakened by this voice from England, especially in view of their subsequent conduct in relation to the exchange of prisoners."[241]

☞ "But to go on with a rapid glance at the progress of events.

"The Federal [U.S.] Congress convened on the 4th of July, according to the Presidential Proclamation. In the Senate, at an early day, on the 10th, a Joint

Resolution was offered to legalize these extraordinary acts of Mr. Lincoln, to which I have referred. This deserves special notice, and is in these words:

> Whereas, since the adjournment of Congress, on the fourth day of March last, a formidable insurrection in certain States of this Union has arrayed itself in armed hostility to the Government of the United States, constitutionally administered; and, whereas, the President of the United States did, under the extraordinary exigencies thus presented, exercise certain powers and adopt certain measures for the preservation of this Government—that is to say: First. He did, on the fifteenth day of April last, issue his Proclamation calling upon the several States for seventy-five thousand men to suppress such insurrectionary combinations, and to cause the laws to be faithfully executed. Secondly. He did, on the nineteenth day of April last, issue a Proclamation setting on foot a blockade of the ports within the States of South Carolina, Georgia, Alabama, Florida, Mississippi, Louisiana, and Texas. Thirdly. He did, on the twenty-seventh day of April last, issue a Proclamation establishing a blockade of the ports within the States of Virginia and North Carolina. Fourthly. He did, by order of the twenty-seventh day of April last, addressed to the Commanding General of the Army of the United States, authorize that officer to suspend the Writ of *Habeas Corpus* at any point on or in the vicinity of any military line between the city of Philadelphia and the city of Washington. Fifthly. He did, on the third day of May last, issue a Proclamation calling into the service of the United States forty-two thousand and thirty-four volunteers, increasing the regular Army by the addition of twenty-two thousand seven hundred and fourteen men, and the Navy by an addition of eighteen thousand seamen. Sixthly. He did, on the tenth day of May last, issue a Proclamation authorizing the Commander of the forces of the United States on the coast of Florida to suspend the Writ of *Habeas Corpus*, if necessary. All of which Proclamations and orders have been submitted to this Congress. Now, therefore,
> Be it resolved by the Senate and House of Representatives of the United States of America in Congress assembled, That all of the extraordinary acts, proclamations, and orders, hereinbefore mentioned, be, and the same are hereby, approved and declared to be in all respects legal and valid, to the same intent, and with the same effect, as if they had been issued and done under the previous express authority and direction of the Congress of the United States.

"*This Resolution deserves to be thus noted, not only from its own extraordinary character in thus attempting to legalize unconstitutional acts and gross usurpations of power by the [U.S.] President, through the means of a joint resolution of both Houses of Congress, but from the fact, also, that up to this time, even a majority of that body was not prepared to sanction or maintain either the monstrous doctrines upon which Mr. Lincoln's acts were based, or this equally monstrous manner of granting him indemnification for them. The resolution was never even acted upon, though parts of the indemnification contained in it, were subsequently inserted in other joint measures, without which even those Senators, who balked at first, saw that the war could not be maintained.*"²⁴² [Emphasis added L.S.]

☛ "On the assembling of this [U.S.] Congress, Mr. Lincoln in his message did not claim that his previous acts, which we have noticed, were all in pursuance of the Constitution or laws, but said, 'whether strictly legal or not,' they 'were ventured upon under what appeared to be a popular demand and a public necessity, and trusted that Congress would readily ratify them.' In it, however, he called for more men and money. [Said Lincoln:]

> 'It is now recommended that you give the legal means for making this contest a short and decisive one; that you place at the control of the Government, for the work, at least four hundred thousand men, and four hundred million dollars!'

"In this message he attempted an argument to show that 'the Southern movement,' as he called it, was a 'Rebellion,' and that the war to suppress it, and to preserve 'the Union,' was perfectly justifiable. This was perhaps more for effect abroad than at home. He stated that 'the whole movement' was based 'upon an ingenious sophism which if conceded was followed by perfectly logical steps through all the incidents to the complete disruption of the Union.'

"That was an important admission. It was virtually giving up the argument in the outset. For the 'sophism' on which it was based in his view, was the incontestable fact, as we have seen, of the Sovereignty of the several States. If this be a fact and not a 'sophism' then according to his own admission, Secession was necessarily a logical sequence and perfectly justifiable. This fact, however, or sophism as it appeared to him, he attempted to refute after this fashion. [Said Lincoln further:]

> 'This sophism derives much, perhaps the whole, of its currency from the assumption that there is some omnipotent and sacred supremacy pertaining to a State—to each State of our Federal Union. Our States have neither more nor less power than that reserved to them in the Union by the Constitution—no one of them ever having been a State out of the Union. The original ones passed into the Union even before they cast off their British colonial dependence; and the new ones each came into the Union directly from a condition of dependence, excepting Texas. And even Texas, in its temporary independence was never designated a State. The new ones only took the designation of States on coming into the Union, while that name was first adopted by the old ones in and by the Declaration of Independence.

Therein the "United Colonies" were declared to be "free and independent States;" but, even then, the object plainly was not to declare their independence of one another, or of the Union, but directly the contrary; as their mutual pledge, and their mutual action, before, at the time, and afterwards, abundantly show. The express plighting of faith by each and all of the original thirteen in the Articles of Confederation, two years later, that the Union shall be perpetual, is most conclusive. Having never been States, either in substance or in name, outside of the Union, whence this magical omnipotence of "State rights," asserting a claim of power to lawfully destroy the Union itself? Much is said about the "Sovereignty" of the States; but the word, even, is not in the national Constitution; nor, as is believed, in any of the State Constitutions. What is "Sovereignty," in the political sense of the term? Would it be far wrong to define it "a political community, without a political superior?" Tested by this, no one of our States, except Texas, ever was a Sovereignty.'

"This argument, if it may be so considered, needs but little comment in the face of the facts apparent in our review of the history of the States, and the formation of the Constitution. By these it has been clearly and fully demonstrated, that *what he styles a 'sophism' is an impregnable truth! What is said about Texas never having been designated during her Independence as a State, is altogether puerile. It is wholly immaterial, whether she was designated as 'the Republic of Texas,' or 'the State of Texas.' Every independent, separate, self-existing Body-Politic, by whatever designation known, whether that of Nation, Empire, Kingdom, or Republic, is a State. Texas, therefore, was certainly a separate, Sovereign and Independent State, when she entered into the Compact of Union with the other United States of America. So of what is said of the other new States only taking the designation of States on entering the Union! They were all admitted on an equal footing with the original Thirteen, and these we have seen were Sovereign!* [Emphasis added L.S.]

"The idea that *the Articles of Confederation of 1778*, by declaring and expressing the plighted faith of each, that the Union thereby entered into was to be perpetual, furnishes 'a most conclusive' argument 'that the States were never severally Sovereign,' is, to say the least, a most singular one; especially in view of the fact that *by the very second one of these Articles, it was expressly declared that each State retained its Sovereignty!* Such an argument does not rise to the dignity of 'an ingenious sophism.' It is really unworthy of notice. Not even so much as one which should maintain for a similar reason, that none of the great Powers of Europe which entered into Articles of Perpetual Alliance—'from this day henceforth'—at Paris, in 1815, for the purpose of quieting the Continent, were ever severally Sovereign, because in the latter case, there was no express declaration that the Parties so entering into the perpetual alliance, did so, as separate Sovereign Powers. *But the strangest position in this most sophistical attempt* to refute an imaginary sophism, is that, wherein it is asserted, that 'the States of the Federal Union have neither more nor less power than that reserved to them in the Union by the Constitution,' as proof that the States are not Sovereign. For even according to this statement, every power was reserved which was not delegated by the States, nor prohibited to them in the Constitution. [Emphasis added L.S.]

"The States, as we have seen, made the Constitution. They formed it by virtue of their several Sovereignties. It was by virtue of the 'omnipotence' of this majestical, if not 'magical' Sovereign power, on their part, severally, that the Constitution and the Union under it was formed. The Federal Government has no inherent power whatever. It has no power except what is delegated to it by the Sovereign States. All the inherent powers of Sovereignty itself not delegated in trust to the General Government, nor prohibited to the States, are, it is true, expressly declared in the Constitution to be reserved to the States. This shows that as Sovereignty was not parted with, it remained with the States by this express reservation! The States derive no power from the Constitution as [Lincoln's] . . . form of expression was intended, perhaps, to imply, while the Federal Government possesses none whatever which is not conferred upon it by the States in the Constitution. [Emphasis added L.S.]

"It is true, the word Sovereignty is not in the 'national Constitution,' nor had it any business there. But the words 'State' and 'States' abound in it. From its Preamble to its close it shows that it was made 'by States' and 'for States,' and to be binding 'between States' only; and binding between them only as all Compacts are between States! The word State of itself imports Sovereignty as fully as the word Nation, Kingdom, or Empire. When the Constitution upon its face showed that it was made 'by States' and 'for States,' it was needless to speak of them as Sovereign States; for there cannot be any such thing as a State, known and recognized by public law, without Sovereignty. [Emphasis added L.S.]

"But the capping climax of this argument requires more special attention. In this we have an attempted definition of Sovereignty, and a most singular definition it is! As if almost satisfied himself of its inaccuracy, Mr. Lincoln asks 'what is Sovereignty in the political sense of the term? Would it be far wrong to define it "a political community, without a political superior?"' It would certainly be very far from right thus to define it. It would, indeed, be no definition at all. Sovereignty is not ' a political community,' but in whatever terms it may be defined, it is the controlling attribute of the political community in which it exists. This is ground we have gone over. With a correct understanding as to what Sovereignty is 'in the political sense of the term,' according to the highest authorities upon the subject, and the true history of these States, his own imaginary sophism vanishes as a fog before the rays of the sun, and leaves in its place, clearly apparent, a great truth which can never be successfully assailed by the most skilfully applied subtleties of logic.

"Further on, in the same argument, [Lincoln] says:

'The principle itself [the Right of Secession] is one of disintegration, and upon which no Government can possibly endure. If all the States, save one, should assert the power to drive that one out of the Union, it is presumed, the whole class of Seceder Politicians would at once deny the power, and denounce the act as the greatest outrage upon State rights. But suppose that precisely the same act, instead of being called, "driving the one out," should be called the "seceding of the others from that one," it would be exactly what the Seceders claim to do,' etc.

"In this he was slightly mistaken. It was not exactly what the Seceders claimed to do. The difference between the cases is the difference between any given number of men getting rid of another one, by driving that one out of a house while they retain it; and the same men, instead of driving the one out, quitting it themselves, aud leaving it to him alone. There is a very marked difference in principle between the two cases."[243]

☞ "But, however logical Mr. Lincoln may have deemed this view of the question, as showing the absurdity of the position of the 'Seceder Politicians,' in rightfully breaking up the Union, under the Constitution, is it not strange that it did not occur to him that this was exactly in principle, what eleven of the original thirteen States did towards two, in breaking up that Union to which all stood pledged in plighted faith, that it should be perpetual? *If eleven States, in 1788, rightfully seceded or withdrew from the Confederation of 1778, which was so declared, 'to be perpetual,' and entered into the new Union, under the present Constitution, leaving North Carolina and Rhode Island out, as they did, why could not the same eleven, or any other eleven, in 1861, just as rightfully withdraw from the Union of 1788, which was not declared to be perpetual? If there was no treason or rebellion in the first 'Secession movement,' it seems to me, that he ought to have seen there could not be in the second, which was based on the same identical principle.* [Emphasis added L.S.]

"Nor is this principle of a Union of States, formed and held together by a voluntary assent, one of 'disintegration upon which no Government can endure.' Upon it many Governments, as we have seen, have been formed, which did endure, and continued to grow and prosper until this principle was departed from by them. It is the principle of real strength as well as aggregation upon which our Government endured and increased in the number of States, from eleven to thirty-three, and prospered as no other Government ever did, for sixty years, under the teachings of Mr. [Thomas] Jefferson! All such Governments will endure and increase by aggregation and accession, and not go to pieces by disintegration or Secession, so long as the cohesive principle of mutual interests and *reciprocal advantages binds the States together. No Federal Government ought to endure or last any longer than this principle is recognized. Mutual interests and reciprocal advantages are the main objects aimed at in the formation of all such Governments. These are the ends for which they are created. It was for these reasons, and to secure these objects, that the original joint Declaration of Independence was made by the several States of our Union. It is true, their joint Declaration was not made with a view of the States being severally independent of each other, but with the view that, by joint and Federal action, all would be better enabled to achieve, establish, and secure, permanently, the Sovereignty of each severally. Continued union on the same principles was doubtlessly expected and desired. But the right of each to its own Sovereignty and Independence was what was achieved.* This is the whole of that matter, and with this notice we will leave Mr. Lincoln's refutation of his fancied sophism on which the Right of Secession is based. [Emphasis added L.S.]

"In the same message he was as pointed against the 'armed neutrality' doctrine of the Union men of Kentucky and other Border States, as he was against the doctrine of the Seceders. 'That,' said he, 'carried out would be disunion completed.' Indeed, *the whole message was based upon principles and doctrines which tend inevitably to Centralized Despotism!*"²⁴⁴ [Emphasis added L.S.]

Victorian Liberals—who like Liberals, socialists, dictators, and racists today—worshipped Lincoln, were shocked to hear Stephens insinuate that America's sixteenth president was a "public usurper who disregarded his oath, was wanting in humanity, was insincere, and cruel," and "whose main object was the overthrow of our Free Institutions, and the establishment of a Despotism in their stead."²⁴⁵ Was he not "eminently distinguished for his frankness, good nature and general kindness of heart"? they asked. To this Stephens replied:

☞ "So were many men who have figured in history, and who have brought the greatest sufferings and miseries upon mankind. [French Revolutionary leaders Georges J.] Danton and [Maximilien de] Robespierre, the bloodiest monsters in the form of men we read of in history, were distinguished for the same qualities. They both had the personal esteem as well as the strong attachment of some of the best men in France, who were utterly opposed to their public acts and policy.

". . . This is the character we have of them. Even Danton was distinguished for ' his frankness' and 'his good nature.' It is said of him, that in private life he was capable 'of melting into tenderness,' and 'of spreading the kindly virtues around him as soft, as lucent, and as penetrating as the light of morning.' 'Nature seemed to pervade him in all her forms, from the woman's heart sleeping in his bosom, to the electric fire of genius which played like a glory around his head,' etc. Such were some of the private virtues of the man, who, in his official character at the head of the Department of Justice, thanked the assassins who committed the horrible massacres of September, 1792, when the streets of Paris are said to have run with blood! It is true, he quieted his conscience by a species of 'casuistry' [dishonest reasoning] which has been styled 'atrocious.' He did not have the face to pretend that these inhuman deeds were either right or just, and hence, in thanking the infamous perpetrators of them, he said he did it 'not as Minister of Justice, but as Minister of the Revolution!'

"Of Robespierre it is said that he was devotedly attached to the principles of liberty. 'He was deeply read in the history of the Grecian and Roman Republics,' and had a high 'admiration for the examples set by the free States and heroes of antiquity.' 'These were the models according to which he had formed the ideal of a State.' 'Trial by jury, the enfranchisement of the slaves, the liberty of the press, the abolition of capital punishment were among the special subjects advocated by him.' These were certainly high and admirable qualities, to say nothing of his many other private virtues. This, however, is the man who in power made such bloody use of the guillotine, without allowing his victims any hearing whatever, not even by a military commission, much less a jury; and for which his name has been associated with everything cruel, inhuman, and execrable! But, in these acts, it is said, he was influenced by 'a sense of justice' which was 'incorruptible in its nature, but statue-like in its frigid insensibility.'

"A man may possess many amiable qualities in private life—many estimable virtues and excellencies of character, and yet in official position commit errors involving not only most unjustifiable usurpations of power, but such as rise to high crimes against society and against humanity. This, too, may be done most conscientiously and with the best intentions. This, at least, is my opinion on that subject. The history of the world abounds with apt instances for illustration. Mr. Lincoln, you say, was kind-hearted. In this, I fully agree. No man I ever knew was more so, but the same was true of Julius Caesar. *All you have said of Mr. Lincoln's good qualities, and a great deal more on the same line, may be truly said of Caesar. He was certainly esteemed by many of the best men of his day for some of the highest qualities which dignify and ennoble human nature. He was a thorough scholar, a profound philosopher, an accomplished orator, and one of the most gifted, as well as polished writers of the age, in which he lived. No man ever had more devoted personal friends, and justly so, too, than he had. And yet, notwithstanding all these distinguishing, amiable and high qualities of his private character, he is by the general consent of mankind looked upon as the destroyer of the liberties of Rome!* [Emphasis added, L.S.]

"The case of Caesar illustrates to some extent my view both of the private character of Mr. Lincoln, and of his public acts. In what I have said of him, I have been speaking only of his official acts—of their immediate effects and ultimate tendencies. I do not think that he intended to overthrow the Institutions of the country. I do not think he understood them or the tendencies of his acts upon them. The Union with him in sentiment, rose to the sublimity of a religious mysticism; while his ideas of its structure and formation in logic, rested upon nothing but the subtleties of a sophism! His many private virtues and excellencies of head and heart, I did esteem. Many of them had my admiration. In nothing I have said, or may say, was it, or will it be my intention to detract from these. In all such cases in estimating character, we must discriminate between the man in private life, and the man in public office. The two spheres somehow, and strangely enough too, appear to be totally different, and men in them, respectively, usually seem to be prompted and governed by motives totally different. Power generally seems to change and transform the characters of those invested with it. Hence, the great necessity for 'those chains' in the Constitution, to bind all Rulers and men in authority, spoken of by Mr. [Thomas] Jefferson.

"[The ancient Aramean king] Hazael, for all we know, may have been highly distinguished, and perhaps beloved, by the virtuous and good of his acquaintance for many excellent traits of character in private life. He was, unquestionably, an eminently representative man. From his knowledge of himself in the lower, he seemed to have not the slightest conception of what he would or could be induced to do when raised to the higher official sphere! No more than a man in this life can conceive of the impulses by which he will be governed in the life hereafter! When he was told by Elisha, the Prophet, that Benhadad, the King of Syria, would surely die, and that he would be elevated to the throne in his stead; and when he was further told of 'the evil' he would do, and the barbarous iniquities he would commit, in this, to him, new sphere, he was so shocked at the announcement that he exclaimed, 'But what, is thy servant a dog, that he should do this great thing?'

"So, perhaps it would have been with Mr. Lincoln, if a like prophetic disclosure had been made to him. *If, for instance, on the evening of his nomination at Chicago, when the two images of himself were presented in his mirror at Springfield, which ever afterwards so haunted him, it had been told to him, that the 'bright' one of these images was but the true likeness of himself in the sphere of private life, and the other—pale, and 'statue-like in its frigid insensibility' to all the gentle promptings of his generous heart—was the future image of himself in that official sphere to which he was soon to be elevated: if the curtain of the future had been further raised, and 'Death upon his pale horse' had been seen doing his tragical work on the rugged grounds of Manassas, at Oak Hill, at Corinth, on the battle fields around Richmond—at Sharpsburg, Fredericksburg, Murfreesboro, Chancellorsville, Gettysburg, Vicksburg, and Chickamauga:*

if the scenes of slaughter and carnage in the Wilderness, at Cold Harbor and Atlanta had been exhibited: if the wails of horror that went up from the crater of the volcanic mine at Petersburg had been heard, even at a distance, commingling with like cries from the dying in the Prisons of Camp Douglas, Rock Island, and Elmira as well as Salisbury and Andersonville, and others of less note; if the devastations in the valley of Virginia by [Philip H.] Sheridan, and the conflagrations and desolations by [Yankee General William T.] Sherman, through Georgia and the two Carolinas, especially at Columbia, had passed in grand panorama before his vision, reflected from that mirror, and he had been then and there told by some inspired prophet, that all these terrible scenes—these sufferings and woes of millions—these convulsive throes of this our 'Nation of Nations' in the days of their agony—would soon be the results of his own acts in his official character, in that higher sphere to which he was to be elevated—represented by the second image thus reflected—he would doubtless have heard the announcement with no little horror—he would indeed have been 'unnerved,' and would have exclaimed, in language of equal surprise and indignation, with that of Hazael to Elisha! He would have believed, and would have said, with all the emphasis he could have commanded, that it was impossible for him to do such things! [Emphasis added, L.S.]

"We are informed, that notwithstanding all Hazael's indignation, yet he did everything which was told to him that he would do; and it is now our sad task to review all those things in the picture just sketched, with many more of a like character, which did result from the public acts of Mr. Lincoln, who, in private life, was truly distinguished for so many estimable virtues."[246]

Stephens' Lincolnite friends countered his comments, asking: "How can you say that these horrible scenes of blood and death are chargeable to the acts of Mr. Lincoln? They were the necessary consequences of the acts of those who resisted the execution of the laws. The responsibility of them, in no way or view, rests upon him. Mr. Lincoln's earnest desire was for peace. His whole soul was filled with an overflowing benevolence. All he did was to maintain the Government." To these stunning remarks Stephens replied:

☛ "That is precisely what Hazael did! All he did was to maintain Government over an unwilling people, though in doing it he put hundreds of thousands to slaughter, because they would not submit to be so governed. Not only this, but in the execution of his high purpose thus to maintain Government over that people, he found it necessary to burn their cities, to destroy their defences, to lay waste their lands, and to show no mercy either to children or 'women in travail.' *Just so with Mr. Lincoln. Hazael, I doubt not, was perfectly conscientious in all that he did. I grant the same to Mr. Lincoln.* [Emphasis added, L.S.]

"But, I ask, what is there about the maintenance of Government, of any sort, which justifies such conduct? Are not Governments made for the security and peace of the people, and not the people for the maintenance of Governments which gives them neither? What other end or object has any just Government, or one that deserves to be maintained, but to afford protection and security to all those for whom it is instituted? The resistance [the Liberals] . . . speak of, was to his acts, and the measures adopted to maintain Government. But for his acts, and these measures thus to maintain Government, this resistance, and the consequences, would not have taken place. These occurrences, therefore, are not to be attributed to the resistance, but to his acts. The resistance itself was but a consequence of his acts. Had he not acted as he did, there would have been no resistance, and none of these scenes and consequences would have followed. This [my Liberal friends] . . . must admit."[247] [Emphasis added, L.S.]

The Liberals of Stephens' day honestly believed that had Lincoln not invaded the South, the U.S. government would have "gone to pieces" and "general anarchy would have ensued, with burnings, slaughters, and butcheries, ad libitum [Latin: 'at one's pleasure']." Stephens was quick to respond to such balderdash:

☛ "Not quite so fast. Let us see. *You say general anarchy would have ensued. How so? Where would it have commenced and how? Was not everything moving on peacefully and quietly throughout the Confederate States? Were there any indications of anarchy there? Were not the changes in their new Constitution all of a conservative character? Did this furnish any evidence of a tendency to anarchy on their part? How was it in the Northern States? What was there to introduce anarchy there? You say no Government would have been left. How so, I again inquire? Would not the Federal Government of all the States that saw fit to remain in the Union as it then stood, have been left? Was there any hostile resistance or opposition to that? There certainly was not, nor was any designed.* [Emphasis added, L.S.]

"But let us see further: *suppose the entire Government—the entire Conventional Federal Government, I mean—had gone to pieces, gone into dissolution temporarily or permanently, who would have been injured even by that? Would anybody have lost anything by it except the officeholders under it? and would any injury have occurred to them in such a catastrophe, further than the loss of their honors and salaries? Would not all the State Governments at the North have remained intact, clothed with all the powers of inherent Sovereignty, to maintain order and law throughout their respective limits, just as they did before the Union was formed? Is it not to the State Governments, under our system, we look for all necessary protection and security against the approaches of anarchy? Had the General Government any right to interfere in any way to prevent anarchy, or even an insurrection in a State, except at the request of the regularly constituted authorities of that State? Was not this Government made by the States, and for their own several well-being? In the event, therefore, of a total dissolution of the Federal Government—in the event that all the Northern States had quit it as well as the Southern, who would have been hurt by it? Whence would have come the anarchy [the Liberals] . . . speak of, with its burnings, slaughters, and butcheries? Would not the*

Southern States have had what the Federal Government was instituted to secure—peace and prosperity, with domestic tranquillity? If not, whose business was it but their own? Would not the Northern States have had the same? If not, whose fault would it have been but their own? What was the Government or the Union made for, but the good, the peace, the prosperity, and the happiness of all the States? And who were the proper judges of the best interests of the people of all the States? Were they the officers of the Federal Government, or the States who made it? If the Northern manufacturing and commercial States had been indirectly injured by the withdrawal of the Southern States, to the extent of the benefits of the Union to them secured by their association under it, who could be justly subject to blame for this loss but themselves, in their breach of the Compact which was the bond of that Union, which had secured these advantages to them?"[248] [Emphasis added, L.S.]

The members of the Lincoln Church defended the president's illegal and barbaric actions, asking: "But what was to become of the public debt? Would not the Government creditors have sustained loss by such a felo de se *[Latin: 'felon of himself']*? Who would have paid that? What would have become of all the public property?" Stephens replied:

☞ "There would have been no *felo de se* in the case. All the States would have continued to live either separately or in a new Confederation or Confederations, as the case might have been. The public debt would have been paid by these living and responsible States. The States were the real debtors. *The public debt was not the debt of the officers of the Federal Government, or of that Government apart from the States. It was the debt of the States. It was the debt of the United States contracted by them in Congress assembled through their official agents. The public securities showed upon their face that the obligation to meet them rested upon the States jointly, not upon the Government or its official agents.* All the States who were joined or united at the time of the contract of any debt, so made by them jointly, would have been bound to pay their pro rata amount of it. All the States would likewise have been entitled to their pro rata share of the public property. If any of them had refused, or failed to pay their just part of the public debt or liabilities, then would have arisen a just cause on the part of the others to make them do it by force, if necessary! But they had no right to resort to such measures, for such an object, in anticipation of such a result, much less had the official agent of these States this right. This is the solution to that problem. But *the Confederate States had, in advance offered to make provision for their portion of the public debt and all joint liabilities. No one doubted their ability and perfect willingness promptly to comply with their offer.* [Emphasis added, L.S.]

"There was, therefore, no necessity for Mr. Lincoln to assume unconstitutional power to maintain the Government for the purpose of paying the public debt. No such act is specified amongst the duties of the President as set forth in the Constitution. If he *assumed the power he did, for such purposes, it was clearly an usurpation.* [Emphasis added, L.S.]

"In what I say of Mr. Lincoln, I repeat, I speak only of his public acts. With his private character I have nothing to do, nor with those personal qualities of which [my Liberal friends speak]. . . . I do not doubt, as I have said, his thorough conscientiousness in all he did. It is quite probable when he surveyed the whole ground, and beheld the scenes to which I have alluded, that he took none of the responsibility of them upon himself. He may have indulged in 'a casuistry' after the sort of that indulged by [Georges J.] Danton. It may be that he thought that he was not the 'Minister of Justice' in these things, but the 'Preserver of the Union.' He may even have come to the conclusion, as I think not improbable, that he was an instrument specially raised up by Providence to enfranchise the Black race in the Southern States—[Note: as Lincoln was an atheist who stalled emancipation and blocked black suffrage throughout his entire life, Stephens' theory cannot be true. L.S.]—an object so dear to the hearts of so many of his Party, as it was so dear to the heart of Robespierre, towards a like population in other parts of the world. All this may be possible, but his acts like Robespierre's, and the acts of all men of like character, belong to history, and with them as such only I now deal. They must, like the acts of all public men, be held up as beacons to warn the present and future generations."[249]

☞ ". . . let us return to the Federal [U.S.] Congress. Neither House of this assemblage of the States which remained in the Union, under the Constitution of 1787, granted Mr. Lincoln the indemnity that he supposed would be so readily accorded, but both, without any positive censure, responded with alacrity to his call for men and means. Instead of 400,000 men, they provided for raising and putting in the field 525,000, and appropriated all necessary amounts of money for equipping this immense force, as well as for fitting out a most formidable Navy. One hundred and thirty-seven additional vessels, suitable for war purposes, were immediately purchased, and fifty-two iron clad steamers, after the most improved models, were ordered to be constructed, besides a number of 'steam floating batteries,' which was an entirely new system of naval warfare. This branch of their service was put upon a footing to compete with any in the world. This Congress, also, by a strange stretch of power, recognized the disaffected counties of Northwestern Virginia as the State of Virginia [i.e., the new illegally formed state of West Virginia], and admitted Senators and Members under a Government set up there, claiming to be the legitimate Government of the State of Virginia.

"The most important measure, however, adopted at this session of that

[U.S.] Congress, in many respects, in that view of the war which we are taking, was a joint resolution which passed both Houses with great unanimity, setting forth the nature and character of the war as they held it to be, and the declaration of the objects for which it was waged. This Resolution was the declaration, not only of the causes of the war in their view, but also the ends for which it was to be prosecuted on their part. It is upon the principles of this Resolution, the whole war must be considered on their side. Hence its great importance in our present view of the conduct of the war and its ultimate results. For this reason, it now requires special notice, and is in these words:

> [Stephens quoting the U.S. Congress:] Re-solved, That the present deplorable civil war has been forced upon the country by the Dis-Unionists of the Southern States now in revolt against the Constitutional Government and in arms around the Capital; that in this National emergency Congress, banishing all feeling of mere passion or resentment, will recollect only its duty to the whole country; that this war is not prosecuted upon our part in any spirit of oppression, nor for any purpose of conquest or subjugation, nor for the purpose of overthrowing or interfering with the rights or established Institutions of those States, but to defend and maintain the supremacy of the Constitution and all laws made in pursuance thereof, and to preserve the Union, with all the dignity, equality, and rights of the several States unimpaired; that as soon as these objects are accomplished the war ought to cease.

"This Resolution was introduced into the Senate, by Mr. Andrew Johnson, of Tennessee. He was the only Southern Senator who retained his seat in that Body after the Secession of his State. The Resolution, therefore, was the more remarkable in view of the source from which it came. It was clearly based upon the principle, that a Federal Union of Sovereign States may be maintained and preserved by force. For, whatever may have been the opinion of others, Mr. Johnson certainly held the United States to be a Union of Sovereign States. He had voted on the 24th of May, 1860, for the first of the Resolutions then offered by Mr. [Jefferson] Davis . . . affirming this fact.

"About the same time that this Resolution was introduced, he also made a speech upon the general subject of the war, as well as upon Mr. Lincoln's Proclamations referred to, which should be considered in connection with this Resolution. This speech was one of the most notable, as it certainly was one of the most effective, ever delivered by any man on any occasion. I know of no instance in history where one speech effected such results, immediate and remote, as this one did. The Resolution, referred to, and this speech especially, gave the war a vigor and real life it had not before, and never would have had without them, on the Northern side. In the speech, Mr. Johnson fully endorsed the doctrines, principles, and acts of Mr. Lincoln, up to this time, not, however, upon Constitutional grounds, but upon the maxims of public necessity. In it he reviewed at length the denunciations of the usurpations of Mr. Lincoln in the matters I have referred to, which had been made by Senators some days before, when the Indemnity Resolution was up for consideration. In the debate on that Resolution, Mr. [John C.] Breckinridge [of Kentucky], who had not yet resigned his seat in that Body, insisted that

> 'Congress by a joint resolution, had no more right to make valid a violation of the Constitution and the laws by the President [of the U.S.], than the President [Lincoln] would have by an entry upon the Executive Journal to make valid a usurpation of the Executive power by the Legislative Department. Congress had no more right to make valid an unconstitutional act of the President, than the President would have to make valid an act of the Supreme Court of the United States encroaching upon Executive power; or, than the Supreme Court would have the right to make valid an act of the Executive encroaching upon the Judicial power.
>
> '. . . Here in Washington, in Kentucky, in Missouri, everywhere where the authority of the President extends, in his discretion he will feel himself warranted, by the action of Congress upon this Resolution, to subordinate the civil to the military power; to imprison citizens without warrant of law; to suspend the writ of *Habeas Corpus*; to establish martial law; to make seizures and searches without warrant; to suppress the press; to do all those acts which rest in the will and hi the authority of a military commander. *In my judgment, Sir, if we pass it, we are upon the eve of putting, so far as we can, in the hands of the President of the United States the power of a Dictator.* [Emphasis added, L.S.]
>
> '. . . The pregnant question, Mr. President [of the Senate], for us to decide is, whether the Constitution is to be respected in this struggle; whether we are to be called upon to follow the flag over the ruins of the Constitution? *Without questioning the motives of any, I believe that the whole tendency of the present proceedings [in the North] is to establish a Government without limitation of powers, and to change radically our frame and character of Government.* [Emphasis added, L.S.]
>
> '. . . *I deny this doctrine of necessity. I deny that the President of the United States may violate the Constitution upon the ground of necessity. The doctrine is utterly subversive of the Constitution; it is utterly subversive of all written limitations of Government; and it substitutes, especially where you make him the ultimate judge of that necessity, and his decision not to be appealed from, the will of one man for a written Constitution. Mr. President, the Government of the United States which draws its life from the Constitution, and which was made by that Instrument, does not rest, as does the Constitution of many other countries, upon usage or upon implied consent. It rests upon express written consent. The Government of the United States may exercise such powers, and such only, as are given in this written form of Government and bond which unites the States; none others. The people of the States conferred upon this agent*

of theirs, just such powers as they deemed necessary, and no more; all others they retained. That Constitution, was made for all contingencies; for peace and for war. They conferred all the powers they deemed necessary, and more cannot be assumed, to carry on the Government. They intended to provide for all contingencies that they thought ought to be provided for, and they retained to the States all the powers not granted by the Instrument. If in any instance it may be supposed that the powers conferred are not sufficient, still none others were granted, and none others can be exercised. Will this be denied, Sir?' [Emphasis added, L.S.]

"It was not denied by Mr. [Andrew] Johnson, in his review of this speech, nor by any other Senator, that any power, not delegated in the Constitution, could be rightfully exercised, except upon the plea of necessity. It was, strangely enough, claimed that power not delegated, might be rightfully exercised under this plea. This was the only answer attempted to be made by him, or any one, to Mr. Breckinridge's position on the Constitutional question. But, in his reply to the argument that the usurpation of undelegated power, under the plea of necessity, would, upon principle, lead ultimately and inevitably to the overthrow of State Institutions, and the establishment of a consolidated Despotism, Mr. Johnson insisted, with great earnestness and zeal, that such would not be the consequences. The ultimate result, he maintained, would be nothing but the overthrow of the Rebellion, and the suppression of the insurrection, leaving all the States with all their rights, dignity, and equality, as set forth in his Resolution. Amongst other things of similar import, [Johnson] . . . asserted:

> 'I know it has been said that the object of this war is to make war on Southern Institutions. I have been in free States and I have been in slave States; and I thank God that, so far as I have seen, there has been one universal disclaimer of any such purpose. It is a war upon no section; it is a war upon no peculiar Institution; but it is a war for the integrity of the Government, for the Constitution and the supremacy of the laws. That is what the Nation understands by it.'

"As to the effect of principles, and the ultimate results of temporary usurpations, as he viewed them—justifiable, as a means to accomplish the great object with him, as it was with Mr. Lincoln, the preservation of an ideal Union—he seems to have been governed far more by impulse than by reason. That the ultimate result would be as he desired it, and not as apprehended by those who took the contrary view, he would not permit himself to doubt, though he confessed that he did not see his way very clearly. This is apparent from the following extract from the same speech [by Andrew Johnson]:

'Yes, we must triumph. Though sometimes I cannot see my way clear in matters of this kind, as in matters of religion, when my facts give out, when my reason fails me, I draw largely upon my faith. My faith is strong based on the eternal principles of right, that a thing so monstrously wrong as this rebellion cannot triumph. Can we submit to it? Is the Senate, are the American people, prepared to give up the graves of [George] Washington and [Andrew] Jackson, to be encircled and governed and controlled by a combination of traitors and rebels? I say, let the battle go on—it is freedom's cause—until the Stars and Stripes (God bless them!) shall again be unfurled upon every cross-road, and from every housetop, throughout the Confederacy, North and South. Let the Union be re-instated; let the law be enforced; let the Constitution be supreme.'

"This speech, throughout, was characterized by extraordinary fervor and eloquence, and, in my judgment, did more to strengthen and arouse the war passions of the people at the North than everything else combined. As I have said, the speech had a special power and influence springing from the very source from which it emanated. The author stood solitary and alone—isolated from every public man throughout the Southern States, and from nearly every public man throughout the Northern States attached to the same political Party to which he belonged, upon the questions involved. [Andrew Johnson] . . . had been brought up in the State Rights Jeffersonian School. *In this very speech, he styled the Union a 'Confederacy.'* In the late Presidential election, he had supported the ticket headed by Breckinridge and [Joseph] Lane, upon the new Territorial plank incorporated into the Platform. This gave potency to his words and position, not only in Tennessee, but throughout the Northern States. [Emphasis added, L.S.]

"I do not doubt [Johnson's] . . . perfect honesty and sincerity in everything that he said, but sentiment and declamation, however sincere, high and lofty, form a very small part of true statesmanship. The errors in principle, as well as policy, both in the speech and in the resolution referred to, he may, perhaps, live to see himself, if he has not already lived to see and fully realize them. He now feels constrained to denounce those who acted with him in departing from the Constitution at that time, on his maxims of public necessity, (and whose avowed disloyalty to the Constitution was the cause of Secession,) in terms quite as broad and as harsh as those which he then used against the Secessionists. He now applies to his allies in the beginning of the war, the epithet of 'traitors' with as much zeal, sincerity, and earnestness, as he then applied it to the disunionists; while in his present efforts to maintain his ideal State Rights, after ignoring the Sovereignty of the States, upon which alone all their Rights depend, he in turn is denounced back by them as a traitor of even blacker dye than any of the then Rebels, so-called! [Editor's note: It is now 1868, midway through 'Reconstruction'.] *The war is over, but the Union is not re-instated; the several members of it are not restored to their proper places with all their dignity, equality, and rights unimpaired! The 'Stars and Stripes' float as he hoped to see them, but the Constitution is not supreme! It is not now regarded by the others any more than it was then regarded by them as well as himself. The same public necessity which in his opinion justified usurpation in the first instance, in their opinion continues still to justify it, and to require them to continue to act 'outside of the Constitution;' and with them, this public necessity will continue to exist, until all ends in Despotism, or until they are removed from power by the people, and others are put in their places, who will administer the Government not upon maxims, but strictly in accordance with the Constitution upon its true Federal principles. It is not improbable if Mr. Lincoln had lived, he would have found himself in the same situation. Danton became a victim of the Monster Revolution, of which he conceived himself to be the special Minister. Robespierre also fell by the same bloody instrument which he had so conscientiously, and with such 'incorruptible justice,' according to his mode of thinking, so frequently and remorselessly applied to others.* But enough upon this subject for the present.[250] [Emphasis added, L.S.]

☞ "We will now turn our attention to events transpiring elsewhere. The Confederate Congress, we have seen, had adjourned to meet in Richmond, the 20th of July. Full Delegations were sent up to this Session of this Congress, from Virginia, North Carolina and Tennessee. The Delegation of Virginia consisted of the following members: Ex-President John Tyler, William Ballard Preston, Robert M. T. Hunter, James A. Seddon, William H. Macfarland, Roger A. Pryor, Thomas S. Bocock, William C. Rives, Robert E. Scott, James M. Mason, J. W. Brockenbrough, Charles W. Russell, Robert Johnson, Waller R. Staples and Walter Preston. The Delegation from North Carolina consisted of George Davis, William W. Avery, William N. H. Smith, Thomas Ruffin, Thomas D. McDowell, Abram W. Venable, John M. Morehead, Robert C. Puryear, Burton Craige and Andrew J. Davidson. The Delegation of Tennessee consisted of W. H. De Witt, Robert L. Caruthers, James H. Thomas, George W. Jones, John F. House, John D. C. Atkins and David M. Currin.

"There was in these new delegations, as appears from their names, (several of whom stood amongst the most distinguished men in the whole country at the time,) a considerable accession of talent to that body; but there was, at the same time, a considerable loss in this particular. Quite a number of the ablest of the members composing this Congress at Montgomery, had entered the military service. It is true that only a very few of them resigned their seats; but the counsels of those who did not, were lost to a considerable extent, by their absence on their duties in the field. Georgia alone had lost largely in this respect. Howell Cobb, the President, was commanding a Regiment. He afterwards became a Major-General. Francis S. Bartow was also in command of a Regiment. While Thomas R. R. Cobb was at the head of his Legion. [Robert A.] Toombs had quit the Department of State, and had taken the commission of Brigadier-General in the Provisional Army. [Louis T.] Wigfall, of Texas, was also at the head of a Brigade. [J. Patton] Anderson, of Florida, had resigned his seat and gone into the Army soon after the organization of the Government. G. T. Ward, who filled his place, soon after raised a Regiment himself. A great deal of the talent of other States had likewise sought Military instead of Civic service at this time. [Thomas L.] Clingman, of North Carolina, for instance, took a command in the Army. So did James L. Orr, Wade Hampton, James Chesnut, Jr., and Milledge L. Bonham, of South Carolina; Felix K. Zollicoffer, of Tennessee; and John B. Floyd and Henry A. Wise, of Virginia—to say nothing of others.

"In the meantime, however, before this meeting of the Confederate Congress, extensive military movements had commenced. So soon as it was apparent to the [U.S.] authorities at Washington, from the expression of public sentiment in its most authoritative channels, that the people of Virginia would [be] at the polls, to be opened on the 23rd of May, [in order to] ratify the Ordinance of Secession by an overwhelming majority, arrangements were made, by a skilful disposition of [Yankee] forces, to crush her immediately, by assaults from several points at once. General [Jacob D.] Cox was to move from Guyaridotte, General [George B.] McClellan from Wheeling, General [Irvin] McDowell from Washington, and General [Benjamin F.] Butler from Fortress Monroe [all Union officers]. These movements were all made at nearly the same time, in the latter part of May. When the Confederate Congress assembled on the 20th of July, therefore, the affairs at Barboursville, Scarrytown, Grafton, Philippi, Laurel Hill, Cheat River, Alexandria, and Big Bethel, had all transpired. In all these operations the result had been favorable to the Confederates, except those under the direction of General McClellan. The signal victory of [Confederate officer] Daniel H. Hill at Big Bethel, however, on the 9th of June, he having then only the commission of Colonel, more than compensated for these in its moral effect. But there were, on the 20th of July, at least forty thousand Federal soldiers in various parts of Northwestern Virginia, to overawe the majority of the people, and sustain the minority, who were attempting to overthrow the rightful Government of the State. The manner in which these troops executed the purposes for which they were designed, as well as the general conduct of the war by the Federals, up to this period, may be judged of from what Mr.[Jefferson] Davis said upon the subject in his Message to the Confederate Congress, upon their assembling at Richmond. Here is on extract from that Message:

'In this war, rapine [by the Yankee] is the rule; private houses, in beautiful rural retreats, are bombarded and burnt; grain crops in the field are consumed by the torch, and, when the torch is not convenient, careful labor is bestowed to render complete the destruction of every article of use or ornament remaining in private dwellings, after their inhabitants have fled from the outrages of brute soldiery. In 1781 Great Britain when invading the revolted Colonies, took possession of every district and county near Fortress Monroe, now occupied by the troops of the United States. The houses then inhabited by the people, after being respected and protected by avowed invaders, are now pillaged and destroyed by men who pretend that Virginians are their fellow-citizens. Mankind will shudder at the tales of the outrages committed on defenceless families by soldiers of the United States, now invading our homes; yet these outrages are prompted by inflamed passions and the madness of intoxication. But who shall depict the horror they entertain for the cool and deliberate malignancy which, under the pretext of suppressing insurrection, (said by themselves to be upheld by a minority only of our people,) makes special war on the sick, including children and women, by carefully devised measures to prevent them from obtaining the medicines necessary for their cure. The sacred claims of humanity, respected even during the fury of actual battle, by careful diversion of attack from hospitals containing wounded enemies, are outraged in cold blood by a Government and people that pretend to desire a continuance of fraternal connections. All these outrages must remain unavenged [except] by the universal reprehension of mankind. In all cases where the actual perpetrators of the wrongs escape capture, they admit of no retaliation. The humanity of our people would shrink instinctively from the bare idea of urging a like war upon the sick, the women, and the children of an enemy. But there are other savage practices which have been resorted to by the Government of the United States, which do admit of repression by retaliation, and I have been driven to the necessity of enforcing the repression. The prisoners of war taken by the enemy on board the armed schooner *Savannah*, sailing under our commission, were, as I was credibly advised, treated like common felons, put in irons, confined in a jail usually appropriated to criminals of the worst dye, and threatened with punishment as such. I had made application for the exchange of these prisoners to the commanding officer of the enemy's squadron off Charleston, but that officer had already sent the prisoners to New York when application was made. I therefore deemed it my duty to renew the proposal for the exchange to the Constitutional Commander-in-Chief of the Army and Navy of the United States, the only officer having control of the prisoners. To this end, I dispatched an officer to him under a flag of truce, and, in making the proposal, I informed President Lincoln of my resolute purpose to check all barbarities on prisoners of war, by such severity of retaliation on prisoners held by us as should secure the abandonment of the practice. This communication was received and read by an officer in command of the United States forces, and a message was brought from him by the bearer of my communication, that a reply would be returned by President Lincoln as soon as possible. I earnestly hope this promised reply (which has not yet been received,) will convey the assurance that Prisoners of War will be treated, in this unhappy contest, with that regard for humanity, which has made such conspicuous progress in the conduct of modern warfare. As measures of precaution, however, and until this promised reply is received, I still retain in close custody some officers captured from the enemy, whom it had been my pleasure previously to set at large on Parole, and whose fate must necessarily depend on that of prisoners held by the enemy. I append a copy of my communication to the President and Commander-in-Chief of the Army and Navy of the United States, and of the report of the officer charged to deliver my communication. [Emphasis added, L.S.]

'There are some other passages in the remarkable paper to which I have directed your attention, having reference to the peculiar relations which exist between this Government and the States usually termed Border Slave States, which cannot properly be withheld from notice. The hearts of our people are animated by sentiments towards the inhabitants of these States, which found expression in your enactment refusing to consider them enemies, or authorize hostilities against them. That a very large portion of the people of these States regard us as brethren; that, if unrestrained by the actual presence of large armies, subversion of civil authority, and declaration of martial law, some of them, at least, would joyfully unite with us; that they are, with almost entire unanimity, opposed to the prosecution of the war waged against us, are facts of which daily recurring events fully warrant the assertion that the President of the United States [Lincoln] refuses to recognize in these our late sister States, the right of refraining from attack upon us, and justifies his refusal by the assertion that the States have no other power than that reserved to them in the Union by the Constitution. Now, this view of the Constitutional relations between the States and the General Government is a fitting introduction to another assertion of the Message, that the Executive possesses power of suspending the writ of *Habeas Corpus*, and of delegating that power to military Commanders at their discretion. And both these propositions claim a respect equal to that which is felt for the additional statement of opinion in the same paper, that it is proper, in order to execute the laws, that some single law, made in such extreme tenderness of citizens' liberty that practically it relieves more of the guilty than the innocent, should to a very limited extent be violated. *We may well rejoice that we have forever severed our connection with a Government that thus tramples on all principles of constitutional liberty, and with a people in whose presence such avowals could be hazarded.*' [Emphasis added, L.S.]

"But we must now take a brief notice of more exciting scenes, with their results."[251]

☛ "The military movements before referred to, were only preliminary to one on a much grander scale. The [U.S.] rapine, pillage, and outrages in Northwestern Virginia, the massacres at Fort Jackson, in Missouri, and the thunders at Big Bethel, Laurel Hill, and Philippi, were only the storm-notes of the coming tempest. By the 1st of July, the Federals had an available force in the field, at various points, ready for duty, of upwards of 300,000 men.

"Over 60,000 of these were concentrated at or near Washington, constituting a column which was expected to make 'short and decisive work' of the Confederates, by an immediate onward march to Richmond, then the 'Headquarters of the Rebellion.' This 'Grand Army' was organized under the direction and inspection of [U.S.] General [Winfield] Scott himself, the Commander-in-Chief. It consisted of nearly sixty regiments, besides several battalions and other organizations, arranged into numerous brigades, and five great divisions. The command of the whole, in the field, however, was assigned to [U.S.] Major-General Irvin McDowell, an officer of great skill and ability. All being ready, this huge command—the largest and best equipped ever before seen in America, perhaps—was put in motion for its intended destination and purpose, on the 16th of July; four days before the time fixed for the meeting of the Confederate Congress in Richmond. The progress of its march, with its immense and unwieldy trains, was slow. On the 18th, the out-posts of the Confederate forces, under the command of General [Pierre G. T.] Beauregard, were encountered at Bull Run, a small stream a few miles from Manassas. Here a considerable engagement ensued, which stopped McDowell for two days. The forces under General Beauregard amounted in all to little, if any, over 20,000 men. Affairs were now exceedingly critical.

"[Confederate] General Joseph E. Johnston, who had an army of about eight thousand men, in the valley of the Shenandoah, beyond the mountains of the Blue Ridge—was immediately informed, by telegraph from the [C.S.] War Department at Richmond, of the situation; and directed to pursue such course as he might think best under the circumstances. He, by a movement with hardly a parallel in the annals of war, joined [Confederate] General Beauregard with his command, in time to meet and drive back the advancing, threatening and formidable hosts! It was on this occasion that [Johnston] . . . displayed those qualities which so distinguished him throughout the war, and which so endeared him to the soldiers and people of the Confederate States. Of this first great battle, between the opposing sides, which may very properly be noticed here somewhat in detail, I will let him give the account himself. He being the senior in command, the control of all subsequent operations devolved on him, so soon as he reached the field. This was on the evening of Saturday the twentieth. The bloody conflict came off on Sunday the twenty-first. In his rapid movement to Manassas, [General Johnston] . . . had pushed forward at the head of only a part of his forces, leaving the others to follow as quickly as possible. . . .

"The result of this battle between forces so unequal in numbers as well as so unequal in arms, and equipments, is to be attributed mainly to the relative spirit by which the officers and men on the opposing sides were moved and animated in the terrible conflict. Great as was the skill of [C.S.] Generals Johnston and Beauregard, in the disposition and movements of their squadrons, that of [U.S.] General [Irvin] McDowell was also very great. His whole plan of operations, from the beginning to the end, showed military genius of the highest order. The result, therefore, did not depend so much upon the superior skill of the commanders on the Confederate side, as upon the high objects and motives with which they, as well as those under them, were inspired. Johnston and Beauregard were both often in the thickest of the fight, leading in person, with colors in hand, on to the charge, regiments whose officers had fallen! *They, and those who followed them, were moved by a profound sense of the glaring usurpations of Mr. Lincoln*, to which I have referred. They were animated by the sentiments uttered by Mr. [Jefferson] Davis in his message at Montgomery, and repeated the day before at Richmond. *The struggle with them was not for power, dominion, or dynasty—nor for Fame; but to resist palpable and dangerous assumptions of power, and to repel wanton aggressions upon long established rights. They fought for those Principles and Institutions of Self-government which were the priceless heritage of their ancestors!*"[252] [Emphasis added, L.S.]

☛ "On the Federal side, thousands of those who were sent on this expedition, set out, not only with reluctance, but with a consciousness that the whole movement was wrong. They had volunteered for no such purpose. They had tendered their services with the sole view of defending the [U.S.] Capital [at Washington, D.C.]. It was under the impression and belief so extensively created at the North, that the Confederates intended to take Washington, that much the greater portion of this immense army had, with very patriotic motives, rushed to the rescue. Their object was to defend their own rights against an expected assault, and not to make aggression upon the rights of others. *This entrapping them into this movement, when once mustered into service, and under military control, was but a part of the sinister purposes of the Federal authorities, which marked their policy throughout the war. The first false cry was to save the Capital, and after that came a second equally false one to save the Union; while their real object all the time was to use these popular catch words to mislead a confiding people, and under these specious pretexts to cover their ulterior designs of subverting and overturning the whole structure of the Government.* A similar solution is to be given to the subsequent battles, some months afterwards, at Lexington and Oak Hill, near Springfield, in Missouri, under Generals [Sterling] Price and [Benjamin] McCulloch; at Belmont in the same State, under Generals [Leonidas] Polk and

[Gideon J.] Pillow; and at Leesburg, in Virginia, under General [Nathan G.] Evans, in all of which great victories were achieved by the Confederates. To this same spirit, indeed, is mainly to be attributed the fact that *in no field engagement during the war did the Confederates fail of success, where they were not overwhelmed, if not 'annihilated' by numbers.* The most signal successes the Federals met with during the first year of the war were at Fort Hatteras, Port Royal, Fort Henry, and Fort Donelson, where, in addition to a vast superiority of numbers, they had also the advantage of bringing their naval forces most efficiently to their aid. [Emphasis added, L.S.]

"[I also include in these remarks about the battles of the first year of the war [U.S.] General [George H.] Thomas's great victory in Kentucky, at the Battle of Fishing Creek, as . . . [we] Confederates call it. This, it is true, was a very important victory to the Federals, especially as it opened up to them an ingress into East Tennessee; but they had not only a great superiority in numbers, but also in the character of their arms. Besides this, the victory there achieved was owing, in no small degree, to the fall, in the early part of the engagement, of General Felix K. Zollicoffer, who lost his life by incautiously approaching a Federal Regiment, supposing it to be one of his own. This, therefore, is no exception to my general remark."[253]

☞ "But to return to the progress of events at the two Seats of Government, which must necessarily be borne in mind for the purposes of our investigation. After the great defeat of the first 'Onward' to Richmond, it must be recollected, then, that the [Yankee] Authorities at Washington set about the organization of another, and a still greater, army at the same place, and for the same purpose. Hundreds of millions of dollars were appropriated.

"General Winfield Scott, the Commander-in-Chief of the Army of the United States, at his own request, on account of age and its infirmities, was relieved from all further active duty. The organization of the new army, under the new levies, therefore, was assigned to another. [U.S.] General George B. McClellan was the officer selected. This high distinction was conferred upon him in consideration of his successes in Northwestern Virginia, in the month of July. He was at this time regarded as the 'coming man.' To him was given the appellation of the 'Young Napoleon.' He was, indeed, an officer of great ability. Very few ever surpassed him in what may be termed the organizing powers of the mind. He went to work slowly, and, notwithstanding the pressure upon him for another attack upon Richmond, contented himself with having all things ready for such a movement early in the ensuing spring. The whole fall and winter were spent in preparation.

"While this was going on at Washington, the [C.S.] Authorities at

Richmond were doing all in their power to bring into the field a force sufficient to repel the second [Union] blow, as they had the first. The [Confederate] Congress provided, by law, for calling out four hundred thousand volunteers. To meet the expenses, they directed the issuing of one hundred and fifty millions of Treasury Notes, in addition to those previously ordered, with a war tax of fifty cents upon the hundred dollars' worth of certain taxable property.

"They also adopted what was known as the 'Paris Agreement of 1856,' touching the International Law of Blockade, and sent two other Commissioners to Europe to present this subject, especially to the Courts of England and France; and to place the Confederates in a favorable position in relation to the rights of Neutral and Belligerents. These Commissioners, Mr. James M. Mason, of Virginia, and Mr. John Slidell, of Louisiana, with their Secretaries, Mr. George Eustis and Mr. James E. Macfarland, were seized on board the British Mail Steamer *Trent*, between Havana and St. Thomas, by Captain [Charles] Wilkes, of the United States Navy, commanding the *San Jacinto*, on the 8th of November, and were carried to Fort Warren, Boston Harbor, where they were confined as prisoners. The report of this indignity to the British Flag, by Captain [James] Moir, of the *Trent*, and Commander Williams, of the Royal Navy, in charge of Her Majesty's mails, created the most intense excitement in England. A war feeling instantly flamed up there. Troops were sent to Canada. A formal demand was immediately made of the [U.S.] Authorities at Washington, by the British Government, for the surrender of the prisoners, and an apology for the outrage upon Neutral Rights in their capture. Both demands were promptly complied with by Mr. [William H.] Seward, [U.S.] Secretary of State, in a very voluminous parade of not very impertinent learning, notwithstanding the House of Representatives had passed a vote of thanks to Captain Wilkes for his conduct in the matter. This affair, therefore, so threatening for a short time, soon passed off quietly, without any serious results. The Commissioners reached their respective destinations, but met with no success in the accomplishment of their objects. All their labors were as fruitless, as had been those of the Commissioners first sent, upon the subjects specially committed to their charge.

"Mr. John T. Pickett, who was the Secretary of the Commissioners at Washington, was sent, in the month of May, to Mexico, to act as Diplomatic Agent of the Confederate States, with that Government. His mission resulted in nothing effectual.

"Mr. [William L.] Yancey, early in the winter, when he saw that nothing could be accomplished on the business upon which he was sent, returned to his home, and was elected by the Legislature of Alabama to the first Confederate States Senate under the Constitution, which had been adopted for their

Permanent Government; and which was to go into operation on the 22nd day of February, 1862. The regular election for President and Vice President, under the Constitution for a Permanent Government, was held on the 6th of November, 1861, when the same persons [i.e., Jefferson Davis and Alexander H. Stephens] holding these offices under the Provisional Organization, were unanimously re-elected to the same positions, for a term of six years, under the other."[254]

☛ "A few other matters only, during the existence of the Provisional [Confederate] Organization, remain to be noted for our purposes. Among these it is proper to state, that before the expiration of this period, events took a turn which led to the admission of the States of Missouri and Kentucky into the Confederacy. Neither Governor [Claiborne F.] Jackson nor Governor [Beriah] Magoffin was permitted by the Federal Authorities to hold the position of neutrality; nor were these States permitted to hold that position.

"In Missouri a Revolutionary State Government was organized, backed by the Federals. Hamilton R. Gamble was declared Provisional Governor; Willard P. Hall, Lieutenant Governor; and Mordecai Oliver, Secretary of State. This Government, and the [Liberal] Party which sustained it, sided with the Federals [Yankees]. The regular Legislature of Missouri, convened at the call of Governor Jackson, appointed Edward C. Cabell and Thomas L. Snead as Commissioners fully empowered to form an alliance with the Confederate States. This resulted in a Convention not dissimilar in its features to those previously entered into by Virginia and Tennessee. The Convention was signed at Richmond, on the 31st of October, 1861, by the Commissioners on the part of the State, and by Robert M. T. Hunter, Secretary of State, on the part of the Confederate States. This Convention was subsequently ratified unanimously by the Legislature. In this way Missouri was recognized as a member of the Confederacy.

"Kentucky became the theatre of similar scenes with similar results, in a reversed order. In this State, as in all where neutrality was attempted, 'a reign of terror' was instituted. During the latter part of September, Ex-Governor Charles S. Morehead, the life-long personal and political friend of Henry Clay, as well as one of the most devoted adherents to the Union under the Constitution who ever lived, was arrested at his residence near Louisville, for nothing but his denunciations of the flagrant usurpations of [President Lincoln and] the Washington Authorities. He was hurried off by the military to Fort La Fayette, where he was immured for months in one of the dungeons of that Bastile, without a hearing and without a charge! Thomas B. Monroe [Sr.], who was District Judge of the United States Court, John C. Breckinridge, Senator and Ex-Vice President of the United States, Humphrey Marshall, Ex-Congressman and Ex-Minister to China, William Preston, Ex-Congressman and Ex-Minister to Spain. Thomas B. Monroe, Jr., Secretary of State at the time, and several other of the most prominent citizens of Kentucky, who occupied positions similar to that of Mr. Morehead, avoided a similar doom, through the good fortune of receiving information, that orders for their arrest had been issued, in time for them to make their escape.

"Mr. Breckinridge issued an address to the people of the State. A Convention was called, which met at Russellville on the 18th of November. This point had not yet been reached by the Federal forces. Sixty-eight counties of the State were represented in the Convention there assembled. The number of delegates was one hundred and twenty. They proclaimed a Declaration of Independence in behalf of the people of Kentucky, and organized a Government upon Revolutionary principles.

"The grounds upon which these proceedings were justified in the opinion of those who instituted them, were thus set forth by Governor [George W.] Johnson, on the 21st of November, 1862:

'The action of the people of this State, in thus organizing a Provisional Government for the protection of their rights of person and property, was based, as a necessity, upon the ultimate right of Revolution possessed by all mankind against perfidious and despotic Governments. A [Liberal] faction, which may be called the "War Party of Kentucky," composed of most of the members of the last Congress, and a minority of the Legislature, after surrounding themselves with an army of 8,000 Lincoln troops, forced a majority of their own body into caucus, and there concocted, and afterwards enacted in the Legislature (against the vetoes of the Governor and the remonstrances of the minority of the Senate and House of Representatives,) a series of oppressive and despotic acts, which have left us no alternatives except abject submission or manly resistance. The constitutional right of Secession by the State, with organized Government, from the ruins of the old Union, was not possible; because the power of adopting such manly and philosophic action was denied us by the enslaved members of the Legislature, who not only submitted, themselves, to the despotism of the army, but betrayed their political opponents who relied upon their honor, and their own constituents and the great body of the people of Kentucky, who relied upon their pledges of neutrality. Secession being thus impossible, we were compelled to plant ourselves on *a doctrine universally recognized by all Nations—that allegiance is due alone to such Governments as protect Society, and upon that right which God himself has given to mankind and which is inalienable—the right to destroy any Government whose existence is incompatible with the interests and liberties of Society. The foundation, therefore, upon which the Provisional Government rests, is a right of Revolution instituted by the people, for the preservation of the liberty, the interests, and the honor of a vast majority of the citizens of Kentucky.'* [Emphasis added, L.S.]

"George W. Johnson was chosen Governor [of Kentucky]. William Preston, Henry C. Burnett, and William E. Simms were appointed Commissioners to negotiate an alliance with the Confederate States. The result was the recognition by the Confederate States of this Organization as the rightful Government of the State of Kentucky; and of her admission under it, as a member of the Confederacy, in the early part of December."[255]

☛ "Another matter of this period to be specially noted is, that during this winter, while the Confederates had a very large excess of Federal prisoners, the Authorities at Washington under very great pressure of public sentiment in the Northern States, were induced to enter into a Cartel for an exchange, upon the basis that the Confederates had offered at the beginning. This arrangement was entered into, on the 14th of February, by General Howell Cobb on the part of the Confederate States, and General John E. Wool on the part of the United States. According to the agreement then made, the Privateersmen were put upon the footing of other prisoners of war. *But no sooner had the Federals an excess of prisoners by the capture of the garrison of about 10,000 officers and men at Fort Donelson, than the terms of this agreement were violated, by their again refusing to send forward the Privateersmen in exchange, as well as by their failing to comply with the Cartel in other respects.* But enough of this now. One or two other matters of smaller import may be here stated."[256] [Emphasis added, L.S.]

☛ "On Mr. [Robert A.] Toombs's taking a commission in the army, Mr. [Robert M. T.] Hunter succeeded him in the State Department. He continued to fill this office until the close of the Provisional Congress. Having been elected to the Confederate Senate, he took his seat in that body on its first organization. The health of Mr. [Leroy P.] Walker failing during the fall, Mr. [Judah P.] Benjamin filled his place as Secretary of War, and Ex-Governor Thomas Bragg, of North Carolina, acted as Attorney-General during the remaining months of the Provisional Government. Mr. Walker afterwards became a Brigadier-General in the [C.S.] Army.

"At this time the Confederates had in the field, distributed at various points, including all branches of service, in round numbers about three hundred thousand men; while the Federals in like manner, and in like round numbers had not less than eight hundred thousand!

"So matters generally stood, in a political as well as military view, on both sides, when the new Organization under the Constitution for a Permanent Government for the Confederate States went into operation, on the 22nd of

February, 1862; which period may be regarded as the close of the first year of the war. . . ."[257]

Civil War Liberals could not understand why Confederate "Generals [Joseph E.] Johnston and [Pierre G. T.] Beauregard remained entirely inactive at Manassas, during the whole fall [season], after the rout of General [Irvin] McDowell's army on the 21st of July. Why did they not push on to Washington? They must have had a very large force early in the fall, and flushed with victory as they were, it has always been a mystery . . . why they stood so perfectly quiet until [George B.] McClellan's new army was organized almost within their sight?" Stephens replied:

☞ "With the military operations . . . it is not my purpose to deal, except in so far as they bear upon the questions which we have directly in hand. A great deal has been said and written upon the subject of [this] . . . inquiry. It has been said that Thomas J. Jackson, who afterwards became so famous under the appellation of 'Stonewall,' and who was the Colonel of that name so favorably mentioned in General Johnston's report of the battle of the 21st of July, was urgent for an immediate pressing forward to Washington. Some think his views were right. My own opinion, from the reports of both General Johnston and General Beauregard, as well as from other sources, is, that such a movement at that time, was altogether impracticable. As to the state of things afterwards, that is a different question. All I know upon that point, and all I can say in answer to your question upon it, is, that General Johnston did wish to make some movement of the sort in the early part of the fall, when he was better prepared. Not, however, with the forces he then had, for they did not exceed forty thousand effective men; while McClellan had over fifty thousand when he took command at Washington on the 27th of July. Johnston's plan was to concentrate, as quickly as possible, at that place, a force sufficient for his purpose, which could be done only by leaving bare remote points then defended. For this object a Council of War was held at Manassas. Mr. [Jefferson] Davis went up from Richmond. He met Generals Johnston and Beauregard, and General Gustavus W. Smith in this Council. General Beauregard had been promoted to the rank of full General, for his gallantry and great services on the 21st of July. General Smith, at the time, commanded a division of this army, with the rank of Major-General. He was a graduate of West Point, and recognized as an officer of great merit.

"The result of the Council of War so held, was the disapproval by Mr. Davis of the policy suggested. Upon the merits of the views presented, for and against its adoption, I have no speculative opinions to express. Of course, all that could now be said on the subject would amount to nothing but speculations. General Beauregard was, not very long afterwards, transferred to a command in the West. This is all the explanation I can give of the matter [that my Liberal friends] . . . inquire about."[258]

Another point on which 19*th*-Century Liberals were mystified was how the Confederates maintained their spirits at the close of the first year of the War. To this end they posed the following question to Stephens: "With the capture of Forts Henry and Donelson, and the opening into East Tennessee, which [U.S. General George H.] Thomas's victory achieved, and the abandonment of Kentucky, as well as Tennessee, by [Confederate] General Albert Sidney Johnston with all his forces, which these victories rendered necessary, to say nothing of the Coast operations in North and South Carolina; and with the utter failure of both the Embassies to effect anything in Europe, or even in Mexico, it seems to . . . [us,] that the more intelligent men at the South must, at that time, have seen that further resistance was useless and hopeless. [We] . . . should like to know, before you leave this point, what your views of the prospect then were?" To this Stephens responded:

☛ "The prospect to me was not at all so gloomy as you seem to imagine. The Confederate reverses, you refer to, were certainly very great. But the immediate results of all the regular field engagements, as before said, had much in them to inspire not only hope, but confidence as to the final results of the Conflict. What I then thought of the prospect, however, can be better understood, from what I said a few months afterwards, in a speech at this place, which was very well reported, and very clearly sets forth my views and feelings on the subject, at the time you inquire of, as well as at the time when it was delivered. Here is the speech. From it as reported and published at the time, I read:

[A reporter speaking:] 'On the general subject of our present conflict, involving as it does our individual as well as State existence, Stephens said all wars were calamities—the greatest that can befall a people, except, perhaps, direct visitations from Providence, such as famines, plagues, and pestilences.

'The greater the war, the greater the calamity. This war is a great calamity to us. We all feel it. It is the greatest war, and waged on the largest scale of any since the birth of Christ. The history of the world—not excepting the Crusades—furnishes no parallel to it in the present era.

'The responsibility and guilt of it must be fearful somewhere. As great calamities as wars are, they are, however, sometimes necessary. Often forced by the highest dictates of patriotism. Like "offences" we are told of, it must needs be, that they sometimes come. They are, however, never right or justifiable on both sides. They may be wrong on both sides, but can never be right on both. Unjust wars, by the unanimous consent of civilized men, are held, as they should be, in condemnation and reprobation. People, therefore, as well as their rulers, to whom such high trusts are confided, should look well to it, and see that they are right before appealing to this last and most terrible arbitrament of arms.

'Some thoughts on this subject, Mr. Stephens said, might not be out of place, even there. These he dwelt upon at some length, showing the justice of our cause and the wanton aggression of the enemy. He traced the history of the controversy between the Southern and Northern States, the principles and nature of our Government, the Independence and Sovereignty of the States, and the right of each to control its own destinies and act for itself in the last resort, as each State might think best for itself. It was wholly immaterial, he said, in considering the question of right and justice, now to look any further than the solemn act of the States of the South, after mature deliberation, each acting for itself in its Sovereign capacity. Each State had the right thus to act, and when each for itself had thus acted, no power on earth had the right justly to gainsay it.

'*The old Union was formed by the States, each acting for itself in its Sovereign character and capacity, with the object and purpose of advancing their interests respectively thereby. Each State was the sole judge in the last resort, whether the future interest, safety and well-being of her people, required her to resume those Sovereign powers, the exercise of which had been delegated to other hands under the old Compact of Union. These principles have ever been held not only true, but sacred, with the friends of Constitutional Liberty in all the States since the old Union was formed. They rest upon that fundamental principle set forth in the Declaration of Independence, that all Governments "derive their just powers from the consent of the governed." The States South, therefore, had done nothing but what was their right—their inalienable right to do, the same as their ancestors did, in common with the North, when they severed their connection with the British Government.* [Emphasis added, L.S.]

'*This war was waged by the North in denial of this Right, and for the purpose of conquest and subjugation! It was, therefore, aggressive, wanton and unjust! Such must be the judgment of mankind, let its results be what they may. The responsibility, therefore, for all its sacrifices of treasure and blood, heretofore, or hereafter to be made in its prosecution, rests not upon us.* [Emphasis added, L.S.]

'Mr. Stephens said that soon after the first great battle of Manassas, duty called him to our camps near that point. He went over the ground on which that conflict had taken place. The evidences of the late terrible strife were still fresh and visible all around. The widespread desolation, the new-made graves, and the putrid animal remains not yet removed by the vultures, fully attested what a scene of blood it had been. While surveying the hills and defiles over which the various columns of our men and the enemy passed and were engaged on that memorable day, amongst many other things that crowded themselves upon his mind, were two dying expressions reported to have been uttered in the midst of the battle. One was by a soldier on the side of the enemy, who, fallen and weltering in his blood, exclaimed, "My God! what is all this for?" The other was by the lamented [Francis S.] Bartow, who said, "Boys, they have killed me, but never give it up!" These two exclamations were made at no great distance apart, and perhaps near the same time.

'"What is all this for?" Mr. Stephens said he could but think the question was pertinent to both sides, and most pertinent from him who uttered it, addressed to all his invading comrades and those who sent them. Well might he there, in the agonies of death, in the din and dust of strife, in the clangor of arms and the thunder of artillery, ask, "What is all this for?" Why this array of armies? Why this fierce meeting in mortal combat? What is all this carnage and slaughter for? The same question is still as pertinent to those who are waging this war against us, as it was then. Why the prolongation of this conflict? Why this immense sacrifice of life in camp, and the numerous battles that have been fought since? Why this lamentation and mourning going up from almost every house and family from Maine to the Rio Grande, and from the Atlantic and Gulf to the Lakes, for friends and dear ones who have fallen by disease and violence in this unparalleled struggle? The question, if replied to by the North, can have but one true answer. What is all this for on their part, but to overturn the principle upon which their own Government, as well as ours, is based—to reverse the doctrine that Governments derive "their just powers from the consent of the governed?" What is it for but to overturn the principles and practice of their own Government from the beginning? That Government was founded and based upon the political axiom that all States and Peoples have the inalienable right to change their forms of Government at will!* [Emphasis added, L.S.]

'This principle was acted on in the recognition by the United States of the South American Republics. It was the principle acted on in the recognition of Mexico. It was acted on in the struggle of Greece, to overthrow the Ottoman rule. On that question, the great Constitutional Expounder of the North, Mr. [Daniel] Webster, gained his first laurels as an American Statesman. This principle was acted on in the recognition of the Government of [King] Louis-Phillippe [I], on the overthrow of Charles X of France; and again in the recognition of the La-martine Government, on the overthrow of Louis Phillippe in 1848. At that time every man at the North in Congress, save one, Mr. Stephens believed, voted for the principle. The same principle was again acted upon without dissent in 1852, in the recognition of the Government of Louis Napoleon [III]. The same principle was acted upon in the recognition of Texas, when she seceded or withdrew from the Government of Mexico.

'Many at the North opposed the admission of Texas, as a State in our then Union. But there was little, if any, opposition to her recognition as an independent outside Republic. Strange to say, many of those who were then fiercest in their opposition to Texas coming into the Union, are now the fiercest in their denial of the unquestioned right acknowledged to her before. Well may any and every one, North or South, exclaim, What is all this for? What have we done to the North? When have we ever wronged them? We quit them, it is true, as our ancestors and their ancestors quit the British Government. We quit as they quit, upon a question of Constitutional Right. That question they determined for themselves, and we have but done the same. What, therefore, is all this for? Why this war on their part against the uniform principles and practice of their own Government? It is a war, *in short, on their part, against right, against reason, against justice, against nature!* [Emphasis added, L.S.]

'*If asked, on our side, what is all this for? the reply from every breast is, that it is for home, for firesides, for our altars, for our birthrights, for property, for honor, for life*—*in a word, for everything for which freemen should live, and for which all deserving to be freemen should be willing, if need be, to die!*' [Emphasis added, L.S.]

"Upon the subject of the failure of our European Embassies, I then expressed myself as follows:

[The reporter continues:] 'On the subject of foreign recognition, Mr. Stephens said he saw no change in the prospect. Foreign Governments, he thought, were very much disposed to stand aloof from this contest. He did not believe they really sympathized with either side—he meant the ruling classes. The masses of the people, and the commercial interests generally, he thought did sympathize with us. Not so with their rulers. They care but little for the success of either the North or the South. Some of our people were disposed to think that their sympathies were with the North, while the Northern papers were charging them with sympathy for us. He thought they had no kind feelings for either, but rather rejoiced to see professed Republicans [i.e., Americans] cutting each others throats! He thought the remark reported to have lately been uttered by [Thomas] Carlyle in his quaint style, embodied in a nutshell the diplomatic feelings of Europe toward the cause on both sides. The remark was that, "It was the foulest chimney that had been on fire for a century, and the best way is to let it burn itself out."

'They [Europeans] were against Republicanism [i.e., a Confederate system of government]! They are hostile to the opinion that man is capable of Self-government! They are doubtless in hope that this principle will be extinguished on both sides of the line before the contest ends! They were wise enough to see that the North (from the course commenced there) would soon run into anarchy or despotism, and they are perhaps looking for the same fate to befall us. This has usually been the fate of Republics; and one of the highest duties we have to perform to ourselves and posterity, was to see that their expectations shall fail so far as we are concerned. We have a high mission to perform; and Mr. Stephens trusted the people of the South would prove themselves equal to the task of its performance. *We have our Independence to maintain, and Constitutional Liberty to preserve!* With us now rest the hopes of the world! *The North has already become a Despotism! The people, there, while nominally free, are in no better condition, practically, than serfs. The only plausibility they have for the war is to make freemen of slaves, and those of an* [culturally] *Inferior race, while their efforts in this unnatural crusade thus far have resulted in nothing but making slaves of themselves. Presidential Proclamations supersede and set aside both laws and the Constitution. Liberty with them is but a* name and a mockery. In separating from them, we quit the Union, but we rescued the Constitution. This was the Ark of the Covenant of our Fathers! It is our high duty to keep it, and hold it, and preserve it forever!' [Emphasis added, L.S.]

"[It is true that my speech was very 'rebellious,' as Yankees term it . . .] and traitorous too, if treason consists in true loyalty to the fundamental principles upon which the Union was based, and upon which alone it can be perpetuated, with the maintenance of Constitutional Liberty on this Continent! But on these points [my Liberal friends,] . . . I believe, [we] agreed to disagree."[259]

28

THE WAR FOR SOUTHERN INDEPENDENCE PART THREE

IN THIS CHAPTER WE EXAMINE more selections from *A Constitutional View*, most which deal specifically with the enormous corpus of Yankee myths that surround Lincoln's War. One by one the Northern falsehoods fall, easily cut down by Stephens' diamond sharp intellect and extensive knowledge of *genuine* American history.

One of the countless Northern myths about the South was that Vice President Stephens had many differences with President Davis, and that, after a "feud" between the two, Stephens "not only withdrew from Richmond, but withdrew his support from the Administration, and headed a Peace Party movement in Georgia, Alabama, and North Carolina, with a view to the abandonment of the war, and a restoration of the Union." Here Stephens corrects these falsities:

☛ "In the first place . . . I must state most explicitly, that there never was any feud, properly speaking, between Mr. Davis and myself. We differed, it is true, very widely upon several matters of policy, as well as upon some principles of Constitutional law. We had differed, as before stated, upon the policy of introducing the new feature into the Democratic [Conservative] Platform in 1860, which caused a disruption of that Party, and lead to the election of Mr. Lincoln. He was, as we have seen, the distinguished leader on that line of policy in the Senate. We differed also upon the policy of Secession, when that course was adopted. After the rejection of the Crittenden proposition, he advised Secession. . . . I did not concur with him in the expediency of that course. But on these and other points of difference there was nothing like a feud between us, nor were our personal relations, or free interchange of views upon public questions, interrupted at all by them. On the same points I differed as widely with Mr. [Robert A.] Toombs, and two-thirds, perhaps, of the Montgomery Congress.

"So, likewise, I differed with Mr. Davis after the organization of the new Confederacy, and the war was waged to overthrow it, upon several matters connected with the proper administration of our affairs. These related to the internal as well as the external policy of the Government—to wielding most efficiently our internal resources, of men and money, as well as proper external agencies, for the success of *the great cause involved in the Conflict—the Sovereignty of the several States*—to which no one could be more devoted than I was. These differences, however wide and thorough as they were . . . caused no personal breach between us. None of them, moreover, related to the general treatment of prisoners. On that point there was no disagreement between us."[260] [Emphasis added, L.S.]

Stephens here addresses the charge that the Confederacy abused, or allowed the abuse of, Yankee soldiers held in Southern prisons:

☞ "This whole subject of the treatment of prisoners which has become so prominent a feature in considering the conduct of the war on both sides, from the turn which has been given to it, I may as well dispose of here, at once and finally. This I do by stating broadly that *the charge of cruelty and inhumanity towards prisoners, which has been so extensively made at the North, against Mr. Davis and the Confederate authorities, is utterly without foundation in fact. From the commencement and throughout the war, the whole course of Mr. Davis towards prisoners shows conclusively the perfect recklessness of the charge. His position on this subject, in the beginning, clearly appears from what we have seen, and that fully sustains this statement. The efforts which have been so industriously made to fix the odium of cruelty and barbarity upon him, and other high officials under the Confederate Government, in the matter of prisoners, in the face of all the facts, constitute one of the boldest and baldest attempted outrages upon the truth of history, which has ever been essayed: not less so than the infamous attempt to fix upon him and other high officials on the Confederate side, the guilt of Mr. Lincoln's assassination! Whatever unnecessary privations and sufferings prisoners on both sides were subjected to, the responsibility of the whole rested not upon Mr. Davis or the Confederate authorities.* It is not my purpose to go into a full history of the subject. This would take more time than is at all necessary. A few leading facts will settle the matter. [Emphasis added, L.S.]

"Let it be borne in mind, then, that the Confederates were ever anxious for a speedy exchange, and that after the interruption of the exchange under the

Cartel first agreed upon, as before stated, another arrangement was entered into by the Federals, under pressure of public sentiment at the North, when the excess was against them. This was, afterwards, likewise broken. It was broken, not by the Confederates, but by the Federals upon some pretext or other. Throughout the struggle, Mr. Davis's conduct and bearing upon this point, not only challenges the severest scrutiny of the fair minded of this day, but will command the admiration of the just and generous for all time to come. In addition to what has been shown heretofore, what higher evidence on this point could be desired than that furnished by his Congratulatory Address to the Army of [Confederate] General [Robert E.] Lee, for the successes achieved in the battles around Richmond, when [U.S. General George B.] McClellan, with his newly organized hosts of at least one hundred and twenty thousand men, made the second unsuccessful attempt to take the Confederate Capital in 1862, and when over ten thousand Federal prisoners had fallen into their hands? In this hour of triumph, mark the significant, as well as magnanimous, and even chivalrous language, which came spontaneously from [President Davis'] . . . heart on that occasion:

> 'You are fighting for all that is dearest to men; and though opposed to a foe who disregards many of the usages of civilized war, your humanity to the wounded and to the prisoners was the fit and crowning glory to your valor.' [Emphasis added, L.S.]

> "[I can say with complete certainty that the] horrors of Libby and Belle Island [prisons], as well as of Salisbury and Andersonville [prisons], so pathetically set forth by many, and great as they really were, were not his fault, or in any way justly chargeable upon him. . . . It was the fault of the Federal [U.S.] authorities in not agreeing to, and carrying out an immediate exchange, which Mr. Davis was, at all times, anxious to do. The [Liberal] men at the head of affairs at Washington were solely responsible for all these sufferings. Upon these officials, and upon them only, can these sufferings be justly charged! Neither Libby, nor Belle Island, nor Salisbury, nor Andersonville would have had a groaning prisoner of war, but for the refusal of the Federal authorities to comply with the earnest desire of the Richmond [C.S.] Government, for an immediate exchange, upon the most liberal and humane principles. Had Mr. Davis's repeated offers been accepted, no prisoner on either side would have been retained in confinement a day. This all the facts clearly show. All the sufferings and loss of life, therefore, during the entire war, growing out of these imprisonments on both sides, and they were great on both sides, (it is not my wish to understate or underrate them on either,) are justly chargeable to but one side, and that is the Federal side."[261] [Emphasis added, L.S.]

Despite these facts, the anti-South movement has kept alive the myth that Davis, Stephens, and other Confederate authorities mistreated the Union soldiers in their prisons, *refused to exchange prisoners with the North, and withheld proper medical remedies, along with other "savage cruelties." To this day pro-North writers lay particular guilt on Confederate Major Henry Wirz, commandant of the infamous Rebel prison at Andersonville, Georgia, where countless horrors occurred. Though completely innocent, U.S. officials had him tried and executed in what must be counted as one of America's most shameful events. In the following excerpts Stephens discusses these issues:*

☛ ". . . it is not true that there was any such thing as the systematic policy [Liberals] . . . speak of, either in starving the well, or withholding medical remedies and attention from the [Yankee] sick and wounded. The policy of the Confederates in these particulars was established by law. *By an act of Congress, passed soon after the war was inaugurated . . . it was provided that prisoners of war should have the same rations in quantity and quality as Confederate soldiers in the field. By an act afterwards passed all hospitals for sick and wounded prisoners, were put upon the same footing with hospitals for sick and wounded Confederates. This policy was never changed. There was no discrimination in either particular between Federal prisoners and Confederate soldiers. Whatever food or fare the Confederate soldiers had, whether good or bad, full or short, the Federal prisoners shared equally with them. Whatever medical attention the sick and wounded Confederate soldiers had, the Federal prisoners in like condition also received. When the supply of the usual standard medicines was exhausted, and could not be replenished in consequence of the action of the Federal Government in holding them to be contraband of war, and in preventing their introduction by blockade and severe penalties—when resort was had to the virtue of the healing herbs of the country as substitutes for more efficient remedial agents, the suffering Federals shared these equally with like suffering Confederates! Did the requirements of perfect justice and right go beyond this? Could humanity ask more?* [Emphasis added, L.S.]

"As for particular instances of cruelty on the part of subordinates who may have been untrue to their trusts, that is a very different matter. There were unquestionably very great wrongs of this sort on both sides. Wirz, to whom you have alluded, may have committed some of these. How this was I really do not know. He, by-the-by, was not one of our people. He was a European by birth, who obtained position in our service through letters of recommendation, which warranted confidence in his intelligence and good character. I know nothing to his discredit in either of these respects, except the allegations you refer to. Whether they were true or false, as I have said, I do not know. It is due to his memory, however, to recollect that his own dying declarations were against the truth of these accusations. This, moreover, I can, and do venture to say, that acts of much greater cruelty and barbarity than any which were proven against him, could have been easily established, and would have been established on his trial, against numerous prisoners, of unquestionable truth and veracity, from Camp Douglas, Rock Island, Elmira, and Point Lookout, of numerous instances which came under their immediate observation of much greater atrocity than anything alleged against Wirz. *These acts, many of which were of the most inhumane and barbarous character, were perpetrated by Federal subordinates, having control of Confederate prisoners at these points.* There may have been, therefore, and I do not question but that there were, great wrongs of this sort on the part of Confederate subordinates, as there certainly were on the part of the Federals. But what I maintain is, that *such conduct never met the approval of the Confederate authorities. They never in a single instance sanctioned, much less ordered well demeaning and unoffending prisoners of war to be confined in unwholesome dungeons, and to be manacled with cuffs and irons as was repeatedly done by orders from the authorities at Washington, in utter violation of the well established usages of modern civilized warfare! But apart from this marked difference between the two Governments, in their highest official character, in sanctioning and ordering acts of wanton cruelty, I insist upon the irrefutable fact that but for the refusal of the Federals to carry out an exchange, none of the wrongs or outrages you speak of, and none of the sufferings incident to prison life on either side, could have occurred.* [Emphasis added, L.S.]

"[It is a fact that thirty thousand Union soldiers were] . . . huddled together at Andersonville, in the . . . region of Southwestern Georgia, where, [the North believes, many of them died due to] . . . the malarious influences prevailing under a burning sun. . . . [While on the topic of Confederate prisons, let me address this as well.]

"Large numbers of them [Yankee prisoners] were taken to Southwestern Georgia in 1864, because it was a section most remote and secure, from the invading Federal Armies, and because, too, it was a country of all others, then within the Confederate limits, not thus threatened with an invasion, most abundant with food, and all resources at command for the health and comfort of prisoners. They were put in one stockade for the want of men to guard more than one. The section of country, moreover, was not regarded as more unhealthy, or more subject to malarious influences, than any in the central part of the State. The Official order for the erection of the stockade enjoined that it should be in 'a healthy locality, plenty of pure water, a running stream, and, if possible, shade trees, and in the immediate neighborhood of grist and saw mills.' The very selection of the locality, so far from being, as [anti-South Liberals] . . . suppose, made with cruel designs against the prisoners, was governed by the most humane considerations.

"*[This] . . . question might, with much more point, be retorted by asking, why were Southern prisoners taken in the dead of winter with their thin clothing to Camp Douglas, Rock Island, and Johnson's Island—icy regions of the North—where it is a notorious fact that many of them actually froze to death?* [Emphasis added, L.S.]

"As far as Mortuary returns afford evidence of the general treatment of prisoners on both sides, the figures show nothing to the disadvantage of the Confederates, notwithstanding their limited supplies of all kinds, and notwithstanding all that has been said of the horrible sacrifice of life at Andersonville.

"It now appears that *a larger number of Confederates died in Northern, than of Federals in Southern prisons, or stockade. The Report of Mr. [Edwin M.] Stanton, as [U.S.] Secretary of War, on the 19th of July, 1866, exhibits the fact that, of the Federal prisoners in Confederate hands during the war, only 22,576 died; while of the Confederate prisoners in Federal hands 26,436 died.* This Report does not set forth the exact number of prisoners held by each side respectively. These facts were given more in detail in a subsequent Report by Surgeon-General [Joseph K.] Barnes, of the United States Army. His Report I have not seen, but according to a statement, editorially, in the 'National Intelligencer'—very high authority—it appears from the Surgeon-General's Report, that the whole number of Federal prisoners captured by the Confederates and held in Southern prisons, from first to last during the war, was, in round numbers, 270,000; while the whole number of Confederates captured and held in prisons by the Federals was, in like round numbers, only 220,000. *From these two Reports it appears that, with 50,000 more prisoners in Southern stockades, or other modes of confinement, the deaths were nearly 4,000 less! According to these figures, the per centum of Federal deaths in Southern prisons was under nine! while the per centum of Confederate deaths in Northern prisons was over twelve! These Mortality statistics are of no small weight in determining on which side there was the most neglect, cruelty, and inhumanity!*"[262] [Emphasis added, L.S.]

Stephens now turns to the subject of Union outrages, illegalities, and other criminal acts perpetrated by U.S. soldiers against, not only C.S. soldiers, but against innocent and usually passive and unarmed Southern civilians:
☛ "But the great question in this matter is, upon whom rests the tremendous responsibility of all this sacrifice of human life, with all its indescribable miseries and sufferings? *The facts, beyond question or doubt, show that it rests entirely upon the [Liberal] Authorities at Washington! It is now well understood to have been a part of their settled policy in conducting the war, not to exchange prisoners. The grounds upon which this extraordinary course was adopted were, that it was humanity to the men in the field, on their side, to let their captured comrades perish in prison, rather than to let an equal number of Confederate soldiers be released on exchange to meet them in battle! Upon the Federal [U.S.] Authorities, and upon them only, with this policy as their excuse, rests the whole of this responsibility.* To avert the indignation which the open avowal of this policy by them, at the time, would have excited throughout the North, and throughout the civilized world, the false cry of cruelty towards prisoners was raised

against the Confederates. This was but a pretext to cover their own violation of the usages of war in this respect among civilized nations. [Emphasis added, L.S.]

"Other monstrous violations of like usages were not attempted to be palliated by them [the Yankees], or even covered by a pretext. These were, as you must admit, open, avowed and notorious! *I refer not only to the general sacking of private houses—the pillaging of money, plate, jewels and other light articles of value, with the destruction of books, works of art, paintings, pictures, private manuscripts and family relics; but I allude, besides these things, especially to the hostile acts directly against property of all kinds, as well as outrages upon non-combatants—to the laying waste of whole sections of country; the attempted annihilation of all the necessaries of life; to the wanton killing, in many instances, of farm stock and domestic animals; the burning of mills, factories and barns, with their contents of grain and forage, not sparing orchards or growing crops, or the implements of husbandry; the mutilation of County and Municipal records of great value; the extraordinary efforts made to stir up servile insurrections, involving the wide-spread slaughter of women and children; the impious profanation of temples of worship, and even the brutish desecration of the sanctuaries of the dead!* [Emphasis added, L.S.]

"*All these enormities of a savage character against the very existence of civilized society, and so revolting to the natural sentiments of mankind, when not thoroughly infuriated by the worst of passions, and in open violation of modern usages in war—were perpetrated by the Federal armies in many places throughout the conflict, as legitimate means in putting down the Rebellion so-called!* [Emphasis added, L.S.]

". . . Yes; these are severe comments, and I must ask . . . for a little indulgence . . . in expressing myself as I do. It is a sad thing to me to think of these subjects, and a still sadder thing to speak of them as I am compelled to do on this occasion. Severe as these comments are, there is, however, nothing extravagant in anything which I have said. *It is all most lamentably true!* All that I have stated, and much more, too, of a like character, were woefully realized by those who suffered from the deeds of [U.S. General Philip H.] Sheridan's men in the valley of Virginia, and by those who came within the range of the atrocities attending [U.S. General William T.] Sherman's conflagrations and devastations in his 'grand march' through Georgia and the Carolinas, as well as by those who were subjected to the merciless ravages of [U.S. General James H.] Wilson's and [U.S. General John M.] Palmer's Marauders afterwards! Facts which have come to my own knowledge, established by indisputable proof, verify the statement in full, both to the letter and spirit. *Private houses were sacked, pillaged, and then burnt; and after all family supplies were destroyed, or rendered unfit for use, helpless women and hungry children were left destitute alike of shelter and food. I know men—old men, non-combatants, men who had nothing to do with the war, further than to indulge in that sympathy which nature prompted—who were seized by a licensed soldiery and put to brutal torture, to compel them to disclose and to deliver up treasure that it was supposed they possessed. They were in many instances hung by the neck until life was nearly extinguished, and then cut down with the promise to desist if their demands were complied with, and threats of repeating the operation to death if they were not!* Judge Hiram Warner, one of the most upright and unoffending, as well as one of the most distinguished citizens of this State [Georgia], was the victim of an outrage of this sort. He had had nothing to do with the war; but it was supposed he had money, and that was what these 'truly loyal' 'Union Restorers,' so-called, were most eager to secure. Specifications, however, are unnecessary. *Instances of a similar character are numerous and notorious. In some cases, where parties resisted, their lives, as well as their purses, watches and other articles of value, were taken!* [Emphasis added, L.S.]

"[*It has been declared by the North that 'the Confederates did a good deal of this kind of work themselves in Maryland and Pennsylvania, to say nothing of other places.'*] . . . *That, to a limited extent, is also most lamentably true! But these acts of the Confederates were, as is well known, committed upon the avowed principle of retaliation. To this savage practice, if you please, and upon this principle only, they were most reluctantly compelled ultimately to resort.* The *"lex talionis"* [Latin: 'law' of 'retaliation'] *is recognized in such cases by the most civilized Nations, though it be savage in its character.* [Emphasis added, L.S.]

"The truth is . . . [that] wars in their most mitigated form—viewed in any light whatever, have a great deal of the savage character about them. They are *most horrible scourges.* They always spring from huge crimes against humanity, on one side or the other. They often, I admit, call forth the exercise of the highest faculties of the human intellect, and sometimes exhibit the noblest qualities of the human heart in the displays of fortitude, endurance, heroism, and the divine virtue of self-sacrifice for the good of others; but they are ever, upon the whole, even when most justifiably waged and humanely conducted, exceedingly demoralizing in their general tendencies and effects. They arouse and put into action the most fiendish elements of man's compound nature. *Their almost universal tendency is to make demons of men.* They are, certainly, the last instrumentalities that any people devoted to Constitutional Liberty, or the principles of Representative Government, should ever resort to for the purpose of maintaining and securing their objects. They are sometimes, as I said in the speech from which I read, necessary evils, looking to these ends. This was the character of this war on the Confederate side. No resistance by arms, in my opinion, could be more just than this was on their part. But the great objects aimed at in all such cases, are much oftener lost than attained by such resorts, even under such circumstances. This is my deliberate judgment. It was my judgment before the States were involved in this war, about which we can now neither speak nor think without the most melancholy reflections. Everything attending it, the long series of antecedents leading to it, as well as its general conduct on both sides, with its results up to this time, without considering the prospect of the future, all tend greatly to confirm me in that judgment. I do most earnestly hope, you may be assured, that the country may never be cursed with another. If the present and future generations in all the States will but profit, as they should by the experience of the last eight years, they certainly never will be again so cursed. *The only way, however, in which this experience can be rendered profitable to those who now live, as well as those who shall come after us, is by fully and clearly understanding and studying the facts and truths which marked and characterized these most pregnant events from the beginning to the end, and by rigidly practising the lessons which they inculcate. Many questions ignored and principles rejected by the leading public men in the Federal Councils of this day, must be considered and reconsidered. The Government, under different counsels, must be brought back to the Principles upon which it was established, if a repetition of this great scourge is to be hereafter averted. This is also my deliberate judgment. The only way in which wars are to be avoided in this country, is for Rulers to abstain from usurpations of power.* [The] *Magna Charter* was trampled under foot for centuries in England; but its principles died not—they lived on, and, though at the cost of the terrible scourge of many sanguinary conflicts, ultimately triumphed. So it may be expected to be with the ever-living, imperishable Principles of American Free Institutions! [Emphasis added, L.S.]

"But what I had in mind to say a moment ago in this connection, and in conclusion on the point now under our immediate consideration, is that, however horrible wars naturally and necessarily are in themselves; yet, in modern times, under the tempering and redeeming influences of the Christian Religion, civilized Nations have, by common consent, agreed upon certain customs and usages to which they conform in this resort, savage as it is, at best. These are the usages of civilized Nations to which I alluded, and which were so wantonly violated by the Federals [U.S. officials and soldiers], not only in their course upon the subject of prisoners, but in the other acts I mentioned.

"Now, what I affirm is, that in no instance that I am aware of throughout the late war did the Confederate Authorities countenance, much less sanction or order a violation of a single one of these recognized Christian and humane usages, not even in the retaliatory burnings in Maryland and Pennsylvania, and elsewhere. A comparison between the acts of the two Governments in these particulars during the whole conduct of the war, will forever clearly exhibit on which side in the contest was the higher standard of 'moral ideas,' and with it the higher type of civilization, if you will excuse me for saying it, at this period in the common history of the Peoples of the United States, so far as these were indicated by those who controlled the conduct of public affairs on the respective sides.

"However disastrous the results were to the Confederates; however extensive the misfortunes, losses, sufferings and sacrifices which attended and befell them in this second bloody conflict for the sovereign Right of local Self-government, on the part of the Peoples of the several States of this Federal Republic, whether composed of thirteen, thirty-three, or any other number; however utterly they failed to maintain this important principle, to which all that is truly great in the former history of the States is mainly attributable, and on which alone all sure hopes for general peace, prosperity and happiness, with good government for the whole in future, must be placed; however fruitless their efforts and blasted were their fondest anticipations in their highest objects of patriotic aim; however deplorable their present condition is, bereft of their estates and outlawed by the Government; and however worse the condition still to come may be for them; yet, notwithstanding all this, they have left to them that which is inestimable in value, far above riches, wealth or power, and of which no oppression or tyranny can deprive them, and that is a Public Character, which after having passed the severest ordeal that can 'try men's souls,' stands forth with that moral grandeur which is ever imparted to the reputation of States as of individuals, by uprightness in conduct, integrity of purpose, truthfulness in words, and the 'crowning glory' of unsullied honor! [Emphasis added, L.S.]

"Whatever other errors, faults, failings or shortcomings they may have had, no act of treachery, of perfidy, of hypocrisy or deceit, of breach of faith, or of turpitude—nothing of a low, mean, sordid or unmanly nature, can ever be justly laid to their charge in their State or Confederate organizations, either before or during the war; neither in the antecedents which led to it, nor in all the fury which marked its progress. Their whole public course shows them to have been a People as true, as brave, as generous, as frank, as refined, as magnanimous, as moral, as religious, and with all as honorable and patriotic, in the highest and noblest sense of these words, as ever struggled against odds, and thus struggling, fell in battling for the Right. So the truth of history stands, and will continue to stand forever! These are facts which time will never obliterate or destroy. This record of their past is no small heritage, if they have nothing else left for them to transmit to their children, and to their children's children, for generations to come!"[263] [Emphasis added, L.S.]

☛ "Now a word or two more . . . in response to [the Liberals'] . . . question upon the subject of prisoners, and my connection with it, before taking final leave of that matter. I did, indeed, . . . feel a profound sympathy for the sufferings of prisoners on both sides, throughout the war, and I made repeated efforts for their alleviation and relief. . . . There was also a difference between myself and some of the Confederate authorities, as to the best course to be pursued towards the Andersonville prisoners, to whom [my Liberal friends] .

. . have especially referred in the year 1864, as well as prisoners of war generally, then held by the Confederates, after the Federals had refused all proffered terms for their relief by exchange. This difference, however, did not relate to their treatment, but to the most politic manner of disposing of them. On this point I thought policy and humanity were united. I did not confer directly with Mr. [Jefferson] Davis upon it, but I did with several officers high in authority. To General Howell Cobb, who, then, as Major General of the Reserves in the Military District of Georgia, had the general control of the custody and safe-keeping of the prisoners at Andersonville, I specially presented my views upon the whole subject.

"The condition of those at Andersonville, at the time, was, indeed, most pitiable and deplorable. A very correct idea of it is given in the Report of Dr. Joseph Jones, the very learned and eminent, as well as Philanthropic Surgeon, who voluntarily devoted months of his time to the alleviation of their maladies and miseries. In speaking of their general condition he says:

> 'Surrounded by these depressing agencies, the postponement of the general exchange of prisoners and the constantly receding hopes of deliverance through the action of their own Government depressed the already desponding spirits, and destroyed those mental and moral energies so necessary for a successful struggle against disease and its agents. Home sickness and disappointment, mental depression and distress, attending the daily longings for an apparently hopeless release, appeared to be as potent agencies in the destruction of these prisoners as the physical causes of actual disease.'

"Now, to [Confederate] General [Howell] Cobb I suggested the propriety and expediency in a political point of view, as well as from the promptings of humanity, of sending these prisoners, as well as those confined at other places, home without any equivalent in return. My views presented to him, and to be presented by him, if he concurred, to Mr. Davis, were that Mr. Davis himself should visit and address the prisoners in person in a way and manner which I knew he was well fitted to do, if he approved the object; and after recapitulating all the facts in relation to exchange—after setting forth the nature of the war and the objects for which we were struggling—after stating distinctly *we were not fighting against the Union, but for the Principles upon which the Union was based*—for the rights of our common ancestors which were as dear to them as to us—in short, after a full review of all the questions in issue by him thus to be presented, for him to extend to the prisoners an unconditional discharge! [Emphasis added, L.S.]

"Such an unexampled act of generosity on his part, with copies of his address given to them by thousands, not only to be read and pondered by them, but to be distributed through the Northern States in the Presidential election pending that fall, I thought would effect a vast deal in determining the doubtful issue between the then opposing Parties there, and upon which the most momentous results, in my judgment, depended; results of no less importance to us than to the friends of Constitutional Liberty there! My sympathies throughout that contest were of course thoroughly with those [Conservatives] who were attempting at the ballot box to put out of power the Centralists [Liberals], whose Executive and Congressional usurpations had already awakened an extensive alarm in most, if not all the Northern States. *The object of the Centralists throughout the war had been, as the object of most of the writers since has been, to impress upon the minds of the people in the Northern States, that the Confederates were but a set of Conspirators, whose chief design was to subvert the Constitution and overthrow the Government. It was my object in this way, and in quarters which could not so well otherwise be reached, to disabuse the public mind there of this very erroneous sentiment; and that, too, by evidences almost as strong as those which the doubting Thomas required.* These very unfortunate suffering prisoners—suffering from the inhumanity of their own high officials, who had beguiled them by false pretexts into this Crusade against unoffending neighbors—so relieved and sent home to the bosom of their families and friends by such an act of mercy on our part, I thought would be the most effective instruments at our command for accomplishing this great end. The humblest one of them might, in my view, be a diplomat with more power for good in the Cause for which we were contending, than either of our able and accomplished Commissioners abroad, seeking sympathy or favor at foreign Courts. [Emphasis added, L.S.]

"The reply of General [Howell] Cobb, as well as that of others to whom I presented these views, for the purpose of bringing them to the consideration of the Administration at Richmond, was in substance, that if the Federal prisoners should be thus discharged, there would be no security for the safety of the gallant and equally suffering Confederates in Northern prisons. They might, he said, be tried and executed for treason, as the privateersmen had been [illegally] tried and condemned to death for piracy. These had been saved only by the retaliatory course, to which the Confederates had been compelled to resort; and that the only security the Confederates had against so monstrous an outrage upon their soldiers, was the Federal prisoners of war in hand to be kept until regularly exchanged, as hostages against such threatened barbarity. General Cobb, as well as all others with whom I conferred on the subject, fully concurred with me in general sympathy for the condition of prisoners on both sides, and expressed an earnest desire to do all in their power for their relief consistent with public security, and with what was considered by them to be due to Confederates then in the hands and power of the Federals, who openly proclaimed their purpose to treat them and deal with them as traitors!

"This was one of the differences between myself and some of the Confederate authorities. It was a difference upon policy only. Whether I was right in the views I took upon this question, must, of course, be but a matter of speculation. In the opinion of a large majority of mankind, it would, doubtless, be considered a very small matter to differ upon, either in Councils of War or of State. I was, however, thoroughly impressed, not only with the expediency of the policy suggested at the time, but with the great importance of its adoption. The results of wars often depend as much upon very small matters as upon great ones. The wavering scales of battle itself frequently turn upon the merest incidents scarcely noticed at the time. Every one at all conversant with the fluctuating tides of public sentiment and opinion, during an exciting and heated political canvass, knows full well how whole multitudes are frequently moved by matters of apparently very little import—by something, ever so small in itself, which strikes the heart and accords with the popular pulse. This, in my judgment, however, was no small matter, looking either to the humanity of the deed, or to its most probable consequences.

"It is proper also to state, that I did not concur, to the full extent, in the apprehensions entertained by General Cobb and others as to the fate of Confederate prisoners, which might result from the course advised. The retention of a few thousand of the officers of the highest grade among the Federal prisoners in Confederate hands, would be ample security, I thought, against the judicial execution of any Confederate prisoner under the charge of piracy or treason; while the unconditional release of so many prisoners of war on our part under all the circumstances of the case, would, in my judgment, then and now, have produced a profound sensation with the masses of the people throughout the entire North, overwhelming in its effects upon the men in authority at Washington! It might have produced a general release of prisoners as well as the removal of these Officials from Place and Power.

"*On this particular point, as I have said, I did not confer directly with Mr. Davis. I was not in Richmond that summer. Not that I had withdrawn from the Seat of Government with any intention of heading an opposition to the Administration, with the object of abandoning the war. Far, indeed, was I from being actuated during that absence by any such motives as these. I was confined at home the greater part of that summer by a protracted attack of severe disease.* Apart from this, it is proper also to state, that I did not think it worth while for me to submit my views on this subject to Mr. Davis, unless some other more efficient influences could be brought to bear upon him, in securing his sanction of the policy recommended. This brings up the consideration of some of the real differences, as I understood them, between myself and him, as well as others connected with the administration of our affairs, as to the true external policy, especially towards the Northern States, to be pursued by the Confederate States, from the time of their separation throughout the war. [Emphasis added, L.S.]

"To present these clearly it is necessary, first, to make [my Liberal friends] . . . fully understand my own position after the new [Southern] Confederation was formed as to the course which should be pursued toward their former associates, and the general ends and objects to be aimed at through the successful operation of the policy of Secession which had been rightfully, though not judiciously, resorted to, in my judgment, as we have seen. This position was very clearly indicated and set forth at an early day in that 'Corner-Stone Speech' from which I have already read in part. It was made . . . on the 21st of March, 1861, and in response to inquiries for my views of the then future. It was an off-hand speech, without any preparation or notes, and not reported with entire accuracy; yet in the report which went to the country, my general views upon all the topics discussed were substantially correct. After stating the political position of the seven Seceded States at that time, and sketching their action at Montgomery; the extent of country occupied by them; their material resources and productions which controlled the commerce of the world; and after showing their full capacity, in my opinion, to maintain a Separate Government, if that were desirable, the following is the language setting forth my views of the ends and objects which ought, however, to be aimed at by our external policy in this particular, as they were then given to the public in that report:

> 'Will everything, commenced so well, continue as it has begun? In reply to this anxious inquiry, I can only say it all depends upon ourselves. A young man starting out in life on his majority, with health, talent, and ability, under a favoring Providence, may be said to be the architect of his own fortunes. His destinies are in his own hands. He may make for himself a name of honor or dishonor, according to his own acts. If he plants himself upon truth, integrity, honor, and uprightness, with industry, patience, and energy, he cannot fail of success. So it is with us. We are a young Republic just entering upon the arena of Nations; we will be the architects of our own fortunes. Our destiny, under Providence, is in our own hands. With wisdom, prudence, and statesmanship on the part of our public men, and intelligence, virtue, and patriotism on the part of the people, success, to the full measure of our most sanguine hopes, may be looked for. But if unwise counsels prevail—if we become divided—if schisms arise—if dissensions spring up—if factions are engendered—if Party spirit, nourished by unholy personal ambition, shall rear its hideous form, I have no good to prophesy for you.

Without intelligence, virtue, integrity, and patriotism on the part of the people, and statesmanship on the part of their Rulers, no Republic or Representative Government can be durable or stable!

'We have intelligence, and virtue, and patriotism on the part of the people. All that is required is to cultivate and perpetuate these. Intelligence will not do without virtue. France was a nation of philosophers. These philosophers became Jacobins. They lacked that virtue, that devotion to moral principle, and that patriotism which is essential to good government. Organized upon principles of perfect Justice and Right—seeking amity and friendship with all other Powers—I see no obstacle in the way of our upward and onward progress. Our growth, by accessions from other States, will depend greatly upon whether we present to the world, as I trust we shall, a better Government than that to which neighboring States belong. If we do this, North Carolina, Tennessee, and Arkansas cannot hesitate long; neither can Virginia, Kentucky, and Missouri. They will necessarily gravitate to us by an imperious law. We made ample provision in our Constitution for the admission of other States; it is more guarded, and wisely so, perhaps, than the old Constitution on the same subject, but not too guarded to receive them as fast as it may be proper. Looking to the distant future, and, perhaps, not very far distant either, it is not beyond the range of possibility, and even probability, that all the great States of the Northwest will gravitate this way, as well as Tennessee, Kentucky, Missouri, and Arkansas.

'The process of disintegration in the old Union may be expected to go on with almost absolute certainty, if we pursue the right course. We are now the nucleus of a growing Power which, if we are true to ourselves, our destiny, and high mission, will become the controlling Power on this Continent. To what extent accessions will go on in the process of time, or where it will end, the future will determine. So far as it concerns States of the old Union, this process will be upon no such principles of Reconstruction as now spoken of, but upon Reorganization and new Assimilation! (Loud applause.) Such are some of the glimpses of the future as I catch them.'

"*The views here expressed showed unmistakably that the leading object with me was not only to secure the accession of the Border States, so-called, but the accession, at no distant day, of all the great Northwestern States so intimately connected with us geographically and politically; and moreover, if possible, by inducing our late derelict Confederates to reconsider their course, also, in the end, to secure the accession of all these States of the old Union into our new Confederacy! To use a common phrase for illustrating the idea, my object was to Nationalize our new Articles of Union, and to cause them to become the common Bond of a new and still more perfect Union of the whole, by bringing all the States to their voluntary adoption through a process not exactly of a Reconstruction of the old Union, but of a Reorganization of its constituent elements, and a new Assimilation upon the basis of our new Constitution, just as the original thirteen States had passed from the first Articles of Confederation of seventeen hundred and seventy-eight to the second of seventeen hundred and eighty-seven!* [Emphasis added, L.S.]

"This great result I considered of the utmost importance for the welfare of all the States and the permanent peace and prosperity of the whole country. I was also thoroughly impressed with the conviction that it could be attained by proper, prudent, and wise statesmanship. But these views, as well received as they were at the time and place they were given, met with no general favor in the Confederacy. They were commented on and condemned by the press in many places, and by several leading public men. The prevailing doctrine then given forth was, 'no more Union with the Northern States'—'the Separation is perfect, complete, and perpetual!' In this doctrine so given forth, I understood Mr. Davis to concur.

"*[In a word, I was quite willing to] make Peace on the basis of a 'Reorganization of the Union,' as [the Liberals] . . . call it, under . . . the Montgomery Constitution, . . . or upon renewed and reliable guarantees on the part of the derelict Northern States to return to the discharge of their obligations, and to maintain the Federal system according to the true spirit and intent of the Constitution of 1787; or I would have been willing to make Peace simply upon the recognition of the principle that lies at the foundation of that System—the absolute Sovereignty of the several States—leaving any Re-union or Unions in the future to their own voluntary choice, according to their own views of their own interests, safety, security, and happiness, as time with the lights of experience, patriotism, and wisdom might determine.* [Emphasis added, L.S.]

"*[I was never in favor of erecting a permanent separate Slave States' Confederacy.] . . . I did not consider such a Confederacy as either desirable in itself, or permanently practicable under the circumstances. The heterogeneousness of the interests of the different States under the Federal [Confederate] system, when administered according to its true principles, in my opinion, gave it real stability. This was the tightening principle which when left to its own free action gave steadiness to all its parts, and that beauty and grandeur exhibited in all its complicated motions.* [Emphasis added, L.S.]

"But to proceed. This general policy stated in the speech from which I have quoted, was what subjected me to the charge of 'Unionism' by some of the presses in the South throughout the war, and by some of them the charge may have gone to the extent of impressing the public mind with the idea, that I was opposed to the further prosecution of the war on our side. A greater mistake, however, was never made. The only difference between me and any other of the most ardent devotees in the cause, was as to the best objects to be aimed at in its prosecution, and the best means to be used for accomplishing whatever object should be resolved upon, as the best, if nothing else but the averting of ultimate subjugation.

"When the higher and grander objects to which I looked, and which I also thought not only attainable but also the surest means of preventing ultimate subjugation—the most disastrous result according to my opinion that could befall us as well as the people of all the States—became, therefore, altogether impracticable, the whole of my energies, heart and soul, were then directed to the next best alternative which was practisable, and that was the establishment of the separate Independence of the Confederacy. This I considered as not only essential to the maintenance of our own liberties; but the surest means of preserving Constitutional Liberty on the Continent. All this, in my judgment, was involved in the issue. The whole depended upon the successful maintenance of the Principle of the Sovereignty of the States. With this principle once recognized in the result of the war, the future, in my opinion, might well be left to itself, so far as related to any further adjustment of the States between themselves, according to the general laws of political affinity founded upon ' reciprocal advantages and mutual convenience.' Looking to the free operation of these laws in the future, under this firmly established principle, my own convictions were strong that our separate Independence would be of but short duration, however strongly so many of our public men at that time might desire that it should be perpetual, and even believe that it would be. My own views, however, I could not publicly repeat and continue to urge, even in vindication and enforcement of their merits, without producing schisms and dissensions, which, as I had said in the speech, would be attended with the most disastrous consequences. *The great object then was the success of the Cause in achieving the recognition of our separate Independence based upon the Sovereignty of the several States.* [Emphasis added, L.S.]

"[Concerning the idea that the Northern States would ever be induced to adopt the Confederate States Constitution] . . . I entertained scarcely a doubt upon the subject, with prudent and wise statesmanship on the part of our Rulers, looking to that end; indeed, but for the war, this result, with a proper policy for its attainment, would have been almost inevitable. *An overwhelming majority of the people of the Northern States was thoroughly opposed to the principles of the Centralists [Liberals].* The repeated popular condemnations of their principles referred to show this conclusively. But for the war the Centralists, then controlling the Federal Government by accident and not popular confidence, would, as a Party, have gone to pieces in ninety days. They would hardly have been sustained in New England at the next elections; the re-action there was already ominously felt by them. The war was a necessity for their continued hold of Power, even in those States. Hence, the conspiracy of the 'seven Governors' who demanded of Mr. Lincoln a change of his policy, as to the withdrawal of the Federal forces from the Southern Forts. War, with bold usurpations which it was to cover and excuse, was their only hope. [Emphasis added, L.S.]

"But even after the war was thus begun, if the Confederate Authorities had desired it, and had directed their energies to the attainment of that object, it could, in my *opinion, have still been accomplished*—*not so speedily or easily, but almost as surely in the end. The real war-spirit at the North, at first, was confined exclusively to the Abolitionists proper, and other Centralists [Liberals], who, from political affinity, cordially co-operated with them. But these two elements combined did not constitute, in the aggregate, much, if any, over one-third of the people of, the Northern States. The great majority of the people of these States, however strongly they were opposed to Slavery, were nevertheless more strongly attached to the Federal [Confederate] System, and utterly opposed to the consolidating principles of the [Liberal] Party then in power. Thousands, and hundreds of thousands of those who rushed to the rescue of the Capital in the manner we have seen, no more approved the usurpations of Power on the part of the Washington Authorities, nor the policy which inaugurated the war, than did the people of the Confederate States. They, it is true, were all opposed to Secession. They belonged to the mercantile and shipping classes, who were opposed to interrupting the old-established channels of trade, and to that very large class throughout the North, of all interests and occupations, who were thoroughly devoted to what they called 'the Union,' without any very well defined ideas of its nature or character. These different elements, actuated by such sentiments, constituted the masses on whom the 'old flag' produced such magical effect in those eventful days; and these were the masses on whom the Party now in power so adroitly used this 'old flag' for their ulterior purposes, though for it they themselves had neither reverence nor respect. It was now held up by them [Northern Liberals] as a sacred emblem of patriotic devotion, though by many of their leaders it had been for years before denounced as 'a flaunting lie' and 'hate's polluted rag.' It now, however, served their purpose, and they understood well how to use it, in misguiding the patriotic impulses of a confiding people. A very large majority, not only of the entire people of the North, but even of those who voluntarily entered the war, were thoroughly wedded to the Institutions of the Country, as established by the [Founding] Fathers. The main object with them was to maintain what they called 'the integrity of the Country.' 'The Union' under the Montgomery Constitution of 1861, would have been just as acceptable to them, as the 'Union' under the Philadelphia Constitution of 1787. Arch-Bishop [John] Hughes was an eminent representative man of this large portion of the Northern population. In this condition of things it seemed to me that the prospect of effecting an adjustment of the differences between the States upon the basis of the Montgomery Constitution was by no means hopeless, notwithstanding the formidable obstacles produced by the war, if the Confederate Authorities could but be induced to approve it, and direct all their civil and military operations with a view to its accomplishment. If our policy and course had been to make common cause with all true friends of the Federal [Confederate] System throughout the United States, upon this basis, against the usurpations and Centralizing principles of the Washington Government, the war, in my opinion, then and now, would have been a short one.* This, it is true, is speculation. [Emphasis added, L.S.]

"But even after this line of policy was not adopted, when the sole object of the recognition of our separate Independence was resolved upon, even then, with the view to this end, *I still thought the widest field for efficient operations in the external policy of the Government was at the North*, amongst our enemies themselves, so-called! There, after all, were to be found the only real sympathizers with the great Cause for which we were contending. These sympathizers were in no way friends or advocates of Disunion. This I well knew. *They were, however, true friends to those principles of Constitutional Liberty for which we were battling. They were utterly opposed to the [Liberal] principles and policy of the men controlling the Government at Washington, which had prompted the course the Seceded States had taken.* While they condemned the act of Secession as a proper mode of redress for acknowledged wrongs, they nevertheless could but sympathize with the sufferers of these acknowledged wrongs. Hundred of thousands, if not millions, in the Northern States were thoroughly devoted to those principles on which the Union of the States was founded, and on which alone they believed it ought to be maintained and preserved. *The war which had been brought on by the real enemies of the Constitution, and the Union under it*, necessarily threw this large class into political antagonism to us. It rendered them technically enemies to us; yet they had as much interest as we had in resisting the principles and usurpations of those who had brought these troubles upon them as well as upon us. The preservation of their liberties required action as well as ours, though upon a different theatre and in a different sphere. *One of the greatest errors in the policy of Secession, as I viewed it, was the separation which it necessarily produced between the real friends of the principles of the Constitution, North and South, in a common contest between them and the Centralists. It was in truth a great battle—the Political Armageddon of America—in which there should have been a concentration of forces instead of that dispersion which of necessity resulted from Secession.* But, still, *true friends of Constitutional Liberty, as true Christians, are animated by the same essential principles everywhere. They can but be allies in the great cause in whatever different organizations they may be placed. It was our true policy, therefore, as it seemed to me, while struggling for our own Independence, to use every possible means of impressing upon the minds of the real friends of liberty at the North, the truth that if we should be overpowered and put under the heel of Centralism, that the same fate would await them sooner or later. That it would be better for them to permit us to enjoy our separate Independence, and for them to do the same, than for both to be subjected to a Consolidated Despotism.*"[264] [Emphasis added, L.S.]

☛ "In illustration of my idea in this connection, though it be in anticipation of a great deal I intended to say upon intervening events during the second and third years of the war—marking its progress on both sides—it may be as well for me here to explain what gave rise to the idea or charge that I had not only grown lukewarm in the Cause, but was heading 'a Peace Party movement,' to which you have referred. This was a series of Resolutions unanimously adopted by the Legislature of Georgia, in March of this same year, 1864, and my thorough endorsement of them in a public speech before both Houses of the General Assembly.

"These Resolutions were drawn up by Linton Stephens, who was a member of the House that session. I had nothing to do with their preparation, but heartily approved both the sentiments announced, and the policy upon which the announcement was made. How far they merited the character attributed to them by the Southern press, to which you refer, others must judge for themselves. I certainly viewed them in no such light. If there was anything in them looking to an abandonment of the war, or of the Confederate Government by separate State action in negotiating Peace, I failed to perceive it; but I did see in them strong marks of that line of policy which I have just indicated. Here are the Resolutions, upon which you can form your own judgment:

> The General Assembly of the State of Georgia do resolve,
> 1st. That to secure the rights of life, liberty, and the pursuit of happiness, 'Governments were instituted among men, deriving their just powers from the consent of the governed; that whenever any form becomes destructive of these ends, it is the right of the people to alter or to abolish it, and to institute a new Government, laying its foundation on such principles, and organizing its powers in such form, as shall seem to them most likely to effect their safety and happiness.'
> 2nd. That the best possible commentary upon this grand text of our fathers of 1770, is their accompanying action, which it was put forth to justify; and that action was the immortal declaration that the former political connection between the Colonies and the State of Great Britain was dissolved, and the thirteen Colonies were, and of right ought to be, not one independent State, but thirteen independent States, each of them being such a "People" as had the right, whenever they chose to exercise it, to separate themselves from a political association and Government of their former choice, and institute a new Government to suit themselves.
> 3rd. That if Rhode Island, with her meagre elements of Nationality, was such a "People" in 1776, when her separation from the Government and people of Great Britain took place, much more was Georgia, and each of the other Seceding States, with their large territories, populations, and resources, such a "People," and entitled to exercise the same right in 1861, when they declared their separation from the Government and the people of the United States; and if the separation was rightful in the first case, it was more clearly so in the last, the right depending, as it does in the case of every "People" for

whom it is claimed, simply upon their fitness and their will to constitute an independent State.

4th. That this right was perfect in each of the States, to be exercised by her at her own pleasure, without challenge or resistance from any other power whatsoever; and *while these Southern States had long had reason enough to justify its assertion against some of their faithless associates, yet, remembering the dictate of "prudence," that, "Governments long established should not be changed for light and transient causes," they forbore a resort to its exercise, until numbers of the Northern States, State after State, through a series of years, and by studied legislation, had arrayed themselves in open hostility against an acknowledged provision of the Constitution, and at last succeeded in the election of a President [Lincoln] who was the avowed exponent and executioner of their faithless designs against the Constitutional rights of their Southern sisters*; rights which had been often adjudicated by the Courts, and which were never denied by the Abolitionists themselves, but upon the ground that the Constitution itself was void whenever it came in conflict with a "higher law," which they could not find among the laws of God, and which depended for its exposition solely upon the elastic consciences of rancorous partisans. The Constitution thus broken, and deliberately and persistently repudiated by several of the States who were Parties to it, ceased, according to universal law, to be binding on any of the rest, and those States who had been wronged by the breach were justified in using their right to provide "new guards for their future security." [Emphasis added, L.S.]

5th. *That the reasons which justified the separation when it took place, have been vindicated and enhanced in force by the subsequent course of the Government of Mr. Lincoln—by his contemptuous rejection of the Confederate Commissioners who were sent to Washington before the war, to settle all matters of difference without a resort to arms; thus evincing his determination to have war—by his armed occupation of the territory of the Confederate States—and especially by his treacherous attempt to reinforce his garrisons in their midst, after they had, in pursuance of their right, withdrawn their people and territory from the jurisdiction of his Government; thus rendering war a necessity, and actually inaugurating the present lamentable war—by his official denunciation of the Confederate States as "rebels" and "disloyal" States, for their rightful withdrawal from their faithless-associate States, whilst no word of censure has ever fallen from him against those faithless States who were truly "disloyal" to the Union and the Constitution, which was the only cement to the Union, and who were the true authors of all the wrong and all the mischief of the Separation, thus insulting the innocent by charging upon them the crimes of his own guilty allies—and finally, by his monstrous usurpations of power and undisguised repudiation of the Constitution, and his mocking scheme of securing a Republican [i.e., Confederate] form of Government to Sovereign States by putting nine-tenths of the people under the dominion of one-tenth, who may be abject enough to swear allegiance to his usurpation, thus betraying his design to subvert true Constitutional Republicanism in the North as well as the South.* [Emphasis added, L.S.]

6th. That while *we regard the present war between these Confederate States and the*

United States as a huge crime, whose beginning and continuance are justly chargeable to the Government of our enemy, yet we do not hesitate to affirm that, if our own Government, and the people of both Governments, would avoid all participation in the guilt of its continuance, it becomes all of them, on all proper occasions, and in all proper ways—the people acting through their State organizations and popular assemblies, and our Government through its appropriate Departments—to use their earnest efforts to put an end to *this unnatural, unchristian, and savage work of carnage and havoc*. And to this end we earnestly recommend that our Government, immediately after signal successes of our arms, and on other occasions, when none can impute its action to alarm, instead of a sincere desire for Peace, shall make to the Government of our enemy an official offer of peace, on the basis of the great principle declared by our common fathers in 1776, accompanied by the distinct expression of a willingness on our part to follow that principle to its true logical consequences, by agreeing that any Border State, whose preference for our association may be doubted (doubts having been expressed as to the wishes of the Border States), shall settle the question for herself, by a Convention to be elected for that purpose, after the withdrawal of all military forces, of both sides, from her limits. [Emphasis added, L.S.]

7th. That we believe this course, on the part of our Government, would constantly weaken, and sooner or later break down the war power of our enemy, by showing to his people the justice of our cause, our willingness to make peace on the principles of 1776, and the shoulders on which rests the responsibility for the continuance of the unnatural strife; that it would be hailed by our people and citizen-soldiery, who are bearing the brunt of the war, as an assurance that peace will not be unnecessarily delayed, nor their sufferings unnecessarily prolonged; and that it would be regretted by nobody, on either side, *except men whose importance or whose gains would be diminished by peace, and men whose ambitious designs would need cover under the ever-recurring plea of the necessities of war*. [Emphasis added, L.S.]

8th. That while the foregoing is an expression of the sentiments of this General Assembly respecting the manner in which peace should be sought, we renew our pledges of the resources and power of this State to the prosecution of the war, *defensive on our part*, until peace is obtained upon just and honorable terms, and until the Independence and Nationality of the Confederate States is established upon a permanent and enduring basis. [Emphasis added, L.S.]

"These Resolutions constituted what was called the Peace Programme of Georgia, and which it was alleged had the effect of dampening the ardor of our soldiery. In my view the legitimate effect was directly to the contrary. Hence, in the speech endorsing these Resolutions I used this language:

'You cannot, therefore, send these gallant defenders of Constitutional

Liberty, a more cheering message than that, while *they are battling for their rights, and the common rights of all in the field*, you are keeping sacred watch and guard over the same in the Public Councils. They will enter the fight with renewed vigor, from the assurance that their toil, and sacrifice, and blood, will not be in vain, but that when the strife is over and Independence is acknowledged, it will not be a bare name, a shadow and a mockery, but that with it, they and their children after them shall enjoy that liberty for which they now peril all. Next to this, the most encouraging message you could send them is, that while all feel that the brunt of the fight must be borne by them, and the only sure hope of success is in the prowess of their arms, yet every possible and honorable effort will be made by the Civil Departments of the Government to terminate the struggle by negotiation and adjustment upon the principles for which they entered the Contest.'

"A main feature in the external policy of these Resolutions, and the object aimed at in that view, was that they should go forth to the North before the opening of the Presidential canvass that year, with the firm belief that the principles announced, and the spirit with which they were announced, could not fail to make a deep impression upon the minds of all true friends of Constitutional Liberty in those States, and lead them to the basis of a just and permanent peace. I then thought, and still think, that if the Southern press had given these Resolutions a cordial indorsement, instead of censuring them as most of them did—if all the Southern States had with equal unanimity passed the same or similar Resolves, and if the Confederate Administration, at Richmond, could have been brought into cordial approval and co-operation with the same principles and policy, and had directed all their energies, civil and military, in the meantime, to the attainment of the object aimed at, the result of the Presidential election in the Northern States, that year, would have been the displacement of the Centralists [Liberals] from power, at Washington, and with that the final results of the war would have been far different from what they were, and, in my judgment, infinitely better for the Southern States as well as for the Northern States.

"All this again it is true is now speculation only. On the question whether my views of policy were the best at the time or not, it is not my purpose, on this occasion, to pass judgment, one way or the other. What has been said on the subject is only in answer to [the Liberals'] . . . question. Much more could be added on the same line. Enough, however, has been presented to show the general character of the difference between Mr. Davis and myself as to this branch of the external policy of the Confederate States."[265]

In an attempt to end the war as quickly as possible, in 1863 Stephens sought a meeting with Lincoln at Washington, D.C. to discuss terms of peace. Naturally, Lincoln, wanting war, refused to receive Stephens. The Confederate vice president describes the scenario for posterity:

☛ ". . . to understand the nature and character of my proposed mission to Washington in 1863, as well as the objects aimed at by it, it is necessary to know the exact military as well as political status at the time the mission was suggested, and my offer to assume it was made. This will require a *resumé* and rapid glance at the progress of events during the second and the early part of the third year of the war. The offer was made on the 12th day of June, 1863, a year and nearly four months after the Confederate Organization had gone into operation under the Constitution for a Permanent Government. That is the period, as we have seen, which I mark as the close of the first year of the war. Meanwhile, very great events had transpired. Let us now, then, review a few of the more important of these, both of a military and political character, as briefly as possible. This is essential to the point in hand.

"First. Beginning with the military, it must be recollected that the campaign of the second year of the war opened early in March, 1862. [U.S. General George B.] McClellan's new grand "Army of the Potomac," organized in Washington—thoroughly drilled, disciplined and equipped—numbering, at least, one hundred and twenty thousand, was put in motion on the 8th day of that month. They were first directed against General Joseph E. Johnston, still at Manassas, with a force of not over thirty thousand, all told. Johnston by great adroitness withdrew his small army towards Richmond and thus eluded the threatened crushing blow. This caused McClellan to change the line of his operations. The plan then adopted by him, was to make his approaches upon Richmond by the Chesapeake Bay up the Peninsula, using the York River as a base for supplies. For this purpose his forces were conveyed by transports to Fortress Monroe. The Peninsula, at that time, was defended by [Rebel] General John B. Magruder, with a small Confederate force, not exceeding eleven thousand. To support these, and to check McClellan's movements, when they were known, Johnston by rapid marches concentrated as soon as possible all available forces he could command at Yorktown or its vicinity. By these manoeuvres considerable delay was caused in McClellan's advance. It was not until early in May that he reached as far as Yorktown. Several encounters took place on his advance before and after he reached that place, as Johnston with consummate strategy retired before his overwhelming numbers. The most important of these engagements was the battle of Williamsburg on the 5th of May, between detachments of the two armies. This resulted very much to the advantage of the Confederates; but while Johnston by his great skill and tactics was thus holding McClellan in check or retarding his advance, very important military operations were going on elsewhere.

"The Missourians under [Confederate] Generals Sterling Price and Benjamin McCulloch, with less than 20,000 men, had, on the 7th day of March, fought the great battle of Elkhorn, against [Union] General Samuel R. Curtis, with a Federal force estimated at upwards of 25,000. The Confederates in this action were commanded by Major General Earl Van Dorn, to whom the chief command over Price had recently been assigned: and notwithstanding the result was not decisive either way, yet it was a great deal for the Confederates to hold the ground against such a disparity of numbers, as well as against the great superiority in arms and equipments brought against them. Their losses were also less than the losses on the side of the Federals. The severest blow the Confederates received in this conflict was that by which the gallant McCulloch fell, at the very time when complete triumph seemed to be in his grasp, and which most probably would have been achieved but for his fall.

"This heavy combat between the two sides west of the Mississippi, was followed not long afterwards by the great and ever memorable battles of the 6th and 7th of April, at Shiloh, near the Tennessee River. These at this time can only be alluded to. It must now suffice to say that in the first, the Confederates sustained what was deemed an irreparable loss in the fall of General Albert Sidney Johnston; but a brilliant victory in arms was achieved notwithstanding this loss by General Beauregard, who succeeded him in the chief command. The Federals, under General [Ulysses S.] Grant, were completely routed, notwithstanding their superiority in numbers, arms and equipments! Nothing saved them from entire capture or utter destruction but the shelter they found on the banks of the river under the protection of the heavy metal of their Gun-boats. With large Federal reinforcements under General [Don C.] Buell, the battle was renewed the next day, and desperately fought on both sides, without any decisive results either way. The Federals regained the ground from which they were driven the day before, while the Confederates continued to hold their original position. These two battles were the bloodiest of the war up to that time. The slaughter on both sides was appalling! The losses of the Confederates in killed, wounded and missing were 10,699, while the like losses of the Federals, according to their own accounts, were not less than 15,000. [Confederate] General Beauregard in his Report estimated them at near 20,000!

"The disparity between the number of the forces on the two sides in these sanguinary conflicts deserves special notice. The whole number of the Confederates, according to official returns, amounted to 40,355, while the number of the Federals, under Grant and Buell united, was according to the most reliable accounts not less than 78,000! Nearly double! To hold their own under such circumstances, rendered their victory of the second day almost as signal as that of the first.

"But, in the meantime, important operations of a like character were going on in another part of Virginia than that which was the theatre of McClellan's and Johnston's manœuvres. These too must not be passed over, though they be but glanced at. I allude to what was doing on the Shenandoah. The wonderful Valley Campaign of 'Stonewall' Jackson, of this year, in that part of the 'Old Dominion,' was opened, on the 23rd day of March, by the bloody conflict between his forces and those of [Union] General [James] Shields at Kernstown. This was followed by his notable victories over [Robert H.] Milroy at McDowell, on the 8th of May; over [Nathaniel P.] Banks at Winchester, on the 25th of May; over [John C.] Frémont at Cross-Keys, on the 8th of June; and over Shields at Port Republic, on the 9th of June.

"This most extraordinary man [Stonewall Jackson] appeared suddenly in the military firmament as a dazzling Meteor, or rather as a blazing and fiery Comet, exciting the highest admiration on one side, and causing profound fear and terror on the other! His biographer says of him, and correctly, I suppose, in substance, that within forty days he marched his little army, of not much above 15,000 men at any one time during this Campaign, over four hundred miles—sent 3,500 prisoners to the rear—left as many more of the enemy dead or disabled on the field, and defeated four separate armies amounting, in the aggregate, to at least three times his numbers!

"This is the man, the thunder of whose guns, seventeen days after his victory at Port Republic, in the evening of the 26th of June, caused such surprise and consternation on the rear right flank of McClellan's army, which had now reached the Chickahominy, within a few miles of Richmond! These were the opening signals of the six days continued fighting around the Confederate Capital, which sent McClellan's besieging hosts reeling to a new base under the shelter of their Gunboats on the James River. The whole of these grand military exploits were now under the immediate and entire direction of General [Robert E.] Lee, to whom the chief command was assigned upon General Joseph E. Johnston's being disabled by a severe wound, received during an engagement between portions of the two armies on the 31st of May. The result of these repeated conflicts was a series of successful victories, which, when the numbers and the equipments on the respective sides are considered, have few parallels in history. Besides the ten thousand prisoners, fifty-two pieces of artillery, with thirty-four thousand stand of small arms, and immense army stores, were captured. The second 'Onward to Richmond' was, therefore, quite as disastrous to the Federals as the first. Thus ended the Peninsula Campaign.

"Then came the third newly organized army for another movement against the Confederate Seat of Government. This was styled 'The Army of Virginia.' Its chief command was assigned to [Yankee] Major-General John Pope, with his

Headquarters announced by himself to be 'in the saddle,' though his geographical location, at the time, was somewhere between the Rappahannock and the Potomac. The remnant of McClellan's forces were ordered to Acquia Creek, to form part of the new organization under the direction of the new chieftain. These movements not only relieved Richmond from immediate danger, but Lee was also relieved by them from his defensive attitude. Renewed aggressive movements, however, were commenced by Pope. The battle of Cedar Run was fought on the 9th of August. Here his advance under Banks was checked by Jackson. When Pope's general plan was thus developed, Lee speedily moved all his forces to meet him. On the 30th of August, the two armies again met on the rolling grounds of Manassas. Here another great victory was achieved by Lee. Pope was completely routed, and driven to the Fortifications near Washington. The Federal loss was not less than thirty thousand. Eight Generals were killed, nine thousand prisoners taken, with thirty pieces of artillery and twenty thousand stand of small arms. After this brief career and sudden exodus of Pope, McClellan was again put in command of all the scattered Federal forces in the vicinity, to save Washington. Then came General Lee's movement into Maryland. Harper's Ferry was taken on the 15th of September. Here 11,000 prisoners were captured, with seventy-three pieces of artillery, and 13,000 stand of small arms. Two days afterwards, on the 17th of September, was fought the great drawn battle, between Lee and McClellan, at Sharpsburg. On Lee's safe and unmolested return to Virginia, McClellan fell out of favor again with the Washington authorities. On the 5th of November, he was removed from his command, and [Union] Major-General Ambrose E. Burnside appointed to take his place.

"This new chief immediately commenced active operations for a fourth 'Onward to Richmond.' His chosen line of attack was by the way of Fredericksburg. Here he found himself confronted by Lee; and here, on the 13th of December, the two armies again tried their strength. The Federals still greatly exceeded the Confederates in numbers. The result was the achievement by Lee of another most brilliant victory. The aggregate loss of the Confederates was 4,201, while that of the Federals was 12,321. Burnside was so crippled and damaged, and his forces became so demoralized by this conflict, that he made no further attempt to advance. He also soon lost favor at Washington, and was superseded by Major-General Joseph Hooker in command. Both armies thus quietly remained confronting each other on the opposite banks of the Rappahannock during the remainder of the second year of the war.

"While these events were transpiring in Virginia, some occurred in the West, which must also be noticed. After the great battles of the 6th and 7th of April, referred to, the armies on both sides were comparatively quiet until mid-summer. Gen. Beauregard's health failed in the meantime. Upon his application for temporary leave of absence, for its restoration, being granted, [Rebel] Gen. Braxton Bragg was appointed to take chief command of the Army of Tennessee, in his stead. About the middle of August, with forces then numbering near 50,000, he projected his most notable campaign through Tennessee into Kentucky. This resulted in the two battles of Richmond and Perryville, in the latter State. The one at Richmond was fought on the 31st day of August, by Gen. Edmund K. Smith, on the Confederate side, and secured all that the most sanguine could have hoped for. His success there and progress Northward excited alarm for the safety of Cincinnati. The battle at Perryville was fought on the 7th of October, under the auspices of Gen. Bragg himself. The result of this was the retirement of Bragg from Kentucky, and his taking position at or near Murfreesboro, Tennessee. Gen. Buell, who commanded the Federal forces against Bragg in this campaign, was superseded on the 30th of October, by [U.S.] Gen. William S. Rosecrans.

"This new commander immediately commenced active operations, with the view to drive Bragg from Murfreesboro. Meantime Bragg commenced active operations for aggressive movements himself. These two armies met on the 31st of December. The result was the bloody conflict known as the battle of Murfreesboro. It lasted two days. The result on the first day was decidedly favorable to the Confederates. At the close of the second both parties seemed to be equally willing to retire from the combat. During another day they continued to confront each other without either manifesting any desire or inclination to renew it, and both very probably were anxious for the other to withdraw first. This Bragg finally did. On the night of the 3rd of January, he retired and fell back towards Tullahoma. The town of Murfreesboro was immediately occupied by Rosecrans, who claimed the victory, which perhaps he never would have done but for this movement of Bragg. These two armies on this occasion, from the most reliable accounts, were not far from being equally matched as to numbers. There were about 40,000 on each side. In arms and equipments, however, the Federals had unquestionably the advantage. The fighting on both sides was heroic and desperate. In speaking of the sequel of it, Mr. [William] Swinton, to whom I have alluded before, with all his sympathies on the Federal side, uses the following language:

> 'This was the issue of the famous battle in the cedar brakes of Stone River, wherein were put *hors de combat* near twenty-five thousand men, of which appalling aggregate the sum of above ten thousand was from the Confederate, and of about fourteen thousand from the Union army.'

"This, coming as it does, from one on the opposite side, is certainly eulogy enough on *the spirit and valor with which the Confederates battled on that sanguinary field for the inestimable right of Self-government.* [Emphasis added, L.S.]

"These constitute some of the military events of the second year of the war, which it is important to keep in mind while considering the matters we are upon."[266]

☛ "After this battle of Murfreesboro everything remained comparatively quiet, both in the West and in Virginia, until the spring of 1863, when the campaigns of the third year of the conflict commenced. These were opened by the Federals, and were mainly directed to two objects—the capture of Richmond in the East, and the taking of Vicksburg in the West. The first and most desired of these objects was, as we have seen, committed to the military skill of [Union] Gen. [Joseph] Hooker. The other was committed to Gen. Grant, who had won great distinction and eclat for his capture of Forts Henry and Donelson in February, 1862. Hooker commenced his movements against Richmond, you will bear in mind, on the 27th day of April. He had had four months for preparation, with unlimited means to make his army everything he could wish it to be. He had massed opposite Fredericksburg at least 132,000 men, thoroughly drilled and instructed in every branch of the service. In artillery he had above 400 guns. Twelve thousand of his forces were well mounted and perfectly equipped as cavalrymen. For efficiency in every respect it was regarded superior, by far, to any military organization which had ever before taken the field in America. He himself pronounced it 'the finest Army on the Planet!'

"To meet this most formidable array, Gen. Lee had an effective force of not exceeding 50,000 men. Hooker seemed to take it for granted that Lee would instantly retire before these frightful odds, or that he was inevitably doomed to speedy capture with his entire command. Lee, however, did not retire. He gave battle for four days, beginning on the 29th, meeting Hooker's Divisions at every point of assault, and by skilful manoeuvres made several most successful assaults himself. The result of the four days terrible conflict was his driving back the entire body of the invading host. Hooker's whole plan was well conceived, and all his operations for an advance were faultlessly arranged. They failed in execution from nothing but the transcendent skill with which they were met, checked and thwarted, at and around Chancellorsville. The military genius displayed by General Lee in his various movements in repelling this advance of General Hooker, will ever place him high in the rank of the First Class of Commanders who have figured in the world's history! His aggregate losses were 10,281. Of Hooker's like aggregate losses no accurate official statement, as far as I have been able to discover, has ever been given to the public. Information upon the subject was expressly prohibited by orders from the War Department at Washington. From the most reliable estimates, however, they could not have been much, if any, under twenty-five thousand!

"But though the Confederates in all these engagements together achieved a grand success, and their arms were crowned with an exceedingly brilliant victory, yet they here met with a loss that could never be repaired! This was the fall of the great Chieftain, 'Stonewall' Jackson, as he was familiarly and endearingly styled by the soldiery and the mass of the people of the Confederate States. Just as he was in the successful accomplishment of one of his masterly flank movements, and one which turned the fortunes of this eventful four days contest, he received a wound that terminated in his death a few days afterwards. The saddest reflection attending so great a loss, was that the shot, which proved so disastrous, came by mistake from his own lines. Pushing ahead, leading his columns on a night attack, with a view to ascertain for himself the exact position of the Federals, whom he knew to be near, he got somewhat in advance of the main body of his troops. One of his staff and several others were with him. On their return, being mounted and riding briskly, they were supposed by those in the Confederate ranks to be an approaching party of Federal cavalry, and under this misapprehension were fired upon by them. The lines of [Lord] Byron on [Henry] Kirke White might well be applied to him:

> 'So the struck eagle, stretch'd upon the plain,
> No more through rolling clouds to soar again,
> View'd his own feather on the fatal dart,
> And wing'd the shaft that quiver'd in his heart.'

"It is said that his own orders were that his troops were not to fire 'unless cavalry approached from the direction of the enemy.' His death caused grief and mourning from the Potomac to the Rio Grande, and from the Ohio and Missouri to the Gulf and the Atlantic."[267]

☛ "But to go on with the matters more directly in hand. Hooker's grand [U.S.] Army was as completely demoralized in the month of May, by what had befallen it, as Burnside's had been from like causes in the month of December before. Lee, however, was in no condition to make an aggressive movement against it, even disordered and crippled as it was. His whole attention for some time was occupied in closely watching every motion of the adversary, and in strengthening his own forces from every available source. The two Divisions of [Confederate] General Longstreet were recalled from the lower part of Virginia. Other re-inforcements were ordered up. So that by the last of May his numbers were increased to about 68,000 men. Hooker was still confronting him with between 70,000 and 80,000.

"In the West, General Grant had been as unsuccessful in all his 'onwards' to Vicksburg, as McDowell, McClellan, Pope, Burnside, and Hooker had all respectively in turn, been in theirs to Richmond. His seven attempts to take that strong-hold—first, by way of Holly Springs—then by Chickasaw Bayou—then by Williams' Canal—then by Lake Providence—then by Yazoo Pass—then by Steele's Bayou—then by Milliken's Bend, and New Carthage Cut-Off, had all utterly failed. He was, at the time I now speak of, making his eighth attempt, by the rear land movement from below, but with no increased prospect of success from the 16th day of April, when this enterprise was entered upon, by his transports safely running the gauntlet of the Confederate batteries on the River.

"The prevailing opinion at the North as well as the South, in the early part of June, was that Grant's campaign against Vicksburg, would end in as complete a failure as Hooker's had against Richmond. Federal presses were severe in their censures against both. Grant especially had come short of public expectation, and his removal was urged by several high in authority at Washington. This was the general military aspect of affairs when the mission referred to, was proposed by me to Mr. Davis.

"Secondly. A like rapid glance at the intervening political events during the same period, to show the status in this respect, is also necessary, before taking up the subject of that mission. *It must be borne in mind, then, that there had been no 'step backward' in Mr. Lincoln's usurpations of power. The only change in this view was bolder and more glaring forward strides in the same direction. Proclamations of even more extraordinary character than these heretofore noticed, had been issued by him during the second year of the war. Two of these deserve special notice in this connection. The first was his celebrated [Preliminary] Emancipation Proclamation, so-called [which contained Lincoln's racist clause asking the U.S. Congress for money to deport all African-Americans out of the country]. It was issued on the 22nd of September, 1862, to take effect on the 1st of January, 1863 [known as the Final Emancipation Proclamation]. In this he avowedly assumed to do what he had repeatedly declared in the most public and solemn manner he had no rightful power to do. No usurpation could be more palpable or flagrant than this. By the other of these edicts, issued two days afterwards, Martial Law throughout the United States was virtually declared, and a new class of officers under military commission for the execution of this high-handed measure, unknown to the laws and Constitution, was created by Imperial orders through the [U.S.] War Department.* [Emphasis added, L.S.]

"These measures, to say nothing of others, had awakened a most serious alarm throughout the entire North, for the stability and security of their own liberties, even amongst those who favored the prosecution of the war for the preservation of 'the Union.' Hon. Benjamin R. Curtis, of Boston, Ex-Associate Justice of the Supreme Court of the United States, was a striking illustration of that class. This eminent Jurist, of the [Joseph] Story and [Daniel] Webster school in Politics, even in his retirement, felt it to be his duty to address his countrymen, in warning admonitions against these dangerous encroachments upon Constitutional Rights and open assaults upon the very Citadel of Liberty itself. Samples of this address, as it appeared in pamphlet form at the time, may properly be noticed as unmistakable *indicia* of the sentiments, at that period, of that large class of people in the Northern States to whom I have alluded before. Here is the Address [from the Autumn of 1862]. The opening words show the character of the apprehensions entertained by the [Yankee] writer, and the earnestness with which he uttered his warnings:

[Stephens quoting Curtis:] 'No citizen can be insensible to the vast importance of the late Proclamations and Orders of the President of the United States [Lincoln]. . . . These are subjects in which the people have vast concern. It is their right, it is their duty, to themselves and to their posterity, to examine and to consider and to decide upon them; and no citizen is faithful to his great trust if he fail to do so, according to the best lights he has, or can obtain. . . . It has been attempted by some partisan journals to raise the cry of "disloyalty" against any one who should question these Executive acts.

'But the people of the United States know that loyalty is not subserviency to a man, or to a Party, or to the opinions of newspapers; but that it is an honest and wise devotion to the safety and welfare of our country, and to the great principles which our Constitution of Government embodies, by which alone that safety and welfare can be secured. And when those principles are put in jeopardy, every true loyal man must interpose according to his ability, or be an unfaithful citizen. This is not a Government of men. It is a Government of laws. And the laws are required by the people to be in conformity to their will, declared by the Constitution. Our loyalty is due to that will. Our obedience is due to those laws, and he who would induce submission to other laws, springing from sources of power not originating in the people, but in casual events, and in the mere will of occupants of places of power, does not exhort us to loyalty, but to a desertion of our trust.'

"These were noble words, aptly and timely uttered! On [Lincoln's] . . . Emancipation Proclamation, [Judge Curtis said]:

'I do not propose to discuss the question whether the first of these Proclamations of the President, if definitively adopted, can have any practical effect on the unhappy race of persons to whom it refers; nor what its practical consequences would be, upon them and upon the white population of the United States, if it should take effect, nor through what scenes of bloodshed, and worse than bloodshed, it may be, we should advance to those final conditions; nor even the lawfulness, in any Christian or civilized sense, of the use of such means to attain any end.

'If the entire social condition of nine millions of people has, in the providence of God, been allowed to depend upon the Executive decree of one man, it will be the most stupendous fact which the history of the race has exhibited. But, for myself, I do not yet perceive that this vast responsibility is placed upon the President of the United States. I do not yet see that it depends upon his Executive decree, whether a servile war shall be invoked to help twenty millions of the white race to assert the rightful authority of the Constitution and laws of their country, over those who refuse to obey them. But I do see that this Proclamation asserts the power of the Executive to make such a decree!

'I do not yet perceive how it is that my neighbors and myself, residing remote from armies and their operations, and where all the laws of the land may be enforced by Constitutional means, should be subjected to the possibility of military arrest and imprisonment, and trial before a Military Commission, and punishment at its discretion for offences unknown to the law; a possibility to be converted into a fact at the mere will of the President, or of some subordinate officer, clothed by him with this power. But I do perceive that this Executive power is asserted.

'. . . And first, let us understand the nature and operation of the Proclamation of Emancipation, as it is termed; then, let us see the character and scope of the other Proclamation, and the Orders of the Secretary of War, designed to give it practical effect, and having done so, let us examine the asserted source of these powers.

'. . . The persons who are the subjects of this Proclamation are held to service by the laws of the respective States in which they reside, enacted by State authority as clear and unquestionable, under our system of Government, as any law passed by any State on any subject.

'This Proclamation, then, by an Executive decree, proposes to repeal and annul valid State laws which regulate the domestic relations of their people. Such is the mode of operation of the decree.' [Emphasis added, L.S.]

"After a good deal of like character upon the first of these Proclamations, [Judge Curtis] . . . is exceedingly pointed and powerful in [his] . . . denunciations of the principles of the other. Take the following as samples:

'The second Proclamation, and the Orders of the Secretary of War, which follow it, place every citizen of the United States under the direct military command and control of the [U.S.] President [Lincoln]. They declare and define new offences not known to any law of the United States. They subject all citizens to be imprisoned upon a military, order, at the pleasure of the President, when, where, and so long as he, or whoever is acting for him, may choose. They hold the citizen to trial before a Military

Commission appointed by the President, or his representative, for such acts or omissions as the President may think proper to decree to be offences; and they subject him to such punishment as such Military Commission may be pleased to inflict. They create new offices, in such number, and whose occupants are to receive such compensation, as the President may direct; and the holders of these offices, scattered through the States, but with one chief inquisitor at Washington, are to inspect and report upon the loyalty of the citizens, with a view to the above described proceedings against them, when deemed suitable by the central authority.

'Such is a plain and accurate statement of the nature and extent of the powers asserted in these Executive Proclamations.

'What is the source of these vast powers? Have they any limit? Are they derived from, or are they utterly inconsistent with, the Constitution of the United States?

'The only supposed source or measure of these vast powers appears to have been designated by the President [emphasis added, L.S.], in his reply to the address of the Chicago clergymen, in the following words:

[Lincoln speaking:] "Understand, I raise no objection against it on legal or Constitutional grounds; for, as Commander-in-Chief of the Army and Navy, in time of war, *I suppose I have a right to take any measure which may best subdue the enemy.*" [Emphasis added, L.S.]

'This is a clear and frank declaration of the opinion of the President respecting the origin and extent of the power he supposes himself to possess; and, so far as I know, no source of these powers other than the authority of Commander-in-Chief in time of war, has ever been suggested. . . .

'It must be obvious to the meanest capacity, that if the President of the United States has an implied Constitutional right, as Commander-in-Chief of the Army and Navy in time of war, to disregard any one positive prohibition of the Constitution, or to exercise any one power not delegated to the United States by the Constitution, because, in his judgment, he may thereby "best subdue the enemy," he has the same right, for the same reason, to disregard each and every provision of the Constitution, and to exercise all power, needful, in his opinion, to enable him "best to subdue the enemy. . . ." [Emphasis added, L.S.]

'The necessary result of this interpretation of the Constitution is, that, in time of war, the President has any and all power, which he may deem it necessary to exercise, to subdue the enemy; and that every private and personal right of individual security against mere Executive control, and every right reserved to the States or the people, rests merely upon Executive discretion. [Emphasis added, L.S.]

'. . . Besides, all the powers of the President are executive merely. He cannot make a law. He cannot repeal one. He can only execute the laws. He can neither make, nor suspend, nor alter them. He cannot even make an article of war. He may govern the army, either by general or special orders, but only in subordination to the Constitution and laws of the United States, and the Articles of War enacted by the Legislative power. [Emphasis added, L.S.]

'The time has certainly come when the people of the United States must understand,

and must apply those great rules of Civil Liberty, which have been arrived at by the self-devoted efforts of thought and action of their ancestors, during seven hundred years of struggle against arbitrary power. If they fail to understand and apply them, if they fail to hold every branch of their Government steadily to them, who can imagine what is to come out of this great and desperate struggle. The military power of eleven of these States being destroyed—what then? What is to be their condition? What is to be our condition?' [Emphasis added, L.S.]

"These samples must suffice to show the general tenor of this address [given by a Northerner]. The whole presents in a clear and strong view the nature of that civic and political contest which had now begun in earnest in the Northern States between the Centralists [Northern Republicans, i.e., Yankee Liberals] and the true friends of Constitutional Liberty there [Northern Democrats, i.e., Yankee Conservatives], while the military contest on the same essential principles was going on, as we have seen, between the States of the two great Sections of the country. This civil and political conflict so commenced there resulted at the fall elections of 1862, generally to the disadvantage of the Centralists. They lost the great State of New York. Pennsylvania, New Jersey, Ohio, Indiana and Illinois gave strong indications that a majority of their people were in full sympathy with the sentiments of Judge Curtis. The 'truly loyal' masses of the people—those loyal to the Constitution [Yankee Conservatives]—everywhere at the North were beginning seriously to inquire if the Southern States should be overthrown by such usurpations, what then? What was to be the condition of these Southern States? What, too, in that event, was to be the condition of the Northern States?"[268]

☛ "The failures of Hooker and Grant in the spring campaigns of 1863, favored a freer discussion of these momentous questions. Even the 'Seven Headed Monster,' the [Liberal] War Party proper at the North, with clotted gore on its hideous front, was grievously despondent in view of the situation. More liberty of speech was allowed than had been during 'the reign of terror.' 'The Old Guard,' a publication by [Yankee Conservative] Charles Chauncey Burr, of the Jefferson school of Politics, was now permitted to make its appearance in unqualified denunciations of the principles and purposes of the Centralists [Liberals]. A public meeting in the City of New York was tolerated, at which Resolutions, favoring Peace, were adopted. In Philadelphia a Peace Convention had been called. [Clement L.] Vallandigham, the ablest member of the Democratic [Conservative] Party at the North, after the death of [Stephen A.] Douglas, had been nominated for the Governorship of Ohio, with every prospect of success. He was the Leader in the lower House of Congress against the usurpations of the Administration, and bold denouncer of the policy of main taming 'the Union' by a subjugation of the Southern States. It is true the prospect of this Tribune of the people becoming Governor of the Giant State of the West was more than the [Liberal] Powers at Washington, dispirited as they were, could bear. [Vallandigham] . . . had been seized and exiled by [Lincoln's] military orders, but that only tended to increase the rising popular enthusiasm in his favor."[269]

☞ "This, then, was the existing Military, as well as Political status, on the 12th day of June, 1863, when I, then here at home, Congress not being in session, addressed Mr. [Jefferson] Davis at Richmond the following letter:

> 'Dear Sir:—I have just seen what purports to be a letter addressed to you by [Union war criminal] Major General David Hunter, commanding the Federal Forces at Port Royal, S.C., bearing date the 23rd of April last. Of the extraordinary character of this paper, its [savage] tone, temper, and import, whether genuine or not, it is not my purpose to speak. It may be a forgery. [It was not. It was genuine. L.S.] All I know of it is from its publication as we have it in our newspapers. But it has occurred to me if it be genuine, this, together with other matters of controversy I see likewise in the papers, in relation to the future exchange of certain classes of prisoners of war, may necessarily lead to a further conference with the authorities at Washington, upon the whole subject. In that event I wish to say to you briefly, that if you think my services in such a mission would be of any avail, in effecting a correct understanding and agreement between the two Governments, upon those questions involving such serious consequences, they are at your command.
>
> 'You will remember while we were at Montgomery, when the first Commissioners were sent to Washington with a view to settle and adjust all matters of difference between us and the United States, without a resort to arms, you desired me to be one of those clothed with this high and responsible trust. I then declined, because I saw no prospect of success—did not think, upon a survey of the whole field, that I could effect anything good or useful in any effort I could then make on that line. You will allow me now to say, that at this time, I think possibly I might be able to do some good—not only on the immediate subject in hand; but were I in conference with the authorities at Washington on any point in relation to the conduct of the war, I am not without hopes, that indirectly, I could now turn attention to a general adjustment, upon such basis as might ultimately be acceptable to both parties, and stop the further effusion of blood in a contest so irrational, unchristian, and so inconsistent with all recognized American principles.
>
> 'The undertaking I know would be a great one. Its magnitude and responsibility I fully realize. I might signally fail. This I also fully comprehend; but still, be assured, I am not without some hopes of success; and whenever or wherever I see any prospect of the possibility of being useful

or of doing good, I am prepared for any risk, any hazards, and all responsibilities commensurate with the object. Of course, I entertain but one idea of the basis of final settlement or adjustment; that is, the recognition of the Sovereignty of the States, and the right of each in its Sovereign capacity to determine its own destiny. This principle lies at the foundation of the American system. It was what was achieved in the first war of Independence, and must be vindicated in the second. The full recognition of this principle covers all that is really involved in the present issue. That the Federal Government is yet ripe for such acknowledgment, I, by no means, believe; but that the time has come for a proper presentation of the question to the authorities at Washington, I do believe. Such presentation as can only be made in a Diplomatic way. While, therefore, a mission might be despatched on a minor point, the greater one could possibly, with prudence, discretion, and skill, be opened to view and brought in discussion, in a way that would lead eventually to successful results. This would depend upon many circumstances, but no little upon the character and efficiency of the agent. It so occurs to me, and so feeling, I have been prompted to address you these lines. My object is, solely, to inform you, that I am ready and willing to undertake such a mission, with a view to such ulterior ends, if any fit opportunity offers in the present state of our affairs in relation to the exchange of prisoners, or any other matter of controversy growing out of the conduct of the war; and if also, you should be of opinion that I could, be useful in such position. I am at your service, heart and soul, at any post you may assign me, where I see any prospect of aiding, assisting or advancing the great cause we are engaged in, and of securing with its success the blessings of permanent peace, prosperity and *Constitutional Liberty*. [Emphasis added, L.S.]

'Should the present position of affairs in your opinion, be suitable, of which I am not so well informed as you are, and this suggestion so far meet your approval as to cause you to wish to advise further with me on the subject, you have but to let me know—otherwise no reply is necessary, and none will be expected.

'With best wishes for you personally, and our common country in this day of her trial, I remain yours,' &c.

"From this letter you see the nature and objects of my proposed mission. You see the line of policy therein indicated. It was not intended as a Peace mission at all. It did not contemplate any overture or direct offer of terms of any sort on that subject. Hence, Mr. Davis at that time, could not have given his consent to any proposition on my part, to make an attempt at negotiations for Peace, as was generally supposed. Mr. Lincoln, as was known, would receive no one commissioned on such an errand. It was exceedingly doubtful whether he would hold a renewed conference through a special Commissioner, even upon the matter of the exchange of prisoners—a subject, at that time, of such pressing importance from considerations of humanity alone; especially in view of the extraordinary character of [U.S.] General Hunter's announcement in his letter referred to. But if Mr. Lincoln could be prevailed on to agree to such a conference, then the object proposed, besides effecting, if possible, the general amelioration of prisoners, and the mitigation of the horrors of war as conducted by the Federals, was to use the occasion for effecting also, if possible, other ulterior results which might open the way for future negotiations that might eventually lead to an amicable adjustment. In the accomplishment of these ulterior ends the idea was not so much to act upon Mr. Lincoln and the then ruling [Liberal] authorities at Washington, as through them, when the correspondence should be published, upon the great mass of the people in the Northern States, who were becoming so sensitively alive, as we have seen, to the great danger of their own liberties.

"It was believed that in a conference of this character that such a course could be pursued in the discussion of the questions directly in hand, as to deeply impress the growing Constitutional Party at the North with a full realization of the true nature and ultimate tendencies of the war, and to lead all who were anxiously inquiring what was to be their condition in case the Southern States should be subjugated to see that *the surest way to maintain their liberties, was to allow us the separate enjoyment of ours—that the surest way to preserve Self-government at the North, was not to allow it to be overthrown at the South*. In my view this result had to be effected in some way, and the Centralists [Northern Liberals] displaced from power at Washington, before there could be any hopeful prospect in offers to negotiate for peace upon a proper basis. The line of policy indicated by me to this end, depended greatly upon the then military condition of affairs."[270] [Emphasis added, L.S.]

☛ *"The result of wars generally depends quite as much upon diplomacy as upon arms—upon the proper use of the pen as of the sword. There is a time for each. It is a matter of the utmost importance to know when and how to use both.* The Confederate armies, officers and men, for two years and upwards, as we have seen, had nobly and gloriously performed their part. With less than five-hundred thousand in all, from the beginning up to this time, they had brought the enemy, numbering more than a million, during the same period, almost to a standstill. Gen. Grant, it is true, was still 'pegging away,' in his slow approaches upon Vicksburg, but on no other line were any active movements being made. I thought the time had now come, in view of the situation, both politically at the North and militarily at the South, as matters stood in the early part of June, 1863, for our Civil authorities to essay something in their department, and on the line indicated in this letter to the President. The entire propriety and expediency, however, in making this essay, in my judgment, depended upon the then military status.

"In this view, Mr. [Jefferson] Davis did not concur. He did not believe that the road to Peace lay in that way. He did not think that anything towards its ultimate obtainment could be effected on this line of external policy, indicated by me. He regarded Mr. Lincoln and his Cabinet as thoroughly representing the fixed principles and sentiments of a majority of the people of the Northern States. He thought, after Mr. Lincoln's conduct towards our first Peace Commissioners, that the surest, if not only means, of securing our rights was the power of our arms. The efficiency of Diplomacy, at the proper time, and in the proper manner, he fully recognized. On these points there was no disagreement between us, except as to time and manner. In this case his opinion was, that Diplomacy and Arms ought to act in conjunction, and that the Commissioner I had suggested ought to go with a victorious and threatening army. The result of my proposed mission, therefore, was the yielding of my views in this particular to his on this occasion, and not of his to mine, as I will now state.

"My letter was responded to by telegram on the 18th or 19th of June. This was received on the 19th. The response was for me to go on immediately to Richmond. This I did. On reaching there on the 22nd or 23rd, I found an entire change in the military aspect of affairs, from my understanding of it on the 12th of June, when my letter was penned, and with a special view to which the line of policy therein set forth was suggested. [Confederate General Robert E.] Lee was no longer resting quietly on the Rappahannock. I knew nothing of the contemplated movement into Pennsylvania. On the 23rd, in an interview with Mr. [James A.] Seddon, [Confederate] Secretary of War, I was informed that a portion of the Confederate army was already across the Potomac. I was, also, then informed by him, greatly to my surprise, that Grant was pressing [Rebel General John C.] Pemberton closely at Vicksburg, and that the surrender of that place was inevitable. It was only a question of time. There was no hope of raising the siege or giving succor, and that the Post could not be held longer than the supplies on hand would last. These were thought to be sufficient for some weeks to come. This was the first intimation I had of any serious apprehensions of any such final result as to Vicksburg.

"I also had an interview with the [C.S.] President, (Mr. Davis,) as soon as it could be obtained. We talked freely over the subject of my letter, as well as the then position of affairs in the military view. I explained to him more fully than I had done in the letter, the ulterior objects I had hopes of effecting when it was written; but stated that the change in the military aspect, since the letter was written, had entirely changed my views as to the propriety or policy, of then undertaking anything on that line. The movement of our army into Pennsylvania would greatly excite the war spirit and strengthen the War Party—effects directly opposite to those which I had hoped to produce, while our armies were remaining quiet after their recent victories, and with the then state of feeling at the North. I stated that it was a question of great doubt with me, when my offer was made, whether I would be received by Mr. Lincoln in the character of such Commissioner as was proposed, but I now considered it almost certain that any application of the sort would be rejected, under existing circumstances; and my judgment, in consequence of the changes referred to, was as decidedly against the policy of making the proposal then, as it was in favor of it when the letter was written.

"He agreed entirely in the doubts expressed by me as to my reception by the [Liberal] Washington authorities to confer or to enter into any agreement upon the subjects proposed; but was very decided in the opinion that the probabilities of the reception were rather increased than lessened by the present position of General Lee's army. He thought Mr. Lincoln would more likely receive such Commissioner if General Lee's army was actually threatening Washington City, than if he was lying quietly south of the Rappahannock. In this view I could not concur, and gave it as my opinion that the proposed mission had better be postponed. He suggested a Cabinet Consultation upon the subject, and requested me to attend it. This consultation was held the same day. Every one of the [Confederate] Cabinet, while expressing doubts as to the reception, were very decided in the opinion expressed, by the President, that the prospect of success was increased by the position and projected movements of General Lee's army. They all thought the existing state of affairs, militarily, both in the East and West, rendered the occasion most opportune for making the effort for the conference suggested.

"They were all indulging in the most hopeful expectations of the results of General Lee's campaign coming in aid of their views. Indeed, their ideas in the matter evidently sprung from these sanguine expectations. Mr. Seddon was particularly anxious that there should be no postponement or delay in the business, but that whatever could be done, if anything, in the matter of prisoners, should be done before the fall of Vicksburg with its garrison of something over thirty thousand men. Urged in this way, my views were yielded to theirs, and I assumed the mission and undertook to do what I could in the matter of prisoners, and the conduct of the war, when it was thought there was a probability as well as a possibility of my being able to effect something on these important subjects; though I stated to Mr. Davis and the Cabinet that I never would have made the offer I did, under such circumstances as I found existing on my arrival at Richmond. The mission undertaken, therefore, was not the one proposed by me, nor was it, as undertaken, in any sense, an attempt to offer terms of negotiation for Peace."²⁷¹

☛ "At first, the arrangement was for me to proceed by land in the route taken by General Lee's army, and communicate with the Washington authorities from his Headquarters. Excessive rains, badness of roads, and tardiness of travelling in consequence, caused a change in this arrangement. A small steamer was put in readiness by orders of Mr. [Stephen R.] Mallory, of the [Confederate] Navy Department, and I, with Mr. Robert Ould, the distinguished Agent for the Exchange of Prisoners on our side, a gentleman of high accomplishments and attainments, who had been appointed Secretary to the Commission, set out in this way directly for Washington City, if we should be permitted to pass the Federal lines at Fortress Monroe.

"The sequel is known. The great battles of Gettysburg were fought before we reached Newport News. There our arrival and proposal were telegraphed to Washington by Acting Rear Admiral Samuel Phillips Lee [a cousin of Robert E. Lee], of the U. S. Navy, commanding the Blockade Squadron at that point. We were detained two days while the proposition for the conference was held under consideration at Washington. In the meantime Vicksburg was surrendered by General Pemberton, on the 4th day of July—earlier than was expected. *The reply from [Lincoln in] Washington then came, that no Special Commissioner, on the subjects embraced in the proposed conference, would be received.* [Emphasis added, L.S.]

"This is the full history of that whole affair. In it you see something more of the differences between Mr. Davis and myself, as to our views of the policy to be pursued towards the people of the Northern States, as well as the manner of conducting it. Whether my views or his, on the occasion just alluded to, were the better, it is not my purpose to pass judgment. In the retrospect, it appears to me that this was the turning point in the fate of the Confederate Cause.

> 'There is a tide in the affairs of men,
> Which, taken at the flood, leads on to fortune;
> Omitted, all the voyage of their life
> Is bound in shallows and in miseries.'

"At the time these events were transpiring I thought, if [Confederate] General [Robert E.] Lee had remained quietly on the defensive south of the Rappahannock; if all the forces he had collected over and above what were necessary to hold his position there, had been sent in aid of the dislodgement of Grant, in his siege of Vicksburg, instead of joining in the movement made into

Pennsylvania; if the cavalry incursion, by [Confederate] General John [H.] Morgan, into Ohio, about the same time, had not taken place, which could have no effect so sure as that of arousing the war spirit at the North then drooping and pining, that it would have been greatly better for us; and in that state of things, I thought that the conference suggested would most probably have been agreed to; and, also, that the results looked to in its projection, would most probably have eventually ensued. Still, I might have been entirely disappointed. The whole might have utterly failed, even if the military operations on our side had been according to my own programme.

"While, on the other hand, if Mr. Davis's expectations of General Lee's operations had been realized; if the Federal armies under [Yankee] Major-General George G. Meade, who took General Hooker's place on his being removed, had been defeated at Gettysburg, and that had not been a drawn battle as it was; if Washington City had actually been put in imminent danger by the approach of the victorious Confederates, then, perhaps, Mr. Lincoln might have been most unwillingly brought to entertain a proposition to treat not only on the exchange of prisoners, but upon terms of Peace, as Mr. Davis hopefully expected, notwithstanding the fall of Vicksburg. Upon these questions others must form their own speculative judgments. Indeed, all that could be said on the subject now, as stated before, would be nothing but speculation.

"In this connection, however, in speaking of these differences between Mr. Davis and myself, on this branch of our external policy, I will add that they became so wide and decided in the following year, during the Presidential canvass at the North between Lincoln and McClellan, as to lead to a correspondence between us on the subject, which excited, perhaps, a little temporary feeling on both sides, but which in no way interfered with our personal relations, or with our full, free, cordial and continued interchange of views upon all matters of public interest. *There was, as I have said before, at no time upon these, or any other questions, a personal breach, or anything like a feud between us.* So much, then, in answer to your inquiry touching our differences, so far as they related to matters of foreign policy. [Emphasis added, L.S.]

"I come now to the differences between us upon those matters of internal policy, and questions of Constitutional law referred to. These I will only state generally, without entering at all into an exposition of the subjects, or a presentation of the opposing views in regard to them. No good at this time could be effected by a discussion of the points involved. These are certainly among the dead issues of the present day; though the principles involved in some of them, can never die. The leading subjects of our differences, however, on the internal policy of the Government, when the questions were living and vital, related entirely to the best, surest and most efficient mode of wielding the resources of the country for the success of the Cause in conformity with the provisions of the Constitution.

"First, I thought our great staples, tobacco and cotton, especially cotton, constituted the greatest elements of financial power at our command—ample for all purposes, and should be promptly and efficiently used in a practicable way in securing to this end the full development of its tremendous agency. The Produce Loan scheme adopted at the instance of the [Confederate] Administration at Montgomery, as before mentioned, came far short of accomplishing what, in my judgment, could be accomplished from this one of our resources in supplying the sinews of war. Indeed, as matters turned out, very little benefit, where a great deal was expected, was ever derived from that measure.

"Next: The support of the armies by a tax in kind on breadstuffs, instead of the issue of Treasury notes for that purpose, was a favorite idea with me from the beginning. All the States were large producers of grain and animal food, besides the great staples referred to produced in some of them. A tithe [tax] on the annual product of provisions, as was shown by statistics, was amply sufficient to support an army greater than the Confederates could possibly raise. This system, it is true, was resorted to after awhile, but not until after the currency, by redundant issue, had become greatly depreciated. Of its mismanagement, after it was adopted, through which, out of over one hundred and thirty millions' worth of provisions contributed by the tax-payers, less than forty millions of the amount ever reached its proper destination, it is not my purpose now to speak. This resulted from the fault, misconduct and short-comings of subalterns.

"But the measures upon which I differed most widely with the [Confederate] Administration were those which authorized the impressment of provisions at arbitrary prices—the suspension of the Writ of *Habeas Corpus*, and the raising of the necessary military forces by Conscription. *These last I considered not only radically wrong in principle, but as violative of the Constitution, and as exceedingly injurious to our Cause in their effects upon the people.*"[272] [Emphasis added, L.S.]

☛ "[My Liberal friends at the North believe that the Confederate military draft saved Richmond in 1862, and even helped sustain the Southern Cause as long as it was.] But [this view] . . . is a very great mistake. Richmond was not saved by Conscription in 1862, or at any time. The great battles fought by the [C.S.] Army of Virginia, first under [Joseph E.] Johnston, then under [Robert E.] Lee, which achieved such brilliant victories in saving Richmond . . . were fought in

May and June of that year. The first act of [Confederate] Conscription was passed the 16th of April before. That Army was composed chiefly, and almost entirely, of volunteers already enlisted, and in the service for three years or the war. It is true a few Regiments whose term of service was for one year, and which had not expired when the act passed, immediately organized under it for the future; but the term of voluntary service, in which they were enlisted, of most, if not all of these few, extended beyond the time in which the fate of Richmond on that occasion was determined. There may have been a very few Regiments whose term would have expired before that time, and composed of men who, without the passage of the act, might have quit the service. But the number of such Regiments as these must have been very small. Indeed, if any such did exist, (composed of men, who would have quit the field at such an hour, without the restraint of that act,) they were certainly not made of that material which caused the turn of the scales of battle in these conflicts. The fact is, very few, if any, of that Army were there under the operation of that act; not a man had been brought there by it. *Ninety per cent, at least of the fighting men of that Army who achieved these victories, were enrolled in Regiments already voluntarily enlisted for three years or the war, when the act of Conscription was passed.* [Emphasis added, L.S.]

"*The idea or belief that there was a necessity for that mode of filling our armies at the tune, is altogether erroneous and unsustained by the facts of the case. I do not know the exact number, but I think I may venture to say that there were near four hundred thousand men then voluntarily enlisted in the Confederate armies, for three years or the war. Upon every call for troops under the regular Constitutional militia system, the call had been responded to by the tender of more volunteers on these terms than the number asked for. Georgia alone had upwards of fifty Regiments, besides several Battalions, then in the field at Richmond, or elsewhere, so enlisted. In the last call before this act was passed, four more Regiments tendered their services on these terms, than were called for from this State. They were not received by the War Department upon the ground that their services were not needed. This was not more than two months before the passage of that act. The other States were in no degree behind Georgia in readiness to respond with a tender of troops under voluntary service, upon the same terms in proportion to population.* [Emphasis added, L.S.]

"Conscription, therefore, was resorted to from no necessity whatever, as a means of raising troops. It was adopted as a policy, mainly with a view to securing a different mode of officering those who were already voluntarily in the service, as well as those who might be called upon to enter it afterwards. Of this military view of the subject, it is not my purpose now to speak. A vast deal might be said upon it on both sides. *All I mean now to say is, that, in my judgment, it plainly violated not only the spirit, but the letter of the Constitution; and, moreover, had a most pernicious effect upon the public mind. The great mass of our people were perfectly willing to fight for their liberties, but they were utterly unwilling to be placed in a position, where it seemed they were required to do it by compulsion. Moreover, if compulsion had been necessary at that time, or at any time, to fill our armies, the war ought to have been immediately abandoned upon the disclosure of the fact; for no people are worthy of liberty, or capable of preserving it, who have to be compelled to fight, either for its establishment, or its defence. Conscripts or men who are used by Rulers barely as machines in war, may overthrow liberty, and prove efficient instruments in erecting Dynasties and Empires; but never have been, and never will be, the means of establishing free Institutions or maintaining them! This was my judgment then, and will be ever! Fortunately for the Confederates, more than half of their arms-bearing people were virtually in for the war, before this very demoralizing act was passed. The glory of their arms from the beginning to the end was achieved by this class of our soldiers. Very few of those who were brought in subsequently through the instrumentality of the Conscription acts, effected anything creditable to themselves or the country.* [Emphasis added, L.S.]

"The desertions so much complained of were almost entirely from the latter class. *I doubt if there were ten thousand conscripts, properly speaking, in all the armies together, at the time of final surrender. The Army of Virginia, which fought until it was literally 'annihilated,' was composed almost exclusively of the surviving remnants of the original voluntary enlistments. The same is true of the Army of Tennessee.* But, as I have stated, it is not my purpose now to discuss or to enlarge, beyond a general statement of my own position on any of these questions of difference, touching the internal policy of the country between myself and the Administration of Mr. [Jefferson] Davis. He, of course, thought these measures, to which I have alluded, were not only constitutional, but timely and expedient. His views upon them in detail, are to be seen in his messages and speeches. Mine, in like manner, as expressed at the time, are to be found in [Henry] Cleveland's collection of letters and speeches, written and made by me during the war. To them I must refer you for the points of difference on these measures in detail.

"These differences, however, wide as they were, in no degree caused me to withhold my cordial support and cooperation, wherever I saw the possibility of effecting any good on that line of policy, which the Administration thought proper to adopt, even though it was against my own judgment. I neither headed nor countenanced anything like factious opposition to the execution of those measures which I thought would be attended with the worst consequences. This would have produced dissensions and divisions, which in my judgment could lead to nothing but the most disastrous results. My views upon them were given to Mr. Davis, the Members of the Cabinet and Members of Congress, in the most earnest and friendly manner. When they were so given, without avail, I remained silent before the country, except in a few instances in which self-vindication became a public duty. Upon the Constitutionality of the Conscript Acts, my views . . . were very similar to those expressed by the Supreme Court of [in the North], . . . upon a similar act, subsequently passed by the Federal Congress, in a case which produced considerable excitement throughout the North at the time. . . . The opinion of Mr. Justice George W. Woodward, in that case, deserves a place in the future history of this Country, side by side with that of Chief Justice [Roger B.] Taney, of the Supreme Court of the United States, on the suspension of the Writ of *Habeas Corpus*. But enough on these subjects. [Let me just say in closing here that] I wish [it] . . . distinctly [understood,] . . . that the differences between Mr. Davis and myself were in no respect, as I understood them, unlike those differences which often occur between the several Members of the same Cabinet, where all are equally earnest and sincere in their efforts to promote a common object; and not unlike differences which probably existed on many other questions, even between Mr. Davis and Members of his own Cabinet."273

29

THE WAR FOR
SOUTHERN INDEPENDENCE
PART FOUR

STEPHENS BEGINS THIS CHAPTER WITH an in-depth discussion of the infamous four-hour long Hampton Roads Conference, attended by Stephens, Robert M. T. Hunter, and John A. Campbell on the Southern side, and Lincoln and William H. Seward on the Northern side. How did this celebrated meeting originate? Whose idea was it, and why did it fail? What actually occurred at the interview between the Confederate Commissioners and Lincoln and Seward?

Many lies about this conference have been fabricated by enemies of the South. However, Stephens, a stalwart Christian whose word was impeccable, was in attendance. And it is from him that we learn the *Truth* of what went on behind closed doors that chilly Virginia day—the only known time that President Lincoln deigned to meet with what he considered to be lowly Southern "Rebels" and "treasonous anarchists."

Though, because of Lincoln's inflexible Hitler-like approach to his War, the meeting was unsuccessful in yielding any results toward ending it with full Southern rights intact (the Confederates' main objective), several remarkable facts emerged; facts that fly in the face of pro-North propaganda:

• Lincoln and Seward admitted that only 200,000 (a mere 5 percent) of the South's 4 million slaves were affected by the Emancipation Proclamation.

• Lincoln admitted that "the people of the North were as responsible for slavery as the people of the South." [Note: Since both the American slave trade and American slavery got their start in the North (Massachusetts, to be precise), and the American abolition movement began in the South,[274] Lincoln is only half correct.]

• Lincoln admitted that the Emancipation Proclamation was nothing more than a military measure (indeed, he openly referred to it as a "military emancipation"[275] and a "military necessity"),[276] and as such, would end with the termination of the War. After that, for all he cared, the Southern states could vote against the upcoming Thirteenth Amendment and continue to practice slavery. His main interest was, and always had been, the reunion of the Southern states—and nothing more. The only stipulation was that slaves who had been freed could not be re-enslaved.

Though Lincoln does not say here why he did not want emancipated servants put back in bondage, we know the two main reasons from his earlier speeches and letters, and Stephens, Hunter, and Campbell, were no doubt well aware of them as well. The reasons:

A) As the Emancipation Proclamation itself intimates, Lincoln desperately needed blacks to fill the vacancies left by the thousands of his white U.S. soldiers who had died, deserted, or were wounded and could no longer fight.

B) As a white racist, white separatist, and black colonizationist (that is, one who wanted America to be a white-only nation), Lincoln had to free the slaves so that he could legally deport them out of the country (preferably, as he put it, "back to their native land") after the War.[277] The mass deportation of African-Americans was impossible as long as they were considered "private property." Lincoln had made his feelings on this topic perfectly clear during a public speech at Springfield, Illinois, on July 17, 1858, when he said: "What I would most desire would be the separation of the white and black races."[278]

☛ "The real objects of the Hampton Roads Conference have never been made fully known to the country, so far as I am aware. *It was not intended in its origin or objects to bring about direct negotiations for Peace.* On this point very erroneous ideas existed at the time, and do yet, I believe. We had no written instructions upon that subject, or any other, except what were contained in the letter of our appointment, which has been published; nor any verbal instructions on that subject inconsistent with the terms of that letter. The Conference, moreover, did not originate in any way with me, as [many] . . . suppose.

"But for a proper understanding of its origin, nature, and objects, as well as my connection with it, it is essentially necessary that we shall first take another rapid glance at the intervening military as well as political events, which occurred between this and the other proposed Conference referred to. I will not worry [the reader] . . . with unnecessary details of battles or other subjects, but confine myself briefly as possible to such points, in both a military and political view, as are essential to a proper understanding of the matter in hand.

"It must be borne in mind, then, that after the great reverses met with by the Confederates at Gettysburg and Vicksburg, and after the withdrawal of Lee's Army from Pennsylvania,—which, with his great skill, was safely effected, though [Yankee General George G.] Meade then had quite two to one at his command against him—everything remained comparatively quiet for some time, in a military point of view. The Political aspect of affairs at the North, however, was greatly changed by what had occurred. The raid of [Confederate General John H.] Morgan into Ohio, as well as the invasion of Pennsylvania by General Lee, gave new life and vigor to the [Liberal] War Party in all the Northern States, but especially in Ohio, Pennsylvania, and New York. Mr. Lincoln, by this, was enabled, easily, to recruit his armies by volunteers in defence of their own homes and firesides, even from the ranks of those who were utterly opposed to the policy of subjugating the Southern States. The result was, that the [Conservative] Anti-War Party at the North—those who had favored Peace movements—were again put to silence under the denunciation of *incivism*, which was hurled against them. The elation caused by these late greatest successes which had attended their arms during the war, came, as might have been expected, to their aid in the fall elections. In the political contest in 1863, therefore, the War Party proper, recovering from its wound, regained all that it had lost the year before. [U.S. Congressman Clement L.] Vallandigham was beaten in Ohio, and in a large majority, if not all of the States, the Centralists [Liberals] were again triumphant. So much for the political aspect just now. Let us leave it a moment to glance further at military operations.

"While Lee was still holding Meade at bay in Virginia, [Yankee General William S.] Rosecrans, at the head of the Army of the Cumberland, greatly reinforced, was projecting an attack upon Chattanooga, and a campaign thence to Atlanta and through Georgia. To defeat this most dangerous movement, Lee sent about 5,000 of his army to the assistance of [Rebel General Braxton] Bragg, who, at the head of the Confederates, was now confronting Rosecrans. The result was the great battle of Chickamauga, fought on the 20th of September, 1863, where the Confederate arms under Bragg, Daniel H. Hill, [James] Longstreet and [John B.] Hood, again achieved a most brilliant victory. Rosecrans was not only checked, but almost routed. His army was saved by seeking protection behind the Fortifications in and around Chattanooga. The united forces on the Confederate side, in the battle of Chickamauga, was about 40,000, while the Federals under Rosecrans, numbered, from the best accounts, fully 55,000. The Confederate loss was heavy—not less than 16,000; while the Federal loss was fully 20,000 men, (8,000 of whom were prisoners,) besides 49 pieces of artillery, and 15,000 small arms.

"After this terrible conflict, Military affairs were again comparatively quiet for a time, both in the East and the West. Rosecrans remained behind his works at Chattanooga, and Bragg confronted him on Missionary Ridge. In Virginia, however, matters were not quite so still. [Yankee General George G.] Meade made several attempts to assail Lee's weakened Army, reduced, as it was, by the absence of Longstreet's Corps. The most noted of these were at Centreville, Bristoe Station, and Mine Run. These resulted in no serious loss to Lee.

"In the meantime, [Yankee General Ulysses S.] Grant, who, from his exploits at Vicksburg, was now fully recognized as 'the coining man,' had been put at the head of all the South-western Federal forces, and given the control of the movement into Georgia from Chattanooga. Rosecrans having fallen out of favor at Washington, had been removed, and Major-General George H. Thomas put in his place at Chattanooga, he being himself, however, now under the chief command of Grant. About this time, most unfortunately for the Confederates, there was a separation of their forces near Missionary Ridge, when there should have been every possible concentration of them. Longstreet was sent upon an expedition against Knoxville, where, on the 17th of November, he made an unsuccessful assault upon the Federals there strongly fortified, sustaining considerable loss, and accomplishing nothing. While Bragg was thus weakened by the absence of Longstreet's command, Grant, very adroitly, and with consummate skill, by a concentration of his forces, planned and executed those movements which resulted in his most memorable victory, known as the Battle of Missionary Ridge. This was fought on the 25th day of November. Bragg's Army was completely routed. This was the greatest disaster which attended the Confederate Arms in a pitched battle, during the war: not so much in the loss of men, (for that was only about 3000,) as in the loss of ground and the demoralization of his broken columns. Having lost the confidence of his men, he was, upon his own application, relieved from the command of the Army of Tennessee. This position was now, upon the earnest remonstrance and entreaty of many persons high in authority, committed to the military genius of General Joseph E. Johnston, who, for some cause not necessary to mention, had theretofore been out of favor with Mr. [Jefferson] Davis. His presence at the head of the shattered forces now composing this Army, gave new hopes and inspired new zeal in the ranks. All his energies were devoted for some months to recruiting and strengthening his command. The winter thus passed off.

"Meantime, the office of Lieutenant-General was created by the Federal authorities, and General Grant was the man who, by almost universal acclaim, was designated to fill it. His nomination to that post by Mr. Lincoln was, of course, confirmed by the Senate. He was thus put at the head of all the Armies of the United States, and had, thereafter, the general control of all military operations on land. His Head Quarters were immediately transferred to the Army of the Potomac. Thus matters stood on both sides, during the remainder of the third year of the war.

"The prospect upon its close, in a military point of view, was gloomier for the Confederates than it had been at the close of any that had preceded it. This heavy gloom, however, did not rest upon their horizon long. The beginning of operations in the fourth year, soon changed the aspect of affairs in this particular, and gave great encouragement to the Confederates. This year was ushered in, even in its dawn, by the splendid victory at Ocean Pond, Florida, on the 20th of February, achieved under the lead of Brigadier-General Alfred H. Colquitt, against General Truman Seymour, commanding the Federals. With less than 5,000 men, Colquitt put Seymour to rout, with more than 6,000, killing, wounding and capturing 2,500 men, and taking three Napoleon guns, two ten-pounder Parrots, and 3,000 stand-of-arms. This was followed immediately by the great victories achieved by [Rebel] General Edmund Kirby Smith and [Rebel] General [Richard] 'Dick' Taylor [son of U.S. President Zachary Taylor], over [Union] General [Nathaniel P.] Banks in the West. In the early part of March, Banks had set out from New Orleans on an expedition to Texas, by way of Shreveport, with forces at his command numbering in all, not less than 40,000. These were attacked in detail by Smith and Taylor at Mansfield and Pleasant Hill, at which places they utterly routed the Federal forces, and drove Banks back as precipitately as he had been driven from Winchester in 1862, by 'Stonewall' Jackson. In this expedition, Banks lost in prisoners, 6,000, in killed and wounded 8,000, in all 14,000 men, besides thirty-five pieces of artillery, 20,000 small arms, one hundred and twenty wagons, one gunboat, and three transports. The Confederate forces operating against Banks, in all, did not exceed 25,000 men.

"A little before this, [Yankee war criminal] General William T. Sherman had set out on his grand projected expedition to Mobile through Mississippi and Alabama. This most formidable and threatening movement was completely checked by several brilliant cavalry exploits of Major-General Nathan B. Forrest—particularly the one at Okolona on the 22nd of February—the opening day of the fourth year of the war. Sherman's army estimated at 50,000, was thus stopped at Meridian, Mississippi. From this point he retraced his steps to Vicksburg, and by Grant was put at the head of a new army to make another 'onward' upon Atlanta and through Georgia.

"Two grand campaigns were now again clearly developed by the Federals, for the summer of 1864, as in 1863—one against Richmond under Grant himself—the other against Atlanta under Sherman. To Grant's movement Lee was opposed in Virginia; and to Sherman's, Johnston in Georgia. To the movements of these two great armies, the chief attention and energies on both sides, were now directed. This was the general military situation in the early part of May, 1864."[279]

☛ "The political aspect, at the same time, requires a brief notice in the same connection. The Presidential Campaign in the Northern States was opening. The Constitutional [Conservative] Party there was again active. They were resolved to make another desperate struggle, and to displace the Centralists [Liberals] from power by votes, if possible. Several circumstances favored the prospect of their success at first. There was considerable division in the ranks of the Centralists, as to who should be their standard-bearer in the contest. Mr. Lincoln had strong and powerful opponents to his nomination in his own Party. These, in Convention on the 31st of May, put in nomination for the Presidency, General John C. Frémont, and for the Vice Presidency, John Cochrane, of New York. The friends of Mr. Lincoln met in Convention at Baltimore, a week afterwards, on the 7th of June, and put him in nomination for re-election, with Andrew Johnson, of Tennessee, for the Vice Presidency. Frémont was subsequently withdrawn, and Lincoln left without opposition from his own Party.

"The Democratic or Constitutional [Conservative] Party postponed their Convention from the 4th of July, when it was to have been held, to the 29th of August, when, at Chicago, as before stated, they put in nomination for the Presidency, General George B. McClellan, and for the Vice Presidency, George H. Pendleton, of Ohio, upon *a Platform boldly denouncing the usurpations of the Washington authorities, opposing the policy of subjugating the Southern States, declaring the war to be a failure in preserving the Union of the States as it was established under the Constitution, and inviting a general Convention of all the States, for a proper adjustment of the relations between them.* [Emphasis added, L.S.]

"It was . . . on the policy of our giving a favorable response to these Resolutions of the Chicago Convention, looking to a general convocation of all the States, as an initiative step for a final adjustment of the matters in conflict, that I so widely differed with Mr. Davis during this year. The contest, however, fierce and bitter as it was, resulted, as is known, in the success of Mr. Lincoln to the Presidency, and Mr. Johnson to the Vice Presidency, at the election which took place on the 8th day of November. The various causes which co-operated in producing this result, we will not now stop to notice."[280]

☛ "Let us return, therefore, to Military movements. Before either of these nominations had taken place, the two great campaigns of this year, before referred to, had commenced; both at or near the same time. This was in the early part of May. The general results of these need be but glanced at. Lee with his most masterly military genius, with less than 60,000 men, not only held Grant in check with an army of over 100,000 present, and as many more, perhaps, in his rear to draw upon for reinforcements, but entirely defeated all the plans and purposes of this favorite General of the Federals. In a series of battles beginning on the 6th of May, and ending the 12th of June—first in the Wilderness, then at Spotsylvania Court House, then at North Anna, and then at Cold Harbor, which will ever stand amongst the most memorable of history, he sent Grant and his hosts, as he had McClellan and his before, swinging around upon the same new base—James River—where the Federal Chief, with his Head Quarters established at City Point, continued ineffectual efforts, first to take Petersburg as a step towards Richmond, until winter closed upon the scenes. In this campaign, according to Mr. [William] Swinton, Grant lost from the 6th of May to the 12th of June, in his progress from the Rapidan to Cold Harbor alone, 54,551 men. His losses by the time he reached Petersburg, were not less than 60,000—a number equal to Lee's entire Army.

"While these operations were going on in Virginia, [Confederate General Joseph E.] Johnston, with equal masterly skill, with about 45,000 men, was checking, delaying and defeating [Yankee General William T.] Sherman in his 'onward' to Atlanta, with an army equal in number and strength to that of Grant's. For more than two months he had been enabled to proceed but about one hundred miles on his grand march, and at a loss not much, if any, inferior to that of Grant; notwithstanding the great disparity of forces on the respective sides, Sherman had been checked, foiled, and balked at various points by the manoeuvres, strategy, and consummate generalship of Johnston. On the 17th day of July, however, Johnston was removed, and Major-General John B. Hood put in his place. Within a few days afterwards—on the 20th and 22nd of July—were fought the great battles of Atlanta. Hood with unequal forces attacked the Federals under great disadvantages, as it turned out, and in two most gallant and bloody assaults lost, in all, about 8,000 men, without carrying any point, or inflicting any serious injury upon his adversary.

"On the 31st of August, he gave up the city and retired towards Newnan. Sherman took possession of his prize on the 2nd of September. Soon after, Hood, in a new position, projected his famous Tennessee Campaign [breaking his promise to President Davis to continue pursuing Sherman]. This was commenced on the 28th day of September. His Army at this time, after all the recruits which could be brought to its ranks, amounted to about 35,000. The result of this Tennessee movement, as is known, was the battles of Franklin [II] and Nashville. The battle of Franklin [II] was fought on the 30th of November. In this, Hood gained a signal victory, though at considerable loss. [Editor's note: Modern Southern historians do not consider Franklin II a 'victory,' but rather a devastating and unnecessary loss for the South.] The battle of Nashville was fought on the 15th and 16th of December. It lasted two days. The Confederates here were, finally, utterly defeated and almost routed by [George H.] Thomas, whom Sherman had left in his rear, with forces amply sufficient to meet this meditated blow of Hood, of which he was fully apprised.

"In the meantime, Sherman, after destroying and burning Atlanta, had set out anew from that point, (on the 15th of November,) on his grand march to the sea, with an army of 65,000 men. As there was no sufficient Confederate force to oppose him, he passed through the State almost unmolested, laying waste the country in a belt of nearly thirty miles in breadth, and reached Savannah on the 22nd of December, 1864. In the meantime, also, [war criminal Philip H.] Sheridan, the most dashing and fiery of the Federal Generals, had made his Valley Campaign in Virginia, defeating the Confederates under [Jubal A.] Early, and laying waste that most beautiful country.

"This rapid glance must suffice for the general aspect of affairs, both Militarily and Politically, up to January, 1865."[281]

☛ "The prospect at this time, it is true, was exceedingly gloomy for us; but I did not then consider our Cause as utterly hopeless, notwithstanding. I thought the great object might even yet be attained, but I was deeply impressed by the conviction, that it could be done only by an immediate and thorough change in the policy of the Administration, both internally and externally. Being requested by the Senate to give them my views on the situation, in a close Session, I complied in a speech of considerable length, which was never reported. The sum and substance of it, however, was, that our policy both internally and externally should be speedily and thoroughly changed. Conscription, Impressments, Suspension of the Writ of *Habeas Corpus*, and all those measures which tended to dispirit our people in the great cause for which they were struggling, should be immediately abandoned. The resources of the country, both of Men and Subsistence, should be better husbanded than they had been. Proclamation should be made inviting back to the army all who had left it without leave, and all who were then subject to Conscription, to come under chosen leaders of their own. In this way I believed [Rebel Generals Sterling] Price and [Joseph E.] Johnston, to say nothing of others, would in thirty days, bring to their ranks more than the Conscript Bureau had by compulsory process brought from the beginning. Men who should so come would never desert, and might be relied on to fight when they did come.

"I reminded them of what they knew had been my opinions upon these subjects from the beginning: that the policy of holding posts or positions against besieging armies, as well as of engaging in pitched-battles, should not be pursued. We could not match our opponents in numbers, and should not attempt to cope with them in direct physical power. War was a collision of forces, and in this, as in Mechanics, the greater momentum must prevail. Momentum, however, was resolvable into two elements—quantity of matter, and velocity. The superior numbers—the quantity of matter in this instance—was on the other side; and to succeed in the end, we must make up the other requisite element of momentum, not only by the spirit, animation, and morale of our unequal numbers, but by their skilful movements, and by other resorts which were at our command. These consisted in the many advantages which an invaded people have over invaders. The policy of Johnston from Dalton to the Chattahoochee was the right one. To preserve the lives of our arms-bearing men, was, itself, a matter of the utmost importance. Our supply of these was limited, while that of our opponents was inexhaustible. They could afford to lose any number of battles, with great losses of men, if they could thereby materially thin our ranks. In this way, by attrition alone, they would ultimately wear us out. The leading object should be, to keep an army in the field, and to keep the Standard up somewhere, wherever it could be done, without offering battle except where the advantages were decidedly in our favor. If, in pursuing this course now, of retiring when necessary, instead of offering or accepting battle, as stated, our whole country should be penetrated, and should even be laid waste, as the Valley of Virginia and the smoking belt in Georgia had been by Sheridan and Sherman, these devastations would be borne by our people, so long as their hearts were kept enlisted in the Cause. On this line of internal policy, our standard might even yet be kept up, for at least a year or two longer—perhaps for a period far beyond that; and, in the meantime, by a change of our external policy towards the masses of the people at the North, a reaction might reasonably be expected to take place there. A financial revulsion there might be certainly expected in less than two years. The depreciation of their currency had already reached a point which was quite alarming to capitalists. Greenbacks had already sold in New York at nearly three for one in gold. When the crash did come, as soon it must, the effects would be, politically, as well as in other respects, tremendous. At that time they could not be even properly conjectured; but when it did come, then with a proper policy towards the million eight hundred thousand and more of the other side, who had so recently and decidedly demonstrated their opposition to the Centralists [Northern Liberals] in the late election, we might through them—thoroughly aroused to a sense of their own danger—look for a peaceful Adjustment upon a basis, which would best secure both their liberties and ours. My opinion was that, by pursuing this course, we might, in the end, succeed in the Cause for which we were struggling, without relying solely upon the sword.

"The policy thus stated necessarily involved the abandonment of a continued attempt to hold Richmond. This, however, I did not state in express terms in my speech to the Senate. I only left all to draw their own inferences. To Mr. Davis alone, I submitted the propriety and necessity of this course; for I knew if he could not first be brought to see it, it would be not only useless, but most probably exceedingly injurious in the then state of the public mind, to mention it to others. When the subject was mentioned to him, his reply in substance was, that the abandonment of Richmond would be a virtual abandonment of the Cause.

"Now, it was in this stage of our affairs, early in January, 1865, in the midst of winter, when everything was comparatively quiet on the lines of defence around Richmond, and before Sherman had set out from Savannah, on his march through the Carolinas, that [Yankee politician] Mr. Francis P. Blair, Sr., made his appearance in the Confederate Capital. The arrival of this distinguished personage, who was, unquestionably, the master spirit—the real Warwick—of the Party then in power at Washington, caused no little sensation. What could have brought him there? And what was his business? These were the inquiries of almost every one. He was immediately in close and private consultation with Mr. Davis. After remaining a few days, he returned. Nothing, however, touching the object of his visit escaped from the Executive closet, or got to the public in any way. The surprise occasioned by his first visit was even increased by a second in a few days afterwards. He was again in consultation with Mr. Davis, and again returned. The same mystery still continued to hang over the object of his mission.

"It was then . . . in these interviews between Mr. Davis and Mr. Blair, which excited so much curiosity and comment at the time, that this Hampton Roads Conference originated; and as to its objects, how I became connected with it, what occurred at it, and its results, I will now proceed to inform [the reader] . . . in regular order:

"1st. Its objects, and how I became connected with it.

"On the day after Mr. Blair's final departure, I was sent for by Mr. Davis, with a request to meet him at a stated hour, on special and important business. He wished the interview to be entirely private, and therefore named the hour when he would be disengaged and ready to receive me. The message came through Mr. [Robert M. T.] Hunter, who told me what the business was. I called at the hour, and found Mr. Davis alone. He said he wished what he should submit to be strictly confidential. He had mentioned it, as yet, to no one, except Mr. Hunter—not even to any member of his Cabinet; but had requested the Cabinet to meet him at four o'clock that evening, in consultation upon it, and wished to be in possession of my views beforehand.

"The substance of what he then stated was, that Mr. Blair, in a verbal and most confidential manner, had suggested to him a course by which a suspension of hostilities might be effected. This was to be done by a Secret Military Convention between the Belligerents embracing another object, which was the maintenance of the Monroe Doctrine, in the prevention of the establishment of the then projected Empire in Mexico by France. Mr. Davis stated that Mr. Blair had given it as his opinion, that the result of what he proposed would be the ultimate restoration of the Union, which he greatly desired; and that it was much more in accordance with his wishes that it should be effected in this way, than by a continued prosecution of the war to its extreme results. Mr. Davis gave me clearly to understand that he understood Mr. Blair to be acting under the firm belief, that the attempt of the Confederate States to establish a separate Independence would certainly fail in the end. This he did that I might be fully informed as to the candidly professed objects of the proposition. He also submitted, somewhat in detail, a programme suggested by Mr. Blair, for carrying the general outlines of his scheme into practical operation. Now, whether Mr. Blair's ideas as to the ultimate result of such Military Convention, if it should be entered into—so far as they related to the restoration of the Union—were correct or not, and whether his wishes in this particular would be finally attained by the line of policy he proposed, was a grave question for mature consideration, as well as the general subject itself; and what Mr. Davis wished to confer with me about was, whether or not it was advisable to enter into the arrangement at all, under the circumstances; and especially in view of the contingency of such a result as that contemplated by Mr. Blair: and if I were of opinion that it was proper to do so, then who would be the most suitable persons to whom the matter should be committed? He showed me the two letters that had passed between Mr. Lincoln and himself through the medium of Mr. Blair, which have been published. These, however, were only intended to cover the other undisclosed object.

"I inquired if he thought Mr. Blair was really in the confidence of the Administration at Washington, and fully represented their views on the subject. He said that Mr. Blair had expressly disclaimed speaking by authority, but assured Mr. Davis that he believed the Administration would be willing to enter into such an arrangement; and Mr. Davis, in reply to my inquiry, said that he felt assured, notwithstanding what Mr. Blair had said of his acting in the matter of his own accord, that the [Lincoln] Administration at Washington did, in fact, fully understand the object of Mr. Blair's mission, and would act in accordance with the views he had presented.

"In that view of the subject, I promptly told him that I thought the programme suggested by Mr. Blair should be acceded to, at least so far as to obtain, if possible, a Conference upon the subject as proposed. Perhaps such a Convention might be obtained, securing a suspension of hostilities, without committing us to an active participation in the maintenance of the Monroe Doctrine. If so, it was an object of very great importance to us; and the agitation of the Monroe Doctrine, and the diversion of the popular mind at the North to the questions involved in it, might, itself, result in great benefit to our Cause. Whether Mr. Blair was right in his ideas as to the ultimate result or not, was, of course, uncertain; but this result, to which he was looking, was not necessarily involved in it. Moreover, if such result should ensue, it would be by the voluntary assent of the Confederate States, and this would secure the success of the Principles for which we were struggling. In every view, this was a matter which could safely be left to the future. Upon the whole, therefore, I was in favor of the Conference, if it could be obtained.

"I went on further to say, that if there was really anything authoritative in the arrangement proposed; if in truth and in fact, Mr. Lincoln were then, or should be on its direct presentation, favorably inclined to the course suggested, such a Convention, it seemed to me, could not be effected without the utmost discretion and the most perfect secrecy. Mr. Davis said in reply to this, that Mr. Blair had been very particular in stating the same thing.

"Well then, said I, Mr. President, looking to the question in all its bearings, in my judgment, you and Mr. Lincoln, yourselves, are the persons who should hold the Conference. You and he can easily be brought together near City Point, without anybody knowing it except Gen. Lee and Gen. Grant. To this he decidedly objected, and said that the matter, if it should be decided to hold the Conference, ought to be put in the hands of at least three Commissioners.

"When he was so decided on that point, after some moments' reflection, I said that the Commission should be composed of men of ability and discretion, and also of persons whose absence from the City would not attract public attention. Looking to these three requisites, I then suggested as the Commissioners, Judge John A. Campbell, of Alabama, then Assistant Secretary of War, Gen. Henry L. Benning, Ex-Justice of the Supreme Court of Georgia, then commanding a Brigade within a few miles of City Point; and Thomas S. Flournoy, of Virginia, a gentleman of distinguished ability, and well known personally to Mr. Lincoln. This gentleman, to my knowledge, I stated, had reached the City the night before, expecting to remain only a day or two, and hence his leaving would give rise to no inquiry or comment.

"To all these suggestions, both as to qualifications and the persons possessing them, he yielded his ready assent, and I supposed the whole matter would be thus arranged, for I did not think the Cabinet would object to what Mr. Davis so cordially approved. Our conversation—begun on this subject and continued on others—lasted until the arrival of the Cabinet was announced.

"I heard nothing more of the matter until next day, when being sent for again by the [Confederate] President [Davis], I then, for the first time, learned that the result of the Cabinet consultation the evening before, was, that the Conference should be proposed, and that Mr. [Robert M. T.] Hunter, Judge Campbell, and myself should be the Commissioners. It is, perhaps, unnecessary to say that I was very much surprised at this. I urged and insisted upon the impropriety of myself and Mr. Hunter being on the Commission—especially myself, for my absence, as the Presiding Officer the Senate, would, of course, be noticed, and inquiries would almost certainly be made as to where I was. The same reason applied to some extent, though not to its full, to Mr. Hunter, who was one of the most prominent as well active members of the Senate; but the objection applied with more than double force to the appointment of us both. For, in case of my absence barely, he, of course, would take the Chair, as he was the President *pro tempore*, and this might, perhaps, pass off without special notice; but for both of us to be absent at the same time—an event which had never occurred—would necessarily create inquiries as to the cause of our absence. The Rules of the Senate would have to be changed to meet the case—a contingency that had not even been provided for, and some satisfactory reason would have to be given for an occurrence so extraordinary.

"I, therefore, with great earnestness, insisted that this arrangement should be abandoned, if anything was expected to be accomplished by it. My efforts to have it changed, however, were of no avail. The President and Cabinet persisted in the selection of the Commissioners, which they had agreed upon; so in this instance, as in the other referred to, my judgment was yielded to theirs."[282]

☛ "The arrangement was, for the Commissioners to set out the next day, by way of Petersburg [Virginia]. I urged upon the President the importance of having it seen to, that no allusion to the Commission should be published in the City papers.

"According to the arrangement stated, the Commissioners next day, the 29th of January, proceeded as far as Petersburg. There we addressed Lieutenant-General Grant the letter of the 30th, which has been published, asking permission to cross the Federal lines. In reply, we received from him a communication, dated at Head Quarters, Army of the United States, January 31st, 1865, signed by him as Lieutenant-General, and addressed to us at Petersburg. This has never yet been published, so far as I know; and as it was upon this we passed the Federal lines at Petersburg, I will read it:

> 'Gentlemen: Your communication of yesterday, requesting an interview with myself, and a safe conduct to Washington and return, is received.
>
> 'I will instruct the commanding officers of the forces near Petersburg, notifying you at what part of the lines, and the time when and where, conveyances will be ready for you.
>
> 'Your letter to me has been telegraphed to Washington for instructions. I have no doubt that before you arrive at my Head Quarters, an answer will be received, directing me to comply with your request. Should a different reply be received, I promise you a safe and immediate return within your own lines.
>
> 'Yours very respectfully. [Lt.-Gen. U.S. Grant]'

"In pursuance of this letter we were met on the evening of the same day, at that part of the lines at which we had, in the meantime, been notified to appear at 4 o'clock, by an escort under the conduct of Lieutenant-Colonel Babcock of General Grant's staff, and were conveyed by railroad to City Point. Upon reaching that place we were immediately taken to the Head Quarters of the Commander-in-Chief. Here, for the first time, I met General Grant himself.

". . . the idea of drawing a comparison between [General Grant and General Robert E. Lee] . . . did not occur to me. I should just as soon have thought of drawing a comparison between Louis Napoleon and [George] Washington. . . . [A]s to what impression [Grant] he made upon me, I will say, in the first place, that I was never so much disappointed in my life, in my previously formed opinions, of either the personal appearance or bearings of any one, about whom I had read and heard so much. The disappointment, moreover, was in every respect favorable and agreeable. I was instantly struck with the great simplicity and perfect naturalness of his manners, and the entire absence of everything like affectation, show, or even the usual military air or mien of men in his position. He was plainly attired, sitting in a log-cabin, busily writing on a small table, by a Kerosene lamp. It was night when we arrived. There was nothing in his appearance or surroundings which indicated his official rank. There were neither guards nor aids about him. Upon Colonel Babcock's rapping at his door, the response, 'Come in,' was given by himself, in a tone of voice, and with a cadence, which I can never forget.

"His conversation was easy and fluent, without the least effort or restraint.

In this, nothing was so closely noticed by me as the point and terseness with which he expressed whatever he said. He did not seem either to court or avoid conversation, but whenever he did speak, what he said was directly to the point, and covered the whole matter in a few words. I saw before being with him long, that he was exceedingly quick in perception, and direct in purpose, with a vast deal more, of brains than tongue, as ready as that was at his command.

"We were here with General Grant two days, as the correspondence referred to shows. He furnished us with comfortable quarters on board one of his despatch boats. The more I became acquainted with him, the more I became thoroughly impressed with the very extraordinary combination of rare elements of character which he exhibited. During the time he met us frequently, and conversed freely upon various subjects, not much upon our mission. I saw, however, very clearly, that he was very anxious for the proposed Conference to take place, and from all that was said I inferred—whether correctly or not, I do not know—that he was fully apprised of its proposed object. He was, without doubt, exceedingly anxious for a termination of our war, and the return of peace and harmony throughout the country. It was through his instrumentality mainly, that Mr. Lincoln finally consented to meet us at Fortress Monroe, as the correspondence referred to shows.

". . . I will add: that upon the whole the result of this first acquaintance with General Grant, beginning with our going to, and ending with our return from Hampton Roads, was, the conviction on my mind, that, taken all in all, he was one of the most remarkable men I had ever met with, and that his career in life, if his days should be prolonged, was hardly entered upon; that his character was not yet fully developed; that he himself was not aware of his own power, and that if he lived, he would, in the future, exert a controlling influence in shaping the destinies of this country, either for good or for evil. Which it would be, time and circumstances alone could disclose. That was the opinion of him then formed, and it is the same which has been uniformly expressed by me ever since."[283] [Note: Stephens, who wrote this in early to mid 1868, was prophetic: later that year, on November 3, Grant would be elected the eighteenth president of the U.S.]

☞ "After Mr. Lincoln's telegram to him that he would meet us at Fortress Monroe, which General Grant brought to us himself, with evident indications of high gratification, he immediately started us on one of his despatch boats. We reached the Roads in the evening of the same day. We remained on board the steamer which anchored near the Fort. Mr. Lincoln arrived in another steamer during the night, which anchored not far off. Mr. Seward, as is known, had been sent on a day or two in advance. So much then for the first point as to the objects, and how I became connected with this Conference."[284]

☞ "2nd. We come now to the Conference itself, and what occurred at it.

"The interview took place in the Saloon of the steamer, on board of which were Mr. Lincoln and Mr. Seward, and which lay at anchor near Fortress Monroe. The Commissioners were conducted into the Saloon first. Soon after, Mr. Lincoln and Mr. Seward entered. After usual salutations on the part of those who were previously acquainted, and introductions of the others who had never met before, conversation was immediately opened by the revival of reminiscences and associations of former days.

"This was commenced by myself addressing Mr. Lincoln, and alluding to some of the incidents of our Congressional acquaintance—especially, to the part we had acted together in effecting the election of General [Zachary] Taylor in 1848. To my remarks he responded in a cheerful and cordial manner, as if the remembrance of those times, and our connection with the incidents referred to, had awakened in him a train of agreeable reflections, extending to others. Mutual inquiries were made after the fate and well-being of several who had been our intimate friends and active associates in a 'Congressional Taylor Club,' well-known at the time. I inquired especially after Mr. Truman Smith, of Connecticut, and he after Mr. [Robert A.] Toombs, William Ballard Preston, Thomas S. Flournoy, and others. With this introduction I said in substance: Well, Mr. President, is there no way of putting an end to the present trouble, and bringing about a restoration of the general good feeling and harmony then existing between the different States and Sections of the country?

"Mr. Seward said: It is understood, gentlemen, that this is to be an informal Conference. There is to be no clerk or secretary—no writing or record of anything that is said. All is to be verbal.

"I, speaking for the Commissioners, said that was our understanding of it. To this all assented, whereupon I repeated the question.

"Mr. Lincoln in reply said, in substance, that there was but one way that he knew of, and that was, for those who were resisting the laws of the Union to cease that resistance. All the trouble came from an armed resistance against the National Authority.

"But, said I, is there no other question that might divert the attention of both Parties, for a time, from the questions involved in their present strife, until the passions on both sides might cool, when they would be in better temper to come to an amicable and proper adjustment of those points of difference out of which the present lamentable collision of arms has arisen? Is there no Continental question, said I, which might thus temporarily engage their attention? We have been induced to believe that there is.

"Mr. Lincoln seemed to understand my allusion instantly, and said in substance: I suppose you refer to something that Mr. [Francis P.] Blair [Sr.] has said. Now it is proper to state at the beginning, that whatever he said was of his own accord, and without the least authority from me. When he applied for a passport to go to Richmond, with certain ideas which he wished to make known to me, I told him flatly that I did not want to hear them. If he desired to go to Richmond of his own accord, I would give him a passport; but he had no authority to speak for me in any way whatever. When he returned and brought me Mr. Davis's letter, I gave him the one to which you alluded in your application for leave to cross the lines. I was always willing to hear propositions for peace on the conditions of this letter and on no other. The restoration of the Union is a *sine qua non* [Latin: 'without which not'; i.e., indispensable] with me, and hence my instructions that no conference was to be held except upon that basis.

"From this I inferred that he simply meant to be understood, in the first place, as disavowing whatever Mr. Blair had said as coming authoritatively from him; and, in the second place, that no arrangement could be made on the line suggested by Mr. Blair, without a previous pledge or assurance being given, that the Union was to be ultimately restored.

"After a short silence, I continued: But suppose, Mr. President, a line of policy should be suggested, which, if adopted, would most probably lead to a restoration of the Union without further bloodshed, would it not be highly advisable to act on it, even without the absolute pledge of ultimate restoration being required to be first given? May not such a policy be found to exist in the line indicated by the interrogatory propounded? Is there not now such a Continental question in which all the parties engaged in our present war feel a deep and similar interest? I allude, of course, to Mexico, and what is called the 'Monroe Doctrine,'—the principles of which are directly involved in the contest now waging there. From the tone of leading Northern papers and from public speeches of prominent men, as well as from other sources, we are under the impression that the Administration at Washington is decidedly opposed to the establishment of an Empire in Mexico by France, and is desirous to prevent it. In other words, they wish to sustain the principles of the Monroe Doctrine, and that, as I understand it, is, that the United States will maintain the right of Self-government to all Peoples on this Continent, against the dominion or control of any European power.

"Mr. Lincoln and Mr. Seward both concurred in the expression of opinion that such was the feeling of a majority of the people of the North.

"Could not both Parties then, said I, in our contest, come to an understanding and agreement to postpone their present strife, by a suspension of hostilities between themselves, until this principle is maintained in behalf of Mexico; and might it not, when successfully sustained there, naturally, and would it not almost inevitably, lead to a peaceful and harmonious solution of their own difficulties? Could any pledge now given, make a permanent restoration or re-organization of the Union more probable, or even so probable, as such a result would?

"Mr. Lincoln replied with considerable earnestness, that he could entertain no proposition for ceasing active military operations, which was not based upon a pledge first given, for the ultimate restoration of the Union. He had considered the question of an Armistice fully, and he could not give his consent to any proposition of that sort, on the basis suggested. The settlement of our existing difficulties was a question now of supreme importance, and the only basis on which he would entertain a proposition for a settlement was the recognition and re-establishment of the National Authority throughout the land.

"These pointed and emphatic responses seemed to put an end to the Conference on the subject contemplated in our Mission, as we had no authority to give any such pledge, even if we had been inclined to do so, nor was it expected that any such would really be required to be given.

"Judge [John A.] Campbell then inquired in what way the settlement for a restoration of the Union was to be made? Supposing the Confederate States should consent to the general terms as stated by Mr. Lincoln, how would the re-establishment of the National Authority take place? He wished to know something as to the details.

"These inquiries were made by him upon the line agreed upon by the Commissioners before, that if we failed in securing an Armistice, we would then endeavor to ascertain on what terms the Administration at Washington would be willing to end the war.

"Mr. Seward said, he desired that any answer to Judge Campbell's inquiries might be postponed, until the general ideas advanced by me might be more fully developed, as they had, as he expressed it, 'a philosophical basis.' All seemed to acquiesce in this suggestion.

"I then went quite at large into the development of my views, which briefly stated in substance amounted to this: That the Monroe Doctrine, as it was called, so far as it commended itself to my favor, assumed the position, that no European Power should impose Governments upon any Peoples on this Continent against their will. This principle of the Sovereign right of local Self-government, was peculiarly and specially sacred to the people of the United States, as well as to the people of the Confederate States. It was the one on which all our Institutions, State and National, were based. At that time, the Emperor of France was attempting to violate this great principle, which was so sacred alike to the Belligerents on both sides of our contest. Now, if we could in any way agree to suspend our present strife, for the maintenance and vindication of this principle as to Mexico, might, and would not, the result most probably be, not only the allowance of time for the blood of our people on both sides to cool towards each other, but the leading of the public mind, on both sides, to a clearer understanding of those principles which ought to constitute the basis of the settlement of our own difficulties, and on which the Union should be ultimately restored?

"A settlement of the Mexican question in this way, it seemed to me, would necessarily lead to a peaceful settlement of our own. I went on to give it as my opinion that, whenever it should be determined and firmly established that this right of local Self-government is the Principle on which all American Institutions rest and shall be maintained, all the States might reasonably be expected, very soon, to return, of their own accord, to their former relations to the Union, just as they came together at first by their own consent, and for their mutual interests. Others, too, would continue to join it in the future, as they had in the past. This great law of the System would effect the same certain results in its organization, as the law of gravitation in the material world.

"In a word, I presented briefly, but substantially in outline, the same view of our system of Government, which I [gave the reader earlier] . . . and showed how we might become, in deed and in truth, an Ocean-bound Federal [Confederate] Republic, under the operation of this Continental Regulator—the ultimate absolute Sovereignty of each State. This inherent and natural right of all States and Peoples, to govern themselves as they please, in my judgment, was not only the foundation upon which our Institutions were based in the beginning, but constituted the only sure ground of permanent peace and harmony in all parts of the country, consistent with the preservation of the liberties of each, even under a re-organized Union of the States. This Mexican question, therefore, might, it seemed to me, afford a very opportune occasion for reaching a proper solution of our own troubles without any further effusion of fraternal blood.

"Mr. Seward said, in substance, that the ideas as presented had something specious about them in theory; but, practically, no system of Government founded upon them could be successfully worked. The Union could never be restored or maintained on that basis. Suppose, said he, a State under such a system, having within her limits and jurisdiction an important point, or port on the sea coast, should be induced by some foreign Power to abandon the Union so sovereignly entered into, and after setting herself up as an Independent Nation, should enter into a treaty with such foreign Power at enmity, or even at war with the other members of the Union—thus giving their enemies an assumed rightful foothold in their vicinity, and by which great and irreparable injuries might be inflicted upon them. Could this be tolerated by them, for a moment? Suppose, for instance, Louisiana, holding the mouth of the Mississippi, and controlling the commerce of its immense Valley, and for which the United States paid so much, should, as she might, under this theory and doctrine, withdraw at pleasure, and form an alliance with a foreign enemy in time of war. Could the United States tolerate, for a moment, the recognition of any such right on her part? Self-defence, if nothing else, would compel them to interfere, and prevent such withdrawal, and the formation of such an alliance. Self-preservation is the first law of Nature, which applies to Nations as well as to individuals. No Government could have any stability or usefulness founded upon any such principle.

"To this I replied, that it was not my purpose to do more than present briefly the outlines of the basis on which a settlement should be made, and how the Mexican question could he made subservient in bringing the public mind to that result. It was not my intention to argue the general principles as matters of fact or feasible theory. I granted that what he said was the legitimate effect of the System with some limitations. But, said I, in the supposed case of the State at the mouth of the Mississippi; if her Confederates would so act towards her as to make it her interest to remain in the Confederation, as it was when she joined it, she would never think of leaving it, or forming any alliance with a foreign inimical Power. She would abhor and spurn such an idea if presented. The object of all such Unions is the best interests of all the States composing them. This was the object of our Union. It was this that caused its formation. So long as this end is attained, there need be no apprehension of Separation, or foreign alliance by any of them; but if the other States so act toward anyone of their Confederates as to render it more to her interest to be out of the Union than in it, then she ought to quit it. The same doctrine stated by him, in reference to all the States jointly, applied with equal force to each State separately. Self-preservation is as much the first law of Nature to any one of the States of the Union as another or all the others combined. The principle of self-preservation applied to every State, singly, in all such associations. It is only with a view to the better securing of the self-preservation of each State separately, that all such associations are formed. It was true, I admitted, if a State should wantonly, and without just cause, quit any association of this sort, and form an alliance with a foreign inimical Nation, and with hostile intent, then that would, of course, be a just cause of war on the part of her former Confederates. All that I granted; but urged that, if perfect justice should be done to the State in the supposed case, the great law of self-preservation and interest would restrain her from any such course. This might be regarded as one of the most immutable of those laws which regulate human societies in their voluntary relations towards each other.

"Dropping further remarks on that point, Mr. Seward proceeded to inquire of me, something of the details of the plan I had in view for effecting the proposed purpose. What would be the general situation of affairs in the meantime, especially in States where there were two sets of Authorities—one recognized by the Confederate States and one adhering to the National Government? How would the laws be administered in the meantime in those States? and how was the object suggested to be practically accomplished?

"What he meant by presenting this question, after Mr. Lincoln had virtually closed all further conference on that subject, I did not perceive, but proceeded to answer him in a general way, by stating that I had no fixed plan, but there were several which might be suggested, and stated one, amongst other ways, by which it might be effected. The suggestions I made on this point, as of my own accord, were the same which had been communicated to me as coming from Mr. Blair. The whole, I said, could be easily arranged by a Military Convention. This could be made to embrace, not only a suspension of actual hostilities on all the frontier lines, but also other matters involving the execution of the laws in the States referred to. Whatever disposition of troops on both sides might be necessary for the purpose, could be easily arranged in the same way. This Convention being known, however, only to the Authorities at Richmond and Washington. All these matters of detail, I said, could be easily adjusted, if we should first determine upon an Armistice for that purpose. If there was a will to do it, a proper way could easily be made clear.

"Mr. Hunter said, that there was not unanimity in the South upon the subject of undertaking the maintenance of the Monroe Doctrine, and it was not probable that any arrangement could be made by which the Confederates would agree to join in sending any portion of their Army into Mexico. In this view he expressed the joint opinion of the Commissioners; indeed, we had determined not to enter into any agreement that would require the Confederate arms to join in any invasion of Mexico.

"Mr. Lincoln and Mr. Seward stated that the feeling in the North was very strong for maintaining the Monroe Doctrine.

"The conversation was again diverted from that view of the subject by Mr. Lincoln. He repeated that he could not entertain a proposition for an Armistice on any terms, while the great and vital question of re-union was undisposed of. That was the first question to be settled. He could enter into no treaty, convention or stipulation, or agreement with the Confederate States, jointly or separately, upon that or any other subject, but upon the basis first settled, that the Union was to be restored. Any such agreement, or stipulation, would be a quasi recognition of the States then in arms against the National Government as a separate Power. That he never could do.

"I stated that as President, being Commander-in-Chief of the Armies of the United States, he might, without doubt, enter into a Military Convention. The arrangement suggested contemplated nothing but a Military Convention between the two Parties at war. All that way suggested could be easily effected in that way, if there was a willingness on both sides.

"Mr. Lincoln admitted that a Military Convention could be properly entered into by him as President for some of the purposes proposed, but repeated his determination to do nothing which would suspend military operations, unless it was first agreed that the National Authority was to be re-established throughout the country.

"Judge Campbell now renewed his inquiry how restoration was to take place, supposing that the Confederate States were consenting to it?

"Mr. Lincoln replied; By disbanding their armies and permitting the National Authorities to resume their functions.

"Mr. Seward interposed and said, that Mr. Lincoln could not express himself more clearly or forcibly in reference to this question, than he had done in his message to Congress in December before, and referred specially to that portion in these words:

> 'In presenting the abandonment of armed resistance to the National Authority, on the part of the insurgents, as the only indispensable condition to ending the war on the part of the Government, I retract nothing heretofore said as to Slavery. I repeat the declaration made a year ago, that, "while I remain in my present position, I shall not attempt to retract or modify the Emancipation Proclamation, nor shall I return to slavery any person who is free by the terms of that Proclamation, or by any of the Acts of Congress." If the people should, by whatever mode or means, make it an Executive duty to reenslave such persons, another, and not I, must be their instrument to perform it.
>
> 'In stating a single condition of peace, I mean simply to say that the war will cease on the part of the Government whenever it shall have ceased on the part of those who began it.'

"After referring to this and stating its substance from memory, Mr. Seward went on to illustrate the meaning, by saying that the war would cease whenever the civil officers of the Federal Government should be permitted to discharge their duties under the laws of the United States—in other words, whenever the due execution of the laws of the United States should be submitted to in the Confederate States.

"Judge Campbell said that the war had necessarily given rise to questions which must, it seemed to him, require stipulation or agreement of some sort, or assurances of some sort, which ought to be adjusted understandingly, before a harmonious restoration of former relations could properly be made. He alluded to the disbandment of the army, which would require time, and the disposition of its supplies. He alluded to the Confiscation Acts on both sides, and stated that property had been sold under them, and the title would be affected by the facts existing when the war ended, unless provided for by stipulations.

"Mr. Seward replied, that as to all questions involving rights of property, the courts would determine; and that Congress would, no doubt, be liberal in making restitution of confiscated property, or providing indemnity, after the excitement of the times had passed off.

"I asked Mr. Lincoln what would be the status of that portion of the Slave population in the Confederate States, which had not then become free under his Proclamation; or in other words, what effect that Proclamation would have upon the entire Black population? Would it be held to emancipate the whole, or only those who had, at the time the war ended, become actually free under it?

"Mr. Lincoln said, that was a judicial question. How the Courts would decide it, he did not know, and could give no answer. *His own opinion was, that as the Proclamation was a war measure, and would have effect only from its being an exercise of the war power, as soon as the war ceased, it would be inoperative for the future. It would be held to apply only to such slaves as had come under its operation while it was in active exercise. This was his individual opinion, but the Courts might decide the other way, and hold that it effectually emancipated all the slaves in the States to which it applied at the time. So far as he was concerned, he should leave it to the Courts to decide. He never would change or modify the terms of the Proclamation in the slightest particular. Mr. Seward said there were only about two hundred thousand slaves, who, up to that time, had come under the actual operation of the Proclamation*, and who were then in the enjoyment of their freedom under it; so, if the war should then cease, the status of much the larger portion of the slaves would be subject to judicial construction. *Mr. Lincoln sustained Mr. Seward as to the number of slaves who were then in the actual enjoyment of their freedom under the Proclamation.* Mr. Seward also said, it might be proper to state to us, that [the U.S.] Congress, a day or two before, had proposed a Constitutional Amendment [what would become the Thirteenth Amendment] for the immediate abolition of slavery throughout the United States, which he produced and read to us from a newspaper. He said this was done as a war measure. If the war were then to cease, it would probably not be adopted by a number of States, sufficient to make it a part of the Constitution; but presented the case in such light as clearly showed his object to be, to impress upon the minds of the Commissioners that, if the war should *not cease, this, as a war measure, would be adopted by a sufficient number of States to become a part of the Constitution, and without saying it in direct words, left the inference very clearly to be perceived by the Commissioners that his opinion was, if the Confederate States would then abandon the war, they could of themselves defeat this amendment, by voting it down as members of the Union. The whole number of States, it was said, being thirty-six, any ten of them could defeat this proposed amendment.* [Emphasis added, L.S.]

"I inquired how this matter could be adjusted, without some understanding as to what position the Confederate States would occupy towards the others, if they were then to abandon the war. Would they be admitted to representation in Congress?

"Mr. Lincoln very promptly replied, that his own individual opinion was, they ought to be. He also thought they would be; but he could not enter into any stipulation upon the subject. His own opinion was that when the resistance ceased and the National Authority was recognized, the States would be immediately restored to their practical relations to the Union. This was a form of expression repeatedly used by him during the conversation, in speaking of the restoration of the Union. He spoke of it as a 'restoration of the States to their practical relations to the Union.'

"Upon my urging the importance of some understanding on this point, even in case the Confederate States should entertain the proposition of a return to the Union, he persisted in asserting that he could not enter into any agreement upon this subject, or upon any other matters of that sort, with parties in arms against the Government.

"Mr. Hunter interposed, and in illustration of the propriety of the Executive entering into agreements with persons in arms against the acknowledged rightful public authority, referred to repeated instances of this character between Charles I, of England, and the people in arms against him.

"Mr. Lincoln in reply to this said: I do not profess to be posted in history. On all such matters I will turn you over to Seward. All I distinctly recollect about the case of Charles I, is, that he lost his head in the end.

"This was the familiar manner in which Mr. Lincoln, throughout the conversation, spoke of and to Mr. Seward. In the same familiar manner he addressed me throughout, as was his custom with all his intimate acquaintances when in Congress.

"I insisted that if he could, as a war measure, issue his Proclamation for Emancipation, which he did not venture to justify under the Constitution on any other grounds, he could certainly, as a like war measure, or as a measure for putting an end to the war rather, enter into some stipulation on this subject.

"*He [Lincoln] then went into a prolonged course of remarks about the Proclamation.*

He said it was not his intention in the beginning to interfere with Slavery in the States; that he never would have done it, if he had not been compelled by necessity to do it, to maintain the Union; that the subject presented many difficult and perplexing questions to him; that he had hesitated for some time, and had resorted to this measure, only when driven to it by public necessity; that he had been in favor of the General Government prohibiting the extension of Slavery into the Territories, but did not think that that Government possessed power over the subject in the States, except as a war measure; and that he had always himself been in favor of emancipation, but not immediate emancipation, even by the States. Many evils attending this appeared to him. [Emphasis added, L.S.]

"After pausing for some time, his head rather bent down, as if in deep reflection, while all were silent, he rose up and used these words, almost, if not, quite identical:

> 'Stephens, if I were in Georgia, and entertained the sentiments I do—though, I suppose, I should not be permitted to stay there long with them; but if I resided in Georgia, with my present sentiments, I'll tell you what I would do, if I were in your place: I would go home and get the Governor of the State to call the Legislature together, and get them to recall all the State troops from the war; elect Senators and Members to Congress, and ratify this Constitutional Amendment prospectively, so as to take effect—say in five years. Such a ratification would be valid in my opinion. I have looked into the subject, and think such a prospective ratification would be valid. Whatever may have been the views of your people before the war, they must be convinced now, that Slavery is doomed. It cannot last long in any event, and the best course, it seems to me, for your public men to pursue, would be to adopt such a policy as will avoid, as far as possible, *the evils of immediate emancipation.* This would be my course, if I were in your place.' [Emphasis added, L.S.]

"Mr. Seward also indulged in remarks at considerable length on the progress of the Anti-Slavery sentiment of the country, and stated that what he had thought would require forty or fifty years of agitation to accomplish, would certainly be attained in a much shorter time.

"Judge Campbell inquired of Mr. Seward if he thought, that agitation upon the subject of the political relations between the two races would cease upon the emancipation of the Blacks—the point to which heretofore it had been entirely confined.

"Mr. Seward replied, perhaps not, or possibly not.

"Other matters were then talked over relating to the evils of immediate emancipation, if that policy should be pressed, especially the sufferings which would necessarily attend the old and the infirm, as well as the women and children, who were unable to support themselves. These were fully admitted by Mr. Lincoln, but in reference to them, in that event, he illustrated all he could say by telling the anecdote, which has been published in the papers, about the Illinois farmer and his hogs.

"[Let me note here that] Mr. Lincoln had a wonderful talent for illustrations of this sort. His genius for Anecdotes was fully equal, if not superior, to that of Æsop for Apologues or Fables. They were his chief resort in conveying his ideas upon almost every question. His resources for producing them, seemed to be inexhaustible, and they were usually exceedingly pointed, apt, and telling in their application. The one on this occasion was far from being entitled to a place on a list of his best and most felicitous hits of this character. The substance of it was this:

"An Illinois farmer was congratulating himself with a neighbor upon a great discovery he had made, by which he would economize much time and labor in gathering and taking care of the food crop for his hogs, as well as trouble in looking after and feeding them during the winter.

'What is it?' said the neighbor.

'Why, it is,' said the farmer, 'to plant plenty of potatoes, and when they are mature, without either digging or housing them, turn the hogs in the field and let them get their own food as they want it.'

'But,' said the neighbor, 'how will they do when the winter comes and the ground is hard frozen?'

'Well,' said the farmer, *'let 'em root!'* [Emphasis added, L.S.]

"The conversation [between Lincoln and the Confederate commissioners] then took another turn.

"Mr. Hunter inquired of Mr. Lincoln, what would be the result of a restoration of the Union, according to his idea, as to Western Virginia. Would the 'Old Dominion' be restored to her ancient boundaries, or would Western Virginia be recognized as a State in the restored Union? [West Virginia had been formed illegally in 1863, urged on by Lincoln in the hopes of accruing additional electoral votes for his upcoming reelection.]

"Mr. Lincoln said he could only give an individual opinion, which was, that Western Virginia would be continued to be recognized as a separate State in the Union.

"Mr. Hunter after this went into a sort of recapitulation of the subjects talked over in the interview, and the conclusions which seemed to be logically deducible from them; which amounted to nothing as a basis of peace, in his judgment, but an unconditional surrender on the part of the Confederate States and their people. There could be no agreement, no treaty, nor even any stipulations as to terms—nothing but unconditional submission. A good deal of force was given to the points in this summation by the tone in which the whole was expressed.

"Mr. Seward promptly replied by insisting that no words like unconditional submission had been used, or any importing, or justly implying degradation, or humiliation even, to the people of the Confederate States. He wished this to be borne in mind.

"Mr. Hunter repeated his view of the subject. What else could be made of it? No treaty, no stipulation, no agreement, either with the Confederate States jointly, or with them separately, as to their future position or security! What was this but unconditional submission to the mercy of conquerors?

"Mr. Seward said they were not conquerors further than they required obedience to the laws. The force used was simply to maintain National Authority in the execution of laws. Nor did he think that in yielding to the execution of the laws under the Constitution of the United States, with all its guarantees and securities for personal and political rights, as they might be declared to be by the Courts, could be properly considered as unconditional submission to conquerors, or as having anything humiliating in it. The Southern people and the Southern States would be under the Constitution of the United States, with all their rights secured thereby, in the same way, and through the same instrumentalities, as the similar rights of the people of the other States were.

"Mr. Hunter said: But you make no agreement that these rights will be so held and secured!

"Mr. Lincoln said that so far as the Confiscation Acts, and other penal acts, were concerned, their enforcement was left entirely with him, and on that point he was perfectly willing to be full and explicit, and on his assurance perfect reliance might be placed. He should exercise the power of the Executive with the utmost liberality. He went on to say that he would be willing to be taxed to remunerate the Southern people for their slaves. *He [Lincoln] believed the people of the North were as responsible for slavery as the people of the South*, and if the war should then cease, with the voluntary abolition of slavery by the States, he should be in favor, individually, of the Government paying a fair indemnity for the loss to the owners. He said he believed this feeling had an extensive existence at the North. He knew some who were in favor of an appropriation as high as Four Hundred Millions of Dollars for this purpose. *I could mention persons, said he, whose names would astonish you, who are willing to do this*, if the war shall now cease without further expense, and with the abolition of slavery as stated. But on this subject he said he could give no assurance—enter into no stipulation. He barely expressed his own feelings and views, and what he believed to be the views of others upon the subject. [Emphasis added, L.S.]

"*Mr. Seward said, that the Northern people were weary of the war. They desired peace and a restoration of harmony*, and he believed would be willing to pay as an indemnity for the slaves, what would be required to continue the war, but stated no amount. [Emphasis added, L.S.]

"After thus going through with all these matters, in a conversation of about four hours, of which I have given you only the prominent leading points, and these in substance only, there was a pause, as if all felt that the interview should close. I arose and stated that it seemed our mission would be entirely fruitless, unless we could do something in the matter of the Exchange of Prisoners. This brought up that subject.

"Mr. Lincoln expressed himself in favor of doing something on it, and concluded by saying that he would put the whole matter in the hands of General [Ulysses S.] Grant, then at City Point, with whom we could interchange views on our return. Some propositions were then made for immediate special exchanges, which were readily agreed to.

"I then said: I wish, Mr. President, you would re-consider the subject of an Armistice on the basis which has been suggested. Great questions, as well as vast interests, are involved in it. If, upon so doing, you shall change your mind, you can make it known through the Military.

"Well, said he, as he was taking my hand for a farewell leave, and with a peculiar manner very characteristic of him: Well, Stephens, I will re-consider it, but I do not think my mind will change, but I will re-consider.

"The two parties then took formal and friendly leave of each other, Mr. Lincoln and Mr. Seward withdrawing first from the saloon together. Col. Babcock, our escort, soon came in to conduct us back to the steamer on which we came.

"During the interview, no person entered the saloon besides the parties named, except a colored servant or steward, who came in occasionally to see if anything was wanted, and to bring in water, cigars, and other refreshments.

"This is as full and accurate an account as I can now give of the origin, the objects, and conduct of this Conference, from its beginning to its end. In giving it, as stated before, I have not undertaken to do more than to present substantially, what verbally passed between all the parties therein mentioned."[285]

☛ "At City Point we again had an interview with Gen. Grant. He evidently regretted very much that nothing had been accomplished by the Conference. The subject of the Exchange of Prisoners was then mentioned to him, and what Mr. Lincoln said about it, when he expressed a like willingness for an immediate and general Exchange. That subject was then left with him and our

Commissioner of Exchange, Col. [Robert] Ould. Thus ended this Mission."[286]

☛ "3rd. It now remains according to the order prescribed, to say something of its results. A consideration of these will necessarily bring us to the close of the war, for the end was now rapidly approaching.

"On the return of the Commissioners to Richmond, everybody was very much disappointed, and no one seemed to be more so than Mr. Davis. *He thought Mr. Lincoln had acted in bad faith in the matter*, and attributed this change in his policy to the fall of Fort Fisher, in North Carolina, which occurred on the 15th of January, after Mr. Blair's first visit to Richmond. The fall of this Fort was one of the greatest disasters which had befallen our Cause from the beginning of the war—not excepting the loss of Vicksburg or Atlanta. Forts Fisher and Caswell guarded the entrance to the Cape Fear River, and prevented the complete blockade of the port of Wilmington, through which a limited Foreign Commerce had been carried on during the whole time. *It was by means of what cotton could thus be carried out, that we had been enabled to get along financially, as well as we had; and at this point also, a considerable number of arms and various munitions of war, as well as large supplies of subsistence, had been introduced.* All other ports, except Wilmington, had long since been closed by Naval siege. Forts Jackson and St. Philip, which guarded the mouth of the Mississippi and the entrance to New Orleans, had been captured in March, 1862. Fort Pulaski, at the mouth of the Savannah, had fallen on the 12th of April, in the same year; and Fort Macon in North Carolina, a month or two earlier. Forts Gaines, Powell, and Morgan, at Mobile, had also fallen in August, 1863. Fort Sumter at Charleston, it is true, had still held out, and had never been taken, but the harbor there had been virtually closed by a strict blockade; so that the closing of the port of Wilmington was the complete shutting out of the Confederate States from all intercourse by sea with Foreign Countries. The respiratory functions of External Trade, so essential to the vitality of all Communities, had been performed for the whole Confederacy, mainly, for nearly three years, through the small aperture of this little Port, choked to wheezing as it was, by a cordon of armed ships, drawn around its neck. The passing in and out of necessary Commerce at this place, all the time, was very much like breathing through a quill in extreme cases of quinsy or croup; still, as such breathing often saves life, so this channel of External Trade was of the utmost importance to us at that time. The closing of this Port, therefore, and the great advantage against us secured by it, was what Mr. Davis supposed to be the cause of a change of policy on the part of the Administration at Washington. [Emphasis added, L.S.]

"We reported to him, verbally, all that had occurred at the Conference, and much more minutely in detail than I have given it . . . [here]. In this report to him, I gave it as my opinion, that if he were not himself mistaken as to Mr. Blair's knowledge of the policy of the Administration at Washington, and of his being in its confidence; in other words, if there was really at that time, entertained by Mr. Lincoln, any such views as those suggested by Mr. Blair, I was not at all disappointed myself at the result of the interview at Fortress Monroe. I thought the publicity of the Mission was enough to account for its failure, without attributing it to any bad faith, either on the part of Mr. Blair or Mr. Lincoln; that I had expressed the opinion to Judge Campbell and Mr. Hunter, when we saw our departure announced in the papers as it was, (the whole North being in a stir upon the subject by the time we reached City Point,) that this would most probably defeat our accomplishing anything, even if Mr. Lincoln really intended to do anything on that line; and that it was in this view of the subject solely, I had made the request of him, at the close of the interview, to reconsider the matter of the Armistice.

"I called Mr. Davis's attention specially to the fact, that in reply to that request Mr. Lincoln declared he would reconsider it; and notwithstanding the qualification with which he made the declaration, yet I thought if there ever had been really anything in the *projèt* [French: 'project'], Mr. Davis would still hear from it in a quiet way through the Military, after all the then 'hubbub' about Peace Negotiations had subsided. In this view of the subject, I gave it to him as my opinion, that there should be no written report by the Commissioners touching the Conference, especially as a full disclosure of its real objects could not, with propriety, then be made; and that any report without this, however consistent with the facts, as far as they should be set forth, would fail to give full information upon the exact posture of the affairs to which it related, by which the public mind in reference to it would be more or less misled.

"He insisted that a written report should be made, and the other Commissioners concurring with him, I again yielded my views on that point, and joined them in the Report which you have seen, believing, as I did, that if I declined, more harm would certainly result from a misconstruction of my course and reasons in the matter, than would by conforming to his views and those of my Colleagues.

"The question then was, what was next to be done?

"Mr. Davis's position was, that inasmuch as it was now settled beyond question, by the decided and pointed declarations of Mr. Lincoln, that there could be no Peace short of Unconditional Submission on the part of the People of the Confederate States, with an entire change of their Social Fabric throughout the South, the People ought to be, and could be, more thoroughly aroused by Appeals through the Press and by Public Addresses, to the full consciousness of the necessity of renewed and more desperate efforts, for the preservation of themselves and their Institutions. By these means they might yet be saved from the most humiliating threatened degradation. In these lay the only hope left of escaping such a Calamity. [President Davis] . . . himself seemed more determined than ever to fight it out on this line, and to risk all upon the issue. By the course he proposed, I understood him to hold the opinion, that Richmond could still be defended, notwithstanding [U.S. General William T.] Sherman had already made considerable progress on his march from Savannah; and that our Cause could still be successfully maintained, without any change in the internal policy upon the subjects referred to before. His general views and purposes at the time, were set forth with that firmness and decision so characteristic of him, in the Message he sent to [the Confederate] Congress on the Report of the Commissioners, and in a speech he made at the African Church, (a noted place for public speaking in the City of Richmond,) on the night of the second day after our return. The newspaper sketches of that speech were meagre, as well as inaccurate, in several particulars, and, upon the whole, came far short of so presenting its substance even, as to give those who did not hear it anything like an adequate conception of its full force and power. It was not only bold, undaunted, and confident in its tone, but had that loftiness of sentiment and rare form of expression, as well as magnetic influence in its delivery, by which the passions of the masses of the people are moved to their profoundest depths, and roused to the highest pitch of excitement. Many who had heard this Master of Oratory in his most brilliant displays in the Senate and on the hustings, said they never before saw Mr. Davis so really majestic! The occasion, and the effects of the speech, as well as all the circumstances under which it was made, caused the minds of not a few to revert to like appeals by [Fourteenth-Century Italian politician Cola di] Rienzi and Demosthenes [of ancient Greece].

"While it was well calculated to awaken associations and suggest comparisons of that sort, it, nevertheless by the character of its policy, equally reminded me of the famous charge of the 'Six Hundred' at Balaklava, of which some one—I forget who—in witnessing it, said, in substance: 'It is brilliant; it is grand; but it is not war!'

"However much I admired the heroism of the sentiments expressed, yet in his general views of policy to be pursued in the then situation, I could not concur. I saw nothing to prevent Sherman himself from proceeding right on to Richmond and attacking Lee in the rear, to say nothing of any movements by Grant, who then had an Army in front, of not much, if any, under 200,000 men. Lee's forces were not over one fourth of that number. Sherman's army, when united with [U.S. General John M.] Schofield's and [Alfred H.] Terry's, which were joining him from Wilmington, North Carolina, would be swelled to near 100,000. To meet these, the Confederates had in his front, nothing but the fragments of shattered armies, amounting in all to not one half the number of the Federals.

"When the progamme of action, thus indicated by Mr. Davis in our interviews, as well as in his Message and the speech referred to, was clearly resolved upon, I, then, for the first time, in view of all the surroundings, considered the Cause as utterly hopeless. It may be that it was utterly hopeless any how; that nothing could have saved it at that time, or at any time. It may be that if the course which I thought would or could then save it, or would or could have saved it at any time, had been adopted, it would have come as far short of success, as the one which was pursued; and it may be, that the one which was taken on this occasion, as well as on all the other occasions, on which I did not agree, was the very best that could have been taken. These are now all matters purely of speculation . . . and it is not my purpose at this time to discuss them, or to pass any judgment in reference to them, one way or the other. I doubt not that all—the President, the Cabinet, and Congress—did the very best they could, from their own convictions of what was best to be done at the time.

"The ablest and truest men often differ upon vital questions; and all are liable to err in judgment. I wish, therefore, in all I say on this occasion touching these and kindred subjects, as well as what I say in relation to the conduct of others in regard to them, to be understood as only presenting the views from which my own convictions sprung, and the motives by which I was actuated throughout, especially in declining, as I did, to appear and speak at the meeting which was addressed by Mr. Davis as stated, and also at another Grand Meeting arranged to take place a few days after, in Capitol Square, for similar purposes. I declined, because I could not undertake to impress upon the minds of the people the idea that they could do what I believed to be impossible, or to inspire in them hopes which I did not believe could ever be realized.

"It was then that I withdrew from Richmond. My last interview with Mr. Davis before leaving, was after my thus declining to address the meetings proposed. He inquired what it was my purpose to do? I told him it was to go home and remain there. I should neither make any speech, nor even make known to the public in any way my views of the general condition of affairs, but quietly abide the issues of fortune, whatever they might be. Differing as we did, at that time, upon these points, as we had upon others, we parted in the same friendship which had on all occasions marked our personal intercourse.

"*I left Richmond in no ill-humor with Mr. Davis, or with any purpose of opposing or obstructing the execution of the designs of the Administration, in any way; but because I could not sanction a Policy which I thought would certainly end in disaster, and I did not wish to be where my opinions might, by possibility, be the cause of divisions and dissensions, which would just as certainly lead to the same result. General confidence in the Administration was essential to success on any line, and this I did not wish to weaken or impair in others at this most critical juncture, though I could not, myself, approve the course which had been taken.* I, therefore, left on the 9th of February [1865], and reached home the 20th, where I remained in perfect retirement, until I was arrested on the 11th of May [1865]. [Emphasis added, L.S.]

"In the meantime was enacted the last scenes in the Grand Drama of this terrible conflict of arms, which we have so rapidly glanced at, in considering the conflict of the principles out of which it arose. Only a few matters now, connected with its closing events, on the same line, remain to be noticed."[287]

☞ "Mr. George Davis, of North Carolina, had succeeded Mr. Thomas H. Watts as Attorney-General. Mr. George A. Trenholm, of South Carolina, had been put at the head of the [Confederate] Treasury Department, upon the resignation of Mr. [Charles G.] Memminger, in June, 1864. Mr. [James A.] Seddon, also, who had succeeded Mr. [George W.] Randolph, as [C.S.] Secretary of War, resigned that position about the time I left Richmond. This position was immediately assigned to Mr. [John C.] Breckinridge, then a [Confederate] Major-General.

"After Sherman had proceeded in his famous march beyond Columbia, leaving a blackened waste in his track, and when our affairs were '*in extremis*'—almost '*in articulo mortis*' [Latin: 'at the point of death']—Gen. Joseph E. Johnston, upon the earnest appeal of Members of [the Confederate] Congress and the Virginia Legislature, was again assigned to the command of the remnants of the shattered Confederate Armies alluded to, in the Carolinas, which did not exceed 35,000 effective men in all. With these he was to oppose the advancing Federal forces in front of not much, if any, under a hundred thousand.

"[U.S. General Ulysses S.] Grant commenced operations as early as the season would permit. On the 2nd of April, he succeeded, by a concentration of forces, in making breaches in [C.S. General Robert E.] Lee's lines of defence near Petersburg [Virginia]. The whole line for the defence of the [Confederate] Capital then extended at least thirty-five miles in length. By these breaches, made in this line on the 2nd of April, Lee was necessarily compelled to retire, and thus give up Richmond at last. Several bloody and heroic struggles ensued. The remaining thinned, but resolute and undaunted columns of the noble Confederate Chief, like the Spartan band at Thermopylae, were now pressed to a death-grapple by the surrounding legions of the Monster Army of the Potomac under Grant. The tragic finale was at hand! On the 9th of April, at

Appomattox Court House, the sword of Lee was surrendered! Not much else pertaining to the 'annihilated' Army of Northern Virginia, was left to be passed under the formula of that ceremony!"[288]

☛ "Mr. Davis and his Cabinet had left Richmond on the night of the 2nd of April, after Lee's lines were thus broken, as stated. They went as far as Danville, Virginia, where they remained for several days, and where Mr. Davis issued another most stirring and animating address; but after being informed of what had occurred at Appomattox Court House, he and the Cabinet proceeded to Greensboro, North Carolina, where some days afterwards, in consultation with [Confederate] Generals [Joseph E.] Johnston and [Pierre G. T.] Beauregard and his Cabinet, Gen. Johnston was authorized by him, to make such terms as he might be able with Gen. Sherman, for a Termination of the war, and a general Pacification. The result of this was the celebrated Sherman and Johnston Convention, which was formally agreed to and signed on the 18th of April, by these two commanding Generals of the respective sides.

"But while these distinguished parties were thus negotiating, little did they know of what had occurred and was going on elsewhere. Four days before, on the night of the 14th of April, Mr. Lincoln had been assassinated, which produced a state of feeling never before known in the country. The Vice President, Mr. Andrew Johnson, immediately succeeded to the Presidential office. From the great excitement created by the horrible act, by which Mr. Lincoln had been taken off, or from some other most unfortunate cause, this Sherman-Johnston Convention was disapproved by the newly installed President [Johnson] at Washington.

"Upon being notified of this fact by Gen. Sherman, Gen. Johnston then did the next best thing in his power. He entered into a stipulation with Gen. Sherman, by which he surrendered all the Confederate forces north of the Chattahoochee River, upon similar terms to those agreed to between Generals Lee and Grant, in reference to the forces under Gen. Lee.

"The course of Gen. Johnston was promptly followed by Gen. 'Dick' Taylor commanding in Alabama, who surrendered his forces to General Edward R. S. Canby, upon similar terms on the 4th of May. A like surrender of all the Confederate forces west of the Mississippi, was made by Gen. Edmund Kirby Smith, to the same Federal officer, on the 26th of the same month. All other smaller detachments of Confederate forces scattered about in various parts of the country, had, in the meantime, been surrendered by their officers in command, upon the same or similar terms. Kirby Smith's surrender was the last.

"The whole number of Confederates thus surrendered, from the 9th of April to the 25th of May, according to the muster rolls, amounted to a little under 175,000 in number. This embraced quite a number who, from disease, were not actively in the field at the time. Making due allowance for these, there was, therefore, then, hardly more than 150,000 Confederates under arms. The whole number of Federal forces then in the field, and afterwards mustered out of service, as their records show, amounted in round numbers to 1,050,000.

"Thus ended this greatest of modern wars—if not the greatest, in some respects, 'known in the history of the human race.' It lasted four years, and a little over, as we have seen, marked throughout by many sanguinary conflicts, with heroic exploits on both sides, which it has not been in the line of our investigation to notice, but all of which deserve to be, if they have not been, duly chronicled in proper place. Even in memory, many of them will be perpetuated as legends, and thus treasured as themes for story and song for ages to come.

"One of the most striking features in it, was the great disparity between the number of the forces on the opposite sides. From its beginning to its end, near, if not quite, two millions more Federals were brought into the field than the entire force of the Confederates. The Federal records show that they had, from first to last, over 2,600,000 men in the service; while the Confederates, all told in like manner, could not have much, if any, exceeded 600,000! *No People on earth ever maintained the great Right of Self-government, so long as the Confederates did in this contest, with such sacrifices of blood and treasure, against such odds!* [Emphasis added, L.S.]

"The entire loss on both sides, including those who were permanently disabled, as well as those killed in battle and who died from wounds received and diseases contracted in the service, amounted, according to Mr. [Horace] Greeley's estimate, which is more likely to be under than over the mark, to the 'stupendous aggregate of One Million of Men!' [Modern *Southern* historians maintain that some 3 million people, of all races, died during Lincoln's war: 2 million in the South, 1 million in the North.]

"The like aggregate of expenditure of money on both sides, including the loss and sacrifice of property, could not have been less than Eight Thousand Millions of Dollars! [i.e., 8 billion dollars; or about 110 billion dollars into today's currency]—a sum fully equal to three-fourths of the assessed value of the taxable property of the entire country, when it commenced!

"In concluding our Review, may we not well ask, as the dying soldier did in the first great battle on the Plains of Manassas: 'What was all this for?'"[289]

30

THE RESULTS OF LINCOLN'S WAR

IN THIS, THE FINAL CHAPTER, Stephens reviews the consequences of Abraham Lincoln's illegal war on the South and the Constitution, beginning with his assassination and the ascendance to the White House of his successor Andrew Johnson, America's seventeenth president. In these last excerpts from his *A Constitutional View of the Late War Between the States*, Stephens discusses the illegalities of the Thirteenth and Fourteenth Amendments, so-called "Reconstruction," and his unlawful arrest and five-month imprisonment at Boston, Massachusetts. He warns of the future dangers to the U.S. of allowing the rights of state sovereignty and secession to erode, while maintaining to the end that: "The Cause which was lost by the surrender of the Confederates, was only the maintenance of this Principle by arms. It was not the Principle itself that they abandoned."

☞ " [I] . . . come now . . . to the consideration of the Results of this terrible Conflict of arms, which grew out of the Conflict of Principles referred to [earlier], especially its effects upon the general character of the Institutions of the States severally, as well as upon the nature and character of their relations to the Union, or upon the Federal System itself. This double conflict, both in the council-chamber and on the field . . . was between the [Conservative] defenders of the Principles of Federation [Confederation] on one side, and the [Liberal] advocates of Consolidation [empire] on the other; or in other words, between the defenders and opposers of the Sovereign Right of local Self-government on the part of the Peoples of the several States engaged in it.

"In considering these Results in this view, up to this time, [I] . . . can, of course, at present, only note existing facts, and actual changes already effected, so far as they bear upon State and Federal affairs; and in connection with them, indulge such speculations as to the future, as these facts seem most reasonably to warrant. The real and permanent results of this War upon our Institutions, and complex system of Governments, are not yet fully developed [Stephens is writing here in mid 1868, three years into so-called "Reconstruction"]. Though Peace has been proclaimed, the smoke from the battle fields still clouds the horizon. President [Andrew] Johnson himself seems to be almost as much in the dark, upon what will be the ultimate consequences of the War, as he was when, as Senator, he offered the celebrated Resolution which we have specially noticed, declaring its objects and purposes. As he then did not 'see his way clearly,' so, at the surrender of the Confederate Armies, he seemed to be quite as incapable of having a clear perception of the legitimate consequences which necessarily and logically followed the doctrines and principles of that Resolution. According to these doctrines and principles, which expressly set forth the objects of the War on the Federal side not to be a subjugation of the Peoples of the Confederate States, nor for the purpose of overthrowing or interfering with their Rights or established Institutions, but to preserve the Union of the States with all their Dignity, Equality and Rights unimpaired, as they then existed under the Constitution, he ought by all means, it seems to me, as President, to have ratified and confirmed the 'Sherman-Johnston Convention,' before alluded to. This, as its terms show, was a complete abandonment of the War, and a formal engagement on the part of the Confederates, no longer to resist the due execution of the laws of the United States. This engagement, as [I have shown], . . . had been entered into on the part of the Confederates, in pursuance of authority from President Davis, Commander-in-Chief of the Armies of the Confederate States.

"In considering the results of the War, therefore, as far as they have as yet developed themselves, and observing to what they have as yet led, in the view it is proposed to take of them, it is not only important, but essential to note specially the most prominent facts bearing upon the subject in hand since the surrender up to this time. These, according to their importance, in my judgment, I will now proceed to state in regular order.

"1. In the first place, then, the most important matter bearing upon the points we have in hand and which claims special attention, was this disapproval by Mr. [Andrew] Johnson of the 'Sherman-Johnston Convention' referred to. *His action on this occasion, in my opinion, must ever be considered as great an error in accomplishing his object, as was his error in the beginning in holding that the Union of the States under the Constitution could be preserved and rightfully maintained by force.* This most extraordinary, if not fatal error of disapproving that Convention, is the more worthy of special notice here, from the fact that this action was so inconsistent with his own avowed principles, as well as with the avowed policy of Mr. Lincoln throughout the war, even down to the Fortress Monroe Conference. . . . General Sherman whether expressly clothed with authority by Mr. Lincoln, to enter into that Convention, or not, in doing it and agreeing to the terms which he did, certainly acted not only in strict conformity with the principles of Mr. Johnson's Resolution, which had been sanctioned by every member of the Senate and by every member of the House with two exceptions, but with the uniformly avowed policy of Mr. Lincoln throughout the war. Indeed, the facts warrant the belief that [U.S.] General [William T.] Sherman, in entering into that Convention, acted under express authority, verbal if not written, from Mr. Lincoln himself: for it is well known that, just before it was entered into, he had gone round to City Point, where he had met, and had a personal interview with Mr. Lincoln; and had consulted him fully as to the course he should take in winding up the war, which he saw was now rapidly approaching its end. On these matters he had consulted him, even down to the minute detail as to what course he should take toward Mr. Davis—whether he should make a point to capture him, or let him escape. This clearly appears from the newspaper accounts of a speech made by General Sherman in Ohio, not long afterwards. It was in this speech he related the very characteristic as well as felicitous anecdote, by which Mr. Lincoln, in that interview, illustrated his position, views, and wishes (exceedingly politic as they were) in regard to the arrest of Mr. Davis. . . .

"This is the newspaper account:

'President Lincoln and Jeff Davis.—General Sherman says he asked President Lincoln explicitly when at City Point, whether he wanted him to capture Jeff Davis or let him escape, but the President gave him no reply except a story about a temperance lecturer, who, one day, after a long ride in the hot sun, stopped at the house of a friend, and was regaled with lemonade. His host insinuatingly asked, if he wouldn't like the least drop of something stronger to brace up his nerves after the exhausting heat and exercise?

"'No,' replied the lecturer. "I couldn't think of it; I'm opposed to it on principle. But," he added, with a longing glance at the black bottle that stood conveniently at hand, "if you could manage to put in a drop unbeknownst to me, I guess it wouldn't hurt me much."

"'Now, General,' said Mr. Lincoln, in conclusion, "I'm bound to oppose the escape of Jeff Davis; but if you could manage to let him slip out unbeknownst like, I guess it wouldn't hurt me much."'

[Editor's note: It is little wonder Lincoln did not want President Davis captured: Davis' trial before a U.S. court would have fully revealed the unconstitutionality of Lincoln's War on the South and states' rights. Even after Lincoln's assassination, for two years Davis begged from his jail cell to be put on trial. A number of other imprisoned Confederate officials asked to be placed on the witness stand as well. All were repeatedly turned down, for—knowing it was a losing proposition, and that the Union's "dirty little secret" would be exposed—no Northern attorneys could be found who would defend the U.S. against any of the former Southern leaders. L.S.]

"Now, if President Johnson had, on this occasion, approved that Convention, he would have carried out his own principles as well as the policy of Mr. Lincoln, and the States would have been immediately restored (whether for better or worse,) to their 'practical relations to the Union,' which was the whole professed object of the war; and he would have saved himself from those inextricable difficulties about 'Reconstruction' in which he has since been involved, by a departure from them. The National Authority, as Mr. Lincoln styled it, would have been immediately restored, and this, according to his idea, was a Restoration of the Union.

"But instead of giving his approval to this Convention, and thus, at once, effecting a complete Restoration of the Union, or of the 'States to their practical relations' to it, Mr. Johnson most strangely directed the war to be pushed to the overthrow of all the existing State Governments in all the Confederate States (except Tennessee, Kentucky and Missouri), and the arrest and imprisonment of all their chief Executive Officers, and the temporary establishment of complete Military rule throughout the entire limits of the Confederacy, with the exception mentioned. *This, therefore, as just stated, must be looked upon as an error of Mr. Johnson, differing in no respect in principle from the error of Mr. Lincoln in the inauguration of the war at the beginning. It was, moreover, a clear violation of the understanding of the Confederates, of the terms upon which their arms had been surrendered. The then existing State Governments and their laws, were clearly recognized in these terms.* [Emphasis added, L.S.]

"2. The next fact to be noticed in this connection, is the Proclamation issued by Mr. Johnson as President, on the 29th of May, which was a virtual announcement of the close of the war, with an offer of Amnesty and Pardon upon certain conditions, to all who had participated in it on the Confederate side, except fourteen designated classes. Now *according to the principles as well as purposes set forth in his own Resolution referred to before, when resistance had ceased, and the last Confederate arm had been surrendered, and when the Federal Civil Officers had been permitted to perform their functions in all the States, without let or hindrance, then the Insurrection, or Rebellion, as he held the war to be on the part of the Confederates, was certainly put down, and the Union was, of course, instantly restored; and all the States should have been so recognized under their then existing State Constitutions; for the war had been professedly waged against individuals and not against organized Communities or States, or against any of their Institutions, much less their Constitutions! The States could be recognized only in their organized character, as they existed by the terms of their fundamental law. But this he did not do.* We are therefore brought to another step in the progress of events to be specially noted. [Emphasis added, L.S.]

"3. On the same day—29th of May—Mr. Johnson, as Commander-in-Chief of the Army of the United States, issued another Proclamation, by which, as such Commander-in-Chief, he appointed Wm. W. Holden Military or Provisional Governor of the State of North Carolina, basing it upon a declaration that no Civil Government then existed in that State. This fact being so announced, the Proclamation went on to set forth the Terms and Conditions upon which certain classes of Electors under the Constitution of North Carolina as it existed when the war commenced to the exclusion of others, might form a new Constitution and State Government, which would be recognized by him as the legitimate Government of that State. Similar Proclamations were subsequently issued by him, in relation to the other Confederate States which were in the same condition.

"Out of the Principles upon which these Proclamations were based and issued, have arisen all those other agitating questions, to which I have just referred, about 'Reconstruction,' in which he, the Congress, and the whole Country are now embroiled.

"But just at this point, let it be borne in mind that, in pursuance of these Proclamations, the classes designated by [U.S. President Johnson] . . . in all the States respectively, did proceed to make new Constitutions, to organize new State Governments, and to elect members of the Senate and House of Representatives of the Congress of the United States. This was all done as speedily as could be done, after the issuance of the Proclamations in reference to each of the States respectively. *In the formation of their new Constitutions, however, two other prominent conditions were subsequently imposed by Executive requisitions not embraced in the Proclamations. One was the Abolition of Slavery, and the other the Repudiation of what was called the War Debt on the part of each State respectively.* The power exercised in the issuance of these Proclamations, and in the imposition of these Executive requisitions upon the State Conventions, must again be looked upon as differing in no respect whatever, so far as principle is concerned, from the powers claimed by Mr. Lincoln in his Proclamations heretofore reviewed. Mr. Johnson, as yet, seems to have been, as Saul of Tarsus [Saint Paul] on his way to Damascus, 'breathing out threatenings and slaughter!' Still, the great majority of the masses of the Southern People, being exceedingly desirous for Peace and Harmony, *notwithstanding the deep wrongs thus inflicted*, were willing to accept the entire situation, and to comply in good faith, with all the terms thus imposed—especially as the whole was avowedly based on the idea, that when those terms should be complied with the States would then be restored 'to their practical relations to the Union.' With these feelings and views, they did thus in good faith comply. Moreover, their Legislatures elected under their new Constitutions, ratified the proposed Thirteenth Amendment to the Constitution of the United States; and by these ratifications on their part, that new provision in the organic law of the Union, was carried and proclaimed to be a part of the Constitution. Without counting their votes, it was lost!

"In their action, throughout, on these subjects, they were influenced mainly by the strong hope that, notwithstanding the Union would be thus restored, somewhat like the violent and unskilful resetting of dislocated joints with some ruptured ligaments, yet, when all the members of the Federal Body-Politic should be once more in their proper places and their normal functions restored, the whole, after awhile would again assume healthful and vigorous action, by which future tranquillity, happiness, and prosperity would be amply secured. These were the feelings and views by which they were influenced in promptly complying with what is known as the President's Policy."[290]

☞ "But now a new obstacle arose in a different quarter, which brings us to the consideration of another important step in the progress of events. The Thirty-ninth Congress assembled in December, 1865. Soon after its assemblage, all the States embraced in these Proclamations, except Texas, were thoroughly reorganized under the Executive Policy, as just stated, with Senators and Members of Congress ready to take their seats, which Mr. Seward, who was Mr. Johnson's as well as Mr. Lincoln's Secretary of State, had declared were still empty and ready for them in the National Councils. *This [U.S.] Congress, both in the Senate and House of Representatives, it must be recollected, refused to admit the Senators and Members elected from the States thus reorganized under the Executive policy. They repudiated not only the Resolution of the 26th of July, 1861, referred to, as Mr. Johnson had done himself, but also repudiated the principles upon which he had acted; not upon the grounds, however,—which consistency required—that the Union was restored when the Insurrection, or Rebellion, so-called, had been put down; but upon the grounds, that Mr. Johnson had not gone far enough in his action towards the great object of Centralism aimed at from the beginning by the [Liberal] Party leaders of this Congress. They turned over the whole subject to a Joint Committee of the two Houses, known as the celebrated 'Reconstruction Committee.' To this grand Joint Committee, organized upon the model of a Jacobin Junto, was given the entire control of the whole subject. The Restoration of the Union as it was, (even with the abolition of Slavery, so-called,) was not what they wanted. They demanded a thorough Reconstruction, so far as the Confederate States were concerned. This [Liberal, Northern, anti-South] Committee now openly proclaimed that the War had been waged, not for the* *preservation of the Union with the Rights, Dignity and Equality of all the several States unimpaired under the Constitution! The mask so long worn by the leading spirits of the War Party at the North, was now partly raised, and Mr. Johnson himself seems to have discovered for the first time, from the disclosures made, what were the real objects and purposes of the controlling leaders of his late associates and allies, from the beginning! The Monster Principle of ultimate complete Centralism, from clear indications, now stood before him in new lights, and as he had never viewed it before! This Committee assumed the position that not only the States reorganized under Mr. Johnson's policy, but even Tennessee, should never more take part in the Public Councils, without being first required not only to change their domestic Institutions so far as concerned the relations of the two races (constituting parts of their population), but without also being shorn of their Rights, Dignity, and Equality as members of the Union under the Constitution! They thus openly repudiated their many most solemn declarations during the war, and in so doing showed clearly that these declarations were nothing but specious pretexts resorted to at the time, by which thousands, and hundreds of thousands, and millions, perhaps, at the North, had been designedly misled and deceived!* [Emphasis added, L.S.]

"This position of the Reconstruction Committee upon these subjects is what led to the open rupture between Mr. Johnson and his late allies, and the mutual denunciations of treason and traitor, which are now [mid 1868] passing between them, and to which I referred some days ago. But, without commenting upon these, *may it not most appropriately be here asked, if anything could more completely show the great wrong and injustice of the war on the part of the Federals throughout, than the position assumed by this Reconstruction Committee, and which was affirmed by Congress? During the whole period of four years' bloody strife, their avowed object was nothing more than to compel the Seceding States to return to a renewal of their obligations under the Constitution; and when this object was entirely effected, they stood before the country with the public declaration that they could not safely permit that to take place for which so much blood and treasure had been expended!* [Emphasis added, L.S.]

"*What a spectacle they thus exhibited! To fully appreciate its monstrous character, it should be considered from two points of view: The war, remember, was waged by them for this avowed object of making other Parties perform their duties under a Compact, while they, themselves, were, at the very time and before, as we have seen, openly and confessedly faithless in the discharge of their own duties under the same Compact! Nay, more, this faithlessness on their part, remember also, was the cause of the Secession on the part of the others. Now, the spectacle would have been bad enough, if they had stopped with what they had, by superior power, been enabled thus to accomplish, and had been satisfied with results so most wrongfully attained! But how infinitely increased is the monstrousness of their conduct, when, not content with the result so wickedly and nefariously reached, they proceeded to make further exactions for their own special advantage and greater power! Is there to be found in the annals of mankind a parallel of such unblushing, double-faced, insolent and infamous iniquity?* [Emphasis added, L.S.]

"One thing which induced this extraordinary course, was doubtless the discovery of the fact that by the abolition of Slavery, so-called, the Confederate States would be entitled to thirteen more members in the House under the then Ratio of Representation, than they had theretofore been under the three-fifths count of their Black population, about which so much false clamor had been raised before the war! It now became clearly apparent, that the just and equal Rights of the South had been curtailed by that clause of the Constitution; and that her political power, in the Federal Government, would be considerably augmented by the change in this respect, which had been effected in the new order of things. The terms at first exacted of the Confederate States by this Reconstruction Committee, whose Report was agreed to in both Houses, were, that these States should agree to and ratify what they proposed to them as a further Amendment to the Constitution of the United States, known as the Fourteenth Amendment, as a condition precedent to their being allowed Representation in either branch of Congress. With these Congressional terms, Tennessee, on the 12th of July, 1866, complied. The other States all failed, or refused to do so. This brings us to that scene in the drama now being enacted. How far it will come short of being the last scene of a like character, the great future alone can determine! To what is at present passing, therefore, on the political boards, and exhibiting the actual Results of the War up to this time, as well as their general tendency to inevitable ultimate results of a far more serious nature, if action upon the line on which the whole has thus far been conducted be not arrested, we must now look. [Emphasis added, L.S.]

"4. The next great fact, therefore, to be here specially noticed, is the adoption by Congress of the 'Reconstruction Measures,' so-called, which are now pending before the people of those States which have been denied Representation in Congress. The first Act of this character passed Congress in February of this year. This Act more clearly shows the tendency of what may be looked to as the Ultimate Results of the War than any of the previous matters noted. The reasons assigned for this most extraordinary measure on the part of Congress, were no less extraordinary than the measure itself. *It is amazing that men with intelligence and any regard for their character, could have had the audaciousness in the face of notorious truths to assign the reasons which they did for their action in this matter!* [Emphasis added, L.S.] These were given in the Preamble to the Act, and are as follows:

> Whereas, no legal State Governments, or adequate protection for life or property, now exists in the Rebel States of Virginia, North Carolina, South Carolina, Georgia, Mississippi, Alabama, Louisiana, Florida, Texas, and Arkansas; and, Whereas, it is necessary that Peace and Good Order should be

enforced in said States, until loyal and Republican State Governments can be legally established! etc.

"*Was ever a solemn public declaration made by any respectable Bodies of intelligent men, so utterly inconsistent with well known facts, and facts, too, which had been previously recognized and acted upon by themselves? Were there not legal State Governments then existing in every one of these 'Rebel States,' so-called? Was not every Department of Civil Government—Legislative, Executive, and Judicial—as regularly administered in them as ever before, and as regularly as in any of the States represented in the Congress which made this declaration? If not, how was it that their acts in ratifying the Thirteenth Amendment to the Constitution of the United States had been regarded as legal and valid by this very Congress which made this declaration? If these State Governments were not legal, how could that Amendment to the Constitution, carried by their action, be held and declared to be valid? Moreover, were not life and property as thoroughly protected in them, as far as they can be protected by efficient laws, as in any of their own States? If there were violations of law, murders and other outrages, committed in some of them, or all of them, was not the same true of all the States? Where is the State in which outrages of like character were not committed? Had Gen. Grant, who had been sent specially to examine into this matter, in his report, intimated that there was any difference in these particulars between the general state of things South and North? He certainly had not!*"²⁹¹ [Emphasis added, L.S.]

☛ "*But, again, how, with any regard for truth, could these States, in February, 1867, be said to be Rebel States? Was there a single man in arms against the General Government within their entire limits? Was not the whole mass of their entire people perfectly submissive, even to the unjust and unconstitutional demands of the [Liberal Lincolnian] Authorities at Washington? How, also, could they be said to be disloyal, in any sense? Had not every officer in them, from their Chief Executives to their lowest Magistrates, in the most bona fide manner, resumed their obligations to support and defend the Constitution of the United States? Is there any other test of loyalty but this known to the Constitution, either for State or Federal officers? This Preamble, thus fixed to this first Reconstruction Act, can be regarded in no other light, than as one of the most reckless perversions of truth ever put upon public record; while the Act itself must ever be regarded as one of the most palpable usurpations of Power to be found in the history of the world!*" [Emphasis added, L.S.] Well did President [Andrew] Johnson, in his Veto of such a monstrous outrage, say:

'I submit to Congress whether this measure is not, in its whole character, scope, and object, without Precedent, and without Authority—in palpable conflict with the plainest provisions of the Constitution, and utterly destructive of those great principles of Liberty and Humanity for which our

ancestors, on both sides of the Atlantic, have shed so much blood, and expended so much treasure?
'. . . Those who advocated the right of Secession alleged in their own justification, that we had no regard for law, and that their rights of Property, Life, and Liberty would not be safe under the Constitution as administered by us. If we now verify their assertion, we prove that they were, in truth and in fact, fighting for their Liberty; and instead of branding their leaders with the dishonoring name of Traitors against a righteous and legal Government, we elevate them in history in the rank of self-sacrificing Patriots, consecrate them to the admiration of the world, and place them by the side of [George] Washington, [John] Hampden and [Algernon] Sydney!'

"Most truthful utterances these [by President Johnson]! And most remarkable, too, coming as they did from him, who had, himself, just before been so full of 'breathing out threatenings and slaughter' against the 'self-sacrificing patriots!' Delivered as they were, and under the circumstances they were, they remind us forcibly of some which came from the same Saul of Tarsus after the scales had fallen from his eyes, and he had been brought to see his persecutions of the disciples of the true faith, in their proper light. Paul, after he was brought to a full realization of his great error in thus warring against them, most bitterly repented of all that he had thus done, and especially that he had consented to the death of the martyred Stephen, and had even held the clothes of those who slew him, even though he had believed at the time that he was doing right!

"It is true, there is nothing in these expressions of Mr. Johnson, which directly shows that he had then as fully reached a perfect realization of error on his part, in any matter connected with the war, as Paul had in the matter of his persecutions, when the utterances referred to by him were given; and yet there is a good deal in the tone and manner in which Mr. Johnson's expressions were given forth, which clearly indicates that he was very near the same point, whether he had then, or has since, or ever shall, actually reach it or not. The expressions as they stand in the context, were presented only as a strong argument to his late associates and allies, to induce them, if possible, to reconsider and abandon the monstrous provisions of their measure. *Still, he must have felt, as his language unmistakably implies, that if they did not so reconsider and abandon, a very great wrong had been done to those who would suffer from them, by other measure to which he had unwittingly given his consent—never supposing that they would lead to such ruinous results and most disastrous consequences! This, his words clearly import.*"[292] [Emphasis added, L.S.]

☛ "But this and other arguments, strong and pointed as they all were, and coming from *the high source they did, produced no effect whatever, but increased rage, upon those to whom they were so conscientiously, earnestly, and truthfully addressed. Deaf in their madness alike to principles, consistency, and all considerations of their own honor, as well as of humanity, [the Northern Liberals] . . . were resolved upon the execution of their purpose, though in it they destroyed every vestige of Civil Liberty, swept away every existing legal barrier for the protection of life and property in ten States, and put nine millions of people in time of profound peace, under absolute military sway! And this too, was done by them under the atrocious pretext of providing for the establishment of peace and good order! They promptly passed this Reconstruction Act, so-called, over the President's veto, by a two-thirds vote in both Houses of Congress!* [Emphasis added, L.S.]

"*There is no necessity for looking into, or examining the provisions of this Act in detail. It is enough to know that under it, all the Civil Authorities of ten States are completely subverted, and their entire population subjected—temporarily, at least—to the despotism of Martial Law! Not even a Federal Judge is permitted to interfere, or redress any wrong, whether small or great, inflicted by either of the five Satraps [rulers], among whom the several Military Districts are divided. The ostensible object of this unparalleled measure, with those which have followed it, (as Amendments or Supplements,) was to compel the Southern States to submit to degrading conditions before being allowed future Representation in either branch of Congress.* [Emphasis added, L.S.]

"These conditions in short are:

"First. That *the States embraced in the Act shall, before being allowed such Representation, agree to the disfranchisement and virtual Attainder of all that class of their White Citizens who had, before the war, received the public confidence so far as to be entrusted with any Civil Office, either Executive, Legislative or Judicial, Federal or State, from the highest to the lowest* [emphasis added, L.S.]; and

"Second. To *the enfranchisement in their stead, of the entire male Black population who have attained the age of twenty-one years.* [Emphasis added, L.S.]

"*To commend this monstrous outrage to the favor of their constituents, it was pretended to be justified by those who voted for it, as a proper measure of punishment for those who had engaged in the Rebellion, so-called, and as a necessary security in the future, for the Loyal States, so-called! But while this is the ostensible object, the real one was doubtless of a very different character. Viewed in its proper light—looking at its real design—it must be considered, with all its wrongs, as but another advanced step, stealthily taken, under false colors, towards that complete ultimate Consolidation of Power at which these leaders have been aiming all the time, but which they are not yet quite prepared openly to declare!* [Emphasis added, L.S.]

"But viewed in that, or any other light, these measures of Congress again most incontestably prove, even in Mr. Johnson's judgment, on which side the

Right lay in that Conflict of arms, which we have so fully reviewed.

"In this connection, a negative error of Mr. Johnson should receive, at least, a passing notice, and the more so from the fact that I believe his sole object now is, to restore the Union and maintain the Federal [Confederate] System established by the Fathers. To this end his every energy seems, at this time, to be most patriotically directed, and however much I may have disagreed with him in the past, he is, in my judgment, now, entitled to the confidence, support, and cordial co-operation, of every friend of Constitutional Liberty throughout the Country. The error, however, to which I here allude was, that (with his views of the Constitution and the powers and duties of the President under it and the nature of the Union) he did not refuse to recognize, as the Congress of the United States, any Bodies in which any one of the States of the Union was denied Representation in the House and an equal voice in the Senate. Had he thus proclaimed and thus acted, when the policy of the Reconstruction Committee was at first openly declared, he might have sustained his own views and prevented the consummation of that most iniquitous policy. There were then in Congress enough Anti-Centralists [Conservatives] in the Senate and House from the Northern States, with the Senators and Representatives [all Conservative] returned from the South, to constitute a majority of a legitimate Congress. By such union, a Constitutional Congress could have been organized; and if Mr. Johnson had invited such union, and recognized such an organization as the only true Congress of the United States, as it would have been, these gross usurpations never would have been perpetrated. But no more of that on this occasion. What has been said very clearly exhibits the present situation, and leads us one step further in the review proposed.

"5. *The next and last great fact to be borne in mind, in considering the Results of the War, and to what it has led thus far in the view we are taking, is that the Centralists [Liberals] have not as yet openly proclaimed their ultimate object, much less have they acted in anything done by them up to this time, upon any claim of the actual consummation of that object, which we have seen, is Consolidation and Empire. They have not as yet openly denied the Federative [Confederate] character of the Government, however in direct war upon its Principles their acts have been covertly aimed. This is an exceedingly important fact to be specially noted and kept in mind. These monstrous Reconstruction Measures, with all their enormities and fatal tendencies towards ultimate complete Centralism and Empire, are still based upon the assumption that the States, as separate integral parts, constitute members of what is still, in words, at least, acknowledged to be a Federal Union! All these bold usurpations of power are, upon their face, nothing but resorts to induce, or to compel, under duress, the Peoples of the several Southern States to go through the forms of adopting the Fourteenth Amendment, as an additional Article to the Constitution. This policy is avowedly based upon the principle of voluntary consent on the part of these States. The programme of the Reconstructionists [anti-South Northern Liberals] thus far, proceeds upon the assumption that the voluntary ratification of all Amendments to the Constitution by at least three-fourths of the integral members of the Union is essential to their validity. It is true, they did not pretend to have any Constitutional power to pass these measures. On the contrary, they openly and avowedly proclaim, that in adopting them they are acting 'outside of the Constitution!' This, too, they so proclaim to the world, immediately after taking solemn oaths to support that instrument!* But not to stop here to comment upon such gross inconsistency, as well as moral dereliction, the point to be noted is, that nothing really affecting the vital principles of the organic structure of our Federative [Confederate] System of Government has yet been accomplished, or is even claimed to have been accomplished. There is, therefore, still hope for the preservation of the essential features of the system, if there is remaining virtue, intelligence, and patriotism enough to save it, on the part of the Peoples of the Northern States. *No system of Representative Government can be long maintained by any People who have not the Intelligence to understand it, the Patriotism to approve it, and the Virtue to maintain inviolate both its form and principles as established."*²⁹³ [Emphasis added, L.S.]

☛ *"The future destiny . . . of the Free Institutions of this Country, is now in the hands of the Peoples of the Northern States. We, at the South, are utterly powerless to do anything in shaping or controlling, at this time, the progress of coming political events. The only hope left to us is, that a reaction on all these questions, in the public mind, in the Northern States, will take place in time to save our Liberties as well as their own. This, [the reader] . . . may be assured, can be done only by driving the usurpers from their places, and bringing back the administration of the Federal Government to those principles on which it was so harmoniously and prosperously conducted for the first sixty years of its existence. This is to be done through the ballot-box alone. Should this take place, and the Judicial Department maintain its integrity, all may yet be well, even though this Fourteenth Amendment should go through the mockery of a ratification under the present programme; for, no Amendment of the Constitution proposed as this has been, and adopted as it must be, if at all, can ever be held to be valid by a firm and upright Judiciary.* [Emphasis added, L.S.] [Note: Northern Liberals, in fact, violently pushed through the ratification of the Fourteenth Amendment without the vote of most of the Southern states. This means that the Fourteenth Amendment was never legally formalized and is today not a legal and official part of the U.S. Constitution. L.S.]

"So, you see, *my opinion is, that the Cause which was lost at Appomattox Court House, was not the Federative [Confederate] Principle upon which American Free Institutions was based, as some have very erroneously supposed. This is far from being one of the Results of the War. The Cause which was lost by the surrender of the Confederates, was only the maintenance of this Principle by arms. It was not the Principle itself that they abandoned. They only abandoned their attempt to maintain it by physical force. This Principle on which rest the hopes of the world for spreading and perpetuating Free Institutions by neighboring States, in my judgment, like the principles of Christianity, ever advances more certainly and safely without resort to arms, than with it. Its teachings are Peace, Harmony and Good-will to all, and is much more sure of attaining its end, when the actions of its advocates are in conformity with its teachings. This Principle, therefore, though abandoned in its maintenance on battle-fields, still continues to live in all its vigor, in the Forums of Reason, Justice and Truth, and will. I trust, there continue to live forever!* Its continued existence in our system, with vital power, is not yet denied, as we have seen, even by its bitterest and most covert enemies, who have been so long making such extraordinary efforts for its destruction and extinction! Obeisance has been done to it by them, even in these despotic Reconstruction Measures. Those [Liberals] who are looking to and desiring ultimate Centralism and Empire, have, as yet, in their progress that way, thus far, reached only to the point of attempting to induce by duress, certain States, as States, and as Sovereign States, to conform to their action under the semblance, at least, of voluntary consent! This is the present position of affairs on that subject."[294] [Emphasis added, L.S.]

☛ "[There are many topics I have not spoken of. Of these] I have been thus silent, simply because I have seen no prospect of being able to do any good by anything that I could say to the public, on any of these questions. I do not see that any Southern man can say or do anything, which will have any effect in arresting the tendency of affairs. I have taken no part in the discussions in this State, because I saw that such course would but lead to divisions amongst our own people, and I did not think there was enough that could possibly be accomplished, even in securing a temporary relief, to cause old friends to grow angry with each other and quarrel about. If [Georgia's Confederate] Governor [Joseph E.] Brown and others see fit 'to take to life-boats' in our stranded condition, I have no quarrel to make with him or them, for pursuing that course; though I believe that he, and all who make similar ventures, will be swamped in the surfs at last. I see no hope in that course, or any other which we can take. My only hope for relief is in a reaction of public sentiment at the North, as stated. If that comes in time, all may yet be well with us. If not, we must all go under any how; and I prefer, without ill-will towards any, to remain in perfect quiet on the Old Craft as long as she is afloat, and at last, if needs must be, go down with her.

"As to the feelings of the people of this State generally upon these measures, I think Mr. Benjamin H. Hill, in one of his stirring 'Notes' . . . gave a very correct statement, in a very few words, when, in speaking of the position of our people in reference to them, he said in substance: 'The complying accept, the resolute reject, none approve, while all despise!'

"This, in my opinion, is as true of Governor Brown as of all the rest. While he accepts, I have no idea that he approves. Few men hold the principles of Constitutional Liberty in higher esteem than he does.

"In reference to my relations with Gov. Brown, while it is true we did agree upon many leading public questions, before as well as during the war, yet it is also true, we differed very widely upon others; and upon no question have we ever differed more widely than upon this one. Personally, however, I have a very high regard for him, and esteem him as a man of very great ability, as well as integrity. He is, in every respect, entitled to high rank among our public men and statesmen."[295]

Stephens' Liberal colleagues commented: "You do not agree, then, with those who think, as [we] . . . see from your [Southern] papers some do, that [Governor Brown's] . . . course has been influenced by motives of ambition, excited by temptations offered to him on the 'High Mountain,' to which he was carried in Washington?" To this Stephens replied:

☛ "No, not at all. I have no idea of that sort. If, when in Washington, he was taken to any of the places mentioned in the good Book, I think it was not to the 'Mountain of Temptations,' but rather to the verge of that other place known as the Bottomless Pit, or so near to it as for him to get a view of its horrors below, where his fears instead of his hopes were operated upon. In other words, in my opinion, his course has been taken more from apprehensions awakened by threats of Attainder, of Confiscation, and the thousands of other ills that might be expected to attend the rejection of the proposed measure, than from any promise of rewards or official position to him, in consideration of his giving them his support. It was to avoid what he considered impending individual as well as public evils, and not to secure special personal benefits or honors to himself that he acted as he did. He came honestly and sincerely, I have no question, to the conclusion that we might all go further and fare much worse; and hence his recommendation to the people to accept the terms proposed by Congress, and to comply with the conditions offered, however unjustly and wrongfully exacted. With his views and feelings he acted under the conviction that we were a conquered people, and, as such, should accept these terms, as there was, in his opinion, no probability of any better ever being offered.

"[I will also add here that I do not think that Governor Brown was untrue to the Southern Cause during the war, and that he is now carrying out the previously cherished purposes of his heart.] Some people may think and write so, but my opinion is, that no truer man to our Cause lived, while its standard was up, than Governor Brown.

"[As far as why he and Governor William W. Holden of North Carolina did not, in their quarrels with President Jefferson Davis, wish to withdraw from the Confederacy and make terms with Mr. Lincoln by separate State action, I will say this:] no . . . never! As to what Governor Holden may have done, or been willing to do in North Carolina, I cannot, of course, speak. I do not even know that gentleman personally, and hence I can say nothing of him. But Governor Brown I do know; and, further, I know that all such statements in regard to him are utterly untrue. It is true, he differed widely with President Davis upon many matters connected with the administration of affairs. This led to what has been called the 'quarrel' between them, but while the published official correspondence shows a very decided disagreement between them, yet it was only a disagreement on points of policy as to the best and surest way of securing ultimate success to our arms. Governor Brown was as true to the Cause as any man in the country. He and Mr. Davis are both men of very strong convictions and great earnestness of purpose. Neither of them are very yielding in their opinions; and while, in my judgment, he sincerely believed that Mr. Davis's policy was not the best to secure success, and endeavored to get him to change it, still, he never for a moment cherished the dastardly idea attributed to him. This clearly appears from his reply to the overture of [Yankee] General [William T.] Sherman to meet him in Atlanta, in September, 1864, after the fall of that place.

"This overture on the part of General Sherman, was doubtless with a view of such separate State action, and sprung perhaps from impressions on his mind produced by charges of this sort against Governor Brown in some of the Confederate newspapers, about that time. In that reply, while Governor Brown claimed, to the fullest extent, the absolute ultimate Sovereignty of the State of Georgia, yet he most emphatically declared that, being then in Confederation with her Southern sisters for the maintenance of the same Sovereignty on the part of each severally, her public faith, thus pledged, should never be violated by him; and that, 'Come weal or come woe,' the State of Georgia should never by his consent withdraw from that Confederation in dishonor. 'She will never make separate terms with the enemy,' said he, 'which may free her territory from invasion, and leave her Confederates in the lurch.'

"Further, upon the nature of the conflict and the principles involved, he said to General Sherman: *The liberties of the people in this country 'rest upon the Sovereignty of the States as their chief corner-stone. Destroy the Sovereignty of the States, and the whole fabric falls to the ground, and centralized power with Military Despotism takes the place of Constitutional Liberty.*' Thus, said he, 'to destroy our Liberties must cost the Northern people their own, and the Republicanism of America must, in future, be regarded as a reproach and a by-word among all nations.' [Emphasis added, L.S.]

"This language sufficiently fixes the character of Governor Brown, and shows the principles by which he was governed throughout the War. If he had entertained such sentiments as were attributed to him; or if he had been a man likely to be influenced by temptations of ambition held out to him, that was certainly an occasion when the weakness and baseness of such a nature would have manifested itself. In my judgment, he then entertained no such views or ideas as were imagined by some; nor is he now influenced by any such as are similarly imputed. This at least is my opinion of him. When the principle involved in the conflict failed to be maintained by arms, he, as I understand him, then gave up, not only the cause, but the principle itself, as lost. His public acts, since, have been governed by this conviction. Our present differences arise from the different views we take of the Results of the War.

"In my view, [Liberals] . . . perceive that *while the maintenance of the principle, or the maintenance of the Right of local Self-government was lost on the battle field; yet on other grounds, and in other Forums, it still lives in all its vigor. The issue decided by the sword, was the attempt on the part of the Confederates to maintain this principle and right, by physical force, in withdrawing from the Union. To this extent alone was the great cause affected by the arbitrament of arms; and to this extent alone was it then settled, by their abandonment of its further maintenance in that way; but the principle itself was not abandoned. It involves questions which cannot be settled by arms*—no more than questions relating to the diurnal rotation of the earth, or its annual circuit round the sun. These are matters which belong exclusively to the domain of Reason and Logic. They belong to other arenas—to those of Thought, of Public Discussions, Council Chambers, and Courts of Justice. They can never be brought under the subjection of physical power. *Force may control human action, and effect settlements so far as that is concerned; but it can never enslave the human intellect, or disarm truth of its inextinguishable power in its appropriate sphere, upon the human understanding. In this way, by its peaceful, quiet, and effective workings, all great advances and high achievements in civilization have heretofore been made: and all true progress in the science of Government—slow as that has been—as well as in all other departments of human knowledge, have been accomplished! Wars, upon the whole, have done much more in retarding than in advancing either the principles of Liberty, the cause of Civilization, or the general amelioration of mankind.* [Emphasis added, L.S.]

"In this connection it must be borne in mind, that notwithstanding all that was said about the treason of the Confederates, about 'traitors,' about the

'Insurrection,' and the 'Atrocious Rebellion,' so-called, the [Liberal] Authorities at Washington have not yet put that question in issue before the Judicial Tribunals. *Immediately after the surrender, as we have seen, numerous arrests were made of high Confederate, as well as State Officials; but as yet not a single one of these has been put upon trial* [and never were!]"[296] [Emphasis added, L.S.]

☛ "I [myself] was arrested on the 11th of May [1865], was taken to Fort Warren, Boston Harbor, as is known, and was discharged on parole the 13th of October thereafter. It affords me pleasure to state that during the whole of that period of five months and two days, I was treated with the utmost respect and kindness by all, both [Yankee] officers and men, who had charge of me; or at least with the utmost respect and kindness consistent with their duties in obedience to orders from superiors. While in Fort Warren I was very much afflicted with neuralgia, and a complication of diseases, greatly aggravated, if not produced, by my being first put upon soldiers' rations, and closely confined in one of the lower rooms connecting with a casemate, which was below the surface of the adjacent grounds, and which was consequently very humid and damp. Through the kind interposition of the officers, a change was soon allowed as to the matter of diet; and I was permitted by [U.S.] General [John A.] Dix, who commanded the District, and whose head-quarters were at New York, to be supplied with such articles in this respect as I might desire from the sutler, at my own expense. All went along very well in that particular after this change.

"But the close confinement in the quarters which had been assigned me by special orders from superiors, operated very injuriously upon the general enfeebled condition of my health. Indeed I think if a change in this particular also had not been allowed, I should have died. This did not take place until late in August. It was at last effected through the kind interposition of Mr. Senator Henry Wilson of Massachusetts. He visited me, and seeing my situation, went to Washington and interceded in my behalf. The order for the change of quarters came under the hands of President [Andrew] Johnson himself. From this it seemed that the [U.S.] Secretary of War, Mr. [Edwin M.] Stanton, would not give his consent to it to the last. It had been in vain that Dr. [Joel] Seaverns, the Surgeon, had for some time recommended and urged the change.

"During all this time Dr. Seaverns had been exceedingly kind and attentive in administering to my relief and comfort in every way in his power. So had been Major [John W.] Appleton, the officer in command of the Fort, and his most estimable wife [Mary]. All that they could do to alleviate actual suffering and mitigate the necessary discomforts of the situation was done. Their charming little daughter, Mabel, (not four years old,) brought me flowers almost daily. She would get the guard to raise her up, and would put them herself, with her little tiny hand, between the bars of the iron grate of the window, where was placed a vase to receive them, when I was unable to take them myself! Lieutenant Wm. H. Woodman, who had special charge of all prisoners, was also exceedingly kind and unremitting in his attention to my wants and comforts. So too was John Geary, the corporal, whose business it was to attend particularly to my room.

"After Major Appleton left the Post, Major Charles F. Livermore, who succeeded him, was equally kind and attentive, as was also his most excellent and amiable wife [Anna].

"The many, many acts of kindness I received from all these parties, as well as from quite a number of the good people of Boston, during my affliction and imprisonment at Fort Warren, can never be forgotten by me, and can never be thought of without the most grateful emotions! But, as I said, it was to Senator Wilson, I think I was chiefly indebted for the change of quarters.

"[Though Henry Wilson is a radical Northern Liberal] I doubt not [that] he possesses many more good qualities besides kindness of heart. *Human nature is a strange compound at best! No person I have ever yet met with was so bad as not to have some good qualities; and no one I have ever seen was so good as not to have some bad ones. Perfection is not the lot of humanity.* However much I have differed with Mr. Wilson, and do now differ with him, upon many public questions—however great, in my opinion, are his errors, on many subjects; yet I believe he possesses many excellencies of both head and heart. He was certainly very kind to me in a time of great need, for which I felt, at the time, and now and ever shall feel, most profoundly thankful! Indeed I did not then, or now, cherish any resentment even towards *Mr. Stanton, whose course and conduct toward me seemed to be so strange as well as cruel*, and which I believed if not changed would soon end in my death. The prevailing sentiment with me towards him, and all who were co-operating with him, then was, 'Father, forgive them; for they know not what they do!' I thought it not improbable that he and they were acting conscientiously; while I thought it not less probable that he and others thus acting would live to repent most bitterly what they were then doing. [Emphasis added, L.S.]

"This . . . is all I can now say upon the subject of my arrest and imprisonment."[297]

☛ "To return, therefore, from this digression to the point I was upon. As I was discharged, so were all the other Confederate and State officials who had been arrested discharged, after an imprisonment more or less prolonged *without any criminal accusation being even lodged against them for their participation in the war*, except Mr. Davis. [Emphasis added, L.S.]

"As to Mr. Davis, it is true, after the infamous charge upon which he was arrested—that is, of complicity in the assassination of Mr. Lincoln—was proven to have had no foundation whatever, except the perjury of suborned witnesses, a *formal Bill of Indictment for Treason*, in the matter of Secession and the War, was brought in against him. *This has not yet been tried, though he has continuously demanded a trial, and urged it in the most earnest manner.* His late enlargement on bail, without a trial, (through the unexampled generosity and magnanimity of Mr. Horace Greeley, Gerrit Smith, Augustus Schell, H. F. Clark, Aristides Welsch, of New York, David J. Jackman, of Pennsylvania, and others, in becoming sureties for his appearance to answer the charge when the Government shall be ready to proceed with it,) may be considered as settling the question, that *the officials at Washington do not intend to allow that point on the principle involved in the issue, decided by the arbitrament of arms, to come before the Judicial Forum for decision and adjudication there.* An arbitrament on the Arena of Reason, Logic, Truth, and Justice, they have, thus far, eschewed and avoided; so that the great fact is to be borne in mind, that up to this time, nothing really affecting this 'Corner-Stone' [states' rights] of our Federal Institutions, as Governor Brown styled the principle in his reply to General Sherman, has, as yet, been definitely settled, except the abandonment of an attempt to maintain it by a resort to arms. [Emphasis added, L.S.]

"This, then, is one of the main differences between Governor Brown and myself. *To his idea that we are a conquered people, and as such should make the best terms we can, my reply is, that this was not the understanding at the time of the surrender.* The States, as States, were distinctly recognized in that surrender, as we have seen; nor have, even, the Reconstructionists [anti-South Liberals] at Washington, as yet, acted upon the avowed assumption that we are thus conquered. *These monstrous measures so proposed by Congress, are acknowledged to be without authority by those who have passed them, and can, therefore, be considered as nothing but gross usurpations.* The Courts have yet to pass upon them. These measures, in my judgment, can never receive the sanction of that Department of the Government—not even in the view that we are a conquered people. *Conquerors must govern their subjects according to the provisions of their own fundamental law. This is well established by the laws of Nations. The fundamental law of Congress, by which the Courts must be governed, is the Constitution of the United States. This gives Congress no power, in time of Peace, to suspend the Writ of* Habeas Corpus, *nor to declare Martial Law, to say nothing of the other enormities of these measures over any class of people, whether citizens, aliens, denizens or subjects.* We are bound to believe, therefore, that the Supreme Court of the United States will hold these measures, when they come before that body, to be gross and palpable usurpations of power, and utterly null and void! [Emphasis added, L.S.]

"But if this Court should not so hold; if this Tribunal should decide not only that we are a conquered people, but further, that Congress, representing the Conquerors, can properly govern us as they see fit, outside of the limitations of the Constitution of the United States; and can properly deny us, if they choose, *the great American Right of Self-government* for the future, then, even in that view, my reply is, let our Conquerors govern us as they see fit! [Emphasis added, L.S.]

"We, it is true, cannot resist, or offer any violent opposition. We can only bear with patience and fortitude, as best we may, what is imposed upon us; but in the name of all that is sacred, do not let us attempt to govern ourselves—not as we see fit, but as our Conquerors see fit! That would be but their government at last, without any of its responsibility. *By every consideration, then, we should not, by giving these measures a formal approval, put ourselves in the position of being told, when the disastrous consequences follow, which will inevitably ensue, that it was we, ourselves, and not they, who brought such ruin upon the country!* [Emphasis added, L.S.]

"*By our thus acting, perhaps after awhile, sooner or later, when the people of the Northern States become thoroughly impressed . . . with the dangerous tendencies of this whole Reconstructive policy to their own Institutions, a similar cry to that which went up from Virginia in Colonial days in regard to the Boston Port Bill, will again be raised and heard from one extent of the land to the other! The cry then was: 'The cause of Boston is the cause of us all!' These, we have seen, were the stirring notes which led to the establishment of our entire system of Constitutional Liberty. The only hope, in my view, now left for its preservation and maintenance on this Continent, is, that another like cry shall hereafter be raised, and go forth from hill-top to valley, from the Coast to the Lakes, from the Atlantic to the Pacific: 'The Cause of the South is the Cause of us all!'* [Emphasis added, L.S.]

"If this comes in time, all may yet be well. In that event, notwithstanding all that has occurred, I see no reason why the States, once more restored, as they will then be, should not enter upon a new career of greatness exciting increased marvel, if not admiration, in the old world, by higher achievements in progress hereafter to be made than any heretofore attained, through the harmonious workings of the true American Principle of the Sovereign Right of local Self-government on the part of each member of our matchless Federal [Confederate] System, when rightly administered! On these principles, *the Union, in my judgment, can be maintained and perpetuated—not by physical power, but by the much stronger attractive principle of 'mutual convenience and reciprocal advantage;*' and this, too, without any apprehensions of centrifugal tendencies in any of its parts, either from the extent of it boundaries, or the number or diversified interests of its members! [Emphasis added, L.S.]

"But if such reaction should not take place in the public sentiment of the Northern people, then our present condition will soon be theirs. No fact in the future may be relied upon with more certainty, than that their liberties cannot long survive the loss of ours! [Editor's note: To this day, Northerners still seem far less concerned with their Constitutional rights than Southerners. This can be, no doubt, fully attributed to the deep liberalism and socialism that has permeated the North. L.S.]

"So much . . . for the present condition of affairs, and the actual practical results thus far, of this gigantic conflict of arms, upon our Institutions, State and Federal, as well as the general prospect before us.

"In the review [I] . . . have taken, *the origin of all these late troubles as well as present ills, and the still greater ones now threatening, have been traced to their proper source—to their primal cause. That, we have seen, was a violation of one of the essential principles of the organic structure of our new and wonderful system of a Federative Union of Sovereign States [i.e., the right of secession]. From this violation of principle, all these direful consequences have come, as effects follow causes.* [Emphasis added, L.S.]

"Here [my] . . . review properly closes.

"It was undertaken . . . not so much with the intention of vindicating the rightfulness of my own course in going with my State in the matter of Secession, as in vindication of the Rightfulness of the great Cause of those with whom my fortunes in the terrible and most lamentable contest were cast.

"Now that we have gone through with the whole, as stated before, I will not ask [the Liberals'] . . . judgment upon the matter. That, I am content, notwithstanding all that is now said about 'traitors' and 'rebels,' to leave to the arbitrament of the intelligent, unbiased, and impartial of all times and countries. This judgment, I feel assured, will be just as Mr. [Andrew] Johnson so clearly foresaw it would be. By it the Confederates, so far from being branded with the epithets of 'rebels' and 'traitors,' will be honored as 'self-sacrificing Patriots,' fighting for their Liberties throughout, and their Heroes and Martyrs in History will take places 'by the side of Washington, Hampden, and Sydney!'

"It affords me pleasure, however, to say, in winding up, that, while in [this] . . . long and social interchange of views, and discussions of the various questions brought up in review, in which [I] . . . have occasionally so widely differed upon some points [with my Liberal friends from the North], yet upon one we are at last all so fully agreed; and that is, in *our abhorrence of the very idea of anything like Imperialism in this Country!* Perfect agreement on this point is the more agreeable to me, because *this presents the only real living issue of paramount importance before the Peoples of the several States.* The great vital question now is: Shall the Federal Government be arrested in its progress, and be brought back to original principles, or shall it be permitted to go on in its present tendencies and rapid strides, until it reaches complete Consolidation! [Emphasis added, L.S.]

"Depend upon it, there is no difference between Consolidation and Empire; no difference between Centralism and Imperialism. The consummation of either must necessarily end in the overthrow of Liberty and the establishment of Despotism. To speak of any Rights as belonging to the States, without the innate and inalienable Sovereign power to maintain them, is but to deal in the shadow of language without the substance. Nominal Rights without Securities are but Mockeries! [Emphasis added, L.S.]

"Nothing can be truer than that the States under our system possess no Rights but Sovereign Rights. All their reserved Rights are necessarily Sovereign Rights. They hold nothing by grant or favor from the Federal Government. On the contrary, the Federal Government itself possesses no Right, and is intrusted with the exercise of no Power, except by delegation from the Sovereignty of the several States. Sovereignty itself, as [I have shown], . . . is, from its very nature, indivisible! There never was a greater truth, more pointedly uttered than that by Mr. [Thomas] Jefferson, that the States of this Union 'are not united upon the principle of unlimited submission to their General Government.' The Administration of our Government, therefore, must be brought back and made to conform in its action, to these principles thus announced by the Great Author of the System [i.e., God], and under which all the great achievements of the past were made. If this is not done, it is utterly vain to look for, or expect anything, but ultimate Centralism and Despotism! [Emphasis added, L.S.]

"These are words of truth, expressed in an earnestness, which I trust [the reader] . . . will excuse; but they are words which, however received or heeded by the people of this day, will be rendered eternally true by the developments of the future!

"But without further speculation upon this subject or any other, let me, in conclusion, barely add: *If the worst is to befall us; if our most serious apprehensions and gloomiest forebodings as to the future, in this respect, are to be realized; if Centralism is ultimately to prevail; if our entire system of free Institutions as established by our common ancestors is to be subverted, and an Empire is to be established in their stead; if that is to be the last scene in the great tragic drama now being enacted: then, be assured, that we of the South will be acquitted, not only in our own consciences, but by the judgment of mankind, of all responsibility for so terrible a catastrophe, and from all the guilt of so great a crime against humanity! Amidst our own ruins, bereft of fortunes and estates, as well as Liberty, with nothing remaining to us but a good name, and a Public Character, unsullied and untarnished, we will, in the common misfortunes, still cling in our affections to 'the Land of Memories,' and find expression for our sentiments when surveying the past, as well as of our distant hopes when looking to the future*, in the grand words of Father [A. J.] Ryan, one of our most eminent Divines, and one of America's best poets:

> 'A land without ruins is a land without memories—a land without memories is a land without liberty! A land that wears a laurel crown may be fair to see, but twine a few sad cypress leaves around the brow of any land, and be that land beautiless and bleak, it becomes lovely in its consecrated coronet of sorrow, and it wins the sympathy of the heart and history!
>   'Crowns of roses fade—crowns of thorns endure! Calvaries and crucifixes take deepest hold of humanity—the triumphs of Might are transient, they pass away and are forgotten—the sufferings of Right are graven deepest on the chronicles of nations!
>   'Yes! give me a land where the ruins are spread, and the living tread light on the hearts of the dead; Yes, give me a land that is blest by the dust, and bright with the deeds of the down-trodden just! Yes, give me the land that hath legend and lays enshrining the memories of long-vanished days; Yes, give me a land that hath story and song, to tell of the strife of the Right with the Wrong; Yes, give me the land with a grave in each spot, and names in the graves that shall not be forgot!
>   'Yes, give me the land of the wreck and the tomb, there's a grandeur in graves—there's a glory in gloom! For out of the gloom future brightness is born, as after the night looms the sunrise of morn; and the graves of the dead, with the grass overgrown, may yet form the footstool of Liberty's throne, and each single wreck in the war-path of Might, shall yet be a rock in the Temple of Right!'[298]

The End

The CONFEDERATE CABINET

IN PICTURES

Jefferson Davis, Confederate President

Alexander Hamilton Stephens, Confederate Vice President

Robert Edward Lee, General-in-Chief of Confederate Forces

Judah Philip Benjamin, Confederate Attorney General

Christopher Gustavus Memminger,
Confederate Secretary of the Treasury

Leroy Pope Walker, Confederate Secretary of War

Robert Augustus Toombs, Confederate Secretary of State

Stephen Russell Mallory, Confederate Secretary of the Navy

John Henninger Reagan, Confederate Postmaster General

NOTES

1. For more on this topic, see Seabrook, ALSV, pp. 15-20.
2. Stephens, CVLWBS, Vol. 2, p. 496.
3. Cleveland, p. 828.
4. Stephens, CVLWBS, Vol. 2, pp. 79-83.
5. Seabrook, ALSV, pp. 120, 122, 248, 362, 389, 530.
6. Seabrook, ALSV, p. 122.
7. Seabrook, L, pp. 918-938.
8. See e.g., Avary, p. 106.
9. Avary, p. 87.
10. See e.g., Cleveland, pp. 97, 235.
11. Avary, p. 109.
12. Avary, p. 109.
13. Avary, p. 109.
14. Stephens, CVLWBS, Vol. 2, pp. 84, 85.
15. Stephens, CVLWBS, Vol. 2, p. 85.
16. Avary, pp. 174-175.
17. See e.g., Avary, p. 87.
18. Stephens, CVLWBS, Vol. 2, p. 706.
19. Stewart, p. 11.
20. Cleveland, p. 130.
21. Seabrook, EYWTACVW, pp. 89, 104.
22. Stephens, CVLWBS, Vol. 1, pp. 540-541.
23. Stewart, p. 58.
24. Seabrook, L, pp. 896-903.
25. Cleveland, pp. 131, 132-133.
26. Cleveland, p. 824.
27. Stephens, CVLWBS, Vol. 2, p. 446.
28. Phillips, p. 713.
29. Seabrook, L, p. 903.
30. See Bennett, passim.
31. Seabrook, L, pp. 584-633.
32. Seabrook, EYWTACVW, pp. 99-101.
33. Avary, p. 114.
34. Avary, pp. 123-124.
35. Stephens, CVLWBS, Vol. 1, p. 543.
36. Cleveland, p. 786.
37. Stewart, pp. 10-11.
38. Stephens, CVLWBS, Vol. 1, p. 480.
39. "The Alexander H. Stephens Institute," by Mrs. Clem G. Moore (UDC), *Confederate Veteran*, Volume 30, 1922, Nashville, TN, p. 76.
40. Cleveland, pp. 51-52.
41. Phillips, pp. 57-58.
42. Phillips, p. 68.
43. Phillips, p. 127.
44. Phillips, p. 184.

45. Phillips, pp. 237, 238.
46. Phillips, pp. 271, 272-274.
47. Phillips, pp. 325, 326.
48. Phillips, pp. 343-344.
49. Cleveland, pp. 459-471.
50. Phillips, p. 384.
51. Phillips, pp. 446-447.
52. Phillips, p. 454.
53. Phillips, pp. 457-458.
54. Phillips, pp. 463-464.
55. Seabrook, EYWTACWW, pp. 74-78.
56. Phillips, p. 467.
57. Stephens, CVLWBS, Vol. 2, pp. 677-684.
58. Stephens, CVLWBS, Vol. 2, pp. 685-691.
59. Phillips, pp. 502-503.
60. Phillips, pp. 526-527.
61. Phillips, pp. 563-564.
62. Stephens, CVLWBS, Vol. 2, pp. 786-788.
63. Cleveland, pp. 786-790.
64. Cleveland, pp. 790-795.
65. Cleveland, pp. 796-804.
66. Phillips, pp. 654-655.
67. Stephens, CVLWBS, Vol. 2, p. 797.
68. Stephens, CVLWBS, Vol. 2, p. 799.
69. Stephens, CVLWBS, Vol. 2, p. 801.
70. Stephens, CVLWBS, Vol. 2, p. 802.
71. Stephens, CVLWBS, Vol. 2, pp. 792-793.
72. Stewart, pp. 10-12.
73. Phillips, p. 681.
74. Phillips, p. 686.
75. Phillips, pp. 686-687.
76. Stewart, pp. 48-58.
77. Phillips, p. 708.
78. Phillips, pp. 713-714.
79. Phillips, p. 743.
80. Cleveland, pp. 65-67.
81. Cleveland, pp. 71-73.
82. Cleveland, pp. 302-320.
83. Cleveland, pp. 84-88.
84. Gideon, pp. 1-14.
85. Cleveland, pp. 358-362.
86. Cleveland, pp. 429-432.
87. *Congressional Globe*, pp. 1-8.
88. Cleveland, pp. 557-560.
89. Cleveland, pp. 571, 572.
90. Cleveland, pp. 626-627.
91. Cleveland, pp. 633-636.
92. Cleveland, pp. 650-651.

93. Stephens, CVLWBS, Vol. 2, pp. 691-710.
94. Trent, p. 198.
95. Beecher, pp. 552-554.
96. Seabrook, EYWTACWW, pp. 83-85.
97. Cleveland, pp. 717-729.
98. Cleveland, pp. 729-745.
99. Stephens, CVLWBS, Vol. 2, pp. 781-786.
100. Cleveland, pp. 761-786.
101. Cleveland, pp. 804-818.
102. Avary, pp. 99-128.
103. Cleveland, pp. 819-833.
104. Stephens, RR, pp. 137-146.
105. Stephens, CHUS, pp. 422-423, 425, 427-429, 462, 463-467.
106. Stephens, CVLWBS, Vol. 1, p. 9.
107. Stephens, CVLWBS, Vol. 1, pp. 9-12.
108. Stephens, CVLWBS, Vol. 1, pp. 18-22.
109. Stephens, CVLWBS, Vol. 1, pp. 25-26, 28-31.
110. Stephens, CVLWBS, Vol. 1, pp. 32-33.
111. Stephens, CVLWBS, Vol. 1, pp. 34, 35-37, 38-44.
112. Stephens, CVLWBS, Vol. 1, pp. 45-49.
113. Stephens, CVLWBS, Vol. 1, p. 51.
114. Stephens, CVLWBS, Vol. 1, pp. 51, 52-59.
115. Stephens, CVLWBS, Vol. 1, pp. 67-81.
116. Stephens, CVLWBS, Vol. 1, pp. 82-87.
117. Stephens, CVLWBS, Vol. 1, pp. 87-114.
118. See Seabrook, ALSV, p. 299.
119. Stephens, CVLWBS, Vol. 1, pp. 116-125.
120. Stephens, CVLWBS, Vol. 1, pp. 125-126.
121. Stephens, CVLWBS, Vol. 1, pp. 126-128.
122. Stephens, CVLWBS, Vol. 1, pp. 128-137.
123. Stephens, CVLWBS, Vol. 1, pp. 138-144.
124. Stephens, CVLWBS, Vol. 1, pp. 144-147.
125. Stephens, CVLWBS, Vol. 1, pp. 148-158.
126. Stephens, CVLWBS, Vol. 1, pp. 158-170.
127. Stephens, CVLWBS, Vol. 1, pp. 171-192.
128. Stephens, CVLWBS, Vol. 1, pp. 193-197.
129. Stephens, CVLWBS, Vol. 1, pp. 197-206.
130. Stephens, CVLWBS, Vol. 1, pp. 207-297.
131. Stephens, CVLWBS, Vol. 1, pp. 318-322.
132. Stephens, CVLWBS, Vol. 1, pp. 336-388.
133. See Seabrook, EYWTACWW, pp. 104-108.
134. Stephens, CVLWBS, Vol. 1, pp. 394-418.
135. Stephens, CVLWBS, Vol. 1, pp. 420-476.
136. Seabrook, L, pp. 123, 287.
137. Stephens, CVLWBS, Vol. 1, pp. 478-522.
138. Stephens, CVLWBS, Vol. 1, pp. 523-524.
139. Stephens, CVLWBS, Vol. 1, pp. 524-543.
140. Stephens, CVLWBS, Vol. 2, pp. 17-18.

141. Stephens, CVLWBS, Vol. 2, pp. 18-19.
142. Stephens, CVLWBS, Vol. 2, pp. 19-21.
143. Stephens, CVLWBS, Vol. 2, pp. 22-23.
144. Stephens, CVLWBS, Vol. 2, pp. 23-24.
145. See Seabrook, EYWTACWW, pp. 69-108.
146. Stephens, CVLWBS, Vol. 2, pp. 24-25.
147. Stephens, CVLWBS, Vol. 2, pp. 25-26.
148. Stephens, CVLWBS, Vol. 2, pp. 26-27.
149. Stephens, CVLWBS, Vol. 2, pp. 27-29.
150. Stephens, CVLWBS, Vol. 2, pp. 29-30.
151. Stephens, CVLWBS, Vol. 2, pp. 30-33.
152. Stephens, CVLWBS, Vol. 2, pp. 33-34.
153. Stephens, CVLWBS, Vol. 2, pp. 35-36.
154. Stephens, CVLWBS, Vol. 2, pp. 36-40.
155. Stephens, CVLWBS, Vol. 2, pp. 40-42.
156. Stephens, CVLWBS, Vol. 2, pp. 42-43.
157. Stephens, CVLWBS, Vol. 2, pp. 43-44.
158. Stephens, CVLWBS, Vol. 2, pp. 44-49.
159. Stephens, CVLWBS, Vol. 2, pp. 49-50.
160. Stephens, CVLWBS, Vol. 2, p. 50.
161. Stephens, CVLWBS, Vol. 2, pp. 52-53.
162. Stephens, CVLWBS, Vol. 2, pp. 62-76.
163. Stephens, CVLWBS, Vol. 2, pp. 76-79.
164. Stephens, CVLWBS, Vol. 2, pp. 79-84.
165. Stephens, CVLWBS, Vol. 2, pp. 84-89.
166. Stephens, CVLWBS, Vol. 2, pp. 89-95.
167. Stephens, CVLWBS, Vol. 2, p. 95.
168. Stephens, CVLWBS, Vol. 2, pp. 95-104.
169. Stephens, CVLWBS, Vol. 2, pp. 104-106.
170. Stephens, CVLWBS, Vol. 2, pp. 106-126.
171. Stephens, CVLWBS, Vol. 2, pp. 126-130.
172. Stephens, CVLWBS, Vol. 2, pp. 131-135.
173. Stephens, CVLWBS, Vol. 2, pp. 135-146.
174. Stephens, CVLWBS, Vol. 2, pp. 146-149.
175. Stephens, CVLWBS, Vol. 2, pp. 149-150.
176. Stephens, CVLWBS, Vol. 2, pp. 150-154.
177. Stephens, CVLWBS, Vol. 2, pp. 155-163.
178. Stephens, CVLWBS, Vol. 2, pp. 163-171.
179. Stephens, CVLWBS, Vol. 2, pp. 171-173.
180. Stephens, CVLWBS, Vol. 2, pp. 173-175.
181. Stephens, CVLWBS, Vol. 2, pp. 176-196.
182. Stephens, CVLWBS, Vol. 2, pp. 196-211.
183. Stephens, CVLWBS, Vol. 2, pp. 211-214.
184. Stephens, CVLWBS, Vol. 2, pp. 214-217.
185. Stephens, CVLWBS, Vol. 2, pp. 217-220.
186. Stephens, CVLWBS, Vol. 2, pp. 220-225.
187. Stephens, CVLWBS, Vol. 2, pp. 225-231.
188. Stephens, CVLWBS, Vol. 2, pp. 231-232.

189. Stephens, CVLWBS, Vol. 2, pp. 232-240.
190. Stephens, CVLWBS, Vol. 2, pp. 241-243.
191. Stephens, CVLWBS, Vol. 2, pp. 243-261.
192. Stephens, CVLWBS, Vol. 2, pp. 261-262.
193. Stephens, CVLWBS, Vol. 2, pp. 264-265.
194. Stephens, CVLWBS, Vol. 2, pp. 265-271.
195. Stephens, CVLWBS, Vol. 2, pp. 271-300.
196. Stephens, CVLWBS, Vol. 2, pp. 300-309.
197. Stephens, CVLWBS, Vol. 2, pp. 310-312.
198. Stephens, CVLWBS, Vol. 2, pp. 312-317.
199. Stephens, CVLWBS, Vol. 2, pp. 317-321.
200. Stephens, CVLWBS, Vol. 2, pp. 321-324.
201. Stephens, CVLWBS, Vol. 2, p. 324.
202. Stephens, CVLWBS, Vol. 2, pp. 324-326.
203. Stephens, CVLWBS, Vol. 2, pp. 326-327.
204. Stephens, CVLWBS, Vol. 2, p. 328.
205. Stephens, CVLWBS, Vol. 2, pp. 328-329.
206. Stephens, CVLWBS, Vol. 2, pp. 329-333.
207. Stephens, CVLWBS, Vol. 2, pp. 333-335.
208. Stephens, CVLWBS, Vol. 2, pp. 335-339.
209. Stephens, CVLWBS, Vol. 2, pp. 339-344.
210. Stephens, CVLWBS, Vol. 2, pp. 344-351.
211. Stephens, CVLWBS, Vol. 2, pp. 351-354.
212. Stephens, CVLWBS, Vol. 2, pp. 354-357.
213. Stephens, CVLWBS, Vol. 2, p. 357.
214. Stephens, CVLWBS, Vol. 2, pp. 358-359.
215. See Seabrook, EYWTACWW, passim.
216. Stephens, CVLWBS, Vol. 2, pp. 361-362.
217. Stephens, CVLWBS, Vol. 2, pp. 363-366.
218. Stephens, CVLWBS, Vol. 2, pp. 366-370.
219. Stephens, CVLWBS, Vol. 2, pp. 370-376.
220. Stephens, CVLWBS, Vol. 2, pp. 376-380.
221. Stephens, CVLWBS, Vol. 2, pp. 380-387.
222. Stephens, CVLWBS, Vol. 2, pp. 387-389.
223. Stephens, CVLWBS, Vol. 2, pp. 389-394.
224. Stephens, CVLWBS, Vol. 2, pp. 394-395.
225. Stephens, CVLWBS, Vol. 2, pp. 395-396.
226. Stephens, CVLWBS, Vol. 2, p. 396.
227. Stephens, CVLWBS, Vol. 2, pp. 396-397.
228. Stephens, CVLWBS, Vol. 2, pp. 398-402.
229. Stephens, CVLWBS, Vol. 2, pp. 402-408.
230. Stephens, CVLWBS, Vol. 2, p. 409.
231. Stephens, CVLWBS, Vol. 2, pp. 409-410.
232. Stephens, CVLWBS, Vol. 2, pp. 411-412.
233. Stephens, CVLWBS, Vol. 2, pp. 412-415.
234. Stephens, CVLWBS, Vol. 2, pp. 415-416.
235. Stephens, CVLWBS, Vol. 2, pp. 416-419.
236. Stephens, CVLWBS, Vol. 2, pp. 419-421.

237. Stephens, CVLWBS, Vol. 2, pp. 421-423.
238. Stephens, CVLWBS, Vol. 2, pp. 423-424.
239. Stephens, CVLWBS, Vol. 2, pp. 425-427.
240. Stephens, CVLWBS, Vol. 2, pp. 427-430.
241. Stephens, CVLWBS, Vol. 2, pp. 430-435.
242. Stephens, CVLWBS, Vol. 2, pp. 435-437.
243. Stephens, CVLWBS, Vol. 2, pp. 437-443.
244. Stephens, CVLWBS, Vol. 2, pp. 443-444.
245. Stephens, CVLWBS, Vol. 2, p. 445.
246. Stephens, CVLWBS, Vol. 2, pp. 444-450.
247. Stephens, CVLWBS, Vol. 2, pp. 451-452.
248. Stephens, CVLWBS, Vol. 2, pp. 452-454.
249. Stephens, CVLWBS, Vol. 2, pp. 454-455.
250. Stephens, CVLWBS, Vol. 2, pp. 455-463.
251. Stephens, CVLWBS, Vol. 2, pp. 463-469.
252. Stephens, CVLWBS, Vol. 2, pp. 469-479.
253. Stephens, CVLWBS, Vol. 2, pp. 479-481.
254. Stephens, CVLWBS, Vol. 2, pp. 481-484.
255. Stephens, CVLWBS, Vol. 2, pp. 484-486.
256. Stephens, CVLWBS, Vol. 2, pp. 486-487.
257. Stephens, CVLWBS, Vol. 2, pp. 487-488.
258. Stephens, CVLWBS, Vol. 2, pp. 488-489.
259. Stephens, CVLWBS, Vol. 2, pp. 490-497.
260. Stephens, CVLWBS, Vol. 2, pp. 498-501.
261. Stephens, CVLWBS, Vol. 2, pp. 501-504.
262. Stephens, CVLWBS, Vol. 2, pp. 504-508.
263. Stephens, CVLWBS, Vol. 2, pp. 508-516.
264. Stephens, CVLWBS, Vol. 2, pp. 516-531.
265. Stephens, CVLWBS, Vol. 2, pp. 531-538.
266. Stephens, CVLWBS, Vol. 2, pp. 539-546.
267. Stephens, CVLWBS, Vol. 2, pp. 546-549.
268. Stephens, CVLWBS, Vol. 2, pp. 549-557.
269. Stephens, CVLWBS, Vol. 2, pp. 557-558.
270. Stephens, CVLWBS, Vol. 2, pp. 558-562.
271. Stephens, CVLWBS, Vol. 2, pp. 562-566.
272. Stephens, CVLWBS, Vol. 2, pp. 566-570.
273. Stephens, CVLWBS, Vol. 2, pp. 570-575.
274. Seabrook, EYWTACWW, passim.
275. Seabrook, L, p. 647.
276. Seabrook, L, pp. 159, 166, 243, 320, 641, 650, 662, 680, 681.
277. Seabrook, ALSV, p. 254.
278. Seabrook, TUAL, p. 91.
279. Stephens, CVLWBS, Vol. 2, pp. 577-583.
280. Stephens, CVLWBS, Vol. 2, pp. 583-584.
281. Stephens, CVLWBS, Vol. 2, pp. 584-586.
282. Stephens, CVLWBS, Vol. 2, pp. 586-595.
283. Stephens, CVLWBS, Vol. 2, pp. 595-598.
284. Stephens, CVLWBS, Vol. 2, pp. 598-599.

285. Stephens, CVLWBS, Vol. 2, pp. 599-619.
286. Stephens, CVLWBS, Vol. 2, p. 619.
287. Stephens, CVLWBS, Vol. 2, pp. 619-626.
288. Stephens, CVLWBS, Vol. 2, pp. 626-627.
289. Stephens, CVLWBS, Vol. 2, pp. 627-630.
290. Stephens, CVLWBS, Vol. 2, pp. 631-638.
291. Stephens, CVLWBS, Vol. 2, pp. 638-644.
292. Stephens, CVLWBS, Vol. 2, pp. 644-647.
293. Stephens, CVLWBS, Vol. 2, pp. 647-651.
294. Stephens, CVLWBS, Vol. 2, pp. 651-652.
295. Stephens, CVLWBS, Vol. 2, pp. 654-655.
296. Stephens, CVLWBS, Vol. 2, pp. 655-659.
297. Stephens, CVLWBS, Vol. 2, pp. 659-662.
298. Stephens, CVLWBS, Vol. 2, pp. 662-670.

BIBLIOGRAPHY

Avary, Myrta Lockett. *Recollections of Alexander H. Stephens: His Diary Kept When A Prisoner at Fort Warren, Boston Harbor, 1865.* New York, NY: Doubleday, Page and Co., 1910.

Beecher, Henry Ward. *Patriotic Addresses in America and England, From 1850 to 1885, on Slavery, the Civil War, and the Development of Civil Liberty in the United States.* New York, NY: Fords, Howard, and Hulbert, 1891.

Bennett, Lerone. *Forced into Glory: Abraham Lincoln's White Dream.* Chicago, IL: Johnson Publishing Co., 2000.

Cleveland, Henry. *Alexander H. Stephens, in Public and Private.* Philadelphia, PA: National Publishing Co., 1866.

Congressional Globe (pub.). *Speech of Hon. Alexander H. Stephens, of Georgia, on the Kansas Election.* Washington, D.C., 1856.

Davis, Jefferson. *The Rise and Fall of the Confederate Government.* 2 vols. New York, NY: D. Appleton and Co., 1881.

——. *A Short History of the Confederate States of America.* New York, NY: Belford, 1890.

Gideon, J. and G. S. (printers). *Speech of Mr. Stephens, of Georgia, on the War and Taxation.* N.p., 1848.

Herskovits, Melville J. *The Myth of the Negro Past.* 1941. Boston, MA: Beacon Press, 1958 ed.

Hill, Charles E. *Leading American Treaties.* New York, NY: Macmillan Co., 1922.

Johnson, Ludwell H. *North Against South: The American Iliad 1848-1877.* 1978. Columbia, SC: Foundation for American Education, 1993 ed.

Johnston, Richard Malcolm, and William Hand Browne. *Life of Alexander H. Stephens.* Philadelphia, PA: J. B. Lippincott and Co., 1884.

ORA (full title: *The War of the Rebellion: A Compilation of the Official Records of the Union and Confederate Armies.* (Multiple volumes.) Washington, D.C.: Government Printing Office, 1880.

Owsley, Frank Lawrence. *King Cotton Diplomacy: Foreign Relations of the Confederate States of America.* 1931. Chicago, IL: University of Chicago Press, 1959 ed.

Pendleton, Louis. *Alexander H. Stephens.* Philadelphia, PA: George W. Jacobs and Co., 1907.

Phillips, Ulrich Bonnell (ed.). *The Correspondence of Robert Toombs, Alexander H. Stephens, and Howell Cobb* (from the "Annual Report of the American Historical Association for the Year 1911"). Vol. 2. Washington, D.C.: N.p., 1913.

Pollard, Edward A. *Southern History of the War.* 2 vols. in 1. New York, NY: Charles B. Richardson, 1866.

———. *The Lost Cause.* 1867. Chicago, IL: E. B. Treat, 1890 ed.

———. *The Lost Cause Regained.* New York, NY: G. W. Carlton and Co., 1868.

———. *Life of Jefferson Davis, With a Secret History of the Southern Confederacy, Gathered "Behind the Scenes in Richmond."* Philadelphia, PA: National Publishing Co., 1869.

Rawle, William. *A View of the Constitution of the United States of America.* Philadelphia, PA: Philip H. Nicklin, 1829.

Rutherford, Mildred Lewis. *A True Estimate of Abraham Lincoln and Vindication of the South.* N.p., n.d.

———. *Truths of History: A Historical Perspective of the Civil War From the Southern Viewpoint.* Confederate Reprint Co., 1920.

———. *The South Must Have Her Rightful Place In History.* Athens, GA, 1923.

Seabrook, Lochlainn. *Carnton Plantation Ghost Stories: True Tales of the Unexplained from Tennessee's Most Haunted Civil War House!* 2005. Franklin, TN, 2016 ed.

———. *Nathan Bedford Forrest: Southern Hero, American Patriot.* 2007. Franklin, TN, 2010 ed.

———. *Abraham Lincoln: The Southern View.* 2007. Franklin, TN: Sea Raven Press, 2013 ed.

———. *The McGavocks of Carnton Plantation: A Southern History - Celebrating One of Dixie's Most Noble Confederate Families and Their Tennessee Home.* 2008. Franklin, TN, 2011 ed.

———. *A Rebel Born: A Defense of Nathan Bedford Forrest.* 2010. Franklin, TN: Sea Raven Press, 2011 ed.

———. *A Rebel Born: The Screenplay* (for the film). 2011. Franklin, TN: Sea Raven Press.

———. *Everything You Were Taught About the Civil War is Wrong, Ask a Southerner!*

2010. Franklin, TN: Sea Raven Press, revised 2014 ed.

——. *The Quotable Jefferson Davis: Selections From the Writings and Speeches of the Confederacy's First President*. Franklin, TN: Sea Raven Press, 2011.

——. *The Quotable Robert E. Lee: Selections From the Writings and Speeches of the South's Most Beloved Civil War General*. Franklin, TN: Sea Raven Press, 2011 Sesquicentennial Civil War Edition.

——. *Lincolnology: The Real Abraham Lincoln Revealed In His Own Words*. Franklin, TN: Sea Raven Press, 2011.

——. *The Unquotable Abraham Lincoln: The President's Quotes They Don't Want You To Know!* Franklin, TN: Sea Raven Press, 2011.

——. *Honest Jeff and Dishonest Abe: A Southern Children's Guide to the Civil War*. Franklin, TN: Sea Raven Press, 2012.

——. *Encyclopedia of the Battle of Franklin - A Comprehensive Guide to the Conflict that Changed the Civil War*. Franklin, TN: Sea Raven Press, 2012.

——. *The Quotable Nathan Bedford Forrest: Selections From the Writings and Speeches of the Confederacy's Most Brilliant Cavalryman*. Spring Hill, TN: Sea Raven Press, 2012.

——. *Forrest! 99 Reasons to Love Nathan Bedford Forrest*. Spring Hill, TN: Sea Raven Press, 2012.

——. *Give 'Em Hell Boys! The Complete Military Correspondence of Nathan Bedford Forrest*. Spring Hill, TN: Sea Raven Press, 2012.

——. *The Constitution of the Confederate States of America Explained: A Clause-by-Clause Study of the South's Magna Carta*. Spring Hill, TN: Sea Raven Press, 2012 Sesquicentennial Civil War Edition.

——. *The Great Impersonator: 99 Reasons to Dislike Abraham Lincoln*. Spring Hill, TN: Sea Raven Press, 2012.

——. *The Old Rebel: Robert E. Lee As He Was Seen By His Contemporaries*. Spring Hill, TN: Sea Raven Press, 2012 Sesquicentennial Civil War Edition.

——. *The Quotable Stonewall Jackson: Selections From the Writings and Speeches of the South's Most Famous General*. Spring Hill, TN: Sea Raven Press, 2012 Sesquicentennial Civil War Edition.

——. *Saddle, Sword, and Gun: A Biography of Nathan Bedford Forrest for Teens*. Spring Hill, TN: Sea Raven Press, 2013.

——. *The Quotable Alexander H. Stephens: Selections From the Writings and Speeches of the Confederacy's First Vice President*. Spring Hill, TN: Sea Raven Press, 2013 Sesquicentennial Civil War Edition.

——. *Give This Book to a Yankee! A Southern Guide to the Civil War for Northerners*. Spring Hill, TN: Sea Raven Press, 2014.

——. *The Articles of Confederation Explained: A Clause-by-Clause Study of*

America's First Constitution. Spring Hill, TN: Sea Raven Press, 2014.

———. *Confederate Blood and Treasure: An Interview With Lochlainn Seabrook.* Spring Hill, TN: Sea Raven Press, 2015.

———. *Nathan Bedford Forrest and the Battle of Fort Pillow: Yankee Myth, Confederate Fact.* Spring Hill, TN: Sea Raven Press, 2015.

———. *Everything You Were Taught About American Slavery War is Wrong, Ask a Southerner!* Spring Hill, TN: Sea Raven Press, 2015.

———. *Confederacy 101: Amazing Facts You Never Knew About America's Oldest Political Tradition.* Spring Hill, TN: Sea Raven Press, 2015.

———. *The Great Yankee Coverup: What the North Doesn't Want You to Know About Lincoln's War!* Spring Hill, TN: Sea Raven Press, 2015.

———. *Slavery 101: Amazing Facts You Never Knew About America's "Peculiar Institution."* Spring Hill, TN: Sea Raven Press, 2015.

———. *Confederate Flag Facts: What Every American Should Know About Dixie's Southern Cross.* Spring Hill, TN: Sea Raven Press, 2016.

———. *Nathan Bedford Forrest and the Ku Klux Klan: Yankee Myth, Confederate Fact.* Spring Hill, TN: Sea Raven Press, 2016.

———. *Seabrook's Bible Dictionary of Traditional and Mystical Christian Doctrines.* Spring Hill, TN: Sea Raven Press, 2016.

———. *Everything You Were Taught About African-Americans and the Civil War is Wrong, Ask a Southerner!* Spring Hill, TN: Sea Raven Press, 2016.

———. *Nathan Bedford Forrest and African-Americans: Yankee Myth, Confederate Fact.* Spring Hill, TN: Sea Raven Press, 2016.

———. *Women in Gray: A Tribute to the Ladies Who Supported the Southern Confederacy.* Spring Hill, TN: Sea Raven Press, 2016.

———. *Lincoln's War: The Real Cause, the Real Winner, the Real Loser.* Spring Hill, TN: Sea Raven Press, 2016.

———. *The Unholy Crusade: Lincoln's Legacy of Destruction in the American South.* Spring Hill, TN: Sea Raven Press, 2017.

———. *Abraham Lincoln Was a Liberal, Jefferson Davis Was a Conservative: The Missing Key to Understanding the American Civil War.* Spring Hill, TN: Sea Raven Press, 2017.

———. *All We Ask is to be Let Alone: The Southern Secession Fact Book.* Spring Hill, TN: Sea Raven Press, 2017.

———. *The Ultimate Civil War Quiz Book: How Much Do You Really Know About America's Most Misunderstood Conflict?* Spring Hill, TN: Sea Raven Press, 2017.

———. *Rise Up and Call Them Blessed: Victorian Tributes to the Confederate Soldier, 1861-1901.* Spring Hill, TN: Sea Raven Press, 2017.

———. *Victorian Confederate Poetry: The Southern Cause in Verse, 1861-1901.* Spring Hill, TN: Sea Raven Press, 2018.

———. *Confederate Monuments: Why Every American Should Honor Confederate Soldiers and Their Memorials.* Spring Hill, TN: Sea Raven Press, 2018.

———. *The God of War: Nathan Bedford Forrest as He Was Seen by His Contemporaries.* Spring Hill, TN: Sea Raven Press, 2018.

Steel, Samuel Augustus. *The South Was Right.* Columbia, SC: R. L. Bryan Co., 1914.

Simpson, Lewis P. (ed.). *I'll Take My Stand: The South and the Agrarian Tradition.* 1930. Baton Rouge, LA: Louisiana State University Press, 1977 ed.

Stephens, Alexander Hamilton. *A Constitutional View of the Late War Between the States; Its Causes, Character, Conduct and Results—Vol. 1.* Philadelphia, PA: National Publishing Co., 1868.

———. *A Constitutional View of the Late War Between the States; Its Causes, Character, Conduct and Results—Vol. 2.* Philadelphia, PA: National Publishing Co., 1870.

———. *The Reviewers Reviewed.* New York, NY: D. Appleton and Co., 1872.

———. *A Compendium of the History of the United States: From the Earliest Settlements to 1872.* New York, NY: E. J. Hale and Son, 1874.

Stewart, James A. *Conservative Views: The Government of the United States, What Is It?* Atlanta, Georgia: Franklin Printing House, 1869.

Trent, William Peterfield. *Southern Statesmen of the Old Régime: Washington, Jefferson, Randolph, Calhoun, Stephens, Toombs, and Jefferson Davis.* New York, NY: Thomas Y. Crowell and Co., 1897.

Warner, Ezra J. *Generals in Gray: Lives of the Confederate Commanders.* 1959. Baton Rouge, LA: Louisiana State University Press, 1989 ed.

———. *Generals in Blue: Lives of the Union Commanders.* 1964. Baton Rouge, LA: Louisiana State University Press, 2006 ed.

INDEX

NOTES
- As he is the subject of this work and his words appear on nearly every page, Alexander H. Stephens is not listed in the Index (except for his Confederate Cabinet photo, and his mention in my biography).
- Throughout his writings and speeches it is not always clear who Stephens is referring to. Many of the individuals he mentions are not listed in his own indexes, and dozens more show up in his works that lack either a first name or a last name. The confusion is compounded by instances in which people share the same last name, but which are not clearly identified by Stephens. In such cases I have indexed the individuals with whatever information is available.
- Titles (e.g., president) and rank (e.g., captain) have been eliminated from the Index. However, if the first or last name is not known, the title or rank is used—if there is one.

Abraham, of the Bible, 163, 165, 638
Abram, of the Bible, 163
Adam, of the Bible, 189, 204, 641, 771
Adams, John, 12, 65, 540, 544, 553, 580, 613, 643, 650, 653
Adams, John Q., 309, 542, 587, 593, 594, 644, 689, 707, 850, 852
Adams, Samuel, 441, 445, 570, 571
Adams, Shelby L., 1048
Africanus, Scipio, 31
Alcibiades, of Greece, 754
Ames, Fisher, 441, 442, 446, 508, 519
Ampudia, Pedro de, 114, 115
Anderson, J. Patton, 792, 879
Anderson, Loni, 1048
Anderson, Robert, 616, 618, 619, 807
Anne, Queen, 70
Anthony (Stephens' servant), 274, 275, 277-281, 284-287
Appleton, John W., 994, 995
Appleton, Mabel, 994
Appleton, Mary, 994
Archer, William S., 685
Arista, Mariano, 111, 113
Aristides, of Greece, 263, 522
Aristotle, 165, 171, 566, 595
Arnold, Benedict, 48, 415
Artemis, of Greece, 124
Arthur, King, 1046
Ashe, William, 726
Ashley, Chester, 121
Ashmun, George, 132, 736
Atkins, Chet, 1048
Atkins, John D. C., 878
Avery, William W., 878
Babcock, Lieutenant Colonel, 954, 968
Badger, George E., 710, 740
Baker, Edward D., 704
Baker, T. Harrison, 858
Baldwin, Abraham, 366, 385
Baldwin, Henry, 642, 676, 682,

687, 702
Baldwin, John B., 832
Baldwin, Roger S., 724
Bancroft, George, 137, 139, 144
Banks, Nathaniel P., 847, 920, 945
Barbour, Philip P., 676
Barnes, Joseph K., 900
Barnwell, Robert W., 733, 793
Barrow, Charles K., 23, 27
Barrow, Washington, 834
Barry, William S., 793
Bartow, Francis S., 792, 879, 891
Baskerville, Mr., 287
Basset, Richard, 372
Bateman, Ephraim, 687
Baxter, Eli H., 787, 789
Bayly, Thomas H., 700, 726
Beauregard, Pierre G. T., 68, 320, 616-619, 807, 853, 882, 883, 889, 919, 922, 974, 1047
Bedford, Gunning, Jr., 372, 385
Bedinger, Henry, 140
Beecher, Henry W., 267, 268
Bell, H. P., 792
Bell, John, 63, 667, 710, 715, 719, 740, 761, 788, 789, 843
Benhadad, King, 869
Benjamin, Judah P., 804, 888, 1005
Benjamin, of the Bible, 248
Benning, Henry L., 792, 952
Benton, Thomas H., 37, 120, 696, 710, 740
Bernstein, Leonard, 1048
Berrien, John M., 710, 719, 740
Bibb, George M., 532, 534, 535, 547, 551, 553
Birdsall, Ausburn, 695
Black, James, 693
Blackstone, William, 429, 497, 514, 579
Blair, Francis P., Sr., 90, 102, 950-952, 957, 961, 969, 970
Bloomfield, Joseph, 682, 687
Blue, Lieutenant, 288
Bob (Davis' servant), 280, 281
Bobbins, Jonathan, 550
Bocock, Thomas S., 878
Bodman, William, 441, 443
Bokee, David A., 727
Bolling, Edith, 1048
Bond, Ellen, 280, 283
Bond, H. L., 823
Bonham, Milledge L., 879
Boone, Daniel, 1047
Boone, Pat, 1048
Booth, John W., 321
Booth, Junius B., 321
Boudinot, Elias, 614
Bouligney, John E., 792
Boutwell, Mr., 291, 294, 303
Bowdoin, James, 368, 441
Bowlegs, Billy, 660
Bowman, Captain, 860
Boyce, William W., 793
Boyd, Linn, 714, 725-727, 730, 732

Bragg, Braxton, 69, 922, 943, 944
Bragg, Thomas, 888
Brearley, David, 370
Breck, Daniel, 705
Breckinridge, John C., 62, 63, 177, 190, 192, 760-762, 766, 780, 789, 810, 819, 875-877, 886, 973, 1047
Breese, Sidney, 692
Bright, Jesse D., 692, 695, 719
Bristow, George F., 287
Brockenbrough, John W., 819, 832, 878
Brodhead, Richard, 693, 695
Brooke, Edward W., 1048
Brooke, Walker, 793
Brooks, Preston S., 1047
Broom, Jacob, 372
Brougham, Henry, 607
Brougham, Lord, 861
Brown, Albert G., 181, 183, 699, 703
Brown, Charles, 695
Brown, George W., 823
Brown, John, 659, 663, 665, 749, 757
Brown, Joseph E., 75, 76, 235, 236, 238, 242, 243, 990-993, 996
Brown, Milton, 107, 108
Brown, Neil S., 833, 843
Brown, William J., 699
Browne, William M., 798
Bruce, James C., 826, 827
Brune, J. C., 823
Brutus, Marcus J., the Younger, 270
Buchanan, James, 121, 130, 133, 312, 543, 585, 616, 620, 669-671, 680, 681, 685, 688, 739, 748-750, 758, 760, 761, 780, 805, 813
Buchanan, Patrick J., 1048
Buell, Don C., 919, 922
Buford, Abraham, 1047
Burke, Edmund, 186
Burke, Mr., 493
Burlamaqui, Jean-Jacques, 341, 490, 498, 569
Burlingame, Anson, 765
Burnett, Henry C., 888
Burns, Anthony, 40
Burnside, Ambrose E., 921, 924
Burr, Charles C., 929
Burt, Armistead, 690, 727, 732
Burton, William, 821, 823
Burwell, W. W., 37
Butler, A. P., 733, 740
Butler, Andrew P., 1048
Butler, Benjamin F., 760, 879
Butler, Josiah, 685
Byrd, P. M., 787
Byron, Lord, 32, 924
Cabell, Edward C., 731, 886
Cabot, George, 584
Cadwallader, Lambert, 614
Caesar, Julius, 270, 868
Cain, of the Bible, 136, 748
Calhoun, James M., 68
Calhoun, John C., 32, 33, 36, 54, 68, 88, 184, 479, 484, 486, 488, 489, 492, 497,

500, 503, 505, 506, 511, 516, 517, 519, 520, 527, 529-532, 539, 541, 547, 691, 693, 710, 715, 718, 722, 779, 785, 805
Cameron, Simon, 695, 848
Campbell, D. C., 792, 821
Campbell, J. A. P., 793
Campbell, John A., 25, 71, 73, 90-92, 755, 806, 807, 810, 941, 942, 952, 958, 962, 965, 970
Campbell, John W., 685
Campbell, Joseph, 1045
Campbell, Lewis D., 645, 728
Canby, Edward R. S., 974
Canning, George, 629
Carlyle, Thomas, 793, 893
Carmichael, R. B., 820
Carroll, Daniel, 373, 651
Carson, Martha, 1048
Carter, Theodrick, 1047
Cartter, David K., 727
Caruthers, Robert L., 878
Casey, Henry R., 52
Cash, Johnny, 1048
Cass, Lewis, 124, 327, 614, 692, 710, 719, 740
Caswell, Richard, 375
Caudill, Benjamin E., 1046
Chambers, Ezekiel F., 820
Chappell, Absalom H., 33
Charles I, King, 242, 261, 964
Charles II, King, 262
Charles V, King, 88
Charles X, King, 150, 892
Charybdis, of Greek mythology, 232
Chase, Salmon P., 622, 624, 625, 636, 637, 710, 724, 740, 741, 743, 819
Chase, Samuel, 98, 340, 416, 484
Cheairs, Nathaniel F., 1047
Chesnut, James, Jr., 793, 879
Chesnut, Mary, 1048
Chilton, William P., 792
Choate, John, 441, 444
Choate, Rufus, 735
Cicero, Marcus Tullius, 125, 421, 566
Clark, H. F., 996
Clark, John H., 724
Clark, William, 1047
Clay, Clement C., 277, 279-282, 284, 285, 287, 740
Clay, Henry, 33, 34, 107, 327, 485, 518-520, 535, 537-540, 614, 646, 680, 685-688, 709-711, 718, 719, 722-724, 734, 740, 785, 805, 886
Clay, Henry, Jr., 140
Clay, Virginia, 279, 280, 283, 285, 287, 288
Clayton, Alexander M., 793
Clayton, John M., 692
Cleveland, Henry, 754, 939
Clingman, Thomas L., 161, 725, 810, 833, 879
Clinton, George, 370
Clouét, Alexander de, 793
Clymer, George, 371

Cobb, Howell, 33, 35, 127, 130, 192, 699, 700, 703, 709, 713, 725, 731, 734, 792, 793, 796-798, 878, 888, 905-907
Cobb, Thomas R. R., 790, 792, 797, 798, 879
Cobb, Thomas W., 685
Cochrane, John, 946
Cocke, Dr., 554, 555
Cohen, J. Barnett, 93, 94, 102, 103
Cohen, Mrs., 94
Coke, Edward, 261, 848
Collins, Thomas, 372
Colquitt, Alfred H., 945
Combs, Bertram T., 1048
Connel, Cosby, 275
Conner, David, 144
Conrad, Charles M., 793
Cooper, James, 719
Cooper, Major, 276, 277
Cooper, Samuel, 247
Corcoran, Michael, 860
Cox, Jacob D., 879
Coxe, Daniel, 352
Craige, Burton, 878
Crawford, Cindy, 1048
Crawford, George W., 785
Crawford, Martin J., 792, 796, 805
Crittenden, John J., 33, 524, 526, 662
Crockett, Davy, 1047
Cruise, Tom, 1048
Cunningham, Francis A., 691, 693

Currin, David M., 878
Curry, Jabez L. M., 792
Curtis, Benjamin R., 926, 927, 929
Curtis, George T., 344, 347, 350, 355, 388, 394, 395, 433
Curtis, Samuel R., 919
Cushing, Mr., 352
Cushing, William, 441
Cyrus, Billy R., 1048
Cyrus, Miley, 1048
Dana, Francis, 368
Dane, Nathan, 584
Daniel, William C., 792
Danton, Georges J., 867, 873, 878
Davidson, Andrew J., 878
Davie, William R., 375, 385, 471, 473
Davis, George, 878, 973
Davis, Jefferson, 12, 15, 20, 24, 25, 68, 75-77, 88, 91, 132, 210, 213, 240, 251, 252, 277-282, 284-287, 312, 320, 522, 524-527, 617, 663, 667, 710, 719, 720, 733, 734, 740, 759, 761, 795-797, 802, 804, 805, 807, 811, 825, 853, 859, 860, 874, 879, 883, 886, 889, 895-897, 905, 907, 910, 917, 925, 930, 931, 933-936, 939, 944, 946, 947, 950, 951, 953, 957, 969-972, 974, 978, 979, 992, 996, 1002, 1045,

1047
Davis, Jefferson C., 280, 283, 285
Davis, John, 724
Davis, Margaret H., 280, 283, 285
Davis, Varina A. "Winnie", 279
Davis, Varina B., 279-281, 283-285, 287, 288
Davis, William H., 280, 283, 285
Dayton, William L., 724, 736
De Witt, W. H., 878
Delolme, Jean-Louis de, 70
Demosthenes, of Greece, 971
Derby, Earl of, 861
Dickinson, Daniel S., 692, 695, 719
Dickinson, Henry, 821
Dickinson, John, 372
Disney, David T., 726
Dix, General, 289
Dix, John A., 994
Dobbin, George W., 823
Dodge, Augustus C., 740, 741
Dodge, Henry, 724
Dollard, Patrick, 449
Donelson, Andrew J., 121, 129
Doolittle, James R., 809
Doty, James D., 712-714, 720, 722, 724
Douglas, Stephen A., 61-63, 173-175, 177, 179-188, 190, 192, 221, 277, 327, 524, 614, 659, 662, 665, 691, 693-695, 709, 710, 714, 718-720, 725, 740-742, 744, 759-761, 776, 789, 809, 810, 839-841, 847, 849, 851, 929
Downs, Solomon W., 719
Dromgoole, George C., 707
DuBose, Mrs. Dudley M., 287
Duer, William, 700, 704, 731
Duncan, John W., 276-278
Duvall, Robert, 1048
Early, Jubal A., 948
Eckert, Thomas T., 91
Eddy, Samuel, 682, 687
Edsall, Joseph E., 693
Edward I, King, 1046
Elisha, of the Bible, 869, 870
Elizabeth I, Queen, 513
Ellis, John W., 824, 833
Ellis, Richard, 121
Ellsworth, Oliver, 369, 381, 382, 385, 398, 411, 436, 437, 483
Elmore, Rush, 160
Elzy, General, 281
Erdman, Jacob, 693
Eustis, George, 885
Eustis, William, 685
Evans, Nathan G., 884
Eve, of the Bible, 771
Everett, Edward, 667, 761, 788
Ezekiel, of the Bible, 171, 595
Fairfield, John, 658
Falkland, Viscount, 261
Fearn, Thomas, 792
Featherstone, W. S., 729
Felix (Toombs' servant), 276, 277

Ferdinand, King, 88
Few, William, 366
Fillmore, Millard, 327, 710, 724, 736, 749, 780, 785
Filmer, Robert, 483
Findley, William, 428, 429, 431, 432
Fitzgerald, Thomas, 695
Fitzpatrick, Benjamin, 63, 760
Fitzsimons, Thomas, 371
Fitzwater, Robert, 491
Flournoy, Thomas S., 952, 956
Floyd, John B., 879
Foot, Samuel, 682
Foote, Henry S., 486, 509, 557, 710, 718, 734
Foote, Shelby, 1045
Forbes, Christopher, 1048
Ford, William D., 685, 687
Forrest, Nathan B., 945, 1045, 1047
Forsyth, John, Jr., 805
Forsyth, John, Sr., 805
Foster, Ira R., 276
Foster, Thomas, 31
Fountain (Stephens' servant), 279
Frailey, Captain, 286, 287, 289
Franklin, Benjamin, 65, 151, 385, 386, 612, 643
Franklin, John E., 820
Frederick, of Prussia, 227
Frémont, John C., 732, 749, 920, 946
Fullerton, David, 682
Gaines, Edmund P., 141
Galileo, 203, 333

Gamaliel, of the Bible, 267
Gamble, Hamilton R., 817, 886
Garland, Augustus H., 835
Garrett, J. W., 824
Garrison, William L., 517
Gayheart, Rebecca, 1048
Geary, John, 995
George (Stephens' servant), 279
George III, King, 442, 574, 602, 765
George IV, King, 628
Gerry, Elbridge T., 368, 385-387, 401, 402, 614
Giddings, Joshua R., 166, 626
Gilmer, Mrs., 66
Gilpin, Captain, 276, 278
Gist, States R., 1047
Glenn, Luther J., 792, 817
God, 2, 39, 41, 47, 110, 115, 129, 136, 162-166, 189, 198, 212, 223, 259, 267, 274, 366, 442, 532, 538, 596, 637-640, 666, 701, 723, 743, 774, 799, 829, 835, 876, 877, 887, 891, 915, 927, 1023
Goode, John, Jr., 819
Goodhue, Benjamin, 614
Gordon, George W., 1047
Gordon, John B., 26
Gore, Mr., 442
Gorham, Nathaniel, 368
Gott, Daniel, 726, 730
Graham, William A., 692
Grant, Ulysses S., 90, 320, 321, 919, 923, 925, 929, 932, 933, 935, 944, 945, 947,

952, 953, 955, 968, 971, 973, 974, 985
Grattan, Miss, 66
Graves, Robert, 1045
Greeley, Horace, 307-312, 314, 315, 331, 586-589, 611-613, 627, 642, 735, 736, 745, 975, 996
Green, Albert C., 724
Green, James S., 720
Gregg, John, 793
Grier, A. G., 276-278
Griffin, Mr., 288, 289
Griffith, Andy, 1048
Grinnell, Joseph, 728
Grotius, Hugo, 566, 661
Grundy, Felix, 532
Guaraldi, Vince, 1048
Gushing, Caleb, 760
Guthrie, James, 836
Guyon, James, 687
Hackley, Aaron, 685, 687
Hale, John P., 710, 724
Hale, Stephen F., 792
Hall, Samuel, 792
Hall, Willard P., 886
Hallam, Henry, 616
Halleck, Henry W., 286
Halloway, Ransom, 727
Hamilcar, of Carthage, 722
Hamilton, Alexander, 48, 337-339, 369, 382-384, 394, 405, 416, 425, 438, 466-468, 470, 471, 478, 483, 484, 508, 578, 583, 595, 610, 613
Hamilton, James P., 52

Hamlin, Hannibal, 332, 612, 760
Hammond, James H., 640
Hampden, John, 261, 986, 998
Hampton, Wade, 879
Hancock, John, 441, 445, 446, 593, 643
Handy, A. H., 820
Hannegan, Edward A., 692, 695
Hannibal, of Carthage, 31
Hardin, John J., 140
Harding, William G., 1047
Harris, Isham G., 818, 824, 833
Harris, Singleton, 275
Harris, Thomas L., 727
Harris, W. P., 793
Harrison, James T., 793
Harrison, Mr., 280, 287
Harrison, William H., 542, 543
Harry (Stephens' servant), 16, 274, 275
Hartley, Thomas, 614
Harvey, William, 203
Harvie, Lewis E., 826, 827
Hastings, Clinton L., 691
Hayne, I. W., 620
Hazel, of the Bible, 39, 79, 191, 869, 870
Heister, Daniel, 614
Hemphill, John, 793
Henry (Stephens' servant), 278-281, 284-287
Henry, Gustavus A., 834
Henry, Patrick, 12, 401, 404, 453, 454, 457-460, 462, 540, 570, 660
Herrera, José Joaquín de,

132-135
Hicks, Thomas H., 820, 823
Hidell, William H., 274, 275, 278, 279
Higginson, Stephen, 651
Hill, Benjamin H., 50, 68, 786, 792, 795, 991
Hill, D. P., 792
Hill, Daniel H., 879, 943
Hill, Mark L., 682, 687
Hillhouse, James, 584
Hilliard, Henry W., 833
Hillyer, Junius, 289
Hitler, Adolf, 941
Hoar, Samuel, 627, 635, 636
Holcombe, James P., 826, 827
Holden, William W., 981, 992
Holmes, John, 673, 676, 678, 681, 682
Holten, Samuel, 651
Homer, of Greece, 770
Hood, John B., 943, 947, 948, 1047
Hooker, Joseph, 921, 923-925, 929, 936
Hooper, J. J., 793
House, John F., 878
Houston, John W., 693, 695
Houston, Samuel, 710, 740
Houston, William, 366
Houston, William C., 370
Howard, John, 152
Howard, Volney E., 729, 731
Howell, Jefferson D., 280
Hudson, Captain, 282
Hughes, John, 912
Hull, Henry, 273

Hull, Robert, 273
Hunter, David, 930, 932
Hunter, Robert M. T., 25, 90-92, 192, 707, 710, 733, 740, 755, 832, 878, 886, 888, 941, 942, 950, 953, 961, 964, 966, 967, 970
Huntington, Benjamin, 614
Huntington, Samuel, 438
Inge, Samuel W., 704-706, 730, 731
Ingersoll, Charles J., 691, 693, 695
Ingersoll, Jared, 371
Isaac (cook), 289
Isaac, of the Bible, 164, 165, 638
Isabella, Queen, 88
Isacks, Mr., 160
Jackman, David J., 996
Jackson, Andrew, 485, 529, 540, 542, 545, 546, 553, 556, 559-561, 564, 567, 646, 773, 780, 805, 842, 877, 1047
Jackson, Claiborne F., 824, 835, 886
Jackson, Henry R., 792, 1047
Jackson, Stonewall, 31, 889, 920, 921, 924, 945, 1047
Jacob, of the Bible, 164, 165, 638
James I, King, 513
James II, King, 442, 491
James VI, King, 513
James, Frank, 1047
James, Jesse, 1047

Janney, John, 819, 828, 843
Jay, John, 405, 469, 489
Jefferson, Thomas, 12, 13, 19, 22, 65, 83, 102, 118, 148, 202, 206, 216, 221, 254, 308, 309, 312, 326, 327, 364, 380, 381, 400, 485, 486, 540-543, 545, 546, 564, 565, 567, 570, 574, 578, 583, 587, 594, 607, 613, 614, 643, 644, 649, 662, 678, 679, 708, 756, 780, 846, 866, 869, 999, 1047
Jenifer, Daniel of St. Thomas, 373
Jent, Elias, Sr., 1047
Jesus, 1046
Jesus, of Nazareth, 64, 127, 162, 164-166, 637-639, 890
Joab, of the Bible, 48
Job, of the Bible, 164, 638
John, Elton, 1048
John, King, 491
Johnson, Andrew, 63, 93, 261, 270, 321, 874, 876, 877, 946, 974, 978-983, 985-988, 994, 998
Johnson, George W., 887, 888
Johnson, Herschel V., 75, 173, 174, 181, 189, 190, 761, 775, 777, 785, 786, 790
Johnson, Robert, 878
Johnson, Robert W., 835
Johnson, Samuel, 407
Johnson, W. C., 707

Johnson, William S., 369
Johnston, Albert S., 890, 919
Johnston, Colonel, 280
Johnston, Joseph E., 73, 320, 321, 882, 889, 918, 920, 937, 944, 946-948, 973, 974, 978
Johnston, Richard M., 275
Jones, George W., 878
Jones, I. D., 820
Jones, Joseph, 905
Jones, Mr., 442
Jones, Walter, 362
Jones, Willie, 375
Judd, Ashley, 1048
Judd, Naomi, 1048
Judd, Wynonna, 1048
Kane, George P., 823
Keffer, Captain, 860
Keitt, Laurence M., 654, 793
Kelly, Captain, 282, 283
Kenan, A. H., 244
Kenan, Augustus H., 792, 796
Kennedy, Captain, 278
Kennedy, John P., 524
Kenner, Duncan F., 793
Kent, Edward, 658
Kent, James, 580
Keough, Riley, 1048
King, Preston, 728
King, Rufus, 368, 382, 405, 425, 441, 445, 478, 483, 648
King, William R., 710, 719, 740
Kingsdown, Lord, 861
Kinsey, Charles, 681, 682

La Fayette, Marquis de, 61
Lamar, Albert R., 785
Lamar, George W., 189
Lamar, Lucius Q. C., 252
Landrum, Mrs., 66
Landrum, Z. P., 60
Lane, Andrew J., 789
Lane, Joseph, 63, 177, 190, 192, 760, 761, 877
Langdon, John, 376, 452
Lansing, John, 468
Lansing, John, Jr., 369, 401
Lanzas, Joaquín María del Castillo y, 134
Latimer, F. H., 787
Law, Richard, 438
Lawrence, William B., 289
Lecompte, S. D., 160
Lee, Colonel, 860
Lee, Fitzhugh, 1047
Lee, G. W., 276
Lee, Henry, III, 344, 453, 455, 828
Lee, Richard H., 348, 649, 828
Lee, Robert E., 31, 216, 225, 291, 320, 321, 348, 784, 827-831, 897, 920, 921, 923, 924, 933-935, 937, 943, 944, 946, 947, 952, 954, 971, 973, 974, 1004, 1047
Lee, Samuel P., 935
Lee, Stephen D., 1047
Lee, William H. F., 1047
Leigh, Benjamin W., 535
Leslie, Frank, 282
Letcher, John, 824, 825

Lewis, David P., 792
Lewis, Meriwether, 1047
Limber, Jim, 280, 283
Lincoln, Abraham, 12, 16, 18, 19, 21, 25, 62, 63, 66-68, 90, 91, 102, 167, 169, 173, 188, 192, 208, 209, 255, 257, 271, 282, 287, 291, 293, 296, 308, 309, 315, 317-319, 321, 325, 327, 331, 332, 379, 479, 526, 542, 544, 545, 586-589, 612, 614, 616, 618, 619, 621, 623-625, 641, 643, 659, 661, 662, 665, 750, 753-756, 758, 760, 762-766, 773, 776, 783, 798, 805, 808, 810, 811, 813, 816, 819, 821-825, 828, 831, 833-841, 843-846, 848-852, 855, 856, 858-863, 865-874, 876, 878, 880, 881, 883, 886, 887, 895, 896, 911, 915, 917, 925-928, 930, 931, 933-936, 941, 943, 945, 946, 951, 952, 955, 957, 958, 961-964, 966-970, 974, 979-982, 992, 996
Lincoln, Benjamin, 344
Lindsay, Matilda M. S., 278
Little, Dr., 277
Livermore, Anna, 995
Livermore, Charles F., 995
Livingston, Edward, 550, 557, 559

Livingston, Robert R., 466, 643
Livingston, William, 370
Locke, John, 429
Long, Crawford W., 23
Longstreet, James, 924, 943, 944, 1047
Loring, Edward G., 40
Louis XVI, King, 150
Louis-Phillippe I, King, 892
Lovejoy, Owen, 626
Loveless, Patty, 1048
Lowe, E. Louis, 820
Lowndes, Rawlins, 449
Lowndes, William, 681, 685
Lubbock, Francis R., 280, 285
Lucas (steward), 284, 285
Lumpkin, Joseph H., 482
Lunt, George, 611
Lyons, Lord, 845
Mace, Daniel, 646
Macfarland, James E., 885
Macfarland, William H., 878
Mackenzie, Alexander S., 144
Macon, Mr., 503
Madison, James, 20, 107, 125, 216, 220, 221, 254, 340, 362, 364, 382, 387, 400, 402, 405, 416-419, 425, 453, 455, 457, 461, 478, 483, 484, 505, 542, 543, 547, 566, 583, 585, 607, 651, 662, 679, 780
Magoffin, Beriah, 817, 824, 836, 886
Magruder, John B., 918
Mallard, Mr., 288
Mallory, Stephen R., 804, 935, 1009
Mangum, Willie P., 710, 719
Manigault, Arthur M., 1047
Manigault, Joseph, 1047
Mann, Ambrose D., 813
Marcy, William L., 113, 137
Marshall, A. E., 231
Marshall, Alexander J., 80
Marshall, Henry, 793
Marshall, Humphrey, 887
Marshall, John, 98, 354, 383, 400, 453, 457, 458, 461, 550, 563, 751
Martin, Alexander, 375
Martin, Luther, 339, 340, 373, 385, 401, 402, 416, 484
Marvin, Lee, 1048
Mary II, Queen, 242
Mason, George, 362, 394, 401, 402, 453, 458, 462
Mason, James M., 710, 715, 719, 733, 740, 878, 885
Mason, Jonathan, 682
Mathews, John, 367
Matthews, George, 367
Maury, Abram P., 1047
McClellan, George B., 879, 884, 889, 897, 918, 920, 921, 925, 936, 946, 947
McClernand, John A., 713, 714, 725, 726, 731
McCulloch, Benjamin, 883, 919
McDonald, Charles J., 734
McDowell, Irvin, 879, 882, 883, 889, 925
McDowell, James, 730
McDowell, Thomas D., 878

McGavock, Caroline E., 1047
McGavock, David H., 1047
McGavock, Emily, 1047
McGavock, Francis, 1047
McGavock, James R., 1047
McGavock, John W., 1047
McGavock, Lysander, 1047
McGavock, Randal W., 1047
McGraw, Tim, 1048
McHenry, James, 373
McKee, William R., 140
McKenzie, George, 483
McLane, Robert M., 127, 128, 130, 820
McLean, F. E., 727, 731
McLean, John, 635, 643
McMahon, Colonel, 289
McQuade, Captain, 860
McRae, Colin J., 792
McRae, Thomas M., 787
Meade, George G., 936, 943, 944
Meade, Richard K., 728
Meigs, Henry, 676, 682, 687
Memminger, Charles G., 793, 794, 804, 973
Memminger, Christopher G., 1006
Mercer, Captain, 859
Mercer, John F., 373
Meriwether, Elizabeth A., 1047
Meriwether, Minor, 1047
Merryman, John, 848
Mifflin, Thomas, 371
Miles, W. P., 793
Miller, Jacob W., 724
Miller, John K., 714

Milroy, Robert H., 920
Minor, William T., 45
Moir, James, 885
Monroe, James, 344, 362, 453, 508, 542, 543, 630, 660, 686, 687, 780, 828
Monroe, Judge, 280
Monroe, Thomas B., Jr., 887
Monroe, Thomas B., Sr., 886
Montesquieu, Baron de, 408, 421, 425, 426, 478, 564, 566, 568, 569, 572, 577, 593
Moody, Captain, 286
Moore, Dr., 65
Moore, Mr., 283
Moore, Samuel, 685, 687
Moore, Samuel M., 826, 827
Morehead, Charles S., 886
Morehead, John M., 878
Morgan, John H., 936, 943, 1047
Morris, Gouverneur, 371, 379, 381, 382, 405, 425, 478, 483, 578
Morris, Robert, 371, 469
Morse (editor), 280
Morse, Samuel F. B., 151, 544
Morton, Jackson, 792
Morton, Jeremiah, 819
Morton, John W., 1047
Mosby, John S., 1047
Moses, of the Bible, 164, 638
Motley, John L., 580
Muhlenberg, Frederick A., 614
Myers, Joseph, 279
M'Culloch, Mr., 508

M'Kean, Mr., 431
Napoleon III, 150, 892, 954
Nash, Thomas, 550
Nason, Samuel, 441
Neilson, John, 370
Nelson, General, 273
Nelson, Justice, 806
Newenham, Edward, 407
Nicholas, George, 453, 457, 459, 461
Nicholas, S. S., 307
Nicholson, A. O. P., 757
Nicias, of Greece, 754
Nisbet, Eugenius A., 777, 785, 786, 792, 796
Noble, James, 680
Norris, Moses, 710, 720
Nugent, Ted, 1048
Oats, John, 249
Ochiltree, W. B., 793
Oglethorpe, James, 54
Oilman, Nicholas, 376, 614
Oldham, Williamson S., 793
Oliver, Mordecai, 886
Onesimus, of the Bible, 166, 639
Orr, James L., 879
Osgood, Samuel, 651
Otis, Harrison G., 584
Ould, Robert, 935, 969
Owen, Robert D., 693
Owens, James B., 792
Painter (purser), 288
Palgrave, Francis, 501
Palmer, John M., 901
Palmerston, Lord, 230
Paredes, Mariano, 113, 132, 134, 135
Parker, Captain, 286
Parker, James, 681
Parker, Samuel H., 249
Parker, Theodore, 521
Parrish, Isaac, 691, 693
Parsons, Theophilus, 441, 442, 444
Parton, Dolly, 1048
Paterson, William, 370, 385, 483
Paul, Saint, 162, 166, 639, 981, 986
Pearce, James A., 524, 710, 740
Pegram, Robert B., 858
Pemberton, John C., 933, 935
Pendleton, Edmund, 453, 454, 461
Pendleton, George H., 946
Pendleton, Nathaniel, 366
Pericles, of Greece, 666, 770
Perkins, John, Jr., 793, 801
Peter, the Hermit, 799
Pettus, Edmund W., 1047
Phelps, John S., 157
Phelps, Samuel S., 710, 719
Philemon, of the Bible, 166, 639
Philip II, King, 237
Pickens, Francis W., 318, 319, 617, 620, 807
Pickering, John, 376
Pickett, John T., 806, 885
Pierce (Stephens' servant), 277
Pierce, Franklin, 36, 37, 543, 737, 740, 780, 836

Pierce, William, 366
Pillow, Gideon J., 884, 1047
Pinckney, Charles C., 341, 367, 400, 450
Pinckney, Thomas, 375
Pinkney, William, 327, 614, 677, 678
Pius IX, Pope, 42, 252
Plato, 171, 566, 595
Polk, James K., 110-112, 120, 124, 127, 128, 131, 132, 135-139, 141, 143-146, 543, 690, 692, 709, 780, 1047
Polk, Leonidas, 883, 1047
Polk, Lucius E., 1047
Pollard, Edward A., 784
Pompey the Great, 270
Pope, John, 920, 925
Porter, David, 769
Porter, Mr., 444
Potter, Emory D., 731
Potter, Major, 860
Powell, Dr., 277
Powell, Mrs., 277
Pratt, Thomas G., 820
Prentiss, Sergeant S., 485
Presley, Elvis, 1048
Presley, Lisa Marie, 1048
Preston, Walter, 878
Preston, William, 887, 888
Preston, William B., 819, 826, 827, 878, 956
Price, Sterling, 883, 919, 948
Pritchard, Colonel, 281-283, 285, 286, 288
Pryor, Roger A., 878

Pufendorf, Samuel von, 566
Puryear, Robert C., 878
Randall, James R., 848
Randolph, Edmund, 362, 379, 381, 382, 385, 400-403, 405, 442, 453, 456, 459, 478, 483
Randolph, Edmund J., 1047
Randolph, George W., 819, 973, 1047
Rawle, William, 334, 580, 582
Ray, Lieutenant, 289
Read, George, 372
Reagan, John H., 280-282, 284-287, 289, 793, 804, 1010
Reagan, Ronald, 1048
Rector, Henry M., 824
Reeder, Andrew H., 155, 157, 159-162
Reid, Robert E., 676
Reid, Samuel C., 65, 66
Revere, Major, 860
Reynolds, Burt, 1048
Rhett, Robert B., 654, 666, 793, 798, 801
Richardson, William A., 714, 721
Rickett, Captain, 860
Rienzi, Cola di, 971
Riley, B., 711
Rives, William C., 819, 832, 843, 878
Robbins, Hargus, 1048
Robert the Bruce, King, 1046
Robespierre, Maximilien de, 867, 873, 878

Robinson, Edward, 165
Rockwood, Captain, 860
Rogers, Thomas J., 687
Roman, A. B., 805
Ronald, William, 362
Root, Joseph M., 725, 727
Rosecrans, William S., 922, 943
Ross, David, 362
Rost, Pierre A., 813
Rucker, Edmund W., 1047
Ruffin, Thomas, 878
Russell, Charles W., 878
Russell, D. R., 817
Russell, Joseph, 693
Rust, Albert, 835
Rutledge, Edward, 385
Rutledge, John, 375, 651
Ryan, A. J., 999
Saint, Captain, 273-276
Sanford, John W. A., 792
Santa Anna, Antonio López de, 140, 144
Sawyer, William, 693
Saxton, Rufus, 283
Schell, Augustus, 996
Schenck, Robert C., 727
Schleiden, Rudolf M., 67
Schofield, John M., 971
Scott, Dred, 58, 178, 185, 760
Scott, George C., 1048
Scott, Robert E., 843, 878
Scott, T. Parker, 820
Scott, Winfield, 143, 317, 736, 809, 828, 829, 849, 860, 882, 884
Scruggs, Earl, 1048
Scylla, of Greek mythology, 232

Seabrook, John L., 1047
Seabrook, Lochlainn, 15, 22-24, 26, 27, 1045, 1047-1049
Seargeant, John, 685
Seaverns, Joel, 994
Sebastian, Senator, 277
Seddon, James A., 71, 819, 878, 933, 934, 973
Sedgwick, Theodore, 614
Seger, Bob, 1048
Semmes, Raphael, 858
Seward, William H., 25, 91, 223, 318, 618, 658, 710, 724, 737, 740, 805-808, 810, 822, 845, 885, 941, 955, 957, 959, 961-965, 967, 968, 982
Seymour, Truman, 945
Shakespeare, William, 32
Shannon, Wilson, 159
Shaw, Henry, 682, 687
Sheridan, Philip H., 320, 870, 901, 948, 949
Sherman, Roger, 369, 398, 411, 436, 438, 614, 643
Sherman, William T., 320, 321, 870, 901, 945-950, 971, 973, 974, 978, 979, 992, 996
Shields, James, 41, 920
Shorter, John G., 792
Shurtliff, Mr., 442
Simmons, Dr., 277
Simmons, James, 787
Simmons, James P., 787
Simms, William E., 888
Singletary, Amos, 441, 444

Skaggs, Ricky, 1048
Slidell, John, 116, 133-136, 142-144, 147, 885
Smilie, Mr., 432
Smith, Adam, 203
Smith, Bernard, 682, 687
Smith, Edmund K., 321, 922, 945, 974
Smith, Gerrit, 996
Smith, Gustavus W., 889
Smith, J. Henly, 50-52, 66, 67, 226
Smith, Meriwether, 362
Smith, Mr., 493
Smith, Robert, 691, 693
Smith, Robert H., 792
Smith, Truman, 724, 956
Smith, William, 685
Smith, William N. H., 878
Smyth, Alexander, 677
Snead, Thomas L., 886
Soulé, Pierre, 722, 723
Southard, Henry, 687
Spaight, Richard D., 375
Sparrow, Edward, 793
Stanton, Edwin M., 900, 994, 995
Stanton, Fred P., 703, 704, 720
Staples, Waller R., 832, 878
Starr, Captain, 249
Stephen, Saint, 189, 986
Stephens, Alexander H., 1003, 1047
Stephens, Andrew B., 23, 278
Stephens, Clarence, 274, 275
Stephens, Edward, 15
Stephens, John A., 25, 278, 281, 287
Stephens, John L., 274
Stephens, Linton, 31, 32, 35, 274, 275, 278, 281, 286, 287, 786-789, 914
Stephens, Linton A., 278, 279
Stephens, Margaret (Grier), 23
Stevens, James, 682, 687
Stevens, Thaddeus, 95, 705, 730
Stewart, Alexander P., 1047
Stewart, James A., 92, 95
Stewart, William M., 297, 302
Storrs, Henry R., 673, 682, 687
Story, Joseph, 100, 367, 380, 576, 579, 584, 586, 611, 926
Stout, Lansing, 63
Stribling, Mr., 282
Strong, Caleb, 368
Stuart, Alexander H. H., 819, 832
Stuart, Jeb, 1047
Sturgeon, Daniel, 695
Sullivan, John, 452
Summers, George W., 819
Sumner, Charles, 444, 626, 740, 741, 743, 745
Swift, Zephenia, 584
Swinton, William, 783, 784, 922, 947
Sydney, Algernon, 986, 998
Tallmadge, James, 672
Taney, Roger B., 317, 614, 751, 848, 940
Taylor, John, 441
Taylor, John (General), 543

Taylor, John W., 673, 681
Taylor, Richard, 945, 974, 1047
Taylor, Sarah K., 1047
Taylor, Thomas, 859, 860
Taylor, Waller, 680
Taylor, Zachary, 34, 111-115, 122, 127, 136, 138, 139, 141, 143, 698, 711, 724, 755, 785, 945, 956, 1047
Terry, Alfred H., 971
Themistocles, of Greece, 263, 522
Thomas, Emmaline, 32
Thomas, George H., 884, 890, 944, 948
Thomas, James, 32, 34, 36
Thomas, James H., 878
Thomas, Jesse B., 680
Thomas, Thomas W., 37, 49
Thomason, W. F., 835
Thompson, Jacob, 726
Thornton, Seth, 116
Thrasher, Mrs., 277
Tillson, Davis, 296
Tim (Stephens' servant), 273, 274
Tocqueville, Alexis de, 565, 566, 568, 585, 606
Todd, Maria K., 34
Tomlinson, Gideon, 685
Tompkins, Patrick W., 143
Toombs, Robert A., 24, 34, 274-277, 287, 526, 656, 666, 667, 693, 699, 700, 703-705, 707, 709, 713, 714, 721, 722, 728, 730, 736, 740, 766-770, 792, 795-797, 801, 804, 879, 888, 896, 956, 1008
Toombs, Sallie, 287
Totten, Archibald O. W., 834
Toucey, Isaac, 740
Travis (servant), 286
Trenholm, George A., 973
Trist, Nicholas P., 146
Trumbull, Lyman, 41, 524
Tucker, St. George, 362, 497, 576, 579, 580, 582
Tyler, John, 32, 33, 364, 521, 780, 819, 826, 827, 834, 878
Tyler, John, Sr., 364
Tynes, Ellen B., 1047
Udree, Daniel, 687
Upham, William, 692, 724
Upton, General, 274, 276-279, 281
Vallandigham, Clement L., 929, 943
Van Buren, Martin, 32, 118, 542, 543, 780
Van Dorn, Earl, 919
Van Dyke, John, 705
Vance, Robert B., 1047
Vance, Zebulon, 1047
Vance, Zebulon B., 1047
Vason, W. J., 792
Vattel, Emerich de, 341, 409, 420, 569, 572, 664, 855
Vega, Romulo Diaz de la, 114
Venable, Abram W., 878
Venable, Charles S., 1047
Verplanck, Gulian C., 535

Victoria, Queen, 845
Vinton, Samuel F., 726
Vogdes, Major, 860
Wade, Benjamin F., 308, 309, 586
Walden, Hiram, 725
Walker, Isaac P., 724
Walker, Leroy P., 68, 158, 618, 804, 848, 851-854, 888, 1007
Walker, Richard W., 792
Wallack, Mr., 277
Wallis, S. Teackle, 820
Walton, George, 366
Ward, G. T., 879
Warner, Hiram, 902
Washburn, Israel, 157
Washington, Bushrod, 400, 453, 514
Washington, George, 12, 76, 119, 140, 146-148, 150, 216, 220, 221, 254, 272, 344, 377, 395, 397, 400, 401, 405-408, 411, 478, 483, 486, 527, 540, 543, 560, 561, 567, 574, 580, 612, 613, 659, 717, 755, 756, 877, 954, 986, 998
Washington, John A., 1047
Washington, Thornton A., 1047
Watkins, W. H., 835
Watts, Thomas H., 973
Waul, Thomas M., 793
Webster, Daniel, 12, 100, 119, 168, 212, 221, 263, 327, 343, 344, 346, 479, 482, 484, 485, 487-489, 493, 494, 502, 503, 506, 509, 511, 515, 518-522, 527, 530, 539, 543, 560, 570, 575, 577, 596, 600, 622, 710, 718, 719, 723, 724, 735, 736, 740, 805, 842, 847, 849, 852, 892, 926
Webster, Noah, 407
Welsch, Aristides, 996
Wentworth, John, 726, 728, 729
West, Benjamin, 376
Wheeler, Henry W., 709
Wheeler, Joseph, 280-282, 284-287
Whelchel, David, 787
White, Henry K., 924
Whitehill, Mr., 432
Whitfield, John W., 155, 156, 159, 162
Whyte, William P., 820
Wick, William W., 693
Widgery, William, 441
Wigfall, Louis T., 793, 879
Wilberforce, William, 326
Wilkes, Charles, 885
Wilkins, William, 531, 532
William III, King, 242
Williams, Commander, 885
Williams, Louis, 707
Williams, Mr., 467
Williamson, Hugh, 651
Wilmot, David, 145, 690, 692
Wilson, Henry, 994, 995
Wilson, James, 371, 382, 387, 405, 417, 425, 427, 428, 431, 432, 478, 648, 651

Wilson, James H., 901
Wilson, John L., 630
Wilson, W. S., 793
Wilson, Woodrow, 25, 1048
Winder, Charles S., 1047
Winder, John H., 1047
Winthrop, Robert C., 699, 709
Wirt, William, 629, 632
Wirz, Henry, 898
Wise, Henry A., 879
Withers, Thomas J., 793
Witherspoon, Reese, 1048
Wolcott, Oliver, 438, 651
Womack, John B., 1047
Womack, Lee Ann, 1048
Wood, A. M., 860
Woodman, Lieutenant, 289
Woodman, William H., 995
Woodruff, Colonel, 860
Woodward, George W., 940
Wool, John E., 888
Worcester, Joseph E., 407
Worth, William J., 114
Wright, Ambrose R., 792, 820
Wright, Augustus R., 792, 795
Xerxes, of Persia, 59
Yancey, William L., 58, 666, 813, 885
Yates, Edward, 380, 385, 401, 402
Yates, Robert, 369
Yell, Archibald, 140
Zollicoffer, Felix K., 684, 833, 843, 879, 884, 1047

MEET THE AUTHOR

"DEMANDING THE PATRIOTIC SOUTH TO STOP HONORING HER CONFEDERATE ANCESTORS IS LIKE DEMANDING THE SUN NOT TO SHINE." — COLONEL LOCHLAINN SEABROOK

LOCHLAINN SEABROOK, a neo-Victorian and world acclaimed man of letters, is a Kentucky Colonel and the winner of the prestigious Jefferson Davis Historical Gold Medal for his "masterpiece," *A Rebel Born: A Defense of Nathan Bedford Forrest*. A classic littérateur and an unreconstructed Southern historian, he is an award-winning author, Civil War scholar, Confederate culture expert, Bible authority, the leading popularizer of American Civil War history, and a traditional Southern Agrarian of Scottish, English, Irish, Dutch, Welsh, German, and Italian extraction.

Above, Colonel Lochlainn Seabrook, "the voice of the traditional South," award-winning Civil War scholar and unreconstructed Southern historian, America's most popular and prolific pro-South author, his many books have introduced hundreds of thousands to the truth about the War for Southern Independence. He coined the phrase "South-shaming" and holds the world record for writing the most books on Nathan Bedford Forrest: ten.

A child prodigy, Seabrook is today a true Renaissance Man whose occupational titles also include encyclopedist, lexicographer, musician, artist, graphic designer, genealogist, photographer, and award-winning poet. Also a songwriter and a screenwriter, he has a 40 year background in historical nonfiction writing and is a member of the Sons of Confederate Veterans, the Civil War Trust, and the National Grange.

Known to his many fans as the "voice of the traditional South," due to similarities in their writing styles, ideas, and literary works, Seabrook is also often referred to as the "new Shelby Foote," the "Southern Joseph Campbell," and the "American Robert Graves" (his English cousin). Seabrook coined the terms "South-shaming" and "Lincolnian liberalism," and holds the world's record for writing the most books on Nathan Bedford Forrest: ten. In addition, Seabrook is the first Civil War scholar to connect the early American nickname for the U.S., "The Confederate States of America," with the Southern Confederacy that arose eight decades later, and the first to note that in 1860 the party platforms of the two major political parties were the opposite of what they are today (Victorian Democrats were Conservatives, Victorian Republicans were Liberals).

The grandson of an Appalachian coal-mining family, Seabrook is a seventh-generation Kentuckian whose European ancestors came from Virginia, North Carolina, and Tennessee, settling in the Bluegrass State in the early 1700s, thereafter spreading into West Virginia, the Midwest, and finally the West.

Seabrook is co-chair of the Jent/Gent Family Committee (Kentucky), founder and director of the Blakeney Family Tree Project, and a board member of the Friends of Colonel Benjamin E. Caudill. His literary works have been endorsed by leading authorities, museum curators, award-winning historians, bestselling authors, celebrities, noted scientists, well regarded educators, TV show hosts and producers, renowned military artists, esteemed Southern organizations, and distinguished academicians from around the world.

Seabrook has authored over 50 popular adult books on the American Civil War, American and international slavery, the U.S. Confederacy (1781), the Southern Confederacy (1861), religion, theology, thealogy, Jesus, the Bible, the Apocrypha, the Law of Attraction, alternative health, spirituality, ghost stories, the paranormal, ufology, social issues, and cross-cultural studies of the family and marriage. His Confederate biographies, pro-South studies, genealogical monographs, family histories, military encyclopedias, self-help guides, and etymological dictionaries have received wide acclaim.

Seabrook's eight children's books include a Southern guide to the Civil War, a biography of Nathan Bedford Forrest, a dictionary of religion and myth, a rewriting of the King Arthur legend (which reinstates the original pre-Christian motifs), two bedtime stories for preschoolers, a naturalist's guidebook to owls, a worldwide look at the family, and an examination of the Near-Death Experience.

Of blue-blooded Southern stock through his Kentucky, Tennessee, Virginia, North Carolina and West Virginia ancestors, he is a direct descendant of European royalty via his 6th great-grandfather, the Earl of Oxford, after which London's famous Harley Street is named. Among his celebrated male Celtic ancestors is Robert the Bruce, King of Scotland, Seabrook's 22nd great-grandfather. The 21st great-grandson of Edward I "Longshanks" Plantagenet), King of England, Seabrook is a 17th-generation Southerner through his descent from the colonists of Jamestown, Virginia

(1607).

The 2nd, 3rd, and 4th great-grandson of dozens of Confederate soldiers, one of his closest connections to Lincoln's War is through his 3rd great-grandfather, Elias Jent, Sr., who fought for the Confederacy in the Thirteenth Cavalry Kentucky under Seabrook's 2nd cousin, Colonel Benjamin E. Caudill. The Thirteenth, also known as "Caudill's Army," fought in numerous conflicts, including the Battles of Saltville, Gladsville, Mill Cliff, Poor Fork, Whitesburg, and Leatherwood.

Seabrook is a direct descendant of the families of Alexander H. Stephens, John Singleton Mosby, William Giles Harding, and Edmund Winchester Rucker, and is related to the following Confederates and other 18th- and 19th-Century luminaries: Robert E. Lee, Stephen Dill Lee, Stonewall Jackson, Nathan Bedford Forrest, James Longstreet, John Hunt Morgan, Jeb Stuart, Pierre G. T. Beauregard (approved the Confederate Battle Flag design), George W. Gordon, John Bell Hood, Alexander Peter Stewart, Arthur M. Manigault, Joseph Manigault, Charles Scott Venable, Thornton A. Washington, John A. Washington, Abraham Buford, Edmund W. Pettus, Theodrick "Tod" Carter, John B. Womack, John H. Winder, Gideon J. Pillow, States Rights Gist, Henry R. Jackson, John Lawton Seabrook, John C. Breckinridge, Leonidas Polk, Zachary Taylor, Sarah Knox Taylor (first wife of Jefferson Davis), Richard Taylor, Davy Crockett, Daniel Boone, Meriwether Lewis (of the Lewis and Clark Expedition) Andrew Jackson, James K. Polk, Abram Poindexter Maury (founder of Franklin, TN), Zebulon Baird Vance, Thomas Jefferson, Edmund Jennings Randolph, George Wythe Randolph (grandson of Jefferson), Felix K. Zollicoffer, Fitzhugh Lee, Nathaniel F. Cheairs, Jesse James, Frank James, Robert Brank Vance, Charles Sidney Winder, John W. McGavock, Caroline E. (Winder) McGavock, David Harding McGavock, Lysander McGavock, James Randal McGavock, Randal William McGavock, Francis McGavock, Emily McGavock, William Henry F. Lee, Lucius E. Polk, Minor Meriwether (husband of noted pro-South author Elizabeth Avery Meriwether), Ellen Bourne Tynes (wife of Forrest's chief of artillery, Captain John W. Morton), South Carolina Senators Preston Smith Brooks and Andrew

(Photo © Lochlainn Seabrook)

Pickens Butler, and famed South Carolina diarist Mary Chesnut.

Seabrook's modern day cousins include: Patrick J. Buchanan (conservative author), Cindy Crawford (model), Shelby Lee Adams (Letcher Co., Kentucky, photographer), Bertram Thomas Combs (Kentucky's 50th governor), Edith Bolling (second wife of President Woodrow Wilson), and actors Andy Griffith, Riley Keough, George C. Scott, Robert Duvall, Reese Witherspoon, Lee Marvin, Rebecca Gayheart, and Tom Cruise.

Seabrook's screenplay, *A Rebel Born*, based on his book of the same name, has been signed with acclaimed filmmaker Christopher Forbes (of Forbes Film). It is now in pre-production, and is set for release in 2018 as a full-length feature film. This will be the first movie ever made of Nathan Bedford Forrest's life story, and as a historically accurate project written from the Southern perspective, is destined to be one of the most talked about Civil War films of all time.

Born with music in his blood, Seabrook is an award-winning, multi-genre, BMI-Nashville songwriter and lyricist who has composed some 3,000 songs (250 albums), and whose original music has been heard in film (*A Rebel Born, Cowgirls 'n Angels, Confederate Cavalry, Billy the Kid: Showdown in Lincoln County, Vengeance Without Mercy, Last Step, County Line, The Mark*) and on TV and radio worldwide. A musician, producer, multi-instrumentalist, and renown performer—whose keyboard work has been variously compared to pianists from Hargus Robbins and Vince Guaraldi to Elton John and Leonard Bernstein—Seabrook has opened for groups such as the Earl Scruggs Review, Ted Nugent, and Bob Seger, and has performed privately for such public figures as President Ronald Reagan, Burt Reynolds, Loni Anderson, and Senator Edward W. Brooke. Seabrook's cousins in the music business include: Johnny Cash, Elvis Presley, Lisa Marie Presley, Billy Ray and Miley Cyrus, Patty Loveless, Tim McGraw, Lee Ann Womack, Dolly Parton, Pat Boone, Naomi, Wynonna, and Ashley Judd, Ricky Skaggs, the Sunshine Sisters, Martha Carson, and Chet Atkins.

Seabrook lives with his wife and family in historic Middle Tennessee, the heart of Forrest country and the Confederacy, where his conservative Southern ancestors fought valiantly against Liberal Lincoln and the progressive North in defense of Jeffersonianism, constitutional government, and personal liberty.

LOCHLAINN SEABROOK ☞ 1049

If you enjoyed this book you will be interested in Colonel Seabrook's other popular related titles:

- ☞ EVERYTHING YOU WERE TAUGHT ABOUT THE CIVIL WAR IS WRONG, ASK A SOUTHERNER!
- ☞ ABRAHAM LINCOLN WAS A LIBERAL, JEFFERSON DAVIS WAS A CONSERVATIVE
- ☞ ALL WE ASK IS TO BE LET ALONE: THE SOUTHERN SECESSION FACT BOOK
- ☞ EVERYTHING YOU WERE TAUGHT ABOUT AMERICAN SLAVERY IS WRONG, ASK A SOUTHERNER!
- ☞ CONFEDERATE FLAG FACTS: WHAT EVERY AMERICAN SHOULD KNOW ABOUT DIXIE'S SOUTHERN CROSS
- ☞ LINCOLN'S WAR: THE REAL CAUSE, THE REAL WINNER, THE REAL LOSER

Available from Sea Raven Press and wherever fine books are sold

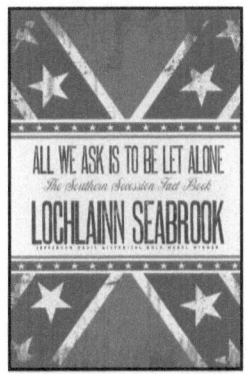

ALL OF OUR BOOK COVERS ARE AVAILABLE AS 11" X 17" POSTERS, SUITABLE FOR FRAMING

SeaRavenPress.com • NathanBedfordForrestBooks.com

www.ingramcontent.com/pod-product-compliance
Lightning Source LLC
Chambersburg PA
CBHW031931290426
44108CB00011B/520